| ACRONYM | FULL NAME |
|---------|-----------|
| GF | General F. |
| GFA | General Fixed Assets |
| GFAAG | General Fixed Assets Account Group |
| GFOA | Government Finance Officers Association |
| GLTD | General Long-Term Debt |
| GLTDAG | General Long-Term Debt Account Group |
| GPFS | General Purpose Financial Statements |
| HFMA | Healthcare Financial Management Association |
| IIA | Institute of Internal Auditors |
| ISF | Internal Service Fund(s) |
| JAG | Joint Accounting Group (Colleges and Universities, NACUBO & NCHEMS) |
| JFMIP | Joint Financial Management Improvement Program |
| MFAP | Major Federal Assistance Program |
| MF/BA | Measurement Focus and Basis of Accounting |
| MFOA | Municipal Finance Officers Association (now GFOA) |
| NACUBO | National Association of College & University Business Officers |
| NCGA | National Council on Governmental Accounting (succeeded by GASB) |
| NCHEMS | National Center for Higher Education Management Systems |
| NETF | Nonexpendable Trust Fund(s) |
| NPO | Nonprofit Organization(s) |
| OMB | Office of Management and Budget (U.S.) |
| ONPO | Other Nonprofit Organization(s) |
| PERISA | Public Employee Retirement Income Security Act |
| PERS | Public Employee Retirement System |
| PG | Primary Government |
| PPB | Planning-Programming-Budgeting |
| PPBS | Planning-Programming-Budgeting System |
| PREF | Plant Replacement and Expansion Fund |
| PTF | Pension Trust Fund(s) |
| RAN | Revenue Anticipation Note |
| RET | Residual Equity Transfer |
| SA | Special Assessment |
| SAS | Statements on Auditing Standards (AICPA) |
| SEC | Securities and Exchange Commission (U.S.) |
| SGL | Standard General Ledger (Federal) |
| SLG | State and Local Government |
| SOP | Statement of Position (AICPA) |
| SRF | Special Revenue Fund(s) |
| T&A | Trust & Agency |
| TAN | Tax Anticipation Note |
| VHWO | Voluntary Health & Welfare Organization |
| ZBB | Zero Base Budget |

# Charles T. Horngren Series in Accounting
*Charles T. Horngren, Consulting Editor*

Advanced Accounting, 7/E
Beams/Brozovsky/Shoulders

Auditing: An Integrated Approach, 7/E
Arens/Loebbecke

Financial Statement Analysis, 2/E
Foster

Governmental and Nonprofit Accounting: Theory and Practice, 6/E
Freeman/Shoulders

Financial Accounting, 3/E
Harrison/Horngren

Cases in Financial Reporting, 2/E
Hirst/McAnally

Cost Accounting: A Managerial Emphasis, 9/E
Horngren/Foster/Datar

Accounting, 4/E
Horngren/Harrison/Bamber

Introduction to Financial Accounting, 7/E
Horngren/Sundem/Elliot

Introduction to Management Accounting, 11/E
Horngren/Sundem/Stratton

Sixth
Edition

# GOVERNMENTAL AND NONPROFIT ACCOUNTING

## Theory and Practice

Robert J. Freeman
*Texas Tech University*

Craig D. Shoulders
*Virginia Polytechnic Institute and State University*

Prentice Hall
Upper Saddle River, New Jersey 07458

Executive Editor: Annie Todd
Editorial Assistant: Fran Toepfer
Editor-in-Chief: PJ Boardman
Executive Marketing Manager: Beth Toland
Production Editor: Lynda Paolucci
Managing Editor: Dee Josephson
Manufacturing Buyer: Lisa DiMaulo
Senior Manufacturing Supervisor: Paul Smolenski
Manufacturing Manager: Vincent Scelta
Design Manager: Patricia Smythe
Cover Designer: Steve Frim
Cover Photo: Courtesy of Jefferson County Public Information
Composition: Omegatype Typography, Inc.

**Library of Congress Cataloging-in-Publication Data**
Freeman, Robert J.
Governmental and nonprofit accounting : theory and practice / by
Robert J. Freeman and Craig D. Shoulders. — 6th ed.
p.    cm. — (Prentice-Hall series in accounting)
Includes bibliographical references and index.
ISBN 0-13-272675-0
1. Municipal finance—United States—Accounting.    2. Local
finance—United States—Accounting.    3. Finance, Public—United
States—Accounting.    4. Fund accounting—United States.
5. Nonprofit organizations—United States—Accounting.
I. Shoulders, Craig D.    II. Title.    III. Series.
HJ9777.A3L95    1999
657'.835'00973—dc21                                          98-11737
                                                             CIP

Prentice-Hall International (UK) Limited, *London*
Prentice-Hall of Australia Pty. Limited, *Sydney*
Prentice-Hall Canada Inc., *Toronto*
Prentice-Hall Hispanoamericana, S.A., *Mexico*
Prentice-Hall of India Private Limited, *New Delhi*
Prentice-Hall of Japan, Inc., *Tokyo*
Pearson Education Asia Pte. Ltd., *Singapore*
Editora Prentice-Hall do Brasil, Ltda., *Rio de Janeiro*

Printed in the United States of America

10 9 8 7 6 5 4 3 2

*Dedicated in Loving Honor*
*of Our Wives*

*Beverly Freeman and Nancy Shoulders*

*Who embody for us*
*the declaration of the Holy Scriptures*
*about a*
*Virtuous Wife*

*. . . For her worth is far above rubies.*
*The heart of her husband safely trusts in her;*
*So he will have no lack of gain.*
*She does him good and not evil all the days of her life. . . .*

*—Proverbs 31:10–12*

# BRIEF CONTENTS

# CONTENTS

# PART III: PUBLIC SECTOR AUDITING

# PREFACE

Governmental and nonprofit accounting, reporting, and auditing continue to evolve rapidly. Indeed, significant changes in the basic state and local government financial reporting model are on the not-too-distant horizon. Moreover, the ever-increasing scrutiny and accountability to which governments and nonprofit organizations are being subjected by the Congress, practitioners, investors and creditors, standards setters, and academicians clearly signal that their accounting, reporting, and auditing concepts, standards, and practices probably will continue to evolve rapidly. One result of this increased attention is that it is now virtually impossible to pass the Uniform CPA Examination without an understanding of governmental and nonprofit accounting.

We have *updated* this sixth edition of our text to incorporate the relevant portions of all authoritative pronouncements issued through mid-1998. This coverage includes GASB Statement 31 which requires fair value accounting for most investments of state and local governments and GASB Statement 32 which changes the reporting of Internal Revenue Code 457 deferred compensation plans to correspond to changes in the legal status of those plans. Too, other key GASB projects—including those on the proposed new financial reporting model and on service efforts and accomplishments reporting—are discussed.

In addition, while retaining the successful approach, comprehensiveness, and other strengths that have long been hallmarks of this text, we have further refined and improved the emphasis on the foundational aspects of governmental accounting and financial reporting—such as the nature and purposes of the various accounting entities—and the *unique approach for teaching* the state and local government accounting and reporting *model* that has proven so successful for students.

## Not-for-Profit Organization Coverage

The sixth edition reorders three chapters to efficiently handle accounting and reporting for not-for-profit organizations, which are the most potentially cumbersome areas to address. This area is challenging not only because SFASs 116 and 117 permit a myriad of alternatives for nongovernment, not-for-profit health care organizations, colleges and universities, voluntary health and welfare organizations, and other nonprofit organizations, but also because GASB standards prohibit government entities from applying those FASB standards. Thus, for each of those types of organizations, there are two or more sets of reporting principles, practices, and/or standards that might apply.

Having found that students learn most effectively if they have an opportunity to master one of these multiple approaches or models before delving into another, we segregated the coverage of the not-for-profit organizations as follows:

- Chapter 16 covers accounting for government colleges and universities. Nongovernment university accounting and reporting are dealt with in an appendix to Chapter 18. This is accomplished by building on the coverage of SFASs 116 and 117 which comprises the core of that chapter and on material learned in Chapter 16 that applies to both nongovernment and government colleges and universities. Addressing government college and university accounting immediately after completing the state and local government coverage should help students receive maximum benefit from the similarity of the two as they learn the uniquenesses of the government college and university model.

- Chapter 17 covers accounting and reporting for government health care organizations. As with colleges and universities, nongovernment health care organizations accounting and reporting are addressed in a separate appendix to Chapter 18. Students who have learned the requirements of SFASs 116 and 117 in Chapter 18 and special health care topics such as accounting for patient service revenues in Chapter 17 can bring that information together efficiently. This approach enables the students to understand nongovernment health care organization accounting and reporting with little additional effort.

- Chapter 18 discusses and illustrates SFASs 116 and 117 thoroughly in the context of nongovernment voluntary health and welfare organizations and other nonprofit organizations. The use of funds is not presumed in this chapter since the focus is on conveying the financial reporting requirements for these organizations. The discussion, diagrams, and illustrations allow students to grasp the key provisions of SFASs 116 and 117 quickly. As noted previously, the appendices facilitate understanding how these standards are applied in nongovernment colleges and universities and in nongovernment health care organizations.

## Updated Single Audit Coverage

Coverage of single audit requirements has been updated for the latest revision of OMB Circular A-133, the 1998 OMB Circular A-133 Compliance Supplement, and the latest AICPA single audit guidance through mid-1998. This coverage includes the risk-based approach to identifying major federal programs and current single audit reporting requirements.

## Problem Material

In addition to the normal adjustment and updating of problem material and questions, the sixth edition incorporates two new features in the end-of-chapter material. The first is the inclusion of a few short, focused exercises in most chapters that should help students master certain specific concepts. The second is the addition of a research problem at the end of most chapters. The Internet can be used to facilitate meeting the requirements of many of these research problems.

## Pedagogical Refinements

Our unique approach to introducing students to the state and local government model—which allows them to understand and apply that model better and more quickly—is still a central feature of the sixth edition. This approach combines a strong emphasis on the underlying nature of the various fund types and account groups with transaction analysis using the accounting equations of the various fund types and account groups to break students out of the "business accounting mindset" and help them understand how the "pieces" of the government model complement one another. Many who have used prior editions of the text have attested to the effectiveness of this approach in the college classroom. This pedagogy **enables students to grasp concepts and principles** at this **early** stage, where without it most would not understand until well into the course. Indeed, for many this approach provides the "key" to unlock the door to understanding state and local government accounting and financial reporting.

## Other Changes

Several other aspects of this revision are noteworthy as well. Among these are the following:

- **Chapter 5** explains and illustrates GASB Statement 31 on accounting for investments.
- **Financial reporting** is covered in two chapters in the sixth edition. Chapter 13, "Financial Reporting: The CAFR and GPFS" covers the basic financial reporting requirements and presumes a simple situation. Chapter 14, "Financial Accounting and Reporting: Complex Reporting Entities and Non-GAAP Bases of Accounting," addresses more advanced reporting issues that are encountered by complex entities or entities that use non-GAAP bases of accounting during the year.
- **Chapter 14** contains an appendix that discusses and illustrates key aspects of government financial statement analysis. This appendix was contributed by Professor David Olson, University of Illinois—Springfield.
- **Chapter 15, "Contemporary Issues"** provides a basis for discussing GASB's key agenda projects and other unresolved state and local government accounting and reporting issues. The GASB's proposed financial reporting model project is a central feature of this chapter.
- **Chapter 19, "Federal Government Accounting,"** has been updated for recent changes in federal financial management and in accounting and reporting for federal agencies. Bruce K. Michelson of the U.S. General Accounting Office provided invaluable assistance in determining the appropriate depth of coverage for this important chapter and in updating for changes since the last edition.

## Acknowledgments

We are grateful for the many excellent suggestions made by the individuals who reviewed the fifth edition in preparation for this edition:

Charles Fazzi, Robert Morris College

Frederk M. Stiner, Jr., University of Delaware

Donald Keller, California State University—Chico

Saleha B. Khumawala, University of Houston

Likewise, we appreciate the reviews of the drafts of various chapters and other significant assistance contributed by the following individuals:

David R. Bean, Director of Research, Governmental Accounting Standards Board

Rob Garner, City of Orlando, Florida

George Hunt, Texas Tech University

Norwood J. (Woody) Jackson, Jr., U.S. Office of Management and Budget

James A. Lampe, Texas Tech University

Bruce K. Michelson, U.S. General Accounting Office

G. Michael (Mickey) Miller, City of Orlando, Florida

David R. Olson, University of Illinois at Springfield

G. Robert Smith, Auburn University

Penelope S. Wardlow, Governmental Accounting Standards Board

George Hunt assisted us throughout the revision process and also searched numerable comprehensive annual financial reports to identify government financial statement examples for the text. Sharendale Bruni not only managed and produced the manuscript for the text in an efficient and professional manner, but also used her professional background and experience to assist in other ways with supplements and other issues that had to be addressed.

Finally, we can never adequately express our love and appreciation to our wives, Beverly Freeman and Nancy Shoulders. Their contributions to all that we do—including the revision of this text—are essential. They encouraged, supported, and advised us as we labored over this revision and took care of many responsibilities that were rightfully ours in order to enable us to have the time and the energy to complete this task. Clearly, they multiply what we are able to accomplish by their help and support. Indeed, Beverly and Nancy are full partners in all that we do.

**Robert J. Freeman**
**Craig D. Shoulders**

# GOVERNMENTAL AND NONPROFIT ACCOUNTING

# 1

# GOVERNMENTAL AND NONPROFIT ACCOUNTING

## Environment and Characteristics

Accounting and financial reporting for governments and nonprofit organizations are based on distinctive concepts, standards, and procedures designed to accommodate their environments and the needs of their financial report users. This book focuses on the most important of these concepts, standards, and procedures applicable to (1) state and local governments—including counties, cities, and school districts, as well as townships, villages, other special districts, and public authorities; (2) the federal government; and (3) nonprofit and governmental universities, hospitals, voluntary health and welfare organizations, and other nonprofit (or not-for-profit) organizations. Financial management and accountability considerations peculiar to government and nonprofit (G&NP) organizations are emphasized throughout the book, and the distinctive aspects of auditing G&NP organizations also are discussed.

## CHARACTERISTICS AND TYPES OF G&NP ORGANIZATIONS

Governments and other nonprofit organizations are **unique** in that:

- They are not organized or operated to earn a profit—and most are exempt from income taxes.
- They are owned collectively by their constituents: Ownership is not evidenced by equity shares that can be sold or traded.
- Those contributing financial resources to the organizations do not necessarily receive a direct or proportionate share of those organizations' services or goods. For example, the welfare recipient (probably) did not pay the taxes from which welfare benefits are paid.
- Their major policy decisions, and perhaps some operating decisions, typically are made by consensus vote of an elected or appointed governing body—for example, a state legislature, a city council, or a hospital board of directors—whose members serve part-time and have diverse backgrounds, philosophies, capabilities, and interests.

A G&NP organization exists because a community or society decides to provide certain goods or services to its group as a whole. Often these goods or services are provided regardless of whether costs incurred will be recovered through charges for the goods or services or whether those paying for the goods or services are those benefiting from them. Many G&NP goods or services could not be produced profitably through private enterprise. In addition, the community or society may deem these goods or services so vital to the public well-being that their provision should be supervised by its elected or appointed representatives.

The major types of government and nonprofit organizations may be classified as:

1. **Governmental:** federal, state, county, municipal, township, village, and other local governmental authorities and special districts
2. **Educational:** kindergartens, elementary and secondary schools, vocational and technical schools, and colleges and universities
3. **Health and welfare:** hospitals, nursing homes, child protection agencies, the American Red Cross, and the USO
4. **Religious:** YMCA, Salvation Army, and other church-related organizations
5. **Charitable:** United Way, Community Chest, and similar fund-raising agencies, related charitable agencies, and other charitable organizations
6. **Foundations:** private trusts and corporations organized for educational, religious, or charitable purposes

This list is a general classification scheme, and much overlap occurs. Many charitable organizations are operated by churches, for example, and governments are deeply involved in education, health, and welfare activities.

## Growth and Importance of the G&NP Sector

Governments and other nonprofit organizations have experienced dramatic growth in recent years and have emerged—individually and collectively—as major economic, political, and social forces in our society. Indeed, the G&NP sector now accounts for more than one-third of all expenditures within the U.S. economy and includes many growth industries. The total value of financial and human resources devoted to this sector is gigantic, both absolutely and relatively.

Sound financial management—including thoughtful budgeting, appropriate accounting, meaningful financial reporting, and timely audits by qualified auditors—is at least as important in the G&NP sector as in the private business sector. Furthermore, because of the scope and diversity of its activities, proper management of the financial affairs of a city or town, for example, may be far more complex than that of a private business with comparable assets or annual expenditures.

As the size and complexity of governments and nonprofit organizations have increased in recent years, so have the number of career employment opportunities in this sector for college graduates majoring in accounting (and other disciplines). Likewise, the number of government and nonprofit organization auditing and consulting engagements with independent public accounting firms have increased significantly. Accordingly, 30% of the Accounting & Reporting–Taxation, Managerial, and Governmental and Not-for-Profit Organizations (ARE) section of the Uniform CPA Examination is on governmental and nonprofit organization accounting concepts, principles, and procedures.

## The G&NP Environment

G&NP organizations are similar in many ways to profit-seeking enterprises. For example:

1. They are integral parts of the same economic system and use financial, capital, and human resources to accomplish their purposes.

2. Both must acquire and convert scarce resources into their respective goods or services.

3. Financial management processes are essentially similar in both. And both must have viable information systems—of which the accounting system is an integral component—for managers, governing bodies, and others to receive relevant and timely data for planning, directing, controlling, and evaluating the use of the scarce resources.

4. Because their resources are scarce, cost analysis and other control and evaluation techniques are essential to ensure that resources are utilized economically, effectively, and efficiently.

5. In some cases, both produce similar products. For example, both governments and private enterprises may own and operate transportation systems, sanitation services, and electric or gas utilities.

There are also significant differences between profit-seeking and G&NP organizations. Broad generalizations about such a diversified group as G&NP organizations are difficult. Nonetheless, the major differences arise from differing (1) organizational objectives, (2) sources of financial resources, and (3) regulation and control.

### Organizational Objectives

Expectation of income or gain is the principal factor motivating investors to provide resources to profit-seeking enterprises. But the objective of most government and nonprofit organizations is to provide as many goods or as much service each year as their financial and other resources permit. G&NP organizations typically operate on a year-to-year basis. They raise as much financial resources each year as possible and then expend them in serving their constituency. They may seek to increase the amount of resources made available to them each year—and most do—but this is to enable the organization to provide more or better goods and services, not to increase its wealth. In sum, private businesses seek to increase their wealth for the benefit of their owners; G&NP organizations seek to expend their available financial resources for the benefit of their constituency. Financial management in the G&NP environment thus typically focuses on acquiring and using financial resources—upon sources and uses of working capital, budget status, and cash flow—rather than on net income or earnings per share.

### Sources of Financial Resources

The sources of financial resources differ between business and G&NP organizations, as well as among G&NP organizations. And, in the absence of a net income determination emphasis, no distinction is generally made between invested capital and revenue of G&NP organizations. A dollar is a financial resource whether acquired through donations, user charges, sales of assets, loans, or some other manner.

The typical nondebt sources of financial resources for business enterprises are investments by owners and sales of goods or services to customers. These sources of financing usually are not the primary sources of G&NP organization financial resources.

Governments have the unique power to force involuntary financial resource contributions through taxation—of property, sales, and income—and all levels rely heavily on this power. Grants and shared revenues from other governments also are important state and local government revenue sources, as are charges levied for goods or services provided, such as utilities.

Religious groups and charitable organizations usually rely heavily on donations, although they may have other revenue sources. Some colleges and universities rely heavily on donations and income from trust funds; others depend primarily on state appropriations and/or tuition charges for support. Hospitals generally charge their clientele, although few admit their patients solely on the basis of ability to pay. Indeed, many G&NP hospitals serve numerous charity patients and/or have large amounts of uncollectible accounts; and some hospitals rely heavily on gifts and bequests.

There are other, more subtle, differences in sources of G&NP organization financial resources as compared with profit-seeking businesses. For example:

- Many services or goods provided by these organizations are monopolistic in nature, and there is no open market in which their value may be objectively appraised or evaluated.
- User charges, where levied, usually are based on the cost of the goods or services provided rather than on supply- and demand-related pricing policies common to private enterprise.
- Charges levied for goods or services often cover only part of the costs incurred to provide them; for example, tuition generally covers only a fraction of the cost of operating state colleges or universities, and token charges (or no charges) may be made to a hospital's indigent patients.

### Regulation and Control

Unregulated profit-seeking enterprises will modify or withdraw unprofitable goods or services offered to the consuming public. The direct relationship between the financial resources each consumer provides and the goods or services that consumer receives from each enterprise essentially dictates the type and quality of goods and services each profit-seeking enterprise will provide. Firms with inept or unresponsive management will be unprofitable and ultimately will be forced out of business. Therefore, the profit motive and profit measurement constitute an automatic allocation and regulating device in the free enterprise segment of our economy.

This profit test/regulator device is not present in the usual G&NP situation, and most G&NP organizations must strive to attain their objectives without its benefits. In addition, as noted earlier, many G&NP organizations provide goods or services having no open market value measurement by which to test consumer satisfaction. This problem exists because the goods and services are unique or are provided to some or all consumers without charge, or at a token charge. Thus, these consumers have no "dollar vote" to cast.

Evaluating the performance and operating results of most G&NP organizations is extremely difficult for several reasons.

1. There is no open market supply and demand test of the value of the goods and services they provide.
2. The relationship, if any, between the resource contributors and the recipients of the goods and services is remote and indirect.
3. Such organizations are not profit oriented in the usual sense and are not expected to operate profitably; thus, the profit test is neither a valid performance indicator nor an automatic regulating device.
4. Governments can force resource contributions through taxation.

Accordingly, other operating results measures and controls must be employed to ensure that G&NP organization resources are used appropriately and to prevent uneconomical or ineffective G&NP organizations from continuing to operate in that manner indefinitely. Governmental and nonprofit organizations, particularly governments, are therefore subject to more stringent legal, regulatory, and other controls than are private businesses.

All facets of a G&NP organization's operations may be affected by legal or quasi-legal requirements (1) imposed externally, such as by federal or state statute, grant regulations, or judicial decrees, or (2) imposed internally by charter, bylaw, ordinance, trust agreement, donor stipulation, or contract. Furthermore, the need to ensure compliance with such extensive legal and contractual requirements often results in more stringent operational and administrative controls than in private enterprise. Aspects of G&NP organization operations that may be regulated or otherwise controlled include:

1. **Organization structure:** form; composition of its governing board; the number and duties of its personnel; lines of authority and responsibility; policies as to which officials or employees are to be elected, appointed, or hired.
2. **Personnel policies and procedures:** who will appoint or hire personnel; tenure of personnel; policies and procedures upon termination; compensation levels; promotion policies; and types and amounts of compensation increments.
3. **Sources of financial resources:** the types and maximum amounts of taxes, licenses, fines, or fees a government may levy; the procedure for setting user charges; tuition rates; debt limits; the purposes for which debt may be incurred; the allowable methods for soliciting charitable contributions.
4. **Uses of financial resources:** the purposes for which resources may be used, including legally restricting certain resources for use only for specific purposes; purchasing procedures to be followed; budgeting methods, forms, or procedures.
5. **Accounting:** any or all phases of the accounting system; for example, chart of accounts, bases of accounting, forms, procedures.
6. **Financial reporting:** type and frequency of financial reports; report format and content; report recipients.
7. **Auditing:** frequency of audit; who is to perform the audit; the scope and type of audit; the time and place for filing the audit report; who is to receive or have access to the audit report.

Thus, managers of G&NP organizations may have limited discretion compared with managers of business enterprises. The role and emphasis of G&NP financial accounting and reporting thus are correspondingly altered as compared with the profit-seeking enterprise environment.

## OBJECTIVES OF G&NP ACCOUNTING AND FINANCIAL REPORTING

A major committee of the American Accounting Association stated that the objectives of accounting for any type of organization are to provide information for:

1. Making decisions concerning the use of limited resources, including the identification of crucial decision areas and determination of objectives and goals.
2. Effectively directing and controlling an organization's human and material resources.
3. Maintaining and reporting on the custodianship of resources.
4. Contributing to the effectiveness of all organizations, whether profit-oriented or not, in fulfilling the desires and demands of all society for social control of their functions.[1]

[1] American Accounting Association, Committee to Prepare a Statement of Basic Accounting Theory, *A Statement of Basic Accounting Theory* (Evanston, Ill.: AAA, 1966), p. 4.

Financial Accounting Standards Board (FASB) *Statement of Financial Accounting Concepts No. 4* (SFAC 4), "Objectives of Financial Reporting by Non-business Organizations," addresses the objectives of **general-purpose external financial reporting** by nonbusiness (nonprofit) organizations. SFAC 4 notes that:

- The objectives stem primarily from the needs of external users who generally cannot prescribe the information they want from an organization.
- In addition to information provided by general purpose external financial reporting, managers and, to some extent, governing bodies need a great deal of internal accounting information to carry out their responsibilities in planning and controlling activities. That information and information directed at meeting the specialized needs of users having the power to obtain the information they need are beyond the scope of this Statement.[2]

The financial reporting objectives set forth in SFAC 4 state that financial reporting by nonbusiness organizations should provide information that is useful to present and potential resource providers and other users in:

- Making rational decisions about the allocation of resources to those organizations.
- Assessing the services that a nonbusiness organization provides and its ability to continue to provide those services.
- Assessing how managers of a nonbusiness organization have discharged their stewardship responsibilities and other aspects of their performance.

Accordingly, nonbusiness organization financial reporting should provide information about:

- The economic resources, obligations, and net resources of an organization and the effects of transactions, events, and circumstances that change resources and interests in those resources.
- The performance of an organization during a period. Periodic measurement of the changes in the amount and nature of the net resources of a nonbusiness organization and information about its service efforts and accomplishments provide the information most useful in assessing its performance.
- How an organization obtains and spends cash or other liquid resources, its borrowing and repayment of debt, and other factors that may affect an organization's liquidity.

In addition, nonbusiness organization financial reporting should include explanations and interpretations to help users understand financial information provided.[3]

## CHARACTERISTICS OF G&NP ACCOUNTING AND FINANCIAL REPORTING

Some G&NP organization activities (such as utilities and public transportation) are similar to those of some profit-seeking enterprises. In such cases the accounting typically parallels that of their privately owned counterparts. In most of their operations, however, governments and nonprofit organizations are not concerned with profit measurement. (Even those G&NP entities that account for revenues, expenses, and net income may not seek to maximize profits, but only to ensure continuity and/or improvement of service.)

[2] Financial Accounting Standards Board, *Statement of Financial Accounting Concepts* No. 4, "Objectives of Financial Reporting by Nonbusiness Organizations" (Stamford, Conn.: FASB, December 1980), p. xii.

[3] Ibid., pp. xiii–xiv.

Accounting is a service function and must meet the information demands in a given environment. In the G&NP environment, decisions concerning financial resource acquisition and allocation, managerial direction and control of financial resource utilization, and custodianship of financial and other resources have traditionally been framed in terms of social and political objectives and constraints rather than profitability. Legal and administrative constraints have been used as society's methods of directing its G&NP institutions in achieving those objectives. Thus, G&NP organization accounting and reporting usually emphasize control of and accountability for expendable financial resources. The two most important types of legal and administrative control provisions affecting accounting in this environment are (1) the use of **funds** and (2) the distinctive role of the **budget.**

## Funds and Fund Accounting

Recall that the financial resources provided to a G&NP organization may be restricted; that is, their use may be limited to specified purposes or activities. For example, a church may receive donations for a building addition; a hospital may receive a grant for adding an intensive care facility; a city may borrow money to construct a sewage treatment plant; a university may receive a federal grant for research purposes. Such **external restrictions** carry significant accountability obligations. Management also may designate specific purposes for which certain resources must be used. For example, management may wish to accumulate resources for equipment replacement or facility enlargement. Because management **designations** are internal plans and may be changed by management, they carry only internal accountability requirements. In any event, using the resources in accordance with stipulations inherent in their receipt and reporting on this compliance to others are essential custodianship obligations.

G&NP organizations establish funds in order to control restricted and designated resources and to both ensure and demonstrate compliance with legal and administrative requirements. **Funds** are separate fiscal and accounting entities, and include both cash and noncash resources—segregated according to the purposes or activities for which they are to be used—as well as related liabilities. A **fund** is:

> . . . a fiscal and accounting entity with a self-balancing set of accounts recording cash and other financial resources, together with all related liabilities, and residual equities or balances, and changes therein, which are segregated for the purpose of carrying on specific activities or attaining certain objectives in accordance with special regulations, restrictions, or limitations.[4]

Two basic types of fund accounting entities are used by G&NP organizations:

1. **Expendable (governmental) funds:** to account for the current assets, related liabilities, changes in net assets, and balances that may be expended in its nonbusiness-type activities (e.g., for fire and police protection).

2. **Nonexpendable (proprietary) funds:** to account for the revenues, expenses, assets, liabilities, and equity of its business-type activities (e.g., utilities, cafeterias, or transportation systems) and some trust funds.

The fund concept involves an accounting segregation—not necessarily the physical separation—of resources; however, resources are often also physically segregated—

---

[4] Governmental Accounting Standards Board, *Codification of Governmental Accounting and Financial Reporting Standards* (Norwalk, Conn.: GASB, 1997), sec. 1100.102 and 1300.

for example, through use of separate checking accounts for cash resources of various funds.

Use of the term *fund* in G&NP situations should be sharply distinguished from its use in private enterprise. A fund of a commercial enterprise is simply a portion of its assets that has been restricted to specific uses, not a separate and distinct accounting entity. Revenues and expenses related to such funds are part of enterprise operations; that is, fund revenue and expense accounts appear side by side in the general ledger with other enterprise revenue and expense accounts. On the other hand, **a fund in the G&NP accounting sense is a self-contained accounting entity with its own asset, liability, revenue, expenditure or expense, and fund balance or other equity accounts**—and with its own ledger(s) (see Figure 1–1). Indeed, a complete set of financial statements may be prepared for each fund of a G&NP organization as well as for the organization as a whole.

Although experts agree that the fund device is essential to sound financial management of most G&NP organizations, its use has a fragmenting effect on their accounting and reporting. Most government organization financial reports consist of a series of fund entity balance sheets and operating statements. Consolidated statements are not in widespread use in government financial reporting.

## Budgets and Appropriations

The creation of an expendable (governmental) fund ordinarily does not carry with it the authority to expend its resources. In most G&NP organizations, especially governments, expenditures may be made only within the authority of appropria-

FIGURE 1–1  **Single Accounting Entity vs. Multiple Accounting Entities**

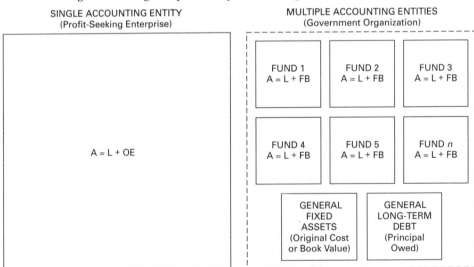

Legend:
A  = Assets—only *current* assets in most expendable (governmental) funds; both current and noncurrent in nonexpendable (proprietary) funds
L  = Liabilities—only current liabilities in most expendable (governmental) funds; both current and noncurrent in nonexpendable (proprietary) funds
OE  = Owner's Equity (of the enterprise)
FB  = Fund Balance (expendable or governmental funds) or Fund Equity (nonexpendable or proprietary funds)
_ _ _  = The government as a whole

tions—which are authorizations to make expenditures for specified purposes—or similar authorizations by the governing body.

A **fixed-dollar budget** is commonly prepared for each expendable fund. That is, the organization's chief executive (or perhaps each department head) asks the governing body for permission to incur a specified ("fixed") amount of expenditures—for salaries, equipment, supplies, and so on—during the budget period to carry out the department's mission. This budget is the vehicle normally used to make and communicate resource allocation decisions establishing the types and quantities of goods and services to be provided during the budget period.

When approved by the governing body, the budgetary expenditure estimates become binding **appropriations**—that both authorize expenditures for specified purposes and limit the amounts that can be expended for each specified purpose. Appropriations must indicate the fund from which the expenditure may be made and specify the purposes, the maximum amount, and the period of time for which the expenditure authority is granted. A department or activity may be financed from several funds. In such cases at least one appropriation must be made from each supporting fund in order to provide the requisite expenditure authority.

In order to control and demonstrate budgetary compliance, it is common— for governments, in particular—to establish **budgetary accounts** within expendable fund ledgers. This technique (explained later) permits managers to determine their remaining expenditure authority at any time during the period. Integrating budgetary accounts into the accounting system is particularly important where budget overruns subject officials to fine, dismissal, or other disciplinary action.

Nonexpendable (proprietary) funds, on the other hand, may be controlled by flexible budgets—such as those used in businesses—rather than by fixed-dollar budgets. Flexible budgets automatically increase authorizations to incur expenses during the year if revenues are greater than planned and decrease expense authorizations if revenues are less than planned. Budgetary accounts are not used with flexible budgets. But budgetary accounts are used by most G&NP organizations that control their nonexpendable funds by fixed-dollar budgets.

Fixed-dollar budgeting of expendable and/or nonexpendable funds often gives rise to a unique dual basis of accounting and reporting for G&NP organizations. This is because (1) generally accepted accounting principles (GAAP) prescribe specific standards for the measurement of revenues, expenditures, expenses, and other amounts reported in financial statements that "present fairly in conformity with GAAP"; but (2) for budgetary purposes, G&NP governing boards may estimate revenues and authorize expenditures on a variety of non-GAAP bases— on the cash receipts and disbursements basis, for example.

Where the budgetary basis differs from the GAAP basis:

1. The accounts are maintained on the budgetary basis during the year to effect budgetary control through the accounts, so that interim and annual budgetary statements may be prepared on the budgetary basis;

2. Adjustments are made at year end—to convert the budgetary basis data in the accounts to the GAAP basis—so that GAAP basis annual statements may be prepared; and

3. The differences between the budgetary basis and the GAAP basis statements are explained and reconciled in the annual financial report of the government or nonprofit organization.

Budgetary accounting and reporting are distinctive characteristics of G&NP organizations, particularly governments, and are discussed and illustrated at numerous points throughout this text.

## Some Other Distinguishing Characteristics

The emphasis on fund and budgetary controls causes the accounting for many G&NP organizations, especially governments, to resemble working capital change analysis—or even cash flow analysis—rather than commercial accounting, in which net income determination is a paramount consideration. **The focal point of most G&NP accounting and reporting is expendable financial resources, accounted for in expendable fund entities and allocated by the budget and appropriation process.**

The cost measurement focus of **nonexpendable (proprietary)** fund accounting of G&NP organizations, like that of business accounting, is **expenses**—the cost of **assets consumed** during the period. In contrast, the cost measurement focus of **expendable (governmental)** fund accounting is **expenditures**—the amount of financial resources expended during the period for:

- **current operations** (e.g., salaries, utilities),
- **capital outlay** (acquiring fixed assets), and
- **long-term debt principal retirement and interest.**

More specifically, **expenditures** has been defined as "the cost of goods delivered or services rendered, whether paid or unpaid, including current operating costs, provision for debt retirement not reported as a liability of the fund from which retired, and capital outlays."[5] Thus, the term *expenditures*—the term that is significant in expendable fund accounting—should not be confused with *expenses* as defined for accounting for profit-seeking enterprises.

Fixed assets normally are not appropriable financial resources and are commonly listed and accounted for separately from the expendable fund accounting entities. Similarly, unmatured long-term debt that is not a liability of a particular fund (but of the government as a whole) may be listed in a separate nonfund accounting entity. Accordingly, the cost of acquiring a fixed asset is considered an expenditure (use of financial resources) in the period in which it occurs, as is the retirement of maturing long-term debt because both reduce the net financial assets of an expendable fund. Furthermore, because net income determination is not a consideration in most G&NP organizations, in expendable funds (1) inventory valuation may receive only passing attention, and (2) depreciation of fixed assets usually is not accounted for because it does not require the use of appropriable financial resources (expenditure) during the current period.

## Summary Comparison with Commercial Accounting

Though commercial-type accounting is employed where G&NP organizations are engaged in commercial-type activities (e.g., electric utilities), accounting and reporting for other G&NP endeavors have evolved largely in view of these key differences from profit-seeking enterprises:

1. **Objectives:** acquiring resources and expending them in a legal and appropriate manner, as opposed to seeking to increase, or even maintain, capital.
2. **Control:** substitution of statutory, fund, and budgetary controls in the absence of the supply and demand and profit regulator/control devices inherent in profit-seeking endeavors.

---

[5] Adapted from National Committee on Governmental Accounting, *Governmental Accounting, Auditing, and Financial Reporting* (Chicago: Municipal Finance Officers Association of the United States and Canada, 1968), p. 160.

These factors—objectives and control—underlie the major differences between commercial and G&NP accounting. The primary consideration in the G&NP environment is on **compliance and accountability**—and G&NP accounting, reporting, and auditing have developed principally as tools of compliance control and accountability demonstration.

The student should constantly note the similarities and differences between commercial and G&NP accounting in concept, approach, and terminology. Note, in particular, those cases where the same concepts and terms are used with different connotations. In G&NP accounting, for example:

1. The **accounting entity** concept relates to the separate fund or fund-type entities, not the organization as a whole; generally, there is no unified accounting entity for the organization in its entirety, which is referred to as the **reporting entity.**

2. The **periodicity** concept relates to the flow of financial resources during the year or other period and to budgetary comparisons, rather than to income determination, in **expendable funds;** it relates to income determination only in **nonexpendable funds.**

3. The **matching** concept as understood in commercial accounting is used similarly for commercial-type activities of G&NP organizations that are accounted for in nonexpendable funds. In all other cases reference is to matching revenues and expenditures—current operating, capital outlay, and debt retirement—and to matching **estimated (budgeted) and actual** revenues and expenditures. **Expendable fund accounting emphasizes the inflows, outflows, and balances of expendable financial resources rather than the determination of revenue, expense, and net income.**

4. The **going-concern** concept usually is considered relevant only when commercial-type or self-supporting activities are involved in G&NP organizations. **Expendable financial resource funds exist on a year-by-year or project-by-project basis and may be intentionally exhausted and "go out of business."**

## AUTHORITATIVE SOURCES OF G&NP ACCOUNTING PRINCIPLES AND REPORTING STANDARDS

Governmental and nonprofit accounting and reporting principles and standards have evolved separately from those for business enterprises. Furthermore, unique principles and standards have evolved separately for each of the several major types of G&NP organizations.

The National Council on Governmental Accounting and several similar predecessor committees led the formulation of accounting principles and standards for state and local governments until the Governmental Accounting Standards Board was created in 1984. The American Hospital Association and the Healthcare Financial Management Association fostered the development of accounting principles and standards for hospitals and other health care institutions; and the American Council on Education and the National Association of College and University Business Officers led the development of those for colleges and universities. Similarly, committees of the American Institute of Certified Public Accountants (AICPA) set forth accounting principles and standards for nonprofit organizations in AICPA audit and accounting guides. The Comptroller General of the United States led the federal government accounting standards effort until the Federal Accounting Standards Advisory Board (FASAB) was established in 1990. In addition, each G&NP field has its own journals, newsletters, and professional societies, and the Financial Accounting Standards Board (FASB) began issuing guidance for *nongovernmental* nonprofit organizations in 1993.

## Evolution of Separate Principles

The separation of business and G&NP accounting principles was formalized in the 1930s when the first accounting standards-setting bodies were established in the United States. The Securities Acts of 1933 and 1934 created the Securities and Exchange Commission (SEC), charged it with overseeing the financial reporting of business enterprises under its jurisdiction, and empowered the SEC to establish accounting and reporting standards for those business enterprises. The American Institute of Accountants (now the American Institute of Certified Public Accountants) then established a senior Committee on Accounting Procedure (CAP), the predecessor to the AICPA's Accounting Principles Board and the Financial Accounting Standards Board. The CAP made recommendations on business accounting and reporting issues, particularly those of concern to the SEC. Indeed, the SEC relied heavily on the CAP in determining what constituted generally accepted accounting principles (GAAP) for business enterprises. In view of its focus on business enterprise financial accounting and reporting, CAP pronouncements were accompanied by the following statement:

> The committee has not directed its attention to accounting problems or procedures of religious, charitable, scientific, educational, and similar non-profit institutions, municipalities, professional firms, and the like. Accordingly . . . its opinions and recommendations are directed primarily to business enterprises organized for profit.[6]

Although the Institute directed the CAP to concentrate on business accounting and reporting, AICPA leaders also recognized the need for nonbusiness accounting and reporting principles to be codified and further developed. Accordingly, the AICPA encouraged the appropriate college and university, hospital, and municipal professional organizations to sponsor committees similar to the CAP to focus on accounting and reporting concerns of those types of G&NP organizations. Thus, several separate G&NP accounting standards-setting bodies were established, each responsible for a specific subset of the G&NP sector. These committees and their successors developed distinctly different subsets of GAAP applicable to hospitals, colleges and universities, and state and local governments.

The AICPA's Accounting Principles Board (APB), which succeeded the CAP in 1959, likewise focused its attention on business enterprises. Only one of its pronouncements (*Opinion 20*, "Disclosure of Accounting Policies") was specifically directed to G&NP organizations as well as for-profit organizations.

## AICPA Audit and Accounting Guides

Several AICPA auditing committees studied the pronouncements of the various G&NP accounting standards bodies in depth in the course of preparing a series of audit guides during the late 1960s and early 1970s. Each of these audit guides—for state and local government, college and university, hospital, and voluntary health and welfare organization audits—recognized the principles set by the several G&NP standards-setting bodies as "authoritative." Although the AICPA audit guides took exception to certain G&NP principles or permitted alternative methods, all substantive differences between the AICPA committees and the various G&NP standards-setting bodies were resolved by the late 1970s.

The AICPA audit guides were of immense significance to the G&NP standards-setting process. Whereas the several G&NP standards-setting bodies had

---

[6] American Institute of Certified Public Accountants, *Accounting Research and Terminology Bulletins,* final ed. (New York: AICPA, 1961), p. 8.

functioned independently of the AICPA for 40 years, now G&NP accounting standards were in essence being established jointly by concurrence of the respective G&NP standards-setting bodies and their counterpart AICPA committees. Furthermore, the AICPA issued a Statement of Position in 1978 (SOP 78–10) setting forth its views with respect to what constituted generally accepted accounting principles and reporting practices for those other types of nonprofit organizations that did not have separate standards-setting bodies and audit guides. These are commonly referred to as other nonprofit organizations (ONP organizations, or ONPOs).

## The FASB

The Financial Accounting Standards Board (FASB), which succeeded the Accounting Principles Board (APB) in 1973, is financed and overseen by a multisponsored Financial Accounting Foundation rather than by the AICPA; and the seven FASB members serve full-time, whereas APB and Committee on Accounting Procedure (CAP) members served only part-time, as did members of the various G&NP accounting standards committees. The FASB was not limited by its original charter or rules of procedure to setting business accounting standards. Indeed, the AICPA recognized the FASB as the body authorized to establish accounting standards—elevating the FASB's authority above that of the several G&NP standards committees. Rule 203 of the AICPA Code of Professional Conduct thus required compliance with FASB pronouncements in virtually all circumstances.

The FASB devoted its efforts almost exclusively to business accounting concepts and standards during its first several years in operation, and deferred the decision on what role, if any, it would play in the G&NP standards area. By 1979, the FASB had decided to issue one or more statements of financial accounting concepts (such as SFAC 4 discussed earlier) but continued to defer the assumption of responsibility for G&NP accounting and reporting standards.

Later in 1979, the FASB agreed to exercise responsibility for all specialized accounting and reporting principles and practices set forth in AICPA statements of position, accounting guides, and audit guides except those dealing with state and local governments *(FASB Statement No. 32)*. The FASB designated the principles and practices described in the AICPA pronouncements—related to colleges and universities, hospitals, voluntary health and welfare organizations, and other nonprofit organizations—as "preferable." Furthermore, the FASB noted that it planned to extract them and issue them as FASB statements. Thereafter, the board would assume responsibility for amending and interpreting such standards in the future. The FASB's "specialized industry" action changed the roles of the AICPA and the various bodies that previously had set standards for nonprofit organizations (other than state and local governments) from setting standards to serving in an advisory capacity to the FASB standards-setting process. More recently, the FASB rescinded *FASB Statement No. 32* and issued standards for nongovernmental not-for-profit organization accounting and financial reporting (discussed in Chapter 18).

The FASB deferred action with respect to state and local government standards. Discussions were under way among representatives of interested organizations, including the National Council on Governmental Accounting and the AICPA, regarding the appropriate structure for setting governmental accounting standards. At issue was whether state and local government accounting standards should continue to be established by the National Council on Governmental Accounting or should be set by the FASB, or perhaps a new standards-setting body. These discussions led to formation of the Governmental Accounting Standards Board in 1984.

FIGURE 1–2 **Financial Reporting Standards-Setting Structure**

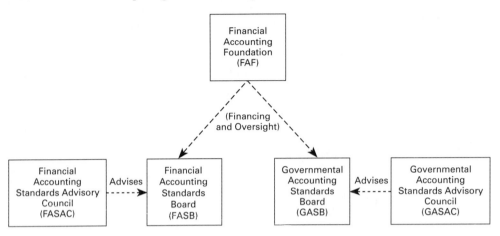

## The GASB

The Governmental Accounting Standards Board (GASB) succeeded the National Council on Governmental Accounting (NCGA) in 1984 as the body authorized to establish accounting standards for state and local governments. (See Figure 1–2.) The GASB is financed and overseen by the Financial Accounting Foundation (FAF), as is the Financial Accounting Standards Board (FASB); and the GASB, FASB, and FAF offices are in the same building in Norwalk, Connecticut. The **GASB** is responsible for establishing accounting standards for activities and transactions of **state and local governments;** the **FASB** sets accounting standards for **all other organizations.**

The GASB has seven members. The chairman serves full-time, whereas the six other members serve part-time. The Board is assisted by a full-time professional staff of about 12 persons, led by the director of research, and meets in open session for two to three days each month. The GASB mission statement is presented in Figure 1–3.

GASB activities center around its agenda topics and projects. While it is researching and analyzing topics, it may issue nonauthoritative invitations to comment, discussion memorandums, preliminary views, and exposure drafts—to obtain viewpoints of practitioners and others—before issuing an authoritative pronouncement. Its authoritative pronouncements are issued as Statements, Interpretations, Technical Bulletins, and Implementation Guides. The GASB issues an *Action Report* newsletter each month to inform interested persons of its activities, and also issues Concepts Statements, research studies, and other nonauthoritative publications from time to time.

GASB *Statement No. 1,* "Authoritative Status of NCGA Pronouncements and AICPA Industry Audit Guide," issued in 1984, provided a transition from the old standards-setting arrangements to the current one. *Statement 1* recognized the then effective NCGA pronouncements and certain accounting and reporting guidance in the then effective AICPA state and local government audit guide (ASLGU, 1974) as authoritative—stating that they are "continued in force until altered, amended, supplemented, revoked, or superseded by a subsequent GASB pronouncement."[7] These NCGA and AICPA pronouncements—now recognized

---

[7] Governmental Accounting Standards Board, *Statement No. 1,* "Authoritative Status of NCGA Pronouncements and AICPA Industry Audit Guide" (GASB, July 1984).

**FIGURE 1–3  The Mission of the Governmental Accounting Standards Board**

**Mission Statement**
The mission of the Governmental Accounting Standards Board is to establish and improve standards of state and local governmental accounting and financial reporting that will:

- Result in useful information for users of financial reports and
- Guide and educate the public, including issuers, auditors, and users of those financial reports.

**Uses and Users of Governmental Accounting and Financial Reporting**
Accounting and financial reporting standards are essential to the efficient and effective functioning of our democratic system of government:

a. Financial reporting plays a major role in fulfilling government's duty to be publicly accountable.
b. Financial reporting by state and local governments is used to assess that accountability and to make economic, social, and political decisions.

The primary users of state and local government financial reports are those:

a. To whom government is primarily accountable—its citizens,
b. Who directly represent the citizens—legislative and oversight bodies, and
c. Who finance government or who participate in the financing process—taxpayers, other governments, investors, creditors, underwriters, and analysts.

Government administrators are also users of financial reports; whether they are considered primary users depends on whether they have ready access to internal information.

**How the Mission Is Accomplished**
To accomplish its mission, the GASB acts to:

a. Issue standards that improve the usefulness of financial reports based on the needs of financial report users; the primary characteristics of understandability, relevance, and reliability; and the qualities of comparability and consistency.
b. Keep standards current to reflect changes in the governmental environment.
c. Provide guidance on implementation of standards.
d. Consider significant areas of accounting and financial reporting that can be improved through the standard-setting process.
e. Improve the common understanding of the nature and purposes of information contained in financial reports.

The GASB develops and uses concepts to guide its work of establishing standards. Those concepts provide a frame of reference, or conceptual framework, for resolving accounting and financial reporting issues. This framework helps to establish reasonable bounds for judgment in preparing and using financial reports; it also helps the public understand the nature and limitations of financial reporting.

The GASB's work on both concepts and standards is based on research conducted by the GASB staff and others. The GASB actively solicits and considers the views of its various constituencies on all accounting and financial reporting issues.

The GASB's activities are open to public participation and observation under the "due process" mandated by its Rules of Procedure.

**Guiding Principles**
In establishing concepts and standards, the GASB exercises its judgment after research, due process, and careful deliberation. It is guided by these principles:

- *To be objective and neutral in its decision making* and to ensure, as much as possible, that the information resulting from its standards is a faithful representation of the effects of state and local government activities. Objective and neutral mean freedom from bias, precluding the GASB from placing any particular interest above the interests of the many who rely on the information contained in financial reports.
- *To weigh carefully the views of its constituents* in developing concepts and standards so that they will:

  a. Meet the accountability and decision-making needs of the users of government financial reports, and
  b. Gain general acceptance among state and local government preparers and auditors of financial reports.

- *To establish standards only when the expected benefits exceed the perceived costs.* The GASB strives to determine that proposed standards (including disclosure requirements) fill a significant need and that the costs they impose, compared with possible alternatives, are justified when compared to the overall public benefit.
- *To consider the applicability of its standards* to the separately issued general purpose financial statements of governmentally owned special entities. The GASB specifically evaluates similarities of special entities and of their activities and transactions in both the public and private sectors, and the need, in certain instances, for comparability with the private sector.
- *To bring about needed changes in ways that minimize disruption of the accounting and financial reporting processes.* Reasonable effective dates and transition provisions are established when new standards are introduced. The GASB considers it desirable that change should be evolutionary to the extent that can be accommodated by the need for understandability, relevance, reliability, comparability, and consistency.
- *To review the effects of past decisions* and interpret, amend, or replace standards when appropriate.

**Due Process**
The GASB is committed to following an open, orderly process for standard setting. The GASB will endeavor at all times to keep the public informed of important developments in its operations and activities.

The due process procedures followed by the GASB are designed to permit timely, thorough, and open study of accounting and financial reporting issues. These procedures encourage broad public participation in the accounting standard-setting process and communication of all points of view and expressions of opinion at all stages of the process. The GASB recognizes that general acceptance of its conclusions is enhanced by demonstrating that the comments received in due process are considered carefully.

*Source:* GASB, *Facts About GASB: 1998.*

as GASB pronouncements—were integrated into one authoritative publication, *Codification of Governmental Accounting and Financial Reporting Standards,* in 1985.[8]

The GASB *Codification* is revised annually to incorporate subsequent GASB pronouncements, as is its companion *Original Pronouncements* volume that contains the complete text of all GASB and NCGA pronouncements. All of the GASB and predecessor literature is available also through the GASB Governmental Accounting Research System (GARS), a readily accessible personal computer disk search and retrieval system that is revised semiannually. The GASB also maintains an informative Internet home page <http://www.GASB.org/>.

## GAAP Hierarchy

The AICPA GAAP hierarchy indicates the relative authoritativeness of the various standards pronouncements and other literature on financial accounting and reporting principles and procedures. Level "a" pronouncements are the most authoritative, followed by the pronouncements and other guidance at levels "b," "c," and "d," respectively. The "other" accounting literature at level "e" is nonauthoritative but may be helpful guidance if no guidance is available at the higher levels of the hierarchy.

The state and local government (SLG) GAAP hierarchy—set forth in AICPA *Statement on Auditing Standards (SAS) No. 69,* "The Meaning of 'Fairly Presents' in the Auditors' Report"—is summarized in Figure 1–4.

---

**FIGURE 1–4  GAAP Hierarchy—State and Local Government Accounting and Financial Reporting**

a. 1. GASB Statements and Interpretations, *and*
   2. AICPA and FASB pronouncements that have been *made applicable to SLGs by GASB* Statements and Interpretations

b. 1. GASB Technical Bulletins, *and*
   2. AICPA Industry Audit and Accounting Guides and AICPA Statements of Position that are
      —specifically *made applicable* to SLGs by the AICPA *and*
      —*cleared* by the GASB

c. 1. Consensus positions of any GASB Emerging Issues Task Force (EITF) that may be established [*no* GASB EITF has been established], *and*
   2. AICPA Accounting Standards Executive Committee (AcSEC) Practice Bulletins *if*
      a. specifically *made applicable* to SLGs by the AcSEC, *and*
      b. *cleared* by the GASB

d. 1. GASB staff Implementation Guides (Question and Answer Guides), *and*
   2. Practices that are *widely recognized and prevalent* in SLGs.

e. Other accounting literature relevant in the circumstances—giving consideration to (1) its relevance to the particular circumstances, (2) the specificity of the guidance, and (3) the general recognition of the issuer or author as an authority.

---

*Source:* Adapted from AICPA, *Statement on Auditing Standards No. 69,* "The Meaning of 'Fairly Presents' in the Auditor's Report," January 1992.

---

[8] Governmental Accounting Standards Board and Governmental Accounting Research Foundation of the Government Finance Officers Association, *Codification of Governmental Accounting and Financial Reporting Standards as of November 1, 1984* (GASB, 1985).

FIGURE 1–5  **Definition of State and Local Government Entities Approved by the GASB and FASB for Use in AICPA Not-for-Profit and Health Care Audit Guides**

Governmental Organizations include [1] public corporations[1] and bodies corporate and politic, and [2] other organizations *if* they have *one or more of* the following characteristics:

- The popular election of officers or appointment (or approval) of a controlling majority of the members of the organization's governing body by officials of one or more state or local governments.

- The potential for unilateral dissolution by a government with the net assets reverting to a government.

- The power to enact and enforce a tax levy.

- The ability to issue directly (rather than through a state or municipal authority) debt that pays interest exempt from federal taxation.[2]

[1] *Black's Law Dictionary* defines a public corporation as: "An artificial person (e.g., [a] municipality or a governmental corporation) created for the administration of public affairs. Unlike a private corporation, it has no protection against legislative acts altering or even repealing its charter. Instrumentalities created by [the] state, formed or owned by it in [the] public interest, supported in whole or part by public funds, and governed by managers deriving their authority from [the] state. . . . A public corporation is an instrumentality of the state, founded and owned in the public interest, supported by public funds and governed by those deriving their authority from the state. . . ."

[2] However, organizations possessing only that ability (to issue tax-exempt debt) and none of the other governmental characteristics may rebut the presumption that they are governmental if their determination is supported by compelling, relevant evidence.

*Source:* Adapted from "FASB and GASB Define 'Government,'" *Journal of Accountancy,* July 1996, pp. 16–17.

Several points are particularly significant with respect to the SLG GAAP hierarchy:

1. Its guidance applies only to state and local government organizations—non-SLGs follow a similar GAAP hierarchy (in which "FASB" is substituted for "GASB").

2. GASB Statements and Interpretations are the highest-ranking authoritative pronouncements for SLGs, followed by certain AICPA guidance that has been cleared by the GASB and certain GASB staff guidance.

3. FASB Statements, Interpretations, and other guidance are not authoritative unless the GASB has recognized them as authoritative.

Most state and local governments—including states, counties, municipalities, townships, and school districts—clearly are "governments" that are subject to the SLG GAAP hierarchy. But it may be difficult to determine whether some not-for-profit and other organizations are government or nongovernment. Accordingly, the GASB and FASB jointly developed a definition of government. This definition— summarized in Figure 1–5—is published in AICPA audit and accounting guides to assist practitioners to determine whether organizations are government or nongovernment, and thus are under GASB jurisdiction or FASB jurisdiction.

## CONCLUDING COMMENTS

There continue to be several sources of authoritative pronouncements concerning G&NP accounting and financial reporting and several distinct subsets of GAAP applicable to the various types of G&NP organizations. This text is based on the most authoritative pronouncements relevant to each of the organizations discussed. Sources of authoritative support are cited throughout the text.

Accounting is often referred to as the "language" of business. It is also the "language" of government and nonprofit organizations. Whereas most terms and their meanings are the same in both, each has some of its own terms and occasionally uses a term with a different connotation than the other. Accordingly, new terms and the occasional use of a familiar term in an unfamiliar way should be noted carefully in reviewing this and later chapters.

State and local government budgeting, accounting, and financial reporting concepts, principles, standards, and procedures are discussed and illustrated in the next several chapters. Federal government accounting and reporting—and that for public sector and nonprofit hospitals, colleges and universities, and other nonprofit organizations—are discussed in later chapters, as is auditing in the G&NP organization environment.

## Questions

**Q 1-1** What characteristics differentiate G&NP organizations from profit-seeking entities?

**Q 1-2** List four factors that cause society to subject G&NP organizations to more stringent legal, regulatory, and other controls than it imposes on private businesses.

**Q 1-3** Discuss (a) the similarities in accounting for profit-seeking and G&NP organizations, and (b) the unique aspects of accounting for G&NP organizations designed to help ensure compliance with budgeted spending limits.

**Q 1-4** (a) Define *fund* as used in not-for-profit organizations. (b) Contrast that definition with the same term as used in a profit-seeking organization. (c) Does the creation of a fund constitute authority to spend or obligate its resources? Explain.

**Q 1-5** Distinguish between expendable funds and nonexpendable funds.

**Q 1-6** Discuss the funds-flow concept as it applies to the operations of G&NP organizations.

**Q 1-7** Contrast the terms *expense* and *expenditure*.

**Q 1-8** Contrast the following concepts as they are used in commercial and G&NP accounting; (a) accounting entity; (b) periodicity; (c) matching; (d) going concern.

**Q 1-9** It was noted in this chapter that most of the differences between commercial accounting and that for G&NP organizations result from differences in (a) organizational objectives and (b) methods of fiscal control employed. Explain.

**Q 1-10** Discuss the roles of the GASB, the FASB, and the AICPA in standards setting for G&NP organizations.

**Q 1-11** Legal and administrative constraints are society's tools for directing G&NP institutions in achieving their objectives. This results in a control of and accountability for expendable financial resources emphasis in G&NP organization accounting and reporting rather than an income determination emphasis. Explain why the profitability measure cannot provide this direction. Also, identify various legal and administrative control provisions unique to G&NP organizations and their impact on accounting and reporting for such organizations.

**Q 1-12** The revenues of profit-seeking organizations are based on user charges. Users may be charged for various services provided by G&NP organizations as well. However, differences often exist in the nature and purpose of user charges of G&NP organizations and those of profit-seeking organizations. Explain.

**Q 1-13** Different sets of accounting and reporting concepts, principles, and procedures have evolved for state and local governments, hospitals, colleges and universities, nonprofit organizations, and business enterprises. Given the differences between and among them, how can they all be considered "generally accepted accounting principles"?

**Q 1-14** (a) What is the purpose of the AICPA GAAP hierarchy guidelines? (b) How would an accountant or auditor use the hierarchy if the guidance given in a GASB Statement and an AICPA audit and accounting guide regarding the proper accounting treatment of a state government transaction or event conflicts?

**Q 1-15**  How can one determine whether a specific not-for-profit organization should follow GASB guidance? FASB guidance?

## Problems

**P 1-1**  Indicate the best answer for each of the following:

1. The body with primary accounting standards-setting authority for state and local governments is the
   a. American Institute of Certified Public Accountants.
   b. Financial Accounting Standards Board.
   c. Government Finance Officers Association.
   d. Governmental Accounting Standards Board.
   e. U.S. General Accounting Office.
2. The body with primary accounting standards-setting authority for colleges and universities is the
   a. National Association of College and University Business Officers.
   b. Financial Accounting Standards Board.
   c. Governmental Accounting Standards Board.
   d. Governmental Accounting Standards Board for governmental colleges and universities and the Financial Accounting Standards Board for all other colleges and universities.
   e. U.S. Department of Education.
3. An expendable fund accounting entity
   a. is often useful in accounting for general government activities but is optional (expendable).
   b. includes only current financial resources and related liabilities and depreciable (expendable) fixed assets. Nondepreciable fixed assets are not reported in expendable funds.
   c. includes only financial resources and liabilities to be repaid from those resources.
   d. has its operating activities measured and reported in terms of revenues and expenses, but the timing of expense recognition differs from that in similar business organizations.
4. In which of the following situations would the amount of expense and expenditure for the period differ?
   a. An entity uses and is billed for utilities but has paid only half of the amount billed at year end.
   b. An entity purchases equipment by issuing a 90-day note that matures in the next period. The purchase occurred on the last day of the fiscal year.
   c. Interest accrued, but was not paid, on a nine-month note payable.
   d. Salaries and wages incurred and paid during the period were $100,000. Additional salaries and wages accrued at year end were $4,000.
   e. The amount of expense and expenditure to be recognized differs in more than one of the preceding situations.
5. Legally adopted budgets of expendable funds of governments are
   a. fixed-dollar budgets which establish expenditure limits that are not to be exceeded.
   b. fixed budgets that cannot be modified during the budget year.
   c. flexible budgets in which the expenditure limits are automatically modified to reflect larger than budgeted levels of various services.
   d. always adopted using the same basis of accounting required by GAAP.
6. Which of the following statements is false? A fund
   a. is an entity for which financial statements can be prepared.
   b. has a self-encompassing, self-balancing accounting equation.
   c. is used to account for a subset of an organization's resources that is to be used for a specific purpose or to achieve a particular objective.

      d. is an accounting entity that is used for one year only. Each year a new set of funds must be established.

      e. None of the above is false.

7. Under SAS 69, with respect to financial reporting for state and local governments, the FASB Statements of Financial Accounting Standards are:

      a. More authoritative than Statements of the GASB.

      b. More authoritative than Statements of Position of the AICPA that have not been "cleared" by the GASB.

      c. More authoritative than GASB Technical Bulletins.

      d. More authoritative than the AICPA state and local government audit guide.

      e. None of the above is true.

      f. None of the above is true unless the GASB has "adopted" the FASB Statement.

8. One unique characteristic of most government and nonprofit organizations is that:

      a. A primary source of financing is sales of services and goods to customers.

      b. Their constituency automatically dictates what the government or nonprofit organization's resources are (to be) used to accomplish.

      c. There is no direct relationship between the amount of goods or services that most resource providers receive and the amount of resources provided by each individual.

      d. These entities sometimes have restrictions placed on what their resources may be used for, whereas such restrictions cannot be placed on business resources.

9. Organizations that are considered to be nonprofit include such organizations as:

      a. Churches

      b. The Boy Scouts and Girl Scouts

      c. Church-supported hospitals

      d. State CPA societies

      e. All of the above

10. A key underlying difference between government or nonprofit organizations and business entities is:

      a. Businesses have scarce resources that must be allocated to different uses; governments and nonprofits are able to command sufficient resources to avoid the need for such allocations.

      b. The absence of the profit motive in most government and nonprofit organizations.

      c. The amount of restricted resources held by governments and nonprofits.

      d. The use of fund accounting by governments and nonprofits.

**P 1-2** (Expenditures vs. Expenses) Family Services, a small social service nonprofit agency, began operations on January 1, 19X1 with $40,000 cash and $150,000 of equipment, on which $60,000 was owed on a note to City Bank. The equipment was expected to have a remaining useful life of 15 years with no salvage value. During its first year of operations ending December 31, 19X1, Family Services paid or accrued the following:

1. Salaries and other personnel costs, $100,000
2. Rent, utilities, and so on, $24,000
3. Debt service—interest, $5,500, and payment on note principal, $10,000
4. Capital outlay—additional equipment purchased January 3, $30,000, expected to last six (6) years and have a $6,000 salvage value
5. Other, $10,500

There were no prepayals or unrecorded accruals at December 31, 19X1, and no additional debt was incurred during the year.

**Required** Compute for the Family Services agency, for the year ended December 31, 19X1, its total (a) expenses and (b) expenditures.

**P 1-3** (Statement of Revenues and Expenditures—Worksheet) Hatcher Township prepares its annual General Fund budget on the cash basis and maintains its accounting records on the cash basis during the year. At the end of Hatcher Township's 19X9 calendar year you determine the following:

| General Fund | Budget (Cash) Basis | | Accruals | |
|---|---|---|---|---|
| | **Budget** | **Actual** | *1/1/X9* | *12/31/X9* |
| Revenues: | | | | |
| Taxes | $600,000 | $595,000 | $  — | $ 6,000 |
| Licenses | 200,000 | 206,000 | — | — |
| Intergovernmental | 100,000 | 110,000 | 9,000 | 1,000 |
| Other | 50,000 | 45,000 | 5,000 | — |
| | 950,000 | 956,000 | 14,000 | 7,000 |
| Expenditures: | | | | |
| Salaries | 700,000 | 704,000 | 17,000 | 11,000 |
| Utilities | 80,000 | 85,000 | — | — |
| Supplies | 70,000 | 64,000 | — | 7,000 |
| Equipment | 60,000 | 58,000 | 2,000 | 12,000 |
| Other | 30,000 | 31,000 | — | — |
| | 940,000 | 942,000 | 19,000 | 30,000 |
| Excess of Revenues Over (Under) Expenditures | $ 10,000 | $ 14,000 | | |

**Required** (1) Prepare a worksheet to derive a GAAP basis (including accruals) statement of revenues and expenditures for the Hatcher Township General Fund for the 19X9 fiscal year.

(2) Might the readers of the budgetary basis and GAAP basis statements get different impressions of the 19X9 operating results of the Hatcher Township General Fund? Explain.

**P 1-4** (SLG GAAP Hierarchy) Mark O. Sleuth, a recent accounting graduate, has been assigned to research several local government accounting and financial reporting issues. Help him rank the several possible sources of guidance he has located for each issue.

1. Issue 1: The AICPA state and local government (SLG) Audit and Accounting Guide, a GASB Technical Bulletin, a leading governmental accounting textbook, a GASB Interpretation, and a FASB Statement.

2. Issue 2: A leading governmental accounting textbook, a GASB Implementation Guide, an article in a leading auditing journal, and a speech by a leading governmental accounting professor.

3. Issue 3: The AICPA SLG Audit and Accounting Guide, a GASB Statement, a journal article that summarizes current practice on the issue in the United States, notes from a telephone conversation on the issue with the GASB director of research, and a FASB Interpretation.

4. Issue 4: An AICPA Statement of Position (cleared by the GASB), an article by the managing partner of an international public accounting firm, a GASB Technical Bulletin, and a FASB Technical Bulletin.

5. Issue 5: The GASB Codification (section on an Implementation Guide), the AICPA SLG Audit and Accounting Guide, four articles from the *Journal of Accountancy,* and a leading governmental accounting textbook.

**P 1-5** (Internet Resources) Locate the home pages for the following organizations and prepare a brief critique (one to three pages, perhaps with attachments) of the contents of each site:

1. Governmental Accounting Standards Board
2. Financial Accounting Standards Board
3. American Institute of Certified Public Accountants

**P 1-6** (Internet Resources) Locate and critique at least six Internet sites (other than those in P 1-5) that may be of informational value to G&NP accountants. Include attachments (e.g., copies of selected pages) as appropriate.

# CHAPTER

# 2

# STATE AND LOCAL GOVERNMENT ACCOUNTING

## Environment, Objectives, and Principles

State and local government is truly "big business." The 50 states and 85,000 local governments within these United States employ more than 15 million persons—over four times as many as are employed by the federal government—and spend about $1 trillion annually. Although the federal government accounts for over half of all government expenditures, state and local governments spend more for nondefense purposes than the federal government. Furthermore, state and local government revenues, expenditures, debt, and employment—both total and per capita—have been increasing at higher rates than those of the federal complex in recent years. Today the state government often is the largest industry within a state, and city hall often houses the biggest business in a town.

The types and numbers of local governments are shown in Figure 2–1. However, the extent of local government jurisdictional overlap is not obvious from that figure. It is common for a given geographic area to be served by a municipality, a school district, a county, and one or more special districts. In fact, many metropolitan areas have 100 or more separate and distinct local government units.

State and local governments have increased both the types and levels of goods and services provided to their citizens in recent years, and many governments have become among the most complex and diversified organizations in ex-

FIGURE 2–1

### Types of Local Governments

| | |
|---|---:|
| Counties | 3,043 |
| Municipalities | 19,279 |
| Townships | 16,656 |
| School districts | 14,422 |
| Special districts | 31,555 |
| Total | 84,955 |

*Source:* U.S. Department of Commerce, number of active governments as of 1/1/92.

istence. No doubt their scope and complexity—as well as their relative importance in our economy and society—will continue to grow as our society becomes increasingly urban and governments at all levels attempt to meet the demands of their constituencies for more and better goods and services.

Two major topics are covered in this introductory chapter to state and local government (SLG) accounting and reporting:

- The SLG environment and the objectives of SLG financial reporting
- The GASB principles (standards) of SLG accounting and financial reporting

Although both topics are important, the "principles" section—which includes "Transaction Analysis and Fund Accounting" discussions and illustrations—is particularly important to understanding SLG accounting and financial reporting.

# ENVIRONMENT AND OBJECTIVES

The discussions of the government and nonprofit (G&NP) organization environment, objectives of G&NP accounting and financial reporting, and characteristics of G&NP accounting in Chapter 1 deal with G&NP organizations generally. This section builds on those discussions and considers similar factors from the state and local government (SLG) perspective, as set forth in GASB *Concepts Statement No. 1*, "Objectives of Financial Reporting." The primary purposes of this section are to

- help the reader understand the most significant features of the SLG environment and how they have influenced the development of SLG accounting and financial reporting objectives, concepts, principles, and standards—particularly when they differ from those of business enterprises; and
- provide background necessary for the reader to understand and apply the GASB's basic principles, which are discussed in the next section of this chapter.

This section is drawn, with permission, primarily from GASB *Concepts Statement No. 1*, "Objectives of Financial Reporting."[1] The environment of SLG accounting and reporting is considered first, followed by a discussion of the users and uses of SLG financial reports. A summary of the objectives of SLG external financial reporting in GASB *Concepts Statement No. 1* concludes this section.

One unique aspect of the SLG environment is that governments may be involved in **both** governmental-type and business-type activities. **Governmental-type activities** include fire and police protection, the courts, and other "general governmental" activities, whereas **business-type activities** include public utilities (e.g., electricity, water) and other activities for which user fees are charged and that are operated similarly to private businesses. The environments of governmental-type and business-type activities may differ, even within one government, as may financial statement user information needs. Thus, the SLG environment, financial statement users, and user information needs are discussed first for governmental-type activities and then are compared with those of business-type activities.

## Environment—Governmental-Type Activities

The governmental-type activity environment is unique in several respects. These include distinctive SLG:

---

[1] Governmental Accounting Standards Board, *Codification of Governmental Accounting and Financial Reporting Standards as of June 30, 1997* (GASB, 1997), Appendix B. Hereafter cited as GASB *Codification.*

1. purpose
2. sources of resources
3. mechanisms for allocating financial resources for various uses
4. accountabilities
5. reporting complexities

### Purpose

A government's primary reason for existence—particularly for its governmental-type activities—differs from that of business enterprises. The key objective and rationale for the existence of businesses is to earn a profit. But the primary goal for governmental-type activities is to provide goods or services that its constituency has agreed should be available to all who need them. These services often are provided without regard to the *individual* service recipient's ability to pay for the goods or services.

Absence of the profit motive in governmental-type activities underlies several other differences between governments and businesses. For instance, the basic performance evaluation measure in business—net income—does not apply to governmental-type activities. Consequently, governments do not attract significant resources for governmental-type activities from

a. investors in equity securities who expect an equity-type return on their investment, or

b. service charges to individual users of SLG services in proportion to the services used.

Because proportionate service charges are not a key source of general government financial resources, the uses of government resources are not automatically allocated to the services for which individual users are willing and able to pay. Indeed, financial resources provided by one person or group may be used to finance services for another person or group. Thus, the market supply and demand allocation mechanism does not function as it does for business.

### Sources of Financial Resources

Because the primary sources of financial resources of businesses are not available to governments for governmental-type activities, governments must raise financial resources from other sources. Two primary examples of these revenue sources are taxes and intergovernmental grants and subsidies.

**Taxation**    The power to tax is unique to governments—and most governmental-type SLG services are financed by taxes. Most general government services—for example, police and fire protection, elementary and secondary education, and streets and highways—usually are financed almost exclusively by tax revenues. Indeed, even when SLGs charge fees for general government services, they often must be subsidized with tax revenues (e.g., many public health clinics).

The power to tax causes taxpayers to be *involuntary* resource providers. Individual taxpayers cannot refuse to pay taxes if they think the government is using the resources improperly, or pay a lesser amount if they do not use as many of the government's services as do others. Rather, the amount of taxes a taxpayer must pay is based on the value of the taxpayer's real and/or personal property (property taxes), the amount of income earned (income taxes), or retail purchases (sales taxes), and so forth—not on the amount or value of services received.

Thus, taxation is a nonexchange transaction or event that eliminates any direct association between

1. the amount and quality of the services a constituent receives from the government, and
2. the amount the constituent pays to the government.

This absence of the market resource allocation mechanism makes it difficult to measure the success of a governmental unit in financial terms.

Many governments also have other powers—similar to taxation—to levy license and permit fees, fines, and other charges. This ability of governments to exact resources from individuals, businesses, and others by taxation and similar levies—without an arm's-length exchange transaction—means that the types, levels, and quality of services that a government provides are not automatically dictated or regulated by what its constituents are willing to pay for the services.

**Intergovernmental Revenues** Grants and subsidies from higher-level governments are another significant source of SLG revenues. The federal government provides several hundred billions of dollars of revenues to SLGs every year and states provide still more resources for local governments. These intergovernmental revenues are not provided as a direct result of services received by the resource provider, but to help finance certain services for the recipient's constituency.

### Resource Allocation Mechanisms

General government resource allocations are derived from processes clearly different from business enterprises. Absence of a direct relationship between the resources provided by an individual taxpayer and the services provided to that individual taxpayer makes it impossible for the resource allocations to be made in the same manner as for business enterprises. Rather, for the most part, the nature of the U.S. system of governance determines how the allocations are made.

**Restrictions on Resource Use** The primary mechanism used for allocating general government resources to various uses is for restrictions to be placed on financial resource use by the resource providers or their representatives. One level of restriction is a broad restriction requiring that certain resources be used for a particular purpose(s) or program(s). Such restrictions arise as a result of:

- Intergovernmental grantors requiring that the resources provided be used for a particular purpose.
- Taxes and similar resources being levied for a specific purpose, such as for roads, education, or debt service.
- Debt proceeds being restricted to a specific purpose(s).

These numerous broad restrictions are the primary reason for the use of funds and account groups—to account for resources segregated according to the purpose(s) for which they may or must be used. The GASB recognizes the importance of the governmental fund structure and the fund accounting control mechanism in the SLG environment, observing that funds and fund accounting controls:

- complement the budgetary process and annual budget in assuring that a government uses its financial resources in compliance with both external restrictions and the annual budget, and
- facilitate fulfilling the SLG's accountability to its constituency, grantors, and so on.

**The Budget** Taxes and other revenues are allocated to various uses by placing more detailed restrictions on their use as well. Theoretically, this could be accomplished by taxpayers meeting and deciding as a group how the various resources are to be used. However, in our representative form of government citizens have delegated that power to public officials through the election process. Too, a system of checks and balances over the potential abuse of power is provided by the separation of powers among the executive, legislative, and judicial branches of government.

These more detailed restrictions thus are placed on the use of resources by elected officials through the budget process. The budget is adopted into law and essentially becomes a contract between the executive branch, the legislative branch, and the citizenry. In most jurisdictions, significant changes in this budget contract should be made only through a process similar to the budget process itself. In the budget process:

- The executive branch typically prepares a proposed budget and submits appropriation requests to the legislative branch.
- The legislative branch has the power to approve those requests, thus authorizing the executive branch to make expenditures within the limits of the appropriations and any laws that may affect programs covered by those appropriations.
- The executive branch is accountable to the legislative branch for operating within those appropriations and laws, and both branches are accountable to the citizenry.

The annual budgetary process and budget are extremely important in the SLG governmental-type activities environment. The budget is an expression of public policy and intent. It also is a financial plan that indicates the proposed expenditures for the year and the means of financing them.

Moreover, an *adopted* budget has the force of law. It *both:*

- *authorizes* amounts to be expended for various specified purposes, *and*
- *limits* (or restricts) the amount that may be expended for each of those purposes. (Budgetary limitations generally cannot be exceeded without due process.)

Thus, the budget is both a form of control and a basis for evaluating performance in a budgetary context. Accordingly, a government must demonstrate its budgetary accountability, which entails reporting whether revenues were obtained and expended as anticipated, and whether authorized expenditure limitations (appropriations) were exceeded.

Furthermore, establishing the budget—determining the types and amounts of taxes and other revenues to be exacted from the citizenry and how those resources will be used—is one of the most important functions that elected representatives perform. Indeed, the citizenry's perception of a representative's budgetary process performance is a significant factor in voting decisions. Hence, the budget process is a vital part of the political process.

### Accountabilities

The numerous environmental features discussed earlier result in distinct SLG accountabilities, which are unique both in terms of (1) to whom SLGs and their officials are accountable and (2) the focuses of their accountability.

**To Whom Accountable**     The need for accountability exists between (1) SLGs and their constituencies, (2) SLGs and other governments, and (3) the SLG's own legislative and executive bodies.

SLGs are accountable to their constituencies for various reasons. Elected officials are in essence empowered by citizens to act on their behalf. Elected officials are evaluated by voters in part on their fiscal and budgetary performance as well as on the perceived efficiency and effectiveness with which the SLG is operated. SLG officials must demonstrate to citizens that revenues or bond proceeds approved for specific purposes were in fact used for those purposes.

The SLG's accountability to other governments arises in part because senior levels of government often have some oversight authority over lower levels of government. It also results when other governments provide grants or other intergovernmental subsidies to the SLG.

Finally, one need for accountability between each SLG's legislative and executive bodies focuses on demonstrating that the budget contract has been complied with and that resources have been used efficiently and effectively.

**Accountability Focuses**     SLG accountabilities have various focuses such as accountability for:

- The use of financial resources from various revenue sources or bond issues in accordance with any restrictions on their use.
- Compliance with the budget.
- Efficient and effective use of SLG resources.
- Maintaining general government capital assets.

### Reporting Problems

The characteristics of the SLG general government environment also create problems that must be dealt with in SLG financial reporting and/or auditing, including:

1. The need to demonstrate compliance with restrictions on the use of financial resources.
2. The need for appropriate budgetary reporting.
3. The impact of restrictions on the use of financial resources (such as from intergovernmental grants) on revenue recognition.
4. The difficulty of measuring and reporting the efficiency and effectiveness of SLGs in providing services.
5. The opportunity to hide or disguise the use or availability of resources for various purposes by (a) improper reporting of transactions between the various SLG accounting entities—funds and account groups—and (b) the misuse of funds by developing an inappropriate fund structure.
6. The lack of comparability that can result between financial reports of two similarly designated governments that perform different functions (which is common in SLGs).
7. The existence of taxation and debt limits.
8. The impact on materiality and reporting judgments caused by (a) overexpenditure of appropriations being a violation of law and (b) failure to follow technical conditions related to intergovernmental revenues, possibly requiring forfeiture of such revenues or loss of future revenues.

Furthermore, financial reporting for governments must be responsive to the temptations that result because the budget process is a vital part of the political process. Elected representatives serve for relatively short terms, and officials may be tempted to employ practices that permit a budget to be technically in balance under many budgetary bases of accounting—including the commonly used cash basis—even when there may not be true budgetary equilibrium.

Accordingly, to appropriately reflect the degree of budgetary equilibrium, the GASB notes that financial reporting should indicate the extent to which:

- current operations were financed by nonrecurring revenues or by incurring long-term liabilities, and

- certain essential costs, such as normal maintenance of government fixed assets, have been deferred to future periods.

This final reporting problem is particularly significant because, as the GASB notes:

> Governmental entities invest large amounts of resources in non-revenue-producing capital assets such as government office buildings, highways, bridges, and sidewalks. Most governmental capital assets have relatively long lives, and an adequate program of maintenance and rehabilitation is needed to ensure that those estimated useful lives will be realized. That is, governments, in essence, *have an implicit commitment to maintain their capital assets,* whether or not they are used directly to produce revenues.[2]

Revenue-producing fixed assets must be maintained in order to continue generating that revenue. But failure to maintain non-revenue-producing capital assets does not affect a government's revenues currently. Indeed, deferring maintenance of its fixed assets can make more financial resources available currently for expenditure for other purposes. However, this practice also causes higher maintenance costs in later years, reduces the useful lives of the fixed assets, or both. Those consequences usually are not apparent until later years, however, and, even then, the resultant additional costs and taxes are not always blamed on the inappropriate maintenance in earlier years.

Governments have an implicit commitment to maintain their capital assets, even if they are not used directly to produce revenues. Thus, maintenance programs should not be neglected because of the competition for limited resources.

## Users of Financial Reports—Governmental-Type Activities

The GASB originally identified three groups of primary users of external financial reports of SLGs,[3] and added a fourth group in its mission statement (Figure 1–3).

1. **The citizenry:** those to whom the government is primarily accountable—including citizens (taxpayers, voters, service recipients), the media, advocate groups, and public finance researchers
2. **Legislative and oversight bodies:** those who directly represent the citizens—including members of state legislatures, county commissions, city councils, boards of trustees and school boards, and executive branch officials with oversight responsibility over other levels of government
3. **Investors and creditors:** those who lend or participate in the lending process—including individual and institutional investors and creditors, municipal security underwriters, bond rating agencies, bond insurers, and financial institutions

The needs of intergovernmental grantors and other users are considered by the GASB to be encompassed within those of these three primary user groups. Furthermore, internal executive branch managers usually have ready access to the SLG's financial information through internal reports—and are not considered primary users of external financial reports. However, if this is not the case, a fourth primary user group is:

4. **Government administrators:** internal executive branch managers—if they do not have ready access to the government's internal information.

---

[2] Ibid., Appen. B, par. 26, emphasis added.
[3] Ibid., Appen. B, pars. 30–31.

## Uses of Financial Reports—Governmental-Type Activities

The GASB notes that financial reporting should provide information useful in making economic and political decisions and in assessing accountability by:[4]

**1.** Comparing actual financial results with the legally adopted budget.

**2.** Assessing financial condition and results of operations.

**3.** Assisting in determining compliance with finance-related laws, rules, and regulations.

**4.** Assisting in evaluating efficiency and effectiveness.

## Environment, Users, and Uses—Business-Type Activities

In contrast to SLG governmental-type activities, a government's business-type activities:

- Provide the same types of services as private-sector businesses.

- Involve exchange relationships—that is, the consumer is charged a fee for services received, and there is a direct relationship between the services provided and the fee charged the consumer.

- Are often separate, legally constituted, self-sufficient organizations—though some resemble governmental-type activities because they are regularly subsidized by the SLG or are operated as departments of the SLG.

### Environment

The GASB contrasts the general government environmental factors discussed earlier with those for the SLG's business-type activities.[5]

**The Relationship between Services Received and Resources Provided by the Consumer** The financial resources raised by general government activities usually are not derived from the specific services rendered. (For example, there is no specific charge for public safety services; they are financed along with many other services from general property or income taxes.) However, business-type activities often involve a direct relationship between the charge and the service. In that relationship—termed an *exchange relationship*—a user fee is charged for a specific service provided, for example, a toll for use of a road, a charge for water, or a fare to ride the bus.

This exchange relationship in a business-type setting causes users of financial reports to focus on measuring the costs (or financial resource outflows, or both) of providing the service, the revenues obtained from the service, and the difference between the two. The difference is particularly important because it may affect future user charges.

Measurement of both the cost of services and financial resource outflows is useful. Whether one is more important than the other depends on various factors, including the way in which user charges are calculated and whether or not subsidies are provided by the general government.

Cost of services information is useful for public policy decisions. For example, the amount a business-type activity charges for its services may be based on recovery of all costs. In other cases, capital assets may be provided by direct subsidies (from the SLG's general government resources or from intergovernmental grants) and therefore not included in calculating user charges. However, in both cases, financial statement users need to know the full cost of operating the business-

---

[4] Ibid., Appen. B, par. 32.

[5] Ibid., Appen. B, pars. 43–50.

type activity; the financial implications of the subsidies or grants need to be understood. At the same time, information about financial resource flows is also useful. For example, user charges may be based on resource flows rather than costs; subsidies from the general government may be based on net cash outflows rather than the net operating deficit after depreciation.

**Revenue-Producing Capital Assets**    Most capital assets of business-type activities are revenue producing. Therefore, the incentive for business-type activities to defer needed maintenance may not be as great as that for governmental-type activities. However, when business-type activities receive general government subsidies, they need to compete for financial resources with governmental-type activities and are subject to the same constraints.

**Similarly Designated Activities and Potential for Comparison**    Governmental business-type activities often perform only a single function. If the function is supplying water, for example, the problems, procedures, and cost elements of obtaining, treating, and delivering it are similar, regardless of whether the function is performed by a private-sector business, a public authority, an Enterprise Fund, or as an activity financed by the government's General Fund. As a result, there is normally a greater potential for comparability among business-type activities performing similar functions than among governmental-type activities, which vary from government to government.

**The Nature of the Political Process**    Some governmental business-type activities are designed to be insulated from the political process—they are not part of the general governmental budgetary process, they have a direct relationship between fees and services rendered, and they are separate, legally constituted agencies. In some instances, however, this insulation from the political process has less substance than appearances suggest. Indeed, especially in subsidized activities, rate setting—even by independent boards—is political in nature. For example, charging mass transit users sufficient fares to pay all costs of the system may be politically or economically undesirable—so subsidies are provided from general tax revenues or grants from other jurisdictions. If operating or capital subsidies are provided, the influences of the political process often are as significant as in governmental-type activities.

**Budgets and Fund Accounting**    The use of multiple-fund accounting and fixed budgets is less common for business-type activities than for governmental-type activities. Unless the business-type activity is operated as a governmental department, budgetary processes and budgets often are internal management processes and tools that lack the force of law. Similarly, because business-type organizations often perform a single function, multiple-fund accounting is not as common as it is in governmental-type activities.

### Users and Uses of Financial Reports

Several similarities and differences between the users and uses of financial reports on the SLG's business-type activities, compared with reports covering its governmental-type activities, are noted in GASB *Concepts Statement No. 1.*[6]

- The users and uses of governmental financial reports typically are essentially the same regardless of whether the activity is business type or governmental type. However, the users and uses of financial reports for business-type activities may differ depending on whether the activity reports separately or as part of a broader general government.

---

[6] Ibid., Appen. B, pars. 51 and 53–55, adapted.

- The uses of financial reports of business-type activities generally differ only in emphasis from the uses of financial reports of governmental-type activities. Users of separate financial reports of business-type activities are concerned primarily with the financial condition and results of operations for that activity; they are often not concerned with comparing actual results with budgeted amounts.

- Investors and creditors are concerned primarily with whether the business-type activity is generating, and will continue to generate, sufficient cash to meet debt service requirements. And many investors and creditors are as concerned with compliance with bond provisions by business-type activities as they are about compliance by governmental-type activities.

- Citizen groups and consumers may use results of operations information primarily to assess the reasonableness of user charges. Legislative and oversight officials and executive branch officials review financial reports of business-type activities from both cash flow and user charge reasonableness perspectives. Legislative and oversight officials also use financial reports to assess the potential need to subsidize the activity with general governmental revenues, or the potential to subsidize the general government with business-type activity resources.

- Both citizen groups and legislative and oversight officials need information about effectiveness, economy, and efficiency, particularly because that information has an effect on user charges.

- Finally, all user groups may be concerned with the relationship between the financial position and operating results of the business-type activity and that of the government as a whole—particularly if the business-type activity is subsidized by, or subsidizes, the general government.

## Objectives of Financial Reporting

Financial reporting objectives set forth what SLG financial statements should accomplish. GASB *Concepts Statement No. 1,* "Objectives of Financial Reporting," does not establish GAAP standards, however, but describes concepts to be used by the GASB as a framework for evaluating present standards and practices and for establishing financial reporting standards in the future.

The GASB notes that its financial reporting objectives are intended to describe broadly the nature of information needed to meet the needs of users of SLG external financial reports, giving consideration to the SLG environment. Furthermore, the GASB concluded that there are no major differences in the financial reporting objectives of governmental-type and business-type activities, though the objectives may apply in differing degrees and with differing emphases to governmental-type and business-type activities of SLGs. For example, budgetary comparisons may be less important in business-type activities, but cost of services information may be more important.

Briefly stated, the GASB concluded in its "Objectives" Concepts Statement that accountability is the "cornerstone"—the paramount objective—of government financial reporting and that interperiod equity is a significant part of accountability. Moreover, the GASB concluded that governmental financial reporting should provide information to assist users in (1) assessing accountability and in (2) making economic, social, and political decisions. Accordingly, SLG financial reporting should provide:

1. A means of demonstrating the SLG's accountability that enables users to assess that accountability. Specifically, the information provided should:
   a. Permit users to determine whether current-year revenues were sufficient to pay for the current year's services and/or whether future-years' citizens must assume burdens for services previously provided.

    b. Demonstrate the SLG's budgetary accountability and compliance with other finance-related legal and contractual requirements.

    c. Assist users in assessing the SLG's service efforts, costs, and accomplishments.

**2.** Information necessary to evaluate the SLG's operating results for the period, including information:

    a. About the sources and uses of financial resources.

    b. On how the SLG financed its activities and met its cash requirements.

    c. Necessary to determine whether the SLG's financial condition improved or deteriorated during the year.

**3.** Information necessary to assess the level of SLG services and its ability to continue to finance its activities and meet its obligations, including:

    a. Information about the SLG's financial position and condition.

    b. Information about the SLG's physical and other nonfinancial resources having useful lives that extend beyond the current year—including information that can be used to assess their service potential.

    c. Disclosure of (1) legal and contractual restrictions on the use of resources and (2) risks of potential loss of resources.[7]

# THE GASB PRINCIPLES

As the GASB indicates in introducing its *Codification of Governmental Accounting and Financial Reporting Standards,* governmental accounting entails many of the same basic concepts, conventions, and characteristics as business accounting. However, the basic objectives of business and government differ. Not surprisingly then, the manner in which we report on each type of entity's progress toward its objectives also differs.

Consequently, the basic accounting and financial reporting principles for government entail many notable differences from those principles that apply to business activities. As noted earlier, those principles applicable to SLGs are established by the GASB. Many of the characteristics of governmental accounting and most of the GASB's guidance relate to the use of multiple-fund accounting entities and account groups to account for and report upon a state or local government. Most other features and GASB authoritative guidance are associated with the general government activities and transactions.

The GASB has to date focused its attention primarily on general government activities and transactions that are accounted for in governmental (expendable) funds and in nonfund account groups for general government fixed assets and long-term debt. The public enterprise and other business-type activities of state and local governments are accounted for in proprietary (nonexpendable) funds using business accounting methods. Indeed, relevant FASB standards usually are applied in accounting for the business-type activities.

The twelve basic GASB principles are divided into the following seven groups for ease of discussion: (1) GAAP and legal compliance, (2) fund accounting, (3) fixed assets and long-term liabilities, (4) basis of accounting, (5) the budget and budgetary accounting, (6) classification and terminology, and (7) financial reporting.

## GAAP and Legal Compliance

Governments must comply with the many legal and contractual requirements, regulations, restrictions, and agreements that affect their financial management and

---

[7] Ibid., Appen. B, pars. 77–79.

accounting; and such compliance must be demonstrable and reported upon regularly. Compliance is necessary even though legal requirements may be archaic, useless, or even detrimental to sound financial management. Governments should also prepare financial statements in conformity with generally accepted accounting principles (GAAP), which provide uniform minimum national standards of and guidelines to financial reporting.

Whereas business accounting systems must provide data both for GAAP reporting and for income tax reporting, the first GASB principle recognizes that governmental accounting systems must provide data both for reporting in conformity with GAAP and for controlling and reporting on finance-related legal compliance matters.

### PRINCIPLE 1
### ACCOUNTING AND REPORTING CAPABILITIES

A governmental accounting system must make it possible both (a) to present fairly and with full disclosure the financial position and results of financial operations of the funds and account groups of the governmental unit in conformity with generally accepted accounting principles and (b) to determine and demonstrate compliance with finance-related legal and contractual provisions.

In some instances the only finance-related legal compliance provision is that the government prepare both its annual operating budget and its financial statements in conformity with GAAP. In such cases, legal compliance provisions and GAAP do not conflict, and the accounting system should be established on a GAAP basis.

In other instances certain finance-related legal provisions conflict with GAAP. The most common GAAP-legal provision conflict occurs where a government's annual operating budget is prepared on a basis significantly different from GAAP. For example:

- A school district may budget on the cash basis, under which revenues are not recorded until cash is received and expenditures are not recognized until cash is disbursed; or

- A city may budget on a cash basis but also consider encumbrances—the estimated cost of goods or services ordered but not yet received—to be expenditures for budgetary purposes, even though encumbrances do not represent expenditures or liabilities under GAAP.

Another common conflict occurs where federal or state grantor agencies require a local government to keep its grant accounting records on a non-GAAP basis.

The requirement that the accounting system must provide data for both legal compliance and GAAP reports does not necessitate two accounting systems. Rather, the accounts will be kept on one basis, and the system will also provide the additional data needed to convert the accounts to the other basis. Because GAAP statements typically are prepared only at year end, the accounts are usually kept on the budgetary (or other legal compliance basis) on which control is exercised daily and on which interim reports must be prepared.

GAAP statements are necessary to ensure proper reporting and a reasonable degree of comparability among the statements of governments across the nation. GAAP reporting also assures that the financial reports of all state and local governments, regardless of their legal provisions and customs, contain the same types of financial statements and disclosures for the same categories and types of funds and account groups, and are based on the same measurement and classification criteria.

## Fund Accounting

The significance the GASB attributes to fund accounting—the most distinctive feature of governmental accounting—is indicated by the fact that three of its twelve principles directly concern this topic. These three principles deal with the need for fund accounting, definition of the term *fund,* and the fund and account group categories (Principle 2); the types of funds recommended for state and local governments (Principle 3); and the need to use an appropriate number of fund entities (Principle 4). Understanding the fund structure, model, and interrelationships described in these principles is essential to mastering the subject matter in this text.

### "Fund"; Fund and Account Group Categories

The second GASB principle is

**PRINCIPLE 2**
**FUND ACCOUNTING SYSTEMS**
[1] Governmental accounting systems should be organized and operated on a fund basis. [2] A fund is defined as a fiscal and accounting entity with a self-balancing set of accounts recording cash and other financial resources, together with all related liabilities and residual equities or balances, and changes therein, which are segregated for the purpose of carrying on specific activities or attaining certain objectives in accordance with special regulations, restrictions, or limitations.

In discussing this principle the GASB notes that the diverse nature of government operations and the necessity of ensuring legal compliance preclude recording and summarizing all governmental financial transactions and balances in a single accounting entity. Thus, from an accounting and financial management viewpoint, a governmental unit is a combination of several distinctly different fiscal and accounting entities, each having a separate set of accounts and functioning independently of the other funds and account groups (see Figure 2–2).

In broad terms a single fund accounting entity is somewhat like a business accounting entity. Each business accounting entity has a self-balancing set of accounts—sufficient to capture all the reported attributes for the whole business and all its transactions. Likewise, each fund of a government has a self-balancing set of accounts sufficient to capture all the reported attributes—for a government fund of this type—of the portion of a government's activities and resources that is accounted for in each particular fund. A key difference is that one accounting entity is used to account for all the activities and resources of a business, whereas each fund accounting entity is used to account for only a certain subset of a government's activities and resources.

Likewise, each business accounting entity has its own journals, its own ledger, its own trial balance, and its own financial statements. Similarly, for each fund of a government there are separate journals and a separate ledger(s) and trial balance; and separate financial statements are prepared and presented.

Four distinct categories of accounting entities—three categories of funds and the nonfund account groups—are employed in governmental accounting. A few points from the state and local government environment discussion should help explain the categories of funds and account groups that are used and the nature of those accounting entities.

First, recall that a general-purpose unit of government has a dual nature. Some of its activities are general government in nature; others are business-type activities. Next, recall that general government activities typically have unique

FIGURE 2–2 **Accounting Entities of State and Local Governments**

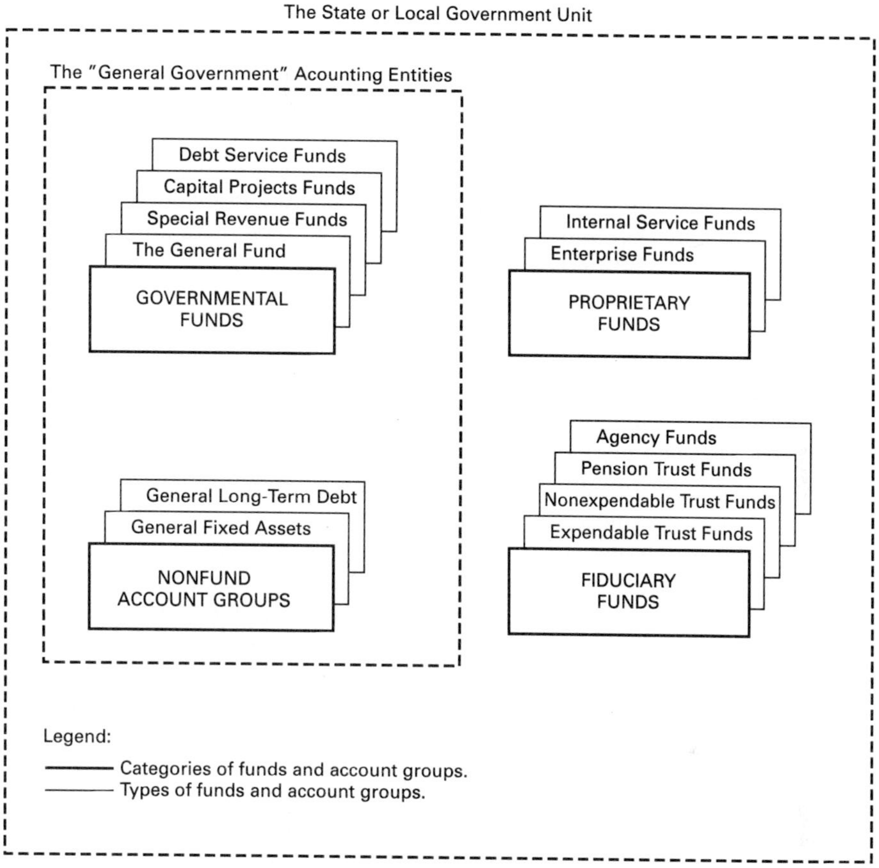

The State or Local Government Unit

The "General Government" Acounting Entities

Debt Service Funds
Capital Projects Funds
Special Revenue Funds
The General Fund
GOVERNMENTAL FUNDS

Internal Service Funds
Enterprise Funds
PROPRIETARY FUNDS

General Long-Term Debt
General Fixed Assets
NONFUND ACCOUNT GROUPS

Agency Funds
Pension Trust Funds
Nonexpendable Trust Funds
Expendable Trust Funds
FIDUCIARY FUNDS

Legend:
———— Categories of funds and account groups.
———— Types of funds and account groups.

Notes:
1. Each fund and account group is an independent accounting entity with a separate self-balancing set of accounts. (There is no single central accounting entity for the state or local government.)
2. As discussed later in "Financial Reporting," financial statements are prepared for each fund (individual fund statements), for all funds of each type (combining statements), and for the government reporting entity (combined statements).

sources of financing such as taxes and grants. The allocation of these resources to various purposes and the control of general government activities focus heavily upon sources and uses of financial resources. The business-type activities function—and may be controlled and evaluated—much like their business counterparts. The information needs of financial report users with respect to these activities are similar to those for similar business activities.

Consistent with these key points, two broad categories of funds and two account groups are used to account for state and local government activities and resources (other than those held in a fiduciary capacity). General government activities and resources are accounted for in governmental funds and the two account groups. Business-type activities are accounted for in proprietary funds.

**Governmental funds** are used to account for the sources, uses, and balances of a government's expendable general government financial resources (and the related current liabilities). In their simplest form governmental funds are in essence segregations of general government working capital according to the purpose(s) for which it is to be used.

The accounting equation for a simple governmental fund is essentially the working capital equation. Expendable assets are assigned to the several governmental funds according to the purposes for which they may (or must) be expended. Current liabilities are accounted for in the fund from which the expenditures giving rise to the liabilities were made, and thus from which they are to be paid. The difference between governmental fund assets and liabilities, the net current assets, is known as the fund balance. In sum, the accounting equation of a simple **governmental fund** is:

$$\text{Current Assets} - \text{Current Liabilities} = \text{Fund Balance}$$

Governmental fund accounting measures fund financial position and changes in fund financial position—sources, uses, and balances of net fund financial resources (working capital)—rather than net income. The statement of revenues, expenditures, and changes in fund balance is the primary governmental fund operating statement. Indeed, it is more similar to a statement of cash flows than to an income statement.

Note that the governmental funds accounting equations do not provide for fixed assets used in general government activities or long-term debt incurred for those activities. However, significant amounts of fixed assets typically are used in general government activities and significant amounts of long-term debt are related to those activities. Accountability for these general government fixed assets and long-term liabilities is maintained in two separate nonfund accounting entities called account groups.

Account groups are essentially lists of a government's general government fixed assets, called *general fixed assets* (General Fixed Assets Account Group) and its general government long-term liabilities, known as *general long-term debt* (General Long-Term Debt Account Group). Offsetting accounts, counterbalancing the list of general fixed assets or of general long-term debt, complete the accounting equation of each account group.

Consequently, the accounting equation for the **General Fixed Assets Account Group** is:

$$\text{Fixed Assets} = \text{Investment in General Fixed Assets}$$

The accounting equation for the **General Long-Term Debt Account Group** is:

| Amount Available in Debt Service Funds to Retire General Long-Term Debt | + | Amount to Be Provided in the Future to Retire General Long-Term Debt | = | Long-Term Liabilities Payable |
|---|---|---|---|---|

The government's general fixed assets—all fixed assets not related to (and hence not accounted for in) proprietary funds or Trust Funds—are not financial resources available to finance governmental fund expenditures. Similarly, the unmatured principal of a government's general obligation long-term debt—long-term liabilities not related to (and hence not accounted for in) proprietary funds or Trust Funds—does not require a governmental fund expenditure (use of financial resources) until the liabilities mature and must be paid, perhaps many years in the future. Thus, neither general fixed assets nor general long-term debt are accounted for in the governmental funds, but in nonfund account groups. These account groups are not funds because they do not contain or account for expendable financial resources and related liabilities. Rather, they are self-balancing sets of accounting records of the general government fixed assets and long-term debt, respectively.

**The governmental funds and the nonfund account groups are the general government accounting entities**—the most unique feature of governmental accounting—whereas the proprietary funds and fiduciary funds are used to account for government organizations and relationships that are similar to those in the private sector. Only those assets, liabilities, transactions, and events that clearly relate specifically to the proprietary funds and fiduciary funds are recorded in those fund categories. All other assets, liabilities, transactions, and events are recorded in the general government accounting entities—the governmental funds and account groups.

Furthermore, given the governmental fund accounting equation, the operating results of governmental funds—and of the general government—are necessarily measured in terms of sources, uses, and balances of net expendable financial resources rather than net income. Recognize that in most situations this means net working capital increases, decreases, and balances. It does not mean net income. Because the nonfund account groups do not account for sources, uses, and balances of net expendable financial resources—but for general government fixed assets and unmatured long-term debt—changes in their accounts do not directly affect the operating results of the general government.

**Proprietary funds** are used to account for a government's continuing business-type organizations and activities. All assets, liabilities, equities, revenues, expenses, and transfers pertaining to these business (and quasi-business) organizations and activities are accounted for through proprietary funds. In other words, the **proprietary fund** accounting equation is:

| Current Assets | | Current Liabilities | | Contributed Capital |
|:---:|:---:|:---:|:---:|:---:|
| + | = | + | + | + |
| Noncurrent (including fixed) Assets | | Long-Term Liabilities | | Retained Earnings |

Proprietary fund accounting therefore measures net income, financial position, and cash flows. Most of the generally accepted accounting principles here are those applicable to similar private businesses.

**Fiduciary funds** are used to account for assets held by a government in a trustee or agency capacity, whether for individuals, private organizations, other governmental units, or other funds of the government. Expendable Trust Fund accounting parallels that for governmental funds; Nonexpendable Trust Fund and Pension Trust Fund accounting is similar to that for proprietary funds. Agency Funds are purely custodial (assets equal liabilities), and Agency Fund accounting is concerned only with recording the changes in fund assets held for others.

### Types of Funds

The third GASB principle recognizes seven specific types of funds within the three broad fund categories. As you study Principle 3, note that the governmental funds are distinguished from one another by the purpose or purposes for which the financial resources accounted for in each fund may or must be used. Therefore, general government resources that are to be used to pay for construction of a major general government capital project are accounted for in a Capital Projects Fund. On the other hand, financial resources to be used to pay principal and interest on general long-term debt are accounted for in a Debt Service Fund. The distinguishing factor in the classification is the purpose for which the resources are to be used. These distinctions are highlighted in Figure 2–3. Note also that the primary

FIGURE 2–3 **Governmental Fund Types: Classification and Typical Types of Expenditures**

### I. Classification

| Purposes for Which General Government Financial Resources May or Must Be Used | Governmental Fund Type to Be Used |
|---|---|
| Available for general SLG uses | General Fund (GF) |
| Specific operating purposes or activities | Special Revenue Fund (SRF) |
| Acquiring major general government capital facilities | Capital Projects Fund (CPF) |
| Payment of general long-term debt principal and interest | Debt Service Fund (DSF) |

### II. Typical Types of Expenditures

|  | GF | SRFs | CPFs | DSFs |
|---|---|---|---|---|
| Operating (e.g., salaries, rent, utilities) | XXX | XXX | | |
| Capital outlay | X | X | XXX | |
| Debt service | X | X | X | XXX |

Legend

**XXX** = Most expenditures are of this type
 **X** = May have some expenditures of this type, usually minor

distinction between the two types of proprietary funds is who the predominant "customers" are—that is, typically the general public for Enterprise Funds and other departments or agencies of the government for Internal Service Funds.

**PRINCIPLE 3**
**TYPES OF FUNDS**
The following types of funds should be used by state and local governments:

**GOVERNMENTAL FUNDS**
1. **The General Fund**—to account for all financial resources except those required to be accounted for in another fund.
2. **Special Revenue Funds**—to account for the proceeds of specific revenue sources (other than expendable trusts or for major capital projects) that are legally restricted to expenditure for specified purposes.
3. **Capital Projects Funds**—to account for financial resources to be used for the acquisition or construction of major capital facilities (other than those financed by proprietary funds and Trust Funds).
4. **Debt Service Funds**—to account for the accumulation of resources for, and the payment of, general long-term debt principal and interest.

**PROPRIETARY FUNDS**
5. **Enterprise Funds**—to account for operations (a) that are financed and operated in a manner similar to private business enterprises—where the intent of the governing body is that the costs (expenses, including depreciation) of providing goods or services to the general public on a continuing basis be financed or recovered primarily through user charges; or (b)where the governing body has decided that periodic determination of revenues earned, expenses incurred, and/or net income is appropriate for capital maintenance, public policy, management control, accountability, or other purposes.
6. **Internal Service Funds**—to account for the financing of goods or services provided by one department or agency to other departments or agencies of the governmental unit, or to other governmental units, on a cost-reimbursement basis.

**FIDUCIARY FUNDS**

7. **Trust and Agency Funds**—to account for assets held by a governmental unit in a trustee capacity or as an agent for individuals, private organizations, other governmental units, and/or other funds. These include (a) **Expendable Trust Funds,** (b) **Nonexpendable Trust Funds,** (c) **Pension Trust Funds,** and (d) **Agency Funds.**

As noted earlier, fund accounting evolved because portions of a government's resources may be restricted as to use. Restrictions may stem from grantor or donor stipulations, laws, contractual agreements, actions by the legislature or council, or other sources. The several fund types recommended by the GASB vary primarily in accordance with (1) whether the resources of the fund may be expended (governmental funds) or are to be maintained on a self-sustaining basis (proprietary funds) and (2) the extent of budgetary control normally employed. Furthermore, the various types of governmental and similar fiduciary funds differ principally according to the uses to which the resources accounted for therein may be put: (1) general operating (unrestricted); (2) special purpose or project, such as for certain services or for capital outlay or debt service; or (3) merely managed for and remitted to those for whom the government is acting as a trustee or agent.

The types of fund and nonfund accounting entities recommended by the GASB are summarized in Figure 2–4; typical governmental and similar fiduciary fund resource flow patterns are indicated in Figure 2–5. Note the purposes of each fund type and account group, and that a state or local government will have only one General Fund, General Fixed Assets Account Group, and General Long-Term Debt Account Group. It may have one, none, several, or many of the other types of funds. Recognize from Figure 2–5 that knowing the source of financial resources available for governmental funds does not allow one to determine in which governmental fund to account for the resources. However, once the purpose(s) for which the resources may be used is known, one can identify the appropriate fund type to use to account for those resources. Note also that at least one chapter of this text is devoted to each fund type and to the nonfund account groups.

## Number of Funds

Finally, the GASB recognizes the need both to maintain those funds necessary to appropriately manage and demonstrate accountability for government resources and to avoid excessive fragmentation of the financial report by establishing unnecessary funds. Accordingly, the GASB cautions against using too few or too many funds in its fourth principle:

**PRINCIPLE 4**
**NUMBER OF FUNDS**

[1] Governmental units should establish and maintain those funds required by [a] law and [b] sound financial administration. [2] Only the minimum number of funds consistent with legal and operating requirements should be established, however, since unnecessary funds result in inflexibility, undue complexity, and inefficient financial administration.

In sum, the government:

- must establish and maintain those funds required by law or contractual agreement, just as it must observe other finance-related legal and contractual provisions.

- should maintain other funds that assist in ensuring effective control over and accountability for its finances.

**FIGURE 2–4 State and Local Government (SLG) Funds, Account Groups, Accounting Equations, and Statements**

| The General Government Funds and Account Groups | |
|---|---|
| **The Governmental Funds**<br><br>General<br>Special Revenue<br>Capital Projects<br>Debt Service<br><br>$CA - CL = FB$ | **The Proprietary Funds**<br><br>Enterprise<br>Internal Service<br><br>$CA + NCA = CL + LTL + CC + RE$ |
| **Statements**<br>Balance Sheet<br>Statement of Revenues, Expenditures, and Changes in Fund Balances—GAAP Basis<br>If budgeted annually, a budgetary comparison statement:<br>Statement of Revenues, Expenditures, and Changes in Fund Balances—Budget and Actual—Budgetary Basis | **Statements**<br>Balance Sheet<br>Statement of Revenues, Expenses, and Changes in Retained Earnings/Equity<br>Statement of Cash Flows |
| **The Account Groups** | **The Fiduciary Funds** |
| **General Fixed Assets**<br>$FA = $ Investment in GFA<br>**General Long-Term Debt**<br>Amount Available in DSF + Amount to Be Provided in Future Years $= LTL$<br><br>**Statement**<br>Balance Sheet<br>(Changes Disclosed in Notes) | Agency        Assets = Liabilities<br>Nonexpendable Trust  $CA + NCA =$<br>                        $CL + LTL + FE$<br>Expendable Trust  $CA - CL = FB$<br>Pension Trust     Assets – Liabilities<br>                          = Net Assets |

**Legend:**

| | |
|---|---|
| CA = Current Assets | FE = Fund Equity |
| CC = Contributed Capital | GFA = General Fixed Assets |
| CL = Current Liabilities | LTL = Long-Term Liabilities |
| FA = Fixed Assets | NCA = Noncurrent Assets |
| FB = Fund Balance | RE = Retained Earnings |

However, maintaining too many funds may be as detrimental as maintaining too few funds.

Selecting the specific funds a government needs requires professional judgment, and the funds in use should be reviewed from time to time to ensure that all funds needed are in use and that no unneeded funds are in use. In amplifying the fourth principle, the GASB offers the following guidance to the exercise of professional judgment in determining the fund structure of a state or local government:

> Some governmental units often need several funds of a single type, such as special revenue or capital projects funds. On the other hand, many governmental units do not need funds of all types at any given time. Some find it necessary to use only a few of the specified types. For example, many small governmental units do not require internal service funds. Moreover, [1] resources restricted to expenditure for purposes normally financed from the general fund may be accounted for through the general fund provided that applicable legal requirements can be appropriately satisfied; and [2] use of special revenue funds is not required unless they are legally mandated. [3] Debt service funds are required if they are legally mandated and/or if financial resources are being accumulated for principal and interest payments maturing in future years.

> The general rule is to establish the minimum number of separate funds consistent with legal specifications, operational requirements, and the principles of fund clas-

FIGURE 2–5  **Typical Resource Flow Pattern Governmental and Similar Fiduciary Funds***

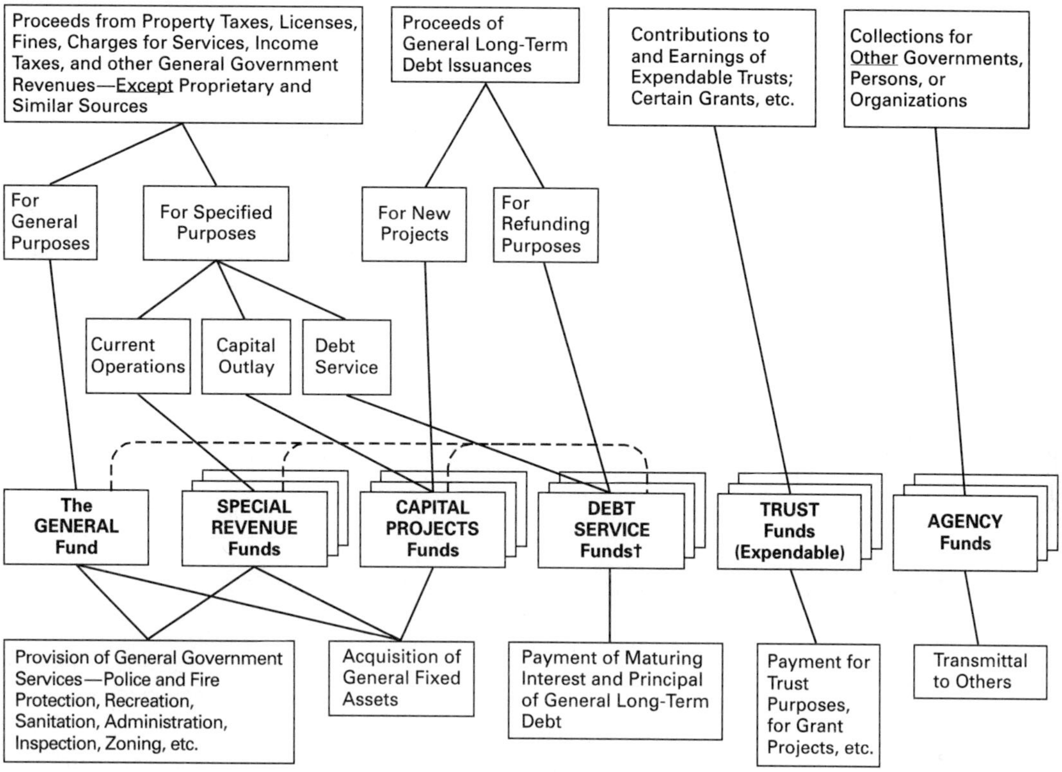

*Flows to and from proprietary and similar fiduciary funds are excluded.
†As indicated by – – –, resources may be transferred to the Debt Service Funds from other funds; also,
  General Long-Term Debt may be serviced directly from other governmental funds.

sification discussed above. Using too many funds causes inflexibility and undue complexity in budgeting, accounting, and other phases of financial management, and is best avoided in the interests of efficient and economical financial administration.[8]

Caution must be exercised in opting to account for resources restricted for current operating or debt service purposes in the General Fund. These resources typically are accounted for in Special Revenue and Debt Service Funds, respectively, to ensure that applicable legal requirements are met. Inadequate accountability may result when these resources are accounted for in the General Fund in governments with less than excellent accounting systems. Accordingly, it is assumed hereafter that these options are not exercised and that restricted resources are accounted for in Special Revenue Funds and Debt Service Funds, for example, rather than in the General Fund.

## Transaction Analysis and Fund Accounting

Understanding the nature and interrelationships of the funds and account groups is critical to understanding the remainder of the principles and, indeed, to understanding governmental accounting. Thus, it is useful at this point to examine fund

[8] Ibid., sec. 1300.107 and 1300.108.

accounting at a practical level to assure that the way the fund accounting model works is understood. To do this, review the analyses of the transactions described in Figure 2–6. Pay particular attention to the first eight transactions, which relate to general government activities. We discuss the first three transactions to help assure that you understand the transaction analysis. Review the others on your own to solidify your understanding of the model.

**Transaction 1** affects two general government accounting entities:

1. $8,000 of General Fund cash is used (hence the decrease in General Fund current assets).
2. The fixed asset acquired does not "fit" in the General Fund accounting equation because fixed assets are not current assets and thus are not part of fund working capital.
3. Because General Fund current assets decreased and its current liabilities did not change, the transaction decreased the General Fund fund balance by $8,000.
4. This decrease in General Fund fund balance will be reported as an expenditure in the General Fund operating statement. (Recall that this statement is somewhat similar in function to a cash flow statement. Similar transactions are reported as decreases in a cash flow statement as well.)
5. The fixed asset is added to the General Fixed Assets Account Group (list of fixed assets) and the offsetting account (Investment in GFA) is increased by a corresponding amount.

Two general government accounting entities also are affected by **Transaction 2:**

1. The cash received from issuing the bonds is to be used to finance construction of a major general government capital facility (fire station). Therefore, this transaction increases the amount of current assets in the Capital Projects Fund.
2. The bonds payable are long-term debt and thus do not "fit" in the accounting equations of any of the governmental funds because long-term debt is not part of fund working capital.
3. Because Capital Projects Fund assets increase $1,000,000 and its liabilities do not change, this transaction increases the Capital Projects Fund fund balance by $1,000,000. The increase in fund balance from issuing the bonds must be reported in the Capital Projects Fund operating statement.
4. Bond proceeds are not revenues. Accordingly, the increase will be reported in a separate "Other Financing Sources" category of fund balance increases. (Again, note the similarity of the operating statement to a cash flow statement—in which such transactions are reported as cash flows from financing activities.)
5. The bonds payable are added to the General Long-Term Debt Account Group (list of general long-term debt). An offsetting balance is recorded in the "Amount to Be Provided in Future Years to Retire Debt Principal" account.

Finally, in **Transaction 3,** note the differences in the effects of issuing long-term debt and issuing short-term general government debt. In this particular case, the borrowing was for General Fund purposes and affects the General Fund as follows:

1. Current assets are increased by $1,000,000.
2. Current liabilities are increased by $1,000,000.
3. Fund balance is unaffected because the changes in Current Assets and Current Liabilities of the fund were equal; that is, working capital did not change.
4. Consequently, this transaction has no effect on the General Fund operating statement.

Note that no other funds or account groups are affected by Transaction 3.

**FIGURE 2–6 Analysis of Transactions**

| Fund Affected | Governmental Funds CA | − CL | = FB | General Fixed Assets Account Group FA | = Investment in GFA | General Long-Term Debt Account Group Amount to Be Provided | + Amount Available | = Long-Term Liabilities | Proprietary Funds CA | + NCA | − CL | − LTL | = CC | + RE |
|---|---|---|---|---|---|---|---|---|---|---|---|---|---|---|
| 1 General | ($8,000) | | ($8,000) | $8,000 | $8,000 | | | | | | | | | |
| 2 Capital Projects | $1,000,000 | | $1,000,000 | | | $1,000,000 | | $1,000,000 | | | | | | |
| 3 General | $1,000,000 | $1,000,000 | | | | | | | | | | | | |
| 4 Capital Projects | | $ 300,000 | ($300,000) | $300,000 | $300,000 | | | | | | | | | |
| 5 General | $7,000 | | $7,000 | ($20,000) | ($20,000) | | | | | | | | | |
| 6a General | ($100,000) | | ($100,000) | | | | | | | | | | | |
| 6b Debt Service | $100,000 | | $100,000 | | | ($100,000) | $100,000 | | | | | | | |
| 7 Debt Service | ($80,000) | | ($80,000) | | | $30,000 | ($80,000) | ($50,000) | | | | | | |
| 8 General | ($1,030,000) | ($1,000,000) | ($30,000) | | | | | | | | | | | |
| 9 Enterprise | | | | | | | | | ($8,000) | $8,000 | | | | |
| 10 Enterprise | | | | | | | | | $1,000,000 | | | $1,000,000 | | |

**Transactions**

1 Purchased a general government fixed asset with General Fund cash, $8,000.
2 Issued $1,000,000 of bonds to finance construction of a fire station.
3 Issued a $1,000,000 six-month note to provide temporary financing for the General Fund.
4 Received a bill from the contractor for $300,000 of construction costs on the fire station.
5 Sold a general fixed asset for $7,000; its original cost was $20,000.
6 Transferred $100,000 of General Fund cash to the fund from which the fire station bonds will be repaid.
7 $50,000 of the fire station bonds and $30,000 of interest matured and were paid.
8 The six-month General Fund note matured and was paid along with $30,000 of interest.
9 Purchased a fixed asset for an Enterprise Fund with Enterprise Fund cash, $8,000.
10 Issued $1,000,000 of Enterprise Fund revenue bonds to finance plant expansion.

**Legend**

| | |
|---|---|
| CA | Current Assets |
| CC | Contributed Capital |
| CL | Current Liabilities |
| FA | Fixed Assets |
| FB | Fund Balance |
| GFA | General Fixed Assets |
| LTL | Long-Term Liabilities |
| NCA | Noncurrent Assets (including fixed assets) |
| RE | Retained Earnings |

> Observe the effects of the remaining transactions (4–10) in Figure 2–6. One who understands the transaction analyses presented in Figure 2–6 is beginning to understand the basics of the governmental accounting model. Indeed, much of the guidance set forth in Principles 5–7, for example, will be intuitively obvious to those who understand the model. Moreover, they will be well on their way to understanding the general government accounting methods discussed in Chapters 3–9.

## Fixed Assets and Long-Term Liabilities

The GASB sets forth three principles of accounting for government fixed assets and long-term liabilities within the fund and account group structure specified in Principles 2 and 3. These three principles relate to (1) distinguishing and accounting differently for specific fund and general fixed assets and long-term liabilities, (2) valuation of fixed assets, and (3) depreciation of fixed assets.

### Specific Fund vs. General Fixed Assets and Long-Term Liabilities

As noted earlier, in a fund accounting environment, specific fund fixed assets and long-term debt, which are accounted for in the appropriate funds, must be distinguished from those related to the government in its entirety, the general government, which are accounted for in the account groups. The fifth GASB principle emphasizes this important distinction:

**PRINCIPLE 5**
**ACCOUNTING FOR FIXED ASSETS AND LONG-TERM LIABILITIES**
A clear distinction should be made between (a) fund fixed assets and general fixed assets and (b) fund long-term liabilities and general long-term debt.

a. Fixed assets related to specific proprietary funds or Trust Funds should be accounted for through those funds. All other fixed assets of a governmental unit should be accounted for through the General Fixed Assets Account Group.
b. Long-term liabilities of proprietary funds and Trust Funds should be accounted for through those funds. All other unmatured general long-term liabilities of the governmental unit, including special assessment debt for which the government is obligated in some manner, should be accounted for through the General Long-Term Debt Account Group.

Thus, the term *general fixed assets* means general government fixed assets, and *general long-term debt* means unmatured general government long-term liabilities.

In discussing the reasons underlying the need to distinguish fund and nonfund fixed assets and long-term debt the GASB notes:

> General fixed assets do not represent financial resources available for expenditure, but are items for which financial resources have been used and for which accountability should be maintained. They are not assets of any fund but of the governmental unit as an instrumentality. Their inclusion in the financial statements of a governmental fund would increase the fund balance, which could mislead users of the fund balance sheet. The primary purposes for governmental fund accounting are to reflect its revenues and expenditures—the sources and uses of its financial resources—and its assets, the related liabilities, and the net financial resources available for subsequent appropriation and

expenditure. These objectives can most readily be achieved by excluding general fixed assets from the governmental fund accounts and recording them in a separate GFAAG.

The general long-term debt of a state or local government is secured by the general credit and revenue-raising powers of the government rather than by the assets acquired or specific fund resources. Further, just as general fixed assets do not represent financial resources available for appropriation and expenditure, the unmatured principal of general long-term debt does not require current appropriation and expenditure of governmental fund financial resources. To include it as a governmental fund liability would be misleading and dysfunctional to the current period management control (for example, budgeting) and accountability functions.[9]

Furthermore, the GASB principles give governments the option to record (or not record) "infrastructure" or public domain general fixed assets in the General Fixed Assets Account Group. (Infrastructure fixed assets of specific proprietary or similar trust funds must be recorded in those funds.) The GASB states:

> Reporting public domain or "infrastructure" [general] fixed assets—roads, bridges, curbs and gutters, streets and sidewalks, drainage systems, lighting systems, and similar items that are immovable and of value only to the governmental unit—is optional.[10]

The theoretical and practical rationale for the infrastructure fixed asset capitalization option is discussed further in Chapter 9.

### Valuation of Fixed Assets

The sixth principle specifies that cost is the basic valuation method for both fund fixed assets and general fixed assets:

> **PRINCIPLE 6**
> **VALUATION OF FIXED ASSETS**
> Fixed assets should be accounted for at cost or, if the cost is not practicably determinable, at estimated cost. Donated fixed assets should be recorded at their estimated fair value at the time received.

Estimated cost (at the time of acquisition) is allowed because some governments have not maintained adequate fixed asset records before beginning to report in conformity with generally accepted accounting principles. This principle (1) allows a government to estimate the original cost of both general fixed assets and specific fund fixed assets for which original costs cannot reasonably be determined but (2) requires that its other fixed assets and all fixed assets acquired subsequently be recorded at cost (or estimated value, if donated).

### Depreciation

Accounting for depreciation of a government's fixed assets is the subject of the seventh principle:

> **PRINCIPLE 7**
> **DEPRECIATION OF FIXED ASSETS**
> a. Depreciation of general fixed assets should not be recorded in the accounts of governmental funds. Depreciation of general fixed assets may be recorded in cost

---

[9] Ibid., sec. 1400.107 and 1500.104.
[10] Ibid., sec. 1400.109.

accounting systems or calculated for cost finding analyses; and accumulated depreciation may be recorded in the General Fixed Assets Account Group.

b. Depreciation of fixed assets accounted for in a proprietary fund should be recorded in the accounts of that fund. Depreciation is also recognized in those Trust Funds where expenses, net income, and/or capital maintenance are measured.

Principle 7 is consistent with the governmental fund and proprietary fund accounting models discussed earlier. The essence of this principle is that (1) depreciation expense should be recorded in those funds where expenses are accounted for—the proprietary funds and similar trust funds—but (2) depreciation expense should not be recorded in those funds where expenditures (not expenses) are accounted for—the governmental funds and similar trust funds—because depreciation expense is not an expenditure.

The GASB rationale for this principle is as follows:

> Depreciation accounting is an important element of the income-determination process. Accordingly, it is recognized in the proprietary funds and in those trust funds where expenses, net income, and/or capital maintenance are measured.
>
> Expenditures, not expenses, are measured in governmental fund accounting. To record depreciation expense in governmental funds would inappropriately mix two fundamentally different measurements—expenses and expenditures. General fixed asset acquisitions require the use of governmental fund financial resources and are recorded as expenditures. General fixed asset sale proceeds provide governmental fund financial resources. Depreciation expense is neither a source nor a use of governmental fund financial resources, and thus is not properly recorded in the accounts of such funds.[11]

## Basis of Accounting

Consistent with its distinction between governmental fund accounting methods and those for proprietary funds, the GASB specifies different methods of applying the accrual concept in accounting for governmental funds and proprietary funds.

**PRINCIPLE 8**
**ACCRUAL BASIS IN GOVERNMENTAL ACCOUNTING**
The modified accrual or accrual basis of accounting, as appropriate, should be utilized in measuring financial position and operating results.

a. **Governmental fund** revenues and expenditures should be recognized on the modified accrual basis. Revenues should be recognized in the accounting period in which they become available and measurable. Expenditures should be recognized in the accounting period in which the fund liability is incurred, if measurable, except for unmatured interest on [and principal of] general long-term debt, which should be recognized when due.

b. **Proprietary fund** revenues and expenses should be recognized on the accrual basis. Revenues should be recognized in the accounting period in which they are earned and become measurable; expenses should be recognized in the period incurred, if measurable.

c. **Fiduciary fund** revenues and expenses or expenditures (as appropriate) should be recognized on the basis consistent with the fund's accounting measurement objective. Nonexpendable Trust and Pension Trust Funds should be accounted for on the accrual basis; Expendable Trust Funds should be accounted for on the modified accrual basis. Agency Fund assets and liabilities should be accounted for on the modified accrual basis.

---

[11] Ibid., sec. 1400.115–116.

    d. **Transfers** should be recognized in the accounting period in which the interfund receivable and payable arise.

The essence of this principle is that, in governmental accounting:

- The **accrual** basis refers to recognition of revenues and expenses of proprietary funds and similar (proprietary-type) trust funds as in business accounting.
- The **modified accrual** basis refers to recognition of revenues and expenditures using the flows of financial resources measurement focus of governmental funds and similar (governmental-type) trust funds:
  1. **Revenues** must be **"available"**—collectible within the period or soon enough thereafter to pay liabilities incurred for expenditures of the period, as well as levied for the period or earned and measurable—or must be deferred (recorded as deferred revenues) and recognized as revenues when "available." (Thus, revenues may be recognized later in governmental-type funds than in proprietary-type funds.)
  2. **Expenditures** (not expenses)—for operations, capital outlay, and debt service—are recognized (1) when operating or capital outlay liabilities to be paid from governmental-type funds are incurred and (2) when general government debt service (principal and interest) payments on long-term debt are due.
- **Transfers** of resources among funds (**interfund transfers**) should be recorded when they occur—when the interfund payable and receivable arise—even though cash (or noncash assets) has not been remitted from one fund to another fund.

The distinction between *expenditures* and *expenses* is extremely important in governmental accounting. **Expenses**—the measurement focus of proprietary fund accounting—are costs expired during a period, including depreciation and other allocations, as in business accounting. **Expenditures**—the measurement focus of governmental fund accounting—are financial resources expended during a period for operations, capital outlay, and long-term debt principal retirement and interest. With the exception of long-term debt principal retirement expenditures, expenditures reflect the cost incurred to acquire goods or services, whereas expenses reflect the cost of goods or services used. This important distinction is illustrated in Figure 2–7.

**FIGURE 2–7  Expenses vs. Expenditures**

| *Expenses*<br>*(Costs Expired)* | | *Expenditures*<br>*(Financial Resources Expended)* | |
|---|---|---|---|
| **Operating:** | Salaries<br>Utilities, etc. | **Operating:** | Salaries<br>Utilities, etc. |
| **Capital:** | Depreciation | **Capital:** | Capital Outlay |
| **Debt Service:** | Interest | **Debt Service:** | Interest<br>Long-Term Debt Retirement |

**Observations**

1. **Operating.** Operating expenses and expenditures often are identical but may differ somewhat because of accrual or allocation differences in expense and expenditure measurement standards.
2. **Capital.** The entire cost of fixed assets acquired during the period is accounted for as a capital outlay expenditure, whereas a portion of all exhaustible fixed asset costs incurred to date is allocated to each period as depreciation expense.
3. **Debt Service.** Interest is both an expenditure and an expense, though not necessarily of the same amount. Long-term debt retirement is an expenditure but not an expense.

In sum, the modified accrual method is, in essence, the accrual method of accounting for the flows and balances of financial resources of governmental funds and similar trust funds, as contrasted with the cash basis of accounting. The term *accrual basis* refers to accounting for revenues earned and expenses incurred, as for business enterprises, in proprietary funds and similar trust funds. The application of the modified accrual and accrual bases is discussed and illustrated throughout this text.

## The Budget and Budgetary Accounting

The importance of budgeting, budgetary control, and budgetary accountability in the governmental-type activities environment is recognized in the ninth GASB principle:

> **PRINCIPLE 9**
> **BUDGETING, BUDGETARY CONTROL, AND BUDGETARY REPORTING**
> a. An annual budget(s) should be adopted by every governmental unit.
> b. The accounting system should provide the basis for appropriate budgetary control.
> c. Budgetary comparisons should be included in the appropriate financial statements and schedules for governmental funds for which an annual budget has been adopted.

Principle 9 is essentially a bridge between

- Principle 1—which requires that government accounting systems make it possible to determine and demonstrate compliance with finance-related legal and contractual provisions—such as the annual operating budget(s)—as well as report in conformity with GAAP; and

- Principle 12—discussed later, which requires presentation of financial statements on both the budgetary basis and the GAAP basis, as well as an explanation and reconciliation of the differences between the budgetary and GAAP bases.

As noted earlier, the annual operating budget of a government—which typically includes the General, Special Revenue, and Debt Service Funds—is a legally enacted plan of fund financial operations. Indeed, as discussed earlier, it is a key allocation mechanism in the general government environment. Its revenue estimates provide legal authority for the levy of taxes, charges for services, fines, and so on for the year. Its appropriations both legally authorize and legally limit the expenditures to be incurred during the year. Thus, budgetary accounting control and accountability are essential aspects of governmental accounting and financial reporting.

Furthermore, governments often budget on a non-GAAP basis. Some governments budget revenues and expenditures on a cash receipts and cash disbursements basis, for example, and some consider encumbrances—the estimated costs of goods and services ordered but not yet received—to be expenditures for budgetary purposes, even though encumbrances are not considered expenditures under GAAP. Because many governments budget on a non-GAAP basis, it is important to identify a government's budgetary basis. If the budgetary basis differs significantly from the GAAP basis, a government must (1) clearly distinguish its budgetary basis from the GAAP basis; (2) maintain budgetary accounting control during the year on the budgetary basis and also accumulate the additional data needed for GAAP reporting; and (3) prepare financial statements on both bases, and explain and reconcile the differences between the budgetary and GAAP bases. Budgeting, budgetary accounting control, and budgetary reporting are considered in depth in Chapter 3 and in the chapters that deal with funds for which budgeting, budgetary control, and budgetary accountability are particularly important.

## Classification and Terminology

The needs (1) to classify accounting data in different ways to meet different information needs, (2) to distinguish internal shifts of resources and long-term borrowings from revenues, expenditures, and expenses, and (3) for consistent classification and terminology are the subjects of the tenth and eleventh GASB principles.

### Transfer, Revenue, Expenditure, and Expense Classification

The tenth GASB principle establishes the broad categories of increases and decreases to be reported in SLG operating statements. It also establishes the revenue and expenditure or expense classifications that may be used. Principle 10 states:

**PRINCIPLE 10**
**TRANSFER, REVENUE, EXPENDITURE, AND EXPENSE**
**ACCOUNT CLASSIFICATION**
a. Interfund transfers and proceeds of general long-term debt issues should be classified separately from fund revenues and expenditures or expenses.
b. Governmental fund revenues should be classified by fund and source. Expenditures should be classified by fund, function (or program), organization unit, activity, character, and principal classes of objects.
c. Proprietary fund revenues and expenses should be classified in essentially the same manner as those of similar business organizations, functions, or activities.

### Interfund Transactions

Five types of interfund transactions commonly encountered in state and local government are defined as follows:

1. **Loans.** Transactions that are loans of cash between funds are expected to be repaid and thus are reported as receivables in the lender fund and as payables in the borrower fund. Examples include a temporary loan from the General Fund to a Capital Projects Fund to provide interim financing pending receipt of bond issue proceeds, from which the loan will be repaid, or a long-term advance from the General Fund to provide working capital to an Enterprise Fund.
2. **Quasi-External Transactions.** Transactions that would be treated as revenues, expenditures, or expenses if they involved organizations external to the governmental unit—e.g., payments in lieu of taxes from an Enterprise Fund to the General Fund; Internal Service Fund billings to departments; routine employer contributions from the General Fund to a Pension Trust Fund; and routine service charges for inspection, engineering, utilities, or similar services provided by a department financed from one fund to a department financed from another fund—should be accounted for as revenues, expenditures, or expenses in the funds involved.
3. **Reimbursements.** Transactions that constitute reimbursements of a fund for expenditures or expenses initially made from it that are properly applicable to another fund—e.g., an expenditure properly chargeable to a Special Revenue Fund was initially made from the General Fund, which is subsequently reimbursed—should be recorded as expenditures or expenses (as appropriate) in the reimbursing fund and as reductions of the expenditure or expense in the fund that it reimbursed.
4. **Residual Equity Transfers.** Nonrecurring or nonroutine transfers of equity between funds—e.g., contribution of Enterprise Fund or Internal Service Fund capital by the General Fund, subsequent return of all or part of such contribution to the General

Fund, and transfers of residual balances of discontinued funds to the General Fund or a Debt Service Fund.

5. **Operating Transfers.** All other interfund transfers—e.g., legally authorized transfers from a fund receiving revenue to the fund through which the resources are to be expended, transfers of tax revenues from a Special Revenue Fund to a Debt Service Fund, transfers from the General Fund to a Special Revenue or Capital Projects Fund, operating subsidy transfers from the General or a Special Revenue Fund to an Enterprise Fund, and transfers from an Enterprise Fund other than payments in lieu of taxes to finance General Fund expenditures.[12]

Proper accounting and reporting for these types of interfund transactions are summarized in Figure 2–8.

**Loans** are the only type of interfund transaction that initially affects only balance sheet accounts. Because interfund loans are expected to be repaid, a loan is reported as a receivable (asset) in the lending fund and as a payable (liability) in the debtor fund. No revenue, expenditure, or expense is recognized except for interest charges, if any, associated with interfund loans.

**Quasi-external transactions** are the only interfund transactions for which it is proper to recognize fund revenues, expenditures, or expenses that are not revenues, expenditures, or expenses of the governmental unit. The GASB views accounting for quasi-external transactions as fund revenues, expenditures, and expenses as essential both (1) to proper determination of proprietary fund operating results and (2) to reporting accurately the revenues and expenditures of programs or activities financed through governmental funds.

**Reimbursements** are necessary when an expenditure attributable to one fund initially was made from another fund. Accounting for interfund reimbursements as specified ensures that such transactions are reflected only once—and in the proper fund—as expenditures or expenses, as appropriate.

All interfund transactions except loans, quasi-external transactions, and reimbursements are transfers:

- **Residual equity transfers** are reported separately after the results of operations—usually immediately before the ending fund balance—in the statement of revenues, expenditures, and changes in fund balances of governmental funds. Residual equity transfers to proprietary funds are reported as additions to contributed capital of the proprietary fund; those from proprietary funds are reported as reductions of retained earnings or contributed capital, as appropriate.

- **Operating transfers** are reported in the "Other Financing Sources (Uses)" section in the statement of revenues, expenditures, and changes in fund balance (governmental funds) and in the "Operating Transfers" section in the statement of revenues, expenses, and changes in retained earnings or equity (proprietary funds). Note that operating transfers increase or decrease proprietary fund net income.

### GLTD Proceeds

The GASB also states that **proceeds of general long-term debt issues** not recorded as fund liabilities—for example, proceeds of general obligation bonds or notes expended through Capital Projects or Debt Service Funds—should be reported as "Bond Issue Proceeds" or "Proceeds of Long-Term Notes" in the **"Other Financing Sources"** section of the operating statement of the recipient **govern-**

---

[12] Ibid., sec. 1800.103 and 1800.106.

FIGURE 2–8  **Summary of Interfund Transactions Reporting**

| | Reporting Treatment | |
|---|---|---|
| *Category of Interfund Transaction* | *Payee (Recipient) Fund* | *Payer Fund* |
| **Loans** | Liability. | Receivable. |
| **Quasi-external transactions** | Revenue. | Expenditure or expense, as appropriate. |
| **Reimbursements** | Reduce expenditures or expenses, as appropriate. | Expenditure or expense, as appropriate. |
| **Residual equity transfers (RETs)** | Residual Equity Transfers In (1) In governmental funds—reported after operations (separate from revenues, bond issue proceeds, and operating transfers in) immediately before ending fund balance. (2) In proprietary funds—increase in contributed capital. | Residual Equity Transfers Out (1) In governmental funds—reported after operations (separate from expenditures or expenses and operating transfers out) immediately before ending fund balance. (2) In proprietary funds—reported as a decrease in retained earnings or contributed capital, depending on circumstances. |
| **Operating transfers** | Operating Transfers In reported (1) As "Other Financing Sources" in the governmental funds operating statement and (2) Separately as "Operating Transfers In" in the proprietary funds operating statement. | Operating Transfers Out reported (1) In "Other Financing Uses" section of the governmental funds operating statement and (2) Separately as "Operating Transfers Out" in the proprietary funds operating statement. (Operating transfers are reported as part of net income of proprietary funds.) |

**mental fund.** (Note that this applies only to GLTD, not to proprietary and similar fiduciary fund long-term debt.)

### Reporting Interfund Transactions and GLTD Proceeds

The GASB classification principles—on quasi-external transactions, reimbursements, residual equity transfers, operating transfers, and general long-term debt issue proceeds—are extremely important in government accounting and financial reporting. Accordingly, they are discussed further and illustrated at numerous points in this text.

The reporting effects of the GASB classification principles are illustrated in Figure 2–9, using comparative, side by side, operating statement format illustrations for governmental and proprietary funds. Essentially, Principle 10 creates three classifications of increases in fund balance—revenues, other financing sources, and residual equity transfers in—to be presented in governmental fund operating statements. Likewise, it requires three categories of fund balance decreases to be presented in those statements—expenditures, other financing uses, and residual equity transfers out. The principle also dictates the major categories in which changes in proprietary fund equity will be reported. In studying Figure 2–9, note (1) the distinct operating statement formats for governmental funds and for proprietary funds and the differences between these formats, (2) the reporting of operating transfers and residual equity transfers in both operating statements and of GLTD issue proceeds in the governmental fund operating statement, and

FIGURE 2–9 **Operating Statement Formats**

## Governmental Funds and Proprietary Funds

| Governmental Fund | Proprietary Fund |
|---|---|
| *Statement of Revenues, Expenditures, and Changes in Fund Balance For Year Ended (Date)* | *Statement of Revenues, Expenses, and Changes in Fund Equity For Year Ended (Date)* |

| Governmental Fund | | | Proprietary Fund | | |
|---|---|---|---|---|---|
| **Revenues:** | | | **Operating Revenues:** | | |
| Taxes | | X | Sales of goods | | X |
| Licenses and permits | | X | Billing for services | | X |
| Intergovernmental | | X | Other | | X |
| Charges for services | | X | | | XX |
| Miscellaneous | | X | | | |
| | | X | **Operating Expenses:** | | |
| | | | Operations | | X |
| **Other Financing Sources:** | | | Depreciation | | X |
| Operating transfers from other funds | | X | Other | | X |
| Bond issue proceeds | | X | | | XX |
| | | X | **Operating Income** | | X |
| Total Revenues and Other Financing Sources | | XX | | | |
| | | | **Nonoperating Revenues (Expenses):** | | |
| | | | Interest revenue | | X |
| **Expenditures:** | | | Interest expense | | (X) |
| Operations | | X | Other | | X |
| Capital outlay | | X | | | X |
| Debt service | | | **Income before Operating Transfers** | | X |
| Bond principal | X | | | | |
| Interest | X | X | **Operating Transfers:** | | |
| | | XX | From other funds | | X |
| | | | To other funds | | (X) |
| **Other Financing Uses:** | | | | | X |
| Operating transfers to other funds | | X | **Net Income (Loss)** | | X |
| Other | | X | | | |
| | | X | Fund Equity—Beginning of Period | | XX |
| Total Expenditures and Other Financing Uses | | XX | **Residual Equity Transfers:** | | |
| | | | From other funds | | X |
| **Excess of Revenues and Other Financing Sources over (under) Expenditures and Other Financing Uses:** | | X | To other funds | | (X) |
| | | | | | X |
| | | | Fund Equity—End of Period | | XX |
| Fund Balance—Beginning of Period | | XX | | | |
| **Residual Equity Transfers:** | | | | | |
| *From* other funds | | X | | | |
| *To* other funds | | (X) | | | |
| Fund Balance—End of Period | | XX | | | |

Notes:

1. Quasi-external transactions and reimbursements are not reported separately because (a) quasi-external transactions are included in the revenues of the payee (recipient) fund and in the expenditures or expenses, as appropriate, of the payer fund; and (b) reimbursements reduce the expenditures or expenses of the payee (recipient) fund and increase the expenditures or expenses of the payer fund.

2. Other acceptable formats for the governmental fund operating statement are discussed later, as are other examples of other financing sources (uses) and reporting restatements of beginning fund balance for prior period error corrections and changes in accounting principles.

3. Governmental fund expenditures are classified by character in this example; classification of expenditures by function or program and other classifications are discussed and illustrated in Chapters 5 and 6.

(3) that neither quasi-external transactions nor reimbursements are separately reported in the operating statements.

### Governmental Fund Expenditure Classification

The GASB recommends classifying governmental fund expenditures by fund, function or program, activity, organization unit, character, and major object classes. These classifications are recommended to facilitate (1) assembling data for internal analysis purposes in manners that cross fund and departmental lines and (2) ready availability of data required for various intergovernmental comparisons and analyses. Classification of governmental fund revenues and expenditures is discussed in detail in Chapters 5 and 6.

### Consistent Classification and Terminology

Consistent classification and terminology among the budget, the accounts, and the budgetary reports is a prerequisite to valid comparisons. In addition, effective budgetary control and accountability require that the accounts and budgetary reports—particularly those related to appropriations and expenditures—be in at least as much detail as appropriation control points. The GASB recognizes the necessity of such consistency and comparability in its eleventh principle:

**PRINCIPLE 11**
**COMMON TERMINOLOGY AND CLASSIFICATION**
A common terminology and classification should be used consistently throughout the budget, the accounts, and the financial reports of each fund.

## Financial Reporting

The final GASB principle emphasizes the importance of both interim internal financial reporting and annual external financial reporting.

**PRINCIPLE 12**
**INTERIM AND ANNUAL FINANCIAL REPORTS**
a. Appropriate interim financial statements and reports of financial position, operating results, and other pertinent information should be prepared to facilitate management control of financial operations, legislative oversight, and, where necessary or desired, for external reporting purposes.
b. A **comprehensive annual financial report [CAFR]** covering all funds and account groups of the reporting entity—including introductory section; appropriate combined, combining, and individual fund statements; notes to the financial statements; required supplementary information; schedules; narrative explanations; and statistical tables—should be prepared and published.
c. **General purpose financial statements [GPFS]** of the reporting entity may be issued separately from the comprehensive annual financial report. Such statements should include the basic financial statements and notes to the financial statements that are essential to fair presentation of financial position and results of operations (and cash flows of proprietary fund types and nonexpendable trust funds). These statements may also be required to be accompanied by required supplementary information. . . .
d. . . .the financial reporting entity consists of (1) the primary government, (2) organizations for which the primary government is financially accountable, and (3) other organizations for which the nature and significance of their relationship with the primary government are such that exclusion would cause the reporting entity's financial statements to be misleading or incomplete. The reporting entity's financial statements should (1) present the fund types and account groups of the primary government (including its blended component units, which are, in substance, part of the

primary government) and (2) provide an overview of the discretely presented component units.

e. The nucleus of a financial reporting entity usually is a primary government. However, a governmental organization other than a primary government (such as a component unit, joint venture, jointly governed organization, or other stand-alone government) serves as the nucleus for its own reporting entity when it issues separate financial statements. For all of these entities, the [GASB financial reporting entity] provisions . . . should be applied in layers "from the bottom up." At each layer, the definition and display provisions should be applied before the layer is included in the financial statements of the next level of the reporting government.

### Annual Reporting Emphasis

No generally accepted accounting principles have been promulgated for monthly, quarterly, or other interim financial reporting, the topic of Principle 12a. Interim reporting is discussed and illustrated at various points throughout the text, although annual financial reporting in conformity with generally accepted accounting principles, the topic of Principles 12b through 12e, is emphasized. Financial reporting is covered comprehensively in a later chapter.

### Individual, Combining, and Combined Statements

A unique feature of state and local government financial reporting is that three categories of financial statements—of balance sheets, operating statements, and other statements—are used: (1) individual fund and account group statements, (2) combining statements, and (3) combined statements:

1. **Individual fund and account group statements,** as the name implies, present status or operating data for a single fund or account group, often in detail and/or with budget-to-actual or current year to prior year comparative data.

2. **Combining fund statements** present, in adjacent columns, data for all funds of a type (e.g., Special Revenue Funds), an "all funds" total, and perhaps a current year to prior year comparative total. Combining statements typically are in less detail than individual fund statements.

3. **Combined fund type and account group statements** present in adjacent columns data by fund type and account group, usually with "memorandum only" total and comparative columns. Combined statements have only one column for each fund type and account group. Where there is more than one fund of a type, the total data from the combining statement for that fund type appear in the combined statement. Combined statements typically are more summarized than combining or individual fund and account group statements.

The distinctions between combined, combining, and individual fund statements are important, and are illustrated in Figure 2–10. Notice that the individual fund financial statements in Figure 2–10 do not contain any information that is not provided in the combining statements. Hence, individual fund financial statements need be presented only if more detail is provided than in the combining statements, or if individual fund prior year comparative data or budgetary comparisons are presented. Combining statements do provide information that is not reported in the combined statements, however, because individual fund information is presented in the combining statements but not in the combined statements. All three types of statements are illustrated in the following chapters.

### Annual Financial Reports and Statements

State and local government units are required to issue an annual comprehensive annual financial report (CAFR), which includes the combined general purpose financial statements (GPFS) as well as (usually) combining, individual

**FIGURE 2–10  Individual Fund vs. Combining vs. Combined Financial Statements**

## Condensed and Simplified Illustrative Governmental Fund Statements of Revenues, Expenditures, and Changes in Fund Balances

**Individual Fund Statements**

| Special Revenue Fund A | |
|---|---|
| Revenues | $500 |
| Other financing sources | 80 |
| Total revenues and other financing sources | 580 |
| Expenditures | 400 |
| Other financing uses | 150 |
| Total expenditures and other financing uses | 550 |
| Excess of revenues and other financing sources over (under) expenditures and other financing uses | 30 |
| Fund balance, beginning | 120 |
| Residual equity transfer in (out) | (90) |
| Fund balance, ending | $ 60 |

| Special Revenue Fund B | |
|---|---|
| Revenues | $300 |
| Other financing sources | 30 |
| Total revenues and other financing sources | 330 |
| Expenditures | 300 |
| Other financing uses | 50 |
| Total expenditures and other financing uses | 350 |
| Excess of revenues and other financing sources over (under) expenditures and other financing uses | (20) |
| Fund balance, beginning | 200 |
| Residual equity transfer in (out) | |
| Fund balance, ending | $180 |

**Combining Statements— All Special Revenue Funds**

### Special Revenue Funds

| | Fund A | Fund B | Total |
|---|---|---|---|
| Revenues | $500 | $300 | $800 |
| Other financing sources | 80 | 30 | 110 |
| Total revenues and other financing sources | 580 | 330 | 910 |
| Expenditures | 400 | 300 | 700 |
| Other financing uses | 150 | 50 | 200 |
| Total expenditures and other financing uses | 550 | 350 | 900 |
| Excess of revenues and other financing sources over (under) expenditures and other financing uses | 30 | (20) | 10 |
| Fund balance, beginning | 120 | 200 | 320 |
| Residual equity transfer in (out) | (90) | | (90) |
| Fund balance, ending | $ 60 | $180 | $240 |

**Combined Statements— All Governmental Funds**

| | General | Special Revenue | Capital Projects | Debt Service | Total (Memorandum only) |
|---|---|---|---|---|---|
| Revenues | $5,000 | $800 | | | $5,800 |
| Other financing sources | 1,200 | 110 | 4,000 | 300 | 5,610 |
| Total revenues and other financing sources | 6,200 | 910 | 4,000 | 300 | 11,410 |
| Expenditures | 4,500 | 700 | 1,500 | 500 | 7,200 |
| Other financing uses | 1,000 | 200 | | | 1,200 |
| Total expenditures and other financing uses | 5,500 | 900 | 1,500 | 500 | 8,400 |
| Excess of revenues and other financing sources over (under) expenditures and other financing uses | 700 | 10 | 2,500 | (200) | 3,010 |
| Fund balance, beginning | 2,000 | 320 | | 400 | 2,720 |
| Residual equity transfer in (out) | | (90) | | | (90) |
| Fund balance, ending | $2,700 | $240 | $2,500 | $200 | $5,640 |

Note: The statements presented here are condensed and otherwise simplified for illustrative purposes—and are not appropriately headed or detailed for GAAP reporting purposes.

fund and account group statements for the reporting entity. The CAFR is viewed as the official annual financial report of the government and includes introductory materials and statistical data as well as financial statements and schedules. The GPFS can be separately issued for readers not requiring the detail in the CAFR, as long as the reader is made aware of the CAFR.

The combined statements that comprise the **general purpose financial statements (GPFS)** are:

1. **Combined Balance Sheet:** All Fund Types and Account Groups
2. **Combined Statement of Revenues, Expenditures, and Changes in Fund Balances:** All Governmental (and Expendable Trust) Fund Types
3. **Combined Statement of Revenues, Expenditures, and Changes in Fund Balances—Budget and Actual:** General and Special Revenue Fund Types (and similar fund types for which annual budgets have been legally adopted)
4. **Combined Statement of Revenues, Expenses, and Changes in Equity (or Retained Earnings):** All Proprietary (and Nonexpendable and Pension Trust) Fund Types
5. **Combined Statement of Cash Flows:** All Proprietary (and Nonexpendable Trust) Fund Types
6. **Combined Statement of Changes in Net Assets:** All Pension Trust Funds

Each of these statements is explained and illustrated in Chapter 13. However, the authors recommend that they be previewed briefly as this "principles" section is concluded.

### Reporting Entity and Component Units

A government's reporting entity may include several separate legal entities—for example, the city per se, a city water and sewer utility, and the city airport. If so, the financial statements of both the city and all of its component units (the utility and the airport) are included in the city CAFR and GPFS. The data for some component units are "blended" with that of the primary government funds and account groups, whereas data for other component units are "discretely presented" in a separate column(s) of the SLG's financial statements.

It also may be necessary to prepare separate, detailed financial statements for some or all of the component units of the city reporting entity. This is often the case where component unit revenue bonds are outstanding—for example, water and sewer revenue bonds—and creditors want detailed financial statements for the component unit. Defining the reporting entity and presenting financial statements for state and local governments with "complex" reporting entities that include component units are discussed and illustrated in Chapter 14. The comprehensive annual financial report (CAFR) and the general purpose financial statements (GPFS) are discussed and illustrated in Chapter 13. Most discussions and examples prior to Chapter 14 assume a reporting entity that does not include discretely presented component units.

## CONCLUDING COMMENTS

Orienting oneself to state and local government accounting and reporting requires that particular attention be given to the GASB principles, fund types, measurement focuses, budgetary control and accountability, and terminology. New and unique terms should be noted carefully. Familiar terminology also deserves analysis, as it may be used with either usual or unique connotations. Definitions of pertinent terms may be found in most chapters.

Adapting to a situation in which there are many accounting entities requires both concentration and practice. The nature, role, and distinguishing characteristics of each of the seven types of funds and the two nonfund account groups recommended by the GASB must be understood thoroughly. Each is discussed in depth in later chapters.

A peculiarity of the multiple-entity approach of fund accounting is that a single transaction may require entries in more than one accounting entity; for example, the purchase of a *general* fixed asset necessitates entries to record both the expenditure in a governmental fund and the asset in the General Fixed Assets Account Group. Furthermore, one must both accept and adapt to virtual personification of the fund accounting entities and the definitions of *revenues* and *expenditures* in a fund accounting context.

Organizational units financed from different funds may buy from and sell to one another (interfund transactions) and resources of one fund may be owed to another (interfund relationships). Too, a fund may have revenues or incur expenditures that are not revenues or expenditures of the government as a whole (quasi-external transactions). For example, payment from the General Fund to the fund through which the government's central repair shop is financed (a quasi-external transaction) constitutes a General Fund expenditure and an Internal Service Fund revenue, even though the transaction does not result in an expenditure or revenue of the government as a whole.

Finally, the budget is of such importance in governments that governmental accounting is often referred to as budgetary accounting. It is appropriate, therefore, to examine the role of the budget and major budgetary approaches, in the next chapter, before delving into the details of fund accounting principles and practices.

## APPENDIX 2–1

## Evolution of Accounting Principles

Although the origin of the profession of accountancy is sometimes traced to ancient governments, modern municipal accounting developed in the twentieth century—its beginning inseparably woven within the municipal reform movement near the turn of the century. About that time, attention was focused on the scandalous practices in the financial administration of many cities; the National Municipal League suggested uniform municipal reporting formats, and the Census Bureau encouraged more uniformity in city accounts and reports.

### Initial Evolution (1900–1933)

A flurry of change in municipal accounting and reporting practices occurred during the first decade of the twentieth century. In 1901, the firm of Haskins and Sells, Certified Public Accountants, investigated the affairs of the city of Chicago at the request of the Merchants' Club. Subsequently, the firm installed a completely new system of accounting for that city. The cities of Newton, Massachusetts, and Baltimore, Maryland, published annual reports during 1901 and 1902 along lines suggested by the National Municipal League, and the states of New York and Massachusetts passed legislation in the areas of uniform accounting and reporting in 1904 and 1906, respectively. There were many other examples of progress during this period as other cities and states followed suit.

During this era Herman A. Metz was elected Comptroller of the city of New York on a "business man for the head of the city's business office" slogan. At that time an estimated one-fourth of New York's $80 million personal services budget was being lost through collusion, idleness, or inefficiency. Too, city departments commonly issued bonds to finance current operating expenditures.

Although Metz was said to have been an outstanding comptroller, his most important contribution was the formation of the Bureau of Municipal Research. One of its purposes was "to promote the adoption of scientific methods of accounting [for] and of reporting the details of municipal business. . . ."[1]

The *Handbook of Municipal Accounting,* commonly referred to as "The Metz Fund Handbook," was called "the most significant contribution of the 1910 decade . . . [because] it brought together for the first time many of the basic characteristics and requirements of municipal accounting and outlined methods of appropriate treatment."[2] Similarly, the bureau's publications were the "first organized materials that could be called a treatise in Municipal Accounting."[3]

Pamphlets, articles, and a few textbooks appeared, as others became more interested in the subject. Municipal leagues were formed in various states and, as Newton expressed it, "we soon began a very serious development of the specialized field of Municipal Accounting."[4]

Interest waned during the 1920s and early 1930s. In a study of Illinois cities during 1931 and 1932, W. E. Karrenbrock found that few had accounting systems adequate to segregate transactions of different activities, and none had budgetary accounts coordinated within the regular accounting system.[5]

Writing in 1933, R. P. Hackett observed:

> The first fact that we are confronted with when searching for recent developments, or any developments, in governmental accounting, particularly that of municipal governments, is the marked absence of any general improvement. . . . it must be admitted that there is very little development in the actual practice of governmental and institutional accounting.[6]

## National Committees on Municipal and Governmental Accounting (1934–1974)

The National Committee on Municipal Accounting was organized in 1934, under the auspices of the Municipal Finance Officers Association, to bring together representatives of various groups concerned with municipal accounting and to put into effect sound principles of accounting, budgeting, and reporting. (Its membership included representatives of the American Association of University Instructors in Accounting, the American Institute of Accountants, the American Municipal Association, the American Society of Certified Public Accountants, the International City Managers' Association, the Municipal Finance Officers Association, the National Association of Cost Accountants, the National Association of State Auditors, Controllers, and Treasurers, the National Municipal League, and the Bureau of the

---

[1] Bureau of Municipal Research, *Making a Municipal Budget: Functional Accounts and Operative Statistics for the Department of Greater New York* (New York: BMR, 1907), p. 5.

[2] Lloyd Morey, "Trends in Governmental Accounting," *Accounting Review,* 23 (July 1948), p. 224.

[3] W. K. Newton, "New Developments and Simplified Approaches to Municipal Accounting," *Accounting Review,* 29 (October 1954), p. 656.

[4] Ibid.

[5] R. P. Hackett, "Recent Developments in Governmental and Institutional Accounting," *Accounting Review,* 8 (June 1933), p. 122.

[6] Ibid., pp. 122, 127.

Census.[7]) Each group represented also had a subcommittee on municipal accounting within its own ranks.

At its organizational meeting, the Committee tentatively adopted certain "principles" of municipal accounting and reporting and began an extensive municipal accounting research program. The Committee's formation was hailed as "the first effort on a national scale to establish principles and standards for municipal accounting and actively promote their use."[8] It was the major event in municipal accounting until that time. Indeed, the Committee's principles were officially recognized by the American Institute of Accountants, predecessor of the American Institute of Certified Public Accountants (AICPA).[9]

Numerous publications defining proper or improved municipal accounting and financial administration practices were issued by the Committee and the Municipal Finance Officers Association (MFOA) in the 1930s and 1940s. In 1948, Morey stated:

> There is no longer any doubt as to what constitutes good accounting, reporting, and auditing for public bodies. The work of the National Committee on Municipal Accounting in particular, in establishing standards and models in these subjects, provides an authority to which officials, accountants, and public may turn with confidence.[10]

In 1951, the committee, by then known as the National Committee on Governmental Accounting, issued *Municipal Accounting and Auditing*.[11] This book combined and revised the major publications of the Committee and became the basis for the major textbooks in the area as well as for many state laws and guides relating to municipal accounting, auditing, and reporting. This "Bible of municipal accounting," as it came to be called, was succeeded in 1968 by *Governmental Accounting, Auditing, and Financial Reporting* (GAAFR), often referred to as the "blue book."[12]

In 1974, the AICPA issued an audit guide, *Audits of State and Local Governmental Units* (ASLGU), to assist its members in the conduct of governmental audits.[13] ASLGU recognized GAAFR as authoritative and stated that, except as modified in ASLGU, the principles in GAAFR constituted generally accepted accounting principles.

The National Committee on Governmental Accounting was not a staff-supported, permanent body that met regularly. Rather, a new committee was formed of appointees of various government agencies, public administration groups, and accounting organizations whenever deemed necessary—historically about every ten years—and served in an advisory and review capacity with respect to revisions proposed by its members and consultants.

---

[7] Carl H. Chatters, "Municipal Accounting Progresses," *Certified Public Accountant*, 14 (February 1934), p. 101.

[8] Ibid.

[9] American Institute of Accountants, *Audits of Governmental Bodies and Accounts of Governmental Bodies* (New York: AIA, 1934 and 1935).

[10] Morey, "Trends in Governmental Accounting," p. 231.

[11] Published by the Municipal Finance Officers Association (Chicago, 1951).

[12] Published by the Municipal Finance Officers Association (Chicago, 1968). Hereafter cited as GAAFR (68).

[13] Committee on Governmental Accounting and Auditing, American Institute of Certified Public Accountants, *Audits of State and Local Governmental Units* (New York: AICPA, 1974).

## National Council on Governmental Accounting (1974–1984)

The National Council on Governmental Accounting (NCGA) was established in 1974 to succeed its predecessor, the National Committee on Governmental Accounting. The MFOA—now the Government Finance Officers Association (GFOA)—established the NCGA as an ongoing body to reconcile the differences between GAAFR and ASLGU and continually evaluate and develop state and local government accounting principles.

The council consisted of 21 members who served four-year terms on a part-time voluntary basis and met for about two days, two to four times each year. The NCGA maintained close liaison with the Financial Accounting Standards Board (FASB), AICPA, and other organizations concerned with state and local government accounting and financial reporting standards.

The NCGA's major agenda project, called the GAAFR Restatement Project, was to develop a statement described as "a modest revision to update, clarify, amplify, and reorder GAAFR." An important related objective was to incorporate pertinent aspects of ASLGU and reconcile any significant differences between GAAFR and ASLGU.

NCGA *Statement 1,* "Governmental Accounting and Financial Reporting Principles," commonly known as the GAAFR Restatement Principles, was issued in 1979. The GAAFR-ASLGU differences had been reconciled during the principles restatement. Accordingly, the AICPA issued a statement of position in 1980 (SOP 80–2)[14] amending ASLGU to incorporate NCGA *Statement 1* by reference and provide additional guidance to auditors of state and local government financial statements.

The NCGA issued seven Statements, eleven Interpretations, and one Concepts Statement during its 1974–1984 tenure. Its early years coincided with a turbulent period marked by the fiscal emergency of the city of New York and by similar financial problems, including debt defaults, in several other major cities and school districts. These crisis situations led to demands that the NCGA issue additional accounting standards. But the NCGA's efforts to provide timely guidance were hampered by the fact that its members served part time, at no pay, and had limited staff support. Thus, leaders of the accounting profession—including members of the NCGA—sought to devise an improved approach to setting accounting standards applicable to state and local governments. Their efforts led to the creation of the Governmental Accounting Standards Board (GASB) in 1984 to succeed the NCGA.

## Questions

**Q 2-1**   The terms *fund* and *funds* are used with varying connotations. For example, a college student may consider his cash and checking account balance to be his *funds* and his savings account his *fund.* Indicate (a) the various meanings associated with these terms in business and (b) the principal manner in which these terms are used in state and local government accounting.

**Q 2-2**   A state or local government may employ only one of certain fund or nonfund account group entities but one, none, or many of other types. Of which would you expect a government to have only one? One, none, or many?

**Q 2-3**   The following are names of funds encountered in governmental reports and the purposes for which these funds have been established. Indicate the corresponding fund type recommended by the Governmental Accounting Standards Board.

---

[14] Audit Standards Division, American Institute of Certified Public Accountants, Inc., *Statement of Position 80–2,* "Accounting and Financial Reporting by Governmental Units" (New York: AICPA, June 30, 1980).

    a. School Fund (to account for special taxes levied by a county to finance the operation of schools)

    b. Bond Redemption Fund (to account for taxes and other revenues to be used in retiring bonds)

    c. Bridge Construction Fund (to account for the proceeds from the sale of bonds)

    d. Park Fund (to account for special taxes levied to finance the operation of parks)

    e. Interdepartmental Printing Shop Fund (to account for revenues received from departments for printing done for them by the interdepartmental printing shop)

    f. City Bus Line Fund (to account for revenues received from the public for transportation services)

    g. Money Collected for the State Fund (to account for money collected as agent for the state)

    h. Operating Fund (to account for unrestricted revenues not related to any other fund)

    i. Electric Fund (to account for revenues received from the sale of electricity to the public)

    j. Federal Fund (to account for federal construction grant proceeds)

    k. Bond Redemption Fund (to account for proceeds of bond refunding issue that are to be used to repay outstanding bonds)

    l. Federal Fund (to account for shared revenue grants that may be used for any of several broad purpose categories)

    m. Bond Proceeds Fund (to account for proceeds of bonds issued to finance street construction)

    n. Employees' Pension and Relief Fund (to provide retirement and disability benefits to employees)

**Q 2-4** Why are a municipality's general fixed assets and general long-term debt accounted for through nonfund account groups rather than within one of its funds, such as the General Fund?

**Q 2-5** What differences would you expect to find between the accounting principles for the General Fund and for Special Revenue Funds?

**Q 2-6** Revenues or expenditures of a specific fund may not represent increases or decreases in the net assets of the government as a whole. Why is this true?

**Q 2-7** It has been asserted that terms such as *sources* and *uses* should be substituted for *revenues* and *expenditures,* respectively, in accounting and reporting for governmental (expendable) funds. Do you agree? Why or why not?

**Q 2-8** The GASB principles classify all of the funds and account groups used in state and local government accounting and financial reporting into four categories: (1) governmental funds, (2) proprietary funds, (3) fiduciary funds, and (4) account groups. What are the major accounting and other commonalities shared by specific funds and account groups in these categories?

**Q 2-9** It is not uncommon to find the terms *expenditures* and *expenses* erroneously used as synonyms. How do expenditures differ from expenses?

**Q 2-10** Governmental fund and proprietary fund operating results are determined differently under GASB standards. Explain.

**Q 2-11** The principal financial statements of business enterprises are the balance sheet, income statement, and statement of cash flows. What similarities are there, if any, among these statements and the operating and position statements of a proprietary (nonexpendable) fund? A governmental (expendable) fund?

**Q 2-12** Fund accounting and budgetary control are deemed of such importance by the GASB that four of its twelve principles deal directly with these topics and most of the others relate to them at least indirectly. Why?

**Q 2-13** In what funds and account groups are (a) fixed assets and (b) long-term debt accounted for? Why are they not accounted for in the other funds and account groups?

**Q 2-14** Harvey Township budgets its resources on the cash basis in accordance with state laws. State law also requires financial statements prepared on the cash basis. To comply with this requirement, Harvey Township prepares the financial statements in its comprehensive annual financial report (CAFR) on the cash basis rather than on the GAAP basis.
a. Discuss the appropriateness of the statements in Harvey Township's CAFR.
b. Explain what, if anything, Harvey Township should change in its CAFR.

**Q 2-15** Define the following interfund transaction terms and explain how each is accounted for and reported by a municipality: (a) reimbursement, (b) quasi-external transaction, (c) residual equity transfer, and (d) operating transfer.

**Q 2-16** The City of Horner's Corner publishes general purpose financial statements (GPFS), but considers it unnecessary to publish a comprehensive annual financial report (CAFR). The city's only funds are a General Fund, three Special Revenue Funds, two Capital Projects Funds, an Internal Service Fund, and two Enterprise Funds. A citizen has asked you if this practice is appropriate according to GASB principles. Discuss.

**Q 2-17** Distinguish between (a) the comprehensive annual financial report and the general purpose financial statements of a government; and (b) combining and combined financial statements of a government.

## Exercises

**E 2-1** (Fund and Account Group Identification) Indicate the fund or account group that should be used to account for each of the following:
1. Tax revenues restricted for road maintenance.
2. Resources restricted to use for construction of a new government office building.
3. Typical water and sewer department.
4. Unrestricted tax revenues.
5. School Buildings.
6. Bonds payable issued for general government purposes.
7. The portion of general government bonds payable that matures in the next fiscal year.
8. Cash and investments of a bond sinking fund established to service general government long-term debt.
9. Fixed assets of a government department that sells services to the public as the primary ongoing source of financing for its operation.
10. Long-term note for the government's central motor pool that "rents" vehicles to other departments and agencies of the government at a rate that reimburses its costs.

**E 2-2** (Fund Identification) Using the appropriate fund abbreviations, indicate which governmental fund(s) might be used to account for the following items and give the reasons for your answer(s).
1. Revenues not restricted as to use
2. Revenues restricted for specified current operating purposes
3. Purchase of equipment, furniture, and fixtures
4. Depreciation of equipment used in general government functions
5. Payment of short-term debt interest and principal
6. Payment of maturing long-term debt interest and principal
7. Construction of a major capital facility or improvement
8. Charges for services
9. Revenues restricted to payment of general obligation long-term debt interest and principal
10. Proceeds of long-term debt issuances

**Solution Format**

| No. | Fund(s) to Be Used | Reason(s) | Fund Abbreviations |
|---|---|---|---|
| | | | GF General Fund |
| | | | SRF Special Revenue Fund |
| | | | CPF Capital Projects Fund |
| | | | DSF Debt Service Fund |

**E 2-3** (Financial Reporting Purposes and Depreciation—Government vs. Business) William Bates is executive vice president of Mavis Industries, Inc., a publicly held industrial corporation. Bates has just been elected to the city council of Gotham City. Prior to assuming office as a city councilman, he asks you to explain the major differences in accounting and financial reporting for a large city as compared to a large industrial corporation.

**Required** (a) Describe the major differences in the purpose of accounting and financial reporting and in the types of financial reports of a large city as compared to a large industrial corporation.

(b) Under what circumstances should depreciation be recognized in accounting for local governmental units? Explain.

(AICPA, adapted)

## Problems

**P 2-1** (Multiple Choice) Select the lettered response that best completes the numbered statements.

1. The operations of a public library receiving the majority of its support from property taxes levied for that purpose should be accounted for in
   a. the General Fund.
   b. a Special Revenue Fund.
   c. an Enterprise Fund.
   d. an Internal Service Fund.
   e. none of the above.

2. The proceeds of a federal grant made to assist in financing the future construction of an adult training center should be recorded in
   a. the General Fund.
   b. a Special Revenue Fund.
   c. a Capital Projects Fund.
   d. a Special Assessment Fund.
   e. none of the above.

3. The receipts from a special tax levy to retire and pay interest on general obligation bonds issued to finance the construction of a new city hall should be recorded in a
   a. Debt Service Fund.
   b. Capital Projects Fund.
   c. Revolving Interest Fund.
   d. Special Revenue Fund.
   e. none of the above.

4. The operations of a municipal swimming pool receiving the majority of its support from charges to users should be accounted for in
   a. a Special Revenue Fund.
   b. the General Fund.
   c. an Internal Service Fund.
   d. an Enterprise Fund.
   e. none of the above.

5. The monthly remittance to an insurance company of the lump sum of hospital-surgical insurance premiums collected as payroll deductions from employees should be recorded in
   a. the General Fund.
   b. an Agency Fund.
   c. a Special Revenue Fund.
   d. an Internal Service Fund.
   e. none of the above.

6. A transaction in which a municipality issued general obligation serial bonds to finance the construction of a fire station requires accounting recognition in the
   a. General Fund.
   b. Capital Projects and General Funds.

    c. Capital Projects Fund and the General Long-Term Debt Account Group.
    d. General Fund and the General Long-Term Debt Account Group.
    e. none of the above.

7. Expenditures of $200,000 were made during the year on the fire station in item 6. This transaction requires accounting recognition in the
    a. General Fund.
    b. Capital Projects Fund and the General Fixed Assets Account Group.
    c. Capital Projects Fund and the General Long-Term Debt Account Group.
    d. General Fund and the General Fixed Assets Account Group.
    e. none of the above.

8. The activities of a central motor pool that provides and services vehicles for the use of municipal employees on official business should be accounted for in
    a. an Agency Fund.         d. a Special Revenue Fund.
    b. the General Fund.        e. none of the above.
    c. an Internal Service Fund.

9. A transaction in which a municipal electric utility paid $150,000 out of its earnings for new equipment requires accounting recognition in
    a. an Enterprise Fund.
    b. the General Fund.
    c. the General Fund and the General Fixed Assets Account Group.
    d. an Enterprise Fund and the General Fixed Assets Account Group.
    e. none of the above.

10. The activities of a municipal employee retirement plan that is financed by equal employer and employee contributions should be accounted for in
    a. an Agency Fund.         d. a Trust Fund.
    b. an Internal Service Fund.    e. none of the above.
    c. a Special Revenue Fund.

11. A city collects property taxes for the benefit of the local sanitary, park, and school districts and periodically remits collections to these units. This activity should be accounted for in
    a. an Agency Fund.         d. a Special Revenue Fund.
    b. the General Fund.        e. none of the above.
    c. an Internal Service Fund.

12. A transaction in which a municipal electric utility issues bonds (to be repaid from its own operations) requires accounting recognition in
    a. the General Fund.
    b. a Debt Service Fund.
    c. Enterprise and Debt Service Funds.
    d. an Enterprise Fund, a Debt Service Fund, and the General Long-Term Debt Account Group.
    e. none of the above.
    (AICPA, adapted)

**P 2-2** (Transaction Analysis—Governmental vs. Proprietary Model)
1. Analyze the following transactions assuming that a business-type activity was involved. (Hint: Use the proprietary fund accounting equation only.)
2. Analyze the following transactions assuming that a general governmental-type activity was involved. (Hint: The governmental fund and account group entities will be required.)
    a. Salaries of $5,100 were incurred and paid during the year. Another $200 of salaries were incurred but not paid as of year end.
    b. Charges for services rendered were billed and received, $3,000.
    c. Borrowed $2,000 on a 1-year, 10%, interest-bearing note, due 3 months after year end. Record borrowing and any accrual.
    d. Principal ($2,000) and interest ($200) on the 1-year note were paid when due.

e. Received a $200 subsidy from another fund in a nonreciprocal transaction.
f. Issued 10-year, 10% bonds payable for par of $1,000.
g. Annual interest on the bonds ($100) was paid when due—at year end.
h. Repaid the principal amount of a 5-year note, $800.
i. Purchased a computer with a 3-year useful life for cash, $900.
j. Straight-line depreciation of the computer is calculated to be $280 per year. The estimated residual value of the computer is $60.
k. The computer is sold at the end of its useful life for $35. Original cost was $900.

**P 2-3** (Transaction Analysis)
a. Analyze the effects of each of the following transactions on each of the funds and account groups of the city of Nancy, Virginia.
b. Indicate how each transaction would be reported in the operating statement for each fund affected.

**EXAMPLE:** Cash received for licenses during 1991, $8,000.

**ANSWER:**

*GENERAL FUND (GF)*
Increases Current Assets (CA) $8,000
Increases Fund Balance (FB) $8,000
Revenues of $8,000 reported

1. Salaries and wages for firefighters and police officers incurred but not paid, $75,000.
2. Borrowed $9,000,000 to finance construction of a new city executive office building by issuing bonds at par.
3. The city paid $5,000,000 to the office building contractor for work performed during the fiscal year.
4. The city purchased a computer by issuing a $5,000, 6%, 6-month note to the vendor. The note is due March 1 of the next fiscal year—which is the calendar year.
5. General Fund resources of $5,000,000 were paid to a newly established Airport Enterprise Fund to provide initial start-up capital.
6. A $3,000,000 personal injury lawsuit has been filed against the city. The controller determines that it is probable that a judgment in that amount will be made in the future but does not expect to have to pay the judgment for another 3 years. The incident relates to general government activities.
7. The city repaid one-half ($10,000,000) of general obligation bonds that had been issued several years before to finance construction of a school building. Interest of $1,000,000 was also paid. All amounts were paid from resources accumulated previously for this purpose.
8. The city sold general fixed assets with an original cost of $50,000 at the end of their useful life for $1,500. There are no restrictions on the use of the money.

**P 2-4** (Transaction Analysis)
a. Analyze the effects of the following transactions on the accounting equations of the various funds and account groups of a state or local government. **(For any borrowing transactions, reflect any necessary year-end interest accruals in your responses.)**
b. Indicate how each transaction would be reported in the operating statement for each fund affected. Be sure to name the operating statement.
  1. A government incurred and paid salaries for general government employees, $500,000.
  2. A government purchased a truck, $38,000, for the use of a general government department that is financed from taxes that can be used only to support that department's programs. The government paid $10,000 in cash and signed a 2-year, 10% note for the $28,000 balance.

3. A government issued $5,000,000 of 6%, 10-year bonds to help finance expansion of a facility used by one of its public utility operations. The bonds were issued at par 3 months before year end and pay interest annually.
4. A government issued a 9-month, 10% note payable for $50,000. The note was issued 6 months before the end of the fiscal year to provide financing for various programs that are financed primarily from general tax revenues.
5. A government issued general obligation bonds at par, $15,000,000, to finance construction of a new school building. The bonds bear interest at 8%, payable annually, and were dated and issued 6 months before the end of the year.
6. The government purchased land for the site of the school, $185,000.
7. The government incurred and paid contruction costs on the school building, which was completed during the year, $14,715,000.
8. The government's governing body ordered that the unused school bond proceeds be set aside for paying principal and interest on the bonds, and those resources were set aside in the appropriate fund.
9. $1,500,000 of general tax revenues was paid over to the fund to be used to pay principal and interest on the school bonds.
10. The first annual interest payment on the school bonds came due and was paid.
11. The 9-month note (from item 4) was repaid with interest when due.
12. The government-owned public utility sold services to the public on account, $1,000,000; 1% is expected to be uncollectible.
13. The government-owned public utility sold services to other departments of the government, $110,000. The other departments have paid all but $10,000.
14. The government sold a police department computer for $4,000. Its original cost (3 years earlier) was $15,000. At the time of purchase the computer was expected to be used for 4 years and have a $7,000 residual value.
15. The government paid $100,000 principal and $10,000 interest on a long-term note that came due midway through the year.

**P 2-5**   (Modified Accrual Basis vs. Accrual Basis) In order to ensure continuous and dependable bus service to its citizens "from now on," Mobiline County acquired the following assets of Mobiline Transit, Inc., a privately owned bus line in financial difficulty:

| Assets | Amount Paid by County |
|---|---|
| Land . . . . . . . . . . . . . . . . . . . . . . . . . . . . . | $ 10,000 |
| Garage and office building . . . . . . . . . . . . . | 30,000 |
| Inventory of tires and parts. . . . . . . . . . . . . | 15,000 |
| Shop equipment. . . . . . . . . . . . . . . . . . . . . . | 5,000 |
| Buses . . . . . . . . . . . . . . . . . . . . . . . . . . . . . | 140,000 |
| Total paid—February 1, 19X3 . . . . . . . . . . | $200,000 |

*Additional Information:*
1. The purchase was financed through the issue of 6% general obligation notes payable, scheduled to mature in amounts of $20,000 each February 1, for ten years. Interest is payable annually each February 1.
2. Bus line revenues and expenditures are accounted for through the General Fund. The fixed assets acquired were recorded in the General Fixed Assets Account Group and the notes payable were recorded in the General Long-Term Debt Account Group.
3. In November 19X3, following the close of the county's fiscal year on October 31, the Mobiline *Daily Banner* published a feature story about the county-owned bus line under the heading "Bus Line Prospers under County Management." The following operating statement, prepared by the county clerk from the General Fund records, appeared within the newspaper article:

**Mobiline County Bus Line**
Operating Statement
For the Nine-Month Period Ending October 31, 19X3

Revenues:

| | | |
|---|---|---|
| Passenger fares—routine route service . . . . . . . . . . . . . . . . | $77,000 | |
| Special charter fees . . . . . . . . . . . . . . . . . . . . . . . . . . . . . . | 3,000 | $80,000 |

Expenditures:

| | | |
|---|---|---|
| Salaries (superintendent, drivers, mechanics) . . . . . . . . . . . . | 52,000 | |
| Fuel and lubrication . . . . . . . . . . . . . . . . . . . . . . . . . . . . . . . | 12,000 | |
| Tires and parts. . . . . . . . . . . . . . . . . . . . . . . . . . . . . . . . . . . | 1,000 | |
| Contracted repairs and maintenance . . . . . . . . . . . . . . . . . . | 8,000 | |
| Miscellaneous . . . . . . . . . . . . . . . . . . . . . . . . . . . . . . . . . . . | 1,000 | 74,000 |
| Net profit . . . . . . . . . . . . . . . . . . . . . . . . . . . . . . . . . . . . . | | $ 6,000 |

The story quoted a county commissioner as saying:

> We are extremely pleased with our bus line operating results to date. Through sound management, we have turned a losing operation into a profitable one—and we expect an even greater profit next year. When we got into the bus line business we determined that the buses would last five years and the building and shop equipment would suffice for ten years—so we do not anticipate any capital outlay expense for some time. In addition, we have $3,000 worth of tires and parts on hand that do not appear in the Operating Statement but will help us hold down our expenses during the next few months, and we should collect another $500 fee for an October charter this week.

*Required*  (a) Prepare an accrual basis statement of revenues and expenses (income statement) for Mobiline County Bus Line for the 9-month period ending October 31, 19X3.

(b) Evaluate the propriety of the information contained within the *Daily Banner* feature story.

**P 2-6**  (Entries Using Different Bases of Accounting) (a) Record each of the following transactions on (1) the cash basis, (2) the modified accrual basis, and (3) the accrual basis.

| | |
|---|---|
| January | 1 Billed customers $400 for services rendered |
| | 3 Purchased $50 of supplies on account |
| | 5 Purchased a truck costing $5,000 (to be paid for on February 3) |
| | 11 Collected $200 from customers on account |
| | 15 Recorded accrued wages to date, $1,000 |
| | 17 Paid for supplies |
| | 21 Paid wages |
| February | 3 Paid for the truck |
| | 5 $20 of supplies have been used |
| | 6 Depreciation on the truck for the month was $100 |

**Solution Format**

| | | Cash Basis | | Modified Accrual Basis | | Accrual Basis | |
|---|---|---|---|---|---|---|---|
| Date | Accounts | Dr. | Cr. | Dr. | Cr. | Dr. | Cr. |

(b) Explain the similarities and differences between the modified accrual and accrual bases of accounting.

**P 2-7**  (Interfund Transactions) (a) Classify each of the transactions according to its type or indicate that it is not an interfund transaction. Indicate why you classified the transaction as you did.

1. $5,000,000 of General Fund cash was contributed to establish an Internal Service Fund.

2. A truck—acquired two years ago with General Fund revenues for $18,000—with a fair market value of $4,000 was contributed to a department financed by an Enterprise Fund.
3. The Sanitation Department, accounted for in the General Fund, billed the Municipal Airport, accounted for in an Enterprise Fund, $4,000 for garbage collection.
4. General Fund cash amounting to $700,000—to be repaid in 90 days—was provided to enable construction to begin on a new courthouse before a bond issue was sold.
5. A $9,000,000 bond issue to finance construction of an addition to the civic center was sold at par.
6. General Fund disbursements during May included a nonloan payment of $300,000 to a Capital Projects Fund to help finance a major capital project.
7. After retirement of the related debt, the remaining net assets of a Debt Service Fund, $1,500,000 were transferred to the General Fund.
8. General Fund cash amounting to $1,000,000 was contributed to a Capital Projects Fund as the city's portion of the cost of the project.
9. An Internal Service Fund department paid $5,000 to the General Fund for Internal Service Fund supplies paid for by, and recorded as expenditures in, the General Fund during the year.
10. $500,000 was allocated and paid from the General Fund to the Enterprise Fund to finance its budgeted operating deficit.

### Solution Format

| No. | Classification | Reason(s) |
| --- | --- | --- |

a. Discuss how each type of interfund transaction should be reported in the statement of revenues, expenditures, and changes in fund balance.
b. Why is it important to distinguish interfund transfers and bond issue proceeds from fund revenues, expenditures, and expenses?

**P 2-8** (Transaction Analysis)

*Required* (a) Analyze the effects of the following transactions on the accounting equations of the various funds and account groups of a state or local government.
(b) Indicate how each transaction would be reported in the operating statement for each fund affected.

1. The government-owned and -operated electric utility billed users $2,000,000 for electricity usage. This included $100,000 billed to general government departments for electricity usage.
2. $50,000 of General Fund money was loaned to a Capital Projects Fund to allow construction on the project to begin before the related bonds were to be issued. The loan is to be repaid in 6 months.
3. $1,000,000 of property taxes were levied during the year to provide financing for the budget of the year of levy. $800,000 was collected by year end. Another $85,000 was collected during the first 60 days of the next fiscal year. An additional $100,000 is expected to be collected during the remainder of the second fiscal year, and $15,000 is estimated to be uncollectible.
4. The government issued a $7,000,000, 6%, 5-year note halfway through the fiscal year to provide partial financing for construction of a bridge.
5. The government issued a $1,000,000, 6%, 1-year note halfway through the fiscal year to provide temporary financing for a special program which will be financed ultimately by reimbursements from a restricted grant awarded to the government for the specific purpose of financing that program. However, no cash has been received from the grantor to date.
6. Purchased a truck for a general government department for $40,000 cash.
7. Repaid outstanding general government bonds, $2,000,000 and $100,000 interest.
8. The government paid $1,000,000 in vacation pay during the year. Employees who do not use their vacation time are paid for unused vacation time upon

termination. The government's liability for accumulated unused vacation pay (measured per GASB Statement No. 16) increased by $250,000 during the year—all of which is considered long term in nature. Half of the costs are for General Fund employees, half are for Enterprise Fund employees.

9. The 1-year note from transaction 5 matured and was paid along with the interest of $60,000.

10. A utility department truck was sold halfway through its useful life for $17,000. The truck, which originally cost $45,000, had an estimated residual value of $5,000.

**P 2-9** (Transaction Analysis)

a. Analyze the effects of each of the following transactions on the accounting equations of any fund or account group of Segelquist County affected by the transaction. (Record any interest accruals that Segelquist would be required to make at year end.)

b. Also indicate if and how each transaction would be reported in the operating statement of each of the affected funds. Be specific.

1. Segelquist County issued $5,000,000 of general obligation, 6% bonds on November 1, 19X5. Bond interest is payable semiannually on April 30 and October 31. The bonds mature in 20 years. December 31 is the end of the county fiscal year. The bonds were issued to finance construction of a new jail annex.

2. The county paid $4,000,000 to Jailbird Construction Company during November and December 19X5 for construction costs incurred on the jail annex. Jailbird billed Segelquist County another $900,000 upon completion of the jail on December 30, 19X5.

3. The Segelquist County board of supervisors voted to set the unused Jail Annex Bonds proceeds aside for future principal and interest payments on the bonds. This action complied with a requirement of the bond indenture and was accomplished on December 31, 19X5, in accordance with the board's directive.

4. The county purchased new furnishings for the jailhouse annex. The total cost of $500,000 was paid from unrestricted resources.

5. The county water and sewer department provides services to county residents at a charge that is established at a level that is intended to recover the costs of providing the goods and services. If the charges prove inadequate, the county subsidizes operations from unrestricted county resources. The county water and sewer department borrowed $5,000,000 on November 1, 19X5, by issuing 6% revenue bonds on November 1, 19X5. Bond interest is payable semiannually on April 30 and October 31. The bonds mature in 20 years. The bonds were issued to finance construction of a new water treatment plant.

6. $200,000 was paid from the General Fund to the fund from which the jail bonds are to be serviced for the purpose of providing for upcoming payments. No repayment is to be made to the General Fund.

7. The county made the first semiannual interest payment on the jail bonds at the due date, April 30, 19X6.

**P 2-10** (Research Problem) Obtain a state or local government comprehensive annual financial report (CAFR) or general purpose financial statements (GPFS) from a government, a library, your professor, the Internet, or elsewhere.

**Required** (a) Identify the CAFR or GPFS and describe its contents.

(b) Describe the contents of the "Summary of Significant Accounting Policies" note to the financial statements and indicate:

1. which notes you were able to understand based on your reading of this chapter of the text, and

2. any notes that you were surprised to find and/or did not understand.

You should attach photocopies or printouts from your CAFR or GPFS, as appropriate, and should also submit your CAFR or GPFS if requested by the instructor.

CHAPTER

# 3

# BUDGETING, BUDGETARY ACCOUNTING, AND BUDGETARY REPORTING

Budgeting is the process of allocating scarce resources to unlimited demands, and a budget is a dollars and cents plan of operation for a specific period of time. At a minimum, such a plan should contain information about the types and amounts of proposed expenditures, the purposes for which they are to be made, and the proposed means of financing them.

Although practices are by no means uniform, budgeting and budgets typically play a far greater role in the planning, control, and evaluation of governmental operations than in those of privately owned businesses. The GASB recognizes the importance of the budget process in the following principle:

9. a. An annual budget(s) should be adopted by every governmental unit.
   b. The accounting system should provide the basis for appropriate budgetary control.
   c. Budgetary comparisons should be included in the appropriate financial statements and schedules for governmental funds for which an annual budget has been adopted.[1]

The adoption of a budget implies that decisions have been made—on the basis of a planning process—as to how the unit is to reach its objectives. The accounting system then assists the administrators to control the activities authorized to carry out the plans and to prepare the statements that permit comparison of actual operations with the budget and evaluation of variances. These three budgetary phases and functions—**planning, control, and evaluation**—are crucial aspects of all budgetary approaches and processes.

Budgeting, budgetary accounting, and budgetary reporting are uniquely important and distinctive features of governmental fund accounting and financial reporting. Indeed, governmental fund accounting is often referred to as *budgetary accounting;* and, as noted in Chapter 2, governmental fund operating statements are prepared on both the GAAP basis and the SLG's budgetary basis. Furthermore, many questions and problems on the Uniform CPA Examination require knowledge of governmental fund budgeting, budgetary accounting, and budgetary reporting.

---

[1] GASB *Codification*, sec. 1100.109.

Accordingly, the first part of this chapter considers the role of the annual budget in governmental fund planning, control, and evaluation; basic budgetary terminology; the major alternative budgeting approaches and emphases found in practice (and on the CPA exam); and the usual procedures in the preparation and enactment of an SLG annual operating budget. The latter part of the chapter is devoted to introductory overview discussions and illustrations of budgetary accounting techniques and budgetary reporting methods. These discussions and illustrations are also designed to provide a bridge to the budgetary accounting entries and budgetary statement examples in the following several chapters.

## BUDGETARY PLANNING, CONTROL, AND EVALUATION

### Planning

The prominence of the budgetary process in government is a natural outgrowth of its environment. Planning is a special concern here because, as noted previously, (1) the type, quantity, and quality of governmental goods and services provided are not normally evaluated and adjusted through the open market mechanism; (2) these goods and services (e.g., education, police and fire protection, and sanitation) are often among the most critical to the public interest; (3) the immense scope and diversity of modern government activities make comprehensive, thoughtful, and systematic planning a prerequisite to orderly decision making; and (4) government planning and decision making is generally a joint process involving its citizens (or "owners"), either individually or in groups, their elected representatives within the legislative branch, and the members of the executive branch.

The legislative-executive division of powers, the so-called checks-and-balances device, is operative in all states and in most local governments. In these and in most manager-council forms of organization, "the executive proposes, the legislature disposes"; that is, the executive is responsible for drafting tentative plans, but final plans are made by the legislative body—often after public hearings in which interested citizens or groups are able to participate. Written budget proposals are essential to communication, discussion, revision, and documentation of plans by those concerned with and responsible for planning.

### Control

Budgets are also widely used control devices in governments, in regard to both (1) legislative branch control over the executive branch and (2) chief executive control over subordinate executive agencies or departments. As observed earlier, when a budget is enacted by the legislative branch, the expenditure estimates become ***appropriations—both authorizations*** to expend ***and*** expenditure ***limitations*** upon the executive branch.

Appropriations may be enacted in very broad categorical terms or in minute detail. When appropriations are enacted in broad categorical terms, the legislature exercises general or policy-level control only—and the executive is given much managerial discretion in the conduct of governmental business. But when appropriations are enacted in minute detail, the chief executive has almost no discretion and is restricted to carrying out various specific, detailed orders from the legislature. Similarly, the chief executive may restrict subordinates by granting agency or departmental expenditure authority in more detailed or specific categories (*allocations*) than those approved by the legislature. Likewise the chief executive may ration expenditure authority to subordinate agencies or departments in terms of monthly or quarterly expenditure ceilings, referred to as *allotments*. Thus, the accounting system must provide information that enables (1) agencies or departments to keep their expenditures within limitations imposed by the chief executive and demonstrate compliance with those limitations, and (2) the chief executive to keep the expenditures of the government as a whole within limitations imposed by the legislative branch and demonstrate such compliance.

### Evaluation

The budgetary authority extended to one branch or level of government by another therefore becomes a standard for measurement of legal and administrative compliance or noncompliance. Appropriate financial reports—that compare the budgeted and actual revenue and expenditure amounts for the period—serve as a basis for evaluating the extent of compliance with standards established by the various "dollar stewardship" accountability relationships in this environment.

## BASIC BUDGETARY TERMINOLOGY

Although the operating budget of each year stands alone from a legal standpoint, *budgeting is a continuous process*. Budget officials will be engaged during any given year in ensuring that the prior year's budgetary reports are properly audited and appropriately distributed, in administering the budget of the current year, and in preparing the budget for the upcoming year(s). The budget for any year (see Figure 3–1) goes through five phases: (1) preparation, (2) legislative enactment, (3) administration, (4) reporting, and (5) postaudit.

State and local governments typically prepare and utilize several types of financial plans referred to as *budgets*. It is important, therefore, to distinguish among various types of budgets, to understand the phases through which each may pass, and to be familiar with commonly used budgetary terminology. For purposes of this discussion, budgets may be classified as:

1. capital or current
2. tentative or enacted
3. general or special
4. fixed or flexible
5. executive or legislative

### Capital vs. Current Budgets

Sound governmental fiscal management requires continual planning for several periods into the future. Most governments are involved in programs to provide certain goods or services continuously (or at least for several years); in acquisitions of buildings, land, or other major items of capital outlay that must be scheduled and financed; and in long-term debt service commitments. Although some prepare comprehensive multiyear plans that include all of these, such multiyear plans most frequently include only the capital outlay plans for the organization. Such a plan generally covers a period of two to six years and is referred to as a *capital program*.

Each year the current segment of the capital program is considered for inclusion as the *capital budget,* in the *current budget*. The current budget also includes

FIGURE 3–1 **The Budget Cycle**

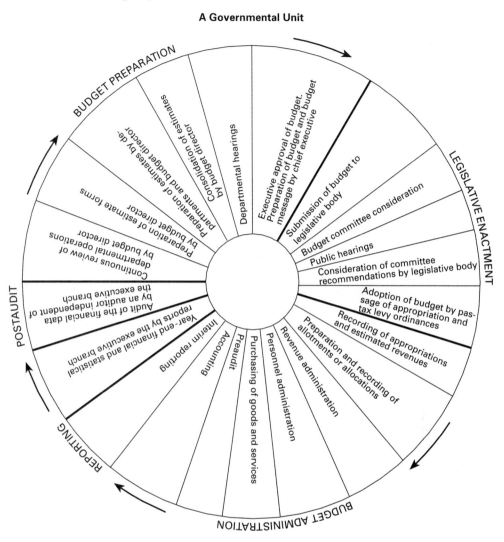

A Governmental Unit

BUDGET PREPARATION

LEGISLATIVE ENACTMENT

BUDGET ADMINISTRATION

REPORTING

POSTAUDIT

Departmental hearings

Consolidation of estimates by budget director

Preparation of estimates by de-partments and budget director

Preparation of estimate forms by budget director

Continuous review of departmental operations by budget director

Audit of the financial data by an auditor independent of the executive branch

Year-end financial and statistical reports by the executive branch

Interim reporting

Accounting

Preaudit

Purchasing of goods and services

Personnel administration

Revenue administration

Preparation and recording of allotments or allocations

Recording of appropriations and estimated revenues

Adoption of budget by pas-sage of appropriation and tax levy ordinances

Consideration of committee recommendations by legislative body

Public hearings

Budget committee consideration

Submission of budget to legislative body

Preparation of budget and budget message by chief executive

Executive approval of budget,

the proposed expenditures for current operations and debt service, as well as esti-mates of all financial resources expected to be available during the current period.

The typical interrelationships of a capital program, capital budget, and cur-rent budget are illustrated in Figure 3–2. The remainder of this chapter is con-cerned primarily with current or operating budgets.

## Tentative vs. Enacted Budgets

One key distinction among budgets is their legal status. Various documents may be called budgets prior to approval by the legislative body. Such documents have vary-ing degrees of finality, but none is a final, legally enacted budget. For example, cap-ital programs represent plans but not requests by the executive branch and are subject to change from year to year. Similarly, whereas a departmental budget re-quest may be called a budget, it may be changed several times by the department head or higher authorities before being included in the chief executive's final bud-get presented to the legislature. Enactment of an appropriation bill by the legisla-

FIGURE 3–2  **Interrelationships of Capital Program—Capital Budget—Operating Budget**

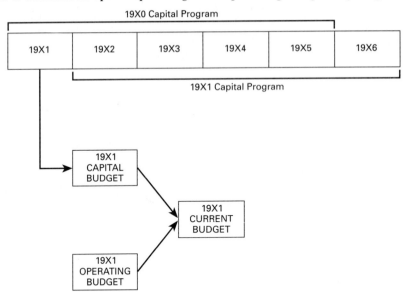

tive branch is the legal basis of its control over the executive branch. Only the legislature may revise the terms or conditions of this final legally enacted budget, which is the basis for executive branch accountability to the legislature.

## General vs. Special Budgets

The budgets of general governmental activities—commonly financed through the General, Special Revenue, and Debt Service Funds—are referred to as *general budgets*. A budget prepared for any other fund is referred to as a *special budget*. Special budgets are commonly limited to those for Capital Projects Funds, though Internal Service and Enterprise Funds are sometimes formally budgeted. Appropriations are not normally required for Trust and Agency Funds because the government usually is acting merely as a fiduciary in such situations; consequently, formal budgets are rarely prepared for these types of funds.

## Fixed vs. Flexible Budgets

Fixed budgets are those in which appropriations are for specific (fixed) dollar amounts of expenditures or expenses. These appropriated amounts may not be exceeded because of changes in demand for governmental goods or services. On the other hand, expenditures or expenses authorized by flexible budgets are fixed per unit of goods or services but are variable in total according to demand for either production or delivery of the goods or services.

Fixed budgets are relatively simple to prepare and administer and are more easily understood than flexible budgets. Additionally, fixed budgets lend themselves to the desire of strong legislatures to limit (control) the discretion of the executive (and his or her subordinates). Finally, fixed budgets are readily adaptable to integrating budgetary control techniques into accounting systems and are consistent with the intent of allocating a fixed amount of financial resources among various departments or programs. Governmental fund budgets are almost invariably fixed expenditure budgets.

Flexible budgets are more realistic when changes in the quantities of goods or services provided directly affect resource availability and expenditure or expense requirements, and when formal budgetary control (in the account structure) is not deemed essential. Flexible budgets—on the expense or expenditure basis—are most appropriate for Enterprise and Internal Service Funds.

## Executive vs. Legislative Budgets

Budgets are also sometimes categorized by preparer. As noted earlier, budget preparation is usually considered an executive function, though the legislature may revise the budget prior to approval. In some instances, however, the legislative branch prepares the budget, possibly subject to executive veto; in other instances, the budget may originate with a joint legislative-executive committee (possibly with citizen representatives) or with a committee composed solely of citizens or constituents. Such budgets are frequently referred to by terms such as *executive budget, legislative budget, joint budget,* and *committee budget,* respectively.

# BUDGETARY APPROACHES AND EMPHASES

Rarely does one find two governments with identical budgetary approaches and procedures. A government's budgetary system should be designed to fit its environmental factors—some of which may be unique—and should provide a budgetary planning, control, and evaluation balance that is appropriate to its circumstances.

## The Budget as Information

Both in practice and in budgetary theory the budget is designed to provide information to decision makers and to indicate the decisions that have been made. Top officials in the executive branch develop policy guidelines for departmental supervisors to use in support of departmental budget requests. The chief executive, with the assistance of the budgetary staff, decides what information and budget requests will go to the legislative body. The ultimate example of the use of the budget to indicate the decisions that have been made is the enacted appropriations bill, a law.

Typically, the expenditure budget proposed by the executive branch includes:

1. Descriptions of programs, functions, and activities carried on by organizational units of the government
2. Objectives of programs, functions, and activities
3. Quantitative data regarding the service efforts (inputs) and accomplishments (outputs) of the programs, functions, and activities
4. Benefits provided at increased (perhaps maximum) and/or decreased (perhaps minimum) levels of service
5. Methods now in use for delivering services; alternative methods for delivering services; and systems analyses and cost-benefit analyses of methods for delivering services
6. Expenditure and/or cost data:
   a. By organization units
   b. By programs, functions, and activities
   c. By object of expenditure
   d. Per unit of service effort (input) or accomplishment (output) at
      • present levels
      • reduced levels
      • expanded levels

Although no budget provides all these kinds of information, every budget provides some of them. The budget approach selected tends to determine the kinds of planning analyses that will be used and the data that will be provided.

## Recommended Budgeting Framework and Practices

The National Advisory Council on State and Local Budgeting (NACSLB) recently made a series of broad recommendations designed to improve state and local government budgeting approaches and practices. Its 1997 report stated that:

- The budget process consists of activities that encompass the development, implementation, and evaluation of a plan for the provision of services and capital assets.
- A good budget process:
  - Incorporates a long-term perspective.
  - Establishes linkages to broad organizational goals.
  - Focuses budget decisions on results and outcomes.
  - Involves and promotes effective communication with stakeholders.
  - Provides incentives to government management and employees.
- The budget process should be strategic in nature, encompassing a multiyear financial and operating plan that allocates resources on the basis of identified goals.
- A good budget process moves beyond the traditional concept of line-item expenditure control, providing incentives and flexibility to managers that can lead to improved program efficiency and effectiveness.

The NACSLB also issued a statement of recommended budget principles, including related elements and practices. These are summarized in Figure 3–3.

## Alternative Expenditure Budgeting Approaches

The several general approaches to governmental budgeting have marked differences in their emphasis on planning, control, and evaluation. As we discuss these approaches in this chapter and in Appendix 3–1, we point out their suitability for planning, control, and evaluation. The principal groups that exercise control are executive branch officials and the legislature. But citizens, creditors, officials of higher governments, and other groups often have control powers that indirectly affect the budgetary planning, control, and evaluation process.

The most common approaches to operating expenditure budgeting may be characterized as follows:

1. Object-of-expenditure
2. Performance
3. Program and planning-programming-budgeting (PPB)
4. Zero-base budgeting (ZBB)

The following section is a brief overview of the key facets of the object-of-expenditure approach. The other three approaches are discussed briefly in Appendix 3–1. A complete discussion of each approach—or possible combinations of approaches—is beyond the scope of this text. Moreover, bear in mind that budgetary nomenclature is not standardized, that each approach may be implemented to varying degrees, that these approaches overlap significantly, and that elements of all four approaches are often found in a single budget system. Furthermore, always look to the substance of a system rather than to the terminology used in reference to it; for example, an object-of-expenditure budget may be referred to publicly as a performance, program, or zero-base budget because these have been considered the more modern approaches in recent years.

FIGURE 3–3  **Recommended Budgeting Principles**

*The National Advisory Council on State and Local Budgeting (NACSLB)*

| | |
|---|---|
| **Principle 1** | **Establish broad goals to guide government decision making.** |
| Element 1 | Assess community needs, priorities, challenges, and opportunities. |
| Element 2 | Identify opportunities and challenges for government services, capital assets, and management. |
| Element 3 | Develop and disseminate broad goals. |
| **Principle 2** | **Develop approaches to achieve goals.** |
| Element 4 | Adopt financial policies. |
| Element 5 | Develop programmatic, operating, and capital policies and plans. |
| Element 6 | Develop programs and services that are consistent with policies and plans. |
| Element 7 | Develop management strategies. |
| **Principle 3** | **Develop a budget consistent with approaches to achieve goals.** |
| Element 8 | Develop a process for preparing and adopting a budget. |
| Element 9 | Develop and evaluate financial options. |

Practices

9.1  Conduct long-range financial planning.

9.2  Prepare revenue projections.

    9.2a  Analyze major revenues.

    9.2b  Evaluate the effect of changes to revenue source rates and bases.

    9.2c  Analyze tax and fee exemptions.

    9.2d  Achieve consensus on revenue forecast.

9.3  Document revenue sources in a revenue manual.

9.4  Prepare expenditure projections.

9.5  Compare revenue and expenditure options.

9.6  Develop a capital improvement plan.

| | |
|---|---|
| Element 10 | Make choices necessary to adopt a budget. |
| **Principle 4** | **Assess performance and make adjustments.** |
| Element 11 | Monitor, measure, and assess performance. |
| Element 12 | Make adjustments as needed. |

*Source:* "A Leap Forward for State and Local Budgeting," *Government Finance Review,* October 1997, p. 38. Used by permission.

## The Object-of-Expenditure Approach

The object-of-expenditure approach to budgeting, often referred to as the traditional approach, has an expenditure control orientation. The object-of-expenditure approach became popular as the basis for legislative control over the executive branch; and it continues to be the most widely used, though elements of newer approaches are often added.

Simply described, the object-of-expenditure method involves three facets. First, subordinate agencies submit budget requests to the chief executive in terms of the type of expenditures to be made. These requests include the number of people to be hired in each specified position and salary level and the specific goods or services to be purchased during the upcoming period. Next, the chief executive compiles and modifies the agency budget requests and submits an overall request for the organization to the legislature in the same object-of-expenditure terms. Finally, the legislature usually makes line-item appropriations, possibly after revising the requests, along object-of-expenditure input lines. Performance or program data may be included in the budget document, but only to supplement or support the object-of-expenditure requests. The basic elements of this approach are illustrated in Figure 3–4.

### Control Points

Various degrees of appropriation control that a legislature might exercise through object-of-expenditure budgets may be illustrated by identifying the possible control points in the example in Figure 3–4. A great degree of legislative control will be typified if appropriations are stated in terms of the most detailed level. For example, the police department appropriation might be in terms of one chief, $137,000; two captains, $139,000; and so on. Alternatively, a lesser amount of control would result if appropriations are stated in terms of object classes, that is, Salaries and Wages, $1,181,000; Supplies, $114,000; Other Services and Charges, $77,000; and Capital Outlay, $71,000. In this case the detailed objects listed would

FIGURE 3–4  **Simplified Object-of-Expenditure Budget**
     **(Classified by Organizational Unit and Object-of-Expenditure)**

**Mayor's Office**

~~~~~~~~~~~~~~~~~~~~~~~~~~~~~~~~~~~~~~~~~~~~~~~~~~~~~~~~~~~~~~~~~~~~~~~~~~~~~~~~~~~~~~~~~~~~~~~~~

**Police Department**

| Salaries and Wages: | Rate | | |
|---|---|---|---|
| 1—Chief | $137,000 | $137,000 | |
| 2—Captains | 69,500 | 139,000 | |
| 3—Sergeants | 47,000 | 141,000 | |
| 22—Patrol officers | 28,000 | 616,000 | |
| 3—Radio operators | 20,000 | 60,000 | |
| 10—School guards (part-time) | 8,800 | 88,000 | $1,181,000 |
| Supplies: | | | |
| Stationery and other office supplies | | 12,200 | |
| Janitorial supplies | | 31,100 | |
| Gasoline and oil | | 43,000 | |
| Uniforms | | 22,200 | |
| Other | | 5,500 | 114,000 |
| Other Services and Charges: | | | |
| Telephone | | 11,400 | |
| Out-of-town travel | | 21,800 | |
| Parking tickets | | 11,600 | |
| Utilities | | 23,000 | |
| Other | | 9,200 | 77,000 |
| Capital Outlay: | | | |
| 2—Motorcycles (net) | | 16,600 | |
| 4—Patrol cars (net) | | 54,400 | 71,000 |
| Total Police Department | | | $1,443,000 |

**Fire Department**

Salaries and Wages:

~~~~~~~~~~~~~~~~~~~~~~~~~~~~~~~~~~~~~~~~~~~~~~~~~~~~~~~~~~~~~~~~~~~~~~~~~~~~~~~~~~~~~~~~~~~~~~~~~

| | |
|---|---|
| Total Budget | $9,801,720 |

be indicative of the types of goods and services to be secured, but the executive branch would have discretion as to an appropriate input mix so long as these expenditure category subtotals were not exceeded. Next, an even greater degree of executive discretion would be granted if appropriations are stated in a lump sum at the departmental level, for example, police department, $1,443,000. Even though all of the supporting details would have been developed during the budget process and likely would have been presented to the legislature, only departmental totals would be legally binding on the executive in such a situation.

In any event, the accounting system must capture data in sufficient detail to permit budgetary control and accountability at the legislative-to-executive budgetary control points.

Furthermore, recall that the chief executive may refine the level of legislative control—and make departmental allotments and/or allocations—in order to achieve the desired degree of fiscal control over subordinates. In such cases, the budgetary accounting system must accumulate data in sufficient detail to permit budgetary control and accountability at the chief executive–department head budgetary control points.

### Advantages

Advocates of the object-of-expenditure approach note its longstanding use, its simplicity, and its ease of preparation and understanding by all concerned. Too, they note that budgeting by organizational units and object-of-expenditure closely fits patterns of responsibility accounting, that this method facilitates accounting control in the budget execution process, and that comparable data may be accumulated for a series of years in order to facilitate trend comparison. In addition, they contend that (1) most programs are of an ongoing nature; (2) most expenditures are relatively unavoidable; (3) decisions must, in the real world, be based on changes in programs, and attention can most readily be given to changes proposed, compared with prior-year data, on this approach; and (4) the object-of-expenditure approach does not preclude supplementing object-of-expenditure data with planning and evaluation information commonly associated with other budgetary approaches. Finally, they observe that where activities are the basis for organizational units, costs of activities are accumulated as costs of the related organizational units. Identification of activity costs permits summations of program and function costs.

### Criticisms

Despite its long-term and widespread use, the object-of-expenditure budget has been severely criticized. In its simplest form it provides no genuine information base for decision makers. Figure 3–4 provides only a list of the proposed personnel to be hired and objects or services to be acquired. Only decision makers familiar with the function and activities of a police department will understand the justifications for such expenditures.

Some critics of the object-of-expenditure approach feel that it is overly control centered, to the detriment of the planning and evaluation processes. They assert that in practice a disproportionate amount of attention is focused on short-term dollar inputs of specific departments (personnel, supplies, and so on); and, consequently, that both long-run considerations and those relevant to the programs of the organization as a whole usually receive inadequate attention. Too, they argue that crucial planning decisions tend to originate at the lowest levels of the organization and flow upward; whereas broad goals, objectives, and policies should originate in the upper echelon and flow downward to be implemented by subordinates. As a result, governmental goals tend to be stated in terms of unco-ordinated aggregations of goals of the various department heads.

Critics also assert that planning may be neglected, budgets being based on re-quests based merely on present expenditure levels and patterns. This "budgeting by default" leads to perpetuation of past activities, whether or not appropriate, fail-ure to set definite goals and objectives, and failure to consider all possible alterna-tives available to the organization in striving to accomplish its purposes.

Furthermore, some assert that the legislative branch is given more object-of-expenditure detail than it can possibly assimilate, yet is not given data pertaining to the functions, programs, activities, and outputs of executive branch agencies. Con-sequently, the legislative branch tends to exercise control over such items as the number of telephones to be permitted or the salary of a particular individual, rather than focusing its attention on broad programs and policies of the organization.

This approach is also criticized as being out of date. Line-item appropriations are encouraged by the approach. But critics assert that in today's complex envi-ronment the executive branch must have reasonable discretion and flexibility to manage diverse and complex programs.

Finally, critics contend that this method encourages spending rather than economizing, and that department heads feel compelled to expend their full ap-propriations—whether needed or not. This philosophy arises because (1) perfor-mance evaluation tends to be focused on spending, and the manager who keeps spending within budgetary limitations is assumed to be "good," and (2) a manager's subsequent budgets may be reduced as a result of spending less than was appro-priated for a given year because legislators often base appropriations on prior ex-penditures and also may consider underexpenditure of appropriations to be indicative of budget request padding.

### Comment

Most of these advantages and criticisms of the object-of-expenditure ap-proach are substantive. However, because budgetary control and accountability are paramount considerations in government—both between the legislative and executive branches and within the executive branch—the control orientation of the object-of-expenditure approach is apt to ensure its continuing predominance. But because of the validity of the criticisms of the object-of-expenditure approach, it is increasingly being supplemented by certain features of the performance, pro-gram, and zero-base budgeting approaches—which are discussed in the appendix to this chapter.

Because of its widespread use and adaptability to budgetary accounting, il-lustrations in the remainder of this text generally assume that an appropriations bill based on organization units and objects of expenditure is in use. The concepts and procedures illustrated apply generally to all budgetary systems, though ex-penditure account classifications may need to be changed and additional data gath-ered to achieve program or performance accountability and reporting.

## BUDGET PREPARATION

A substantial part of most government budgeting textbooks is devoted to design-ing, planning, and implementing appropriate budget preparation procedures. In ad-dition, many SLGs have developed extensive and detailed budget preparation procedures manuals. Our budget preparation discussions are not comparably exhaustive and detailed but summarize the usual budget preparation process from the perspective of the governmental accountant and auditor.

## Overview

Sound financial planning requires that budget preparation begin in time for its adoption before the beginning of the budget period. To ensure that adequate time will be allowed, a budget calendar listing each step in the budgetary process and the time allowed for its completion should be prepared. The budget preparation then proceeds in a manner similar to that shown in Figure 3–5.

## Preliminary Steps

The budget officer and chief executive typically begin preliminary work on the budget for the upcoming year before the steps indicated in the budget cycle (Figure 3–1) are begun in order to:

- Make preliminary estimates of the overall budgetary outlook and parameters—such as the overall levels of expected revenues and appropriations that might be made, including the probable ranges of overall appropriations increases and decreases.

- Inform department heads and others involved in the budgeting process of the plausible ranges of appropriation requests, the chief executive's priorities for the upcoming year, and related matters.

The preliminary estimates of the ideal levels of appropriations and expenditures during the upcoming year almost always exceed the financial resources to be available. Thus, budgeting has been described "as the process of allocating scarce resources to unlimited demands."

FIGURE 3–5  **Traditional Information Flows—Budget Preparation**

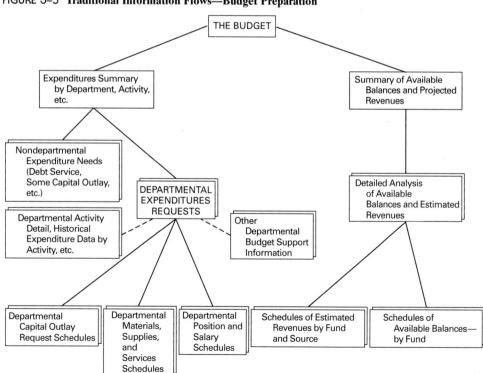

The basic formula for budget decision makers is:

| | | |
|---|---|---|
| Estimated fund balance, beginning of budget year ....................... | $ | X |
| Add: Estimated revenues and other financing sources (e.g., transfers from other funds), budget year......................... | | Y |
| Total appropriable resources, budget year ............................. | $ | X + Y |
| Deduct: Estimated expenditures (appropriations) and other uses of financial resources (e.g., transfers to other funds), budget year.................................................. | | Z |
| Estimated fund balance, end of year................................ | | $X + Y − Z |

After estimating the fund balance to be available at the beginning of the up-coming budget year, the budget officer must obtain estimates of (1) the revenues that will be produced by all revenue sources at current rates of taxes, fees, and other charges; (2) any other sources of appropriable resources (e.g., transfers from other funds); and (3) the fund balance needed at the end of the upcoming budget year for carryover to the next year. Having produced such estimates, the budget officer and the chief executive can compare them with revenues, expenditures, and interfund transfers of prior years and with their knowledge of changes in demands on the government and its programs. Such comparisons should provide an impression of the adequacy of estimated revenues to meet the needs for expenditures.

## Preparing the Budget

Preparation of the annual budget for the upcoming year now proceeds along lines indicated in the budget cycle (Figure 3–1). The chief executive and department heads typically interact frequently during the budget preparation process. For example:

- The chief executive indicates the overall parameters and ranges of plausible departmental appropriation requests—for example, that appropriations will only be increased up to 3%—as well as budget priorities, and so forth.
- The department heads usually confer informally with the budget officer or chief executive during the budget preparation process—possibly seeking exceptions to the overall budget guidelines for certain activities or to persuade the chief executive to place special priority on certain programs.
- After reviewing the departmental appropriation requests, the budget officer or chief executive may confer with department heads to revise these requests in preparing the final executive budget.

### Revenue Estimates

Each revenue source is analyzed in detail—in terms of past amounts, trends, factors apt to affect it next year, and expected level in the upcoming year—in preparing the budget. Because most revenues relate to the government as a whole—for example, property taxes, sales taxes, and interest—the budget officer makes most revenue estimates. However, the various departments often estimate the revenues that relate to specific departments—such as inspections, permits, and charges for services.

In order to simplify the illustrations here and in Chapter 4, we assume that the budget is presented, approved, controlled, accounted for, and reported in broad revenue source categories such as

- Taxes
- Licenses and Permits

- Intergovernmental
- Fines and Forfeits
- Other

Revenues typically are controlled, accounted for, and reported on in more detail in practice.

### Expenditure Estimates

Each departmental expenditure category is likewise analyzed in detail—in terms of past amounts, trends, factors apt to affect it next year, and its necessary level in the upcoming year—in preparing the budget. As noted earlier, much interaction may occur between and among the department heads, budget officer, and chief executive in determining the appropriation proposals for the upcoming year.

For purposes of illustration here and in Chapter 4, we assume that the appropriation requests are approved, controlled, accounted for, and reported in broad functional expenditure categories such as

- General Government
- Public Safety
- Highways and Streets
- Culture and Recreation
- Other

Appropriations usually would be made in more detail in practice—typically by major category of expenditure (e.g., personal services, supplies, capital outlay) within each department.

### Other Estimates

The budget officer and chief executive might also include other proposed sources and uses of financial resources in the executive budget. For example, interfund operating transfers or residual equity transfers might be proposed. For illustrative purposes here and in Chapter 4, it is assumed that interfund transfers are not included in the annual operating budget, but are separately authorized nonbudgeted sources and uses of financial resources.

### The Budget Document

Given these simplifying assumptions, assume also that the executive budget proposed (and subsequently approved) for a governmental fund (e.g., the General Fund) of A Governmental Unit for the 19X2 fiscal year is that presented in Figure 3–6.

## LEGISLATIVE CONSIDERATION AND ACTION

After receiving the executive budget document, the legislative body must adopt an official budget. A legislature of a state or large city usually turns the proposed budget over to a committee or committees to make investigations, to call on department heads and the chief executive for justifications of their requests, and to conduct public hearings. The committee then makes its recommendations to the legislature. In smaller municipalities the council or board of supervisors may act as a committee of the whole in its consideration of the budget.

After completing the budget hearings and investigations, the legislative body adopts the budget, as revised, by passing an appropriations act or ordinance. The

FIGURE 3–6

**ANNUAL OPERATING BUDGET**
Governmental Fund
A Governmental Unit
19X2 Fiscal Year

Estimated Revenues:

| | |
|---|---:|
| Taxes | $ 900,000 |
| Licenses and permits | 400,000 |
| Intergovernmental | 350,000 |
| Charges for services | 50,000 |
| Fines and forfeits | 100,000 |
| Other | 200,000 |
| | 2,000,000 |

Appropriations:

| | |
|---|---:|
| General government | 250,000 |
| Public safety | 575,000 |
| Highways and streets | 500,000 |
| Health and sanitation | 375,000 |
| Culture and recreation | 200,000 |
| Other | 50,000 |
| | 1,950,000 |
| Excess of Estimated Revenues over Appropriations | 50,000 |
| Estimated Fund Balance—Beginning of 19X2 | 450,000 |
| Estimated Fund Balance—End of 19X2 | $ 500,000 |

Note: In practice, the estimated revenue and revenue accounts would be established in more detailed source categories, and the appropriation and expenditure accounts would be established by department and object-of-expenditure category.

amount of detail adopted in the act determines the flexibility granted to the executive branch by the legislative body. Lump-sum appropriations may be made for functions or activities, or, more likely, for organization units. If proper internal control, accounting, reporting, and postaudit procedures are used, the legislative body can retain control of operations without recourse to detailed appropriations. However, most legislative bodies insist on fairly detailed object-of-expenditure data in the executive budget, and they may be appropriated in comparable detail.

The appropriations act or ordinance merely authorizes expenditures. It is also necessary to provide the means of financing them. Some revenues (e.g., interest on investments) will accrue to the governmental unit without any legal action on its part. Other revenues will come as a result of legal action taken in the past. Examples of these are licenses and fees, income taxes, and sales taxes, the rates for which continue until the legislative body changes them. A third type of revenue—for example, the general property tax—usually requires new legal action each year. Accordingly, as soon as the legislative body has passed the appropriations ordinance or act, it proceeds to levy general property taxes.

# BUDGET EXECUTION

Just as the budget approved by the legislative body expresses in financial terms the government's planned activities, the process of budget execution includes every operating decision and transaction made during the budget period. For this reason Figure 3–1, "The Budget Cycle," lists the many activities of administration as aspects of budget execution. Accounting keeps a record of the results of the transactions and permits their summarization, reporting, and comparison with plans (the budget). Therefore, the following chapters that describe the accounting and reporting for the governmental funds are all related to budget execution.

The legally adopted revenue estimates and appropriations are such a controlling influence in government that, contrary to business practice, the budget is recorded as an integral part of the accounting system. Among other benefits, this practice helps governments avoid inadvertent overexpenditure of appropriations. In the general ledger, as well as in the subsidiary ledgers for revenues and expenditures, budgeted amounts are recorded and can be directly compared with their actual counterparts. Similarly, accountability for budget compliance is reported in the financial statements together with the appropriate GAAP-basis information. Accordingly, the remainder of this chapter is devoted to brief illustrative overviews of governmental fund budgetary accounting and budgetary reporting.

## BUDGETARY ACCOUNTING OVERVIEW

Effecting budgetary control in the accounting system requires that budgetary accounts—for total estimated revenues, appropriations, and encumbrances—be included in the general ledger of a governmental fund, and subsidiary ledgers be established to account for each revenue source and each expenditure category in at least as much detail as in the legally adopted budget. The manner in which this is accomplished is illustrated in Figure 3–7, "Budgetary Accounting Overview." Alternatively, only the detailed accounts may be maintained and the totals derived through summation.

### General Ledger

The integration of budgetary accounts into the general ledger does not affect the asset and liability accounts, which record only actual assets and liabilities. Rather, it involves the use of both:

1. Estimated Revenues and Revenues (actual) control accounts to record the total estimated and actual revenues at any time during the year; and

2. Accounts for total Appropriations (authorized estimated expenditures), actual Expenditures, and Encumbrances—the estimated cost of goods and services ordered but not received—to indicate the total appropriations, expenditures, and encumbrances outstanding at any point during the year.

In addition to providing data on total budgeted and actual revenues and expenditures to date and on encumbrances (expenditures in process), these general ledger accounts serve as control accounts over the more detailed revenues and expenditures subsidiary ledgers.

### Revenues and Expenditures Subsidiary Ledgers

Revenues and expenditures subsidiary ledgers are established to effect detailed budgetary control over each revenue source and each appropriation category. Note the relationships between these subsidiary ledgers and the general ledger, as illustrated in Figure 3–7, as well as the column headings of the accounts of each subsidiary ledger. Note also that a separate account is established for each revenue source and appropriation category in the legally adopted budget.

FIGURE 3–7 **Budgetary Accounting Overview**

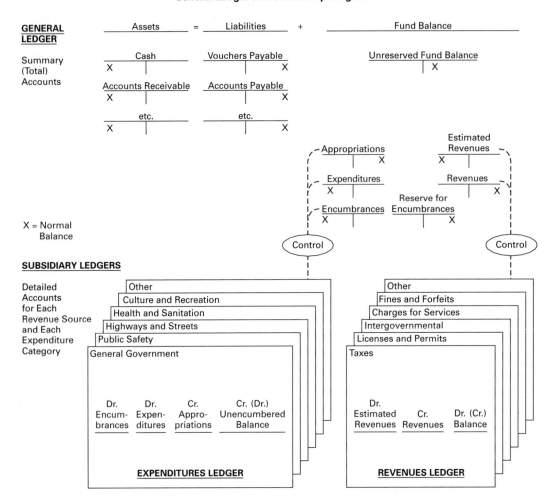

**Governmental Fund
General Ledger and Subsidiary Ledgers**

## Revenues Subsidiary Ledger

Responsible persons or departments can monitor individual revenue sources using the data accumulated in the Revenues Subsidiary Ledger. These data include both estimated and actual revenues for each significant revenue source. Furthermore, such data help the finance officer monitor the revenue management process, and may signal a need to revise the budget during the year. For example, significant shortfalls in budgeted revenue sources may necessitate both lowering revenue estimates for the year and reducing appropriations.

The relationship of the Estimated Revenues and Revenues general ledger control accounts and the more detailed Revenues Subsidiary Ledger accounts is illustrated in Figure 3–8. Note the following in studying Figure 3–8:

1. **When the budget is adopted:**
   a. The total of the estimated revenues for the year is debited to the Estimated Revenues general ledger control account when the annual budget is adopted.

FIGURE 3–8  **Relationship of General Ledger Estimated Revenues and Revenues Control
Accounts and the Revenues Subsidiary Ledger Accounts**

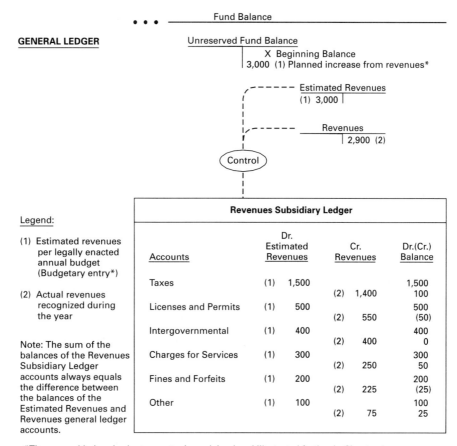

**Governmental Fund**

*The general ledger budgetary entry is explained and illustrated further in Chapter 4.
Note: Only one estimated revenue entry and one actual revenue entry are illustrated. In practice,
several estimated revenue entries and many actual revenue entries are made each year.

    b. Each individual revenue source estimate is posted to the "Estimated Revenues" column of its Revenues Subsidiary Ledger account.

    c. At this point the balances of the Revenues Subsidiary Ledger accounts represent the amounts of revenues expected to be recognized during the year.

  **2. When revenues are recognized:**

    a. The total of the actual revenues is credited to the Revenues general ledger control account as revenues are recognized.

    b. Each individual actual revenue source amount is posted to the "Revenues" (actual) column of its Revenues Subsidiary Ledger account.

    c. The balances of the Revenues Subsidiary Ledger accounts now represent the differences between budgeted and actual revenues to date.

  **3. Control relationship:** At any time during the year the sum of the balances of the Revenues Subsidiary Ledger accounts should equal the difference between the balances of the Estimated Revenues and Revenues general ledger accounts.

Only six revenue accounts are included in the Revenues Subsidiary Ledger illustrated in Figure 3–8. In practice, 50 to 100 or more Revenues Subsidiary Ledger accounts may be necessary to properly control and monitor the various revenue sources. For example, instead of a single Taxes revenue account, it may be appropriate to establish separate revenue accounts for

| | |
|---|---|
| Real Property Taxes—Residential | Sales Taxes |
| Real Property Taxes—Commercial | Income Taxes—Individuals |
| Personal Property Taxes—Residential | Income Taxes—Corporations |
| Personal Property Taxes—Commercial | |

Furthermore, while only one estimated revenue entry and one actual revenue entry are illustrated in Figure 3–8, many entries are made during the year in practice. Estimated revenue entries are made only upon the adoption or revision of the official revenue estimates—so only a few estimated revenue entries may be made annually. But one or more actual revenue entries may be made daily.

### Expenditures Subsidiary Ledger

The Expenditures Subsidiary Ledger accumulates data during the year on each appropriation, including the related (1) expenditures to date, (2) encumbrances outstanding, and (3) unencumbered balance. The Expenditures Subsidiary Ledger thus facilitates the monitoring and control of each appropriation by the department head responsible and by the finance officer. For example, proposed purchase orders for public safety purposes are compared with the unencumbered balance of the public safety appropriation (against which the related expenditures will be charged) before approval. Approved purchase orders are charged as encumbrances against the appropriation. This ensures that sufficient appropriations will be available as authority for the subsequent expenditure for the goods or services ordered and, correspondingly, reduces the unencumbered balance of the related Expenditures Subsidiary Ledger account.

The relationship of the Appropriations, Expenditures, and Encumbrances general ledger control accounts and the more detailed Expenditures Subsidiary Ledger accounts is illustrated in Figure 3–9. Note the following in studying Figure 3–9:

1. **When the budget is adopted:**
   a. The total of the appropriations—the total authorized and estimated expenditures for the year—is credited to the Appropriations general ledger control account when the annual budget is adopted.
   b. Each individual appropriation is posted to the "Appropriations" column of its Expenditures Subsidiary Ledger account.
   c. At this point, the balances of the Expenditures Subsidiary Ledger accounts represent the amounts of expenditures authorized to be incurred during the year.

2. **When encumbrances are incurred (by ordering goods or contracting for services):**
   a. The total amounts of encumbrances—expenditures expected to be incurred for goods or services ordered or contracted for—are recorded in offsetting general ledger Encumbrances and Reserve for Encumbrances accounts.
   b. Each encumbrance is posted to the "Encumbrances" column of the Expenditures Subsidiary Ledger account against which the resulting expenditures will be charged, thus reducing its Unencumbered Balance available for expenditure.
   c. This effectively reserves a sufficient balance of each appropriation for the expenditures expected to result from the encumbrances; hence, the term *reserve for encumbrances*.

3. **When encumbrances result in expenditures:** When goods or services ordered are received, the government no longer has an encumbrance, but an expenditure. Accordingly,
   a. the encumbrances are reversed (removed from the accounts).

b. the expenditures are recorded in the accounts.
c. the unencumbered balance of the Expenditures Subsidiary Ledger accounts is adjusted for any difference between the estimated expenditures (encumbrances) and actual expenditures.

**FIGURE 3–9 Relationship of General Ledger Appropriations, Expenditures, and Encumbrances Accounts and the Expenditures Subsidiary Ledger Accounts**

**Governmental Fund**

**GENERAL LEDGER**

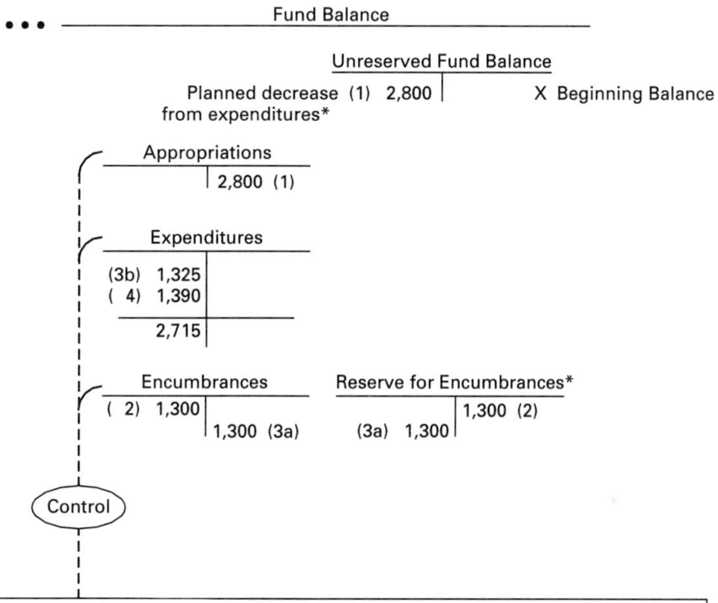


**Expenditures Subsidiary Ledger**

| Accounts | Dr. Encumbrances | Dr. Expenditures | Cr. Appropriations | Cr. (Dr.) Unencumbered Balance |
|---|---|---|---|---|
| General Government | | | (1) 500 | 500 |
| | (2) 200 | | | 300 |
| | (3a) (200) | (3b) 225 | | 275 |
| | | (4) 260 | | 15 |
| Public Safety | | | (1) 1,300 | 1,300 |
| | (2) 600 | | | 700 |
| | (3a) (600) | (3b) 575 | | 725 |
| | | (4) 700 | | 25 |
| Highways and Streets | | | (1) 400 | 400 |
| | (2) 300 | | | 100 |
| | (3a) (300) | (3b) 300 | | 100 |
| | | (4) 100 | | 0 |
| Health and Sanitation | | | (1) 300 | 300 |
| | (2) 100 | | | 200 |
| | (3a) (100) | (3b) 125 | | 175 |
| | | (4) 160 | | 15 |
| Culture and Recreation | | | (1) 200 | 200 |
| | (2) 75 | | | 125 |
| | (3a) (75) | (3b) 75 | | 125 |
| | | (4) 100 | | 25 |
| Other | | | (1) 100 | 100 |
| | (2) 25 | | | 75 |
| | (3a) (25) | (3b) 25 | | 75 |
| | | (4) 70 | | 5 |

Legend:

(1) Appropriations (estimated and authorized expenditures) per legally enacted annual budget. (Budget entry*)
(2) Encumbrances incurred for estimated costs of goods and services ordered (purchase orders) or contracted for (contracts).
(3) Goods and services ordered where received; actual costs sometimes more or less than estimated. (Entry 3a reverses the encumbrance entry (2); Entry 3b records the actual expenditures.)
(4) Expenditures incurred that were not previously encumbered (e.g., salaries, utilities)

*The general ledger budgetary entry and the Reserve for Encumbrances account are explained and illustrated in Chapter 4.

4. **When unencumbered expenditures are incurred:**
   a. Expenditures not resulting from purchase orders or other contracts—for example, salaries and utilities—are recorded when incurred.
   b. No encumbrance reversal entry is needed.
   c. All expenditures, whether or not previously encumbered, reduce the unencumbered balance of the related Expenditures Subsidiary Ledger accounts.

5. **Control relationship:**
   a. At any time during the year, the sum of the "Unencumbered Balance" column amounts of the Expenditures Subsidiary Ledger accounts should equal the difference between the balance of the Appropriations general ledger account and the sum of the Expenditures and Encumbrances general ledger accounts.
   b. Furthermore, to ensure proper budgetary control and avoid appropriation overruns, most computerized accounting systems are programmed to reject (not process) any encumbrance or expenditure transaction that would cause the "Unencumbered Balance" column of an Expenditures Subsidiary Ledger account to have a debit balance.

Only six expenditures accounts are included in the Expenditures Subsidiary Ledger illustrated in Figure 3–9. In practice several hundred Expenditures Subsidiary Ledger accounts may be necessary to monitor and control the numerous appropriations properly. For example, instead of a single General Government expenditures account it usually is necessary to establish more detailed accounts, such as:

General Government—Legislative Branch

General Government—Executive Branch

General Government—Judicial Branch

General Government—Elections

General Government—Financial Administration

General Government—Other

Furthermore, depending on the level of detail at which the appropriations are enacted, it is often necessary to establish even more detailed object-of-expenditure accounts for each departmental and other appropriation, such as:

General Government—Legislative Branch—Personal Services

General Government—Legislative Branch—Supplies

General Government—Legislative Branch—Other Services and Charges

General Government—Legislative Branch—Capital Outlay

Finally, although only a few appropriations, encumbrances, and expenditures entries are illustrated in Figure 3–9, many entries are made each year in practice. Appropriations entries are made only upon adoption or revision of the budget—so only a few appropriations entries may be made annually. But several encumbrances and expenditures entries may be made daily.

## BUDGETARY REPORTING OVERVIEW

Because of the unique importance of budgeting, budgetary control, and budgetary accountability in the state and local government environment, both interim (e.g., monthly) and annual budgetary statements are prepared. Furthermore, the GASB requires extensive budgetary reporting in the comprehensive annual financial report (CAFR), which includes the general purpose financial statements (GPFS). These requirements include:

1. a summary budgetary comparison statement by function or program—prepared on the unit's budgetary basis—for its annually budgeted governmental funds;

2. a similar individual fund(s) budgetary basis schedule(s) at the legislative-to-executive branch budgetary control points level of detail; and

3. an explanation of the unit's budgetary basis and a reconciliation of the budgetary basis data and the GAAP basis data.

## The Budgetary Basis

Another unique feature of governmental budgeting, budgetary control, and budgetary accountability is that the governing body can choose the basis on which its annual budget will be prepared and adopted, controlled, and reported upon. Accordingly, whereas some governments budget their governmental funds on the modified accrual (GAAP) basis, others budget revenues and expenditures on the cash basis. That is, for budgetary accounting and reporting purposes they do not recognize revenues and expenditures until the related cash is received or disbursed, respectively. In either event, most governments maintain their accounts on the budgetary basis during the year—for budgetary control and for interim and annual budgetary reporting purposes—then adjust the accounts to the GAAP basis at year end for annual GAAP basis reporting purposes.

Furthermore, some governments consider encumbrances outstanding to be the equivalent of expenditures for budgetary reporting purposes—and compare the sum of expenditures and encumbrances with appropriations. This is known as the *encumbrances method.* But other governments consider encumbrance accounting to be only an internal budgetary control technique to avoid incurring expenditures in excess of appropriations. Because these governments do not consider encumbrances to be equivalent to expenditures for budgetary reporting purposes, they (1) compare budgetary basis expenditures (only) with appropriations and report the unexpended (not unencumbered) appropriation balances, and (2) disclose encumbrances outstanding in the notes to the financial statements or in a fund balance reserve (discussed later).

Because of the variation of budgetary bases in practice, the need for effective budgetary control, and GAAP requirements related to budgetary reporting, the governmental accountant and auditor must:

- Carefully identify the budgetary basis used by each state or local government, particularly for its annually budgeted governmental funds, and

- Ensure that the budgetary basis is appropriately used in budgetary accounting and reporting, and that the differences between the budgetary basis and the GAAP basis are adequately explained and reconciled in the CAFR and GPFS.

## Interim Budgetary Statements

Monthly or quarterly interim budgetary statements typically are prepared directly from the Revenues and Expenditures Subsidiary Ledger accounts illustrated in Figures 3–8 and 3–9. Because GAAP require only that interim statements be "appropriate" for their management control, legislative oversight, or other purposes—that is, the GASB has not established interim financial statement formats, contents, and so on—interim budgetary reports may contain whatever statements, schedules, and other information management deems appropriate.

### Interim Revenues Statements

Interim revenues statements typically include, as a minimum, data from the Revenues Subsidiary Ledger accounts (Figure 3–8) on (1) the revenues recognized to date and (2) the estimated revenues for the year. Too, interim statements often include the difference between the two.

Furthermore, percentage data are frequently presented—such as the percent of the estimated annual revenues realized to date, by revenue category and in total, and the percent of each revenue source and total revenues that had been realized at this time last year. For example, a monthly budgetary revenues statement might present—for each revenue source and in total:

| *Revenues Year to Date* | *Estimated Revenues for the Year* | *Percent Realized to Date* ||
| --- | --- | --- | --- |
| | | *Current Year* | *Prior Year* |

In addition, management commentary accompanying the interim revenue statement should describe any significant factors affecting revenues to date or apt to affect the revenues in the upcoming months and for the year. Indeed, evaluations of budgetary reports are often the basis on which the governing body revises the estimated revenues budget during the year.

### Interim Expenditures Statements

Interim expenditures statements typically include, as a minimum, data drawn from the Expenditures Subsidiary Ledger accounts (Figure 3–9) at the interim statement date on

1. appropriations for the year,
2. expenditures to date,
3. encumbrances outstanding at the interim date, and
4. the unencumbered balance of each appropriation.

For example, a monthly budgetary expenditures statement might present—for each appropriation and in total:

| *Year to Date* ||| | |
| --- | --- | --- | --- | --- |
| *Expenditures* | *Encumbrances* | *Total* | *Annual Appropriations* | *Unencumbered Balance* |

Governments using monthly allotments controls would also include data for the allotment period; and those budgeting on the encumbrances method may present only the expenditures and encumbrances total. Further, as in interim revenues budgetary reporting, interim expenditure budgetary statements (1) may contain year-to-date and/or prior year comparative percentage data; (2) should contain management commentary on any significant factors affecting expenditures and encumbrances to date or apt to affect total expenditures for the year or encumbrances outstanding at year end; and (3) often serve as the basis for governing body revisions of appropriations during the year.

### Interim Revenues and Expenditures Statements

Although interim budgetary statements for revenues and expenditures may be presented separately, they often are presented in the same statement. This type of interim budgetary comparison statement is illustrated in Figure 3–10. Further,

FIGURE 3-10

**INTERIM BUDGETARY COMPARISON STATEMENT**
**(Budgetary Basis)**
A Governmental Unit
Governmental Fund
At End of (Month), 19X2

| | *Actual*<br>*(To Date)* | *Annual*<br>*Budget* | *Unrealized/*<br>*Unencumbered* | *Percent (%)*<br>*Actual to Date*<br>*to Total* | |
| --- | --- | --- | --- | --- | --- |
| | | | | *19X2* | *19X1* |
| Revenues: | | | | | |
| Taxes | $ 550,000 | $ 900,000 | $ 350,000 | 61.1 | 66.0 |
| Licenses and permits | 150,000 | 400,000 | 250,000 | 37.5 | 31.0 |
| Intergovernmental | 200,000 | 350,000 | 150,000 | 57.1 | 60.7 |
| Charges for services | 25,000 | 50,000 | 25,000 | 50.0 | 45.4 |
| Fines and forfeits | 40,000 | 100,000 | 60,000 | 40.0 | 35.6 |
| Other | 70,000 | 200,000 | 130,000 | 35.0 | 33.3 |
| | 1,035,000 | 2,000,000 | 965,000 | 51.8 | 49.7 |
| Expenditures | | | | | |
| and Encumbrances: | | | | | |
| General government | 120,000 | 250,000 | 130,000 | 48.0 | 51.3 |
| Public safety | 300,000 | 575,000 | 275,000 | 52.2 | 48.0 |
| Highways and streets | 175,000 | 500,000 | 325,000 | 35.0 | 55.0 |
| Health and sanitation | 225,000 | 375,000 | 150,000 | 60.0 | 51.4 |
| Culture and recreation | 70,000 | 200,000 | 130,000 | 35.0 | 41.6 |
| Other | 60,000 | 50,000 | (10,000) | 120.0 | 55.4 |
| | 950,000 | 1,950,000 | 1,000,000 | 48.7 | 46.0 |
| Excess of Revenues | | | | | |
| over (under) Expenditures | | | | | |
| and Encumbrances | $ 85,000 | $ 50,000 | | | |

Notes:
1. This statement may also contain beginning fund balance and anticipated ending fund balance amounts.
2. Expenditures and encumbrances may be presented separately as well as in total.
3. If encumbrances are not viewed as equivalent to expenditures for budgetary purposes, only expenditures (not encumbrances) are presented in this statement.

the budgetary comparison data may be summarized in the budgetary comparison statement, which may be supported by separate, more detailed revenues and expenditures budgetary schedules.

## Annual Budgetary Statements

As noted earlier, GASB standards require extensive budgetary reporting presentations in the governmental unit's CAFR (which includes the GPFS). The CAFR budgetary reporting requirements include:

1. A summary budgetary comparison statement—prepared on the unit's budgetary basis—for its annually budgeted governmental funds (Figure 3–11);
2. A similar budgetary basis schedule(s) at the legislative-to-executive branch "budgetary control points" level of detail;
3. An explanation of the unit's budgetary basis; and
4. A reconciliation of the unit's budgetary basis and GAAP basis operating data.

Furthermore, the GASB *Codification* includes illustrative examples of a summary budgetary comparison statement—the Statement of Revenues, Expenditures, and Changes in Fund Balances—Budget and Actual—as well as guidance to (1) preparing and presenting the more detailed budgetary control points schedules(s) and (2) explaining the budgetary basis and reconciling the budgetary basis and GAAP basis operating data.

An example of a summary annual budgetary comparison statement—in this case, the Statement of Revenues, Expenditures and Encumbrances, and Changes in Fund Balance—Budget and Actual—is presented in Figure 3–11. This statement is prepared on the budgetary basis—here assumed to consider encumbrances the

FIGURE 3–11

**STATEMENT OF REVENUES, EXPENDITURES AND ENCUMBRANCES, AND CHANGES IN FUND BALANCE—BUDGET AND ACTUAL**
**(Budgetary Basis)**
A Governmental Unit
Governmental Fund
For Fiscal Year Ended (Date)

|  | Budget (As Revised) | Actual | Variance— Favorable (Unfavorable) |
|---|---|---|---|
| Revenues: |  |  |  |
| Taxes | $ 900,000 | $ 918,000 | $ 18,000 |
| Licenses and permits | 400,000 | 395,000 | (5,000) |
| Intergovernmental | 350,000 | 364,000 | 14,000 |
| Charges for services | 50,000 | 49,000 | (1,000) |
| Fines and forfeits | 100,000 | 102,000 | 2,000 |
| Other | 200,000 | 197,000 | (3,000) |
|  | 2,000,000 | 2,025,000 | 25,000 |
|  |  |  |  |
| Expenditures and Encumbrances: |  |  |  |
| General government | 250,000 | 249,000 | 1,000 |
| Public safety | 575,000 | 570,000 | 5,000 |
| Highways and streets | 500,000 | 490,000 | 10,000 |
| Health and sanitation | 375,000 | 371,000 | 4,000 |
| Culture and recreation | 200,000 | 194,000 | 6,000 |
| Other | 50,000 | 65,000 | (15,000) |
|  | 1,950,000 | 1,939,000 | 11,000 |
| Excess of Revenues over Expenditures and Encumbrances | 50,000 | 86,000 | 36,000 |
| Fund Balance—Beginning of Period | 450,000 | 450,000 | — |
| Fund Balance—End of Period | $ 500,000 | $ 536,000 | $ 36,000 |

Notes:

1. Data on the original budget, before revisions, may be presented in a "Budget (Original)" column preceding the "Budget (As Revised)" column of this statement. (For illustrative simplicity, the examples in this chapter assume that no budget revisions were enacted.)

2. This statement assumes that the budgetary basis in use considers encumbrances outstanding equivalent to expenditures for budgetary control, accountability, and evaluation purposes. Thus, expenditures and encumbrances are reported rather than only expenditures.

3. The GASB requires that published financial statements include an explanation of the unit's budgetary basis and a reconciliation of the differences between its budgetary basis and GAAP basis operating data.

budgetary equivalent of expenditures—and would be accompanied by a budgetary-GAAP basis explanation and reconciliation. Variations of this format, other approaches to preparing the summary budgetary comparison statement (e.g., for a GAAP basis budget and for budgets on other budgetary bases), preparing detailed budgetary schedules, and presenting budgetary-GAAP basis explanations and reconciliations are discussed and illustrated in later chapters of this text.

## CONCLUDING COMMENTS

Budgeting, budgetary accounting, and budgetary reporting are uniquely important features of the governmental fund accounting and financial reporting environment. Indeed, governmental fund accounting is sometimes referred to as budgetary accounting; and budgeting, budgetary accounting, and budgetary reporting are recurring topics on the Uniform CPA Examination.

Accordingly, much of this chapter is devoted to discussions of budgetary terminology, the major budgetary approaches and emphases, and preparation of the annual operating budget. The budgetary accounting and reporting overview discussions and illustrations that conclude this chapter both introduce these important topics and provide a bridge to the budgetary accounting entries and budgetary statement examples in the next several chapters. Thus, these overview discussions and illustrations should be reviewed before proceeding to Chapter 4, "General and Special Revenue Funds," and reviewed again while studying that chapter.

### APPENDIX 3-1

## Alternative Expenditure Budgeting Approaches

As noted in Chapter 3, the most common approaches to *operating expenditure budgeting* may be characterized as:

1. Object-of-expenditure
2. Performance
3. Program and planning-programming-budgeting (PPB)
4. Zero-base budgeting (ZBB)

The object-of-expenditure or line-item approach is discussed and illustrated in Chapter 3. This appendix focuses on the remaining three alternative expenditure budgeting approaches.

## THE PERFORMANCE APPROACH

Although the performance approach originated in the early 1900s, it received its biggest impetus from the report of the first Hoover Commission in 1949 and came into popular usage in the 1950s. The Hoover Commission report included the statement:

> We recommend that the whole budgetary concept of the federal government should be refashioned by the adoption of a budget based on functions, activities, and projects: this we designate a "performance budget."[1]

---
[1] Commission on Organization of the Executive Branch of the Government, *Budgeting and Accounting* (Washington, D.C.: U.S. Government Printing Office, 1949), p. 8.

Confusion accompanied the report of the Commission's Task Force, however, because it used the terms *performance* and *program* synonymously:

> A program or performance budget should be substituted for the present budget, thus presenting a document . . . in terms of services, activities, and work projects rather than in terms of the things bought.[2]

Although these terms have been used synonymously by many eminent authorities, the term *program budgeting* has taken on different connotations from that of *performance budgeting* and these terms will be distinguished here.[3] A performance budget is

> . . . a budget that bases expenditures primarily upon measurable performance of activities and work programs. A performance budget may also incorporate other bases of expenditure classification, such as character and object class, but these are given a subordinate status to activity performance.[4]

This approach shifts budgeting emphasis from objects of expenditure to "measurable performance of activities and work programs." The primary focus is on evaluation of the efficiency with which existing activities are being carried out; its primary tools are cost accounting and work measurement. The gist of this method may be summarized as (1) classifying budgetary accounts by function and activity, as well as by organization unit and object of expenditure, (2) investigating and measuring existing activities in order to obtain maximum efficiency and to establish cost standards, and (3) basing the budget of the succeeding period on unit cost standards multiplied by the expected number of units of the activity estimated to be required in that period. The total budget for an agency would be the sum of the products of its unit cost standards multiplied by the expected units of activity in the upcoming period. The enacted budget is viewed somewhat as a performance contract between the legislative branch and the chief executive.

## Advantages

Probably the most important contributions of the performance approach have been (1) its emphasis on including a narrative description of each proposed activity within the proposed budget, (2) organization of the budget by activities, with requests supported by estimates of costs and accomplishments in quantitative terms, and (3) its emphasis on the need to measure output as well as input. The performance budget thus emphasizes the activities for which appropriations are requested rather than merely how much will be spent, and requires answers to questions such as these:

1. What are the agency's objectives; for what reason does the agency ask for appropriations; what services does the agency render to justify its existence?

---

[2] Task Force Report, *Fiscal, Budgeting, and Accounting Activities* (Washington, D.C.: U.S. Government Printing Office, 1949), p. 43.

[3] The confusion has arisen primarily over differing uses of the term *program*. In performance budgeting the term has been applied generally to specific activities within a single department (street sweeping, police patrol, and so on), whereas in program or planning-programming-budgeting (PPB) the term usually has a broader connotation (preservation of life and property, alleviation of pain and suffering, and so on), which may include activities of many departments of a government.

[4] Government Finance Officers Association, *Governmental Accounting, Auditing and Financial Reporting* (Chicago: GFOA, 1994), p. 346.

2. What programs or activities does the agency use to achieve its objectives?
3. What volume of work is required in each of the activities?
4. What levels of services have past appropriations provided?
5. What level of activity or service may legislators and the taxpayers expect if the requested amounts are appropriated?

To provide the legislative body with a reasonable justification for its budget request, each department must do some clear thinking about what it is trying to do and how it can do it best. In addition, when the legislators fully understand the department's work, its objectives, and its problems, the appropriation ordinance achieves its full meaning as a contract between the executive and legislative branches.

Performance data also provide legislators additional freedom to reduce or expand the amounts requested for particular functions or activities. Where information is available as to particular functions and activities, these may be readily expanded or contracted at the will of the legislature. On the other hand, where only object-of-expenditure data are available, the legislature must deal with minute details and may be tempted to make arbitrary changes such as slashing all requests a given percentage. When final appropriations under the performance approach differ from the requested amounts for certain functions or activities, the executive branch must, of course, revise its plans in order to make the most effective use of amounts appropriated.

The performance approach also provides the chief executive with an additional avenue of control over subordinates. Rather than being restricted merely to how much subordinates spend, the chief executive may evaluate the performance of activities in terms of both dollar and activity unit standards.

## Limitations

Although much has been written about the performance approach, it does not appear to have often been adopted in its pure state. The approach is fundamentally sound, but (1) few state and local governments have sufficient budgetary or accounting staffs to identify units of measurement, perform cost analyses, and so on; (2) many government services and activities do not appear readily measurable in meaningful output units or unit cost terms; and (3) accounts of governments have typically been maintained on a budgetary expenditure basis, rather than on a full cost basis, making data gathering difficult if not impossible. In practice, expenditure data often have been substituted indiscriminately for cost (expense) data; and input measures have been used in place of output measures. In addition, activities sometimes have been costed and measured in great detail without sufficient consideration being given to the necessity or desirability of the activities themselves—that is, without concern for whether the activity was the best means (or even contributed) to achieving the government's goals. For these and other reasons, most attempts to install comprehensive performance budgeting systems were disappointing and no doubt discouraged others from experimenting with the approach. Advocates of the performance approach feel that it has helped instill an attitude of cost consciousness in government, however, and note the many governmental activities now being measured objectively.

## Comment

Although the performance budgeting approach never achieved widespread use in its entirety, the approach has proved extremely helpful—especially when its application has been limited to discrete, tangible, routine types of activities such as street sweeping, police patrol, and garbage collection. Furthermore, performance data are frequently used to supplement or support object-of-expenditure budget requests and are essential to program budgeting.

# THE PROGRAM AND PLANNING-PROGRAMMING-BUDGETING (PPB) APPROACHES

Another reason for the apparent demise of the performance budget (as such) was the shift in emphasis in the late 1950s and early 1960s to the program approach and then, in the mid-1960s, to what has come to be known as the planning-programming-budgeting system, often referred to as PPB or PPBS. Here again, terminology is a problem. The term *program budget* is sometimes used to refer to PPB systems or approaches and at other times is used in distinctly different ways. The GFOA, for example, defines a program budget as:

> . . . a budget wherein expenditures are based primarily on programs of work and secondarily on character and object class, on the one hand, and performance, on the other.[5]

Others distinguish between *full program* and *modified program* budgetary approaches, the latter being essentially a performance approach in which unit cost measurement is attempted only selectively. The following definition is preferred by the authors:

> Program budgets deal principally with broad planning and the costs of functions or activities. A full program approach to budgeting would require that the full cost of a function, e.g., juvenile delinquency control, would be set forth under the *program* regardless of the organizational units that may be involved in carrying such programs into execution. Thus, in the juvenile delinquency "program," certain activities of the welfare agency, the police department, the juvenile courts, the law department, and the district attorney would be included. . . .
>
> A modified program budget approach would be organized solely within major organizational units, e.g., departments.[6]

As the term is used here, *program budgeting* refers to a planning-oriented approach which emphasizes programs, functions, and activities—with much less emphasis on evaluation or control. Also, the program approach is communication oriented, with budgetary requests and reports summarized in terms of a few broad programs rather than in myriad object-of-expenditure or departmental activity detail—though such details may be provided in the executive budget and the final appropriation may be on a line-item basis.

The most elaborate version of program budgeting has come to be known as the planning-programming-budgeting system (PPB or PPBS). As with performance budgeting, the PPB emphasis originated with the federal government when concepts developed in the early part of this century were refined by the Rand Corporation in the late 1950s and experimented with in the Department of Defense in

---

[5] Ibid., p. 347.

[6] L. Moak and K. Killian, *Operating Budget Manual* (Chicago: Municipal Finance Officers Association, 1963), pp. 11–12.

the early 1960s. The movement to PPB received its greatest impetus in 1965 when President Johnson instructed most federal departments and agencies to apply this approach to their program planning and budgeting.

PPB or PPBS is not so much a new system or approach as a reordered synthesis of time-honored budgetary concepts and techniques, with additional emphasis on long-run considerations, systems analyses, and cost-benefit analyses of alternative courses of action. As Hatry observed:

> Its essence is development and presentation of information as to the full implications, the costs and benefits, of the major alternative courses of action relevant to major resource allocation decisions.
>
> The main contribution of PPBS lies in the *planning* process, i.e., the process of making program policy decisions that lead to a specific budget and specific multi-year plans. The *budget* is a detailed short term resource plan for implementing the program decisions. PPBS does not replace the need for careful budget analysis to assure that approved programs will be carried out in an efficient and cost-conscious manner, nor does it remove the need for the preparation of the detailed, line-item type of information to *support* budget submission.[7]

The major distinctive characteristics of PPB, as described by Hatry, are:

1. It focuses on identifying the fundamental objectives of the government and then relating all activities to these (regardless of organizational placement).
2. Future year implications are explicitly identified.
3. All pertinent costs are considered.
4. Systematic analysis of alternatives is performed [e.g., cost-benefit analysis and systems analysis and operations research].[8]

## Advantages

Those closely associated with PPB do not claim it to be a panacea. But this approach is designed to overcome criticisms that have been made of object-of-expenditure and performance budgeting. Both of these other approaches are based principally on historical data and focus on a single period. On the other hand, PPB emphasizes long-range planning in which (1) ultimate goals and intermediate objectives must be explicitly stated, and (2) the costs and benefits of major alternative courses to achieve these goals and objectives are to be explicitly evaluated—in quantitative terms where practicable and narratively in all cases.

PPB theory assumes that all programs are to be evaluated annually, so that poor ones may be weeded out and new ones added. Changes in existing programs are evaluated in terms of discounted marginal costs (and benefits), whereas object-of-expenditure budgets focus on total expenditures, and performance budgets are based on an average cost or average expenditure concept.

Program decisions are to be formulated at upper management levels under PPB, and department or agency heads are expected to gear their activities to fulfilling those agreed-upon objectives and goals. Finally, though PPB can be adapted to any level of appropriation specificity, many of its advocates hope to encourage (1) decision making and appropriations by legislatures in broader policy terms, and (2) increased executive powers by use of lump-sum appropriations.

---

[7] Harry P. Hatry and John F. Cotton, *Program Planning for State, County, City* (Washington, D.C.: George Washington University, 1967), pp. 14–15.

[8] Ibid., p. 15.

## Limitations

Although the logic of PPB is convincing, many barriers impede implementation of a complete PPB system. For example:

1. It is quite difficult to formulate a meaningful, explicit statement of a government's goals and objectives that can be agreed upon by all concerned—regardless of how worthwhile such a statement may be.

2. Not only do goals change, but elected officials, in particular, often prefer not to commit themselves to more than very general statements lest they be precluded from changing their positions when politics dictates.

3. The time period considered relevant by an elected official may be limited to that remaining prior to the expiration of his or her current term of office—resulting perhaps, at least subconsciously, in a greater interest in short-run costs and results than in long-run costs or results.

4. PPB, like performance budgeting, assumes both an adequate data base and a high level of analytical ability to be readily available to the government. Relatively few state or local governments have sophisticated program data or the luxury of sophisticated staff analysts. Thus, there has been little or no accounting follow-up for comparisons of PPBS plans with results. Governmental accounting systems are geared first to typical departmental object-of-expenditure budgetary accounting and only secondarily to supplemental data.

5. Objective measurement is even more of a problem here than in the performance approach because both costs and benefits, over a period of several years, must be estimated. Both are often quite difficult to measure and the ratio or relationship between two such estimates is apt to imply far more precision than actually exists.

6. Despite its planning strengths, the PPBS focus on programs differs from the departmental object-of-expenditure control orientations of most legislatures and chief executives. Indeed, many of these officials view PPBS as a threat to their "power of the purse strings."

## Comments

The full PPBS approach requires the consideration of government-wide programs and their evaluation without regard to departmental assignments. That requirement—together with the habits of years of object-of-expenditure budgeting and a jealously guarded legislative power of the purse strings—has required that PPBS budgets contain explanations of the relationships between programs, program plans, and program budget requests, on the one hand, and units of government (agencies) and objects of expenditure, on the other. Such "crosswalks" are illustrated in Figure 3–12. Appropriations typically continue to be made on the basis of organization units and objects of expenditure rather than in lump sum by program.

PPBS thus is generally viewed as more useful for planning than for operation and control. Accordingly, PPBS information appears to be used in practice more to supplement and support traditional budget information than vice versa.

# ZERO-BASE BUDGETING

The newest approach to budgetary planning is zero-base budgeting (ZBB). It came on the scene about 1970 from the profit-seeking sector of the economy, was adopted by a few governments, and was popularized when President Carter required its use for the federal government.

The essential idea of ZBB is that the continued existence of programs or activities is not taken for granted; each service must be justified in its entirety every year. The basic processes of ZBB are as follows:

FIGURE 3–12

**PPBS CROSSWALK**

19X1 Budget, All Departments

Programs

| Department or Agency and/or Object of Expenditure | Total | Public Safety | Health | Education | Trans-portation | Recreation and Culture | Social Services | Legal, Fiscal Manage-ment | Community Welfare | Non-program Items |
|---|---|---|---|---|---|---|---|---|---|---|
| Mayor/Council | | | | | | | | | | |
| City Clerk | | | | | | | | | | |
| City Attorney | | | | | | | | | | |
| Personnel | | | | | | | | | | |
| City Planning | | | | | | | | | | |
| Retirement Administration | | | | | | | | | | |
| Office of Finance | | | | | | | | | | |
| Office of Budget | | | | | | | | | | |
| Police Department | | | | | | | | | | |
| Fire Department | | | | | | | | | | |

Note: Totals of each column indicate program sums; totals for each organization unit indicate the amounts requested for each. If necessary or desired, the amounts requested for each unit may be listed by classes of objects in varying degrees of detail.

1. Divide all the operations of the government into decision units. These are programs, activities, or relatively low-level organization units. In general, ZBB does not attempt to go outside major organizational units in its definition of programs, though it can be combined with PPBS in this respect.

2. Divide the operations of each decision unit into decision packages. The bases for these may be specific activities, specific services rendered, organizational subunits of the decision unit, or alternative activities to be carried out to achieve, say, program goals.

3. Select the best option for providing service based on cost-benefit or other analysis (or on a political basis).

4. Divide the selected option into levels of service to be provided, such as last year's level, minimal, reduced, increased, or maximum. The levels of service should be costed and the costs compared with the services to be provided.

5. Rank the decision packages. As the budget requests move upward through the executive branch, managers at each level rank the decision packages in terms of governmental priorities. These priorities may have been developed through PPB; if not, priorities set at the highest levels should be used as assumptions in ranking decision packages. The chief executive, having the priorities assigned by those below him or her in the administrative hierarchy, makes the ultimate decisions required to produce the executive budget.

ZBB is designed to force an annual review of all programs, activities, and expenditures; to save money by identifying outdated programs and unnecessarily high levels of service; to concentrate the attention of officials on the costs and benefits of services; to cause a search for new ways of providing services and achieving objectives; to improve the abilities of management to plan and evaluate; to provide better justification for the budget; and, finally, to improve the decisions made by the executive and legislative branches of the government. But it requires a great deal of paperwork, staff time, and effort to identify and rank decision units and decision packages. Furthermore, it is difficult to obtain the data to compute costs of alternative methods of achieving objectives and of alternative levels of service. Accordingly, ZBB usage appears to lead to reductions in the rigor of the theory. For instance, some have determined that full justification need be required of specific activities only once every few years rather than for every budget (periodic sunset reviews of agencies fit nicely with this adaptation). Furthermore, a government may decide that some or all of the services provided by agencies must be provided at some minimum level and that crucial judgments need be applied only to the levels of service to be provided. Indeed, the primary use of ZBB appears to be to supplement the object-of-expenditure approach—particularly where the overall level of spending must be reduced by a specified percentage, and in periodic sunset reviews of agencies and programs.

## IN SUM

The budgetary approaches outlined here represent, in theory, a record of changes from devices (object-of-expenditure budget and line-item appropriations) designed primarily to authorize and fiscally control expenditures. These changes have sought to bring program planning, analysis (systems, cost-benefit), and performance measurement into the process. The primarily incremental approach has given way to the consideration of complete programs and activities (program budgets, PPBS, ZBB). Techniques encouraging executive branch managerial control have been developed. Legislative involvement has, in many instances, moved from minute control of details to broad control of functions, programs, and activities. Emphasis has shifted from input to output.

In practice the changes have not been as dramatic. Few budgets, no matter what their planning bases may have been, have avoided specification of objects of expenditures. Program planning on a government-wide basis, as in PPBS, must be related to agencies responsible for elements of the programs. The relationship may be stated in the executive budget or in the appropriation bill, but few legislative bodies are willing to appropriate without identifying agencies and objects of expenditure. PPBS has proved useful for planning, but not for execution, and has not been considered successful. Performance budgeting has led to gradual increases in the number of activities having defined units of output. Nonetheless, it has proved feasible in a relatively small number of such activities. ZBB, concentrating at the decision package level, may prove to be more easily convertible into appropriation bills and legislative control on program or activity bases within specific agencies. But the organization unit and objects of expenditure continue to be the primary basis for budgetary reporting and accountability.

The typical "good" budget for a municipality at this time, then, probably consists of program or activity descriptions *within organization units,* quantitative descriptions of levels of program activity where units of service effort (input) or accomplishment (output) have been defined, and object-of-expenditure units of input in dollars and numbers of employees.

## SELECTING AN APPROPRIATE APPROACH

Designing an appropriate approach to expenditure budgeting for a specific government requires (1) knowledge of the various general approaches that have been developed, (2) insight into the history and activities of the organization in question and the attitudes and capabilities of its personnel, in order to assess the proper planning-control-evaluation balance to be sought, (3) originality in combining the strengths of the object-of-expenditure, performance, program, and ZBB approaches, while avoiding their weaknesses, and (4) patience in system design and implementation and the ability to adapt the system to changed circumstances. Experimentation with PPBS and ZBB analyses is highly desirable in the hope that they will be suited or adaptable to state and local government needs.

## Questions

**Q 3-1**  Governmental budgeting and budgetary control are deemed so important by the GASB that it devotes an entire principle to the subject. Why?

**Q 3-2**  Distinguish between the following types of budgets: (a) capital and current; (b) tentative and enacted; (c) general and special; (d) fixed and flexible; and (e) executive and legislative.

**Q 3-3**  Budgeting is a continuous process. Explain.

**Q 3-4**  What are budgetary control points? How do they affect budgetary accounting and reporting?

**Q 3-5**  A municipality's budget is prepared on a cash basis. What basis of accounting would you recommend? Explain.

**Q 3-6**  Why are General, Special Revenue, and other governmental (expendable) funds typically controlled by fixed budgets integrated within the account structure, while Enterprise and other proprietary (nonexpendable) funds may be subject to less formal control through flexible budgets not integrated within the account structure?

**Q 3-7** Some persons contend that an inherent limitation of the line-item department or object-of-expenditure budget is that it is based on a backwards or reverse decision-making process. Explain and evaluate this assertion.

**Q 3-8** A General Fund balanced budget has been amended to increase the total appropriations. From what sources may the increase be financed?

**Q 3-9** Discuss the meaning and implications of the following statements pertaining to budgeting:
  a. "A budget is just a means of getting money."
  b. "*Never* underexpend an appropriation—the more you spend, the more you get next year."
  c. "Budgeting is easy! You just take last year's budget and add 10%—or twice what you think you might need. The council will cut your request in half and you'll wind up getting what you wanted in the first place."
  d. "The traditional line-item budget only appears to provide an orderly and seemingly objective approach to financial planning and control. In too many instances, all it really provides is a uniform framework for establishing and maintaining a set of orderly records which comply with legal requirements, but which provide very little in the way of useful management information."

**Q 3-10** Revenue estimates and appropriations enacted are standards against which performance is subsequently measured. What implications can be drawn at year end if there are variances from these standards? If there are no variances?

**Q 3-11** In business accounting a single general ledger account—such as Cash, Accounts Receivable, Investments, or Accounts Payable—typically controls the related subsidiary ledger accounts. Referring to Figure 3–7; explain how in governmental fund accounting the general ledger accounts control (a) the Revenues Subsidiary Ledger accounts, and (b) the Expenditures Subsidiary Ledger accounts.

**Q 3-12** Figures 3–7 through 3–9 illustrate Revenues Subsidiary Ledger accounts classified by major revenue source category and Expenditures Subsidiary Ledger accounts classified by function. Might more detailed subsidiary ledger accounts be necessary in practice? Explain.

**Q 3-13** An interim budgetary comparison statement for a governmental fund is illustrated in Figure 3–10. (a) Should this statement be prepared on the unit's budgetary basis or on the GAAP basis? Why? (b) Why are interim budgetary comparison statements important to effective management control and legislative oversight?

**Q 3-14** An annual budgetary comparison statement for a governmental fund is illustrated in Figure 3–11. (a) Should this statement be prepared on the unit's budgetary basis or on the GAAP basis? (b) Why does the GASB require that a state or local government's CAFR and GPFS include budgetary comparison statements and schedules for governmental funds that are budgeted annually? (c) Some governments include both original and revised budget data in budgetary comparison statements. Why?

**Q 3-15** (Appendix) Behavioral scientists tell us that "the measurement employed affects the performance of the person or group measured." What implications for performance and program budgeting are contained in this statement?

**Q 3-16** (Appendix) What major strengths and weaknesses are generally associated with the (a) line-item or object-of-expenditure, (b) performance, and (c) program approaches to budgeting?

**Q 3-17** (Appendix) (a) What are the major distinctive characteristics of the PPB approach to budgeting? (b) What is a budgetary crosswalk?

**Q 3-18** (Appendix) (a) What is the essential idea of ZBB? (b) What benefits is ZBB designed to produce?

**Q 3-19** (Appendix) (a) What are the processes required to produce a ZBB? (b) What are the difficulties that may prevent ZBB from achieving success and continuing application?

**Q 3-20** (Appendix) Most performance measures (number of arrests made, tons of garbage collected, miles of street cleaned, and so on) do not adequately measure the quantity or quality of performance but are only indicators of certain aspects of performance. Discuss (a) the validity of this statement and (b) how performance measures or indicators may be properly and beneficially employed in evaluating performance.

**Q 3-21** (Appendix) Proponents of zero-based budgeting contend that a government's budgetary process should begin each year with the assumption that no program or department has a vested interest—that each should comprehensively justify its existence, its activities, and its appropriation requests annually as if it were a proposed program or department not in existence previously. Evaluate the merits of this approach.

## Problems

**P 3-1** (Operating Budget Preparation) The finance director of the Bethandy Independent School District is making preliminary estimates of the budget outlook for the 19X8 fiscal year so that the superintendent can properly advise the department heads when budget instructions and forms are distributed. She has assembled the following information:

| 1. Revenues | *Estimated* *19X7* | *Expected* *Change—19X8* |
|---|---|---|
| Property taxes | $2,000,000 | +6% |
| State aid | 1,000,000 | +3% |
| Federal grants | 500,000 | −$40,000 |
| Other | 300,000 | +$10,000 |
| | $3,800,000 | |

| 2. Expenditures | | |
|---|---|---|
| Salaries and wages | $2,700,000 | ? |
| Utilities | 400,000 | +4% |
| Maintenance | 300,000 | +$24,000 |
| Capital outlay | 200,000 | −$15,000 |
| Debt service | 100,000 | +$20,000 |
| Other | 50,000 | +$5,000 |
| | $3,750,000 | |

3. Fund balance at the end of 19X7 is expected to be $1,600,000; at least $1,500,000 must be available at the end of 19X8 for carryover to help finance 19X9 operations.

**Required**  (a) Prepare a draft operating budget for the Bethandy Independent School District for the 19X8 fiscal year—including 19X7 comparative data and expected change computations—assuming the budget is to be balanced in the sense that 19X8 appropriations are to equal 19X8 estimated revenues.

(b) What total salaries and wages amount and average percentage increase or decrease are implied in the draft operating budget prepared in part (a)? What are the maximum salary and wage amount and percentage increase that seem to be feasible in 19X8?

**P 3-2** (Expenditures Subsidiary Ledger) Refer to Figure 3–4, "Simplified Object-of-Expenditure Budget."

**Required**  (1) What would be the minimum number of Expenditures Subsidiary Ledger accounts required for the Police Department if:
(a) The council enacted the appropriations ordinance by department?
(b) The council enacted the appropriations by department and broad object-of-expenditure category (e.g., supplies)?
(c) Same as (a) except the mayor apportioned the appropriations by broad object-of-expenditure category?

    (d) The council enacted appropriations by department and specific object class (e.g., gasoline and oil)?

    (e) Same as (b) except the controller wants to accumulate accounting data by specific object-of-expenditure classes?

(2) Refer also to Figure 3–9. "Relationship of General Ledger Appropriations, Expenditures, and Encumbrances Accounts and the Expenditures Subsidiary Ledger Accounts," and set up the Police Department Expenditures Subsidiary Ledger accounts. Then record directly in the subsidiary ledger accounts:

    (a) The Police Department appropriations, assuming they were made at the broad object-of-expenditure level.

    (b) Issuance of purchase orders for office supplies (estimated cost, $800) and a motorcycle (estimated cost, $8,400).

    (c) Payment of monthly salaries ($97,000) and utilities ($1,800).

    (d) Delivery of the office supplies (cost, $790) and motorcycle (cost, $8,500, including freight, and so on).

    (e) Council approval of the police chief's request to use $4,800 appropriated for telephone costs to employ a part-time radio operator.

**P 3-3**  (Budgetary and Other Entries—General and Subsidiary Ledgers) The Murphy County Commissioners adopted the following General Fund budget for the 19X3 fiscal year:

**General Fund**
**Murphy County**
Budget—19X3

Estimated Revenues:

| | |
|---|---:|
| Taxes | $ 8,000,000 |
| Licenses and Permits | 800,000 |
| Intergovernmental | 2,000,000 |
| Charges for Services | 200,000 |
| Fines and Forfeits | 400,000 |
| Other | 600,000 |
| | 12,000,000 |

Appropriations:

| | |
|---|---:|
| General Government | 1,000,000 |
| Public Safety | 4,000,000 |
| Highways and Streets | 5,000,000 |
| Health and Sanitation | 900,000 |
| Culture and Recreation | 400,000 |
| Other | 600,000 |
| | 11,900,000 |

| | |
|---|---:|
| Excess of Estimated Revenues over Appropriations | 100,000 |
| Fund Balance—Beginning | 1,400,000 |
| Fund Balance—Ending (Anticipated) | $ 1,500,000 |

The following events occurred during 19X3:

1. Purchase orders issued and contracts let were expected to cost:

| | |
|---|---:|
| General Government | $ 300,000 |
| Public Safety | 1,200,000 |
| Highways and Streets | 2,500,000 |
| Health and Sanitation | 500,000 |
| Culture and Recreation | 300,000 |
| Other | 200,000 |
| | $ 5,000,000 |

2. The commissioners reviewed the budget during the year and (a) revised the estimate of Intergovernmental Revenues to $1,500,000 and reduced the Public Safety and Highways and Streets appropriations by $225,000 each to partially compensate for the anticipated decline in intergovernmental revenues; and (b) increased the Health and Sanitation appropriation by $70,000 because of costs incurred in connection with an unusual outbreak of Tasmanian flu.
3. Revenues (actual) for 19X3 were:

| | |
|---|---:|
| Taxes...................................... | $ 8,150,000 |
| Licenses and Permits........................ | 785,000 |
| Intergovernmental........................... | 1,520,000 |
| Charges for Services ........................ | 210,000 |
| Fines and Forfeits .......................... | 395,000 |
| Other ..................................... | 500,000 |
| | $11,560,000 |

4. Goods and services under purchase orders and contracts were received:

| | Estimated Cost | Actual Cost |
|---|---:|---:|
| General Government ...................... | $ 280,000 | $ 278,000 |
| Public Safety ............................. | 900,000 | 910,000 |
| Highways and Streets ...................... | 2,500,000 | 2,500,000 |
| Health and Sanitation...................... | 440,000 | 440,000 |
| Culture and Recreation..................... | 300,000 | 295,000 |
| Other ..................................... | 180,000 | 181,000 |
| | $ 4,600,000 | $4,604,000 |

The remaining orders are still outstanding.

5. Other expenditures incurred were:

| | |
|---|---:|
| General Government ...................... | $ 700,000 |
| Public Safety ............................. | 2,560,000 |
| Highways and Streets ...................... | 2,271,000 |
| Health and Sanitation...................... | 485,000 |
| Culture and Recreation..................... | 45,000 |
| Other ..................................... | 391,000 |
| | $ 6,452,000 |

***Required*** (1) Set up general ledger T-accounts like those in Figure 3–7 and revenues and expenditures subsidiary ledgers like those in Figures 3–8 and 3–9.
(2) Record the Murphy County 19X3 General Fund budget in the general ledger and subsidiary ledger accounts, keying these entries "B" (for budget). Then record the numbered transactions and events, keying these entries by those numbers.

**P 3-4** (Budgetary Comparison Statement) This problem is based on the information about the Murphy County General Fund budgeted and actual transactions and events described in Problem 3-3.

***Required*** (1) Prepare a budgetary comparison statement for the General Fund of Murphy County for the 19X3 fiscal year. The statement should present revenues (by source category), expenditures and encumbrances (by function), and the excess of revenues over (under) expenditures and encumbrances. Use these column headings:

Budget (Revised)

Actual

Variance—Favorable (Unfavorable)

Assume that no encumbrances were outstanding at the beginning of 19X3.

(2) Because encumbrances do not constitute expenditures, some governmental fund budgetary comparison statements omit data on encumbrances. (a) Assuming no encumbrances were outstanding at the beginning of 19X3, what effects would omission of encumbrances data have on the Murphy County General Fund budgetary comparison statement for the 19X3 fiscal year? (b) In what circumstances would including or excluding encumbrances data mislead users of a governmental fund budgetary comparison statement?

(3) What may have caused the variations between the appropriations and the actual expenditures and encumbrances reported in the 19X3 Murphy County General Fund budgetary comparison statement for (a) Health and Sanitation? (b) Culture and Recreation?

**P 3-5** (Property Tax Levy Computation) The comptroller of the city of Helmaville recently resigned. In his absence, the deputy comptroller attempted to calculate the amount of money required to be raised from property taxes for the General Fund for the fiscal year ending June 30, 19X7. The calculation is to be made as of January 1, 19X6, to serve as a basis for setting the property tax rate for the following fiscal year. The mayor has requested you to review the deputy comptroller's calculations and obtain other necessary information to prepare a formal statement for the General Fund, which will disclose the amount of money required to be raised from property taxes for the fiscal year ending June 30, 19X7. Following are the calculations prepared by the deputy comptroller:

City resources other than proposed tax levy:

| | |
|---|---|
| Estimated General Fund working balance, January 1, 19X6 | $   352,000 |
| Estimated receipts from property taxes (January 1, 19X6–June 30, 19X6) | 2,222,000 |
| Estimated revenue from investments (January 1, 19X6–June 30, 19X7) | 442,000 |
| Estimated proceeds from sale of general obligation bonds in August 19X6 | 3,000,000 |
| | $ 6,016,000 |

General Fund requirements:

| | |
|---|---|
| Estimated expenditures (January 1, 19X6–June 30, 19X6) | $ 1,900,000 |
| Proposed appropriations (July 1, 19X6–June 30, 19X7) | 4,300,000 |
| | $ 6,200,000 |

*Additional information:*

1. The General Fund carryover balance required by the city council for July 1, 19X6, is $175,000.
2. Property tax collections are due in March and September of each year. Your review indicates that during the month of February 19X6 estimated expenditures will exceed available funds by $200,000. Pending collection of property taxes in March 19X6, this deficiency will have to be met by the issuance of 30-day tax anticipation notes of $200,000 at an estimated interest rate of 9% per annum.

3. The proposed general obligation bonds will be issued by the City Water Enterprise Fund and will be used for the construction of a new water pumping station.

*Required*  Prepare a statement as of January 1, 19X6, calculating the property tax levy required for the city of Helmaville General Fund for the fiscal year ending June 30, 19X7. (*Hint:* Requirements – Resources Other Than Property Tax Levy = Amount of the Required Levy.)

(AICPA, adapted)

**P 3-6**  (Research and Analysis) Obtain a recent state or local government annual operating budget from a library, your professor, the Internet, or elsewhere and submit a brief report on this research assignment.

*Required*  (1) Identify the government and describe the budget type (e.g., line item, program, performance).
(2) Which aspects of the budget document(s) were like what you expected based on Chapter 3? Explain.
(3) Which aspects of the budget document(s) were different from what you expected based on Chapter 3? Explain.
(4) Submit photocopies or printouts of relevant pages of the budget to support and illustrate your analyses.
(5) Submit the budget document if requested by the instructor.

**P 3-7**  (Research and Analysis) Obtain at least two recent annual operating budgets of similar state or local governments (e.g., two cities, three states) from the governments, a library, your professor, the Internet, or elsewhere. Submit a brief report consistent with these requirements.

*Required*  (1) Describe how the budget documents are similar.
(2) Describe how the budget documents differ.
(3) Submit photocopies or Internet printouts of relevant pages in each budget document to support and illustrate your analysis.
(4) Submit the budget documents if requested by the instructor.

**P 3-8**  (Research and Analysis) Obtain a recent comprehensive annual financial report (CAFR) of a state or local government from the government, a library, your professor, the Internet, or elsewhere.

*Required*  (1) Identify and describe each reference to, presentation of, and disclosure of budgetary and budget-related information in the (a) introductory section, (b) financial section, and (c) statistical section. Attach photocopies or printouts of the most significant items.
(2) Evaluate and discuss the clarity and usefulness of these references, presentations, and disclosures.
(3) Submit a brief report summarizing your research and analyses. You should attach photocopies or printouts of relevant CAFR pages to support and illustrate your report.

**P 3-9**  (Appendix: Program to Object-of-Expenditure Crosswalk) The following is a portion of a draft of the 19X5 budget for the city of Woodbridge, which is being compiled by its administrator. The major programs and subprograms are indicated by notations in brackets; the departmental responsibility for program elements is indicated in parentheses.

**City of Woodbridge**
19X5 Budget (Draft)

Public Safety [Program]:
  Prevent and Prosecute Crime [Subprogram]:
    Community Police Surveillance (Police Department):

| | |
|---|---:|
| Salaries and Wages | $399,796 |
| Materials and Supplies | 34,023 |
| Contractual Services | 41,905 |
| Permanent Property | 1,734 |
| | $477,458 |

Investigate and Prosecute Adult Crimes
(Police Department):

| | |
|---|---:|
| Salaries and Wages | $258,944 |
| Materials and Supplies | 7,760 |
| Contractual Services | 7,750 |
| | $274,454 |

Investigate and Prosecute Juvenile Crimes
(Police Department):

| | |
|---|---:|
| Salaries and Wages | $207,450 |
| Materials and Supplies | 1,100 |
| Contractual Services | 2,150 |
| | $210,700 |

Detain Accused Law Violators (Police Department):

| | |
|---|---:|
| Materials and Supplies | $    50 |
| Contractual Services | 750 |
| | $   800 |

Cooperate with Regional Law Enforcement Agencies
(Police Department):

| | | |
|---|---:|---:|
| Materials and Supplies | $    50 | |
| Total | | $  963,462 |

Adjudication of Crimes [Subprogram]:

Litigate Civil Cases (Municipal Court):

| | |
|---|---:|
| Salaries and Wages | $  6,468 |
| Materials and Supplies | 200 |
| Contractual Services | 494 |
| | $  7,162 |

Penalize Criminal Violators (Municipal Court):

| | | |
|---|---:|---:|
| Salaries and Wages | $ 14,325 | |
| Materials and Supplies | 575 | |
| Contractual Services | 644 | |
| Permanent Property | 400 | |
| | $ 15,944 | |
| Total | | $   23,106 |

~~~~~~~~~~~~~~~~~~~~~~~~~~~~~~~~~~~~~~~~~~~~~~

| | |
|---|---:|
| Grand Total—Public Safety [Program] | $7,261,500 |

Community Development and Environmental Control
[Program]:

Community Development [Subprogram]:

Planning Land Use (Director of Planning):

| | |
|---|---:|
| Salaries and Wages | $ 54,439 |
| Materials and Supplies | 2,422 |
| Contractual Services | 7,825 |
| | $ 64,686 |

~~~~~~~~~~~~~~~~~~~~~~~~~~~~~~~~~~~~~~~~~~~~~~

The grand total budgeted (all programs) for the object-of-expenditure classifications included above was:

| | |
|---|---:|
| Salaries and Wages .................................. | $5,126,197 |
| Materials and Supplies .............................. | 1,817,923 |
| Contractual Services................................ | 291,060 |
| Permanent Property ................................. | 2,140,781 |
| | $9,375,961 |

**Required**  Using the data given, prepare a budget presentation in a program to object-of-expenditure crosswalk format, with subprogram and program element detail.

**P 3-10**  (Appendix: Program to Department Crosswalk) Using the information contained in Problem 3–9, prepare a crosswalk budgetary presentation relating programs, subprograms, and program elements to departments. (You need not include object-of-expenditure detail.) The grand total budgeted for the departments with which this problem deals are as follows:

| | |
|---|---:|
| Police ............................................. | $1,717,476 |
| Municipal Court .................................... | 81,050 |
| Director of Planning................................ | 124,292 |

# CHAPTER

# 4

# GENERAL AND SPECIAL REVENUE FUNDS

The General Fund and Special Revenue Funds typically are used to finance and account for most general government activities of state and local governments. General government activities include police protection, fire protection, central administration, street maintenance, and similar general operating activities of independent school districts and nonproprietary special districts. They are discussed together because accounting and reporting for General and Special Revenue Funds are identical.

Special Revenue Funds are established to account for general government financial resources that are restricted by law or by contractual agreement to specific purposes. The General Fund is used to account for all financial resources that are not restricted to specific purposes or otherwise required to be accounted for in another fund. The General Fund is established at the inception of a government and exists throughout the government's life. Special Revenue Funds exist as long as the government has resources dedicated to specific purposes. In the typical case, most of the resources of both types of funds are expended each year and are replenished on an annual basis.

The financial resources of the General Fund and Special Revenue Funds typically are expended primarily for current operating purposes (e.g., salaries, supplies) rather than for capital outlay or debt service. Significant amounts to be expended for capital outlay or debt service from these funds usually are transferred to Capital Projects and Debt Service Funds, respectively, and expended through those funds. But routine capital outlay expenditures (e.g., for vehicles and equipment) and debt service expenditures (e.g., for capital leases and equipment notes payable) generally are made directly from the General and Special Revenue Funds.

Furthermore, recall from the discussion of the GASB principles in Chapter 2 that:

1. Resources restricted to expenditure for purposes normally financed from the General Fund may be accounted for through the General Fund as long as applicable legal requirements are met, and

2. Use of Special Revenue Funds is not required unless they are legally mandated.

Thus, some restricted resources may be accounted for through the General Fund rather than through Special Revenue Funds. This option is not assumed in Chapter 4.

## Measurement Focus

Because of the recurring nature of their revenues and commitments, and the necessity of meeting current commitments from the currently expendable (appropriable) financial resources, the accounting principles for General and Special Revenue Funds are based on the flows and balances of financial resources concept rather than on the income determination concept of business accounting. Consistent with this measurement focus, recall that General and Special Revenue Funds are working capital entities. The basic accounting equation for each is Current Assets – Current Liabilities = Fund Balance. Accordingly, purchases of fixed assets with the financial resources of these funds decrease their fund balance. Expenditures for fixed assets thus have the same effect in these funds as expenditures for wages and salaries because fixed assets are not capitalized in the General or Special Revenue Funds but in the General Fixed Assets Account Group. Similarly, if maturing general obligation bonds of the government—which are carried as liabilities in the General Long-Term Debt Account Group prior to maturity—are paid from the resources of these funds, the expenditure decreases fund balance in the same manner as expenditures for salaries and wages.

As a result of the flows and balances of financial resources concept, the General or Special Revenue Fund year-end balance sheet presents the financial resources on hand, any related current liabilities, and the fund balance—the net financial resources of the fund. Furthermore, if some of the fund's net assets are not available for expenditure—as when a three-year interfund loan has been made from the General Fund to another fund—this is indicated by reserving a portion of the total fund balance. This treatment segregates total fund balance between its reserved fund balance and unreserved fund balance components. Accordingly, the unreserved fund balance at year end is expected to be available, together with the revenues and other financing sources of the following year, to meet the needs of that year. Additional references to this concept—and to the unreserved and reserved components of total fund balance—will be made as transactions and statements of these funds are discussed.

## Purposes and Assumptions of This Chapter

This chapter discusses and illustrates the basic accounting procedures and financial statements for the General Fund and Special Revenue Funds. Accordingly, except where stated otherwise, the discussions and illustrations in this chapter assume that:

1. The annual operating budget is prepared and adopted on a GAAP basis, and
2. The accounts are maintained on a GAAP basis during the year.

Most Uniform CPA Examination questions are based on these assumptions, though they are not typical in practice.

The discussions and illustrations in this chapter focus on demonstrating one way a transaction or event may properly be accounted for and reported—typically the manner in which it might appear in unofficial solutions to CPA exam questions and problems—even though there may be acceptable alternatives. Some of these alternatives are discussed and illustrated in later chapters.

Furthermore, to enhance illustrative clarity, small numerical dollar amounts are used in the illustrative journal entries, trial balances, and financial statements.

Likewise, only a few Revenues Subsidiary Ledger accounts (by broad revenue source category) and a few Expenditures Subsidiary Ledger accounts (by function) are used. Hundreds of subsidiary ledger accounts may be needed in practice—at least one account for each significant revenue source and appropriation line item in the adopted budget (as discussed in Chapter 3).

Because accounting and reporting for the General Fund and Special Revenue Funds are identical, this chapter deals primarily with General Fund accounting and reporting, with only occasional reference to Special Revenue Funds. The principles, procedures, and illustrations are equally applicable to Special Revenue Funds, however.

## GENERAL FUND ACCOUNTING ILLUSTRATIVE EXAMPLE

To illustrate the essential aspects of General and Special Revenue Fund accounting, assume that a new local governmental unit, a city which we shall call A Governmental Unit, was founded late in 19X0. A Governmental Unit uses revenues and expenditures subsidiary ledgers like those illustrated in Figures 3–7, 3–8, and 3–9, and the trial balance of its General Fund at January 1, 19X1, appears in Figure 4–1.

Note that the "Unreserved Fund Balance" in Figure 4–1 is also the total fund balance, and might be called simply "Fund Balance." However, because total fund balance may have both reserved and unreserved components, the "Unreserved Fund Balance" title is preferable.

The annual operating budget adopted for the General Fund of A Governmental Unit for the fiscal year beginning January 1, 19X1—the government's first full year of operation—is summarized in Figure 4–2.

Note that the General Fund budget illustrated in Figure 4–2 assumes that:

1. The annual budget is adopted on the modified accrual, or GAAP, basis, as indicated earlier, and thus there are not any budgetary-GAAP basis differences.

2. Appropriations are made for operating expenditures by function and for capital outlay and debt service expenditures to be made directly from the General Fund.

3. The budget does not include appropriations for interfund transfers—though it might—but assumes that any interfund transfers will be *separately* authorized by the governing body.

The accounting implications of this budget are that (1) the accounts should be maintained during the year on the modified accrual (GAAP) basis, (2) accounts

FIGURE 4–1 **General Ledger Trial Balance—Beginning of 19X1**

A Governmental Unit
General Fund

**General Ledger Trial Balance**
January 1, 19X1

|  | Debit | Credit |
|---|---|---|
| Cash .................... | $14,000 | |
| Accounts Receivable ........ | 12,000 | |
| Vouchers Payable .......... | | $15,000 |
| Unreserved Fund Balance..... | | 11,000 |
| | $26,000 | $26,000 |

FIGURE 4–2  **Annual Operating Budget for 19X1**

A Governmental Unit
General Fund
**Annual Operating Budget**
For 19X1 Fiscal Year
(Budgetary Basis Is the Modified Accrual GAAP Basis)

Estimated Revenues:

| | |
|---|---|
| Taxes | $250,000 |
| Licenses and permits | 70,000 |
| Intergovernmental | 50,000 |
| Charges for services | 40,000 |
| Fines and forfeits | 20,000 |
| Other | 1,000 |
| | 431,000 |

Appropriations:
Current operating

| | |
|---|---|
| General government | 40,000 |
| Public safety | 150,000 |
| Highways and streets | 120,000 |
| Health and sanitation | 60,000 |
| Other | 25,000 |
| | 395,000 |
| Capital outlay | 30,000 |
| Debt service | 1,000 |
| | 426,000 |

| | |
|---|---|
| Excess of Estimated Revenues over Appropriations | $ 5,000 |

Notes:

1. The enacted budget appropriates operating expenditures by function but includes separate appropriations for the capital outlay and debt service expenditures of this fund. (Major capital outlay and debt service expenditures typically are financed by interfund transfers to Capital Projects and Debt Service Funds.)

2. The governmental unit may (and will) separately authorize interfund transfers during the year and, if appropriate, revise this original budget.

3. Because the budgetary basis is the modified accrual (GAAP) basis, there will be no differences between the budgetary basis and the GAAP basis in this example.

should be established in the Revenues Subsidiary Ledger and Expenditures Subsidiary Ledger at the level of detail (at least) of the official budget, and (3) any interfund transfers or other fund balance changes will be recorded in appropriately titled General Ledger accounts, but will not be recorded in subsidiary ledger accounts because only revenues and expenditures are subject to formal budgetary accounting control procedures.

## Entries During 19X1

### Budgetary Entry

The operation of the General Fund of A Governmental Unit begins with the adoption of the budget. The appropriations it contains, together with the revenue

estimates on which the appropriations are based, provide the basis for the following **budgetary entry** on the first day of the new year:

| (1) **Estimated Revenues** | $431,000 | |
|---|---|---|
| **Appropriations** | | $426,000 |
| **Unreserved Fund Balance** | | 5,000 |

To record appropriations and revenue estimates.

**Revenues Ledger (Estimated Revenues):**

| | |
|---|---|
| Taxes | $250,000 |
| Licenses and Permits | 70,000 |
| Intergovernmental | 50,000 |
| Charges for Services | 40,000 |
| Fines and Forfeits | 20,000 |
| Other | 1,000 |
| | $431,000 |

**Expenditures Ledger (Appropriations):**

| | |
|---|---|
| General Government | $ 40,000 |
| Public Safety | 150,000 |
| Highways and Streets | 120,000 |
| Health and Sanitation | 60,000 |
| Other | 25,000 |
| Capital Outlay | 30,000 |
| Debt Service | 1,000 |
| | $426,000 |

Note the format of this entry:

- The General Ledger entry appears first, followed by the subsidiary ledger entries.
- The subsidiary ledger entries do not balance but sum to the related Estimated Revenues and Appropriations control account entry amounts in the General Ledger.

Note also that the General Ledger budgetary entry causes the Unreserved Fund Balance account to be stated at its $16,000 ($11,000 beginning balance plus $5,000 planned increase) planned end-of-year balance. This is the manner by which the Estimated Revenues and Appropriations budgetary accounts traditionally have been incorporated into the General Ledger and subsidiary ledgers in order to effect budgetary control during the period. Alternatively, the budgeted changes in unreserved fund balance ($5,000 here) may be recorded in a separate Budgetary Fund Balance account, discussed later in this chapter.

The budgetary accounts do not affect the actual asset, liability, revenue, or expenditure General Ledger accounts. Furthermore, carrying the Unreserved Fund Balance account at its planned end-of-year balance focuses attention during the year on the target ending fund balance ("where we want to be") rather than on the beginning-of-period fund balance ("where we used to be"). In any event, neither the Estimated Revenues and Appropriations accounts nor the budgetary entry permanently affects the Unreserved Fund Balance account. At year end—having effected budgetary control during the year—the budgetary entry is reversed in the closing entries.

Entry 1 compounds two possible separate General Ledger budgetary entries:

| (1a) Estimated Revenues | $431,000 | |
|---|---|---|
| Unreserved Fund Balance | | $431,000 |

To record estimated revenues and the expected fund balance
increase to result during the period.

(1b) Unreserved Fund Balance............................ $426,000

    Appropriations....................................           $426,000

       To record appropriations and the expected fund balance
       decrease to result during the period.

Should the revenue estimate be revised upward during the period, the increase would be debited to Estimated Revenues and credited to Unreserved Fund Balance. A decrease in estimated revenues would be recorded by debiting the expected decrease to Unreserved Fund Balance and crediting Estimated Revenues. Similarly, if additional appropriations are made during the year, Unreserved Fund Balance would be debited and Appropriations credited for the increase. The opposite would be true should appropriations be decreased.

    Therefore, if during the year the governing body had increased the official estimate of tax revenues by $1,000 and also increased the public safety appropriations by $3,000, thus reducing the year-end Unreserved Fund Balance estimate by $2,000, the entry would be:

Estimated Revenues..................................... $1,000

Unreserved Fund Balance .............................. 2,000

    Appropriations .......................................           $3,000

    To record budget revisions.

    <u>Revenues Ledger (Estimated Revenues):</u>

Taxes .................................................. <u>$1,000</u>

    <u>Expenditures Ledger (Appropriations):</u>

Public Safety...........................................           <u>$3,000</u>

    The illustrative example in this chapter assumes that no budget revisions were made during the year. Budget revisions are discussed further in Chapters 5 and 6.

### Property Tax Levy

    Property taxes usually are a major revenue source of local governments. They accrue when they are formally levied by the legislative body of the city. (The assessment date is the date on which the value and ownership of property are determined for purposes of assigning tax liability and usually precedes the date of levy by a substantial period.) On the date that A Governmental Unit's current-year taxes are levied, assuming the taxes are considered available—that is, are expected to be collected during the year or soon thereafter—the following entry is made:

(2) Taxes Receivable—Current ........................... $200,000

    Allowance for Uncollectible Current Taxes..............      $  3,000

    Revenues .........................................      197,000

    To record levy of property taxes.

    <u>Revenues Ledger (Revenues):</u>

Taxes...............................................      <u>$197,000</u>

    The Allowance for Uncollectible Current Taxes amount is the portion of the tax levy not expected to be collected. At this time the city does not know which specific tax bills will not be collected. As specific amounts are determined to be uncollectible, they are written off by charging the Allowance for Uncollectible Current Taxes account and crediting Taxes Receivable. Because such taxes are a primary lien on the property, no loss is incurred until the city has gone through foreclosure proceedings that result in the sale of the property for taxes. The accounting for tax liens and for dispositions of such property is discussed in Chapter 5.

Observe in entry 2 that only the net expected tax collections are credited to Revenues. This net revenue approach differs from business accounting, where the gross receivable ($200,000) is credited to revenues and the estimated uncollectible amounts ($3,000) are debited to expense. But governmental funds account for expenditures, not expenses; and the amount of taxes levied that is uncollectible does not constitute an expenditure. Furthermore, uncollectible taxes will never meet the "available" revenue recognition criteria.

### Other Revenues Billed or Accrued

As other revenues are billed or accrue, the following entries are made:

| | | |
|---|---|---|
| (3) Accounts Receivable.................................. | $36,000 | |
|     Allowance for Uncollectible Accounts Receivable........ | | $ 1,000 |
|     Revenues ...................................... | | 35,000 |
|     To record accrual of revenues and related allowance for estimated losses. | | |
|     Revenues Ledger (Revenues): | | |
|     Charges for Services .................................. | | $35,000 |

The foregoing charges for services revenues might represent charges for court costs and fees, inspection fees, or parking fees, for example. Those revenues that do not accrue, or are not deemed sufficiently measurable to be accrued in the accounts prior to collection, are debited to Cash and credited to Revenues at the time of collection. Also, note that the net revenue approach is used with various types of governmental fund revenues—not only for tax revenues.

### Encumbrances and Related Expenditures

A primary objective of governmental accounting is to assist the administration in controlling the expenditures, including avoiding overexpenditure of appropriations. Thus, accounts must be kept both for total expenditures (General Ledger) and for expenditures chargeable to each appropriation (Expenditures Subsidiary Ledger). Usually a record of the estimated expenditures in process is maintained—in total in the General Ledger and by each appropriation in the Expenditures Subsidiary Ledger—through the use of an Encumbrances account. Encumbrances are recorded when purchase orders are issued for goods and services. Thus, if we assume that orders are placed for materials and equipment estimated to cost $30,000 for the functions indicated, the entry at the time the orders are placed would be:

| | | |
|---|---|---|
| (4) **Encumbrances** ....................................... | $30,000 | |
|     **Reserve for Encumbrances** .......................... | | $30,000 |
|     To record encumbering appropriations. | | |
|     Expenditures Ledger (Encumbrances): | | |
|     General Government .................................. | $ 2,000 | |
|     Public Safety ........................................ | 8,000 | |
|     Highways and Streets ................................. | 10,000 | |
|     Other .............................................. | 4,000 | |
|     Capital Outlay ...................................... | 6,000 | |
| | $30,000 | |

Comparison of appropriations with expenditures and encumbrances shows the amount of uncommitted (unencumbered) appropriations available for expenditure. When the actual expenditure occurs, the entry setting up the encumbrances is reversed and the actual expenditure is recorded.

If the materials and equipment subsequently received cost only $29,900, the entries will be:

(5a) **Reserve for Encumbrances** .......................... $30,000

      **Encumbrances**................................. $30,000

    To reverse the entry encumbering the Appropriations account.

    Expenditures Ledger (Encumbrances):

| | |
|---|---|
| General Government................................ | $ 2,000 |
| Public Safety..................................... | 8,000 |
| Highways and Streets.............................. | 10,000 |
| Other............................................ | 4,000 |
| Capital Outlay................................... | 6,000 |
| | $30,000 |

(5b) **Expenditures**.................................... $29,900

      Vouchers Payable ............................... $29,900

    To record expenditures.

    Expenditures Ledger (Expenditures):

| | |
|---|---|
| General Government.............................. | $ 1,700 |
| Public Safety..................................... | 8,000 |
| Highways and Streets.............................. | 10,100 |
| Other............................................ | 4,000 |
| Capital Outlay................................... | 6,100 |
| | $29,900 |

These entries accomplish two things. The unencumbered balance of the Appropriations, Expenditures, and Encumbrances accounts in the General Ledger, and of the individual accounts in the Expenditures Subsidiary Ledger, against which the expenditures for materials and equipment are chargeable, was temporarily reduced—while the order was outstanding—by the estimated amount of the expenditures, the encumbrance. Now, however, the exact amount of the expenditures is known; accordingly, the entry setting up the encumbrances is reversed and the actual expenditures are recorded. The General Ledger effects of these entries are as follows:

| | After Entry 1 | After Entry 4 | After Entries 5a and 5b |
|---|---|---|---|
| Appropriations ................ | $426,000 | $426,000 | $426,000 |
| Less: Expenditures ............. | -0- | -0- | 29,900 |
| Unexpended balance ........... | 426,000 | 426,000 | 396,100 |
| Less: Encumbrances ............ | -0- | 30,000 | -0- |
| Unencumbered Balance ......... | $426,000 | $396,000 | $396,100 |

Note again, as discussed in Chapter 3, that the sum of the "Unencumbered Balance" column amounts of the several Expenditures Subsidiary Ledger accounts should always equal the total unencumbered balance computed from the General Ledger accounts.

Note also from entries 5a and 5b that encumbrances are estimates of subsequent expenditures—and that the resulting actual expenditures may be more than, less than, or equal to the encumbrances. In this case the Public Safety and Other expenditures were exactly as planned—perhaps the result of an exact price quotation or bid on a firm price purchase order. But the General Government order cost less than anticipated—perhaps because of a price decline but also possibly because part of the order could not be filled or was canceled. On the other hand, the Highways and Streets and Capital Outlay expenditures were more than originally estimated—

possibly because of freight, delivery, or similar costs that were not anticipated or because of an approved change in specifications after the purchase order was issued. In any case, the accounting upon receipt of encumbered goods or services is simply: Reverse the encumbrance entry and record the actual expenditure.

Finally, recall from Chapter 2 that the purchase of equipment also impacts the General Fixed Assets Account Group. The equipment would be accounted for in the GFAAG, resulting in the following changes in the GFAAG accounting equation:

$$\text{Equipment} = \text{Investment in GFA}$$
$$+\,\$6{,}100 \qquad +\,\$6{,}100$$

### Unencumbered Expenditures

If an expenditure is controlled by devices other than encumbrances, the appropriation is not encumbered. Rather, the amount of the available appropriation is reduced only at the time of the expenditure. This is usually true with payrolls, for example, which are controlled by specified employment procedures and payroll system controls. Thus, if the payroll at the end of a pay period was $40,000, the entry at the time the payroll was approved for payment would be:

| | | |
|---|---:|---:|
| (6) Expenditures ........................................ | $40,000 | |
| Vouchers Payable.................................. | | $40,000 |

To record approval of payroll.

Expenditures Ledger (Expenditures):

| | |
|---|---:|
| General Government ................................. | $ 5,000 |
| Public Safety .......................................... | 16,000 |
| Highways and Streets ............................... | 13,000 |
| Health and Sanitation ............................... | 4,000 |
| Other ................................................. | 2,000 |
| | $40,000 |

### Other Transactions and Events

Additional entries illustrating the operation of the General Fund of A Governmental Unit follow. Note that entries are made in the Revenues Subsidiary Ledger or Expenditures Subsidiary Ledger only when the General Ledger entries affect the Revenues or Expenditures accounts or the related Estimated Revenues, Appropriations, or Encumbrances budgetary accounts. **(All amounts are assumed.)**

| | | |
|---|---:|---:|
| (7) Cash.............................................. | $175,000 | |
| Taxes Receivable—Current......................... | | $160,000 |
| Accounts Receivable ............................. | | 15,000 |

To record collection of taxes receivable and accounts receivable.

| | | |
|---|---:|---:|
| (8) Taxes Receivable—Delinquent........................ | $ 40,000 | |
| Taxes Receivable—Current......................... | | $ 40,000 |

To record reclassification of taxes receivable not collected by the due date.

[Total levy of $200,000 (transaction 2) less collections of current taxes of $160,000 (transaction 7).]

| | | |
|---|---:|---:|
| (9) Allowance for Uncollectible Current Taxes .............. | $ 3,000 | |
| Allowance for Uncollectible Delinquent Taxes ......... | | $ 3,000 |

To record reclassification of allowance for estimated losses on taxes (to correspond with the reclassification of the taxes receivable in entry 8).

(10)   Cash.......................................... $205,000

        Revenues......................................                      $205,000

        To record receipt of revenues not previously accrued.

        Revenues Ledger (Revenues):

        Taxes ..................................... $ 58,000

        Licenses and Permits ............................... 68,000

        Intergovernmental ................................. 52,500

        Charges for Services................................. 6,000

        Fines and Forfeits................................... 19,000

        Other........................................      1,500

                                                 $205,000

(11)   Vouchers Payable................................. $ 40,000

        Cash.........................................         $ 40,000

        To record payment of payroll voucher.

(12)   Encumbrances ...................................... $ 20,000

        Reserve for Encumbrances .......................      $ 20,000

        To record reduction of appropriation available for future expenditure by amount of estimated cost of purchase orders issued.

        Expenditures Ledger (Encumbrances):

        Public Safety..................................... $  7,000

        Health and Sanitation .............................   13,000

                                          $ 20,000

(13)   Cash.......................................... $ 20,200

        Taxes Receivable—Delinquent ......................     $ 20,000

        Revenues......................................           200

        To record collection of delinquent taxes, together with interest and penalties thereon that had not been accrued.

        Revenues Ledger (Revenues):

        Other.........................................          $    200

(14)   Investments..................................... $ 10,000

        Cash.........................................         $ 10,000

        To record temporary investment of excess cash.

        Investment accounting and reporting under GASB *Statement No. 31* are discussed and illustrated in Chapter 5 and in later chapters.

(15)   Expenditures..................................... $ 30,000

        Due to Stores Fund .............................      $ 30,000

        To record supplies provided by an Internal Service Fund.

        Expenditures Ledger (Expenditures):

        General Government............................... $  4,000

        Public Safety..................................... 6,000

        Highways and Streets.............................. 10,000

        Health and Sanitation ............................. 7,000

        Other.........................................    3,000

                                      $ 30,000

This **quasi-external transaction** would have the following impact on the Stores Internal Service Fund:

Assets – Liabilities = Contributed Capital + Retained Earnings

+$30,000                                     + $30,000 (Revenues)

| | | | |
|---|---|---|---|
| (16) | Due from Special Revenue Fund . . . . . . . . . . . . . . . . . . . . . | $ 1,500 | |
| | Expenditures. . . . . . . . . . . . . . . . . . . . . . . . . . . . . . . . . . . . | | $ 1,500 |
| | To record reimbursement due from Special Revenue Fund for expenditure made initially from the General Fund. | | |
| | <u>Expenditures Ledger (Expenditures):</u> | | |
| | General Government . . . . . . . . . . . . . . . . . . . . . . . . . . . . . . . | | <u>$  1,500</u> |

This **reimbursement** transaction would have the following effect on the specific Special Revenue Fund accounting equation:

$$\text{Current Assets} - \text{Current Liabilities} = \text{Fund Balance}$$
$$+\ \$1{,}500 \qquad\qquad -\ \$1{,}500\ (\text{Expenditures})$$

| | | | |
|---|---|---|---|
| (17) | Operating Transfer to Debt Service Fund. . . . . . . . . . . . . . | $ 5,000 | |
| | Due to Debt Service Fund . . . . . . . . . . . . . . . . . . . . . . . . . | | $ 5,000 |
| | To record annual transfer to Debt Service Fund to meet debt service and fiscal charges. | | |

Note that interfund operating transfers must be reported separately from Revenues and Expenditures, and that this transfer effects the Debt Service Fund as follows:

$$\text{Current Assets} - \text{Current Liabilities} = \text{Fund Balance}$$
$$+\ \$5{,}000 \qquad\qquad\qquad +\ \$5{,}000\ (\text{Other Financing Sources})$$

Likewise, the "Amount Available" and "Amount to Be Provided" balances in the General Long-Term Debt Account Group will be affected.

| | | | |
|---|---|---|---|
| (18) | Due from Special Revenue Fund . . . . . . . . . . . . . . . . . . . . . | $ 10,000 | |
| | Operating Transfer from Special Revenue Fund . . . . . . . . | | $ 10,000 |
| | To record interfund transfer from Special Revenue Fund ordered by governing board. | | |
| | The impact of this transfer on the Special Revenue Fund accounting equation is: | | |

$$\text{Current Assets} - \text{Current Liabilities} = \text{Fund Balance}$$
$$+\ \$10{,}000 \qquad\qquad -\ \$10{,}000\ (\text{Other Financing Uses})$$

| | | | |
|---|---|---|---|
| (19) | Residual Equity Transfer to Enterprise Fund. . . . . . . . . . . . | $ 6,000 | |
| | Cash. . . . . . . . . . . . . . . . . . . . . . . . . . . . . . . . . . . . . . . . . . . | | $ 6,000 |
| | To record residual equity transfer to provide contributed capital to a new Enterprise Fund. | | |

Note that interfund residual equity transfers must be reported separately from Revenues, Expenditures, and Operating Transfers. This residual equity transfer impacts the Enterprise Fund accounting equation as follows:

$$\text{Assets} - \text{Liabilities} = \text{Contributed Capital} + \text{Retained Earnings}$$
$$+\ \$6{,}000 \qquad\qquad +\ \$6{,}000\ (\text{Residual}$$
$$\text{Equity Transfer})$$

| | | | |
|---|---|---|---|
| (20) | Expenditures. . . . . . . . . . . . . . . . . . . . . . . . . . . . . . . . . . . . | $300,000 | |
| | Vouchers Payable . . . . . . . . . . . . . . . . . . . . . . . . . . . . . . . . | | $300,000 |
| | To record unencumbered expenditures. | | |
| | <u>Expenditures Ledger (Expenditures):</u> | | |
| | General Government . . . . . . . . . . . . . . . . . . . . . . . . . . . . . . . | $ 30,000 | |
| | Public Safety . . . . . . . . . . . . . . . . . . . . . . . . . . . . . . . . . . . . | 112,000 | |
| | Highways and Streets. . . . . . . . . . . . . . . . . . . . . . . . . . . . . . | 90,000 | |
| | Health and Sanitation . . . . . . . . . . . . . . . . . . . . . . . . . . . . | 35,400 | |
| | Other. . . . . . . . . . . . . . . . . . . . . . . . . . . . . . . . . . . . . . . . . . | 9,600 | |
| | Capital Outlay . . . . . . . . . . . . . . . . . . . . . . . . . . . . . . . . . . . | <u>23,000</u> | |
| | | <u>$300,000</u> | |

The capital outlay expenditures ($23,000) increase the fixed asset accounts and the Investment in General Fixed Assets balance in the General Fixed Assets Account Group.

(21) Vouchers Payable................................. $320,000
    Cash.........................................             $320,000
    To record payment of vouchers.

(22) Cash.......................................... $ 20,000
    Notes Payable.................................    $ 20,000
    To record borrowing on short-term note at bank to
    maintain an adequate cash balance.

(23) Due to Stores Fund ............................. $ 22,500
    Cash.........................................    $ 22,500
    To record partial payment of amount due the Stores Fund.

This transaction also results in a corresponding increase in "Cash" and decrease in "Due from General Fund" in the Stores Internal Service Fund.

(24) Cash.......................................... $ 13,000
    Accounts Receivable ............................    $ 13,000
    To record collections of accounts receivable.

(25) Allowance for Uncollectible Accounts Receivable ........ $ 400
    Accounts Receivable ............................    $ 400
    To record write-off of accounts receivable determined to
    be uncollectible.

(26) Notes Payable................................. $ 5,000
    Expenditures.................................. 600
    Cash.........................................    $ 5,600
    To record payment of part of the short-term note principal
    and interest to date.
    Expenditures Ledger (Expenditures):
    Debt Service (Interest) ............................ $ 600

Note that the General Long-Term Debt Account Group is not affected because the note payable was a short-term fund liability.

(27) Correction of Prior Year Error ....................... $ 300
    Vouchers Payable...............................    $ 300
    To record correction of prior period (19X0) error (failure to
    record 19X0 expenditure and liability at December 31, 19X0).

In reviewing the foregoing illustrative general journal entries, note particularly entries 15 through 19. Entry 15 records an interfund quasi-external transaction, while entry 16 reflects an interfund reimbursement; entries 17 and 18 are for interfund operating transfers, and entry 19 records an interfund residual equity transfer. Also note entries 22 and 26, which record issuance of a short-term note payable as a current liability of the General Fund and the payment of part of the note principal and interest, respectively, and entry 27, which records the correction of a prior year error.

## Alternative Account Structure and Entries

As noted in Chapter 3, many governments no longer use the traditional General Ledger—subsidiary ledger account structure and entry approach illustrated in this chapter. Modern computerized systems facilitate the use of detailed General Ledger accounts in lieu of the General Ledger control accounts supported by detailed subsidiary ledgers. To familiarize readers with this approach—which is preferred by some practitioners and professors and is sometimes useful on the CPA Examination—entries using the detailed General Ledger accounts approach are presented next for transactions 1, 5, and 10. This approach also is used in selected subsequent chapters.

| | | | |
|---|---|---|---|
| (1) | Estimated Revenues—Taxes . . . . . . . . . . . . . . . . . . . . . . . . . . | $250,000 | |
| | Estimated Revenues—Licenses and Permits . . . . . . . . . . . | 70,000 | |
| | Estimated Revenues—Intergovernmental . . . . . . . . . . . . . . | 50,000 | |
| | Estimated Revenues—Charges for Services. . . . . . . . . . . . . | 40,000 | |
| | Estimated Revenues—Fines and Forfeits. . . . . . . . . . . . . . . | 20,000 | |
| | Estimated Revenues—Other. . . . . . . . . . . . . . . . . . . . . . . . . | 1,000 | |
| | Appropriations—General Government . . . . . . . . . . . . . . | | $ 40,000 |
| | Appropriations—Public Safety . . . . . . . . . . . . . . . . . . . . | | 150,000 |
| | Appropriations—Highways and Streets . . . . . . . . . . . . . | | 120,000 |
| | Appropriations—Health and Sanitation. . . . . . . . . . . . . | | 60,000 |
| | Appropriations—Other . . . . . . . . . . . . . . . . . . . . . . . . . . | | 25,000 |
| | Appropriations—Capital Outlay. . . . . . . . . . . . . . . . . . . | | 30,000 |
| | Appropriations—Debt Service . . . . . . . . . . . . . . . . . . . . | | 1,000 |
| | Unreserved Fund Balance . . . . . . . . . . . . . . . . . . . . . . . . | | 5,000 |
| | To record appropriations and revenue estimates. | | |
| (5a) | Reserve for Encumbrances . . . . . . . . . . . . . . . . . . . . . . . . . | $ 30,000 | |
| | Encumbrances—General Government. . . . . . . . . . . . . . . | | $ 2,000 |
| | Encumbrances—Public Safety. . . . . . . . . . . . . . . . . . . . . | | 8,000 |
| | Encumbrances—Highways and Streets. . . . . . . . . . . . . . | | 10,000 |
| | Encumbrances—Other. . . . . . . . . . . . . . . . . . . . . . . . . . . | | 4,000 |
| | Encumbrances—Capital Outlay . . . . . . . . . . . . . . . . . . . | | 6,000 |
| | To reverse the entry encumbering the Appropriations account. | | |
| (5b) | Expenditures—General Government. . . . . . . . . . . . . . . . . . | $ 1,700 | |
| | Expenditures—Public Safety. . . . . . . . . . . . . . . . . . . . . . . | 8,000 | |
| | Expenditures—Highways and Streets. . . . . . . . . . . . . . . . | 10,100 | |
| | Expenditures—Other. . . . . . . . . . . . . . . . . . . . . . . . . . . . . | 4,000 | |
| | Expenditures—Capital Outlay . . . . . . . . . . . . . . . . . . . . . | 6,100 | |
| | Vouchers Payable . . . . . . . . . . . . . . . . . . . . . . . . . . . . . . | | $ 29,900 |
| | To record expenditures. | | |
| (10) | Cash. . . . . . . . . . . . . . . . . . . . . . . . . . . . . . . . . . . . . . . . . . . | $205,000 | |
| | Revenues—Taxes . . . . . . . . . . . . . . . . . . . . . . . . . . . . . . | | $ 58,000 |
| | Revenues—Licenses and Permits . . . . . . . . . . . . . . . . . . | | 68,000 |
| | Revenues—Intergovernmental . . . . . . . . . . . . . . . . . . . . | | 52,500 |
| | Revenues—Charges for Services. . . . . . . . . . . . . . . . . . . | | 6,000 |
| | Revenues—Fines and Forfeits. . . . . . . . . . . . . . . . . . . . . | | 19,000 |
| | Revenues—Other. . . . . . . . . . . . . . . . . . . . . . . . . . . . . . . | | 1,500 |
| | To record receipt of revenues not previously accrued. | | |

Some instructors prefer this approach and require its use in solving problems requiring both General Ledger and subsidiary ledger entries. It may also be required or preferred on some CPA examination questions.

## Adjusting Entries at Year End

Regardless of the account structure and entry approach used, the accounts should be reviewed at year end to determine whether any adjusting entries are needed to properly reflect fund operating results and financial position. Among the types of revenues that might be accrued in adjusting entries are interest on investments and delinquent taxes, unbilled charges for services, and unrestricted intergovernmental grants that are due but have not been received by year end. Expenditures that might need to be accrued in adjusting entries include interest on short-term debt, accrued payroll, and amounts recorded as encumbrances that have become expenditures by year end.

To illustrate year-end adjusting entries, assume that A Governmental Unit had no significant payroll accruals, but that two revenue accruals and one expenditure accrual are in order:

| | | |
|---|---|---|
| (A1) Interest and Penalties Receivable—Delinquent Taxes ..... | $550 | |
|     Allowance for Uncollectible Interest and Penalties...... | | $ 50 |
|     Revenues..................................... | | 500 |

To record interest and penalties accrued on delinquent
taxes outstanding and to provide for estimated losses.
Revenues Ledger (Revenues):
Other........................................... <u>$500</u>

| | | |
|---|---|---|
| (A2) Accrued Interest Receivable......................... | $400 | |
|     Revenues..................................... | | $400 |

To record interest accrued on investments.
Revenues Ledger (Revenues):
Other........................................... <u>$400</u>

| | | |
|---|---|---|
| (A3) Expenditures..................................... | $250 | |
|     Accrued Interest Payable...................... | | $250 |

To record interest accrued on short-term notes payable.
Expenditures Ledger (Expenditures):
Debt Service (Interest) ............................ <u>$250</u>

## Preclosing Trial Balances—End of 19X1

Figure 4–3 presents the **preclosing** trial balance of the **General Ledger** accounts after the preceding illustrative journal entries are posted. Figure 4–4 presents the **preclosing** trial balances of the **Revenues Subsidiary Ledger and Expenditures Subsidiary Ledger.** These trial balances are the basis for the closing entries discussed in the following section and for the statements later in the chapter. Appendix 4–1 includes for the General Fund of A Governmental Unit for the year ended December 31, 19X1:

1. Figure 4–13—General Ledger Worksheet
2. Figure 4–14—Revenues Subsidiary Ledger (Preclosing)
3. Figure 4–15—Expenditures Subsidiary Ledger (Preclosing)

## Closing Entries—End of 19X1

At the end of the fiscal year, entries are made closing the accounts. The closing process summarizes the results of operations in the Unreserved Fund Balance account. More specifically, the purposes of closing entries are to:

1. **Close the budgetary** (e.g., Estimated Revenues and Appropriations) **and related actual** (e.g., Revenues and Expenditures) **operating accounts** in the **General Ledger** so they will begin the next year with zero balances—ready to record that year's budgetary and actual operations.
2. **Close the other General Ledger operating accounts**—for example, the transfer and restatement (correction of prior year error) accounts—to zero out these accounts and have them ready to record the next year's transfers and restatements.
3. **Update the Unreserved Fund Balance account** to its actual end-of-year balance—which is accomplished simultaneously with (1) and (2).
4. Usually, as assumed here, **convert the Reserve for Encumbrances account** from a memorandum offset General Ledger account **to a true reserve** of fund balance by closing the Encumbrances account to Unreserved Fund Balance—thus reducing the Unreserved Fund Balance account and, because the Reserve for Encumbrances is no longer offset by the Encumbrances account, making it a true fund balance reserve.
5. **Close the Revenues Subsidiary Ledger and Expenditures Subsidiary Ledger accounts** so they are ready to record the next year's detailed budgetary and actual operating data.

These purposes may be accomplished in differing sequences of entries—depending on personal preferences of accountants or on how the computer software is

FIGURE 4–3 **Preclosing Trial Balance—General Ledger—End of 19X1**

A Governmental Unit
General Fund

**Preclosing Trial Balance**
**General Ledger**

December 31, 19X1

| | Debit | Credit |
|---|---|---|
| Cash . . . . . . . . . . . . . . . . . . . . . . . . . . . . . . . . . . . . . . . . . . . . . . . | $ 43,100 | |
| Investments . . . . . . . . . . . . . . . . . . . . . . . . . . . . . . . . . . . . . . | 10,000 | |
| Accrued Interest Receivable . . . . . . . . . . . . . . . . . . . . . . . . | 400 | |
| Taxes Receivable—Delinquent . . . . . . . . . . . . . . . . . . . . . . . . | 20,000 | |
| Allowance for Uncollectible Delinquent Taxes . . . . . . . . . . . . . . . . . | | $ 3,000 |
| Interest and Penalties Receivable—Delinquent Taxes . . . . . . . . . . . | 550 | |
| Allowance for Uncollectible Interest and Penalties . . . . . . . . . . . . . . | | 50 |
| Accounts Receivable . . . . . . . . . . . . . . . . . . . . . . . . . . . . . . . . | 19,600 | |
| Allowance for Uncollectible Accounts Receivable . . . . . . . . . . . . . . | | 600 |
| Due from Special Revenue Fund . . . . . . . . . . . . . . . . . . . . . . . . | 11,500 | |
| Vouchers Payable . . . . . . . . . . . . . . . . . . . . . . . . . . . . . . . . . . | | 25,200 |
| Notes Payable . . . . . . . . . . . . . . . . . . . . . . . . . . . . . . . . . . . . | | 15,000 |
| Accrued Interest Payable . . . . . . . . . . . . . . . . . . . . . . . . . . . . | | 250 |
| Due to Stores Fund . . . . . . . . . . . . . . . . . . . . . . . . . . . . . . . | | 7,500 |
| Due to Debt Service Fund . . . . . . . . . . . . . . . . . . . . . . . . . . . | | 5,000 |
| Reserve for Encumbrances . . . . . . . . . . . . . . . . . . . . . . . . . . . | | 20,000 |
| Unreserved Fund Balance ($11,000 + $5,000) . . . . . . . . . . . . . . . | | 16,000 |
| Estimated Revenues . . . . . . . . . . . . . . . . . . . . . . . . . . . . . . . . | 431,000 | |
| Revenues . . . . . . . . . . . . . . . . . . . . . . . . . . . . . . . . . . . . . . . | | 438,100 |
| Appropriations . . . . . . . . . . . . . . . . . . . . . . . . . . . . . . . . . . . | | 426,000 |
| Expenditures . . . . . . . . . . . . . . . . . . . . . . . . . . . . . . . . . . . . | 399,250 | |
| Encumbrances . . . . . . . . . . . . . . . . . . . . . . . . . . . . . . . . . . . | 20,000 | |
| Operating Transfer to Debt Service Fund . . . . . . . . . . . . . . . . . | 5,000 | |
| Operating Transfer from Special Revenue Fund . . . . . . . . . . . . . . | | 10,000 |
| Residual Equity Transfer to Enterprise Fund . . . . . . . . . . . . . . . . | 6,000 | |
| Correction of Prior Year Error . . . . . . . . . . . . . . . . . . . . . . . . | 300 | |
| | $966,700 | $966,700 |

designed—but any proper closing entry sequence must accomplish all of these purposes.

### Closing the Encumbrances Account

Whether or not the Encumbrances account is closed at year end and the appropriate closing procedures (when required) are determined by the government's legal and policy provisions pertaining to the lapsing of appropriations and to the treatment of encumbrances outstanding at year end. An appropriation is said to lapse when it terminates, that is, when it no longer is an authorization to make an expenditure.

The illustration of A Governmental Unit is completed on the assumption that the law and policy state that:

**1.** All unexpended appropriations lapse at the end of the year, even if encumbered;

**2.** The unit is committed to accepting the goods or services on order (encumbered) at year end;

**3.** Expenditures resulting from encumbrances outstanding at the end of the year must be charged against appropriations of the next year; and

**4.** The closing entry should leave on the books a Reserve for Encumbrances account to indicate the commitment of the resources of the fund.

This assumption is the most common in practice with respect to annually budgeted governmental funds, and is the usual assumption in Uniform CPA Examination

FIGURE 4–4   **Preclosing Trial Balances—Revenues and Expenditures Subsidiary Ledgers—End of 19X1**

A Governmental Unit
General Fund

**Preclosing Trial Balances**
**Revenues and Expenditures Subsidiary Ledgers**

December 31, 19X1

**Revenues Subsidiary Ledger**

| | | |
|---|---:|---:|
| Taxes | | $ 5,000 |
| Licenses and Permits | $2,000 | |
| Intergovernmental | | 2,500 |
| Charges for Services | | 1,000 |
| Fines and Forfeits | 1,000 | |
| Other | | 1,600 |
| | $3,000 | $10,100 |

*Proof:* $10,100 – $3,000 =  $ 7,100

Compare to General
Ledger control accounts:

| | | |
|---|---:|---:|
| Revenues | $438,100 | |
| Estimated Revenues | 431,000 | |
| Difference | $ 7,100 | |

**Expenditures Subsidiary Ledger**

| | | |
|---|---:|---:|
| General Government | | $ 800 |
| Public Safety | | 1,000 |
| Highways and Streets | $3,100 | |
| Health and Sanitation | | 600 |
| Other | | 6,400 |
| Capital Outlay | | 900 |
| Debt Service | | 150 |
| | $3,100 | $ 9,850 |

*Proof:* $ 9,850 – $3,100 =  $ 6,750

Compare to General
Ledger control accounts:

| | | |
|---|---:|---:|
| Appropriations | | $426,000 |
| Expenditures | $399,250 | |
| Encumbrances | 20,000 | 419,250 |
| Difference | | $ 6,750 |

questions and problems. We shall call this Assumption A1; other types of laws and policies relating to appropriations and encumbrances are discussed in Chapter 6.

### Closing Entry Approaches

Three closing entry sequences—referred to as the *reverse the budget—close the actual, variance,* and *compound entry* approaches—are commonly encountered on the Uniform CPA Examination and in practice. All achieve the same end result. The reverse the budget—close the actual and compound entry approaches are discussed and illustrated in this chapter. All three approaches, including the variance approach, are illustrated in later chapters.

### Reverse the Budget—Close the Actual Approach

The reverse the budget—close the actual closing entry sequence approach focuses first on closing the General Ledger accounts, then on closing the subsidiary ledger accounts in a separate entry or entries. The rationale of this approach—with respect to the General Ledger accounts—is that:

- The budgetary entry (and any budget revision entries) caused the Unreserved Fund Balance account to be carried at its planned end-of-year balance during the year.
- Because the budgetary control purposes of the budgetary entry (or entries) have been served by year end—and the revenue estimates and appropriations in the annual operating budget typically expire at year end—the first closing entry should reverse the budgetary entry (including any revisions), which changes the amount in the Unreserved Fund Balance account from its planned end-of-year balance to its actual preclosing balance.
- Next, closing the actual revenues, expenditures, transfers, and restatement accounts updates the Unreserved Fund Balance account from its actual preclosing amount to its actual year-end balance.
- Finally, a portion of the Unreserved Fund Balance may be reserved for encumbrances (or other reasons).

### General Ledger Closing Entries

The General Ledger closing entries using the reverse the budget—close the actual closing entry sequence (see Figure 4–13) are:

**Reverse the Budgetary Entry:**

| | | | |
|---|---|---:|---:|
| (C1) | Appropriations.................................... | $426,000 | |
| | Unreserved Fund Balance........................... | 5,000 | |
| | Estimated Revenues................................ | | $431,000 |
| | To close the budgetary accounts and bring the Unreserved Fund Balance account to its actual preclosing balance. | | |

**Close the Revenue and Expenditure Accounts:**

| | | | |
|---|---|---:|---:|
| (C2) | Revenues......................................... | $438,100 | |
| | Unreserved Fund Balance........................... | | $ 38,850 |
| | Expenditures..................................... | | 399,250 |
| | To close the Revenues and Expenditures accounts to Unreserved Fund Balance. | | |

**Close the Transfer and Restatement Accounts:**

| | | | |
|---|---|---:|---:|
| (C3) | Operating Transfer from Special Revenue Fund.......... | $ 10,000 | |
| | Unreserved Fund Balance........................... | 1,300 | |
| | Operating Transfer to Debt Service Fund............. | | $ 5,000 |
| | Residual Equity Transfer to Enterprise Fund........... | | 6,000 |
| | Correction of Prior Year Error...................... | | 300 |
| | To close the transfer and restatement accounts. | | |

**Close the Encumbrances Account to Reserve Fund Balance:**

| | | | |
|---|---|---:|---:|
| (C4) | Unreserved Fund Balance[1]......................... | $ 20,000 | |
| | Encumbrances.................................... | | $ 20,000 |
| | To close the Encumbrances account and establish the Reserve for Encumbrances account as a reservation of fund balance. | | |

---

[1] Entry C4 is in essence a compounding of the following two General Ledger entries:

| | | | |
|---|---|---:|---:|
| (C4a) | Reserve for Encumbrances............................... | $20,000 | |
| | Encumbrances...................................... | | $20,000 |
| | To close the offsetting encumbrances and reserve for encumbrances memorandum accounts. | | |
| (C4b) | Unreserved Fund Balance............................... | $20,000 | |
| | Reserve for Encumbrances.......................... | | $20,000 |
| | To reduce unreserved fund balance and increase reserved fund balance (for encumbrances). | | |

Note that because closing entry C1 reverses the budgetary entry, closing entries C2 and C3 summarize the actual change in **total** fund balance during the year, $37,550 ($38,850 − $1,300). Furthermore, entries C2, C3, and C4 summarize the actual change in **unreserved** fund balance during the year, $17,550 ($37,550 − $20,000). These amounts are not so readily apparent in the other closing entry approaches, though all yield the same end result.

This illustration assumes that only revenues and expenditures are subject to formal budgetary accounting control procedures. This is often the case because the governing board directly controls interfund transfers. Alternatively, budgetary accounts such as Estimated Operating Transfers In, Estimated Operating Transfers Out, and Estimated Residual Equity Transfers Out could have been used and would be closed at this time. Accounting procedures where interfund transfers and debt issue proceeds are subject to formal budgetary accounting control are considered in later chapters.

### Subsidiary Ledger Closing Entries

Under the reverse the budget—close the actual approach, the accounts in the Revenues Subsidiary Ledger and the Expenditures Subsidiary Ledger are closed by simply debiting the credit balances and crediting the debit balances—thus bringing all accounts to a zero balance. This may be done automatically in computerized systems or manually by observing the preclosing account balances (see Figures 4–4, 4–14, and 4–15):

(C) **Revenues Ledger (Balance):**

| | | |
|---|---|---|
| Taxes | $ 5,000 | |
| Licenses and Permits | | $2,000 |
| Intergovernmental | 2,500 | |
| Charges for Services | 1,000 | |
| Fines and Forfeits | | 1,000 |
| Other | 1,600 | |
| | $10,100 | $3,000 |

| | | |
|---|---|---|
| *Proof:* $10,100 − $3,000 = | $ 7,100 | |
| Compare to General Ledger control accounts: | | |
| Revenues | $438,100 | |
| Estimated Revenues | 431,000 | |
| Difference | $ 7,100 | |

(C) **Expenditures Ledger (Balance):**

| | | |
|---|---|---|
| General Government | $ 800 | |
| Public Safety | 1,000 | |
| Highways and Streets | | $3,100 |
| Health and Sanitation | 600 | |
| Other | 6,400 | |
| Capital Outlay | 900 | |
| Debt Service | 150 | |
| | $ 9,850 | $3,100 |

| | | |
|---|---|---|
| *Proof:* $9,850 − $3,100 = | | $ 6,750 |
| Compare to General Ledger control accounts: | | |
| Appropriations | | $426,000 |
| Expenditures | $399,250 | |
| Encumbrances | 20,000 | 419,250 |
| Difference | | $ 6,750 |

### Compound Entry Approach

Although the reverse the budget—close the actual and other closing entry approaches are based on different rationales and involve different closing entry sequences, all have precisely the same result. That is, the accounts that should be closed are closed, the Unreserved Fund Balance account is updated to its actual year-end balance, and the accounts that should be left open are left open. The post-closing trial balance account balances are the same in either event. Thus, some accountants prefer to prepare a single compound closing entry.

A compound General Fund general ledger closing entry for A Governmental Unit at December 31, 19X1, under the assumptions illustrated so far, would appear as follows:

| | | |
|---|---:|---:|
| (C) Revenues . . . . . . . . . . . . . . . . . . . . . . . . . . . . . . . . . . . . . . . . . . . | $438,100 | |
| Appropriations. . . . . . . . . . . . . . . . . . . . . . . . . . . . . . . . . . . . . | 426,000 | |
| Operating Transfer from Special Revenue Fund. . . . . . . . . . . . | 10,000 | |
| Unreserved Fund Balance. . . . . . . . . . . . . . . . . . . . . . . . . . . | | $ 12,550 |
| Estimated Revenues . . . . . . . . . . . . . . . . . . . . . . . . . . . . . . | | 431,000 |
| Expenditures . . . . . . . . . . . . . . . . . . . . . . . . . . . . . . . . . . . . | | 399,250 |
| Encumbrances . . . . . . . . . . . . . . . . . . . . . . . . . . . . . . . . . . . | | 20,000 |
| Operating Transfer to Debt Service Fund . . . . . . . . . . . . . . . | | 5,000 |
| Residual Equity Transfer to Enterprise Fund . . . . . . . . . . . . | | 6,000 |
| Correction of Prior Year Error . . . . . . . . . . . . . . . . . . . . . . . | | 300 |
| To close the general ledger accounts. | | |

The subsidiary ledger closing entries under the compound closing entry approach would be identical to those illustrated for the reverse the budget—close the actual approach.

### Reserve for Encumbrances

At this point a review of the nature of the Reserve for Encumbrances account is appropriate. It started life as an offset to the Encumbrances account in the General Ledger. Throughout 19X1 both accounts contained a balance representing the amount (with Expenditures) to be deducted from the Appropriations account, to arrive at the estimated spendable balance of appropriations. In other words, the Encumbrances and Reserve for Encumbrances accounts were offsetting memorandum budgetary accounts in the General Ledger. The closing entry for expenditure accounts closed the Encumbrances account but not the Reserve for Encumbrances; the Reserve for Encumbrances was converted into a reservation of fund balance. Thus, the Reserve for Encumbrances, any other reserve accounts, and the Unreserved Fund Balance account should be added to obtain the total fund balance at year end.

Reserves usually indicate that a portion of the total fund balance is not available for appropriation, that only the unreserved fund balance may be appropriated. Under Assumption A1, however, the Reserve for Encumbrances indicates the amount of total fund balance that must be appropriated next year (19X2) to authorize completion of transactions in process at year end (19X1). Thus, under Assumption A1 the amount in the Reserve for Encumbrances is available for 19X2 appropriation, but only to provide for past commitments, whereas the unreserved fund balance is available to finance new 19X2 expenditure commitments.

Because the amount represented by the Reserve for Encumbrances is available for appropriation under Assumption A1, some accountants prefer to disclose encumbrances outstanding at year end in the notes to the financial statements rather than in a Reserve for Encumbrances account in the balance sheet. Assumption A2, discussed in Chapter 6, provides for disclosure of encumbrances outstanding at year end in the notes to the financial statements rather than by reporting a Reserve for Encumbrances in the balance sheet.

## The Budgetary Fund Balance Account

One variation in budgetary accounting methodology is the use of the Budgetary Fund Balance account. Some prescribed governmental fund accounting systems require—and some SLG accountants prefer—that the budgeted increase or decrease in fund balance for the year be recorded in a Budgetary Fund Balance (or similarly titled) general ledger account rather than in the Unreserved Fund Balance account. Use of the Budgetary Fund Balance account is an acceptable practice. Indeed, it probably should be used in some circumstances.

To illustrate the use of the Budgetary Fund Balance account, the general ledger budgetary entry earlier in this chapter (entry 1) using the Budgetary Fund Balance account would be:

| | | |
|---|---|---|
| (1) Estimated Revenues | $431,000 | |
|     Appropriations | | $426,000 |
|     Budgetary Fund Balance | | 5,000 |

To record appropriations and revenue estimates (the annual budget).

The closing entry under the reverse the budget—close the actual approach would be:

| | | |
|---|---|---|
| (C1) Appropriations | $426,000 | |
|     Budgetary Fund Balance | 5,000 | |
|       Estimated Revenues | | $431,000 |

To close the budgetary accounts.

Use of the Budgetary Fund Balance account does not affect the fund's financial statements because (1) the general ledger budgetary entry is reversed in the closing entry process, so the budgeted change in fund balance does not affect the (actual) year-end balance of the Unreserved Fund Balance reported in the financial statements; and (2) the budgetary comparison statement will not be changed by the use of either the traditional budgetary entry or the Budgetary Fund Balance account budgetary entry.

The primary reason some SLG accountants prefer the Budgetary Fund Balance account approach is that some annual SLG budgets are extremely optimistic. That is, they are based on unrealistic or extremely uncertain projections of high revenue levels and/or low levels of expenditures. Similarly, some annual budgets are hurried "guesstimates" that are not based on proper budgetary analyses and estimates by qualified personnel or consultants; and others may be purposefully biased optimistically for political reasons. In cases such as these, the SLG accountant may properly balk at reporting an inflated estimate of the year-end Unreserved Fund Balance and insist on using a Budgetary Fund Balance account to segregate the actual beginning balance and planned change components in the accounts and interim budgetary (and other) financial statements.

If a government's environment gives rise to the Budgetary Fund Balance approach, that approach probably should be used. But otherwise the advantages of the traditional Unreserved Fund Balance budgetary entry approach should be weighed carefully before making the decision. The primary advantage of the Unreserved Fund Balance budgetary entry approach—given a sound budget—is that it focuses the attention of the governing body and managers on "where they plan to be by year end" rather than on "where they were at the beginning of the year." Thus, the Unreserved Fund Balance account balance is a target year-end balance—assuming no further budget revisions—and indicates to what extent additional appropriations may be made and financed by year end. Furthermore, if the budget is regularly and properly revised during the year, the Unreserved Fund Balance account automatically signals if an impending deficit is projected by year end. Such targets and signals are not as readily apparent under the Budgetary Fund Balance budgetary entry approach.

## Postclosing Trial Balance—End of 19X1

Following the posting of the 19X1 closing entries (see Figure 4–13), the trial balance of the General Fund appears as in Figure 4–5.

**FIGURE 4–5  Postclosing Trial Balance—General Ledger—End of 19X1**

A Governmental Unit
General Fund

**Postclosing Trial Balance**
**General Ledger**

December 31, 19X1

|  | Debit | Credit |
|---|---|---|
| Cash | $ 43,100 | |
| Investments | 10,000 | |
| Accrued Interest Receivable | 400 | |
| Taxes Receivable—Delinquent | 20,000 | |
| Allowance for Uncollectible Delinquent Taxes | | $ 3,000 |
| Interest and Penalties Receivable— | | |
| Delinquent Taxes | 550 | |
| Allowance for Uncollectible Interest and | | |
| Penalties | | 50 |
| Accounts Receivable | 19,600 | |
| Allowance for Uncollectible Accounts | | |
| Receivable | | 600 |
| Due from Special Revenue Fund | 11,500 | |
| Vouchers Payable | | 25,200 |
| Notes Payable | | 15,000 |
| Accrued Interest Payable | | 250 |
| Due to Stores Fund | | 7,500 |
| Due to Debt Service Fund | | 5,000 |
| Reserve for Encumbrances | | 20,000 |
| Unreserved Fund Balance | | 28,550 |
| | $105,150 | $105,150 |

# BALANCE SHEETS

The essential character of the General Fund should be kept constantly in mind as balance sheets and balance sheet accounts are discussed. Though the General Fund presumably will exist as long as the governmental unit exists, the operation of the fund is on a year-to-year basis. Each year the problem of financing a new year's operations with financial resources on hand and the new year's revenues and other financial resource inflows (e.g., transfers) is the central concern of those managing the finances of the fund. The balance sheet is prepared to provide information that assists in addressing this problem.

## The Interim Balance Sheet

Interim balance sheets may be prepared monthly, quarterly, or when needed for bond issue or other purposes. SLGs rarely issue audited interim balance sheets. Accordingly, the GASB *Codification* provides balance sheet standards and guidance only for year-end balance sheets.

## The Year-End Balance Sheet

The balance sheet of the General Fund of A Governmental Unit at December 31, 19X1 (Figure 4–6) is based on the postclosing trial balance at that date after the closing entries illustrated. The statement is largely self-explanatory, but comments on

FIGURE 4–6 **Balance Sheet—End of 19X1**

A Governmental Unit
General Fund
**Balance Sheet**
December 31, 19X1

### Assets

| | | |
|---|---:|---:|
| Cash | | $ 43,100 |
| Investments | | 10,000 |
| Accrued interest receivable | | 400 |
| Taxes receivable—delinquent | $20,000 | |
| Less: Allowance for uncollectible delinquent taxes | 3,000 | 17,000 |
| Interest and penalties receivable on taxes | 550 | |
| Less: Allowance for uncollectible interest and penalties | 50 | 500 |
| Accounts receivable | 19,600 | |
| Less: Allowance for uncollectible accounts | 600 | 19,000 |
| Due from Special Revenue Fund | | 11,500 |
| Total Assets | | $101,500 |

### Liabilities and Fund Balance

| | | |
|---|---:|---:|
| Liabilities: | | |
| Vouchers payable | $25,200 | |
| Notes payable | 15,000 | |
| Accrued interest payable | 250 | |
| Due to Stores Fund | 7,500 | |
| Due to Debt Service Fund | 5,000 | $ 52,950 |
| Fund Balance: | | |
| Reserved for encumbrances | 20,000 | |
| Unreserved | 28,550 | 48,550 |
| Total Liabilities and Fund Balance | | $101,500 |

some of the accounts should help clarify its characteristics. The comments deal with (1) the significance of the Unreserved Fund Balance account, (2) the nature of several fund balance reserve accounts, (3) interfund receivables and payables, and (4) the exclusion of fixed assets and long-term (noncurrent) liabilities from the General Fund accounts and its balance sheet.

## Unreserved Fund Balance

As previously indicated, the General Fund is a current fund. Its fiscal operations are concerned with the current-year revenues and other financing sources and the current-year expenditures and other uses of financial resources. As a general rule the fund is intended to show neither a surplus nor a deficit. A credit balance in the Unreserved Fund Balance account after closing entries does not in any sense represent retained earnings. Rather, it indicates an excess of the assets of the fund over its liabilities and fund balance reservations, if any, and would more properly be titled "Unreserved, Unappropriated Fund Balance." Accordingly, the legislative body is likely to use the available assets, as indicated by the credit balance, in financing the budget for the succeeding year. But, as noted earlier, under Assumption A1 the budget officials and the legislative body should realize that the Reserve for Encumbrances also is available for 19X2 appropriation for the 19X1 commitments.

During a fiscal year the balance of the Unreserved Fund Balance account may be of a nature substantially different from that of the year-end balance. Suppose that the year-end Unreserved Fund Balance (postclosing) is $5,000, and that in the following year budgeted revenues are $100,000 and appropriations total $97,000. The Unreserved Fund Balance account will be carried at the planned end-of-year balance of $8,000 after the recording of the budget. The exact nature of the balance during the year can be determined only by examining all the facts. Its balance is neither exclusively budgetary nor exclusively proprietary.

If the General Fund has a deficit, the amount of the deficit should be exhibited on the balance sheet in the same position as the Unreserved Fund Balance and called a deficit. Typical municipal financial administration policy requires that the deficit be eliminated in the following fiscal year and that the necessary revenues for this purpose be provided in the budget.

## Fund Balance Reserves

Assets in an amount equal to the Unreserved Fund Balance account are assumed to be available to finance appropriations for expenditures of the current year and/or succeeding year. Thus, it is desirable to remove from that account any portions that are not available for that purpose. Fund balance reserves are essentially tags attached to part of total fund balance to indicate that some of the fund net assets are not available for discretionary appropriation and expenditure.

The reserve for encumbrances left in the accounts by the closing entries made has already been discussed as a fund balance reserve at the end of the year. This reserve indicates that some of the General Fund assets are not available to finance new purchase commitments in 19X2 because they will be needed to pay for the 19X2 expenditures that result from the outstanding 19X1 purchase commitments. It also reminds those preparing the 19X2 budget to provide sufficient appropriations for the expenditures to result in 19X2 from the 19X1 commitments.

Frequently, some of the General Fund assets need to be maintained at a certain level rather than expended. For example, such assets as petty cash and inventories of materials and supplies may not be available for financing expenditures of a subsequent period because they must be maintained at or near the required level. The entries to account for materials and supplies and the related Reserve for Inventories are discussed in Chapter 6. Entries for petty cash are as follows:

| | | |
|---|---|---|
| Petty Cash . . . . . . . . . . . . . . . . . . . . . . . . . . . . . . . . . . . . . . . . . . | $2,000 | |
|   Cash . . . . . . . . . . . . . . . . . . . . . . . . . . . . . . . . . . . . . . . . . . . . | | $2,000 |

To record the creation of a petty cash fund out of general cash.

| | | |
|---|---|---|
| Unreserved Fund Balance . . . . . . . . . . . . . . . . . . . . . . . . . . . . . . . | $2,000 | |
|   Reserve for Petty Cash Fund . . . . . . . . . . . . . . . . . . . . . . . . . . . | | $2,000 |

To record a reservation of fund balance in the amount of the petty cash fund.

As another example, suppose that a $5,000 loan to be repaid in 19X3 had been made from the General Fund to a Special Revenue Fund at the end of 19X1. The General Fund entries at the end of 19X1 would be:

| | | |
|---|---|---|
| Advance to Special Revenue Fund . . . . . . . . . . . . . . . . . . . . . . . . . | $5,000 | |
|   Cash . . . . . . . . . . . . . . . . . . . . . . . . . . . . . . . . . . . . . . . . . . . . | | $5,000 |

To record interfund loan to be repaid in 19X3.

| | | |
|---|---|---|
| Unreserved Fund Balance . . . . . . . . . . . . . . . . . . . . . . . . . . . . . . . | $5,000 | |
|   Reserve for Advance to Special Revenue Fund . . . . . . . . . . . . . . | | $5,000 |

To record a reservation of fund balance in the amount of the interfund advance.

The Reserve for Advance to Special Revenue Fund indicates that the General Fund asset represented by the Advance to Special Revenue Fund is not available to finance 19X2 expenditures. The Reserve for Advance to Special Revenue Fund will be canceled at the end of 19X2 because the loan will be repaid in 19X3.

Similar reservations may be made for other assets that are not expected to be available to finance current operations. Fund balance reserves are reported in the "Fund Balance" section of the balance sheet as shown in Figure 4–6. Alternatively, separate "Reserved Fund Balance" and "Unreserved Fund Balance" categories may be used, especially when there are several reserves. But a "Total Fund Balance" amount should be reported and reserves should not be reported with liabilities or between the liabilities and fund balance sections of the balance sheet.

## Unreserved Fund Balance Designations

Governments may also tag a portion of the unreserved fund balance of a governmental fund to indicate tentative management plans to use specified amounts of fund financial resources for certain specified purposes. This partitioning of unreserved fund balance to indicate management intent is referred to as *designation* of unreserved fund balance.

The general journal entry to record a designation would be:

| | | |
|---|---|---|
| Unreserved Fund Balance . . . . . . . . . . . . . . . . . . . . . . . . . . . . . . . | $8,000 | |
|   **Designated for Equipment Replacement** . . . . . . . . . . . . . . . . . . | | $8,000 |

To record a designation of unreserved fund balance for equipment replacement.

The entry would be reversed to remove the designation.

The use of such designations is optional. But if designations are used, they should be:

- clearly distinguished from reserves, and
- reported as part of the unreserved fund balance designated for the specified purpose or disclosed parenthetically or in the notes to the financial statements.

### Due To/From and Advance To/From

The illustration of the interfund advance in the discussion of fund balance reserves points out a significant terminology distinction that warrants further discussion. The illustrative example entries earlier in the chapter recorded interfund receivables and payables in Due from (Fund) and Due to (Fund) accounts. Yet, in the case of a two-year interfund loan, the term *advance to (fund)* was used and a corresponding fund balance reserve was established.

The terms *due to (fund)* and *due from (fund)* should be used only to describe currently receivable and currently payable interfund balances. During the year, *currently* means collectible or payable within the year or soon thereafter. At year end, amounts to be received or paid in the next year may properly be classified as current and thus recorded as due from and due to other funds.

Any noncurrent interfund receivable or payable should be recorded as advance to (fund) or advance from (fund). Furthermore, any governmental fund advance to another fund requires that a corresponding reserve be established to indicate that the fund financial resources that are loaned on a noncurrent basis are not currently available for expenditure and thus should not be appropriated. An interfund advance for which repayment is expected in the next fiscal year is not reclassified as a Due from (Fund) or Due to (Fund) account. But any corresponding governmental fund fund balance reserve for advances should be eliminated because the advance is now available.

### Exclusion of Fixed Assets and Long-Term Debt

Although some General Fund expenditures represent outlays that should be capitalized, fixed assets are not included in the balance sheet of the General Fund. For example, $6,100 of the total expenditures of $29,900 shown in entry 5b on page 119 was for equipment. In commercial accounting this $6,100 would be shown in the general balance sheet as part of the assets. In governmental fund accounting the fixed assets are capitalized in a separate nonfund (General Fixed Assets) account group rather than as assets of the General Fund (see Chapter 9).

Similarly, even if general obligation long-term debt (such as bonds) is ultimately payable out of the General Fund, and even if it has been issued to eliminate a deficit in the General Fund, unmatured general obligation long-term debt is not recorded as a liability of the General Fund but in a separate nonfund (General Long-Term Debt) account group (see Chapter 9). The only long-term debt included in the General Fund is that which has matured and is payable from the current resources of the General Fund (an unusual occurrence, except for capital leases because matured bonds and other long-term debts are ordinarily repaid from a Debt Service Fund[2]).

---

[2] Taxes designated for debt service usually are treated as revenues of a Debt Service Fund and do not affect the General Fund. In specific cases, however, the taxes may be collected through the General Fund and used to service debt directly from the General Fund. Alternatively, such taxes may be transferred to the Debt Service Fund. In the latter case, they would be accounted for as General Fund revenues and as an operating transfer to the Debt Service Fund.

Fixed assets are excluded from the General Fund balance sheet because they do not represent financial resources with which the government intends to finance its current activities or pay its liabilities. These assets are not acquired for resale but for the purpose of rendering service over a relatively long period of time.

Bonds and other long-term general obligation debts payable are not included as part of the liabilities of the General Fund because the existing resources of the fund are not expected to be used for their payment. The governmental unit's future taxing power will ultimately provide resources to pay them.

# STATEMENT OF REVENUES, EXPENDITURES, AND CHANGES IN FUND BALANCE

The second major General and Special Revenue Fund financial statement is the Statement of Revenues, Expenditures, and Changes in Fund Balance. As its title indicates, this operating statement presents the revenues, expenditures, and other increases and decreases in fund balance during a year (or other time period), and reconciles the beginning and ending fund balances. (Recall from Chapter 2 that increases and decreases in fund balance are essentially changes in working capital.) It is prepared on the GAAP basis, regardless of the basis of the budget, and is the GAAP basis operating statement.

The Statement of Revenues, Expenditures, and Changes in Fund Balance may present data pertaining to *either* the Unreserved Fund Balance account or the *total* fund balance, including reserves. The unreserved fund balance approach reconciles the beginning and ending Unreserved Fund Balance account balances and, thus, has a "changes in reserves" section. The more widely used total fund balance approach, illustrated here (Figure 4–7), presents only the items that changed total fund balance, and reconciles beginning and ending total fund balances. Significant changes in reserves are disclosed in the notes to the financial statements.

## Total Fund Balance Approach

A Statement of Revenues, Expenditures, and Changes in Fund Balance for the General Fund of A Governmental Unit for the 19X1 fiscal year is presented in Figure 4–7. Although the Statement of Revenues, Expenditures, and Changes in Fund Balance is largely self-explanatory, it should be studied carefully. Observe the major components of this statement and the order in which they appear:

Revenues
– Expenditures
———————————————————————————————
Excess of revenues over (under) expenditures
± Other financing sources (uses)
———————————————————————————————
Excess of revenues and other sources over (under) expenditures and other uses
+ Fund balance, beginning of period
± Residual equity transfers
———————————————————————————————
Fund balance, end of period
═══════════════════════════════════

Observe also in Figure 4–7 that (1) the beginning fund balance is reported as previously reported, followed by the error correction and the restated amount; (2) operating transfers are reported separately from revenues and expenditures—as Other Financing Sources (Uses); (3) residual equity transfers are reported separately from operating transfers; and (4) the statement explains the changes in total fund balance during the period.

FIGURE 4–7 **Statement of Revenues, Expenditures, and Changes in Fund Balance—For 19X1**
(GAAP Operating Statement)

A Governmental Unit
General Fund
**Statement of Revenues, Expenditures,
and Changes in [Total] Fund Balance**
For the 19X1 Fiscal Year

| | | |
|---|---:|---:|
| Revenues | | |
| Taxes | $255,000 | |
| Licenses and permits | 68,000 | |
| Intergovernmental | 52,500 | |
| Charges for services | 41,000 | |
| Fines and forfeits | 19,000 | |
| Other | 2,600 | |
| Total Revenues | | $438,100 |
| Expenditures | | |
| Current Operating: | | |
| General government | 39,200 | |
| Public safety | 142,000 | |
| Highways and streets | 123,100 | |
| Health and sanitation | 46,400 | |
| Other | 18,600 | |
| Total Current Operating Expenditures | 369,300 | |
| Capital Outlay | 29,100 | |
| Debt Service (interest) | 850 | |
| Total Expenditures | | 399,250 |
| Excess of Revenues over Expenditures | | 38,850 |
| Other Financing Sources (Uses) | | |
| Operating transfer from Special Revenue Fund | 10,000 | |
| Operating transfer to Debt Service Fund | (5,000) | 5,000 |
| Excess of Revenues and Other Financing Sources Over Expenditures and Other Uses | | 43,850 |
| Fund Balance—Beginning of 19X1—As Restated | | |
| As previously reported | 11,000 | |
| Correction of prior year error | (300) | 10,700 |
| Residual equity transfer to Enterprise Fund | | (6,000) |
| Fund Balance—End of 19X1 | | $ 48,550 |

The Statement of Revenues, Expenditures, and Changes in Fund Balance may be presented in at least three acceptable alternate formats. The format outlined in this section and illustrated in Figure 4–7—known as Format A and as Presentation 1—is the most common in practice. The other major alternative statement arrangement—known as Format B and as Presentation 2—is equally acceptable. Format B (Presentation 2), which is preferred by many practitioners and instructors, is illustrated in Figure 4–11.

## Residual Equity Transfers

The GASB *Codification* says at one point that "residual equity transfers should be reported as additions to or deductions from the beginning fund balance of governmental funds."[3] At another point it says that "residual equity transfers should

---

[3] GASB *Codification*, sec. 1800.107.

be reported after the results of operations"[4] and illustrates presentation of residual equity transfers after "excess of revenues and other sources over (under) expenditures and other uses" and immediately before ending fund balance. Either presentation approach is acceptable: (1) as the last item in the Statement of Revenues, Expenditures, and Changes in Fund Balance before the Fund Balance section, or (2) as the last item before the ending Fund Balance. We have chosen to illustrate the latter approach because it seems preferable in the GASB *Codification* and is most in keeping with current practice.

### Restatements

Occasionally, a governmental fund Statement of Revenues, Expenditures, and Changes in Fund Balance for an accounting period must report a restatement of the beginning fund balance because of an error correction or the change to a preferable accounting principle. The restatement may be reported in either of two ways. The beginning fund balance in the statement can be noted as being "as previously reported," as in Figure 4–7, and followed by the restatement amount and a restated beginning fund balance, presented as follows:

Fund balance, beginning of period, as previously reported
±   Restatements (e.g., correction of prior period errors)
Fund balance, beginning of period, as restated

Or only the restated beginning fund balance may be presented in the statement, noted as being "as restated," with reference made to the explanation of the restatement contained in the notes to the financial statements:

Fund balance, beginning of period, as restated (Note X)

Note X would contain the information presented on the face of the statement in the first method and in Figure 4–7.

In comparative statements covering two or more periods (1) the cumulative restatement effect on periods prior to the earliest period being reported on should be reported as a restatement of the beginning fund balance of that period, and (2) the data reported for later periods should be restated to reflect the changed accounting principle or error correction.

# STATEMENT OF REVENUES, EXPENDITURES, AND CHANGES IN FUND BALANCE—BUDGET AND ACTUAL

A third statement required for General and Special Revenue Funds (and for similar governmental funds with legally adopted annual budgets) compares budgeted and actual operating results. This Statement of Revenues, Expenditures, and Changes in Fund Balance—Budget and Actual is prepared on the budgetary basis—which often differs from GAAP—and thus is the budgetary operating statement.

---

[4] Ibid., sec. 2200.126.

Whereas the GAAP basis operating statement must comply with GAAP standards and guidelines, the budgetary basis operating statement must demonstrate budgetary accountability in terms of the government's own methods of budgeting, including its budgetary basis and format. Thus, the budgetary operating statement may be presented in any of the alternative formats for the Statement of Revenues, Expenditures, and Changes in Fund Balance, or in the format in which the budget is adopted. However, regardless of basis or format, it usually has columns headed:

|  |  | Variance |
|---|---|---|
|  |  | Favorable |
| **Budget** | **Actual** | **(Unfavorable)** |

The "Budget" column should contain the revised budget data. The revised budget means the originally adopted budget adjusted for all budget amendments adopted throughout the fiscal year. This revised budget sometimes differs significantly from the originally adopted budget. Similarly, terms other than *Variance—Favorable (Unfavorable)* may be used to describe the "Variance" column. Indeed, some governments omit the "Variance" column to conserve space in combining statements or because the variance is deemed obvious from the data in the "Budget" and "Actual" columns.

If the legally adopted budget is prepared on a basis consistent with GAAP, the actual data in this statement will correspond with the data presented in the Statement of Revenues, Expenditures, and Changes in Fund Balance (Figure 4–7). However, if the budget is prepared on a basis other than GAAP—for example, on the cash receipts and disbursements or an encumbrances basis—both the budget data and the actual data should be presented on the budgetary basis. Using the budgetary basis results in an accurate budgetary comparison and a meaningful variance—favorable (unfavorable) comparison.

If the budget and budgetary statement are prepared on a basis other than GAAP, the actual data in the budgetary comparison statement will differ from the data presented in the GAAP basis operating statement. In such cases, the notes to the financial statements should explain the budgetary basis employed and reconcile the budgetary data with the GAAP data.

Alternatively, the budgetary basis may be explained in the notes and the reconciliation of the budgetary-basis and GAAP basis data included in the Statement of Revenues, Expenditures, and Changes in Fund Balance—Budget and Actual. Preparing the budgetary statement where the budget is not prepared on the GAAP basis and reconciling the budgetary basis-GAAP basis differences are discussed in Chapter 14.

A Statement of Revenues, Expenditures, and Changes in Fund Balance—Budget and Actual for the General Fund of A Governmental Unit for the 19X1 fiscal year is presented in Figure 4–8. Because the illustrative example in this chapter assumes that the budget is prepared on the GAAP basis, this budgetary operating statement is prepared on the GAAP basis—which in this case is also the budgetary basis. Note in studying Figure 4–8 that:

- The title of the statement includes the term *budget and actual* and indicates the budgetary basis on which the statement is prepared.
- Had there been budget revisions during the year, the revised budgetary data would be presented, although both the original and revised budgets may be presented (in adjacent columns) in the budgetary comparison statement.

FIGURE 4–8 **Statement of Revenues, Expenditures, and Changes in Fund Balance— Budget and Actual—For 19X1 (Budgetary Comparison Statement)**

A Governmental Unit
General Fund

**Statement of Revenues, Expenditures, and Changes in Fund Balance— Budget and Actual (Budgetary Basis Is Modified Accrual Basis)**

For the 19X1 Fiscal Year

|  | Revised Budget (Note 1) | Actual | Variance— Favorable (Unfavorable) |
|---|---|---|---|
| **Revenues** | | | |
| Taxes | $250,000 | $255,000 | $5,000 |
| Licenses and permits | 70,000 | 68,000 | (2,000) |
| Intergovernmental | 50,000 | 52,500 | 2,500 |
| Charges for services | 40,000 | 41,000 | 1,000 |
| Fines and forfeits | 20,000 | 19,000 | (1,000) |
| Other | 1,000 | 2,600 | 1,600 |
| Total Revenues | 431,000 | 438,100 | 7,100 |
| **Expenditures (Note 2)** | | | |
| Current Operating: | | | |
| General government | 40,000 | 39,200 | 800 |
| Public safety | 150,000 | 142,000 | 8,000 |
| Highways and streets | 120,000 | 123,100 | (3,100) |
| Health and sanitation | 60,000 | 46,400 | 13,600 |
| Other | 25,000 | 18,600 | 6,400 |
| Total Current Operating Expenditures | 395,000 | 369,300 | 25,700 |
| Capital outlay | 30,000 | 29,100 | 900 |
| Debt service | 1,000 | 850 | 150 |
| Total Expenditures | 426,000 | 399,250 | 26,750 |
| Excess of Revenues over Expenditures | 5,000 | 38,850 | 33,850 |
| **Other Financing Sources (Uses)** | | | |
| Operating transfer from Special Revenue Fund | — | 10,000 | 10,000 |
| Operating transfer to Debt Service Fund | — | (5,000) | (5,000) |
|  | — | 5,000 | 5,000 |
| Excess of Revenues and Other Financing Sources over Expenditures and Other Uses | 5,000 | 43,850 | 38,850 |
| Fund Balance—Beginning of 19X1—As Restated (Note X) | 11,000 | 10,700 | (300) |
| Residual equity transfer to Enterprise Fund | — | (6,000) | (6,000) |
| Fund Balance—End of 19X1 | $ 16,000 | $ 48,550 | $ 32,550 |

Notes:

1. This column should reflect the revised budget amounts, if there are budget revisions. In this example the governing body authorized interfund transfers that were not included in the original budget.

2. Because this illustrative example assumes that the budget is prepared and adopted on the modified accrual (GAAP) basis, only expenditures are reported (encumbrances are excluded).

- Encumbrances are not reported (only expenditures) because encumbrances are not considered equivalent to expenditures for budgetary or other purposes on the modified accrual basis.

- Because the interfund transfers were not included in the fiscal budget but were separately authorized, no budget amounts are presented for interfund transfers.

## ENTRIES DURING 19X2

The only additional information needed to account for the General Fund in 19X2 is the treatment of the Reserve for Encumbrances account and the related expenditures made in 19X2. The first entry of 19X2 is to reverse the 19X1 entry that closed Encumbrances to Unreserved Fund Balance and established the Reserve for Encumbrances as a true fund balance reserve:

| | | |
|---|---|---|
| Encumbrances . . . . . . . . . . . . . . . . . . . . . . . . . . . . . . . . . . . . | $20,000 | |
|     Unreserved Fund Balance . . . . . . . . . . . . . . . . . . . . . . . . . . . | | $20,000 |

To return the Encumbrances account to its usual offset
    relationship with the Reserve for Encumbrances and
    increase Unreserved Fund Balance accordingly.

Expenditures Ledger (Encumbrances):

| | |
|---|---|
| Public Safety. . . . . . . . . . . . . . . . . . . . . . . . . . . . . . . . . . . . . . . | $ 7,000 |
| Health and Sanitation . . . . . . . . . . . . . . . . . . . . . . . . . . . . . . . . | 13,000 |
| | $20,000 |

(Note that this is the reverse of entry C4.)

This entry restores the Encumbrances and Reserve for Encumbrances accounts to the balances that were in them before the 19X1 closing entries. Hence, this entry reestablishes the usual offset relationship between the Encumbrances and Reserve for Encumbrances accounts, causing the Reserve for Encumbrances to no longer be a true fund balance reserve. The entry also increases the Unreserved Fund Balance account to the total appropriable fund balance amount so that 19X2 appropriations for encumbrances outstanding at the end of 19X1 can be recorded.

When the goods or services ordered in 19X1 are received in 19X2, the usual entries to reverse the encumbrances and record the actual expenditures are made. The expenditures are charged against the 19X2 appropriations. Assuming that the goods or services actually cost $21,000, the entry to record their receipt is:

| | | |
|---|---|---|
| Reserve for Encumbrances . . . . . . . . . . . . . . . . . . . . . . . . . . . . | $20,000 | |
| Expenditures. . . . . . . . . . . . . . . . . . . . . . . . . . . . . . . . . . . . . . . . | 21,000 | |
|     Encumbrances. . . . . . . . . . . . . . . . . . . . . . . . . . . . . . . . . . . . . | | $20,000 |
|     Vouchers Payable . . . . . . . . . . . . . . . . . . . . . . . . . . . . . . . . . . | | 21,000 |

To record expenditures for goods and services and to reverse the
    related encumbrance entry.

Expenditures Ledger (Encumbrances):

| | |
|---|---|
| Public Safety. . . . . . . . . . . . . . . . . . . . . . . . . . . . . . . . . . . . . . . | $ 7,000 |
| Health and Sanitation . . . . . . . . . . . . . . . . . . . . . . . . . . . . . . . . | 13,000 |
| | $20,000 |

Expenditures Ledger (Expenditures):

| | |
|---|---|
| Public Safety. . . . . . . . . . . . . . . . . . . . . . . . . . . . . . . . . . . . . . . | $ 7,400 |
| Health and Sanitation . . . . . . . . . . . . . . . . . . . . . . . . . . . . . . . . | 13,600 |
| | $21,000 |

If the government wanted to account separately for the goods or services received during 19X2 that were ordered in 19X1, it could use separate General Ledger and/or Expenditures Subsidiary Ledger accounts classified by the year in which the appropriations were made. Furthermore, some or all of the year-end 19X1 adjusting entries may be reversed at the beginning of 19X2 to facilitate the 19X2 accounting process and routine.

## COMBINING SRF STATEMENTS

Recall from the "principles" discussions in Chapter 2 that combining financial statements should be prepared when a government has two or more funds of a type, such as Special Revenue Funds. Excerpts from a city of Memphis comprehensive annual financial report (CAFR) are presented in the final four figures of this chapter to illustrate the presentation of combining Special Revenue Fund financial statements:

- Figure 4–9: Narrative Explanations—Special Revenue Funds, which are concise descriptions of each Special Revenue Fund used by the city of Memphis.
- Figure 4–10: All Special Revenue Funds—Combining Balance Sheet—which is like individual fund financial statements presented side by side, as are combining financial statements.
- Figure 4–11: All Special Revenue Funds—Combining Statement of Revenues, Expenditures, and Changes in Fund Balances—which is presented in Format B, or Presentation 2.
- Figure 4–12: All Special Revenue Funds—Combining Schedule of Revenues and Expenditures—Budget and Actual on Budgetary Basis—which is presented vertically in a "pancake" format. Some Special Revenue Funds are budgeted on a non-GAAP basis.

FIGURE 4–9  **Narrative Explanations—Special Revenue Funds**

### PRIMARY GOVERNMENT—GOVERNMENTAL FUNDS

# CITY OF MEMPHIS

T E N N E S S E E

## SPECIAL REVENUE FUNDS

Special Revenue Funds are used to account for the proceeds of specific revenue sources (other than expendable trusts or major capital projects) that are legally restricted to expenditures for specific purposes. Included in the Special Revenue Funds are:

**Municipal State Aid** – This fund is used to account for the funds received from the local share of the tax on motor fuel. Funds are restricted for use only on street and road construction and maintenance.

**Community Development** – This fund is used to account for the Community Development Block Grant and other related grants. Funds are restricted to uses approved under federal guidelines.

**Job Training Partnership Act** – This fund is used to account for the funds received from the federal Department of Labor for use in the training of qualified individuals.

**Miscellaneous Grants** – This fund is used to account for several unrelated federal and state grants.

**Midtown Corridor** – This fund is used to account for the revenues and expenditures related to the sale of undeveloped residential lots located within the Midtown Corridor West Redevelopment Plan.

**Solid Waste Management** – This fund is used to account for the revenues and expenditures related to the collection and disposal of solid waste.

FIGURE 4–10 **Combining Balance Sheet—All Special Revenue Funds**

**ALL SPECIAL REVENUE FUNDS**
**COMBINING BALANCE SHEET**
(Thousands of Dollars)
June 30, 19X6 (With Comparative Totals for 19X5—as Restated)

**CITY OF MEMPHIS, TENNESSEE**
**EXHIBIT C-1**

| | Municipal State Aid | Community Development | Job Training Partnership Act | Miscellaneous Grants | Midtown Corridor | Solid Waste Management | TOTALS 19X6 | 19X5 |
|---|---|---|---|---|---|---|---|---|
| **ASSETS** | | | | | | | | |
| Cash and cash equivalents | $ — | 1,066 | — | 646 | — | 4 | 1,716 | 1,084 |
| Equity in cash and investment pool | — | — | — | — | 207 | 3,270 | 3,477 | 723 |
| Receivables (net of allowance for uncollectibles): | | | | | | | | |
| Federal grants and entitlements | — | 3,151 | 1,875 | 572 | — | — | 5,598 | 4,858 |
| State grants and entitlements | 2,973 | 15 | — | 156 | — | 36 | 3,180 | 4,070 |
| Interest on investments | — | 85 | — | — | — | 5 | 90 | 66 |
| Housing and other rehabilitation loans | — | 33,839 | — | — | — | — | 33,839 | 28,175 |
| Other | — | 161 | 10 | 519 | — | 48 | 738 | 627 |
| Due from other funds | — | — | — | — | — | — | — | 612 |
| Due from other agencies and governments | — | — | — | — | — | 1,530 | 1,530 | 1,530 |
| **Total Assets** | $2,973 | 38,317 | 1,885 | 1,893 | 207 | 4,893 | 50,168 | 41,745 |
| **LIABILITIES AND FUND BALANCES** | | | | | | | | |
| **Liabilities:** | | | | | | | | |
| Accounts payable | $ — | 1,218 | 509 | 585 | 17 | 1,350 | 3,679 | 3,364 |
| Accrued liabilities | — | 346 | 1 | — | — | — | 347 | 1 |
| Due to other funds | 2,973 | 1,588 | 1,375 | — | — | 1,149 | 7,085 | 6,060 |
| Deferred revenue | — | 35,165 | — | 1,308 | — | — | 36,473 | 30,122 |
| Vacation, sick, and other leave benefits | — | — | — | — | — | 516 | 516 | 420 |
| **Total liabilities** | $2,973 | 38,317 | 1,885 | 1,893 | 17 | 3,015 | 48,100 | 39,967 |
| **Fund balances:** | | | | | | | | |
| Reserved for encumbrances | — | — | — | — | — | 1,878 | 1,878 | 1,650 |
| Undesignated | — | — | — | — | 190 | — | 190 | 128 |
| **Total fund balances** | — | — | — | — | 190 | 1,878 | 2,068 | 1,778 |
| **Total liabilities and fund balances** | $2,973 | 38,317 | 1,885 | 1,893 | 207 | 4,893 | 50,168 | 41,745 |

**ALL SPECIAL REVENUE FUNDS**
**COMBINING STATEMENT OF REVENUES,**
**EXPENDITURES, AND CHANGES IN FUND BALANCES**
(Thousands of Dollars)
For the fiscal year ended June 30, 19X6 (With Comparative Totals for 19X5—as Restated)

**CITY OF MEMPHIS, TENNESSEE**
**EXHIBIT C-2**

| | Municipal State Aid | Community Development | Job Training Partnership Act | Miscellaneous Grants | Midtown Corridor | Solid Waste Management | TOTALS 19X6 | TOTALS 19X5 |
|---|---|---|---|---|---|---|---|---|
| **REVENUES AND OTHER SOURCES** | | | | | | | | |
| **Revenues:** | | | | | | | | |
| State taxes (local share) | $17,284 | — | — | — | — | — | 17,284 | 17,266 |
| Charges for services | — | — | — | — | — | 18,358 | 18,358 | 18,345 |
| Use of money and property | — | — | — | 174 | — | 46 | 220 | 149 |
| Federal grants and entitlements | — | 17,166 | 7,478 | 2,503 | — | — | 27,147 | 30,567 |
| State grants | — | 452 | — | 3,474 | — | 723 | 4,649 | 3,714 |
| Other | — | 3,470 | 177 | 1,493 | 111 | — | 5,251 | 3,987 |
| Total revenues | 17,284 | 21,088 | 7,655 | 7,644 | 111 | 19,127 | 72,909 | 74,028 |
| **Other sources:** | | | | | | | | |
| Operating transfer in: | | | | | | | | |
| General Fund | — | — | — | 517 | — | 17,868 | 18,385 | 16,759 |
| Total other sources | — | — | — | 517 | — | 17,868 | 18,385 | 16,759 |
| **Total revenues and other sources** | 17,284 | 21,088 | 7,655 | 8,161 | 111 | 36,995 | 91,294 | 90,787 |
| **EXPENDITURES AND OTHER USES** | | | | | | | | |
| **Expenditures:** | | | | | | | | |
| General government | — | 21,088 | — | 6,214 | 49 | — | 27,351 | 27,484 |
| Instruction and administration | — | — | — | 232 | — | — | 232 | 86 |
| Community service | — | — | 7,655 | — | — | — | 7,655 | 8,414 |
| Transportation and environment | — | — | — | — | — | 36,767 | 36,767 | 36,802 |
| Food service | — | — | — | 1,280 | — | — | 1,280 | 1,158 |
| Capital outlay | — | — | — | 435 | — | — | 435 | 891 |
| Total expenditures | — | 21,088 | 7,655 | 8,161 | 49 | 36,767 | 73,720 | 74,835 |
| **Other uses—operating transfers out:** | | | | | | | | |
| General fund | 5,997 | — | — | — | — | — | 5,997 | 8,127 |
| Debt service fund | 11,287 | — | — | — | — | — | 11,287 | 9,139 |
| Total other uses | 17,284 | — | — | — | — | — | 17,284 | 17,266 |
| **Total expenditures and other uses** | 17,284 | 21,088 | 7,655 | 8,161 | 49 | 36,767 | 91,004 | 92,101 |
| Revenues and other sources over (under) expenditures and other uses | — | — | — | — | 62 | 228 | 290 | (1,314) |
| Fund balances—beginning of year | — | — | — | — | 128 | 1,650 | 1,778 | 3,092 |
| **Fund balances—end of year** | $ — | — | — | — | 190 | 1,878 | 2,068 | 1,778 |

**ALL SPECIAL REVENUE FUNDS (WITH ANNUAL BUDGETS)**
**COMBINING SCHEDULE OF REVENUES AND EXPENDITURES**
**BUDGET AND ACTUAL ON BUDGETARY BASIS (NON-GAAP)**

**CITY OF MEMPHIS, TENNESSEE**
**EXHIBIT C-3**

(Thousands of Dollars)
For the fiscal year ended June 30, 19X6 (With Comparative Totals for 19X5—as Restated)

| | *19X6* | | | *19X5* |
|---|---|---|---|---|
| | *Actual on Budgetary Basis* | *Budget* | *Variance— Favorable (Unfavorable)* | *Actual on Budgetary Basis* |
| **MUNICIPAL STATE AID FUND** | | | | |
| **Revenues:** | | | | |
| State gasoline tax (local share) | $ 17,284 | 17,220 | 64 | 17,266 |
| Total revenue | 17,284 | 17,220 | 64 | 17,266 |
| **Uses—operating transfers out:** | | | | |
| General fund | 5,997 | 5,933 | (64) | 8,127 |
| Debt service fund | 11,287 | 11,287 | — | 9,139 |
| Total uses | 17,284 | 17,220 | (64) | 17,266 |
| Revenues over (under) uses | $ — | — | — | — |
| **JOB TRAINING PARTNERSHIP ACT FUND** | | | | |
| **Revenues—federal grants** | $ 7,655 | 14,262 | (6,607) | 8,414 |
| **Expenditures—payments to subgrantees** | 7,655 | 14,262 | 6,607 | 8,414 |
| Revenues over (under) expenditures | $ — | — | — | — |
| **MISCELLANEOUS GRANTS** | | | | |
| **Revenues:** | | | | |
| Federal grants | $ 2,502 | 16,349 | (13,847) | 1,852 |
| State grants | 3,474 | 3,007 | 467 | 3,321 |
| Other | 1,668 | 2,227 | (559) | 1,463 |
| Total revenues | 7,644 | 21,583 | (13,939) | 6,636 |
| **Other sources:** | | | | |
| **Operating transfer in—general fund** | 517 | 898 | (381) | 147 |
| Total revenues and other sources | 8,161 | 22,481 | (14,320) | 6,783 |
| **Expenditures:** | | | | |
| General government | 6,214 | 9,767 | 3,553 | 4,648 |
| Instruction and administration | 232 | 933 | 701 | 86 |
| Food service | 1,280 | 1,267 | (13) | 1,158 |
| Capital outlay | 435 | 10,514 | 10,079 | 891 |
| Total expenditures | 8,161 | 22,481 | 14,320 | 6,783 |
| Revenues and other sources over (under) expenditures | $ — | — | — | — |
| **SOLID WASTE MANAGEMENT FUND** | | | | |
| **Revenues:** | | | | |
| Charges for services | $ 18,358 | 18,392 | (34) | 18,345 |
| Use of money and property | 46 | — | 46 | 5 |
| Federal grants and entitlements | — | — | — | 226 |
| State grants | 723 | 390 | 333 | 320 |
| Total revenues | 19,127 | 18,782 | 345 | 18,896 |
| **Other sources:** | | | | |
| **Operating transfer in—general fund** | 17,868 | 20,243 | (2,375) | 16,612 |
| Total revenues and other sources | 36,995 | 39,025 | (2,030) | 35,508 |
| **Expenditures:** | | | | |
| Transportation and environment | 36,767 | 40,853 | 4,086 | 36,802 |
| Total expenditures | 36,767 | 40,853 | 4,086 | 36,802 |
| Revenues and other sources over (under) expenditures | $ 228 | (1,828) | 2,056 | (1,294) |

## CONCLUDING COMMENTS

The General and Special Revenue Funds typically account for significant portions of the financial resources of state and local government units. Thus, a thorough understanding of General and Special Revenue Fund accounting is important to governmental accountants, auditors, and systems specialists.

Moreover, accounting and reporting for the other governmental funds (Capital Projects, Debt Service, and Expendable Trust Funds) closely parallel that for the General and Special Revenue Funds and can be understood largely by analogy. Thus, a firm foundation in General and Special Revenue Fund accounting and reporting is essential for both students and practitioners.

This chapter discusses and illustrates the basic accounting and reporting procedures for the General Fund and Special Revenue Funds—which apply also to other governmental funds—and necessarily includes several simplifying assumptions. For example, we assumed that:

- The annual budget was prepared and legally enacted on the modified accrual (GAAP) basis.

- The accounts were accordingly maintained on a GAAP basis during the year, and there were no budgetary basis versus GAAP basis differences in the accounts or in the financial statements.

- Where alternative methods of accounting for certain transactions and events are acceptable, only one acceptable method should be discussed and illustrated in this "basics" chapter.

The chapters that follow build on this chapter. The next two chapters refine and expand the basic discussions in this chapter on revenue accounting and expenditure accounting, respectively. Then the other governmental funds are considered.

### APPENDIX 4–1

## General Ledger Worksheet and Subsidiary Ledgers

As noted in Chapter 4, this appendix presents, for the General Fund of A Governmental Unit, for the year ended December 31, 19X1:

- Figure 4–13—General Ledger Worksheet
- Figure 4–14—Revenues Subsidiary Ledger (Preclosing)
- Figure 4–15—Expenditures Subsidiary Ledger (Preclosing)

# FIGURE 4-13   General Ledger Worksheet—General Fund

## GENERAL LEDGER WORKSHEET
## A GOVERNMENTAL UNIT—GENERAL FUND
## FOR THE YEAR ENDED DECEMBER 31, 19X1

| Accounts | Transactions Debit | # | Credit | # | Preclosing Trial Balance Debit | Credit | Closing Entries Debit | # | Credit | # | Postclosing Trial Balance Debit | Credit |
|---|---|---|---|---|---|---|---|---|---|---|---|---|
| Cash | $ 14,000 | (BB) | $ 40,000 | (11) | | | | | | | | |
| | 175,000 | (7) | 10,000 | (14) | | | | | | | | |
| | 205,000 | (10) | 6,000 | (19) | | | | | | | | |
| | 20,200 | (13) | 320,000 | (21) | | | | | | | | |
| | 20,000 | (22) | 22,500 | (23) | | | | | | | | |
| | 13,000 | (24) | 5,600 | (26) | $43,100 | | | | | | $43,100 | |
| Investments | 10,000 | (14) | | | 10,000 | | | | | | 10,000 | |
| Accrued Interest Receivable | 400 | (A2) | | | 400 | | | | | | 400 | |
| Taxes Receivable—Current | 200,000 | (2) | 160,000 | (7) | | | | | | | | |
| | | | 40,000 | (8) | | | | | | | | |
| Allowance for Uncollectible Current Taxes | 3,000 | (9) | 3,000 | (2) | | | | | | | | |
| Taxes Receivable—Delinquent | 40,000 | (8) | 20,000 | (13) | 20,000 | | | | | | 20,000 | |
| Allowance for Uncollectible Delinquent Taxes | | | 3,000 | (9) | | $3,000 | | | | | | $3,000 |
| Interest and Penalties Receivable—Delinquent Taxes | 550 | (A1) | | | 550 | | | | | | 550 | |
| Allowance for Uncollectible Interest and Penalties | | | 50 | (A1) | | 50 | | | | | | 50 |
| Accounts Receivable | 12,000 | (BB) | 15,000 | (7) | | | | | | | | |
| | 36,000 | (3) | 13,000 | (24) | | | | | | | | |
| | | | 400 | (25) | 19,600 | | | | | | 19,600 | |
| Allowance for Uncollectible Accounts Receivable | 400 | (25) | 1,000 | (3) | | 600 | | | | | | 600 |
| Due from Special Revenue Fund | 1,500 | (16) | | | | | | | | | | |
| | 10,000 | (18) | | | 11,500 | | | | | | 11,500 | |
| Vouchers Payable | 40,000 | (11) | 15,000 | (BB) | | | | | | | | |
| | 320,000 | (21) | 29,900 | (5b) | | | | | | | | |
| | | | 40,000 | (6) | | | | | | | | |
| | | | 300,000 | (20) | | | | | | | | |
| | | | 300 | (27) | | 25,200 | | | | | | 25,200 |
| Notes Payable | 5,000 | (26) | 20,000 | (22) | | 15,000 | | | | | | 15,000 |
| Accrued Interest Payable | | | 250 | (A3) | | 250 | | | | | | 250 |
| Due to Stores Fund | 22,500 | (23) | 30,000 | (15) | | 7,500 | | | | | | 7,500 |
| Due to Debt Service Fund | | | 5,000 | (17) | | 5,000 | | | | | | 5,000 |
| Reserve for Encumbrances | 30,000 | (5a) | 30,000 | (4) | | | | | | | | |
| | | | 20,000 | (12) | | 20,000 | | | | | | 20,000 |
| Unreserved Fund Balance | | | 11,000 | (BB) | | | | | | | | |
| | | | 5,000 | (1) | | 16,000 | $ 5,000 | (C1) | $ 38,850 | (C2) | | |
| | | | | | | | 1,300 | (C3) | | | | |
| | | | | | | | 20,000 | (C4) | | | | 28,550 |
| Estimated Revenues | 431,000 | (1) | | | 431,000 | | | | 431,000 | (C1) | | |
| Revenues | | | 197,000 | (2) | | | | | | | | |
| | | | 35,000 | (3) | | | | | | | | |
| | | | 205,000 | (10) | | | | | | | | |
| | | | 200 | (13) | | | | | | | | |
| | | | 500 | (A1) | | | | | | | | |
| | | | 400 | (A2) | | 438,100 | 438,100 | (C2) | | | | |
| Appropriations | | | 426,000 | (1) | | 426,000 | 426,000 | (C1) | | | | |
| Expenditures | 29,900 | (5b) | 1,500 | (16) | | | | | | | | |
| | 40,000 | (6) | | | | | | | | | | |
| | 30,000 | (15) | | | | | | | | | | |
| | 300,000 | (20) | | | | | | | | | | |
| | 600 | (26) | | | | | | | | | | |
| | 250 | (A3) | | | 399,250 | | | | 399,250 | (C2) | | |
| Encumbrances | 30,000 | (4) | 30,000 | (5a) | | | | | | | | |
| | 20,000 | (12) | | | 20,000 | | | | 20,000 | (C4) | | |
| Operating Transfer to Debt Service Fund | 5,000 | (17) | | | 5,000 | | | | 5,000 | (C3) | | |
| Operating Transfer from Special Revenue Fund | | | 10,000 | (18) | | 10,000 | 10,000 | (C3) | | | | |
| Residual Equity Transfer to Enterprise Fund | 6,000 | (19) | | | 6,000 | | | | 6,000 | (C3) | | |
| Correction of Prior Year Error | 300 | (27) | | | 300 | | | | 300 | (C3) | | |
| | $2,071,600 | | $2,071,600 | | $966,700 | $966,700 | $900,400 | | $900,400 | | $105,150 | $105,150 |

**FIGURE 4–14 Revenues Subsidiary Ledger—General Fund**

**REVENUES SUBSIDIARY LEDGER**
**GENERAL FUND**
**A GOVERNMENTAL UNIT**
**FOR THE YEAR ENDED DECEMBER 31, 19X1: PRECLOSING**

**Revenues Ledger**

| | Dr. Estimated Revenues | Cr. Revenues | Dr. (Cr.) Balance |
|---|---|---|---|
| **Taxes** | $250,000 (1) | | $250,000 |
| | | $197,000 (2) | 53,000 |
| | | 58,000 (10) | (5,000) |
| Totals/Balance | 250,000 | 255,000 | (5,000) |
| **Licenses and Permits** | 70,000 (1) | | 70,000 |
| | | 68,000 (10) | 2,000 |
| Totals/Balance | 70,000 | 68,000 | 2,000 |
| **Intergovernmental** | 50,000 (1) | | 50,000 |
| | | 52,500 (10) | (2,500) |
| Totals/Balance | 50,000 | 52,500 | (2,500) |
| **Charges for Services** | 40,000 (1) | | 40,000 |
| | | 35,000 (3) | 5,000 |
| | | 6,000 (10) | (1,000) |
| Totals/Balance | 40,000 | 41,000 | (1,000) |
| **Fines and Forfeits** | 20,000 (1) | | 20,000 |
| | | 19,000 (10) | 1,000 |
| Totals/Balance | 20,000 | 19,000 | 1,000 |
| **Other** | 1,000 (1) | | 1,000 |
| | | 1,500 (10) | (500) |
| | | 200 (13) | (700) |
| | | 500 (A1) | (1,200) |
| | | 400 (A2) | (1,600) |
| Totals/Balance | 1,000 | 2,600 | (1,600) |

**FIGURE 4–15 Expenditures Subsidiary Ledger—General Fund**

**EXPENDITURES SUBSIDIARY LEDGER**
**GENERAL FUND**
**A GOVERNMENTAL UNIT**
**FOR THE YEAR ENDED DECEMBER 31, 19X1: PRECLOSING**

**Expenditures Ledger**

| | Dr. Encumbrances | | Dr. Expenditures | | Cr. Appropriations | Cr. (Dr.) Unencumbered Balance |
|---|---|---|---|---|---|---|
| **General Government** | | | | | $ 40,000 (1) | $ 40,000 |
| | $ 2,000 | (4) | | | | 38,000 |
| | (2,000) | (5a) | $ 1,700 | (5b) | | 38,300 |
| | | | 5,000 | (6) | | 33,300 |
| | | | 4,000 | (15) | | 29,300 |
| | | | (1,500) | (16) | | 30,800 |
| | | | 30,000 | (20) | | 800 |
| Totals/Balance | 0 | | 39,200 | | 40,000 | 800 |
| **Public Safety** | | | | | 150,000 (1) | 150,000 |
| | 8,000 | (4) | | | | 142,000 |
| | (8,000) | (5a) | 8,000 | (5b) | | 142,000 |
| | | | 16,000 | (6) | | 126,000 |
| | 7,000 | (12) | | | | 119,000 |
| | | | 6,000 | (15) | | 113,000 |
| | | | 112,000 | (20) | | 1,000 |
| Totals/Balance | 7,000 | | 142,000 | | 150,000 | 1,000 |
| **Highways and Streets** | | | | | 120,000 (1) | 120,000 |
| | 10,000 | (4) | | | | 110,000 |
| | (10,000) | (5a) | 10,100 | (5b) | | 109,900 |
| | | | 13,000 | (6) | | 96,900 |
| | | | 10,000 | (15) | | 86,900 |
| | | | 90,000 | (20) | | (3,100) |
| Totals/Balance | 0 | | 123,100 | | 120,000 | (3,100) |
| **Health and Sanitation** | | | | | 60,000 (1) | 60,000 |
| | | | 4,000 | (6) | | 56,000 |
| | 13,000 | (12) | | | | 43,000 |
| | | | 7,000 | (15) | | 36,000 |
| | | | 35,400 | (20) | | 600 |
| Totals/Balance | 13,000 | | 46,400 | | 60,000 | 600 |
| **Other** | | | | | 25,000 (1) | 25,000 |
| | 4,000 | (4) | | | | 21,000 |
| | (4,000) | (5a) | 4,000 | (5b) | | 21,000 |
| | | | 2,000 | (6) | | 19,000 |
| | | | 3,000 | (15) | | 16,000 |
| | | | 9,600 | (20) | | 6,400 |
| Totals/Balance | 0 | | 18,600 | | 25,000 | 6,400 |
| **Capital Outlay** | | | | | 30,000 (1) | 30,000 |
| | 6,000 | (4) | | | | 24,000 |
| | (6,000) | (5a) | 6,100 | (5b) | | 23,900 |
| | 0 | | 23,000 | (20) | | 900 |
| Totals/Balance | 0 | | 29,100 | | 30,000 | 900 |
| **Debt Service** | | | | | 1,000 (1) | 1,000 |
| | | | 600 | (26) | | 400 |
| | | | 250 | (A3) | | 150 |
| Totals/Balance | 0 | | 850 | | 1,000 | 150 |

## Questions

**Q 4-1**  Why is there no chapter in this text devoted to describing operations and accounting procedures of Special Revenue Funds?

**Q 4-2**  What are the characteristics of expenditures that distinguish them from expenses in the financial accounting sense?

**Q 4-3**  Why are encumbrances not considered expenditures under the modified accrual (GAAP) basis of governmental fund accounting?

**Q 4-4**  Although the illustrative examples in this chapter use only a few Revenues Subsidiary Ledger and Expenditures Subsidiary Ledger accounts, a state or local government probably will use hundreds or even thousands of such accounts in practice. Why?

**Q 4-5**  Why might a local government not prepare and adopt its General Fund annual operating budget on the modified accrual (GAAP) basis?

**Q 4-6**  Explain what is meant by General Ledger control over the Revenues Subsidiary Ledger and the Expenditures Subsidiary Ledger.

**Q 4-7**  The illustrative example in this chapter uses the term *unreserved fund balance* to describe the Unreserved Fund Balance account. Yet in practice one often sees that account titled simply "Fund Balance," even though it is accompanied by a reserve for encumbrances, reserve for interfund advances, and perhaps other reserve accounts. Is this acceptable?

**Q 4-8**  Explain the net revenue approach to revenue recognition employed in General and Special Revenue Fund (and other governmental fund) accounting and reporting, including why it is used.

**Q 4-9**  Why might a General Fund reserve be established?

**Q 4-10**  Why are nonrevenue financing sources and nonexpenditure uses of financial resources distinguished from governmental fund revenues and expenditures?

**Q 4-11**  Explain the nature and purpose of the Reserve for Encumbrances account (a) during the year and (b) at year end.

**Q 4-12**  The terms *advance to (from) other funds* and *due from (to) other funds* have distinct meanings in governmental fund accounting and financial reporting. Explain.

**Q 4-13**  Explain the purpose, nature, and effect of the entry reestablishing encumbrances in the accounts at the beginning of a new year.

**Q 4-14**  The budget was assumed to be enacted on the GAAP basis in this chapter. What differences in the General Fund financial statements and disclosures would result from adopting the budget on the cash basis or another non-GAAP basis?

**Q 4-15**  (a) Distinguish between unreserved fund balance and total fund balance. (b) How does a governmental fund Statement of Revenues, Expenditures, and Changes in Fund Balance prepared on the usual total fund balance approach differ from such a statement prepared on the unreserved fund balance approach?

**Q 4-16**  Explain (a) which of the illustrative entries in this chapter would change—and how they would change—if budgeted changes were recorded in a Budgetary Fund Balance account rather than in the Unreserved Fund Balance account, and (b) why an accountant might prefer that approach over the traditional approach illustrated in this chapter.

## Exercises

**E 4-1**  (Budgetary Entries—General Ledger) The city of Cherokee Hill adopted its fiscal year 20X1 General Fund budget on January 1, 20X1. Budgeted revenues were $17 million; budgeted expenditures were $16,500,000.

1. On August 5, 20X1, the Cherokee Hill city council adopted a motion by Mayor Clyde Fisher to increase the police department appropriation by $200,000. All other budgeted items remained unchanged.

2. On September 1, the city council revised the estimate of sales tax revenues upward by $60,000.

**Required**  (a) Record the foregoing transactions. Do not use a Budgetary Fund Balance account.

(b) Close the General Fund accounts. In addition to the foregoing transactions, assume the following information:

- Actual revenues for the year totaled $17,300,000.
- Expenditures for the year totaled $16,600,000.
- Operating transfers to Debt Service Funds totaled $800,000.
- Encumbrances of $80,000 were outstanding at year end.

(c) Repeat parts (a) and (b) using the Budgetary Fund Balance account.

**E 4-2**  (General Ledger Entries) Record the following transactions in the general ledger accounts of the Tegarden County General Fund.

1. Tegarden County levied its 20X0 property taxes on January 1, 20X0. The total tax levy was $80,000,000; 2% is expected to be uncollectible.
2. Tegarden collected $55,000,000 of property taxes before the due date. The remaining taxes are past due.
3. Interest and penalties of $2,500,000 were assessed on the past due taxes; 6% is expected to be uncollectible.
4. Tegarden County collected $20,000,000 of delinquent taxes and $2,000,000 of interest and penalties. At the end of 20X0, Tegarden estimates that it will collect $3,000,000 of the delinquent taxes and $300,000 of the previously accrued interest and penalties in the first 60 days of 20X1.

**E 4-3**  (General Ledger Entries) Record the following transactions in the general ledger accounts of the General Fund of the Keffer Independent School District.

1. Ordered textbooks with an estimated cost of $80,000.
2. Ordered laboratory supplies with an estimated cost of $25,000.
3. Signed a contract with Victory Transportation Services for athletic team transportation. The estimated total cost of the services was $7,000.
4. Hired a new clerk and approved a salary of $18,000 per year.
5. The textbooks were received at an actual cost of $80,400.
6. Half of the laboratory supplies were received and vouchered at an actual cost of $12,000. (Estimated cost was $12,000.)
7. Actual transportation costs billed to Keffer School District by Victory Transportation Services were $8,000.

**E 4-4**  (Financial Statement Presentation) (a) Prepare using good form a skeleton statement of revenues, expenditures, and changes in fund balance. Use the format for the statement that presents two operations subtotals. (b) Next insert the number representing each of the following items in the appropriate location in the statement. If any item is not reported in the statement, explain why not.

1. Property taxes levied for and collected in the current year
2. Estimated cost of goods ordered but not received by year end
3. Operating transfer to another fund
4. Salary costs incurred during the year
5. Payment to retire long-term note principal
6. Payment of interest on long-term note
7. Accrued interest on long-term note
8. Receipt of proceeds of short-term note
9. Payment of interest on short-term note
10. Accrued interest on short-term note
11. Payment to retire principal of short-term note
12. Payment to establish an Enterprise Fund activity; no repayment expected
13. Long-term loan from General Fund to Internal Service Fund
14. Short-term loan from General Fund to Capital Projects Fund

15. Purchase of equipment
16. Purchase of temporary investment in securities
17. Receipt of proceeds from sale of fixed asset
18. Property taxes collected in advance on next year's tax levy
19. Depreciation of equipment
20. Purchase of electricity from Electric Enterprise Fund

## Problems

**P 4-1**   (Multiple Choice) Indicate the best answer to each question.

1. A city levies property taxes of $500,000 for its General Fund for a year and expects to collect all except the estimated uncollectible amount of $5,500 by year end. To reflect this information, the city should record General Fund revenues of
   a. $500,000 and General Fund expenses of $5,500.
   b. $500,000 and General Fund expenditures of $5,500.
   c. $500,000 and no General Fund expenses or expenditures.
   d. $494,500 and no General Fund expenses or expenditures.
   e. None of the above. The correct answer is _____.

2. At year end, a school district purchases instructional equipment costing $10,000 by issuing a 6-month note to be repaid from General Fund resources. This transaction should be reflected in the General Fund as
   a. expenditures of $10,000 and a $10,000 liability.
   b. expenditures of $10,000 and a $10,000 other financing source from the issuance of the note.
   c. a fixed asset of $10,000 and a liability of $10,000.
   d. expenditures of $10,000 and revenues of $10,000 from issuance of the note.

3. Which of the following statements is true?
   a. Encumbrances are equivalent to expenditures, and encumbrances outstanding at the end of a year should be reported as liabilities.
   b. No expenditure can be reported without first being encumbered.
   c. Encumbrances are recorded at the estimated cost of goods ordered or services contracted for. The subsequent amount recognized as expenditures upon receipt of the goods or services must be equal to the encumbered amount.
   d. Encumbrances are recorded at the estimated cost of goods ordered or services contracted for. The subsequent amount recognized as expenditures upon receipt of the goods or services may differ from the encumbered amount.

4. A state borrowed $10,000,000 on a nine-month, 9% note payable to provide temporary financing for the General Fund. At year end, the note has been outstanding for six months. The state should report General Fund interest expenditures and interest payable on the note in its financial statements in the amount of
   a. $0, the interest will be recognized when it matures.
   b. $450,000.
   c. $450,000 unless the state does not expect to be able to pay the interest when it matures—in which case no interest expenditures should be reported for the current year.
   d. $675,000.

5. Charges for services rendered by a county's General Fund departments totaled $500,000—of which $5,500 is expected to be uncollectible. The county expects to collect $494,500 by year end. To reflect this information, the county should record General Fund revenues of
   a. $500,000 and General Fund expenses of $5,500.
   b. $500,000 and General Fund expenditures of $5,500.
   c. $500,000 and no General Fund expenses or expenditures.
   d. $494,500 and no General Fund expenses or expenditures.
   e. none of the above. The correct answer is _____.

6. Which of the following transactions requires entries in an Expenditures Subsidiary Ledger?
   a. Legal adoption of the General Fund budget.
   b. Purchase of equipment on account.
   c. Accrual of salaries and wages.
   d. Order of supplies.
   e. All of the above.

7. If a Warren County Special Revenue Fund has a long-term receivable from another county fund, the receivable will be reported as a(n)
   a. advance from other funds with an equivalent amount of fund balance reserved for advances from other funds.
   b. advance from other funds with no fund balance reserve needed.
   c. advance to other funds with an equivalent amount of fund balance reserved for advances to other funds.
   d. advance to other funds with no fund balance reserve needed.
   e. due from other funds.
   f. due to other funds.

8. Which of the following items is reported differently in a statement of revenues, expenditures, and changes in unreserved fund balance than it is in a statement of revenues, expenditures, and changes in total fund balance?
   a. Personal services expenditures.
   b. Encumbrances outstanding.
   c. Changes in fund balance reserves.
   d. Proceeds of general long-term debt issuances.
   e. Residual equity transfers.

9. The budget data presented in a school district General Fund statement of revenues, expenditures, and changes in fund balance—budget and actual are to be
   a. the original, legally adopted budget.
   b. the original, legally adopted budget, as amended.
   c. presented on the modified accrual basis of accounting even if the budget is adopted on the cash basis.
   d. adjusted to equal the actual in the expenditure portion of the statement to avoid any overexpenditures of budget being presented.

10. In the statement of revenues, expenditures, and changes in fund balance, operating transfers in must be reported
    a. in a separate section immediately following revenues.
    b. in a section immediately following the excess of revenues over (under) expenditures.
    c. either a or b is permissible.
    d. immediately following beginning fund balance.

**P 4-2** (General Ledger Entries) Prepare the general journal entries to:
1. Record the following transactions in the general ledger accounts of the Kessinger County General Fund.
   a. Paid $500,000 to the Bridge Bond Debt Service Fund to provide for upcoming principal and interest payments.
   b. Paid $5,000,000 to the Kessinger County Airport Fund to provide financing for a major expansion project. $2,000,000 is not required to be repaid, but $3,000,000 is to be repaid at the end of five years.
   c. Loaned $320,000 to the Holstein Skywalk Capital Projects Fund—to be repaid in 90 days.
   d. Paid $22,000 to the Highways Special Revenue Fund to repay it for General Fund employee salaries that were inadvertently recorded as expenditures of that fund.
   e. Received a bill from the County Electric Utility Enterprise Fund for electricity usage charged to General Fund departments and agencies, $3,000.

2. Explain how each of the foregoing transactions is reported in the Kessinger County General Fund Statement of Revenues, Expenditures, and Changes in Fund Balance.

**P 4-3** (General Ledger Entries) (a) Prepare general journal entries to record the following transactions in the general ledger of the General Fund or a Special Revenue Fund, as appropriate. (b) Explain how these transactions and events are reported in the General or Special Revenue Fund statement of revenues, expenditures, and changes in fund balance.

1. $100,000 of General Fund cash was contributed to establish a new Internal Service Fund.
2. A truck—acquired two years ago with General Fund revenues for $19,000—with a fair value of $10,000 was contributed to a department financed by an Enterprise Fund. Record the contribution of the asset to the Enterprise Fund—not the purchase.
3. The Sanitation Department, accounted for in the General Fund, billed the Municipal Airport, accounted for in an Enterprise Fund, $800 for garbage collection.
4. General Fund cash of $50,000—to be repaid in 90 days—was provided to enable construction to begin on a new courthouse before a bond issue was sold.
5. A $9,000,000 bond issue to finance construction of a major addition to the civic center was sold at par. The civic center is accounted for in the governmental funds and account groups.
6. General Fund disbursements during May included a contribution of $35,000 to a Capital Projects Fund to help finance a major capital project.
7. After retirement of the related debt, the balance of the net assets of a Debt Service Fund, $8,500, was transferred to the General Fund.
8. General Fund cash of $70,000 was loaned to an Enterprise Fund. The loan is to be repaid in three years.
9. An accounting error made during the prior accounting period caused the General Fund cash balance at the beginning of the current year to be understated by $6,500.
10. Another accounting error was discovered: expenditures of $4,000, properly chargeable to a Capital Projects Fund, were inadvertently charged to a Special Revenue Fund during the current year.

**P 4-4** (Property Tax Entries) Prepare the general journal entries to record the following transactions of the Baker School District General Fund.

1. On January 1 the school district levied property taxes of $8,000,000. The due date for the taxes is March 31. The school district expects to collect all except $200,000 either by the end of the fiscal year or within 60 days thereafter. The other $200,000 is expected to prove uncollectible.
2. During the first quarter (ending March 31) the school district collected $6,800,000 of its current year property taxes. The rest of the taxes are past due.
3. On June 12 the school district wrote off $88,000 of property taxes as uncollectible.
4. From March 31 to December 31 the school district collected $700,000 of the property taxes that were levied on January 1. The school district expects to collect an additional $300,000 of these taxes during the first two months of the next fiscal year.

**P 4-5** (Debt-related Transactions) Prepare the general journal entries to record the following transactions of the Quinones County General Fund.

1. Quinones County borrowed $1,000,000 by issuing 6-month tax anticipation notes bearing interest at 6%. The notes are to be repaid from property tax collections during the fiscal year.
2. The county repaid the tax anticipation notes, along with $30,000 interest, at the due date.
3. The county ordered a new patrol car for the Sheriff's Department. The purchase order was for $35,000.

4. The county received the new patrol car two months before the end of the fiscal year. Its actual cost was $35,000. The county paid $5,000 upon receipt and signed a 6-month, 9% note payable for the balance.
5. The county services one of its general obligation serial bond issues directly from the General Fund—that is, a Debt Service Fund is not used. The annual principal and interest payment, which is due two months before year end, was paid. The principal payment was $200,000 and the interest was $120,000. (Next year's interest payment will be $108,000.)
6. Record all appropriate interest accruals.

**P 4-6, Part I** (Closing Entries) The preclosing trial balance of a Special Revenue Fund of Mesa County at the end of its 19X3 fiscal year is:

| | | |
|---|---:|---:|
| Cash | $ 25,000 | |
| Taxes Receivable—Delinquent | 70,000 | |
| Allowance for Uncollectible Delinquent Taxes | | $ 10,000 |
| Due from General Fund | 16,000 | |
| Advance to Enterprise Fund | 45,000 | |
| Accrued Receivables | 9,000 | |
| Vouchers Payable | | 21,000 |
| Due to Internal Service Fund | | 4,000 |
| Accrued Payables | | 6,000 |
| Reserve for Interfund Advance | | 45,000 |
| Reserve for Encumbrances | | 20,000 |
| Unreserved Fund Balance | | 52,000 |
| Estimated Revenues | 800,000 | |
| Appropriations | | 810,000 |
| Revenues | | 798,000 |
| Expenditures | 789,000 | |
| Encumbrances | 20,000 | |
| Operating Transfer to Debt Service Fund | 15,000 | |
| Residual Equity Transfer from Capital Projects Fund | | 35,000 |
| Correction of Prior Year Error | 12,000 | |
| | $1,801,000 | $1,801,000 |

Revenues Ledger:

| | | |
|---|---:|---:|
| Taxes | $ 3,000 | |
| Intergovernmental | | $ 4,000 |
| Charges for Services | 1,000 | |
| Other | 2,000 | |
| | $ 6,000 | $ 4,000 |

Expenditures Ledger:

| | | |
|---|---:|---:|
| General Government | | $ 1,500 |
| Parks and Recreation | | 2,500 |
| Social Services | $ 3,500 | |
| Other | | 500 |
| | $ 3,500 | $ 4,500 |

**Required** (a) Prepare the entry or entries to close the General Ledger and subsidiary ledger accounts at the end of the 19X3 fiscal year.
(b) Prepare any related entry(ies) needed at the beginning of the 19X4 fiscal year.

**P 4-6, Part II** (Financial Statements) Based on the preclosing trial balance in P 4-6, Part I, prepare in good form for the Mesa County Special Revenue Fund:

(a) A balance sheet at the end of the 19X3 fiscal year.
(b) A statement of revenues, expenditures, and changes in fund balance (total) for the 19X3 fiscal year. In completing requirement b, assume the following actual revenues and expenditures:

Revenues:

| | |
|---|---|
| Taxes ......................................... | $550,000 |
| Intergovernmental ................................ | 150,000 |
| Charges for Services ............................. | 80,000 |
| Other ......................................... | 18,000 |

Expenditures:

| | |
|---|---|
| General Government ............................... | $330,000 |
| Parks and Recreation ............................. | 200,000 |
| Social Services................................. | 250,000 |
| Other ......................................... | 9,000 |

Furthermore, assume that all outstanding encumbrances relate to parks and recreation and that the only reserve at the beginning of the year was a reserve for encumbrances of $33,000.

**P 4-7**  (GL and SL Entries) Prepare the journal entries to record the following transactions and events either (a) in the General Ledger, Revenues Ledger, and Expenditures Ledger of a local government General Fund or (b) in detailed General Ledger accounts (with no subsidiary ledgers).

1. The annual budget was adopted as follows:

Estimated Revenues:

| | |
|---|---|
| Property taxes..................................... | $400,000 |
| Sales taxes....................................... | 200,000 |
| Charges for services ............................. | 100,000 |
| Other ......................................... | 50,000 |
| | $750,000 |

Appropriations:

| | |
|---|---|
| General administration............................. | $ 80,000 |
| Police ......................................... | 310,000 |
| Fire............................................ | 320,000 |
| Other ......................................... | 30,000 |
| | $740,000 |

2. Property taxes of $408,000 were levied. $7,000 are expected to be uncollectible.
3. Purchase orders and contracts were approved for goods and services expected to cost:

| | |
|---|---|
| Police ......................................... | $ 50,000 |
| Fire............................................ | 90,000 |
| | $140,000 |

4. Most of the goods and services ordered were received.

| | Encumbered For | Actual Cost |
|---|---|---|
| Police ......................................... | $ 40,000 | $ 41,000 |
| Fire............................................ | 70,000 | 68,500 |
| | $110,000 | $109,500 |

5. The budget was revised during the year to decrease the sales tax revenue estimate by $5,000 and increase the police appropriation by $7,000.
6. Interfund transfers were ordered as follows:

From the General Fund

| | |
|---|---|
| To provide for principal and interest payments on GLTD.... | $30,000 |
| To establish a new data processing Internal Service Fund.... | 50,000 |
| | $80,000 |

To the General Fund

| | |
|---|---|
| Balance of Capital Projects Fund terminated upon project completion ................................ | $60,000 |
| Routine annual transfer from a Special Revenue Fund...... | 25,000 |
| | $85,000 |

All of the transfers were paid or received except that from the Special Revenue Fund, which will be paid soon.

7. It was discovered that $2,000 of supplies charged to Police in transaction 4 should be charged to Parks, which is financed through a Special Revenue Fund.

**P 4-8** (GL and SL Entries) Prepare the journal entries to record the following transactions and events either (a) in the General Ledger, Revenues Ledger, and Expenditures Ledger of a Special Revenue Fund of a local independent school district or (b) in detailed General Ledger accounts (with no subsidiary ledgers).

1. The annual operating budget provides for:

Estimated Revenues:

| | |
|---|---|
| State appropriation................................. | $500,000 |
| Property taxes..................................... | 300,000 |
| Other............................................. | 100,000 |
| | $900,000 |

Appropriations:

| | |
|---|---|
| Administration .................................... | $100,000 |
| Instruction....................................... | 750,000 |
| Other............................................. | 40,000 |
| | $890,000 |

2. Purchase orders and contracts for goods and services were approved at estimated costs of:

| | |
|---|---|
| Administration .................................... | $ 15,000 |
| Instruction....................................... | 60,000 |
| Other............................................. | 20,000 |
| | $ 95,000 |

3. Property taxes were levied, $320,000. $15,000 of the taxes are estimated to be uncollectible.
4. Most of the goods and services ordered at 2 arrived and the invoices were approved and vouchered for payment:

| | Encumbered At | Actual Cost |
|---|---|---|
| Administration ....................................... | $15,000 | $14,800 |
| Instruction.......................................... | 40,000 | 40,000 |
| Other............................................... | 20,000 | 20,300 |
| | $75,000 | $75,100 |

5. Cash receipts and year-end revenue accruals were:

|  | Cash Receipts | Year-End Accrued Receivable |
|---|---|---|
| State appropriation | $460,000 | $ 38,000 |
| Current property taxes | 290,000 | — |
| Delinquent property taxes | 15,000 | — |
| Accrued revenue receivable (beginning) | 30,000 | — |
| Other | 41,000 | 2,000 |
|  | $836,000 | $ 40,000 |

6. Cash disbursements, including payment of payroll and other unencumbered expenditures, and year-end expenditure accruals were:

|  | Cash Disbursements | Year-End Accrued Payable |
|---|---|---|
| Administration | $ 84,000 | $ 1,000 |
| Instruction | 700,000 | 8,000 |
| Other | 20,000 | — |
| Accrued expenditures payable (beginning) | 30,000 | — |
|  | $834,000 | $ 9,000 |

7. Interfund transfers were ordered (not yet paid) as follows: (a) $25,000 to the Debt Service Fund to be used to pay general long-term debt principal and interest, and (b) $40,000 from an Internal Service Fund that is being discontinued.
8. It was discovered that $1,500 charged to Instruction (in 6) should be charged to Transportation, which is financed through the General Fund.

**P 4-9, Part I** (General Ledger Entries) The trial balance of the General Fund of the city of Claire on January 1, 19X0, was as follows:

| | | |
|---|---|---|
| Cash | $15,000 | |
| Taxes Receivable—Delinquent | 20,000 | |
| Allowance for Uncollectible Taxes—Delinquent | | $ 3,000 |
| Interest and Penalties Receivable on Taxes | 1,000 | |
| Allowance for Uncollectible Interest and Penalties | | 75 |
| Accounts Receivable | 10,000 | |
| Allowance for Uncollectible Accounts | | 1,000 |
| Vouchers Payable | | 20,500 |
| Reserve for Encumbrances (Assumption A1) | | 10,000 |
| Unreserved Fund Balance | | 11,425 |
| | $46,000 | $46,000 |

The following transactions and events took place during 19X0:
1. Revenues were estimated at $110,000; appropriations of $108,000 were made.
2. An order for materials placed at the end of the preceding year and estimated to cost $10,000 was received; the invoice indicated an actual cost of $9,500.
3. Taxes of $110,000 accrued; an allowance of 5% was made for possible losses.
4. Collections were made as follows:

| | |
|---|---|
| Current Taxes | $90,000 |
| Delinquent Taxes | 10,000 |
| Interest and Penalties Receivable on Taxes | 300 |
| Accounts Receivable | 5,000 |

5. Taxes amounting to $20,000 have become delinquent; the balance of Allowance for Uncollectible Taxes—Current was transferred to Allowance for Uncollectible Taxes—Delinquent.
6. Delinquent taxes amounting to $2,000 were written off; interest and penalties receivable on taxes of $20 were also written off.
7. Orders were placed for (a) materials estimated to cost $20,000 and (b) a truck estimated to cost $8,000.
8. Delinquent taxes amounting to $200, which were written off in preceding years, were collected with interest and penalties of $35 ($25 of which had been previously accrued and written off).
9. Payments were made as follows:

| | |
|---|---|
| Vouchers Payable.................................. | $15,500 |
| Payrolls........................................... | 45,000 |

10. The materials and truck ordered (in 7) were received; bills for $21,000 and $8,000, respectively, were also received.
11. Operating lease payments of $15,000 were paid.
12. Interest of $600 accrued on delinquent taxes, and an allowance for uncollectible losses thereon of 10% was provided.
13. An order was placed for materials estimated to cost $19,000.

*Required* (a) Complete a worksheet headed as follows:

| Columns | Heading |
|---|---|
| 1–2 | Trial Balance, 1/1/19X0 |
| 3–4 | 19X0 Transactions |
| 5–6 | Preclosing Trial Balance, 12/31/19X0 |
| 7–8 | 19X0 Closing Entries |
| 9–10 | Postclosing Trial Balance, 12/31/19X0 |

(b) In lieu of requirement (a) you may:
   1. Post the opening trial balance to T-accounts.
   2. Prepare journal entries.
   3. Post to T-accounts.
   4. Prepare closing entries.
   5. Post to T-accounts.
   6. Prepare a postclosing trial balance at December 31, 19X0.

*Instructor's Note* P 4-9, Part II should be assigned only if P 4-9, Part I also is assigned.

**P 4-9, Part II** (Financial Statements) Based on your solution to P 4-9, Part I, prepare for the city of Claire General Fund:
(a) A statement of revenues, expenditures, and changes in fund balance (total) for the year ended December 31, 19X0.
(b) A balance sheet at December 31, 19X0.

**P 4-10, Part I** (General Ledger Entries) The following is a trial balance of the General Fund of the city of Lynnville as of December 31, 19X0, after closing entries:

| | | |
|---|---|---|
| Cash ............................................. | $33,600 | |
| Taxes Receivable—Delinquent ......................... | 25,400 | |
| Allowance for Uncollectible Delinquent Taxes.............. | | $ 5,900 |
| Accounts Receivable................................. | 15,500 | |
| Allowance for Uncollectible Accounts .................... | | 2,500 |
| Vouchers Payable ................................... | | 42,000 |
| Reserve for Encumbrances............................. | | 16,000 |
| Unreserved Fund Balance ............................. | | 8,100 |
| | $74,500 | $74,500 |

(Because interest and penalties on taxes are not material, they are not accrued.)

The following transactions took place during 19X1:

1. The budget for the year was adopted. Revenues were estimated at $216,000; appropriations of $229,000 were made, including an appropriation of $16,000 for materials ordered in 19X0, covered by the Reserve for Encumbrances.
2. Delinquent taxes of $2,800 were declared uncollectible and written off.
3. Property taxes of $210,000 were levied; a 3% allowance for estimated losses was provided.
4. Uniforms estimated to cost $15,000 were ordered, as was a snowplow estimated to cost $3,500.
5. The materials ordered in 19X0 and set up as an encumbrance of that year for $16,000 were received; the actual cost, $15,000, was vouchered for later payment.
6. Collections were made as follows:

| | |
|---|---:|
| Current Taxes ........................................ | $182,000 |
| Delinquent Taxes ................................... | 8,500 |
| Interest and Penalties on Taxes ....................... | 200 |
| Accounts Receivable ............................... | 7,300 |
| | $198,000 |

7. Received a bill for $3,000 from the city central printing shop.
8. Payroll vouchers for $100,000 were approved and paid, as was a transfer of $38,000 to a Debt Service Fund to cover serial bond debt service.
9. The uniforms and snowplow (ordered in 4) were received; the invoices were for $16,000 and $3,800, respectively.
10. Delinquent taxes of $350, written off in preceding years, were collected.
11. Current taxes receivable became delinquent.
12. Paid $200 to the Special Revenue Fund for supplies acquired for General Fund purposes, but originally paid for from (and recorded as expenditures in) the Special Revenue Fund; and paid $60,000 of vouchers payable.
13. An order was placed for civil defense equipment estimated to cost $24,000.
14. Miscellaneous revenues of $5,000 were collected and $5,000 was received from a discontinued Capital Projects Fund.

*Required*  (a) Complete a worksheet headed as follows:

| Columns | Heading |
|---|---|
| 1–2 | Trial Balance, 1/1/19X1 |
| 3–4 | 19X1 Transactions |
| 5–6 | Preclosing Trial Balance, 12/31/19X1 |
| 7–8 | Closing Entries 12/31/19X1 |
| 9–10 | Postclosing Trial Balance, 12/31/19X1 |

(b) In lieu of requirement (a) you may:
   1. Post the opening trial balance to T-accounts.
   2. Prepare journal entries.
   3. Post to T-accounts.
   4. Prepare preclosing trial balance at December 31, 19X1.
   5. Prepare closing entries.
   6. Post to T-accounts.
   7. Prepare a postclosing trial balance at December 31, 19X1.

*Instructor's Note*  P 4-10, Part II should be assigned only if P 4-10, Part I also is assigned.

**P 4-10, Part II**  (Financial Statements) Based on your solution to P 4-10, Part I, prepare for the city of Lynnville General Fund:
   (a) A statement of revenues, expenditures, and changes in fund balance (total) for the year ended December 31, 19X1.
   (b) A balance sheet at December 31, 19X1.

**P 4-11** (GL and SL Entries) Marcus County adopted the following budget for one of its Special Revenue Funds for the 19X9 fiscal year, its first year in operation:

Revenues:

| | |
|---|---:|
| Property taxes | $500,000 |
| Sales taxes | 200,000 |
| Federal grants | 100,000 |
| Service charges | 80,000 |
| Fines | 50,000 |
| Other | 20,000 |
| | $950,000 |

Expenditures:

| | |
|---|---:|
| Manager | $110,000 |
| Commission | 90,000 |
| Roads and bridges | 400,000 |
| Courts | 60,000 |
| Sheriff | 180,000 |
| Jail | 70,000 |
| Other | 30,000 |
| | 940,000 |
| Budgeted Excess of Revenues over Expenditures | $ 10,000 |

The following transactions and events occurred during 19X9.
1. The property taxes were levied, $530,000, of which $25,000 is expected to be uncollectible.
2. Purchase orders and contracts were approved at the following estimated costs:

| | |
|---|---:|
| Manager | $ 20,000 |
| Roads and bridges | 200,000 |
| Sheriff | 40,000 |
| Jail | 10,000 |
| | $270,000 |

3. The goods and services ordered on these purchase orders and contracts were delivered at the following actual costs which were approved as vouchers payable:

| | |
|---|---:|
| Manager | $ 19,500 |
| Roads and bridges | 200,000 |
| Sheriff | 40,300 |
| Jail | 9,900 |
| | $269,700 |

4. Property taxes collected during 19X9 totaled $503,000. The balance of the uncollected taxes became delinquent.
5. Other cash receipts during 19X9 were:

| | |
|---|---:|
| Sales taxes | $180,000 |
| Federal grants | 106,000 |
| Service charges | 74,000 |
| Fines | 52,000 |
| Other | 18,000 |
| | $430,000 |

6. Cash was disbursed for payroll and other unencumbered expenditures as follows:

| | |
|---|---:|
| Manager........................................... | $ 88,700 |
| Commission........................................ | 84,300 |
| Roads and bridges ................................. | 197,000 |
| Courts ............................................ | 56,000 |
| Sheriff ........................................... | 133,000 |
| Jail .............................................. | 61,500 |
| Other............................................. | 29,500 |
| | $650,000 |

Vouchers payable of $260,000 also were paid.

7. Additional purchase orders and contracts were issued at these estimated costs:

| | |
|---|---:|
| Commission........................................ | $ 4,000 |
| Roads and bridges ................................. | 2,000 |
| Courts ............................................ | 3,700 |
| Sheriff ........................................... | 5,800 |
| | $15,500 |

8. Accrued receivables and payables at year end were:

a. Revenues receivable:

| | |
|---|---:|
| Sales taxes ................................... | $19,000 |
| Service charges................................ | 4,000 |
| Other ......................................... | 1,000 |
| | $24,000 |

b. Expenditures payable:

| | |
|---|---:|
| Manager ...................................... | $ 500 |
| Commission ................................... | 1,200 |
| Other ........................................ | 300 |
| | $ 2,000 |

***Required*** Prepare the journal entries required to record the adoption of the budget and the numbered transactions and events in the General Ledger and in the Revenues and Expenditures Subsidiary Ledgers of the Marcus County Special Revenue Fund for the 19X9 fiscal year. Key the budgetary entry "B" and key the numbered transactions and events by number.

**P 4-12, Part I** (GL Worksheet and SL Accounts)

***Instructor's Note*** This problem may be assigned either as a continuation of or instead of Problem 4-11.

***Required*** Based on the information about the Marcus County Special Revenue Fund in Problem 4-11:
(a) Record the effects of the 19X9 budget adoption and the numbered transactions and events in an appropriate General Ledger worksheet and in Revenues Subsidiary Ledger and Expenditures Subsidiary Ledger accounts.
(b) Prepare the entries to close the accounts at the end of 19X9 and record them on the General Ledger worksheet and in the subsidiary ledger accounts.

**P 4-12, Part II** (Financial Statements; Encumbrances)

***Required*** Based on the solution to Part I of this problem:
(a) Prepare the year end 19X9 Balance Sheet and the Statement of Revenues, Expenditures, and Changes in Fund Balance—Budget and Actual for the 19X9 fiscal year for the Marcus County Special Revenue Fund.
(b) Briefly explain why the actual excess of revenues over expenditures differed from that budgeted.

(c) How would the budgetary comparison statement prepared in part (a) differ if the Marcus County commissioners considered encumbrances equivalent to expenditures for budgetary compliance evaluation purposes?

(d) Prepare the entry necessary to reestablish the encumbrances in the accounts at the beginning of the next year, 19Y0.

**P 4-13** (GL and SL Entries) The trial balance of the General Fund of Mann Independent School District at the beginning of its 19X5 fiscal year was:

|  | Dr. | Cr. |
|---|---|---|
| Cash | $20,000 | |
| Taxes Receivable—Delinquent | 15,000 | |
| Allowance for Uncollectible Delinquent Taxes | | $ 8,000 |
| Accrued Receivables | 43,000 | |
| Vouchers Payable | | 12,000 |
| Accrued Payables | | 10,000 |
| Unreserved Fund Balance | | 48,000 |
| | $78,000 | $78,000 |

The following transactions and events affected the Mann Independent School District General Fund during 19X5:

1. The annual budget (GAAP basis) adopted provided for:

Estimated Revenues:

| Property taxes | $400,000 |
|---|---|
| State assistance | 300,000 |
| Federal grants | 200,000 |
| Other | 50,000 |
| | 950,000 |

Appropriations:

| Administration | 100,000 |
|---|---|
| Instruction | 700,000 |
| Maintenance | 90,000 |
| Other | 55,000 |
| | 945,000 |
| Planned Increase in Fund Balance | $ 5,000 |

2. Property taxes totaling $420,000 were levied. $15,000 were expected to prove uncollectible.

3. Cash receipts during 19X5 and additional accrued receivables at the end of 19X5 were as follows:

| | Cash Receipts | Accrued at End of 19X5 |
|---|---|---|
| Property taxes—current | $391,000 | $ — |
| Property taxes—delinquent | 6,000 | — |
| State assistance | 260,000 | 38,000 |
| Federal grants | 190,000 | 14,000 |
| Other | 47,000 | — |
| Accrued receivables (beginning) | 43,000 | — |
| | $937,000 | $52,000 |

4. Delinquent property taxes totaling $16,000 were written off during 19X5 by action of the school board, and the uncollected current property taxes became delinquent at year end.

5. Purchase orders and contracts were issued and related goods and services were delivered and vouchered as payable as follows:

| | Orders and Contracts | Goods and Services Received | |
| --- | --- | --- | --- |
| | Encumbered For | Encumbered For | Actual Cost |
| Administration ................... | $ 20,000 | $ 15,000 | $ 14,800 |
| Instruction ...................... | 80,000 | 80,000 | 79,200 |
| Maintenance ..................... | 50,000 | 50,000 | 50,000 |
| Other ........................... | 25,000 | 21,000 | 21,500 |
| | $175,000 | $166,000 | $165,500 |

6. Cash disbursements—for payroll, other unencumbered expenditures, and vouchers payable—during 19X5 and additional accrued expenditures at the end of 19X5 were as follows:

| | Cash Disbursements | Accrued at End of 19X5 |
| --- | --- | --- |
| Administration ................................. | $ 79,000 | — |
| Instruction .................................... | 617,000 | 2,800 |
| Maintenance ................................... | 38,000 | 2,700 |
| Other .......................................... | 27,000 | 2,000 |
| Vouchers Payable .............................. | 163,000 | — |
| Accrued Payables (beginning) ................... | 10,000 | — |
| | $934,000 | $7,500 |

**Required** Prepare the journal entries to record the numbered transactions and events in the General Ledger, Revenues Subsidiary Ledger, and Expenditures Subsidiary Ledger.

**P 4-14, Part I** (GL Worksheet and SL Accounts)

***Instructor's Note*** This problem may be assigned either as a continuation of or instead of Problem 4-13.

**Required** Based on the information about the General Fund of the Mann Independent School District in Problem 4-13:

(a) Record the beginning trial balance and the numbered transactions and events in an appropriate General Ledger worksheet and in Revenues Subsidiary Ledger and Expenditures Subsidiary Ledger accounts.

(b) Prepare the entry or entries to close the accounts at the end of 19X5 and record it (them) on the General Ledger worksheet and in the subsidiary ledger accounts. (The Reserve for Encumbrances should become a true reservation of fund balance.)

**P 4-14, Part II** (Financial Statements; Encumbrances)

**Required** (a) Prepare a Statement of Revenues, Expenditures, and Changes in Fund Balance—Budget and Actual—for the General Fund of Mann Independent School District for the 19X5 fiscal year and a balance sheet as of the end of 19X5.

(b) How would the Statement of Revenues, Expenditures, and Changes in Fund Balance—Budget and Actual differ from (a) if the Mann Independent School District budgetary basis considered both encumbrances and expenditures to be uses of appropriation authority?

(c) Prepare the entry to reestablish encumbrances in the accounts at the beginning of 19X6.

**P 4-15** (GL and SL Entries; Statements) The following financial activities affecting Judbury City's General Fund took place during the year ended June 30, 19X1:

1. The following budget was adopted:

Estimated revenues:

| | |
|---|---:|
| Property taxes | $4,500,000 |
| Licenses and permits | 300,000 |
| Fines | 200,000 |
| Total | $5,000,000 |

Appropriations:

| | |
|---|---:|
| General government | $1,500,000 |
| Police services | 1,200,000 |
| Fire department services | 900,000 |
| Public works services | 800,000 |
| Acquisition of fire engines | 400,000 |
| Total | $4,800,000 |

2. Property tax bills totaling $4,650,000 were mailed. It was estimated that $300,000 of this amount will be delinquent, and $150,000 will be uncollectible.
3. Property taxes totaling $3,900,000 were collected. The $150,000 previously estimated to be uncollectible remained unchanged, but $750,000 was reclassified as delinquent. It is estimated that delinquent taxes will be collected soon enough after June 30, 19X1, to make these taxes available to finance obligations incurred during the year ended June 30, 19X1. There was no balance of uncollected taxes at July 1, 19X0.
4. Tax anticipation notes in the face amount of $300,000 were issued.
5. Other cash collections were as follows:

| | |
|---|---:|
| Licenses and permits | $270,000 |
| Fines | 200,000 |
| Sale of public works equipment (original cost, $75,000) | 15,000 |
| Total | $485,000 |

6. The following purchase orders were executed:

| | Total | Outstanding at 6/30/X1 |
|---|---:|---:|
| General government | $1,050,000 | $ 60,000 |
| Police services | 300,000 | 30,000 |
| Fire department services | 150,000 | 15,000 |
| Public works services | 250,000 | 10,000 |
| Fire engines | 400,000 | — |
| Totals | $2,150,000 | $115,000 |

No encumbrances were outstanding at June 30, 19X0.

7. The following vouchers were approved:

| | |
|---|---:|
| General government | $1,440,000 |
| Police services | 1,155,000 |
| Fire department services | 870,000 |
| Public works services | 700,000 |
| Fire engines | 400,000 |
| Totals | $4,565,000 |

8. Vouchers totaling $4,600,000 were paid.

**Required** (a) Prepare journal entries to record the foregoing financial activities in the General Fund General Ledger and in the Revenues and Expenditures Subsidiary Ledgers. Omit explanations. Ignore interest accruals.

(b) Prepare a Statement of Revenues, Expenditures, and Changes in Fund Balance for the General Fund of Judbury City for the fiscal year ended June 30, 19X1. Assume that the beginning total fund balance was $80,000. (AICPA, adapted)

**P 4-16** (Statement of Revenues, Expenditures, and Changes in Fund Balance) Using the following information, prepare the Statement of Revenues, Expenditures, and Changes in (Total) Fund Balance for the city of Nancy General Fund for the fiscal year ended December 31, 19X1.

1. Unreserved Fund Balance, January 1, 19X1, was $150,000.
2. Fund balance reserves, January 1, 19X1, were for:

| | |
|---|---:|
| Encumbrances........................................ | $25,000 |
| Advances........................................... | 50,000 |

The advance is due in 19X2.

3. Revenues for 19X1 totaled $2,500,000, including:

| | |
|---|---:|
| Property taxes...................................... | $1,800,000 |
| Licenses and permits ............................... | 190,000 |
| Intergovernmental revenues .......................... | 310,000 |
| Proceeds from short-term note ....................... | 50,000 |
| Other.............................................. | 150,000 |

Other revenues include $40,000 received from a Capital Projects Fund upon completion of the project and termination of the fund and a $65,000 routine annual transfer from the city's Water Enterprise Fund.

4. Expenditures for 19X1 totaled $2,600,000, including:

| | |
|---|---:|
| General government................................. | $ 800,000 |
| Public safety ...................................... | 1,000,000 |
| Highways and streets ............................... | 600,000 |
| Health and sanitation............................... | 150,000 |
| Other.............................................. | 50,000 |

Included in the public safety expenditures is $85,000 for the estimated cost of a fire truck that has been ordered but not received. A second truck costing $55,000 was received during 19X1.

Also, the highways and streets expenditures include $42,000 for work contracted out to independent contractors but not performed as of year end.

**P 4-17** (Statement of Revenues, Expenditures, and Changes in Fund Balance) The following information regarding the fiscal year ended December 31, 19X4 was drawn from the accounts and records of the Reach City General Fund.

Cash Receipts:

| | |
|---|---:|
| Taxes ............................................. | $5,000,000 |
| Licenses and fees .................................. | 1,000,000 |
| Intergovernmental grants............................ | 2,000,000 |
| Fines and forfeits .................................. | 1,000,000 |
| Short-term note issuances .......................... | 3,000,000 |
| Long-term note issuances............................ | 8,000,000 |
| Collection of interfund advance to other fund........ | 3,500,000 |
| Net assets of terminated Capital Projects Fund ...... | 800,000 |

Cash Disbursements:

| | |
|---|---:|
| Salaries and wages . . . . . . . . . . . . . . . . . . . . . . . . . . . . . . . . . . . . | $4,000,000 |
| Consulting services . . . . . . . . . . . . . . . . . . . . . . . . . . . . . . . . . . . | 750,000 |
| Material and supplies . . . . . . . . . . . . . . . . . . . . . . . . . . . . . . . . . . | 1,000,000 |
| Equipment purchases . . . . . . . . . . . . . . . . . . . . . . . . . . . . . . . . . . | 3,500,000 |
| Short-term note retirements . . . . . . . . . . . . . . . . . . . . . . . . . . . | 2,800,000 |
| Interest on short-term notes . . . . . . . . . . . . . . . . . . . . . . . . . . . | 200,000 |
| Interest on long-term notes . . . . . . . . . . . . . . . . . . . . . . . . . . . . | 400,000 |
| Paid to Debt Service Fund to provide for required payments for bonded debt . . . . . . . . . . . . . . . . . . . . . . . . . . . . . . . . . . . | 1,200,000 |
| Purchases of services from Enterprise and Internal Service Fund departments. . . . . . . . . . . . . . . . . . . . . . . . . . . . . . . . . . . | 2,300,000 |
| Payments of compensated absences . . . . . . . . . . . . . . . . . . . . . . | 1,500,000 |

***Other Information***
1. Taxes receivable decreased by $80,000 during the year. 19X3 taxes of $75,000 were collected in January and February of 19X4. 19X4 taxes of $95,000 were collected in January and February 19X5.
2. Unpaid interest on short-term notes at the end of 19X4 was $18,000; at the end of 19X3, it was $10,000.
3. Unmatured interest incurred to date on long-term notes at the end of 19X4 was $100,000; at the end of 19X3 it was zero.
4. Due to other funds (for services purchased) increased by $50,000 during the year.
5. The liability for compensated absences (all long term) increased by $900,000 during the year.
6. Salaries and wages payable was $200,000 less at year end than at the beginning of the year.
7. The inventory of materials and supplies did not change during the fiscal year. Accounts payable for materials and supplies increased by $50,000 during the year.
8. The beginning balance of unreserved fund balance was $4,000,000. The beginning balance of the fund balance reserved for advances was $3,500,000 and that of the reserve for encumbrances, $1,000,000. Encumbrances outstanding at the end of the fiscal year amounted to $850,000.

***Required*** Prepare the GAAP-basis Statement of Revenues, Expenditures, and Changes in Fund Balance for the Reach City General Fund for the fiscal year ended December 31, 19X4. The statement should be in proper form and supporting computations should be included in an easy-to-follow manner.

**P 4-18** (Research) Obtain copies of the General Fund and Special Revenue Funds financial statements from a state or local government, the Internet, your professor, a library, or elsewhere.

***Required*** (a) Study the General Fund financial statements and compare them with those discussed and illustrated in this chapter, noting
   (1) similarities,
   (2) differences, and
   (3) other matters that come to your attention, such as formats and accounts not discussed in the text.
(b) Study the Special Revenue Fund financial statements, noting
   (1) the nature and purpose of each fund, and
   (2) the similarities, differences, and other matters as in requirement (a).
(c) Prepare a brief report on requirements (a) and (b), including photocopies or printouts of unusual or otherwise interesting presentations, explanations, and the like.
(d) Submit your financial statements also if requested by your instructor.

# CHAPTER

# 5

# REVENUE ACCOUNTING— GOVERNMENTAL FUNDS

Revenue accounting in government parallels that for business enterprises in many respects. In both, revenues must be distinguished from nonrevenue resource inflows, and accounting guidelines have been established regarding the timing of revenue recognition. Proprietary fund revenue recognition is virtually identical to that in business accounting.

Significant differences and unique considerations are also involved, however, particularly in revenue accounting for governmental (expendable) funds. These differences and special considerations are the principal focus of this chapter. Specifically, this chapter addresses

1. The definition of revenue in the governmental environment and the revenue recognition criteria used;
2. Classification of revenue accounts;
3. Accounting for revenue sources that are unique to governments, such as taxes and intergovernmental grants; and
4. Other revenue-related accounting topics, including budget revisions, changes in accounting principles, and restatements.

The discussions and illustrations in this chapter focus primarily on GAAP-basis revenue accounting and reporting. Thus, as in Chapter 4, we assume that the SLG governmental fund budgetary basis is the GAAP basis, except where noted otherwise, and that the governmental fund revenue accounts are maintained on (or near) the GAAP basis during the year. Non-GAAP budgetary basis accounting and reporting, including adjustment of non-GAAP revenue account data to the GAAP basis, are discussed and illustrated in Chapter 14.

## REVENUE DEFINITION AND RECOGNITION

Governmental fund revenues are increases in the net assets of a governmental fund that either

a. result in a corresponding increase in the net assets of the governmental unit as a whole, *or*
b. result from quasi-external interfund transactions.

Revenues may be operationally defined in a governmental fund accounting context as all increases in fund net assets except those arising from interfund reimbursements, interfund operating and residual equity transfers, sale of or compensation for loss of fixed assets, or long-term debt issues.

Governments have a wide variety of revenue sources. Some revenues, such as property taxes, are levied in known amounts prior to collection and uncollectible amounts usually can be estimated with reasonable accuracy. Such revenues are recorded on the modified accrual basis, as are other revenues billed by the government. On the other hand, it often is not practicable to accrue other types of government revenues. For example, sales taxes theoretically accrue to the government as retail merchants sell goods and collect sales taxes on behalf of the government. But the government does not know the amount of the sales taxes until merchants file sales tax returns. Thus, sales tax revenues usually cannot be accrued prior to receipt of the sales tax returns, which normally coincides with payment of the taxes due. Similarly, the amounts of self-assessed income taxes and business licenses are not known prior to receipt of the tax return or license application by the government, and typically are not accrued until then.

The modified accrual basis of governmental fund revenue recognition takes into account the diverse government revenue sources and the varying degrees to which government revenues can be recorded on the accrual basis. Under the modified accrual basis, only those revenues that are susceptible to accrual are recognized on the accrual basis; others are recognized on the cash basis or are recorded initially as deferred revenues.

Revenues are considered *susceptible to accrual* if they are both (1) objectively measurable and (2) available to finance current period expenditures. An item is available only if it

**a.** is legally available (usable) to finance current period expenditures *and*

**b.** is collected in the current period or soon enough thereafter to be used to pay liabilities of the current period. (This cut-off period for revenue recognition is typically limited to a 60-day maximum.)

Revenues are legally available if the government's legal claim to the resources has been established by the end of the period and the resources were raised for the purpose of financing the expenditures of the current period or prior periods. A government's legal claim to revenues is established in different ways depending upon the nature of the revenues.

- For taxes assessed by a government, the tax levy establishes the government's claim to the resources.
- A government's claim to charges for services of general government departments is established by performing the service.
- Its claim to sales taxes is established by a business making a taxable sale.
- Its claim to income taxes results from taxpayers earning taxable income.

Taxes collected before the year for which they are levied or that will not be collected until a later year are recorded initially as *deferred revenues,* a liability. Unearned revenues such as restricted grants that are received before qualifying expenditures are made also are recorded as deferred revenues. Thus, governmental fund revenues are recognized conservatively on a cash or near cash approach under the modified accrual basis.

The GASB notes that application of the susceptibility to accrual criteria requires (1) judgment, (2) consideration of the materiality of the item in question, (3) due regard for the practicality of accrual, and (4) consistency in application.[1] In commenting further on revenue accrual the GASB observes that:

> . . . some revenues are assessed and collected in such a manner that they can appropriately be accrued, whereas others cannot. Revenues and other increases in governmental fund financial resources that usually can and should be recorded on the accrual [modified accrual] basis include property taxes, regularly billed charges for inspection or other routinely provided services, most grants from other governments, interfund transfers and other transactions, and sales and income taxes where taxpayer liability has been established and collectibility is assured or losses can be reasonably estimated.[2]

The GASB also states:

> The susceptibility to accrual of the various revenue sources of a governmental unit may differ significantly. Likewise, the susceptibility to accrual of similar revenue sources (for example, property taxes) differs among governmental units. Thus, each governmental unit should [1] adopt revenue accounting policies that appropriately implement the susceptibility to accrual criteria, [2] apply them consistently, and [3] disclose them in the Summary of Significant Accounting Policies.[3]

Applying the susceptibility to accrual criteria—particularly the availability criterion—often proves difficult in practice. Application of the criteria is discussed further at several points in this chapter and in later chapters dealing with specific governmental fund types.

## CLASSIFICATION OF REVENUE ACCOUNTS

A chart of accounts is designed to provide a vehicle for summarizing information in a useful form. Revenues are classified by source in the accounts in order to produce information that management may use to (1) prepare and control the budget, (2) control the collection of revenues, (3) prepare financial statements and schedules for reporting to the public, and (4) prepare financial statistics. The revenue accounts provide the basic data for revenue reports used for all these purposes.

### General Fund Revenues

The following typically are the main revenue source classes for a city or county General Fund:

- **Taxes** (including property, sales, income, and other taxes; penalties and interest on delinquent taxes)
- **Licenses and permits**
- **Intergovernmental revenues** (including grants, shared revenues, and payments by other governments in lieu of taxes)
- **Charges for services** (for general government activities)

---

[1] GASB *Codification,* sec. 1600.106.
[2] Ibid., sec. 1600.107.
[3] Ibid., sec. 1600.108.

- **Fines and forfeits**
- **Miscellaneous revenues** (including interest earnings, rents and royalties, contributions in lieu of taxes from the government's enterprise fund activities, escheats, and contributions and donations from private sources)

The preceding classes are not account titles. Rather, they are broad revenue source categories that are useful for reporting purposes just as Current Assets and Fixed Assets are category groupings on the balance sheet of a private enterprise. For example, though we do so for illustrative purposes, no account would be set up for fines and forfeits. Instead, individual accounts would be provided for each type of revenue falling in that class, including court fines, library fines, and forfeits. The total revenues accrued or received from fines and forfeits would be the sum of the balances of these accounts.

## Revenues of Other Funds

The revenue classes described for the General Fund also are suitable for the other governmental funds of a governmental unit. For example, taxes may be a revenue source of Special Revenue Funds and Debt Service Funds, and interest earnings are likely to be a revenue source of all governmental funds. Clearly, no other fund is likely to have as many different revenue sources as the General Fund. Enterprise and Internal Service Funds use revenue accounts and revenue recognition principles similar to those of business enterprises.

## Revenues of a Fund versus Revenues of the Governmental Unit

A distinction must be made between the revenues of a fund and the revenues of the governmental unit as a whole. As noted earlier, interfund transfers and reimbursements are not reported as revenues. However, quasi-external transaction receipts or accruals are reported as fund revenues even though they are not revenues of the governmental unit. To illustrate, charges for services rendered to departments financed out of the General Fund are revenues of the Internal Service Fund but not of the governmental unit as a whole because these charges must be paid from the General Fund. Quasi-external transactions are the only instance where fund revenues (and related expenditures or expenses, as appropriate) should be recognized when they are not revenues of the government as a whole.

In classifying revenues for the purpose of statewide or national financial statistics, only those revenues of the governmental unit as a whole should be included. Ideally, any material amounts arising from quasi-external transactions would be eliminated.

This chapter is concerned with accounting for the principal revenue sources of the General Fund, Special Revenue Funds, and other governmental funds. Those types of revenues that are peculiar to another fund type are discussed in the chapter on that fund type.

## TAXES

As noted earlier, taxes are forced contributions to a government to meet public needs. Typically, the amount of a tax bears no direct relationship to any benefit received by the taxpayer.

The amount of any tax is computed by applying a rate or rates set by the governmental unit to a defined base, such as value of property, amount of income, or number of units. From the standpoint of administration, taxes may be divided into two groups—those that are **taxpayer assessed** and those that are **levied.** For the levied group the governmental unit establishes the amount of the tax base to which the rate or rates will be applied. The general property tax on real property and personal property is the chief representative of this group. Taxes on income, inheritance, severance of natural resources, gasoline, general sales, tobacco, alcoholic beverages, and chain stores are taxpayer assessed (also called self-assessed). For these taxes, the taxpayer is expected to determine the amount of the tax base, apply the proper rate or rates thereto, and submit the payment with the return that shows the computation.

## Taxpayer-Assessed Taxes

When taxpayers assess their own tax, verifying the amount of tax requires (1) determining that the tax base has been properly reported by the taxpayer and (2) determining that the proper rates have been applied accurately to the tax base to arrive at the total amount of the tax. The first is the most difficult problem. For example, for income taxes this requires ascertaining that all income that should have been reported has been reported. Furthermore, investigations should *not* be limited to those taxpayers who file returns. The governmental unit must also make certain that all taxpayers who should pay taxes have filed returns.

The GASB notes with regard to taxpayer-assessed taxes that:

> Revenues from taxpayer-assessed taxes, such as sales and income taxes, net of estimated refunds, should be recognized in the accounting period in which they become susceptible to accrual—that is, when they become both measurable and available to finance expenditures of the fiscal period. . . .[4]

In practice, taxpayer-assessed taxes usually are accounted for on a cash basis because the return and the remittance are ordinarily received at the same time. Furthermore, there may be no objectively measurable basis upon which to set up accruals because the amount of tax is not known before the return is filed.

Furthermore, the GASB states with respect to sales taxes that:

> Sales taxes collected by merchants but not yet required to be remitted to the taxing authority at the end of the fiscal year and taxes collected and held by one government agency for another at year-end should be accrued if they are to be remitted in time to be used as a resource for payment of obligations incurred during the preceding fiscal year.[5]

Being remitted "in time" to be used to pay liabilities for current operations is not defined by the GASB but is generally considered to mean collected by the government during the year or within not more than 60 days after year end.

Finally, the GASB indicates that year-to-year comparability should be considered in determining whether to recognize sales taxes and other self-assessed revenues:

> . . . material revenues otherwise not recorded until received should be accrued if receipt is delayed beyond the normal time of receipt. . . . Material revenues received prior to the normal time of receipt should be recorded as deferred revenue.[6]

---

[4] Ibid., sec. 1600.110.

[5] Ibid., sec. 1600.111.

[6] Ibid., secs. 1600.116 and 1600.117.

Many cities, counties, and states with income taxes have continually improved their ability to reasonably estimate income tax revenues for the year and the related income tax receivables and refund liabilities. Although this is often an extremely difficult task, the GASB requires income tax revenues of governmental funds to be recognized in the period that the measurability and availability criteria are first met. In some jurisdictions income tax returns are filed at a specified time and the tax is paid currently in installments. In such a case, because the amount of the tax is known, the receivables are accrued and revenue (or deferred revenue) is reported as soon as the return is filed.

Some taxes require the attachment of stamps to an article to indicate that the tax has been paid. For example, liquor taxes and tobacco taxes are frequently paid through the purchase of stamps to be affixed to bottles or packages. In such cases the taxes are considered to be revenue as soon as the stamps are sold to the manufacturer, dealer, or other business, even though the articles to which the stamps are affixed may not be sold for an indefinite period following the purchase of the tax stamps.

## Property Taxes

Property taxes are ad valorem taxes in proportion to the assessed valuation of real or personal property. The procedure for administering general property taxes is as follows: (1) The assessed valuation of each piece of real property and of the taxable personal property of each taxpayer is determined by the local tax assessor; (2) a local board of review hears complaints regarding assessments; (3) county and state boards of equalization assign equalized values to taxing districts; (4) the legislative body levies the total amount of taxes it needs, but not in excess of the amount permitted by law; (5) the tax levy is distributed among taxpayers on the basis of the assessed value of property owned by them; (6) taxpayers are billed; (7) tax collections are credited to taxpayers' accounts; and (8) tax collections are enforced by the imposition of penalties, interest, and the sale of property for taxes. Each of these steps in general property tax administration is discussed briefly in the following sections.

### Assessment of Property

Valuing property for purposes of taxation is called assessment. Assessment of property for local taxes usually is performed by an elected or appointed official known as an assessor. The **assessed value** of each piece of real property or of the personal property of every taxpayer is recorded on an assessment roll. The tax roll of real property typically contains columns entitled:

Taxpayer's Name and General Description of Property

Block and Lot Number

Value of Land

Value of Improvements

Total Assessed Valuation

Not all real and personal property in the jurisdiction of a government will be subject to real or personal property assessment and taxation. Properties owned by governments and religious organizations usually are exempt from such taxes and are referred to as exempt properties.

On the other hand, several governmental units with overlapping jurisdictions, such as a state, county, city, and school district, may tax many of the same pieces of property. Ordinarily only one of these jurisdictions will have the assessment responsibility, and separate assessment rolls are prepared for each of the governmental units for the property within its jurisdiction.

### Review of Assessment

Individual property owners are notified of the assessments on their properties and are permitted to protest (appeal) the assessments to a local reviewing board. This board may be composed of officials of the government or of other residents of the governmental unit. The board hears objections to assessments, weighs the evidence, and changes the assessments if deemed appropriate. Taxpayers may appeal the board action to the courts.

### Equalization of Assessments

In most states the assessment of property is made by a local government. The taxes of the state and perhaps even the county are, therefore, levied on the basis of assessments made by a number of different assessors. Each assessor may have different ideas as to the valuations that should be assigned to property. The law usually requires that the assessment be the equivalent of *fair market value* in the accountant's terminology, but in practice the actual valuations in a state or even a county will cover a wide range of percentages of market value. Lack of equalization or poor equalization leads to competitive underassessment in the several assessing districts and to widespread dissatisfaction with the property tax as a revenue source. Thus, both state and county equalization boards may attempt to ensure that assessments are made equitably—that is, at fair market value or at the same percentage of fair market value—among and within the counties.

### Levying the Tax

Taxes are levied through the passage of a tax levy act or ordinance, usually passed at the time the appropriation act or ordinance is passed. The levy is ordinarily applicable to only one year.

Tax levies vary in detail and restrictiveness. Some governments levy taxes in one or two lump sums for unrestricted general government purposes or perhaps also for one or two broad specified purposes (e.g., schools). Other tax levies are very detailed and restricted. A statute or even a charter may require that certain taxes are to be levied for specific identified purposes. In that event the legislative body must indicate specifically the amount levied for each purpose. Another effect of detailed tax levies is to require the creation of Special Revenue Funds. For example, if a special levy is made for parks, a Special Revenue Fund for parks normally must be established to ensure that the taxes collected are used only for parks.[7]

---

[7] Recall that the GASB *Codification* (sec. 1300.107) states that "use of special revenue funds is not required unless they are legally mandated." Property tax authorization legislation typically specifies that a separate fund be maintained, and many accountants feel that Special Revenue Funds are needed to assure sound financial administration of restricted property taxes even if not legally mandated.

**Determining the Tax Rate**     The tax rate is determined by dividing the amount of taxes levied by the assessed valuation. Thus, if a government has an assessed valuation of $10,000,000 and its total tax levy is $250,000, the tax rate is 2.5% of, or 25 **mills** per dollar ($0.025) of, assessed value ($250,000 ÷ $10,000,000). The total tax rate consists of the tax rate for general purposes and special tax rates, if any, for particular purposes. For example, if we assume that the total levy of $250,000 consisted of $150,000 for general purposes, $10,000 for parks, $50,000 for schools, and $40,000 for debt service, the tax rates would be as follows:

| *Purpose* | *Rate* (mills per dollar of assessed value) |
|---|---|
| General | 15 |
| Parks | 1 |
| Schools | 5 |
| Debt Service | 4 |
| | 25 |

Maximum tax rates are frequently prescribed for governmental units by the constitution, statutes, or charters. The legislative body must recognize such limitations as it plans the total levy. If the amount the legislative body would like to produce from the tax will require a rate higher than the maximum permitted by law, the amount of the levy must be reduced. When a government finds itself thus limited in the amount of taxes it can levy, it would ordinarily review the assessment process in the hope that the total assessed valuation, the tax base, could be increased.

**Determining the Amount Due from Each Taxpayer**     The amount of tax due from each taxpayer is derived by multiplying the assessed value of the taxpayer's property by the tax rate. For example, a taxpayer who owns real estate with an assessed value of $8,000 during a year when the city tax rate is 25 mills per dollar of assessed value will owe taxes of $200 ($8,000 × 0.025).

### Setting Up Taxes Receivable and Billing Taxpayers

As soon as the amount due from each taxpayer is determined, it is entered on the tax roll.

**The Tax Roll**     A tax roll is a record showing the amount of taxes levied against each piece of real property and against each owner of personal property. The tax roll provides a record of each parcel of real or personal property—including its assessed value, taxes levied against the property, and property tax collections and balances owed with respect to the property. The tax roll also serves as a subsidiary ledger supporting the Taxes Receivable control accounts in the General Ledger. If interest and penalties on delinquent taxes are accrued at the end of each year, provision is made for showing the accruals.

**Recording Taxes in the Accounts**     Some of the entries to record taxes in the accounts were introduced in Chapter 4. For example, when taxes are levied, the usual entry in each fund is a debit to Taxes Receivable—Current and credits to Allowance for Uncollectible Current Taxes and to Revenues. (If the tax is levied prior to the year to which it applies, a Deferred Revenues account is credited initially.) Later, if the taxes become delinquent, a reclassification entry is made debiting Taxes Receivable—Delinquent and Allowance for Uncollectible Current Taxes and crediting Taxes Receivable—Current and Allowance for Uncollectible Delinquent Taxes. This latter entry essentially renames the receivables and related allowance balances to indicate the delinquent (past due) status of the receivables.

Separate Taxes Receivable accounts should be set up for each kind of taxes, such as real property taxes, personal property taxes, and income taxes that may have been accrued. Furthermore, all these taxes should be recorded in a way that identifies the amount applicable to each year. One way to accomplish this objective is to set up control accounts for each kind of taxes receivable by years.

Because the proportion of the total tax levy made for each purpose may vary from year to year, each year's levy must be identified so that the proper Taxes Receivable accounts may be credited and the cash collected may be allocated to the proper fund(s). For example, suppose that the property tax levy is $100,000 both for this year and for last year but that the levies are divided as follows:

| Fund | This Year Amount Levied | This Year Percentage of Total | Last Year Amount Levied | Last Year Percentage of Total |
|---|---|---|---|---|
| General Fund................. | $ 46,700 | 46.7 | $ 40,000 | 40.0 |
| Parks Fund.................... | 13,300 | 13.3 | 13,300 | 13.3 |
| School Fund.................. | 26,700 | 26.7 | 33,400 | 33.4 |
| Debt Service Fund ............ | 13,300 | 13.3 | 13,300 | 13.3 |
| | $100,000 | 100.00 | $100,000 | 100.00 |

The General Fund portion of the proceeds of this year's tax levy is found by multiplying the amount collected from the levy by 46.7%. Thus, if $90,000 of this year's taxes is collected, $42,030 is allocated to the General Fund ($90,000 × 46.7%). On the other hand, the amount of collections from last year's levy that is for General Fund purposes is obtained by multiplying the collections from that levy by 40%. For example, if collections of last year's taxes total $10,000, $4,000 ($10,000 × 40%) is for the General Fund. Collections from other years' levies are allocated to the proper funds in the same manner.

### Recording Tax Collections

Assume that the preceding $100,000 property tax levy was for 19Y0 and that the delinquent receivables and related allowance are as follows:

Property Taxes Receivable—Delinquent:

| | |
|---|---|
| Levy of 19X9 ........................................ | $30,000 |
| 19X8 ........................................... | 20,000 |
| 19X7 ........................................... | 10,000 |
| 19X6 ........................................... | 5,000 |
| 19X5 and prior ................................... | 3,000 |
| | 68,000 |
| Less: Allowance for Uncollectible Delinquent Taxes .......... | 10,000 |
| | $58,000 |

As taxes are collected, the entry in the recipient fund is as follows:

| | | |
|---|---|---|
| Cash.................................................. | $100,000 | |
| Taxes Receivable—Current ............................ | | $80,000 |
| Taxes Receivable—Delinquent ......................... | | 20,000 |

To record collection of current and delinquent taxes in the following assumed amounts:

| Year of Levy | Amount |
|---|---|
| 19Y0 ............................ | $ 80,000 |
| 19X9 ............................ | 10,000 |
| 19X8 ............................ | 5,000 |
| 19X7 ............................ | 3,000 |
| 19X6 ............................ | 1,000 |
| 19X5 ............................ | 500 |
| 19X4 ............................ | 500 |
| | $100,000 |

**Collection of a Government's Taxes by Another Unit**     Frequently, one governmental unit acts as collecting agent for other units. In that case, each governmental unit certifies its tax levy to the collecting unit, which in turn bills the taxpayers. The collecting unit accounts for these taxes is an Agency Fund, which is discussed in Chapter 10.

The accounting procedures outlined thus far for governmental units that collect their own taxes also apply to those that do not. In the latter case the collecting unit transmits a report indicating the amount collected for each year's levy of real property taxes and of personal property taxes. The receiving unit, on the basis of this report, distributes the proceeds among the various funds and credits the proper General Ledger accounts. However, a governmental unit that does not collect its own taxes does not prepare a tax roll and probably does not keep a record of the amounts paid or owed by the individual taxpayers. Those records are kept for it by the collecting governmental unit.

**Discounts on Taxes**     Some governmental units allow discounts on taxes paid before a certain date. These discounts usually are considered as **revenue deductions** rather than interest expenditures. An Allowance for Discounts on Taxes account should be established and the tax revenues recognized should equal only the net amount of the tax. For example, a tax levy of $300,000, including $9,000 expected to be uncollectible and $2,000 of discounts expected to be taken, would be recorded as follows:

| | | |
|---|---|---|
| Taxes Receivable—Current................................ | $300,000 | |
| Allowance for Uncollectible Current Taxes ................ | | $ 9,000 |
| **Allowance for Discounts on Taxes** ...................... | | 2,000 |
| Revenues......................................... | | 289,000 |

To record levy of taxes, estimated uncollectible taxes, and estimated discounts to be taken.

Revenues Ledger (Revenues):

| | |
|---|---|
| Taxes ................................................. | $289,000 |

As taxes are collected and discounts are taken, the discounts are charged against the Allowance for Discounts on Taxes account. For example, tax collections of $150,000 and discounts taken of $1,500 are recorded as:

| | | |
|---|---|---|
| Cash............................................... | $150,000 | |
| Allowance for Discounts on Taxes ........................ | 1,500 | |
| Taxes Receivable—Current ............................. | | $151,500 |

To record collection of taxes net of discounts.

When the discount period expires, the following entry is made:

| | | |
|---|---|---|
| Allowance for Discounts on Taxes ........................ | $500 | |
| Revenues........................................ | | $500 |

To record increase in revenues by amount of estimated discounts
which were not taken.

Revenues Ledger (Revenues):

| | |
|---|---|
| Taxes ........................................... | $500 |

When discounts taken exceed the balance of the Allowance for Discounts on Taxes
account, the excess is debited to Revenues.

**Taxes Levied But Not Available**     In some governments taxes are levied in one
year but are not available, and hence not revenue, in that year. Revenue recognition
is deferred when either (1) the taxes were levied to finance the next year's operations and, thus, are not legally available in the year of levy, or (2) the taxes will not be
collected until well into the next period and, thus, are not available to finance
current-year expenditures.[8] The entry upon levy of taxes in either case would be:

| | | |
|---|---|---|
| Taxes Receivable—Current............................... | $100,000 | |
| Allowance for Uncollectible Current Taxes ................ | | $ 3,000 |
| Deferred Revenues.................................... | | 97,000 |

To record levy of taxes not available to finance current-period
expenditures.

At the beginning of the next period the deferred revenues would be reclassified as
revenues by the following entry:

| | | |
|---|---|---|
| Deferred Revenues .................................... | $97,000 | |
| Revenues........................................ | | $97,000 |

To record the taxes levied last period becoming available.

Revenues Ledger (Revenues):

| | |
|---|---|
| Taxes ........................................... | $97,000 |

Deferred revenues for property taxes may also need to be recorded in the
year-end adjusting entry process. Whenever a government records the property tax
levy under the assumption that the revenues are available—as in the illustrative
example in Chapter 4—the related amounts in the preclosing trial balance (Figure
4–3) should be examined to determine whether significant amounts are not available at year end. The amount of the current property tax levy that has been
recorded as revenues during the period but is not expected to be collected within
about 60 days after year end should be reclassified as deferred revenues as follows:

| | | |
|---|---|---|
| Revenues.......................................... | $12,000 | |
| Deferred Revenues.................................... | | $12,000 |

To adjust the accounts for property taxes that are not available
at year end.

Revenues Ledger (Revenues):

| | |
|---|---|
| Taxes ........................................... | $12,000 |

---

[8] The GASB *Codification* (sec. P70.103) states that "legally available" property taxes collected within approximately 60 days after year end would be considered "available" at year end and thus recognized as revenue in the year preceding collection.

This adjusting entry is reversed at the beginning of the next year.

Some governments that recognize property tax revenues on the cash basis during the year use a similar deferred revenue accounting technique. They record the property tax levy as deferred revenue, as described previously, then recognize revenue (and reduce deferred revenue) as property taxes are collected.

**Taxes Collected in Advance**    Sometimes a taxpayer will pay the subsequent year's taxes before the tax has been levied or billed. Such tax collections are subsequent period revenue, not revenue of the period in which they are collected, and may be recorded initially in a Trust or Agency Fund. If they are recorded in the General Fund or another governmental fund, the entry is:

| | | |
|---|---|---|
| Cash. | $2,500 | |
|    **Taxes Collected in Advance** | | $2,500 |

To record collection of taxes ($2,500) on next year's roll.

These tax collections represent a deferred credit to revenues, and the Taxes Collected in Advance account is, therefore, reported as deferred revenues in the balance sheet.

The deferred revenues are recognized as revenues of the next (or subsequent) year. After the taxes have been officially levied and the usual tax levy entry has been made recording the Taxes Receivable—Current, the related allowance(s), and Revenues—which includes those collected and deferred previously—the entry in the General Fund or other governmental fund is:

| | | |
|---|---|---|
| Taxes Collected in Advance | $2,500 | |
|    Taxes Receivable—Current | | $2,500 |

To record application of taxes collected in advance to reduce
   General Fund taxes receivable.

If the amount of taxes collected in advance exceeds the amount levied, the excess is either refunded or continues as deferred revenues until the next levy is made. If the amount collected is less than the amount levied, the taxpayer is billed for the difference.

### Enforcing the Collection of Taxes

The laws for most jurisdictions prescribe a date after which unpaid taxes become delinquent and are subject to specified penalties and interest. Taxes, interest, and penalties in most states become a **lien** against property without any action by the governmental unit. After a specified period of time, the governmental unit can sell the property to satisfy its lien.[9] Sale proceeds in excess of the lien for taxes, interest, penalties, and the cost of holding the sale are paid to the property owner. If the sale proceeds are less than the amount due, the property owner may or may not be legally liable for the difference. Furthermore, the SLG may bid in (retain) the property at the tax sale rather than sell it.

The property owner usually is given the privilege of redeeming the property within a certain period of time. If the property was purchased by an individual, it can be redeemed by payment to the buyer of the purchase price plus interest. If it was bid in by the governmental unit, the property can be redeemed by payment of the taxes, interest, penalties, and other charges to the governmental unit. If the property is not redeemed by the specified date, the acquirer secures title.

---

[9] In some states the state government pays the delinquent taxes and related amounts to the local governments, obtains their liens on the properties, and disposes of the properties at tax sales.

Typically, more than one governmental unit has liens against property that is being sold for delinquent taxes. If each government were left to enforce its own lien and sell the property for taxes, the cost of sale would greatly increase and considerable confusion would result. Accordingly, the statutes ordinarily provide for transferring delinquent tax rolls to a single governmental unit. This unit attempts to collect the delinquent taxes and performs all the steps necessary to enforce the lien. In the absence of statutory provisions, each unit receives from the collecting unit its proportionate share of tax collections, net of collection costs.

**Recording Interest and Penalties on Taxes**     Some governmental units accrue interest and penalties on delinquent taxes, whereas others do not record them until they are collected. They should be accrued if material, of course, and added to the tax roll or other subsidiary record. The entry to record the accrual of interest and penalties is:

| | | |
|---|---:|---:|
| Interest and Penalties Receivable—Delinquent Taxes........... | $15,000 | |
| Allowance for Uncollectible Interest and Penalties........... | | $ 1,000 |
| Revenues........................................ | | 14,000 |
| To record interest and penalties revenues on delinquent taxes net of the estimated uncollectible. | | |
| Revenues Ledger (Revenues): | | |
| Interest and Penalties.................................... | | $14,000 |

If the available criterion is not met when interest and penalties receivable are accrued, Deferred Revenues would be credited (rather than Revenues) and revenue would be recognized when the receivable becomes available, usually upon collection.

In any event, it is essential to identify the revenues from interest and penalties with the particular tax levy to which they apply. The reasons for this distinction are the same as those for recording taxes receivable by year of levy.

**Accounting for Tax Sales**     After the legally specified period has passed without payment of taxes, penalties, and interest, the assets are converted into tax liens:

| | | |
|---|---:|---:|
| **Tax Liens Receivable** ..................................... | $28,000 | |
| Taxes Receivable—Delinquent .......................... | | $25,000 |
| Interest and Penalties Receivable—Delinquent Taxes......... | | 3,000 |
| To record conversion of delinquent taxes and of interest and penalties thereon to tax liens as follows: | | |

| Levy of | Taxes | Interest and Penalties | Total |
|---|---|---|---|
| 19X8 | $10,000 | $1,000 | $11,000 |
| 19X7 | 15,000 | 2,000 | 17,000 |
| | $25,000 | $3,000 | $28,000 |

Subsidiary taxes receivable records (including penalties and interest) for each piece of property are credited at this time, and subsidiary records of the individual tax liens are established.

Court and other costs are ordinarily incurred in the process of converting property into tax liens and in selling the properties. In some jurisdictions the law provides that the costs of holding a tax sale are covered by interest and penalties levied against the property. Such costs are charged to expenditures in those jurisdictions. In most cases, however, the costs are recoverable from the taxpayer and should be added to the amount of the tax lien:

| | | |
|---|---|---|
| Tax Liens Receivable .................................... | $1,000 | |
| Cash ............................................ | | $1,000 |

To record court costs and other costs incurred in the conversion of delinquent taxes and related interest and penalties into tax liens.

When the assets are converted into tax liens, appropriate amounts of the related allowance for uncollectible accounts are converted into an Allowance for Uncollectible Tax Liens. The amount to be reclassified is determined by comparing the tax liens receivable and the estimated salable value of each property. Only some (perhaps none) of the allowance may need to be reclassified.

| | | |
|---|---|---|
| Allowance for Uncollectible Delinquent Taxes ............... | $2,000 | |
| Allowance for Uncollectible Interest and Penalties............ | 100 | |
| Allowance for Uncollectible Tax Liens .................... | | $2,100 |

To reclassify the allowances for estimated uncollectible taxes, interest, and penalties to the allowance for uncollectible tax liens.

If the proceeds from the sale of a property equal the amount of the tax lien against it, there is simply a debit to Cash and a credit to Tax Liens Receivable. If a property is sold for more than the amount of the liens, the excess is paid to the property owner. On the other hand, if the cash received from the sale of a property is not sufficient to cover the tax liens, and if taxes are a lien only against the property, the difference is charged to Allowance for Uncollectible Tax Liens.

If the governmental unit bids in (retains) properties at the time of the sale, it becomes, as is any other purchaser, subject to the redemption privilege by the property owners. As properties are redeemed, an entry is made debiting Cash and crediting Tax Liens Receivable.

If some of the properties are not redeemed and the governmental unit decides to use them for its own purposes—for example, for neighborhood parks—the Tax Liens Receivable accounts are removed from the funds in which they are carried through the following entry:

| | | |
|---|---|---|
| Expenditures.......................................... | $4,000 | |
| Allowance for Uncollectible Tax Liens...................... | 2,000 | |
| Tax Liens Receivable .................................. | | $6,000 |

To record the expenditure for tax sale property retained.

Expenditures Ledger (Expenditures):

| | |
|---|---|
| Capital Outlay ......................................... | $4,000 |

The debit to Expenditures is for the estimated salable value of the property, whereas the debit to Allowance for Uncollectible Tax Liens is the difference between the salable value of the property and the liens receivable against it. If the property's salable value is more than the receivable, only the amount of the receivable—the government's cost—is charged to Expenditures. Thus, the amount charged to Expenditures when a government retains bid-in property is the lesser of its salable value and the Tax Liens Receivable.

The bid-in property retained usually becomes a general fixed asset and must be recorded in the General Fixed Assets Account Group. Such fixed assets are capitalized at the lower of cost (i.e., the tax liens) or market value of the property (in this case, $4,000). The joint cost incurred should be allocated between the land and building in proportion to their relative fair values.

If several governmental units have liens on the same piece of property, the accounting procedure for the sale of the property is the same as that for property sold to satisfy the lien of only one governmental unit. The proceeds from the sale of the property are distributed among the various units to satisfy their liens, and any remaining cash is turned over to the property owner. If the proceeds are not sufficient to cover all the liens, each governmental unit receives a proportionate share of the money realized, unless statutes specify another basis of distribution.

## Property Tax Statements

Several types of property tax statements and schedules usually are prepared to provide adequate disclosure of the details of property taxes. These statements and schedules may be divided into two classes: (1) those related to the financial statements of the current period and (2) those showing data for other periods as well as for this period.

Some property tax statements and schedules are prepared primarily for internal use. Others are included in either the financial section or the statistical section of the comprehensive annual financial report (CAFR) of a state or local government (see Chapter 13). The general property tax statements and schedules that are directly related to the financial statements of the current period belong in the financial section of the annual report, whereas those that show data for a number of periods are known as statistical statements and appear in the statistical section.

# LICENSES AND PERMITS

Governments have the right to permit, control, or forbid many activities of individuals or corporations. Governments issue licenses or permits to grant the privilege of performing acts that would otherwise be illegal. Licenses and permits revenues may be divided into business and nonbusiness categories. In the business category are alcoholic beverages, health, corporations, public utilities, professional and occupational, and amusements licenses, among others. The nonbusiness category may include building permits and motor vehicle, motor vehicle operator, hunting and fishing, marriage, burial, and animal licenses.

The rates for licenses and permits are established by ordinance or statute. In contrast to property taxes, however, new rates need not be established each year. Instead, the legislative body usually adjusts the rates of particular licenses from time to time.

Revenues from most licenses and permits are not recognized until received in cash. This is because the amount is not known until the licenses and permits are issued, and cash is collected upon their issuance.

Proper control over these revenues must ensure not only that the revenues actually collected are handled properly but also that all the revenues that should be collected are collected. In other words, the governmental unit must see that all those who should secure licenses or permits do so. For example, if a license is required to operate a motor vehicle, no vehicle should be operated without one. Of course, the governmental unit must also institute controls to ensure that the revenues actually collected are recorded. This is accomplished in part by using sequentially numbered licenses, permits, and similar documents.

## INTERGOVERNMENTAL REVENUES

Intergovernmental revenues consist of grants and other financial assistance received from other governmental units. The GASB literature defines grants, entitlements, and shared revenues as follows:

- **Grants.** A grant is a contribution or gift of cash or other assets from another government to be used or expended for a specified purpose, activity, or facility. **Capital grants** are restricted by the grantor for the acquisition and/or construction of fixed (capital) assets. All other grants are **operating grants.**
- **Entitlements and Shared Revenues.** An **entitlement** is the amount of payment to which a state or local government is entitled as determined by the federal government or other (e.g., state) government pursuant to an allocation formula contained in applicable statutes. A **shared revenue** is a revenue levied by one government but shared on a predetermined basis, often in proportion to the amount collected at the local level, with another government or class of government.[10]

Federal or state grants for buses, subway systems, and wastewater treatment systems are examples of capital grants. All other grants—such as those for the operation of social welfare programs—are operating grants.

The primary distinction between entitlements and shared revenues lies in the difference between the nature of the amounts being allocated by formula. Entitlements are portions of a fixed, appropriated amount of money—for example, a federal or state revenue-sharing appropriation—that are allocated among eligible state or local governments by some formula, such as according to their relative populations. Shared revenues, on the other hand, are portions of a federal or state revenue source that varies in amount each month, quarter, or year—for example, gasoline, sales, liquor, and tobacco taxes. Shared revenues also are allocated among eligible state or local governments according to some formula, such as by relative number of vehicles registered or by relative sales of the products or services taxed at the federal or state level. This distinction is often confused in practice and in political rhetoric. For example, federal and state revenue-sharing programs usually are actually entitlements, and state tax-sharing programs are often referred to as entitlements. State-collected, locally shared taxes should be identified in the Revenues Subsidiary Ledger according to the kind of tax being received.

**Payments in lieu of taxes**—a significant intergovernmental revenue source of some local government public school systems—are amounts paid to one government by another to reimburse the payee for revenues lost because the payer government does not pay taxes. The maximum amount usually would be computed by determining the amount that the receiving government would have collected had the property of the paying government been subject to taxation.

Payments in lieu of taxes are particularly significant where the federal government makes payments in lieu of taxes to local governments and school districts near its major military bases. Presumably, the receiving government would record payments in lieu of taxes in the same fund(s) and manner as it records its tax revenues.

### Intergovernmental Revenue Account Classifications

Twelve possible classifications of intergovernmental revenues may be prepared for a municipality by listing the four kinds of intergovernmental revenue under fed-

---

[10] Adapted from GASB *Codification*, secs. G60.501–.505 and NCGA *Statement 2,* pars. 3–4. (Emphasis added.)

eral, state, and local unit categories. For example, there would be federal grants, state grants, local grants, federal entitlements, and so on.

As already indicated, grants ordinarily are made for a specified purpose(s). Entitlements and shared revenues may also be restricted as to use but frequently are not. Accordingly, restricted grants, entitlements, and shared revenues—whether from federal, state, or local government sources—should be recorded in the appropriate fund and classified both by source and according to the function for which the grants are to be spent (e.g., general government, public safety, highways and streets, sanitation, and health). On the other hand, unrestricted entitlements and shared revenues should be classified into accounts according to the source of the revenues because they may be used for a variety of purposes. Similarly, payments in lieu of taxes are classified only by governmental source—federal, state, or local unit—because they ordinarily are not restricted as to use.

## Accounting for Intergovernmental Revenues

The section of the GASB *Codification* on "Grants and Other Financial Assistance" emphasizes that:

> This section establishes standards of accounting and financial reporting for grants and other financial assistance, including entitlements, shared revenues, pass-through grants, food stamps, and on-behalf payments for fringe benefits and salaries. This section does not apply to unrestricted resources received from other governmental entities. Except as provided [for on-behalf payments] this section also does not apply to resources received from private contributors such as individuals, commercial enterprises, and foundations or to interfund transactions.[11]

This section of this text has the same intergovernmental restricted resource focus and, likewise, the guidance here should not be applied to any other resources.

### Fund Identification

The purpose and requirements of each grant, entitlement, or shared revenue must be analyzed to identify the proper fund(s) to be utilized. Existing funds should be used where possible; it is not always necessary to establish a separate fund for each grant, entitlement, or shared revenue. Indeed, the GASB *Codification* provides that:

> [1] Grants, entitlements, or shared revenues received for purposes normally financed through the general fund may be accounted for within that fund provided that applicable legal requirements can be appropriately satisfied; use of special revenue funds is not required unless they are legally mandated. [2] Such resources received for the payment of principal and/or interest on general long-term debt should be accounted for in a debt service fund. [3] Capital grants or shared revenues restricted for capital acquisitions or construction, other than those associated with enterprise and internal service funds, should be accounted for in a capital projects fund.
>
> [4] Grants, entitlements, or shared revenues received or utilized for enterprise or internal service fund operations and/or capital assets should be accounted for in those fund types.
>
> [5] A trust fund should be used for such resources that establish a continuing trustee relationship.[12]

---

[11] GASB *Codification,* sec. G60.101.

[12] Ibid., sec. G60.105–.106.

Furthermore, the GASB *Codification* observes that:

> Some grants, entitlements, and shared revenues may be used in more than one fund at the discretion of the recipient. Pending determination of the fund(s) to be financed, such resources should be accounted for in an agency fund. When the decision is made about the fund(s) to be financed, the asset(s) and revenues should be recognized in the fund(s) financed and removed from the agency fund. Revenues and expenditures or expenses are not recognized in agency funds. Assets being held in agency funds pending a determination of the fund(s) to be financed should be disclosed in the notes to the financial statements.[13]

### Pass-Through Grants

The distinction between pass-through and other types of grants is important. A **pass-through** grant is where

- The **primary recipient,** such as a state government, receives the grant—say, from the federal government.
- The primary recipient cannot spend the resources for its own purposes, but must "pass through" the resources to a **secondary recipient**—say, a local government or public school district—which is referred to as the **subrecipient.**
- The subrecipient then spends the grant resources for the specified purposes—perhaps under both federal and state regulations and oversight—or may "pass through" some or all of the resources, if permitted, to its subrecipients, or sub-subrecipients.

State governments, in particular, are primary recipients of significant pass-through grants for public education and other purposes.

The GASB notes with respect to pass-through grants:

> . . . All cash pass-through grants received by a governmental entity (referred to as a recipient government) should be reported in its financial statements. As a general rule, cash pass-through grants should be recognized as revenue and expenditures or expenses in a governmental, proprietary, or trust fund. In those infrequent cases in which a recipient government serves only as a cash conduit, the grant should be reported in an agency fund. A recipient government serves only as a cash conduit if it merely transmits grantor-supplied moneys without having administrative or direct financial involvement in the program.[14]

### Revenue Recognition

Regarding governmental fund revenue recognition for grants, entitlements, and shared revenues, the GASB *Codification* states that:

> [1] Grants, entitlements, or shared revenues recorded in governmental funds should be recognized as revenue in the accounting period when they become susceptible to accrual, that is, both measurable and available (modified accrual basis). [2] In applying this definition, legal and contractual requirements should be carefully reviewed for guidance. [3] Some such resources, usually entitlements or shared revenues, are restricted more in form than in substance. Only a failure on the part of the recipient to

---

[13] Ibid., sec. G60.108.

[14] Ibid., sec. G60.107. The GASB also notes that a recipient government has **administrative involvement** if, for example, it (a) monitors secondary recipients for compliance with program-specific requirements, (b) determines eligible secondary recipients or projects, even if using grantor-established criteria, or (c) has the ability to exercise discretion in how the funds are allocated. A recipient government has **direct financial involvement** if, for example, it finances some direct program costs because of a grantor-imposed matching requirement or is liable for disallowed costs.

comply with prescribed regulations will cause a forfeiture of the resources. Such resources should be recorded as revenue at the time of receipt or earlier if the susceptible to accrual criteria are met. [4] For other such resources, usually grants, expenditure is the prime factor for determining eligibility, and revenue should be recognized when the expenditure is made. Similarly, if cost sharing or matching requirements exist, revenue recognition depends on compliance with these requirements.[15]

Whereas unrestricted grants, entitlements, and shared revenues are recognized immediately as revenues of governmental funds, if available, restricted grants are not recognized as revenue until they are earned. In the usual case a restricted grant must be expended for the specified purposes to be considered earned. Thus, such grants are often referred to as **expenditure-driven grants** because deferred grant revenue is recorded initially and the grant revenue is recognized only when qualifying expenditures are incurred. That is, grant revenue recognition is driven by grant-related expenditures being incurred. Furthermore, if a restricted grant has been awarded to a governmental unit but (1) has not been received and (2) has not been earned by the SLG making qualifying expenditures, the grant awarded is not reported in the financial statements, though it may be disclosed in the notes to the financial statements. This situation is essentially equivalent to an executory contract.

**Grant Received Before Earned**     Where revenues should not be recognized at the time the grant, entitlement, or shared revenue is received, the following entry is appropriate:

| | | |
|---|---|---|
| Cash | $100,000 | |
| Deferred Revenues | | $100,000 |

To record receipt of grant, entitlement, or shared revenue prior to revenue recognition.

This entry also would be appropriate where an entitlement or shared revenue applicable to the next year is received currently, as well as when a restricted cash grant has been received but is not yet earned.

When the conditions of the grant, entitlement, or shared revenue restrictions have been met, the deferred revenue is recognized as revenue. For example, assuming that any local matching requirements have been met and the remaining requirement is that the resources be expended for a specified purpose(s), the following entries are made upon incurring a qualifying expenditure:

| | | |
|---|---|---|
| (1) Expenditures | $40,000 | |
| Vouchers Payable | | $40,000 |

To record expenditures qualifying under restricted grant program.

Expenditures Ledger (Expenditures):

| | | |
|---|---|---|
| Grant (Specify type) | $40,000 | |

| | | |
|---|---|---|
| (2) Deferred Revenues | | $40,000 |
| Revenues | | $40,000 |

To record recognition of revenues concurrent with expenditures meeting grant restrictions.

Revenues Ledger (Revenues):

| | | |
|---|---|---|
| Intergovernmental | | $40,000 |

[15] Ibid., sec. G60.111.

A more detailed subsidiary ledger account title—such as Federal Grants or even by grant name and number—would be used in practice. Broad account titles such as Intergovernmental are used only for illustrative purposes.

**Grant Earned Before Received**     A state or local government may make qualifying expenditures under a grant before the grant cash is received. Although this may occur in many grant programs, some grants—known as reimbursement grants—specify that the government must first incur qualifying expenditures, then file for reimbursement under the grant program.

A government that makes an expenditure that qualifies for reimbursement under an approved grant should record both (1) the expenditure and (2) the corresponding grant revenue accrual:

| | | |
|---|---:|---:|
| (1) Expenditures .......................................... | $75,000 | |
|     Vouchers Payable ................................... | | $75,000 |
|     To record expenditure that qualifies for reimbursement under approved grant. | | |
|     Expenditures Ledger (Expenditures): | | |
|     Grant X (Specify type) .............................. | <u>$75,000</u> | |
| (2) Due from Grantor ..................................... | $75,000 | |
|     Revenues ......................................... | | $75,000 |
|     To record grant revenues earned and receivable under reimbursement grant. | | |
|     Revenues Ledger (Revenues): | | |
|     Intergovernmental—Grant X ......................... | | <u>$75,000</u> |

This entry assumes both that the grant is a pure reimbursement grant—that is, only the actual direct expenditures are reimbursed under the grant—and that collection of the receivable is expected soon enough for the revenue to be considered available.

- If the reimbursement grant pays more or less than the direct expenditures incurred, the amount reimbursed is recorded as the grant receivable and revenue.
- If the grant receivable is not expected to be collected soon enough for the related revenue to be considered available, Deferred Revenues (not Revenues) is credited initially, and revenue is recognized when the grant receivable becomes available.

The qualifying expenditure entry and the entry to accrue the related grant revenue are not always made simultaneously in practice. For example, the total qualifying expenditures for several days, a month, or a quarter may be accumulated, then filed for reimbursement. Thus, controls should be established to ensure that all qualifying expenditures are properly filed for reimbursement and are indeed reimbursed. Furthermore, qualifying expenditure entries should be reviewed at year end to ensure that revenues have been properly accrued or are accrued in the year-end adjusting entries.

Revenue recognition for grants, entitlements, and shared revenues restricted for proprietary fund purposes is discussed in Chapters 11 and 12.

### Compliance Accounting

Grant, entitlement, and shared revenue provisions often require that special accounting procedures be followed and certain special reports that are not in conformity with generally accepted accounting principles be made to grantors. Also, they may specify that reports be prepared for a fiscal year different from that of the recipient government or for a period other than a fiscal year, for example, the duration of the grant. In this regard, the GASB *Codification* states that:

> In some instances, it may be necessary or desirable to record grant, entitlement, or shared revenue transactions in an agency fund in order to provide an audit trail and/or to facilitate the preparation of special purpose financial statements. The transactions are recorded as they occur in the agency fund utilizing "memoranda" revenue and expenditure accounts coded in accordance with specialized needs. The same transactions are subsequently recorded as revenues or contributed capital and expenditures or expenses, as appropriate, in conformity with GAAP in the fund(s) financed. The agency fund memoranda accounts are not reported as operating accounts. This "dual" recording approach may be especially helpful where a grant is received for multiple purposes and/or where the grant accounting period is different from that of the fund(s) financed, i.e., multi-year or different operating year awards. This "dual" recording approach is suggested only when a beneficial purpose is served. When an agency fund is used for this purpose, fund assets and liabilities should be combined with those of the fund(s) financed for financial statement presentation.[16]

Accounting for grants, entitlements, and shared revenues initially through an agency fund in this manner is discussed further in Chapter 10.

## CHARGES FOR SERVICES

Revenues from charges for services consist of charges made by various general government departments for goods or services rendered by them to the public, other departments of the government, or other governments. Similarly, special assessments for current services are considered departmental charges for services revenues.

It is important to distinguish between revenues derived from departmental earnings and those from licenses and permits. Only those charges that result directly from the activity of the department and are made for the purpose of recovering part of the costs of the department are considered charges for current services. Some of these charges may involve the issuance of permits, but the revenues should be classed as charges for services, not as from permits.

### Distinguishing Quasi-External Transactions and Reimbursements

It is also important to distinguish charges for services rendered by one department to other departments, which constitute quasi-external transactions, from reimbursements.

- **Quasi-external transactions** result in (1) revenues being recognized in the fund financing the provider department and (2) expenditures or expenses being recognized in the fund financing the department receiving the goods or services.
- **Reimbursements** result in expenditures or expenses being recognized in the fund from which the department receiving the goods or services is financed but a reduction (recovery) of expenditures or expenses being recorded in the fund through which the provider department is financed.

---

[16] Ibid., sec. G60.110.

A quasi-external transaction should be deemed to occur only when interdepartmental services (or goods) of the type routinely rendered to external parties are provided in the equivalent of an interdepartmental arm's-length transaction and charged for at established rates. Such instances are uncommon except between departments financed from governmental funds and those financed through Internal Service and Enterprise Funds. Therefore, most governmental fund interdepartmental charges for goods and services should be accounted for as reimbursements.

### Accounting for Charges for Services

Some charges for services are collected when the services are rendered and are recorded as revenues at that time. If not collected at the time services are rendered or immediately thereafter, revenues should be recorded as the persons or governments served are billed or, if not yet billed at year end, in adjusting entries. The following entries illustrate some transactions that result in revenues being recorded as soon as they are earned:

| | | |
|---|---:|---:|
| Due from Other Governmental Units ..................... | $25,000 | |
|     Revenues ............................................. | | $25,000 |

To record earnings resulting from charges to other governmental units for patients in mental hospitals and for inmates in prisons.

Revenues Ledger (Revenues):

| | |
|---|---:|
| Hospital Fees ................................................. | $10,000 |
| Prison Fees ................................................... | 15,000 |
| | $25,000 |

| | | |
|---|---:|---:|
| Accounts Receivable ...................................... | $20,000 | |
|     Revenues............................................. | | $20,000 |

To record street lighting, street sprinkling, and trash collection charges made to property owners.

Revenues Ledger (Revenues):

| | |
|---|---:|
| Street Light Charges......................................... | $ 5,000 |
| Street Sanitation Charges .................................. | 8,000 |
| Refuse Collection Fees...................................... | 7,000 |
| | $20,000 |

The following entry illustrates some of the transactions in which revenues typically are recorded only as cash is collected (i.e., are not billed or accrued):

| | | |
|---|---:|---:|
| Cash ........................................................ | $38,200 | |
|     Revenues ............................................. | | $38,200 |

To record receipt of cash representing charges for services.

Revenues Ledger (Revenues):

| | |
|---|---:|
| Sale of Maps and Publications............................. | $ 4,200 |
| Building Inspection Fees .................................. | 9,000 |
| Plumbing Inspection Fees ................................. | 5,000 |
| Swimming Pool Inspection Fees .......................... | 2,000 |
| Golf Fees..................................................... | 7,000 |
| Fees for Recording Legal Instruments ..................... | 6,000 |
| Animal Control and Shelter Fees .......................... | 5,000 |
| | $38,200 |

Finally, some government services may be provided in one period, billed to service recipients, and collected in a later period. Thus, expenditures may be recognized before the related revenues are recognized. A common example is street maintenance or improvement programs financed by special assessments against benefited properties or citizens. Some assessments are essentially taxes; others are charges for services. The following entries illustrate transactions in which governments render services and bill service recipients in one period but collect the charges (say, special assessments) and recognize revenues during one or more future periods. (Subsidiary ledger entries are omitted.)

Mid-19X1: Assessment-financed services rendered; service recipients billed—charges payable in five annual installments, with 6% interest, beginning in mid-19X2:

| | | |
|---|---|---|
| Expenditures......................................... | $100,000 | |
|   Vouchers Payable................................... | | $100,000 |
| To record expenditures incurred. | | |
| Assessments Receivable—Deferred........................ | $100,000 | |
|   Deferred Revenues.................................. | | $100,000 |
| To record levy of special assessments. | | |

Mid-19X2: One-fifth of the deferred receivables became due and reminder notices were mailed.

| | | |
|---|---|---|
| Assessments Receivable—Current........................ | $ 20,000 | |
|   Assessments Receivable—Deferred..................... | | $ 20,000 |
| To record currently maturing special assessment receivables. | | |
| Deferred Revenues .................................... | $ 20,000 | |
|   Revenues—Special Assessments........................ | | $ 20,000 |
| To recognize special assessment revenues. | | |
| Interest Receivable on Special Assessments (6%).............. | $ 6,000 | |
|   Revenues—Interest on Special Assessments ............... | | $ 6,000 |
| To record current interest billed on special assessments. | | |

The special assessments would mature and be collected during 19X2–19X6, with interest on the unpaid balances. This example is highly simplified, of course; more complex special assessment situations are addressed in Chapters 7 and 8.

As implied by the foregoing discussions and illustrations, the chart of accounts for charges for services should be based on the activity for which the charge is made. These activities can be classified according to the function of the government in which the activity is carried on. For example, under the general government function we would expect to find accounts for the following:

- Court costs, fees, and charges
- Recording of legal instruments
- Zoning and subdivision fees
- Plan checking fees
- Sale of maps and publications
- Building inspection fees

# FINES AND FORFEITS

Revenues from fines and forfeits are not usually an important source of a governmental unit's income. Because they often are not susceptible to accrual prior to collection, these revenues usually are accounted for on a cash basis. Fines are penalties imposed for the commission of statutory offenses or for violation of lawful administrative rules. Penalties for the delinquent payment of taxes are not included in this category of revenue because they are considered part of tax revenues. Similarly, penalties for late payment of utility bills are considered utility operating revenues. Fines and other penalties included in this section are primarily those imposed by the courts.

Where courts accept cash bonds or fine payments, adequate cash receipt and related controls are essential. In any event, all activities of the court should be documented so that there is an appropriate record of all cases brought before the court, the cash or property bond or bail related to each case, and the disposition of each case, including any bond or bail forfeitures ordered and fines levied.

Similar types of controls are essential when any police department, sheriff's office, or other law enforcement agency accepts cash for any reason. Effective cash and related controls, such as over traffic and parking tickets, are essential. Even small improprieties within courts and law enforcement agencies damage their credibility, public image, and effectiveness.

The money from forfeits of cash bonds and bail is often first accounted for in a Trust or Agency Fund (Chapter 10). Unless the law provides otherwise, forfeited bail money is paid from the Trust or Agency Fund to the General Fund, where it is recorded:

| | | |
|---|---|---|
| Cash............................................... | $5,000 | |
|    Revenues......................................... | | $5,000 |

To record receipt of money representing forfeited bail.
<u>Revenues Ledger (Revenues):</u>

| | |
|---|---|
| Fines and Forfeits....................................... | <u>$5,000</u> |

## MISCELLANEOUS REVENUES

Included in the miscellaneous category are such sources of revenues as investment earnings, rents and royalties, certain nontransfer payments from the government's public enterprises, escheats, and contributions and donations from private sources. All of the revenues discussed in this chapter may be found in General and Special Revenue Funds; some of them may also appear in other funds. In addition, other funds may have sources of revenues that have not been described here but will be treated in subsequent chapters. Most of the revenues in the miscellaneous category are self-explanatory, but a discussion of some of them may prove useful.

### Investment Earnings

Short-term investment of cash available in excess of current needs is authorized by legislative bodies throughout the country. Indeed, many state and local governments have highly sophisticated cash management systems. Thus, in addition to interest on long-term investments of Debt Service and Trust Funds, for example, interest earned on short-term investments of idle cash is a substantial general revenue source in many municipalities. Interest receivable should be accrued as it is earned by the governmental unit and recognized as revenue if it will be received (or constructively received) during the period or soon enough thereafter to be considered available.

GASB *Statement No. 31* establishes fair value[17] standards for investments in (a) participating interest-earning investment contracts, (b) external investment pools, (c) open-end mutual funds, (d) debt securities, and (e) equity securities, option contracts, stock warrants, and stock rights that have readily determinable fair values.

---

[17] Governmental Accounting Standards Board, *Statement No. 31,* "Accounting and Financial Reporting for Certain Investments and for External Investment Pools" (GASB, March 1997).

- **Participating** investment contracts are investments whose value is affected by market (interest rate) changes because they are (1) negotiable or transferable, or (2) their redemption value considers market rates.
- **Fair value** is the amount at which a financial instrument could be exchanged in a current transaction between willing parties, other than in a forced or liquidation sale.

GASB *Statement No. 31* requires that:

1. Governmental entities report *most types* of investments at fair value in the balance sheet.
2. All investment income—including changes in the fair value of investments—usually should be reported as revenue in the operating statements.

However, *Statement No. 31* permits governmental units to continue reporting *certain* investments at amortized cost, including lower of amortized cost or fair value, rather than at fair value. These *exempted* investments include:

- Nonparticipating interest-earning investment contracts.
- Money market investments and participating interest-earning investment contracts that have a remaining maturity *when purchased* of one year or less.[18]

These *Statement No. 31* exceptions exempt significant amounts of the general government investments of many local governments from the fair value standards. These exemptions also may result in some governmental unit investments being accounted for under the fair value approach and other investments being accounted for using the amortized cost method.

To illustrate the differences in amortized cost and fair value accounting for investments, consider these facts: A Governmental Unit made two, two-year $500,000 investments on July 1, 19X1, the beginning of its fiscal year, in 6% interest-earning contracts. Each investment was purchased at a discount of $4,000. The fair value of each investment at June 30, 19X2 was $497,000.

1. One investment, **Investment A,** is exempt from the fair value requirements of GASB *Statement No. 31* and will be accounted for on the **amortized cost method.**
2. The other investment, **Investment B,** is to be accounted for on the **fair value method.**

The governmental fund entries to record the investment acquisition and interest received are identical for Investments A and B:

**Investment (Same for Investments A and B)**

| | | | |
|---|---|---|---|
| 7/1/X1 | Investments. . . . . . . . . . . . . . . . . . . . . . . . . . . . . . . . . . . . . | $496,000 | |
| | Cash. . . . . . . . . . . . . . . . . . . . . . . . . . . . . . . . . . . . . . . | | $496,000 |
| | To record investments purchased. | | |

**Interest Received (Same for Investments A and B)**

| | | | |
|---|---|---|---|
| 6/30/X2 | Cash . . . . . . . . . . . . . . . . . . . . . . . . . . . . . . . . . . . . . . . | $ 30,000 | |
| | Revenues—Interest . . . . . . . . . . . . . . . . . . . . . . . . . | | $ 30,000 |
| | To record interest received. | | |

---

[18] Ibid., par. 22. The terms *interest-earning investment contract* and *money market investment* are defined as:
- **Interest-earning investment contract.** A direct contract, other than a mortgage or other loan, that a government enters into as a creditor of a financial institution, broker-dealer, investment company, insurance company, or other financial services company and for which it receives, directly or indirectly, interest payments. Interest-earning investment contracts include time deposits with financial institutions (such as certificates of deposit), repurchase agreements, and guaranteed and bank investment contracts (GICs and BICs).
- **Money market investment.** A short-term, highly liquid debt instrument, including commercial paper, banker's acceptances, and U.S. Treasury and agency obligations.

The amortized cost and fair value entries at June 30, 19X2 differ:

**Amortized Cost (Investment A)**

| | | | |
|---|---|---|---|
| 6/30/X2 | Investments. . . . . . . . . . . . . . . . . . . . . . . . . . . . . . . . . | $2,000 | |
| | Revenues—Interest . . . . . . . . . . . . . . . . . . . . . . . | | $2,000 |
| | To amortize unamortized investment discount. | | |

Investment income reported: $30,000 + $2,000 = $32,000

**Fair Value (Investment B)**

| | | | |
|---|---|---|---|
| 6/30/X2 | Investments[19] . . . . . . . . . . . . . . . . . . . . . . . . . . . . . . | $1,000 | |
| | Revenues—Increase in Fair Value of Investments. . | | $1,000 |
| | To record change in fair value of investments. | | |
| | (Fair value of investments is $497,000.) | | |

Investment income reported: $30,000 + $1,000 = $31,000

These entries are summarized in Figure 5–1.

Note that the fair value approach is affected by interest rate changes, whereas the amortized cost approach assumes the interest rate was established when the investments were acquired. Note also that the change in fair value of investments is reported in **revenue.** A net loss would not be reported unless the decrease in investment fair value exceeded all interest and other investment revenue received and accrued, and would be reported as *negative* revenue rather than as an expenditure.

GASB *Statement No. 31* includes illustrations of computing changes in fair values of investments—the difference between the fair value of investments at the beginning of the year and at the end of the year, taking into consideration investment purchases, sales, and redemptions—under both the specific identification method and the aggregate method. Both approaches are illustrated in Figure 5–2.

FIGURE 5–1   **Investment Accounting Methods—Interest-Bearing Debt Securities**

| | Amortized Cost | | Fair Value | |
|---|---|---|---|---|
| **When Acquired** | Investments      $496,000<br>  Cash                   $496,000 | | Investments      $496,000<br>  Cash                   $496,000 | |
| **Interest Received** | Cash                  $ 30,000<br>  Revenues—Interest      $ 30,000 | | Cash                  $ 30,000<br>  Revenues—Interest      $ 30,000 | |
| **Discount Amortized** | Investments         $  2,000<br>  Revenues—Interest       $  2,000 | | No entry | |
| **Change in Fair Value Recognized** | No entry—unless<br>apparently permanent<br>decline in fair value | | Investments            $  1,000<br>  Revenues—Increase<br>    in Fair Value<br>    of Investments         $  1,000 | |
| **Investment Income Reported** | $32,000 | | $31,000 | |

---

[19] Some governments maintain the Investments account at cost. These governments record the difference between the cost and fair value in a valuation allowance account.

**FIGURE 5–2  Investment Fair Value Changes Analysis Approaches**

**1. Fair Value Analysis of Investment Activity—Specific Identification Method**

| | | | | | | | |
|---|---|---|---|---|---|---|---|
| | | | | | **Fair Value** | | |
| | | *A* | *B* | *C* | *D\** | *E* | *F\*\** |
| *Security* | *Cost* | *Beginning Fair Value 1/1/X1* | *Purchases* | *Sales* | *Subtotal* | *Ending Fair Value 12/31/X1* | *Changes in Fair Value* |
| 1 | $100 | $100 | — | — | $100 | $120 | $20 |
| 2 | 520 | 540 | — | — | 540 | 510 | (30) |
| 3 | 200 | 240 | — | $250 | (10) | 0 | 10 |
| 4 | 330 | — | $330 | — | 330 | 315 | (15) |
| | $880 | $880 | $330 | $250 | $960 | $945 | ($15) |

**2. Calculation of the Net Change in the Fair Value of Investments—Aggregate Method**

| | |
|---|---|
| Fair Value at December 31, 19X1 | $945 |
| Add: Proceeds of investments sold in 19X1 | 250 |
| Less: Cost of investments purchased in 19X1 | (330) |
| Less: Fair value at December 31, 19X0 | (880) |
| Change in fair value of investments | ($15) |

  \* Column D = Columns A + B – Column C.
\*\* Column F = Column E – Column D.
*Source:* GASB *Statement No. 31,* "Accounting and Financial Reporting for Certain Investments and for External Investment Pools" (GASB, March 1997), par. 78.

Finally, GASB *Statement No. 31* permits governments to:

- report investment income either in one summary amount, with details disclosed in the notes to the financial statements, or in detail, such as:

| | |
|---|---|
| Investment income | |
|   Interest | $30,000 |
|   Net increase in the fair value of investments | 1,000 |
|   Total investment income | $31,000 |

- disclose details of realized and unrealized investment gains and losses in the notes to the financial statements.

Government finance officers, accountants, and auditors should ensure that any state or local regulations relating to short-term investments are observed, as well as those of the federal government with respect to **arbitrage** in the Internal Revenue Code (IRC) and related regulations. Briefly, the IRC provides that a state or local government **investing tax-exempt debt issue proceeds** (interest exempt from federal income taxes) in non-tax-exempt investments at rates higher than that being paid on the debt may have to rebate the excess interest earned to the U.S. Treasury. SLGs that do not comply may be assessed a 50% penalty. Or they may have the tax-exempt status of their debt issues revoked. Although the immediate and direct impact of such revocation would adversely affect the investors in those debt securities rather than the government, its future debt issues would probably be difficult to sell and carry much higher interest rates than formerly. Furthermore, GASB *Statement No. 3* requires numerous disclosures about each government's investment activities in the notes to its financial statements.[20]

### Sales and Compensation for Loss of Fixed Assets

Fixed assets financed from General and Special Revenue Funds resources are not assets of those funds. Financial resources received from disposition of general fixed assets are governmental fund assets, however. Therefore, the net proceeds from the sale and compensation for loss of these fixed assets are reported as either revenues or other financing sources of these funds. Net general fixed asset sales proceeds and loss compensation traditionally have been reported as revenues, which parallels the reporting of general fixed asset acquisitions as expenditures. It has also become acceptable recently to report such sale and loss compensation proceeds as nonrevenue other financing sources because they may be viewed as resulting from the conversion of general fixed assets to financial resources rather than as revenue transactions.

Ideally, general fixed asset sale and loss compensation proceeds should be recorded in the fund that financed the acquisition of the asset that has been sold or destroyed. But identifying the source from which assets were financed may be difficult—and in many instances the funds that financed the purchase of assets are abolished before the assets are disposed of. Accordingly, the net proceeds from the sale and compensation for loss of general fixed assets usually flow into the General Fund, and thus are reported as revenues or other financing sources of that fund. Proceeds from the sale and compensation for loss of assets carried in Internal Service Funds, Enterprise Funds, and Trust Funds ordinarily are accounted for in those funds rather than in the General Fund.

### Nontransfer Payments from Public Enterprises

Payments made to the government by a publicly owned enterprise in lieu of property or other taxes from which they are legally exempt may be reported either as miscellaneous revenues or as tax revenues. Other contributions made by its Enterprise Funds should be classified as operating transfers or residual equity transfers, as appropriate in the circumstances.

### Escheats

The laws of most states specify that the net assets of deceased persons who died intestate (without having a valid will) and with no known relatives revert to the state. Similarly, most state laws specify that amounts in inactive checking accounts (and perhaps other accounts) in banks revert to the state after a period of time, often seven years. Such laws result in what are referred to as **escheats** to the state. The cash or equivalent values of financial resources (e.g., cash, stocks, and bonds) received by escheat—net of any amounts expected to be claimed by heirs—are recognized as revenues by the recipient state.[21] Fixed assets received by escheat and retained for use by the government should be recorded in the General Fixed Assets Account Group at their fair value at time of receipt by the state.

---

[20] Ibid., sec. C20.
[21] Ibid., sec. E70.

### Private Contributions

Occasionally, a government will receive contributions or donations from private sources. Unrestricted contributions, which are rare, would be recognized as General Fund revenues. Restricted donations (except those in trust) usually would be recognized as Special Revenue or Capital Projects Fund revenue, as appropriate to the operating or capital purpose; those in trust would be accounted for initially in a Trust Fund as discussed in Chapter 10.

# REVENUE BUDGET REVISIONS

Budgets usually are prepared several months before the beginning of the year to which they apply based on the best information available at that time. While preliminary estimates often are revised prior to formal adoption of the budget, revisions may also be appropriate after the budget has been adopted. For example, the government may find it is not going to receive a sizable grant it had expected during the budget year, or it may be granted a significantly different amount than planned. Such an event may well signal a need to revise appropriations also, as discussed in Chapter 6.

The entry to record formal approval of a revenue estimate increase would parallel the original budgetary entry for estimated revenues:

| | | |
|---|---|---|
| Estimated Revenues............................................. | $75,000 | |
| Unreserved Fund Balance................................. | | $75,000 |
| To record an increase in estimated revenues. | | |
| Revenues Ledger (Estimated Revenues): | | |
| Intergovernmental......................................... | $75,000 | |

The entry to record a formally authorized decrease in estimated revenues would be the reverse:

| | | |
|---|---|---|
| Unreserved Fund Balance................................. | $50,000 | |
| Estimated Revenues..................................... | | $50,000 |
| To record a decrease in estimated revenues. | | |
| Revenues Ledger (Estimated Revenues): | | |
| Intergovernmental......................................... | | $50,000 |

In the event that two or more revenue estimate revisions net to zero—for example, the estimate of general property tax revenues is reduced $30,000 but those for income taxes and for sales taxes are increased $20,000 and $10,000, respectively—the following entry is required:

| | | |
|---|---|---|
| Estimated Revenues............................................. | $30,000 | |
| Estimated Revenues..................................... | | $30,000 |
| To record offsetting revenue estimate revisions. | | |
| Revenues Ledger (Estimated Revenues): | | |
| Income Taxes ................................................ | $20,000 | |
| Sales Taxes ................................................... | 10,000 | |
| Property Taxes .............................................. | | $30,000 |
| | $30,000 | $30,000 |

The only effect of this entry, of course, is to change the estimated revenue amounts in the several revenues subsidiary ledger accounts affected. The offsetting estimated revenues entries in the general ledger are needed because the subsidiary ledger is normally accessed, in both manual and automated systems, through the general ledger.

## CHANGES IN ACCOUNTING PRINCIPLES

Restatement of the beginning fund balance of a governmental fund to correct a prior year error was illustrated briefly in Chapter 4. Restatements may also be necessary to report the cumulative effect of changes in accounting principles. Three types of events that might cause a government to change its governmental fund revenue recognition principles are:

- Management decides to change from one acceptable revenue recognition principle or policy to another acceptable alternative revenue recognition principle or policy. (This is not common in governmental fund accounting.)
- Changed circumstances require a change in the method of applying the acceptable principle in use. For example, a revenue source not previously deemed objectively measurable and/or available is now considered to be both objectively measurable and available at year end. (This type of change is common in governmental fund accounting.)
- The GASB or another recognized standards-setting body issues a new revenue recognition standard that requires a different revenue accounting policy than that presently used.

In any event, (1) changes in accounting principles are made effective at the beginning of the year in which the change occurs, the current year; (2) the cumulative effect of the change—computed by comparing the revenues recognized and effects on fund balance of the governmental fund under the old accounting policy with the effects as if the new accounting policy had been in effect—are reported as a restatement of the beginning fund balance of the earliest year presented; (3) revenues are reported under the new accounting policy for each year presented; and (4) the change in accounting principle is disclosed and explained in the notes to the current year financial statements.

### Changed GASB Standards

Most changes in governmental fund accounting principles occur because the GASB—or another recognized standards-setting body discussed in Chapter 2—issues a new revenue recognition standard or revises an existing standard. If the new or revised revenue recognition standard requires a different revenue recognition policy than that presently being used in its governmental fund accounting, a state or local government must change its accounting policy to comply with the new or revised standard.

GASB statements and interpretations include an "Effective Date and Transition" section that specifies when and how the new standards are to be implemented, as do FASB and AICPA pronouncements. Furthermore, such standards typically encourage (but do not require) early application, that is, implementation prior to the effective date specified.

## Prospective Application

Occasionally the transition instructions are that a new accounting policy is to be applied prospectively—that is, applied only to transactions occurring on or after the effective date or, if implemented earlier, the implementation date. For example, a revised standard might require that a type of transaction previously recognized as revenues be reported as other financing sources in the future; or a new standard might specify that transactions previously reported as giving rise to gains and losses by some governments (e.g., advance refundings of GLTD) be reported as other financing sources (uses) in the future, with no gain or loss recognized. Because changed standards that are implemented prospectively apply only to transactions and events occurring on or after the implementation date—that is, they do not require retroactive application as if the new standard had been in effect earlier—they do not require restatement of governmental fund assets, liabilities, and fund balance. Thus, new standards that are applied prospectively do not give rise to cumulative effect of changes in accounting principles restatements.

## Retroactive Application

Most new and revised GASB and other standards are required to be implemented retroactively—that is, as if the new standard had been in effect earlier. Thus, they require that (1) assets, liabilities, and fund balance at the beginning of the year in which the new standard is implemented be restated as if the new standard had been applied earlier, and (2) the cumulative effect of applying the changed accounting principle retroactively be reported as a restatement of the beginning fund balance of that year. The logic and approach involved in implementing a new accounting principle are identical to those for correcting errors that require retroactive restatement.

## CONCLUDING COMMENTS

Proper revenue administration, including revenue accounting and reporting, has never been more important to state and local governments. During periods of rapid economic growth, some governments become lax on revenue administration, assuming that growth in revenues will compensate for any administrative shortcoming. Well-managed governments, however, place equal emphasis on excellent revenue administration and expenditure administration.

Several important revenue sources were discussed in this chapter, and additional types of revenue accounting entries were illustrated. Current rules for governmental fund revenue recognition require that revenue(s) be both measurable and available before being recognized. Applying these criteria in practice requires judgment, consistency in application, and disclosure of the major judgments made in the notes to the financial statements. Too, investment income and intergovernmental grant revenues are subject to special revenue recognition criteria. Furthermore, it is important to distinguish revenues from reimbursements, bond issue proceeds, operating transfers in, and residual equity transfers in.

Finally, revenues subsidiary ledger accounting, revenue budgetary revision entries, and entries to effect changes in revenue accounting principles were discussed and illustrated. These procedures and the concepts and procedures discussed earlier are essential in practice and will be applied throughout subsequent chapters.

## Questions

**Q 5-1**    What is the meaning of the term *available* as used in governmental fund revenue recognition?

**Q 5-2**    A revenue item must be objectively measurable as well as available to be accrued as governmental fund revenue. (a) What is meant by the term *objectively measurable* in this context? (b) Might revenue items be available but not objectively measurable prior to collection? Explain.

**Q 5-3**    The controller of a school district had recorded the entire property tax levy, $20,000,000, as revenues when levied during the first month of the year. At year end the auditor states that $3,000,000 must be reclassified as deferred revenues because that amount of the property tax levy will not be collected until more than 60 days into the next year or later. The controller objects, noting that the property tax receivables are as available as cash because the school district regularly uses them as the basis for borrowing on tax anticipation notes at local banks. Furthermore, the penalties and interest charged on delinquent taxes exceed the interest charges on the tax anticipation notes. With whom do you agree? Why?

**Q 5-4**    The term *deferred revenues* seems out of place in governmental fund accounting. It would seem that a government either has or does not have expendable financial resources as a result of a property tax, grant, or other revenue transaction. Furthermore, deferred working capital is not reported in business accounting. Explain the use of the term *deferred revenues* in governmental fund accounting.

**Q 5-5**    (a) Should estimated uncollectible amounts of taxes be accounted for as direct deductions from revenues or as expenditures? Why? (b) Should discounts on taxes be accounted for as direct deductions from revenues or as expenditures? Why?

**Q 5-6**    (a) What are expenditure-driven intergovernmental grants? (b) When and how are revenues from such grants recognized?

**Q 5-7**    The taxes of City A are collected by County C, whereas City B collects its own taxes. In what respects will the tax accounting procedures for the two cities differ?

**Q 5-8**    For which of the following would you set up accounts in the revenues subsidiary ledger?

| Case 1: Taxes | Case 2: Intergovernmental Revenue |
|---|---|
| General Property Taxes | State-Shared Revenues |
| Real Property | Property Taxes |
| Personal Property | Individual Income Taxes |
| Tangible Personal | Corporate Income Taxes |
| Intangible Personal | |

**Q 5-9**    The controller of the city of F, who is independent of the chief executive, purposely underestimates revenues and publishes revenue statements that show actual revenues only. (a) How can one discover the controller's practice? (b) The controller, when discovered in the practice, points with pride to the city's solvency and states that his underestimates have kept the city from overspending. Comment.

**Q 5-10**    What purposes do revenue statements serve in the administration of the General Fund?

**Q 5-11**    A recently elected city council member of the city of Lynne has returned from a two-day course on governmental accounting that she attended to assist her in understanding the city financial statements and budgeting process. She is perplexed by a point the instructor emphasized during the course, however, and asks the city finance officer about it. "Why did the instructor keep harping about the need to distinguish between fund revenues and the revenues of the governmental unit? It seems to me that if the governmental unit as a whole has a net increase in resources, one or more of the funds has to recognize net increases totaling the same amount. So, what's the big problem?" Respond.

**Q 5-12** A county decided to keep land it bid in at its property tax sale to use for parks and recreation purposes. The redemption period has passed and the county has a valid deed to the land. Taxes, interest, penalties, and sheriff's sale costs applicable to the land total $15,000, and the land could have been sold for $12,000. The Tax Liens Receivable account in the General Fund has been charged to the Allowance for Uncollectible Tax Liens Receivable account and the land has been capitalized (recorded) at $15,000 in the General Fixed Assets Account Group. (a) Do you agree with the recording of this transaction? (b) Would your answer differ if the land could be sold for $18,000?

**Q 5-13** During the course of your audit of a city, you noted an $800,000 payment to the General Fund from an Enterprise Fund. The payment was recorded in both funds as a payment in lieu of property taxes, as similar payments had been in past years. Your inquiries at the local tax appraisal and assessment offices indicate that, if taxed, the Enterprise Fund property taxes would be $450,000 annually. What should you do?

**Q 5-14** Some state laws prohibit revisions of a government's annual operating budget, perhaps because it is an official, legally enacted document. (a) What is wrong with such a law? (b) What might you do in view of such a law if you were the chief finance officer of a county in one of these states?

**Q 5-15** What is arbitrage? Why is an awareness of arbitrage important to a government finance officer?

**Q 5-16** One county might properly account for its investments at fair value, whereas another county might properly account for its investments at amortized cost or the lower of amortized cost or fair value. Explain.

## Exercises

**E 5-1** (Investments) Aslan County purchased $3,000,000 of bonds as a General Fund investment on March 1, 20X1 for $3,060,000 plus four months' accrued interest of $80,000. The bonds mature in four years and two months.
1. The county received the semiannual interest payment on the bonds ($120,000) on April 30, 20X1.
2. The county received the October 31 semiannual interest payment ($120,000).
3. On December 31, the end of Aslan's fiscal year, the fair value of its bond investment was $3,065,000.

*Required* (a) Record these transactions in the general ledger accounts of the Aslan County General Fund.
(b) Compute the investment income that should be reported for this investment.

**E 5-2** (Property Tax Entries) Prepare the general journal entries to record the following transactions in the general ledger accounts of a General or Special Revenue Fund of a city:
1. The city levied current year property taxes of $1,000,000, of which 5% is estimated to be uncollectible. Also, 70% of the taxes levied normally are collected within the 2% discount period; and all collectible taxes are expected to be collected during the year.
2. Current property taxes billed at $600,000 (gross) were collected within the recently expired discount period.
3. Assume current property taxes billed at $720,000 (instead of $600,000 in item 2) were collected before the discount period expired.
4. After item 3, $80,000 of current taxes (not collected in item 3) were collected after the discount period and the balance of current property taxes became delinquent. Interest and penalties of $5,000—one-quarter of which is estimated to be uncollectible—were assessed on delinquent taxes.
5. $110,000 of delinquent taxes and $1,400 of previously accrued interest and penalties were collected and $30,000 was collected on taxes not to be levied or due until the next fiscal year.

6. A taxpayer is protesting a delinquent property tax billing of $2,000, on which $50 of interest and penalties were assessed in item 4. Although the city expects to collect the taxes, interest, and penalties, the protest process will probably delay the collection until late in the following year.

**E 5-3** (Property Tax Allocation) (a) The 19X7, 19X6, and 19X5 tax rates for the city of Yonker are:

|  | Rate per $100 of Assessed Value | | |
|---|---|---|---|
|  | **19X7** | **19X6** | **19X5** |
| General Fund ................... | $1.00 | $1.10 | $1.20 |
| Library Fund ................... | .09 | .09 | .09 |
| Municipal Bonds—Redemptions ... | .20 | .18 | .16 |
|  | $1.29 | $1.37 | $1.45 |

The total assessed value for 19X7 was $88,400,000.

**Required**   Compute the amount of taxes levied for each fund for 19X7.

(b) Collections were made in 19X7 as follows:

| | |
|---|---|
| 19X7 levy..................................... | $1,000,000 |
| 19X6 levy..................................... | 100,000 |
| 19X5 levy..................................... | 50,000 |
| | $1,150,000 |

Compute the amount of collections applicable to each fund for each year.

## Problems

**P 5-1** (Multiple Choice) Indicate the best answer to each question.
1. Which of the following is not to be reported as governmental fund revenue?
   a. Taxes
   b. Fines and forfeitures
   c. Special assessments
   d. Payments in lieu of taxes
   e. All of the above are properly reported as governmental fund revenues.
2. Generally, sales tax revenues should be recognized by a local government in the period
   a. in which the local government receives the cash.
   b. that the underlying sale occurs, whether or not the local government receives the cash in that period.
   c. in which the state—which collects all sales taxes in the state—receives the cash from the collecting merchants.
   d. in which the state—which collects all sales taxes in the state—receives the cash from the collecting merchants if the local government collects the taxes from the state in that period or soon enough in the next period to be used as a resource for payment of liabilities incurred in the first period.
3. On June 1, 19X4 a school district levies the property taxes for its fiscal year that will end on June 30, 19X5. The total amount of the levy is $1,000,000 and it is expected that 1% will prove uncollectible. Of the levy, $250,000 is collected in June 19X4 and another $500,000 is collected in July and August 19X4. What amount of property tax revenue associated with the June 1, 19X4 levy should be reported as revenue in the fiscal year ending June 30, 19X4?
   a. $0                                            c. $760,000
   b. $750,000                                      d. $990,000

4. A city levied $2,000,000 of property taxes for its current fiscal year. The city collected $1,700,000 cash on its taxes receivable during the year and granted $72,000 in discounts to taxpayers who paid within the legally established discount period. It is expected that the city will collect another $88,000 on these taxes receivable during the first two months of the next fiscal year. One percent of the tax levy is expected to be uncollectible. What amount of property tax revenues should the city report for the current fiscal year?
   a. $1,788,000
   c. $1,980,000
   b. $1,860,000
   d. $2,000,000

5. What would the answer to 4 be if the city also collected $100,000 of prior year taxes during the first two months of the current fiscal year and another $53,000 of prior year taxes during the remainder of the current year?
   a. $1,788,000
   c. $1,941,000
   b. $1,860,000
   d. $1,980,000
   e. None of the above. The correct answer is $_____.

6. A county received $3,000,000 from the state. Of the $3,000,000, $1,500,000 was received under an entitlement program and was not restricted as to use. The other $1,500,000 was received under a grant agreement, which requires the funds to be used for specific health and welfare programs. The county accounts for the resources from both of these programs in a Special Revenue Fund. Expenditures of that fund that qualified under the grant agreement totaled $900,000 in the year that the grant and entitlement were received. What amount of revenues should the county recognize in that year with respect to the entitlement and the grant?
   a. $0
   d. $1,800,000
   b. $900,000
   e. $2,400,000
   c. $1,500,000

7. A Special Revenue Fund expenditure of $40,000 was initially paid for through and recorded in the General Fund. The General Fund is now being reimbursed. The General Fund should report
   a. revenues of $40,000.
   b. other financing sources of $40,000.
   c. a $40,000 reduction in expenditures.
   d. other changes in fund balance of $40,000.
   e. residual equity transfers in of $40,000.

8. A state acquired $80,000 of equipment through the enforcement of escheat laws. The General Fund statement of revenues, expenditures, and changes in fund balance should report
   a. revenues from escheat of $80,000.
   b. an other financing source of $80,000.
   c. both capital outlay expenditures and revenues from escheat of $80,000.
   d. nothing—it is not affected if the state plans to retain the equipment for its use because no financial resources were involved.

9. A city has formalized tax liens of $50,000 against a property on which there are delinquent taxes receivable. The estimated salable value of the property is $39,000. The remaining *total* balances in property taxes receivable—delinquent and the related allowance are $113,000 and $28,000, respectively. What amount should be reclassified from allowance for uncollectible delinquent taxes to allowance for uncollectible tax liens?
   a. $0
   c. $28,000
   b. $11,000
   d. $8,589

10. If the city in 9 decides to keep the property for its own use, what amount of expenditures should be recognized?
   a. $0
   c. $50,000
   b. $39,000
   d. none of the above

**P 5-2** (GL and SL Entries; SL Trial Balance) The city of Asher had the following transactions, among others, in 19X7:

1. The council estimated that revenues of $210,000 would be generated for the General Fund in 19X7. The sources and amounts of expected revenues are as follows:

| | |
|---|---:|
| Property taxes . . . . . . . . . . . . . . . . . . . . . . . . . . . . . . . . . . . . | $150,000 |
| Parking meters . . . . . . . . . . . . . . . . . . . . . . . . . . . . . . . . . . . | 5,000 |
| Business licenses . . . . . . . . . . . . . . . . . . . . . . . . . . . . . . . . . . | 30,000 |
| Amusement licenses . . . . . . . . . . . . . . . . . . . . . . . . . . . . . . . . | 10,000 |
| Charges for services . . . . . . . . . . . . . . . . . . . . . . . . . . . . . . . | 8,000 |
| Other revenues . . . . . . . . . . . . . . . . . . . . . . . . . . . . . . . . . . . . | 7,000 |
| | $210,000 |

2. Property taxes of $152,000 were levied by the council; $2,000 of these taxes are expected to be uncollectible.
3. The council adopted a budget revision increasing the estimate of amusement licenses revenues by $2,000 and decreasing the estimate for business licenses revenues by $2,000.
4. The following collections were made by the city:

| | |
|---|---:|
| Property taxes . . . . . . . . . . . . . . . . . . . . . . . . . . . . . . . . . . . . | $140,000 |
| Parking meters . . . . . . . . . . . . . . . . . . . . . . . . . . . . . . . . . . . | 5,500 |
| Business licenses . . . . . . . . . . . . . . . . . . . . . . . . . . . . . . . . . . | 28,000 |
| Amusement licenses . . . . . . . . . . . . . . . . . . . . . . . . . . . . . . . . | 9,500 |
| Charges for services (not previously accrued) . . . . . . . . . . . . | 9,000 |
| Other revenues . . . . . . . . . . . . . . . . . . . . . . . . . . . . . . . . . . . . | 10,000 |
| | $202,000 |

5. The resources of a Capital Projects Fund being discontinued were transferred to the General Fund, $4,800.
6. Enterprise Fund cash of $5,000 was paid to the General Fund to subsidize its operations.

*Required* (a) Prepare general journal entries to record the transactions in the General Ledger and Revenues Subsidiary Ledger accounts.
(b) Prepare a trial balance of the Revenues Ledger after posting the general journal entries prepared in item 1. Show agreement with the control accounts.
(c) Prepare the general journal entry(ies) to close the revenue accounts in the General and Revenues Ledgers.

**P 5-3** (Tax Penalties, Interest, and Discounts)

**Situation A.** Interest and penalties assessed on late payments.
1. On January 1 a county levies property taxes for the year of $5,000,000. $50,000 are expected to prove uncollectible.
2. Before the due date, the county collects $4,000,000 of taxes. Interest and penalties of 10% are assessed on the uncollected taxes on the due date; 5% of the interest and penalties are expected to be uncollectible.
3. The county writes off $50,000 of delinquent taxes and $5,000 of interest and penalties receivable as uncollectible.
4. The remainder of the receivables is collected by year end.

**Situation B.** Discounts awarded for on-time payments.
1. On January 1 a city levies property taxes for the year of $5,500,000. $55,000 of the taxes are expected to prove uncollectible. Additionally, property owners who pay on or before the due date for taxes receive a discount of one-eleventh of their tax bill. It is expected that 80% of the taxes will be collected by the due date.
2. Taxes receivable of $4,400,000 are collected by the city on or before the due date. The balance of the taxes are declared delinquent.

3. The city writes off $55,000 of the delinquent taxes as uncollectible.
4. The remainder of the taxes is collected by year end.

**Required** (a) Prepare the journal entries to record the transactions for each preceding situation.
(b) Compute the amount of revenues to be reported for the year for each situation.

**P 5-4** (GL and SL Entries; Statement) The following are the estimated revenues for a Special Revenue Fund of the city of Marcelle at January 1, 19X0:

| | |
|---|---|
| Taxes | $175,000 |
| Interest and penalties | 2,000 |
| Fines and fees | 700 |
| Permits | 300 |
| Animal licenses | 900 |
| Rents | 500 |
| Other licenses | 3,500 |
| Interest | 1,000 |
| | $183,900 |

The city records its transactions on a cash basis during the year and adjusts to the modified accrual basis at year end. At the end of January, the following SRF collections had been made.

| | |
|---|---|
| Taxes | $90,000 |
| Interest and penalties | 1,000 |
| Fines and fees | 50 |
| Permits | 140 |
| Animal licenses | 800 |
| Rents | 45 |
| Other licenses | 2,000 |
| | $94,035 |

An unanticipated grant-in-aid of $5,000 was received from the state on February 1.

SRF collections for the remaining 11 months were as follows:

| | |
|---|---|
| Taxes | $70,000 |
| Interest and penalties | 800 |
| Fines and fees | 400 |
| Permits | 30 |
| Animal licenses | 70 |
| Rents | 455 |
| Other licenses | 300 |
| Interest | 900 |
| | $72,955 |

Accrued SRF receivables at year end were as follows:

| | |
|---|---|
| Taxes | $20,000 |
| Interest and penalties | 300 |
| Rents | 10 |
| Interest | 50 |
| | $20,360 |

Only half of the taxes and interest and penalties receivable is expected to be collected during the first 60 days of 19X1. All of the rent and interest receivable should be received in January 19X1.

*Required* (a) Prepare the general and subsidiary ledger entries necessary to record the SRF estimated revenues, revenue collections, and revenue accruals.
 (b) Post to SRF General Ledger worksheet (or T-accounts) and to subsidiary revenue accounts.
 (c) Prepare SRF closing entries for both the General and Revenues Subsidiary Ledgers.
 (d) Post to the SRF General Ledger worksheet (or T-accounts) and to the subsidiary revenue accounts.
 (e) Prepare a SRF statement of estimated revenues compared with actual revenues for 19X0.

**P 5-5** (GL and SL Entries; Trial Balance) The city of Coralen's Corner had the following transactions, among others, in 19X3:

1. The city council estimated that revenues of $212,000 would be generated for the General Fund in 19X3, as follows:

| | |
|---|---:|
| Property tax | $120,000 |
| City sales tax | 40,000 |
| Parking meters | 8,000 |
| Business licenses | 20,000 |
| Amusement licenses | 10,000 |
| Fines and forfeitures | 12,000 |
| Interest earnings | 2,000 |
| | $212,000 |

2. Property taxes of $124,000 were levied by the council; $2,500 of these taxes are expected to be uncollectible and discounts of $1,500 are expected to be taken.

3. The following General Fund collections were made by the city:

| | |
|---|---:|
| Property taxes—current | $105,000 |
| City sales tax | 41,000 |
| Parking meters | 7,900 |
| Business licenses | 29,000 |
| Amusement licenses | 7,000 |
| Fines and forfeitures | 12,200 |
| Interest earnings | 1,100 |
| Proceeds of five-year note | 25,000 |
| Annual transfer from Special Revenue Fund | 12,000 |
| | $240,200 |

4. Discounts of $1,400 were taken on property taxes before the discount period lapsed. Of the remaining balance of 19X3 taxes, $12,000 is expected to be collected by February of 19X4; the remainder is expected to be collected in 19X5 or later, or not collected.

5. A 30-day $3,000 note, dated September 30, 19X3, was issued to provide cash needed temporarily in the General Fund.

*Required* (a) Prepare general journal entries to record the 19X3 transactions in the General Ledger and in the Revenues Ledger accounts.
 (b) Prepare a trial balance of the Revenues Ledger after posting the entries in (a). Prove its agreement with the control accounts.
 (c) Prepare general journal entries to close the revenue accounts in the General Ledger and in the Revenues Ledger at the end of 19X3.

**P 5-6** (Revenue Recognition) In auditing the city of Pippa Passes General Fund a staff member asks whether the following items should be reported as calendar year 19X4 revenues:

1. Property taxes—which are levied in December and due the following April 30
 a. Levied in 19X3 and collected in April 19X4, $800,000
 b. Levied in 19X4 and collected in May 19X5, $850,000

    c. Levied in 19X2 and collected in January 19X4, $8,000

    d. Levied in 19X3 and collected in January 19X5, $137,000

    e. Collected in 19X4 on taxes levied for 19X5, $22,000

    f. Levied in 19X3, not expected to be collected until late 19X5 or 19X6, $12,000

2. Proceeds of 6%, ten-year general obligation bond issued December 28, 19X4, $540,000

3. Income taxes
    a. 19X3 returns filed during 19X4 and taxes collected in mid-19X4, $150,000
    b. 19X4 returns filed in 19X4 and taxes collected in 19X4, $18,000
    c. 19X4 returns filed in 19X4 and taxes not collected until mid-19X5, $4,000

4. Payment from the Capital Projects Fund of net assets after completion of the project, $3,000

5. Sales taxes
    a. Returns filed and taxes collected in 19X4, $42,000
    b. Returns filed in 19X3 and taxes collected in June 19X4, $7,400
    c. Returns filed in 19X4 and taxes collected in the first week of 19X5, $6,200

6. Proceeds of 10% note payable, dated November 1, 19X4, and due March 1, 19X5, $15,000

7. Grant awarded in 19X4—received in full in mid-19X4 (portion not used for designated purposes by 19X7 must be refunded)
    a. Total amount of award, $250,000
    b. Qualifying expenditures made in 19X4, $172,000

8. Repayment in 19X4 of an advance made to the Internal Service Fund in 19X0, $72,300

9. 19X4 payment from Enterprise Fund in lieu of taxes, $2,500

10. 19X4 payment from a Special Revenue Fund to finance street improvements, $12,000

11. Interest and penalties
    a. Accruing and collected during 19X4, $2,200
    b. Accruing, but not recorded in the accounts, during 19X0–X3 and collected in mid-19X4, $7,800
    c. Accruing during 19X4 and expected to be collected in early 19X5, $3,400
    d. Accruing during 19X4 and expected to be collected in 19X6 and later, $1,200

***Required*** (a) What is your recommendation for each of the preceding items? (Indicate how each item not reported as 19X4 revenue should be reported.) Explain your recommendation using this format:

| *Item* | *Recommendation(s)* | *Reason(s)* |
| --- | --- | --- |

(b) What total revenue amount should Pippa Passes report for 19X4?

**P 5-7** (Grants) The Sinking Creek School District was notified that the federal government has awarded it a $5,000,000 grant to finance a special program that the school had developed to teach math to a select group meeting specified criteria. **Record the following transactions in a Special Revenue Fund general journal.**

Situation A. Cash received in advance of incurring expenditures.
1. The school district received the grant in cash on January 22, 19X8.
2. The school purchased 10 computers and related software for use in the program, $75,000.
3. The school paid salaries for the three instructors who are assigned to the program, $112,000.
4. The school purchased materials for students for the program, $1,420,000.
5. December 31 is the end of the school's fiscal year. All of the foregoing expenditures qualify as expenditures payable from the grant resources.

Situation B. Cash received to reimburse expenditures after they are incurred.
1. Received a 1-year loan from the General Fund, $1,700,000.

2. The school purchased 10 computers and related software for use in the program, $75,000.
3. The school paid salaries for the three instructors who are assigned to the program, $112,000.
4. The school purchased materials for students for the program, $1,420,000.
5. The school filed for and received reimbursement of $1,300,000.
6. As of year end, the school had filed for reimbursement for all but $30,000 of the expenditures. It will file for reimbursement for the remaining $30,000 of qualifying expenditures early in the next year. It should receive all amounts for which it has already filed within 45 days after year end. The remaining $30,000 will likely not be received until the end of the first quarter of the next year.

**P 5-8** (Tax Liens and Tax Sales) On February 4, 19X6, selected accounts for the city of Hayden General Fund had the following balances:

|  | Debit | Credit |
|---|---|---|
| Taxes Receivable—Delinquent ......................... | $83,000 | |
| Allowance for Uncollectible Delinquent Taxes ............ | | $26,500 |
| Interest and Penalties Receivable ..................... | 4,000 | |
| Allowance for Uncollectible Interest and Penalties......... | | 1,500 |

*Required*  Prepare general journal entries to record the following transactions in the general ledger of the city of Hayden General Fund:

(1) Hayden formalized tax liens against properties with delinquent taxes of $9,000 and related interest and penalties of $1,000. The estimated salable value of the properties was $11,500.

(2) Hayden sold the properties at a tax sale for $11,000. Costs of selling the property totaled $400.

(3) How would your answers to items 1 and 2 differ if the estimated fair value of the properties was $9,000 and the property sold for $9,400?

(4) How would your answers to items 1 and 2 differ if the estimated fair value of the property was $9,000 and the city of Hayden decided to use it for a playground development?

**P 5-9** (GL and SL Entries) The following Special Revenue Fund transactions and events occurred in Annette County during 19X1.

1. The annual budget adopted included these estimated revenues:

| | |
|---|---|
| Property taxes ....................................... | $ 500,000 |
| Payment in lieu of taxes ............................. | 200,000 |
| Federal grants ...................................... | 150,000 |
| State grants ........................................ | 50,000 |
| Interest ........................................... | 10,000 |
| Other ............................................. | 90,000 |
| | $1,000,000 |

2. Property taxes of $520,000 were levied for 19X1. It was estimated that 3% discounts for early payment would total $8,000, and that $12,000 of the taxes would never be collected; but the balance is expected to be available to finance 19X1 expenditures.

3. Property taxes billed at $280,000 in transaction 2 were collected within the 3% discount period.

4. Cash was received (drawn down) on a restricted federal grant for which no expenditures had been made, $50,000.

5. A restricted state grant of $60,000 was awarded, but no related expenditures have been made; nor has any grant cash been received.

6. Qualifying expenditures incurred were vouchered: (a) $45,000 for the federal grant program (transaction 4) and (b) $30,000 for the state grant program. The federal grant program reimburses 80% of qualifying costs, whereas the state grant pays cost plus a 20% of cost overhead allowance.

7. An annual payment in lieu of property taxes from the water, sewer, and electricity utility fund was received, $300,000. The property taxes that would be paid if these properties were taxable would be $225,000.

8. The revenue estimates in the original budget adopted (transaction 1) were revised. The estimate for federal grants was reduced by $5,000, and that for interest earnings was increased by $2,000.

9. It was discovered that the 19X1 beginning Accounts Receivable balance was overstated by $15,000, and that $4,000 of 19X1 revenues had improperly been credited to the Federal Grants revenue account rather than to the State Grants revenue account.

10. At the end of 19X1, the following information was learned in the adjusting entry process:
    a. Some $30,000 of collectible 19X1 property tax receivables will not be collected until mid-19X2.
    b. Additional qualifying expenditures of $10,000 on the state grant program (transactions 5 and 6) have been incurred and recorded, but no related revenues have been recognized.
    c. Unrecorded interest earnings accrued at year end were $1,000.

**Required** Prepare the general journal entries to record these 19X1 transactions and events in the General Ledger, Revenues Subsidiary Ledger, and Expenditures Subsidiary Ledger of the Special Revenue Fund of Annette County.

**P 5-10** (Error Correction, Change in Accounting Principle, and Adjusting Entries) The following transactions and events affected a Special Revenue Fund of Stem Independent School District during 19X4.

1. The chief accountant discovered that (a) the $20,000 proceeds of a sale of used educational equipment in 19X3 had been recorded as 19X4 revenues when received in early 19X4, and (b) $150,000 of property taxes receivable were not available at the end of 19X3 but were reported as revenues in 19X3.

2. Because of a change in the timing of the payments of the state minimum education program assistance grants to school districts, the related revenue recognition policy was changed. Substantial amounts of the state payments for the prior fiscal year previously were accrued as deferred revenue at year end under the old policy, but most will now be considered available revenue. The comparative Deferred State Assistance account balances at the end of the current year and prior year under the old and new policies were determined to be:

| *Deferred State Assistance* | *Old Policy* | *New Policy* |
| --- | --- | --- |
| End of 19X3 .................................... | $300,000 | $ 75,000 |
| End of 19X4 .................................... | 400,000 | 100,000 |

3. The auditor discovered the following errors:
   a. Special instruction fees of $8,000 paid for the hearing-impaired education program, properly charged to the 19X4 Education—Hearing-Impaired account in the General Fund, were charged to that account in this Special Revenue Fund.
   b. Some $130,000 of federal grant revenues were earned by incurring qualifying expenditures during 19X3, but no grant cash had been received and no revenues were recorded in 19X3. Furthermore, the federal grantor agency has not been billed for this payment.
   c. An operating transfer from the General Fund during 19X4, $85,000, was credited to the Revenues—Other account in this Special Revenue Fund.

d. Interest revenue earned and received during 19X4, $15,000, was improperly recorded as other revenues, whereas a separate Revenues—Interest account is maintained.

e. A 19X4 payment in lieu of taxes by the federal government was erroneously credited to the Education—General and Administrative expenditures account, $50,000.

4. The following adjusting entries were determined to be necessary at the end of 19X4:

a. State special education grants received during 19X4 and recorded as 19X4 revenues, $800,000, were only 75% earned by incurring qualifying expenditures during 19X4.

b. The Stem Independent School District was notified that the state had collected $300,000 of sales taxes for its benefit and would remit them early in 19X5.

**Required** Prepare the journal entries to record these error corrections, changes in accounting principle, and adjustments in the general ledger and subsidiary ledger accounts of the Special Revenue Fund of Stem Independent School District.

**P 5-11** (Investments Fair Value Analysis) The fair values of the Bruni Independent School District (BISD) General Fund investments, all subject to the fair value provisions of GASB *Statement No. 31*, were:

|  | Fair Value | |
|---|---|---|
| Investment | 7/1/X3 | 6/30/X4 |
| A | $10,000 | $ 4,000 |
| B | 5,000 | 29,000 |
| C | 20,000 | — |
| D | — | 15,000 |
| E | — | 40,000 |

During the X3–X4 fiscal year, the BISD had purchased and sold securities as follows:

| Investment | Cost of Purchases | Sales Proceeds |
|---|---|---|
| A | $ — | $ 7,000 |
| B | 20,000 | — |
| C | — | 19,000 |
| D | 13,000 | — |
| E | 43,000 | — |

**Required** (1) Compute the net change in the fair value of the BISD investments using (a) the specific identification method, and (b) the aggregate method.

(2) Prepare the general journal entry required to record the net change in the fair value of the General Fund investment portfolio.

**P 5-12** Obtain a copy of a recent comprehensive annual financial report (CAFR) of a state or local government from the government, the Internet, your professor, or a library.

**Required** (1) Letter of Transmittal. Review the revenue-related discussions and presentations. What were the most significant general government revenue sources? Which general government revenues increased (decreased) significantly from the previous year?

(2) Financial Statements. Indicate the sources of general government revenues. Did any revenue sources differ from what you expected based on your study of Chapters 2–5? Explain.

(3) Summary of Significant Accounting Policies (SOSAP). Review the general government revenue-related SOSAP disclosures. Were any of these disclosures different from, or in addition to, those you expected based on your study of Chapters 2–5? Explain.

(4) <u>Statistical Section.</u> Review the general government revenue-related statistical presentations. Explain how these might be useful in evaluating the general government financial position and changes in financial position.

(5) <u>Reporting.</u> Include photocopies or printouts of relevant excerpts from the CAFR with your brief written report on items 1–4 and submit your CAFR if required by your instructor.

CHAPTER

# 6

# EXPENDITURE ACCOUNTING— GOVERNMENTAL FUNDS

The annual operating budget prepared by the executive branch contains the activity and expenditure plans the chief executive wants to carry out during a fiscal year. The legislative branch reviews the plans, and by providing appropriations it enters into a contract with the executive branch for putting into effect those plans—or as much of the plans as it endorses. The executive branch is then charged with the responsibility of carrying out the contract in a legal and efficient manner.

The primary measurement focus of governmental funds is on financial position and changes in financial position. Therefore, activities financed through such funds are usually planned, authorized, controlled, and evaluated in terms of expenditures—the primary outflow measurement in governmental fund accounting. Expenditures is a different measurement concept than expenses in that **expenditures** is a measure of fund liabilities incurred (or fund financial resources used) during a period for operations, capital outlay, and debt service. **Expenses** is a measure of costs expired or consumed during a period.

This chapter focuses on **expenditure accounting** for **governmental funds.** Specifically, it addresses:

1. The definition of expenditures in the governmental fund accounting environment and the expenditure recognition criteria used;
2. Expenditure accounting controls and procedures;
3. Classification of expenditure accounts; and
4. Several important expenditure accounting topics—including claims and judgments, compensated absences, unfunded and underfunded pension contributions, appropriations revisions, and changes in expenditure accounting principles.

Three appendices to this chapter discuss and illustrate multiple classifications of expenditure accounts, accounting for annual appropriations under differing encumbrance-lapsing provisions, and accounting for multiyear or continuing appropriations.

The discussions and illustrations in this chapter, like those in Chapters 4 and 5, assume that there are no significant differences between the SLG's budgetary basis and the GAAP basis. Also, except where noted otherwise, the accounts are maintained on (or near) the GAAP basis during the year. Non-GAAP basis budgetary accounting and reporting, adjustment of non-GAAP basis accounting data to the GAAP basis, and related topics are discussed and illustrated in Chapter 14.

## EXPENDITURE DEFINITION AND RECOGNITION

Expenditures may be defined in a governmental fund accounting context as all decreases in fund net assets—for current operations, capital outlay, or debt service—except those arising from operating and residual equity transfers to other funds. Only quasi-external transactions result in the recognition of fund expenditures that are not expenditures of the government as a whole.

The GASB *Codification* states that:

> The **measurement focus** of governmental fund accounting is upon **expenditures**—decreases in net financial resources—rather than expenses.[1]

The *Codification* observes that most expenditures and transfers out are objectively measurable and should be recorded when the related fund liability is incurred. Specifically, it provides that:

> Expenditures should be recognized in the accounting period in which the **fund liability** is **incurred,** if measurable, **except** for **unmatured** interest [and principal] on general long-term debt, which should be recognized **when due.**[2]

The reasons why principal and interest expenditures on general long-term debt usually are not accrued at year end, and when they should be accrued, are explained as follows:

> The **major exception** to the general rule of **expenditure accrual** relates to **unmatured principal and interest** on **general obligation long-term debt**. . . . Financial resources usually are appropriated in other funds for transfer to a debt service fund in the period in which maturing debt principal and interest must be paid. Such amounts thus are not current liabilities of the debt service fund as their settlement will not require expenditure of existing fund assets.[3]

Thus, both GLTD principal retirement expenditures and related interest expenditures usually are recorded when they are due to be paid rather than being accrued at year end. But the *Codification* also states that:

> On the other hand, **if** debt service fund **resources have been provided** during the current year for payment of principal and interest **due early in the following year,** the expenditure and related liability **may** be recognized in the debt service fund and the debt

---

[1] GASB *Codification,* sec. 1600.118. (Emphasis added.)
[2] Ibid., sec. 1100.108. (Emphasis added.)
[3] Ibid., sec. 1600.123. (Emphasis added.)

principal amount removed from the GLTDAG (General Long-Term Debt Account Group).[4]

Furthermore, the *Codification* provides two other expenditure recognition alternatives:

1. **Inventory** items (for example, materials and supplies) may be considered expenditures **either** when purchased (**purchases method**) or when used (**consumption method**), but significant amounts of inventory should be reported in the balance sheet.
2. Expenditures for **insurance and similar services** extending over more than one accounting period [prepayments] need not be allocated between or among accounting periods, but may be accounted for as expenditures of the period of acquisition.[5]

### Capital Outlay Expenditures

Accounting for capital outlay expenditures typically financed from the General Fund and Special Revenue Funds—such as for equipment, machinery, and vehicles—was discussed and illustrated in Chapter 4. One additional type of capital outlay transaction that may be accounted for in the General Fund and Special Revenue Funds—the acquisition of fixed assets by capital lease—is discussed and illustrated later in this chapter. Most major general government capital outlay expenditures usually are accounted for through Capital Projects Funds, though many are at least partially financed by interfund transfers from the General or Special Revenue Funds. Accordingly, accounting for major capital expenditures is discussed and illustrated further in Chapter 7, "Capital Projects Funds."

### Debt Service Expenditures

The main reason for the usual "when due" recognition of GLTD principal and interest expenditures is that most governments budget on a **"when due"** basis. Thus, the appropriations for GLTD principal and interest expenditures equal the payments to be made during the year, irrespective of any accruals at year end. Permitting governments to account and report for GAAP purposes on the basis on which the budget is prepared avoids a significant GAAP-budgetary difference that would have to be explained and reconciled in almost every governmental fund financial statement. There also are other practical and theoretical reasons for this "when due" approach.

Most GLTD debt service is accounted for through Debt Service Funds, though (1) capital lease debt service may be accounted for in the General Fund and in Special Revenue Funds, and (2) financial resources may be transferred from the General Fund and Special Revenue Funds to finance debt service payments accounted for in Debt Service Funds. Accordingly, accounting for capital lease debt service is discussed and illustrated in this chapter; and both "when due" recognition of GLTD principal and interest expenditures and the alternative "before due" recognition for payments due early in the following year are discussed and illustrated further in Chapter 8, "Debt Service Funds."

### Intergovernmental Expenditures

State governments, in particular, often incur intergovernmental expenditures under state revenue-sharing, grant, and other financial assistance programs to counties, cities, school districts, and other local governments. State gasoline taxes

---

[4] Ibid. (Emphasis added.)
[5] Ibid., sec. 1600.124. (Emphasis added.)

may be shared with cities and counties, for example, and program grants and other aid may be provided to school districts within the state. The intergovernmental expenditure classification signals that these state-level expenditures were not for goods and services at that level, but were payments to local governments for local-level expenditure.

### Current Operating Expenditures

All governmental fund expenditures other than those for capital outlay, GLTD debt service, or intergovernmental purposes are referred to as *current operating* expenditures or simply *operating* expenditures.

Payroll and related personnel costs are the largest current operating expenditures of most state and local governments. Indeed, payroll and related costs often compose 65–75% of the General and Special Revenue Fund expenditures of cities, counties, and other local governments and 75–85% of public school system expenditures of these fund types. Accordingly, accounting procedures for personal services expenditures are discussed in this chapter, as are those for inventories and prepayments.

### Inventories and Prepayments

The GASB permits inventories and prepayments to be charged as expenditures immediately because—from a cash or convertible to cash perspective—such items are not financial resources available for financing future expenditures. In essence, this alternative permits those governments that wish to do so to follow a quick assets concept of working capital in accounting for fund balance and changes in fund financial position. Also, many governments make appropriations in terms of the inventory to be acquired or insurance to be purchased during a fiscal year. Permitting them to report such items on the budgetary basis in the governmental fund Statement of Revenues, Expenditures, and Changes in Fund Balance avoids a potential conflict between budgetary accounting procedures and generally accepted accounting principles that would have to be explained and reconciled in the notes to the financial statements. Governmental fund inventory accounting procedures are discussed and illustrated further later in this chapter.

## EXPENDITURE ACCOUNTING CONTROLS

The accounting system is a powerful tool for control of both the legality and efficiency of expenditures. Though its obvious role is financial, it may also be used to record and report quantitative data of all kinds. Indeed, the statistical data that must be estimated and accumulated to plan and control virtually all the operations of a government are best used in conjunction with financial data, and frequently the two kinds of data can be accumulated simultaneously. The accounting system also plays important *managerial* roles with respect to the following problems and controls:

- Misapplication of assets
- Illegal expenditures
  —Overspending of appropriations
  —Spending for illegal purposes
- Use of improper methods and procedures

- Unwise or inappropriate expenditures
- Allocation and allotment of appropriations

In general the expenditure control principles are internal control principles and procedures, and an exhaustive discussion of that topic is not presented here.[6]

## EXPENDITURE ACCOUNTING PROCEDURES

Expenditures are classified and coded during the preaudit step of the expenditure control process. Preaudit consists of approving transactions before they occur, as in the case of purchase order encumbrances, or before they are recorded, as in the case of expenditures. The chief accounting officer is usually responsible for this function, although large departments may have accountants who perform some or all of the preaudit functions. The goals of the preaudit of expenditures are to control the methods and procedures involved in the expenditure process as well as to prevent illegal expenditures.

Most governmental units use some form of the voucher system, which requires that all disbursements be authorized by an approved voucher. The voucher itself constitutes an outline of the steps that must be performed in making sure that appropriate procedures have been followed in the process of requisitioning, purchasing, receiving, and approving invoices for payment.

Vouchers usually provide a space by each step in the approval and preaudit process for the persons responsible for each step to sign or initial after completing that step. These signature blocks also are an important part of the postaudit trail of transactions that is evaluated both in the study of internal controls and as transactions are tested in the postaudit process.

All governmental fund expenditures—whether current operating, capital outlay, debt service, or intergovernmental—should be properly controlled through the voucher and preaudit processes and included in the scope of the postaudit. Because most accounting procedures for capital outlay and debt service expenditures are discussed in the Capital Projects Funds and Debt Service Funds chapters, this chapter focuses primarily on accounting for current operating expenditures.

### Personal Services

The steps in accounting for personal services are (1) ensuring that the person is a bona fide employee, (2) determining rates of pay, (3) establishing the amounts earned by employees, (4) recording payments made to employees, and (5) charging the resultant expenditures to the proper accounts.

The personal services expenditures charged against the departmental appropriations properly include employee fringe benefit costs—such as employer payroll taxes, insurance costs, pension and other retirement benefit costs, and the costs of compensated absences such as vacation and sick leave time—as well as employee salaries and wages. However, many governments make separate appropriations for fringe benefit expenditures, and charge the expenditures against such

---

[6] See Auditing Standards Board, American Institute of Certified Public Accountants, *Codification of Statements on Auditing Standards,* sec. 319, and related interpretations.

separate appropriations rather than as departmental expenditures. Although such expenditures are preferably appropriated and recorded as department or activity costs, the use of separate fringe benefit appropriations and expenditure accounts is an accepted alternative in practice.

### Pension Cost Expenditure Recognition

Most state and local governments contribute to a pension or retirement plan for the benefit of their employees. Some participate in statewide or other group plans, but others manage their own plans. Transactions between a government and its self-managed pension plans are considered quasi-external transactions. Therefore, properly determined pension contributions are recognized as expenditures, not transfers, in the employer governmental funds. A few smaller governments have no pension plans or have informal arrangements where certain employees receive retirement benefits that are charged as expenditures on a pay-as-you-go cash basis. But most governments have or participate in either defined contribution or defined benefit pension plans.

### Defined Contribution Plans

The government employer's obligation under a defined contribution pension plan is limited to making the contributions required to the plan. Retiree benefits are determined by the total contributions to the defined contribution plan on the retiree's behalf and by the plan's investment performance over time. Benefits are not guaranteed by the employer government. Governments with defined contribution plans should charge the required contribution amount—including current accruals at year end—to expenditures in the year it was earned by the general government employees.[7] Noncurrent liabilities for underpayments are considered general long-term debt. Most state and local governments comply with this expenditure recognition requirement. Once the appropriate contribution is paid, these governments have no further liability under the defined contribution pension plan.

### Defined Benefit Plans

Most state and local government pension and retirement plans are defined benefit plans. Under a defined benefit plan, the government guarantees the employee-retiree a determinable pension benefit, which is usually based on a formula such as:

1. number of years service ×
2. average compensation during the highest 3–5 years ×
3. a percentage, such as 1½–2% =
4. annual pension or retirement benefit.

The annual benefit is divided by 12 to determine the monthly benefit.

Defined benefit pension plan contributions must of necessity be based on numerous actuarial estimates. Such estimates include the number of years an employee will serve; levels of inflation and pay rates over time; employee turnover; retiree life spans and mortality rates; and plan funding, investment returns, and

---

[7] GASB *Codification,* sec. P20.121.

administrative costs. Furthermore, plan provisions may be changed in the future or other events may occur that necessitate major revisions of actuarial estimates of the government employer's ultimate liabilities under the defined benefit pension plan. Thus, the amount that should properly be recognized as governmental fund expenditures and liabilities (current and noncurrent) each year under defined benefit pension plans is difficult to estimate.

GASB *Statement No. 27,* "Accounting for Pensions by State and Local Governmental Employers," provides extensive guidance—including specific actuarial parameters that must be met—to determine the employer's annual required contribution (ARC). The ARC typically is paid during the year or any unpaid portion is considered a current liability at year end. For most governments, then, the ARC equals the annual pension expenditure. However, GASBS 27 specifies that, consistent with the modified accrual basis, any noncurrent underpayment liability should be recorded in the General Long-Term Debt Account Group.[8]

Accounting for pension plan contributions—including dividing the pension cost and liability recognition between the governmental funds and the GLTD Account Group—is discussed and illustrated later in the "Adjusting Entries" section of this chapter. Pension Trust Fund accounting and reporting are discussed and illustrated in Chapter 10.

### Materials and Supplies

The accounting procedures for materials and supplies may be divided into two parts: (1) accounting for purchases and (2) accounting for the use of materials and supplies.

#### Accounting for Purchases

The details of purchasing procedures vary according to whether

1. the materials and supplies are purchased directly by individual departments or through a central purchasing agency, and
2. the materials and supplies are purchased for a central storeroom or directly for departments.

Nearly all city, county, and state governments, as well as the federal government, use varying degrees of central purchasing. Throughout this chapter purchases are assumed to be made through a central agency. If a central storeroom is not used, all materials and supplies are delivered directly to the departments; and, even if a storeroom is used, many deliveries will be made directly to departments.

The purchasing procedure and the related accounting procedures consist of the following steps:

1. preparing purchase requisitions and placing them with the purchasing agent,
2. securing prices or bids,
3. placing orders,
4. receiving the materials and supplies,
5. receiving the invoice and approving the liability, and
6. paying the liability.

---

[8] Ibid., sec. P20.113.

### Accounting for Materials and Supplies Used

As in all governmental activities, the law may to some degree determine the practices a government uses to provide and account for materials and supplies used by its departments, but the law and policy may allow substantial latitude. Two legal assumptions are dealt with in the following paragraphs:

1. The Expenditures account is to be charged with the amount of materials and supplies consumed (consumption method).

2. The Expenditures account is to be charged with the amount of materials and supplies purchased (purchases method).

Both are recognized as acceptable alternatives in the GASB *Codification,* and a state or local government typically selects the alternative that corresponds with the inventory appropriations method in its annual operating budget in order to avoid a budget-GAAP basis difference. Moreover, the consumption method can be used with either a periodic or perpetual inventory system, whereas the purchases method is invariably used with the periodic inventory system. The essence of governmental fund inventory accounting and reporting is summarized in Figure 6–1.

### Consumption Method

When stores accounting is on the consumption method, the inventory-related appropriations are provided on the basis of estimated usage and the Expenditures account is charged with actual usage. As noted earlier, inventory may be kept on the consumption method using either a periodic or a perpetual system.

FIGURE 6–1  **Inventory Accounting Methods Overview**

| | Consumption Method | | Purchases Method |
|---|---|---|---|
| | **Periodic System** | **Perpetual System** | |
| **When Purchased** | Expenditures    XX<br>  Vouchers Payable    XX | Inventory of Supplies    XX<br>  Vouchers Payable    XX | Expenditures    XX<br>  Vouchers Payable    XX |
| **When Issued** | No entry | Expenditures    XX<br>  Inventory of Supplies    XX | No entry |
| **End of Year** | Inventory of Supplies  XX<br>  Expenditures    XX<br><br>(To record increase in inventory during the year. If inventory decreased, accounts would be reversed.) | **No entry required—unless there is:**<br><br>• a shortage (increase expenditures and decrease inventory)<br>or<br>• an overage (decrease expenditures and increase inventory) | **If inventory level increases:**<br><br>Inventory of Supplies    X<br>  OFS—Inventory Increase    X<br>Unreserved Fund Balance    X<br>  Reserve for Inventory<br>    of Supplies    X<br><br>**If inventory level decreases:**<br><br>OFU—Inventory Decrease    X<br>  Inventory of Supplies    X<br>Reserve for Inventory<br>  of Supplies    X<br>  Unreserved Fund Balance    X |
| **Reserve for Inventory of Supplies** | Not required—optional | Not required—optional | Required—as shown above |

**Periodic System**     When the periodic inventory system is used with the **consumption** method, typical entries (encumbrances and subsidiary ledger entries omitted) are as follows:

**When Purchased:**

| | | |
|---|---|---|
| Expenditures . . . . . . . . . . . . . . . . . . . . . . . . . . . . . . . . . . . . . . . . . . . . . . . | $850,000 | |
|    Vouchers Payable . . . . . . . . . . . . . . . . . . . . . . . . . . . . . . . . . . . . | | $850,000 |

To record inventory purchases during the year.

**When Issued:**

No entry

**End of Year:**

| | | |
|---|---|---|
| Inventory of Supplies . . . . . . . . . . . . . . . . . . . . . . . . . . . . . . . . . . . | $72,500 | |
|    Expenditures . . . . . . . . . . . . . . . . . . . . . . . . . . . . . . . . . . . . . . . | | $72,500 |

To record the increase in inventory during the fiscal period, or
to record the inventory at the end of the first year of the fund's
existence, and reduce expenditures accordingly.

These entries may be accompanied by an entry to adjust the reserve account because inventory is not an expendable financial resource—even though the supplies are available to finance subsequent period expenditures because (1) having the inventory obviates the need to buy the items later, and (2) inventory costs are not charged to Expenditures until the items are used. The entry to adjust the Reserve for Inventory of Supplies to fully reserve fund balance for the inventory on hand—as is usually assumed in Uniform CPA Examination Unofficial Solutions—would be:

| | | |
|---|---|---|
| Unreserved Fund Balance . . . . . . . . . . . . . . . . . . . . . . . . . . . . . . . | $72,500 | |
|    **Reserve for Inventory of Supplies** . . . . . . . . . . . . . . . . . . . . . . . | | $72,500 |

To adjust the reserve to equal the valuation of the supplies on hand.

The debits and credits in the last two entries would be reversed if the inventory had decreased.

Some accountants would not routinely fully reserve fund balance for inventory under the consumption method. They believe that inventory is as available to finance future expenditures as is cash—because inventory on hand is an asset, is not charged to Expenditures until issued, and obviates future cash disbursements. Thus, they do not reserve fund balance unless some of the inventory is not available. For example, if a minimum base stock of $15,000 of inventory must be maintained at all times, they would reserve $15,000 of fund balance because that amount of the inventory is not available for issuance to finance expenditures or avoid future cash disbursements.

Practice varies with regard to reserving fund balance under the consumption method. Indeed, fully reserving, not reserving, and partially reserving inventory all are common in practice. The authors believe that the partial reserving approach is most in keeping with the theory underlying the consumption method of inventory accounting.

**Perpetual System**     When a perpetual inventory system is used with the **consumption** method, the entries are as follows (encumbrances and subsidiary ledger entries again omitted):

**When Purchased:**

| | | |
|---|---|---|
| Inventory of Supplies .................................... | $850,000 | |
|    Vouchers Payable ...................................... | | $850,000 |

To record the purchases of supplies.

**When Issued:**

| | | |
|---|---|---|
| Expenditures ......................................... | $774,000 | |
|    Inventory of Supplies ................................. | | $774,000 |

To charge Expenditures for the supplies issued.

**End of Year:**

| | | |
|---|---|---|
| Expenditures ......................................... | $3,500 | |
|    Inventory of Supplies ................................. | | $3,500 |

To record inventory shortage, per physical inventory. (If there is an overage, the accounts debited and credited in this entry are reversed.)

**If Inventory Fully Reserved:**

| | | |
|---|---|---|
| Unreserved Fund Balance ............................... | $72,500 | |
|    Reserve for Inventory of Supplies ....................... | | $72,500 |

To adjust the reserve for the increase in inventory during the period. (If there has been a decrease in inventory during the period, the entry is reversed.)

Note that the entry affecting the Reserve for Inventory of Supplies is based on the assumption that the Reserve for Inventory of Supplies is to be maintained at an amount equal to the inventory. Again, although this fully reserving practice is common, theoretically only the normal minimum (base stock) amount of inventory should be reserved—because under the consumption method of inventory accounting, inventory is not charged to Expenditures until consumed and, hence, may be viewed as a financial resource available to finance future expenditures.

The primary advantage of the perpetual system is that the government knows both (1) the inventory that should have been on hand at year end and (2) by comparison with what actually is on hand, the amount of the inventory overage or shortage at year end. Under the periodic system, the government knows only what is on hand at year end and cannot distinguish what was used from what was stolen, damaged, or improperly accounted for. Thus, as in business accounting, under the periodic inventory system what is termed *cost of goods sold* is in fact "cost of goods sold, stolen, or otherwise mysteriously disappeared or not accounted for properly."

Ideally, then, all governments (and other organizations) would use a perpetual inventory system. But, whereas perpetual inventory systems provide better accounting control and information, they also add accounting system implementation and operating costs. Thus, accounting system decisions, like other decisions, must be evaluated from a cost-benefit perspective. The usual result is that (1) the perpetual inventory system is used to account for large amounts of supplies and other inventories that justify the accounting control costs involved from an asset management and/or expenditure accounting perspective; but (2) lesser amounts of inventory, inventories that do not lend themselves to perpetual systems (e.g., sand and gravel), and inventories that may be controlled otherwise (e.g., by department personnel) are accounted for on the periodic system—on either the consumption method or the purchases method.

## Purchases Method

The purchases method is used when the inventory-related appropriations are based on estimated purchases. Its use is limited to the **periodic** system because it is not compatible with the perpetual inventory system. Under the purchases method, the Expenditures account is charged with inventory purchases during the year.

Assuming the same dollar amounts used in the preceding consumption basis illustration (and again omitting encumbrance and subsidiary ledger entries), the entries under the purchases method would be:

**When Purchased:**

Expenditures . . . . . . . . . . . . . . . . . . . . . . . . . . . . . . . . . . . . . . . . $850,000

   Vouchers Payable . . . . . . . . . . . . . . . . . . . . . . . . . . . . . . . .            $850,000

To record the purchase of supplies.

**During the Year:**

No entry

**End of Year:**

(a) Inventory of Supplies . . . . . . . . . . . . . . . . . . . . . . . . . . . . . . $72,500

     **Other Financing Sources—Inventory Increase**

       (or Unreserved Fund Balance) . . . . . . . . . . . . . . . . . . . . .          $72,500

    To record the increase in inventory during the year, or to record the inventory at the end of the first year of the fund's existence.

(b) Unreserved Fund Balance . . . . . . . . . . . . . . . . . . . . . . . . . . . . $72,500

     Reserve for Inventory of Supplies . . . . . . . . . . . . . . . . . . . . .          $72,500

    To fully reserve the inventory of supplies.

Note that under the purchases method all inventory purchases are charged to Expenditures and no inventory-related entries are made during the year. In these ways it is like the consumption system using the periodic inventory system. However, at year end, the increase in the inventory is debited to Inventory of Supplies in both cases but is:

- Credited to Expenditures under the consumption method, adjusting that account to the cost of goods used (assuming no shortage or overage because of theft, accounting errors, and so on).
- Credited to Other Financing Sources—Inventory Increase (or Unreserved Fund Balance) rather than to Expenditures under the purchases method, leaving the total cost of inventory purchased charged to Expenditures.

The credit to Other Financing Sources—Inventory Increase (or Unreserved Fund Balance) in entry (a) at year end results from the fact that GAAP permits use of the purchases method only for expenditure accounting. Any significant amounts of inventory must be reported in the governmental fund balance sheet. Because, as compared with the consumption method, the purchases method overstates Expenditures—in this case, by $72,500—the Unreserved Fund Balance account will be understated $72,500 after the Expenditures account is closed. Thus, the $72,500 credit to Other Financing Sources—Inventory Increase—which is closed at year end to Unreserved Fund Balance—or directly to Unreserved Fund Balance may be viewed as correcting for the understatement of Unreserved Fund Balance caused by the Expenditures overstatement.

The inventory must be fully reserved under the purchases method. This is because it has already been charged to Expenditures, even though reported as an asset on the balance sheet, and thus is not available to finance future expenditures. Accordingly, inventory is not considered a financial resource under the purchases method and is always fully reserved.

The change in the inventory and reserve must be reported as an Other Financing Source (Use) or as a Fund Balance Increase (Decrease) in the governmental fund Statement of Revenues, Expenditures, and Changes in Fund Balance when the purchases method is used. This is because the Expenditures and Unreserved Fund Balance misstatements noted earlier were corrected not only by debiting the Inventory of Supplies account but by crediting either the Other Financing Sources—Inventory Increase or the Unreserved Fund Balance account, thus increasing total fund balance. Thus, the increase in the Unreserved Fund Balance because of the inventory increase must be reported as an other financing source, and a decrease in inventory would be reported as an other financing use—under the purchases method (only)—in the Statement of Revenues, Expenditures, and Changes in Fund Balance. Furthermore, the beginning and ending fund balance amounts will not reconcile otherwise.

Finally, note that the foregoing end-of-year entries (a) and (b) are often compounded:

| | | |
|---|---|---|
| Inventory of Supplies . . . . . . . . . . . . . . . . . . . . . . . . . . . . . . . . . . . . . | $72,500 | |
| Reserve for Inventory of Supplies . . . . . . . . . . . . . . . . . . . . . . . . | | $72,500 |

To record the increase in and fully reserve the inventory of supplies.

This may be one reason that some governmental accountants view the purchases method end-of-year inventory adjustment as a "balance sheet plug" and do not realize that it must be reported as an other financing source (use).

## Other Services and Charges

When services are being acquired under contract, an entry is made encumbering appropriations for the amount of the estimated ultimate contractual liability at the time the contract is awarded. As services and the related invoices are received, the encumbering entries are reversed and the actual expenditures are recorded.

Whereas the accounting for most other services and charges is apparent from the discussions in this text, several specific types of other services and charges expenditures warrant at least brief mention. Two types are discussed here: (1) prepayments and (2) capital leases. Related topics—including (a) interest on short-term governmental fund debt, (b) claims and judgments, (c) compensated absences, and (d) pension contribution underfunding—are discussed in the "Adjusting Entries" section later in this chapter.

**Prepayments**    Governments may prepay costs that benefit two or more accounting periods. For example, a two-year insurance policy may be purchased or rental on a building may be paid for a year in advance at midyear. As in the case of inventories, governments are permitted to use **either** the **consumption** method **or** the **purchases** method in accounting for prepayments (prepayals).[9] Moreover, those using the purchases method need not report prepayments on the balance

---

[9] Ibid., sec. 1600.124.

sheet. Thus, if a two-year insurance policy were purchased at the beginning of 19X1, the entries (omitting subsidiary ledger entries) would be:

**When Purchased:**

| | | |
|---|---|---|
| Expenditures | $88,000 | |
| Vouchers Payable | | $88,000 |

To record payment for two-year insurance policy at beginning of 19X1.

**End of 19X1:**

(a) **Purchases Method**—No entry.

(b) **Consumption Method**—

| | | |
|---|---|---|
| Prepaid Insurance | $44,000 | |
| Expenditures | | $44,000 |

To record prepaid insurance.

**Beginning of 19X2:**

(a) **Purchases Method**—No entry.

(b) **Consumption Method**—

| | | |
|---|---|---|
| Expenditures | $44,000 | |
| Prepaid Insurance | | $44,000 |

To reverse the 19X1 adjusting entry and charge the applicable insurance cost to 19X2 expenditures.

**Capital Leases and Certificates of Participation**    Many governments lease assets—such as vehicles, computers, photocopy machines, other equipment, and buildings—rather than buying them. When such leases are ordinary rentals, for example, monthly rentals that may be canceled with little notice, the rents paid or accrued usually are recorded as rental expenditures. (Advance rental payments might be initially recorded as prepayments, as discussed earlier.) However, if the government is in substance buying the assets or is leasing them for most or all of their useful lives, GAAP requires that the accounting for such capital leases reflect their substance instead of their legal form.

Accordingly, GASB requirements adapt the FASB *Statement No. 13* capital lease accounting requirements, as amended and interpreted, for governmental accounting.[10] The GASB *Codification* requires that:

- General fixed assets acquired in capital lease agreements should be capitalized in the GFAAG at the inception of the lease at the present value of the future lease payments, as determined under FASB *Statement No. 13;* and a general long-term debt liability in the same amount (less any payment at inception) should be recorded concurrently in the GLTDAG.
- When a general fixed asset is acquired by capital lease, its acquisition should be reported in an appropriate governmental fund as both (1) a capital outlay expenditure for a fixed asset and (2) an other financing source, as if long-term debt had been issued to finance the fixed asset acquisition.[11]
- Capital lease proceeds need not be accounted for through a Capital Projects Fund, nor does capital lease debt service have to be accounted for through a Debt Service Fund, unless use of such funds is legally or contractually required.

Figure 6–2 presents an overview of general government capital lease accounting. The General Fixed Assets Account Group (GFAAG) and General Long-Term Debt Account Group (GLTDAG) entries are illustrated in Chapter 9. The key points here are that (1) a governmental fund expenditure and other financing source must be recognized at the inception of the lease; (2) neither use of a Capi-

---

[10] These requirements are discussed in intermediate accounting textbooks.

[11] GASB *Codification*, sec. L20.115.

FIGURE 6–2  **Capital Lease Accounting Overview**

| | General Fund (or other fund paying for capital lease) | General Fixed Assets Account Group | General Long-Term Debt Account Group |
|---|---|---|---|
| **Inception of the lease** | Expenditures— <br>    Capital Outlay   XX <br>    OFS—Capital Lease    XX <br><br> **Recorded at <u>present value</u> of the <u>future lease payments.</u>** | Equipment under <br>    Capital Lease    XX <br> Investment in GFA— <br>    Capital Lease    XX <br><br> **Recorded at <u>present value</u> of the <u>future lease payments.</u>** | Amount to Be Provided   XX <br>    Capital Leases Payable    XX <br><br><br> **Recorded at <u>present value</u> of the <u>future lease payments.</u>** |
| **Annual lease payment** | Expenditures—Capital <br>    Lease—Principal   XX <br> Expenditures—Capital <br>    Lease—Interest   XX <br> Cash (or Vouchers <br>    Payable)    XX <br><br> **Principal and interest amounts determined using the <u>effective interest</u> rate method.** | None | Capital Leases Payable   XX <br>    Amount to Be Provided    XX <br><br><br><br> **For principal amounts <u>only.</u>** |
| **Termination of lease** | Process last lease payment as above. | Equipment    XX <br>    Equipment under Capital <br>     Lease    XX <br><br> **Asset acquired at end of lease term.** | After last lease payment, balance of the above accounts will be 0 (zero). |

tal Projects Fund at the inception of the capital lease nor use of a Debt Service Fund to service the capital lease debt is required unless legally or contractually required, which is rare; and thus (3) both the governmental fund expenditure and other financing source and the related debt service on the capital lease may be accounted for in the General Fund or perhaps a Special Revenue Fund.

To illustrate, assume that a general government department entered into a capital lease of equipment. The capitalizable cost of the equipment per FASB *Statement No. 13* is $900,000 and the government makes a $50,000 down payment at the inception of the lease. The first monthly lease payment after inception is for $17,821, including $5,250 of interest.

Regardless of the governmental fund in which the capital lease transaction and debt service are recorded, the entries are:

**Inception of Capital Lease:**

| | | |
|---|---|---|
| Expenditures . . . . . . . . . . . . . . . . . . . . . . . . . . . . . . . . . . . . . . . . . . . . | $900,000 | |
|    **Other Financing Sources—Capital Lease** . . . . . . . . . . . . . . . . . . | | $850,000 |
|    Cash . . . . . . . . . . . . . . . . . . . . . . . . . . . . . . . . . . . . . . . . . . . . . . | | 50,000 |

To record capital lease expenditure and related other financing source.

Expenditures Ledger (Expenditures):

| | | |
|---|---|---|
| Capital Outlay . . . . . . . . . . . . . . . . . . . . . . . . . . . . . . . . . . . . . . . . | <u>$900,000</u> | |

**First Debt Service Payment:**

| | | |
|---|---|---|
| Expenditures . . . . . . . . . . . . . . . . . . . . . . . . . . . . . . . . . . . . . . . . . . | $17,821 | |
|    Vouchers Payable . . . . . . . . . . . . . . . . . . . . . . . . . . . . . . . . . . . . | | $17,821 |

To record capital lease debt service payment due.

Expenditures Ledger (Expenditures):

| | | |
|---|---|---|
| Debt Service—Interest (Capital Lease) . . . . . . . . . . . . . . . . . . . . | $ 5,250 | |
| Debt Service—Principal (Capital Lease) . . . . . . . . . . . . . . . . . . . | <u>12,571</u> | |
| | <u>$17,821</u> | |

Note that the effect of the entry at the inception of the lease on the fund balance of the governmental fund is equal to the decrease in fund financial resources of $50,000. This is the net effect of the $850,000 other financing source and the $900,000 expenditure. $900,000 is also the amount of the fair market value of the fixed asset acquired, that is, the present value of the capital lease. Note too that the capital lease debt service payment must be allocated between interest expenditures and debt principal reduction based on the effective interest rate of the capital lease agreement. The effective interest amount for the first payment is computed by multiplying the effective interest rate for the lease by the carrying amount (book value) of the lease liability, initially $850,000, and dividing by 12.

Several variations of the traditional capital lease have appeared recently. Certificates of participation (COPs) typically involve governments dealing with brokerage firms rather than product manufacturers or banks—and receiving cash that is used to purchase the computers, vehicles, or other equipment. COPs are otherwise like traditional leases and are accounted for in the same manner.

## CLASSIFICATION OF EXPENDITURES

A governmental unit's expenditures are classified in several ways to serve several managerial and financial reporting purposes. As observed in the GASB *Codification:*

> Multiple classification of governmental fund expenditure data is important from both internal and external management control and accountability standpoints. It facilitates the aggregation and analysis of data in different ways for different purposes and in manners that cross fund and organizational lines, for internal evaluation, external reporting, and intergovernmental comparison purposes. The major accounting classifications of expenditures are by fund, function (or program), organization unit, activity, character, and object class.[12]

Because appropriations are made in terms of specified funds, the basic classification of expenditures is by fund. To produce all the required information, the expenditures of a fund are also classified by function or program, activity, organization unit, character, and object class.

The GASB *Codification* does not contain a detailed chart of expenditure accounts for state and local governments. However, the National Committee on Governmental Accounting, the predecessor of the National Council on Governmental Accounting and the GASB, prepared a standard classification of accounts, including expenditure accounts.[13] Although no longer required to be used, that classification of accounts, as updated by the GFOA in the 1994 edition of its *Governmental Accounting, Auditing and Financial Reporting,*[14] is widely used (and adapted) in practice.

The budgeting, accounting, and reporting systems of a governmental unit should be based on the same structure of accounts. Some state and local governments have accounting systems and charts of accounts that classify every expenditure transaction by fund, function or program, organization unit, activity, character, and object class. On the other hand, others use systems and charts of accounts that record expenditure data only in certain essential classifications—such as by fund,

---

[12] Ibid., sec. 1800.116.

[13] GAAFR (68), "Appendix B: Use of Account Classifications," pp. 175–201.

[14] GAAFR (94), Appendix C, pp. 361–410.

organization unit, and object class—and compile these data at year end to derive data for the other expenditure classifications.

Classification of expenditures by fund has been discussed earlier in this text, and is discussed further in later chapters. Appendix 6–1 discusses and illustrates governmental fund expenditure classification by (1) function or program, (2) activity, (3) organization unit, (4) character, and (5) object class.

## ACCOUNTING FOR ALLOCATIONS AND ALLOTMENTS

**Allocations** are executive branch subdivisions of legislative appropriations. Allocations do not cause any unique accounting procedures. Rather, they are accommodated in the Expenditures Ledger by establishing subsidiary accounts in at least as much detail as the allocations. To illustrate, assume that the legislative body made a lump-sum appropriation for the police department, but the executive branch then allocated specific maximum amounts by object-of-expenditure class. Only one subsidiary account (Police Department) would be needed to satisfy legislative budgetary control and accountability requirements in this instance, but a series of more detailed accounts (Police Department—Personal Services, etc.) would be needed to meet the more stringent executive branch budgetary control and accountability requirements. Hence, the subsidiary accounts must provide at least as much detail as is required to meet the more stringent requirements.

The chief executive may not allocate all the appropriations to the agencies immediately but may hold back some expenditure authority for contingencies that might arise during the year. In such cases an account such as Unallocated Appropriations should be established in either the General Ledger or the Expenditures Ledger.

**Allotments**—divisions of appropriations authority by time period, usually months or quarters—require modification of the General Ledger accounts and accounting procedures discussed so far. To illustrate, assume that the annual General Fund appropriations of A Governmental Unit—now made by organization unit and object class rather than by function—are allotted on a monthly basis, that $35,000 was allotted for the month of January 19X1, and that $350 of the total allotment was allotted to the fire department for supplies expenditures during January 19X1. Because only allotted appropriations constitute valid expenditure authority at the department or agency level, separate Unallotted Appropriations and Allotments (or Allotted Appropriations) control accounts are established in the General Ledger. The Allotted Appropriations account serves as a control account for the Expenditures Ledger. The Unallotted Appropriations account is not a control account for the subsidiary ledger. Therefore, the budgetary entry to record appropriations for the year and the allotments for January 19X1 would appear:

| | | |
|---|---:|---:|
| Unreserved Fund Balance ................................ | $426,000 | |
| **Unallotted Appropriations** ............................... | | $391,000 |
| **Allotments** (or **Allotted Appropriations**) ................... | | 35,000 |
| To record the 19X1 appropriations and January 19X1 allotments. | | |
| Expenditures Ledger (**Allotments**): | | |
| Fire Department—Firefighting Supplies ..................... | | $    350 |
| Fire Department—Other ................................... | | XX |
| Other Departments ....................................... | | XX |
| | | $ 35,000 |

As noted, the Allotments (or Allotted Appropriations), Expenditures, and Encumbrances accounts in the General Ledger control the Expenditures Ledger accounts where formal allotments are used. Thus, as noted earlier, the "Appropriations" column of the subsidiary ledger account is retitled "Allotments" (or Allotted Appropriations) and the "Unencumbered Balance" column—which previously contained the unencumbered balance of the annual appropriation—is retitled "Unencumbered Allotments."

At the beginning of each month or quarter (1) an appropriate amount will be reclassified from the Unallotted Appropriations account to the Allotments (or Allotted Appropriations) account in the General Ledger and, correspondingly, (2) appropriate amounts will be credited to the "Allotments" columns of the various Expenditures Ledger accounts. Assuming that all appropriations have been allotted by the end of 19X1, the Unallotted Appropriations account will have a zero balance and will require no closing entry at the end of 19X1.

Some governments do not allot all of the appropriations so that they have a cushion in the event that contingencies occur. If some appropriations have not been allotted, the balance of the Unallotted Appropriations account is closed at year end unless unexpended or unencumbered appropriations do not lapse (discussed in Appendix 6–3).

## APPROPRIATIONS REVISIONS

Appropriations may be revised during the year for a variety of reasons. Increases in revenues over those estimated—whether from regular sources or because of unanticipated special grants—may either permit or require additional expenditures that must be authorized by appropriations. Or, conversely, declines in revenues as compared with the original expectations may necessitate that appropriations be reduced to avoid a fund balance deficit.

Appropriations revisions may also arise because of utility cost increases, damage to streets caused by unusually cold or wet weather, unanticipated costs of patrolling and cleaning up the town after the hometown university won the national football championship, or for an infinite variety of other reasons. Appropriations increases are not necessarily bad, of course, nor are appropriations decreases necessarily good.

The continuing process of reviewing budgeted and actual revenues and comparing appropriations, expenditures, and encumbrances—and revising the budget as needed in view of changing circumstances—is considered good financial management. Thus, as noted earlier, an annual budget that may have been enacted well before the beginning of the current year should not be considered unchangeable but should be continually reviewed and appropriately revised throughout the year.

The accounting for appropriations revisions during the year parallels that discussed and illustrated in Chapter 5 for revenue budget revisions. Thus, it seems sufficient at this point to illustrate three common types of appropriations revisions and entries:

**Appropriations Increased:**

| | | |
|---|---:|---:|
| Unreserved Fund Balance ............................... | $10,000 | |
|    Appropriations ........................................ | | $10,000 |
| To record increase in appropriations. | | |

Expenditures Ledger (Appropriations):

| | |
|---|---:|
| Police Department—Salaries ............................. | $10,000 |

(The entry would be reversed if the appropriations were decreased.)

**Both Estimated Revenues and Appropriations Decreased:**

| | | |
|---|---|---|
| Appropriations ......................................... | $10,000 | |
|    Estimated Revenues .................................... | | $10,000 |

To record reduction in appropriations because of reduction in
estimated revenues.

Expenditures Ledger (Appropriations):

| | | |
|---|---|---|
| Parks and Recreation—Supplies ........................... | $ 4,000 | |
| Mayor's Office—Equipment .............................. | 6,000 | |
| | $10,000 | |

Revenues Ledger (Estimated Revenues):

| | | |
|---|---|---|
| Sales Taxes .......................................... | | $10,000 |

**Appropriations Shift between Departments:**

| | | |
|---|---|---|
| Appropriations ......................................... | $10,000 | |
|    Appropriations ......................................... | | $10,000 |

To record shift of appropriations from police department to fire
department.

Expenditures Ledger (Appropriations):

| | | |
|---|---|---|
| Police Department—Equipment ........................... | $10,000 | |
| Fire Department—Supplies ............................... | | $10,000 |

## ADJUSTING ENTRIES

Most of the expenditure-related adjusting entries that may be required in a governmental fund at year end are similar to those covered in intermediate accounting courses. That is, the accountant must ensure that there is a proper year-end cutoff of expenditures for payrolls, utilities, and similar costs.

The available revenue recognition criterion is not applicable in governmental fund expenditure accounting, and an expenditure payable beyond 60 days into the next year may be considered a current liability that should be recorded as a governmental fund expenditure and liability. However, the governmental fund expenditure recognition criteria are not as clearly defined as the available revenue recognition criterion. The general rule is that any expenditure and related liability applicable to a fund are recorded as a fund expenditure and liability unless the liability is a noncurrent liability that is properly classified as general long-term debt, and thus is recorded in the GLTDAG. In this regard the GASB *Codification* states that:

> ... general long-term debt is not limited to liabilities arising from debt issuances *per se*, but it **may also include noncurrent liabilities for other commitments** that are **not current liabilities properly recorded in governmental funds.**[15]

This paragraph of the *Codification* concludes with the statement that:

> ... in governmental funds, liabilities usually are **not** considered **current** [and thus fund expenditures] **until** they are **normally expected to be liquidated with expendable available financial resources.**[16]

This expenditure recognition criterion does not define the term *expendable available financial resources,* which seems to refer to the ending fund balance of the governmental fund, and has proven to be difficult to implement in practice.

---

[15] GASB *Codification*, sec. C60.111. (Emphasis added.)

[16] Ibid. (Emphasis added.)

Furthermore, differing interpretations of the criterion and varying levels of governmental fund expendable available financial resources have resulted in expenditure recognition inconsistencies among governments.

The notion of "to be liquidated with expendable available financial resources" is not an issue in most routine adjusting entries made at year end. Such accrued expenditure liabilities as payroll, utilities, and similar costs usually are presumed to be payable from existing fund resources and are accrued. Rather, the **"to be liquidated with expendable available financial resources"** notion relates primarily to accruing expenditures for (1) debt service, (2) claims and judgments, (3) accrued vacation and sick leave, referred to as compensated absences, and (4) pension plan contributions. These are the main topics of this section and are considered after a brief discussion of encumbrances.

## Encumbrances

The encumbrances outstanding at year end should be reviewed because, as noted in the GASB *Codification:*

> If performance on an executory contract is complete, or virtually complete, an expenditure and liability should be recognized rather than an encumbrance.[17]

A failure to record completed contracts as governmental fund expenditures and liabilities (rather than encumbrances) may be unintentional. Invoices for the goods or services may not have arrived at the government's offices by year end, for example, and they are inadvertently recorded as expenditures in the next year. On the other hand, it may be intentional—as when recording expenditures for an encumbered order would cause departmental expenditures to exceed appropriations. This might occur where the budgetary basis is the modified accrual basis—on which encumbrances are not considered equivalent to expenditures and thus are not charged against appropriations—or where the budgetary basis includes encumbrances but the encumbrance recorded is significantly less than the actual expenditure incurred.

In any event, the encumbrances outstanding against a governmental fund at year end should be analyzed. If any are found to be expenditures misclassified as encumbrances, the adjusting entry (omitting subsidiary ledger entries) would be:

| | | |
|---|---:|---:|
| Reserve for Encumbrances ............................... | $19,000 | |
| Expenditures ........................................... | 20,000 | |
|     Encumbrances ...................................... | | $19,000 |
|     Accounts Payable (or Accrued Liabilities) ................. | | 20,000 |

To record reclassifying encumbrances as expenditures at year end.

## Debt Service

As noted earlier, debt service on general long-term debt typically is not accrued at year end. This usually is consistent with the "to be liquidated with expendable available financial resources" criterion because the property tax rates of many state and local governments are set to provide the financial resources required for the GLTD debt service payments due each year. Thus, the financial resources available at the end of a year ordinarily need not be used for the following year's debt

---

[17] Ibid., sec. 1700.129(c).

service because those resources will be provided by that year's tax levy. On the other hand, if resources have been provided currently to pay GLTD debt service payments due early in the next year, those debt service payments (principal and interest) may be accrued at year end as governmental fund expenditures and liabilities. Clearly, the SLG should adopt an appropriate debt service expenditure accounting policy and apply it consistently each year.

It was noted earlier that state and local governments may borrow on **short-term** notes such as tax anticipation notes (TANs), revenue anticipation notes (RANs), and similar debt instruments. The GASB *Codification* states that TANs, RANs, and similar short-term debt instruments should be accounted for as a **fund liability** of the governmental fund that receives the proceeds.[18] Also, the short-term note and interest usually would be paid from that fund. Thus, whereas interest on general long-term debt is ordinarily recorded when due rather than accrued at year end, interest on governmental fund (non-GLTD) short-term notes and other debts is accrued at year end:

| | | |
|---|---|---|
| Expenditures ............................................... | $36,000 | |
|    Accrued Interest Payable ................................ | | $36,000 |

To record interest accrued at year end on **short-term** notes payable.

Expenditures Ledger (Expenditures):

| | |
|---|---|
| Interest ............................................... | <u>$36,000</u> |

## Claims and Judgments

Lawsuits and other claims for personal injury, property damage, employee compensation, or other reasons have increasingly been filed against states and local governments in recent years. Such claims include—but are by no means limited to—those arising from:

- Employment—such as worker compensation and unemployment claims;
- Contractual actions—such as claims for delays or inadequate specifications;
- Actions of government personnel—such as claims for medical malpractice, damage to privately owned vehicles by government-owned vehicles, and improper police arrest; and
- Government properties—such as claims relating to personal injuries and property damage.

Many claims filed against state and local governments are characterized by conditions that make it extremely difficult to reasonably estimate the ultimate liability, if any, that will result:

- *Unreasonably high claims.* Some claims may be filed in amounts far greater than those reasonably expected to be agreed to by the government and the claimant or awarded by a court.
- *Time between occurrence and filing.* The time permitted (e.g., by law) between the occurrence of an event giving rise to a claim and the actual filing of the claim may be lengthy. (An event leading to a claim may occur during a year but the claim may not be filed by year end; thus, the government may not be aware of the claim at year end.)
- *Time between filing, settlement, and payment.* Likewise, many months or even years may elapse between (1) the filing of the claim and its ultimate settlement, perhaps after court appeals, and (2) the settlement of the claim and its ultimate payment because adjudicated or agreed settlement amounts may be paid over a period of years after settlement.

---

[18] Ibid., sec. B50.101.

On the other hand, the outcome of some claims may be readily estimable (1) such as when a court has entered a judgment against the government that will not be appealed, or (2) because the government has appropriate estimates by its attorneys and/or sufficient data regarding past settlements of similar claims to reasonably estimate the ultimate liabilities to result from such claims, either individually or by type of claim.

### GASB Standards

Claims outstanding against a government are contingencies, regardless of whether the claims have been filed, are being negotiated or arbitrated, or have resulted in judgments for or against the government that will be appealed by either the claimant or the government. Accordingly, the contingencies accounting standards of FASB *Statement No. 5* have been adapted to state and local governments. The GASB *Codification* requires that the liability for claims and judgments (CJ) outstanding be recognized in the accounts if information available prior to issuance of the financial statements indicates that:

1. It is probable that an asset has been impaired or a liability has been incurred—as of the date of the financial statements—*and*
2. The amount of the loss can be reasonably estimated.

If these contingencies recognition criteria are not met, the claims and judgments outstanding would be disclosed in the notes to the government's financial statements but would not be recorded in the accounts or presented in the financial statements.

If the CJ recognition criteria are met, CJ expenditures and related liabilities are to be accounted for as follows:

> The amount calculated in accordance with the provisions of FASB *Statement No. 5* should be recognized as expenditures and fund liabilities to the extent that the amounts are payable with expendable available financial resources. Any remaining accrued liabilities . . . should be reported in the general long-term debt account group (GLTDAG).[19]

### Adjusting Entry(ies)—CJ

During the year a government typically will record the amounts paid or vouchered as payable for claims and judgments as expenditures. To illustrate CJ adjusting entries at year end, assume that CJ expenditures and current liabilities are recorded in the General Fund, that no CJ current liabilities were accrued at the end of the prior year (19X0), and that the following entry summarizes the CJ entries during 19X1:

**During the Year (19X1)**

| | | |
|---|---|---|
| Expenditures . . . . . . . . . . . . . . . . . . . . . . . . . . . . . . . . . . . . . . . . . . . . . | $300,000 | |
|    Cash or Vouchers Payable . . . . . . . . . . . . . . . . . . . . . . . . . . . . . | | $300,000 |

To record CJ expenditures paid or vouchered during 19X1.
   (None accrued at end of 19X0.)

Expenditures Ledger (Expenditures):

| | |
|---|---|
| Claims and Judgments . . . . . . . . . . . . . . . . . . . . . . . . . . . . . . . . . . | $300,000 |

Assume also at the end of 19X1 that:

1. Claims and judgments totaling $900,000 are outstanding.

---

[19] Ibid., sec. C50, fn. 3.

2. It is reasonably estimated that the ultimate CJ liabilities resulting—including legal fees and net of insurance recoveries—will be $200,000.

3. $50,000 of the $200,000 total unrecorded CJ liability is reasonably expected to be paid from General Fund net assets available at the end of 19X1.

The $50,000 expected to be paid from existing available General Fund net assets typically represents amounts that must be paid in 19X2 on claims settled by the end of 19X1 or immediately thereafter. (The government and its auditor often use information learned early in 19X2 to assist in estimating the liabilities at the end of 19X1 and when, and from which governmental fund, they will be paid.)

Given these facts, this CJ adjusting entry would be made in the General Fund accounts at the end of 19X1:

**End of Year (19X1)**

| | | |
|---|---|---|
| Expenditures | $50,000 | |
|   Accrued Liabilities (CJ) | | $50,000 |

To record additional 19X1 expenditures for CJ current liabilities expected to be paid from existing fund assets.

Expenditures Ledger (Expenditures):

| | |
|---|---|
| Claims and Judgments | $50,000 |

The $150,000 noncurrent CJ liability would be recorded directly in the General Long-Term Debt Account Group (GLTDAG) accounts. Furthermore, all of the outstanding claims and judgments ($900,000) would be disclosed in the notes to the 19X1 financial statements.

In sum, $350,000 of CJ expenditures would be reported in the General Fund during 19X1, and a $50,000 CJ current liability would be reported at the end of 19X1; a $150,000 CJ noncurrent liability would be added to the GLTDAG; and all CJ contingencies, including those not recorded in the accounts, would be disclosed in the notes to the 19X1 financial statements.

The 19X1 year-end adjusting entry usually would be reversed at the beginning of 19X2:

**Beginning of Year (19X2)**

| | | |
|---|---|---|
| Accrued Liabilities (CJ) | $50,000 | |
|   Expenditures | | $50,000 |

To reverse CJ accrual adjusting entry made at end of 19X1.

Expenditures Ledger (Expenditures):

| | |
|---|---|
| Claims and Judgments | $50,000 |

To continue the illustration, assume that the following entry summarizes the General Fund CJ expenditures paid or accrued during 19X2:

**During the Year (19X2)**

| | | |
|---|---|---|
| Expenditures | $450,000 | |
|   Cash or Vouchers Payable | | $450,000 |

To record CJ expenditures paid or vouchered during 19X2.

Expenditures Ledger (Expenditures):

| | |
|---|---|
| Claims and Judgments | $450,000 |

This summary entry presumably includes payment or vouchering of the 19X1 year-end CJ accruals of $50,000.

Assume at the end of 19X2 that (1) claims and judgments totaling $1,200,000 are outstanding, (2) it is reasonably estimated that the ultimate CJ liabilities resulting—including legal and other related costs but net of insurance recoveries—

will be $325,000, and (3) $75,000 of that $325,000 is reasonably expected to be paid from existing General Fund financial resources. The General Fund 19X2 year-end CJ adjusting entry in this case would be:

**End of Year (19X2)**

| | | |
|---|---:|---:|
| Expenditures . . . . . . . . . . . . . . . . . . . . . . . . . . . . . . . . . . . . . . . . . . . | $75,000 | |
|   Accrued Liabilities (CJ) . . . . . . . . . . . . . . . . . . . . . . . . . . . . . . . . | | $75,000 |

To record expenditures for CJ current liabilities expected to be
  paid from existing fund assets.

Expenditures Ledger (Expenditures):

| | |
|---|---:|
| Claims and Judgments . . . . . . . . . . . . . . . . . . . . . . . . . . . . . . . . . | $75,000 |

This adjusting entry increases the 19X2 CJ expenditures recognized to $475,000:

**19X2 CJ Expenditures:**

| | |
|---|---:|
| Paid or accrued during 19X2 . . . . . . . . . . . . . . . . . . . . . . . . . . . . . | $450,000 |
| 19X1 CJ expenditures—reversing entry . . . . . . . . . . . . . . . . . . . . | (50,000) |
| 19X2 accrual at year end . . . . . . . . . . . . . . . . . . . . . . . . . . . . . . . | 75,000 |
| | $475,000 |

Furthermore, the GLTDAG noncurrent CJ liability account would be increased by $100,000—from the $150,000 year-end 19X1 balance to the $250,000 ($325,000 total less $75,000 recorded in the General Fund) balance at the end of 19X2. All outstanding CJ contingencies would be disclosed in the notes to the financial statements, including those not recorded in the General Fund and GLTDAG accounts.

To summarize, the CJ liabilities arising during a year that are paid or vouchered (as payable) during the year—plus any other CJ liabilities that are considered current liabilities at year end—are accounted for and reported as governmental fund CJ expenditures of that year. Thus, CJ liabilities are not necessarily recorded as governmental fund expenditures of the year in which they arise. Rather, noncurrent CJ liabilities are recorded initially in the GLTDAG and are recorded as governmental fund CJ expenditures in the year during which the CJ liabilities mature or become current liabilities, as defined in a governmental fund context. All significant contingencies—whether or not recorded in the governmental fund or GLTD accounts—should be disclosed appropriately in the notes to the financial statements.

### Insurance, Self-Insurance, and No Insurance

The discussions of CJ liability estimation noted that the final estimate of a CJ liability should include legal and other related costs, as well as the settled or adjudicated claim amount, but should be net of any insurance or similar recoveries. Thus, if a currently payable claim was settled in 19X1 for $250,000 but related insurance reimbursed the government for $200,000 of that amount, the governmental fund entry (omitting subsidiary ledger entries) would be:

**During 19X1:**

| | | |
|---|---:|---:|
| Expenditures . . . . . . . . . . . . . . . . . . . . . . . . . . . . . . . . . . . . . . . | $ 50,000 | |
| Cash or Receivable from Insurance Company . . . . . . . . . . . . . . . . | 200,000 | |
|   Cash or Vouchers Payable . . . . . . . . . . . . . . . . . . . . . . . . . . . . . | | $250,000 |

To record settlement of claim net of related insurance recovery.

The insurance company and the insured government may occasionally disagree on the amount of a CJ expenditure to be reimbursed, however, and thus the insurance recovery might not be reasonably estimable or its receipt might be delayed until a subsequent year.

Suppose, for example, that the $200,000 insurance recovery in this example is reasonably estimable but will not be received until late in 19X2. Because the available criterion does not apply to expenditure recognition, the preceding entry would be made; furthermore, no fund balance reserve is required at the end of 19X1 because the insurance recovery proceeds will be collected during 19X2. (But if the insurance recovery was not expected until 19X3, a fund balance reserve would be required during 19X2 to indicate that the receivable did not represent expendable financial resources during 19X2.)

On the other hand, suppose that (1) the insurance recovery amount was in dispute and was not reasonably estimable at the end of 19X1, but (2) was agreed to and received in 19X2, after the 19X1 financial statements were issued by the government. In this situation the entries would be:

**During 19X1**

| | | |
|---|---|---|
| Expenditures . . . . . . . . . . . . . . . . . . . . . . . . . . . . . . . . . . . . . . . | $250,000 | |
|    Cash or Vouchers Payable . . . . . . . . . . . . . . . . . . . . . . . . . . . | | $250,000 |

To record settlement of claim. (Insurance recovery not reasonably estimable.)

**During 19X2**

| | | |
|---|---|---|
| Receivable from Insurance Company . . . . . . . . . . . . . . . . . . . . . . | $200,000 | |
|    **Insurance Recovery Proceeds** . . . . . . . . . . . . . . . . . . . . . . . . . | | $200,000 |

To record insurance recovery on 19X1 claim expenditures.

The Insurance Recovery Proceeds account might be reported as a deduction from 19X2 CJ Expenditures, but—because the $250,000 (gross) related expenditures were reported in 19X1—is more often reported as an other financing source in 19X2.

Liability insurance premiums have increased rapidly in recent years, and some governments have been unable to obtain adequate levels of insurance for what they consider reasonable or affordable premiums. Thus, many state and local governments have instituted self-insured plans—alone or in pools with other governments—or are uninsured. Self-insurance plans are discussed and illustrated in Chapter 11, "Internal Service Funds."

Governments that are uninsured assume more CJ risk than those that are insured or self-insured. Accordingly, some establish governmental fund reserves of fund balance to indicate that some net assets must be maintained in view of the uninsured CJ contingencies, and others obtain umbrella insurance policies—with large deductibles but covering large amounts above the deductibles—to insure partially against possible catastrophic CJ liabilities being incurred.

## Compensated Absences

The accounting and reporting for compensated absences (CA)—such as accumulated vacation and sick leave—parallel that for claims and judgments. Accordingly, the GASB standards require government employers to accrue a liability for future **vacation and similar** compensated absences that meet both of these conditions:

a. The employees' rights to receive compensation for future absences are attributable to services already rendered.
b. It is probable that the employer will compensate the employees for the benefits through paid time off or by some other means, such as cash payments at termination or retirement.[20]

---

[20] Ibid., sec. C60.104.

Sick leave and similar payments during employees' working years are considered expenditures of the years during which the employees are ill. Whether or not employees become ill during their working years is viewed as an uncertain future event beyond the control of the employee or the employer. Thus, **sick leave and similar** compensated absences are accrued only to the extent they are expected to be paid when employees retire or otherwise terminate employment.

To determine whether an adjusting entry is required and (if so) the amount of the adjustment, the accumulated vacation and similar CA liabilities at year end should be inventoried at current salary levels. Only the hours or days of each employee's accumulated CA time that carry over to the next year should be inventoried. For example, an employee may have accumulated 36 days of vacation. But if only 24 days may be carried forward to the next year—that is, the other 12 days are lost if not taken currently—then only 24 days are inventoried. Sick leave calculations can be made similarly—but must be capped at the amount expected to be paid upon employee retirement or other termination. Alternatively, sick leave calculations may be based on overall estimates of expected termination payments. The estimated liabilities for compensated absences must include salary-related payments (e.g., payroll taxes) as well as base compensation levels.

### Adjusting Entry(ies)—CA

To illustrate CA accounting, we use the 19X1 and 19X2 General Fund assumptions and amounts used in the claims and judgment (CJ) illustration earlier in this section. The General Fund CA entries—assuming reversing entries are not made and omitting subsidiary ledger entries—are as follows:

**During the Year (19X1)**

| | | |
|---|---|---|
| Expenditures . . . . . . . . . . . . . . . . . . . . . . . . . . . . . . . . . . . . . . . . . . . . . . | $300,000 | |
|    Cash or Vouchers Payable . . . . . . . . . . . . . . . . . . . . . . . . . . . . . | | $300,000 |

To record CA expenditures paid or vouchered during 19X1.
  (None accrued at the end of 19X0.)

**End of Year (19X1)**

| | | |
|---|---|---|
| Expenditures . . . . . . . . . . . . . . . . . . . . . . . . . . . . . . . . . . . . . . . . . . . . . . | $ 50,000 | |
|   **Accrued Vacation and Sick Leave Payable** . . . . . . . . . . . . . . . . . | | $ 50,000 |

To record additional 19X1 expenditures for current CA liabilities
  expected to be paid from existing fund assets.

**During the Year (19X2)**

| | | |
|---|---|---|
| Expenditures . . . . . . . . . . . . . . . . . . . . . . . . . . . . . . . . . . . . . . . . . . . . . . | $450,000 | |
|   Cash or Vouchers Payable . . . . . . . . . . . . . . . . . . . . . . . . . . . . . | | $450,000 |

To record CA expenditures paid or vouchered during 19X2. (Note:
  This entry assumes that the Accrued Vacation and Sick Leave
  Payable account is not changed during the year.)

**End of Year (19X2)**

| | | |
|---|---|---|
| Expenditures . . . . . . . . . . . . . . . . . . . . . . . . . . . . . . . . . . . . . . . . . . . . . . | $ 25,000 | |
|   Accrued Vacation and Sick Leave Payable . . . . . . . . . . . . . . . . . | | $ 25,000 |

To record additional 19X2 expenditures for the increase in current
  CA liabilities expected to be paid from existing fund assets.

    Computation:

| | |
|---|---|
| CA current (fund) liability at end of 19X2 . . . . . . . . . . . . . . . | $ 75,000 |
| CA current liability recorded at end of 19X1 . . . . . . . . . . . . . | 50,000 |
| Increase in current CA liability during 19X2 . . . . . . . . . . . . . | $ 25,000 |

The "no reversing entry" approach has the advantage of clearly emphasizing that it is the change in the current CA or CJ liability that is recorded as an additional governmental fund expenditure and liability in the year-end adjusting entry.

### Rationale

The rationale of CA accounting and reporting is largely the same as that for CJ accounting and reporting. Only the measurement differs because of the differing natures of CJ and CA liabilities. Thus, the noncurrent CA liabilities recognized would be recorded in the GLTDAG—not in a governmental fund—and the notes to the financial statements would describe both the unit's vacation, sick leave, and other CA policies and the related CA accounting and reporting policies.

## Pension Plan Contributions

GASB *Statement No. 27,* "Accounting for Pensions by State and Local Governmental Employers," provides specific actuarial parameters and other guidance for computing employer pension expenditures and liabilities. GASB *Statement No. 27* requires that state and local government employers use acceptable actuarial methods in computing employer contribution liabilities under most **defined benefit** pension plans and enforce statutory or contractual requirements for **defined contribution** pension plans. Furthermore, GASB requires that the pension contribution expenditures and liabilities be recognized in the same manner they are recognized for claims and judgments and compensated absences (CJCA). Thus, if some of the actuarially required pension plan contributions for the year have not been paid or vouchered as payable at year end,

1. the amount that would normally be liquidated with expendable available financial resources of a governmental fund would be recorded as a fund expenditure and liability, and
2. the remaining amount would be recorded as a liability in the GLTDAG.

Most statewide and other group plans require that participating employer governments pay the required contributions promptly to both defined contribution and defined benefit pension plans. However, some governments that manage their own single employer pension plans do not make the required contributions. This may occur regularly, as when the legislative body routinely fails to appropriate the actuarially required amount, or only occasionally during financial crises. In any event, the amounts involved may be large—in the millions or even billions of dollars—both currently and cumulatively.

Because the accounting and reporting for underfunded required pension contributions parallels that for CJCA, a brief example should suffice here. Thus, if a government that (1) had no unfunded pension contribution liability at the beginning of the year, (2) had charged the pension contributions paid during the year to Expenditures, and (3) had an additional (unrecorded) unfunded actuarially required pension contribution of $800,000, of which $100,000 is considered a current liability of the General Fund, the adjusting entry (omitting subsidiary ledger entries) in the General Fund at year end would be:

| | | |
|---|---|---|
| Expenditures . . . . . . . . . . . . . . . . . . . . . . . . . . . . . . . . . . . . . . . . . . . . | $100,000 | |
| Current Liability—Pension Contribution . . . . . . . . . . . . . . . . . . . | | $100,000 |

To record additional expenditures for the current portion of the unfunded actuarially required pension contribution at year end.

The remaining $700,000 would be recorded as a liability in the GLTDAG.

As with claims, judgments, and compensated absences, a government must determine the current portion, if any, of its underfunded pension contributions in order to recognize the appropriate amount of pension expenditures for a governmental fund. Local governments frequently participate in state retirement plans, which require the local governments to contribute the **actuarially required contribution (ARC)** each period. In these cases, assuming the contribution required by the pension plan meets the GASB *Statement No. 27* parameters, the government will not have a current unfunded pension liability. The expenditures recognized will equal the contribution, which equals the ARC. However, practices regarding how to determine the current portion of the unfunded actuarially required pension plan contributions for those governments that do not fully fund their ARC vary even more widely than for CJCA liabilities.

## CHANGES IN ACCOUNTING PRINCIPLES

Restatements may be required to report the cumulative effect of changes in accounting principles. Four types of events that might cause, or result from, a change in the expenditure recognition accounting principles of a governmental fund are:

- A type of expenditure not previously deemed to be objectively measurable—such as claims and judgments—may now be considered reasonably estimable.
- Where there are acceptable alternative expenditure recognition principles—such as the purchases and consumption methods of inventory and prepayment expenditure recognition—management might change from one acceptable alternative principle to the other.
- Where there are two or more acceptable methods of applying an accounting principle—such as the FIFO, LIFO, and average cost methods of inventory accounting on the consumption basis using a periodic method—management might change the method of applying the principle.
- The GASB or another recognized standards-setting body may issue a new expenditure recognition standard that requires a different expenditure accounting policy than that presently used.

Two of these types of events and changes in accounting principles and the methods of applying principles are discussed briefly in this section.

### Changes between Alternative Principles

To illustrate the implementation of changes between acceptable alternative principles, assume that a government decides to change from the purchases to the consumption method of General Fund inventory accounting. The fully reserved purchases method inventory at the end of the prior year was $100,000. The entry at the beginning of the current year to implement the change to the consumption method would be:

| | | |
|---|---|---|
| Reserve for Inventory | $100,000 | |
|    Cumulative Effect of Change in Accounting Principle | | $100,000 |
| To effect change in inventory accounting from purchases to consumption basis. | | |

The logic underlying this entry is that (1) under the purchases method the inventory purchases had been charged to expenditures, resulting in an understatement of Unreserved Fund Balance, and (2) recording inventory as required under the purchases method results in crediting Unreserved Fund Balance, correcting its misstatement, but also requires that a reserve for inventory be established. Thus, assuming no reserve is needed under the consumption method, the consumption method may be implemented by the preceding entry. If a reserve were desired, it could be established after this entry or compounded with it—for example, if a $30,000 reserve were desired, the Reserve for Inventory account would be debited $70,000 (instead of $100,000) and Unreserved Fund Balance would be debited $30,000.

### Changed GASB Standards

Changes in accounting principles may also occur because the GASB (or another recognized standards-setting body discussed in Chapter 2) issues a new expenditure recognition standard or revises an existing standard. If the new or revised expenditure recognition standard requires a different expenditure recognition principle than that presently being used in its governmental fund accounting, a state or local government must change its accounting policy to comply with the new or revised standard.

As noted in the discussion on revenue-related accounting changes in Chapter 5, GASB and other standards pronouncements specify when (at the latest) and how the new standards are to be implemented. If a new standard is to be applied prospectively—that is, only to transactions and events occurring on or after the implementation date—the change will not have a cumulative effect on the beginning fund balance. For example, such a standard might specify that, from the implementation date forward, certain transactions that had previously been reported as expenditures be reported as other financing uses.

Most new or revised standards require retroactive application, however. That is, the new expenditure recognition standard is to be implemented as if it had been applied in prior periods. Accordingly, the entry to implement new retroactive application expenditure recognition standards resembles a correction entry—as do those illustrated earlier in this section—except that the cumulative effect is reported as the cumulative effect of change(s) in accounting principles.

## CONCLUDING COMMENTS

Several significant conceptual, standards, and procedural considerations are important in governmental fund expenditure accounting and reporting. Most are discussed at least briefly in this chapter and some are discussed in detail and illustrated.

The concept and definition of expenditures in a governmental fund context were considered initially and at several points throughout the chapter, as were related GASB standards. Brief discussions of expenditure accounting controls and procedures—over personal services, purchases of materials and supplies, and other services and charges—included discussions and illustrations of related matters such as the purchases and consumption methods of inventory and prepayment accounting and accounting for capital leases and certificates of participation. Other important expenditure accounting topics—including claims and judgments, compensated absences, unfunded pension contributions, debt service, and encumbrances—were discussed and illustrated in the section on adjusting entries. In addition, several other important expenditure accounting topics were discussed and illustrated—such as accounting for appropriations revisions, allocations and allotments, and changes in expenditure-related accounting principles—as was expenditure account classification, which is discussed further in Appendix 6–1. Varying annual appropriations and encumbrance assumptions—and continuing appropriations—are discussed and illustrated in Appendices 6–2, 6–3, and 6–4.

Some of the unresolved governmental fund expenditure-related issues also were noted. The most significant relate to the definitions of *fund liability* and *fund expenditure,* particularly the definition of *current liability* (in the governmental fund context) as the amount accrued during the year that would normally be liquidated with expendable available financial resources of a governmental fund. The GASB has adopted several significant changes in recognition and expenditure recognition and is working intensely on other major related issues, including the overall financial reporting model for SLGs. The GASB's reporting model project and proposals are discussed and illustrated in Chapter 15.

## APPENDIX 6–1

## Classification of Expenditures

The GASB *Codification* states that governmental fund expenditures should be classified by (1) function or program, (2) activity, (3) organization unit, (4) character, and (5) object class, as well as by fund. Each of these expenditure classifications is discussed and illustrated here.

## CLASSIFICATION BY FUNCTION OR PROGRAM

According to the GASB *Codification:*

> Function or program classification provides information on the **overall purposes** or **objectives** of expenditures. **Functions** group related activities that are aimed at accomplishing a major service or regulatory responsibility. **Programs** group activities, operations, or organizational units that are directed to the attainment of specific purposes or objectives.[1]

A government may choose between function and program classification but should use one or the other. The reason for this is that some governments are organized and budgeted by functions, whereas others are organized and budgeted by programs (as noted in Chapter 3), so this option permits governments to use the corresponding functional or program classification in accounting and financial reporting.

A typical governmental unit provides a wide spectrum of services; many provide services that are also provided by other governmental units. For example, typical city, county, and state governments all provide for public safety. If they all select the accounts necessary to record their expenditures for public safety from a standard classification, a total figure may be accumulated for a state or for the nation as a whole. Furthermore, it makes possible comparisons of expenditure data between and among cities and counties of comparable size that have similar problems. Thus, the functional classification provides the basic structure for the classification of expenditures in the general purpose financial statements (GPFS).

---

[1] GASB *Codification*, sec. 1800.117. (Emphasis added.)

Figure 6–3 presents a condensed standard classification of expenditures by function. Observe the relationship between the broad functional classifications and the more detailed functional classifications. Both have been used for illustrative purposes in budgets and journal entries earlier in the text with the caveat that more detailed department or other organization unit and object class accounts would be used in practice.

Note also that the more detailed functional classifications summarize the organizational structure of many governments. Many governments may have several departments within at least some of the functions, but many smaller governments have only one department, at most, in each function. For example, in many smaller governments the police department is the police protection function. Thus, many governmental budgets, accounting systems, and charts of accounts are classified by departments or other organization units, rather than by functions, and the function or functional data are derived by aggregating the expenditure data by organizational unit.

**FIGURE 6–3 Expenditure Classification By Functions**

| *Broad Functions or Functional Classifications* | | | *Functions* | |
|---|---|---|---|---|
| *Code\** | *Title* | | *Code\** | *Title* |
| 1000–1999 | General Government | | 1000 | Legislative Branch |
| | | | 1100 | Executive Branch |
| | | | 1200 | Judicial Branch |
| | | | 1300 | Elections |
| | | | 1400 | Financial Administration |
| | | | 1500 | Other |
| 2000–2999 | Public Safety | | 2000 | Police Protection |
| | | | 2100 | Fire Protection |
| | | | 2200 | Correction |
| | | | 2300 | Protective Inspection |
| 3000–4999 | Public Works | | 3000 | Highways and Streets |
| | | | 4000 | Sanitation |
| 5000–6999 | Health and Welfare | | 5000 | Health |
| | | | 6000 | Welfare |
| 7000–7999 | Education (Schools) | | | |
| 8000–9999 | Culture and Recreation | | 8000 | Libraries |
| | | | 9000 | Parks |
| 10000–14999 | Conservation of Natural Resources | | 10000 | Water Resources |
| | | | 11000 | Agricultural Resources |
| | | | 12000 | Mineral Resources |
| | | | 13000 | Fish and Game Resources |
| | | | 14000 | Other Natural Resources |
| 15000–15999 | Urban Redevelopment and Housing | | | |
| 16000–16999 | Economic Development and Assistance | | | |
| 17000–17999 | Economic Opportunity | | | |
| 18000–19999 | Debt Service | | 18000 | Interest |
| | | | 19000 | Principal |
| | | | 19500 | Paying Agent's Fees |
| 20000–20999 | Intergovernmental | | | |
| 21000–21999 | Miscellaneous | | | |

\*Code numbers are illustrative only.

## CLASSIFICATION BY ORGANIZATION UNIT

The GASB *Codification* states that:

> Classification of expenditures by **organization unit** is essential to responsibility accounting. This classification **corresponds with** the governmental unit's **organization structure.** A particular organization unit may be charged with carrying out one or several activities or programs. Moreover, the same activity or program is sometimes carried on by several organization units because of its inherent nature or because of faulty organization structure.[2]

Sound budgetary control requires that authority and responsibility for the activities of the government be assigned in a definite fashion to its officials and employees. Assignment of appropriations and related expenditures to organization units is essential if department heads are to be held responsible for planning their activities and for controlling those activities authorized by the legislative body through the appropriations process. Classifying expenditures by organization unit is, therefore, important because it provides the means for controlling expenditures and for definitively allocating and evaluating expenditure responsibility. Stated differently, classifying expenditures by organizational unit is a prerequisite to effective responsibility accounting and to ensuring and evaluating proper stewardship of public funds.

There is no standard classification of expenditure accounts by organization unit. Rather, this expenditure classification should correspond with however the government is organized into departments or other units and subunits. Thus, in a government where the police, fire, and jail are separate departments—organizationally and budgetarily—this department structure would be the basis for expenditure classification by organization unit. But, if in another government the jail is organized as an integral part of the police department, the jail would be budgeted and accounted for as a subunit of the police department.

Furthermore, except in the smallest governments, departments may contain two or more subunits. For example, a police department may be organized by such subunits as street patrol, vehicle patrol, detectives, and vice and drug abuse control—each having separate appropriations line items or executive allocations. In all cases the expenditure accounts should be set up in at least as much detail as is necessary for appropriations and allocations control and accountability.

If the planning and execution of government functions, programs, and activities are to be properly controlled, activities must be properly allocated to departments. Ideally, a major department would be assigned responsibility for a function or program and its subunits would be assigned responsibility for the several activities necessary to carry out the function or program.

## CLASSIFICATION BY ACTIVITY

An **activity** is a specific line of work performed by a governmental unit as part of one of its functions or programs. Ordinarily, several activities are required to fulfill a function or program.

---

[2] Ibid., sec. 1800.118. (Emphasis added.)

A minimum requirement is that responsibility for an activity should be assigned to only one organization unit. Those units that cover more than one activity should have their budgeting, accounting, reporting, and administration arranged so that assignments or allocations of costs can be made by activity. Organization by activity is highly desirable because it facilitates precise assignment of authority and responsibility and because it simplifies accounting for and controlling activities.

The typical classifications of activities (and illustrative account codes) for the police protection function are:

2000 Police Protection Function
    2010 Police Administration
    2020 Crime Control and Investigation
        2021 Criminal Investigation
        2022 Vice Control
        2023 Patrol
        2024 Records and Identification
        2025 Youth Investigation and Control
        2026 Custody of Prisoners
        2027 Custody of Property
        2028 Crime Laboratory
    2030 Traffic Control
        2031 Motor Vehicle Inspection and Regulation
    2040 Police Training
    2050 Support Services
        2051 Communications Services
        2052 Automotive Services
        2053 Ambulance Services
        2054 Medical Services
        2055 Special Detail Services
        2056 Police Stations and Buildings

Expenditure data classified by activity are not required to be presented in published financial statements but are intended primarily for managerial use. The GASB *Codification* observes that:

> Activity classification is particularly significant because it **facilitates evaluation of the economy and efficiency** of operations by providing data for calculating expenditures per unit of activity. That is, the expenditure requirements of performing a given unit of work can be determined by classifying expenditures by activities and providing for performance measurement where such techniques are practicable. These expenditure data, in turn, can be used in preparing future budgets and in setting standards against which future expenditure levels can be evaluated.[3]

In addition, it notes the usefulness of activity expenditure data when expense data need to be derived for managerial decision-making purposes:

> Further, activity expenditure data provide a convenient **starting point for calculating total and/or unit expenses of activities** where that is desired, for example, for "make or buy" or

---

[3] Ibid., sec. 1800.119. (Emphasis added.)

"do or contract out" decisions. Current operating expenditures (total expenditures less those for capital outlay and debt service) may be adjusted by depreciation and amortization data derived from the account group records to determine activity expense.[4]

Many services traditionally provided by state and local governments are being outsourced or privatized, that is, contracted for from private firms or even relocated to the private sector. Thus, while not required for external financial reporting, expenditure data classified by activity may be very important for internal uses.

Classifying expenditures by activity is essential to secure cost (expenditure basis) data for budget preparation and managerial control. Unit cost accounting (expenditure or expense basis) is possible only if (1) expenditures are classified by activities and (2) statistics concerning units of output are accumulated. Even if unit costs are not to be computed, the costs (expenditure and/or expense bases) of an activity should be compared with the benefits expected from it as a basis for deciding whether the scope of the activity should be increased, decreased, or left unchanged. Accumulating cost data by activities also permits comparing such costs between governmental units and accumulating cost data by function or program.

This discussion of activity classification also illustrates the need to distinguish the expenditure and expense measurement concepts, both conceptually and in practice, and to use appropriate terminology. Too often, the term *expense* is used (e.g., operating expense) when the measurement being described is *expenditures*. Using these terms improperly, or interchangeably as if they were synonymous, causes confusion and should be avoided.

## CLASSIFICATION BY CHARACTER

The **character** classification, which has been used in earlier illustrative examples, identifies expenditures by the **period benefited.** The three main character classifications are current operating, capital outlay, and debt service. A fourth category, intergovernmental, is needed where one government transfers resources to another, as when states transfer shared revenues to local governments. (As noted earlier, a state should account for pass-through grants for which it serves only as a cash conduit in an Agency Fund. In these limited instances, pass-through grants would not be recognized as state revenues nor expenditures.)

Current operating expenditures are those expenditures expected to benefit primarily the current period, such as for salaries and utilities. Capital outlays are those expenditures expected to benefit not only the current period but also future periods. Purchases of desks, vehicles, and buildings are examples of capital outlays. Maturing long-term debt principal, interest on debt, and related service charges are debt service expenditures. Payments made from the General Fund or Special Revenue Funds to Debt Service Funds for these purposes are operating transfers that ultimately will finance Debt Service Fund expenditures, perhaps many years hence. Though debt service expenditures are sometimes said to be expenditures that are made for past benefits, where debt proceeds were used to acquire capital outlay items, the expenditures may benefit past, present, and future periods.

Just as expenditure data by function or program can be derived by summarizing departmental (organization unit) expenditure data, data by character can be

---

[4] Ibid. (Emphasis added.)

derived by aggregating data by object classes (discussed later). Thus, some accounting systems and charts of accounts do not provide for expenditure classification by character but obtain it by rolling up the expenditure data classified by object classes.

## CLASSIFICATION BY OBJECT CLASSES

The **object class (object-of-expenditure)** classification groups expenditures according to the type of article purchased or service obtained. The following is a standard classification of object classes related to the character classification as indicated:

| Character | Object Class |
|---|---|
| 01–03* Current Operating | 01 Personal Services |
| | 02 Supplies |
| | 03 Other Services and Charges |
| 04–07  Capital Outlay | 04 Land |
| | 05 Buildings |
| | 06 Improvements Other Than Buildings |
| | 07 Machinery and Equipment |
| 08–10  Debt Service | 08 Debt Principal |
| | 09 Interest |
| | 10 Debt Service Charges |
| 11       Intergovernmental | 11 Intergovernmental |

*Code numbers are illustrative only.

The preceding object classes under "Current Operating" are major classifications. A small municipality, or a small organization unit in a larger municipality, might find that "Personal Services," "Supplies," and "Other Services and Charges" provide enough detail for administrative and reporting purposes. In most cases, however, each of these classifications would be subdivided into more detailed classifications. Personal services could be subdivided into salaries, wages, employer contributions to the retirement system, insurance, sick leave, terminal pay, and the like. Supplies may be detailed in whatever way proves useful: at a minimum as among office supplies, operating supplies, and repair and maintenance supplies. Other services and charges include such costs as professional services, communications, transportation, advertising, printing, and binding. In certain circumstances it might be very useful to the administration to further subdivide some or all of the foregoing into even greater detail. For example, it might be useful to divide communications into such categories as telephone, telegraph, and postage.

The main object classes ordinarily provide sufficient detail for the GPFS and other summarized reports to the public, including the budgetary comparison statement of the GPFS. Classification by the main object classes also may provide sufficient detail to demonstrate budgetary compliance. This depends, of course, on the detail in which the appropriations by the legislative body are considered binding on the executive branch. If budgetary compliance is at a more detailed level, then a budgetary compliance schedule must be presented at the more detailed level and the accounts must be classified at the more detailed level. Thus, providing greater amounts of detail by object-of-expenditure in the accounts should be based on administrative need for such information for planning, controlling, and evaluating the operations of the governmental unit.

**APPENDIX 6–2**

## Accounting for Annual Appropriations—Various Encumbrances Assumptions

The discussions and illustrations in Chapter 4 assumed that the annual appropriations lapse at the end of each year but that the Encumbrances account should be closed to Unreserved Fund Balance to establish the Reserve for Encumbrances account as a true reservation of fund balance. We referred to this assumption as Assumption A1. This assumption is reviewed and two other assumptions that may be encountered in accounting for encumbrances of annually budgeted governmental funds in which appropriations lapse at year end are discussed and illustrated briefly in this appendix. Only General Ledger entries are presented because the Expenditures Subsidiary Ledger entries would be the same in all cases. These assumptions are summarized in Figure 6–4, along with other assumptions relating to continuing appropriations, which are discussed in the next appendix to this chapter.

**FIGURE 6–4  Reporting Encumbrances and Continuing Appropriations**

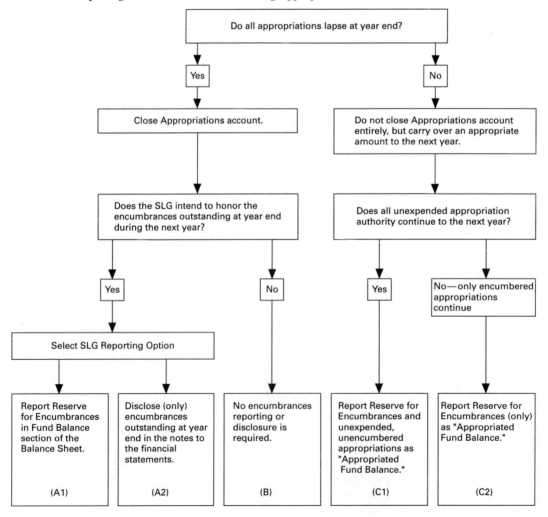

## ASSUMPTION A1

The General Fund closing entries illustrated in Chapter 4 (pages 125–130) were based on certain assumptions about the laws and policies of A Governmental Unit:

> Assumption A1. (1) All unexpended appropriations lapse at year end, even if encumbered; (2) the unit is committed to accept the goods or services on order at year end; (3) expenditures resulting from encumbrances outstanding at the end of a year must be charged against the next year's appropriations; and (4) the Reserve for Encumbrances should be left open and be reported as a reservation of fund balance in the year-end balance sheet.

Recall that the reserve entry at the end of 19X1 was:

Unreserved Fund Balance .................................. $20,000
   Encumbrances ..........................................          $20,000
To close the Encumbrances account and cause the Reserve for
   Encumbrances to be a true reservation of fund balance.

Under Assumption A1, the Reserve for Encumbrances balance reported in the 19X1 year-end balance sheet serves (1) to remind those preparing the 19X2 budget to include $20,000 appropriations for 19X2 expenditures expected to result from encumbrances outstanding at the end of 19X1 as well as (2) to inform readers of the financial statements of the commitments outstanding at the end of 19X1 that are expected to result in expenditures in 19X2. The entry at the start of 19X2 returns the Encumbrances and Reserve for Encumbrances accounts to their usual offsetting relationship in the General Ledger, causing the Reserve for Encumbrances to no longer be a true fund balance reserve, and increases the Unreserved Fund Balance account accordingly. In essence, this entry restores the affected accounts to the balances and relationships that would have existed if encumbrances had never been closed.

Encumbrances ......................................... $20,000
   Unreserved Fund Balance .............................          $20,000
To reestablish Encumbrances in the accounts and return
   Encumbrances and Reserve for Encumbrances to offsetting
   memorandum accounts.

## ASSUMPTION A2

Another legal and policy situation that may be encountered is where all appropriations lapse, whether or not encumbered, as in Assumption A1, but there is no statutory or policy requirement that the Reserve for Encumbrances be reported in the balance sheet. This variation of Assumption A1, which we shall call Assumption A2, may be summarized:

> Assumption A2. (1) All unexpended appropriations lapse at year end, even if encumbered; (2) the unit is committed to accept the goods or services on order at year end; (3) expenditures resulting from encumbrances outstanding at the end of a year must be authorized by and charged against the next year's appropriations; and (4) a Reserve for Encumbrances is not required to be reported in the year-end balance sheet.

Under Assumption A2, management may choose to report the Reserve for Encumbrances in the balance sheet as required by Assumption A1. If so, the entries illustrated earlier for the end of 19X1 and the beginning of 19X2 are applicable. Alternatively, management may choose to report the encumbrances outstanding only in the notes to the financial statements and not by a Reserve for Encumbrances in the 19X1 year-end balance sheet. In this case both the Encumbrances and Reserve for Encumbrances accounts usually are closed. Accordingly, the General Ledger closing entry for the General Fund appropriations, expenditures, and encumbrances would be:

| | | |
|---|---|---|
| Appropriations | $426,000 | |
| Reserve for Encumbrances | 20,000 | |
| Expenditures | | $399,250 |
| Encumbrances | | 20,000 |
| Unreserved Fund Balance | | 26,750 |

To close the accounts at year end.

Note that the Unreserved Fund Balance account would reflect total fund balance (except for any other reserves) in this case, and no Reserve for Encumbrances would be reported in the General Fund balance sheet. Note also that if both Encumbrances and Reserve for Encumbrances are closed at the end of 19X1, both must be reestablished in the accounts, by the reverse of the closing entry, at the start of 19X2:

| | | |
|---|---|---|
| Encumbrances | $20,000 | |
| Reserve for Encumbrances | | $20,000 |

To reestablish these accounts at the beginning of 19X2.

## ASSUMPTION B

A third variation in the legal status of appropriations at year end, which we shall call Assumption B, may be summarized:

> Assumption B. (1) All unexpended appropriations lapse, even if encumbered; and (2) all encumbrances are null and void after year end.

The essence of this legal circumstance is that each year stands clearly apart. Vendors must perform by 19X1 year end or seek new 19X2 contracts, which may or may not be approved, to provide the goods or services in 19X2. Purchase orders typically carry a prominent notice to this effect in this situation. Whereas the essence of Assumption B differs markedly from that of Assumptions A1 and A2, the General Fund accounting entries at the end of 19X1 are the same as those for Assumption A2, illustrated previously. Under Assumption B both the Encumbrances and Reserve for Encumbrances accounts should be closed at the end of 19X1, and neither Encumbrances nor Reserve for Encumbrances is reported or disclosed in the General Fund statements at year end. There would be no Encumbrances and Reserve for Encumbrances entry in 19X2 until new 19X2 encumbrances were incurred.

APPENDIX 6–3

## Accounting for Continuing Appropriations

To this point we have assumed that annual appropriations of governmental funds are made for a year and that the appropriation authority lapses at year end. This is the usual case with appropriations of General, Special Revenue, and Debt Service Funds, and usually is the case with other annually budgeted governmental funds. However, the appropriations of Capital Projects Funds, in particular, are often made for the project—and thus continue as valid appropriation authority until expended or the project has been completed—and thus do not lapse at the end of each fiscal year. Continuing appropriations also may be made for all other governmental fund types—for specified purposes and for two years or longer periods, or until expended—particularly by state governments.

Two variations in the legal provisions and policies where some or all of the unexpended appropriations continue as expenditure authority until at least the following year are discussed and illustrated in this section. They are referred to as Assumption C1 and Assumption C2. Although only one of these assumptions is commonly used in General Fund accounting, we illustrate them in the General Fund context of Chapter 4 so that the effects of all five assumptions may readily be compared.

# ASSUMPTION C1

This assumption is commonly used with Capital Projects Fund and other appropriations made on a project basis rather than an annual basis. Appropriations made under Assumption C1 thus continue as valid expenditure authority until expended or the project is completed. This assumption may be summarized succinctly:

> Assumption C1. Unexpended appropriations continue (do not lapse at year end) to the next period(s); that is, only expended appropriations lapse at year end.

In this situation—because only the expended appropriations lapse at year end—only the Expenditures, $399,250, should be closed against Appropriations. That is, the 19X1 year-end General Fund closing entry for A Governmental Unit under Assumption C1 should leave a $26,750 balance in the Appropriations account, and would be:

| | | |
|---|---|---|
| Appropriations [$26,750 left] .............................. | $399,250 | |
|     Expenditures ......................................... | | $399,250 |
| To close the accounts at year end. | | |

Furthermore, when appropriations continue, the "Fund Balance" section of the governmental fund balance sheet must include a Reserve for Encumbrances for the encumbrances against the continuing appropriations. Accordingly, the Encumbrances account should be closed as in Assumption A1. But, because it now relates to the continuing appropriation (rather than to Unreserved Fund Balance), the Encumbrances account is closed to the Appropriations account.

| Appropriations | $20,000 | |
| Encumbrances | | $20,000 |

To close encumbrances against continuing appropriations at
year end.

Note that the postclosing balance of the Appropriations account does not represent the total appropriation, but only the unencumbered appropriation, and that the fund balance section of the General Fund balance sheet (Figure 4–6) prepared under Assumption C1 at the end of 19X1 would appear as:

Fund Balance:
 Appropriated:
  Reserved for encumbrances (or Encumbered) ............. $20,000
  Unencumbered ...................................... 6,750   $26,750
 Unappropriated ...................................... 21,800
                                                        $48,550

The encumbrances closing entry would be reversed at the beginning of 19X2:

| Encumbrances | $20,000 | |
| Appropriations | | $20,000 |

To reverse the 19X1 entry closing the encumbrances account.

This reversing entry restores the Appropriations account to its full $26,750 unexpended balance, returns the Encumbrances and Reserve for Encumbrances accounts to their usual offsetting relationship, and records the encumbrances in the appropriate Expenditures Subsidiary Ledger accounts (omitted here).

## ASSUMPTION C2

The policy of some governments is that encumbered appropriations continue to the next period. In some cases the encumbered appropriations continue throughout the following year; but in other cases they continue for only a short period considered sufficient for the goods and services encumbered during the prior year to be delivered and billed—often 60–90 days—and then lapse. At that time the unexpended balance is restored to the Unreserved Fund Balance.

Assumption C2 may be summarized succinctly:

Assumption C2. Encumbered appropriations continue (do not lapse at year end) to the next period; that is, only unencumbered appropriations lapse at year end.

In this case—because encumbered appropriations do not lapse—the closing entry should leave on the books Appropriations, Encumbrances, and Reserve for Encumbrances in the $20,000 amount of the encumbrances outstanding. Thus, the General Ledger 19X1 closing entry for appropriations, expenditures, and encumbrances would appear as:

| Appropriations [$20,000 left] | $406,000 | |
| Expenditures | | $399,250 |
| Unreserved Fund Balance | | 6,750 |

To close the accounts at year end.

Furthermore, as in Assumption C1, the Encumbrances account would be closed against the Appropriations account to reserve fund balance:

| Appropriations ........................................ | $20,000 | |
| Encumbrances ........................................ | | $20,000 |

To close encumbrances against continuing appropriations at year end.

This leaves a zero balance in the postclosing Appropriations account—obviously the correct unencumbered balance under Assumption C2 because only encumbered appropriations continue (i.e., unencumbered appropriations lapse). The fund balance section of the General Fund balance sheet at the end of 19X1 under Assumption C2 would appear as:

Fund Balance:
  Appropriated:
    Reserved for Encumbrances .......................... $20,000
    Unappropriated ...................................... <u>28,550</u>
                                   <u>$48,550</u>

Then at the beginning of 19X2 the encumbrance closing entry will be reversed, as in Assumption C1, returning the Appropriations account to its full $20,000 balance, restoring the Encumbrances–Reserve for Encumbrances offsetting relationship, and recording the encumbrances in the related Expenditures Subsidiary Ledger accounts (omitted here):

| Encumbrances ........................................ | $20,000 | |
| Appropriations ........................................ | | $20,000 |

To reverse the 19X1 entry closing the Encumbrances account.

Finally, recall that a government's budgetary basis may be a non-GAAP basis that treats encumbrances as expenditures for budgetary purposes. If so, the substance of the budgetary and appropriations laws and policies must be recognized. Thus, if an SLG adopts an annual operating budget on a modified accrual plus encumbrances basis, it is in substance under Assumption C2 because (1) no new appropriation authority need be provided to complete the encumbered transactions and (2) some of the net assets on hand at year end are needed to complete these transactions and are, therefore, not available to finance expenditures arising from future year appropriations.

## Questions

**Q 6-1** Distinguish between an expenditure in the governmental accounting sense and an expense in the commercial accounting sense.

**Q 6-2** When should General Fund expenditures be recognized? What are the major exceptions?

**Q 6-3** What expenditures-related General Ledger control accounts might be used in the General Fund?

**Q 6-4** The appropriations of a certain government for current expenditures lapse at the end of the fiscal year, whereas appropriations for capital outlay lapse two years later. Discuss the desirability of this dual arrangement.

**Q 6-5** On January 2, 19X1, materials costing $100 were issued from perpetual inventory to the police department. What General Ledger journal entry or entries should be made?

**Q 6-6** A governmental unit takes advantage of purchase discounts by paying its bills promptly. Should the full purchase price be recorded in the records with the discounts treated as revenues, or should the purchases be recorded at their net cost (i.e., after deduction of discounts)?

**Q 6-7** Some argue that General Fund payments to a pension fund for the city's share of pension fund contributions should be charged to the departments in which the covered employees work. Do you agree? Explain.

**Q 6-8** In one municipality vouchers must be approved not only by the finance officer but also by the finance committee of the city council. Is the approval of the finance committee desirable? Give reasons.

**Q 6-9** Explain how you would decide whether or not to encumber a planned expenditure.

**Q 6-10** The newly elected mayor of the town of Dewey is a well-respected businessman. He is perplexed because the town's finance director has given him an interim financial statement that reports repayment of a ten-year note through the General Fund as an expenditure. The mayor is aware that several short-term notes were repaid during the interim period as well, and these are not reported. "Two things puzzle me," says the mayor. "First, why should repayment of a note be reported as an expenditure? We decreased our assets and liabilities by equal amounts; therefore, the city's equity did not change. Second, why is only part of the principal retirement reported as expenditures if such a practice is appropriate?" Respond to the mayor.

**Q 6-11** Why would an executive branch make allocations and/or allotments of appropriations authorized by the legislative branch? How do (a) allocations and (b) allotments of appropriations affect accounting for a governmental fund's expenditures?

**Q 6-12** An accountant for the town of Don's Grove previously worked for the city of Victorville. Don's Grove records purchases of materials and supplies as expenditures and reports any change in the inventory of materials and supplies in its Statement of Revenues, Expenditures, and Changes in (Total) Fund Balance. The accountant recalls, however, that the city of Victorville recorded expenditures for materials and supplies when they were used, not when they were purchased. Also, Victorville did not report changes in inventory in its Statement of Revenues, Expenditures, and Changes in (Total) Fund Balance. The accountant asks his supervisors which way is correct. Respond.

**Q 6-13** When is fully reserving fund balance for inventory on hand appropriate? Explain.

**Q 6-14** Why do governmental fund accounting standards allow both the consumption method and the purchases method of inventory accounting?

**Q 6-15** Why might a school district change from using certain expenditure recognition principles to different expenditure recognition principles?

**Q 6-16** Why are adjusting entries often required in governmental funds at year end in accounting for claims and judgments?

**Q 6-17** Why does the GASB require employers to recognize sick leave liabilities only to the extent they will be paid upon employee termination or retirement, but require vacation leave liabilities to be recognized as earned—regardless of whether the employees will receive paid time off or be paid for the leave upon retirement or other termination?

**Q 6-18** (Appendix 6–1) Distinguish between and among the four character-of-expenditures classifications.

**Q 6-19** (Appendix 6–1) Explain how an accounting system can be designed to produce information for all the bases of expenditure classification and still produce information useful for managerial purposes.

**Q 6-20** (Appendix 6–1) The clerk of the city of Wilmaton is revising the city accounting system so that she can report expenditures by function, organization unit, activity, character, and object class as well as by fund. Her assistant is perturbed because he considers all these classifications unnecessary and, he states: "It will take five extra sets of books to record expenditures this way. Every expenditure will have to be recorded six times!" Explain to the assistant (a) the purpose of each expenditure classification and (b) how to implement the multiple classification scheme without multiplying the work required to record expenditures.

**Q 6-21** (Appendices 6–2 and 6–3) Discuss the several common legal assumptions as to the lapsing of appropriations for the benefit of a committee to write the charter for a newly incorporated village.

**Q 6-22**  (Appendices 6–2 and 6–3) The postclosing trial balance of the General Fund contains, in three different cases, balances for the following accounts, among others:

Case 1: Reserve for Encumbrances, Unreserved Fund Balance, and Appropriations

Case 2: Unreserved Fund Balance

Case 3: Reserve for Encumbrances and Unreserved Fund Balance

On which legal assumption may the closing entries have been based in each case?

## Exercises

**E 6-1**  (Various Entries) Record the following transactions in the General Fund of a city.
1. Salaries were incurred, $300,000, $280,000 of which were paid.
2. Long-term note ($400,000 face value) matured. The interest of $40,000 was paid but the principal was not.
3. Purchased computers with a cost of $45,000. $22,000 was paid, but the balance is due and expected to be paid at the end of the first quarter of the next fiscal year.
4. Purchased materials for cash, $19,000. Assume purchases method of accounting for inventory.
5. Received bill from the water and sewer department for services, $7,500. $4,000 was paid.
6. Ordered, but not yet received, materials costing $70,000.
7. Paid required annual contribution to pension plan, $250,000.
8. Determined that the Capital Projects Fund should be reimbursed $3,000 for wages that should have been charged to General Fund departments but were paid from the Capital Projects Fund.
9. Repaid a six-month note (face value, $50,000) and interest on the note ($2,500).
10. Paid $75,000 to the Golf Course Enterprise Fund to cover its operating deficit for the year.

**E 6-2**  (Purchases versus Consumption Method) The city of Bettinger's Bend General Fund had a beginning inventory of materials and supplies of $86,000. The beginning fund balance reserved for inventory was also $86,000.
1. Materials and supplies costing $740,000 were ordered during the year.
2. The materials and supplies ordered were received; actual cost, $741,000.
3. According to the physical inventory, $90,000 of materials and supplies were on hand at year end.

*Required*  (a) Prepare general journal entries to record the foregoing information using the **purchases** method of accounting for inventories.
(b) Prepare general journal entries to record the foregoing information using the **consumption** method assuming (1) a perpetual inventory system is used and (2) an inventory reserve is not maintained.

**E 6-3**  (Capital Lease Entries)
(a) Record the following 19X8 transactions in the town of Colin General Fund General Ledger.
1. The town of Colin entered into a capital lease for firefighting equipment. The capitalizable cost of the equipment was $3,800,000 and the town made a 10% down payment at the inception of the lease. The effective interest rate implicit in the lease was 10%, compounded semiannually.
2. The town paid its first semiannual lease payment of $240,000.
3. The second semiannual lease payment of $240,000, due one day before the end of the town fiscal year, was paid.
(b) What amount of capital outlay expenditures should the town of Colin General Fund report for 19X8?
(c) What amount of debt service expenditures should be reported for the General Fund for 19X8?

**E 6-4**   (Pension Entries) Assume that the actuarially required contribution for a county for its general government employees is $8,000,000. Compute the pension expenditures to be reported in each of the following situations.

1. The county contributed $5,000,000 to the pension plan. Its unfunded pension liability increased by $3,000,000 (all classified as noncurrent).
2. The county contributed $4,500,000 to the pension plan. Its unfunded pension liability increased to $3,500,000 (all classified as current).
3. The county contributed $4,200,000 to the pension plan. The current portion of unfunded pension liability increased $150,000.
4. The county contributed $9,000,000 to the pension plan. The current portion of unfunded pension liability decreased $200,000.

## Problems

**P 6-1**   (Multiple Choice) Indicate the best answer to each question.

1. A county entered into a capital lease on June 30, 19X8 for equipment to be used by General Fund departments. The capitalizable cost of the leased asset was $200,000. An initial payment of $20,000 was made at the inception of the lease. The first annual lease payment of $35,000 is due on July 1, 19X9. Assuming a 10% implicit rate of interest on the lease, the county should report General Fund expenditures in the fiscal year ended December 31, 19X8 as follows:
   a. capital outlay expenditures of $20,000
   b. capital outlay expenditures of $200,000
   c. capital outlay expenditures of $20,000 and interest expenditures of $9,000
   d. capital outlay expenditures of $200,000 and interest expenditures of $9,000
   e. rent expenditures of $20,000 and no capital outlay or debt service expenditures

2. The county in 1 paid its first $35,000 lease payment as scheduled on July 1, 19X9. The county should report General Fund expenditures for the fiscal year ended December 31, 19X9 as follows:
   a. rent expenditures of $35,000
   b. interest expenditures of $35,000
   c. principal retirement expenditures of $35,000
   d. interest expenditures of $9,000 and principal retirement expenditures of $28,000
   e. interest expenditures of $18,000 and principal retirement expenditures of $17,000
   f. interest expenditures of $9,000 and principal retirement expenditures of $17,000

3. A city paid General Fund claims and judgments incurred during 19X1 of $20,000. Additional General Fund claims were incurred during 19X1 that are deemed probable to result in judgments against the city totaling $180,000. It is likely that these claims will not result in required payments for at least two years, however. The city General Fund expenditures reported for claims and judgments in 19X1 should be:
   a. $20,000
   b. $200,000
   c. $20,000 with $180,000 of other financing uses reported
   d. $200,000 with $180,000 of other financing sources reported

The following information pertains to questions 4 and 5.

A school district Special Revenue Fund's beginning materials inventory was $100,000; its ending materials inventory was $120,000. Materials costing $400,000 were purchased for the fund during the year. Accounts payable for the fund's materials were $17,000 at the beginning of the year and $7,000 at year end.

4. The school district should report expenditures for materials in its Special Revenue Fund of:

| | If the School District Uses | |
| --- | --- | --- |
| | *Purchases Method* | *Consumption Method* |
| a. | $400,000 | $400,000 |
| b. | $400,000 | $380,000 |
| c. | $410,000 | $380,000 |
| d. | $400,000 | $420,000 |
| e. | $410,000 | $420,000 |

5. If the school district presents its Special Revenue Fund statement of revenues, expenditures, and changes in fund balance in terms of changes in total fund balance, what amount(s) besides expenditures must be reported in that statement related to materials?

| | *Purchases Method* | *Consumption Method* |
| --- | --- | --- |
| a. | Nothing. | Nothing. |
| b. | Other financing source of $20,000. | Other financing source of $20,000. |
| c. | Nothing. | Other financing source of $20,000. |
| d. | Other financing source of $20,000. | Nothing. |

e. None of the above is correct.

6. A state pays salaries and wages of $118 million to General Fund employees during a year. Unpaid, accrued salaries were $3 million at the beginning of the year and $6 million at year end. General Fund salary expenditures should be reported for the year in the amount of
   a. $115 million.
   b. $118 million.
   c. $121 million.
   d. $124 million.

7. Equipment purchased for county General Fund departments on a line of credit with a supplier cost $800,000. $200,000 had been paid by year end, including $4,000 interest. The county expects to repay another $300,000, including $7,000 interest, during the first two months of the next fiscal year. The remaining balance is to be repaid by midyear. Capital outlay expenditures should be reported for the county General Fund in the amount of
   a. $196,000.
   b. $200,000.
   c. $489,000.
   d. $493,000.
   e. $800,000.

8. The minimum expenditure classifications required in the general purpose financial statements for governmental funds are
   a. fund and function or program
   b. fund, character, and function or program
   c. fund, character, and department
   d. none of the above. The minimum required classifications are _____ .

9. How should the purchase of land for General Fund purposes by issuing a three-year, $80,000, interest-bearing note be reported in the General Fund statement of revenues, expenditures, and changes in fund balance?
   a. no effect
   b. expenditures of $80,000
   c. expenditures of $80,000 and other financing sources of $80,000
   d. other financing uses of $80,000 and other financing sources of $80,000

10. Which of the following should be reported as expenditures in a county General Fund?
    1. reimbursement of a Special Revenue Fund for General Fund expenditures inadvertently paid for from and recorded in the Special Revenue Fund
    2. water services received from the town Water Enterprise Fund
    3. payment of the federal income tax withheld from employee paychecks to the federal government
    4. payment to a Debt Service Fund to provide resources for principal and interest payments that matured and were paid during the year
       a. 1 only
       b. 2 only
       c. 3 only
       d. 4 only
       e. 1 and 2 only
       f. none of the above. The correct answer is _____ .

**P 6-2** (GL and SL Budgetary Entries, Balances) The following General Fund appropriations were made for 19X4 by the city of Dulaney:

| | |
|---|---:|
| City Council | $ 15,000 |
| Mayor | 15,000 |
| Courts | 30,000 |
| City Clerk | 15,000 |
| Department of Finance | 30,000 |
| Department of Police | 75,000 |
| Department of Fire | 60,000 |
| Department of Public Works | 30,000 |
| Interest | 15,000 |
| Retirement of long-term notes | 15,000 |
| | $300,000 |

Estimated revenues are $350,000; the council reserved $30,000 for contingencies.

The following appropriations revisions and additional appropriations were subsequently authorized:

| Reductions (from): | Increases (to): | Amount |
|---|---|---:|
| City Council | City Clerk | $ 750 |
| City Clerk | Mayor | 1,500 |
| Department of Finance | Department of Public Works | 1,500 |
| Department of Public Works | Courts | 1,000 |

| Additional Appropriations | Appropriated for: | Amount |
|---|---|---:|
| | Department of Police | $1,500 |
| | Department of Fire | 2,200 |
| Reserve for Contingencies | City Council | 750 |
| | Department of Public Works | 3,000 |

**Required** (a) Prepare the GF journal entry necessary to record the adoption of the budget, showing both the General Ledger and the Expenditures Subsidiary Ledger accounts.
(b) Prepare the GF journal entry to record the revised and additional appropriations, showing both the General Ledger and the Subsidiary Ledger accounts involved.
(c) Prepare a statement showing the appropriation balances after the appropriations revisions and additional appropriations.

**P 6-3** (Allotments) The following appropriations and first quarter allotments for 19X4 were made by Dogwood City's council and manager, respectively:

|  | 19X4 Appropriations | First Quarter Allotments |
|---|---|---|
| City Council | $ 12,000 | $ 3,000 |
| Manager | 40,000 | 11,000 |
| Courts | 30,000 | 7,000 |
| City Clerk | 20,000 | 5,000 |
| Finance Department | 35,000 | 10,000 |
| Police Department | 80,000 | 20,000 |
| Fire Department | 75,000 | 16,000 |
| Public Works Department | 45,000 | 12,000 |
| Interest | 15,000 | — |
| Retirement of Notes | 25,000 | — |
|  | $377,000 | $84,000 |

**Required** (a) Prepare the journal entry necessary to record the appropriations and first quarter allotments in both the General Ledger and the Expenditures Subsidiary Ledger accounts.

(b) If first quarter expenditures for the City Council account total $2,800 and another $150 is encumbered for that purpose, what is the balance in the City Council account in the Expenditures Subsidiary Ledger?

**P 6-4** (GL and SL Entries, Reconciliation) The city of Beverly Heights General Fund had the following transactions, among others, in 19X7:

1. Appropriations were made as follows:

| | |
|---|---|
| Personal Services | $111,400 |
| Contractual Services | 8,700 |
| Materials and Supplies | 8,500 |
| New Patrol Cars | 21,000 |
| Other | 12,000 |
| | $161,600 |

2. $2,000 of General Fund cash was paid to the Debt Service Fund to provide for debt service.

3. A long-term note of $8,300, including interest of $1,300, and a short-term note of $2,500 (including $150 interest) came due. The Beverly Heights Council had not made appropriations for these items. The necessary action was taken and the notes and interest were paid.

4. $100,000 of General Fund cash was paid to the Enterprise Fund to finance construction of a new auxiliary generator and $50,000 was contributed to establish a central motor pool facility. The Enterprise Fund will repay the General Fund in ten equal annual installments beginning January 1, 19X9.

5. The council increased the appropriation for personal services by $500.

6. Materials and supplies are accounted for on the purchases method. The beginning inventory was $200; $8,500 of materials and supplies were ordered during the year. New patrol cars costing $20,000 were also ordered.

7. The following expenditures were made by the city:

| | | |
|---|---|---|
| Personal Services | $111,700 | |
| Contractual Services | 8,700 | |
| Materials and Supplies | 7,500 | (encumbered for $7,600) |
| New Patrol Cars | 21,200 | (encumbered for $20,000) |
| Other | 11,800 | |
| | $160,900 | |

The council passed the amendments to its appropriations necessary to make the foregoing expenditures legal.

8. Materials and supplies on hand at year end amounted to $1,000.

*Required* (a) Prepare and post the general journal entries required to record the transactions in the General Ledger and in the Expenditures Ledger. Assume that there were no outstanding encumbrances at the beginning of 19X7.

(b) Prepare a trial balance of the Expenditures Ledger and prove its agreement with the control accounts.

(c) Prepare the general journal entries required to close the expenditure accounts in the General and Expenditures Ledgers. Assume that all appropriations lapse, but a reserve is reported for encumbrances outstanding at year end.

(d) Prepare the general journal entries required to close the expenditures accounts in the General and Expenditures Ledgers assuming that unexpended appropriations do not lapse.

**P 6-5** (GL and SL Entries—Allotments) The town of Dee's Junction General Fund was affected by the following transactions, among others, during its calendar 19X4 fiscal year:

1. Appropriations were made as follows:

| | |
|---|---|
| Personal Services | $222,800 |
| Contractual Services | 17,400 |
| Materials and Supplies | 17,000 |
| Firefighting Equipment | 42,000 |
| Other | 24,000 |
| | $323,200 |

The appropriation for materials and supplies covers a $1,800 order outstanding at the end of 19X3. An appropriate fund balance reserve is on the books (Assumption A1).

**January transactions (2–8):**

2. Allotments for the month of January were:

| | |
|---|---|
| Personal Services | $20,800 |
| Contractual Services | 1,600 |
| Materials and Supplies | 3,000 |
| Firefighting Equipment | 35,000 |
| Other | 500 |
| | $60,900 |

3. $15,000 of General Fund cash was paid to the Debt Service Fund to provide for debt service.

4. The Dee's Junction Council amended the budget, increasing the contractual services appropriation by $5,000 and decreasing the materials and supplies appropriation by $1,700. These budget amendments did not affect the January allotments.

5. Materials and supplies of $200 were acquired for cash and $1,200 of supplies were ordered during January. Materials ordered in 19X3 were received on January 8 at their estimated cost of $1,800. Materials and supplies are accounted for on the purchases method.

6. The supplies ordered were received, with an invoice for $1,180.

7. Firefighting equipment costing $35,000 was ordered.

8. Other expenditures during January 19X4 were:

| | |
|---|---|
| Personal Services | $20,800 |
| Firefighting Equipment (included in January order—estimated cost $31,800) | 32,000 |
| Other | 400 |
| | $53,200 |

**February through December transactions (9–11):**

9. Allotments for the remainder of the year were:

| | |
|---|---:|
| Personal Services | $202,000 |
| Contractual Services | 15,800 |
| Materials and Supplies | 12,000 |
| Firefighting Equipment | 7,000 |
| Other | 11,500 |
| | $248,300 |

10. Expenditures for the remainder of the year were:

| | |
|---|---:|
| Personal Services | $200,000 |
| Contractual Services | 12,000 |
| Materials and Supplies | 11,000 |
| Firefighting Equipment | 1,000 |
| Other | 11,500 |
| | $235,500 |

11. In addition to the encumbrances for firefighting equipment, encumbrances of $1,000 for materials and supplies and $2,000 for contractual services were outstanding at year end. The inventory of materials and supplies decreased by $1,100 during the year.

*Required* (a) Prepare the general journal entries to record the transactions in the General Ledger and in the Expenditures Ledger and post the Expenditures Ledger accounts.

(b) Prepare a trial balance of the January 31, 19X4, balances in the Expenditures Ledger. Show its agreement with the General Ledger control accounts.

(c) Prepare a preclosing trial balance of the year-end balances in the Expenditures Ledger and show its agreement with the General Ledger control accounts.

(d) Prepare the general journal entries to close the expenditure accounts in the General and Expenditures Ledgers at year end.

**P 6-6** (GL and SL Entries—Errors, Pensions, Changes, Leases, CJ, etc.) The following transactions and events relate to the General Fund of Antonio County for the 19X6 fiscal year.

1. Early in 19X6 it was discovered that at the end of 19X5 (a) the inventory of supplies was overstated $30,000, and (b) interest payable of $11,000 was not accrued.

2. Appropriations were revised as follows:

| | |
|---|---:|
| Increased Appropriations: | |
| Police Department—Supplies | $10,000 |
| Streets Department—Equipment | 50,000 |
| Decreased Appropriations: | |
| Parks Department—Wages | 20,000 |

3. The county entered a capital lease for equipment that could have been purchased for $850,000 (which is also the net present value of the lease) for the Roads and Bridges Department.

4. An equipment capital lease payment, $80,000 (including $45,000 interest), was made.

5. Antonio County changed its method of inventory accounting from the purchases method to the consumption method (perpetual system) at the beginning of 19X6. The inventory of supplies at the end of 19X5 was $150,000; no inventory reserve is considered necessary under the consumption method.

6. During the year it was found that (a) $12,000 charged to Fire Department—Contractual Services should have been charged to that account in the Police Department, and (b) $16,000 charged to salaries and wages in a Capital Projects Fund

7. should have been charged to the Streets Department, which is financed from the General Fund.

7. At year end it was determined that the county had estimated liabilities (including legal fees and related costs and net of insurance reimbursements) for unsettled claims and judgments of $400,000, of which $100,000 is considered a current liability. The comparable estimated liability amounts (which had been properly recorded) at the end of 19X5 were $350,000 and $60,000, respectively.

8. The year-end physical count of the inventory of supplies revealed that $25,000 of supplies had been stolen; $20,000 will be recovered from the insurance company that bonds employees.

9. Although the actuarially required defined benefit pension plan contribution for 19X6 was $600,000, Antonio County made contributions of only $200,000. The County Commission voted to appropriate an additional $100,000 in the 19X7 budget—to be paid early in 19X7 and applied to the 19X6 contribution deficiency—but made no provision with respect to the remaining unfunded balance of the 19X6 contribution.

**Required** Prepare the journal entries to record these transactions and events in the General Ledger and Expenditures Subsidiary Ledger of the General Fund of Antonio County assuming that the county's accountant:

(a) makes reversing entries at the beginning of the year for most prior year-end adjusting entries.

(b) does not make reversing entries at the beginning of each year for prior year-end adjusting entries. (Make only those entries that differ from part a.)

**P 6-7** (GL and SL Entries—Errors, Changes, Leases, Pensions, CJ, etc.) The following transactions and events relate to the General Fund of Harmer Township for the 19X8 fiscal year.

1. Early in 19X8 it was discovered that at the end of 19X7 (a) encumbrances recorded for equipment, $30,000, should have been recorded as an expenditure and liability, $31,000, and the liability was vouchered for payment; and (b) interest payable on tax anticipation notes, $16,000, was not accrued.

2. Appropriations were revised as follows:

Appropriations Decreased

| | |
|---|---:|
| Recreation Department—Salaries . . . . . . . . . . . . . . . . . . . . . . | $25,000 |
| Parks Department—Equipment . . . . . . . . . . . . . . . . . . . . . . | 30,000 |

Appropriations Increased

| | |
|---|---:|
| Fire Department—Equipment . . . . . . . . . . . . . . . . . . . . . . . . | 70,000 |

3. The township entered into a capital lease for computer equipment with a fair market value (and net present value) of $500,000.

4. A capital lease payment on the computer equipment, $60,000 (including $40,000 interest), was vouchered for payment.

5. Harmer Township changed its method of materials inventory accounting to the purchases method from the consumption method (no related reserve) at the beginning of 19X8. The beginning inventory of materials was $90,000.

6. During the year it was realized that (a) $44,000 of salaries and wages charged to the General Fund Parks Department appropriation should have been charged to a Special Revenue Fund, and (b) $19,000 charged to Police Department—Equipment should have been charged to the Fire Department.

7. At year end it was determined that the township had estimated liabilities (including legal and related costs and net of insurance recoveries) for unsettled claims and judgments of $700,000, of which $160,000 is considered a current liability. This is the first year the township has recorded such liabilities—they had not been considered reasonably estimable in prior years.

8. An internal audit during the year revealed that $30,000 had been embezzled and the Cash account was overstated by that amount. The insurance company that bonds employees has agreed to reimburse the township $25,000 on this embezzlement.

9. Harmer Township paid only $150,000 to the trustee of its defined benefit pension plan during 19X8, even though the actuarially required contribution for 19X8 was $400,000. The governing board agreed to pay another $75,000 early in 19X9, but it is uncertain when the remaining pension plan underfunded contribution will be paid.

*Required* Prepare the journal entries to record these transactions and events in the General Ledger and Expenditures Ledger of the General Fund of Harmer Township for the 19X8 fiscal year.

**P 6-8** (Appendices 6–2 and 6–3) (Various Appropriations and Encumbrances Assumptions) At December 31, 19X1, the city of X had in certain of its accounts the following balances: Appropriations, $200,000; Expenditures, $190,000; Encumbrances, $7,500; Reserve for Encumbrances, $7,500. On February 15, 19X2, the only item represented by the $7,500 encumbrance was billed to the city at $7,350. On the basis of the preceding information, prepare the closing entry, December 31, 19X1; entries required to be made January 1, 19X2, and February 15, 19X2; and the closing entry December 31, 19X2, for each of the five law and policy assumptions pertaining to the lapsing of appropriations and encumbrances outstanding at year end. Assume that continuing 19X1 appropriations lapse at the end of 19X2.

**P 6-9** (Appendices 6–2 and 6–3) (Various Appropriations and Encumbrances Assumptions) The balances of selected accounts of the town of Bettinger's Haven General Fund at December 31, 19X5 before preparing year-end closing entries are as follows:

| | |
|---|---:|
| Unreserved Fund Balance | $ 85,000 |
| Appropriations | 1,000,000 |
| Estimated Revenues | 1,020,000 |
| Expenditures | 920,000 |
| Encumbrances | 50,000 |
| Operating Transfers In | 30,000 |
| Revenues | 980,000 |
| Reserve for Advances | 10,000 |
| Reserve for Encumbrances | 50,000 |

*Required* (a) Prepare the closing entry(ies) under each of the five law and policy assumptions pertaining to the lapsing of appropriations and encumbrances outstanding at year end.

(b) Prepare the fund balance section of the year-end balance sheet under each of the five assumptions.

(c) Indicate the footnote disclosures related to encumbrances that are required under each assumption.

(d) Assuming the goods on order at year end were received January 15, 19X6, at an invoice price of $50,900, prepare any general journal entries required on January 1 and January 15, 19X6, under each of the five assumptions.

**P 6-10** (Worksheets and Statements) The following information summarizes the operation of the Library Fund, a Special Revenue Fund of the city of Hillsdale:

1. The account balances at December 31, 19X0, were as follows:

| | |
|---|---:|
| Cash | $ 2,350 |
| Reserve for Encumbrances | 1,000 |
| Unreserved Fund Balance | 1,350 |

2. Effective January 1, 19X1, the city council dedicated a portion of the property taxes of the city, together with all receipts from parking meters, to the Library Fund. The council's estimate of revenues from these sources follows:

| | |
|---|---:|
| Property Taxes | $ 50,000 |
| Parking Meters | 135,000 |
| | $185,000 |

3. Planned expenditures for 19X1 were as follows:

| | |
|---|---:|
| General Administration ............................... | $ 50,000 |
| Library-on-Wheels .................................... | 40,000 |
| Books ................................................ | 90,000 |
| | $180,000 |

The council's approval of expenditures included $1,000 for books ordered in 19X0.

4. Taxes of $52,500 were levied. It was expected that $2,000 would prove uncollectible.

5. Receipts during the year consisted of the following items:

| | |
|---|---:|
| Property Taxes ....................................... | $ 51,500 |
| Parking Meter Collections ........................... | 136,000 |
| Refund on Books Bought This Year .................... | 300 |
| | $187,800 |

6. The following purchase orders were placed:

| | |
|---|---:|
| General Administration ............................... | $ 30,000 |
| Library-on-Wheels .................................... | 10,000 |
| Books ................................................ | 80,000 |
| | $120,000 |

7. Certain of the orders placed in 19X0 and 19X1 were received. The vouchers, together with the amount of the related purchase orders are summarized as follows:

| | *Ordered* | *Vouchered* |
|---|---:|---:|
| General Administration .................... | $ 20,000 | $ 21,500 |
| Library-on-Wheels ....................... | 10,000 | 10,000 |
| Books .................................. | 80,000 | 85,000 |
| | $110,000 | $116,500 |

8. Additional vouchers were prepared for the following purposes:

| | |
|---|---:|
| General Administration ............................... | $27,000 |
| Library-on-Wheels .................................... | 30,000 |
| Books ................................................ | 6,000 |
| Refund of Overpayment of Taxes ...................... | 400 |
| | $63,400 |

9. Vouchers were paid in the total amount of $178,000.

10. A physical inventory of $2,000 was taken on December 31, 19X1, and the city council directed that it be properly recorded. (Use the purchases method.) The $2,000 is applicable to General Administration.

11. Expenditures must be charged against appropriations of the year in which the expenditures are made. Any outstanding orders at year end must be honored, however, and are to be reported as fund balance reserves.

*Required* (a) Prepare a worksheet(s) that will show the Library Fund General Ledger and subsidiary ledger closing entries and balance sheet information at December 31, 19X1, and will summarize the information needed for the Statement of Revenues, Expenditures, and Changes in Fund Balance.

(b) Prepare the statements just mentioned.

**P 6-11** (Worksheets, Closing Entries, Operating Statement) Waynesville had the following General Fund trial balance on January 1, 19X1, after the reversing entry for the 19X0 encumbrances closing entry was made:

| | | |
|---|---:|---:|
| Cash | $ 7,000 | |
| Taxes Receivable–Delinquent | 48,000 | |
| Allowance for Uncollectible Delinquent Taxes | | $ 4,000 |
| Due from Water Fund | 500 | |
| Vouchers Payable | | 11,000 |
| Due to Taxpayers | | 1,000 |
| Encumbrances | 3,000 | |
| Reserve for Encumbrances | | 3,000 |
| Appropriations (Police Department) | | 3,000 |
| Unreserved Fund Balance | | 36,500 |
| | $58,500 | $58,500 |

The following information summarizes the transactions of the General Fund during 19X1:

1. The city council approved the following budget for 19X1:

| | |
|---|---:|
| Expenditures: | |
| City Manager | $20,000 |
| Police Department | 10,000 |
| Fire Department | 10,000 |
| Streets and Roads | 20,000 |
| | $60,000 |
| Revenues: | |
| Property Taxes | $75,000 |
| Fines and Fees | 5,000 |
| Miscellaneous | 5,000 |
| | $85,000 |

2. The council levied property taxes of $75,000. It was estimated that $2,000 of the amount would never be collected.

3. Cash collected during the year may be summarized as follows:

| | |
|---|---:|
| Prior years' levies | $45,000 |
| 19X1 levy | 46,000 |
| Fines and Fees | 4,000 |
| Taxes written off in prior years | 500 |
| Interest | 500 |
| Service charges | 2,000 |
| | $98,000 |

4. With council approval, $5,000 was borrowed on a 90-day note.

5. Orders placed during the year were as follows:

| | |
|---|---:|
| City Manager | $ 4,000 |
| Police Department | 3,000 |
| Fire Department | 3,000 |
| Streets and Roads | 5,000 |
| | $15,000 |

6. Payrolls vouchered during the year were as follows:

| | |
|---|---:|
| City Manager | $15,000 |
| Police Department | 7,000 |
| Fire Department | 6,500 |
| Streets and Roads | 14,000 |
| | $42,500 |

7. Invoices vouchered during the year were as follows:

| | |
|---|---:|
| City Manager | $ 4,500 |
| Police Department | 6,100 |
| Fire Department | 3,000 |
| Streets and Roads | 4,000 |
| Repayment of note plus interest (see item 4) | 5,200 |
| | $22,800 |

The preceding invoices completed all orders except one, dated June 1, 19X1, for an attachment for a Streets and Roads road grader for $950.

8. Payments to other funds:

| Fund | Purpose | Amount |
|---|---|---:|
| Debt Service | Provide for payment of bond principal and interest | $ 8,000 |
| Capital Projects | City contribution to construction of city park facilities | 15,000 |
| Water Fund | Water supply for Streets and Roads Department | 1,500 |
| | | $24,500 |

9. Analysis of collections revealed that taxpayer A, to whom the city owed $1,000 on January 1, 19X1, for overpayment of taxes, had paid his tax for 19X1 less $1,000.
10. The Streets and Roads Department rendered services in the amount of $250 to the Water Fund.
11. The city council made an additional appropriation in the amount of $5,000 (including $600 interest) for a long-term note maturity which was overlooked in preparing the budget.
12. The note matured and was vouchered.
13. Vouchers of $70,000 were paid.
14. Delinquent taxes in the amount of $500 were written off on the authority of the council.
15. Current taxes became delinquent.

*Required* (a) Prepare a worksheet or worksheets summarizing the year's operations in such a way that the General Ledger and subsidiary ledger closing entries and required statements may be easily prepared.

(b) Prepare the required closing entry(ies) for the General Ledger and subsidiary ledger accounts at year end.

(c) Prepare a Statement of Revenues, Expenditures, and Changes in Fund Balance for the General Fund of Waynesville for the year ended December 31, 19X1.

**P 6-12** (Research and Analysis) Obtain a copy of a recent comprehensive annual financial report (CAFR) of a state or local government from the government, the Internet, your professor, or a library.

*Required* (1) **Letter of Transmittal.** Review the expenditure-related discussions and presentations. What were the most significant general government expenditure categories? Which general government expenditures increased (decreased) significantly from the previous year?

(2) **Financial Statements.** Indicate the types of general government expenditures reported. Did any expenditure types differ from those you expected based on your study of Chapters 2–5? Explain.

(3) **Summary of Significant Accounting Policies (SOSAP).** Review the general government expenditure-related SOSAP disclosures. Were any of these disclosures different from, or in addition to, those you expected based on your study of Chapters 2–5? Explain.

(4) **Statistical Section.** Review the general government expenditure-related statistical presentations. Explain how these might be useful in evaluating the general government financial position and changes in financial position.

(5) **Reporting.** Include photocopies or printouts of relevant excerpts from the CAFR with your brief written report on items 1–4, and submit your CAFR if required by your instructor.

# CHAPTER

# 7

# CAPITAL PROJECTS FUNDS

Capital Projects Funds are established to account for financial resources that are to be used to construct or otherwise acquire **major** long-lived **general government capital facilities**—such as buildings, highways, storm sewer systems, and bridges. Their principal purpose is to ensure the economical and legal expenditure of the resources, but they also serve as cost accounting mechanisms for controlling and accumulating the costs of major capital outlay projects. Furthermore, Capital Projects Funds must be used whenever they are legally or contractually required for nonmajor capital asset acquisitions. Indeed, they may be used to account for any general government fixed asset acquisition.

Not all general government fixed asset acquisitions are financed through Capital Projects Funds. Routine fixed asset purchases—for example, school buses and photocopy equipment—may be financed with resources of the General Fund or Special Revenue Funds, unless prohibited by legal or contractual provisions. Likewise, capital leases usually do not involve projects and are reported in the General Fund or a Special Revenue Fund as discussed and illustrated in Chapter 6. And acquisitions of specific fund fixed assets are accounted for through proprietary funds and Trust Funds.

But major general government capital projects usually must be financed at least partly with bond issue proceeds or intergovernmental grants. And both bond covenants and grant agreements—as well as GAAP—often require that a Capital Projects Fund be used to account for the related projects. Furthermore, many state and local government finance officers prefer to account for most general government capital projects through Capital Projects Funds—even when their use is not required—in order to better control and account for each project and its related resources. That is, because the accounting systems of Capital Projects Funds are designed to control the expenditure of resources for major capital assets, some prefer to transfer resources of General and Special Revenue Funds to Capital Projects Funds rather than to account for capital expenditures through systems oriented to current operations.

Similarly, not all long-term debt issue proceeds are accounted for in Capital Projects Funds. The GASB standards recommend accounting for the proceeds of bonds and other long-term debt issues in the following funds:

- Proceeds that are to be used to acquire capital assets should be accounted for in a Capital Projects Fund.

- Proceeds of refunding issues should be accounted for in a Debt Service Fund.

- Proceeds of proprietary and Trust Funds issues should be accounted for in those funds because such liabilities are the primary responsibility of and will be serviced by the issuing funds.

The GASB standards do not address debt issued for other purposes. But it seems appropriate for proceeds of debt issued to finance a deficit to be accounted for in the fund that has the deficit. Furthermore, it would seem that the proceeds of debt issued to provide disaster relief might properly be accounted for in Capital Projects or Special Revenue Funds, or even the General Fund.

The terms **major** and **project**—as used in determining when Capital Projects Funds are required—are not defined in the GASB *Codification* and are subject to interpretation in practice. A $10,000,000 street improvement program would be a major capital project in a small town, for example, but might be considered a non-major, routine activity of a state highway department. Thus, assuming no legal or contractual provisions require a Capital Projects Fund, (1) the town would nonetheless use a Capital Projects Fund, whereas (2) the state might account for the capital expenditure through a Special Revenue Fund. Unless noted otherwise, we assume that the capital asset acquisitions discussed here are major capital projects that should be accounted for in Capital Projects Funds.

Furthermore, some capital projects—such as neighborhood street construction or improvement projects—are financed by **special assessments** levied against the properties improved. Special assessments are essentially a special tax imposed only upon those properties or taxpayers benefited by the capital improvement or service financed by the assessment. Special assessments for capital improvements normally are payable, along with related interest, over a period of five to ten years or longer. Therefore, long-term debt typically is issued to finance construction of the improvements. The special assessment collections are used to service the debt issued. The proceeds of long-term special assessment debt issued to finance general government capital improvement special assessment projects should be reported in the Capital Projects Fund financial statements. Any related debt service transactions and balances, including the special assessments receivable, normally should be reported in a Debt Service Fund.

This chapter begins with brief discussions of Capital Projects Fund (CPF) operations and accounting standards. These discussions are followed by a CPF accounting and reporting illustrative case example. Finally, several other CPF operations, accounting, and reporting matters are considered at the conclusion of the chapter.

# CPF OPERATIONS AND ACCOUNTING STANDARDS

Capital Projects Fund operations and accounting standards are discussed briefly under these topic headings:

1. Sources of Financial Resources
2. Number of Funds Required
3. Capital Projects Fund Life Cycle
4. The Budget
5. Interim Financing
6. Costs Charged to Projects
7. Intergovernmental Revenues
8. Bond Premiums, Discounts, and Issuance Costs

## Sources of Financial Resources

Typical sources of Capital Projects Fund financial resources are bond issues or other long-term general obligation debt issues, special assessment indebtedness, grants or shared revenues from other governments, transfers from other funds, and interest earned on temporary investments of project resources. The classification of resource inflows is significant for reporting purposes because the government as a whole should be considered the entity for which financial statements are presented.

Capital Projects Fund inflows from intergovernmental grants and from interest on investments should be considered revenues when earned and available. But two typical financing sources do not represent revenues to the government as a whole: (1) Interfund transfers should be classified as operating transfers or as residual equity transfers, as appropriate, and (2) proceeds of the issue of long-term debt should be labeled as other financing sources because they are not revenue. Operating transfers and bond issue proceeds are reported in the "Other Financing Sources" section of the Capital Projects Fund statement of revenues, expenditures, and changes in fund balance.

## Number of Funds Required

Separate Capital Projects Funds are usually established for each project or debt issue. Separate funds are used because the nature of such projects varies widely, they typically involve significant amounts of financial resources, they are usually budgeted on an individual project or debt issue basis, and legal and contractual requirements differ significantly among projects. Where debt issues or grants are involved, a major purpose of the Capital Projects Funds is to show that the proceeds were used only for authorized purposes and that unexpended balances or deficits have been handled in accordance with applicable contractual agreements or legal provisions.

A single Capital Projects Fund will suffice, however, where a single debt issue is used to finance several projects or a series of closely related projects is financed through a single grant or by internal transfers from the General Fund or Special Revenue Funds. Combining statements are used to present financial operation or position data where a government has more than one Capital Projects Fund in operation during a given year.

Some state or local governments properly use a single Capital Projects Fund accounting entity even when several restricted financing sources (e.g., bonds, grants) and several different capital projects are involved. This is done through what is known as a "funds within a fund" or "subfund" approach under which each capital project is accounted for as a separate subfund of the overall Capital Projects Fund.[1] This "funds within a fund" or "subfund" approach should be used only where the substance of separate Capital Projects Fund accounting and control is achieved and the compliance reporting objectives of Capital Projects Funds are met.

## Capital Projects Fund Life Cycle

A Capital Projects Fund is authorized by action of the legislative body on either the project or debt issue. The accrual and inflows, expenditures and encumbrances, and balances of project-related resources are then recorded in the fund accounting records. The fund is abolished at the conclusion of the project and the ac-

---

[1] That is, the overall Capital Projects Fund is assigned a number in the governmental fund chart of accounts, say, 300, and each separate capital project is assigned a separate "300" number, such as 319 or 368. Thus, every subfund asset, liability, and fund balance—and every subfund revenue, expenditure, other financing source, and so on—is identified (coded) by subfund within the overall Capital Projects Fund.

counting records are retained to evidence the fiscal stewardship of the government. A Capital Projects Fund life cycle overview is illustrated in Figure 7–1.

In extremely simple situations, such as where the project consists of purchasing existing facilities for a single payment, the life of the Capital Projects Fund may be brief and its entries uncomplicated: (1) Receipts of all financial resources will occur and revenues or other financing sources will be credited, (2) expenditures will be recorded and paid, (3) the temporary fund balance accounts will be closed to Unreserved Fund Balance, and (4) any remaining financial resources and the balance of the fund will be closed out when the assets are transferred to another fund (or disposed of in some other way as required by law or contract).

In other cases, however, a Capital Projects Fund is used to finance construction projects where the government acts as a general contractor, possibly using its own employees and equipment for part or all of the work. In this situation accounting procedures are more complicated and closely resemble those of the General Fund.

Laws or contracts will determine the disposition of any unused balance remaining in the Capital Projects Fund at completion of its mission. It may, for example, have to be refunded on a pro rata basis to the grantors who participated in financing the project. The city's portion is usually transferred to the Debt Service Fund that will service the debt incurred to finance the project. If any bond premium is kept in the Capital Projects Fund in conformity with legal provisions or debt indenture requirements, it typically will be transferred to a Debt Service Fund when the Capital Projects Fund is closed.

## The Budget

The projects financed through Capital Projects Funds (1) usually are planned in the government's long-term capital budget and (2) are appropriated for on a project basis; that is, appropriations do not lapse at the end of each fiscal year (Assumption C1, Appendix 6–3). If annual reappropriations are made of project appropriations, they are considered to be allotments.

FIGURE 7–1    **Capital Projects Fund Life Cycle: An Overview**

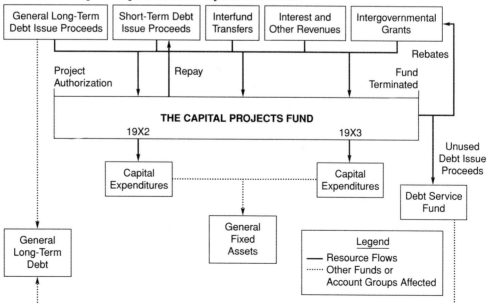

In some cases adequate control is provided without the budgetary process, and appropriations are not made. In substance, the entire CPF is appropriated for the project in such cases. Reasons for not budgeting capital projects include (1) only one project is financed from a single fund; and (2) control is provided by specifications, bids, inspections, and the like.

On the other hand, budgetary control is important where several projects are accounted for through a single CPF, where the government budgets the CPF in detail, where the government uses its own employees to construct a major capital asset, and where the CPF is budgeted annually. The case illustration in this chapter assumes that the capital project is appropriated on a project basis (Assumption C1, Appendix 6–3) and full budgetary control is desirable.

## Interim Financing

Cash may be borrowed in the short term, especially during the early stages of the CPF life cycle, to pay for project expenditures incurred before the bond issue proceeds or other CPF financial resources are received. Governments may use short-term financing to allow them to issue long-term debt close to the time that the bulk of the resources will be expended, to take advantage of anticipated improvements in bond market conditions, or to avoid delaying a project while technical details associated with a debt issuance are addressed. Such short-term borrowing may be from other funds of the governmental unit or by bond anticipation notes (BANs), revenue anticipation notes, or other notes issued to local banks or other creditors. The short-term borrowing ordinarily is repaid when the bond issue proceeds or other CPF resources are received.

Most types of interim borrowing are considered current liabilities of the CPF. Accordingly, Cash is debited and Notes Payable or Due to General (or other) Fund is credited—not a debt proceeds Other Financing Source account—to record the short-term loan. The entries are reversed when the loan is repaid and any interest (but not note principal) paid is recorded as Expenditures of the CPF. For example, if at midyear a government issued a one-year, $500,000, 6% bond anticipation note payable to provide temporary financing for a major general government capital project, and expended 90% of the proceeds on the project by year end, the following Capital Projects Fund entries would be required:

| | | |
|---|---|---|
| Cash . . . . . . . . . . . . . . . . . . . . . . . . . . . . . . . . . . . . . . . . . . . . . . . | $500,000 | |
|    Notes Payable . . . . . . . . . . . . . . . . . . . . . . . . . . . . . . . . . . . . . . | | $500,000 |
| To record issuance of the notes at par. | | |
| Expenditures—Capital Outlay . . . . . . . . . . . . . . . . . . . . . . . . . . . . | $450,000 | |
|    Cash or Payables . . . . . . . . . . . . . . . . . . . . . . . . . . . . . . . . . . . . | | $450,000 |
| To record expenditures incurred on the project. | | |
| Expenditures—Debt Service . . . . . . . . . . . . . . . . . . . . . . . . . . . . . | $ 15,000 | |
|    Accrued Interest Payable . . . . . . . . . . . . . . . . . . . . . . . . . . . . . . | | $ 15,000 |
| To record accrual of interest on the short-term, bond anticipation notes. | | |
| Unreserved Fund Balance . . . . . . . . . . . . . . . . . . . . . . . . . . . . . . . | $465,000 | |
|    Expenditures—Capital Outlay . . . . . . . . . . . . . . . . . . . . . . . . . . | | $450,000 |
|    Expenditures—Debt Service . . . . . . . . . . . . . . . . . . . . . . . . . . . | | 15,000 |
| To close the CPF accounts at year end. | | |

Note that this sequence of events results in a fund balance deficit in the Capital Projects Fund at year end.

An exception to this general rule of recording short-term loans as CPF fund liabilities is made with respect to certain bond anticipation notes (BANs). The GASB *Codification* states that BANs are treated as long-term debt if both: (1) the BANs are issued in relation to a bond issue that is legally authorized and definitely issuable, and (2) two specific GASB BAN refinancing criteria (discussed later) are met. BANs not meeting these criteria are considered CPF liabilities. When BANs that qualify for long-term debt treatment are issued, a BAN proceeds other financing source is reported in the Capital Projects Fund and the BAN liability is recorded in the GLTDAG—not the CPF. The logic underlying the treatment of qualifying BANs as general long-term debt is that they definitely will be repaid from the related bond issue proceeds, and thus their repayment will not require the use of existing CPF financial resources.

To illustrate, assume that the one-year BANs in the previous example meet these criteria. The following entries would be made in the Capital Projects Fund to record the transactions described:

| | | |
|---|---|---|
| Cash | $500,000 | |
|     Other Financing Sources—BAN Proceeds | | $500,000 |
| To record issuance of the BANs. | | |
| Expenditures—Capital Outlay | $450,000 | |
|     Cash or Payables | | $450,000 |
| To record expenditures incurred on the project. | | |
| Other Financing Sources—BAN Proceeds | $500,000 | |
|     Expenditures—Capital Outlay | | $450,000 |
|     Unreserved Fund Balance | | 50,000 |

Note that (1) the note payable is not recorded in the CPF—but in the General Long-Term Debt Account Group, (2) interest is not accrued at year end—because the BANs are treated as general long-term debt, and (3) the CPF fund balance at year end is positive.

The accounting for CPF interim financing described previously is based on the "Bond, Tax, and Revenue Anticipation Notes" section of the GASB *Codification*. That guidance states that in accounting for governmental funds:

> . . . If [1] all legal steps have been taken to refinance the bond anticipation notes and [2] the intent is supported by an ability to consummate refinancing the short-term note on a long-term basis in accordance with the criteria set forth in FASB Statement No. 6, *Classification of Short-Term Obligations Expected to Be Refinanced,* they should be shown as part of the general long-term debt account group.[2]

BANs that do not meet both criteria must be reported as a fund liability of the fund in which the proceeds are recorded, as are tax anticipation notes (TANs) and revenue anticipation notes (RANs).[3]

## Costs Charged to Projects

All expenditures necessary to bring the capital facility to a state of readiness for its intended purpose are properly chargeable as Capital Projects Fund expenditures. Clearly, the direct cost of items such as land, buildings, materials, and labor would

---

[2] GASB *Codification*, sec. B50.101.

[3] Ibid.

be included. Additionally, the total project cost would include such related items as engineering and architect fees, transportation costs, damages occasioned by the project, and other costs associated with the endeavor.

### Overhead

General government overhead is rarely charged to the project unless it is reimbursable, such as under terms of the grant through which the project is financed. Where costs such as overhead are reimbursable, the reimbursable amount is frequently calculated in accordance with a predetermined formula rather than by being derived from cost accounting or similar records.

This is not to say that no overhead costs are charged to the project unless reimbursable. Overhead is charged to the project, for example, to the extent that such costs are included in charges for goods or services provided for the project through Internal Service Funds. And additional overhead costs caused by the project are properly charged to the CPF. Because of past abuses, however, and because intergovernmental grants are often intended only to supplement existing resources, charges for overhead may be specifically excluded from project cost as defined by statute, contractual agreement, or administrative determination.

### Interest

Interest expenditures on interim **short-term** CPF notes are usually paid from the fund and accounted for as project costs. But interest expenditures for bonds and other **long-term** debt issued to finance capital projects typically are financed and accounted for through a Debt Service Fund, and are not accounted for as project costs in the CPF. Interest earned by investing Capital Projects Fund cash is recognized as CPF revenue. However, interest earned by investing bond issue proceeds may be transferred to the appropriate Debt Service Fund to help finance the related bond interest expenditures.

Both interest revenues and interest expenditures related to capital projects must be carefully planned, controlled, and accounted for in the Capital Projects and Debt Service Funds. Although this is true from sound financial management and accountability perspectives generally, both interest expenditures and interest revenues amounts are used in determining whether the state or local government has complied with federal **"arbitrage"** provisions. These provisions require the interest earnings from investing tax-exempt bond issue proceeds that are in excess of the related interest costs to be remitted to the federal government. Both interest expenditures and interest revenues also may be used in computing the cost of the project to be capitalized in the General Fixed Assets Account Group (GFAAG).

## Intergovernmental Revenues

Because grants, shared revenues, and contributions from other governments are revenues, they are subject to the modified accrual basis specified by the GASB for governmental funds. Thus, to be recognized as revenues, they must be both measurable and available. These two qualities are determined by the legal and contractual requirements of each case.

Both unrestricted grants received or receivable and those restricted to a specific purpose (but not to capital outlay) usually are recognized as assets and revenues of the General Fund or a Special Revenue Fund, as appropriate. Subsequently, they might be transferred to a Capital Projects Fund if authorized by the governing body. But some intergovernmental grants and other contributions are restricted to capital project use. Most such **capital grants** are **expenditure-driven**—that is, earned by the grantee's incurring of expenditures that qualify under the terms of the grant or other contribution agreement.

If restricted capital grant resources are received before appropriate expenditures have been made, both the assets and deferred revenue are recognized in the CPF. Thereafter, revenue is recognized as appropriate expenditures are made. But, if qualifying expenditures are made before the grant resources are received, the grant receivable and revenue should be accrued, assuming the receivable is available. Finally, if an expenditure-driven grant has been awarded but no cash has been received and no revenue has been earned by incurring qualifying expenditures, (1) neither the asset nor the deferred revenue are reported in the financial statements, but (2) the grant award and the related potential resources may be disclosed in the notes to the financial statements.

## Bond Premiums, Discounts, and Issuance Costs

Bond issue proceeds are recorded at the amount received, including any premium and net of any discount. Bond issuance costs typically are recorded as expenditures. Because interest on the bonds typically will be paid from a Debt Service Fund, the premium and any payment received for accrued interest usually are transferred to that fund. The project authorization must be reduced unless bond discounts and/or issuance costs are made up by acquiring additional financial resources—from other funds, for example—or from interest earned on temporary investments of the Capital Projects Fund.

## CPF CASE ILLUSTRATION BEGUN—19X1

To illustrate Capital Projects Fund accounting, assume that in 19X1 the governing body of A Governmental Unit decided to construct a bridge expected to cost $3,000,000. The bridge construction and related costs are to be financed as follows:

|  | Total | Percent |
|---|---|---|
| Federal grant | $1,200,000 | 40 |
| State grant | 600,000 | 20 |
| Bond issue proceeds | 900,000 | 30 |
| Transfer from General Fund | 300,000 | 10 |
|  | $3,000,000 | 100 |

The $600,000 state grant is a fixed sum irrevocably granted for the bridge project and will revert to the state only if the bridge is not built. But the federal grant is for 40% of the qualifying project expenditures, with a maximum grant limit of $1,200,000; any excess grant cash received would revert to the federal government. Thus, the federal grant is an expenditure-driven grant and federal grant revenues will be recognized accordingly.

The bridge is to be constructed by a private contracting firm, Bean Bridge Builders, Inc., doing business as Bean & Co., selected by sealed bids based on engineering specifications; the government's work force will do related earth-moving and landscape work. The estimated costs of the bridge project are:

Bridge Structure:

| | | |
|---|---|---|
| Bean & Co. contract ..................................... | | $2,400,000 |
| Earthmoving and Landscaping (Government Roads Department): | | |
| Labor ............................................. | $300,000 | |
| Machine time ........................................ | 200,000 | |
| Fuel and materials .................................. | 100,000 | 600,000 |
| | | $3,000,000 |

Bean & Co. has posted a performance bond guaranteeing the quality and timeliness of its work. In addition, 5% of the amounts payable to Bean & Co. under the contract will be retained as a further guarantee of the quality of the work. This retainage will be remitted upon final inspection of the bridge and its acceptance by the governing body of A Governmental Unit. The bridge construction will begin in 19X1 and should be completed in 19X2.

## Alternative Account Structure and Entries

In Chapters 3 and 4 we demonstrated the traditional General Ledger, Revenues Ledger, and Expenditures Ledger account structure and journal entries. That approach can also be used for Capital Projects Fund and Debt Service Fund accounting.

We also noted in Chapters 3 and 4 that many governments no longer use the traditional General Ledger–Subsidiary Ledger approach. Modern computerized systems facilitate the use of detailed General Ledger accounts in lieu of the General Ledger control accounts supported by detailed subsidiary ledgers. We briefly illustrated the detailed General Ledger approach at "Alternative Account Structures and Entries" in Chapter 4.

To more thoroughly familiarize readers with the detailed General Ledger approach, which is preferred by some practitioners and professors and is sometimes useful on the CPA examination, the CPF case illustration entries are presented using the **detailed General Ledger approach.** The 19X1 entries are summarized in Appendix 7–1. CPF case illustration entries are presented in the more familiar General Ledger–Subsidiary Ledger approach in Appendix 7–2.

## Budgetary Entry

When the governing body officially authorized the bridge capital project by ordinance, which included the estimated financing sources and appropriations as outlined earlier, the government's controller made the following budgetary entry:

| | | |
|---|---|---|
| (B) Estimated Revenues—Federal Grant .................... | $1,200,000 | |
| Estimated Revenues—State Grant ...................... | 600,000 | |
| Estimated Other Financing Sources—Bond Proceeds ....... | 900,000 | |
| Estimated Other Financing Sources—Operating Transfer from General Fund | 300,000 | |
| Appropriations—Bean & Co. Contract ................. | | $2,400,000 |
| Appropriations—Labor ............................. | | 300,000 |
| Appropriations—Machine Time ...................... | | 200,000 |
| Appropriations—Fuel and Materials .................. | | 100,000 |
| To record project budget. | | |

Note that budgetary control is to be achieved over all financing sources, not just revenues. The examples in earlier chapters assumed use of a Revenues Ledger and that interfund transfers and long-term debt issues were separately authorized and, thus, were not included in the budget or budgetary accounts. This pure Revenues Ledger approach may also be used in Capital Projects Fund accounting. But the detailed General Ledger account approach better fits the typical Capital Projects Fund financing situation.

Note also that the controller established detailed General Ledger Expenditures accounts. Because all appropriations, expenditures, and encumbrances relate to the same bridge project and only one government department is involved, the accounts are set up to control and account for the appropriations for the most significant bridge costs: (1) the Bean & Co. construction contract and (2) the government's labor, machine time, and fuel and materials related to the bridge, which are assumed to be charged directly to this CPF. The following Expenditures accounts would more appropriately be titled "Expenditures—Roads Department—Labor," and so on, but are shortened for illustrative purposes because only one department is involved. Were several contracts and/or departments involved, Appropriations, Expenditures, and Encumbrances accounts for each contract and for each government department participating in the project would be used. In such cases some or all of the expenditures might be recorded initially in other funds, which would be reimbursed from the CPF.

## 19X1 Transactions and Events

The following entries summarize the several Capital Projects Fund transactions and events that occurred during 19X1.

(1) The contract with Bean & Co. was signed and work began on the bridge.

| | | |
|---|---|---|
| Encumbrances—Bean & Co. Contract | $2,400,000 | |
|   Reserve for Encumbrances | | $2,400,000 |
| To record signing of bridge contract. | | |

(2) The bonds were sold at a slight premium (101) for $909,000.

| | | |
|---|---|---|
| Cash | $909,000 | |
|   **Other Financing Sources—Bond Proceeds** | | $909,000 |
| To record sale of bonds at a premium. | | |

(3) Fuel and materials ordered during the year totaled $55,000.

| | | |
|---|---|---|
| Encumbrances—Fuel and Materials | $55,000 | |
|   Reserve for Encumbrances | | $55,000 |
| To record encumbrances incurred. | | |

(4) The state grant was received. The governing body authorized a $130,000 transfer from the General Fund during 19X1, which was received, and will authorize the remainder in 19X2.

| | | |
|---|---|---|
| Cash | $730,000 | |
|   Revenues—State Grant | | $600,000 |
|   Other Financing Sources—Operating Transfer | | |
|     from General Fund | | 130,000 |
| To record receipt of state grant and partial General Fund transfer. | | |

(5) Invoices were received and vouchered for fuel and materials, $49,000 (encumbered at $48,000); machine time, $81,000; and the Bean & Co. contract, $1,000,000 (as encumbered).

| | | | |
|---|---|---|---|
| (a) Reserve for Encumbrances | $1,048,000 | | |
| Encumbrances—Fuel and Materials | | $ 48,000 | |
| Encumbrances—Bean & Co. Contract | | 1,000,000 | |
| To reverse encumbrances. | | | |
| (b) Expenditures—Fuel and Materials | $ 49,000 | | |
| Expenditures—Machine Time | 81,000 | | |
| Expenditures—Bean & Co. Contract | 1,000,000 | | |
| **Contracts Payable—Retained Percentage** | | $ 50,000 | |
| Vouchers Payable | | 1,080,000 | |
| To record vouchering expenditures for payment and 5% retainage on Bean & Co. contract. | | | |

(6) Cash disbursements during 19X1 were:

| | |
|---|---|
| Vouchers Payable | $ 970,000 |
| Investments | 400,000 |
| Payroll | 140,000 |
| | $1,510,000 |

| | | |
|---|---|---|
| Vouchers Payable | $970,000 | |
| Investments | 400,000 | |
| Expenditures—Labor | 140,000 | |
| Cash | | $1,510,000 |
| To record vouchers and payroll paid. | | |

(7) Filed for federal grant reimbursement for 40% of the expenditures (transactions 5 and 6) incurred for the project during 19X1:

| | | |
|---|---|---|
| Due from Federal Government | $508,000 | |
| Revenues—Federal Grant | | $508,000 |
| To record filing for federal grant reimbursement for qualifying expenditures. | | |
| Calculation: 0.4 ($1,130,000 + $140,000) | | |

(8) Accrued interest receivable on investments at year end was $18,000.

| | | |
|---|---|---|
| Accrued Interest Receivable | $18,000 | |
| Revenues—Interest | | $18,000 |
| To record accrued interest at year end. | | |

## Preclosing Trial Balance—End of 19X1—Project Incomplete

The preclosing trial balance of the bridge project Capital Projects Fund General Ledger accounts at the end of 19X1 appears in the first two columns of the worksheet illustrated in Figure 7–2. It differs from the preclosing trial balance for the General Fund example in Chapter 4 because detailed General Ledger accounts are used instead of Revenues and Expenditures Subsidiary Ledgers. These two approaches are illustrated in Appendices 7–1 and 7–2.

## Closing Entries—End of 19X1—Project Incomplete

As illustrated in Figure 7–3, the most relevant time frame in Capital Projects Fund accounting is that between its inception and its termination after the project is completed. Appropriations are made on a project life basis in this example, as is

**FIGURE 7–2**  **Worksheet—Preclosing General Ledger Trial Balance, Closing Entries, and Postclosing Trial Balance—End of 19X1 (Project Incomplete)**

A Governmental Unit
Capital Projects Fund
(Bridge Project)
**Preclosing General Ledger Trial Balance, Closing Entries, and Postclosing Trial Balance Worksheet**
End of 19X1
(Project Incomplete)

| Accounts | Preclosing Trial Balance Dr. | Preclosing Trial Balance Cr. | Closing Entries (Actual or Worksheet Only) Dr. | Closing Entries (Actual or Worksheet Only) Cr. | Postclosing Trial Balance Dr. | Postclosing Trial Balance Cr. |
|---|---|---|---|---|---|---|
| Cash | $ 129,000 | | | | $ 129,000 | |
| Investments | 400,000 | | | | 400,000 | |
| Accrued Interest Receivable | 18,000 | | | | 18,000 | |
| Due from Federal Government | 508,000 | | | | 508,000 | |
| Vouchers Payable | | $ 110,000 | | | | $ 110,000 |
| Contracts Payable—Retained Percentage | | 50,000 | | | | 50,000 |
| Estimated Revenues—Federal Grant | 1,200,000 | | | $1,200,000 (C1) | | |
| Estimated Revenues—State Grant | 600,000 | | | 600,000 (C1) | | |
| Estimated Other Financing Sources—Bond Issue Proceeds | 900,000 | | | 900,000 (C1) | | |
| Estimated Other Financing Sources—Operating Transfer from General Fund | 300,000 | | | 300,000 (C1) | | |
| Appropriations—Bean & Co. Contract | | 2,400,000 | $1,000,000 (C2) 1,400,000 (C3) | | | |
| Appropriations—Labor | | 300,000 | 140,000 (C2) | | | 160,000 |
| Appropriations—Machine Time | | 200,000 | 81,000 (C2) | | | 119,000 |
| Appropriations—Fuel and Materials | | 100,000 | 49,000 (C2) 7,000 (C3) | | | 44,000 |
| Revenues—Federal Grant | | 508,000 | 508,000 (CI) | | | |
| Revenues—State Grant | | 600,000 | 600,000 (C1) | | | |
| Revenues—Interest | | 18,000 | 18,000 (C1) | | | |
| Other Financing Sources—Bond Proceeds | | 909,000 | 909,000 (C1) | | | |
| Other Financing Sources—Operating Transfer from General Fund | | 130,000 | 130,000 (C1) | | | |
| Expenditures—Bean & Co. Contract | 1,000,000 | | | 1,000,000 (C2) | | |
| Expenditures—Labor | 140,000 | | | 140,000 (C2) | | |
| Expenditures—Machine Time | 81,000 | | | 81,000 (C2) | | |
| Expenditures—Fuel and Materials | 49,000 | | | 49,000 (C2) | | |
| Encumbrances—Bean & Co. Contract | 1,400,000 | | | 1,400,000 (C3) | | |
| Encumbrances—Fuel and Materials | 7,000 | | | 7,000 (C3) | | |
| Reserve for Encumbrances | | 1,407,000 | | | | 1,407,000 |
| | $6,732,000 | $6,732,000 | | | | |
| Unreserved Fund Balance | | | 835,000 (C1) | | 835,000 | |
| | | | | | $1,890,000 | $1,890,000 |

typical, and all budgetary compliance, project cost, and similar determinations are made when the project has been completed. Thus, whereas the Capital Projects Fund accounts must be closed at its termination, the end of a government's fiscal year within the Capital Projects Fund life cycle is an interim date that is not particularly significant from a CPF perspective.

FIGURE 7–3  **Capital Projects Fund Life Cycle versus Fiscal Year**

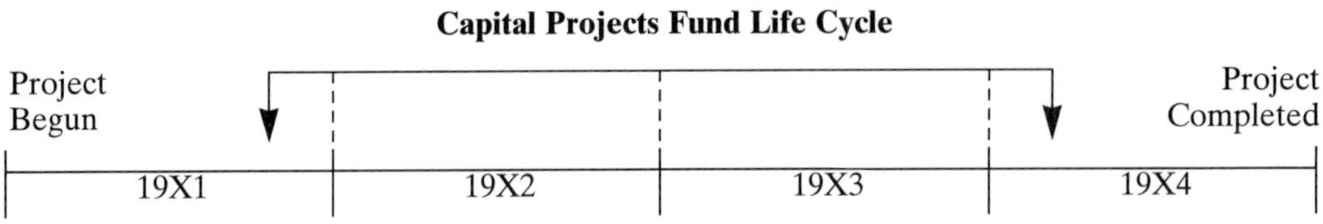

**Capital Projects Fund Life Cycle**

| Project Begun | 19X1 | 19X2 | 19X3 | 19X4 | Project Completed |

- - - - - - - - - -    Financial statements prepared for a government at the end of each fiscal year in conformity with GAAP are *interim* statements from a Capital Projects Fund perspective.

————————▶    The most relevant statements from a Capital Projects Fund are for its entire life cycle—from inception to termination.

*Note:* Although project life cycle financial statements are not required by GAAP, they often are essential to demonstrate compliance with budgetary, grant, and bond indenture requirements as well as to report all transactions and balances of the entire project.

Financial statements must be prepared for state and local governments at the end of each year, however. Accordingly, Capital Projects Fund financial statements must be prepared at the end of a government's fiscal year—even though they are interim statements from a Capital Projects Fund standpoint (Figure 7–3).

The Capital Projects Fund accounts need not be closed at the end of a government's fiscal year, however, and may or may not be closed in practice. Both closing the accounts and not closing them have advantages and disadvantages.

### Accounts Not Closed

If the CPF accounts are not closed at fiscal year end, a worksheet giving effect to pro forma ("as if") closing entries is prepared. This type of worksheet, like the worksheet illustrated in Figure 7–2, begins with the preclosing trial balance (columns 1 and 2), from which are derived the pro forma closing entries (columns 3 and 4) and the postclosing trial balance (columns 5 and 6).

The pro forma closing entries are not journalized and posted to the accounts under this approach. Rather, the information needed to prepare the Capital Projects Fund financial statements is obtained from the General Ledger closing entries (operating statement) and postclosing trial balance (balance sheet) worksheet columns.

The primary advantage of this "no closing entry" worksheet approach is that it saves time otherwise spent in journalizing Capital Projects Fund closing entries, posting them to the several CPF ledgers, and then reestablishing the appropriate amounts in those several CPF ledgers at the beginning of the next year. The primary disadvantage of the "no closing entry" approach is that it precludes the use of reversing entries to facilitate the accounting for accruals made at the end of one year during the next year. Furthermore, some accountants and auditors prefer that worksheets not be used as a bridge between the ledger accounts and the financial statements. Accordingly, they prefer to close the accounts at year end so that the ledger account balances correspond with the amounts reported in the financial statements.

### Accounts Are Closed

If the accounts are closed, they may be closed using the reverse the budget—close the actual or compound entry approaches illustrated in Chapter 4, or using the variance approach. The **General Ledger** closing entries (see Figure 7–2)—using the **variance approach**—are:

| | | | |
|---|---|---:|---:|
| (C1) | Revenues—Federal Grant .......................... | $ 508,000 | |
| | Revenues—State Grant ............................. | 600,000 | |
| | Revenues—Interest .................................. | 18,000 | |
| | Other Financing Sources—Bond Proceeds .............. | 909,000 | |
| | Other Financing Sources—Operating Transfer from General Fund ................................ | 130,000 | |
| | Unreserved Fund Balance .......................... | 835,000 | |
| |    Estimated Revenues—Federal Grant ................. | | $1,200,000 |
| |    Estimated Revenues—State Grant ................... | | 600,000 |
| |    Estimated Other Financing Sources—Bond Proceeds .... | | 900,000 |
| |    Estimated Other Financing Sources—Operating Transfer from General Fund ............................. | | 300,000 |
| | To close the estimated and actual revenues and other financing sources accounts at year end. | | |
| (C2) | Appropriations—Bean & Co. Contract ............... | $1,000,000 | |
| | Appropriations—Labor ............................ | 140,000 | |
| | Appropriations—Machine Time ..................... | 81,000 | |
| | Appropriations—Fuel and Materials ................... | 49,000 | |
| |    Expenditures—Bean & Co. Contract ................. | | $1,000,000 |
| |    Expenditures—Labor .............................. | | 140,000 |
| |    Expenditures—Machine Time ....................... | | 81,000 |
| |    Expenditures—Fuel and Materials ................... | | 49,000 |
| | To close the expenditures at year end and reduce the continuing appropriations. | | |
| (C3) | Appropriations—Bean & Co. Contract ............... | $1,400,000 | |
| | Appropriations—Fuel and Materials ................... | 7,000 | |
| |    Encumbrances—Bean & Co. Contract ................ | | $1,400,000 |
| |    Encumbrances—Fuel and Materials ................. | | 7,000 |
| | To close the encumbrances accounts and establish corresponding reserves of appropriated fund balance. | | |

These variance approach closing entries update the budgeted (planned) Unreserved Fund Balance amount to its actual year-end balance by adding (or deducting) the differences (variances) between the budgeted and actual amounts to date.

Note that entry C1 closes the entire balance of the Estimated Revenues and Estimated Other Financing Sources accounts—even though those amounts relate to the entire project rather than to only this fiscal year—which causes Unreserved Fund Balance to be debited $835,000. The reason is that the Estimated Revenues and Estimated Other Financing Sources accounts are budgetary resource accounts and their balances are not assets properly reported in the CPF balance sheet at year end. Thus, whereas the CPF statements are in substance interim statements, they must be reported on a basis consistent with the General Fund and other governmental funds in the government's year-end financial statements. This often gives rise to artificial deficits being reported in Capital Projects Fund financial statements (as is the case here), which is discussed further later in this section.

Entries C2 and C3 are consistent with the "unexpended appropriations continue" assumption of this case example, which are discussed and illustrated (Assumption C1) in Appendix 6–3. Entry C2 closes the various Expenditures accounts to the related Appropriations accounts so the remaining Appropriations balances represent the unexpended balances, whereas entry C3 closes the various Encumbrances accounts to the unexpended balance of the related Appropriations accounts, reducing them to their unencumbered balances. Entry C3 will be reversed, of course, at the beginning of 19X2.

### Financial Statements—End of 19X1—Project Incomplete

Two annual financial statements are required for a Capital Projects Fund that is budgeted for the project, as in this case example: (1) a balance sheet (Figure 7–4) and (2) a Statement of Revenues, Expenditures, and Changes in Fund Balance (Figure 7–5). A budgetary comparison statement would also be required if the CPF were budgeted annually.

#### Balance Sheet

The balance sheet for the Capital Projects Fund at the end of 19X1 (Figure 7–4) is like that presented for the General Fund except for the "Fund Balance" section. The CPF appropriations are for the project, and thus the unexpended appro-

FIGURE 7–4  **Balance Sheet—End of 19X1 (Project Incomplete)**

A Governmental Unit
Capital Projects Fund
(Bridge Project)
**Balance Sheet**

**Assets**

| | |
|---|---:|
| Cash | $ 129,000 |
| Investments | 400,000 |
| Accrued interest receivable | 18,000 |
| Due from federal government | 508,000 |
| | $1,055,000 |

**Liabilities and Fund Balance***

| | | |
|---|---:|---:|
| Liabilities | | |
| Vouchers payable | $ 110,000 | |
| Contracts payable—retained percentage | 50,000 | $ 160,000 |
| Fund Balance: | | |
| Appropriated— | | |
| Reserved for encumbrances | 1,407,000 | |
| Unencumbered | 323,000 | |
| | 1,730,000 | |
| Unappropriated—Unreserved | (835,000) | 895,000 |
| | | $1,055,000 |

*Alternatively, the Fund Balance section may be presented as follows:

Fund Balance:
    Appropriated and encumbered (note X)....    895,000
and the details explained in a note to the financial statements. This approach avoids reporting the potentially misleading artificial Unreserved Fund Balance deficit in the balance sheet in many situations.

priations do not lapse at the end of 19X1, but continue as expenditure authority into 19X2. In this situation (1) the "Fund Balance" section should be classified as between its appropriated and unappropriated components, and (2) the Reserve for Encumbrances should be presented as a reservation of appropriated fund balance.

But whereas the appropriations are for the project, the unrealized estimated financial resources are not properly reported as assets in a GAAP-basis year-end balance sheet. The net effect, as noted at closing entry C1, is that the unrealized estimated financial resources decrease the Unreserved Fund Balance reported in what is in substance an interim CPF balance sheet included in A Governmental Unit's financial statements prepared at the end of 19X1. In this example there was no Unreserved Fund Balance prior to the pro forma or actual closing entries. Thus, the difference between estimated financial resources for the project and those realized to date is reported as an Unreserved Fund Balance deficit.

This Unreserved Fund Balance deficit is an **artificial deficit,** however, because the Capital Projects Fund is not expected to be in a deficit situation at the conclusion of the project. Again, this occurs because the year-end CPF balance sheet is an interim statement from a CPF perspective. The artificial deficit reported is unfortunate. It may mislead users of the government's financial statements—who could understandably get the impression that the bridge Capital Projects Fund is $835,000 "in the red" even though the total fund balance is positive, $895,000 "in the black." At the least the Unreserved Fund Balance artificial deficit may confuse readers of the financial statements, and its origin and temporary nature should be explained in the notes to the financial statements. Indeed, many practitioners present the "Fund Balance" section of the CPF balance sheet as shown in the note to Figure 7–4.

### Operating Statement

The GAAP basis operating statement for the Capital Projects Fund at the end of 19X1 is presented in Figure 7–5. The format of this CPF Statement of Revenues, Expenditures, and Changes in Fund Balance is the same as that of the corresponding statement presented for the General Fund in Chapter 4.

Note that the CPF operating statement in Figure 7–5 presents an excess of expenditures over revenues of $144,000. Readers may interpret this negative excess—which may be many millions of dollars in practice—as being "bad," even though there is an excess of revenues and other financing sources over expenditures and other uses. Like the artificial deficit in the Unreserved Fund Balance account, this excess of expenditures over revenues is attributable (partly) to the fact that this CPF operating statement is indeed an interim statement.

The excess of expenditures over revenues also arises from the fact that Capital Projects Funds typically are financed differently than are General and Special Revenue Funds. Bond issue proceeds are usually major CPF financing sources, for example, whereas they are rarely used to finance General Fund operations except in times of financial distress.

The format for the Statement of Revenues, Expenditures, and Changes in Fund Balance presented in Figure 7–5, like that presented in Chapter 4—known as format A or presentation 1—is by far the most widely used in practice. However, an acceptable alternate format—known as format B or presentation 2—is preferred by some state and local governments because it helps avoid reporting artificial excesses of expenditures over revenues in the operating statements of Capital Projects Funds, in particular, as well as in other governmental funds.

FIGURE 7–5  **Operating Statement for 19X1 Fiscal Year (Project Incomplete)**

**Format A/Presentation 1**

A Governmental Unit
Capital Projects Fund
(Bridge Project)

**Statement of Revenues, Expenditures, and Changes in Fund Balance**
For 19X1 Fiscal Year
(Project Incomplete)

Revenues:
| | | |
|---|---|---|
| Federal grant | $ 508,000 | |
| State grant | 600,000 | |
| Interest | 18,000 | $1,126,000 |

Expenditures:*
| | | |
|---|---|---|
| Bean & Co. contract | 1,000,000 | |
| Labor | 140,000 | |
| Machine time | 81,000 | |
| Fuel and materials | 49,000 | 1,270,000 |
| Excess of Revenues Over (Under) Expenditures | | (144,000) |

Other Financing Sources (Uses)
| | | |
|---|---|---|
| Bond proceeds | 909,000 | |
| Operating transfer from General Fund | 130,000 | 1,039,000 |

Excess of Revenues and Other Financing Sources Over (Under)
| | |
|---|---|
| Expenditures and Other Uses | 895,000 |
| Fund Balance—Beginning of 19X1 | — |
| Fund Balance—End of 19X1 | $ 895,000 |

*All are capital outlay expenditures and in practice may be reported in a single capital outlay total expenditures amount.

An alternate format Statement of Revenues, Expenditures, and Changes in Fund Balance for the Capital Projects Fund at the end of 19X1—in the Format B or Presentation 2 arrangement—is presented in Figure 7–6. The difference between this format and that in Figure 7–5 is that (1) the Other (Nonrevenue) Financing Sources are presented immediately after the revenues and lead to a Total Revenues and Other Financing Sources subtotal; (2) any Other (Nonexpenditure) Financing Uses are presented after expenditures and lead to a total expenditures and other uses subtotal—though in the absence of other uses, as in this example, the Total Expenditures amount is reported; and (3) the optional Excess of Revenues over (under) Expenditures amount in the format A Statement (Figure 7–5) is not presented—only the Excess of Revenues and Other Financing Sources Over (Under) Expenditures and Other Financing Uses. This latter subtotal is required by GAAP.

### No Budgetary Comparison Statement Required

The budgetary comparison statement, the Statement of Revenues, Expenditures, and Changes in Fund Balance—Budget and Actual, is not required here because this example assumes that the Capital Projects Fund is budgeted for the project life span, not annually. (The budgetary comparison statement is required

FIGURE 7–6  **Operating Statement for 19X1 Fiscal Year (Project Incomplete)**

**Format B/Presentation 2**

A Governmental Unit
Capital Projects Fund
(Bridge Project)

**Statement of Revenues, Expenditures, and Changes in Fund Balance**

For 19X1 Fiscal Year
(Project Incomplete)

| | | |
|---|---:|---:|
| Revenues: | | |
| Federal grant | $ 508,000 | |
| State grant | 600,000 | |
| Interest | 18,000 | $1,126,000 |
| Other Financing Sources: | | |
| Bond proceeds | 909,000 | |
| Operating transfer from General Fund | 130,000 | 1,039,000 |
| Total Revenues and Other Financing Sources | | 2,165,000 |
| Expenditures:* | | |
| Bean & Co. contract | 1,000,000 | |
| Labor | 140,000 | |
| Machine time | 81,000 | |
| Fuel and materials | 49,000 | 1,270,000 |
| Excess of Revenues and Other Financing Sources Over Expenditures† | | 895,000 |
| Fund Balance—Beginning of 19X1 | | — |
| Fund Balance—End of 19X1 | | $ 895,000 |

*All are capital outlay expenditures and in practice may be reported in a single Capital Outlay total expenditures amount. The detailed expenditure amounts reported here would be for internal use, and are presented here for illustrative purposes.

†If there had been other (nonexpenditure) financing uses during 19X1, they would have been reported in an "Other Financing Uses" section immediately after the "Expenditures" section and the "Excess of Revenues and Other Financing Sources Over (Under) Expenditures and Other Uses" would have been reported.

only for governmental funds that are budgeted annually.) Furthermore, note that a budgetary comparison statement prepared at an interim point in the life of a Capital Projects Fund might be misleading because (1) the estimated financing sources and appropriations are for the entire project life cycle, but (2) the actual financing sources, expenditures, and encumbrances data are for a portion of the project life or at an interim point during the project life cycle. Thus, the GASB standards require budgetary comparison statements only for annually budgeted governmental funds.

## CPF CASE ILLUSTRATION CONCLUDED—19X2

Whether any preliminary entries are required at the beginning of 19X2—before recording the 19X2 transactions and events—depends on whether closing entries were made at the end of 19X1. Furthermore, if closing entries were made, the preliminary entries depend on whether reversing entries are used.

### Accounts Closed in 19X1

If the General Ledger accounts were closed at the end of 19X1, three entries are needed at the beginning of 19X2:

(R1) Estimated Revenues—Federal Grant .................. $ 692,000

    Estimated Other Financing Sources—Operating Transfer
        from General Fund ............................ 170,000

      Unreserved Fund Balance ......................... $ 862,000

    To record the budgeted revenues and other financing
    sources not received in 19X1.

(R2) Encumbrances—Bean & Co. Contract .................. $1,400,000

    Encumbrances—Fuel and Materials ................... 7,000

      Appropriations—Bean & Co. Contract ............... $1,400,000

      Appropriations—Fuel and Materials ................ 7,000

    To reverse the entry closing encumbrances made at the
    end of 19X1.

(R3) Revenues—Interest ................................. $ 18,000

    Accrued Interest Receivable ...................... $ 18,000

    To reverse the interest accrual entry made at the end
    of 19X1.

Entry R1 reestablishes the Estimated Revenues and Estimated Other Financing Sources budgetary accounts at the amount of project financial resources yet to be realized and removes the artificial deficit in the Unreserved Fund Balance account. Entry R2 restores the Appropriations account to its unexpended balance, while returning the various Encumbrances and Reserve for Encumbrances accounts to their usual offsetting status. Entry R3 records the 19X1 interest revenues as a debit (deduction) to the 19X2 Revenues—Interest account, thus permitting all interest received or accrued during 19X2 to be credited to the Revenues—Interest account.

Note that the entry recording the federal grant earned in 19X1 was not reversed. This is because that receivable was recorded as billed and the Due from Federal Government account presumably is used to control the unpaid billings throughout the years the Capital Projects Fund exists. But had some unbilled federal grant revenue been accrued at the end of 19X1, that accrual entry would have been reversed at the beginning of 19X2.

### Accounts Not Closed in 19X1

If the Capital Projects Fund General Ledger accounts were not closed at the end of 19X1, no reversing entries would be made at the beginning of 19X2. Again, many accountants consider the inability to use usual reversing entries a significant disadvantage of the "no closing entry" approach. However, not all SLG accountants use reversing entries. Furthermore, some CPFs have only a relatively few (but large) transactions, and so reversing entries are not as useful as in governmental funds with numerous transactions.

### Case Illustration Assumptions

The General Ledger accounting for 19X2 transactions is essentially the same (except reversing entries) regardless of whether or not the General Ledger accounts were closed at the end of 19X1. But the temporary accounts will accumulate (1) total project data if they were not closed at the end of 19X1, or (2) if they were closed at the end of 19X1, either total project data or 19X2 data, depending on whether gross balances or net remaining balances of budgetary accounts are reestablished at the beginning of 19X2. Our example assumes that only net remaining balances of the budgetary accounts are reestablished.

## 19X2 Transactions and Events

To conclude the bridge project Capital Projects Fund illustration, assume that the following entries summarize the transactions and events that occurred during 19X2.

(1) Invoices were received and vouchered for fuel and materials, $43,000 (partially encumbered at $7,000); machine time, $108,000; and the Bean & Co. contract, $1,410,000 (encumbered at $1,400,000), including a $10,000 adjustment in the contract, approved by the governing body, for necessary work not anticipated in the contract specifications. No other encumbrances were incurred or outstanding.

(a) Reserve for Encumbrances ........................... $1,407,000
    Encumbrances—Bean & Co. Contract ................. $1,400,000
    Encumbrances—Fuel and Materials ................... 7,000
To reverse encumbrances outstanding.

(b) Expenditures—Bean & Co. Contract .................... $1,410,000
Expenditures—Fuel and Materials ..................... 43,000
Expenditures—Machine Time ......................... 108,000
    Contracts Payable—Retained Percentage .............. $   70,500
    Vouchers Payable .................................. 1,490,500
To record expenditures incurred.

(2) Cash receipts during 19X2 were from:

Federal grant ........................... $1,198,000
Investments (including interest) ............. 430,000
Operating Transfer from General Fund ....... 170,000
                                     $1,798,000

Cash ......................................... $1,798,000
    Due from Federal Government ...................... $  508,000
    Revenues—Federal Grant .......................... 690,000
    Investments ...................................... 400,000
    Revenues—Interest ................................ 30,000
    Other Financing Sources—Operating Transfer
      from General Fund .............................. 170,000
To record cash receipts.

(3) Cash disbursements made during 19X2 included:

Vouchers payable ........................ $1,600,500
Payroll ............................... 129,000
                               $1,729,500

Vouchers Payable ..................................... $1,600,500
Expenditures—Labor ................................. 129,000
    Cash ........................................... $1,729,500
To record cash disbursements.

(4) Under terms of the federal grant: (a) the $10,000 additional payment to Bean & Co. is not an allowable cost; (b) only the actual costs for earthmoving and landscaping are allowable; and (c) the otherwise allowable costs must be reduced by the interest earned by investing project monies. Accordingly, $30,000 was recorded as payable to the federal government, pending final inspection of the completed bridge.

| Revenues—Federal Grant | $30,000 | |
| Due to Federal Government | | $30,000 |

To record liability for unallowable federal grant costs
previously reimbursed.

Calculation:

Allowable costs and reimbursement—

| | |
|---|---|
| Bean & Co. Contract | $2,400,000 |
| Labor | 269,000 |
| Machine Time | 189,000 |
| Fuel and Materials | 92,000 |
| | 2,950,000 |
| Less: Interest earned | 30,000 |
| Allowable costs | 2,920,000 |
| Federal grant share (40%) | .4 |
| Reimbursement | 1,168,000 |
| Federal grant revenue recognized to date | 1,198,000 |
| Due to federal government | $ 30,000 |

(5) The new bridge was approved by the inspectors and accepted by the governing body, which ordered that (a) the retained percentage be paid to the contractor, (b) the federal government be repaid (transaction 4), and (c) the remaining CPF fund balance be transferred to the related Debt Service Fund.

| Contracts Payable—Retained Percentage | $120,500 | |
| Due to Federal Government | 30,000 | |
| Residual Equity Transfer to Debt Service Fund | 47,000 | |
| Cash | | $197,500 |

To record payment of retained percentage, reimbursement to
federal government, and transfer of remaining net assets.

(6) The accounts were closed and the bridge project Capital Projects Fund was terminated.

| Revenues—Federal Grant | $ 660,000 | |
| Revenues—Interest | 12,000 | |
| Other Financing Sources—Operating Transfer from General Fund | 170,000 | |
| Appropriations—Bean & Co. Contract | 1,400,000 | |
| Appropriations—Labor | 160,000 | |
| Appropriations—Machine Time | 119,000 | |
| Appropriations—Fuel and Materials | 51,000 | |
| Unreserved Fund Balance | 27,000 | |
| Estimated Revenues—Federal Grant | | $ 692,000 |
| Estimated Other Financing Sources—Operating Transfer from General Fund | | 170,000 |
| Expenditures—Bean & Co. Contract | | 1,410,000 |
| Expenditures—Labor | | 129,000 |
| Expenditures—Machine Time | | 108,000 |
| Expenditures—Fuel and Materials | | 43,000 |
| Residual Equity Transfer to Debt Service Fund | | 47,000 |

Note that the $47,000 residual equity transfer to the Debt Service Fund (transaction 5) is no doubt partially attributable to the $9,000 premium received upon sale of the bonds in 19X1. Had that bond premium been separately identified as a transfer to the Debt Service Fund, say, during 19X1, it would have been accounted for as an operating transfer. However, the transfer at the conclusion of a project is classified as a residual equity transfer because (1) the identity of the bond premium has been lost—because money is homogeneous, one cannot tell whether the bond premium dollars were spent on construction and the interest earned led to the transfer, for example, or vice versa; and (2) the GASB *Codification* requires that interfund transfers of residual balances of discontinued funds be classified as residual equity transfers.

## Financial Statements—End of 19X2—Project Complete

Because the capital project is complete and the Capital Projects Fund has been terminated, no CPF balance sheet is prepared at the end of 19X2. The only statement required in this example, because the CPF was not budgeted annually, is a Statement of Revenues, Expenditures, and Changes in Fund Balance. Only the 19X2 operating statement need be presented in the government's annual financial report. But an operating statement for the project is prepared for internal use and may also be included in the annual financial report.

### Project Operating Statement

A Statement of Revenues, Expenditures, and Changes in Fund Balances for the 19X1–19X2 project period is presented as Figure 7–7. Like the 19X1 operating statement in Figure 7–6, it is presented in Format B and thus does not include the

**FIGURE 7–7  Operating Statement for the Project—19X1 and 19X2 Fiscal Years (Project Complete)**

**Format B/Presentation 2**
A Governmental Unit
Capital Projects Fund
(Bridge Project)
**Statement of Revenues, Expenditures, and Changes in Fund Balance**
For the Project—19X1 and 19X2 Fiscal Years
(Project Complete)

|  | *19X2* | *19X1* | *Total* |
|---|---|---|---|
| Revenues: |  |  |  |
| Federal grant ....................... | $ 660,000 | $ 508,000 | $1,168,000 |
| State grant ......................... | — | 600,000 | 600,000 |
| Interest ............................ | 12,000 | 18,000 | 30,000 |
|  | 672,000 | 1,126,000 | 1,798,000 |
| Other Financing Sources: |  |  |  |
| Bond proceeds ...................... | — | 909,000 | 909,000 |
| Operating transfer from General Fund ... | 170,000 | 130,000 | 300,000 |
|  | 170,000 | 1,039,000 | 1,209,000 |
| Total Revenues and Other Financing |  |  |  |
| Sources ......................... | 842,000 | 2,165,000 | 3,007,000 |
| Expenditures: |  |  |  |
| Bean & Co. contract .................. | 1,410,000 | 1,000,000 | 2,410,000 |
| Labor ............................. | 129,000 | 140,000 | 269,000 |
| Machine time ....................... | 108,000 | 81,000 | 189,000 |
| Fuel and materials ................... | 43,000 | 49,000 | 92,000 |
|  | 1,690,000 | 1,270,000 | 2,960,000 |
| Excess of Revenues and Other Financing |  |  |  |
| Sources Over (Under) Expenditures ...... | (848,000) | 895,000 | 47,000 |
| Fund Balance—Beginning of Year ........ | 895,000 | — | — |
| Residual equity transfer to Debt Service |  |  |  |
| Fund ................................. | (47,000) | — | (47,000) |
| Fund Balance—End of Year ............. | $  — | $ 895,000 | $  — |

"Excess of Revenues over Expenditures" subtotal. Although only the data in the 19X2 column need to be presented in the government's annual financial statements, this operating statement for the project obviously is more useful than a single-year statement and, accordingly, some governments include it in the annual financial report.

### Project Budgetary Comparison Statement

Although not required for external reporting, government accountants usually prepare a budgetary comparison statement at the conclusion of a capital project. The CPF budgetary comparison statement is used primarily for internal purposes, but may also be required by project creditors and grantors.

A Statement of Revenues, Expenditures, and Changes in Fund Balance—Budget and Actual—for the bridge project Capital Projects Fund is illustrated in Figure 7–8. Clearly, this project budgetary comparison statement and the 19X1–19X2

**FIGURE 7–8 Budgetary Comparison Statement for the Project 19X1 and 19X2 Fiscal Years (Project Complete)**

**Format B/Presentation**

A Governmental Unit

Capital Projects Fund

(Bridge Project)

**Statement of Revenues, Expenditures, and Changes in Fund Balance—Budget and Actual**

For the Project—19X1 and 19X2 Fiscal Years

(Project Complete)

|  | Budget | Actual | Variance—Favorable (Unfavorable) |
|---|---|---|---|
| Revenues: |  |  |  |
| Federal grant | $1,200,000 | $1,168,000 | $ (32,000) |
| State grant | 600,000 | 600,000 | — |
| Interest | — | 30,000 | 30,000 |
|  | 1,800,000 | 1,798,000 | (2,000) |
| Other Financing Sources: |  |  |  |
| Bond proceeds | 900,000 | 909,000 | 9,000 |
| Operating transfer from General Fund | 300,000 | 300,000 | — |
|  | 1,200,000 | 1,209,000 | 9,000 |
| Total Revenues and Other Financing Sources | 3,000,000 | 3,007,000 | 7,000 |
| Expenditures: |  |  |  |
| Bean & Co. contract | 2,400,000 | 2,410,000 | (10,000) |
| Labor | 300,000 | 269,000 | 31,000 |
| Machine time | 200,000 | 189,000 | 11,000 |
| Fuel and materials | 100,000 | 92,000 | 8,000 |
|  | 3,000,000 | 2,960,000 | 40,000 |
| Excess of Revenues and Other Financing Sources Over (Under) Expenditures | — | 47,000 | 47,000 |
| Fund Balance—Beginning of 19X1 | — | — | — |
| Residual equity transfer to Debt Service Fund | — | (47,000) | (47,000) |
| Fund Balance—End of 19X2 | $    — | $    — | $    — |

operating statement for the project (such as that in Figure 7–7) provide the data managers and others need to evaluate the fiscal and budgetary management of the capital project, determine the cost of the fixed assets acquired, and understand the sources and uses of the Capital Projects Fund financial resources. Indeed, the data in Figures 7–7 and 7–8 are sometimes included in a single CPF summary operating and budgetary comparison statement with columns headed:

| *Actual* | | *Total Project* | | *Variance–* |
|---|---|---|---|---|
| | | | | *Favorable* |
| *19X1* | *19X2* | *Actual* | *Budget* | *(Unfavorable)* |

## OTHER CPF OPERATIONS, ACCOUNTING, AND REPORTING MATTERS

Several other CPF operations, accounting, and reporting matters warrant at least brief attention as we conclude this chapter. These include (1) bond anticipation notes, (2) investment of idle cash, (3) disposing of fund balance or deficit, (4) reporting several projects financed through one fund, and (5) combining CPF statements.

### Bond Anticipation Notes (BANs)

We noted earlier in the chapter that bond anticipation notes (BANs) may be issued to provide interim financing for Capital Projects Funds prior to the issuance of authorized bonds. BANs may be issued for two main reasons: (1) Even though the bonds have been authorized, the bond issue process (including legal procedures, bond ratings, and so on) may take several weeks or months, yet CPF cash is required immediately; and (2) if long-term bond interest rates are expected to decline in the months ahead, the bond issue may be purposefully delayed to take advantage of the lower long-term interest rates. In any event, the BANs should be repaid from the bond issue proceeds.

To illustrate the issuance and repayment of BANs, suppose that A Governmental Unit has issued $500,000 of BANs in 19X1 prior to issuing the bonds (entry 2). As noted earlier, assuming the BANs met the GASB *Codification* noncurrent criteria, the entry to record the BAN issue proceeds in the Capital Projects Fund would be:

| | | |
|---|---|---|
| Cash . . . . . . . . . . . . . . . . . . . . . . . . . . . . . . . . . . . . . . . . . . . . . . . | $500,000 | |
| Other Financing Sources—BAN Proceeds . . . . . . . . . . . . . . . . . | | $500,000 |

To record issuance of noncurrent BANs.

Because these are noncurrent liability BANs, the related liability would be recorded in the General Long-Term Debt Account Group (GLTDAG) rather than in the CPF. Assume further that interest on the BANs ($30,000) was paid from the Capital Projects Fund rather than from a Debt Service Fund or the General Fund.

The issuance of the bonds would be recorded in the Capital Projects Fund, as illustrated in entry 2 earlier in the chapter:

| | | |
|---|---|---|
| Cash . . . . . . . . . . . . . . . . . . . . . . . . . . . . . . . . . . . . . . . . . . . . . . . | $909,000 | |
| Other Financing Sources—Bond Proceeds . . . . . . . . . . . . . . . . . | | $909,000 |

To record sale of bonds at a premium.

The liability for the bonds would be recorded in the GLTDAG. Then the BAN retirement would be recorded in the Capital Projects Fund as follows:

| | | |
|---|---:|---:|
| Other Financing Uses—BAN Principal Retirement | $500,000 | |
| Expenditures—Interest on BAN | 30,000 | |
|   Cash | | $530,000 |

To record retirement of BANs.

Also, the BAN liability would be removed from the GLTDAG. (Alternatively, the $530,000 might have been transferred to a Debt Service Fund through which the BANs were retired.)

As illustrated earlier, had the BANs not met the noncurrent criteria in the GASB *Codification,* a BAN Payable liability account—not the BAN Proceeds Other Financing Source account—would be credited in the Capital Projects Fund upon BAN issuance. In that case, the BAN Payable liability account would be debited upon their retirement—not the BAN Principal Retirement other financing use account.

## Investment of Idle Cash; Arbitrage

Significant sums of cash are commonly involved in capital project fiscal management. Cash receipt, investment, and disbursement, therefore, warrant careful planning, timing, and control.

Prudent financial management typically requires that loan transactions not be closed (and interest charges begun) until the cash is needed. There are exceptions to this rule, of course, as where statutes require that bonds be issued before the project begins, loan interest rates are expected to rise soon, or investments yield the government more than enough to cover the related interest costs. Similarly, significant sums should not be permitted to remain on demand deposit, but should be invested until such time as they are to be disbursed.

State and local governments that issue tax-exempt bonds or other debt issues must carefully observe the federal government's **arbitrage** regulations. Generally, the arbitrage regulations require that state and local governments that issue **tax-exempt** debt securities (the interest on which is not subject to federal income tax) and invest the tax-exempt debt proceeds in **taxable** investments must **rebate** the arbitrage—the excess interest earned—to the federal government. The arbitrage rules and regulations are complex—much like the federal income tax code and regulations—and contain several exemptions and exceptions. In any event, investment revenues should be reduced and arbitrage rebate liabilities should be established when calculations indicate that arbitrage liabilities have been incurred during a period. Similarly, state and local governments that draw down federal grant money before it is expended for the grant project may owe interest to the federal government.

Both the authority to invest idle cash and the disposition of net investment earnings should be agreed upon and documented in the project authorization ordinance and in contractual agreements. Investment earnings might be used, for example, to reduce the government's share of the project cost or to increase the project expenditure authorization. Where monies have been borrowed and interest expenditures are being incurred, investment earnings usually are transferred to the appropriate Debt Service Fund.

## Disposing of Fund Balance or Deficit

Frequently, the governing body specifies what shall be done with any remaining CPF fund balance, as assumed in the case illustration. In the absence of legal or contractual restrictions, however, the balance is usually transferred to the Debt Service Fund from which the bonds or other related debt will be retired. The rationale for such action is that the balance arose because project expenditure requirements were overestimated, with the result that a larger amount than necessary was borrowed. Where resources were provided by intergovernmental grants or intragovernmental transfers, it may be either necessary or appropriate to refund a portion of these resources in disposing of the fund balance.

Government managers should provide in project authorizations, bond indentures, grant agreements, or otherwise for the possibility that costs have been overestimated and a fund balance might need to be disposed of at the conclusion of the project. In the absence of written authorization to rebate unneeded monies or transfer them to the related Debt Service Fund, officials may be precluded from doing so. Indeed, they might be forced to hold them, possibly indefinitely, until they are needed for the express purpose for which they were secured. (Such situations have arisen, for example, where money was borrowed "for the sole and exclusive purpose of extending existing waterlines and no other purposes.") Moreover, in the absence of such an agreement, grantors may insist that any remaining balance be returned to them—even though a project is only partially financed by grants.

A Capital Projects Fund deficit would ordinarily be disposed of in one of two ways. If small, it would probably be eliminated by transferring money from the General Fund; if large, it would probably be financed by additional general government borrowing.

## Reporting Several Projects Financed Through One Fund

Earlier in this chapter it was noted that a single Capital Projects Fund may be used to finance several projects where only one debt issue or grant is involved or the projects are financed through internal transfers from other funds. For example, the capital project may consist of several general improvements, possibly financed through one general obligation bond issue. It was also noted that several Capital Projects Funds may be accounted for on a "funds within a fund" or "subfund" approach within a single overall Capital Projects Fund accounting entity. Each project undertaken may be separately budgeted in such cases and, in any event, each must be separately controlled and accounted for within the CPF accounts.

Separate project control and accounting within a single CPF is best done by using distinctively titled (and coded) Estimated Revenues and Other Financing Sources, Revenues and Other Financing Sources, Appropriations, Expenditures, and Encumbrances control accounts and a set of appropriately named and coded subsidiary ledger accounts. Accounting for this type of fund corresponds with procedures discussed previously.

Financial statements for such composite CPFs, where the subfunds are in substance a series of separate Capital Projects Funds, often are presented as a series of separate fund statements—individually and/or in combining statements—as if each were accounted for separately. Financial statements for a multiproject fund thus would show data for each project. If assets, liabilities, and fund balance are identified by projects, the balance sheet may be presented in this columnar form, particularly for internal use:

**A GOVERNMENTAL UNIT**

Capital Projects Fund
Balance Sheet
(Date)

| Total | Completed Projects Project A | Incomplete Projects Project B | Projects Not Yet Determined |
|---|---|---|---|

A supplemental schedule like that shown in Figure 7–9 may be prepared in "pancake" form—also primarily for internal use—to show operating data for individual projects. Information for this supplemental schedule is in the Expenditures Ledger.

## Combining CPF Statements

In order to focus attention on capital projects activities as a whole and to reduce the number of separate statements required, statements of the several Capital Projects Funds of a government are usually presented in combining form. With adequate disclosure, such combining statements fulfill the requirement for separate statements for each fund. In general, combining totals should be shown with the details applicable to each fund either being presented in the statement itself or being incorporated by reference therein to a statement or schedule containing the separate fund details. (The totals are properly presented alone only in certain combined statements discussed and illustrated in Chapter 13.)

**FIGURE 7–9  Multiple Project Budgetary Comparison Schedule**

A Governmental Unit

Capital Projects Fund
Schedule of Appropriations, Expenditures, and Encumbrances
For the Fiscal Year Ended (Date)

| | Appropriations | Expenditures | Encumbrances | Unencumbered Balance |
|---|---|---|---|---|
| Project A | | | | |
| Total Project A | $ 500,000 | $200,000 | $ 10,000 | $290,000 |
| Project B | | | | |
| Total Project B | $ 700,000 | $600,000 | $ 90,000 | $ 10,000 |
| Total—All Projects | $1,200,000 | $800,000 | $100,000 | $300,000 |

Combining CPF balance sheets and operating statements are presented in the formats illustrated earlier in this chapter, but the column headings might appear as:

| *Completed Projects* | | *Incomplete Projects* | | *Totals* | |
|---|---|---|---|---|---|
| *Bridge Fund* | *Sewer System Fund* | *Civic Center Fund* | *General Improvements Fund* | *This Period* | *Last Period* |

The distinction between completed and incomplete projects is made more often in combining statements prepared for internal use than in those published in the government's annual financial report. Likewise, the prior period comparative data are optional in combining statements. The combining Capital Projects Fund operating statement from a recent annual financial report of the city of Sioux City, Iowa, is presented in Figure 7–10.

**FIGURE 7–10  Combining Capital Projects Funds Operating Statement**

City of Sioux City, Iowa

**Combining Statement of Revenues, Expenditures, and Changes in Fund Balances—All Capital Project Funds**

For the Year Ended June 30, 19X1

| | Street Improvement | Storm Sewer Improvement | Special Improvement | Park Improvement | Miscellaneous Improvement | Totals |
|---|---|---|---|---|---|---|
| **Revenues** | | | | | | |
| Special Assessments | $  29,591 | | | | | $  29,591 |
| Regulatory Fees | | | | | $    150 | 150 |
| Intergovernmental Revenue | 1,071,137 | $   3,474 | $  50,000 | $ 424,154 | 1,743,573 | 3,292,338 |
| Revenue from Use of Property | | | 324,424 | | 579,753 | 904,177 |
| Charges for Services | | | | | 8,949 | 8,949 |
| Interest | 10,382 | | 5,756 | 27,606 | 82,052 | 125,796 |
| Contributions | | | 1,000 | 33,437 | 47,893 | 82,330 |
| Miscellaneous | 16,891 | 8,144 | 332 | 3,382 | | 28,749 |
| Total Revenues | 1,128,001 | 11,618 | 381,512 | 488,579 | 2,462,370 | 4,472,080 |
| **Expenditures** | | | | | | |
| Capital Outlay | 4,507,769 | 567,592 | 1,178,754 | 3,508,438 | 3,311,889 | 13,074,442 |
| Total Expenditures | 4,507,769 | 567,592 | 1,178,754 | 3,508,438 | 3,311,889 | 13,074,442 |
| (Deficiency) of Revenues Over Expenditures | (3,379,768) | (555,974) | (797,242) | (3,019,859) | (849,519) | (8,602,362) |
| **Other Financing Sources (Uses)** | | | | | | |
| Proceeds from Issuance of Bonds | 2,163,950 | 82,000 | 263,200 | 1,380,000 | 601,350 | 4,490,500 |
| Operating Transfers In | 1,732,860 | 652,000 | 15,986 | 366,655 | 1,265,727 | 4,033,228 |
| Operating Transfers Out | (2,500) | | (13,301) | | (104,797) | (120,598) |
| Total Other Financing Sources (Uses) | 3,894,310 | 734,000 | 265,885 | 1,746,655 | 1,762,280 | 8,403,130 |
| Excess (Deficiency) of Revenues and Other Sources over Expenditures and Other Uses | 514,542 | 178,026 | (531,357) | (1,273,204) | 912,761 | (199,232) |
| **Fund Balances—Beginning of Year** | 2,221,479 | 875,648 | 420,647 | 917,160 | 1,342,089 | 5,777,023 |
| Residual Equity Transfers In/(Out) | 48,000 | | | | (111,960) | (63,960) |
| **Fund Balances—End of Year** | $2,784,021 | $1,053,674 | ($  110,710) | ($  356,044) | $2,142,890 | $ 5,513,831 |

The notes to the financial statements are an integral part of this statement.

*Source:* Adapted from a recent annual financial report of the city of Sioux City, Iowa.

If a government has numerous Capital Projects Funds (i.e., more than six or seven), it may be desirable to prepare combining schedules for groups of funds and use such combining data, appropriately described and referenced to the schedules, in preparing the combining balance sheet for all Capital Projects Funds. A similar technique often proves useful in connection with statements of multi-project funds.

## CONCLUDING COMMENTS

Capital Projects Funds are used to account for a state or local government's major general government capital outlays for buildings, highways, storm sewer systems, bridges, and other fixed assets. Accordingly, they often involve millions of dollars (even hundreds of millions of dollars) of financial resources and expenditures.

The main aspects of Capital Projects Fund financing, financial management, and accounting discussed in this chapter include sources of CPF resources, number of funds required, CPF life cycle, interim financing, the CPF budget, costs charged to projects, investment of idle cash, and disposing of the CPF fund balance or deficit upon its termination. In addition, a Capital Projects Fund case illustration and illustrative financial statements were presented.

Although this chapter illustrates the financing of Capital Projects Funds with general long-term bond proceeds, it does not address the repayment of that debt or the related interest and fiscal charges. Those topics are covered in Chapter 8 on "Debt Service Funds."

## APPENDIX 7–1

### Detailed General Ledger Worksheet

The 19X1 CPF illustration entries presented in entries B and 1–8 in Chapter 7 are summarized in the worksheet in Figure 7–11.

## APPENDIX 7–2

### General Ledger Worksheet and Subsidiary Ledgers

As noted in the section "Alternative Account Structure and Entries" in Chapter 7, this appendix presents the 19X1 CPF illustration entries in the General Ledger, Revenues Ledger, Expenditures Ledger context illustrated in Chapters 3 and 4. Note that the Revenues Ledger has been expanded to a Revenues and Other Financing Sources Ledger since non-revenue financing sources are common in CPFs. This change is not essential, but facilitates CPF accounting procedures.

- Figure 7–12—General Ledger Worksheet
- Figure 7–13—Revenues and Other Financing Sources Subsidiary Ledger (Preclosing)
- Figure 7–14-Expenditures Subsidiary Ledger (Preclosing)

**FIGURE 7–11 Detailed General Ledger Worksheet—Capital Projects Fund**

## GENERAL LEDGER WORKSHEET
A Governmental Unit
Capital Projects Fund
(Bridge Project)
For 19X1 (Project Incomplete)

| Accounts | Worksheet Entries | | Preclosing Trial Balance | |
|---|---|---|---|---|
| | *Debit* | *Credit* | *Debit* | *Credit* |
| Cash .......................... | $ 909,000 (2) | | | |
| | 730,000 (4) | | | |
| | | $1,510,000 (6) | $ 129,000 | |
| Investments ..................... | 400,000 (6) | | 400,000 | |
| Accrued Interest Receivable .......... | 18,000 (8) | | 18,000 | |
| Due from Federal Government ........ | 508,000 (7) | | 508,000 | |
| Vouchers Payable ................... | | 1,080,000 (5b) | | |
| | 970,000 (6) | | | $ 110,000 |
| Contracts Payable—Retained | | | | |
| Percentage ...................... | | 50,000 (5b) | | 50,000 |
| Estimated Revenues—Federal Grants ... | 1,200,000 (B) | | 1,200,000 | |
| Estimated Revenues—State Grant ...... | 600,000 (B) | | 600,000 | |
| Estimated Other Financing Sources— | | | | |
| Bond Issue Proceeds .............. | 900,000 (B) | | 900,000 | |
| Estimated Other Financing Sources— | | | | |
| Operating Transfer from General | | | | |
| Fund .......................... | 300,000 (B) | | 300,000 | |
| Appropriations—Bean & Co. Contract ... | | 2,400,000 (B) | | 2,400,000 |
| Appropriations—Labor .............. | | 300,000 (B) | | 300,000 |
| Appropriations—Machine Time ........ | | 200,000 (B) | | 200,000 |
| Appropriations—Fuel and Materials ..... | | 100,000 (B) | | 100,000 |
| Revenues—Federal Grant ............ | | 508,000 (7) | | 508,000 |
| Revenues—State Grant .............. | | 600,000 (4) | | 600,000 |
| Revenues—Interest ................. | | 18,000 (8) | | 18,000 |
| Other Financing Sources—Bond Proceeds | | 909,000 (2) | | 909,000 |
| Other Financing Sources—Operating | | | | |
| Transfers from General Fund ......... | | 130,000 (4) | | 130,000 |
| Expenditures—Bean & Co. Contract .... | 1,000,000 (5b) | | 1,000,000 | |
| Expenditures—Labor ................ | 140,000 (6) | | 140,000 | |
| Expenditures—Machine Time .......... | 81,000 (5b) | | 81,000 | |
| Expenditures—Fuel and Materials ...... | 49,000 (5b) | | 49,000 | |
| Encumbrances—Bean & Co. Contract ... | 2,400,000 (1) | | | |
| | | 1,000,000 (5a) | 1,400,000 | |
| Encumbrances—Fuel and Materials ..... | 55,000 (3) | | | |
| | | 48,000 (5a) | 7,000 | |
| Reserve for Encumbrances ........... | | 2,400,000 (1) | | |
| | | 55,000 (3) | | |
| | 1,048,000 (5a) | | | 1,407,000 |
| | $11,308,000 | $11,308,000 | $6,732,000 | $6,732,000 |

FIGURE 7–12  Summary General Ledger Worksheet—Capital Projects Fund

**GENERAL LEDGER WORKSHEET**
A Governmental Unit
Capital Projects Fund (Bridge Project)
For 19X1 (Project Incomplete)

| Accounts | Transactions Debit | # | Transactions Credit | # | Preclosing Trial Balance Debit | Preclosing Trial Balance Credit | Closing Entries Debit | # | Closing Entries Credit | # | Postclosing Trial Balance Debit | Postclosing Trial Balance Credit |
|---|---|---|---|---|---|---|---|---|---|---|---|---|
| Cash | $ 909,000<br>730,000 | (2)<br>(4) | $ 1,510,000 | (6) | $ 129,000 | | | | | | $ 129,000 | |
| Investments | 400,000 | (6) | | | 400,000 | | | | | | 400,000 | |
| Accrued Interest Receivable | 18,000 | (8) | | | 18,000 | | | | | | 18,000 | |
| Due from Federal Government | 508,000 | (7) | | | 508,000 | | | | | | 508,000 | |
| Vouchers Payable | 970,000 | (6) | 1,080,000 | (5b) | | $ 110,000 | | | | | | $ 110,000 |
| Contracts Payable—Retained Percentage | | | 50,000 | (5b) | | 50,000 | | | | | | 50,000 |
| Estimated Revenues | 1,800,000 | (B) | | | 1,800,000 | | | | $1,800,000 | (C1) | | |
| Estimated Other Financing Sources | 1,200,000 | (B) | | | 1,200,000 | | | | 1,200,000 | (C1) | | |
| Appropriations | | | 3,000,000 | (B) | | 3,000,000 | $1,270,000<br>1,407,000 | (C2)<br>(C3) | | | | 323,000 |
| Revenues | | | 600,000<br>508,000<br>18,000 | (4)<br>(7)<br>(8) | | 1,126,000 | 1,126,000 | (C1) | | | | |
| Other Financing Sources | | | 909,000<br>130,000 | (2)<br>(4) | | 1,039,000 | 1,039,000 | (C1) | | | | |
| Expenditures | 1,130,000<br>140,000 | (5b)<br>(6) | | | 1,270,000 | | | | 1,270,000 | (C2) | | |
| Encumbrances | 2,400,000<br>55,000 | (1)<br>(3) | 1,048,000 | (5a) | 1,407,000 | | | | 1,407,000 | (C3) | | |
| Reserve for Encumbrances | 1,048,000 | (5a) | 2,400,000<br>55,000 | (1)<br>(3) | | 1,407,000 | | | | | | 1,407,000 |
| Unreserved Fund Balance | | | | | | | 835,000 | (C1) | | | 835,000 | |
| | $11,308,000 | | $11,308,000 | | $6,732,000 | $6,732,000 | $5,677,000 | | $5,677,000 | | $1,890,000 | $1,890,000 |

# Exercises

**E 7-1** (Bond Anticipation Notes) Record the following transactions in the Capital Projects Fund of a county. Reflect all required accruals.

1. The county issues $3,000,000 of 10%, 9-month bond anticipation notes at midyear to allow it to begin construction of a new library addition. The bond anticipation notes meet the criteria for treatment as long-term debt.
2. The county signs a contract for construction of the library addition for $3,000,000.
3. The contractor billed the county $2,000,000 for work completed by the **end of the fiscal year.**
4. The bonds, which have a par value of $10,000,000, were issued at par.
5. The bond anticipation notes and interest were paid at maturity.

**E 7-2** (General Ledger Entries) The following transactions and events occurred in Lanesburg Township during 19X4:

1. The township assembly agreed that a new police and fire department building would be constructed at a cost not to exceed $1,500,000, on land owned by the township.
2. Cash with which to finance the project was received from the following sources:

| | |
|---|---|
| Transfer from General Fund ......................... | $ 100,000 |
| State–Federal grant ................................ | 500,000 |
| Bank of Lanesburg (long-term note) .................... | 900,000 |
| | $1,500,000 |

   The state–federal grant is for one-third of the project cost, not to exceed $500,000, and any unearned balance must be returned to the state.
3. Cash was disbursed for building costs from the Capital Projects Fund as follows:

| | |
|---|---|
| Construction contract .................................... | $1,400,000 |
| Architect fees ...................................... | 50,000 |
| Engineering charges ................................. | 20,000 |
| | $1,470,000 |

4. The unearned portion of the grant was refunded to the state, the remaining cash was transferred to the General Fund, and the Capital Projects Fund was terminated.

*Required* Prepare general journal entries to record the foregoing facts in the Capital Projects Fund General Ledger assuming that budgetary accounts and subsidiary ledgers are not used.

# Problems

**P 7-1** (Multiple Choice) Indicate the best answer to each question.

1. The city of Nancy is installing a lighting system in the Harvey Subdivision. The system is being financed by the issuance of $500,000 of five-year, 6%, special assessment notes payable. The notes and interest thereon are to be repaid from collections of special assessments levied against the properties in the Harvey Subdivision. The construction and acquisition of the lighting system is deemed a major general government capital project for the city. The proceeds from the issuance of the notes would increase the fund balance of the city's Lighting System Capital Projects Fund by
   a. $0. There should be no CPF for the lighting system. The proceeds are to be accounted for in a different fund type.
   b. $0. The notes payable should be reported as liabilities of the Lighting System CPF because the debt is special assessment debt. Therefore, the fund's fund balance does not increase.

c. $500,000. The proceeds from the issuance of the note should be reported as Revenues—Special Assessment Note Proceeds.

d. $500,000. The proceeds from the issuance of the note should be reported as Other Financing Sources—Special Assessment Note Proceeds, essentially the same as any other general government long-term debt issuance for a general government capital project.

2. If the city of Nancy levies special assessments of $500,000—$100,000 of which is due and collected during the current year—what amount of special assessment revenues should be recognized in the Lighting System CPF in the current year?

   a. $0. The special assessments should be reported in a Debt Service Fund because collections of the assessments are to be used to pay principal and interest on the special assessment notes payable.

   b. $100,000

   c. $500,000

   d. $0. Special assessments are reported as other financing sources, not as revenues.

3. Assume the city of Nancy is financing construction of the lighting system directly from its special assessment levy (i.e., no debt is being incurred). If, as in 2, the city of Nancy levies special assessments of $500,000—$100,000 of which is due and collected during the current year—what amount of special assessment revenues should be recognized in the Lighting System CPF in the current year?

   a. $0. The special assessments should be reported in a special revenue fund.

   b. $100,000

   c. $500,000

   d. $0. Special assessments are reported as other financing sources, not as revenues.

4. The city of Joni Fire Station Capital Project Fund has an excess of expenditures over revenues of $5,000,000 reported in its statement of revenues, expenditures, and changes in fund balances. Which of the following explanations for that excess are plausible?

   a. The city financed a substantial portion of the fire station project by issuing bonded indebtedness; therefore, its expenditures are likely to exceed its revenues.

   b. The city financed a substantial portion of the fire station project with a federal block grant, which was recognized in the last year's revenues. Therefore, minimal revenues are being recognized this year, but a substantial fund balance exists as a result of the federal grant.

   c. The city has incurred significant cost overruns on the project. This is the only reason that an excess of expenditures over revenues should be reported in a CPF operating statement.

   d. None of the above is a plausible explanation.

5. Matthew County issued a six-month, 6%, $1,000,000 bond anticipation note to provide temporary financing for a major general government capital project. The bonds have not been authorized by the voters yet, but approval is anticipated by the county board of supervisors. In any event, the county has other financing sources that it can use to finance the project in the event that the voters reject the bond issue in the bond referendum election. What would be the fund balance of the Capital Projects Fund used to account for this project if the county incurred $800,000 of construction costs on the project by year end, which is three months before the bond anticipation note maturity date?

   a. $185,000                    c. ($815,000)

   b. $200,000                    d. ($800,000)

6. If Matthew County already had voter approval of the bond issue in 5 and intended to refinance the bond anticipation note from the bond proceeds, what would the CPF fund balance be?

   a. $185,000                    c. ($800,000)

   b. $200,000                    d. ($815,000)

7. If Matthew County already had voter approval of the bond issue in 5 and intended to refinance the bond anticipation note from the bond proceeds, what amount of expenditures would be reported for the CPF as a result of the repayment of the bond anticipation principal and interest in year 2?

   a. $0
   c. $1,000,000
   b. $1,030,000
   d. $30,000

8. Luke County issued $20,000,000 par of capital improvement bonds for a general government project. The bonds were issued at a premium of 2% of par. The bond indenture requires that any premium be set aside for debt service. This transaction should be reflected in Luke's CPF as

   a. other financing sources—bond proceeds, $20,000,000.
   b. other financing sources—bond proceeds, $20,400,000 and expenditures, $400,000.
   c. other financing sources—bond proceeds, $20,400,000 and other financing uses—operating transfers out, $400,000.
   d. other financing sources—bond proceeds, $20,000,000 and bond premium, $400,000.

9. Upon completion of its new city office building, the city of Caleb had net assets of $880,000 remaining in its City Hall CPF. Council approves use of these net assets for future debt service on the City Hall bonds. The reclassification of these assets as Debt Service Fund assets will be reflected in the CPF statement of revenues, expenditures, and changes in fund balances as

   a. expenditures.
   b. operating transfers out.
   c. residual equity transfers out.
   d. reductions of revenues for the final project period.

10. A county's Courthouse CPF has the following balances in selected accounts at the end of its first year:

    | | |
    |---|---|
    | Revenues, $1,500,000 | Encumbrances, $8,000,000 |
    | Bond proceeds, $5,000,000 | Appropriations, $9,500,000 |
    | Expenditures, $1,500,000 | |

    The appropriation authority for the project continues from year to year. At the end of the first year of the project, what amount of Unreserved Fund Balance should be reported in the Courthouse CPF balance sheet?

    a. $0
    c. ($3,000,000)
    b. $5,000,000
    d. None of the above are correct.

**P 7-2, Part I** (General Ledger Entries; Statements) The following transactions took place in the village of Burchette during 19A:

1. A bond issue of $12,000,000 was authorized for the construction of a library, and the estimated bond issue proceeds and related appropriations were recorded in the General Ledger accounts of a new Capital Projects Fund.
2. The bonds were sold at a premium of $90,000.
3. The cost of issuing the bonds, $80,000, was paid.
4. An order was placed for materials estimated to cost $6,500,000.
5. Salaries and wages amounting to $500,000 were paid.
6. The premium, net of bond issuance costs, was transferred to a Debt Service Fund.

**Required** (a) Prepare all entries, including closing entries, to record the Capital Projects Fund transactions for 19A.

(b) Post to T-accounts.

(c) Prepare a CPF balance sheet as of December 31, 19A.

(d) Prepare a CPF Statement of Revenues, Expenditures, and Changes in Fund Balance for the year ended December 31, 19A.

**P 7-2, Part II** (General Ledger Entries; Project Operating Statement) The following transactions took place during 19B:

7. The materials were received; the actual cost was $6,585,000.

8. Salaries and wages amounting to $4,010,000 were paid.
9. All outstanding bills were paid.
10. The project was completed. The accounts were closed, and the remaining balance was transferred to a Debt Service Fund.

**Required**   (a) Prepare all journal entries, including closing entries, to record the CPF transactions for 19B.
(b) Post to T-accounts.
(c) Prepare a CPF Statement of Revenues, Expenditures, and Changes in Fund Balance for the project, including (a) the years ended December 31, 19A and 19B, and (b) budgetary comparisons for the project.

**P 7-3**   (General Ledger Worksheet) From the data in Problem 7–2, Parts I and II, prepare a columnar worksheet for the two-year period ending December 31, 19B, using the following columnar headings:
1. 19A Transactions
2. Closing Entries, 12/31/19A
3. Postclosing Trial Balance, 12/31/19A
4. 19B Transactions
5. Closing Entries, 12/31/19B
6. Postclosing Trial Balance, 12/31/19B

**P 7-4, Part I**   (General Ledger Entries; Statements) The following transactions took place in Mills County during 19X4.
1. A bond issue of $5,000,000 was authorized for the construction of a bridge, and the estimated bond issue proceeds and appropriations were recorded in the General Ledger accounts of a new Bridge CPF.
2. One-half of the bonds were sold at par.
3. The cost of issuing the bonds, $7,000, was paid from the Capital Projects Fund.
4. A contract was entered into with White & Company for the construction of the bridge at a cost of $4,200,000.
5. A bill for $1,750,000 was received from White & Company for work done on the bridge to date.
6. Salaries of state engineers amounting to $53,500 were paid to the state.

**Required**   (a) Prepare CPF General Ledger entries.
(b) Post to T-accounts.
(c) Prepare CPF financial statements as of December 31, 19X4.

**P 7-4, Part II**   (General Ledger Entries; Subfunds; Combining Statements) The following transactions took place during 19X5:
7. A bond issue of $4,000,000 was authorized at the beginning of 19X5 for the purpose of constructing a garage. As permitted by the bond indentures, both the bridge project (Bridge Fund) and the garage project (Garage Fund) are to be accounted for in the same Capital Projects Fund on a "funds within a fund" or "subfund" approach. Accordingly, "Bridge" was added to all existing Bridge Fund accounts and "Garage" is to be added to all Garage Fund accounts. The garage bond issue authorization was recorded in the accounts.
8. The bill due White & Company was paid.
9. Bonds (garage) of $2,000,000 were sold at a $40,000 premium.
10. The cost of issuing the garage bonds, $25,000, was paid.
11. Orders were placed for materials (garage project) estimated to cost $520,000.
12. A bill for $1,250,000 was received from White & Company for further work performed on the bridge contract.
13. Salaries and wages paid amounted to $511,000; of this total $40,000 applies to the bridge project and the remainder to the garage project.
14. The materials ordered (in 11) were received; the actual cost, $530,000, was vouchered for later payment.

15. An order was placed for materials (garage project) estimated to cost $1,000,000.
16. The net garage bond premium was transferred to the appropriate Debt Service Fund.

**Required** (a) Prepare CPF General Ledger journal entries.
(b) Post to T-accounts.
(c) Prepare a combining balance sheet for the Capital Projects Funds as of December 31, 19X5.
(d) Prepare a CPF combining statement of revenues, expenditures, and changes in fund balances for the year ended December 31, 19X5.

**P 7-5** (General Ledger Worksheet) From the data in Problem 7–4, Parts I and II, prepare columnar worksheets for each fund for the two-year period ended December 31, 19X5. The worksheet for the Bridge (Capital Projects) Fund should have columnar headings as follows:

| 19X4 Transactions | | Trial Balance, 12/31/19X4 | | 19X5 Transactions | | Trial Balance, 12/31/19X5 | |
|---|---|---|---|---|---|---|---|
| Debit | Credit | Debit | Credit | Debit | Credit | Debit | Credit |

The worksheet for the Garage (Capital Projects) Fund should contain similar headings relating to 19X5 transactions and balances. Entries should be keyed to the numbered items in Problem 7–4. (If statements were not prepared for Problem 7–4, they may be assigned here.)

**P 7-6** (GL Entries; Bond Anticipation Notes) Rhea County issued $2,000,000 of nine-month, 9% notes in anticipation of bonds being issued to provide ultimate financing for construction of a county baseball stadium. This prevented undesirable delays in beginning the project, which had been approved at an estimated cost of $4,000,000. December 31 is the end of the county's fiscal year. The following transactions occurred during 19X8 and 19X9:

1. The bond anticipation notes were issued at par on July 1, 19X8.
2. The county signed a contract on July 1, 19X8 with the King of Swat Construction Company to build the stadium. The contract price was $4,000,000.
3. The King of Swat Construction Company billed the county $1,800,000 during 19X8 for work completed on the project. The county paid the amount billed less a 5% retainage to be remitted upon final inspection and approval of the stadium.
4. On February 20, 19X9 the county issued the baseball stadium bonds ($4,000,000 par) at a price of $4,180,000, net of bond issue costs.
5. The county repaid the bond anticipation notes and interest from the bond proceeds upon maturity.
6. The King of Swat Construction Company billed Rhea County $2,200,000 for work performed in 19X9 to complete the baseball stadium. The project was approved by the county and the King of Swat Construction Company was paid in full.

**Required** (a) Prepare the general journal entries to record the preceding transactions for Rhea County.
Prepare 19X8 and 19X9 financial statements for the county's Baseball Stadium CPF. Assume that the bond issue had not yet received voter approval in 19X8.
(b) Repeat the requirements in (a) under the assumption that the bond anticipation notes meet the criteria for being treated as general long-term debt.

**P 7-7** (GL Entries; Statement) Minars County undertook a major highway improvement project during 19X7 using both independent contractors and its own Highway Department. The following transactions and events affected the related Capital Projects Fund.

1. The county commission approved the following financial plan and appropriations:

Financial Plan

| | |
|---|---:|
| Bond issue proceeds | $ 4,000,000 |
| Federal grant | 3,000,000 |
| State grant | 2,000,000 |
| Transfer from General Fund | 1,000,000 |
| | $10,000,000 |

Appropriations

| | |
|---|---:|
| Contract #1 | $ 3,500,000 |
| Contract #2 | 2,700,000 |
| Contract #3 | 1,300,000 |
| Highway Department | 2,500,000 |
| | $10,000,000 |

The federal grant is for 30% of the actual allowable costs incurred, up to a maximum of $3,000,000, whereas the state grant is a fixed sum $2,000,000 grant.

2. The county commission let highway construction contracts as follows:

| | |
|---|---:|
| Contract #1 | $3,300,000 |
| Contract #2 | 2,800,000 |
| Contract #3 | 1,300,000 |
| | $7,400,000 |

The contract appropriations were revised accordingly. Also, the county Highway Department ordered materials estimated to cost $1,100,000.

3. Expenditures vouchered during 19X7 included:

| | |
|---|---:|
| Contract #1 | $3,350,000 |
| Contract #2 | 2,800,000 |
| Contract #3 | 1,325,000 |
| Highway Department | 1,475,000 |
| | $8,950,000 |

A billing for $50,000 of supplies for the Highway Department also was received from an Internal Service Fund. No encumbrances were outstanding at year end. The county retains 5% of contract billings pending final inspection and approval of contract projects, and revised the contract project appropriations to authorize the approved additional work reflected in the contractor billings.

4. Cash receipts during 19X7 included:

| | |
|---|---:|
| Bond issue proceeds | $4,100,000 |
| Federal grant | 2,600,000 |
| State grant | 2,000,000 |
| Transfer from General Fund | 800,000 |
| | $9,500,000 |

5. Cash disbursements during 19X7 included:

| | |
|---|---:|
| Vouchers payable | $8,576,250 |
| Transfer of bond premium to Debt Service Fund | 100,000 |
| Highway Department payroll | 730,750 |
| Internal Service Fund | 50,000 |
| | $9,457,000 |

6. Expenditures of $85,250 recorded previously in the General Fund were found to relate to Highway Department CPF activities. The expenditures were not reimbursed, but were recorded as an in-substance operating transfer to the CPF from the General Fund.

7. The federal government was billed for its remaining share of the total project costs.
8. The final federal grant payment was received as billed, except for a $1,800 reimbursement disallowed because $6,000 of project costs incurred were unallowable under terms of the grant.
9. The highway improvement projects were inspected, approved, and accepted by the county commission. Accordingly, the retained percentages were paid to the contractors, and the remaining balance of the CPF was transferred to a Debt Service Fund.
10. The Capital Projects Fund accounts were closed, and the fund was terminated.

***Required*** (a) Prepare the journal entries to record the budgetary and actual transactions and events that affected the Minars County Highway Improvement Capital Projects Fund during 19X7 in the CPF General Ledger, Revenues Ledger, and Expenditures Ledger.

(b) Prepare a Statement of Revenues, Expenditures, and Changes in Fund Balance—Budget and Actual for the Minars County Highway Improvement Capital Projects Fund for 19X7.

**P 7-8** (GL Worksheet and SLs) This problem requires an alternate solution approach to Problem 7–7 on the Minars County Highway Improvement Capital Projects Fund.

***Required*** (a) Prepare a General Ledger worksheet and the Revenues Ledger and Expenditures Ledger accounts to record the budgetary and actual transactions and events that affected the Minars County Highway Improvement Capital Projects Fund during 19X7. The General Ledger worksheet should be headed

| Columns | Heading |
|---------|---------|
| 1–2 | 19X7 Budgetary and Transaction Entries |
| 3–4 | Closing Entries—End of 19X7 |

(b) Prepare a Statement of Revenues, Expenditures, and Changes in Fund Balance—Budget and Actual for the Minars County Highway Improvement Capital Projects Fund.

**P 7-9 Part I** (GL and SL Entries; Trial Balances; Statements) The following transactions and events relate to the Harmer Independent School District high school building Capital Projects Fund during 19X3.

1. The school board appropriated $9,000,000 to construct and landscape a new regional high school building to be financed as follows:

| | |
|---|---:|
| Bond issue proceeds ................................. | $6,000,000 |
| Federal grant (for 20% of cost) ........................ | 1,800,000 |
| State grant ......................................... | 700,000 |
| Transfer from General Fund ......................... | 500,000 |
| | $9,000,000 |

The appropriations made for the high school building were:

| | |
|---|---:|
| Structure ......................................... | $5,000,000 |
| Plumbing and heating ............................... | 1,800,000 |
| Electrical ......................................... | 1,300,000 |
| Landscaping ...................................... | 700,000 |
| Other ............................................. | 200,000 |
| | $9,000,000 |

2. Contracts were let to private contractors:

| | |
|---|---:|
| Structure ......................................... | $4,700,000 |
| Plumbing and heating ............................... | 1,825,000 |
| Electrical ......................................... | 1,300,000 |
| | $7,825,000 |

Thus, the plumbing and heating appropriation was increased $25,000, and the structure appropriation was decreased $300,000.

3. Cash receipts during 19X3 included:

| | |
|---|---|
| Federal grant | $ 250,000 |
| State grant | 350,000 |
| Bond issue proceeds (par $2,000,000) | 2,020,000 |
| Transfer from General Fund | 100,000 |
| | $2,720,000 |

The federal grant is for 20% of actual qualifying costs incurred (expenditure-driven) up to its $1,800,000 maximum, but the state grant is an outright contribution to the project. The remaining bonds authorized will be issued as needed, depending on market conditions; and the board authorized only part of the General Fund transfer but is expected to authorize the remainder during 19X4.

4. Invoices from contractors were received, approved, and vouchered for payment less a 5% retained percentage:

| | |
|---|---|
| Structure | $2,000,000 |
| Plumbing and heating | 500,000 |
| Electrical | 700,000 |
| Other (not encumbered) | 50,000 |
| | $3,250,000 |

5. Borrowed $150,000 on a short-term note from First State Bank of Harmer.

6. Cash disbursements during 19X3 included:

| | | |
|---|---|---|
| Vouchers Payable | | $2,600,000 |
| Payroll: | | |
| Landscaping | $120,000 | |
| Other | 80,000 | 200,000 |
| Machinery charges—Landscaping | | 50,000 |
| | | $2,850,000 |

7. Billed the federal government for the balance of its share of project costs incurred to date.

8. Accrued interest payable on the note at year end, $4,000. Interest expenditures on this note are considered a project cost (other) but are not reimbursable under terms of the federal grant.

*Required*
(a) Prepare the journal entries to record the preceding transactions and events in the General Ledger, Revenues Ledger, and Expenditures Ledger of the Harmer Independent School District High School Building Capital Projects Fund during 19X3.

(b) Prepare a preclosing trial balance of the General, Revenues, and Expenditures Ledgers accounts at the end of 19X3.

(c) Prepare the journal entry(ies) to close the General Ledger accounts at the end of 19X3. (Do not close the subsidiary ledgers accounts.)

(d) Prepare a balance sheet for the Harmer Independent School District Capital Projects Fund at the end of 19X3 and a Statement of Revenues, Expenditures, and Changes in Fund Balance for the 19X3 fiscal year.

(e) Does it appear that the deficits reported are real or artificial? Explain.

**P 7-9, Part II** (GL and SL Entries; Statement) The following transactions and events relate to the Harmer Independent School District High School Building Capital Projects Fund during 19X4.

1. The Estimated Revenues and Estimated Other Financing Sources accounts were reestablished at their remaining balances, and the Encumbrances account was

reestablished. (The interest expenditure accrual entry made at the end of 19X3 was not reversed.)

2. Cash receipts during 19X4 included:

| | |
|---|---:|
| Bond issue proceeds ($4,000,000 par) . . . . . . . . . . . . . . . . . . . | $3,985,000 |
| Federal grant . . . . . . . . . . . . . . . . . . . . . . . . . . . . . . . . . . . . | 1,440,000 |
| State grant . . . . . . . . . . . . . . . . . . . . . . . . . . . . . . . . . . . . . . | 350,000 |
| Transfer from General Fund . . . . . . . . . . . . . . . . . . . . . . . . . | 375,000 |
| | $6,150,000 |

3. Final invoices from contractors were received, approved, and vouchered for payment less a 5% retained percentage:

| | |
|---|---:|
| Structure . . . . . . . . . . . . . . . . . . . . . . . . . . . . . . . . . . . . . . . . | $2,750,000 |
| Plumbing and heating . . . . . . . . . . . . . . . . . . . . . . . . . . . . . . | 1,325,000 |
| Electrical . . . . . . . . . . . . . . . . . . . . . . . . . . . . . . . . . . . . . . . . | 600,000 |
| Landscaping (not encumbered) . . . . . . . . . . . . . . . . . . . . . . . | 400,000 |
| | $5,075,000 |

4. Cash disbursements during 19X4 included:

| | | |
|---|---:|---:|
| Vouchers Payable . . . . . . . . . . . . . . . . . . . . . . . . . . . . . . . . . | | $5,308,750 |
| Short-term note payable (including interest) . . . . . . . . . . . . . | | 160,000 |
| Transfer of net bond issue premium to Debt Service Fund . . . | | 5,000 |
| Payroll: | | |
|     Landscaping . . . . . . . . . . . . . . . . . . . . . . . . . . . . . . . . . . . . | $75,000 | |
|     Other . . . . . . . . . . . . . . . . . . . . . . . . . . . . . . . . . . . . . . . . . | 62,000 | 137,000 |
| Machinery charges—Landscaping . . . . . . . . . . . . . . . . . . . . . | | 60,000 |
| | | $5,670,750 |

5. Billed the federal government for the balance of its share of qualifying project costs (excluding interest expenditures).
6. Received final payment on the federal grant as billed, except for $400 disallowed because of a $2,000 unallowable cost included in the billing.
7. The high school building was inspected, approved, and accepted by the school board. Accordingly, the retained percentages were paid to the contractors.
8. The remaining cash was transferred to the Debt Service Fund.
9. The High School Building Capital Projects Fund accounts were closed and the fund was terminated.

***Required*** (a) Prepare the journal entries to record the 19X4 transactions and events in the General Ledger, Revenues Ledger, and Expenditures Ledger of the Harmer Independent School District High School Building Capital Projects Fund.

(b) Prepare a Statement of Revenues, Expenditures, and Changes in Fund Balance—Budget and Actual for the High School Building Capital Projects Fund for the 19X3–19X4 period. The columns of the statement should be headed:

| *Actual* | | | *Budget* | *Variance—* |
|---|---|---|---|---|
| *19X4* | *19X3* | *Total* | *(Revised)* | *Favorable (Unfavorable)* |

**P 7-10** (GL Worksheet, Subsidiary Ledgers, and Statements) This problem requires an alternate solution approach to Problem 7–9, Parts I and II.

***Required*** (a) Prepare a General Ledger worksheet, accompanied by Revenues and Expenditures Ledgers accounts, for the Harmer Independent School District Capital

Projects Fund for the 19X3 and 19X4 fiscal years. Your General Ledger worksheet should be headed:

| Columns | Heading |
|---|---|
| 1–2 | 19X3 Budgetary and Transaction Entries |
| 3–4 | Preclosing Trial Balance—End of 19X3 |
| 5–6 | Closing Entries—End of 19X3 |
| 7–8 | Postclosing Trial Balance—End of 19X3 |
| 9–10 | 19X4 Budgetary and Transaction Entries |
| 11–12 | Closing Entries—End of 19X4 |

(b) Prepare a balance sheet for the Harmer Independent School District Capital Projects Fund at the end of 19X3 and a Statement of Revenues, Expenditures, and Changes in Fund Balance for the 19X3 fiscal year.

(c) Prepare a Statement of Revenues, Expenditures, and Changes in Fund Balance—Budget and Actual for the Harmer Independent School District Capital Projects Fund for the 19X3–19X4 period. The columns of the statement should be headed:

| Actual | | | Budget | Variance—Favorable |
|---|---|---|---|---|
| 19X4 | 19X3 | Total | (Revised) | (Unfavorable) |

**P 7-11, Part I** (SA Project Entries) The city council of Johnson City authorized special assessment #13 during 19X1 to improve neighborhood storm drainage systems. The project is expected to cost $2,000,000, to be financed by a city contribution and by assessments. Johnson City uses private contractors on special assessment contracts and does not use budgetary accounts (except Encumbrances) in its special assessment accounting.

The following transactions and events relate to the Johnson City special assessment project during 19X1 and 19X2.

### 19X1 TRANSACTIONS AND EVENTS

1. Awarded construction contracts to ABC Company, $1,200,000, and XYZ, Inc., $800,000.
2. Received the city's contribution, $200,000.
3. The improvements were completed and bills were received and approved for payment, less a 10% retainage pending final inspection, from ABC Company ($1,200,000) and from XYZ, Inc. ($850,000). The increase in the XYZ, Inc. billing was caused by change orders approved during the course of construction.
4. Borrowed $1,900,000 on a five-year, 10% installment note at the Johnson City National Bank. (The note is guaranteed by Johnson City.)
5. Paid the contractor billings, net of the retained percentage.
6. Levied assessments of $1,900,000, based on appraisals of property value increments. The assessments are due in five equal annual installments, with 10% interest, beginning in 19X2.
7. Some property owners paid their entire assessments immediately, $100,000.
8. Paid interest to date on the note, $70,000.
9. The accounts were closed at the end of 19X1.

### 19X2 TRANSACTIONS AND EVENTS

10. The project improvements passed final inspection and the contractors were paid the retainages.
11. The city council ordered that the net assets remaining at the end of the construction phase of the project be dedicated to project debt service.

12. Billings were mailed to property owners for the assessments due in 19X2 and the related annual interest to date.

13. Collections from property owners were:

| | |
|---|---|
| Assessments ........................................ | $350,000 |
| Interest on Assessments ............................. | 107,400 |

14. The annual note debt service payment was made.

15. The accounts were closed at the end of 19X2.

***Required***   Prepare the journal entries necessary to record the preceding transactions and events in the general ledger accounts of the appropriate governmental funds of Johnson City in conformity with GAAP.

**P 7-11, Part II**   (SA Project Statements) Based on your solution to Part I, prepare a Statement of Revenues, Expenditures, and Changes in Fund Balance for each of the governmental funds in which the Johnson City special assessment project #13 transactions and events were recorded. The statements should be for the 19X1 and 19X2 fiscal years and should include a 19X1–19X2 total column.

**P 7-12**   (Research and Analysis) Obtain a copy of a recent comprehensive annual financial report (CAFR) of a state or local government from the government, the Internet, your instructor, or a library.

***Required***   (1) **Letter of Transmittal.** Review the capital projects–related discussions and presentations. Which were the most significant general government capital projects? Which planned capital projects (if any) were discussed?

(2) **Financial Statements.** What were the major types of Capital Projects Funds total revenues, other financing sources, expenditures, and other financing uses? Were any reported that were not discussed in Chapter 7 or in earlier chapters? Discuss.

(3) **Narrative Explanation.** Which individual Capital Projects Funds were reported? (Attach a photocopy of the narrative explanations.) Were any of these funds different than you expected based on your study of Chapter 7? Explain.

(4) **Combining and Individual Fund Statements.** Review the combining and individual fund statements for the Capital Projects Funds. What additional information is apparent compared with the combined general purpose financial statements?

(5) **Statistical Section.** What information in the statistical section might be relevant in planning and financing future general government capital projects?

# CHAPTER

# 8

# DEBT SERVICE FUNDS

The purpose of Debt Service Funds (DSFs) is "to account for the accumulation of resources for, and the payment of, *general long-term debt* principal and interest."[1] Thus, only general government long-term debt that is recorded in the General Long-Term Debt Account Group (GLTDAG) is serviced through Debt Service Funds.

Furthermore, not all general long-term debt must be serviced through Debt Service Funds. The GASB *Codification* provides that "Debt Service Funds are required [only] if they are legally mandated and/or if financial resources are being accumulated for principal and interest payments maturing in future years."[2]

Thus, capital lease and serial bond debt might properly be serviced directly from the General Fund or a Special Revenue Fund—rather than from a Debt Service Fund—if a Debt Service Fund is not required legally or contractually and debt service resources are not being accumulated beyond those needed currently. Of course, such debt *could* be serviced through a Debt Service Fund, and many government accountants prefer to account for all general long-term debt service through one or more Debt Service Funds (1) so that all general long-term debt is serviced through the same fund type, and (2) to enhance control over and accountability for debt service resources.

The responsibility of providing for the retirement of long-term general obligation debt is ordinarily indicated by the terms of the debt indenture or other contract. The term *general obligation* indicates that the "full faith and credit" of the governmental unit has been pledged to the repayment of the debt. The term *revenue debt* indicates that a specific revenue source—such as special assessments or tolls—is dedicated to repayment of the debt.

Liabilities of specific funds are not general long-term debt, even if "full faith and credit" debt; and they are normally serviced through those funds rather than the Debt Service Fund(s). For example, when general obligation bonds are issued for the benefit of a public enterprise, the enterprise frequently has primary responsibility for repayment of the bonds (Chapter 12). The same is true of Internal Service Fund debt (Chapter 11). Similarly, some Trust Funds (Chapter 10) may have long-term debt. In these situations the debt is specific fund debt—not general long-term debt—and is accounted for in and serviced through those funds.

This chapter includes discussions and illustrations of (1) the general government Debt Service Fund (DSF) environment, including its unique terminology and

---

[1] GASB *Codification,* sec. 1300.104.
[2] Ibid., sec. 1500.109.

debt service financing and expenditure recognition; (2) accounting and reporting for conventional serial bond DSFs and term bond DSFs; (3) accounting for and reporting debt service on general government special assessment debt—debt that is issued to finance special capital improvements and is serviced by assessments levied against the owners of the properties benefited; and (4) general long-term debt refundings and the accounting and reporting for DSFs for refundings. We begin with brief discussions of several important DSF environment, terminology, financing, and expenditure recognition matters.

## DSF ENVIRONMENT, FINANCING, AND EXPENDITURE RECOGNITION

Several features of SLG long-term debt and debt service should be noted at this point. Some are similar to the business environment, but others are unique to the SLG environment.

### Types of Long-Term Debt

Four types of long-term debt are frequently incurred by state and local governments: bonds; notes; time warrants; and capital leases, lease-purchase agreements, and installment purchase contracts.

A *bond* is a written promise to pay a specified principal sum at a specified future date, usually with interest at a specified rate. Bond issues often are for many millions of dollars because bonds are a major source of long-term financing of capital improvements of most governments. Bonds usually are issued in $1,000 and $5,000 denominations with maturities scheduled over 15 to 25 years and interest paid semiannually or annually. *Term bonds* are those for which all of the principal is payable at a single specified maturity date. *Serial bonds,* by far the most widely used, provide for periodic maturities ranging up to the maximum period permitted by law in the respective states. Specific arrangements of maturities vary widely. Regular serial bonds are repayable in equal annual installments over the life of the issue. In some cases the beginning of the repayment series is deferred several years into the future, after which equal annual installments are to be paid. In other cases the indenture provides for increasing amounts of annual principal payments, computed so that the total annual payment of interest and principal is constant over the life of the issue. Other arrangements also may be provided in the bond indenture.

*Notes* are less formal documents than bonds that indicate an obligation to repay borrowed money at interest. Notes typically have a single maturity date, as do term bonds, but their maturity typically ranges from as soon as 30 to 90 days to as long as three to five years after issuance. Too, a single note usually evidences the borrowing transaction, whereas bonds are generally issued in $1,000 and $5,000 denominations. General obligation notes to be repaid not more than one year from the date of issue normally are carried as liabilities of the General Fund, whereas those to be repaid over a longer period are carried in the General Long-Term Debt Account Group and may be serviced through Debt Service Funds.

*Warrants* are orders by authorized legislative or executive officials directing the treasurer to pay a specific sum to order or bearer. If these warrants are to be paid more than one year after the date of issue, they also are recorded in the General Long-Term Debt Account Group and may be serviced through a Debt Service Fund.

*Capital leases, lease-purchase agreements, and installment purchase contracts* have come into widespread use in government. A variation of lease agreements that has grown more common recently is the "carving up" of leases into shares, called *certificates of participation,* which are sold to individual investors. Where the substance of these transactions indicates that a general government purchase (or capital lease) and liability exist, they should be recorded as General Fixed Assets and General Long-Term Debt, and may require a Debt Service Fund.

Arrangements of maturity dates of notes, warrants, leases, and similar debt may have substantial diversity. Indeed, some long-term debt issues have abnormally low (even zero) stated interest rates and are issued or sold at significant discounts from par. Such deep discount debt requires little or no interest payments during the life of the debt. But the entire par amount, which includes balloon payment of prior period interest, must be paid at maturity. Most deep discount debt is issued in relatively small amounts in conjunction with serial debt issues, rather than as stand-alone issues. Indeed stand-alone issuance of deep discount debt often is prohibited by state or local law. Debt Service Funds for notes, warrants, and other types of general long-term debt are not discussed separately because the accounting for them is similar to that for DSFs for bonds. However, deep discount debt security debt service is discussed later in this chapter.

## Fixed vs. Variable Interest Rates

Municipal bonds issued by state and local governments traditionally have been fixed rate bonds. That is, the annual interest rate, say 6%, is determined upon issuance of the bonds and remains the same throughout the period the bonds are outstanding.

In recent years, some variable rate municipal bonds have been issued. In variable rate bond issues the interest rate is set initially, say at 6%. But the interest rate varies periodically while the bonds are outstanding—perhaps annually or semiannually—according to an agreed index such as a certain bank's prime rate or a specified federal security interest rate. Furthermore, some variable rate bonds have interest floor (minimum) and ceiling (maximum or cap) rates, which limit the range within which the interest rate can vary.

Government interest expenditure planning, budgeting, and appropriating obviously is simpler and more precise where fixed rate bonds are issued. However, initial interest rates are often lower on variable rate bonds because the SLG bears some or all of the interest rate change risk. Indeed, it is extremely difficult to predict whether a SLG will obtain lower interest costs over the life of a fixed rate or a variable rate issue, all other factors being equal. The examples in this chapter assume fixed interest rate bonds for the sake of illustrative simplicity.

## Planning Debt Service Payments

Interest expenditure is an annual cost and is directly proportional to the principal amount of debt outstanding. Because a common debt service planning objective is to keep the drain on each year's resources relatively constant, the pattern of debt service payments for long-term debt usually is designed so that total annual debt service requirements will not fluctuate materially.

Regular fixed rate serial bonds meet the objective fairly well, and both serial bond issues and lease agreements may be structured to meet the objective extremely well, as do most term bonds. A term bond or deep discount debt security maturing 20 years in the future requires the governmental unit to accumulate the par amount due 20 years hence through annual contributions to a Debt Service Fund that, together with earnings on the invested contributions, will equal the par amount.

## Bond Registration and Fiscal Agents

Both serial bonds and term bonds may be either registered or bearer bonds. All municipal bonds issued since the mid-1980s are registered bonds—that is, the bonds are registered in the name of the investor-creditor, whose name appears on the bond, and bond principal and interest payments are made by checks issued to each investor-creditor. On the other hand, bearer bonds—which are no longer issued—are not registered but are presumed to belong to whomever has possession of them (the bearer). Each bearer bond has dated interest coupons attached, which the bearer clips and deposits at a bank—which processes it like a check. (The bond is deposited and processed similarly upon its maturity.) Thus, bearer bonds are sometimes referred to as coupon bonds.

A few state and local governments perform all bond-related registration and debt service payment functions internally. That is, they register and reregister their bonds, prepare individual interest and principal payment checks, and prepare required annual reports of their debt service activities and payments to the federal and state governments. However, most state and local governments retain a registration agent and/or a paying agent (fiscal agent) to perform such bond-related functions. A SLG that retains a bond registrar and paying agent—usually a large bank—sends its debt service checks (including a fiscal agent fee) to the fiscal agent. The fiscal agent prepares and processes the individual investor-creditor checks, registers and reregisters bonds as ownership changes, prepares and files the necessary federal and state reports on the SLG's debt service payments, and sends the SLG regular reports summarizing its activities on behalf of the SLG.

## Required DSF Reserves

Many SLG bond indentures require the SLGs to maintain a specified level of Debt Service Fund reserves or funded reserves. A common provision is that net assets in the amount of the highest year's principal and interest requirements of the bond issue be maintained in the DSF and be fully reserved. A certain dollar amount, say, $2,000,000, may also be specified; and in some agreements the SLG can accumulate the funded reserve amounts over two to five years. Such funded reserve amounts typically may be expended only for (1) debt service payments in the event the SLG encounters financial difficulty during the time the bonds are outstanding, or (2) payment of the final year's debt service. Any amount remaining after the bonds are retired reverts to the SLG.

Such DSF reserves or funded reserves go by many names—such as Reserve for Financial Exigencies, Reserve for Contingencies, and Reserve for Debt Service Assurance—and the net assets may be held by the SLG or by the trustee for the bondholders, depending on the agreement. In any event, their purpose is to provide bondholders additional assurance that they will be paid promptly—even if the SLG encounters financial difficulty—and that the bonds will not be allowed to go into default. Such agreements are important contractual agreements that must be observed by SLG officials, and compliance with these agreements must be examined by the external auditor. Existence of such reserves also dictates that a Debt

Service Fund—not the General or a Special Revenue Fund—be used to account for debt service for the debt issue. A DSF is required when "financial resources are being accumulated for principal and interest payments maturing in future years."[3]

## Bond Ratings

Several private firms—including Standard & Poors, Moody's, and Fitch Investment Services—may be retained by bond and other debt issuers to rate debt issues as to the certainty of the payments of interest and principal by the debtor. These ratings are signified by letters and/or numerals: AAA typically is the best rating.

Higher-rated bonds and other debt securities command lower interest rates—and thus cost borrowers less—than lower-rated securities. In addition, investors in lower-rated securities may demand that the debtor maintain large funded reserves to ensure timely debt service payments. Finally, securities that are not rated high enough to be considered investment grade may not be purchased or held by certain banks, insurance companies, and other investor firms.

## Bond Insurance

Several private firms—including MBIA and AMBAC—issue insurance policies that guarantee timely payment of bond and other debt principal and interest payments to investors. Bond issuers must pay premiums for such insurance, of course, but their bonds or other debt instruments usually are rated AAA and can be issued at lower interest costs than otherwise. Moreover, investors typically do not insist on large funded reserves being established for insured bonds or other debt instruments.

Bond insurance has become popular in recent years because governments issuing debt often can save enough interest costs and funded reserve costs to more than pay the insurance premiums. Too, some governments would not be able to issue debt securities at a reasonable cost—without insuring their bonds or other debt securities.

## Sources of Financing

The money for repaying long-term debt may come from numerous sources with varying legal restrictions. The typical source is property taxes. A special tax rate may be assessed for a single bond issue, or a total annual rate may be used with the proceeds prorated to several debt issues. Legislative bodies may earmark a tax for a specified purpose, with a provision that the proceeds may be used for current operating expenditures, capital outlay, or to repay debt incurred to finance the specified purpose. In such cases the proceeds of the tax would be accounted for in a Special Revenue Fund; the portion of the proceeds allocated to debt service would be transferred to a Debt Service Fund.

Some SLGs levy a sales tax—in addition to or instead of a property tax—to service some of their general long-term debt. Also, general government special assessment debt service typically is financed from special assessments levied on benefited properties and interest charged on the unpaid assessments.

Still another method of providing for debt service is required by bond indentures or other contracts that specify that the debt shall be repaid out of "the first

---

[3] Ibid.

revenues accruing to the treasury." Such agreements require the government to contribute the necessary amounts to the Debt Service Fund from the General Fund; the obligation has first claim on the revenues of the General Fund.

When a term bond issue is to be repaid through a fund in which resources are being accumulated to retire the principal at maturity, the assets of the fund will be invested in income-producing securities. Similarly, some serial bond Debt Service Funds have investable resources. The income from these securities—net of any arbitrage—constitutes still another form of Debt Service Fund revenue.

Finally, maturing bonds may be refunded, that is, they may be retired by either (1) exchanging new bonds for old ones or (2) selling a new bond issue and using the proceeds to retire an old issue. The new bond issue constitutes the financing source in refunding transactions.

## DSF Investments

The financial resources of Debt Service Funds are invested until such time as they are needed to pay maturing debt service. State laws and/or bond indenture requirements often specify the types of DSF investments that may be made, and such provisions must be complied with and audited for compliance.

The federal arbitrage regulations, discussed earlier, also may influence the SLG's Debt Service Fund investments. Recall that these federal arbitrage regulations generally limit the yield the SLG may earn when investing the proceeds of tax-exempt debt issues—and usually require that any excess be paid (rebated) to the U.S. Treasury. In turn, the U.S. Treasury makes available to SLGs a special type of investment security—known as State and Local Governments (SLUGs)—which yield rates of return that are acceptable under federal arbitrage regulations.

Most SLG Debt Service Fund investments are in certificates of deposit, U.S. Treasury bills, SLUGs, or other high-grade debt securities, though some may be in marketable equity securities. Investments are initially accounted for at cost, including any investment-related fees. Thereafter, investments are accounted for at fair value, as discussed in Chapter 5, unless they are exempt from the provisions of GASB *Statement No. 31*.

## Debt Service Expenditure Recognition

Debt service payments are made routinely for three types of debt-related expenditures: (1) interest on long-term debt outstanding, (2) retirement of debt principal as it matures, and (3) fiscal agent fees charged by a bank or other institution for preparing and processing debt service checks, registering and reregistering bonds, and related services. Assuming a fiscal agent is used, a SLG typically issues only one annual or semiannual check—to its fiscal agent—for all debt service expenditures for each bond issue.

As discussed in detail early in Chapter 6, GLTD debt service expenditures usually are *not* accrued at year end, but are recorded as expenditures when due, that is, when they mature and are due and payable. Several practical and conceptual reasons are the basis for the "when due" recording:

1. Most SLGs budget and appropriate on the basis of how much debt service must be paid during the year directly to bondholders or through fiscal agents. Permitting SLGs to report debt service expenditures when due avoids a potential budgetary basis–GAAP basis difference that otherwise would have to be reported, explained, and reconciled in the financial statements and notes.

2. Few government budgets separate the bond interest—the main potentially accruable debt service component—from the bond principal payments and related fiscal agent fees. Rather, they view the total required payments as the debt service expenditures.

3. Many governments transfer resources from the General Fund or Special Revenue Funds to the Debt Service Fund(s) when debt service payments are due. Thus, to accrue interest expenditures and liabilities in the Debt Service Fund prior to the debt service due date could cause an artificial fund balance deficit to be reported in the Debt Service Fund.

4. Where financial resources are transferred from other funds to the Debt Service Fund, as in 3, payment of the unmatured debt service will not require the use of existing financial resources of the Debt Service Fund. Thus, such amounts are not current liabilities properly recorded as expenditures in the Debt Service Fund. Similarly, where governments levy property taxes sufficient to pay each year's debt service requirements, the debt service payments to be made in the following year do not require the expenditure of existing year-end resources of any governmental fund and, thus, are not current year expenditures and liabilities.

Although most SLGs recognize debt service expenditures on the "when due" approach, recall that the GASB *Codification* provides this option:

> ... if debt service fund resources have been provided during the current year for payment of principal and interest due early in the following year, the [debt service] expenditure and related liability may be recognized [at year end] in the debt service fund and the debt principal amount removed from the GLTDAG.[4]

This option has arisen because some SLGs budget and appropriate in this manner. Note that under this option the entire next debt service payment—not just the interest expenditure accrued at year end—would be recorded as a current year expenditure and liability.

A SLG can combine the "when due" approach and "if due early next year" option by using the former for most issues and using the latter for those issues that meet its criteria. However, each SLG should adopt appropriate debt service expenditure recognition policies and apply them consistently so that 12 months' debt service is reported in each fiscal year.

## DEBT SERVICE FUND FOR A SERIAL BOND ISSUE

To illustrate the operation of a Debt Service Fund for a serial issue assume that A Governmental Unit issued $1,000,000 of 5% Flores Park Serial Bonds on January 1, 19X1, to finance the purchase and development of a park. The bond indenture requires annual payments of $100,000 to retire the principal and additional amounts for annual payments of interest to date. The debt service requirements (principal and interest) are to be financed by a property tax levied for that purpose.

The bond indenture requires that a $150,000 funded and invested reserve for fiscal exigencies be accumulated—$80,000 in 19X1 and $70,000 in 19X2. The purpose of the reserve is to provide added assurance of timely payments to bondholders. The governing body of A Governmental Unit agreed to transfer such amounts from the General Fund to the Flores Park Serial Bonds Debt Service Fund.

[4] Ibid., sec. 1600.123.

The Third State Bank was retained as the bond registrar and paying agent (fiscal agent) for the Flores Park serial bond issue. The 19X1 fiscal agent fee will be $10,000.

The governing body of A Governmental Unit adopted the following budget for the Flores Park Serial Bonds Debt Service Fund for 19X1:

**Estimated Revenues and Transfers In:**

| | |
|---|---:|
| Property taxes . . . . . . . . . . . . . . . . . . . . . . . . . . . . . . . . . . . . . . . . . . . | $162,000 |
| Investment income . . . . . . . . . . . . . . . . . . . . . . . . . . . . . . . . . . . . . . | 6,000 |
| Operating transfer from General Fund . . . . . . . . . . . . . . . . . . . . . . | 80,000 |
| | 248,000 |

**Appropriations:**

| | |
|---|---:|
| Bond principal retirement . . . . . . . . . . . . . . . . . . . . . . . . . . . . . . . | 100,000 |
| Interest on bonds . . . . . . . . . . . . . . . . . . . . . . . . . . . . . . . . . . . . . . . . | 50,000 |
| Fiscal agent fees . . . . . . . . . . . . . . . . . . . . . . . . . . . . . . . . . . . . . . . . . | 10,000 |
| | 160,000 |
| Budgeted increase in fund balance . . . . . . . . . . . . . . . . . . . . . . . . | $ 88,000 |

Furthermore, it ordered that the $80,000 transferred from the General Fund be invested and fully reserved.

## Illustrative Entries

The following journal entries record the 19X1 transactions and events affecting the Flores Park Serial Bonds Debt Service Fund assuming revenues and expenditures subsidiary ledgers and budgetary accounts are used. (The nature of the transactions being recorded and the amounts involved are clear from the journal entry explanations and the recorded amounts; therefore, transaction descriptions are not stated separately before each entry.)

**Entries during 19X1**

| | | | |
|---|---|---:|---:|
| (1) | Estimated Revenues . . . . . . . . . . . . . . . . . . . . . . . . . . . . . . . . . . . | $168,000 | |
| | Estimated Operating Transfer from General Fund . . . . . . . . . | 80,000 | |
| |    Appropriations . . . . . . . . . . . . . . . . . . . . . . . . . . . . . . . . . . . . . | | $160,000 |
| |    Unreserved Fund Balance . . . . . . . . . . . . . . . . . . . . . . . . . . . | | 88,000 |
| | To record 19X1 budget. | | |

Revenues Ledger (Estimated Revenues):

| | |
|---|---:|
| Property Taxes . . . . . . . . . . . . . . . . . . . . . . . . . . . . . . . . . . . . . . . . . . | $162,000 |
| Investment Income . . . . . . . . . . . . . . . . . . . . . . . . . . . . . . . . . . . . . . | 6,000 |
| | $168,000 |

Expenditures Ledger (Appropriations):

| | |
|---|---:|
| Bond Principal Retirement . . . . . . . . . . . . . . . . . . . . . . . . . . . . . | $100,000 |
| Interest on Bonds . . . . . . . . . . . . . . . . . . . . . . . . . . . . . . . . . . . . . . . | 50,000 |
| Fiscal Agent Fees . . . . . . . . . . . . . . . . . . . . . . . . . . . . . . . . . . . . . . . | 10,000 |
| | $160,000 |

| | | | |
|---|---|---:|---:|
| (2) | Cash . . . . . . . . . . . . . . . . . . . . . . . . . . . . . . . . . . . . . . . . . . . . . . . . . . . | $ 80,000 | |
| |    Operating Transfer from General Fund . . . . . . . . . . . . . . . . | | $ 80,000 |
| | To record transfer received. | | |
| (3) | Investments . . . . . . . . . . . . . . . . . . . . . . . . . . . . . . . . . . . . . . . . . . . | $ 80,000 | |
| | Unreserved Fund Balance . . . . . . . . . . . . . . . . . . . . . . . . . . . . . . | 80,000 | |
| |    Cash . . . . . . . . . . . . . . . . . . . . . . . . . . . . . . . . . . . . . . . . . . . . . . . . | | $ 80,000 |
| |    Reserve for Fiscal Exigencies . . . . . . . . . . . . . . . . . . . . . . . . . . | | 80,000 |
| | To record establishing invested reserve as required by bond indenture. | | |

| | | | |
|---|---|---|---|
| (4) | Taxes Receivable—Current .......................... | $165,000 | |
| | Allowance for Uncollectible Current Taxes ............ | | $ 3,000 |
| | Revenues ....................................... | | 162,000 |
| | To record property tax levy of $165,000 (estimated uncollectible taxes are $3,000). | | |
| | Revenues Ledger (Revenues): | | |
| | Property Taxes ................................... | | $162,000 |
| (5) | Cash ........................................... | $158,000 | |
| | Taxes Receivable—Current ........................ | | $158,000 |
| | To record property tax collections. | | |
| (6) | Cash ........................................... | $ 4,000 | |
| | Revenues ....................................... | | $ 4,000 |
| | To record receipt of interest on investments. | | |
| | Revenues Ledger (Revenues): | | |
| | Investment Income ............................... | | $ 4,000 |
| (7) | Expenditures .................................... | $160,000 | |
| | Matured Bonds Payable ........................... | | $100,000 |
| | Matured Interest Payable .......................... | | 50,000 |
| | Fiscal Agent Fees Payable ......................... | | 10,000 |
| | To record liability for first annual serial bond maturity. | | |
| | Expenditures Ledger (Expenditures): | | |
| | Bond Principal Retirement ......................... | $100,000 | |
| | Interest on Bonds ................................. | 50,000 | |
| | Fiscal Agent Fees ................................. | 10,000 | |
| | | $160,000 | |
| (8) | Matured Bonds Payable ............................ | $100,000 | |
| | Matured Interest Payable .......................... | 50,000 | |
| | Fiscal Agent Fees Payable ......................... | 10,000 | |
| | Cash .......................................... | | $160,000 |
| | To record payment of matured debt service liabilities. | | |

Note: Many governments pay the debt service to the paying agent several days before or upon its maturity. Therefore, entries 7 and 8 are often compounded into one expenditures and cash disbursement entry in practice.

| | | | |
|---|---|---|---|
| (9a) | Taxes Receivable—Delinquent ....................... | $ 7,000 | |
| | Allowance for Uncollectible Current Taxes ............. | 3,000 | |
| | Taxes Receivable—Current ........................ | | $ 7,000 |
| | Allowance for Uncollectible Delinquent Taxes ......... | | 3,000 |
| | To reclassify taxes receivable and related allowance accounts from current to delinquent. | | |
| (9b) | Revenues ....................................... | $ 2,000 | |
| | Deferred Property Tax Revenue ..................... | | $ 2,000 |
| | To record deferred revenue for the portion of the current levy not expected to be collected within the first 60 days of the next fiscal year (i.e., not considered available). | | |
| | Revenues Ledger (Revenues): | | |
| | Property Taxes ................................... | | $ 2,000 |
| (10) | Investments ..................................... | $ 300 | |
| | Accrued Interest Receivable ........................ | 2,700 | |
| | Revenues ....................................... | | $ 3,000 |
| | To record net increase in fair value of investments and accrued interest on investments at year end. | | |
| | Revenues Ledger (Revenues): | | |
| | Investment Income ............................... | | $ 3,000 |

**Closing Entries—End of 19X1**

**General Ledger**

| | | | |
|---|---|---|---|
| (C1) | Appropriations .................................... | $160,000 | |
| | Unreserved Fund Balance ........................... | 88,000 | |
| | Estimated Revenues .............................. | | $168,000 |
| | Estimated Operating Transfer from General Fund ...... | | 80,000 |
| | To reverse budgetary entry. | | |
| (C2) | Revenues ....................................... | $167,000 | |
| | Operating Transfer from General Fund ................ | 80,000 | |
| | Expenditures ................................... | | $160,000 |
| | Unreserved Fund Balance ........................ | | 87,000 |
| | To close operating accounts. | | |

**Revenues Subsidiary Ledger**

| | | | |
|---|---|---|---|
| Property Taxes ..................................... | | | $ 2,000 |
| Investment Income ................................. | | $ 1,000 | |

Note that so few operating accounts were needed that this fund could readily have been accounted for entirely in the DSF General Ledger. Use of a series of detailed General Ledger accounts—as illustrated in Chapter 7—would negate the need for the Revenues Subsidiary Ledger and Expenditures Subsidiary Ledger. Both approaches may be found in practice and on the Uniform CPA Examination.

Note also that there were few variances between budget and actual during 19X1. Indeed, the Expenditures Ledger accounts had zero preclosing balances, so no entry was required to close those accounts. Debt Service Fund expenditures usually can be budgeted precisely. Thus, especially where DSFs have little revenue—as when they are financed largely by interfund transfers—budgetary control accounts might not be used in practice in simple DSF situations.

Finally, observe that a single Investment Income account is used in these illustrative entries rather than the separate Interest on Investments and Net Increase (Decrease) in Fair Value of Investments accounts illustrated in Chapter 5. Although the more detailed approach would be preferable in accounting for large interest-bearing security investment portfolios, both methods are acceptable.

## Financial Statements

As for all governmental funds, the annual financial statements required for Debt Service Funds are:

- Balance Sheet
- Statement of Revenues, Expenditures, and Changes in Fund Balance (GAAP operating statement)
- Statement of Revenues, Expenditures, and Changes in Fund Balance—Budget and Actual (budgetary operating statement) if budgeted annually, as is usual with Debt Service Funds.

The balance sheet at the end of 19X1 for the Flores Park Serial Bonds Debt Service Fund is presented in Figure 8–1, and its Statement of Revenues, Expenditures, and Changes in Fund Balance—Budget and Actual (budgetary operating statement) is presented in Figure 8–2. Because the budget is prepared on the GAAP basis in this example, the data in the GAAP operating statement are the same as the actual data in Figure 8–2.

FIGURE 8–1  **Serial Bonds Debt Service Fund Balance Sheet**

A Governmental Unit
Flores Park Serial Bonds Debt Service Fund
**Balance Sheet**
December 31, 19X1

**Assets**

| | | |
|---|---:|---:|
| Cash | | $ 2,000 |
| Taxes receivable—delinquent | $ 7,000 | |
| Less: Allowance for uncollectible delinquent taxes | 3,000 | 4,000 |
| Investments | | 80,300 |
| Accrued interest receivable | | 2,700 |
| | | $89,000 |

**Liabilities and Fund Balance**

| | | |
|---|---:|---:|
| Liabilities: | | |
| Deferred property tax revenue | | $ 2,000 |
| Fund Balance: | | |
| Reserved for exigencies | $80,000 | |
| Unreserved | 7,000 | 87,000 |
| | | $89,000 |

FIGURE 8–2  **Serial Bonds Debt Service Fund Budgetary Operating Statement**

A Governmental Unit
Flores Park Serial Bonds Debt Service Fund
**Statement of Revenues, Expenditures, and
Changes in Fund Balance—Budget and Actual**
For the Year Ended December 31, 19X1

| | Budget | Actual | Variance— Favorable (Unfavorable) |
|---|---:|---:|---:|
| Revenues: | | | |
| Property taxes | $162,000 | $160,000 | ($2,000) |
| Investment income | 6,000 | 7,000 | 1,000 |
| | 168,000 | 167,000 | (1,000) |
| Other Financing Sources: | | | |
| Operating transfer from General Fund | 80,000 | 80,000 | — |
| Total Revenues and Other Financing Sources | 248,000 | 247,000 | (1,000) |
| Expenditures: | | | |
| Bond principal retirement | 100,000 | 100,000 | — |
| Interest on bonds | 50,000 | 50,000 | — |
| Fiscal agent fees | 10,000 | 10,000 | — |
| | 160,000 | 160,000 | — |
| Excess of Revenues and Other Financing Sources Over Expenditures | 88,000 | 87,000 | (1,000) |
| Fund Balance—January 1 | — | — | — |
| Fund Balance—December 31 | $ 88,000 | $ 87,000 | ($1,000) |

Note: Under terms of the bond indenture, $80,000 of the total fund balance is invested and reserved for exigencies.

## SPECIAL ASSESSMENT DEBT SERVICE FUNDS

One unique type of Debt Service Fund, referred to as a Special Assessment Debt Service Fund, is used to account for servicing general long-term debt issued to finance special assessment capital improvement projects. As noted in previous chapters, a special assessment is, in substance, a special property tax that is levied only on properties or property owners benefited by a particular capital project—such as sidewalk construction in a new subdivision. The projects are referred to as special assessment projects because of the underlying financing source—the special assessments.

In the typical special assessment project, the benefited area is made a special assessment district, and the local government serves as the general contractor and financing agent for the project. As the general contractor, the government oversees the project, arranges for the necessary engineering studies, prepares specifications for the project, and so on. As the financing agent, the government:

- Provides interim financing for construction. The government may issue its own bonds or notes or issue special assessment bonds or notes, which it typically guarantees.

- Levies assessments against the properties or property owners benefited upon completion, inspection, and approval of the project. Each property owner is billed for a proportionate share of the project costs but is allowed to pay in installments over a period of years. The government charges interest on the unpaid assessment receivable balances.

- Bills and collects the special assessments and related interest.

- Services the general long-term debt associated with the project using the special assessment collections. If the government is responsible for part of the cost of the project, some general government cash may be transferred to the special assessment Debt Service Fund for this purpose as well.

The primary uniqueness of a special assessment Debt Service Fund is that most of the portion of the receivables that is not yet due and payable is noncurrent. Indeed, the key differences between special assessments and property taxes are that special assessments are (1) for amounts that are payable over several years and (2) levied only on a subset of properties in a government's jurisdiction. Given the similarities, revenue accounting for special assessments follows the same principles as that for property taxes. Revenue is recognized when it is measurable and available; therefore, the long-term special assessments receivable, called special assessments receivable—deferred, are offset by deferred revenues. Additionally, any portion of current or delinquent special assessments receivable that does not meet the revenue recognition criteria will result in additional deferred revenues—and less revenues—being reported.

Debt Service Funds are not used to account for debt service on all special assessment indebtedness. Enterprise-related special assessment indebtedness may be accounted for entirely in the appropriate Enterprise Fund if the government chooses to do so, as discussed in Chapter 12. Also, if the government is not obligated in some manner on special assessment revenue debt:

- The debt is not viewed as debt of the government.

- No Debt Service Fund is used, because the debt is not an obligation of the government.

- An Agency Fund will be used to reflect the government's fiduciary responsibility as the fiscal agent for the special assessment district. This is illustrated in Chapter 10.

In most cases, governments are obligated in some manner for the debt issued to finance special assessment projects for their constituency. Indeed, in describing the intended breadth of this criterion, the GASB notes that:

> . . . the phrase "obligated in some manner" . . . is intended to include all situations other than those in which (a) the government is prohibited (by constitution, charter, statute, ordinance, or contract) from assuming the debt in the event of default by the property owner or (b) the government is not legally liable for assuming the debt and makes no statement, or gives no indication, that it will, or may, honor the debt in the event of default.[5]

Note that when a general government special assessment project is financed with special assessment debt for which the government is not obligated in any manner, the construction costs still are reported in a Capital Projects Fund. This is required because the fixed asset will become the property of the government when completed. The primary difference in the Capital Projects Fund reporting under these circumstances is that the other financing source reported for proceeds from issuance of the special assessment indebtedness is called "Contributions from property owners" rather than "General long-term debt issue proceeds."

## Illustrative Entries

To illustrate the accounting and reporting for a Special Assessment Debt Service Fund, assume that A Governmental Unit financed a general government special assessment capital project by issuing special assessment bonds backed by the full faith and credit of A Governmental Unit. General revenues are to be used for the first principal and interest payment on the special assessment bonds. This covers the portion of the project cost that the government agreed to contribute. The remaining costs are to be recovered through special assessments levied against benefited properties.

The par value of the five-year, 6%, special assessment bonds was $1,000,000 and the bonds were issued at par on July 1, 19X0. Interest and one-fifth of the principal are due each June 30, beginning June 30, 19X1. The project was completed during 19X0 at the budgeted cost of $1,000,000.

The bond proceeds and the construction phase of the project would be accounted for like any other major general government capital project—in a Capital Projects Fund. The fixed assets constructed would be reported in the General Fixed Assets Account Group (Chapter 9) and the bonds payable would be reported in the General Long-Term Debt Account Group (Chapter 9).

The following transactions are used to illustrate the accounting for and reporting of the Special Assessment Debt Service Fund. Assume that the government adopted a project budget for this fund and, therefore, does not need to present budgetary statements each year. Moreover, budgetary entries are omitted to focus on the entries for the actual transactions and events.

1. Special assessments of $800,000 were levied on benefited properties upon completion of the project on **December 31, 19X0.** One-fourth of the levy, along with 7½% interest on the uncollected balance, is due each of the next four years beginning December 31, 19X1.

| | | |
|---|---|---|
| Assessments Receivable—Deferred | $800,000 | |
|     Deferred Revenues—Assessments | | $800,000 |
| To record levy of special assessments. | | |

---
[5] Ibid, sec. 540.116.

Note that the Special Assessment DSF financial statements at December 31, 19X0, would consist only of a balance sheet reporting the accounts and amounts from the preceding entry.

**The following transactions occurred in 19X1.**

**2.** $200,000 of special assessments became current in 19X1.

| | | |
|---|---|---|
| Assessments Receivable—Current .................... | $200,000 | |
| Assessments Receivable—Deferred ................. | | $200,000 |
| To reclassify deferred assessments that are due in 19X1. | | |
| Deferred Revenues—Assessments .................... | $200,000 | |
| Revenues—Assessments .......................... | | $200,000 |
| To recognize assessment revenues for current assessments. | | |

Note that this entry assumes that the $200,000 is available, that is, will be collected by year end or within 60 days thereafter.

**3.** A $260,000 operating transfer is received from the General Fund.

| | | |
|---|---|---|
| Cash ......................................... | $260,000 | |
| Operating Transfer from General Fund .............. | | $260,000 |
| To record receipt of General Fund transfer. | | |

**4.** The principal and interest on the special assessment bonds matured and were paid.

| | | |
|---|---|---|
| Expenditures—Principal Retirement ................... | $200,000 | |
| Expenditures—Interest ............................ | 60,000 | |
| Cash ......................................... | | $260,000 |
| To record payment of debt service. | | |

**5.** Collections of special assessments included $185,000 principal and $55,000 interest.

| | | |
|---|---|---|
| Cash ......................................... | $240,000 | |
| Assessments Receivable—Current ................... | | $185,000 |
| Revenues—Interest .............................. | | 55,000 |
| To record collections during 19X1. | | |

**6.** The uncollected assessments receivable that were due in 19X1 were reclassified as delinquent and the uncollected interest ($5,000) was accrued. It is expected that all amounts except $1,500 of interest will be collected within the first 60 days of 19X2.

| | | |
|---|---|---|
| Assessments Receivable—Delinquent ................. | $15,000 | |
| Accrued Interest Receivable ........................ | 5,000 | |
| Assessments Receivable—Current ................... | | $15,000 |
| Revenues—Interest .............................. | | 3,500 |
| Deferred Revenues—Interest ...................... | | 1,500 |
| To accrue interest receivable and reclassify assessment receivables. | | |

**7.** The accounts were closed.

| | | |
|---|---|---|
| Revenues—Assessments ........................... | $200,000 | |
| Revenues—Interest .............................. | 58,500 | |
| Operating Transfer from General Fund ................ | 260,000 | |
| Expenditures—Principal Retirement ................. | | $200,000 |
| Expenditures—Interest ........................... | | 60,000 |
| Unreserved Fund Balance ......................... | | 258,500 |
| To close the accounts at the end of 19X1. | | |

## Financial Statements

The balance sheet for the Special Assessment Bonds Debt Service Fund of A Governmental Unit at the end of 19X1 is presented in Figure 8–3. The 19X1 Statement of Revenues, Expenditures, and Changes in Fund Balance is presented in Figure 8–4. The balance sheet continues to be quite simple as in the serial bond example, though it is complicated somewhat by the reporting of the special assessments receivable and deferred revenues. Note that only the assessments that meet the property tax revenue recognition criteria are reported in the operating statement.

**FIGURE 8–3  Special Assessment Debt Service Fund Balance Sheet**

A Governmental Unit
Special Assessment Bonds Debt Service Fund
**Balance Sheet**
December 31, 19X1

**Assets**

| | |
|---|---:|
| Cash | $240,000 |
| Special assessments receivable—deferred | 600,000 |
| Special assessments receivable—delinquent | 15,000 |
| Interest receivable on assessments | 5,000 |
| Total assets | $860,000 |

**Liabilities and Fund Balance**

| | |
|---|---:|
| Liabilities: | |
| Deferred assessment revenues | $600,000 |
| Deferred interest revenues | 1,500 |
| Total liabilities | 601,500 |
| Unreserved fund balance | 258,500 |
| Total liabilities and fund balance | $860,000 |

**FIGURE 8–4  Special Assessment Debt Service Fund Operating Statement**

A Governmental Unit
Special Assessment Bonds Debt Service Fund
**Statement of Revenues, Expenditures, and Changes in Fund Balance**
For the Year Ended December 31, 19X1

| | | |
|---|---:|---:|
| Revenues: | | |
| Special assessments | $200,000 | |
| Interest | 58,500 | $258,500 |
| Other Financing Sources: | | |
| Operating transfer from General Fund | | 260,000 |
| Total Revenues and Other Financing Sources | | 518,500 |
| Expenditures: | | |
| Principal retirement | $200,000 | |
| Interest | 60,000 | 260,000 |
| Excess of Revenues and Other Financing Sources over Expenditures | | 258,500 |
| Fund Balance—January 1 | | — |
| Fund Balance—December 31 | | $258,500 |

# OTHER CONVENTIONAL DSF CONSIDERATIONS

Several other accounting and reporting considerations should be noted or reviewed briefly at this point. These include (1) nonaccrual of interest payable, (2) the combining DSF balance sheet, (3) the combining DSF operating statement, (4) use of a single DSF for several bond issues, and (5) pooling of DSF investments.

## Nonaccrual of Interest Payable

Recall that the GASB *Codification* does not permit—much less require—accrual of the year-end balances of interest payable on conventional bonds or other general long-term debt unless (1) the resources to pay the interest have been accrued or received in the Debt Service Fund and (2) the debt service payment is due early in the next year. If a fund is on a calendar year basis and the annual interest on its bonds was paid as scheduled on October 31, 19X1, the government clearly would be obligated, as of December 31, 19X1, for the interest for the last two months of 19X1. On the other hand, the 19X1 tax levy and budget typically would provide for the payment of the interest expenditure falling due in the current year, and the following year's tax levy and budget would provide for payment of interest due in 19X2. Because the resources that will be used to pay the interest for the months of November and December 19X1 cannot be accrued as of December 31, 19X1, accruing that interest expenditure and liability could result in (1) an unwarranted deficit being reported in serial bond Debt Service Funds and (2) an unwarranted fund balance deficiency being reported in term bond Debt Service Funds. Thus, interest payable at year end normally is not recorded in Debt Service Funds.

On the other hand, if Debt Service Fund taxes or other financial resources have been made available at the end of 19X1 to pay debt interest and/or principal maturing early in 19X2, the expenditure and related liability may be recorded in the Debt Service Fund in 19X1. In this case the amount of the debt principal that is recorded as a Debt Service Fund expenditure and liability should be removed from the General Long-Term Debt accounts.

## Combining Balance Sheet

Separate balance sheets are prepared for each of the Debt Service Funds of A Governmental Unit, as in Figures 8–1 and 8–3, and may be sent to bond trustees. But if there are two or more funds, they are presented in a combining balance sheet, as shown in Figure 8–5, and the total data are presented in the SLG's combined balance sheet.

Debt Service Fund balance sheets might include such additional assets as Cash with Fiscal Agents, Taxes Receivable—Current, Tax Liens Receivable, and Interest and Penalties Receivable on Taxes. In addition, the unamortized premiums and discounts on investments not reported at fair value may be presented separately in the combining balance sheet rather than showing the investment figure at net amortized cost. Similarly, there may be such liability accounts as Matured Bonds Payable and Matured Interest Payable.

If a government has more than seven or eight Debt Service Funds, the format of Figure 8–5 becomes unwieldy. One option in such cases is to present a combining Debt Service Funds balance sheet with a column for each major Debt Service Fund and an "Other Debt Service Funds" column presenting the combined data for the other Debt Service Funds. This should be accompanied by a combining balance

FIGURE 8–5  **Debt Service Funds Combining Balance Sheet**

A Governmental Unit
Debt Service Funds
**Combining Balance Sheet**
December 31, 19X1

| | Flores Park Serial Bonds | Special Assessment Bonds | Total |
|---|---:|---:|---:|
| **Assets** | | | |
| Cash .......................................... | $ 2,000 | $240,000 | $242,000 |
| Special assessments receivable—deferred .......... | — | 600,000 | 600,000 |
| Special assessments receivable—delinquent ........ | — | 15,000 | 15,000 |
| Taxes receivable—delinquent | | | |
| (net of estimated uncollectible taxes) ........... | 4,000 | — | 4,000 |
| Investments .................................. | 80,300 | — | 80,300 |
| Interest receivable on investments .............. | 2,700 | — | 2,700 |
| Interest receivable on assessments .............. | — | 5,000 | 5,000 |
| Total assets ............................. | $89,000 | $860,000 | $949,000 |
| **Liabilities and Fund Balances** | | | |
| Liabilities: | | | |
| Deferred property tax revenues .............. | $ 2,000 | $    — | $  2,000 |
| Deferred assessment revenues ................ | — | 600,000 | 600,000 |
| Deferred interest revenues .................. | — | 1,500 | 1,500 |
| Total liabilities .......................... | 2,000 | 601,500 | 603,500 |
| Fund Balances: | | | |
| Reserved for exigencies ..................... | 80,000 | — | 80,000 |
| Unreserved .............................. | 7,000 | 258,500 | 265,500 |
| Total fund balances ....................... | 87,000 | 258,500 | 345,500 |
| Total liabilities and fund balances ........... | $89,000 | $860,000 | $949,000 |

sheet (or schedule) for the other Debt Service Funds, the total of which agrees with the "Other Debt Service Funds" column of the main combining balance sheet.

## Combining Operating Statement

A Combining Statement of Revenues, Expenditures, and Changes in Fund Balances for the Debt Service Funds of A Governmental Unit is presented in Figure 8–6. Combining budgetary comparison statements also are presented by governments with two or more Debt Service Funds.

Additional revenue accounts that might appear in the statement include Interest and Penalties on Property Taxes; Revenue from Other Agencies, such as shared taxes from higher governments; and Gains or Losses on Disposition of Investments not reported at fair value. Also, additional operating transfers and residual equity transfers may have increased the fund balance during the period.

## Single Debt Service Fund for Several Bond Issues

As a general rule, the number of Debt Service Funds should be held to a minimum. The law or contractual requirements may in some cases require a separate Debt Service Fund for each bond issue; in other cases they permit a single Debt Service Fund to service several or all issues.

**FIGURE 8–6 Debt Service Funds Combining Operating Statement**

A Governmental Unit
Debt Service Funds
**Combining Statement of Revenues, Expenditures, and Changes in Fund Balances**
For the Year Ended December 31, 19X1

|  | Flores Park Serial Bonds | Special Assessment Bonds | Total |
|---|---|---|---|
| Revenues: |  |  |  |
| Property taxes | $160,000 | $ — | $160,000 |
| Special assessments | — | 200,000 | 200,000 |
| Investment income | 7,000 | — | 7,000 |
| Interest on assessments | — | 58,500 | 58,500 |
|  | 167,000 | 258,500 | 425,500 |
| Other Financing Sources: |  |  |  |
| Operating transfer from General Fund | 80,000 | 260,000 | 340,000 |
| Total Revenues and Other Financing Sources | 247,000 | 518,500 | 765,500 |
| Expenditures: |  |  |  |
| Bond principal retirement | 100,000 | 200,000 | 300,000 |
| Interest on bonds | 50,000 | 60,000 | 110,000 |
| Fiscal agent fees | 10,000 | — | 10,000 |
|  | 160,000 | 260,000 | 420,000 |
| Excess of Revenues and Other Financing Sources Over Expenditures | 87,000 | 258,500 | 345,500 |
| Fund Balances—January 1 | — | — | — |
| Fund Balances—December 31 | $ 87,000 | $258,500 | $345,500 |

A single Debt Service Fund is particularly desirable for all debt issues financed from the general property tax. The budget for the single Debt Service Fund is prepared by analyzing the debt service requirements for each bond issue, and the Estimated Transfers In, Estimated Revenues, and Appropriations accounts are recorded in total. Revenues and transfers in are not allocated to specific issues in such cases, nor are assets and liabilities segregated by bond issue, though fund balances may be. Indeed, some SLGs prefer to account for single DSFs on a "funds within a fund" approach that distinguishes all DSF transactions and balances by bond issue.

## Pooling of Investments

Even though the law, contractual agreements, or administrative judgment may require several Debt Service Funds, it may be feasible to pool the investments of the Debt Service Funds to achieve maximum efficiency and safety in the investment program. For example, a single investment counsel may be able to serve more effectively for a major investment than for several minor ones. More important, the investments may be diversified when a substantial sum is involved and economies of purchase may result from investing large sums rather than small ones.

Also, higher yields may be earned and less of the total assets of all of the funds may need to be kept in cash (nonearning) if the investable assets of the Debt Service Funds are pooled. In such cases well-defined rules for determining the equity of each Debt Service Fund in the assets and in the profits and losses from investments must be established and detailed records must be maintained.

Recall that the GASB *Codification* (sec. 1300.109) provides for practices such as pooling of investments—assuming they are permitted by a government's legal and contractual provisions—by stating that the GAAP requirement for a complete set of accounts for each fund refers to identification of accounts in the accounting records—and does not necessarily require physical segregation of assets. However, that *Codification* statement presumes that a sound accounting system is in place—which is a prerequisite both to "funds within a fund" accounting (discussed earlier) and pooling of investments.

## DEBT SERVICE FUNDS FOR DEEP DISCOUNT ISSUES

Although most state and local government bond and note issues are conventional serial or term issues, some recent issues are nonconventional deep discount bonds and notes. The pure deep discount issue—the zero coupon bond—has a 0% stated interest rate and provides that neither interest nor principal will be paid during the term the bond issue is outstanding. Rather, both the principal and accumulated effective interest, compounded at the effective rate for the life of the bonds—typically ranging from 10 to 25 years—are paid in a lump-sum payment of the par (face) amount upon maturity of the zero coupon bonds. Thus, zero coupon bonds are like term bonds except that the total compound interest for the term of the bond—as well as the principal—is included in the single balloon payment of the par (face) amount upon maturity of the bonds 10 to 25 years or more after issuance.

A variation of the pure zero coupon deep discount bond, the low-interest bond, may bear an interest rate of 1% to 2% when the market rate—the effective interest rate—is 6% to 8%.

Both zero coupon bonds and low-interest bonds and notes are discounted from issuance until maturity at the effective interest rate by investors, so their issue proceeds are only a fraction of their par or face value. The discount from par (face) thus represents the interest (or additional interest) on the bonds that will not be paid until their maturity.

Deep discount bonds and notes are generally defined as those issued with a stated (or face) interest rate less than 75% of the effective interest rate. Such deep discount debt issued as general long-term debt presents debt service accounting problems because either (1) current liabilities are not incurred until the maturity of the debt or (2) the current liabilities incurred on low-interest debt are not a reasonable measure of the interest cost of such debt issues.

The GASB *Codification* does not contain guidance on accounting for and reporting these relatively new, nonconventional deep discount bond and note issues. Thus, most governments with deep discount debt appear to recognize debt service expenditures and liabilities on such debt—for both interest and principal retirement—on the "when due" or "due early next year" approaches discussed and illustrated earlier for conventional interest-bearing (at market rates) bonds and notes. The result is that most or all of the interest expenditures—as well as the principal retirement expenditures—are reported in the year the deep discount debt matures, perhaps 15 to 25 years after issuance of the debt instrument.

Although such practices are consistent with the current GASB standards—and most governments with deep discount debt make extensive disclosures—the propriety of lumping all or most interest expenditures, in particular, in the year of debt maturity is questionable. Accordingly, the GASB plans to specify a method of accounting for deep discount general long-term debt.

# DEBT SERVICE FUND FOR A TERM BOND ISSUE

Although most recent bond issues have been serial issues, term and deep discount debt issues may be found occasionally in practice. Term bond issues differ from serial issues in that, whereas some serial bond principal matures each year (or most years)—and, thus, some serial bond principal is paid each year, together with interest on the remaining outstanding principal balance—the entire principal of a term bond issue matures at the end of the bond issue term, say, 20 years. Thus, in term bond issues (1) interest is paid on the entire principal (par or face) balance throughout the life of the issue, and (2) all of the principal is paid at the end of the bond issue term. In deep discount debt issues, most or all of the interest—as well as the principal—is paid at the end of the debt issue term.

To ensure timely payment of term bond interest and principal (at maturity), most term bond issue indentures require the issuing government to establish a Debt Service Fund that provides for:

1. Accumulation of any required funded reserves.
2. Payment of interest (and fiscal agent charges) during each year the term bonds are outstanding.
3. Systematic accumulation of a sinking fund (savings subfund) within the Debt Service Fund that will be sufficient to retire the term bond principal upon its maturity at the end of the bond issue term.

Because of the sinking fund (subfund) provision, term Debt Service Funds are often referred to as sinking funds. Deep discount debt DSFs are similar except that most or all interest (2 above) must be accumulated like principal requirements (3 above).

The sinking fund assets and funded reserves may be held and invested by the issuing government or by a trustee for the bondholders, depending on terms of the bond issue indenture. In either event, the sinking fund requirements must be computed at the origination of the issue and the term Debt Service Fund must be maintained in compliance with the bond indenture provisions throughout the life of the issue.

# SINKING FUND REQUIREMENTS

As noted earlier, term bonds ordinarily are repaid from a debt service sinking (savings) fund in which resources are accumulated over the life of the bonds by means of annual additions to the fund and by earnings of the fund assets. A schedule of sinking fund requirements (Figure 8–7) has been prepared for the city hall bonds of A Governmental Unit. These are 9%, 20-year term bonds, $1,000,000 par, issued January 1, 19X0, to be repaid out of the first revenues accruing to the treasury. Recall that the latter terminology indicates that the source of financing for the Debt Service Fund for these bonds is the General Fund of A Governmental Unit.

The first payment to the sinking fund is scheduled for the end of year 1 (19X0). A similar payment will be made at the end of each succeeding year until, when the twentieth payment has been made, fund resources should total $1,000,000—the amount required to pay the term bond principal upon its maturity.

An estimated earnings rate of 10% has been used in developing Figure 8–7. The amount of the required annual additions was determined by selecting from a table the amount of an ordinary annuity of $1 per period at 10% for 20 periods. As

**FIGURE 8–7  Schedule of Sinking Fund Requirements**

Schedule of Sinking Fund Requirements
$1 Million 20-Year Term Bond Issue
(Assuming an Annual Earnings Rate of 10%)

| Year | *(1)* Required Annual Additions | *(2)* Required Fund Earnings (4PY) × 10% | *(3)* Required Fund Increases (1) + (2) | *(4)* Required Fund Balances (3) + (4PY) |
|---|---|---|---|---|
| 1 (19X0) | $ 17,460 | | $    17,460 | $    17,460 |
| 2 (19X1) | 17,460 | $   1,746 | 19,206 | 36,666 |
| 3 (19X2) | 17,460 | 3,667 | 21,127 | 57,793 |
| 4 (19X3) | 17,460 | 5,779 | 23,239 | 81,032 |
| 5 (19X4) | 17,460 | 8,103 | 25,563 | 106,595 |
| 6 (19X5) | 17,460 | 10,660 | 28,120 | 134,715 |
| 7 (19X6) | 17,460 | 13,472 | 30,932 | 165,647 |
| 8 (19X7) | 17,460 | 16,565 | 34,025 | 199,672 |
| 9 (19X8) | 17,460 | 19,967 | 37,427 | 237,099 |
| 10 (19X9) | 17,460 | 23,710 | 41,170 | 278,269 |
| 11 (19Y0) | 17,460 | 27,827 | 45,287 | 323,556 |
| 12 (19Y1) | 17,460 | 32,356 | 49,816 | 373,372 |
| 13 (19Y2) | 17,460 | 37,337 | 54,797 | 428,169 |
| 14 (19Y3) | 17,460 | 42,817 | 60,277 | 488,446 |
| 15 (19Y4) | 17,460 | 48,845 | 66,305 | 554,751 |
| 16 (19Y5) | 17,460 | 55,475 | 72,935 | 627,686 |
| 17 (19Y6) | 17,460 | 62,769 | 80,229 | 707,915 |
| 18 (19Y7) | 17,460 | 70,792 | 88,252 | 796,167 |
| 19 (19Y8) | 17,460 | 79,617 | 97,077 | 893,244 |
| 20 (19Y9) | 17,432* | 89,324 | 106,756 | 1,000,000 |
| | $349,172 | $650,828 | $1,000,000 | |

\* The last year's addition needs to be only $17,432 because of rounding errors.
PY = Prior year end required fund balance.

indicated in the schedule, the last addition is somewhat less than the preceding ones because of rounding errors. In any event, the final payment in 19Y9 will be in the amount that brings the sinking fund resources to the $1,000,000 required to retire the term bonds.

The schedule of sinking fund requirements provides the amounts of the budgetary requirements for the Debt Service Fund for the duration of the fund, provided the accumulation process proceeds as planned or departs from the plan by immaterial amounts. The required fund balance at the end of each year (Figure 8–7) provides a standard against which the actual accumulation may be compared—and may be a required minimum amount under terms of the bond indenture.

The primary uniqueness in reporting term debt service funds is the need to report a fund balance reserve equal to the accumulated net assets at the end of each fiscal year that are required by the bond indenture. Failure to maintain the required fund balance may violate the bond issue covenants and—if not waived (permitted) by the bond trustee—could cause the bond issue to be in default and the entire principal balance to become due immediately. Thus, compliance with bond indenture provisions must be monitored closely by internal managers and auditors and examined by external auditors.

# REFUNDINGS

The term and serial Debt Service Fund examples presented earlier in the chapter are based on the usual assumptions of conventional Debt Service Funds, that during the life of the debt issue (1) financial resources are accumulated in DSFs from non-GLTD sources—such as property taxes, special assessments, interest earned on investments, and interfund transfers; (2) DSF financial resources are expended to pay GLTD principal and interest at their scheduled maturities; and (3) the payments or accruals of GLTD principal and interest from non-GLTD financial resources as they mature are reported in accounts such as Expenditures—Bond Principal Retirement, to reflect the extinguishment of the GLTD principal, and Expenditures—Interest on Bonds, respectively.

But governments may issue new GLTD to pay (or service) old GLTD prior to its maturity—thus effectively substituting the new GLTD issue for the old GLTD issue. Accordingly, such transactions—known as advance refundings—are accounted for as substitutions of GLTD rather than as extinguishments of GLTD.

## Reasons for Refundings

State and local governments may issue new debt to refund old debt for a variety of reasons, including:

1. **Lower effective interest rates.** The SLG may be able to issue new bonds or notes at interest rates sufficiently lower than those being paid on the old bonds or notes that—even after paying the related refunding costs—it obtains lower net effective interest rates (and costs) and, thus, has an economic gain as a result of the advance refunding.

2. **Extend maturity dates.** Where old debt principal matures soon, perhaps without adequate financial resources having been accumulated, the SLG may effectively extend the maturity date of the old debt by a refunding.

3. **Revise payment schedules.** If the total debt service requirements—including both interest and principal—of the old debt are not relatively stable for each future year, the SLG may effectively rearrange its debt service payment schedule by an advance refunding.

4. **Remove or modify restrictions.** Onerous restrictions of old debt indentures, covenants, or other agreements—such as those requiring large funded reserves or specifying that no (or limited) new debt may be incurred while the old debt is outstanding—may be removed or modified by issuing new advance refunding debt with different indenture provisions.

In sum, certain refundings are undertaken to obtain an economic advantage—such as lower net effective interest rates and interest costs—but other refundings are designed to obtain noneconomic advantages such as to extend maturity dates, revise debt service payment schedules, and remove or modify debt-related restrictions.

## Refundings Defined

The GASB states that:

> **Refundings** involve the issuance of new debt whose proceeds are used to repay previously issued ("old") debt. The new debt proceeds may be used to repay the old debt immediately (a *current refunding*); or the new debt proceeds may be placed with an escrow agent and invested until they are used to pay principal and interest on an old debt at a future time (an *advance refunding*).[6]

Both types of refundings are illustrated in Figure 8–8.

------

[6] Ibid., sec. D20.102. (Emphasis added.)

FIGURE 8–8 **Debt Refundings**

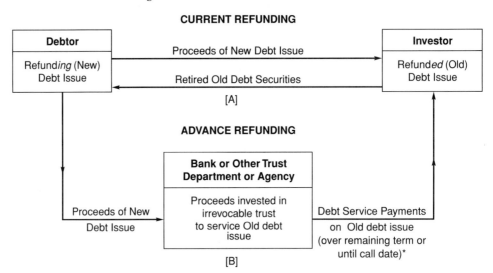

**CURRENT REFUNDING**

| Debtor | | Investor |
|---|---|---|
| Refund*ing* (New) Debt Issue | Proceeds of New Debt Issue → Retired Old Debt Securities ← | Refund*ed* (Old) Debt Issue |

[A]

**ADVANCE REFUNDING**

**Bank or Other Trust Department or Agency**

Proceeds of New Debt Issue

Proceeds invested in irrevocable trust to service Old debt issue

Debt Service Payments on Old debt issue (over remaining term or until call date)*

[B]

*Debt securities are eventually retired and returned to the debtor.

In some advance refundings, the SLG uses the proceeds of the new GLTD issue to retire the old GLTD issue directly within a few weeks or months. This may occur, for example, when the new GLTD is issued to refund an old term bond or deep discount note that matures soon but for which adequate resources have not been accumulated in a DSF sinking fund. These refundings are similar to current refundings—which are accounted for as new debt issuances and old debt retirements—as illustrated in Figure 8–8[A].

Advance refundings (Figure 8–8[B]) do not result in immediate, direct retirement of the old GLTD issue, however. Rather, in advance refunding transactions (1) the proceeds of the new GLTD issue are placed in escrow—in an irrevocable trust—with a bank or other financial institution trust department for the benefit of the old GLTD investors-creditors; (2) the proceeds are invested in appropriate securities that are acceptable under the terms of the old GLTD issue indenture, covenant, or other agreement and in compliance with applicable federal arbitrage and other regulations; and (3) the invested proceeds and related earnings are used to pay interest and principal on the old debt—which remains outstanding—at the regularly scheduled maturities or, if the old debt is called for early redemption, until (and at) the call date.

## Defeasance of Old Debt

The term *defeased* means "terminated" or "rendered null and void." Debt that has been defeased is considered to be extinguished and is removed from the GLTD accounts and is not reported in the SLG's balance sheet.

In conventional serial and term Debt Service Funds, the debt is defeased by being paid off directly at its scheduled maturity. An expenditure account such as Expenditures—Debt Principal Retirement is recorded in the DSF, the liability is removed from the GLTDAG accounts, the debt instrument is marked "paid" and canceled, and the debt is no longer reported in the balance sheet.

But in advance refundings it may not be possible or advantageous to actually pay off the old debt with the proceeds of the new substitute debt. Instead, the old debt may remain outstanding for much or all of its originally scheduled life and be serviced by the resources of an irrevocable trust financed (entirely or partly) by the proceeds of the new refunding debt issue. In such cases the old debt is considered to be extinguished—and is removed from the GLTDAG accounts and the SLG's balance sheet—if it is either legally defeased or is defeased in substance.

### Legal Defeasance

In law, a debt may be considered defeased—terminated and rendered null and void—by being legally defeased when the debtor fulfills the defeasance provisions of the debt indenture or other agreement. Defeasance provisions of bond indentures may specify, for example, that if a sufficient sum is placed in an irrevocable trust with a specified trustee and invested for the benefit of the bondholders, the debt will be considered to have been paid—that is, legally defeased.

### In-Substance Defeasance

All bond and note agreements do not contain defeasance provisions, however. Indeed, many agreements are silent; that is, they do not contain provisions that either permit or prohibit defeasance. The GASB has established highly restrictive and specific standards for in-substance defeasance.[7] If the conditions of these in-substance defeasance standards are met in an advance refunding or otherwise, the old debt is considered to be defeased in substance—for accounting and financial reporting purposes—even though a legal defeasance has not occurred. Accordingly, the old debt is removed from the GLTDAG accounts and from the SLG's balance sheet as in a legal defeasance.

### Nondefeasance

Most advance refundings are carefully planned and conducted to result in either legal defeasance or in-substance defeasance of the old debt. However, in the event the old debt is not defeased legally or in substance, (1) both the old debt and the new debt must be recorded in the GLTDAG and reported as liabilities in the SLG's balance sheet, and (2) amounts deposited in escrow (trust) are reported as investments in a Debt Service Fund.

## DEBT SERVICE FUNDS FOR REFUNDINGS

Debt Service Funds for refundings that result in retirement or defeasance of the old debt are usually simple and short-lived. Indeed, they may involve only two transaction entries—one for the receipt of the refunding bond proceeds and another for the payment to the escrow trustee—and, after a closing entry, be terminated.

The accounting for refunding DSFs differs from that for conventional serial and term DSFs also in that the defeasance of the old debt is not considered an extinguishment but a substitution of the new debt for the old debt. Thus, whereas the payment of bond principal in a conventional serial or term DSF is recorded as Expenditures—Bond Principal Retirement, the defeasance of the old debt in a refunding is recorded as a nonexpenditure Other Financing Use, rather than as an expenditure, to the extent the defeasance is financed by issuance of new refunding

---

[7] Ibid., sec. D20.

debt. In other words, debt principal retirement or defeasance is accounted for as an expenditure only if it is financed by non-GLTD financial resources. Debt principal retirement or defeasance that financed by issuing new GLTD is accounted for as an Other Financing Use to signal that new debt has been substituted for old debt.

Three types of refunding transactions are discussed and illustrated in this section. These transactions involve (1) retirement of the old issue (current refunding), (2) legal or in-substance defeasance of the old issue (advance refunding), and (3) use of both existing financial resources and new debt proceeds to effect an advance refunding.

## Current Refunding—Retirement of Old Debt

A government may not have accumulated sufficient sinking fund resources to retire a term bond upon its impending maturity. Thus, it may issue new current refunding bonds (or notes) to pay the maturing term bond principal—effectively refinancing the term bond to extend its debt service over the life of the new refunding issue.

To illustrate, assume that a $2,000,000 term bond issue will mature soon. Assume also that the SLG has already paid the $55,000 interest due upon maturity of the term bonds, and will refund the principal of the term bonds by issuing $2,000,000 of refunding bonds. Assuming the new refunding bonds are issued at 101, bond issue costs of $15,000 are withheld by the bond underwriter, and the old term bonds are retired at par before or upon maturity, the DSF General Ledger entries for these current refunding transactions are:

**Issuance of Refunding Bonds:**

| | | |
|---|---|---|
| Cash . . . . . . . . . . . . . . . . . . . . . . . . . . . . . . . . . . . . . . . . . . . . . . . . . . . . . . | $2,005,000 | |
| Expenditures—Bond Issue Costs . . . . . . . . . . . . . . . . . . . . . . . . . . . | 15,000 | |
|    Other Financing Source—Proceeds of Refunding Bonds . . . . . . | | $2,020,000 |

To record issuance of advance refunding bonds.

Calculations:

| | | |
|---|---|---|
| (1) | Gross refunding bond proceeds | |
| |   $2,000,000 × 1.01 = . . . . . . . . . . . . . . . . . . . . . . | $2,020,000 |
| (2) | Bond issue costs . . . . . . . . . . . . . . . . . . . . . . . . | 15,000 |
| (3) | Net refunding bond proceeds . . . . . . . . . . . . . . | $2,005,000 |

**Retirement of Old Bonds:**

| | | |
|---|---|---|
| Other Financing Use—Retirement of Refunded Term Bonds . . . . | $2,000,000 | |
|   Cash . . . . . . . . . . . . . . . . . . . . . . . . . . . . . . . . . . . . . . . . . . . . . . . . . | | $2,000,000 |

To record payment of term bond principal before or upon its maturity.

Note in this entry that the bond issue costs are reported as an expenditure rather than netted from the gross bond issue proceeds. This is the usual practice, though issue costs may be netted and the proceeds of refunding bonds reported at $2,005,000.

Note also that no revenue, expenditure, gain, or loss is recorded in accounting for this current refunding. This is consistent both with the funds flow DSF accounting model and the substitution of the new debt for the old debt. The DSF Statement of Revenues, Expenditures, and Changes in Fund Balance reports these refunding transactions as affecting other financing sources and uses of DSF financial resources rather than as revenues, expenditures, gains, and/or losses from refunding.

The old term bond debt will be removed from the GLTDAG accounts, of course, and the new refunding debt will be recorded in the GLTDAG accounts. Then, when the $5,000 remaining fund balance has been disposed of—probably by transfer to the DSF for the new debt—the final closing entry will be made and the term bond principal refunding DSF will be terminated.

## Advance Refunding—Legal and In-Substance Defeasance of Old Debt

To illustrate DSF accounting for the legal and in-substance defeasance of an old debt, assume the same facts as noted earlier except:

1. The new advance refunding bonds ($2,000,000) were issued at a discount of $85,000, and $15,000 of bond issuance costs were withheld by the bond underwriter.

2. The old term bonds mature several years hence and the amount necessary to be invested at this time to service them, $1,900,000, was placed in an escrow trust that was properly invested in accordance with the bond indenture defeasance provisions or the GASB's in-substance defeasance standards.

The DSF entries to record this legal or in-substance defeasance are:

**Issuance of Refunding Bonds:**

| | | |
|---|---|---|
| Cash | $1,900,000 | |
| Expenditures—Bond Issue Costs | 15,000 | |
|    Other Financing Source—Proceeds of Refunding Bonds | | $1,915,000 |

To record issuance of advance refunding bonds.

Calculations:

| | | |
|---|---|---|
| (1) | Refunding bond proceeds $2,000,000 at par less discount of $85,000 | $1,915,000 |
| (2) | Bond issue costs | 15,000 |
| (3) | Net refunding bond proceeds | $1,900,000 |

**Defeasance of Old Bonds:**

| | | |
|---|---|---|
| Other Financing Use—Payment to Refunded Bond | | |
|    Escrow Agent | $1,900,000 | |
|    Cash | | $1,900,000 |

To record payment to escrow agent to defease old bonds.

Note that the first entry is essentially the same in all cases. The second entry differs from that for a direct retirement, however, in that the amount expended to defease the debt is distinctly reported as an Other Financing Use—Payment to Refunded Bond Escrow Agent. The amount paid to the escrow trustee being less than the par (face) of the old bonds indicates that the amount paid can be invested at an interest rate higher than the rate the SLG is paying on the old defeased issue. However, U.S. government arbitrage regulations limit the amount of arbitrage permissible in advance refunding investment portfolios.

    The legal or in-substance defeasance of an old debt is considered to be a settlement that terminates the old debt. Thus, the old debt is removed from the GLTDAG accounts and the new refunding debt is recorded in the GLTDAG accounts. Furthermore, neither the assets nor the operations of the escrow trustee's investment portfolio are reported in the SLG's financial statements.

## Use of Both Existing Resources and New Debt Proceeds in Refundings

As a final example, assume the same facts as the legal or in-substance defeasance example except:

1. The SLG has $600,000 of net assets in an existing DSF for the old debt; and

2. The remaining $1,300,000 ($1,900,000 – $600,000) will be financed by (a) a $300,000 transfer to the DSF from the General Fund, and (b) a $1,000,000 advance refunding bond issue that is sold to net par (face) after issuance costs.

The advance refunding DSF entries in this situation are:

**Transfer and Refunding Bond Issuance:**

Cash . . . . . . . . . . . . . . . . . . . . . . . . . . . . . . . . . . . . . . . . . . . . . . . $1,300,000

    Other Financing Source—Operating Transfer from
        General Fund . . . . . . . . . . . . . . . . . . . . . . . . . . . . . . . . . . . . . .     $ 300,000

    Other Financing Source—Proceeds of Refunding Bonds . . . . . .     1,000,000

To record interfund transfer and issuance of refunding bonds.

**Defeasance of Old Bonds:**

Expenditures—Payment to Refunded Bond Escrow Agent . . . . . .  $ 900,000

Other Financing Use—Payment to Refunded Bond
        Escrow Agent . . . . . . . . . . . . . . . . . . . . . . . . . . . . . . . . . . .   1,000,000

    Cash . . . . . . . . . . . . . . . . . . . . . . . . . . . . . . . . . . . . . . . . . . . . . .     $1,900,000

To record payment to escrow agent to defease bonds.

The key point here is that payments from existing financial resources—to retire bonds directly or to an escrow agent—are accounted for as expenditures, whereas such payments from refunding debt issue proceeds are accounted for as other financing uses rather than as expenditures. This applies to both current and advance refundings.

    Like the DSFs illustrated earlier, this fund is short-lived. Because its function is accomplished and the fund has no remaining balance, the DSF accounts will now be closed and the fund terminated.

## Financial Statement Presentation of Refundings

The substitution aspect underlying the typical treatment of general government refunding transactions is reflected well in DSF operating statements. Indeed, note the equal amounts of advance refunding debt proceeds and other financing uses reported in the Streets and Highways DSF in the city of Phoenix Combining Statement of Revenues, Expenditures, and Changes in Fund Balances for its DSFs (Figure 8–9). Also note the types of DSFs reported, the statement content and format, and the details presented in Figure 8–9 and in Figure 8–10, the city of Garden Grove DSF Combining Statement of Revenues, Expenditures, and Changes in Fund Balances.

## Advance Refunding Disclosures

The GASB requires SLGs to make certain disclosures about their advance refundings in the notes to their financial statements. Most of these disclosures are made only in the year the advance refunding occurs, but one must be made each year as long as any old in-substance defeased debt remains outstanding.

    The major GASB advance refunding disclosure requirements are:

**I. In the Year of the Advance Refunding**

    **A. General Description.** The advance refunding transaction(s) should be described generally—for example, which debt issues were advance refunded, what par (face) amounts were refunded, how the advance refundings were financed (e.g., refunding bonds, some existing resources), which defeasances were legal defeasances and which were in-substance defeasance transactions, and the name of the bank or other institution that serves as the escrow agent trustee.

    **B. Difference in Debt Service Requirements.** SLGs should disclose the difference between (1) the total of the remaining debt service requirements of the old defeased issue and (2) the total debt service requirements of the new

**FIGURE 8–9  Combining Statement of Revenues, Expenditures, and Changes in Fund Balances—Debt Service Funds—City of Phoenix**

**CITY OF PHOENIX, ARIZONA**
**Debt Service Funds**
**Combining Statement of Revenues, Expenditures,**
**and Changes in Fund Balances**
**For the Fiscal Year Ended June 30, 19X4**
**With Comparative Totals For The Fiscal Year Ended June 30, 19X3 (In Thousands)**

| | General Obligation/ Secondary Property Tax | Streets and Highways | Public Housing | City Improve- ment | Special Assess- ment | Totals 19X4 | Totals 19X3 |
|---|---|---|---|---|---|---|---|
| **SOURCES OF FINANCIAL RESOURCES** | | | | | | | |
| Revenues | | | | | | | |
| Secondary Property Taxes | $ 51,902 | $ — | $ — | $ — | $ — | $ 51,902 | $ 56,078 |
| Special Assessments | — | — | — | — | 1,749 | 1,749 | 1,661 |
| Interest on Assessments | — | — | — | — | 1,182 | 1,182 | 916 |
| Interest on Investments | 7,679 | 2 | 42 | 44 | 56 | 7,823 | 4,086 |
| Other | 477 | 369 | — | 329 | — | 1,175 | 785 |
| Total Revenues | 60,058 | 371 | 42 | 373 | 2,987 | 63,831 | 63,526 |
| | | | | | | | |
| Other Sources | | | | | | | |
| Operating Transfers from Other Funds | | | | | | | |
| General Fund | 380 | — | — | 1,987 | — | 2,367 | 1,503 |
| Excise Tax | 900 | — | — | 5,646 | — | 6,546 | 7,769 |
| Highway User Revenue | 2,000 | 30,214 | — | — | — | 32,214 | 35,982 |
| Public Housing Special Revenue | — | — | 866 | 27 | — | 893 | 875 |
| Sports Facilities | 1,295 | — | — | 4,556 | — | 5,851 | 5,388 |
| Capital Projects | — | — | — | 518 | 7 | 525 | 1,637 |
| Proceeds from Refunding Bonds | 41,006 | 63,422 | — | 24,076 | — | 128,504 | 239,140 |
| Total Other Sources | 45,581 | 93,636 | 866 | 36,810 | 7 | 176,900 | 292,294 |
| Total Sources of Financial Resources | 105,639 | 94,007 | 908 | 37,183 | 2,994 | 240,731 | 355,820 |
| | | | | | | | |
| **USES OF FINANCIAL RESOURCES** | | | | | | | |
| Expenditures | | | | | | | |
| Debt Service | | | | | | | |
| Principal | 21,047 | 10,965 | 485 | 3,503 | 1,901 | 37,901 | 31,535 |
| Interest | 26,503 | 19,620 | 381 | 8,997 | 1,169 | 56,670 | 55,065 |
| Arbitrage Rebate and Fiscal Agent Fees | 16 | — | — | 21 | — | 37 | 1,622 |
| Total Expenditures | 47,566 | 30,585 | 866 | 12,521 | 3,070 | 94,608 | 88,222 |
| | | | | | | | |
| Other Uses | | | | | | | |
| Operating Transfers to Other Funds | | | | | | | |
| General Fund | — | — | — | — | 201 | 201 | 259 |
| Deposit to Refunding Escrow | 41,039 | 63,422 | — | 26,362 | — | 130,823 | 239,491 |
| Total Other Uses | 41,039 | 63,422 | — | 26,362 | 201 | 131,024 | 239,750 |
| Total Uses of Financial Resources | 88,605 | 94,007 | 866 | 38,883 | 3,271 | 225,632 | 327,972 |
| Net Increase (Decrease) in Fund Balances | 17,034 | — | 42 | (1,700) | (277) | 15,099 | 27,848 |
| **FUND BALANCES, JULY 1, as Previously Reported** | 96,711 | — | 1,424 | 1,825 | 1,991 | 101,951 | 74,103 |
| Prior Period Adjustments | — | — | — | — | 275 | 275 | 275 |
| **FUND BALANCES, JULY 1, as Restated** | 96,711 | — | 1,424 | 1,825 | 2,266 | 102,226 | 74,378 |
| **FUND BALANCES, JUNE 30** | $113,745 | $ — | $1,466 | $ 125 | $1,989 | $117,325 | $102,226 |

The accompanying notes are an integral part of these financial statements.

FIGURE 8–10 **Combining Statement of Revenues, Expenditures, and Changes in Fund Balances— Debt Service Funds—City of Garden Grove**

**CITY OF GARDEN GROVE
DEBT SERVICE FUNDS
COMBINING STATEMENT OF REVENUES, EXPENDITURES,
AND CHANGES IN FUND BALANCES
YEAR ENDED JUNE 30, 19X4
WITH COMPARATIVE TOTALS FOR YEAR ENDED JUNE 30, 19X3**

| | Community Project | Buena-Clinton Project | Totals 19X4 | 19X3 |
|---|---|---|---|---|
| **Revenues:** | | | | |
| Taxes | $ 8,329,996 | $220,669 | $ 8,550,665 | $9,083,893 |
| From use of money and property | 200,447 | — | 200,447 | 74,718 |
| From other agencies | 42,580 | 33 | 42,613 | 38,337 |
| Total revenues | 8,573,023 | 220,702 | 8,793,725 | 9,196,948 |
| **Expenditures:** | | | | |
| Bond issue costs | 784,635 | — | 784,635 | — |
| Principal retirement | — | — | — | 1,400,000 |
| Interest and fiscal charges | 2,482,526 | — | 2,482,526 | 2,342,351 |
| Total expenditures | 3,267,161 | — | 3,267,161 | 3,742,351 |
| Excess of revenues over expenditures | 5,305,862 | 220,702 | 5,526,564 | 5,454,597 |
| **Other Financing Sources (Uses):** | | | | |
| Bond proceeds, net | 35,194,851 | — | 35,194,851 | — |
| Payment to refunded bond escrow agent | (33,849,672) | — | (33,849,672) | — |
| Transfer to other funds | (5,534,224) | (257,387) | (5,791,611) | (5,431,319) |
| Total other financing sources (uses) | (4,189,045) | (257,387) | (4,446,432) | (5,431,319) |
| Excess (deficiency) of revenues and other financing sources over expenditures and other financing uses | 1,116,817 | (36,685) | 1,080,132 | 23,278 |
| **Fund balances at beginning of year** | 3,827,919 | 38,677 | 3,866,596 | 3,843,318 |
| **Fund balances at end of year** | $ 4,944,736 | $ 1,992 | $ 4,946,728 | $3,866,596 |

issue, adjusted for any additional cash received or paid. These totals and the difference are computed using scheduled debt service amounts derived from the respective debt service requirement schedules—not present values—and indicate the overall cash flow consequences of the advance refundings without regard to the time value of money or present values.

C. **Economic Gain or Loss.** The present value of the net debt service savings or cost of the advance refunding transaction—referred to as the economic gain or loss—must also be disclosed. The economic gain or loss is the difference between (1) the present value of the *new* advance refunding debt issue debt service requirements, adjusted for any additional cash paid or received in the advance refunding transaction, and (2) the present value of the *old* defeased debt's debt service requirements. Both present values are calculated using the net effective interest rate (considering premiums, discounts, issuance costs, and so on) of the new refunding issue.

    **II. As Long as In-Substance Defeased Debt Is Outstanding**

        **D. Amount of In-Substance Defeased Debt Outstanding.** Any debt defeased in substance in an advance refunding—as opposed to being retired or legally defeased—must be disclosed as long as it is outstanding. This is because the SLG remains a guarantor of the debt, in effect, even though the possibility of its having to pay any of the debt is remote.

## CONCLUDING COMMENTS

Most government bond issues in recent years have been serial issues; term bond issues have been less popular, though they still are encountered in practice. Likewise, most SLG bond issues have been traditional fixed rate issues, though some have been variable rate issues. Furthermore, because many serial bonds have been serviced by annual transfers from the General or a Special Revenue Fund(s)to a Debt Service Fund(s)—and Debt Service Funds are not required legally or by GAAP in some cases—some governments now record such debt service directly in the General Fund and Special Revenue Funds instead of making annual operating transfers to Debt Service Funds. On the other hand, the law or contractual agreements usually require Debt Service Funds for bonds and other long-term debt, and many finance officers prefer to control and account for all general government general obligation debt service through Debt Service Funds.

    The use of various forms of lease arrangements has increased significantly in recent years. Some finance officers who prefer to centralize the control of and accounting for general long-term debt service in Debt Service Funds use them to service major capital leases, at least, and possibly other significant lease arrangements. Those finance officers who prefer to control and account for as much of the general operations of government as possible through the General Fund and Special Revenue Funds do not use Debt Service Funds to service any lease arrangements unless required to do so by law or contractual agreement. Thus, the use of Debt Service Funds for leases varies widely among state and local governmental units.

    Finally, the issuance of nonconventional deep discount bonds and notes by state and local governments has increased in recent years, as have SLG refundings of outstanding long-term debt. Accordingly, the GASB has issued new and revised standards—and plans to issue more standards—to ensure that deep discount debt issues, refundings, and other debt- and debt service-related transactions of state and local governments are appropriately accounted for, reported, and disclosed in the notes to the financial statements.

## Questions

**Q 8-1**  What is the nature of the fund balance account(s) in a Debt Service Fund at year end?

**Q 8-2**  A sinking fund was established for the purpose of retiring Dorchester Street Bridge bonds, which have a 20-year maturity. In the fifth year $10,000 of Dorchester Street Bridge bonds were acquired by the Debt Service Fund. Should these bonds be retired, or should they be held alive until maturity? Why?

**Q 8-3**  Why might a governmental unit want to refund an outstanding bond issue (a) at maturity? (b) prior to maturity?

**Q 8-4** Interest on its city hall bonds is paid from Allen City's Debt Service Fund on February 1 and August 1. Should interest payable be accrued at December 31, the end of the fund's fiscal year? Why?

**Q 8-5** (a) General sinking fund investment securities have risen in value. Should the appreciation in value be recorded in the accounts of the Debt Service Fund? (b) Would your answer be different if the securities had declined in value?

**Q 8-6** Distinguish (a) between fixed and variable rate debt issues, and (b) between conventional serial and term bond issues and deep discount bond issues.

**Q 8-7** What disposition should be made of the balance remaining in a Debt Service Fund after the bonds mature and are paid?

**Q 8-8** What is meant by defeasance? What conditions are necessary to achieve legal defeasance or in-substance defeasance?

**Q 8-9** What are the advantages of pooling the investments of a city's Debt Service Funds?

**Q 8-10** What are the main sources of assets for a Debt Service Fund?

**Q 8-11** Some accountants believe that budgetary control of Debt Service Fund operations such as illustrated in this chapter is unnecessary unless required by law. Others disagree. What is your opinion?

**Q 8-12** When would bond interest or principal due soon in the next year be accrued as expenditures and current liabilities of a Debt Service Fund? When would they not be accrued?

**Q 8-13** Why might a government use a Debt Service Fund for a serial bond issue when it is not required to do so?

**Q 8-14** Distinguish between a current refunding and an advance refunding.

**Q 8-15** The town of Sinking Creek has a semiannual debt service payment of $1,300,000 (including $1,000,000 interest) due on January 3, 20X1. The finance director transferred $1,500,000 from the General Fund to the Debt Service Fund on December 15, 20X0. Mayor Arnold Mills asks you if Sinking Creek is required to accrue the $1,000,000 of interest at December 31, 20X0, the end of its fiscal year. Respond.

## Exercises

**E 8-1** (Use of Debt Service Fund) For which of the following would a government typically use a Debt Service Fund?
1. Repayment of term bonds issued to finance construction of a general government office building.
2. Amounts paid to settle long-term claims and judgments liabilities associated with general government operations.
3. Accumulation of resources to be used to repay zero coupon bonds issued to finance construction of courtroom annex.
4. Payments required by general government capital leases.
5. Repayment of general government special assessment debt that the government does not guarantee.
6. Payment upon retirement to a general government employee of an amount reported as a long-term vacation pay liability in the General Long-Term Debt Account Group.
7. Repayment of general obligation bonds issued for Enterprise Fund purposes. Enterprise Fund revenues are intended to be used to service the debt.
8. Repayment (from bond proceeds) of bond anticipation notes issued for a general government project.

**E 8-2** (Refunding) Record the following transactions in the Debt Service Fund of Perfaterville.
1. The city issued $50,000,000 of refunding bonds at par to provide most of the financing to refund $60,000,000 of outstanding bonds.
2. The city transferred $5,000,000 from the General Fund to the fund from which the outstanding bonds are to be defeased.
3. The city paid $55,000,000 into an irrevocable trust established in a manner that defeased in substance the $60,000,000 of previously outstanding bonds.

# Problems

**P 8-1** (Multiple Choice) Indicate the best answer to each of the following questions. Use the following information in responding to questions 1 through 3.

The city of Lora issued $5,000,000 of general government, general obligation, 8%, 20-year bonds at 103 on April 1, 19X1, to finance a major general government capital project. Interest is payable semiannually on each October 1 and April 1 during the term of the bonds. In addition, $250,000 of principal matures each April 1.
1. If Lora's fiscal year end is December 31, what amount of debt service expenditures should be reported for this DSF for the 19X1 fiscal year?
   a. $0           c. $300,000
   b. $200,000      d. $400,000
2. If Lora's fiscal year end is March 31 and Lora has a policy of accumulating resources in the DSF by fiscal year end sufficient to pay the principal and interest due on April 1 of the subsequent fiscal year, what amount of debt service expenditures must Lora report for the fiscal year ended March 31, 19X2?
   a. $200,000
   b. $400,000
   c. $650,000
   d. $200,000 or $650,000, depending on the city's policy on accrual of debt service
3. Assume the same information as in 1, except that Lora has not made the October 1, 19X1 interest payment as of the fiscal year end. What amount of debt service expenditures should be reported for this DSF for the 19X1 fiscal year?
   a. $0           c. $300,000
   b. $200,000      d. $400,000
4. A county had borrowed $18,000,000 to finance construction of a general government capital project. The debt will be serviced from collections of a special assessment levy made for the project. The county levied the special assessments in 19X8. Ten percent of the assessments are due in 19X8. The 19X8 and early 19X9 collections on the assessments total $1,500,000. The amount of special assessments revenue that should be recognized in the county's Special Assessments DSF for 19X8 is
   a. $0. Special assessments are reported as other financing sources.
   b. $1,500,000
   c. $1,800,000
   d. $18,000,000
   Assume for questions 5 to 8 that:
   The state of Exuberance issued $10,000,000 of 5%, 20-year refunding bonds in 19X5 at par.
5. If the state used the proceeds to retire $10 million of general long-term debt upon its maturity, the state should report
   a. revenues of $10,000,000 and expenditures of $10,000,000.
   b. other financing sources of $10,000,000 and expenditures of $10,000,000.

     c. revenues of $10,000,000 and other financing uses of $10,000,000.

     d. other financing sources of $10,000,000 and other financing uses of $10,000,000.

6. If the state placed the $10,000,000 in an irrevocable trust that is to be used to service an outstanding $9,000,000 general obligation bond issue and those bonds are deemed defeased in substance, the state should report

     a. expenditures of $9,000,000 and other financing uses of $1,000,000.

     b. expenditures of $10,000,000.

     c. expenditures of $1,000,000 and other financing uses of $9,000,000.

     d. other financing uses of $10,000,000.

     e. no expenditures or other financing uses.

7. If the state placed the $10,000,000 in an irrevocable trust as in 6, but the transaction did not meet the defeasance in substance criteria, the state should report

     a. expenditures of $9,000,000 and other financing uses of $1,000,000.

     b. expenditures of $10,000,000.

     c. expenditures of $1,000,000 and other financing uses of $9,000,000.

     d. other financing uses of $10,000,000.

     e. no expenditures or other financing uses.

8. If the state placed $12,000,000 (the $10,000,000 from the advance refunding plus $2,000,000 from previously accumulated DSF resources) in the irrevocable trust in 6 and the debt were deemed defeased in substance, the state should report

     a. expenditures of $9,000,000 and other financing uses of $3,000,000.

     b. expenditures of $3,000,000 and other financing uses of $9,000,000.

     c. expenditures of $2,000,000 and other financing uses of $10,000,000.

     d. expenditures of $12,000,000.

     e. other financing uses of $12,000,000.

9. If the state of Exuberance defeased its $9,000,000 debt in substance as in 8 except that there was no advance refunding debt issued, the state should report

     a. expenditures of $9,000,000 and other financing uses of $3,000,000.

     b. expenditures of $3,000,000 and other financing uses of $9,000,000.

     c. expenditures of $2,000,000 and other financing uses of $10,000,000.

     d. expenditures of $12,000,000.

     e. other financing uses of $12,000,000.

10. A government paid $3,500,000 to its fiscal agent on June 30, 19X6, to provide for principal ($2,000,000) and interest payments due on July 1, 19X6. The fiscal agent will make payments to bondholders on July 1. The payment to the fiscal agent does not constitute legal or in-substance defeasance of the principal and interest payments. If the government uses the option of accruing its principal and interest expenditures due early in the next year, which of the following assets and liabilities should be reported in the government's DSF balance sheet at June 30, 19X6?

     a. No assets or liabilities from the preceding information would be reported because the government has paid the fiscal agent.

     b. Cash with fiscal agent, $3,500,000

     c. Cash with fiscal agent, $3,500,000
       Matured bonds payable, $2,000,000
       Matured interest payable, $1,500,000

     d. Cash with fiscal agent, $3,500,000
       Accrued interest payable, $1,500,000

**P 8-2** (General Ledger Entries) Gotham City issued $500,000 of 8% regular serial bonds at par (no accrued interest) on January 2, 20X0, to finance a capital improvement project. Interest is payable semiannually on January 2 and July 2 and $50,000 of the principal matures each January 2 beginning in 20X1. Resources for servicing the debt will be made available through a special tax levy for this purpose and transfers as needed from a Special Revenue Fund. The required transfers typically will be made on January 1 and July 1, respectively. The Debt Service Fund is not under formal budget control; the city's fiscal year begins October 1.

***Required*** Prepare general journal entries to record the following transactions and events in the General Ledger of the Debt Service Fund.

(1) June 28, 20X0—The first installment of the special tax was received, $52,000.

(2) June 29, 20X0—A Special Revenue Fund transfer of $38,000 was received.

(3) July 2, 20X0—The semiannual interest payment on the bonds was made.

(4) July 3, 20X0—The remaining cash was invested.

(5) December 30, 20X0—The investments matured, and $73,000 cash was received.

(6) January 2, 20X1—The semiannual interest payment and the bond payment were made.

(7) January 2, 20Y0—At the beginning of 20Y0, the Debt Service Fund had accumulated $30,000 in investments (from transfers) and $25,000 in cash (from taxes). The investments were liquidated at face value, and the final interest and principal payment on the bonds was made.

(8) January 3, 20Y0—The Debt Service Fund's purpose having been served, the council ordered the residual assets transferred to the Special Revenue Fund and the Debt Service Fund terminated.

**P 8-3** (GL Entries and Statements) Hatcher Village, which operates on the calendar year, issued a 5-year, 8%, $100,000 note to the Bank of Hatcher on January 5, 19X4. The proceeds of the note were recorded in a Capital Projects Fund. Interest and one-tenth of the principal are due semiannually, on January 5 and July 5, beginning July 5, 19X4. A Debt Service Fund has been established to service this debt; financing will come from General Fund transfers and a small debt service tax levied several years ago.

***Required*** (a) Prepare the general journal entries needed to record the following transactions and events.

(b) Prepare a balance sheet at December 31, 19X4, and a statement of revenues, expenditures, and changes in fund balance for the year then ended for the Debt Service Fund.

### Transactions and Events

(1) January 6—The Debt Service Fund budget for 19X4 was adopted. The General Fund contribution was estimated at $10,000; the tax levy was expected to yield $18,000. The appropriations included the January 5, 19X5 debt service payment.

(2) The tax levy was received, $20,000.

(3) The July 5, 19X4, payment of principal and interest was made.

(4) The General Fund contribution of $10,000 was received.

(5) The residual balance of a discontinued Capital Projects Fund, $6,000, was transferred to the Debt Service Fund.

(6) The January 5, 19X5, payment was accrued.

(7) Closing entries were prepared at December 31, 19X4.

**P 8-4** (Special Assessment DSF; Entries, Statements) On September 30, 20X3, Duncan Township issued $100,000 of 5-year, 6%, Zachary Addition Special Assessment Bonds to finance construction of storm sewers in the Zachary Addition. Duncan Township guarantees the bonds in the event that collections of the special assessments are inadequate to service the debt. Interest and $20,000 of principal are due and payable each September 30 beginning September 30, 20X4. The Duncan Township fiscal year ends on December 31. The following transactions related to servicing the Zachary Addition bonds occurred in 20X4 and 20X5.

1. On January 1, 20X4, Duncan Township levied special assessments totaling $100,000 on properties in the Zachary Addition Special Assessment District. Interest of 7% on the unpaid balance at the beginning of each year and $20,000 of principal are due each June 30.

2. Between January 1 and June 30, 20X4, Duncan Township collected $24,300 from the special assessments, including interest of $6,300. Uncollected current assessments became delinquent.

3. The town collected one-half of the delinquent assessments and interest on September 30, 20X4. The balance should be collected in the first month of 20X5.

4. Duncan Township loaned $1,000 from its General Fund to the Zachary Addition DSF on September 30, 20X4. Repayment is due in 9 months.
5. The bond principal and interest, along with $100 of fiscal agent fees, were paid to the township's fiscal agent on September 30, 20X4.
6. In May and June 20X5 the town collected:

| | |
|---|---:|
| Current assessments | $19,000 |
| Delinquent assessments | 1,000 |
| Interest on assessments | 5,740 |
| Total | $25,740 |

7. The amount borrowed from the General Fund was repaid on June 30, 20X5. Uncollected current assessments became delinquent.
8. The bond principal and interest, along with $100 of fiscal agent fees, were paid to the township's fiscal agent on September 30, 20X5.

*Required* (a) Prepare the journal entries to record the preceding transactions, assuming that the fiscal agent paid all principal and interest on the debt when it matured.
(b) Prepare the 20X4 financial statements for the Zachary Addition DSF.

**P 8-5 Part I** (Advance Refunding) The state of Artexva advance refunded $8,000,000 par of 19X2 10% serial bonds by issuing $9,000,000 par of 19Y6 6% serial bonds.

*Required* Prepare the entries required to record the following advance refunding transactions, which occurred during 19Y6, in the Artexva Advance Refunding Debt Service Fund.
1. The new $9,000,000, 6%, 19Y6 serial bonds were issued at 101 (no accrued interest) less $290,000 issuance costs, and the net proceeds were accounted for in a new advance refunding Debt Service Fund.
2. The net proceeds of the 19Y6 serial bond issue were paid to the Second National Bank of Artexva as escrow agent of an irrevocable trust for the benefit of the holders of the 19X2 10% serial bonds. That amount is sufficient under terms of the defeasance provisions in the 19X2 10% serial bond covenant, as invested, to legally defease that issue.
3. The advance refunding Debt Service Fund accounts were closed, and, its purpose having been served, the fund was discontinued.

**P 8-5 Part II** (Advance Refunding)
a. Assume that the state of Artexva advance refunding bonds yielded only $7,800,000, net of issuance costs; an additional $1,000,000 was transferred from the General Fund to the advance refunding DSF; and $8,800,000 was paid to the escrow agent. Prepare the entry necessary to record the payment to the escrow agent.
b. Assume the facts in part (a) except (1) the 19X2 10% serial bonds matured soon after the 19Y6 6% serial bonds were issued, and (2) the $8,800,000 payment was to retire the $8,000,000 of 19X2 serial bonds and to pay the $800,000 19Y6 interest on those bonds. Prepare the entry to record the bond principal and interest payment.

**P 8-6** (Advance Refunding) The city of Andrew had outstanding $1,000,000 par of 12% Series A bonds issued several years ago when interest rates were high. The finance officer proposes to refinance the issue with a new 8% Series B issue and some cash to be transferred from the General Fund. Because the Series A bonds are now selling at a substantial premium and, in any event, it does not appear feasible to buy all of them back, the finance officer proposed to place sufficient monies in an irrevocable trust and meet all other conditions as set forth in the Internal Revenue Code and Regulations and in the GASB standards to achieve defeasance in substance. The council approved the plan and the following transactions occurred during 19X8:
1. A new 8% Series B serial bond issue was sold at par, $1,000,000.
2. A General Fund transfer of $145,000 was made to the Debt Service Fund.
3. It was determined that the amount that must be placed in the irrevocable trust to service the Series A issue until maturity and pay the principal at that time was

$1,140,000. The payment to the trustee was made, as were payments of $5,000 of consultation fees and travel costs necessary to consummate the transaction.

*Required*  (a) Prepare the general journal entries required in the Debt Service Fund to record the transactions and events described previously.

(b) Assume, instead, that the trust did not meet the conditions of the GASB defeasance in-substance standards.

(1) Prepare the general journal entries to record the preceding transactions and events under this assumption.

(2) Identify any differences in the accounting and reporting for the preceding transactions and events in the various governmental funds and account groups under these two differing assumptions.

**P 8-7**  (GL and SL Entries; Statements) The Leslie Independent School District (LISD) services all of its long-term debt through a single Debt Service Fund. The LISD DSF balance sheet at December 31, 19X4 appeared as:

## LESLIE INDEPENDENT SCHOOL DISTRICT
### Debt Service Fund
### Balance Sheet
### December 31, 19X4

**Assets**

| | |
|---|---:|
| Cash | $220,000 |
| Investments | 670,000 |
| Accrued interest receivable | 10,000 |
| | $900,000 |

**Liabilities and Fund Balance**

| | | |
|---|---:|---:|
| Liabilities: | | |
| Matured interest payable | $101,500 | |
| Matured serial bonds payable | 50,000 | |
| Accrued fiscal agent fees payable | 1,005 | $152,505 |
| Fund Balance: | | |
| Reserved for term bond principal | 315,285 | |
| Reserved for serial bond service assurance | 350,000 | |
| | 665,285 | |
| Unreserved | 82,210 | 747,495 |
| | | $900,000 |

1. The LISD adopted the following DSF budget for its 19X5 calendar fiscal year:

**Appropriations:**

| | | |
|---|---:|---:|
| (1) Serial bonds (8%, $2,500,000 unmatured at 1/1/X5): | | |
| (a) 7/5/X5—Principal | $ 50,000 | |
| Interest | 100,000 | |
| Fiscal agent fees | 1,000 | $151,000 |
| (b) 1/5/X6—Principal | $ 50,000 | |
| Interest | 98,000 | |
| Fiscal agent fees | 995 | 148,995 |
| | | $299,995 |

[The 1/5/X5 debt service payment was accrued at 12/31/X4 because resources were provided for that payment during 19X4.]

(2) <u>Term bonds</u> (6%, $1,000,000 unmatured at 1/1/X5):

    (a) 4/15/X5—Interest ...............................     30,000

    (b) 10/15/X5—Interest ..............................     <u>30,000</u>

                                                60,000

[The board also approved a $21,019 addition to the sinking fund Reserve for Term Bond Principal as required by the term bond indenture.]

(3) <u>Capital lease</u> (7%, $400,000 book value at 1/1/X5):

    Annual payment (including interest) due 3/25/X5 ..........     <u>38,986</u>

      Total Appropriations ................................     $398,981

**Required Financing:**

Appropriations .........................................     $398,981

Addition to term bond sinking fund ........................     <u>21,019</u>

                                              $420,000

**Authorized Financing Sources:**

Estimated property tax revenue .........................     $250,000

Estimated interest revenues .............................     52,000

Authorized operating transfer from General Fund .............     <u>118,000</u>

                                              $420,000

2. All debt service payment transactions occurred during 19X5 as they were budgeted and scheduled. Investments were liquidated—in $1,000 blocks—the day before cash was required; the cash balance was never permitted to be less than $5,000.

3. The General Fund transfer was made on 2/12/X5, was invested (at par); the sinking fund Reserve for Term Bond Principal was also adjusted on that date.

4. Investment earnings during 19X5 were $54,000, $15,000 of accrued interest receivable at 12/31/X5. The ending cash balance at 12/31/X5 was $13,509. (Record all investment earnings transactions and events at 12/31/X5.)

5. Property taxes for the year, all received on 5/8/X5, totaled $256,000.

*Required* (a) Prepare the summary journal entries necessary to record these transactions and events in the General Ledger, Revenues Ledger, and Expenditures Ledger of the Leslie Independent School District during 19X5, including closing entries. Key the entries by date.

(b) Prepare a balance sheet at 12/31/19X5 and a Statement of Revenues, Expenditures, and Changes in Fund Balance—Budget and Actual for the year then ended for the LISD Debt Service Fund.

**P 8-8** (GL Worksheet: SLs; Statements) This problem requires an alternate solution approach to Problem 8–7 on the Leslie Independent School District Debt Service Fund.

*Required* (a) Based on the information in Problem 8–7, prepare a General Ledger worksheet and Revenues Ledger and Expenditures Ledger accounts for the LISD Debt Service Fund for the year 19X5. The General Ledger worksheet should be designed as follows:

| Columns | Heading |
|---|---|
| 1–2 | Trial Balance, 1/1/X5 |
| 3–4 | 19X5 Reversing (optional), Transaction, and Adjusting Entries |
| 5–6 | Preclosing Trial Balance, 12/31/X5 |
| 7–8 | Closing Entry(ies), 12/31/X5 |
| 9–10 | Postclosing Trial Balance, 12/31/X5 |

(b) Prepare a balance sheet at 12/31/X5 and a Statement of Revenues, Expenditures, and Changes in Fund Balance—Budget and Actual for the year then ended for the LISD Debt Service Fund.

**P 8-9**  (GL and SL Entries, Statements) A serial Debt Service Fund of the state of Texona had the following postclosing trial balance at September 30, 19X7, the end of its fiscal year:

**State of Texona**
**Serial Debt Service Fund No. 2**
**Postclosing Trial Balance**
**September 30, 19X7**

| | | |
|---|---:|---:|
| Cash .................................................... | $10,600,000 | |
| Investments ........................................... | 7,600,000 | |
| Matured Bonds Payable ................................. | | $ 5,000,000 |
| Matured Notes Payable ................................. | | 2,000,000 |
| Matured Interest Payable .............................. | | 3,500,000 |
| Reserved for Bond Debt Service ........................ | | 6,000,000 |
| Unreserved Fund Balance ............................... | | 1,700,000 |
| | $18,200,000 | $18,200,000 |

The Debt Service Fund is financed by a share of state sales tax revenues, transfers from other funds, and interest earnings. Significant debt service payments fall due on October 1 each year and are provided for in the appropriations of the previous year. The following transactions and events affected the State of Texona Serial Debt Service Fund No. 2 during the 19X7–X8 fiscal year:

1. The matured bonds, notes, and interest payable were paid.
2. State sales taxes collected for the Debt Service Fund totaled $12,000,000.
3. All but $10,000 of the cash was invested.
4. The Reserve for Bond Debt Service was increased to $7,000,000 as required by the bond indenture.
5. Debt service maturities on April 1, 19X8 were:

| | |
|---|---:|
| Bonds ............................................... | $5,000,000 |
| Notes ............................................... | 2,000,000 |
| Interest ............................................ | 3,000,000 |

6. Temporary investments of $9,200,000 were liquidated to pay the debt service due; the proceeds were $10,500,000. (Accrued interest receivable is debited to the Investments account at year end.)
7. The debt service payments due were made.
8. A $1,400,000 transfer was received upon termination of Debt Service Fund No. 6.
9. An $8,000,000 transfer was received from the General Fund.
10. A capital lease obligation, $1,500,000, was paid (includes $600,000 interest).
11. Debt service maturities at year end, on which payment is due October 1, 19X8, were:

| | |
|---|---:|
| Bonds ............................................... | $5,000,000 |
| Notes ............................................... | 2,000,000 |
| Interest ............................................ | 2,500,000 |

12. Accrued interest receivable on investments at year end, $900,000.

**Required**  (1) Prepare DSF general journal entries to record the preceding transactions and events in the General, Revenues, and Expenditures Ledgers.
(2) Prepare a preclosing trial balance for the Debt Service Fund at September 30, 19X8.
(3) Prepare DSF closing entries at September 30, 19X8.
(4) Prepare a balance sheet for the Debt Service Fund at September 30, 19X8.
(5) Prepare a statement of revenues, expenditures, and changes in fund balance for the Debt Service Fund for the 19X7–X8 fiscal year.

Alternatively, in lieu of requirements 1–4, prepare a worksheet headed as follows:

| Columns | Heading |
|---------|---------|
| 1–2 | Postclosing Trial Balance, 9/30/19X7 |
| 3–4 | 19X7–X8 Transactions |
| 5–6 | Closing Entries, 9/30/19X8 |
| 7–8 | Postclosing Trial Balance, 9/30/19X8 |

**P 8-10** (Research and Analysis) Obtain a comprehensive annual financial report (CAFR) of a state or local government (SLG). Familiarize yourself with the financial statements and disclosures with respect to the SLG's Debt Service Funds.

*Required* (1) How many DSFs are maintained by the SLG? What is the purpose of each DSF? (Attach a copy of the DSF narrative explanations.)

(2) Does this SLG employ a type of DSF you were not expecting based on the DSF coverage of this chapter? If so, explain.

(3) Note the format and content of the combining DSF balance sheet. Are any format features or contents different than you expected? If so, explain.

(4) Note the format and content of the DSF Statement of Revenues, Expenditures, and Changes in Fund Balances. Is it format A? Format B? Another format? Are any format features or contents different than you expected? If so, explain.

(5) Attach a copy of the combining DSF financial statements (or, if no combining statements, the combined statements).

# 9

# GENERAL FIXED ASSETS; GENERAL LONG-TERM DEBT

## Introduction to Interfund-Account Group Accounting

The governmental funds for which accounting principles have been presented thus far are separate, self-balancing entities that may have seemed unrelated to one another. Fixed assets purchased through these governmental funds have been recorded as fund expenditures rather than as fund assets; and fixed asset sale proceeds have been recorded as fund revenues or other financing sources. Likewise, the proceeds of general long-term debt issues have been recorded as other financing sources in governmental funds (e.g., Capital Projects Funds), and the retirement of such debt has been accounted for as expenditures or other financing uses in these funds (e.g., Debt Service Funds). Thus, both the general government fixed assets acquired through governmental funds and the general government long-term debt may seem to have mysteriously disappeared from the accounts.

These mysteries were dealt with briefly in Chapter 2 and are explained in depth in this chapter. The chapter begins by discussing the accounting procedures for general fixed assets (GFA) and the roles and interrelationships of the General Fixed Assets Account Group and the funds from which the fixed assets are financed. Next the chapter addresses the accounting procedures for a government's general obligation long-term debt—its general long-term debt (GLTD)—and points out the relationship of that indebtedness to the four governmental fund types. The chapter concludes with a formal introduction to accounting for interfund and interfund-account group transactions and relationships, or interfund-account group accounting.

## GENERAL FIXED ASSETS

Governments use many durable, long-term assets in their operations. Examples are land, buildings, and equipment. They possess physical substance and are expected to provide service for periods that extend beyond the year of acquisition. They are not physically consumed by their use, though their economic usefulness typically declines over their lifetimes. Their proper recording and control are necessary for efficient management and for financial reporting.

## General Fixed Assets Defined

A clear-cut distinction is maintained between accounting for general fixed assets in the General Fixed Assets Account Group (GFAAG) and for fixed assets in specific fund entities. The GASB *Codification* defines **general fixed assets** as all fixed assets other than those accounted for in proprietary or Trust Funds.[1] In some Trust Funds and in Internal Service and Enterprise Funds, fixed assets are accounted for in the same manner as in profit-seeking enterprises.

The governmental funds, discussed in preceding chapters, are used to account for the sources and uses of expendable, general government, financial resources. Recall that the governmental funds are essentially working capital entities. Therefore, acquiring fixed assets uses governmental fund financial resources because the fixed assets are not expendable financial resources. Furthermore, these assets belong to the organization as a whole, not to any specific fund. (The assets may or may not be used by agencies financed by the acquiring fund.) Thus, capital assets are not recorded as governmental fund assets. Rather, acquisition of fixed assets is an expenditure of governmental fund resources. The assets are capitalized in the General Fixed Assets Account Group.

## Acquisition and Initial Valuation

A government may purchase or construct general fixed assets (GFA) or may acquire them by capital lease, gift, or escheat. Most GFA are recorded at cost.

### Cost

General fixed assets should be recorded at cost. The cost principle used in state and local government accounting is essentially the same as that included in generally accepted accounting principles (GAAP) for business enterprises. Cost is generally defined as the value of consideration given or consideration received, whichever is more clearly determinable. Cost includes all normal and necessary outlays incurred to bring the asset into a state of readiness for its intended use.

The GASB *Codification* specifically states that general fixed assets include those acquired, in substance, through noncancellable leases.[2] Furthermore, it contains extensive guidance on accounting for and reporting SLG capital leases.

### Estimated Cost

In the past, many governments failed to maintain adequate records of fixed assets. Today most SLGs accumulate and record fixed asset cost data. However, original records are not available in some cases and reconstruction of records may be impossible or prohibitively expensive. In such cases, the GASB *Codification* permits recording **estimated original cost** on the basis of available information. Specifically, the GASB *Codification* states that:

> Initial costs of fixed assets usually are readily ascertainable from contracts, purchase vouchers, and other transaction documents at the time of acquisition or construction.

---

[1] GASB *Codification*, sec. 1400.106.
[2] Ibid., sec. 1400.108.

However, governmental units are sometimes faced with the task of establishing appropriate fixed asset accounting records and valuations after many years of operation without such records. In such situations, the original purchase documents may not be available, or an inordinate expenditure of resources may be required to establish original asset costs precisely. It may therefore be necessary to *estimate* the original cost of such assets on the basis of such documentary evidence as may be available, including price levels at the time of acquisition, and to record these estimated costs in the appropriate fixed asset accounts.[3]

Although these estimates are less objective than the information usually available for recording cost, errors are gradually eliminated as the older assets are retired. The basis of fixed asset valuation, whether actual or estimated cost, should be disclosed in the financial statements.

### Gifts, Foreclosures, Eminent Domain, and Escheat

Governments may acquire fixed assets by gift as well as by purchase, construction, or capital lease. Fixed assets acquired by gift are recorded at their fair value when received, which is the value of the consideration received under the cost principle discussed earlier.

In addition, governments acquire assets by three methods not customary for business enterprises: foreclosure, eminent domain, and escheat. In cases of **foreclosure,** the valuation should normally be the lower of (1) the amount due for taxes or special assessments, related penalties and interest, and applicable foreclosure costs, or (2) the appraised fair value of the property. Both amounts should be recorded in the fixed asset records. **Eminent domain** is the power of government to seize private property for public use, compensation to the owner normally being determined through the courts. Property thus acquired is accounted for in the same manner as that acquired in a negotiated purchase. Acquisition by **escheat** occurs when title to property is vested in or reverts to the government because the rightful owner does not come forward to claim it or dies without known heirs. Fixed assets obtained in this manner are accounted for in the same manner as gifts; that is, they are capitalized in the general fixed assets accounts at estimated fair value at acquisition.

## Classification

Classification of general fixed assets involves classifying both (1) the general fixed assets and (2) the sources by which the GFA were financed.

### Fixed Assets

The GASB has not specified a standard (uniform) classification of general fixed assets accounts. However, many SLGs follow or adapt the recommendation of the Government Finance Officers Association (GFOA) that fixed assets be classified as (1) land, (2) buildings, (3) infrastructure or improvements other than buildings, (4) machinery and equipment, or (5) construction in progress.

1. **Land.** The cost of land includes the amount paid for the land itself, costs incidental to the acquisition of land, and expenditures incurred in preparing the land for use (e.g., for storm water drainage and for water and sewer connection charges).

2. **Buildings or Buildings and Improvements.** The "buildings" or "buildings and improvements" classification includes (1) relatively permanent structures used to house persons or property, and (2) fixtures that are permanently attached to and made a part of buildings

---

[3] Ibid., sec. 1400.112.

and that cannot be removed without cutting into walls, ceilings, or floors or without in some way damaging the building.

3. **Infrastructure or Improvements Other Than Buildings.** Long-lived improvements (other than buildings) that add value (including use value) to land. Examples of items in this category are bridges, sidewalks, streets, dams, tunnels, and fences. (Capitalization of GFA infrastructure assets is optional, as discussed momentarily.)

4. **Machinery and Equipment.** Examples are trucks, automobiles, pumps, desks, typewriters, computers, and bookcases. Because much machinery and equipment are movable, they must be accounted for with particular care.

5. **Construction in Progress.** The cost of construction work undertaken but incomplete at a balance sheet date. These costs are appropriately reclassified upon project completion.

These general fixed asset classifications are not all inclusive. For example, a county public school system might report Library Books, and a city museum might include Museum Collections.

### GFA Financing Sources

In order to record and report the manner in which fixed assets were acquired, both currently and cumulatively, the GASB *Codification* recommends classifying the accounts on the credit side of the General Fixed Assets Account Group according to the sources by which the fixed assets were financed. This information indicates, to some degree, the extent to which the government is financing its fixed asset acquisitions from its current taxes, gifts, borrowings, and so on. It also provides insight into how dependent the government is on other governments to finance its capital program.

In previous chapters, we have observed that general fixed asset acquisitions may be financed through three major fund types:

- **Capital Projects Funds:** major facilities acquired through long-term borrowing, special assessments, intergovermental grants-in-aid, interfund transfers, or some combination of sources.

- **The General Fund and Special Revenue Funds:** various general fixed assets, particularly equipment, acquired from general or special revenues.

It is not sufficient merely to classify fixed asset sources by fund or fund type. Identifying the financing fund or fund type does not always definitively identify the underlying GFA financing source. Furthermore, (1) general or special revenues may be transferred to Capital Projects Funds, (2) Capital Projects Funds may have several sources of financing, (3) some fixed assets are acquired by gift or in other non-purchase manners, and (4) other governments often assist in fixed asset acquisition. Rather, GFA financing sources should be classified by the original funding source—such as (1) general obligation bonds, (2) federal grants, (3) state grants, (4) general (or unrestricted) revenues, (5) special (or restricted) revenues, (6) special assessments, and (7) gifts, or in summary classifications such as (1) federal grants and entitlements, (2) state grants and entitlements, and (3) local taxes and other revenues. Therefore, a single acquisition may require credits to several Investment in General Fixed Assets (source) accounts. Figure 9–1 presents an overview of the accounting equation applicable to general fixed assets accounting.

Although some question the usefulness of the GFA financing sources data from a cost-benefit perspective, GAAP require these data. State statutes or regulations often require GFA financing sources data also. Furthermore, the terms of many federal grants virtually require that federally financed fixed assets be readily identifiable in the fixed asset and/or GFA financing sources accounts. For example,

FIGURE 9–1  **General Fixed Assets Accounting**

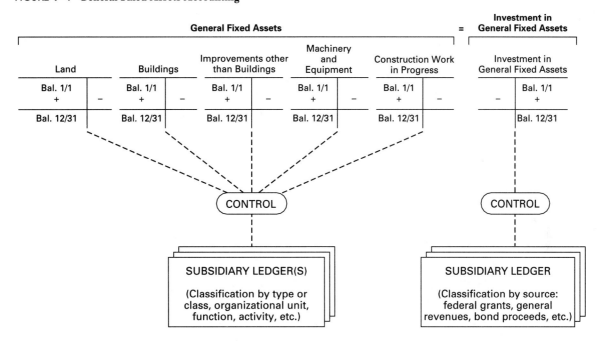

some grants require that proceeds of the sale of federally financed fixed assets be reinvested in similar program assets or be returned to the federal government.

## Infrastructure GFA

The GASB *Codification* states that:

> Reporting public domain or "infrastructure" fixed assets—roads, bridges, curbs and gutters, streets and sidewalks, drainage systems, lighting systems, and similar assets that are immovable and of value only to the governmental unit—is optional. The accounting policy in this respect should be consistently applied and should be disclosed in the Summary of Significant Accounting Policies. Appropriate legal and descriptive records (for example, deeds, maps, and listings) should be maintained for *all* fixed assets, however, for both management and accountability purposes.[4]

This option, like the permission to use estimated costs where necessary, resulted from a standards-setting judgment that the costs involved in establishing and maintaining cost and financing source records for infrastructure GFA might well exceed the benefits of such data.

Determining either actual or estimated costs and financing sources of infrastructure GFA can be very difficult. Indeed, it may be equally difficult to classify infrastructure expenditures between capitalizable capital outlay expenditures and maintenance and repair expenditures. Thus, many SLGs have excellent accounting records of all GFA *except* infrastructure fixed assets. Requiring them to establish and maintain cost and financing source records on infrastructure GFA to comply with GAAP was not deemed appropriate from a SLG cost-benefit perspective.

---

[4] Ibid.,sec. 1400.109.

The GFA infrastructure option permits those SLGs that want to maintain complete accounting records of infrastructure GFA—including cost and financing source data—to do so and to include infrastructure cost data in their GFA-related statements and schedules and in the SLG balance sheet. On the other hand, those SLGs that do not want to establish and maintain complete cost and financing source records on infrastructure GFA need not do so. But these governments should be able to identify all GFA, including infrastructure GFA. Likewise, they should keep relevant legal and descriptive records such as deeds, maps, and listings for all GFA. In either event, the SLG's infrastructure GFA accounting policy should be consistently applied and disclosed in the notes to the SLG's financial statements.

## Capitalization Policy

Before establishing GFA property records, most SLGs establish a GFA capitalization policy. One aspect of a SLG's GFA capitalization policy obviously will be its decision on whether to capitalize infrastructure GFA, the primary GFA accounting option under present GAAP. Furthermore, its capitalization policy must meet legal requirements and control needs. Thus, because GAAP applies only to items that are material and significant in the circumstances, the SLG may establish additional GFA accounting policies based on legal compliance, materiality, and control considerations.

### Legal Compliance

Some state and local ordinances require every fixed asset costing a certain amount—say $1,500, $500, or even $100—or more to be capitalized in the accounts. Whereas the wisdom of such laws may be questioned from materiality and cost-benefit perspectives—particularly when assets such as highways, right-of-ways, buildings, and building improvements are involved—the SLG must comply with the laws. However, certain capitalization policies may be permissible even under such laws—for example, which expenditures are considered capital outlay and, thus, are capitalized if equal to or greater than the specified amount, and which are considered maintenance or repairs. Also, it may be acceptable to capitalize certain fixed assets in groups (e.g., 100 folding chairs in an auditorium) rather than individually, and it may be acceptable to apply the capitalization policy to each item in a lot or group (say, to each chair) rather than to the total. If in doubt in such respects, practitioners should seek appropriate legal advice—for example, from the SLG attorney, the state attorney general, or perhaps the state auditor.

### Materiality and Control Considerations

In accounting and auditing, an item is considered material if *either* (1) its dollar magnitude is significant to the financial statements, *or* (2) its nature is such that proper accounting is required regardless of its dollar magnitude. Thus, both the relative dollar amount and its nature must be considered in determining its materiality.

Materiality is important in GAAP accounting and reporting because, although items that are material must be accounted for and reported strictly in accordance with GAAP, those that are not material need not be. Thus, within the confines of legal constraints, SLGs can set GFA accounting policies in a materiality context.

GFA capitalization materiality judgments, thus, may be made in terms of the various classifications of GFA—Land, Buildings and Improvements, Infrastructure (if capitalized), Machinery and Equipment, and Construction in Progress—and different capitalization policies may be established for each GFA classification. But, again, the nature of the items, as well as their dollar magnitude, should be considered in establishing GFA capitalization policies.

Control considerations may dictate capitalization of certain types of GFA even if their cost is less than the legal or other materiality thresholds. This often occurs in the case of movable machinery and equipment—such as personal computers, guns, and communication devices (e.g., two-way radios, pagers)—that may readily be converted to personal use, pawned, or sold.

## GFA Property Records

After the GFA capitalization policies have been established and the cost or other valuation of a fixed asset to be capitalized has been determined, it is recorded in an individual GFA property record. A separate record is established for each unit of property. (A unit of property is any item that can be readily identified and accounted for separately, but may be a group of similar items, such as folding chairs.) These records of individual assets or groups of similar minor assets constitute the subsidiary accounts that support the general fixed assets accounts in the general ledger, and include information on each unit of property such as:

1. Property system identification number, including any serial number, etc.
2. Abbreviated description
3. Date of acquisition
4. Name and address of vendor
5. Payment voucher number
6. Fund and account from which purchased
7. Federal financing, if any
8. Cost
9. Department, division, or unit charged with custody
10. Location
11. Estimated life
12. Date, method, and authorization of disposition

These subsidiary records must provide for classification in a number of ways:

- **General Ledger–Subsidiary Ledger Control.** They should permit a reconciliation of the detailed subsidiary ledger account amounts with the summary amounts in the Land, Buildings, and other control accounts in the general ledger.
- **Organizational Accountability.** The assets in use by the several organizational units of a government are the responsibility of the agencies, bureaus, departments, and so on. The system should permit identification of such assets by organization unit for custodial control, cost finding, and accountability purposes.
- **Availability.** Assets not in use should be easily identifiable so that requests for assets may be filled from assets on hand and unnecessary purchases can be avoided.
- **Location.** Assets should be classifiable by location so that custodial control by physical inventory will be feasible.

## Inventory of Fixed Assets

Land, buildings, infrastructure, and other immovable GFA need not be inventoried annually, though their records should be reviewed regularly for accuracy and completeness. However, a physical inventory of machinery, equipment, and other movable GFA should be taken on a regular basis for internal control, accounting, and accountability purposes. The physical count can then be compared with recorded descriptions and quantities. All differences between counts and records should be investigated. Missing assets must be removed from the accounts, and significant shortages should be disclosed in the statements or notes. Management should correct the weaknesses in internal control or accounting systems revealed by the shortages and related investigations.

Inventories of machinery, equipment, and other movable GFA may be taken annually or on a cycle approach throughout the year. GFA property records classified by organization unit responsible and location are essential to such an inventory. The usual procedure is for the SLG finance officer to send a list of the machinery and equipment for which each department is responsible to that department, asking that the inventory be made and any discrepancies noted. After the department has conducted the inventory, which may be observed or reviewed by the SLG's internal auditors and/or external auditors, the department head and finance officer (or their representatives) determine if any adjustments and corrective actions are necessary. Thereafter, the department head takes any needed corrective actions, and the finance officer adjusts the GFA records as necessary.

## Additions, Betterments, and Renewals

The costs of additions, betterments, and renewals are additional costs of general fixed assets. The costs may be incurred in one of the governmental funds, where the distinction between expenditures to be capitalized and those to be treated as repair or maintenance costs must be made. Because expenditures for both purposes must be authorized by appropriations, the distinction should first be made in the budget.

As noted earlier, the distinction between capital outlay and repair and maintenance expenditures is often difficult in practice. Moreover, it is common to find in practice that (1) amounts that do not meet the GFA capitalization criteria are recorded as capital outlay expenditures in governmental funds, but (2) amounts that should be recorded as capital outlay expenditures in governmental funds and capitalized in the GFAAG are misclassified—usually unintentionally—as repairs and maintenance or as other operating expenditures (e.g., capital leases recorded as rentals) in the governmental funds. The first situation presents no problems—the GFAAG accountant need only select those capital outlay expenditures to be capitalized and perhaps prepare a reconciliation of the governmental fund capital outlay expenditures and those capitalized in the GFAAG. But the second situation may require extensive analysis and evaluation of the governmental fund operating expenditure accounts to determine additional amounts that should be capitalized in the GFAAG accounts.

Additions to fixed assets are not classified according to whether they are buildings, other improvements, or equipment until the additions are completed. As noted earlier, costs incurred are accumulated in the Construction Work in Progress account during the construction period and are reclassified by asset type following completion of the project.

## Depreciation/Accumulated Depreciation

A major distinction between the accounting for governmental funds and that for proprietary funds and for profit-seeking enterprises results from GASB Principle 7a:

> Depreciation [expense] of general fixed assets should not be recorded in the accounts of governmental funds. Depreciation [expense] of general fixed assets may be recorded in cost accounting systems or calculated for cost finding analyses, and **accumulated** depreciation **may** be recorded in the General Fixed Assets Account Group.[5]

---
[5] Ibid., sec. 1100.107. (Emphasis added.)

If accumulated depreciation is recorded in the General Fixed Assets Account Group—which is not common in practice—it should be reported with the asset type for which it is being recorded. The corresponding debit would reduce the related investment in general fixed assets financing source account(s).

The GFAAG is not a fund, but an account group—a management control and accountability listing of a government's general fixed assets balanced by accounts indicating the sources by which the GFA were financed.[6] And, as discussed and illustrated later in this chapter, the GFAAG accounts are reported only in the SLG balance sheet; no operating statement is prepared for the GFAAG. Thus, depreciation expense is not recorded in the GFAAG accounts, though accumulated depreciation may be recorded in the GFAAG accounts and reported in the SLG's balance sheet.

Figure 9–2 summarizes the key financial reporting provisions discussed to this point. The next section illustrates the accounting for fixed asset acquisitions of various types.

## Recording Fixed Asset Acquisitions

Practice varies considerably as to both (1) the updating of the General Fixed Assets Account Group, and (2) the extent of subsidiary account use.

Computerized systems may be programmed to generate GFAAG entries continually, periodically, or at year end. In systems that are not fully automated (1) some accountants prefer to update the GFA ledger whenever a relevant transaction occurs—which typically is assumed in Uniform CPA Exam questions and problems; (2) others maintain a GFA journal that is posted to the GFA ledger periodically during the year or at year end; and (3) still others update the GFA ledger only at year end, perhaps based on worksheet analyses of fund capital outlay expenditures. Regardless of individual preference, there should be an established, workable system for updating the general fixed assets subsidiary records and the account group at least annually prior to statement preparation.

FIGURE 9–2  **General Fixed Assets Reporting Summary**

| | |
|---|---|
| A. Valuation of GFA acquired via: | |
|    Purchase | Cost |
|    Gift | Fair value when received |
|    Eminent domain | Cost (established by court) |
|    Escheat | Fair value when escheat occurs |
|    Foreclosure | Lower of (1) government's claims against the property or (2) the property's fair value at foreclosure |
| B. Use of estimated costs | Permitted when: (1) establishing initial GFA records and (2) actual costs are not practicably determinable |
| C. Capitalization of infrastructure fixed assets | Optional |
| D. Reporting of accumulated depreciation | Optional |
| E. Classification of Investment in GFA | By original sources of financing |

---

[6] Ibid., sec. 1400.110.

Similarly, the extent to which subsidiary ledgers are employed is a matter of accounting system design, individual preference, and the detailed information desired or required. As illustrated in Figure 9–1, the Land, Buildings, Improvements Other Than Buildings (Infrastructure), Machinery and Equipment, Construction in Progress, and Investment in General Fixed Assets accounts typically are **controlling** accounts and details of assets owned and the sources by which they were financed are maintained in subsidiary ledgers.

Figure 9–1 illustrates the accounting equation (see "Classification" earlier in this chapter) applicable to the General Fixed Assets accounts and the subsidiary information necessary to support the principal accounts. The following trial balance further illustrates the account relationships:

**General Fixed Assets Accounts**
Trial Balance
(Date)

| | | |
|---|---:|---:|
| Land | $ 700,000 | |
| Buildings | 2,500,000 | |
| Improvements Other Than Buildings (Infrastructure) | 1,100,000 | |
| Machinery and Equipment | 619,200 | |
| Construction in Progress | 480,800 | |
| Investment in General Fixed Assets from: | | |
| General Obligation Bonds | | $2,500,000 |
| Federal Grants | | 1,500,000 |
| General Revenues | | 1,150,000 |
| Special Assessments | | 250,000 |
| | $5,400,000 | $5,400,000 |

The entries to record the capital expenditures in each governmental fund have already been given. In order to highlight the relationship between these funds and the General Fixed Assets accounts, some of the fund general ledger entries will be repeated and the corresponding general ledger and Investment in GFA subsidiary ledger entries in the General Fixed Assets Account will be indicated. A series of Land, Machinery and Equipment, and similar fixed asset subsidiary ledgers also would be used, of course. But these are not unique to governmental accounting and are not illustrated here.

### Assets Financed from the General Fund or Special Revenue Funds

If the $29,100 of capital outlay expenditures in the General Fund illustrative example (entries 5b and 20, Chapter 4) had been made for equipment **purchases,** the entry in the **General Fund** would be:

| | | |
|---|---:|---:|
| Expenditures—Capital Outlay | $29,100 | |
| Vouchers Payable | | $29,100 |

To record purchase of equipment.
Expenditures Ledger(Expenditures):

| | |
|---|---:|
| Capital Outlay | $29,100 |

A companion entry would be made in the **General Fixed Assets Account Group:**

| | | |
|---|---:|---:|
| Machinery and Equipment | $29,100 | |
| Investment in General Fixed Assets | | $29,100 |

To record cost of fixed assets financed from current revenues.
Investment in GFA Ledger:

| | |
|---|---:|
| General Revenues | $29,100 |

General fixed assets acquired by **capital lease** are recorded similarly. Recall that the **governmental fund** general ledger entry (Chapter 6, page 225) upon the inception of a capital lease was:

| | | |
|---|---:|---:|
| Expenditures—Capital Outlay | $900,000 | |
| Other Financing Sources—Capital Lease | | $850,000 |
| Cash | | 50,000 |
| To record capital lease expenditure and related other financing source. | | |
| Expenditures Ledger (Expenditures): | | |
| Capital Outlay | | $900,000 |

The companion entry in the **General Fixed Assets Account Group**—assuming the lease was for land and a building—would be:

| | | |
|---|---:|---:|
| Land—Under Capital Lease | $100,000 | |
| Building—Under Capital Lease | 800,000 | |
| Investment in General Fixed Assets | | $900,000 |
| To record land and building acquired by capital lease. | | |
| Investment in GFA Ledger: | | |
| Capital Leases (or General Revenues) | | $900,000 |

Note that the fixed assets are identified as "under capital lease" during the term of the lease. Then, if the government takes title to the fixed assets, they are re-classified to the usual accounts (e.g., Land and Buildings). The usual financing source description is "Capital Leases" because capital leasing is often an alternative to bond issue financing, though some governments classify capital lease transactions according to the source of the capital lease payments (e.g., general revenues).

### Assets Financed through Capital Projects Funds and Special Assessments

Regardless of whether construction expenditures accounts are closed at the end of each year or only when the bridge construction is completed, this **Capital Projects Fund** general ledger entry (Chapter 7) is made—in the accounts or in the year-end worksheets—at the end of the first year:

| | | |
|---|---:|---:|
| Appropriations—Bean & Co. Contract | $1,000,000 | |
| Appropriations—Labor | 140,000 | |
| Appropriations—Machine Time | 81,000 | |
| Appropriations—Fuel and Materials | 49,000 | |
| Expenditures—Bean & Co. Contract | | $1,000,000 |
| Expenditures—Labor | | 140,000 |
| Expenditures—Machine Time | | 81,000 |
| Expenditures—Fuel and Materials | | 49,000 |
| To close the expenditures to date (project incomplete). | | |

The following entry is required in the **General Fixed Assets Account Group**:

| | | |
|---|---:|---:|
| Construction in Progress | $1,270,000 | |
| Investment in General Fixed Assets | | $1,270,000 |
| To record construction in progress financed through Capital Projects Fund. | | |
| Investment in GFA Ledger: | | |
| General Revenues [10%] | | $ 127,000 |
| State Grants [20%] | | 254,000 |
| Federal Grants [40%] | | 508,000 |
| General Obligation Bonds [30%] | | 381,000 |
| | | $1,270,000 |

The distribution of sources among general revenues (10%), state grants (20%), federal grants (40%), and issuance of general obligation bonds (30%) would be made in proportion to the expected total contribution of each to the project. Note also that encumbered amounts, whether or not closed out at year end, are not capitalized; only expended amounts are capitalized.

When the project is completed, during the second year in our example, the general ledger expenditures closing entry in the **Capital Projects Fund**—assuming the accounts are closed annually—is:

| | | |
|---|---:|---:|
| Appropriations—Bean & Co. Contract | $1,400,000 | |
| Appropriations—Labor | 160,000 | |
| Appropriations—Machine Time | 119,000 | |
| Appropriations—Fuel and Materials | 51,000 | |
|     Expenditures—Bean & Co. Contract | | $1,410,000 |
|     Expenditures—Labor | | 129,000 |
|     Expenditures—Machine Time | | 108,000 |
|     Expenditures—Fuel and Materials | | 43,000 |
|     Unreserved Fund Balance | | 40,000 |

To close the accounts (project completed).

In the **General Fixed Assets Account Group** the entry is:

| | | |
|---|---:|---:|
| Improvements Other Than Buildings | $2,960,000 | |
|     Construction in Progress | | $1,270,000 |
|     Investment in General Fixed Assets | | 1,690,000 |

To record the cost of completed bridge project financed through Capital Projects Fund and to close the Construction in Progress account.

Investment in GFA Ledger:

| | |
|---|---:|
| General Revenues | $ 203,000 |
| State Grants | 346,000 |
| Federal Grants | 660,000 |
| General Obligation Bonds | 481,000 |
| | $1,690,000 |

The **subsidiary entry** pertaining to **financing sources** was determined (see Figure 7–7) by the following calculation:

| | Total | General Revenues | State Grant | Federal Grant | Bond Issue |
|---|---:|---:|---:|---:|---:|
| Final project revenues and other financing sources | $3,007,000 | $330,000 | $600,000 | $1,168,000 | $909,000 |
| Less: Fund balance transferred to Debt Service Fund | (47,000) | | | | (47,000) |
| Final project cost/sources | 2,960,000 | 330,000 | 600,000 | 1,168,000 | 862,000 |
| Less: Amounts credited to sources in previous Construction in Progress entry(ies) | (1,270,000) | (127,000) | (254,000) | (508,000) | (381,000) |
| Balance to be credited to Investment in General Fixed Assets subsidiary ledger source accounts | $1,690,000 | $203,000 | $346,000 | $ 660,000 | $481,000 |

As noted in Chapter 7, most special assessment projects are accounted for in Capital Projects Funds. In any event, the procedure for recording general fixed assets acquired through special assessments parallels that illustrated for Capital Projects

Funds. However, the financing source may be reported as special assessments instead of general long-term debt proceeds when special assessments are the underlying source of financing for a project—even if interim financing debt is issued initially.

### Assets Acquired through Foreclosure

We noted earlier that fixed assets acquired through foreclosure should be recorded at the lower of (1) fair value or (2) the amount of taxes or assessments, penalties, and interest due on the property, and costs of foreclosure and sale. To illustrate, assume that land with an estimated value of $2,000 was acquired through foreclosure. At the time of foreclosure, the following were due a Special Revenue Fund:

| | |
|---|---:|
| Taxes | $ 900 |
| Penalties | 100 |
| Interest | 75 |
| Costs of foreclosure and sale | 25 |
| | $1,100 |

Further assuming that these receivables had been reclassified as tax liens receivable prior to the decision to retain the property for the government's use, the following entry should be made in the **Special Revenue Fund:**

| | | |
|---|---:|---:|
| Expenditures | $1,100 | |
| Tax Liens Receivable | | $1,100 |

To record acquisition of land through foreclosure; estimated fair value, $2,000.

Expenditures Ledger(Expenditures):

| | |
|---|---:|
| Capital Outlay | $1,100 |

The accompanying entry in the **General Fixed Assets Account Group** would be:

| | | |
|---|---:|---:|
| Land | $1,100 | |
| Investment in General Fixed Assets | | $1,100 |

To record acquisition of land through foreclosure of tax lien.

Investment in GFA Ledger:

| | |
|---|---:|
| Special Revenues | $1,100 |

Note that the Investment in General Fixed Assets subsidiary ledger credit is to Special Revenues rather than to Foreclosures (or some similar account). Note also that had the fair value of the property been less than charges against it, say $800, the Special Revenue Fund expenditure would be recorded at $800 and $300 would be charged against the allowance for uncollectible taxes and interest (or tax liens) receivable.

Most of the examples cited thus far have provided a clear-cut indication within a fund ledger that a fixed asset has been acquired and should be capitalized; that is, there has been a charge to the Expenditures account of some fund. Laws or custom in some jurisdictions do not permit charging fixed asset acquisitions through foreclosure to the Expenditures account, however. Rather, for these or other reasons, the uncollectible amount may have been improperly charged as a bad debt, and the following **non-GAAP** entry would appear in the governmental fund ledger of, for example, a **Special Revenue Fund:**

| | | |
|---|---:|---:|
| Allowance for Uncollectible Tax Liens | $1,100 | |
| Tax Liens Receivable | | $1,100 |

To record write-off of uncollectible account and the acquisition of property through foreclosure, estimated fair value, $2,000.

Such non-GAAP bad debt entries must be examined because they may call for a **General Fixed Assets** entry:

| | | |
|---|---|---|
| Land ............................................... | $1,100 | |
|    Investment in General Fixed Assets ...................... | | $1,100 |
| To record land acquired by tax lien foreclosure. | | |

Investment in GFA Ledger:

| | |
|---|---|
| Special Revenues ........................................ | <u>$1,100</u> |

Likewise, the Special Revenue Fund accounts and GAAP statements would need to be corrected to record properly the expenditures (and allowance for uncollectible tax liens) in conformity with GAAP.

### Assets Acquired through Gifts

No governmental fund assets are relinquished in acquiring property donated to the government. Thus, general government fixed assets acquired by gift are recorded only in the General Fixed Assets Account Group. Donated property should be recorded in the GFA accounts at estimated fair value at the time of donation:

| | | |
|---|---|---|
| Land ............................................... | $1,500 | |
|    Investment in General Fixed Assets ...................... | | $1,500 |
| To record land received by gift at estimated fair value. | | |

Investment in GFA Ledger:

| | |
|---|---|
| Private Gifts .......................................... | <u>$1,500</u> |

## Sale, Retirement, or Replacement

General fixed assets may be disposed of in sale, retirement, or replacement transactions with other governments, nongovernment organizations, and individuals. If accumulated depreciation of General Fixed Assets is not recorded, as is the usual case, an asset's carrying value in the accounts remains at original cost plus the cost of any additions and betterments made throughout the period of its use. Removal of the asset's carrying value upon its disposal requires the reverse of the usual acquisition entry. The accounting procedure upon **disposal** is, in sum:

1. **General Fixed Assets Account Group.** Remove the asset carrying value by debiting the Investment in General Fixed Assets account(s) and crediting the asset account(s) in the general and subsidiary ledgers. If a replacement asset is acquired, record it properly in the GFAAG.

2. **Fund receiving proceeds of sale.** Record any salvage value, insurance proceeds, or other receipts as other financing sources (or as revenues) in the accounts of the recipient governmental fund.

If a government has adopted the policy of recording accumulated depreciation on assets of the General Fixed Assets Account Group, the entries to record removal of an asset from the group, for whatever reason, would include removal of the accumulated depreciation related to the asset being removed.

The preceding GFAAG illustrative entries assumed that an Investment in GFA subsidiary ledger was used to account for the GFA financing sources. **The GFAAG entries that follow illustrate how a series of general ledger Investment in General Fixed Assets accounts may be used instead of a subsidiary ledger.** They also illustrate the use of several Revenues and Expenditures accounts in governmental funds rather than Revenues and Expenditures control accounts and a Revenues Ledger and Expenditures Ledger.

### Sale

If a fire truck with a book value of $100,000 is sold for $20,000, the following entries are made:

**General Fund:**

| | | |
|---|---|---|
| Cash . . . . . . . . . . . . . . . . . . . . . . . . . . . . . . . . . . . . . . . . . . . . . . | $ 20,000 | |
| Other Financing Sources—Sales of Equipment . . . . . . . . . . . . . . | | $ 20,000 |
| To record sale of fire truck. | | |

**General Fixed Assets Account Group:**

| | | |
|---|---|---|
| Investment in General Fixed Assets—General Revenues . . . . . . . . | $100,000 | |
| Machinery and Equipment . . . . . . . . . . . . . . . . . . . . . . . . . . . . . | | $100,000 |
| To record sale of fire truck with book value of $100,000. | | |

### Replacement (Trade-In)

If the fire truck is traded in on a new one costing $120,000 (fair value), and an allowance of $30,000 is made for the old truck, the transaction is recorded as:

**General Fund:**

| | | |
|---|---|---|
| Expenditures—Capital Outlay . . . . . . . . . . . . . . . . . . . . . . . . . . . | $ 90,000 | |
| Cash . . . . . . . . . . . . . . . . . . . . . . . . . . . . . . . . . . . . . . . . . . . . . . | | $ 90,000 |
| To record purchase of fire truck costing $120,000, net of trade-in allowance of $30,000. | | |

**General Fixed Assets Account Group:**

| | | |
|---|---|---|
| Investment in General Fixed Assets—General Revenues . . . . . . . . | $100,000 | |
| Machinery and Equipment . . . . . . . . . . . . . . . . . . . . . . . . . . . . . | | $100,000 |
| To record disposal (trade-in) of old fire truck with book value of $100,000. | | |
| Machinery and Equipment . . . . . . . . . . . . . . . . . . . . . . . . . . . . . | $120,000 | |
| Investment in General Fixed Assets—General Revenues . . . . . . | | $120,000 |
| To record purchase of fire truck at a cost of $120,000 less $30,000 trade-in allowance on old fire truck. | | |

Note that the book value of the old fire truck traded in should be removed from the GFAAG accounts, as in a sale, and the new fire truck should be recorded at its fair value in the GFAAG accounts. (One of the most common GFA accounting errors in practice is that the new fixed asset may erroneously be capitalized at the amount of the "boot" given in an exchange—the amount of the governmental fund expenditure—rather than at its fair value.)

### Retirement

The entries to record retirements may be more complicated than other fixed asset sales because the cost of retirement, as well as the proceeds received from the sale of salvage, must be taken into account. For example, assume that a fire station with a book value of $150,000 was torn down. The cost of tearing it down was $10,000, and $15,000 was realized from the sale of salvage. The entries to record these transactions are:

**General Fixed Assets Account Group:**

| | | |
|---|---|---|
| Investment in General Fixed Assets—Bond Issues | $150,000 | |
| Buildings | | $150,000 |

To record retirement of fire station.

**General Fund:**

| | | |
|---|---|---|
| Expenditures—Other | $ 10,000 | |
| Cash | | $ 10,000 |

To record cost of dismantling building—to be reimbursed from
sale of salvage.

| | | |
|---|---|---|
| Cash | $ 15,000 | |
| Expenditures—Other | | $ 10,000 |
| Revenues—Salvage Proceeds | | 5,000 |

To record sale of salvage.

Note that while the salvage costs are temporarily recorded as expenditures, those costs are netted against the gross salvage proceeds and the net amount is reported as Revenues—Salvage Proceeds.

## Intragovernmental Sale, Transfer, and Reclassification

Thus far we have assumed that the assets were sold or traded to private non-SLG organizations or persons. Sometimes property accounted for in a proprietary or similar Trust Fund is sold to a department financed through a governmental fund. Fixed assets may also be transferred among agencies of the government.

### Intragovernmental Sale

Assume that an enterprise (Enterprise Fund) sells equipment at book value to the public works department, which is financed from the General Fund, in a quasi-external transaction. The following entries would be made:

**Enterprise Fund:**

| | | |
|---|---|---|
| Due from General Fund | $15,000 | |
| Accumulated Depreciation—Equipment | 1,000 | |
| Equipment | | $16,000 |

To record sale of equipment to department of public works
at net book value.

**General Fund:**

| | | |
|---|---|---|
| Expenditures—Capital Outlay | $15,000 | |
| Due to Enterprise Fund | | $15,000 |

To record purchase of equipment from Enterprise Fund for
department of public works and liability to that fund.

**General Fixed Assets Account Group:**

| | | |
|---|---|---|
| Machinery and Equipment | $15,000 | |
| Investment in General Fixed Assets—General Revenues | | $15,000 |

To record purchase of equipment for public works department.

If the sale were for more or less than book value, a gain or loss would be recognized in the Enterprise Fund.

Interagency sales of fixed assets in quasi-external transactions appear to occur most often in state governments and in large local governments with rather autonomous departments and agencies. Fixed assets may also be transferred and reclassified (rather than sold) between agencies.

### Intragovernmental Transfer

Fixed assets may be transferred both (1) between general government departments, financed by governmental funds, and (2) between general government departments and proprietary fund departments or agencies. The accounting procedures differ for each type of transfer and reclassification.

**General Government Transfer**　　When fixed assets are transferred from one general government department or agency to another general government department or agency, or even from one location to another, a written authorization for the transfer should be issued by the proper authority. The authorization will be the basis for changes in the GFA subsidiary records—reclassifications of departmental responsibility and/or location—to permit continuing control. The GFA general ledger accounts will not be affected.

Note that such GFA transfers are not interfund transfers. Rather, whereas they may be referred to informally as *transfers,* they are simply *reclassifications* within the GFAAG accounts.

**Proprietary Fund–General Government Transfer**　　Transfers of capital assets between agencies financed by governmental funds and agencies financed by proprietary funds affect both the general ledger and the subsidiary property records of both the GFAAG and the proprietary fund. For example, if equipment is transferred from the Water Fund to the fire, police, and public works departments—which are general government departments financed from governmental funds—the entries to record this transaction are as follows:

**Water (Enterprise) Fund:**

| | | |
|---|---|---|
| Retained Earnings (or Governmental Unit's Contribution) . . . . . . | $10,000 | |
| Accumulated Depreciation—Equipment . . . . . . . . . . . . . . . . . . . . | 20,000 | |
|   Equipment . . . . . . . . . . . . . . . . . . . . . . . . . . . . . . . . . . . . . . . . . . | | $30,000 |

To record transfer of equipment to other departments as follows:

| Department | Cost of Equipment | Accumulated Depreciation | Net Book Value |
|---|---|---|---|
| Police . . . . . . . . . . . . . . . . . . . . . . . . | $ 5,000 | $ 3,000 | $ 2,000 |
| Fire . . . . . . . . . . . . . . . . . . . . . . . . . . . | 10,000 | 6,500 | 3,500 |
| Public Works . . . . . . . . . . . . . . . . . . | 15,000 | 10,500 | 4,500 |
| | $30,000 | $20,000 | $10,000 |

**General Fixed Assets Account Group:**

| | | |
|---|---|---|
| Machinery and Equipment . . . . . . . . . . . . . . . . . . . . . . . . . . . . . . | $10,000 | |
|   Investment in General Fixed Assets—Enterprise | | |
|     Fund Contributions . . . . . . . . . . . . . . . . . . . . . . . . . . . . . . . . . . | | $10,000 |

To record receipt of equipment.

Observe that this transfer is recorded in the Enterprise Fund (1) at book value—no gain or loss usually is recognized because such transfers are not considered to be quasi-external transactions, and (2) as a direct deduction from retained earnings or contributed capital—depending on whether it is viewed as a dividend or as a return of contributed capital—and not as an operating transfer or residual equity transfer. Although the substance of the transaction may be identical to that of an operating transfer or a residual equity transfer, a fixed asset transfer is not an interfund transfer but a fund–account group transfer or reclassification. Furthermore, operating statements are not presented for the account groups in the GPFS. So if a transfer out were reported in the proprietary fund, no corresponding transfer in would be reported—and the transfers out reported would not agree with the transfers in. In any event, such direct deductions from and additions to proprietary fund equity accounts are reported similarly to interfund transfers and are illustrated in later chapters.

Note also that the fixed assets are recorded in the GFAAG accounts at the net book value at which they were carried in the Enterprise Fund. A separate GFA property record is established for each unit of equipment in each department, of course. No entry is made in the General Fund accounts, however, because (1) no appropriable General Fund assets were either provided or used as a result of the transfer, and (2) this is a proprietary fund–GFAAG transfer rather than an interfund transfer.

**General Government–Proprietary Fund Transfer**   Fixed assets may also be transferred from the general government departments to proprietary fund departments or agencies. The GFAAG accounting required is to remove the fixed asset accounts as in any fixed asset disposal. The fixed assets are then recorded in the proprietary fund at the *lower* of their depreciated cost—as if they had been originally acquired for proprietary fund use—or their use value to the proprietary fund activity. Furthermore, that amount is credited directly to proprietary fund contributed capital rather than being reported as an interfund transfer.

## Property Damaged or Destroyed

Expenditures for repairs necessary to restore damaged property to its former condition are reported as current operating expenditures in the fund from which the cost of repairs is financed. Insurance proceeds are reported as revenues. To illustrate, assume that the total book value of a police station is $800,000, that the station is destroyed by fire, and that the governmental unit collects insurance of $200,000. The following entries would be made in the General Fixed Assets Account Group and in the General Fund, respectively, to record these transactions.

**General Fixed Assets Account Group:**

| | | |
|---|---|---|
| Investment in General Fixed Assets—Bond Issue . . . . . . . . . . . . . . | $800,000 | |
|   Buildings . . . . . . . . . . . . . . . . . . . . . . . . . . . . . . . . . . . . . . . . . . . | | $800,000 |

To record destruction of police station by fire.

**General Fund:**

| | | |
|---|---|---|
| Cash . . . . . . . . . . . . . . . . . . . . . . . . . . . . . . . . . . . . . . . . . . . . . . . . . | $200,000 | |
|   Revenues—Insurance Proceeds . . . . . . . . . . . . . . . . . . . . . . . . . . | | $200,000 |

To record receipt of proceeds of insurance policy on police station.

If the government intends to use some or all of the proceeds for replacement purposes, a Reserve for New Police Station could be created in the General Fund. Repair expenditures are classified as current operating; only betterment expenditures are reported as capital outlay. No entries are made in the GFAAG for repair expenditures. But the cost of betterments—improvements over an asset's original design—are to be capitalized in the GFAAG.

The GASB *Codification* does not mention write-downs of general fixed assets because of damage, obsolescence, or abandonment. It would seem reasonable to write down an asset (say, a 1926 fire engine) to a much lower figure if it is now used for a purpose for which it was not purchased (say, a display in a park). Similarly, assets that are to be sold for scrap probably should be carried at salvage value.

## General Fixed Assets Statements and Schedules

The purpose of financial statements and schedules for the General Fixed Assets Account Group is to provide reports on what the GASB *Codification* calls "a management control and accountability listing." The statements and schedules discussed in the following paragraphs are usually prepared.

### Statement (or Schedule) of General Fixed Assets

General fixed assets must be presented in the combined balance sheet. A more detailed statement (or schedule) of general fixed assets also is required when it is considered necessary to present fairly the financial position of the account group.

Some governments present detailed general fixed assets data—such as those in the GFAAG trial balance presented earlier—in the combined balance sheet. These governments do not need to present a separate statement (or schedule) of general fixed assets. But larger governments, in particular, often report a single amount for general fixed assets and investment in general fixed assets in their combined balance sheet—to keep that statement as brief as practicable. These governments must include a more detailed schedule of general fixed assets and of the sources of investment in general fixed assets in the notes to the financial statements.

The statement (or schedule) of general fixed assets presents a summary of the assets by major category and source. Most SLGs also present a schedule of general fixed assets—by functions and activities—as supplemental information. To be more useful to management, this schedule may be prepared on the basis of organizational units rather than by function and activity. It then indicates departmental use of and responsibility for assets.

### Statement (or Schedule) of Changes in General Fixed Assets

The GASB *Codification* also requires that either a statement or a schedule (in the notes) of changes in general fixed assets be presented in the annual financial statements. The GASB does not require or illustrate a specific format for the statement (or schedule).

Most SLGs present a highly summarized schedule of changes in general fixed assets—such as that in Figure 9–3—in the notes to the financial statements. This presentation fulfills the minimum GASB requirements. Some also present a more detailed statement or schedule of changes in GFA—such as that presented in Figure 9–4—usually as supplemental information. Furthermore, some SLGs present a supplemental statement or schedule of changes in GFA by functions and activities—or by organization units—primarily for managerial accountability purposes.

FIGURE 9–3  **Statement (or Schedule) of Changes in General Fixed Assets**

A Governmental Unit

Statement (or Schedule) of Changes in General Fixed Assets
For the Fiscal Year Ended (Date)

| | Beginning Balance | Additions | Deductions | Ending Balance |
|---|---|---|---|---|
| Land . . . . . . . . . . . . . . . . . . . . . . . . . . . . | $  700,000 | $    9,600 | | $  709,600 |
| Buildings . . . . . . . . . . . . . . . . . . . . . . . . | 2,500,000 | 37,200 | $ 50,000 | 2,487,200 |
| Improvements other than buildings . . . . | 1,100,000 | 878,200 | | 1,978,200 |
| Machinery and equipment . . . . . . . . . . . | 619,200 | 59,100 | 35,200 | 643,100 |
| Construction work in process . . . . . . . . . | 480,800 | 100,000 | 280,800 | 300,000 |
| | $5,400,000 | $1,084,100 | $366,000 | $6,118,100 |

**FIGURE 9–4 Detailed Statement (or Schedule) of Changes in General Fixed Assets**

A Governmental Unit

Detailed Statement (or Schedule) of Changes in General Fixed Assets—By Sources

For the Fiscal Year Ended (Date)

| | Total | Land | Buildings | Improve-ments Other Than Buildings | Machinery and Equipment | Construction Work in Progress |
|---|---|---|---|---|---|---|
| General fixed assets (beginning of year) . | $5,400,000 | $700,000 | $2,500,000 | $1,100,000 | $619,200 | $480,800 |
| Additions from: | | | | | | |
|   General obligation bonds . . . . . . . . . . | 168,200 | | | 93,200 | | 75,000 |
|   Federal grants . . . . . . . . . . . . . . . . . . | 225,000 | | | 200,000 | | 25,000 |
|   County grants . . . . . . . . . . . . . . . . . . . | 50,000 | | | 50,000 | | |
|   Special assessments . . . . . . . . . . . . . . | 400,000 | | | 400,000 | | |
|   General revenues* . . . . . . . . . . . . . . . | 238,300 | 7,000 | 37,200 | 135,000 | 59,100 | |
|   Special revenues* . . . . . . . . . . . . . . | 1,100 | 1,100 | | | | |
|   Private gifts . . . . . . . . . . . . . . . . . . . | 1,500 | 1,500 | | | | |
|     Total additions . . . . . . . . . . . . . . . | 1,084,100 | 9,600 | 37,200 | 878,200 | 59,100 | 100,000 |
| Total balance and additions . . . . . . . . . . | 6,484,100 | 709,600 | 2,537,200 | 1,978,200 | 678,300 | 580,800 |
| Deductions: | | | | | | |
|   Cost of assets sold or traded . . . . . . . . | 32,800 | | | | 32,800 | |
|   Cost of assets lost by fire . . . . . . . . . . . | 50,000 | | 50,000 | | | |
|   Cost of assets worn out and | | | | | | |
|     written off . . . . . . . . . . . . . . . . . . . . | 2,400 | | | | 2,400 | |
|   Cost of construction work in progress | | | | | | |
|     of prior year completed† . . . . . . . . . | 280,800 | | | | | 280,800 |
|     Total deductions . . . . . . . . . . . . . . | 366,000 | | 50,000 | | 35,200 | 280,800 |
| General fixed assets (end of year) . . . . . . | $6,118,100 | $709,600 | $2,487,200 | $1,978,200 | $643,100 | $300,000 |

*Includes amounts transferred to and expended through Capital Projects Funds.

†Included in costs capitalized to Land, Buildings, Improvements Other Than Buildings, and Machinery and Equipment.

# GENERAL LONG-TERM DEBT

**General** long-term debt of a government is defined in the GASB *Codification* as **all** of its **unmatured** long-term debt **except** that of proprietary funds or Trust Funds.[7] General long-term debt (GLTD) thus includes the unmatured principal of bonds, warrants, notes, capital leases, certificates of participation, underfunded pension plan contributions, claims and judgments, compensated absences, landfill closure and postclosure care, and other forms of general government debt that is not a primary obligation of any fund. Special assessment debt is included in GLTD if the government is obligated in any manner on the debt and it is not being serviced through a specific Enterprise Fund, as noted in Chapter 8.

Matured general obligation debt that has been recorded in and will be paid from a Debt Service Fund is excluded from the GLTD definition, as are all debts to be paid by proprietary funds or Trust Funds. The excluded debt is not recorded in the General Long-Term Debt Account Group (GLTDAG), but if non-GLTD

---

[7] Ibid., sec. 1500.103.

debt is guaranteed by the government, the government's contingent liability should be disclosed.

Thus, the same type of clear-cut distinction maintained between fixed assets of specific funds and general fixed assets is maintained between (1) long-term debt that is the primary responsibility of specific funds and (2) general long-term debt. The liability for unmatured general long-term debt is recorded in the General Long-Term Debt Account Group, not in the fund used to account for the proceeds from its issuance (e.g., the Capital Projects Fund) or the fund from which it will eventually be paid (e.g., the Debt Service Fund).

## Overview of General Long-Term Debt Accounting

Accounting for general long-term debt may be divided into three phases:

1. **When debt is incurred.** The **principal** of the debt owed is credited to an appropriate liability account; the corresponding debit is to an "Amount to Be Provided for Payment of Debt Principal" or similar account, indicating the extent to which future revenues are committed to the retirement of debt principal.

2. **While unmatured debt is outstanding.** As resources for the retirement of general long-term debt principal are accumulated in Debt Service Funds, the "Amount to be Provided . . . " account is reduced and an "Amount Available in DSFs for Payment of Debt Principal" account is increased to reflect their availability.

3. **When debt matures.** The matured debt is established as a liability of the fund through which it is to be paid—usually a Debt Service Fund—and the liability and related "Amount Available in DSFs . . . " and/or "Amount to Be Provided . . . " accounts are reversed from the General Long-Term Debt Account Group.

The accounting process for general long-term debt is summarized in Figure 9–5.

FIGURE 9–5 **General Long-Term Debt Account Group Accounting Equation**

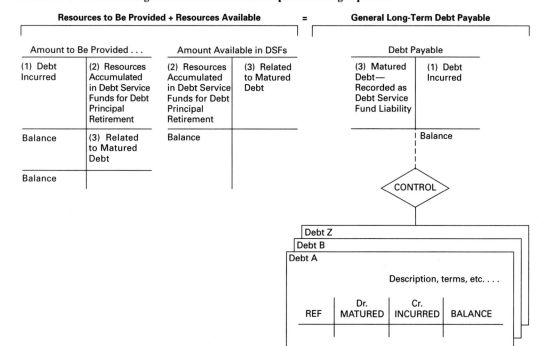

Practice varies somewhat as to the timing of the entries in the General Long-Term Debt Account Group. As a general rule (1) entries to record incurrence of debt are made immediately upon its incurrence, (2) entries to record accumulation of debt retirement resources are made in the course of the year-end adjustment process (but should be made immediately on the CPA exam), and (3) entries to record debt maturity are prepared at the date the debt is due. Furthermore, unless some of the Debt Service Fund resources are restricted for interest payments—or otherwise must be used for interest payments—the entire fund balance typically is considered to be available for debt principal retirement. Thus, the "Amount Available in DSF ... " related to a specific long-term liability typically equals the fund balance of the related DSF.

### Relationship to Debt Service and Capital Projects Funds

To illustrate the relationship among the Capital Projects and Debt Service Funds and the General Long-Term Debt Account Group, recall the Flores Park bonds example in Chapter 8. Upon issuance of the debt instruments in 19X1 at par, entries would have been made as follows:

**Capital Projects Fund:**

| | | |
|---|---|---|
| Cash | $1,000,000 | |
|   Other Financing Sources—Bond Issue Proceeds | | $1,000,000 |
| To record receipt of bond issue proceeds. | | |

**General Long-Term Debt Account Group:**

| | | |
|---|---|---|
| Amount to Be Provided for Payment of Serial Bonds | $1,000,000 | |
|   Serial Bonds Payable | | $1,000,000 |
| To record issuance of serial bonds. | | |

Traditional debt issues are recorded at par or maturity value in the GLTD accounts, even if the debt is issued at a premium or discount. The proceeds are expended through the Capital Projects Fund and the fixed assets acquired are capitalized in the General Fixed Assets Account Group.

Recall, however, that a Flores Park Serial Bonds Debt Service Fund was established to service this debt. When the 19X1 principal ($100,000) and interest ($50,000) payment on the Flores Park bonds became due along with $10,000 of fiscal agent fees, the following entries were required:

**Debt Service Fund:**

| | | |
|---|---|---|
| Expenditures | $160,000 | |
|   Matured Bonds Payable | | $100,000 |
|   Matured Interest Payable | | 50,000 |
|   Fiscal Agent Fees Payable | | 10,000 |
| To record maturity of bonds and interest along with fiscal agent fees. | | |

**General Long-Term Debt Account Group:**

| | | |
|---|---|---|
| Serial Bonds Payable | $100,000 | |
|   Amount to Be Provided for Payment of Serial Bonds | | $100,000 |
| To record serial bonds maturing and being recorded as a DSF liability. | | |

At the end of 19X1 there was a balance of $87,000 in the Flores Park Serial Bond DSF—which was accumulated to protect bondholders—requiring the following adjustment to be made at year end in the GLTD accounts:

**General Long-Term Debt Account Group:**

| | | |
|---|---|---|
| Amount Available in Debt Service Funds—Serial Bonds . . . . . . . . | $87,000 | |
| Amount to Be Provided for Payment of Serial Bonds . . . . . . . . . | | $87,000 |

To record amount available for retirement of serial bonds.

When the 19X2 principal ($100,000) and interest ($45,000) payment on the Flores Park bonds became due along with $10,000 of fiscal agent fees, the following entries were required:

**Debt Service Fund:**

| | | |
|---|---|---|
| Expenditures . . . . . . . . . . . . . . . . . . . . . . . . . . . . . . . . . . . . . . . | $155,000 | |
| Matured Bonds Payable . . . . . . . . . . . . . . . . . . . . . . . . . . . . . | | $100,000 |
| Matured Interest Payable . . . . . . . . . . . . . . . . . . . . . . . . . . . . | | 45,000 |
| Fiscal Agent Fees Payable . . . . . . . . . . . . . . . . . . . . . . . . . . . | | 10,000 |

To record maturity of bonds and interest along with fiscal agent fees.

**General Long-Term Debt Account Group:**

| | | |
|---|---|---|
| Serial Bonds Payable . . . . . . . . . . . . . . . . . . . . . . . . . . . . . . . . | $100,000 | |
| Amount to Be Provided for Payment of Serial Bonds . . . . . . . . . | | $100,000 |

To record serial bonds maturing and being recorded as a DSF liability.

Similarly, if at the end of 19X2 the Flores Park Serial Bonds Debt Service Fund had net assets (fund balance) of $150,000, the following GLTD adjustment would be required for the amount of the increase:

**General Long-Term Debt Account Group:**

| | | |
|---|---|---|
| Amount Available in Debt Service Funds—Serial Bonds . . . . . . . . | $63,000 | |
| Amount to Be Provided for Payment of Serial Bonds . . . . . . . . . | | $63,000 |

To record increase in the amount available for retirement of serial bonds from $87,000 to $150,000.

Similar entries would be made at least annually throughout the life of the Debt Service Fund and the debt issue.

## Relation to Serial Debt

Some serial Debt Service Funds closely parallel the Flores Park Serial Bonds Debt Service Fund example from Chapter 8 that was used in the previous section. Others are essentially flow-through vehicles through which current period principal and interest requirements and payments are accounted for. Many such funds have minimal (or zero) balances at year end and do not normally require entries in the General Long-Term Debt Account Group except when debt principal matures. For example, capital leases and long-term notes payable usually do not have funded reserve or other requirements that amounts in excess of the annual debt service requirements be accumulated in a Debt Service Fund. Furthermore, any related Debt Service Funds often are financed by interfund transfers in the amount of the annual debt service requirements. Hence, no excess resources are accumulated in the DSF in such cases, and no amount is reported as "Amount Available in DSF . . . " in the General Long-Term Debt Account Group. The appropriate GLTD entry upon maturity of debt principal in such situations is simply the reverse of the entry made to record debt incurrence.

In the case of regular serial bonds with *funded reserve* requirements—like the Flores Park serial bonds—an amount at least equal to the requirement(s) should be accumulated in the related Debt Service Fund, of course. Those resources typically are available for either principal or interest payments upon the occurrence of some contingency—such as a fiscal emergency—and, in any event, may be used to make the final debt service payments on the issue. Thus, they are reported as "Amount Available in DSF . . . " in the GLTDAG and should be reversed from the GLTDAG accounts when they are used for either purpose or, if not needed, are transferred to another fund after the related debt issue has been retired.

Where debt principal maturities are staggered over a period of years, the government may equalize its annual debt service provisions, thereby accumulating resources in low-requirement years for use during high-requirement years. Where a significant excess of serial Debt Service Fund assets over current year principal and interest requirements exists, the serial bond Debt Service Fund becomes similar to a term bond Debt Service Fund and should be accounted for similarly. The required annual adjustment to the GLTD accounts in such cases is simply a matter of reclassifying from the "Amount to Be Provided . . . " account to the "Amount Available . . . " account—or vice versa—an amount sufficient to bring the latter into agreement with the fund balance of the serial bond Debt Service Fund that is available for debt principal retirement. Again, unless some of the DSF fund balance has been restricted for interest payments—or otherwise must be used for interest payments—the total fund balance of the DSF typically is considered to be available for debt principal retirement.

### Relation to Special Assessment Debt

Recall from Chapter 8 that the GASB *Codification* (sec. S40) requires a government to report unmatured special assessment bonds, notes, or other debt in its GLTDAG if the government is even remotely contingently obligated in any manner on the debt. Thus, whereas other contingent liabilities are disclosed in the notes to the financial statements—rather than reported as liabilities in the financial statements—the GASB requires a unique exception with respect to special assessment indebtedness.

Recognizing the unusual nature of this requirement, the Board also specified that the special assessment liability be distinguished from other GLTD by being reported as "Special Assessment Debt with Governmental Commitment." Thus, issuance of $900,000 of special assessment bonds that are expected to be serviced by related special assessments—but on which a government is obligated in some manner—would be recorded in the **General Long-Term Debt Account Group** as follows:

| | | |
|---|---|---|
| Amount to Be Provided by Special Assessments .............. | $900,000 | |
|   Special Assessment Bonds [or Debt] with Governmental | | |
|     Commitment ........................................ | | $900,000 |

To record issuance of special assessment debt on which the government is obligated in some manner.

With this exception, the GLTDAG entries parallel those discussed earlier.

### Relation to Other General Government Liabilities

Recall that the GASB *Codification* definition of the modified accrual basis of governmental (and similar trust) fund accounting states that a fund expenditure is recognized when a fund liability is incurred. Recall also that the *Codification* provides that all unmatured noncurrent indebtedness except specific fund indebtedness is GLTD; and that GLTD "is not limited to liabilities arising from debt issuances per se, but may also include . . . other commitments that are not current liabilities properly recorded in governmental [or similar trust] funds."[8]

Furthermore, the *Codification* states—with regard to claims and judgments, compensated absences, and unfunded actuarially required pension plan contributions—that "in governmental (and similar trust) funds, liabilities usually are **not** considered **current** until they are normally expected to be liquidated with expendable available financial resources."[9] It then provides direction for determining the liability for general government underfunded pension contributions, claims and judgments, and compensated absences liabilities—and changes therein—and directs that (1) the amount of the liability that would normally be expected to be liquidated with available expendable financial resources be recorded as a governmental (or similar trust) fund expenditure and liability, and (2) the excess be recorded in the GLTD accounts.

Thus, the GLTDAG may account for numerous types of unmatured "general government" liabilities—such as claims and judgments; accumulated vacation, sick leave, and other compensated absences; landfill closure and postclosure care; and underfunded pension contributions—as well as unmatured bonds, notes, and capital leases payable. "Amounts available" for such other liabilities typically are not accumulated in related Debt Service Funds. However, any resources accumulated in DSFs for such other liabilities would be accounted for and reported as discussed and illustrated previously.

To illustrate, recall the claims and judgments expenditures example from Chapter 6 (pages 232–234). This example assumed the following key information:

| Year | Transaction/Information Summary | Amount |
|------|--------------------------------|--------|
| 19X1 | Claims and judgments (CJ) paid during year | $300,000 |
| 19X1 | Total accruable CJ liabilities outstanding at year end | 200,000 |
| 19X1 | Portion of CJ liabilities considered current at year end | 50,000 |
| 19X2 | Claims and judgments paid during year | 450,000 |
| 19X2 | Total accruable CJ liabilities outstanding at year end | 325,000 |
| 19X2 | Portion of CJ liabilities considered current at year end | 75,000 |

The entries required to record the preceding information in the General Fund and in the General Long-Term Debt Account Group are:

### 19X1 Entries

**General Fund:**

| | | |
|---|---|---|
| Expenditures—Claims and Judgments ..................... | $300,000 | |
| Cash ............................................... | | $300,000 |

To record payment of CJ expenditures.

**General Fund:**

| | | |
|---|---|---|
| Expenditures—Claims and Judgments ..................... | $ 50,000 | |
| Accrued CJ Liabilities ................................ | | $ 50,000 |

To record additional expenditures for current CJ liabilities expected to be paid from existing fund assets.

**General Long-Term Debt Account Group:**

| | | |
|---|---|---|
| Amount to Be Provided for Payment of CJ Liabilities .......... | $150,000 | |
| Accrued CJ Liabilities ................................ | | $150,000 |

To record the increase in the long-term portion of CJ liabilities.

---

[8] Ibid.

[9] Ibid., secs. C50.110, C60.109–.111, and P20.113.

**19X2 Entries**

**General Fund:**

| | | |
|---|---|---|
| Expenditures | $400,000 | |
| Accrued CJ Liabilities | 50,000 | |
| Cash | | $450,000 |

To record payment of CJ expenditures and accrued fund liabilities from 19X1.

**General Fund:**

| | | |
|---|---|---|
| Expenditures | $ 75,000 | |
| Accrued CJ Liabilities | | $ 75,000 |

To record additional expenditures for current CJ liabilities expected to be paid from existing fund assets.

**General Long-Term Debt Account Group:**

| | | |
|---|---|---|
| Amount to Be Provided for Payment of CJ Liabilities | $100,000 | |
| Accrued CJ Liabilities | | $100,000 |

To record the increase in the long-term portion of CJ liabilities.

As an additional example, recall the capital lease transactions discussed in Chapter 6, pages 225–226. The General Fund entry to record the inception of the lease and the General Fixed Assets Account Group entry to record the leased asset are shown in this chapter on page 359. In addition to those entries, the following **General Long-Term Debt Account Group entry** is required at the inception of the lease to record the resulting capital lease liability of $850,000.

| | | |
|---|---|---|
| Amount to Be Provided for Capital Lease Liabilities | $850,000 | |
| Capital Lease Liability | | $850,000 |

To record liability for capital lease resulting from entering into a capital lease agreement.

Next, recall that the **General Fund** entry to record the first lease payment of $17,821 (including interest of $5,250) was:

| | | |
|---|---|---|
| Expenditures—Interest | $ 5,250 | |
| Expenditures—Principal | 12,571 | |
| Cash | | $17,821 |

To record capital lease debt service payment due and paid.

The companion entry in the **General Long-Term Debt Account Group** would be:

| | | |
|---|---|---|
| Capital Lease Liability | $12,571 | |
| Amount to Be Provided for Capital Lease Liabilities | | $12,571 |

To record reduction of outstanding capital lease liability.

Similar entries would be required to record each subsequent lease payment.

## Defaulted Bonds

The GASB *Codification* does not provide specific guidance for reporting if a government defaults on its general long-term debt, but does provide guidance where proprietary fund or trust fund long-term debt on which the unit is contingently liable is in (or near) default:

> In the event that **fund liabilities** for which the unit is **contingently liable** are **in default—or** where for other reasons it appears probable that they will not be paid on a timely

basis from the resources of these funds and **default is imminent**—these liabilities should be reported separately from other liabilities in the fund balance sheet.[10]

Furthermore, all significant facts concerning the government's contingent liability on the proprietary fund or trust fund debt in default, or which will soon be in default, should be disclosed in the notes to the financial statements.

The authors believe that the preferred approach is to record the maturity and default in a Debt Service Fund or the General Fund. The government should remove the debt from the GLTDAG on the grounds that GLTD is, by definition, the unmatured principal of general government long-term debt. Likewise, the matured debt should be removed from the GLTDAG and recorded as a Debt Service Fund or General Fund expenditure—whether or not the related liability can be paid. If it is not paid, the government should report "Defaulted Bonds Payable" (and any resulting deficit) in the DSF or General Fund to draw attention to the default. The government also should disclose the default in a note to the financial statements and/or in the statement of general long-term debt.

## In-Substance Defeasance

As discussed in Chapter 8, governments may set aside resources in an irrevocable trust to provide for future debt service requirements for a particular debt issue. Where certain conditions are met as outlined in Chapter 8, the debt is deemed to be defeased in substance. General long-term debt (GLTD) that has been defeased in substance should be removed from a government's general long-term debt accounts as if it had been retired. This treatment is followed regardless of whether the defeasance was achieved using advance refunding bond proceeds or other government financial resources. If long-term advance refunding bonds were issued, the liability for the refunding bonds would be recorded in the GLTD Account Group.

Sometimes governments fail to meet all the technical requirements for defeasance in substance of general long-term debt that the government desires to defease. If the in-substance defeasance criteria are not met, the old debt cannot be removed from the account group. The assets placed in trust would be accounted for as investments of the DSF servicing the old debt, resulting in a need to increase the "Amount Available . . . " account in the General Long-Term Debt Account Group. Any new advance refunding debt issued in such situations also would be recorded and reported in the GLTDAG.

## GLTD Records

A file should be established for each debt issue at any early date, preferably while it is in the planning stage. The file should contain copies of, or references to, all pertinent correspondence, ordinances or resolutions, advertisements for the authorization referendum, advertisements or calls for bids, bond indentures or other agreements, debt service schedules, and the like.

Subsidiary records should be established and maintained for each liability in the account group. The exact nature of each record will vary with the pertinent details of the debt, but typical information would include title and amount of

---

[10] GASB *Codification*, sec. 1500.110. (Emphasis added.)

the issue; nature of the debt; dates of issue, required interest payments, and maturity; denominations; nominal and effective interest rates; and premium or discount. Furthermore, if the issue is registered, provision must be made to record owners' names and addresses. The subsidiary record will support the liabilities recorded in the account group, as well as the related debt service payments.

The debt instruments should be prenumbered and carefully controlled at all stages of their life cycle. Most government bonds issued before the mid-1980s are bearer instruments with interest coupons attached, which makes strict control essential.

As debt principal and interest are paid, whether by the government or through a fiscal agent, paid coupons and bonds should be marked "Paid" or "Canceled," reconciled with reports of payments, and retained at least until the records have been audited. Paid bonds and coupons are typically destroyed periodically, usually by cremation, to conserve storage space and avoid even the slightest possibility of reissue or double payment. The number of each bond or coupon destroyed should be recorded, attested to by two or more responsible officials who have verified the accuracy of the list and witnessed the bond and coupon destruction, and filed for reference. Bonds and interest coupons may be destroyed by the fiscal agent. In this case, the certified statement of items destroyed (provided by the fiscal agent) should be recorded and filed for reference. As an extra safeguard, some governments microfilm canceled bonds and interest coupons before destroying them.

## GLTD Statements, Schedules, and Statistical Tables

A statement (or schedule) of general long-term debt (Figure 9–6) is prepared at each statement date in accordance with GASB standards. It is essentially a balance sheet of the GLTD Account Group, and may be presented in the combined balance sheet. Like the GFAAG data, the GLTDAG data presented in the combined balance sheet may be more summarized than that in Figure 9–6, with the details presented in a separate statement of general long-term debt or in a schedule in the notes to the financial statements. Footnotes should disclose any obligations that, although primarily the responsibilities of some specific fund, are also full faith and credit responsibilities of the government as a whole.

The GASB *Codification* also requires presentation of a statement of changes in general long-term debt unless sufficiently disclosed in a schedule of changes in general long-term debt (Figure 9–7) in the notes to the financial statements. This statement or schedule forms a connecting link between statements (or schedules) of general long-term debt at successive statement dates.

In order to present the resources requirements of the existing debt structure, for each future year and in total, the GASB *Codification* requires that a summary of **debt service requirements to maturity** be presented in the notes to the financial statements (the usual practice) or as a separate schedule to the general purpose financial statements. Figure 9–8 is a typical summary schedule, though some governments present detailed data for only five to ten years and summarize the data for later years.

In addition to these GLTD financial statements or schedules, the comprehensive annual financial report ordinarily includes a number of detailed schedules that are designed to provide additional (usually unaudited) financial data. Several examples are presented in Chapter 13, "Financial Reporting."

**FIGURE 9–6  Statement of General Long-Term Debt**

**Statement of General Long-Term Debt**
**Broward County, Florida**
September 30, 19X1
(In Thousands)

Amount Available and to Be Provided for the Payment of
General Long-Term Debt:

| | |
|---|---:|
| Amount Available | $ 34,295 |
| Amount to Be Provided: | |
| Tourist Tax Revenue Bonds | 28,817 |
| Gas Tax Revenue Bonds | 66,316 |
| General Obligation Bonds | 388,947 |
| Special Obligation Bonds | 46,273 |
| Loans Payable and Capital Lease Obligations | 104,276 |
| Compensated Absences | 25,811 |
| **Total Available and to Be Provided** | **$694,735** |
| General Long-Term Debt Payable: | |
| Tourist Tax Revenue Bonds | $ 35,156 |
| Gas Tax Revenue Bonds | 74,845 |
| General Obligation Bonds | 390,130 |
| Special Obligation Bonds | 51,070 |
| Loans Payable and Capital Lease Obligations | 115,177 |
| Compensated Absences | 25,811 |
| Liability for Arbitrage | 2,546 |
| **Total General Long-Term Debt Payable** | **$694,735** |

**FIGURE 9–7  Schedule of Changes in General Long-Term Debt**

**Schedule of Changes in General Long-Term Debt**

**Shelby County, Tennessee**

Notes to Financial Statements

June 30, 19X6

Note (H)—General Long-Term Liabilities

Changes in general long-term liabilities:
Changes in general long-term debt during the year were:

| | Balance July 1, 19X5 | Debt Issues | Debt Retirements/ Defeasance | Increase (Decrease) in Accruals | Balance June 30, 19X6 |
|---|---:|---:|---:|---:|---:|
| Bonds payable | $755,023,599 | $30,150,000 | $49,080,000 | $4,265,368 | $740,358,967 |
| Capitalized lease obligations | 530,615 | — | 283,138 | — | 247,477 |
| Claims and judgments | 7,124,600 | — | 1,337,500 | (287,100) | 5,500,000 |
| Unfunded employer pension contributions | 12,066,651 | — | — | — | 12,066,651 |
| Landfill postclosure care costs | 3,752,194 | — | — | 42,506 | 3,794,700 |
| Sick and annual leave | 29,040,911 | — | — | 2,771,107 | 31,812,018 |
| Total | $807,538,570 | $30,150,000 | $50,700,638 | $6,791,881 | $793,779,813 |

FIGURE 9–8 **Schedule of Debt Service Requirements to Maturity**

**Schedule of Debt Service Requirements
to Maturity**

**Shelby County, Tennessee**
Notes to Financial Statements
June 30, 19X1

Note (H)—General Obligation Bonds
The County is indebted for serial bonds with interest rates varying from 4.25% to 8.75%, variable rate bonds, and notes. The County has no legal debt limit. Debt service requirements for principal and interest in future years, using the actual rate on fixed rate bonds and notes and 8.4% for the variable rate issue, are as follows:

| Years Ending June 30 | Principal | Interest | Total |
|---|---|---|---|
| 19X2 | $ 23,155,000 | $ 28,294,819 | $ 51,449,819 |
| 19X3 | 25,905,000 | 26,940,566 | 52,845,566 |
| 19X4 | 27,605,000 | 25,176,331 | 52,781,331 |
| 19X5 | 29,405,000 | 23,371,704 | 52,776,704 |
| 19X6 | 30,895,000 | 21,405,220 | 52,300,220 |
| 19X7 | 32,750,000 | 19,318,796 | 52,068,796 |
| 19X8 | 33,775,000 | 17,095,697 | 50,870,697 |
| 19X9 | 36,200,000 | 14,697,179 | 50,897,179 |
| 20Y0 | 25,565,000 | 12,469,599 | 38,034,599 |
| 20Y1 | 24,455,000 | 10,647,588 | 35,102,588 |
| 20Y2 | 19,035,000 | 9,045,054 | 28,080,054 |
| 20Y3 | 19,075,000 | 7,705,550 | 26,780,550 |
| 20Y4 | 22,304,138 | 8,654,349 | 30,958,487 |
| 20Y5 | 17,157,040 | 13,967,329 | 31,124,369 |
| 20Y6 | 17,730,033 | 13,458,506 | 31,188,539 |
| 20Y7 | 15,391,684 | 7,077,053 | 22,468,737 |
| 20Y8 | 16,333,709 | 6,174,878 | 22,508,587 |
| 20Y9 | 13,173,163 | 5,347,700 | 18,520,863 |
| 20Z0 | 10,970,000 | 734,778 | 11,704,778 |
| 20Z1 | 3,945,000 | 256,426 | 4,201,426 |
| | $444,824,767 | $271,839,122 | $716,663,889 |

These obligations are backed by the full faith and credit of the County and represent borrowings for the following:

| | |
|---|---|
| General Government ........... | $332,575,103 |
| Education .................... | 112,094,664 |
| Utility Bonds ................ | 155,000 |
| | $444,824,767 |

*Source:* A recent annual financial report of Shelby County, Tennessee.

# INTRODUCTION TO INTERFUND-ACCOUNT GROUP ACCOUNTING

Thus far in this chapter we have indicated how the transactions in the various governmental funds affect the General Fixed Assets and General Long-Term Debt Account Groups. The following entries illustrate interfund-account group accounting when transactions in one fund affect another fund or account group:

1. A $500,000 serial bond issue to finance capital improvements was issued at a $5,000 premium.

   **Capital Projects Fund:**

   | | | |
   |---|---|---|
   | Cash .......................................... | $505,000 | |
   |   Bond Proceeds ................................... | | $505,000 |

   To record bond issue at a $5,000 premium.

   **Note:** Some accountants prefer to use a more detailed account such as other Financing Sources—Bond Proceeds.

   **General Long-Term Debt Account Group:**

   | | | |
   |---|---|---|
   | Amount to Be Provided for Retirement of Serial Bonds ..... | $500,000 | |
   |   Serial Bonds Payable ............................. | | $500,000 |

   To record liability for serial bond issue.

2. The bond premium was transferred to the Debt Service Fund for either principal or interest payments on the serial bonds.

   **Capital Projects Fund:**

   | | | |
   |---|---|---|
   | Operating Transfer to Debt Service Fund ................ | $5,000 | |
   |   Cash .......................................... | | $5,000 |

   To record transfer of cash representing premium on bonds to the Debt Service Fund.

   **Debt Service Fund:**

   | | | |
   |---|---|---|
   | Cash .......................................... | $5,000 | |
   |   Operating Transfer from Capital Projects Fund .......... | | $5,000 |

   To record receipt of cash representing premium on bonds.

   **Note:** Some accountants prefer to use more detailed accounts such as Other Financing Uses—Operating Transfer to Debt Service Fund and Other Financing Sources—Operating Transfer from Capital Projects Fund when recording operating transfers.

   **General Long-Term Debt Account Group:**

   | | | |
   |---|---|---|
   | Amount Available for Retirement of Serial Bonds ......... | $5,000 | |
   |   Amount to Be Provided for Retirement of Serial Bonds ... | | $5,000 |

   To record additional amount available in Debt Service Fund.

3. An $80,000 contribution was made from the General Fund to the Debt Service Fund: $30,000 for interest payments and $50,000 for serial bond principal payments.

   **General Fund:**

   | | | |
   |---|---|---|
   | Operating Transfer to Debt Service Fund ................ | $80,000 | |
   |   Cash .......................................... | | $80,000 |

   To record payment of contribution to Debt Service Fund.

   **Debt Service Fund:**

   | | | |
   |---|---|---|
   | Cash .......................................... | $80,000 | |
   |   Operating Transfer from General Fund ................ | | $80,000 |

   To record receipt of contribution from General Fund.

   **General Long-Term Debt Account Group:**

   | | | |
   |---|---|---|
   | Amount Available for Retirement of Serial Bonds ......... | $50,000 | |
   |   Amount to Be Provided for Retirement of Serial Bonds ... | | $50,000 |

   To decrease amount to be provided and to increase the amount available for the retirement of serial bonds.

4. Bond-financed Capital Projects Fund capital outlay expenditures were made, $496,000, for improvements.

   **Capital Projects Fund:**

   | | | |
   |---|---|---|
   | Expenditures—Capital Outlay ......................... | $496,000 | |
   |   Vouchers Payable ................................. | | $496,000 |

   To record capital improvement expenditures.

**General Fixed Assets Account Group:**

| | | |
|---|---:|---:|
| Improvements Other Than Buildings .................... | $496,000 | |
|    Investment in General Fixed Assets—Bond Issues ....... | | $496,000 |

To record capital improvements made.

5. The $4,000 remaining balance of a terminated Capital Projects Fund was transferred to the Debt Service Fund for use as needed.

**Capital Projects Fund:**

| | | |
|---|---:|---:|
| Residual Equity Transfer to Debt Service Fund ............ | $4,000 | |
|    Cash ........................................... | | $4,000 |

To record transfer of balance of Capital Projects Fund to Debt Service Fund.

**Debt Service Fund:**

| | | |
|---|---:|---:|
| Cash ............................................... | $4,000 | |
|    Residual Equity Transfer from Capital Projects Fund ..... | | $4,000 |

To record receipts of Capital Projects Fund balance.

**General Long-Term Debt Account Group:**

| | | |
|---|---:|---:|
| Amount Available for Retirement of (Type of) Bonds ...... | $4,000 | |
|    Amount to Be Provided for Retirement of (Type of) Bonds . | | $4,000 |

To record receipt of Capital Projects Fund Balance by Debt Service Fund and corresponding increase in amount available for retirement of bonds.

6. Maturing serial bonds ($50,000) and interest ($30,000) were paid from the Debt Service Fund.

**Debt Service Fund:**

| | | |
|---|---:|---:|
| Expenditures—Bond Principal ....................... | $50,000 | |
| Expenditures—Interest on Bonds ...................... | 30,000 | |
|    Cash ........................................... | | $80,000 |

To record payment of serial bond debt service.

**General Long-Term Debt Account Group:**

| | | |
|---|---:|---:|
| Serial Bonds Payable .............................. | $50,000 | |
|    Amount Available for Retirement of Serial Bonds ....... | | $50,000 |

To record retirement of serial bonds.

7. A General Fund department entered into a capital lease of equipment with a capitalizable cost of $250,000. A $25,000 down payment was made at the inception of the lease.

**General Fund:**

| | | |
|---|---:|---:|
| Expenditures—Capital Outlay ...................... | $250,000 | |
|    Other Financing Sources—Increase in Capital Lease | | |
|       Liability .......................................... | | $225,000 |
|    Cash ........................................... | | 25,000 |

To record the inception of a capital lease and the initial down payment.

**General Long-Term Debt Account Group:**

| | | |
|---|---:|---:|
| Amount to Be Provided for Retirement of Capital Lease | | |
|    Liabilities ....................................... | $225,000 | |
|    Capital Lease Liabilities ............................ | | $225,000 |

To record capital lease liabilities.

**General Fixed Assets Account Group:**

| | | |
|---|---:|---:|
| Equipment Under Capital Lease ...................... | $250,000 | |
|    Investment in General Fixed Assets—Capital Leases ..... | | $250,000 |

To record leased assets.

8. Lease payments of $50,000, including $20,000 interest, were paid.

   **General Fund:**

   | | | |
   |---|---|---|
   | Expenditures—Capital Lease Principal | $30,000 | |
   | Expenditures—Interest on Capital Lease | 20,000 | |
   | Cash | | $50,000 |

   To record periodic lease payments.

   **General Long-Term Debt Account Group:**

   | | | |
   |---|---|---|
   | Capital Lease Liabilities | $30,000 | |
   | Amount to Be Provided for Retirement of Capital Lease Liabilities | | $30,000 |

   To record retirement of a portion of the capital lease liabilities.

9. The government unit accrued its liability to pay part of the cost of special assessment improvements being accounted for in a Capital Projects Fund from the General Fund.

   **General Fund:**

   | | | |
   |---|---|---|
   | Operating Transfer to Capital Projects Fund | $100,000 | |
   | Due to Capital Projects Fund | | $100,000 |

   To record governmental unit's liability for contribution toward construction of special assessment improvements.

   **Capital Projects Fund:**

   | | | |
   |---|---|---|
   | Due from General Fund | $100,000 | |
   | Operating Transfer from General Fund | | $100,000 |

   To record amount due from General Fund for governmental unit's share of cost of project.

10. Special assessments of $100,000 became current and $20,000 interest on special assessments was accrued. The full amount of the current assessments and interest is expected to be collected by the end of the current fiscal year and is to be used to service general government special assessment bonds that the government guarantees.

    **Debt Service Fund:**

    | | | |
    |---|---|---|
    | Special Assessments Receivable—Current | $100,000 | |
    | Interest Receivable on Assessments | 20,000 | |
    | Special Assessments Receivable—Deferred | | $100,000 |
    | Revenues—Interest | | 20,000 |

    To reclassify deferred receivables as current and accrue interest.

    | | | |
    |---|---|---|
    | Deferred Revenues—Assessments | $100,000 | |
    | Revenues—Assessments | | $100,000 |

    To recognize current assessments revenues.

    **General Long-Term Debt Account Group:**

    | | | |
    |---|---|---|
    | Amount Available for Retirement of Special Assessment Bonds | $120,000 | |
    | Amount to Be Provided for Retirement of Special Assessment Bonds | | $120,000 |

    To reflect increase in Special Assessment Debt Service Fund fund balance available for retirement of special assessment debt.

11. Inspection services were performed (**quasi-external transaction**) by a department financed through the General Fund for a capital project.

**General Fund:**

| | | |
|---|---|---|
| Due from Capital Projects Fund | $8,000 | |
|     Revenues—Inspection Services | | $8,000 |

To record revenues for inspection services rendered on capital projects.

**Capital Projects Fund:**

| | | |
|---|---|---|
| Expenditures—Capital Outlay | $8,000 | |
|     Due to General Fund | | $8,000 |

To record cost of inspection services performed by a department financed through the General Fund.

**General Fixed Assets Account Group:**

| | | |
|---|---|---|
| Construction in Progress | $8,000 | |
|     Investment in General Fixed Assets—Bond Issues | | $8,000 |

To record inspection cost as capital asset cost.

12. Services were rendered by workers paid from a Capital Projects Fund for a department financed through the General Fund (**reimbursement**).

**Capital Projects Fund:**

| | | |
|---|---|---|
| Due from General Fund | $5,000 | |
|     Expenditures—Capital Outlay | | $5,000 |

To record reduction of construction expenditures by cost of services rendered Department X.

**General Fixed Assets Account Group:**

| | | |
|---|---|---|
| Investment in General Fixed Assets—Bond Issues | $5,000 | |
|     Construction in Progress | | $5,000 |

To record reduction of construction cost by reimbursement. (This entry assumes that Capital Projects Fund expenditures were recorded previously in construction in progress.)

**General Fund:**

| | | |
|---|---|---|
| Expenditures—Current Operating | $5,000 | |
|     Due to Capital Projects Fund | | $5,000 |

To record amount due to Capital Projects Fund on account of services rendered Department X.

13. A short-term (e.g., 90-day) loan was made from the General Fund to the Debt Service Fund.

**General Fund:**

| | | |
|---|---|---|
| Due from Debt Service Fund | $40,000 | |
|     Cash | | $40,000 |

To record short-term loan to Debt Service Fund.

**Debt Service Fund:**

| | | |
|---|---|---|
| Cash | $40,000 | |
|     Due to General Fund | | $40,000 |

To record short-term loan from General Fund.

14. A noncurrent loan (e.g., two-year advance) was made from the General Fund to a Capital Projects Fund.

**General Fund:**

| | | |
|---|---|---|
| Advance to Capital Projects Fund | $75,000 | |
| Unreserved Fund Balance | 75,000 | |
|     Cash | | $75,000 |
|     Reserve for Interfund Advance | | 75,000 |

To record two-year advance to Capital Projects Fund.

**Capital Projects Fund:**

| | | |
|---|---|---|
| Cash ............................................ | $75,000 | |
|   Advance from General Fund ......................... | | $75,000 |

To record two-year advance from General Fund.

15. Cash payments for vacation and sick leave totaled $400,000. The payable for current vacation and sick leave increased $20,000 to $45,000. The noncurrent portion of the payable decreased by $67,000.

**General Fund:**

| | | |
|---|---|---|
| Expenditures—Vacation and Sick Leave ................. | $375,000 | |
| Current Liability for Vacation and Sick Leave ............. | 25,000 | |
|   Cash ......................................... | | $400,000 |

To record payments of vacation and sick leave.

| | | |
|---|---|---|
| Expenditures—Vacation and Sick Leave ................. | $ 45,000 | |
|   Current Liability for Vacation and Sick Leave ........... | | $ 45,000 |

To accrue current liability for vacation and sick leave.

**General Long-Term Debt Account Group:**

| | | |
|---|---|---|
| Noncurrent Liability for Vacation and Sick Leave .......... | $ 67,000 | |
|   Amount to Be Provided for Retirement of Liability for Vacation and Sick Leave .......................... | | $ 67,000 |

To record the decrease in the noncurrent portion of the vacation and sick leave liability.

16. A government sold computers used by its Department of Comptroller for $13,000. The computers originally cost $45,000 when purchased three years before. The proceeds are unrestricted.

**General Fund:**

| | | |
|---|---|---|
| Cash ............................................ | $13,000 | |
|   Other Financing Sources—General Fixed Asset Sale Proceeds ................................... | | $13,000 |

To record proceeds from sale of general fixed assets.

**General Fixed Assets Account Group:**

| | | |
|---|---|---|
| Investment in General Fixed Assets—General Revenues .... | $45,000 | |
|   Equipment ...................................... | | $45,000 |

To remove fixed assets upon sale.

## CONCLUDING COMMENTS

These discussions and illustrations of general fixed assets, general long-term debt, and interfund-account group accounting and reporting conclude the several general government accounting and reporting chapters of this text. This general government accounting model—the governmental funds and account groups—clearly constitutes the most distinctive aspect of state and local government accounting and reporting.

The remaining parts of the governmental accounting model—the fiduciary funds and proprietary funds—are discussed and illustrated in Chapters 10–12. As these additional funds are presented, typical interfund transactions and relationships of each type of fund with other funds are illustrated. Finally, a comprehensive summary of interfund and interfund-account group accounting is presented in Chapter 12.

## Questions

**Q 9-1**   Distinguish between *interfund transactions* and *interfund relationships*.

**Q 9-2**   Distinguish between a *fund* and an *account group*.

**Q 9-3**   What criteria must be met for an asset to be classified as a *fixed* asset? A *general* fixed asset?

**Q 9-4**   Generally speaking, what is meant by the term *cost* when determining what costs should be assigned to a fixed asset?

**Q 9-5**   A governmental unit acquired land, buildings, other improvements, and certain equipment for a single lump-sum purchase price. How should the portion of the total cost attributable to the various assets acquired be determined?

**Q 9-6**   Fixed assets may be acquired through exercise of a government's power of *eminent domain* and by *escheat*. Distinguish between these terms.

**Q 9-7**   A municipality was granted certain land for use as a playground. The property was appraised at $400,000 at the time of the grant. Subsequently, all land in the neighborhood rose in value by 30%. Should the increase be reflected in the GFA accounts?

**Q 9-8**   A municipality owns a fire station and is required to pay assessments of $10,000 as an owner of property in the benefited area. As a result of the improvements, the property in the benefited area has risen in value by 15%. Should the asset be written up, and, if so, by how much?

**Q 9-9**   Why does the GASB *Codification* not require the capitalization and reporting of infrastructure general fixed assets?

**Q 9-10**  What liabilities are accounted for through the General Long-Term Debt Account Group? Which items of long-term debt are excluded?

**Q 9-11**  In earlier years, general fixed assets and general long-term debt were both accounted for in a single Capital Fund. Why do you suppose general fixed assets and general long-term debt are not now accounted for and reported in the same account group?

**Q 9-12**  An asset originally financed out of a Special Revenue Fund and accounted for in the General Fixed Assets Account Group was sold. To which fund would you credit the proceeds? Why?

**Q 9-13**  Assume that the asset referred to in the preceding question was financed from a Special Assessment Capital Projects Fund. To which fund should the proceeds from the sale of this asset be credited? Explain.

**Q 9-14**  On June 1, 19W3, $300,000 par value of 20-year term general obligation sinking fund bonds were issued by a governmental unit. Only $50,000 had been accumulated in the Debt Service (Sinking) Fund by May 30, 19Y4, the end of the unit's fiscal year, and there was no possibility of retiring the bonds from resources of other funds during that year. Should the matured bonds be reported in the General Fund or in the Debt Service Fund, or should they continue to be accounted for in the General Long-Term Debt Account Group? Why?

**Q 9-15**  What effect might funded reserve requirements of serial bond covenants have on the General Long-Term Debt Account Group?

**Q 9-16**  Unmatured general government liabilities are recorded in the General Long-Term Debt Account Group. Neither special assessment debt that is expected to be serviced by special assessments, but on which the government is obligated in some manner, nor underfunded pension contributions seem to fit this definition—yet both are recorded in the GLTDAG. Why do you suppose this is so?

**Q 9-17**  Records of fixed assets owned by Lucas County have never been maintained in a systematic manner. The auditor has recommended that an inventory be taken and that a General Fixed Assets Account Group be established and maintained. The governing board agrees that it needs better fixed asset control but has tentatively concluded that no action will be taken in this regard because the appraisal fee estimates provided by reputable appraisal firms far exceed the amount of resources available for such an undertaking. What suggestions or comments, if any, would you offer upon your advice being sought by members of the board?

**Q 9-18**   Near the end of 20X5, a city purchased an automobile at a cost of $12,000. The vehicle was wrecked during 20X6 and sold for salvage for $1,000. Assuming that the automobile was purchased from General Fund resources and the salvage proceeds were also recorded there, what entries would be made in 20X5 and 20X6 to reflect these facts? Might misleading inferences be drawn from the General Fund statements for 20X6?

**Q 9-19**   Why is there no operating statement equivalent to that for governmental funds for either the General Fixed Assets Account Group or the General Long-Term Debt Account Group?

**Q 9-20**   It has been proposed that (1) all general fixed assets, including "infrastructure" assets, be recorded, (2) only fixed asset–related noncurrent debt be considered general long-term debt—and all other general government liabilities be considered fund liabilities— and (3) the redefined general fixed assets and general long-term debt be accounted for and reported in a single Capital Fund. What do you consider the advantages and disadvantages of this proposal to be?

## Problems

**P 9-1**   (Multiple Choice)

1. Ariel Village issued the following bonds during the year ended June 30, 20X1:

| | |
|---|---|
| Revenue bonds to be repaid from admission fees collected by the Ariel Zoo enterprise fund ....................... | $200,000 |
| General obligation bonds issued for the Ariel water and sewer enterprise fund which will service the debt ............. | 300,000 |

How much of these bonds should be accounted for in Ariel's General Long-Term Debt Account Group?
   a. $500,000        c. $300,000
   b. $200,000        d. $0

2. The following assets are among those owned by the city of Foster:

| | |
|---|---|
| Apartment building (part of the principal of a Nonexpendable Trust Fund) ..................................... | $  200,000 |
| City hall ........................................ | 800,000 |
| Three fire stations ................................ | 1,000,000 |
| City streets and sidewalks .......................... | 5,000,000 |

How much should be included in Foster's General Fixed Assets Account Group?
   a. $2,000,000 or $7,000,000, depending on city policy
   b. $1,800,000 or $6,800,000, depending on city policy
   c. $6,800,000
   d. $7,000,000

3. The Amount Available in Debt Service Funds is an account of a governmental unit that would be included in the
   a. liability section of the Debt Service Fund.
   b. liability section of the General Long-Term Debt Account Group.
   c. asset section of the Debt Service Fund.
   d. "Other Debits" section of the General Long-Term Debt Account Group.

4. Penn City's Capital Projects Fund incurred expenditures of $4,000,000 on a project in 20X0. $3,600,000 has been paid on these expenditures. Additionally,

encumbrances outstanding on the project at December 31, 20X0 total $8,000,000. What amount should be recorded in Penn City's General Fixed Assets Account Group at December 31, 20X0 for this project?

a. $3,600,000          c. $11,600,000
b. $4,000,000          d. $12,000,000

5. Fred Bosin donated a building to Palma City in 19X3. Bosin's original cost of the property was $100,000. Accumulated depreciation at the date of the gift amounted to $60,000. Fair value at the date of the gift was $300,000. In the General Fixed Assets Account Group, at what amount should Palma City record this donated fixed asset?

a. $300,000          c. $40,000
b. $100,000          d. $0

6. Harris Village issued the following bonds during the year ended June 30, 19X3:

| | |
|---|---|
| For installation of general government street lights, to be assessed against properties benefited .................. | $300,000 |
| For construction of public swimming pool; bonds to be paid from pledged fees collected from pool users ......... | 400,000 |

How much should be accounted for through Debt Service Funds for payments of principal over the life of the bonds?

a. $0          c. $400,000
b. $300,000          d. $700,000

7. The following items were among Payne Township's General Fund expenditures during the year ended July 31, 19X3:

| | |
|---|---|
| Computer for tax collector's office ..................... | $44,000 |
| Equipment for Township Hall ........................ | 80,000 |

How much should be classified as fixed assets in Payne's General Fund balance sheet at July 31, 19X3?

a. $124,000          c. $44,000
b. $80,000          d. $0

8. Proceeds of General Obligation Bonds is an account of A Governmental Unit that would be included in the

a. Enterprise Fund.          d. Debt Service Fund.
b. Internal Service Fund.          e. General Long-Term Debt
c. Capital Projects Fund.                 Account Group.

9. The following balances are included in the subsidiary records of Burwood Village's Parks and Recreation Department at March 31, 19X2:

| | |
|---|---|
| Appropriations—supplies ............................. | $7,500 |
| Expenditures—supplies ............................... | 4,500 |
| Encumbrances—supply orders ......................... | 750 |

How much does the department have available for additional purchases of supplies?

a. $0          c. $3,000
b. $2,250          d. $6,750

10. When fixed assets purchased from General Fund revenues were received, the appropriate journal entry was made in the General Fixed Assets Account Group. What account, if any, should have been debited in the General Fund?

a. No journal entry should have been made in the General Fund.
b. Fixed Assets
c. Expenditures
d. Due from General Fixed Assets Account Group

(AICPA, adapted)

**P 9-2** (GFA Account Group Entries) Prepare the general ledger entries required in the General Fixed Assets Account Group of Meyer County to record the following transactions.

1. Purchased computer equipment needed to update the library's cataloging system and to interface it with the Internet. The equipment costing $320,000 was purchased through the county's Library Special Revenue Fund. Half of the cost was paid upon delivery and the balance is due in 90 days. Resources for this fund come from a special property tax levied for the library.

2. Construction costs incurred during the year on a new county park totaled $2,000,000. $1,900,000 has been paid. Encumbrances for contracted work that is still underway at year end totaled $1,000,000. The project is financed from bond proceeds.

3. In a recent drug arrest the county confiscated a new sports car valued at $65,000. The county has kept the car for use by undercover agents in future drug investigations.

4. Computers previously used by the Water and Sewer Enterprise Fund were given to General Fund departments. The Water and Sewer Department originally purchased the computers three years earlier for $17,000. Accumulated depreciation of $10,000 has been recorded in the Enterprise Fund on the computers to date. The fair value of the computers at the date of the exchange was approximately $7,300.

5. The county traded in an old fire truck for a new one. In addition, the county paid $300,000 cash. The original cost of the old truck was $150,000. Its fair value at the trade-in date was $58,000.

**P 9-3** (GFA Account Group Entries) Prepare general journal entries to record the effects on the General Fixed Assets Account Group of the following transactions. The transactions are independent of each other unless otherwise noted. Assume straight-line depreciation is used when depreciation is required and that no depreciation is recorded or reported unless required.

1. A government leased computers with a capitalizable cost of $150,000, including $30,000 paid at the inception of the lease agreement. The lease is properly classified as a capital lease, and the computers are for the use of the government's finance and accounting division.

2. A government foreclosed on land against which it had tax liens amounting to $20,000. The estimated salable value of the land is $18,500. The government decided to use the land as the site for a new baseball park.

3. Construction costs billed during the year on a new addition to city hall totaled $8,000,000. $7,600,000 was paid to the contractors. Encumbrances of $10,000,000 were outstanding at year end related to the project. $3,000,000 of general revenues were transferred to the City Hall Addition Capital Projects Fund; the remainder of the construction costs are being financed from bond proceeds.

4. In the next year, the city hall addition in 3 was completed at an additional cost of $9,800,000. The building was inspected and approved, but $2,000,000 of the construction costs still have not been paid.

5. General government fixed assets with an original cost of $300,000 were sold three-fourths of the way through their useful lives for $65,000. The assets were originally financed half from general revenues and half from bond proceeds.

6. An uninsured storage building used by general government departments was destroyed by a tornado. Its original cost was $92,000. Its useful life was only half over, and it is estimated that it will cost $250,000 to replace the building.

7. A dump truck originally purchased for and used by a city Enterprise Fund has been transferred to the streets and roads department—a general government department. The truck originally cost $80,000 and is halfway through its estimated useful life. Its residual value is $18,000.

8. Computers with an original cost of $40,000 and estimated residual value of $5,000 were transferred out of General Fund departments to the municipal golf course,

which is accounted for in an Enterprise Fund. The transfer occurred at the end of the estimated useful life of the computers.

**P 9-4** (GLTD Account Group Entries) Prepare the general ledger entries required in the General Long-Term Debt Account Group of Barger County to record the following transactions.
1. Barger County issued $20,000,000 of 8%, 5-year refunding bonds to help finance an in-substance defeasance of its $28,000,000 face value courthouse bonds.
2. The county paid $30,000,000 to an irrevocable trust established at New Castle National Bank to accomplish the in-substance defeasance of the courthouse bonds.
3. Repeat parts 1 and 2. Assume that the payment to the trust does not constitute an in-substance defeasance of the courthouse bonds.
4. Midway through the fiscal year, the county leased buses for its school system under a capital lease agreement. A down payment of $300,000 was paid. The total capitalizable cost of the leased buses was $2,500,000, including the down payment. The interest rate implicit in the lease is 15%.
5. The county made its first annual payment under the lease agreement for the buses, $900,000.
6. The county paid $2,000,000 for claims and judgments related to general government activities during the year. Its current liability for claims and judgments increased by $50,000. The long-term portion of this obligation decreased by $200,000 during the year.

**P 9-5** (GLTD Account Group Entries) Prepare general journal entries to record the effects on the General Long-Term Debt Account Group of the following transactions. The transactions are independent of each other unless otherwise noted.
1. The fund balance of the Municipal Arts Center Debt Service Fund increased by $90,000 during the year. The entire fund balance is available for retirement of the Municipal Arts Center General Obligation Bonds.
2. Special assessment bonds guaranteed by the government matured and were paid during the year. $50,000 principal and $30,000 interest were paid. The beginning fund balance of the Special Assessment Debt Service Fund was $48,000—all of which was deemed available for principal retirement. The ending fund balance of that fund was $45,000.
3. Principal and interest on the County Courthouse Serial Bonds matured during the year. There was no beginning fund balance in the related Debt Service Fund. The maturing interest ($200,000) was paid but the maturing principal ($75,000) had not been paid by year end. General Fund revenues were transferred to cover the interest payments.
4. General Fund expenditures accounts included a Rent Expenditures account with a balance of $200,000. Further investigation of the account indicated that the balance resulted from the payment of $40,000 on operating leases and $160,000 of lease payments on a capital lease (of which $90,000 was for imputed interest).
5. The total general government underfunded pension liability at the beginning of the fiscal year was $14,000,000. Of this, $1,500,000 was considered current. The total general government underfunded pension liability at the end of the fiscal year was $14,500,000. Of this, $2,500,000 was considered current.
6. Advance refunding bonds ($10,000,000 par) were issued. The proceeds of the refunding and $2,000,000 of previously accumulated Debt Service Fund resources were set aside in an irrevocable trust to defease in substance $11,500,000 of School Bonds.
7. Assume the same information as in 6, except that the School Bonds are not defeased in substance as a result of the transaction described.
8. Bond anticipation notes that meet the criteria for noncurrent treatment were issued to provide financing for a general government capital project. The notes, which have a par value of $5,000,000, are issued at 101.

**P 9-6**  (Interfund-Account Group Entries) Prepare all journal entries required in all funds and/or account groups to record the following transactions and events.

1. A state issued $50,000,000 of 4% term bonds at 105 to provide financing for construction of a new state legislative office building. The premium, which is to be used for debt service, was transferred to the appropriate fund.
2. The state signed contracts for $55,000,000 for construction of the building. Costs incurred for construction of the office building during Year 1 amounted to $18,000,000, all but 10% of which was paid.
3. Interest of $2,000,000 was paid on the bonds in Year 1.
4. General Fund resources, $5,000,000, were transferred to the Legislative Office Building Capital Projects Fund during Year 2 for use on the project.
5. The project was completed. Expenditures in Year 2 totaled $36,500,000, and all fund liabilities were paid. The remaining resources, to be used for debt service, were paid to the appropriate fund.
6. $3,300,000 was transferred from the General Fund to service the bonds in Year 2.
7. Interest of $2,000,000 was paid in Year 2.
8. The bonds were paid in Year 20. $46,000,000 had been accumulated previously in the Debt Service Fund to retire the bonds; the remainder needed to retire the bonds and make the last $2,000,000 interest payment was transferred from the General Fund in Year 20.

**P 9-7**  (Interfund-Account Group Entries) Prepare all journal entries required in all funds and/or account groups to record the following transactions and events.

1. The county sold old equipment, original cost $800,000, for $127,000. The equipment was included in the General Fixed Assets Account Group.
2. The county leased equipment for use by departments financed through the General Fund under a capital lease. The capitalizable cost was $780,000; an initial payment of $100,000 was made.
3. The county ordered new patrol cars estimated to cost $100,000.
4. The county received the patrol cars along with an invoice for $101,200.
5. Land with a fair value of $90,000 was donated to the county. The donor had paid $37,000 for the land when he acquired it 4 years ago.
6. Bonds of $2,000,000 were issued at par for Enterprise Fund purposes. The bonds are to be repaid from the revenues of the Enterprise Fund. However, they are backed by the full faith and credit of the county; if the bonds cannot be repaid from the Enterprise Fund, general revenues must be used to repay them.

**P 9-8**  (Interfund-Account Group Entries) Record the following transactions in all the affected funds and account groups of a county. Reflect all required accruals as well.

1. A county transferred $2,000,000 of general revenues to the fund to be used to pay principal and interest on its outstanding bonds.
2. Principal of $10,000,000 and interest of $2,000,000 became due and payable on the bonds referred to in the preceding transaction. Only the interest was paid.
3. The government sold a building that has been used to house government offices. The building, which originally cost $1,500,000, was sold for $2,000,000.
4. The county entered into a capital lease for police vehicles. The capitalizable cost of the vehicles was $550,000, including a $50,000 down payment. The lease was initiated at midyear and the first annual payment is due in 1 year. The implicit interest rate on the lease was 20%.
5. In the next year, the county paid the first annual lease payment, $150,000.
6. The actuarially required payment from the county to its pension plan for its general government employees was $3,000,000. The county only paid $1,000,000. It is not likely that the balance will be paid in the near future.
7. The county completed construction of a general government building at a total cost of $18,000,000, all but 10% of which has been paid. Construction billings for the current year totaled $10,000,000.

**P 9-9** (Interfund-Account Group Entries) The following transactions and events (among others) affected the state of Texva during 19X3. (The state updates the account group accounts throughout the year.)

1. It was discovered that in 19X2 $440,000 of expenditures properly chargeable to Highway Patrol—Salaries and Wages in the General Fund had been inadvertently charged to the Highway Department—Salaries and Wages account in Special Revenue Fund #4. The amount was repaid during 19X3.

2. The Health Department, which is financed from Special Revenue Fund #2, entered a capital lease for equipment that could have been purchased outright for $600,000. (The capital lease has a 6% effective interest rate.)

3. Special Revenue Fund #4 was reimbursed for $700,000 of 19X3 salaries and wages for Highway Department employees working on a bridge construction project, which is financed by serial bonds and accounted for in Capital Projects Fund #7.

4. The first annual $100,000 payment on the Health Department equipment capital lease (transaction 2) was made.

5. A three-year advance was made from the General Fund to Debt Service Fund #12, $500,000.

6. Serial bonds, $4,000,000, were issued at 96 to finance a construction project being financed from Capital Projects Fund #7.

7. After its accounts were closed for 19X3, the $375,000 net assets (cash) of term bond Debt Service Fund #1 were transferred to establish Debt Service Fund #14 to service the serial bonds issued at transaction 6, and Debt Service Fund #1 was abolished.

8. Health department land and buildings—originally purchased through Special Revenue Fund #2 for $50,000 and $450,000, respectively—were sold for $12,000,000, and the proceeds were recorded in Special Revenue Fund #2.

9. Although the actuarially required payment from the General Fund to the state pension plan was $15,000,000, only $6,000,000 was paid during 19X3. The 19X4 appropriation bill enacted recently provides for another $2,000,000 payment on the 19X3 contribution—which normally would have been paid from assets on hand at the end of 19X3. The $2,000,000 payment was provided for by continuing the 19X3 appropriations for that purpose, but it is uncertain when (if ever) the remaining 19X3 contributions will be made.

*Required* Prepare the journal entries to record these transactions and events in the general ledgers of the various governmental funds and account groups of the state of Texva. Assume that an appropriate series of Revenues, Expenditures, and Investment in General Fixed Assets accounts was used in each general ledger.

**P 9-10** (Interfund-Account Group Entries—Review) The following selected transactions and events (among others) affected the Vatexona Independent School District during the 19X8 and 19X9 fiscal years. (The Vatexona ISD updates the General Long-Term Debt Account Group accounts throughout the year, but updates the General Fixed Assets Account Group accounts only at year end.)

### 19X8 Transactions and Events

1. A $1,000,000 serial bond issue was issued at 102 during 19X8 to partially finance a new elementary school building that is expected to cost, and be financed, as follows:

| | |
|---|---:|
| Bond issue | $1,000,000 |
| State grant | 400,000 |
| General Fund transfer | 200,000 |
| | $1,600,000 |

(Assume that project appropriations and estimated financing sources were authorized previously, but budgetary accounts other than Encumbrances are not recorded in the CPF accounts.)

2. The bond premium was immediately transferred to the Debt Service Fund for the bond issue, and was ordered to be fully reserved for debt principal retirement.
3. Capital outlay expenditures incurred for the new elementary school building during 19X8 of $1,000,000, as encumbered, were vouchered for payment net of a 5% retained percentage.
4. The state grantor agency was billed for its share of the 19X8 elementary school building expenditures (25%) on the expenditure-driven reimbursement grant. (The billing is expected to be collected in 30 to 45 days.)
5. Transfers were made from the General Fund during 19X8 as follows:

**Debt Service Fund**

| | |
|---|---|
| For bond principal retirement ........................ | $ 50,000 |
| For interest and fiscal agent charges .................... | 65,000 |
| | 115,000 |

**Capital Projects Fund**

| | |
|---|---|
| For elementary school building (only $80,000 paid during 19X8) ...................................... | 200,000 |
| | $315,000 |

6. Debt Service Fund expenditures paid during 19X8 on the elementary school building bonds were:

| | |
|---|---|
| Bond principal ...................................... | $ 50,000 |
| Interest and fiscal agent charges ....................... | 64,000 |
| | $114,000 |

7. The Capital Projects Fund accounts were closed at the end of 19X8.

### *19X9 Transactions and Events*

8. The elementary school building was completed during 19X9. The remaining state grant was billed and received; the contractor was paid in full, as was the General Fund transfer; and all other preclosing transactions and events were recorded. After all of these transactions and events were properly recorded (do not record them), the preclosing balances of the Capital Projects Fund at the end of 19X9 included Cash, Unreserved Fund Balance, and these operating amounts:

| | |
|---|---|
| Revenues—State Grant .............................. | $145,000 |
| Expenditures—Capital Outlay ......................... | 580,000 |

   The remaining Capital Projects Fund balance was transferred to the Debt Service Fund and the CPF accounts were closed.
9. The Vatexona ISD estimates that it had these unrecorded estimated liabilities at the end of 19X9:

| | Total | Current Portion |
|---|---|---|
| Claims and judgments ................................ | $300,000 | $50,000 |
| Vacation and sick leave .............................. | 450,000 | 80,000 |

   None of these amounts related to prior years, during which related amounts had been properly recorded. The current portion will be paid from the General Fund.

***Required*** Prepare the entries required to record these transactions and events in the general ledger accounts of the affected funds and account groups of Vatexona Independent School District. Assume that an appropriate series of Revenues, Expenditures, and

Investment in General Fixed Assets accounts is used in the general ledgers of the funds and account groups.

**P 9-11** (Interfund-Account Group GL Error Correction Entries) You have been engaged by the town of Rego to examine its June 30, 19X8 balance sheet. You are the first CPA to be engaged by the town and find that acceptable methods of municipal accounting have not been employed. The town clerk stated that the books had not been closed and presented the following preclosing trial balance of the General Fund as of June 30, 19X8:

| | Debit | Credit |
|---|---|---|
| Cash | $150,000 | |
| Taxes Receivable—Current | 59,200 | |
| Allowance for Uncollectible Current Taxes | | $18,000 |
| Taxes Receivable—Delinquent | 8,000 | |
| Allowance for Uncollectible Delinquent Taxes | | 10,200 |
| Estimated Revenues | 310,000 | |
| Appropriations | | 348,000 |
| Donated Land | 27,000 | |
| Building Addition | 50,000 | |
| Serial Bonds Paid | 16,000 | |
| Expenditures | 280,000 | |
| Special Assessment Bonds Payable | | 100,000 |
| Revenues | | 354,000 |
| Accounts Payable | | 26,000 |
| Fund Balance | | 44,000 |
| | $900,200 | $900,200 |

**Additional Information:**
1. The estimated losses of $18,000 for current taxes receivable were determined to be a reasonable estimate. Current taxes become delinquent on June 30 of each year.
2. Included in the Revenues account is a credit of $27,000 representing the value of land donated by the state as a grant-in-aid for construction of a municipal park.
3. The Building Addition account balance is the cost of an addition to the town hall building. This addition was constructed and completed in June 19X8. The payment was recorded in the General Fund as authorized.
4. The Serial Bonds Paid account reflects the annual retirement of general obligation bonds issued to finance the construction of the town hall. Interest payments of $7,000 for this bond issue are included in Expenditures.
5. Operating supplies ordered in the prior fiscal year ($8,800) were received, recorded, and consumed in July 19X7. (Encumbered appropriations lapse one year after the end of the fiscal year for which they are made.)
6. Outstanding purchase orders at June 30, 19X8 for operating supplies totaled $2,100. These purchase orders were not recorded in the accounts.
7. The special assessment bonds are guaranteed by the town of Rego and were sold in June 19X8 to finance a street-paving project. No contracts have been signed for this project and no expenditures have been made.
8. The balance in the Revenues account includes credits for $20,000 for a note issued to a bank to obtain cash in anticipation of tax collections. The note was still outstanding at June 30, 19X8.

*Required* (a) Prepare the formal adjusting and closing journal entries for the General Fund for the fiscal year ended June 30, 19X8.

(b) The foregoing information disclosed by your examination was recorded only in the General Fund even though other funds or account groups were involved. Prepare the formal adjusting journal entries for any other funds or account groups involved. (AICPA, adapted)

**P 9-12** (Research and Analysis) Obtain a recent comprehensive annual financial report (CAFR) from a state or local government and note its presentations and disclosures with respect to general fixed assets (GFA) and general long-term debt (GLTD).

*Required* (1) **Table of Contents.** What indications of GFA and GLTD presentations and disclosures are evident from the CAFR table of contents? (Attach a copy of the table of contents.)

(2) **General Purpose Financial Statements (GPFS).** Describe the GFA and GLTD information presented in the GPFS—including the categories of GFA and GLTD, the relative aggregation or disaggregation of the GFA and GLTD information, and the other significant matters that come to your attention as you review the GPFS. (Attach copies of GPFS that include GFA and/or GLTD presentations.)

(3) **Notes.** Describe the GFA and GLTD information presented in the notes to the GPFS—including the type of information, the relative aggregation or disaggregation of the information, and other matters coming to your attention as you review the notes. (Attach copies of the GFA and GLTD note presentations and disclosures.)

(4) **Combining and Individual Fund/Account Group Statements and Schedules.** Describe the GFA and GLTD information presented in the combining and individual fund and account group statements and schedules—including whether the CAFR has separate sections (perhaps tabbed) for GFA and GLTD information, the nature of the presentations and disclosures, and other matters coming to your attention during your review. (Attach copies of the more significant GFA and GLTD presentations and disclosures in this CAFR section.)

CHAPTER

# 10

# TRUST AND AGENCY (FIDUCIARY) FUNDS

A **Trust Fund** is established to account for assets received and held by a government acting in the capacity of trustee or custodian. **Agency Funds** are used to account for assets received by a government in its capacity as an agent for individuals, businesses, or other governments.

The government acts in a **fiduciary** capacity in all trust or agency relationships. Typically, the government is managing assets that belong to another agency or individual, and how the assets must be handled and used is directed by that agency or individual. The difference between trust and agency relationships often is one of degree. Trust Funds may be subject to complex administrative and financial provisions set forth in trust agreements, may exist for long periods of time, and may involve investment or other management of trust assets. Thus, Trust Fund management and accounting may be very complex. Agency Funds, on the other hand, are primarily clearance devices for cash collected for others, held briefly, and then disbursed to authorized recipients. The essential equation for Agency Funds is that assets equal liabilities.

Trust Funds and Agency Funds comprise the fiduciary category of funds. Most trust and agency activities of governments are accounted for in Trust Funds or Agency Funds. The principal exception is that some enterprise trust and agency relationships (such as customer deposits) are accounted for in Enterprise Funds (Chapter 12). Too, minor agency relationships of general government activities may be handled in the governmental funds, if desired, as long as the government maintains appropriate accountability and does not violate any laws or regulations.

## THE ACCOUNTABILITY FOCUS

General Fund and Special Revenue Fund accounting focuses primarily on operating budget compliance during a specified fiscal year. Capital Projects Fund accounting generally focuses mainly on the project rather than a specific year, and on the capital program or capital budget. The accountability focus in Trust and Agency Fund accounting, on the other hand, is on the government's fulfillment of its fiduciary responsibilities during a specified period and on its remaining responsibilities at the end of the period.

Trust Fund accounting, therefore, must ensure that the money or other resources are handled in accordance with the terms of the trust agreement and/or applicable trust laws. The accounting for Agency Funds must ensure proper handling of collections and prompt payments to those for whom they are collected. The net amount of resources in a Trust Fund is usually indicated in a Fund Balance account. This account reflects the government's accountability as trustee for the use and disposition of the resources in its care. In the case of the Agency Fund the accountability concept is the liability concept, and even in the Trust Fund there is an obligation for the government to use fund resources to discharge the assigned function. Violating trust terms could result in litigation, civil penalties, or even forfeiture of fund resources.

# TRUST FUNDS

The GASB classifies Trust Funds as expendable, nonexpendable, and pension. **Expendable Trust Funds** are similar to **governmental** funds. They are oriented to the inflow, outflow, and balances of resources much as are the General and Special Revenue Funds. In fact, Expendable Trust Funds operate very much like Special Revenue Funds. An example is a trust fund established to account for the use of endowment income as specified by a donor.

**Nonexpendable Trust Funds** require fund principal to be maintained. Net income (or a similar figure) also must be reported. Such funds are operated and accounted for essentially like their private sector counterparts, and hence are **proprietary** in nature. An endowment fund whose principal must be kept intact is a good example of a proprietary or nonexpendable fund. If the earnings are available to support a specified governmental activity, they should be transferred to and accounted for in an expendable trust fund. Another nonexpendable trust fund example is a loan fund whose principal and earnings must be kept intact.

**Pension Trust Funds** are used to account for government pension plans. The activities of the plan include receiving and investing contributions made by the government, its employees, or others to finance pensions, and paying pensions to beneficiaries. In its investment activities, the pension fund is similar to the nonexpendable fund, but in its pension payment activities it is like the expendable fund.

An exhaustive treatment of trust law and accounting is beyond the scope of this text. Rather, the more usual types of Trust Funds found in state and local governments are briefly considered and illustrated here. Determining appropriate systems and procedures in specific cases may require a search of the more technical accounting, legal, and insurance literature or the assistance of specialists within one or more of these fields.

The authoritative literature provides relatively little specific guidance for Trust and Agency Funds (other than Pension Trust Funds). This lack of specific guidance is probably because (1) Agency Funds have no "operations" and (2) Trust Funds other than Pension Trust Funds are essentially accounted for either (a) like governmental funds (Expendable Trust Funds) or (b) like proprietary funds (Nonexpendable Trust Funds).

## Budgetary Considerations

Because of the differences in complexity and purpose of Trust Funds, some should be formally budgeted and controlled by budgetary control accounts and some should not. In many cases the government manages or transmits fund resources in accordance with specific instructions or customary trust practices and does not need a formal budget. A flexible (business-type) budget may be useful for nonexpendable (proprietary-type) funds with complex operations. Furthermore, because most expendable (governmental) funds are in essence Special Revenue Funds, their resources may properly be budgeted as part of the government's operating budget and be subjected to formal budgetary control. No major budgetary problems are posed by Trust Funds; therefore, their budgetary accounting is not illustrated.

## Expendable Trust Funds

The most common type of Expendable Trust Fund results from governments accepting resources that they agree to spend as specified by the donor. Examples include assets donated to support the operations of a library or to provide food, shelter, or health care to the needy. These assets should be recorded in a separate fund. Additionally, a budget should be adopted for the fund (frequently as a part of the government's operating budget), and expenditures should be controlled and recorded. Another common example of an activity accounted for in Expendable Trust Funds is deferred compensation plans for employees. These plans are accounted for in Expendable Trust Funds if the government has fiduciary responsibility for the assets.[1] Expendable Trust Funds operate **like Special Revenue Funds,** and are illustrated briefly in the section on Endowment Funds.

## Nonexpendable Trust Funds

There are two types of Nonexpendable Trust Funds. In one type, neither the principal nor the earnings of the fund may be expended. In the other type, the earnings may be expended but principal must be kept intact. A loan fund is an example of the first type. Some common forms of endowment funds are examples of the second type. In the second type of trust—with expendable earnings—principal (corpus) and income must be distinguished carefully. Also, the "earnings" that are expendable may be uniquely defined by the trust instrument or applicable laws. The same principles and distinctions apply as in trust accounting generally. The creator or donor can specify the items of revenue, expense, gain, or loss that affect trust principal and those that are treated as trust earnings. A Nonexpendable Trust Fund is used to account for the nonexpendable portions of such partially expendable trusts. The income/loss of the trust is also measured and reported in this fund. Then, the expendable resources of the trust are transferred to a separate Expendable Trust Fund established to account for the expendable resources of the trust.

### Loan Funds

The following transactions and entries illustrate the operation of a loan fund. Both principal and earnings are nonexpendable.

**Transactions and Entries**

**1.** A cash donation of $100,000 was received to establish a loan fund.

(1)  Cash . . . . . . . . . . . . . . . . . . . . . . . . . . . . . . . . . . . . . . . . .    $100,000
       **Fund Balance—Nonexpendable**  . . . . . . . . . . . . . . . . .              $100,000
       To record receipt of cash to establish a loan fund.

---

[1] GASB *Statement No. 32,* "Accounting and Financial Reporting for Internal Revenue Code Section 457 Deferred Compensation Plans" (Norwalk, Conn.: GASB, 1997).

**2.** Loans of $60,000 were made.

| (2) Loans Receivable | $60,000 | |
|---|---|---|
|     Cash | | $60,000 |

To record loans made.

**3.** A loan of $1,000 was collected with interest of $20.

| (3) Cash | $1,020 | |
|---|---|---|
|     Loans Receivable | | $1,000 |
|     Interest Revenues | | 20 |

To record collection of loan with interest.

**4.** Interest receivable, $2,300, was accrued at year end.

| (4) Interest Receivable | $2,300 | |
|---|---|---|
|     Interest Revenues | | $2,300 |

To accrue interest receivable at year end.

**5.** Several loans and the related interest receivable were written off as uncollectible.

| (5) Uncollectible Accounts Expense | $2,100 | |
|---|---|---|
|     Loans Receivable | | $1,800 |
|     Interest Receivable | | 300 |

To write off uncollectible loans and interest receivable.

**6.** The accounts were closed.

| (6) Interest Revenues | $2,320 | |
|---|---|---|
|     Uncollectible Accounts Expense | | $2,100 |
|     Fund Balance—Nonexpendable | | 220 |

To close the accounts.

The year end balance sheet for this Loan Fund reports cash and loans receivable as assets and reports a fund balance of $100,220. Only one fund balance amount appears. There is no need to distinguish between the original capital and the $220 increase during the period because both are nonexpendable and are available for loans.

If the costs of administration are payable out of a loan fund, administration expenses would reduce its earnings and, consequently, the available balance of fund resources. Note also that though theoretically the loan fund illustrated is non-expendable, uncollectible loans may reduce the fund balance.

### Endowment Funds

We noted earlier that some trusts are best accounted for by using both an **Expendable** (governmental type) Trust Fund and a **Nonexpendable** (proprietary type) Trust Fund. For example, assume an individual who donates money and other property stipulates that the income earned on those assets be used to finance certain activities. Because the donor intended the principal to be held intact and only the income expended, two funds are established: (1) A Nonexpendable Trust Fund is used to account for the principal and to measure and report the amount of earnings; (2) An Expendable Trust Fund is used to account for the expendable earnings.[2]

---

[2] Alternatively, a single Trust Fund having separate Fund Balance—Principal and Fund Balance—Earnings accounts may be established. In this case, the gains, losses, revenues, and expenses attributed to principal (corpus) are closed to the Fund Balance—Principal account; those entering into the determination of trust income and expenditures of earnings for their designated uses are closed to Fund Balance—Earnings. Even under this accounting approach, however, the trust should be reported as if it were accounted for in two separate funds.

Significant legal and accounting issues may be associated with trust agreements of this type. As noted earlier, a discussion of the principles of trust accounting is beyond the scope of this book. Selected principles are illustrated in the following transactions and entries for an endowment fund.

**Transactions and Entries**

**1.** Cash of $210,000 was received to establish a fund whose income is to be used to grant scholarships.

**(1) Endowment Principal Fund**

| | | |
|---|---|---|
| Cash | $210,000 | |
| Fund Balance—Nonexpendable | | $210,000 |

To record establishment of endowment fund.

Note that the Endowment Principal Fund is a Nonexpendable Trust Fund.

**2.** Investments, par value $200,000, were purchased at a premium of $3,000 plus accrued interest of $400.

**(2) Endowment Principal Fund**

| | | |
|---|---|---|
| Investments | $203,000 | |
| Accrued Interest Receivable | 400 | |
| Cash | | $203,400 |

To record purchase of investments.

**3.** A check for $3,000 was received for interest on the investments.

**(3) Endowment Principal Fund**

| | | |
|---|---|---|
| Cash | $3,000 | |
| Accrued Interest Receivable | | $ 400 |
| Interest Revenues | | 2,600 |

To record collection of interest on investments.

**4.** Securities with a carrying value of $3,042 were sold for $3,055 plus accrued (previously unrecorded) interest of $35.

**(4) Endowment Principal Fund**

| | | |
|---|---|---|
| Cash | $3,090 | |
| Investments | | $3,042 |
| Interest Revenues | | 35 |
| Gain on Sale of Investments | | 13 |

To record sale of investments at a gain of $13, and related interest income of $35.

Note: In this example Endowment Principal Fund investments are assumed to be exempt from the fair value provisions of GASB *Statement No. 31*.

**5.** Interest receivable, $2,600, was recorded.

**(5) Endowment Principal Fund**

| | | |
|---|---|---|
| Interest Receivable on Investments | $2,600 | |
| Interest Revenues | | $2,600 |

To record interest accrued on investments and related premium amortization.

**6.** The total interest earnings to date were recorded as a liability of the Endowment Principal Fund to the Endowment Earnings Fund. (Note that the Endowment Earnings Fund is an Expendable Trust Fund.)

**(6) (a) Endowment Principal Fund**

| | | |
|---|---|---|
| Operating Transfer to Endowment Earnings Fund .... | $5,235 | |
| Due to Endowment Earnings Fund .............. | | $5,235 |

To record transfer of endowment earnings to date.

**(6) (b) Endowment Earnings Fund**

| | | |
|---|---|---|
| Due from Endowment Principal Fund ............. | $5,235 | |
| Operating Transfer from Endowment Principal Fund .. | | $5,235 |

To record amount due from endowment principal fund for earnings to date.

**7.** A $2,500 payment was made from the Endowment Principal Fund to the Endowment Earnings Fund.

**(7) (a) Endowment Principal Fund**

| | | |
|---|---|---|
| Due to Endowment Earnings Fund ................ | $2,500 | |
| Cash ....................................... | | $2,500 |

To record partial payment of liability to endowment earnings fund.

**(7) (b) Endowment Earnings Fund**

| | | |
|---|---|---|
| Cash ....................................... | $2,500 | |
| Due from Endowment Principal Fund ............ | | $2,500 |

To record receipt of part of receivable from endowment principal fund.

**8.** A $2,000 scholarship grant was made from the Endowment Earnings Fund.

**(8) Endowment Earnings Fund**

| | | |
|---|---|---|
| Expenditures—Scholarship Grant ................. | $2,000 | |
| Cash ....................................... | | $2,000 |

To record payment of scholarship.

**9.** Closing entries were prepared for both funds.

**(9) (a) Endowment Principal Fund**

| | | |
|---|---|---|
| Interest Revenues ............................. | $5,235 | |
| Gain on Sale of Investments ..................... | 13 | |
| Operating Transfer to Endowment Earnings Fund .. | | $5,235 |
| Fund Balance—Nonexpendable ................. | | 13 |

To close accounts.

The gain on sale of investments is added to the fund balance of the Endowment Principal Fund either because it resulted from sale of investments of the original corpus of the trust or because the trust agreement specifies that gains and losses affect the trust principal and are not expendable. If the trust agreement or applicable laws specify that gains and losses are part of the expendable income from a trust, the net gains or losses affect the amount transferred to the Expendable Trust Fund instead of affecting the fund balance of the Nonexpendable (Principal) Trust Fund.

**(9) (b) Endowment Earnings Fund**

| | | |
|---|---|---|
| Operating Transfer from Endowment Principal Fund .. | $5,235 | |
| Expenditures—Scholarship Grant ................ | | $2,000 |
| Unreserved Fund Balance ...................... | | 3,235 |

To close accounts.

The Endowment Fund balance sheets for these funds are in Figures 10–1 and 10–2. A statement of revenues, expenditures, and changes in fund balance should be prepared for the Endowment Earnings Fund. Both a statement of revenues, expenses, and changes in fund balance and a statement of cash flows should be prepared for the Endowment Principal Fund.

If endowments are in the form of fixed assets, these constitute the principal fund and the net income therefrom is transferred to an expendable fund. Both the revenues and the expenses of administering the property—for example, depreciation, rents, repairs, decorating expenses, and janitor's wages—are accounted for in the principal fund. The net earnings are transferred to the earnings fund and expended for the purpose designated—for example, granting scholarships.

In such cases, governments must carefully account for the revenues and expenses of the principal fund so that the income may be properly computed. Too, the provisions of the trust document or the implied intent of the donor determine whether income before or after depreciation is expendable. If the trust instrument is silent as to depreciation of fixed assets held in trust, and the donor's intent in this regard is unclear, state statutes control. Competent legal advice should be sought whenever such questions are not explicitly treated in the trust document.

**FIGURE 10–1  Nonexpendable Trust Fund Balance Sheet**

A Governmental Unit
**Endowment Principal Trust Fund
Balance Sheet**
At End of Fiscal Year

**Assets**

| | |
|---|---:|
| Cash | $ 10,190 |
| Investments | 199,958 |
| Interest receivable on investments | 2,600 |
| | $212,748 |

**Liabilities and Fund Balance**

| | |
|---|---:|
| Due to Endowment Earnings Fund | $  2,735 |
| Fund balance—nonexpendable | 210,013 |
| | $212,748 |

**FIGURE 10–2  Expendable Trust Fund Balance Sheet**

A Governmental Unit
**Endowment Earnings Trust Fund
Balance Sheet**
At End of Fiscal Year

**Assets**

| | |
|---|---:|
| Cash | $  500 |
| Due from Endowment Principal Fund | 2,735 |
| | $3,235 |

**Fund Balance**

| | |
|---|---:|
| Unreserved fund balance | $3,235 |

# AGENCY FUNDS

Agency Funds are conduit or clearinghouse funds established to account for assets (usually cash) received for and paid to other funds, individuals, or organizations. The assets thus received are usually held only briefly; investment or other fiscal management complexities are rarely involved, except in situations such as that of the Tax Agency and Special Assessment Agency Funds illustrated later in this chapter.

The GASB *Codification* requires an Agency Fund to be used to account for and report the debt service transactions for projects financed with special assessment debt for which the government is not obligated in any manner. However, not all agency relationships arising in the conduct of a government's business require an Agency Fund. For example, payroll deductions for such items as insurance premiums and income tax withholdings create agency responsibilities that often are accounted for (as liabilities) in the fund used to pay the payroll. On the other hand, if payrolls are paid from several funds it may be more convenient to pay withheld amounts to an Agency Fund. This permits forwarding a single check and remittance report to the recipient. As a general rule, Agency Funds should be used whenever the volume of agency transactions, the magnitude of the sums involved, and/or the management and accounting capabilities of government personnel make it either unwieldy or unwise to account for agency responsibilities through other funds. Likewise, Agency Funds may be used to expedite financial management or accounting for interfund transactions or relationships.

## Simpler Agency Funds

Though agency relationships are commonly viewed as arising between the government and individuals or organizations external to it, recall that each fund of the government is a distinct fiscal and accounting entity. **Intragovernmental Agency Funds** are used to alleviate some of the awkwardness caused by using numerous fund accounting entities in governments. These internal Agency Funds also are used to establish clear-cut audit trails where a single transaction affects several funds. Thus, though a special imprest[3] bank account will often suffice, some governments establish an Agency Fund where (1) receipts must be allocated among several funds or (2) a single expenditure is financed through several funds. In the first case, a single check may be deposited in an Agency Fund and separate checks payable to the various funds drawn against it. In the latter, checks drawn against several funds are placed in an Agency Fund and a single check drawn against it in payment for the total expenditure. Judgment is required to decide whether an Agency Fund is useful in such cases. A special imprest checking account may serve the government's needs adequately and avoid unneeded additional record keeping.

The GASB *Codification* notes three other situations where Agency Funds may be employed:

1. Where a government receives **"pass-through" grants**—grants that the recipient government must transfer to, or spend on behalf of, another governmental unit for which it serves only as a "cash conduit" (i.e., has no administrative or direct financial involvement in the grant program)—an Agency Fund is required. The government should record the receipt

---

[3] An imprest bank account is one to which deposits are made periodically in an amount equal to the sum of the checks written thereon: When all checks written have cleared, the bank account balance will equal a predetermined amount, often zero. Imprest bank accounts are often used to enhance cash control and/or to facilitate bank-book reconciliations.

and disbursement of the "pass-through" grant in an **Agency Fund** rather than as revenues and expenditures.

2. Where a government receives a **grant, entitlement, or shared revenue that may be used, at its discretion, for programs or projects financed through more than one fund,** the resources should initially be accounted for in an Agency Fund. When decisions have been made as to which programs or projects—financed by which governmental and/or proprietary funds—the resources will be allocated to, the resources are removed from the Agency Fund and recorded in the governmental and/or proprietary fund(s). There they will be accounted for as revenues and as expenditures or expenses at the appropriate time.

3. When a **grant, entitlement, or shared revenue must be accounted for in a prescribed way that differs from GAAP** for purposes of reporting to the grantor government, the resources may be initially accounted for in an Agency Fund. The transactions are accounted for in the Agency Fund using "memoranda" accounts that accumulate data for the prescribed special purpose reports but are not reported in the GAAP financial statements, then are accounted for in the fund(s) financed as revenues or contributed capital and as expenditures or expenses, as appropriate, in conformity with GAAP.[4]

Whether the agency relationship is external or internal, the accounting in situations discussed thus far is not complicated. Agency Fund entries such as the following are prepared upon receipt and disbursement of cash or other assets:

| | | |
|---|---|---|
| Cash (or other assets) . . . . . . . . . . . . . . . . . . . . . . . . . . . . . . . . . . . . . | $100,000 | |
|     Due to individual (or fund or organization) . . . . . . . . . . . . . . . . . | | $100,000 |
| To record receipt of assets. | | |
| Due to individual (or fund or organization) . . . . . . . . . . . . . . . . . . | $100,000 | |
|     Cash (or other assets) . . . . . . . . . . . . . . . . . . . . . . . . . . . . . . . . . . | | $100,000 |
| To record payment of assets. | | |

Note that ***all Agency Fund assets are owed*** to some person, fund, or organization. The ***government has no distinct equity*** in the Agency Fund's assets.

## Tax Agency Funds

The Agency Funds cited in the preceding examples require little management action or expertise. Other Agency Funds, such as Tax Agency Funds, may involve significant management responsibilities and more complex accounting procedures.

Often several entities levy taxes on properties within a state, county, or other geographic area. One of the taxing governments typically bills and collects all the taxes levied on the properties in that jurisdiction. This practice avoids duplicating assessment and collection efforts and facilitates enforcement of equitable and economical tax laws. The billing and collecting unit is an agent for the other taxing units and establishes an Agency Fund such as the Tax Agency Fund described here. In the usual case, the several taxing bodies (e.g., the state, county, school district) certify the amounts or rates of taxes to be levied for them. The billing and collecting unit then levies the total tax, including its own, against specific properties and proceeds to collect the tax. It normally makes pro rata payments of collections to the various taxing bodies during the year, often quarterly. Finally, it charges a collection or service fee to the other units.

The following example illustrates the general approach to Tax Agency Fund accounting. Though not illustrated here, detailed records of levies and collections for each property taxed, by year of levy, are required. Collections from each year's levy are distributed among the taxing bodies in the ratio of each unit's levy to the total levy of that year.

---

[4] See GASB *Codification*, sec. G60.107–.110. (Emphasis added.)

To illustrate Tax Agency Fund accounting, assume that City A serves as the **property tax collecting agent** for several governmental units. The city charges the other units a collection fee equal to 2% of the taxes collected for them. City A's levies and those of the other units for 19X2 and 19X3 are as follows:

| | 19X3 | | 19X2 | |
|---|---|---|---|---|
| | *Amount Levied* | *Percentage of Total* | *Amount Levied* | *Percentage of Total* |
| City A* ................... | $100,000 | 25.0 | $ 91,200 | 24.0 |
| School District B ............ | 200,000 | 50.0 | 188,100 | 49.5 |
| Park District X ............. | 50,000 | 12.5 | 49,400 | 13.0 |
| Sanitary District Y........... | 50,000 | 12.5 | 51,300 | 13.5 |
| | $400,000 | 100.0 | $380,000 | 100.0 |

*Although these taxes are the taxes of the collecting governmental unit, they are treated in the same manner as if they were being collected for it by another unit, except no collection fees are charged on those collections.

The Tax Agency Fund trial balance at December 31, 19X2 consists of $75,000 of Taxes Receivable for Taxing Units and Due to Taxing Units, $75,000. These amounts are from the 19X2 levy. Transactions and entries illustrated for the General Fund of City A are similar to those of the other recipient governmental units.

**Transactions and Entries**

1. The 19X3 levies are placed on the tax roll and recorded on the books.

   **(1)(a) Tax Agency Fund**

   | | | |
   |---|---|---|
   | **Taxes Receivable for Taxing Units** .................... | $400,000 | |
   | **Due to Taxing Units** ............................. | | $400,000 |

   To record 19X3 taxes placed on the tax roll.

   Due to Taxing Units Ledger (Uncollected):

   | | |
   |---|---|
   | City A ........................................ | $100,000 |
   | School District B ................................. | 200,000 |
   | Park District X ................................... | 50,000 |
   | Sanitary District Y ............................... | 50,000 |
   | | $400,000 |

   **(1)(b) General Fund**

   | | | |
   |---|---|---|
   | Taxes Receivable—Current ......................... | $100,000 | |
   | Allowance for Uncollectible Current Taxes ............ | | $ 1,000 |
   | Revenues ....................................... | | 99,000 |

   To record the 19X3 tax levy.

   Revenues Ledger (Revenues):

   | | |
   |---|---|
   | Taxes ......................................... | $ 99,000 |

Taxes Receivable for Taxing Units may be classified into two accounts, Current and Delinquent, if desired. The distinction would be apparent in the subsidiary records, however, because (1) taxes are levied by year, and (2) a separate ledger account or column would be provided for each year's levy against each property. Appropriate subsidiary records for Taxes Receivable for Taxing Units by taxpayer would be maintained.

2. Taxes of $300,000 and interest and penalties (not previously accrued) of $15,000 are collected. Collections should be identified by type, year, and governmental unit to enable distributions in accordance with the original levies. (This detail is not provided here, so **assume the following amounts are correct.**)

**(2) Tax Agency Fund**

| | | |
|---|---:|---:|
| Cash ........................................... | $315,000 | |
|    Taxes Receivable for Taxing Units .................... | | $300,000 |
|    Due to Taxing Units ............................... | | 15,000 |
| To record collections of taxes and interest and penalties. | | |

Due to Taxing Units Ledger (Uncollected):

| | | |
|---|---:|---|
| City A ........................................... | $ 74,250 | |
| School District B ............................... | 149,625 | |
| Park District X ................................. | 37,875 | |
| Sanitary District Y ............................. | 38,250 | |
| | $300,000 | |

Due to Taxing Units Ledger (**Tax Collections**):

| | | |
|---|---:|---|
| City A ........................................... | | $ 77,850 |
| School District B ............................... | | 157,050 |
| Park District X ................................. | | 39,825 |
| Sanitary District Y ............................. | | 40,275 |
| | | $315,000* |

*Note that this amount includes collections of previously recorded taxes receivable for taxing units ($300,000) and the previously unrecorded interest and penalties that were collected ($15,000).

The balances in the **"Tax Collections"** subsidiary ledger accounts are currently payable to the taxing units. The **"Uncollected"** balances reflect amounts not yet payable to the taxing units because these amounts have not been collected.

**3.** The collections (transaction 2) are paid from the Tax Agency Fund to the respective governmental units, except for a 2% collection charge levied upon the **other** governments.

**(3) Tax Agency Fund**

| | | |
|---|---:|---:|
| Due to Taxing Units ............................. | $315,000 | |
|    Cash ........................................... | | $310,257 |
|    Due to General Fund ............................ | | 4,743 |
| To record payment of amounts collected, less a 2% collection charge for taxes collected for other governmental units. | | |

Due to Taxing Units Ledger (**Tax Collections**):

| | | |
|---|---:|---|
| City A ........................................... | $ 77,850 | |
| School District B ............................... | 157,050 | |
| Park District X ................................. | 39,825 | |
| Sanitary District Y ............................. | 40,275 | |
| | $315,000 | |

**(3)(a) General Fund**

| | | |
|---|---:|---:|
| Cash ........................................... | $ 77,850 | |
|    Taxes Receivable—Current ........................ | | $ 56,250 |
|    Taxes Receivable—Delinquent ..................... | | 18,000 |
|    Revenues ....................................... | | 3,600 |
| To record receipt of collections of taxes and interest and penalties from Tax Agency Fund. | | |

Revenues Ledger (Revenues):

| | | |
|---|---:|---|
| Interest and Penalties .............................. | | $ 3,600 |

Note that interest and penalties receivable would be credited instead of revenues if the interest and penalties were previously accrued.

**(3)(b) General Fund**

| | | |
|---|---:|---:|
| Due from Tax Agency Fund ......................... | $ 4,743 | |
|    Revenues ....................................... | | $ 4,743 |
| To record revenues for collection fees charged to other governments. | | |

Revenues Ledger (Revenues):

| | | |
|---|---:|---|
| Tax Collection Fees ................................ | | $ 4,743 |

The collection fee and the amounts paid to the other governments were calculated as follows:

|  | Collections | 2% Collection Fee | Net |
|---|---|---|---|
| City A ........................ | $ 77,850 | $ — | $ 77,850 |
| School District B ............... | 157,050 | 3,141 | 153,909 |
| Park District X .................. | 39,825 | 796 | 39,029 |
| Sanitary District Y .............. | 40,275 | 806 | 39,469 |
|  | $315,000 | $4,743 | $310,257 |

Preparing the tax roll, accounting for taxes, and handling the collections involve considerable costs, and the collecting unit usually charges for these services. The charges are legitimate financial expenditures of the various taxing units and are provided for in their budgets. The usual practice, illustrated earlier, is for the collecting unit to retain a portion of the taxes and interest and penalties collected. This practice avoids the process of billing the charges to the several governmental units. To illustrate the procedure further, the journal entry that **School District B** makes to record receipt of cash from the Tax Agency Fund **(preceding transaction 3)** follows:

**(3) School District B—General Fund**

| | | |
|---|---|---|
| Cash ............................................. | $153,909 | |
| Expenditures ...................................... | 3,141 | |
|    Taxes Receivable—Current ............................ | | $112,500 |
|    Taxes Receivable—Delinquent .......................... | | 37,125 |
|    Revenues ........................................ | | 7,425 |

To record receipt of amounts collected by City A less collection charge of 2%.

Expenditures Ledger (Expenditures):

| | |
|---|---|
| Tax Collection Fees ...................................... | $  3,141 |

Revenues Ledger (Revenues):

| | |
|---|---|
| Interest and Penalties ..................................... | $  7,425 |

Note again that revenues from interest and penalties are recognized in this entry because they were not accrued previously.

The December 31, 19X3 Balance Sheet of the Tax Agency Fund of City A is presented in Figure 10–3.

A Statement of Changes in Assets and Liabilities for the Tax Agency Fund is presented in Figure 10–4. Note that this statement does not report "operating results," but simply reports, in summary form, the changes in each of the fund's assets and liabilities. This reporting reflects that Agency funds have no "operations."

**FIGURE 10–3  Agency Fund Balance Sheet**

City A

**Tax Agency Fund**
**Balance Sheet**

December 31, 19X3

**Assets**

| | |
|---|---|
| Cash ................................................. | $  4,743 |
| Taxes receivable for taxing units .............................. | 175,000 |
| | $179,743 |

**Liabilities**

| | |
|---|---|
| Due to General Fund ...................................... | $  4,743 |
| Due to taxing units (for uncollected taxes)..................... | 175,000 |
| | $179,743 |

FIGURE 10–4  **Agency Fund Statement of Changes in Assets and Liabilities**

City A
**Tax Agency Fund**
**Statement of Changes in Assets and Liabilities**
For the Year Ended December 31, 19X3

|  | Balances, January 1, 19X3 | Additions | Deductions | Balances, December 31, 19X3 |
|---|---|---|---|---|
| **Assets** | | | | |
| Cash ..................... |  | $315,000 | $310,257 | $  4,743 |
| Taxes receivable for taxing units . | $75,000 | 400,000 | 300,000 | 175,000 |
| Total assets ................. | $75,000 | $715,000 | $610,257 | $179,743 |
| **Liabilities** | | | | |
| Due to General Fund .......... |  | $  4,743 |  | $  4,743 |
| Due to taxing units for uncollected taxes .......... | $75,000 | 415,000 | $315,000 | 175,000 |
| Total liabilities .............. | $75,000 | $419,743 | $315,000 | $179,743 |

## Special Assessment Debt Service Agency Funds

As discussed in Chapters 7 and 8, most special assessment projects—and any related debt and debt service—are accounted for and reported essentially like other capital projects, long-term debt, and related debt service. This is not true, however, for special assessment capital improvements financed by issuing special assessment debt for which the government is not obligated in any manner.

In these cases, the government is merely acting as an agent for the property owners and would not honor the debt if default occurred. Therefore, the debt is not reported in the government's financial statements. The construction or acquisition of the fixed assets is reported in a Capital Projects Fund (or Enterprise Fund, if appropriate) because the government is acquiring a fixed asset. However, the proceeds from the special assessment debt should not be called "bond proceeds" because the government is not incurring debt. Rather, the GASB suggests a title such as "Contributions from Property Owners." Likewise, the fixed assets constructed or acquired will be reported in the General Fixed Assets Account Group (or an Enterprise Fund if for Enterprise Fund use).

Even when the government is not obligated in any manner for special assessment debt, the government usually acts as a debt service agent for the special assessment district. In this capacity, the government (1) collects the special assessments levied for the project, and (2) pays the debt service costs for the property owners from collections of these receivables (and perhaps, any remaining construction phase assets). The government has a fiduciary responsibility to collect the special assessments and to remit the collections to the bondholders when debt service payments come due. Again, however, if collections do not cover required debt service payments, the government is not obligated to pay the difference and probably does not intend to do so. Thus, the government is acting purely in an agency capacity with respect to the debt service transactions, and these transactions are accounted for in an Agency Fund.

To illustrate a **Special Assessment Agency Fund,** assume that Norwood Village approves a project in 19X1 to construct sidewalks in a subdivision. The project will be financed by issuing ten-year, 6% notes for $1,000,000, when the project is finished. The government is **not** obligated in any manner for payment of the debt or related interest. Both are payable solely from special assessments to be levied against the properties and the related interest of 6% annually on unpaid special assessment balances. One-tenth of the notes are payable at the end of each year, beginning one year after issuance.

1. Expenditures incurred to complete the sidewalks during the year totaled $1,000,000.

   **(1)(a) Capital Projects Fund**

   | | | |
   |---|---|---|
   | Expenditures—Capital Outlay ....................... | $1,000,000 | |
   | Vouchers Payable ................................ | | $1,000,000 |

   To record expenditures for sidewalk construction.

   **(1)(b) General Fixed Assets Account Group**

   | | | |
   |---|---|---|
   | Improvements Other Than Buildings ................... | $1,000,000 | |
   | Investment in General Fixed Assets—Special Assessments .................................. | | $1,000,000 |

   To record cost of sidewalks constructed.

2. The notes were issued at par at the end of 19X1.

   **(2) Capital Projects Fund**

   | | | |
   |---|---|---|
   | Cash ........................................... | $1,000,000 | |
   | **Other Financing Sources—Contributions from Property Owners** ............................... | | $1,000,000 |

   To record issuance of special assessment debt for which the government is not obligated in any manner.

   Note that (1) the **note proceeds** are **not** recorded as debt proceeds but as contributions from property owners, and (2) the government does *not* record the debt.

3. Special assessments of $1,000,000 are levied at the end of 19X1. One-tenth of the principal is due each year as is 6% interest on the uncollected assessments. Collections are invested at 6% interest.

   **(3) Agency Fund**

   | | | |
   |---|---|---|
   | Assessments Receivable—Current .................... | $100,000 | |
   | Assessments Receivable—Deferred ................... | 900,000 | |
   | **Due to Special Assessment Note Creditors** ............ | | $1,000,000 |

   To record levy of special assessments.

   Note that Assessments Receivable—Deferred is essentially the long-term portion of the receivable.

4. The accounts are closed at the end of 19X1.

   **(4) Capital Projects Fund**

   | | | |
   |---|---|---|
   | Other Financing Sources—Contributions from Property Owners ............................... | $1,000,000 | |
   | Expenditures—Capital Outlay ..................... | | $1,000,000 |

   To close the accounts.

5. Special assessment collections during 19X2 totaled $160,000, including $60,000 interest.

   **(5) Agency Fund**

   | | | |
   |---|---|---|
   | Cash ........................................... | $160,000 | |
   | Assessments Receivable—Current ................... | | $100,000 |
   | Due to Special Assessment Note Creditors ............ | | 60,000 |

   To record collections of current assessments and interest.

6. The first installment of the note, including interest, was paid at the end of 19X2.

**(6) Agency Fund**

| | | |
|---|---|---|
| Due to Special Assessment Note Creditors | $160,000 | |
| Cash | | $160,000 |

To record debt service payment on special assessment note.

7. The appropriate portion of assessments receivable was reclassified as current at the end of 19X2.

**(7) Agency Fund**

| | | |
|---|---|---|
| Assessments Receivable—Current | $100,000 | |
| Assessments Receivable—Deferred | | $100,000 |

To reclassify deferred assessments as current.

The 19X2 Balance Sheet for this Special Assessment Agency Fund would report the assessments receivable as assets and the (equal) liability for amounts due to the project creditors. The government never recognizes revenues from the special assessments and interest. Likewise, the government never recognizes debt service expenditures on the debt.

In the preceding example, Norwood Village paid for the sidewalk construction from one of its Capital Projects Funds, which was reimbursed when the notes were issued. Alternatively, the notes might have been issued at the start of the project and all cash receipts and disbursements might have been recorded in the Special Assessment Agency Fund. Note that only the first two preceding entries would differ in this case:

1. The notes were issued at par at the beginning of 19X1.

**(1) Special Assessment Agency Fund**

| | | |
|---|---|---|
| Cash | $1,000,000 | |
| Due to Special Assessment Note Creditors | | $1,000,000 |

To record issuance of notes for cash to finance sidewalk special assessment project construction.

2. Expenditures of $1,000,000 for sidewalk construction were paid.

**(2)(a) Special Assessment Agency Fund**

| | | |
|---|---|---|
| Due to Special Assessment Note Creditors | $1,000,000 | |
| Cash | | $1,000,000 |

To record payment of SA project expenditures.

**(2)(b) Capital Projects Fund (or General Fund)**

| | | |
|---|---|---|
| Expenditures—Capital Outlay | $1,000,000 | |
| Other Financing Sources—Contributions from Property Owners | | $1,000,000 |

To record expenditures for general fixed assets financed by special assessments.

**Note:** This records the **substance** of the events—as if the village had levied the assessments and constructed the sidewalks.

**(2)(c) General Fixed Assets Account Group**

| | | |
|---|---|---|
| Improvements Other than Buildings | $1,000,000 | |
| Investment in General Fixed Assets—Special Assessments | | $1,000,000 |

To record cost of sidewalks constructed.

Entries 3–7 are the same as those illustrated previously.

## PENSION TRUST FUNDS

Pension Trust Funds (PTFs) are likely to be the largest Trust Funds of many governments. They are growing rapidly, and the cost to governments of contributions to them is significant. Their ability to pay pensions on schedule is vitally important to individual retirees and to work force morale.

Many types of retirement plans exist in governments. Both state and local governments often have retirement plans, though in some states employees of all governmental units of a certain type (e.g., municipalities) or all employees within certain functional fields (e.g., teachers, police, fire fighters) are included in a plan within a statewide retirement system. In some cases these plans are integrated with federal social security benefits; in others, employees are not covered under that program. The administrative mechanisms established also differ widely. Some retirement plans are managed and accounted for by the finance department or some other executive agency of the government. In other cases an independent board, or even a separate corporation, is charged with retirement system management and accountability. These entities often are referred to as public employee retirement systems (PERS).

Plans also are classified according to whether they are for (1) the employees of only one unit of government, **single-employer plans,** or (2) the employees of more than one employer government, **multiple-employer plans.** The GASB further categorizes **multiple-employer plans** based upon the extent to which the interests and risks of the various employer governments are integrated:

> Some multiple-employer PERS [plans] are aggregations of single-employer PERS, with pooled administrative and investment functions; that is, the PERS acts as a common investment and administrative agent for each employer. These PERS are referred to as agent PERS. . . . Each entity participating in an agent PERS receives a separate actuarial valuation to determine its required periodic contribution. . . .
>
> Other multiple-employer PERS [plans] are essentially one large pension plan with cost-sharing arrangements; that is, all risks and costs, including benefits costs, are shared proportionately by the participating entities. One actuarial valuation is performed for the PERS as a whole, and the same contribution rate applies to each participating entity. These PERS are referred to as "cost-sharing" PERS. . . .[5]

Of far more consequence to sound public finance policy and to the public interest generally is the disparate array of financial management practices relating to retirement systems. Government plans are not subject to the Federal ERISA (Employee Retirement Income Security Act) regulations on vesting, funding, and the like, though various PERISA (Public Employee Retirement Income Security Act) and similar bills have been proposed in Congress in recent years. Some governments are on a pay-as-you-go basis—pension payments are paid from current revenues. In such cases pensioners must depend on the flow of revenues and other demands for appropriations and thus on the uncertainties of the budget process. At the other extreme, some governments have overfunded retirement systems. Most government pension plans fall between these extremes and are actuarially sound.

Accounting and reporting for pension **plans** and PTFs must be **distinguished** from accounting and reporting for the pension costs and liabilities of **employer**

---

[5] GASB *Codification*, sec. Pe6.109–110.

funds and the account groups of the employer government(s). Reporting in the financial statements, per se, required supplementary information, and disclosures required in the notes to the financial statements are each distinct and important as well. Accounting and reporting for pension plans are the primary focus of the discussion of pensions in this chapter, though accounting and reporting requirements for the employer governments are outlined briefly. Too, the discussion here assumes that the pension plans are **defined benefit plans,** in which the amounts of benefits to be paid under the plan are specified, rather than **defined contribution plans,** which specify a level of contributions to be made but do not guarantee a specific level of benefits.

## Accounting Standards

In 1994, the GASB completed a long-term project on pensions and issued three statements: GASB *Statement No. 25,* "Financial Reporting for Defined Benefit Pension Plans and Note Disclosures for Defined Contribution Plans"; GASB *Statement No. 26,* "Financial Reporting for Postemployment Healthcare Plans Administered by Defined Benefit Pension Plans"; and GASB *Statement No. 27,* "Accounting for Pensions by State and Local Governmental Employers." These pronouncements superseded all previous government pension standards.

The primary accounting and reporting requirements of GASB *Statement No. 25* are as follows:

- Plan assets and liabilities (primarily short term) are presented in a **Statement of Plan Net Assets.** Additions and deductions to plan net assets are presented in a **Statement of Changes in Plan Net Assets.**
- **The Statement of Changes in Plan Net Assets** categorizes changes as additions or as deductions rather than as revenues, expenses, gains, or losses.
- **Investments** (excluding insurance contracts) are reported **at fair value.** Fixed income securities are *not* amortized.
- Fixed assets used in plan operations are reported at historical cost and depreciated.
- **Actuarial information** generally is not reported in the basic financial statements or the notes to the financial statements. These data are **reported as required supplementary information.**
- **Parameters** (e.g., acceptable actuarial assumptions) are **established** for actuarially determined information.
- A standardized pension benefit obligation measurement is *not* required.

Actuarial information is reported in two schedules included in required supplementary information. Actuarial information is not reported in the Statement of Plan Net Assets or the Statement of Changes in Plan Net Assets. The two required schedules are a Schedule of Funding Progress and a Schedule of Employer Contributions.

## Retirement Fund Example

To illustrate the accounting for a pension plan—whether it is a single-employer, agent, or cost-sharing plan—assume that a fund is already in operation and its beginning trial balance appears as in Figure 10–5. Assume also that (1) the plan is fi-

FIGURE 10–5 **Pension Trust Fund Trial Balance Traditional Approach**

A Governmental Unit

**Pension Trust Fund**

**Trial Balance**

At Beginning of Fiscal Year (Date)

| | Debit | Credit |
|---|---|---|
| Cash | $ 56,000 | |
| Due from General Fund | 8,000 | |
| Interest Receivable | 3,000 | |
| Investments | 985,000 | |
| Due to Resigned Employees | | $ 3,000 |
| Annuities Payable | | 2,800 |
| Net Assets Held in Trust for Pension Benefits | | 1,046,200 |
| | $1,052,000 | $1,052,000 |

nanced by employer contributions, employee contributions, and investment earnings, and (2) the equities of employees resigning or dying prior to retirement are returned to them or to their estates, but employer contributions on their behalf remain in the fund.

The nature and purposes of most of the accounts in the beginning trial balance will become evident in the course of the illustration. The Net Assets Held in Trust for Pension Benefits account is the residual balance of the pension plan assets less its liabilities.

The following transactions and events occurred during the year and would be recorded in the **Pension Trust Fund** as indicated.

**Transactions and Entries**

**1.** Employer ($50,000) and employee ($125,000) contributions were accrued in the General Fund (a quasi-external transaction).

| (1) Due from General Fund | $175,000 | |
|---|---|---|
| **Employee Contributions** | | $125,000 |
| **Employer Contributions** | | 50,000 |

To record employee and employer contributions due from the General Fund.

Although the employer contribution would be budgeted in the fund through which payrolls are paid, the plan in this example is not under formal budgetary accounting control. The levels of its activity are determined by factors such as levels of employment in the government and the changes in status of participants in the system.

**2.** A check for $170,000 was received from the General Fund.

| (2) Cash | $170,000 | |
|---|---|---|
| Due from General Fund | | $170,000 |

To record receipt of contributions from the General Fund.

**3.** Accrued interest of $45,000 on investments was recorded.

| | | |
|---|---|---|
| (3) Interest Receivable .............................. | $45,000 | |
| Interest Income ............................... | | $45,000 |
| To record accrued interest receivable on investments. | | |

**4.** Interest receivable of $40,000 was collected.

| | | |
|---|---|---|
| (4) Cash ......................................... | $40,000 | |
| Interest Receivable ........................... | | $40,000 |
| To record receipt of interest receivable. | | |

**5.** Three nonvested employees resigned and one died prior to retirement. The accumulated balances of their contributions totaled $16,000 and $9,000, respectively.

| | | |
|---|---|---|
| (5) Payments to Deceased Employees' Estates .......... | $ 9,000 | |
| Payments to Resigned Employees ................. | 16,000 | |
| Due to Deceased Employees' Estates ............. | | $ 9,000 |
| Due to Resigned Employees .................... | | 16,000 |
| To record amounts due upon employee resignations and the death of one employee prior to retirement. | | |

**6.** Checks were mailed to two of the resigned employees ($13,000) and to the estate of the deceased employee ($9,000).

| | | |
|---|---|---|
| (6) Due to Deceased Employees' Estates ............... | $ 9,000 | |
| Due to Resigned Employees ..................... | 13,000 | |
| Cash ........................................ | | $22,000 |
| To record payments to former employees and to the estate of a deceased employee. | | |

**7.** Annuities payable of $24,000 were accrued.

| | | |
|---|---|---|
| (7) **Annuity Payments** ............................. | $24,000 | |
| Annuities Payable ............................. | | $24,000 |
| To record accrual of liability for annuities payable. | | |

**8.** Annuities payable were paid except for that owed to one retiree who is out of the country.

| | | |
|---|---|---|
| (8) Annuities Payable ............................... | $23,000 | |
| Cash ........................................ | | $23,000 |
| To record payment of annuities. | | |

**9.** Additional investments were made for $150,000 less a discount of $7,000.

| | | |
|---|---|---|
| (9) Investments ..................................... | $143,000 | |
| Cash ......................................... | | $143,000 |
| To record investments. | | |

**10.** At year end the following adjusting and closing entries were made. The fair value of the fund's investments had decreased by $20,000 during the year.

| | | |
|---|---|---|
| (10) Net Increase (Decrease) in Fair Value of Investments .. | $20,000 | |
| Investments ................................... | | $20,000 |
| To record the change in the fair value of the investments of the fund. | | |

All PTF additions and deductions to net assets are closed to Net Assets Held in Trust for Pension Benefits.

The closing entry for the illustrative PTF is:

**Closing Entries**

(C1)  Employee Contributions ............................. $125,000

     Employer Contributions ............................. 50,000

     Interest ........................................... 45,000

          Net Increase (Decrease) in Fair Value of Investments .... $ 20,000

          Payments to Deceased Employees' Estates ............ 9,000

          Payments to Resigned Employees .................... 16,000

          Annuity Benefits .................................. 24,000

          Net Assets Held in Trust for Pension Benefits .......... 151,000

     To close the accounts.

The postclosing trial balance for the illustrative PTF is presented in Figure 10–6. Figures 10–7 and 10–8 illustrate the plan's basic financial statements.

**FIGURE 10–6  Pension Trust Fund Postclosing Trial Balance**

A Governmental Unit

**Pension Trust Fund**

**Postclosing Trial Balance**

At Close of Fiscal Year (Date)

| | | |
|---|---:|---:|
| Cash ................................................. | $   78,000 | |
| Due from General Fund ............................... | 13,000 | |
| Interest Receivable ................................. | 8,000 | |
| Investments ......................................... | 1,108,000 | |
| Due to Resigned Employees ........................... | | $    6,000 |
| Annuities Payable ................................... | | 3,800 |
| Net Assets Held in Trust for Pension Benefits ........ | | 1,197,200 |
| | $1,207,000 | $1,207,000 |

**FIGURE 10–7  Statement of Plan Net Assets**

Plan A

**Statement of Plan Net Assets**

As of Fiscal Year (Date)

**Assets:**

| | | |
|---|---:|---:|
| Cash ............................................... | | $   78,000 |
| Receivables: | | |
|   Employer ....................................... | $ 13,000 | |
|   Interest ....................................... | 8,000 | |
|     Total Receivables .................... | | 21,000 |
| **Investments at Fair Value:** | | |
|   U.S. Government Obligations .......................... | 325,300 | |
|   Municipal Bonds ...................................... | 220,300 | |
|   Stocks ............................................... | 562,400 | |
|     Total Investments ...................... | | 1,108,000 |
|     Total Assets ........................... | | 1,207,000 |
| **Liabilities:** | | |
|   Refunds Payable ...................................... | | 6,000 |
|   Annuities Payable .................................... | | 3,800 |
|     Total Liabilities ...................... | | 9,800 |
| Net Assets Held in Trust for Pension Benefits | | |
|   (See Schedule of Funding Progress) ................... | | $1,197,200 |

**FIGURE 10–8  Statement of Changes in Plan Net Assets**

Plan A

**Statement of Changes in Plan Net Assets**

For the Fiscal Year Ended (Date)

**Additions:**

Contributions:

| | | |
|---|---:|---:|
| Employee | $125,000 | |
| Employer | 50,000 | |
| Total Contributions | | $ 175,000 |
| Investment Income: | | |
| Net Decrease in Fair Value of Investments | (20,000) | |
| Interest | 45,000 | |
| Total Investment Income | | 25,000 |
| Total Additions | | 200,000 |
| **Deductions:** | | |
| Benefits | 24,000 | |
| Refunds | 25,000 | |
| Total Deductions | | 49,000 |
| Net Increase for the Year | | 151,000 |
| Net Assets Held in Trust for Pension Benefits | | |
| Beginning of Year | | 1,046,200 |
| End of Year | | $1,197,200 |

GASB *Statement No. 27* requires governments to measure their annual pension costs, or APC. The APC is measured differently by employer governments that participate in cost-sharing defined benefit plans than by those participating in single-employer or agent plans. The APC for an employer government involved in a cost-sharing plan is simply the contractually required contribution to the plan. For employers with single-employer plans or participating in agent plans, the APC is:

- measured as the employer's actuarially determined annual required contribution (ARC),

- adjusted for interest on any beginning net pension obligation (NPO) balance (the net pension obligation is the cumulative difference between the APC and the employer's contributions to the plan), and

- an adjustment to the annual required contribution to eliminate any actuarial amortization resulting from past contribution deficiencies or past excess contributions.

*Statement No. 27* also requires that the actuarially required contribution for governments participating in single-employer or agent plans be measured using the same parameters, or guidelines, as required for pension plan accounting and reporting by *Statement No. 25*.

Parameters are established for such things as actuarial assumptions, actuarial cost methods that may be used, and length of amortization periods. If a government's annual contribution is computed in a manner that fails to meet these parameters, it cannot be used as the basis for reporting the government's pension liability, expenditure, and expense. The pension amounts will have to be computed using an approach that meets the *Statement No. 27* parameters. This statement applies to both governmental and proprietary funds.

**Employer fund/employer government** accounting and reporting are addressed in GASB *Statement No. 27*. As discussed in Chapter 6:

1. Governmental fund employers must report as expenditures the portion of the annual pension cost that has been or will be funded with expendable available financial resources of the fund.

2. If a portion of the annual pension cost of governmental fund employers is not payable from expendable available financial resources, the unfunded portion is to be reported as an unfunded pension liability in the General Long-Term Debt Account Group.

3. For proprietary and nonexpendable trust fund employers, the APC is reported as pension expense.

Most of the data presented in the Schedule of Funding Progress and the Schedule of Employer Contributions are not derived from the accounting system but are provided by the actuary. Examples of these schedules for our illustrative PTF are presented in Figure 10–9. The data are assumed, but note the dramatic difference between what is reported in the financial statements and in the actuarial schedules. Even actuarially underfunded pension plans typically have significant net assets held in trust for pension benefits. This is because the obligation for future benefits is not included in determining this amount.

**FIGURE 10–9  Required Supplementary Information**

Plan A
**Schedule of Funding Progress**
(in thousands)
As of Fiscal Year (Date)

| Actuarial Valuation Date | Actuarial Value of Assets (a) | Actuarial Accrued Liability (AAL) Entry Age (b) | Unfunded AAL (UAAL) (b − a) | Funded Ratio (a/b) | Covered Payroll (c) | UAAL as a Percentage of Covered Payroll [(b − a)/c] |
|---|---|---|---|---|---|---|
| 12/31/W6 | $ 990 | $1,233 | $243 | 80.3% | $433 | 56.1% |
| 12/31/W7 | 1,025 | 1,173 | 148 | 87.4 | 396 | 37.4 |
| 12/31/W8 | 1,175 | 1,373 | 198 | 85.6 | 419 | 47.3 |
| 12/31/W9 | 1,200 | 1,370 | 170 | 87.6 | 408 | 41.7 |
| 12/31/X0 | 1,280 | 1,421 | 141 | 90.1 | 406 | 34.7 |
| 12/31/X1* | 1,300 | 1,448 | 148 | 89.8 | 401 | 36.9 |

**Schedule of Employer Contributions**
(in thousands)

| Year Ended June 30 | Employer Contributions | |
|---|---|---|
| | Annual Required Contribution | Percentage Contributed |
| 19W6 | $46 | 100% |
| 19W7 | 40 | 100 |
| 19W8 | 42 | 100 |
| 19W9 | 41 | 100 |
| 19X0 | 42 | 100 |
| 19X1* | 44 | 100 |

*Assume X1 is the current year.

## COMBINING TRUST AND AGENCY FUND FINANCIAL STATEMENTS

In the comprehensive annual financial report (CAFR) of an SLG, the fiduciary funds should be reported in the combined financial statements as explained in Chapter 13. In addition, assuming there is more than one each of the various types of trust funds, several combining financial statements are required for these funds as well. They include:

| *Expendable Trust Funds* | *Nonexpendable Trust Funds* | *Pension Trust Funds*[6] |
|---|---|---|
| Combining Balance Sheet | Combining Balance Sheet | Combining Statement of Plan Net Assets |
| Combining Statement of Revenues, Expenditures, and Changes in Fund Balances | Combining Statement of Revenues, Expenses, and Changes in Fund Balances | Combining Statement of Changes in Plan Net Assets |
| | Combining Statement of Cash Flows (nonexpendable trust funds only) | |

Because the combining statements are illustrated for various fund types in other chapters, the combining trust fund statements are not illustrated or discussed here.

A Combining Statement of Changes in Assets and Liabilities—All Agency Funds should be presented if an SLG has more than one Agency Fund. A Combining Statement of Changes in Assets and Liabilities—All Agency Funds is illustrated in Figure 10–10. This illustration is from the CAFR of Pima County, Arizona. Note that the statement is not an operating statement because, as discussed earlier, Agency Funds do not have operations per se. Rather, this statement simply discloses the changes in the unit's custodial responsibilities. Note also that this statement is not a required statement in the general purpose financial statements (GPFS). It usually is presented in the notes to the GPFS and may be presented in the combining and individual fund statements section of the CAFR.

## CONCLUDING COMMENTS

Trust and Agency Funds are used to account for the fiduciary responsibilities of state and local governments. Although there is relatively little specific guidance regarding accounting and reporting for this fund type (other than Pension Trust Funds), most are similar in nature to and, thus, are accounted for much like either governmental funds or proprietary funds.

Expendable Trust Funds are similar in nature to governmental funds, and governmental fund accounting and reporting principles apply to those funds. The Nonexpendable Trust Funds are similar to proprietary funds in that these funds are to be self-sustaining. Thus, for the most part, proprietary fund accounting and reporting principles apply to these funds. Agency Funds differ from proprietary funds and from governmental funds in that Agency Funds have no equity and, thus,

---

[6]These statements are required for investment trust funds also. Investment trust funds are used to account for the external portions of an investment pool operated by a government.

**FIGURE 10–10  Combining Statement of Changes in Assets and Liabilities**

Pima County

**Combining Statement of Changes in Assets and Liabilities—Agency Funds**

For the Year Ended June 30, 19X7

(in thousands)

| _Payroll Clearing_ | Balance 06/30/X6 | Additions | Deductions | Balance 06/30/X7 |
|---|---|---|---|---|
| Assets | | | | |
| Cash and cash equivalents | $    1,076 | $    403,728 | $    403,731 | $    1,073 |
| Liabilities | | | | |
| Deposits and rebates | $    1,076 | $    403,728 | $    403,731 | $    1,073 |
| _Treasurer's Clearing_ | | | | |
| Assets | | | | |
| Cash and cash equivalents | $    1,241 | $1,479,380 | $1,479,233 | $    1,388 |
| Due from other funds | 2 | | 2 | |
| Total assets | $    1,243 | $1,479,380 | $1,479,235 | $    1,388 |
| Liabilities | | | | |
| Deposits and rebates | $    1,011 | $    434,547 | $    434,214 | $    1,344 |
| Due to other governments | 230 | 1,044,833 | 1,045,019 | 44 |
| Due to other funds | 2 | | 2 | |
| Total liabilities | $    1,243 | $1,479,380 | $1,479,235 | $    1,388 |
| _School Districts_ | | | | |
| Assets | | | | |
| Cash and cash equivalents | $179,956 | $6,456,993 | $6,490,779 | $146,170 |
| Liabilities | | | | |
| Due to other governments | $179,956 | $6,456,993 | $6,490,779 | $146,170 |
| _Other_ | | | | |
| Assets | | | | |
| Cash and cash equivalents | $  20,727 | $    518,911 | $    519,892 | $  19,746 |
| Due from other funds | | 1 | | 1 |
| Total assets | $  20,727 | $    518,912 | $    519,892 | $  19,747 |
| Liabilities | | | | |
| Due to other governments | $    6,694 | $    200,090 | $    201,588 | $    5,196 |
| Deposits and rebates | 13,988 | 318,822 | 318,259 | 14,551 |
| Due to other funds | 45 | | 45 | |
| Total liabilities | $  20,727 | $    518,912 | $    519,892 | $  19,747 |
| _Totals—All Agency Funds_ | | | | |
| Assets | | | | |
| Cash and cash equivalents | $203,000 | $8,859,012 | $8,893,635 | $168,377 |
| Due from other funds | 2 | 1 | 2 | 1 |
| Total assets | $203,002 | $8,859,013 | $8,893,637 | $168,378 |
| Liabilities | | | | |
| Due to other governments | $186,880 | $7,701,916 | $7,737,386 | $151,410 |
| Deposits and rebates | 16,075 | 1,157,097 | 1,156,204 | 16,968 |
| Due to other funds | 47 | | 47 | |
| Total liabilities | $203,002 | $8,859,013 | $8,893,637 | $168,378 |

no "operating results." Each increase in Agency Fund total assets is accompanied by a corresponding increase in its liabilities. Not all agency relationships require use of Agency Funds.

Pension Trust Fund reporting requirements distinguish between the need to report the current status of the plan and the plan's long-term viability. The financial statements are used to reflect the current status of the plan. The schedules presented as required supplementary information disclose a longer-term perspective.

Note that while earlier chapters focus on governmental fund accounting and reporting, this chapter includes both governmental fund and proprietary fund accounting and reporting—as noted earlier—because of the differences in the nature of the various types of Trust and Agency Funds. The next two chapters discuss accounting and reporting principles and concepts for proprietary funds—Internal Service Funds and Enterprise Funds, respectively. These chapters complete the coverage of the current SLG accounting and reporting model; then Chapter 13 discusses and illustrates basic SLG financial reporting concepts and the Comprehensive Annual Financial Report.

## Questions

**Q 10-1** Trust Funds and Agency Funds, though separate fund types, are treated in the same chapter in this text and are often spoken of collectively. In what ways are they similar and how do they differ?

**Q 10-2** Compare the primary forms of accountability as among (1) the General and Special Revenue Funds, (2) Capital Projects Funds, and (3) Trust and Agency Funds.

**Q 10-3** A single trust agreement often gives rise to two separate Trust Funds. When is this so, and may a single trust agreement result in the establishment of three, four, or more separate funds?

**Q 10-4** In certain situations an Expendable (governmental) Trust Fund may be virtually identical to a Special Revenue Fund and should be budgeted and accounted for as though it were a Special Revenue Fund. Explain.

**Q 10-5** What is the difference between a Nonexpendable (proprietary) Trust Fund and an Agency Fund?

**Q 10-6** Accounting for separate Trust and Agency Funds on a "funds within a fund" approach was not illustrated in this chapter. Is it possible and/or permissible to account for more than one type of trust or agency relationship within a single Trust or Agency Fund?

**Q 10-7** Classify the following as to whether they are Expendable Trust Funds, Nonexpendable Trust Funds, or Agency Funds:
a. A fund established to handle tax collections by a governmental unit for other governments
b. A loan fund
c. A fund whose principal and income are both to be used in granting scholarships
d. A fund whose principal is to be held intact but whose income must be expended for bravery awards
e. A fund established to handle bidder deposits received by a county
f. A fund established to handle that part of the proceeds from the sale of property for taxes that is to be refunded to the property owner

**Q 10-8** The status of a pension plan as reported in its financial statements typically differs significantly from its status as presented in the required supplementary information for the plan. Why? Do you agree with providing this "dual presentation"?

**Q 10-9** When should an Agency Fund be used to account for special assessments? Why?

**Q 10-10** How might *internal* (interfund or intragovernmental) Agency Funds be used to facilitate a governmental unit's financial management and accounting processes?

**Q 10-11**   In accounting for a Tax Agency Fund, why is it necessary to maintain records of taxes levied and collected for each taxing authority involved by year of levy?

**Q 10-12**   According to the terms of A's will, the city is to become the owner of an apartment building. The net income from the building is to be added to the Policemen's Pension Fund. (a) Is this new fund an Expendable or a Nonexpendable Trust Fund? (b) Suppose that net income before depreciation is to be added to the Pension Fund. Is the fund expendable or nonexpendable?

**Q 10-13**   The earnings of a proprietary (nonexpendable as to corpus) Trust Fund are used to support the operation of a municipal museum, art gallery, and park complex. Should these activities be accounted for through the General Fund, a Special Revenue Fund, or a Trust Fund?

**Q 10-14**   Should the financial statements of PTFs be included in the combined statements issued as the GPFS of the governmental unit?

**Q 10-15**   A trust indenture states that the principal (corpus) of the trust is to be maintained intact in perpetuity. Yet, although the governmental trustee did not violate the terms of the trust agreement—and it was not subsequently revised—the principal (corpus) had decreased to less than half its original amount five years after the trust was created. Why or how might this have happened?

**Q 10-16**   What financial statements should be presented for (a) an Expendable Trust Fund, (b) a Nonexpendable Trust Fund, (c) an Agency Fund, and (d) a Pension Trust Fund under GASB *Statement No. 25*?

**Q 10-17**   Explain how the annual pension cost is used in determining employer government expenses, expenditures, and liabilities.

## Exercises

**E 10-1**   (Nonexpendable and Expendable Trust Funds) Prepare journal entries to record the following transactions in a city's accounts. Include any required adjustments.
1.  The city received a $3,000,000 gift in the form of cash ($1,000,000) and investments ($2,000,000). The donor stipulated that the principal of the gift be maintained intact. Earnings of the trust may be used only to restore historic buildings in the community.
2.  Interest and dividends received on the investments during the year totaled $300,000.
3.  At year end the expendable earnings were transferred to a fund established to account for the use of those resources for restoration of historic buildings.
4.  In the next year the city spent $65,000 to restore a historic church building that had been donated to the city in a prior year.

**E 10-2**   (Property Tax Agency Fund) Prepare general journal entries for the following transactions in the appropriate funds or account groups of a county, the county school district, and a town within the county. The county serves as the tax collection agent for the county, the county school district, and the town.
1.  Taxes were levied and bills were sent to taxpayers. The county tax levy was for $4,000,000; the school district tax levy was for $5,000,000; the town tax levy was for $2,000,000; 2% of the taxes are expected to be uncollectible. The county charges the school district and the town a collection fee of 1% of the taxes collected.
2.  Tax collections for the year totaled $8,960,000—$3,200,000 for the county, $4,000,000 for the school district, and $1,760,000 for the town.
3.  The amounts due to the county General Fund, the school district, and the town were paid from the Tax Agency Fund.

**E 10-3**   1.  A cash donation of $80,000 was received by Joyce County. The donor stipulated that the resources were to be used solely for 4-H purposes.
2.  Rent for an auditorium used for a 4-H conference and training session was paid, $800.

3. Travel and registration costs for 4-H members and staff to attend a regional 4-H camp were incurred and paid, $2,000.
4. A computer was purchased for the use of the 4-H coordinator and leaders, $5,000.

**Required**   Record the transactions in all the Joyce County funds and account groups affected.

**E 10-4**   Prepare the journal entries required in a county tax agency fund to record the following transactions.
1. Levy of taxes for the various taxing units, $3,000,000; 1% is expected to be uncollectible, 10% is expected to be collected after the cutoff date for revenue recognition.
2. Collection of taxes during the year, $2,600,000.
3. Write-off of taxes receivable of $12,000.
4. Remittance of amounts due to various taxing units, $2,600,000.

## Problems

**P 10-1**   (Multiple Choice)
1. Which of the following statements is required to be prepared for Agency Funds?
   a. statement of revenues, expenses, and changes in fund equity
   b. statement of revenues, expenditures, and changes in fund balances
   c. balance sheet
   d. statement of changes in agency fund assets and liabilities
   e. both c and d
2. Which of the following items should be accounted for in an Agency Fund when a special assessment project is financed by issuing special assessment debt for which the government is not obligated in any manner?
   a. the bond proceeds and construction costs
   b. the debt service transactions
   c. the long-term debt issued
   d. the fixed asset constructed or acquired
   e. none of the above
   f. all of the above
3. The long-term debt issued in a situation like that described in item 2 should be reported by the government in
   a. an Agency Fund.
   b. a Capital Projects Fund.
   c. a Debt Service Fund.
   d. the General Long-Term Debt Account Group.
   e. none of the above
4. Expenditures for an Agency Fund are recognized in the period
   a. the fund incurs a liability.
   b. the fund pays the amount owed for the expenditure.
   c. the expenditure is incurred.
   d. none of the above
5. When a Tax Agency Fund is used, the funds in which the taxes should ultimately be accounted for should report tax revenues
   a. when levied.
   b. when received by year end or not more than 60 days thereafter.
   c. in the year for which the taxes are levied or later.
   d. when both c and d are true.
6. Employer governments must measure their annual pension contribution
   a. using a standardized approach.
   b. in accordance with certain guidelines, but not in a standardized way.
   c. using the unit credit method.
   d. none of the above
7. In general, governmental fund accounting principles apply to
   a. trusts of which the corpus and earnings are expendable.

    b. trusts of which the corpus and earnings are nonexpendable.

    c. trusts of which the corpus is nonexpendable and the earnings are expendable.

    d. none of the above

    e. more than one of the above (explain)

8. Which of the following statements is not required to be presented for a Nonexpendable Trust Fund?

    a. balance sheet

    b. statement of revenues, expenses, and changes in fund balance

    c. statement of cash flows

    d. All of the above are required.

9. Which of the following statements about a Pension Trust Fund Statement of Plan Net Assets is not true?

    a. Investments are reported at fair value.

    b. Fixed assets are reported.

    c. The actuarial present value of future benefits payable is reported as a liability, not as an equity component.

    d. All of the above are true.

**P 10-2**  (Nonexpendable and Expendable Trust Funds) The following is a trial balance of the Child Welfare Principal Trust Fund of the city of Slusher's Ridge as of January 1, 19X3:

| | | |
|---|---:|---:|
| Cash | $ 98,000 | |
| Land | 70,000 | |
| Buildings | 162,000 | |
| Accumulated Depreciation | | $ 65,000 |
| Accrued Wages Payable | | 150 |
| Accrued Taxes Payable | | 1,800 |
| Due to Child Welfare Earnings Trust Fund | | 15,000 |
| Fund Balance—Trust Principal | | 248,050 |
| | $330,000 | $330,000 |

The endowment was in the form of an apartment building. Endowment principal is to be kept intact, and the net earnings are to be used in financing child welfare activities.

    The following transactions took place during the year:

1. Expenses and accrued liabilities paid in cash were as follows:

| | |
|---|---:|
| Heat, light, and power | $5,200 |
| Janitor's wages (including $150 previously accrued) | 3,000 |
| Painting and decorating | 3,750 |
| Repairs | 1,500 |
| Taxes (including $1,800 previously accrued) | 3,750 |
| Management fees | 4,500 |
| Miscellaneous expenses | 1,500 |
| | $23,200 |

2. A land improvement of $2,000 was constructed by an outside contractor who was paid in full.

3. Rents for 19X3 (all collected) amounted to $45,000.

4. The amount due to the Child Welfare Earnings Trust Fund at January 1, 19X3, was paid.

5. Expenditures of $13,500 were paid from the Child Welfare Earnings Trust Fund to finance 19X3 summer camp activities.

6. The following adjustments were made at the close of the year:

| | |
|---|---:|
| Depreciation | $6,000 |
| Accrued Taxes | 1,900 |
| Accrued Wages | 170 |

**Required** (a) Prepare a balance sheet as of December 31, 19X3, and a Statement of Revenues, Expenses, and Changes in Fund Balance for the fiscal year ended December 31, 19X3, for the Child Welfare Principal Trust Fund. (Support these statements with a worksheet, T-account, or other analysis.)

(b) Prepare a balance sheet as of December 31, 19X3, for the Child Welfare Earnings Trust Fund and a Statement of Revenues, Expenditures, and Changes in Fund Balance for the year then ended. (Assume that the Child Welfare Earnings Trust Fund had no activities or balances other than those indicated in the problem.)

**P 10-3** (Tax Agency Fund) Prepare the general journal entries required to record the following transactions in the general ledgers of the state, the County General Fund, and the County Tax Agency Fund. You may omit formal entry explanations but should key the entries to the numbered items in this problem.

1. The County Tax Agency Fund has been established to account for the county's duties of collecting the county and state property taxes. The levies for the year 19X0 were $600,000 for the County General Fund and $480,000 for the state. It is expected that uncollectible taxes will be $10,000 for the state and $15,000 for the county.
2. Collections were $300,000 for the county and $240,000 for the state.
3. The county is entitled to a fee of 1% of taxes collected for other governments. The amounts due to the state and to the County General Fund are paid except for the collection fee due to the County General Fund.
4. The fee is transmitted from the Tax Agency Fund to the County General Fund.
5. Uncollectible taxes in the amount of $5,000 for the state and $6,000 for the county are written off.

**P 10-4** (Tax Agency Fund) The following is a trial balance of the Tax Agency Fund of Cranor City as of June 30, 19X0:

| | | |
|---|---|---|
| Cash . . . . . . . . . . . . . . . . . . . . . . . . . . . . . . . . . . . . . . . . . . . . . | $ 90,000 | |
| Taxes Receivable for Teekell County . . . . . . . . . . . . . . . . . . . . . . . | 22,500 | |
| Taxes Receivable for Cranor City General Fund . . . . . . . . . . . . . . | 48,000 | |
| Taxes Receivable for Bonham School District . . . . . . . . . . . . . . . . | 69,000 | |
| Due to Teekell County . . . . . . . . . . . . . . . . . . . . . . . . . . . . . . . . . | | $ 37,500 |
| Due to General Fund . . . . . . . . . . . . . . . . . . . . . . . . . . . . . . . . . . | | 78,000 |
| Due to Bonham School District . . . . . . . . . . . . . . . . . . . . . . . . . . | | 114,000 |
| | $229,500 | $229,500 |

The following transactions took place:
1. Cash, $89,600, was paid over as follows:

| Unit | Amount Due | Collection Fee | Amount Paid Over |
|---|---|---|---|
| Teekell County | $15,000 | $100 | $14,900 |
| Cranor City General Fund | 30,000 | — | 30,000 |
| Bonham School District | 45,000 | 300 | 44,700 |

2. The collection fees were paid over to the General Fund.
3. Taxes were levied as follows:

| Unit | Amount Levied |
|---|---|
| Teekell County | $ 50,000 |
| Cranor City General Fund | 100,000 |
| Bonham School District | 150,000 |

*Required*   (a) Prepare journal entries.
        (b) Post to T-accounts.
        (c) Prepare a balance sheet as of June 30, 19X1.
        (d) Or in lieu of (a)–(c) prepare a worksheet from which requirement (c) might easily be fulfilled.

**P 10-5**   (Special Assessment Project—Government Not Obligated)
       1. The city of Robinsburg approved a $750,000 special assessment project in 19X5.
       2. A $740,000 contract was let to M & M Murphy Company for construction of the project.
       3. The project was completed and approved in 19X5, and the contractor billed the city accordingly for $740,000.
       4. The city issued $740,000 of 7%, 10-year special assessment bonds at par and used the proceeds to pay the contractor. The debt is secured solely by the assessment liens against the benefited properties, and the government will not repay the bonds in the case of default. One-tenth of the bonds mature each year.
       5. Assessments of $740,000 were levied in 19X5 upon completion of the project. Interest of 7% is charged on the balance of unpaid assessments. One-tenth of the assessments is due each year.
       6. Assessments collected during 19X6 totaled $74,000. Related interest collected was $51,800.
       7. The first debt service payment on the special assessment bonds was made in 19X6.

*Required*   (a) Prepare all the general ledger entries required in all of the funds and account groups of the city of Robinsburg to record the preceding transactions.
        (b) Repeat the entries assuming that Robinsburg is obligated in some manner on the debt.

**P 10-6**   (Pension Trust Fund Journal Entries) The following is a trial balance of the Policemen's Retirement Fund of the City of Cherrydale at January 1, 19X0:

| | | |
|---|---:|---:|
| Cash | $ 6,000 | |
| Interest Receivable | 450 | |
| Investments | 52,000 | |
| Pensions Payable | | $ 150 |
| Net Assets Held in Trust for Pension Benefits | | 58,300 |
| | $58,450 | $58,450 |

The following transactions took place during the year:
       1. Contributions became due from the General Fund, $38,000, and a Special Revenue Fund, $6,000. One-half of these amounts represents the employees' share of contributions.
       2. Payments were received from the General Fund, $30,000, and the Special Revenue Fund, $4,000.
       3. Securities were acquired for cash as follows:

| | | |
|---|---|---:|
| a. | First Purchase: | |
| | Par value | $20,000 |
| | Premiums | 300 |
| | Interest accrued at purchase | 200 |
| b. | Second Purchase: | |
| | Par value | 15,000 |
| | Discounts | 150 |

       4. Interest received on investments amounted to $3,000, including interest receivable on January 1, 19X0, and the accrued interest purchased.

5. An employee resigned prior to retirement and was paid $300, which is the amount of her contributions and interest thereon. Employer contributions do not vest until retirement.
6. Retirement payments of $600 were made; pensions payable of $200 remained at year end.
7. An actuary indicated that the actuarial deficiency at year end was $19,000.
8. The fair value of the pension plan investments was $200 more than the carrying value at year end.

**Required**  Prepare journal entries—including closing entries—to record the transactions in the general ledger of the Policemen's Retirement Fund.

**P 10-7**  (Pension Trust Fund Entries and Statements) The following is a trial balance of the McCarthy County Public Employees Retirement Fund, a multiple-employer pension plan in which the cities of Mooresville and Sutherland's Gap participate as well as the county.

| | | |
|---|---:|---:|
| Cash . . . . . . . . . . . . . . . . . . . . . . . . . . . . . . . . . . . . . . . . . . . . . . . . . . . | $   76,000 | |
| Due from Sutherland's Gap . . . . . . . . . . . . . . . . . . . . . . . . . . . . . . | 12,000 | |
| Interest Receivable . . . . . . . . . . . . . . . . . . . . . . . . . . . . . . . . . . . . | 14,200 | |
| Investments . . . . . . . . . . . . . . . . . . . . . . . . . . . . . . . . . . . . . . . . . . | 1,456,000 | |
| Due to Resigned Employees . . . . . . . . . . . . . . . . . . . . . . . . . . . . . | | $   14,500 |
| Due to Estates of Deceased Employees . . . . . . . . . . . . . . . . . . . . | | 3,000 |
| Annuities Payable  . . . . . . . . . . . . . . . . . . . . . . . . . . . . . . . . . . . . | | 1,700 |
| Net Assets Held in Trust for Pension Benefits . . . . . . . . . . . . . . . | | 1,539,000 |
| | $1,558,200 | $1,558,200 |

The employees' contributions are returned to them or to their estates upon resignation or death, respectively; vesting of employers' matching contributions occurs only at retirement.

During 19X4 the following transactions occurred:
1. Employee contributions for the year were as follows:

| Employees Of: | Contributions |
|---|---|
| McCarthy County | $60,000 |
| Mooresville | 35,000 |
| Sutherland's Gap | 25,000 |

2. All amounts due the McCarthy County plan were collected except $20,000 each still due from the cities.
3. Interest accrued in the amount of $169,000.
4. Interest receivable of $168,400 was collected.
5. Five employees resigned; their contributions were determined to have been $24,000. Two employees died prior to retirement; their contributions were determined to have been $36,000.
6. Checks mailed to resigned employees during the year amounted to $34,500. Checks mailed to the estates of deceased employees totaled $33,000.
7. Annuities were accrued in the amount of $63,000; annuities in the amount of $62,700 were paid.
8. Additional investments were made as follows:

| | |
|---|---:|
| Bonds (at par) . . . . . . . . . . . . . . . . | $160,000 |
| Accrued interest . . . . . . . . . . . . . . . | 30,000 |
| Discounts . . . . . . . . . . . . . . . . . . . . | (8,000) |
| | $182,000 |

9. The fair value of investments at year end exceeded the carrying value by $3,000.

**Required**   (a) Prepare a worksheet (or journal entries and T-accounts) showing transactions, adjustments, and closing entries for the Retirement Fund for 19X4.

(b) Prepare a statement of plan net assets as of December 31, 19X4; and a statement of changes in plan net assets for the year ended December 31, 19X4.

**P 10-8, Part I**   (Trust Fund Worksheet) Nancy Township had not been operating a public library prior to October 1, 19X1. On October 1, 19X1, James Jones died, having made a valid will that provided for the gift of his residence and various securities to the town for the establishment and operation of a free public library. The gift was accepted, and the library funds and operations were placed under the control of trustees. The terms of the gift provided that not more than $5,000 of the principal of the fund could be used for the purchase of equipment, building rearrangement, and purchase of such standard library reference books as, in the opinion of the trustees, were needed for starting the library. Except for this $5,000, the principal of the fund is to be invested and the income therefrom used to operate the library in accordance with appropriations made by the trustees. The property received from the estate by the trustees included:

| Description | Face or Par | Appraised Value |
|---|---|---|
| Residence of James Jones: | | |
|   Land | | $ 2,500 |
|   Building (25-year estimated life) | | 20,000 |
| Bonds: | | |
|   Wirt Company | $34,000 | 32,000 |
|   Bromley Company | 10,000 | 11,200 |
|   Covey Company | 20,000 | 20,000 |
| Stocks: | | |
|   Eames Company, 6% preferred | 12,000 | 12,600 |
|   Elliott Company, 5% preferred | 10,000 | 9,600 |
|   Thurman Company, common (300 shares) | No par | 12,900 |
|   Wright Company (200 shares) | 4,000 | 14,500 |

The following events occurred in connection with the library operations up to June 30, 19X2:

1. 100 shares of Wright Company stock were sold on November 17, 19X1 for $6,875.
2. Cash payments were made for (a) alteration of the house—$1,310, (b) general reference books—$725, (c) equipment having an estimated life of 10 years—$2,180. The trustees state that these amounts are to be charged to principal under the applicable provision of the gift.
3. The library started operation on January 1, 19X2. The trustees adopted the following budget for the year ended December 31, 19X2:

| | |
|---|---|
| Estimated income from Trust Principal Fund earnings transfers | $5,000 |
| Estimated income from fines, etc. | 200 |
| Appropriation for salaries | 3,600 |
| Appropriation for subscriptions | 300 |
| Appropriation for purchase of books | 800 |
| Appropriation for utilities, supplies, etc. | 400 |

4. The following cash receipts were reported during the 6 months to June 30, 19X2:

| | | |
|---|---|---|
| a. Sale of Bromley Company bonds, including | | |
|     accrued interest of $80 | $11,550 | |
| b. Interest and dividends | 3,100 | |
| c. Fines | 20 | |
| d. Gift for purchase of books | 200 | |
|     Total | $14,870 | |

5. The following cash payments were made during the 6 months to June 30, 19X2:

| | |
|---|---:|
| a. Purchase of 100 shares of no-par common stock of Daniels Company, including commission and tax cost of $50 .... | $ 9,655 |
| b. Payment of salaries .............................. | 1,500 |
| c. Payment of property taxes applicable to the year ended December 31, 19X1 based on an assessment of June 30, 19X1 ................................... | 200 |
| d. Purchase of books ............................... | 900 |
| e. Magazine subscriptions ........................... | 230 |
| f. Supplies and other expenses ....................... | 260 |
| Total ....................................... | $12,745 |

6. On June 30, 19X2, there were miscellaneous library expenses unpaid, but accrued, amounting to $90. Also, there were outstanding purchase orders for books in the amount of $70.

**Required** Assuming that the township records budgetary accounts with respect to library operations, prepare in detail the worksheet(s) necessary to show the results of operations to June 30, 19X2 and the financial position of the Trust Fund(s) related to the library as of June 30, 19X2. Where alternative treatments of an item are acceptable, explain the alternative treatments and state the justification for your treatment. In designing your worksheet(s), you should observe the requirements of Part II of this problem in order that those requirements may be fulfilled readily from the worksheet(s) prepared here.

**P 10-8, Part II** (Trust Fund Financial Statements) From the worksheet(s) prepared in Part I, construct the following formal statements relative to Nancy Township's library endowment and library operations:
(a) A Balance Sheet(s) for the Trust Fund(s) at June 30, 19X2.
(b) A Statement of Revenues, Expenditures, and Changes in Fund Balance—Budget and Actual—for the Library Endowment Earnings Trust Fund for the six months ended June 30, 19X2.

**P 10-9** (Research Problem) Obtain copies of the Trust and Agency Fund financial statements of a state or local government.

**Required** (a) Study the Trust and Agency Fund financial statements and compare them with those discussed and illustrated in this chapter, noting
(1) similarities,
(2) differences, and
(3) other matters that come to your attention.
(b) Study the authoritative literature to determine the following:
(1) What is an investment pool?
(2) What is meant by the "internal portion" of an investment pool?
(3) What is meant by the "external portion" of an investment pool?
(4) How are the assets of the investment pool reported in the financial statements of the government that operates the pool?
(c) Prepare a brief report on requirements (a) and (b).

# C H A P T E R

# 11

# INTERNAL SERVICE FUNDS

Internal Service (IS) Funds are established in order to finance, administer, and account for departments or agencies of a government whose exclusive or nearly exclusive purpose is to provide goods and services (e.g., printing services) to the government's other departments on a **cost-reimbursement** basis. (The break-even objective has caused such funds to be referred to as "working capital" or "revolving" funds in many jurisdictions.)

Internal Service Fund departments may provide a limited portion of their services to other governments in some instances. But, when providing services to other governments (or to other customers) is a significant purpose of the department, an Enterprise Fund should be used, not an Internal Service Fund. Enterprise Funds are used to account for and finance the provision of goods or services for compensation primarily to the general public and to outside entities rather than to other departments of the government.

IS Funds are internal intermediary fiscal and accounting entities through which some of the expenditures of other departments are made. They are used (1) to attain greater economy, efficiency, and effectiveness in the acquisition and distribution of common goods or services utilized by several or all departments within the organization; and (2) to facilitate an equitable sharing of costs among the various departments served and, hence, among the funds of the organization. They also may be used to provide interim financing for capital projects.

The type and complexity of activities accounted for through IS Funds vary widely in practice. Among the simpler types are those used (1) to distribute common or joint costs—such as the cost of telephone, two-way radio, or other communication facilities—among departments; (2) to acquire, distribute, and allocate costs of selected items of inventory, such as office supplies or gasoline; or (3) to provide temporary loans to other funds. More complex activities accounted for through IS Funds include motor pools; data processing activities; duplicating and printing facilities; repair shops and garages; cement and asphalt plants; purchasing, warehousing, and distribution services; and insurance and other risk management services.

## OVERVIEW OF ACCOUNTING PRINCIPLES

IS Funds are **proprietary** (nonexpendable) funds. Their accounting is essentially the same as that for a profit-seeking enterprise in the same business. Accordingly, the accrual basis of accounting is used. Too, both the related fixed assets—which

427

normally are replaced from IS Fund resources—and any long-term debt to be serviced through the fund are recorded as "fund" assets and liabilities in the IS Fund. Depreciation expense is recorded and net income or loss is computed. In sum, the capital maintenance measurement focus of proprietary funds is used. Therefore, most transactions and events are accounted for and reported just as for business enterprises. Leases, for example, are classified and reported virtually the same as in business accounting. Pension costs and liabilities are not accounted for in the same manner as for businesses, however. Instead, pension costs and liabilities are reported in accordance with GASB *Statement No. 27,* as discussed in Chapter 10. The GASB either requires or permits governments to apply most FASB standards and interpretations to their proprietary activities unless they conflict with a GASB pronouncement, as detailed in the next chapter.

The application of generally accepted business accounting principles is consistent with the funds' typical objectives. First, the usual policy requires break-even pricing and the maintenance of the invested capital. (As mentioned earlier, IS Funds sometimes are referred to as revolving funds because the fund resources are used to provide goods or services and are subsequently replenished by charges to other funds. Then those resources are used to provide goods and services, and so on.) Information on revenues and expenses is essential to fulfilling this policy. Second, full costing provides appropriate information for "make or buy" decisions and for determining equitable charges to the departments that use the services of the IS Fund.

## Creation of the IS Fund

Ordinarily an IS Fund will be created by constitutional, charter, or legislative action. However, in some instances the chief executive may be empowered to create an IS Fund. Capital to finance IS Fund activities may come from various sources. Examples include appropriations from the General Fund, the issue of general obligation bonds or other debt instruments, transfers from other funds, or advances from another government. Capital may also be provided by contributing all, or excessive, inventories of materials and supplies that a fund's future "clients" (a governmental unit's departments) may have on hand at a specified time. Likewise, general fixed assets may be reclassified for use in IS Fund operations as IS Fund assets. The sources of capital used to finance a specific IS Fund depend to some extent on whether the IS Fund is being established to account for a new activity or for an activity previously accounted for in other funds.

If the General Fund provides permanent capital ($50,000) for the IS Fund, the following entries are made:

**General Fund**

| | | |
|---|---|---|
| Residual Equity Transfer to IS Fund | $50,000 | |
|   Cash | | $50,000 |
| To record capital provided to IS Fund. | | |

**IS Fund**

| | | |
|---|---|---|
| Cash | $50,000 | |
|   Residual Equity Transfer from General Fund | | $50,000 |
| To record receipt of capital from General Fund. | | |

Residual equity transfers from other funds should be closed to an IS Fund contributed capital account such as "Contributed Capital—Governmental Unit."

Capital contributions must be distinguished from loans and advances. If the IS Fund ultimately must repay the General Fund, the following entries would be made rather than the preceding entries:

**General Fund**

| | | |
|---|---|---|
| Advance to IS Fund ..................................... | $50,000 | |
|   Cash ................................................. | | $50,000 |
| To record advance to IS Fund. | | |
| Unreserved Fund Balance ............................... | $50,000 | |
|   Reserve for Advance to IS Fund ......................... | | $50,000 |
| To record reservation of fund balance for advance to IS Fund. | | |

**IS Fund**

| | | |
|---|---|---|
| Cash .................................................. | $50,000 | |
|   Advance from General Fund ............................. | | $50,000 |
| To record advance from General Fund. | | |

The terms *advance to* and *advance from* indicate intermediate- and long-term receivables and payables. *Due to* and *due from* connote short-term relationships. The reserve established in the General Fund indicates that the asset "Advance to IS Fund" does not represent currently appropriable resources.

If general obligation bonds ($100,000) intended to be repaid from the IS Fund are issued at par to finance an IS Fund, the following entry is made:

**IS Fund**

| | | |
|---|---|---|
| Cash .................................................. | $100,000 | |
|   Bonds Payable ........................................ | | $100,000 |
| To record bond issue. | | |

In this case the contingent "general government" liability for the bonds need only be disclosed in the notes to the financial statements. If the bonds were not intended to be repaid from the IS Fund and receipt of the bond proceeds were recorded in the General Fund, the following entries are made:

**General Fund**

| | | |
|---|---|---|
| Cash .................................................. | $100,000 | |
|   Bond Issue Proceeds ................................... | | $100,000 |
| To record issuance of bonds. | | |
| Residual Equity Transfer to IS Fund ....................... | $100,000 | |
|   Due to IS Fund ....................................... | | $100,000 |
| To record transfer of bond proceeds to IS Fund. | | |

**General Long-Term Debt Account Group**

| | | |
|---|---|---|
| Amount to Be Provided for Retirement of Bonds .............. | $100,000 | |
|   Bonds Payable ........................................ | | $100,000 |
| To record issuance of bonds to finance IS Fund but to be repaid from general revenues. | | |

**IS Fund**

| | | |
|---|---|---|
| Due from General Fund ................................. | $100,000 | |
|   Residual Equity Transfer from General Fund .............. | | $100,000 |
| To record residual equity transfer from General Fund. | | |

When an IS Fund is established to account for an activity previously financed and accounted for through the governmental funds, inventories or general fixed assets often are contributed to the IS Fund. If equipment with a five-year estimated useful life that was acquired for $30,000 two years prior to creation of an IS Fund is contributed to the IS Fund when it is created, the following entries are required:

**General Fixed Assets Account Group**

| | | |
|---|---|---|
| Investment in General Fixed Assets—General Revenues . . . . . . . . | $30,000 | |
| Equipment . . . . . . . . . . . . . . . . . . . . . . . . . . . . . . . . . . . . . . . . . . . . | | $30,000 |

To record reclassification of equipment to IS Fund.

**IS Fund**

| | | |
|---|---|---|
| Equipment . . . . . . . . . . . . . . . . . . . . . . . . . . . . . . . . . . . . . . . . . . . | $30,000 | |
| Accumulated Depreciation—Equipment . . . . . . . . . . . . . . . . . . | | $12,000 |
| Contributed Capital—Governmental Unit . . . . . . . . . . . . . . . . | | 18,000 |

To record fixed assets reclassified from General Fixed Assets
Account Group.

Note that the equipment is recorded at its original cost less the accumulated depreciation that would have been recorded to date if the asset had been accounted for in the IS Fund all along (as discussed in Chapter 9). Also, no entry is required in the General Fund because General Fund resources are not involved in the transaction. Recall that if the asset's net utility value is less than the book value recorded in this entry, the asset is written down further to its net utility value. Finally, note that this contributed capital increase will be reported in the same manner for the IS Fund as residual equity transfers in.

## Pricing Policies

The preceding discussions relative to pricing assumed that the prices charged by the IS Fund would be based on (historical) cost. Most authorities agree that cost is the proper pricing basis. IS Fund activities that are very modest in scope, have no full-time personnel, and do not incur other significant costs sometimes base charges to user departments on direct costs. This might be the case, for example, where (1) very limited group purchasing and warehousing is done only occasionally or as a small part of the overall purchasing operation, or (2) where the IS Fund is essentially a flow-through or clearance device for common costs, such as two-way radio facility rentals. More commonly, however, IS Fund activities involve substantial amounts of personnel, space, materials, and other overhead costs that are recovered through billing user departments for more than the direct cost of the goods or services provided.

The IS Fund usually has a captive clientele. In most governments the departments may not use another source of supply if a service or material is available through an IS Fund. The lack of outside competition can lead to inefficiencies. Therefore, the economy, efficiency, and effectiveness of IS Fund activities should be monitored closely under such circumstances. Without such precautions, the convenience of having an "in-house" supplier may result in significantly higher costs than otherwise necessary.

Being the sole source of a particular good or service also permits IS Fund prices to be set at levels that will produce profit or loss. In some cases IS Fund capital has been built up by means of substantial annual profits. The increase in capital was paid for, of course, by the funds that financed the expenditures used to buy IS Fund services or supplies. There have even been instances in which the retained earnings of an IS Fund provided the basis for a cash "dividend" that was transferred as "revenue" to the General Fund. To the extent that IS Fund revenues were derived from departments financed by the General Fund, the profit thus transferred merely had the effect of offsetting excessive charges to it previously. But, if departments or activities financed through other funds patronized the IS Fund, the effect of over-charging was to transfer resources from these other funds to the General Fund.

Overcharging user departments sometimes results in diverting restricted re-sources to other purposes. This use of IS Fund charges cannot be condoned. Such a practice erodes confidence in the organization's administrators and in the ac-counting system. It also constitutes indirect fraud at best, and at worst results in il-legal use of intergovernmental grant, trust, or other restricted resources. Excessive charges for IS Fund goods or services to federally (or state) financed programs are properly disallowed for reimbursement. The government also risks being penalized by having to repay the grantor government and not receiving such financial assis-tance in the future.

## Pricing Methods

The pricing method used by an IS Fund is usually based on estimates of total costs and total consumption of goods or services. From these two estimates a rate is de-veloped that is applied to each purchase. Assume that the cost of materials to be issued by a Stores Fund during the coming year was expected to be $300,000 and that other costs of fund operation were estimated at $12,000. Goods would be priced to departments at $1.04 for every $1.00 of direct cost of materials issued. Similarly, rental rates for automotive equipment may be based on time or mileage, or both. If a truck was expected to be driven 12,000 miles during the year at a total cost of $2,400, the departments would be charged $0.20 per mile.

The alternative to using predetermined rates is to charge the departments on the basis of actual costs determined at the end of each month, quarter, or year. Though this method is sometimes used for uncomplicated IS Funds, a predeter-mined charge rate is generally used for more complex operations. This practice is preferable because (1) some IS Fund expenses may not be determinable until the end of the month (or later), whereas it may be desirable to bill departments promptly so that they know how much expense or expenditure is charged to their jobs and activities at any time, and (2) charges based on actual monthly costs are likely to spread the burden inequitably among departments. For example, assume that the costs of extensive equipment repairs made in June are included in the charges to the departments using the equipment during that month. In this situa-tion, those departments that used the equipment in June would be billed for costs more properly allocated to several months or years. The departments that used the equipment in previous or succeeding months would not bear their fair share of these costs. Furthermore, even if one department used the equipment throughout the year, charges based on actual monthly costs often would result in an unequitable distribution of costs among jobs and activities carried on by the department.

IS Fund expenses, including overhead, should be recorded in appropriatcly titled expense accounts. IS Fund charges for the goods or services provided are credited to a revenue account such as Billings to Departments or Intragovern-mental Sales, and corresponding receivables from (due from) other funds or other governments are recorded.

## Relation to the Budget

The level of activity of an IS Fund will be determined by the demand of the user departments for its services. IS Fund appropriations often are not made, and formal budgetary control may not be employed in IS Fund accounts. These controls are often not used because (1) the IS activity must be able to respond to service demands, not constrained by inflexible appropriation levels, and (2) the appropriations to the various user departments place an indirect budgetary ceiling on the IS activities.

Sound management requires the use of flexible budgetary techniques in planning and conducting major IS Fund activities. Although the budget developed with these techniques may be formally approved, the expense element is not considered to be appropriated. Budgetary control is exercised as in a business. The expenses incurred are compared with estimated expenses at the level of activity actually achieved.

Laws or custom in some cases prohibit the incurrence of obligations against or disbursement of cash from IS Funds without appropriation authority. Where this is the case, it is necessary to record not only those transactions that affect the actual position and operations of the fund (i.e., those transactions that affect the actual revenues, expenses, assets, liabilities, and capital) but also those relating to appropriations, expenditures, and encumbrances. Because this is the unusual case rather than the usual one, the examples that follow illustrate the accounting for proprietary accounts only. Budgetary accounting for proprietary funds typically is accomplished using self-balancing budgetary accounts in which the budgetary effects of transactions are recorded. Accounting for the proprietary accounts is not affected by the budgetary accounting entries under this approach.

## Financial Statements

The required IS Fund financial statements parallel those for businesses. The same financial statements are required for Enterprise Funds and Nonexpendable Trust Funds. The three required financial statements for these fund types are the:

- Balance sheet
- Statement of revenues, expenses, and changes in fund equity (or retained earnings)
- Statement of cash flows

### Balance Sheet

The balance sheet of a proprietary fund is like that of a similar business entity. Fixed assets, intangible assets, and similar accounts that are not included in governmental fund balance sheets are reported in proprietary fund balance sheets. This is consistent with the application of the business accounting model to proprietary funds as discussed in Chapter 2. Likewise, long-term liabilities payable from the resources of a proprietary fund are reported in the balance sheet of that proprietary fund. An IS Fund balance sheet is illustrated later in this chapter.

### Statement of Revenues, Expenses, and Changes in Fund Equity (Retained Earnings)

As discussed in Chapter 2, the proprietary fund basic operating statement is the statement of revenues, expenses, and changes in fund equity (or in retained earnings). This statement closely resembles a business income statement. A simple example of this statement is provided later in this chapter. A more in-depth discussion of the statement of revenues, expenses, and changes in fund equity (or in retained earnings) is presented in Chapter 12.

### Statement of Cash Flows

The statement of cash flows for proprietary funds serves essentially the same purposes as the business statement of cash flows. However, cash flows resulting from similar or identical transactions and events are often required to be classified differently in proprietary fund cash flow statements than in business cash flow statements. Instead of the three classifications of cash flows used in business cash flow statements (operating, financing, and investing), the GASB requires four cash flow categories:

- Cash flows from operating activities
- Cash flows from noncapital financing activities
- Cash flows from capital and related financing activities
- Cash flows from investing activities

The proprietary fund cash flows from operating activities classification differs from the business cash flows from operating activities primarily in that it generally incorporates only the cash effects of transactions and events that enter into operating income rather than net income. Consequently, the cash effects associated with nonoperating revenues and expenses such as interest revenue and interest expense are not included in cash flows from operating activities. The GASB *Codification* states that:

> Operating activities generally result from providing services and producing and delivering goods, and include all transactions and other events that are not defined as capital and related financing, noncapital financing, or investing activities. . . .[1]

The *Codification* further states that the direct method of presenting cash flows from operating activities is preferred. But governments are permitted to use the indirect (reconciliation) method. If the direct method is used, certain operating cash flows must be reported as separate line items. Also, if the direct method is used, a reconciliation of operating income and cash flows from operating activities—that is, the indirect method presentation of cash flows from operating activities—must be presented either at the bottom of the cash flow statement or as a separate schedule.

Noncapital financing activities and capital and related financing activities are distinguished by whether the cash flow is clearly attributable to the financing of capital asset (i.e., fixed asset) acquisition, construction, or improvement. Cash flows from issuing (or repaying) debt, interest payments, interfund transfers from other funds, and certain other transactions will be classified as capital and related financing activities if clearly attributable to capital asset financing. Otherwise, they are classified as noncapital financing activities. For example, cash received from issuing bonds that are clearly issued for the explicit purpose of financing construction of a fixed asset is reported as cash flows from capital and related financing activities. Cash payments of interest or principal on those bonds also will be classified as capital and related financing activities. The cash effects of issuing or servicing all other debt issuances (not clearly related to capital asset financing) would be noncapital financing activities.

One striking difference from the business cash flow statement classifications is that cash payments to acquire fixed assets are reported as capital and related financing activities, not as investing activities. Likewise, cash received from the sale or disposal of fixed assets is reported as capital and related financing activities.

Investing activities include (a) making and collecting most loans, (b) making or disposing of investments in debt or equity instruments, and (c) the related interest and dividends received. As noted earlier, acquisition and disposition of capital assets are not reported as investing activities in government cash flow statements. The government cash flow classifications appear to center more on distinguishing capital asset-related cash flows from noncapital asset-related cash

---

[1] GASB *Codification*, sec. 2450.113.

flows, whereas the business cash flow classifications focus on distinguishing financing cash flows and investing cash flows.

As in business cash flow statements, the GASB requires disclosure of information about significant noncash financing and investing activities. This information is to be presented in a schedule either on the face of the statement or separately.

Figure 11–1 summarizes the common classifications of the typical cash flows of proprietary funds. As indicated in the figure, some of the transactions resulting in these cash flows are discussed in the next chapter. A simple cash flow statement is presented in this chapter, while a more complex statement of cash flows is illustrated in Chapter 12.

**FIGURE 11–1  Cash Flow Classifications Summary**

*Cash Flows from Operating Activities*
- Cash received from sales of goods or services
- Cash paid for materials used in providing services or manufacturing goods for resale
- Cash paid to suppliers for other goods or services
- Cash paid to employees for services
- Cash received or paid resulting from quasi-external transactions
- Cash received from other funds for reimbursement of operating transactions
- Cash payments for taxes
- Cash received or paid from grants for specific activities that are part of grantor governments' operating activities
- Other cash flows that are not properly reported in the other classifications

*Cash Flows from Noncapital Financing Activities*
- Cash received from issuing (or paid to repay) borrowings not clearly attributable to capital assets
- Cash paid for interest on those borrowings
- Cash received from operating grants (discussed in Chapter 12) not included in operating activities
- Cash paid for grants or subsidies to other governments that are not included in operating activities

- Cash paid for transfers out and for interfund reimbursements not included in operating activities
- Cash received from transfers not clearly made for capital asset purposes

*Cash Flows from Capital and Related Financing Activities*
- Cash received from issuing (or paid to repay) borrowings clearly attributable to capital assets
- Cash paid for interest on those borrowings
- Cash received from capital grants (discussed in Chapter 12)
- Cash paid or received from acquisition or disposal of capital assets
- Cash received from transfers from other funds for the specific purpose of financing capital assets
- Cash received from special assessments or taxes levied to finance capital assets

*Cash Flows from Investing Activities*
- Cash paid or received for the acquisition or disposal of investments in debt or equity securities
- Cash paid or received from loans made to others
- Cash received from interest and dividends

Note: This figure is not intended to be comprehensive. Many transactions and situations are beyond the scope of this text.

## IS FUND ACCOUNTING ILLUSTRATED

Three illustrations of IS Fund activities, accounting, and reporting make up this section of this chapter. The fund activities illustrated are a central automotive equipment operation, a Stores Fund, and a Self-Insurance Fund. Only general ledger entries are illustrated in the examples. Subsidiary ledgers and cost accounting systems are maintained for IS Funds but are not illustrated because they should be identical to those for similar business operations.

### A Central Automotive Equipment Unit

Assume that a Central Automotive Equipment Fund has been created and that some of the assets needed have been acquired. The IS Fund balance sheet prior to beginning operations is presented in Figure 11–2. Fund resources will be used to buy automobiles, trucks, tractors, and the like. The use of each machine and the cost of operation on a per mile or per hour basis will be estimated. Records of actual cost will be kept for comparison with the estimates and for making estimates for coming years. Such records also are useful in evaluating the efficiency of management and economy of operation of various types and brands of equipment.

The following transactions and entries illustrate how a typical IS Fund equipment bureau operates. Note that in this case every transaction is substantially the same as it would have been for a business enterprise.

**Transactions and Entries**

**1.** Purchased equipment by paying $25,000 cash and issuing a two-year, 6% note for $15,000 on October 1.

| | | |
|---|---|---|
| (1) Machinery and Equipment | $40,000 | |
| Notes Payable | | $15,000 |
| Cash | | 25,000 |

To record purchase of equipment.

Note that the long-term note is recorded and reported in the IS Fund as is the equipment.

**2.** Materials and supplies purchased on credit, $10,000.

| | | |
|---|---|---|
| (2) Inventory of Materials and Supplies | $10,000 | |
| Vouchers Payable | | $10,000 |

To record purchase of materials and supplies.

**FIGURE 11–2** **Beginning Balance Sheet**

A Governmental Unit

**Central Automotive Equipment (IS) Fund**
**Balance Sheet**
(Date)

**Assets**

| | | |
|---|---|---|
| Current assets: | | |
|   Cash | | $ 75,000 |
| Fixed assets | | |
|   Land | $10,000 | |
|   Buildings | 40,000 | |
|   Machinery and equipment | 10,000 | 60,000 |
| | | $135,000 |

**Contributed Capital**

| | | |
|---|---|---|
| Contributed capital—governmental unit | | $135,000 |

**3.** Salaries and wages paid, $19,000, distributed as follows:

| | |
|---|---|
| Mechanics' Wages | $ 9,000 |
| Indirect Labor | 3,000 |
| Superintendent's Salary | 3,500 |
| Office Salaries | 3,500 |
| | $19,000 |

| | | |
|---|---|---|
| (3) Expenses—Mechanics' Wages | $ 9,000 | |
| Expenses—Indirect Labor | 3,000 | |
| Expenses—Superintendent's Salary | 3,500 | |
| Expenses—Office Salaries | 3,500 | |
| Cash | | $19,000 |

To record salaries and wages expenses.

**4.** Heat, light, and power paid, $2,000.

| | | |
|---|---|---|
| (4) Expenses—Heat, Light, and Power | $ 2,000 | |
| Cash | | $ 2,000 |

To record heat, light, and power expenses.

**5.** Depreciation:

| | |
|---|---|
| Buildings | $2,400 |
| Machinery and Equipment | 9,200 |

| | | |
|---|---|---|
| (5) Expenses—Depreciation—Buildings | $ 2,400 | |
| Expenses—Depreciation—Machinery and Equipment | 9,200 | |
| Accumulated Depreciation—Buildings | | $ 2,400 |
| Accumulated Depreciation—Machinery and Equipment | | 9,200 |

To record depreciation expense.

**6.** Total billings to departments for services rendered, $42,800, of which $30,000 is payable from the General Fund and $12,800 is payable from the Enterprise Fund.

| | | |
|---|---|---|
| (6) Due from General Fund | $30,000 | |
| Due from Enterprise Fund | 12,800 | |
| **Revenues—Billings to Departments** | | $42,800 |

To record billings to departments.

This transaction is a quasi-external transaction. Expenditures will be charged in the General Fund and an expense account will be charged in the Enterprise Fund. In both cases, the credit will be to Due to Central Automotive Equipment (Internal Service) Fund.

The "Billings to Departments" revenues account often is used by governments for IS Fund charges to user departments. Some accountants consider the title to be more descriptive than "Sales." Others consider titles such as "Sales" to connote the inclusion of a "profit" element in the charges, which should not be true with IS Fund charges. Still other accountants prefer to use the account title "Sales" (or "Revenues from Sales").

**7.** Vouchers payable of $7,500 were paid.

| | | |
|---|---|---|
| (7) Vouchers Payable | $ 7,500 | |
| Cash | | $ 7,500 |

To record payment of vouchers payable.

**8.** Cash collected from the General Fund, $29,000, and from the Enterprise Fund, $10,000.

| | | |
|---|---|---|
| (8) Cash | $39,000 | |
| Due from General Fund | | $29,000 |
| Due from Enterprise Fund | | 10,000 |

To record collections on interfund receivables.

**9.** Office maintenance expenses paid, $200.

| | | |
|---|---|---|
| (9) Expenses—Office Maintenance | $ 200 | |
| Cash | | $ 200 |

To record miscellaneous office expenses.

**10.** Materials and supplies issued during the period, $7,000.

| | | |
|---|---|---|
| (10) Expenses—Cost of Materials and Supplies Used . . . . . . | $7,000 | |
|   Inventory of Materials and Supplies . . . . . . . . . . . . . | | $7,000 |
|   To record cost of materials and supplies used. | | |

**11.** Accrued salaries and wages, $1,000, distributed as follows:

| | |
|---|---|
| Mechanics' Wages . . . . . . . . . . . . . . . . . . . . | $500 |
| Indirect Labor . . . . . . . . . . . . . . . . . . . . . . | 150 |
| Superintendent's Salary . . . . . . . . . . . . . . . . | 175 |
| Office Salaries . . . . . . . . . . . . . . . . . . . . . . | 175 |

Also, interest was accrued on notes payable, $400.

| | | |
|---|---|---|
| (11) Expenses—Interest . . . . . . . . . . . . . . . . . . . . . . . . . . . | $ 400 | |
|   Expenses—Mechanics' Wages . . . . . . . . . . . . . . . . . . . . | 500 | |
|   Expenses—Indirect Labor . . . . . . . . . . . . . . . . . . . . . . . | 150 | |
|   Expenses—Superintendent's Salary . . . . . . . . . . . . . . . . | 175 | |
|   Expenses—Office Salaries . . . . . . . . . . . . . . . . . . . . . . . | 175 | |
|     Accrued Interest Payable . . . . . . . . . . . . . . . . . . . . . . | | $ 400 |
|     Accrued Salaries and Wages Payables . . . . . . . . . . . . | | 1,000 |
|   To record accrued salaries, wages, and interest. | | |

After these entries have been posted, the trial balance of the accounts of the IS Fund will appear as follows:

A Governmental Unit
**Central Automotive Equipment (IS) Fund**
**Preclosing Trial Balance**
**(Date)**

| | | |
|---|---:|---:|
| Cash . . . . . . . . . . . . . . . . . . . . . . . . . . . . . . . . . . . . . . . . . . . | $60,300 | |
| Due from General Fund . . . . . . . . . . . . . . . . . . . . . . . . . . . . | 1,000 | |
| Due from Enterprise Fund . . . . . . . . . . . . . . . . . . . . . . . . . . | 2,800 | |
| Inventory of Materials and Supplies . . . . . . . . . . . . . . . . . . . | 3,000 | |
| Land . . . . . . . . . . . . . . . . . . . . . . . . . . . . . . . . . . . . . . . . . | 10,000 | |
| Buildings . . . . . . . . . . . . . . . . . . . . . . . . . . . . . . . . . . . . . . | 40,000 | |
| Accumulated Depreciation—Buildings . . . . . . . . . . . . . . . . . | | $ 2,400 |
| Machinery and Equipment . . . . . . . . . . . . . . . . . . . . . . . . . . | 50,000 | |
| Accumulated Depreciation—Machinery and Equipment . . . . . . . . | | 9,200 |
| Vouchers Payable . . . . . . . . . . . . . . . . . . . . . . . . . . . . . . . . | | 2,500 |
| Accrued Salaries and Wages Payable . . . . . . . . . . . . . . . . . . | | 1,000 |
| Accrued Interest Payable . . . . . . . . . . . . . . . . . . . . . . . . . . . | | 400 |
| Notes Payable . . . . . . . . . . . . . . . . . . . . . . . . . . . . . . . . . . . | | 15,000 |
| Contributed Capital—Governmental Unit . . . . . . . . . . . . . . . . | | 135,000 |
| Revenues—Billings to Departments . . . . . . . . . . . . . . . . . . . . | | 42,800 |
| Expenses—Cost of Materials and Supplies Used . . . . . . . . . . . . | 7,000 | |
| Expenses—Mechanics' Wages . . . . . . . . . . . . . . . . . . . . . . . | 9,500 | |
| Expenses—Indirect Labor . . . . . . . . . . . . . . . . . . . . . . . . . . | 3,150 | |
| Expenses—Superintendent's Salary . . . . . . . . . . . . . . . . . . . | 3,675 | |
| Expenses—Depreciation—Buildings . . . . . . . . . . . . . . . . . . . | 2,400 | |
| Expenses—Depreciation—Machinery and Equipment . . . . . . . . . | 9,200 | |
| Expenses—Heat, Light, and Power . . . . . . . . . . . . . . . . . . . . | 2,000 | |
| Expenses—Office Salaries . . . . . . . . . . . . . . . . . . . . . . . . . . | 3,675 | |
| Expenses—Office Maintenance . . . . . . . . . . . . . . . . . . . . . . . | 200 | |
| Expenses—Interest . . . . . . . . . . . . . . . . . . . . . . . . . . . . . . . | 400 | |
| | $208,300 | $208,300 |

Closing entries may be made in a variety of methods. Some accountants prefer to make one compound entry closing all revenue and expense accounts directly to Retained Earnings. Any reasonable closing entry or combination of entries will suffice that (1) updates the Retained Earnings account to its period end balance and (2) brings the temporary proprietary accounts to a zero balance so that they are ready for use during the next period.

| | | | |
|---|---|---|---|
| (C1) | Revenues—Billings to Departments .................... | $42,800 | |
| | Expenses—Cost of Materials and Supplies Used ........ | | $7,000 |
| | Expenses—Mechanics' Wages ...................... | | 9,500 |
| | Expenses—Indirect Labor ......................... | | 3,150 |
| | Expenses—Superintendent's Salary .................. | | 3,675 |
| | Expenses—Depreciation—Buildings ................. | | 2,400 |
| | Expenses—Depreciation—Machinery and Equipment ... | | 9,200 |
| | Expenses—Heat, Light, and Power ................... | | 2,000 |
| | Expenses—Office Salaries ......................... | | 3,675 |
| | Expenses—Office Maintenance ...................... | | 200 |
| | Expenses—Interest ............................... | | 400 |
| | Excess of Net Billings to Departments over Costs ....... | | 1,600 |
| | To close revenue and expense accounts and determine the excess of net charges over costs of services for the period. | | |
| (C2) | Excess of Net Billings to Departments over Costs ......... | $ 1,600 | |
| | Retained Earnings ............................... | | $1,600 |
| | To close net income for the period to Retained Earnings. | | |

Figures 11–3, 11–4, and 11–5 present the Balance Sheet, the Statement of Revenues, Expenses, and Changes in Fund Equity, and the Statement of Cash Flows for the illustrative Central Automotive Equipment Fund. Note that the fixed assets of the fund and the related accumulated depreciation accounts appear in the balance sheet. Because departments are billed for overhead charges, including depreciation, part of the money received from departments represents depreciation charges. The money representing depreciation charges may be debited to a restricted cash account (set up in a separate "fund") to ensure its availability to replace assets; or it may be included in the fund's general cash and used for various purposes pending the replacement of the assets. In the present case, it is assumed that no segregation is made, nor is a retained earnings reserve established.

Long-term debt incurred for IS Fund purposes is reported in the fund balance sheet if the resources of the fund are to be used to service and retire the debt. Certain types of long-term debt such as capital lease obligations and the long-term portion of the liability for compensated absences typically will be repaid from IS Fund resources. Others may be intended to be paid out of general taxation or other sources, such as enterprise earnings in the case of IS Funds furnishing services to a utility department. In such cases the debt should be reported in the General Long-Term Debt Account Group or in an Enterprise Fund, whichever is appropriate in the circumstances.

## A Central Stores Fund

Many departments and agencies of a government often use similar or identical materials and supplies. In some governments each department or agency is responsible for acquiring and maintaining a sufficient inventory of the needed materials and

**FIGURE 11–3  Ending Balance Sheet**

A Governmental Unit
**Central Automotive Equipment (IS) Fund**
**Balance Sheet**
At Close of Fiscal Year (Date)

**Assets**

Current Assets:

| | | |
|---|---:|---:|
| Cash . . . . . . . . . . . . . . . . . . . . . . . . . . . . . . . . . . . . . . . . | $60,300 | |
| Due from General Fund . . . . . . . . . . . . . . . . . . . . . . | 1,000 | |
| Due from Enterprise Fund . . . . . . . . . . . . . . . . . . . . | 2,800 | |
| Inventory of materials and supplies . . . . . . . . . . . . | 3,000 | $ 67,100 |

Fixed Assets:

| | | | |
|---|---:|---:|---:|
| Land . . . . . . . . . . . . . . . . . . . . . . . . . . . . . . . . . . . . . . | | 10,000 | |
| Buildings . . . . . . . . . . . . . . . . . . . . . . . . . . . . . . . . . . | $40,000 | | |
| Less: Accumulated depreciation . . . . . . . . . . . . . | 2,400 | 37,600 | |
| Machinery and equipment . . . . . . . . . . . . . . . . . . . | 50,000 | | |
| Less: Accumulated depreciation . . . . . . . . . . . . | 9,200 | 40,800 | 88,400 |
| Total Assets . . . . . . . . . . . . . . . . . . . . . . . . . . . . . | | | $155,500 |

**Liabilities and Fund Equity**

Current Liabilities:

| | | |
|---|---:|---:|
| Vouchers payable . . . . . . . . . . . . . . . . . . . . . . . . . . . | $ 2,500 | |
| Accrued salaries and wages payable . . . . . . . . . . . . | 1,000 | |
| Accrued interest payable . . . . . . . . . . . . . . . . . . . . . | 400 | $  3,900 |

Long-Term Liabilities:

| | | |
|---|---:|---:|
| Notes payable . . . . . . . . . . . . . . . . . . . . . . . . . . . . . . | | 15,000 |
| Total Liabilities . . . . . . . . . . . . . . . . . . . . . . . . . . . | | 18,900 |

Fund Equity:

| | | |
|---|---:|---:|
| Contributed capital—governmental unit . . . . . . . . . | | 135,000 |
| Retained earnings . . . . . . . . . . . . . . . . . . . . . . . . . . . | | 1,600 |
| Total Fund Equity . . . . . . . . . . . . . . . . . . . . . . . . | | 136,600 |
| Total Liabilities and Fund Equity . . . . . . . . . . . . | | $155,500 |

supplies. However, many other governments centralize their purchasing and warehousing operations and operate them as an IS Fund activity to enhance economy, efficiency, and control in these activities. In these latter governments the materials and supplies are purchased and stored by the personnel in the central stores operation. Then, the central stores department eventually distributes them to user departments when requisitioned by those departments. Departmental billings are usually based on direct inventory cost plus an overhead factor. To simplify the discussion, it is again assumed that appropriations are not required for Fund expenditures.

### Inventory Acquisition

The first step in the accounting process occurs here when an invoice for supplies of inventory items ($20,000) is approved for payment. At that time, an entry is made to record the purchase and to set up the liability. The entry is as follows:

| | | |
|---|---:|---:|
| Inventory of Materials and Supplies . . . . . . . . . . . . . . . . . . . . . . . . | $20,000 | |
| Vouchers Payable . . . . . . . . . . . . . . . . . . . . . . . . . . . . . . . . . . . . | | $20,000 |

To record the purchase of materials and supplies.

FIGURE 11–4  **Operating Statement**

A Governmental Unit

**Central Automotive Equipment (IS) Fund**
**Statement of Revenues, Expenses, and Changes in Fund Equity**
For (Period)

| | | |
|---|---:|---:|
| Operating Revenues: | | |
| Billings to departments ................................... | | $42,800 |
| Operating Expenses: | | |
| Cost of materials and supplies used ...................... | $ 7,000 | |
| Other operating costs: | | |
| Mechanics' wages .................................. | 9,500 | |
| Indirect labor ...................................... | 3,150 | |
| Superintendent's salary ........................... | 3,675 | |
| Depreciation—building ........................... | 2,400 | |
| Depreciation—machinery and equipment ............... | 9,200 | |
| Heat, light, and power ............................ | 2,000 | |
| Office salaries .................................... | 3,675 | |
| Office maintenance ................................. | 200 | |
| Total other operating costs ...................... | 33,800 | |
| Total Operating Expenses ............................... | | 40,800 |
| Operating Income ....................................... | | 2,000 |
| Nonoperating Expenses: | | |
| Interest expense ...................................... | | (400) |
| Net income ............................................. | | 1,600 |
| Fund equity, beginning of the period ...................... | | 135,000 |
| Fund equity, end of the period .............................. | | $136,600 |

Note that a Purchases account is not used. The purchases are recorded directly in an Inventory of Materials and Supplies account. The reason is that perpetual inventory records should be kept for a central storeroom operation.

### Perpetual Inventory Procedures

Materials or supplies purchased for central storerooms are not charged against departmental appropriations until the materials or supplies are withdrawn from the storeroom. One procedure in withdrawing materials and charging appropriations is as follows: When a department needs materials, it prepares a stores requisition (in duplicate at least) and presents it to the storekeeper. The storekeeper issues the items called for on the requisition and has the employee receiving them sign one copy of the requisition. The storekeeper retains this copy as evidence that the materials have been withdrawn and as the basis for posting the individual stock records to reduce the amount shown to be on hand. Subsequently, individual items on the requisition are priced and the total cost of materials withdrawn on that requisition is computed. Sometimes requisitions are priced before they are filled. When practicable, this procedure ensures that the cost of materials requisitioned does not exceed a department's unencumbered appropriation.

### Billing Rates

In the perpetual inventory record, the unit cost should include the purchase price plus transportation expenses. To keep the IS Fund capital intact, overhead costs also must be recovered. Overhead costs include such costs as the salary of the purchasing agent, wages of storekeepers, and amounts expended for heat, light, and

FIGURE 11–5  **Statement of Cash Flows**

A Governmental Unit

**Central Automotive Equipment (IS) Fund**
**Statement of Cash Flows**
For (Period)

**Cash Flows from Operating Activities:**

| | | |
|---|---:|---:|
| Cash received from user departments ..................... | $39,000 | |
| Cash paid to suppliers for goods and services ............... | (9,700) | |
| Cash paid to employees .................................. | (19,000) | |
| Net cash provided by operating activities ................ | | $10,300 |
| **Cash Flows from Capital and Related Financing Activities:** | | |
| Acquisition of equipment ............................... | | (25,000) |
| Net decrease in cash ...................................... | | (14,700) |
| Cash and cash equivalents at beginning of year ................ | | 75,000 |
| Cash and cash equivalents at end of year .................... | | $60,300* |
| **Reconciliation of Operating Income to Net Cash Provided by** | | |
| **Operating Activities:** | | |
| Operating income ....................................... | | $ 2,000 |
| Adjustments to reconcile operating income to net cash provided by | | |
| operating activities: | | |
| Depreciation ........................................ | $11,600 | |
| Increase in vouchers payable .......................... | 2,500 | |
| Increase in accrued salaries and wages payable ............ | 1,000 | |
| Increase in billings receivable ........................ | (3,800) | |
| Increase in inventories ............................... | (3,000) | |
| Total adjustments .................................... | | 8,300 |
| Net cash provided by operating activities .................. | | $10,300 |

* A schedule describing the fund's noncash financing and investing activities would also be presented in the government's financial report.

power. As noted earlier, these expenses usually are allocated to each requisition based on a predetermined percentage of the cost of the materials withdrawn. The percentage is determined by dividing the estimated total stores overhead expenses for the year by the total estimated costs of materials to be issued. Assume that total estimated stores overhead expenses for the forthcoming year are $20,000 and that the estimated cost of the materials to be withdrawn during the period is $500,000. The overhead rate applicable to materials issued is 4% ($20,000 ÷ $500,000). The overhead charge upon the issue of materials that cost the Stores Fund $2,585 is $103.40 (4% of $2,585).

### Inventory Issued

Once the requisition is priced, the department withdrawing the materials is billed. The entry to record the issue and billing is:

| | | |
|---|---:|---:|
| Due from General Fund ..................................... | $2,688.40 | |
| Cost of Materials and Supplies Issued ...................... | 2,585.00 | |
| Billings to Departments ................................... | | $2,688.40 |
| Inventory of Materials and Supplies ....................... | | 2,585.00 |

To record the billing and cost of materials issued to Department of Public Works on Requisition 1405.

Note that the General Fund is billed for both the cost of the materials and a portion of the estimated overhead expenses ($2,585.00 + $103.40).

### Overhead Expenses

Entries to record actual overhead expenses in the IS Fund are made at the time the expenses are incurred rather than when materials are issued. For example, at the time that storekeepers' salaries ($1,000) are approved for payment, the following entry is made:

| | | |
|---|---|---|
| Salaries and Wages Expenses | $1,000 | |
|   Vouchers Payable | | $1,000 |

To record storekeepers' salaries.

### Physical Inventory

Under the system of accounting for materials described here, the inventory of materials and supplies on hand is available from the records at any time. To ensure that the recorded balances of materials and supplies are actually on hand, a physical inventory should be taken at least annually. Usually the actual amount on hand will be smaller than the amount shown by the records. The shortage may result from such things as shrinkage, breakage, theft, or improper recording. The records must be adjusted to equal the actual physical count by making entries on each perpetual inventory record affected. The Inventory of Materials and Supplies account in the general ledger must also be adjusted, of course. If the physical count indicates $2,000 less inventory than shown on the records, the entry is as follows:

| | | |
|---|---|---|
| Inventory Losses | $2,000 | |
|   Inventory of Materials and Supplies | | $2,000 |

To record inventory losses as revealed by actual physical count.

Inventory losses must be recovered to keep the IS Fund capital intact. Hence, such losses should be included when estimating the overhead expenses of the central storeroom and establishing the overhead rate to be charged.

### Closing Entries

Closing entries for the Stores Fund would parallel those illustrated earlier for the Central Automotive Equipment Fund. Similarly, a balance sheet, statement of revenues, expenses, and changes in fund equity, and statement of cash flows like those illustrated in Figures 11–3 to 11–5 should be prepared at least annually.

### Entries in Other Funds

Thus far we have discussed the entries to be made in the IS Fund. Corresponding entries are, of course, made for the departments receiving the materials. In the case of a public works department financed from the General Fund, the entry is as follows:

**General Fund**

| | | |
|---|---|---|
| Expenditures—Materials | $2,688.40 | |
|   Due to IS Fund | | $2,688.40 |

To record receipt of materials by the Department of Public Works and liability to IS Fund.

## A Self-Insurance Fund

State and local governments sometimes find insurance coverage for some types of risks to be overly expensive or unavailable. Partly as a result of this, some governments "self-insure" a part or all of their properties, potential liabilities for claims and judgments, and other risks. Often a government that self-insures part (or all) of its risks also centralizes its risk financing activities. The government then establishes a program designed to provide for potential losses—other than those covered by outside insurers—from its own resources. The amount of resources to be set aside must be actuarially determined to help ensure that it will cover actual losses. Also, if the government is partially insured by third-party insurers, insurance premiums will have to be paid to outside insurers for such coverage.

Other governments do not centralize their risk financing activities. These governments account for claims and judgments associated with general government activities in the various governmental fund(s) and account groups affected in accordance with the guidance illustrated in Chapter 6.

Governments that centralize their risk financing activities should use either the General Fund or an Internal Service Fund to account for those activities. If the General Fund is used, all covered claims and judgments are recorded as General Fund expenditures and any amounts charged to other (user) funds are reported as reductions of General Fund expenditures (as reimbursements—not as revenues). Use of Self-Insurance IS Funds is illustrated next.

### Use of Self-Insurance IS Funds

In practice, self-insurance plans are often established by charging the various departments and agencies of the government for their share of the cost of the self-insurance coverage. Some governments use actuarially determined rates or the amount that an insurance policy would have cost. Other governments base the cost on other techniques that do not ensure as appropriate an allocation of self-insurance costs either over time or among departments as do actuarially based costing methods.

Governments that use an Internal Service Fund to account for centralized risk financing activities are required to:

- Recognize all claims and judgments liabilities and expenses in the ISF.

- Charge the other funds amounts that are reasonable and equitable—preferably actuarially based—such that Self-Insurance IS Fund revenues and expenses are approximately equal. In addition charges may include a reasonable provision for expected future catastrophic losses.

- Reserve or designate any retained earnings resulting from incremental charges made to provide for expected future catastrophic losses.

- Determine whether payments to the Self-Insurance Fund that differ from the required amounts are in-substance interfund transfers or loans.

### Accounting for Self-Insurance IS Funds

Accounting for Self-Insurance IS Funds entails primarily three aspects. The first is accounting for the revenues from billings to departments for the actuarially determined contributions or premiums to be paid to the fund. The second is accounting for investment of the fund's resources. The final aspect is accounting for the recognition and settlement of claims and judgments against the fund for self-insured losses.

**Revenues**     Amounts paid to or accrued by Self-Insurance IS Funds based on actuarial or other acceptable estimates should be reported as revenues. Amounts paid to the Self-Insurance IS Funds that differ from these charges should be evaluated carefully to determine the substance of the transaction or event. For instance, overpayments in one year may be in-substance prepayals of subsequent years' "premiums"—if the intent is to reduce or eliminate the need for a particular department or agency to contribute to the fund in the next year. In such cases these overpayments should be treated as IS Fund deferred revenues and as prepayments in the payer fund(s).

In other cases overpayments are made to the Self-Insurance Fund from one or more other funds with no intention of payments being reduced or avoided in subsequent years. Rather, these payments might be interfund loans or advances. Or, they might be made to provide contributed capital from which losses in excess of those provided for through departmental billings can be financed temporarily until made up through increased charges to insured departments or agencies in subsequent years. In the latter case residual equity transfers should be recorded for the overpayment received. If routine, recurring overpayments are made, the overpayments should be reported as operating transfers.

**Expenses**     Claims and judgments for covered losses should be recorded as expenses in the Self-Insurance IS Fund—not in the insured funds. The expenses should be recognized when both of the following conditions are met:

1. Information prior to the issuance of the financial statements indicates that it is probable that an asset was impaired or a liability incurred at the date of the financial statements; and

2. The amount of the loss can be reasonably estimated.

### Illustrative Transactions and Entries

These principles are illustrated in the following transactions and entries for a newly established Self-Insurance IS Fund of A Governmental Unit.

**Transactions and Entries**

1. General Fund resources of $500,000 were transferred to establish a Self-Insurance IS Fund. The IS Fund is (a) to acquire insurance from third-party insurers, where available at reasonable cost, and (b) to self-insure other risks.

**General Fund**

| | | |
|---|---|---|
| (1a) Residual Equity Transfer to IS Fund . . . . . . . . . . . . . . . | $500,000 | |
| Cash . . . . . . . . . . . . . . . . . . . . . . . . . . . . . . . . . . . . . . . . . | | $500,000 |
| To record contribution of resources to establish a self-insurance fund. | | |

**Internal Service Fund**

| | | |
|---|---|---|
| (1b) Cash . . . . . . . . . . . . . . . . . . . . . . . . . . . . . . . . . . . . . . . . | $500,000 | |
| Residual Equity Transfer from General Fund . . . . . . . | | $500,000 |
| To record contribution from General Fund. | | |

(Note that the residual equity transfer will be closed to Contributed Capital— Governmental Unit at the end of the year.)

**2.** Actuarially determined charges of $80,000 to the General Fund and $20,000 to the Enterprise Fund were billed for insurance or self-insurance.

**General Fund**

(2a) Expenditures ................................. $ 80,000

    Due to Self-Insurance IS Fund .................. $ 80,000

    To record billings for insurance coverage and self-
    insurance for General Fund departments.

**Enterprise Fund**

(2b) Expenses ...................................... $ 20,000

    Due to Self-Insurance IS Fund ................. $ 20,000

    To record billings for insurance coverage and self-
    insurance for the enterprise activity.

**Internal Service Fund**

(2c) Due from General Fund ........................ $ 80,000

    Due from Enterprise Fund ...................... 20,000

       Revenues—Billings to Departments (or Premiums) .. $100,000

    To record revenues from billings to departments
    "insured" through the IS Fund.

**3.** Three-fourths of the amounts due from the other funds were collected.

**General Fund**

(3a) Due to Self-Insurance IS Fund .................. $ 60,000

    Cash ....................................... $ 60,000

    To record payment of interfund payable.

**Enterprise Fund**

(3b) Due to Self-Insurance IS Fund .................. $ 15,000

    Cash ....................................... $ 15,000

    To record payment of interfund payable.

**Internal Service Fund**

(3c) Cash ......................................... $ 75,000

    Due from General Fund ....................... $ 60,000

    Due from Enterprise Fund .................... 15,000

    To record collection of interfund receivables.

Note again that if more than the actuarially determined amount had been paid to the IS Fund, only the actuarially required amounts are recorded as expenditures or expenses in the "insured" funds and as revenues in the Self-Insurance IS Fund. Any additional payments should be treated as discussed previously. Underpayments should be recorded as interfund payables/receivables, as in this example—if they are to be settled in some definite time frame. Otherwise, underpayments are interfund transfers out of the IS Fund.

**4.** Investments with a par value of $470,000 were purchased at a discount of $10,000.

**Internal Service Fund**

(4) Investments ................................... $460,000

    Cash ....................................... $460,000

    To record purchase of investments.

**5.** Premiums paid to third-party insurers were $8,000, of which $500 was for coverage for the next fiscal year.

**Internal Service Fund**

| | | |
|---|---:|---:|
| (5) Expenses—Insurance Premiums ................... | $7,500 | |
| Prepaid Insurance ............................... | 500 | |
| Cash ........................................ | | $8,000 |

To record payment of insurance premiums.

6. Payments in settlement of claims and judgments incurred during the year amounted to $22,000, net of insurance recovery.

**Internal Service Fund**

| | | |
|---|---:|---:|
| (6) Expenses—Claims and Judgments ................ | $22,000 | |
| Cash ........................................ | | $22,000 |

To record settlement of claims and judgments.

7. The accrued liability for probable losses for claims and judgments is estimated to total $70,000 at year end, net of expected insurance recovery. (The accrued liability was zero at the beginning of the year.) Administrative expenses paid totaled $3,800. Half of the liabilities for claims and judgments are expected to be settled in the next fiscal year and the remainder in subsequent periods.

**Internal Service Fund**

| | | |
|---|---:|---:|
| (7) Expenses—Claims and Judgments ................ | $70,000 | |
| Expenses—Administrative ....................... | 3,800 | |
| Liability for Claims and Judgments—Current ...... | | $35,000 |
| Liability for Claims and Judgments—Long-Term .... | | 35,000 |
| Cash ........................................ | | 3,800 |

To adjust the accrued liabilities for claims and judgments to their appropriate year-end balances and record administrative expenses incurred.

Note that recognition of the expenses for claims and judgments is not affected by whether the liability is current or long term.

8. Interest of $27,600 was accrued on investments at year end.

**Internal Service Fund**

| | | |
|---|---:|---:|
| (8) Accrued Interest Receivable ..................... | $27,600 | |
| Revenues—Interest ........................... | | $27,600 |

To record accrual of interest.

9. The fair value of the investments increased $1,200 during the year.

**Internal Service Fund**

| | | |
|---|---:|---:|
| (9) Investments .................................... | $1,200 | |
| Net Increase (Decrease) in Fair Value of Investments .. | | $1,200 |

To adjust investments to fair value.

10. The Self-Insurance Fund accounts were closed and the actuarially required balance was recorded in a reserve for losses.

**Internal Service Fund**

| | | |
|---|---:|---:|
| (10) (a) Revenues—Billings to Departments ............ | $100,000 | |
| Revenues—Interest ......................... | 27,600 | |
| Net Increase (Decrease) in Fair Value of Investments . | 1,200 | |
| Losses—Claims and Judgments .............. | | $92,000 |
| Expenses—Administrative .................. | | 3,800 |
| Unreserved Retained Earnings .............. | | 33,000 |

To close the accounts.

(10) (b) Unreserved Retained Earnings . . . . . . . . . . . . . . . .    $26,000

        Retained Earnings Reserved for Losses . . . . . . .    $26,000

        To adjust the reserve for losses to its actuarially
        determined required balance.

The financial statements required for the Self-Insurance IS Fund are a Balance Sheet, a Statement of Revenues, Expenses, and Changes in Fund Equity (or Retained Earnings), and a Statement of Cash Flows. These statements would be similar to those illustrated in Figures 11–3 to 11–5 for the Central Automotive Repair IS Fund and are not presented here.

## DISPOSITION OF PROFIT OR LOSS

Because charges to departments must be based on estimates, an IS Fund usually has a profit or loss at the end of a year. The profit or loss may be disposed of in one of the following ways:

1. It may be charged or credited to the billed departments in accordance with their usage. If the intent is for the fund to break even, this procedure is theoretically the correct one.

2. The amount may be closed to Retained Earnings with the intent of adjusting the following year's billings to eliminate the balance. This procedure is a practical substitute for the first.

3. The amount may be closed to and left in Retained Earnings without subsequent adjustment of billing rates—on the theory that the fund will break even over a period of several years.

In the absence of specific instructions, the profit or loss should be closed to Retained Earnings. No refunds, supplemental billings, or transfers should be made in the absence of specific authorization or instructions in this regard.

## RETAINED EARNINGS

The cost-reimbursement focus of IS Funds would seem to indicate that significant retained earnings should not exist over the long term in IS Funds. Indeed, the AICPA audit guide, *Audits of State and Local Governmental Units*, states,

> . . . rates should not be established at confiscatory levels that siphon off assets earmarked for other purposes. Likewise, rates should not be set so low as to incur significant losses that result in retained earnings deficits. . . . Because the intent of these funds is to facilitate cost allocation, accumulation of resources or deficits over a long term is considered inappropriate.[2]

---

[2] AICPA, *Audits of State and Local Governmental Units*, 1998, par. 13.28.

The intent of an IS Fund implies that significant retained earnings should not exist in IS Funds except for Self-Insurance IS Funds where charges to cover future catastrophic losses have been made. However, other exceptions exist. In practice many governments have significant retained earnings balances in various traditional IS Funds. Such balances may have resulted from overcharging user funds for goods or services provided in order to permit replacement of fund fixed assets at higher replacement costs. As mentioned earlier, such excessive charges are not considered proper—particularly if the charges are passed on to federally financed or state-financed programs, where they may not be allowable and may be illegal. On the other hand, the balance could result from routine operating transfers from the General Fund or other funds to provide additional financing needed to replace fund fixed assets or gradually expand operations—which would be entirely appropriate even given the cost allocation focus of IS Funds.

## DISSOLUTION OF AN IS FUND

An IS Fund is dissolved when the services provided through it are no longer needed, or a preferable method of providing the services is found. The net current assets of a dissolved fund are usually transferred to the funds from which the capital was originally secured. However, if capital was generated by incurring general obligation long-term debt, the net current assets usually are transferred to the Debt Service Fund that will retire the debt.

Fixed assets usually are transferred to departments financed from the funds that contributed the capital or to the departments that can best use them. Unless they are transferred to one of the governmental unit's other proprietary funds, the assets are recorded in the General Fixed Assets Account Group accounts. If transferred to an enterprise, they are recorded in the Enterprise Fund.

## COMBINING IS FUND FINANCIAL STATEMENTS

As with other fund types, combining financial statements must be prepared for IS Funds by governments having more than one IS Fund. Typically, individual fund statements for individual IS Funds are not necessary. Sufficient individual fund detail is usually provided in the individual fund columns of the combining statements and any schedules accompanying those statements. The total columns of the combining statements are included in the combined financial statements—which make up the general purpose financial statements (GPFS) of a government as discussed and illustrated in Chapter 13.

The combining Internal Service Fund statements included in a recent Comprehensive Annual Financial Report for Arlington County, Virginia, are presented in Figures 11–6, 11–7, and 11–8.

**FIGURE 11–6**

**ARLINGTON COUNTY, VIRGINIA**
**INTERNAL SERVICE FUNDS**
**COMBINING BALANCE SHEET**
JUNE 30, 19X4
(WITH COMPARATIVE TOTALS FOR 19X3)

| | *Automotive Equipment* | *Technology and Information Systems* | *Printing* | *Totals June 30 19X4* | *June 30 19X3* |
|---|---|---|---|---|---|
| **ASSETS** | | | | | |
| CURRENT ASSETS: | | | | | |
| Equity in pooled cash and investments | $ 4,772,020 | $ 953,152 | $626,839 | $ 6,352,011 | $6,061,546 |
| Accounts receivable | 24,544 | 242,715 | 11,610 | 278,869 | 282,351 |
| Inventories | 475,495 | — | 52,199 | 527,694 | 553,818 |
| Due from other funds | — | — | — | — | 99 |
| Total Current Assets | 5,272,059 | 1,195,867 | 690,648 | 7,158,574 | 6,897,814 |
| FIXED ASSETS, at cost: | | | | | |
| Equipment and other fixed assets | 21,127,904 | 13,028,701 | 799,325 | 34,955,930 | 33,103,622 |
| Less—accumulated depreciation | (11,666,348) | (9,814,583) | (565,048) | (22,045,979) | (20,060,420) |
| Net Fixed Assets | 9,461,556 | 3,214,118 | 234,277 | 12,909,951 | 13,043,202 |
| Total Assets | $14,733,615 | $4,409,985 | $924,925 | $20,068,525 | $19,941,016 |
| **LIABILITIES AND EQUITY** | | | | | |
| CURRENT LIABILITIES: | | | | | |
| Vouchers payable | $ 160,729 | $ 279,674 | $ 70,165 | $ 510,568 | $ 1,132,683 |
| Current portion—capital leases | — | — | 77,460 | 77,460 | 76,207 |
| Compensated absences | 294,107 | 701,221 | 97,019 | 1,092,347 | 861,491 |
| Due to other funds | 88,156 | 4,343,363 | 18,992 | 4,450,511 | 4,321,264 |
| Total Current Liabilities | 542,992 | 5,324,258 | 263,636 | 6,130,886 | 6,391,645 |
| LONG-TERM LIABILITIES: | | | | | |
| Capital leases | — | — | 23,250 | 23,250 | 103,601 |
| Total Liabilities | 542,992 | 5,324,258 | 286,886 | 6,154,136 | 6,495,246 |
| **EQUITY** | | | | | |
| Contributed capital | 3,015,288 | 129,702 | 169,908 | 3,314,898 | 3,314,898 |
| Retained earnings | 11,175,335 | (1,043,975) | 468,131 | 10,599,491 | 10,130,872 |
| Total Equity | 14,190,623 | (914,273) | 638,039 | 13,914,389 | 13,445,770 |
| Total Liabilities and Equity | $14,733,615 | $4,409,985 | $924,925 | $20,068,525 | $19,941,016 |

The notes to the financial statements are an integral part of this statement.

*Source:* Adapted from a recent comprehensive annual financial report of Arlington County, Virginia.

FIGURE 11–7

**ARLINGTON COUNTY, VIRGINIA**
**INTERNAL SERVICE FUNDS**
**COMBINING STATEMENT OF REVENUES, EXPENSES, AND CHANGES IN EQUITY**
FOR THE YEAR ENDED JUNE 30, 19X4
(WITH COMPARATIVE TOTALS FOR 19X3)

| | *Automotive Equipment* | *Technology and Information Systems* | *Printing* | *Totals June 30 19X4* | *June 30 19X3* |
|---|---|---|---|---|---|
| **OPERATING REVENUES:** | | | | | |
| Charges for services | $ 8,680,022 | $8,069,330 | $1,756,432 | $18,505,784 | $19,072,271 |
| **OPERATING EXPENSES:** | | | | | |
| Cost of store issuances | 1,620,973 | — | 799,042 | 2,420,015 | 2,497,393 |
| Personnel services | 1,905,457 | 3,087,238 | 391,413 | 5,384,108 | 4,895,631 |
| Fringe benefits | 590,885 | 822,367 | 108,085 | 1,521,337 | 1,450,868 |
| Material and supplies | 750,416 | 480,127 | 226,440 | 1,456,983 | 2,748,503 |
| Utilities | 79,503 | 1,132,014 | 4,913 | 1,216,430 | 1,194,258 |
| Outside services | 167,035 | 1,651,877 | 186,332 | 2,005,244 | 1,502,204 |
| Depreciation | 2,151,500 | 1,727,669 | 99,881 | 3,979,050 | 4,107,422 |
| Insurance and other | 555,962 | 44,849 | 1,908 | 602,719 | 1,373,391 |
| Total Operating Expenses | 7,821,731 | 8,946,141 | 1,818,014 | 18,585,886 | 19,769,670 |
| Operating Income (Loss) | 858,291 | (876,811) | (61,582) | (80,102) | (697,399) |
| **NONOPERATING REVENUES (EXPENSES):** | | | | | |
| Interest expense | — | — | (1,917) | (1,917) | (11,013) |
| Gain on disposal of assets | 91,832 | — | — | 91,832 | 126,094 |
| Total Nonoperating Revenues (Expenses) | 91,832 | — | (1,917) | 89,915 | 115,081 |
| Income Before Operating Transfers | 950,123 | (876,811) | (63,499) | 9,813 | (582,318) |
| **OPERATING TRANSFERS IN (OUT):** | | | | | |
| Operating transfers in | 9,207 | 528,428 | 51,171 | 588,806 | 686,899 |
| Operating transfers out | (130,000) | — | — | (130,000) | (730,000) |
| Total Operating Transfers | (120,793) | 528,428 | 51,171 | 458,806 | (43,101) |
| Net Income (Loss) | 829,330 | (348,383) | (12,328) | 468,619 | (625,419) |
| **EQUITY:** | | | | | |
| Retained earnings, beginning of year | 10,346,005 | (695,592) | 480,459 | 10,130,872 | 10,756,291 |
| Retained earnings, end of year | 11,175,335 | (1,043,975) | 468,131 | 10,599,491 | 10,130,872 |
| Contributed capital | 3,015,288 | 129,702 | 169,908 | 3,314,898 | 3,314,898 |
| Total Equity | $14,190,623 | ($  914,273) | $  638,039 | $13,914,389 | $13,445,770 |

The notes to the financial statements are an integral part of this statement.

*Source:* Adapted from a recent comprehensive annual financial report of Arlington County, Virginia.

FIGURE 11–8

# ARLINGTON COUNTY VIRGINIA
## INTERNAL SERVICE FUNDS
## COMBINING STATEMENT OF CASH FLOWS
### FOR THE YEAR ENDED JUNE 30, 19X4
### (WITH COMPARATIVE TOTALS FOR 19X3)

| | Automotive Equipment | Technology and Information Systems | Printing | Totals June 30 19X4 | Totals June 30 19X3 |
|---|---|---|---|---|---|
| **CASH FLOWS FROM OPERATING ACTIVITIES** | | | | | |
| Cash received from customers | $ 447,470 | $ 817,057 | $ 47,380 | $ 1,311,907 | $ 1,347,239 |
| Cash received from interfund charges | 8,354,278 | 7,128,484 | 1,714,596 | 17,197,358 | 17,660,516 |
| Cash paid to suppliers | (3,791,747) | (3,294,484) | (1,211,150) | (8,297,381) | (8,867,951) |
| Cash paid to employees | (2,435,870) | (3,757,493) | (481,226) | (6,674,589) | (6,346,499) |
| Net cash provided by operating activities | 2,574,131 | 893,564 | 69,600 | 3,537,295 | 3,793,305 |
| **CASH FLOWS FROM NONCAPITAL FINANCING ACTIVITIES:** | | | | | |
| Cash received from other funds | 99 | — | — | 99 | (114,404) |
| Cash paid to other funds | 83,980 | 26,275 | 18,992 | 129,247 | — |
| Operating transfers in (out) | (120,793) | 528,428 | 51,171 | 458,806 | (43,101) |
| Net cash provided by financing activities | (36,714) | 554,703 | 70,163 | 588,152 | (157,505) |
| **CASH FLOWS FROM CAPITAL AND RELATED FINANCING ACTIVITIES:** | | | | | |
| Principal payments under capital leases | — | — | (79,098) | (79,098) | (417,025) |
| Purchases of equipment and other fixed assets | (2,934,735) | (938,722) | (53,290) | (3,926,747) | (2,515,997) |
| Proceeds from sale of equipment | 172,779 | — | — | 172,779 | 158,811 |
| Interest paid | — | — | (1,917) | (1,917) | (11,011) |
| Net cash used by capital and related financing activities | (2,761,956) | (938,722) | (134,305) | (3,834,983) | (2,785,222) |
| Net increase (decrease) in cash and cash equivalents | (224,539) | 509,545 | 5,458 | 290,464 | 850,578 |
| Cash and cash equivalents at beginning of year | 4,996,559 | 443,607 | 621,381 | 6,061,547 | 5,210,968 |
| Cash and cash equivalents at end of period | $4,772,020 | $ 953,152 | $ 626,839 | $ 6,352,011 | $ 6,061,546 |
| Reconciliation of operating income to net cash provided by operating activities | | | | | |
| Operating income (loss) | $ 858,291 | ($ 876,811) | ($ 61,582) | ($ 80,102) | ($ 697,399) |
| Adjustments to reconcile operating income to net cash provided by operating activities: | | | | | |
| Depreciation | 2,151,500 | 1,727,669 | 99,881 | 3,979,050 | 4,107,422 |
| (Increase) Decrease in accounts receivable | 121,727 | (123,788) | 5,544 | 3,483 | (64,516) |
| (Increase) Decrease in inventories | 8,074 | — | 18,050 | 26,124 | 27,499 |
| Increase (Decrease) in vouchers payable | (625,933) | 14,382 | (10,564) | (622,115) | 369,178 |
| Increase (Decrease) in compensated absences | 60,472 | 152,112 | 18,271 | 230,855 | 51,121 |
| Net cash provided by operating activities | $2,574,131 | $ 893,564 | $ 69,600 | $ 3,537,295 | $ 3,793,305 |

Supplemental Disclosure of Noncash Capital and Related Financing Activities:

The Printing Fund purchased assets in 19X3 under a capital lease agreement for $49,406.

The notes to the financial statements are an integral part of this statement.

*Source:* Adapted from a recent comprehensive annual financial report of Arlington County, Virginia.

## CONCLUDING COMMENTS

Internal Service Funds are used to account for departments or agencies of a state or local government that provide goods or services to its other departments or agencies or to other governments on a cost-reimbursement basis. Such activities are intended to be self-sustaining. Therefore, net income determination and capital maintenance are important aspects of accounting and financial reporting for such funds. Accordingly, the accounting and reporting principles that apply are typically identical to those for similar business operations and the same financial statements are prepared.

Activities commonly managed and accounted for through IS Funds include communications, data processing, printing and duplication, motor pools and maintenance services, central purchasing and stores operations, and self-insurance programs. Such activities often involve millions of dollars of government resources, as indicated in the Arlington County, Virginia, financial statements presented in Figures 11–6 through 11–8.

Appropriately classifying activities that should be reported in Internal Service Funds rather than in the governmental funds and account groups is essential. Significantly different accounting and reporting principles apply, and different financial statements are prepared under the two treatments. Indeed, misclassifying an Internal Service Fund activity as a general government operation would result in reporting its assets, liabilities, and equities in several governmental funds and account groups, using the wrong basis of accounting, and presenting the wrong financial statements.

## Questions

**Q 11-1**  Why might IS Funds be thought of as revolving or working capital funds?

**Q 11-2**  IS Funds are proprietary (nonexpendable) funds. How does this cause IS Fund accounting to differ from that for governmental (expendable) funds?

**Q 11-3**  Many governments use titles such as "Billings to Departments" and "Excess of Net Billings to Departments Over Costs" in IS Fund accounting and reporting rather than more familiar titles such as "Sales" and "Net Income." Why?

**Q 11-4**  Why is an IS Fund typically not subject to fixed budgetary control?

**Q 11-5**  Accounting for an IS Fund that is controlled by a fixed budget may be referred to as double accounting. Why?

**Q 11-6**  In what ways might the original capital required to establish an IS Fund be acquired?

**Q 11-7**  What advantages might a governmental unit expect from the use of an IS Fund to account for the acquisition, storage, and provision of supplies for the various departments?

**Q 11-8**  What major benefits should accrue from accurate cost data being maintained for activities accounted for through the IS Fund?

**Q 11-9**  Under what circumstances would the *direct* cost of the goods or services provided (with no additions to acquisition cost for items such as depreciation or overhead) be the appropriate basis for IS Fund reimbursement? Explain.

**Q 11-10**  Why are predetermined price schedules or overhead rates commonly used in IS Fund billings to user departments?

**Q 11-11**  An IS Fund established by a county is intended to operate on a break-even basis. How might profits or losses (or a retained earnings balance remaining at year end) be disposed of?

**Q 11-12**  A city operates a motor pool as an IS Fund. List and evaluate the ways that over- or under-absorbed overhead may be treated.

**Q 11-13**  An IS Fund was established ten years ago through the sale of 20-year bonds. What disposition should be made of the assets of the fund if it is dissolved?

**Q 11-14**  The mayor wants to increase the size of an IS Fund by setting a higher-than-cost rate of reimbursement. What response would you make to his suggestion?

**Q 11-15**  How should overtime premiums incurred in the conduct of IS Fund activities be charged to user departments where IS Fund charges are based on direct cost plus overhead? (AICPA, adapted)

**Q 11-16**  What are the major classifications of cash flows required to be presented for a proprietary or nonexpendable trust fund? Distinguish between them.

**Q 11-17**  What are the key differences between the cash flow statement requirements for IS Funds and those for business enterprises?

**Q 11-18**  When are cash flows from *operating* transfers from an IS Fund to other funds reported as capital and related financing activities in the IS Fund statement of cash flows?

**Q 11-19**  What determines whether cash received from a borrowing is reported as cash flows from noncapital financing activities or from capital and related financing activities?

**Q 11-20**  What financial statements must a government present for an Internal Service Fund?

## Exercises

**E 11-1**  Indicate which of the following should be reported as cash flows from capital and related financing activities.
1. Purchase of IS Fund fixed assets for cash
2. Sale of IS Fund fixed assets for cash
3. Operating transfers from other funds for the sole and specific purpose of financing IS Fund fixed asset purchases
4. Residual equity transfers from other funds for the sole and specific purpose of financing IS Fund fixed asset purchases
5. Operating transfers to other funds for the sole and specific purpose of financing fixed asset purchases of departments financed from those funds
6. Residual equity transfers to other funds for the sole and specific purpose of financing fixed asset purchases of departments financed from those funds
7. Proceeds of bonds issued to finance construction of IS Fund fixed assets
8. Interest paid on bonds issued to finance construction of IS Fund fixed assets
9. Principal retirement payments on bonds issued to finance construction of IS Fund fixed assets
10. Purchases of investments with cash received from issuing bonds to finance construction of IS Fund fixed assets

**E 11-2**  Prepare journal entries to record the following transactions of an IS Fund.
1. Salaries of $10,000 were paid. Additional salaries accrued but not paid totaled $300.
2. Purchased equipment costing $50,000 by issuing a 3-year, $45,000 note and making a down payment of $5,000.
3. Billed users for services, $100,000. $90,000 was collected during the year; $1,000 is expected to be uncollectible; and $9,000 is expected to be collected during the second quarter of the next fiscal year.
4. Incurred a probable loss from claims and judgments of $25,000. Nothing is expected to be paid for at least 2 years, however.

## Problems

**P 11-1**  (Multiple Choice)
1. Which of the following liabilities are not accounted for and reported in the same manner by an Internal Service Fund and a business enterprise?
   a. capital leases
   b. compensated absences
   c. contingent liabilities
   d. pension liabilities
   e. both c and d
2. Initial financing for Internal Service Fund activities may be obtained from
   a. advances from another fund.

    b. profits from the provision of goods or services to departments within the government.
    c. appropriation of related materials held by governmental departments.
    d. both a and c
    e. all of the above

3. The Yourtown Motor Pool Fund estimates that the cost of operating and maintaining its fleet of 20 vehicles during 19X8 will be $150,000. On the basis of past experience, each vehicle can be expected to be used 150 days during the year and can be expected to be driven 3,000 miles during the year. The other costs of operating the fund are estimated at $15,000 for the year. The price that the Motor Pool Fund should charge other Yourtown government departments for use of a motor pool vehicle is
    a. $50 per day.              d. $2.75 per mile.
    b. $55 per day.              e. a or c
    c. $2.50 per mile.           f. b or d

4. Residual equity transfers are always reported in an IS Fund operating statement if it reports revenues, expenses, and changes in
    a. unreserved retained earnings.        d. all of the above
    b. total retained earnings.           e. none of the above
    c. total fund equity.

5. If a computer previously recorded in the General Fixed Assets Account Group is contributed to a department accounted for in an IS Fund, the computer will be recorded in the IS Fund accounts
    a. at the historical cost recorded in the GFAAG accounts.
    b. at the historical cost, less the amount of depreciation that would have been recorded if it had originally been purchased for the Internal Service Fund.
    c. at the computer's fair market value on the contribution date.
    d. at the computer's replacement value on the contribution date.
    e. either a or b

6. The charge by an Internal Service Fund department to other departments for a service should include
    a. the direct cost to the fund of providing the service.
    b. the direct cost to the fund of providing the service, plus a proportionate share of the fund's variable overhead costs.
    c. the direct cost to the fund of providing the service, plus a proportionate share of the fund's total overhead costs.
    d. the direct cost to the fund of providing the service, plus a proportionate share of the fund's variable overhead costs, plus a reasonable cushion for contingencies and capital growth.
    e. the direct cost to the fund of providing the service, plus a proportionate share of the fund's total overhead costs, plus a reasonable cushion for contingencies and capital growth.

7. The activity level of an Internal Service Fund is normally controlled by
    a. the appropriations made by its controlling legislative body.
    b. the flexible budget enacted by its controlling legislative body.
    c. the formal budget enacted by its controlling legislative body.
    d. the needs of the various governmental departments using its services.

8. The actuarially based charges to the General Fund from a Self-Insurance IS Fund should be reported in the IS Fund as
    a. operating transfers.
    b. revenues.
    c. residual equity transfers.
    d. deferred revenues until claims and judgments are incurred.
    e. revenues only if the required payment is made.

9. Loans to an Internal Service Fund from another fund are reported in the Internal Service Fund cash flow statement as
    a. cash flows from operating activities.

  b. cash flows from noncapital financing activities.
  c. cash flows from capital and related financing activities.
  d. cash flows from capital and related financing activities if clearly and solely for the purpose of financing acquisition, construction, or improvement of the IS Fund's fixed assets and as cash flows from noncapital financing activities in all other cases.

10. Residual equity transfers from an Internal Service Fund to another fund are reported in the Internal Service Fund cash flow statement as
   a. cash flows from operating activities.
   b. cash flows from noncapital financing activities.
   c. cash flows from capital and related financing activities.
   d. cash flows from investing activities.

**P 11-2** (Cash Flow Statement Classifications) Use the letter beside the appropriate cash flow statement classification to indicate the section of the cash flow statement in which each of the following transactions of an IS Fund should be reported.
  a. Cash flows from operating activities
  b. Cash flows from noncapital financing activities
  c. Cash flows from capital and related financing activities
  d. Cash flows from investing activities
  e. Either b or c, additional information required. Explain.
  f. None of the above. Explain.
   1. Cash purchase of equipment
   2. Operating transfer received from the General Fund
   3. Payment of accounts payable created by the acquisition of supplies on credit
   4. A cash contribution by the General Fund for the purpose of financing half the cost of new equipment
   5. Payment of capital lease payments
   6. Cash received from the collection of billings to other departments
   7. Cash paid for investments in bonds of other governments
   8. Residual equity transfer to another fund
   9. Cash received from borrowing on a short-term basis for operations
   10. Interest paid on the short-term borrowing

**P 11-3** (Self-Insurance Fund Entries)
   1. Sorenson County established a self-insurance program in 19X8 by transferring $2,000,000 of General Fund resources to an Internal Service Fund that is to be used to account for the county's self-insurance program.
   2. An actuarial study indicated that to provide the appropriate loss reserve for the county's self-insurance program for risks self-insured for various departments, $75,000 should be charged to the General Fund for the year and $15,000 to the various Enterprise Funds of the county. The $75,000 General Fund payment was made to the Self-Insurance Fund, and $30,500 was paid from the Enterprise Funds to cover the estimated cost chargeable to those funds for the next fiscal year as well as the current year's cost.
   3. Administrative expenses payable from the IS Fund totaled $3,600.
   4. Claims filed against the county during the year were settled for $42,000 (paid).
   5. The county attorney estimated that it is probable that the county will incur additional losses from current year incidents giving rise to claims and judgments of $36,000. Of those claims, $22,000 probably will be settled and paid within 30 to 60 days after the end of the year; the remainder most likely will not be finally settled for at least 2 to 3 years. In addition, it is reasonably likely that other claims for events occurring during 19X8 will result in additional losses of $4,200.

***Required*** (a) Prepare the journal entries required in 19X8 for the Sorenson County Self-Insurance Fund.
   (b) Prepare the IS Fund journal entries that would have been required in transactions 4 and 5 if (1) there were no Self-Insurance IS Fund—and thus transactions 1, 2, and 3 had not occurred, and (2) all of the claims relate to the Central Printing ISF.

**P 11-4** (Worksheet) The trial balance for the Metro School District Repair Shop at January 1, 19X6 was as follows:

| | | |
|---|---:|---:|
| Cash ......................................................... | $ 30,000 | |
| Due from Other Funds ................................. | 40,000 | |
| Inventory .................................................. | 10,000 | |
| Building .................................................... | 35,000 | |
| Equipment ................................................ | 100,000 | |
| Accumulated Depreciation—Building ...................... | | $ 12,000 |
| Accumulated Depreciation—Equipment ................... | | 30,000 |
| Vouchers Payable ........................................ | | 35,000 |
| Contributed Capital ...................................... | | 136,000 |
| Retained Earnings ....................................... | | 2,000 |
| | $215,000 | $215,000 |

The Repair Shop Fund had the following transactions during 19X6:
1. Materials purchased on account, $20,000.
2. Materials used, $7,000.
3. Payroll paid, $12,000.
4. Utilities paid, $3,500.
5. Billings to departments for repair services, $29,500.
6. Collections from departments, $27,900.
7. Equipment acquired under a capital lease; capitalizable cost, $8,000, and initial payment, $300.
8. Subsequent lease payments, $1,000, including $100 interest.
9. Depreciation on:

| | |
|---|---:|
| Buildings ...................... | $2,000 |
| Equipment .................... | 4,000 |
| | $6,000 |

10. Payments on vouchers payable (for materials), $30,000.

***Required*** Prepare a worksheet for the Metro School District Repair Shop Fund for 19X6 with columns for the beginning trial balance, transactions and adjustments, adjusted trial balance, closing entries (operating statement), and year-end balance sheet.

**P 11-5** From the information in Problem 11-4, prepare the statement of cash flows (direct method) for the Metro School District Repair Shop Internal Service Fund for the year ended December 31, 19X6. (Omit schedules.)

**P 11-6** (Entries and Trial Balance) The city of Morristown operates a printing shop through an Internal Service Fund to provide printing services for all departments. The Central Printing Fund was established by a contribution of $30,000 from the General Fund on January 1, 19X5, at which time the equipment was purchased. The postclosing trial balance on June 30, 19X8 was as follows:

| | *Debits* | *Credits* |
|---|---:|---:|
| Cash ......................................................... | $35,000 | |
| Due from General Fund ................................. | 2,000 | |
| Accounts Receivable ..................................... | 1,500 | |
| Supplies Inventory ....................................... | 3,000 | |
| Equipment ................................................ | 25,000 | |
| Accumulated Depreciation—Equipment ...................... | | $ 8,750 |
| Accounts Payable ........................................ | | 4,750 |
| Advance from General Fund ............................ | | 20,000 |
| Contributed Capital—City ............................... | | 30,000 |
| Retained Earnings ....................................... | | 3,000 |
| | $66,500 | $66,500 |

The following transactions occurred during fiscal year 19X9:

1. The publicity bureau, financed by the General Fund, ordered 30,000 multicolor travel brochures printed at a cost of $1.20 each. The brochures were delivered.
2. Supplies were purchased on account for $13,000.
3. Employee salaries were $30,000. One-sixth of this amount was withheld for taxes and is to be paid to the City's Tax Fund; the employees were paid.
4. Taxes withheld were remitted to the Tax Fund.
5. Utility charges for the year, billed by the Enterprise Fund, were $2,200.
6. Supplies used during the year cost $10,050.
7. Other billings during the period were Electric Enterprise Fund, $300; Special Revenue Fund, $4,750.
8. The inventory of supplies at year end was $5,900.
9. Collections from other funds on account during the year ended June 30, 19X9 were General Fund, $35,000; Special Revenue Fund, $4,000; and Enterprise Fund, $300.
10. Printing press number 3 was repaired by the central repair shop, operated from the Maintenance Fund. A statement for $75 was received but has not been paid.
11. The accounts receivable at June 30, 19X8 were collected in full.
12. $14,950 was paid on accounts payable.
13. Depreciation expense was recorded, $2,500.

***Required***  (a) Journalize all transactions and adjustments required in the Central Printing Fund accounts.

(b) Prepare closing entries for the Central Printing Fund accounts as of June 30, 19X9.

(c) Prepare a postclosing trial balance for the Central Printing Fund as of June 30, 19X9.

**P 11-7**  (Worksheet) From the information in Problem 11-6, prepare a columnar worksheet to reflect the beginning balances, transactions and adjustments, closing entries (results of operations), and ending balances of the Central Printing Fund of the city of Morristown for the year ended June 30, 19X9.

**P 11-8**  (Transaction and Closing Entries) The city of Merlot operates a central garage through an Internal Service Fund to provide garage space and repairs for all city-owned and -operated vehicles. The Central Garage Fund was established by a contribution of $500,000 from the General Fund on July 1, 19X7, at which time the building was acquired. The postclosing trial balance at June 30, 19X9, was as follows:

|  | *Debit* | *Credit* |
|---|---|---|
| Cash . . . . . . . . . . . . . . . . . . . . . . . . . . . . . . . . . . . . . . . . . . . . . . . . . . . | $150,000 |  |
| Due from General Fund . . . . . . . . . . . . . . . . . . . . . . . . . . . . . . . | 20,000 |  |
| Inventory of Materials and Supplies . . . . . . . . . . . . . . . . . . . . . . . | 80,000 |  |
| Land . . . . . . . . . . . . . . . . . . . . . . . . . . . . . . . . . . . . . . . . . . . . . . | 60,000 |  |
| Building . . . . . . . . . . . . . . . . . . . . . . . . . . . . . . . . . . . . . . . . . . . . | 200,000 |  |
| Accumulated Depreciation—Building . . . . . . . . . . . . . . . . . . . . . |  | $ 10,000 |
| Machinery and Equipment . . . . . . . . . . . . . . . . . . . . . . . . . . . . . | 56,000 |  |
| Accumulated Depreciation—Machinery and Equipment . . . . . . . . |  | 12,000 |
| Vouchers Payable . . . . . . . . . . . . . . . . . . . . . . . . . . . . . . . . . . . . |  | 38,000 |
| Contribution from General Fund . . . . . . . . . . . . . . . . . . . . . . . . . |  | 500,000 |
| Retained Earnings . . . . . . . . . . . . . . . . . . . . . . . . . . . . . . . . . . . |  | 6,000 |
|  | $566,000 | $566,000 |

The following information applies to the fiscal year ended June 30, 19Y0:

1. Materials and supplies were purchased on account for $74,000.
2. The inventory of materials and supplies at June 30, 19Y0 was $58,000, which agreed with the physical count taken.
3. Salaries and wages paid to employees totaled $230,000, including related costs.
4. A billing from the Enterprise Fund for utility charges totaling $30,000 was received and paid.

5. Depreciation of the building was recorded in the amount of $5,000. Depreciation of the machinery and equipment amounted to $8,000.
6. Billings to other departments for services rendered to them were as follows:

General Fund .......................................... $262,000
Water and Sewer Fund ................................ 84,000
Special Revenue Fund ................................ 32,000

7. Unpaid interfund receivable balances at June 30, 19Y0 were as follows:

General Fund .......................................... $ 6,000
Special Revenue Fund ................................ 16,000

8. Vouchers payable at June 30, 19Y0 were $14,000.

*Required* (a) For the period July 1, 19X9 through June 30, 19Y0, prepare journal entries to record all of the transactions in the Central Garage Fund accounts.
(b) Prepare closing entries for the Central Garage Fund at June 30, 19Y0. (AICPA, adapted)

**P 11-9** (Transaction and Adjusting Entries)
1. Frederic County established a Central Data Processing Internal Service Fund in 19X7. Data processing services had previously been financed via General Fund appropriations. To establish the fund, $750,000 (original cost) of computers and peripheral equipment were provided to the IS Fund from general fixed assets. The equipment, on average, had two-thirds of its 6-year useful life remaining (estimated residual value, $90,000). Also, computer paper and other supplies costing $32,000 were transferred to the IS Fund from the General Fund. General Fund inventories are accounted for on the consumption basis. In addition, $65,000 of General Fund cash was contributed to the Central Data Processing Fund to provide needed working capital.
2. Electric bills of $17,000 and payrolls of $41,000 were paid.
3. Insurance premiums of $6,400 were paid for a policy covering both the current and the next fiscal years.
4. Supplies purchased on account cost $65,000.
5. Cost of supplies used was $72,000.
6. Billings to departments for data processing services were $260,000.
7. Vouchers payable of $57,000 were paid.
8. Depreciation on equipment was recorded, $100,000.
9. Collections of amounts due from other funds for billings were $235,000.
10. Other information:
   a. Salaries and wages payable at year end were $1,100.
   b. Inventory of supplies on hand at year end was $24,700.

*Required* Prepare the general journal entries required to record all transactions and adjustments for the Central Data Processing Fund for 19X7.

**P 11-10** (Leases and Claims and Judgments) Prepare the journal entries required for the following selected transactions of the Reese County Central Data Processing Internal Service Fund.
1. The county entered into a long-term capital lease to purchase equipment midway through its fiscal year. The capitalizable cost of the equipment was $500,000. An initial payment of $100,000 was made at the inception of the lease. The implicit rate of interest on the lease is 10%, and lease payments are to be made from the resources of the Central Data Processing Fund.
2. The county paid the semiannual lease payment of $100,000. Assume that the economic useful life of the equipment is 5 years.
3. The county Central Data Processing Fund has had a $300,000 claim filed against it. It is probable that the claim will have to be paid by the county Central Data Processing Fund, but it is expected to be 2 years or more before payment is required. The county does not have a self-insurance Internal Service Fund.

# CHAPTER

# 12 | ENTERPRISE FUNDS

## Summary of Interfund- Account Group Accounting

Enterprise Funds are established to account for activities of a government that provide goods or services primarily to the public at large on a consumer charge basis. Enterprise Funds should be distinguished from Internal Service Funds, which account for activities that provide goods or services to other departments of the governmental unit, and from general government activities that charge the public for incidental services such as libraries and museums.[1]

The GASB states that Enterprise Funds should be used:

> to account for operations (a) that are financed and operated in a manner similar to private business enterprises—where the intent of the governing body is that the costs (expenses, including depreciation) of providing goods or services to the general public on a continuing basis be financed or recovered primarily through user charges; or (b) where the governing body has decided that periodic determination of revenues earned, expenses incurred, and/or net income is appropriate for capital maintenance, public policy, management control, accountability, or other purposes.[2]

This definition provides much flexibility. The first part (a) may be described as mandatory, because meeting this criterion requires the use of Enterprise Funds. The three key elements in the mandatory criterion are:

- The purpose of the activity is to provide goods or services to the public (primarily).
- A fee is charged to the users of the goods or services.
- Fee revenue is intended to cover (primarily) the full cost (expenses) of providing the goods or services.

Governments must use an Enterprise Fund to account for organizations that have all of these characteristics. The most common examples of government activities or

---

[1] The key distinction between Internal Service Funds and Enterprise Funds is straightforward. Other departments or agencies are the predominant, if not the only, customers of Internal Service Fund activities. Although many Enterprise Fund departments serve other departments or agencies of the government, such internal customers are not the predominant or sole set of customers.

[2] GASB *Codification,* sec. 1300.104b(1).

organizations that typically meet the mandatory criterion are public utilities, including:

- Water and sewer departments
- Government electric utilities
- Government gas utilities
- Government sanitary sewer operations
- Government garbage and other solid waste collection and disposal services
- Off-street parking lots and garages

Note that the mandatory criterion may not be met for all of the preceding examples in all governments. Likewise, the mandatory criterion sometimes is met for other activities or services of some governments. If the mandatory criterion is not met, the government could still choose to use an Enterprise Fund to account for the activity because of Part (b) of the Enterprise Fund definition.

Part (b), often described as permissive, provides wide discretion to the governing body in determining when to use an Enterprise Fund. This permissive part of the Enterprise Fund definition allows a government to use an Enterprise Fund to account for an operation that does not meet the conditions of the mandatory criterion. The only requirements are:

- The operation can be accounted for separately from other government operations.
- The operation primarily involves providing goods or services to the public (or other outside customers).
- The governing body desires net income or capital maintenance information to be provided for the activity.

The logic for allowing this optional use of Enterprise Funds appears to be threefold. First, it permits a government to use an Enterprise Fund consistently for an activity that sometimes meets the mandatory criterion, but at other times does not appear to meet the criterion. Second, it permits an activity that never meets the mandatory criterion—as is true with some transit systems and civic centers—to be reported in a manner that indicates its profit or loss, more fully discloses a government's subsidy of the activity, and is more comparable to reporting of similar nongovernment activities. Third, whereas most governments operate certain activities (such as public water systems) in a manner that meets the mandatory criterion, others do not. The optional criterion allows the latter governments to report their water departments, for instance, in a manner that is comparable with other governments and consistent with the norm.

Common examples of activities sometimes accounted for in Enterprise Funds under the Part (b) option criterion are:

- Mass transit operations
- Civic centers
- Toll highways and bridges
- Public housing
- Public school food services

As implied by the previous discussion, state and local governments engage in a seemingly unlimited variety of businesses. Besides the preceding examples, other government activities financed through Enterprise Funds include public docks and wharves, hospitals, nursing homes and other health care facilities, airports, lotteries, liquor wholesaling and retailing operations, swimming pools, and golf courses.

Enterprise Fund accounting and reporting principles and procedures are the principal topic of this chapter. A summary review of interfund (or multifund) and account group accounting concepts concludes the chapter. This review assists the reader to (1) review the material covered thus far, (2) integrate the knowledge of appropriate accounting principles and procedures for the various types of funds and account groups commonly employed by state and local governments, and (3) gain conceptual dexterity in applying appropriate accounting principles and procedures in the multiple-entity accounting environment of governments.

# ENTERPRISE FUND ACCOUNTING

Most enterprise activities are administered through a department of a general purpose government. Others are administered by a separate board or commission under the jurisdiction of a general purpose government. Still others are operated by an independent special district or corporation not under a general purpose government's jurisdiction. Certain characteristics, principles, and procedures are common to all Enterprise Fund accounting.

## Characteristics of Enterprise Fund Accounting

For discussion purposes, we categorize the major distinguishing characteristics of Enterprise Fund accounting under the following headings: (1) accounting principles, (2) restricted asset accounts, and (3) budgeting and appropriations. Other features of certain enterprise situations, such as payments in lieu of taxes, are discussed later in the chapter.

### Accounting Principles

Enterprise Funds, like Internal Service Funds, are proprietary (nonexpendable) funds. Thus, it is essential to distinguish between capital contributions and revenues. Likewise, revenues and expenses are accounted for on an accrual basis so that periodic net income or loss can be determined. Fixed assets and long-term debt related to enterprise activities are accounted for in the Enterprise Fund, as are depreciation and amortization.

More specifically, the pertinent accounting principles or standards typically are those used in accounting for privately owned enterprises of similar types and sizes. Indeed, many municipally owned utilities are required by supervisory commissions to follow the same accounting as that prescribed for privately owned utilities of the same class.

For external financial reporting purposes, all pertinent pronouncements of the Financial Accounting Standards Board (and its predecessor bodies) through Statement of Financial Accounting Standards No. 102 are applied, unless GASB pronouncements indicate otherwise. For later FASB pronouncements (No. 103 and later), each government must make an election for each of its proprietary activities.[3] For each proprietary fund a government must choose to either (1) apply all those subsequent FASB standards that do not relate solely or primarily to not-for-profit organizations and that do not conflict with GASB standards or (2) not apply any of those subsequent FASB standards unless they have been adopted by the

---

[3] GASB *Codification*, sec. P80.104–107.

GASB. This latter option reduces comparability among proprietary activities of different governments (and perhaps among a government's own proprietary activities). It was issued as temporary guidance and is expected to be changed. Legal or contractual reporting requirements that differ from GAAP must be met in supplemental schedules presented in the Comprehensive Annual Financial Report or by issuing special purpose reports.

Most transactions between the enterprise and other government departments should be accounted for in the same manner as "outsider" transactions, that is, as quasi-external transactions. Therefore, goods or services provided by an Enterprise Fund department or activity to other departments of the government should be billed at regular, predetermined rates. Likewise, all goods or services provided to the enterprise by other government departments should be billed to it on the same basis that other users are charged. Failure to do this distorts the operating and position statements of all funds involved.

A separate fund usually should be established for each government enterprise. Too, all transactions or events relating to a specific enterprise should be recorded in the appropriate Enterprise Fund records. However, closely related activities, such as water and sewer utilities, are sometimes merged because of their complementary nature or because joint revenue bonds often are used in financing such operations.

### Restricted Asset Accounts

Enterprise activities may involve transactions or relationships that, if encountered in a general government situation, would require the use of several separate and distinct fund entities. Thus, utilities may require customers to post deposits (Trust or Agency), may acquire or construct major capital facilities (Capital Projects), or may have funded reserves or other debt-related resources (Debt Service). In some cases, certain enterprise-related intrafund "funds" are required to be established under terms of bond indentures or similar agreements.

In keeping with its recommendation that governmental enterprises follow appropriate commercial accounting principles, the term *funds* is interpreted in this instance in the usual commercial accounting connotation of restricted assets. Thus, Enterprise Funds may contain several "funds within a fund." These "funds" are simply distinctively titled intrafund restricted asset accounts (accompanied by related liability and, if desired, by equity reserve accounts). This practice is preferable to the use of a series of separate fund entities in Enterprise Fund accounting. The "funds within a fund" approach is demonstrated in the illustrative example in this chapter.

### Budgeting and Appropriations

As with Internal Service Funds, careful planning and realistic budgeting are prerequisites to sound Enterprise Fund management. Clearly, if flexible budgets are adopted, they are guides to action and means of managerial control, as in business enterprises. These flexible budgets are not fixed limitations as are the budgets of governmental funds. However, fixed budgets often are adopted because of legal requirements or because the executive or legislative body desires to control some (e.g., capital outlay) or all expenditures. In these cases, the Enterprise Fund accounts may be maintained on the budgetary basis during the year, then converted to GAAP at year end. Alternatively, the budget may be incorporated into the chart of accounts.

## Enterprise Fund Accounting Illustrated

Services of the type generally referred to as public utilities are among the most common enterprise activities undertaken by local governments. Such activities invariably involve significant amounts of assets, liabilities, revenues, and expenses and are seldom considered in contemporary undergraduate accounting courses. For these reasons, we have chosen an electric utility example to illustrate Enterprise Fund accounting procedures. The illustrative utility is assumed to be nonregulated. Regulated utilities are subject to special accounting and reporting requirements not discussed here. The illustrative example is presented in several phases.

### Establishment of Fund and Acquisition of Plant

The acquisition of a utility may be financed from various sources. Possible sources include the sale of bonds to be retired from utility earnings, contributions or grants from the governmental unit, intergovernmental grants, intergovernmental or intragovernmental loans, and contributions from subdivision developers and prospective customers.

Assume that the acquisition of the illustrative utility plant is financed through a General Fund contribution.

**1.** The entry to record the receipt of a contribution of $400,000 and to establish the fund at the end of 19X1 is:

(1)  Cash ........................................... $400,000
         Residual Equity Transfer from General Fund ....... $400,000
      To record governmental unit's contribution for acquisition of utility.

**2.** The net assets of an existing private electricity generation and distribution plant are acquired by the government at the end of 19X1. The government is to pay $280,000. This amount equals the fair value of the assets acquired less the fair value of the liabilities assumed.

The entry to record the acquisition of the plant and the assumption of the liabilities (assume that all the amounts in the entries are the correct fair values) is:

(2)  Land ........................................... $ 50,000
      Buildings ...................................... 90,000
      Improvements Other Than Buildings ............... 480,000
      Machinery and Equipment ........................ 110,000
      Accounts Receivable ........................... 62,000
      Inventory of Materials and Supplies ............... 10,000
         Allowance for Uncollectible Accounts ............ $ 12,000
         Bonds Payable ................................ 500,000
         Vouchers Payable ............................ 10,000
         Due to ABC Electric Company ................. 280,000
      To record the acquisition of the assets and liabilities of the ABC Electric Company.

**3.** Payment of the amount due to ABC Electric Company is recorded as follows:

(3)  Due to ABC Electric Company ................... $280,000
         Cash ....................................... $280,000
      To record payment to ABC Electric Company.

**4.** At the end of 19X1, the Residual Equity Transfer account would be closed with the following entry:

| | | | |
|---|---|---|---|
| (4) | Residual Equity Transfer from General Fund ........ | $400,000 | |
| | Contributed Capital—Governmental Unit ........ | | $400,000 |
| | To close residual equity transfer from General Fund. | | |

### Accounting for Routine Operating Transactions

The following transactions and entries illustrate the operation of an Enterprise Fund for a utility. These transactions occur in 19X2, the first year of operations. The accounting procedures for (1) the receipt and expenditure of bond proceeds, (2) utility debt service and related "funds," and (3) customers' deposits require use of intrafund restricted asset accounts and are discussed in a subsequent phase of the example.

For simplicity, all revenues, except interest and other nonoperating revenues, are credited to an Operating Revenues control account. Likewise, all expenses are charged to either an Operating Expenses or a Nonoperating Expenses control account. A detailed operating expense statement is illustrated in Figure 12–4.

**Transactions and Entries—During 19X2**

**5.** Materials costing $59,000 were received.

| | | | |
|---|---|---|---|
| (5) | Inventory of Materials and Supplies ............... | $ 59,000 | |
| | Vouchers Payable .......................... | | $ 59,000 |
| | To record purchase of materials. | | |

**6.** Revenues billed during the year totaled $300,000.

| | | | |
|---|---|---|---|
| (6) | Accounts Receivable .......................... | $300,000 | |
| | Operating Revenues ........................ | | $300,000 |
| | To record operating revenue. | | |

**7.** Equipment costing $50,500 was purchased on account.

| | | | |
|---|---|---|---|
| (7) | Machinery and Equipment ...................... | $ 50,500 | |
| | Vouchers Payable .......................... | | $ 50,500 |
| | To record purchase of equipment. | | |

**8.** Rental due on equipment rented to the State Public Works Department totaled $7,000.

| | | | |
|---|---|---|---|
| (8) | Due from State Public Works Department .......... | $ 7,000 | |
| | Nonoperating Revenues—Equipment Rental ...... | | $ 7,000 |
| | To record rental of equipment to State Public Works Department. | | |

**9.** Collections on accounts receivable were $290,000. Interest received totaled $1,000.

| | | | |
|---|---|---|---|
| (9) | Cash ......................................... | $291,000 | |
| | Accounts Receivable .......................... | | $290,000 |
| | Nonoperating Revenues—Interest .............. | | 1,000 |
| | To record collection of accounts receivable and interest revenues. | | |

**10.** A bill was received from an Internal Service Fund for services used, $12,800.

| | | | |
|---|---|---|---|
| (10) | Operating Expenses .......................... | $ 12,800 | |
| | Due to Internal Service Fund .................. | | $ 12,800 |
| | To record cost of services used by Internal Service Fund. | | |

**11.** Bond principal ($50,000) and interest ($20,000) were paid.

| | | |
|---|---|---|
| (11) Bonds Payable | $ 50,000 | |
| Nonoperating Expenses—Interest | 20,000 | |
| Cash | | $ 70,000 |
| To record debt service payment | | |

**12.** Other cash payments were made during the year for:

| | |
|---|---|
| Salaries and wages | $127,200 |
| Telephone and Internet services | 500 |
| Fire insurance premiums (two-year policy) | 1,000 |
| Utilities | 10,500 |
| Vouchers payable (including $30,000 on the equipment from Transaction 7) | 70,000 |
| | $209,200 |

| | | |
|---|---|---|
| (12) Operating Expenses | $139,200 | |
| Vouchers Payable | 70,000 | |
| Cash | | $209,200 |
| To record payments of various expenses and liabilities. | | |

(Prepaid insurance, $600, is recorded in an adjusting entry later in the example.)

**13.** $10,000 was paid from the Enterprise Fund to the General Fund to subsidize General Fund operations.

| | | |
|---|---|---|
| (13) Operating Transfer to General Fund | $ 10,000 | |
| Cash | | $ 10,000 |
| To record payment of operating transfer to General Fund. | | |

**14.** A subdivision developer donated a subdivision electricity system (fair value $30,000) to the utility.

| | | |
|---|---|---|
| (14) Improvements Other Than Buildings | $ 30,000 | |
| Contributed Capital—Contributions from Subdividers | | $ 30,000 |
| To record dedication of subdivision distribution lines to the utility. | | |

(Hookup, tapping, or tap fees and similar charges paid by customers also preferably should be credited to a contributed capital account, such as Contributed Capital—Contributions from Customers, to the extent they exceed recovery of hookup costs.)

Note that (1) contributed capital changes are carefully distinguished from revenues, expenses, gains, and losses and (2) operating and nonoperating revenues and expenses are carefully distinguished in the illustrative entries. In Enterprise Fund (as in IS Fund) accounting and reporting the distinction between contributed capital and retained earnings is significant. Proprietary-type activities typically are intended to be self-sustaining. The extent to which the activity is self-sustaining is reflected by its Retained Earnings account if increases and decreases in equity are classified appropriately over time.

Likewise, the distinction between operating and nonoperating revenues and expenses is significant. If significant nonoperating revenues are needed to cover operating expenses, the full cost of services provided is not being charged to users of Enterprise Fund services. This implies that the activity may not be able to sustain itself in the future without rate increases if (1) the nonoperating revenue is reduced significantly or (2) the demand for the department's (underpriced) services increases significantly.

Finally, note and review the other key differences between governmental fund and proprietary fund accounting. These include the required use of the consumption method of inventory accounting (entry 5) and the gross revenue approach (entry 6) in proprietary funds, reporting fixed assets and noncurrent liabilities in proprietary funds (entries 2 and 7), and accounting for expenses (rather than expenditures) in proprietary funds.

### Adjusting Entries—End of 19X2

**15.** Necessary adjusting entries at the end of 19X2 were based on the following data.

|   |   |   |   |
|---|---|---|---|
| a. | Accrued salaries and wages payable | ........ | $ 6,000 |
|   | Accrued interest payable | ................ | 2,000 |
|   | Accrued utilities payable | ................ | 7,500 |
| b. | Prepaid insurance | ........................ | 600 |
| c. | Ending inventory of materials and supplies | .. | 30,000 |
| d. | Estimated losses on accounts receivable | ..... | 1,500 |
| e. | Depreciation: | | |
|   | Buildings | ........................... | 5,000 |
|   | Improvements other than buildings | ....... | 15,000 |
|   | Machinery and equipment | ............. | 16,000 |
| f. | Unbilled receivables | ..................... | 21,000 |
|   | Accrued interest receivable | ............. | 200 |

| (15) | (a) Operating Expenses | .............................. | $13,500 | |
|---|---|---|---|---|
|   | Nonoperating Expenses—Interest | .................. | 2,000 | |
|   | Accrued Salaries and Wages Payable | .............. | | $ 6,000 |
|   | Accrued Interest Payable | ........................ | | 2,000 |
|   | Accrued Utilities Payable | ........................ | | 7,500 |
|   | To record accrued expenses. | | | |
|   | (b) Prepaid Insurance | .............................. | $ 600 | |
|   | Operating Expenses | ........................... | | $ 600 |
|   | To record unexpired insurance. | | | |
|   | (c) Operating Expenses | .............................. | $39,000 | |
|   | Inventory of Materials and Supplies | .............. | | $39,000 |
|   | To record operating expenses for materials used during year. | | | |
|   | (d) Operating Expenses | .............................. | $ 1,500 | |
|   | Allowance for Uncollectible Accounts | ............ | | $ 1,500 |
|   | To record estimated losses on accounts receivable. | | | |
|   | (e) Operating Expenses | .............................. | $36,000 | |
|   | Accumulated Depreciation—Buildings | ............. | | $ 5,000 |
|   | Accumulated Depreciation—Improvements Other Than Buildings | ........................ | | 15,000 |
|   | Accumulated Depreciation—Machinery and Equipment | .................................. | | 16,000 |
|   | To record depreciation for fiscal year. | | | |
|   | (f) Unbilled Accounts Receivable | ..................... | $21,000 | |
|   | Accrued Interest Receivable | ..................... | 200 | |
|   | Operating Revenues | ........................... | | $21,000 |
|   | Nonoperating Revenues—Interest | ............... | | 200 |
|   | To record unbilled receivables and revenues and accrued interest receivable on customer accounts at year end. | | | |

## Accounting for Restricted Asset Accounts

As indicated earlier, an enterprise's restricted assets are accounted for in the Enterprise Fund accounts rather than through separate fund entities. Restricted asset, liability, and, if desired, equity reserve accounts are distinctively titled to establish "funds" within the Enterprise Fund. In this way, a single fund serves the purpose of several separate fund entities. Before studying the procedures that follow, note how the Trial Balance (Figure 12–1) and the Balance Sheet (Figure 12–2) at the conclusion of this example separate those intrafund "funds" from the unrestricted assets and other liabilities and equities.

The types of restricted asset situations encountered in practice vary widely. They range from simple customer deposits "funds" to complex series of "funds" required under terms of bond indentures, through legislative decree, or for administrative purposes. Several common restricted asset situations are used here to illustrate intrafund restricted asset accounting, sometimes referred to as secondary account groups, in Enterprise Fund accounting.

The following illustrations use distinctively titled asset and liability accounts for each "fund." The appropriate reserve accounts are adjusted by inspection at period end. (The reserve accounts are commonly used but are not required by GAAP.) "Fund" revenues and expenses are recorded in the Electric (Enterprise) Fund revenue and expense control accounts. Any "fund" detail needed is assumed to be maintained in subsidiary records. Alternatively, we might have used detailed "fund" revenue and expense accounts and closed them at period end either (1) directly to the appropriate reserve account, or (2) to the Retained Earnings account, followed by an entry adjusting the appropriate reserve account. If needed, special purpose reports are issued for these restricted subfunds to satisfy legal or contractual reporting requirements.

**Customer Deposits Trust or Agency Subfund** A utility usually requires its customers to post deposits as a partial protection against bad debt losses. The utility typically pays interest on the deposits. The following transactions and entries illustrate the key aspects of accounting for customer deposits.

Transactions and Entries—During 19X2

**16.** Deposits of $11,000 were received.

| | | | |
|---|---|---|---|
| (16) | **Customer Deposits—Cash** . . . . . . . . . . . . . . . . . . . . . . . . . . . . . | $11,000 | |
| | **Customer Deposits—Deposits Payable** . . . . . . . . . . . . . . | | $11,000 |
| | To record receipt of customer deposits. | | |

**17.** Deposits of $10,000 were invested (assume that no accrued interest was involved).

| | | | |
|---|---|---|---|
| (17) | **Customer Deposits—Investments** . . . . . . . . . . . . . . . . . . . . . | $10,000 | |
| | **Customer Deposits—Cash** . . . . . . . . . . . . . . . . . . . . . . . . . . | | $10,000 |
| | To record investment of customer deposits. | | |

**18.** Interest accrued on investments but not received totaled $200.

| | | | |
|---|---|---|---|
| (18) | **Customer Deposits—Accrued Interest Receivable** . . . . . . . . | $    200 | |
| | Nonoperating Revenues—Interest . . . . . . . . . . . . . . . . . . | | $    200 |
| | To record interest revenues. | | |

Note that not all accounts affected by these transactions are subfund accounts. The subfund accounts are in boldface type to emphasize the effects of the transactions on the subfund.

**19.** Interest accrued on deposits at year end, $150.

| (19) Nonoperating Expenses—Interest ................. | $150 | |
|---|---|---|
| Customer Deposits—Accrued Interest Payable .... | | $150 |
| To record interest expense. | | |

**20.** A customer's deposit was declared forfeited for nonpayment of his account.

| (20) (a) **Customer Deposits—Deposits Payable** .......... | $ 12 | |
|---|---|---|
| **Customer Deposits—Accrued Interest Payable** ... | 2 | |
| Allowance for Uncollectible Accounts .......... | 8 | |
| Accounts Receivable ..................... | | $ 22 |
| To record forfeiture of customer's deposit, offset against overdue receivable, and write-off of the uncollectible balance. | | |
| (b) Cash ...................................... | $ 14 | |
| Customer Deposits—Cash ................. | | $ 14 |
| To reclassify forfeited customer deposit cash to unrestricted cash. | | |

Note that entry 20(b) reclassifies the forfeited customer deposits as unrestricted cash. The customer no longer has a valid claim against the assets—as reflected in entry 20(a); therefore, use of the assets is no longer restricted.

**21.** A customer moving to another town requested that her service be disconnected. Her final bill was offset against her deposit, and the balance was remitted to her.

| (21) (a) **Customer Deposits—Deposits Payable** .......... | $ 15 | |
|---|---|---|
| **Customer Deposits—Accrued Interest Payable** ... | 3 | |
| Accounts Receivable ..................... | | $ 10 |
| Customer Deposits—Cash ................. | | 8 |
| To record offsetting of customer's final bill against her deposit account and remittance of the balance due her. | | |
| (b) Cash ...................................... | $ 10 | |
| Customer Deposits—Cash ................. | | $ 10 |
| To reclassify customer deposit cash applied to final bill as unrestricted cash. | | |

**Adjusting Entries—End of 19X2**

**22.** The fair value of the subfund investments at year end was $10,100.

| (22) **Customer Deposits—Investments** ................. | $100 | |
|---|---|---|
| **Nonoperating Revenues—Net Increase (Decrease) in Fair Value of Investments** ................. | | $100 |
| To adjust investments to fair value. | | |

**23.** The appropriate reserve account was adjusted at period end to equal the net assets of the "fund."

| (23) Retained Earnings ............................. | $150 | |
|---|---|---|
| **Reserve for Earnings on Customer Deposits** ...... | | $150 |
| To reserve Retained Earnings to indicate that net assets of the Customer Deposits subfund are used only for customer deposit interest requirements. | | |

This entry assumes that subfund revenues are restricted for paying interest on deposits. Under these conditions, some accountants prefer to use distinctively titled subfund revenue and expense accounts to facilitate preparation of this entry. If the revenues from the restricted assets are unrestricted, no reserve would be established and the Customer Deposits subfund would be an Agency subfund rather than a Trust subfund.

**Construction Financed by Bond Issue (CPF Subfund)**     Accounting for Enterprise Fund construction financed through the sale of bonds is not unlike that for private construction. Both the authorization of the bond issue and appropriations, if any, are normally recorded in memorandum form rather than formally within the accounts. However, Enterprise Fund bond indentures may require accounting for proceeds of the bond issue in Capital Projects Fund and/or accounting for resources required to be set aside for debt service in a Debt Service Fund. The "funds within a fund" approach illustrated here usually satisfies these legal or contractual requirements.

The following transactions and entries illustrate appropriate procedures in the typical case.

Transactions and Entries—During 19X2

**24.** Bonds ($200,000 par) were sold at a premium of $2,000 to provide financing for expanding and modernizing the utility's distribution system. The premium cash was restricted for debt service.

| | | | |
|---|---|---:|---:|
| (24) | **Construction—Cash** | $200,000 | |
| | **Debt Service—Cash** | 2,000 | |
| | Unamortized Premiums on Bonds | | $  2,000 |
| | Bonds Payable | | 200,000 |
| | To record sale of bonds at a premium. | | |

**25.** A contract was entered into with Smith & Company to construct part of the project at a cost of $100,000.

(25)  No entry is necessary to record the contract; a narrative memorandum entry may be made.

**26.** Materials costing $41,000 were purchased by the utility and delivered to the construction site.

| | | | |
|---|---|---:|---:|
| (26) | Construction Work in Progress | $ 41,000 | |
| | **Construction—Vouchers Payable** | | $ 41,000 |
| | To record cost of construction materials. | | |

**27.** A bill for $30,000 was received from Smith & Company.

| | | | |
|---|---|---:|---:|
| (27) | Construction Work in Progress | $ 30,000 | |
| | **Construction—Contracts Payable** | | $ 30,000 |
| | To record receipt of bill from Smith & Company for part of cost of contract. | | |

**28.** The amount due Smith & Company and the bill for materials were paid.

| | | | |
|---|---|---:|---:|
| (28) | **Construction—Vouchers Payable** | $ 41,000 | |
| | **Construction—Contracts Payable** | 30,000 | |
| | **Construction—Cash** | | $ 71,000 |
| | To record payment of amount now due on contract and of bill for materials. | | |

**29.** Construction labor and supervisory expenses of $56,000 were paid.

| | | |
|---|---|---|
| (29) Construction Work in Progress ................. | $ 56,000 | |
| Construction—Cash ......................... | | $ 56,000 |
| To record cost of labor and supervisory expenses. | | |

**30.** Smith & Company completed its part of the construction project and submitted its bill for $70,000. The completed project was found to be satisfactory.

| | | |
|---|---|---|
| (30) (a) Construction Work in Progress ............... | $ 70,000 | |
| Construction—Contracts Payable ............ | | $ 70,000 |
| To record receipt of bill from Smith & Company to cover remaining cost of contract. | | |
| (b) Improvements Other Than Buildings ........... | $197,000 | |
| Construction Work in Progress ............. | | $197,000 |
| To close Construction Work in Progress account and to record the cost of completed improvements. | | |

**31.** Smith & Company was paid in full, and the remaining bond cash was transferred to the Enterprise debt service "fund."

| | | |
|---|---|---|
| (31) Construction—Contracts Payable ................. | $ 70,000 | |
| Debt Service—Cash ........................... | 3,000 | |
| Construction—Cash ......................... | | $ 73,000 |
| To record final payment to contractor and transfer of unused bond proceeds to Debt Service "fund." | | |

This entry assumes that the bond indenture requires unused bond proceeds to be used for debt service on the bonds.

**Debt Service and Related Accounts**     A variety of intrafund "funds" related to bond issues may be required (in addition to a construction or Capital Projects "fund") under terms found in contemporary bond indentures. Among the most usual of these are:

**1.** *Term Bond Principal Sinking Fund.* Often referred to merely as a "sinking" fund, its purpose is to accumulate specified amounts of assets, and earnings thereon, for the eventual retirement of term bond principal. These usually are for older issues because most recent issues are serial bonds rather than term bonds.

**2.** *Serial Bond Debt Service Fund.* This type of intrafund "fund," may be referred to as an Interest and Redemption, Interest and Sinking, or Bond and Interest fund. It is often required to assure timely payment of serial bond interest and principal. A common indenture provision is that one-sixth of the next semiannual interest payment, plus one-twelfth of the next annual principal payment, be deposited monthly in a "fund" of this type.

**3.** *Principal and Interest Reserve Fund.* Often referred to simply as a Reserve fund, these intrafund "funds" are often required to provide bondholders an additional cushion or safety margin. "Funds" of this sort are usually required to be accumulated to a specific sum immediately or within the first 60 months after bonds are issued. The "fund" resources are used (1) to pay matured bonds and interest if the resources in the Debt Service "fund" prove inadequate, or (2) if not required earlier to cover deficiencies, to retire the final bond principal and interest maturities.

**4.** *Contingencies Fund.* This intrafund "fund," sometimes referred to as the Emergency Repair or Operating Reserve fund, affords bondholders even more security by providing in advance for emergency expenditures or for operating asset renewal or replacement. Thus, the bondholder receives additional assurance (1) that the operating facilities will not be permitted to deteriorate in order that bond principal and interest requirements be met and

(2) that the utility will not be forced into receivership because of such unforeseen expenditure requirements. Like the Principal and Interest Reserve "fund," the Contingencies "fund" is usually required to be accumulated in a specific amount early in the life of the bond issue.

To illustrate the operation and accounting for debt service-related "funds" within an Enterprise Fund, assume that Debt Service, Principal and Interest Reserve, and Contingencies "funds," as described previously, are required by an enterprise bond indenture. A total of $5,000 has already been classified as Debt Service—Cash (Construction "fund" transactions 24 and 31) as a result of a bond issue premium ($2,000) and unused bond issue proceeds ($3,000). The following transactions illustrate typical activities related to these restricted asset accounts:

**Transactions and Entries—During 19X2**

**32.** The Debt Service "fund" was increased by $25,000. $10,000 was added to the Principal and Interest Reserve "fund" and to the Contingencies "fund."

| | | |
|---|---|---|
| (32) **Debt Service—Cash** | $25,000 | |
| **Principal and Interest Reserve—Cash** | 10,000 | |
| **Contingencies—Cash** | 10,000 | |
| Cash | | $45,000 |
| To record amounts restricted and set aside for these "funds." | | |

**33.** Interest on bonds, $15,000, was paid.

| | | |
|---|---|---|
| (33) Nonoperating Expenses—Interest | $15,000 | |
| **Debt Service—Cash** | | $15,000 |
| To record payment of bond interest. | | |

**34.** A $7,000 unforeseen emergency repair expense to be paid from the Contingencies "fund" was incurred.

| | | |
|---|---|---|
| (34) Operating Expenses | $ 7,000 | |
| **Contingencies—Vouchers Payable** | | $ 7,000 |
| To record liability for emergency repair expense. | | |

**35.** Principal and Interest Reserve "fund" cash, $9,000, was invested.

| | | |
|---|---|---|
| (35) **Principal and Interest Reserve—Investments** | $ 9,000 | |
| **Principal and Interest Reserve—Cash** | | $ 9,000 |
| To record investment of fund cash. | | |

**36.** Interest of $430 was earned on the investment. $300 was collected.

| | | |
|---|---|---|
| (36) **Principal and Interest Reserve—Cash** | $ 300 | |
| **Principal and Interest Reserve—Accrued Interest Receivable** | 130 | |
| Nonoperating Revenues—Interest | | $ 430 |
| To record interest earned and received. | | |

**37.** Bond interest payable had accrued at year end, $6,000; premium of $300 was amortized.

| | | |
|---|---|---|
| (37) Nonoperating Expenses—Interest | $ 5,700 | |
| Unamortized Premium on Bonds | 300 | |
| **Debt Service—Accrued Bond Interest Payable** | | $ 6,000 |
| To record bond interest accrued and amortization of bond premium. | | |

**38.** The investments of the Principal and Interest Reserve "funds" are participating, interest-earning investment contracts that are subject to fair value accounting requirements. The fair value of the investments increased by $20 during the year.

| | | | |
|---|---|---|---|
| (38) | **Principal and Interest Reserve—Investments** . . . . . . . . | $ 20 | |
| | **Nonoperating Revenues—Net Increase (Decrease)** | | |
| | **in Fair Value of Investments** . . . . . . . . . . . . . . . . | | $ 20 |
| | To record increase in fair value of investments. | | |

### Adjusting Entry—End of 19X2

**39.** The appropriate reserve accounts were adjusted at year end to equal the net assets of the funds.

| | | | |
|---|---|---|---|
| (39) | Retained Earnings . . . . . . . . . . . . . . . . . . . . . . . . . . . . | $22,450 | |
| | **Reserve for Bond Debt Service** . . . . . . . . . . . . . . . . | | $ 9,000 |
| | **Reserve for Bond Principal and Interest Payments** | | |
| | **Guarantee** . . . . . . . . . . . . . . . . . . . . . . . . . . . . . | | 10,450 |
| | **Reserve for Contingencies** . . . . . . . . . . . . . . . . . . . | | 3,000 |
| | To adjust reserve accounts at year end. | | |

The purpose of the Retained Earnings reserves is to indicate that restricted intrafund "fund" net assets are not available for "dividends" to the General Fund or for other purposes. The reserves also constitute the balancing accounts of the self-balancing "funds within a fund." Finally, as noted earlier, GAAP does not require that the reserves be maintained unless they are legally or contractually required. However, maintaining the reserves makes the "funds" self-balancing.

## Special Assessment Improvements Affecting Enterprise Funds

Though used most commonly for general government capital projects or services, special assessments are sometimes a source of financing for Enterprise Fund services or capital assets. Service-type special assessments for Enterprise Fund services should be treated like Enterprise Fund user fees. Accounting for capital-type special assessment projects that result in Enterprise Fund capital assets being acquired or constructed depends upon whether or not the project is administered by the enterprise activity.

**SA Project Administered Separately** Special assessment (SA) projects that result in construction or acquisition of Enterprise Fund fixed assets may be accounted for in Capital Projects and Debt Service Funds, respectively. In such cases, the long-term debt that is not to be repaid from Enterprise Fund resources is included in the General Long-Term Debt Account Group. The fixed assets constructed or acquired and any portion of the debt that is to be repaid from the Enterprise Fund are recorded in the Enterprise Fund. The net amount is accounted for as contributed capital. For example, if improvements costing $900,000 were constructed in a special assessment project for Enterprise Fund use, and $100,000 of related notes payable are to be repaid from the Enterprise Fund, the entry in the Enterprise Fund would be:

| | | |
|---|---|---|
| Improvements Other Than Buildings . . . . . . . . . . . . . . . . . . . . . . | $900,000 | |
| Notes Payable . . . . . . . . . . . . . . . . . . . . . . . . . . . . . . . . . . . . | | $100,000 |
| Contributed Capital—Contributions from Property Owners . . . | | 800,000 |
| To record construction of improvements via special assessment | | |
| projects, including Enterprise Fund share of project liabilities. | | |

**SA Project Administered by Enterprise Activity**     Special assessment projects that result in Enterprise Fund fixed assets may be administered by the Enterprise Fund department or activity. If so, all of the assets, liabilities, and transactions for the special assessment project may be accounted for in the Enterprise Fund using proprietary fund accounting principles. Hence, the debt issued is recorded as a payable in the Enterprise Fund. Costs incurred on the construction of the project are recorded as Enterprise Fund fixed assets. Segregation of special assessment project cash, investments, receivables, payables, and so on would be accomplished by using restricted asset accounting. For instance, the bond proceeds to be used for construction would be accounted for in a Special Assessment Construction "fund" within the Enterprise Fund like the construction fund illustrated earlier.

### Unbilled Receivables

For ease of illustration, most of the required adjusting entries were included in the various phases of the example. Most of the adjusting entries required are similar to those common in commercial accounting; and, as in commercial accounting, those of an accrual nature typically would be reversed at the beginning of the subsequent period. The adjusting entry for unbilled receivables may be less familiar to the reader. Accurately determining the revenue earned during a year requires that significant amounts of unbilled receivables be accrued at year end, particularly if the amount of such receivables varies materially from year to year.

### Interest Capitalization

State and local governments may issue both taxable and tax-exempt bonds and other debt securities to finance Enterprise Fund fixed assets. Capitalization of interest cost on taxable debt follows the same guidance as for commercial entities. When feasible, SLGs will finance their major construction activities with tax-exempt debt and/or grants that are restricted for construction of a capital facility. Interest capitalization differs significantly when these sources of financing are used. First, no interest cost should be capitalized on asset costs financed by restricted gifts or grants. Second, interest capitalization associated with tax-exempt debt is computed differently than for taxable debt. The interest capitalization period begins when tax-exempt debt restricted for construction of a qualifying asset is issued. Also, the interest cost capitalized is computed as all interest costs of the borrowing during the capitalization period less any investment earnings on temporary investment of the bond proceeds during that period.

### Preclosing Trial Balance

An adjusted, preclosing trial balance for the Electric (Enterprise) Fund, based on the numbered illustrative journal entries in this chapter, appears as Figure 12–1. To emphasize the "funds within a fund" approach common to Enterprise Fund accounting, this trial balance has been modified from the usual trial balance format. It is divided into two major sections, entitled "General Accounts" and "Restricted Accounts," respectively, and (2) subtotals are included to indicate the self-balancing nature of many Enterprise Fund intrafund "funds."

Recall that not all intrafund restricted account groups need be self-balancing. Thus, had we not assumed in our example that the net assets of the Customer

FIGURE 12-1 Preclosing Trial Balance

A Governmental Unit
Electric (Enterprise) Fund
**Preclosing (Adjusted) Trial Balance**
(Date)

**General Accounts:**

| | | |
|---|---:|---:|
| Cash | $ 76,824 | |
| Accounts Receivable | 71,968 | |
| Allowance for Uncollectible Accounts | | $ 13,492 |
| Unbilled Accounts Receivable | 21,000 | |
| Accrued Interest Receivable | 200 | |
| Due from State Public Works Department | 7,000 | |
| Inventory of Materials and Supplies | 30,000 | |
| Prepaid Insurance | 600 | |
| Land | 50,000 | |
| Buildings | 90,000 | |
| Accumulated Depreciation—Buildings | | 5,000 |
| Improvements Other Than Buildings | 707,000 | |
| Accumulated Depreciation—Improvements Other Than Buildings | | 15,000 |
| Machinery and Equipment | 160,500 | |
| Accumulated Depreciation—Machinery and Equipment | | 16,000 |
| Vouchers Payable | | 49,500 |
| Due to Internal Service Fund | | 12,800 |
| Accrued Salaries and Wages Payable | | 6,000 |
| Accrued Interest Payable | | 2,000 |
| Accrued Utilities Payable | | 7,500 |
| Bonds Payable | | 650,000 |
| Unamortized Premiums on Bonds | | 1,700 |
| Contributed Capital—Governmental Unit | | 400,000 |
| Contributed Capital—Contributions from Subdividers | | 30,000 |
| Retained Earnings | 22,600 | |
| Operating Revenues | | 321,000 |
| Operating Expenses | 248,400 | |
| Nonoperating Revenues—Equipment Rental | | 7,000 |
| Nonoperating Revenues—Interest | | 1,830 |
| Nonoperating Revenues—Increase (Decrease) in Fair Value of Investments | | 120 |
| Nonoperating Expenses—Interest | 42,850 | |
| Operating Transfer to General Fund | 10,000 | |
| Subtotal | 1,538,942 | 1,538,942 |

**Restricted or Secondary Accounts:**

| | | | |
|---|---|---:|---:|
| **Customer Deposits "Fund"** | Customer Deposits—Cash | 968 | |
| | Customer Deposits—Investments | 10,100 | |
| | Customer Deposits—Accrued Interest Receivable | 200 | |
| | Customer Deposits—Deposits Payable | | 10,973 |
| | Customer Deposits—Interest Payable | | 145 |
| | Reserve for Earnings on Customer Deposits | | 150 |
| | Subtotal | 11,268 | 11,268 |
| **Debt Service "Fund"** | Debt Service—Cash | 15,000 | |
| | Debt Service—Accrued Interest Payable | | 6,000 |
| | Reserve for Bond Debt Service | | 9,000 |
| | Subtotal | 15,000 | 15,000 |
| **Principal And Interest "Fund"** | Principal and Interest Reserve—Cash | 1,300 | |
| | Principal and Interest Reserve—Investments | 9,020 | |
| | Principal and Interest Reserve—Accrued Interest Receivable | 130 | |
| | Reserve for Bond Principal and Interest Payments Guarantee | | 10,450 |
| | Subtotal | 10,450 | 10,450 |
| **Contingencies "Fund"** | Contingencies—Cash | 10,000 | |
| | Contingencies—Vouchers Payable | | 7,000 |
| | Reserve for Contingencies | | 3,000 |
| | Subtotal | 10,000 | 10,000 |
| | Total | $1,585,660 | $1,585,660 |

Deposits "fund" were restricted to guarantee future interest liabilities to customers (1) no Reserve for Earnings on Customer Deposits would be needed, and (2) this "fund" would not be self-balancing.

### Closing Entries

As observed earlier, any reasonable closing entry combination that brings the temporary accounts to a zero balance and updates the Contributed Capital and Retained Earnings accounts is acceptable. A multiple-step closing approach was illustrated in Chapter 11; the compound closing entry approach is demonstrated here:

| | | |
|---|---:|---:|
| (40) Operating Revenues | $321,000 | |
| Nonoperating Revenues—Equipment Rental | 7,000 | |
| Nonoperating Revenues—Interest | 1,830 | |
| Nonoperating Revenues—Net Increase (Decrease) in Fair Value of Investments | 120 | |
| Operating Expenses | | $248,400 |
| Nonoperating Expenses—Interest | | 42,850 |
| Operating Transfer to General Fund | | 10,000 |
| Retained Earnings | | 28,700 |

To close the temporary accounts and update the Retained Earnings account.

### Financial Statements

The three required primary statements for Enterprise Funds are the balance sheet; statement of revenues, expenses, and changes in total fund equity (or retained earnings); and statement of cash flows. These often include prior year data columns, which have been omitted here in order to emphasize the essential aspects of these financial statements.

Supplemental schedules may be used to present the details of any segments of the principal statements that need additional explanation. Typical schedules of this type are for budgeted versus actual operating expenses and for fixed assets and depreciation, including changes therein. Schedules describing aspects of intra-fund restricted account groups may also be desirable or required. For example, contractual requirements may dictate a statement of assets restricted for bond debt service. Schedules detailing changes in the cash and investment accounts of other intrafund restricted asset account groups may be useful as well. Also, schedules demonstrating compliance with any pertinent legal requirements may be needed.

**Balance Sheet**  A balance sheet for the Electric (Enterprise) Fund is illustrated in Figure 12–2. Note that the balance sheet is similar to that of a profit-seeking public utility. Like the balance sheet of a business enterprise or of many Nonexpendable Trust and Internal Service Funds, this statement contains both fixed assets and long-term liabilities of the government enterprise.

Notice the asset categorization as among current assets, restricted assets, and plant and equipment in the Balance Sheet in Figure 12–2 and the parallel division of liabilities into current liabilities payable from current assets, liabilities payable from restricted assets, and long-term liabilities. Such intrastatement categorization

**FIGURE 12–2  Balance Sheet**

A Governmental Unit
Electric (Enterprise) Fund
**Balance Sheet**
December 31, 19X2

| *Assets* | | |
|---|---:|---:|
| **Current Assets:** | | |
| Cash .......................... | $ | 76,824 |
| Accounts receivable (less allowance | | |
| for doubtful accounts of $13,492) | | 58,476 |
| Unbilled accounts receivable ...... | | 21,000 |
| Accrued interest receivable ....... | | 200 |
| Due from State Public Works | | |
| Department ................ | | 7,000 |
| Inventory of materials and supplies . | | 30,000 |
| Prepaid insurance .............. | | 600 |
| Total Current Assets .......... | | 194,100 |
| | | |
| **Restricted Assets:** | | |
| *Customer deposits:* | | |
| Cash .......................... | | 968 |
| Investments .................... | | 10,100 |
| Accrued interest receivable ....... | | 200 |
| | | 11,268 |
| *Debt service:* | | |
| Cash .......................... | | 15,000 |
| *Principal and interest reserve:* | | |
| Cash .......................... | | 1,300 |
| Investments .................... | | 9,020 |
| Accrued interest receivable ....... | | 130 |
| | | 10,450 |
| *Contingencies:* | | |
| Cash .......................... | | 10,000 |
| Total Restricted Assets ......... | | 46,718 |
| | | |
| **Property, Plant, and Equipment:** | | |
| Land .......................... | | 50,000 |
| Buildings (less accumulated | | |
| depreciation of $5,000) ........ | | 85,000 |
| Improvements other than buildings | | |
| (less accumulated depreciation of | | |
| $15,000) .................... | | 692,000 |
| Machinery and Equipment (less | | |
| accumulated depreciation of | | |
| $16,000) .................... | | 144,500 |
| Total Property, Plant, and | | |
| Equipment .............. | | 971,500 |
| Total Assets ........... | | $1,212,318 |

| *Liabilities and Fund Equity* | | |
|---|---:|---:|
| **Current Liabilities (Payable from Current Assets):** | | |
| Vouchers payable .............. | $ | 49,500 |
| Due to Internal Service Fund ...... | | 12,800 |
| Accrued salaries and wages payable | | 6,000 |
| Accrued interest payable ......... | | 2,000 |
| Accrued utilities payable ......... | | 7,500 |
| Total Current Liabilities (Payable | | |
| from Current Assets) ........ | | 77,800 |
| **Liabilities Payable from Restricted Assets:** | | |
| *Customer deposits:* | | |
| Deposits payable ................ | | 10,973 |
| Interest payable ................ | | 145 |
| | | 11,118 |
| *Debt service:* | | |
| Accrued bond interest payable ..... | | 6,000 |
| *Contingencies:* | | |
| Vouchers payable .............. | | 7,000 |
| Total Liabilities Payable from | | |
| Restricted Assets ............. | | 24,118 |
| **Long-Term Liabilities:** | | |
| Bonds payable .................. | | 650,000 |
| Unamortized premium on bonds ... | | 1,700 |
| Total Long-Term Liabilities ...... | | 651,700 |
| Total Liabilities .............. | | 753,618 |
| **Fund Equity:** | | |
| **Retained Earnings:** | | |
| Reserved: | | |
| Reserve for earnings on customer | | |
| deposits .................... | | 150 |
| Reserve for bond debt service ... | | 9,000 |
| Reserve for bond principal and | | |
| interest guarantee ........... | | 10,450 |
| Reserve for contingencies ....... | | 3,000 |
| Total reserved .............. | | 22,600 |
| Unreserved ................. | | 6,100 |
| Total Retained Earnings ...... | | 28,700 |
| **Contributed Capital:** | | |
| Contributed capital—governmental | | |
| unit ........................ | | 400,000 |
| Contributions from subdividers .... | | 30,000 |
| Total Contributed Capital ...... | | 430,000 |
| Total Fund Equity ........... | | 458,700 |
| Total Liabilities and Fund | | |
| Equity .................. | | $1,212,318 |

permits ready "across the balance sheet" comparisons and analyses. The use of distinctively titled restricted asset and liability accounts and related retained earnings reserves distinguishes the restricted subfund assets, liabilities, and equity from unrestricted amounts. Use of these subfunds does not impact revenues, expenses, net income, or total fund equity. Rather, it simply communicates the restrictions on the use of a portion of the Enterprise Fund's net assets.

The Contributed Capital—Governmental Unit account shows the amount of capital invested in the utility by the governmental unit. As indicated earlier, this account is credited for the amount expended by the governmental unit in acquiring the utility. Similarly, the account is credited for subsequent capital contributions made by the governmental unit to the utility, such as those to increase its capital. The GASB position is that the Contributed Capital—Governmental Unit account should not be reduced by amounts routinely transferred each year from the Enterprise Fund to the General Fund, such as routine transfers of all or a portion of utility profits to the General Fund each year. Such transfers typically are classified as operating transfers that reduce net income and retained earnings rather than disinvestments of capital. Only when the Retained Earnings account has been reduced to zero do such routine transfers reduce the governmental unit's capital contribution. However, major disinvestments of capital are residual equity transfers that reduce the Contributed Capital—Governmental Unit account balance.

**Statement of Revenues, Expenses, and Changes in Fund Equity**    A statement of revenues, expenses, and changes in fund equity (or in retained earnings) should be prepared annually. The statement should also be prepared on an interim basis as necessary. The statement for the Electric Fund shown in Figure 12–3 is prepared in the format specified in the GASB *Codification.* Operating revenues and expenses and nonoperating revenues and expenses are distinguished in the statement. In this example operating revenues are presented in detail because there are relatively few revenue sources. However, operating expenses are reported in summary form and supported by a Detailed Statement of Operating Expenses (Figure 12–4). Had there been many significant types of operating revenues, these too might have been reported in summary and supported by a detailed schedule. If the Electric (Enterprise) Fund had extraordinary gains (losses) or a cumulative effect of a change in accounting principles, they would be reported as the last item(s) before net income. In other words, the placement of these items is the same as in a business income statement.

Note that the statement explains changes in total fund equity. The authors prefer this approach because all changes in fund equity are presented, including all Enterprise Fund residual equity transfers in or out. Contributed capital changes, such as those resulting from capital grants and residual equity transfers, are not reported in the statement if it explains only changes in retained earnings (either total or unreserved retained earnings). Thus, the interfund residual equity transfers in and out reported in the government's financial statements will not balance when there are Enterprise Fund residual equity transfers if the statement explains only changes in retained earnings. Also, the statement will not be comprehensive in nature. The retained earnings approaches are permitted by the GASB, however.

FIGURE 12–3 **Operating Statement**

A Governmental Unit
Electric (Enterprise) Fund
**Statement of Revenues, Expenses, and Changes in Fund Equity**
For the Year Ended December 31, 19X2

**Operating Revenues:**

| | |
|---|---:|
| Residential sales........................................... | $155,200 |
| Commercial sales........................................... | 91,300 |
| Industrial sales............................................ | 62,500 |
| Public street lighting ...................................... | 12,000 |
|    Total Operating Revenues ............................... | 321,000 |

**Operating Expenses:**

| | |
|---|---:|
| Production ................................................ | 144,400 |
| Distribution .............................................. | 49,200 |
| Accounting and collection.................................. | 15,300 |
| Sales promotion ........................................... | 1,000 |
| Administrative and general................................. | 38,500 |
|    Total Operating Expenses............................... | 248,400 |

| | |
|---|---:|
| **Operating Income** ......................................... | 72,600 |

**Nonoperating Revenues (Expenses):**

| | |
|---|---:|
| Equipment rental........................................... | 7,000 |
| Investment income......................................... | 1,950 |
| Interest expense........................................... | (42,850) |
|    Net Nonoperating Revenues (Expenses)..................... | (33,900) |

**Income before Operating Transfers**

| | |
|---|---:|
| Operating transfer to General Fund........................... | (10,000) |

| | |
|---|---:|
| **Net Income**................................................ | 28,700 |
| Fund equity, January 1 ..................................... | 400,000 |
| Contributions from subdividers.............................. | 30,000 |
| Fund Equity, December 31 ................................... | $458,700 |

The principal causes of changes in the Retained Earnings account are, as in commercial accounting, (1) net income or loss, after operating transfers to or from other funds of the governmental unit, (2) increases or decreases in reserved retained earnings accounts (when using the unreserved retained earnings approach), and (3) corrections of prior year errors. When the statement explains changes in retained earnings, contributed capital changes are disclosed by footnote or in a separate statement of changes in contributed capital.

**Statement of Cash Flows**    The third primary statement required for Enterprise Funds is the statement of cash flows. This statement was discussed in Chapter 11. A Statement of Cash Flows is presented in Figure 12–5. For review purposes, note that:

**FIGURE 12–4  Detailed Operating Expenses Statement**

A Governmental Unit
Electric (Enterprise) Fund
**Detailed Statement\* of Operating Expenses**
For the Fiscal Year Ended (Date)

**Production Expenses:**

Electric generating:

| | | |
|---|---:|---:|
| Supervision | $ 8,000 | |
| Station labor | 15,000 | |
| Fuel | 54,000 | |
| Water | 4,000 | |
| Depreciation | 20,000 | |
| Supplies and other | 8,400 | $109,400 |

Maintenance of plant and equipment:

| | | |
|---|---:|---:|
| Supervision | 4,000 | |
| Maintenance of structures and improvements | 8,000 | |
| Maintenance of boiler plant equipment | 10,000 | |
| Maintenance of generating and electric plant equipment .... | 10,000 | |
| Depreciation | 1,000 | 33,000 |
| Power purchased | | 2,000 |
| Total production expenses | | 144,400 |

**Distribution Expenses:**

| | | |
|---|---:|---:|
| Supervision | 2,500 | |
| Services on consumers' premises | 4,500 | |
| Street lighting and signal system | 4,000 | |
| Overhead system | 18,200 | |
| Depreciation | 13,000 | |
| Maintenance and servicing of mobile equipment | 3,000 | |
| Utility storeroom expenses | 4,000 | |
| Total distribution expenses | | 49,200 |

**Accounting and Collection Expenses:**

| | | |
|---|---:|---:|
| Customers' contracts and orders | 2,500 | |
| Meter reading | 3,500 | |
| Collecting offices | 1,000 | |
| Delinquent accounts—collection expense | 2,000 | |
| Customers' billing and accounting | 4,000 | |
| Provision for doubtful accounts | 1,800 | |
| Depreciation | 500 | |
| Total accounting and collection expenses | | 15,300 |

| | | |
|---|---:|---:|
| **Sales Promotion Expenses** | | 1,000 |

**Administrative and General Expenses:**

| | | |
|---|---:|---:|
| Salaries of executives | 8,000 | |
| Other general office salaries | 3,500 | |
| General office supplies and expenses | 400 | |
| Insurance | 2,000 | |
| Employees' welfare expenses | 1,500 | |
| Pension fund contributions | 2,800 | |
| Utilities | 18,000 | |
| Depreciation | 1,500 | |
| Miscellaneous general expenses | 800 | |
| Total administrative and general expenses | | 38,500 |
| Total operating expenses | | $248,400 |

\*The detailed amounts in this statement cannot be derived from the example in the chapter. They have been hypothesized for illustrative purposes only. Note: This statement would be prepared in comparative form when data for the prior year are available.

FIGURE 12–5 **Statement of Cash Flows**

A Governmental Unit
Electric (Enterprise) Fund
**Statement of Cash Flows**
For the Year Ended December 31, 19X2

**Cash Flows from Operating Activities:**

| | |
|---|---:|
| Cash received from customers | $301,000 |
| Cash paid to suppliers of goods and services | (41,500) |
| Cash paid to employees | (127,200) |
| Cash paid for utilities | (10,500) |
| Cash deposits refunded to customers | (5) |
| Net cash provided by operating activities | 121,795 |

**Cash Flows from Noncapital Financing Activities:**

| | |
|---|---:|
| Cash paid for operating transfers | (10,000) |
| Cash paid for interest on customer deposits | (3) |
| Net cash flows from noncapital financing activities | (10,003) |

**Cash Flows from Capital and Related Financing Activities:**

| | |
|---|---:|
| Cash received from issuing bonds | 202,000 |
| Cash paid for retirement of bonds | (50,000) |
| Cash paid for interest | (35,000) |
| Cash paid for property, plant, and equipment | (30,000) |
| Cash paid for construction of fixed assets | (197,000) |
| Net cash flows from capital and related financing activities | (110,000) |

**Cash Flows from Investing Activities:**

| | |
|---|---:|
| Cash paid for investments | (19,000) |
| Cash received from interest | 1,300 |
| Net cash flows from investing activities | (17,700) |

| | |
|---|---:|
| **Net increase (decrease) in cash** | (15,908) |
| Cash at beginning of year* | 120,000 |
| Cash at end of year* | $104,092 |

**Reconciliation of operating income to net cash flows**
 **from operating activities:**

| | |
|---|---:|
| Operating income | $ 72,600 |
| Adjustments to reconcile operating income to cash flows<br> from operating activities: | |
| Depreciation | 36,000 |
| Increase in vouchers payable (associated with operating activities) | 26,000 |
| Increase in interfund payable | 12,800 |
| Increase in salaries and wages payable | 6,000 |
| Increase in utilities payable | 7,500 |
| Increase in customer deposits payable | 10,973 |
| Increase in accounts receivable (adjusted for noncash decrease from offset<br> against customer deposits interest payable—transaction 20) | (29,478) |
| Increase in inventories | (20,000) |
| Increase in prepaid insurance | (600) |
| Net adjustments | 49,195 |
| Net cash provided by operating activities | $121,795 |

**Noncash Financing and Investing Activities:**

| | |
|---|---:|
| Subdivision electricity system donation (Transaction 14) | $ 30,000 |

*Includes both unrestricted and restricted cash.

- The statement has four classifications of cash flows.

- Cash paid for interest is *not* an operating activity as it is in business cash flow statements. Cash paid for interest associated with long-term debt issued clearly and specifically for the purpose of capital asset acquisition, construction, or improvement is reported as cash flows from capital and related financing activities. Cash paid for interest on all other indebtedness is classified as cash flows from noncapital financing activities.

- Cash paid for capital asset acquisition, construction, or improvement and cash received from selling capital assets are classified as capital and related financing activities, not as investing activities.

- As is typical in a government cash flow statement, the only activities resulting in investing cash flows are buying and selling investments and receipt of earnings on investments.

- Cash includes not only unrestricted cash balances but also the fund's restricted cash balances.

## COMBINING ENTERPRISE FUND FINANCIAL STATEMENTS

If a government has more than one Enterprise Fund, combining Enterprise Fund financial statements are required in its Comprehensive Annual Financial Report. Individual fund statements may also be presented if additional detail, individual fund comparative data, or other additional information is deemed appropriate.

The total columns of the combining statements are included in the appropriate combined financial statements. Too, segment information on individual Enterprise Funds is typically required in the notes to the combined statements, as discussed in Chapter 13.

The combining Enterprise Fund financial statements in a recent city of Des Moines, Iowa, annual financial report were preceded by these narrative explanations:

The funds included in this fund type and their purposes are as follows:

Airport—to account for the operation and maintenance of the city's airport facility, including airport parking.

Convention Center—to account for the construction, operation, and maintenance of the city's convention center facility.

Golf Courses—to account for the operation and maintenance of the city's three golf courses—Waveland, Grandview, and A. H. Blank.

Parking Facilities System—to account for the operation and maintenance of all the city's on- and off-street public parking facilities, except for those facilities operated by the airport.

Sewer System—to account for the operation and maintenance of the city's sanitary sewer system.

Solid Waste System—to account for the operation and maintenance of the city's solid waste collection system.

Veterans' Memorial Auditorium—to account for the operation and maintenance of Veterans' Memorial Auditorium.

**FIGURE 12–6  Combining Balance Sheet**

City of Des Moines, Iowa
**All Enterprise Funds**
**Combining Balance Sheet**
June 30, 19X1

| ASSETS | Airport | Convention Center | Golf Courses |
|---|---|---|---|
| **Current Assets:** | | | |
| Cash and pooled cash investments .................. | $ 2,398,174 | $    4,106 | $  147,715 |
| Accounts receivable ............................. | 487,806 | 32,038 | 37,507 |
| Due from other governmental units ............... | 302,895 | — | — |
| Inventory, at cost .................................... | 22,725 | — | — |
| Total Current Assets ............................ | 3,211,600 | 36,144 | 185,222 |
| **Restricted Assets:** | | | |
| Cash and pooled cash investments .................. | 37,940 | 52,539 | 608,156 |
| Investments ....................................... | — | — | — |
| Accrued interest receivable ...................... | — | — | — |
| Total Restricted Assets .......................... | 37,940 | 52,539 | 608,156 |
| Land | 6,835,164 | — | 106,829 |
| Buildings | 12,294,058 | 13,727,650 | 213,114 |
| Improvements other than buildings | 59,485,132 | 516,903 | 1,682,667 |
| Machinery and equipment | 4,271,231 | 815,341 | 572,723 |
| Accumulated depreciation | (38,145,625) | (1,960,316) | (460,001) |
| Construction in progress | 731,746 | — | 819,811 |
| Investment in joint venture | — | — | — |
| Due from other governmental units | — | — | — |
| **Total Assets** | $48,721,246 | $13,188,261 | $3,728,521 |
| **LIABILITIES AND FUND EQUITY** | | | |
| **Current Liabilities:** | | | |
| Warrants payable ............................. | $     64,308 | $    4,106 | $    1,988 |
| Accrued wages payable ......................... | 37,764 | 9,054 | 15,774 |
| Accrued employee benefits ...................... | 28,230 | 6,125 | 11,860 |
| Accounts payable .............................. | 95,936 | 30,943 | 6,599 |
| Accrued interest payable ...................... | 66,198 | — | — |
| Due to other funds ............................ | 29,737 | 301 | 8,459 |
| Due to other governmental units .................. | — | — | — |
| Advance from other funds ....................... | — | — | 16,115 |
| Notes payable ................................ | 110,598 | — | — |
| Revenue bonds payable .......................... | — | — | — |
| General obligation bonds payable .................... | 735,000 | — | — |
| Total Current Liabilities ......................... | 1,167,771 | 50,529 | 60,795 |
| **Liabilities Payable from Restricted Assets:** | | | |
| Warrants payable .............................. | 6,677 | — | 1,707 |
| Construction contracts .......................... | 31,263 | — | 283,060 |
| Revenue bonds payable .......................... | — | — | 75,995 |
| Accrued interest ............................... | — | — | 8,856 |
| Total Liabilities Payable from Restricted Assets ....... | 37,940 | — | 369,618 |
| **Long-Term Liabilities:** | | | |
| Accrued employee benefits ...................... | 207,018 | 44,919 | 86,971 |
| Revenue bonds payable .......................... | — | — | 1,319,115 |
| General obligation bonds payable .................. | 9,969,450 | — | — |
| Advance from other funds ....................... | — | — | 463,042 |
| Deferred revenue ............................. | — | — | — |
| Total Liabilities ................................. | 11,382,179 | 95,448 | 2,299,541 |
| **Fund Equity:** | | | |
| Contributed capital ............................ | 45,237,247 | 14,792,155 | 540,358 |
| Retained earnings (deficit): | | | |
| Reserved for: | | | |
| Revenue bond retirement ...................... | — | — | 103,434 |
| Unreserved .................................... | (7,898,180) | (1,699,342) | 785,188 |
| Total Fund Equity ............................... | 37,339,067 | 13,092,813 | 1,428,980 |
| **Total Liabilities and Fund Equity** .................. | $48,721,246 | $13,188,261 | $3,728,521 |

The notes to the financial statements are an integral part of this statement.

*Source:* Adapted from a recent comprehensive annual financial report of the city of Des Moines, Iowa.

The city of Des Moines combining Enterprise Fund financial statements are reproduced in part (Airport, Convention Center, and Golf Courses columns) as follows:

- Figure 12–6, Combining Balance Sheet
- Figure 12–7, Combining Statement of Revenues, Expenses, and Changes in Fund Equity
- Figure 12–8, Combining Statement of Cash Flows

**FIGURE 12–7  Combining Statement of Revenues, Expenses, and Changes in Fund Equity**

City of Des Moines, Iowa

**All Enterprise Funds**
**Combining Statement of Revenues,**
**Expenses, and Changes in Fund Equity**
For the Fiscal Year Ended June 30, 19X1

|  | Airport | Convention Center | Golf Courses |
|---|---|---|---|
| **Operating Revenues:** | | | |
| Charges for services | $ 7,514,212 | $ 633,243 | $ 926,061 |
| **Operating Expenses:** | | | |
| Personal services | 1,895,144 | 586,434 | 381,276 |
| Contractual services | 2,479,168 | 478,531 | 228,831 |
| Supplies | 414,201 | 28,294 | 121,362 |
| Depreciation | 2,914,632 | 335,734 | 86,303 |
| Total Operating Expenses | 7,703,145 | 1,428,993 | 817,772 |
| Operating Income (Loss) | (188,933) | (795,750) | 108,289 |
| **Nonoperating Revenues (Expenses):** | | | |
| Loss on joint venture | — | — | — |
| Interest revenue | 269,805 | — | 519 |
| Interest expense and fiscal charges | (906,821) | — | (70,725) |
| Gain on sale of fixed assets | — | — | — |
| Total Nonoperating Revenues (Expenses) | (637,016) | — | (70,206) |
| Income (Loss) before Operating Transfers | (825,949) | (795,750) | 38,083 |
| Operating transfers in | — | 484,469 | — |
| Operating transfers out | — | — | — |
| Net Income (Loss) | (825,949) | (311,281) | 38,083 |
| Retained earnings (deficit) at beginning of year (as restated) | (7,072,231) | (1,388,061) | 850,539 |
| Retained earnings (deficit) at end of year | (7,898,180) | (1,699,342) | 888,622 |
| Contributed capital at beginning of year | 44,820,578 | 14,792,155 | 471,431 |
| Contributions from other governmental units | 217,140 | — | 10,887 |
| Contributions from other sources | 199,529 | — | 58,040 |
| Contributed capital at end of year | 45,237,247 | 14,792,155 | 540,358 |
| Total Fund Equity | $37,339,067 | $13,092,813 | $1,428,980 |

The notes to the financial statements are an integral part of this statement.

*Source:* Adapted from a recent comprehensive annual financial report of the city of Des Moines, Iowa.

# FIGURE 12–8 Combining Statement of Cash Flows

**City of Des Moines, Iowa**
**All Enterprise Funds**
**Combining Statement of Cash Flows**
For the Fiscal Year Ended June 30, 19X1

| | Airport | Convention Center | Golf Courses |
|---|---|---|---|
| **Cash Flows from Operating Activities:** | | | |
| Cash received from customers | $7,619,745 | $ 630,082 | $ 889,162 |
| Cash paid to suppliers | (3,177,178) | (501,953) | (570,672) |
| Cash paid to employees | (1,878,620) | (581,021) | (360,292) |
| Net cash provided (used) by operating activities | 2,563,947 | (452,892) | (41,802) |
| **Cash Flows from Noncapital Financing Activities:** | | | |
| Operating transfers | — | 484,469 | — |
| Net cash provided (used) by noncapital financing activities | — | 484,469 | — |
| **Cash Flows from Capital and Related Financing Activities:** | | | |
| Contributed capital | 611,465 | — | 68,927 |
| Advance from other funds | — | — | (13,821) |
| Interest paid | (899,374) | — | (61,869) |
| Notes payable (issued) | 110,598 | — | — |
| Acquisition and construction of capital assets | (3,833,533) | (23,928) | (761,311) |
| Principal paid on revenue bond maturities | — | — | (29,890) |
| Proceeds from sale of revenue bonds | — | — | 1,425,000 |
| Proceeds from other city revenue bonds | — | — | — |
| Principal paid on general obligation bond maturities | (693,000) | — | — |
| Proceeds from sale of general obligation bonds | 2,004,250 | — | — |
| Proceeds from other city general obligation bonds | — | — | — |
| Net cash provided (used) by capital and related financing activities | (2,699,594) | (23,928) | 627,036 |
| **Cash Flows from Investing Activities:** | | | |
| Interest on investments | 269,805 | — | 519 |
| Investment in joint venture | — | — | — |
| Restricted asset investment maturities/sales | — | — | — |
| Restricted asset investment purchases | — | — | — |
| Net cash provided (used) by investing activities | 269,805 | — | 519 |
| Net change in cash and cash equivalents | 134,158 | 7,649 | 585,753 |
| Cash and cash equivalents, beginning of year | 2,301,956 | 48,996 | 170,118 |
| Cash and cash equivalents, end of year | $2,436,114 | $ 56,645 | $ 755,871 |
| **Reconciliation of Operating Income (Loss) to Net Cash Provided (Used) by Operating Activities:** | | | |
| Operating income (loss) | (188,933) | (795,750) | 108,289 |
| Adjustments to reconcile operating income (loss) to net cash provided (used) by operating activities: | | | |
| Depreciation | 2,914,632 | 335,734 | 86,303 |
| Change in assets and liabilities: | | | |
| Change in accounts receivable | 105,532 | (3,161) | (36,899) |
| Change in inventory | (11,153) | — | (1,747) |
| Change in warrants payable | 4,061 | (569) | (1,747) |
| Change in wages payable | 4,035 | (600) | 6,255 |
| Change in accrued employee benefits | 10,409 | 2,523 | 5,131 |
| Change in accounts payable | (296,116) | 5,599 | 2,944 |
| Change in long-term benefits payable | 2,080 | 3,490 | 9,598 |
| Change in amount owed other funds | 19,400 | (158) | (221,676) |
| Change in deferred revenue | — | — | — |
| Total adjustments | 2,752,880 | 342,858 | (150,091) |
| Net cash provided (used) by operating activities | $2,563,947 | $(452,892) | $ (41,802) |

The notes to the financial statements are an integral part of this statement.

*Source:* Adapted from a recent comprehensive annual financial report of the city of Des Moines, Iowa.

# INTERGOVERNMENTAL GRANT REPORTING

The GASB *Codification* provides general guidelines for reporting for all proprietary funds with respect to grants, entitlements, and shared revenues. Restricted intergovernmental grants are classified as either capital grants or operating grants. Capital grants are intergovernmental grants that must be used solely for construction, acquisition, or improvement of capital assets. All other intergovernmental grants are operating grants.

The usual criteria for recognizing grants—fulfilling all significant grant conditions, including incurring qualifying costs—apply to the timing of recognition of both operating and capital grants. If grant resources are received before the recognition criteria are met, deferred revenues or deferred capital grants (i.e., liabilities) must be reported in the proprietary fund. When the recognition criteria are met, operating grants are reported as nonoperating revenues, and capital grants are reported as increases in contributed capital. An appropriately descriptive caption should be used in the latter case, such as "Contributed Capital—Capital Grants."[4] Recognize, therefore, that capital grants do not affect revenues, net income, or retained earnings.

All fixed assets except land, including those acquired via intergovernmental capital grants, are subject to depreciation. Likewise, depreciation of all depreciable assets is a part of operating expenses. However, the GASB permits—but does not require[5]—the depreciation of assets acquired with intergovernmental capital grant resources to be closed to the related Contributed Capital account, thus effectively reclassifying a portion of contributed capital as retained earnings. When the assets are fully depreciated, the related contributed capital would be eliminated.

This reclassification process should not be used for similarly acquired nondepreciable fixed assets, nor for depreciable fixed assets acquired with other resources. Indeed, because the using up of depreciable assets has no bearing on the fact of the contribution, there seems to be no theoretical justification for the process. But many Enterprise Funds were heavily capital grant financed and had both large contributed capital balances and large retained earnings deficits. Officials with such funds argued that (1) they would not have acquired the depreciable fixed assets, and thereby incurred the related depreciation expenses, if such capital grants had not been available, and (2) they would not replace the fixed assets unless additional capital grants were available. The special capital grant accounting procedures for proprietary funds are permitted because of these arguments. The example in Figure 12–9 compares proprietary fund accounting for an operating grant (assuming resources were used to buy equipment), a capital grant for which the reclassification alternative is not used, and a capital grant for which the reclassification alternative is used.

To illustrate the effects of the alternative process on the financial statements, assume the following for a proprietary fund of a government:

| | |
|---|---|
| Gross amount of contributed capital from capital grants as of the beginning of the year | $ 810,000 |
| Contributed capital from governmental unit at beginning of the year | 1,085,000 |
| Retained earnings, beginning of year | 200,000 |
| Operating revenues | 4,000,000 |
| Operating expenses | 3,159,500 |
| (Includes $500,000 of depreciation expense, of which $175,000 is on fixed assets acquired with restricted capital grants) | |

---

[4] GASB *Codification*, sec. G60.114.

[5] Ibid., sec. G60.116.

FIGURE 12–9 **Proprietary Fund Accounting: Operating Grants and Capital Grants**

| Transaction (in thousands) | Operating Grant | | Capital Grant for Equipment (Depreciation on grant assets closed to Retained Earnings) | | Capital Grant for Equipment (Depreciation on grant assets closed to Contributed Capital) | |
|---|---|---|---|---|---|---|
| Received $1,000 intergovernmental grant | Cash<br>   Deferred Revenue | 1,000<br>1,000 | Cash<br>   Deferred Capital Grant | 1,000<br>1,000 | Cash<br>   Deferred Capital Grant | 1,000<br>1,000 |
| Purchased $1,000 of equipment with grant resources | Equipment<br>   Cash<br>Deferred Revenues<br>   Nonoperating Revenues | 1,000<br>1,000<br>1,000<br>1,000 | Equipment<br>   Cash<br>Deferred Capital Grant<br>   Contributed Capital—<br>     Capital Grants | 1,000<br>1,000<br>1,000<br><br>1,000 | Equipment<br>   Cash<br>Deferred Capital Grant<br>   Contributed Capital—<br>     Capital Grants | 1,000<br>1,000<br>1,000<br><br>1,000 |
| Depreciation on all fixed assets of the fund ($500) included depreciation of $175 on fixed assets purchased with grant resources | Depreciation Expense<br>   Accumulated Depreciation | 500<br>500 | Depreciation Expense<br>   Accumulated Depreciation | 500<br>500 | Depreciation Expense<br>   Accumulated Depreciation | 500<br>500 |
| Close the accounts. | Close all revenues and expenses, including depreciation of $500 to retained earnings. | | Close all revenues and expenses, including depreciation of $500 to retained earnings. Recognize that the amount of income closed to retained earnings will be $1,000 less than if the grant were an operating grant because capital grants are not recognized as revenues or as retained earnings increases. | | Initially, close all revenues and expenses, including depreciation of $500 to retained earnings. Recognize that the amount of income closed to retained earnings will be $1,000 less than if the grant were an operating grant because capital grants are not recognized as revenues or as retained earnings increases. To effect the charging of depreciation on intergovernmental capital grant financed fixed assets against contributed capital, make the following reclassification entry:<br><br>Contributed Capital—<br>   Capital Grants   175<br>   Retained Earnings      175 | |

The proprietary fund operating statement is presented in Figure 12–10 and the equity section of its balance sheet is presented in Figure 12–11.

Note in Figure 12–10 that depreciation on all of a proprietary fund's fixed assets is deducted in arriving at net income. However, the depreciation on fixed assets acquired with restricted capital grants is added back to net income to arrive at the change in retained earnings. Under the optional reclassification treatment, this portion of depreciation expense reduces contributed capital—capital grants, not retained earnings. Also, note in Figure 12–11 that the contributed capital—capital grants is reported net of accumulated depreciation on the assets acquired with the capital grants when the optional treatment of depreciation is used.

FIGURE 12–10 **Proprietary Fund Operating Statement—with Optional Treatment of Depreciation on Assets Acquired with Intergovernmental Capital Grants**

A Governmental Unit

A Proprietary Fund

**Statement of Revenues, Expenses, and Changes in Retained Earnings**

For the Fiscal Year Ended (Date)

| | |
|---|---:|
| **Operating Revenues:** | |
| (Detailed) . . . . . . . . . . . . . . . . . . . . . . . . . . . . . . . . . . . . . . . . . . . . . . . . . . . . . . . | $ 4,000,000 |
| **Operating Expenses:** | |
| (Detailed—includes depreciation on all depreciable fixed assets) . . . . . . . . . . | (3,159,500) |
| Operating Income (Loss) . . . . . . . . . . . . . . . . . . . . . . . . . . . . . . . . . . . . . . . | 840,500 |
| **Nonoperating Revenues (Expenses):** | |
| (Detailed—nonoperating revenues include intergovernmental grants, entitlements, and shared revenues received for operations and/or such resources that may be used for either operations or capital outlay at the discretion of the recipient) . . . . . . . . . . . . . . . . . . . . . . . . . . . . . . . . . . . | — |
| Income (Loss) before Operating Transfers . . . . . . . . . . . . . . . . . . . . . . . . | 840,500 |
| **Operating Transfers:** | |
| (Detailed) . . . . . . . . . . . . . . . . . . . . . . . . . . . . . . . . . . . . . . . . . . . . . . . . . . . . | — |
| Net Income (Loss) . . . . . . . . . . . . . . . . . . . . . . . . . . . . . . . . . . . . . . . . . . . . | 840,500 |
| Add depreciation on fixed assets acquired by intergovernmental grants, entitlements, and shared revenues externally restricted for capital acquisitions and construction that reduces contributed capital [Optional] . | 175,000 |
| Increase (Decrease) in Retained Earnings . . . . . . . . . . . . . . . . . . . . . . . . . | 1,015,500 |
| **Retained Earnings—Beginning of Period** . . . . . . . . . . . . . . . . . . . . . . . . . . . | 200,000 |
| **Retained Earnings—End of Period** . . . . . . . . . . . . . . . . . . . . . . . . . . . . . . . . | $ 1,215,500 |

FIGURE 12–11

**PROPRIETARY FUND BALANCE SHEET EQUITY SECTION—WITH OPTIONAL TREATMENT OF DEPRECIATION ON ASSETS ACQUIRED WITH INTERGOVERNMENTAL CAPITAL GRANTS**

| | | | |
|---|---:|---:|---:|
| **Fund Equity:** | | | |
| Contributed capital: | | | |
| Intergovernmental capital grants . . . . . . . . | $1,810,000 | | |
| Less: amortization [Optional] . . . . . . . . . . | 175,000 | $1,635,000 | |
| Governmental unit . . . . . . . . . . . . . . . . . . . . | | 1,085,000 | $2,720,000 |
| Retained earnings . . . . . . . . . . . . . . . . . . . . . . . | | | 1,215,500 |
| Total Fund Equity . . . . . . . . . . . . . . . . . . | | | $3,935,500 |

# REFUNDINGS OF PROPRIETARY FUND LONG-TERM DEBT

Refundings of general long-term debt were discussed and illustrated in Chapter 8, "Debt Service Funds." But refundings of proprietary fund long-term debt are reported differently than those of either general government or business entities. There is one key difference from reporting refunding transactions of businesses. Businesses report the difference between the carrying amount of debt retired prior to its maturity date and the amount paid to retire it as an extraordinary gain or loss in the period that the debt is retired—whether or not a refunding is involved. This extraordinary gain or loss treatment also is required for government proprietary activities when refunding issues are not the source of resources used to retire or defease the old debt.

When refunding proceeds are used to retire or defease proprietary fund debt prior to its maturity date, however, the difference is treated as an adjustment of future interest expense rather than as a gain or a loss. The difference must be amortized as a component of interest expense over the shorter of the remaining term of the old debt or the term of the refunding issue. The amortization method must be systematic and rational—the effective interest method, the straight-line method, and other systematic and rational methods are all permitted. The unamortized deferred amount is added to or deducted from the carrying value of the refunding debt to determine the carrying value to report in the balance sheet. Refunding bond issue costs should be amortized in a systematic manner over the life of the refunding bonds.

To illustrate these requirements, assume that a county Airport Enterprise Fund refunded a $1,935,000 bond issue that had been outstanding for several years on its call date, December 31, 19X4. The call premium was $50,000, and the scheduled maturity of the old bonds was in five years—December 31, 19X9. The unamortized bond discount on the old debt at the call date was $35,000 and the unamortized bond issue costs on the old debt were $1,582. The county issued $2,000,000 of 4%, ten-year Airport Refunding Bonds on December 31, 19X4 to finance retirement of the old bonds. The refunding bonds were issued at par and $15,000 of bond issue costs were incurred and paid from the bond proceeds. The entries to record these transactions on December 31, 19X4, which is also the fiscal year end, are:

| | | |
|---|---|---|
| Cash .............................................. | $1,985,000 | |
| Unamortized Refunding Bond Issue Costs (New bonds) ........ | 15,000 | |
|    Refunding Bonds Payable (New bonds) .................... | | $2,000,000 |
| To record issuance of refunding bonds at par, net of issue costs. | | |

| | | |
|---|---|---|
| Bonds Payable ........................................ | $1,935,000 | |
| Deferred Interest Expense Adjustment—Refunding Bonds ...... | 86,582 | |
|    Unamortized Discount on Bonds Payable (Old bonds) ........ | | $   35,000 |
|    Unamortized Bond Issue Cost (Old bonds) ................ | | 1,582 |
|    Cash .............................................. | | 1,985,000 |
| To record retirement of refunded bonds payable. | | |

No gain or loss from the retirement of debt is reported in the Airport Enterprise Fund Statement of Revenues, Expenses, and Changes in Fund Equity for 19X4. The liability for the refunding bonds payable would be reported net of the unamortized Deferred Interest Expense Adjustment—Refunding Bonds, at $1,913,418 ($2,000,000 less $86,582).

In this example the term of the refunding bonds is longer than the remaining life of the old bonds. Therefore, the amortization period for the deferred amount on the refunding is the remaining term of the old bonds, five years. If the county uses the straight-line method to amortize the deferred amount on refunding, it will simply add one-fifth of the original amount of the deferred interest expense adjustment to interest expense for each of the next five years, 19X5 through 19X9. Therefore, the interest expense reported on the refunding bonds each of those years would be $97,316 (rounded). This is the cash interest of $80,000 ($2,000,000 × .04 × 1) plus the amortization of the deferred interest expense adjustment, $17,316 (rounded). The interest expense and deferred interest expense adjustment amortization would be recorded as follows:

| | | |
|---|---|---|
| Interest Expense . . . . . . . . . . . . . . . . . . . . . . . . . . . . . . . . . . . . . . . . . . | $80,000 | |
|     Cash . . . . . . . . . . . . . . . . . . . . . . . . . . . . . . . . . . . . . . . . . . . . . . . | | $80,000 |

To record payment of interest on refunding bonds.

| | | |
|---|---|---|
| Interest Expense . . . . . . . . . . . . . . . . . . . . . . . . . . . . . . . . . . . . . . . . . . | $17,316 | |
|     Deferred Interest Expense Adjustment—Refunding Bonds . . . . | | $17,316 |

To record amortization of deferred amount on refunding.

The carrying value of the bonds will be increased each year by the amortization. The amount reported for the refunding bonds payable in the December 31, 19X5 balance sheet, for instance, would be $1,930,734.

    If a refunding results in deferral of a credit balance Interest Expense Adjustment ("gain"), the effect on interest expense and the carrying value of the liability would be opposite from that illustrated previously. The unamortized deferred amount would increase the carrying value reported for the refunding bonds payable in the balance sheet. Amortization of the deferred amount would reduce the interest expense that would otherwise be reported.

    Again, the refunding bond issuance costs would be amortized over the life of the refunding (new) bond issue rather than over the remaining (shorter) life of the refunded (old) issue. In this illustration—assuming straight-line amortization for simplicity—the refunded bond issue costs ($15,000) would be amortized over the ten-year life of the refunding bonds. This entry would be made each year:

| | | |
|---|---|---|
| Interest Expense . . . . . . . . . . . . . . . . . . . . . . . . . . . . . . . . . . . . . . . . . . | $1,500 | |
|     Unamortized Refunding Bond Issue Costs . . . . . . . . . . . . . . . . . | | $1,500 |

To record annual amortization of refunding bond issue costs.

# ADDITIONAL INTERFUND-ACCOUNT GROUP ACCOUNTING ILLUSTRATIONS

At this point all the types of funds and nonfund account groups commonly employed in state and local government accounting have been presented and discussed. Additionally, recording and reporting of representative types of transactions have been illustrated for each individual fund type and account group. Recall that at the end of Chapter 9, accounting for representative transactions that affect more than one governmental fund and/or account group was illustrated to crystallize the reader's understanding of the various interrelationships between and among the governmental funds and account groups. This section extends the Chapter 9 illustration by presenting entries for additional interfund-account group transactions—those that involve at least one proprietary or fiduciary fund.

**1.** Seventy percent of the actuarially required contributions from the General Fund and an Enterprise Fund were paid to the government's Pension Trust Fund. The actuarially required contribution was $800,000 for each fund. The balance of the required contributions has not been scheduled for payment in the near future.

**Pension Trust Fund**

| | | |
|---|---|---|
| Cash . . . . . . . . . . . . . . . . . . . . . . . . . . . . . . . . . . . . . . . . . . . . . . . . . . | $1,120,000 | |
|     Revenues—Employer Contributions . . . . . . . . . . . . . . . . . | | $1,120,000 |

To record receipt of employer fund contributions.

**Enterprise Fund**

| | | |
|---|---|---|
| Expenses—Pensions | $800,000 | |
| Cash | | $560,000 |
| Unfunded Pension Liability | | 240,000 |

To record the pension expense for the year.

**General Fund**

| | | |
|---|---|---|
| Expenditures—Pensions | $560,000 | |
| Cash | | $560,000 |

To record payment of budgeted pension fund contributions.

**General Long-Term Debt Account Group**

| | | |
|---|---|---|
| Amount to Be Provided for Retirement of Pension Liabilities | $240,000 | |
| Unfunded Pension Liabilities | | $240,000 |

To record the long-term portion of the underfunding of the General Fund actuarially required pension contribution.

2. A "payment in lieu of tax" of $900,000 was made from an Enterprise Fund to the General Fund. If the Enterprise Fund had been a private entity, its taxes would have been approximately $600,000.

**General Fund**

| | | |
|---|---|---|
| Cash | $900,000 | |
| Revenues—Payment in Lieu of Taxes | | $600,000 |
| Operating Transfer from Enterprise Fund | | 300,000 |

To record receipt of payment in lieu of taxes and operating transfer from Enterprise Fund.

**Enterprise Fund**

| | | |
|---|---|---|
| Expenses—Payment in Lieu of Taxes | $600,000 | |
| Operating Transfer to General Fund | 300,000 | |
| Cash | | $900,000 |

To record payment in lieu of taxes and operating transfer to General Fund.

3. Water Enterprise Fund billings to other funds for services was as follows:

| | |
|---|---|
| General Fund | $300,000 |
| Special Revenue Fund | 20,000 |
| Internal Service Fund | 50,000 |
| Total | $370,000 |

**Water Enterprise Fund**

| | | |
|---|---|---|
| Due from Other Funds | $370,000 | |
| Revenues—Charges for Services | | $370,000 |

To record interfund billings for services.

**General Fund**

| | | |
|---|---|---|
| Expenditures—Utilities | $300,000 | |
| Due to Enterprise Fund | | $300,000 |

To record billings for water used.

**Special Revenue Fund**

| | | |
|---|---|---|
| Expenditures—Utilities | $ 20,000 | |
| Due to Enterprise Fund | | $ 20,000 |

To record billings for water used.

**Internal Service Fund**

| | | |
|---|---|---|
| Expenses—Utilities | $ 50,000 | |
| Due to Enterprise Fund | | $ 50,000 |

To record billings for water used.

4. A $500,000 two-year advance was made from an Internal Service Fund to a Capital Projects Fund.

**Internal Service Fund**

| | | |
|---|---|---|
| Advance to Capital Projects Fund .................... | $ 500,000 | |
| Cash ......................................... | | $ 500,000 |

To record advance to Capital Projects Fund.

**Capital Projects Fund**

| | | |
|---|---|---|
| Cash ......................................... | $ 500,000 | |
| Advance from Internal Service Fund ................ | | $ 500,000 |

To record advance received from Internal Service Fund.

5. Because of insufficient Enterprise Fund revenues, debt service payments on long-term Enterprise Fund notes payable regularly have been paid from general government resources. The government determines that the Enterprise Fund will never be able to finance the debt service on the notes ($2,000,000) and reclassifies the notes payable to the General Long-Term Debt Account Group to be serviced from general revenues.

**Enterprise Fund**

| | | |
|---|---|---|
| Notes Payable ...................................... | $2,000,000 | |
| Contributed Capital—Governmental Unit ............. | | $2,000,000 |

To record reclassification of Enterprise Fund notes.

**General Long-Term Debt Account Group**

| | | |
|---|---|---|
| Amount to Be Provided for Retirement of Notes ......... | $2,000,000 | |
| Notes Payable .................................... | | $2,000,000 |

To record reclassification of notes payable from Enterprise Fund.

6. $2,500,000 was transferred from the General Fund to provide initial financing for an Internal Service Fund.

**General Fund**

| | | |
|---|---|---|
| Residual Equity to Internal Service Fund .............. | $2,500,000 | |
| Cash ......................................... | | $2,500,000 |

To record residual equity transfer to Internal Service Fund.

**Internal Service Fund**

| | | |
|---|---|---|
| Cash ......................................... | $2,500,000 | |
| Residual Equity Transfer from General Fund .......... | | $2,500,000 |

To record receipt of residual equity transfer from General Fund.

7. Equipment with an original cost of $20,000 (fair market value, $12,000) was transferred from a General Fund department to an Enterprise Fund department halfway through its useful life.

**General Fixed Assets Account Group**

| | | |
|---|---|---|
| Investment in General Fixed Assets ................... | $  20,000 | |
| Equipment ....................................... | | $  20,000 |

To record reclassification of equipment as Enterprise Fund asset.

**Enterprise Fund**

| | | |
|---|---|---|
| Equipment ....................................... | $  20,000 | |
| Accumulated depreciation ......................... | | $  10,000 |
| Contributed Capital—Governmental Unit ............ | | 10,000 |

To record general government contribution of fixed asset.

8. General obligation bonds were issued several years ago to provide the contributed capital of an Enterprise Fund. The bonds have been serviced from general government taxes and

other revenues. However, the Enterprise Fund activity has been sufficiently profitable that the governing body has decided to transfer money as a "dividend" each six months from the Enterprise Fund to the Debt Service Fund to pay the semiannual debt service on the bonds. The first dividend was paid, $70,000.

**Enterprise Fund**

| | | |
|---|---|---|
| Operating Transfer to Debt Service Fund | $70,000 | |
|    Cash | | $70,000 |
| To record payment of dividend transfer to Debt Service Fund. | | |

**Debt Service Fund**

| | | |
|---|---|---|
| Cash | $70,000 | |
|    Operating Transfer from Enterprise Fund | | $70,000 |
| To record receipt of dividend transfer from Enterprise Fund. | | |

9. Assume the same facts as in transaction 8 except that the transfers are viewed as a return of contributed capital from the Enterprise Fund to the general government.

**Enterprise Fund**

| | | |
|---|---|---|
| Residual Equity Transfer to Debt Service Fund | $70,000 | |
|    Cash | | $70,000 |
| To record return of contributed capital transfer to the Debt Service Fund. | | |

**Debt Service Fund**

| | | |
|---|---|---|
| Cash | $70,000 | |
|    Residual Equity Transfer from Enterprise Fund | | $70,000 |
| To record return of contributed capital transfer from Enterprise Fund. | | |

10. Additional claims and judgment liabilities were recognized, of which 10% are considered current liabilities:

| | |
|---|---|
| Enterprise Fund | $ 80,000 |
| General government (70% General Fund, 30% Capital Projects Fund #3) | 100,000 |

**Enterprise Fund**

| | | |
|---|---|---|
| Expenses—Claims and Judgments | $80,000 | |
|    Current Liabilities—Claims and Judgments | | $ 8,000 |
|    Noncurrent Liabilities—Claims and Judgments | | 72,000 |
| To record additional estimated claims and judgments liabilities. | | |

**General Fund**

| | | |
|---|---|---|
| Expenditures (0.1 × 0.7 × $100,000) | $ 7,000 | |
|    Current Liabilities—Claims and Judgments | | $ 7,000 |
| To record additional estimated current liabilities for claims and judgments. | | |

**Capital Projects Fund #3**

| | | |
|---|---|---|
| Expenditures (0.1 × 0.3 × $100,000) | $ 3,000 | |
|    Current Liabilities—Claims and Judgments | | $ 3,000 |
| To record additional estimated current liabilities for claims and judgments. | | |

**General Long-Term Debt Account Group**

| | | |
|---|---|---|
| Amount to Be Provided for Claims and Judgments | $90,000 | |
|    Noncurrent Liabilities—Claims and Judgments | | $90,000 |
| To record additional estimated noncurrent liabilities for general government claims and judgments. | | |

11. A four-year interest-free loan was made from the General Fund to an Enterprise Fund, $160,000.

**General Fund**

| | | |
|---|---|---|
| Advance to Enterprise Fund | $160,000 | |
| Unreserved Fund Balance | 160,000 | |
|    Cash | | $160,000 |
|    Reserve for Interfund Advance | | 160,000 |

To record four-year loan to Enterprise Fund and related
reserve for nonavailable financial asset.

**Enterprise Fund**

| | | |
|---|---|---|
| Cash | $160,000 | |
|    Advance from General Fund | | $160,000 |

To record four-year loan from General Fund.

**12.** During the following year, $40,000 of the loan in transaction 11 was repaid.

**Enterprise Fund**

| | | |
|---|---|---|
| Advance from General Fund | $ 40,000 | |
|    Cash | | $ 40,000 |

To record partial repayment of loan from the General Fund.

**General Fund**

| | | |
|---|---|---|
| Cash | $ 40,000 | |
| Reserve for Interfund Advance | 40,000 | |
|    Advance to Enterprise Fund | | $ 40,000 |
|    Unreserved Fund Balance | | 40,000 |

To record partial repayment of interfund loan and reduction
of related reserves.

**13.** During the next year (after transaction 12), it became apparent that the Enterprise Fund
was undercapitalized, and the governing body ordered the interfund advance from the
General Fund to the Enterprise Fund to be forgiven.

**Enterprise Fund**

| | | |
|---|---|---|
| Advance from General Fund | $120,000 | |
|    Residual Equity Transfer from General Fund | | $120,000 |

To record forgiveness of loan to provide additional
capitalization to this fund.

**General Fund**

| | | |
|---|---|---|
| Residual Equity Transfer to Enterprise Fund | $120,000 | |
| Reserve for Interfund Advance | 120,000 | |
|    Advance to Enterprise Fund | | $120,000 |
|    Unreserved Fund Balance | | 120,000 |

To record forgiveness of loan to provide additional capital
to Enterprise Fund.

**14.** Analyses of the current year Operating Expenses account indicated that $19,000 charged
to the Enterprise Fund should be charged to a Special Revenue Fund ($8,000) and an In-
ternal Service Fund ($11,000).

**Enterprise Fund**

| | | |
|---|---|---|
| Due from Special Revenue Fund | $ 8,000 | |
| Due from Internal Service Fund | 11,000 | |
|    Operating Expenses | | $ 19,000 |

To record reimbursements as indicated.

**Special Revenue Fund**

| | | |
|---|---|---|
| Expenditures | $ 8,000 | |
|    Due to Enterprise Fund | | $ 8,000 |

To record reimbursement due to Enterprise Fund.

**Internal Service Fund**

| | | |
|---|---|---|
| Expenses .......................................... | $11,000 | |
|     Due to Enterprise Fund ............................ | | $11,000 |
| To record reimbursement due to Enterprise Fund. | | |

15. The Inspection Department (financed from the General Fund) charged the Electric Department (financed from an Enterprise Fund) $7,000 for inspecting construction projects in process and $3,000 for routine semiannual inspections of electricity generation equipment.

**General Fund**

| | | |
|---|---|---|
| Due from Enterprise Fund ......................... | $10,000 | |
|     Revenues ...................................... | | $10,000 |
| To record billings for inspection fees. | | |

**Enterprise Fund**

| | | |
|---|---|---|
| Construction in Progress ............................ | $ 7,000 | |
| Operating Expenses ................................ | 3,000 | |
|     Due to General Fund ............................ | | $10,000 |
| To record inspection charges owed to General Fund. | | |

# CONCLUDING COMMENTS

Enterprise Funds are used to account for goods or services that a government provides to the public for a fee that is intended to cover the cost of providing the goods or services, including depreciation. The accounting equation for Enterprise Funds is the same as that for business enterprises, and accounting and reporting for Enterprise Funds parallels, in most respects, that of similar businesses.

Some unique aspects of Enterprise Fund accounting were discussed and illustrated. Most notable were (1) the extensive use of restricted asset accounting, using a "funds within a fund" approach, found in many SLG enterprise activities, (2) accounting for intergovernmental grants, and (3) accounting for refundings of debt. The chapter dealt primarily with principles applicable to a broad spectrum of Enterprise Fund activities as opposed to industry-specific applications such as Enterprise Fund accounting for municipal solid waste landfills, which is covered in GASB *Statement No. 18.*

This chapter concludes our discussion of specific SLG fund types and account groups. The next chapter concerns financial reporting for all the fund types and account groups of a government. The structure, content, and logic of a government's Comprehensive Annual Financial Report are explained in that chapter. Then Chapter 14 addresses certain unique government financial reporting issues in greater detail.

## Questions

**Q 12-1**  How should one determine whether to use an Enterprise Fund to account for a particular activity?

**Q 12-2**  The garbage collection and disposal services of a local government might be accounted for through the General Fund, a Special Revenue Fund, or an Enterprise Fund. Indicate the circumstances in which each of these fund types might be appropriate.

**Q 12-3**  How does one distinguish between an Internal Service Fund and an Enterprise Fund?

**Q 12-4** Contrast and explain the accounting distinction between revenues and capital investments (or disinvestments) in a nonexpendable (proprietary) fund such as an Enterprise Fund with that made in an expendable (governmental) fund.

**Q 12-5** What is the purpose of reserves in Enterprise Fund accounting?

**Q 12-6** An asset costing $10,000 was reclassified from the General Fixed Assets Account Group of a governmental unit to the governmental unit's enterprise. What effect would this reclassification have on the General Fund and the Enterprise Fund, respectively?

**Q 12-7** The city of Cherokee Hills is located adjacent to a freeway leading to a nearby metropolitan area and has grown rapidly from a small village to a city of 75,000. Its population is expected to double every ten years in the foreseeable future. The city has owned and operated the local electricity generation and distribution system since its inception many years ago and has never charged itself for electricity consumption. The newly employed comptroller of Cherokee Hills seeks your advice in this regard. What is your response?

**Q 12-8** It is sometimes claimed that to include depreciation among the expenses and to provide money out of earnings to retire bonds that were used to finance the acquisition of the assets being depreciated is to overcharge the current generation of customers. Through retiring the debt, the customers are paying for the old plant, and through depreciation charges they are paying for a new plant. Is this claim correct? Explain.

**Q 12-9** Virgie Township is retiring Enterprise Fund bonds before their maturity date. How does the difference between the amount paid to retire the debt and the carrying value of the debt affect interest expense reported in future years if Virgie does not borrow to accomplish the early retirement? If Virgie does retire the old debt with new debt proceeds, how is future years' interest expense affected by the difference in the payment and the carrying value?

**Q 12-10** Why is it not necessary to reserve Enterprise Fund retained earnings to the extent that assets are set aside in an equipment replacement intrafund "fund"? (Note particularly that this procedure is contrary to the practice followed in the case of a sinking fund, where an amount corresponding to the addition made to the sinking fund is added to the appropriate reserve account.)

**Q 12-11** Having been told repeatedly during his many years of service that depreciation was charged "in order to provide for the replacement of fixed assets," a member of a government's electric utility (Enterprise Fund) board of directors was visibly upset upon being advised by the controller that it would be necessary for the utility to go deeply in debt "in order to replace some of our fixed assets." "How can it be true," he asks, "that we have operated profitably each year, have an $850,000 Retained Earnings balance and total Accumulated Depreciation account balances of $6,000,000, have never made transfers to the General Fund, and yet have cash and investments totaling only $100,000?"

**Q 12-12** It is sometimes suggested that the amount contributed to a municipally owned enterprise by the municipality or donated to it by others should be amortized to the Retained Earnings as the property thereby acquired is depreciated in the accounts. Proponents of the amortization procedure believe that, in its absence, the Retained Earnings account is understated. Do you agree with the procedure proposed? Why?

**Q 12-13** Why does the GASB recommend the modified accrual basis of accounting for some funds and the accrual basis for others? Is this not inconsistent?

**Q 12-14** A city controller has expressed his desire to convert the city's fund and nonfund account group records, now maintained in separate ledgers, to a system in which all accounts would be maintained within a single general ledger. Is this permissible? Explain.

**Q 12-15** In what funds may Buildings properly appear as an account title? For which types of funds are profit and loss (income determination) accounting procedures employed?

**Q 12-16** Contrast and explain the differences in the accounting for bond premiums or discounts related to general obligation construction bonds and to enterprise revenue bonds.

## Exercises

**E 12-1**  Prepare the journal entries required to record the following transactions of an Enterprise Fund. (Ignore bond issue costs.)

1. Issued refunding bonds at par, $4,000,000. The refunding bonds have an interest rate of 7% payable annually. The term of the bonds is 8 years, and a portion of the principal is to be repaid each year beginning in the third year of the bond term.
2. Paid the proceeds of the refunding bonds to an escrow agent to defease other outstanding bonds. The bonds that are defeased have a par value of $4,200,000, 4 years remaining to maturity, no unamortized premium or discount, and an interest rate of 6% payable annually.
3. Paid interest on the refunding bonds, $280,000. Make any necessary adjusting entries at this point as well.

**E 12-2**  A government's Enterprise Fund received 2 intergovernmental restricted grants in cash—a capital grant of $3,000,000 and an operating grant of $1,000,000. The government incurred and paid construction costs of $1,200,000 payable from the capital grant and operating costs of $300,000 payable from the operating grant. Additionally, the government acquired and paid for $50,000 of equipment payable from the operating grant.

1. What amount of operating revenues should be reported by the Enterprise Fund based on the above information?
2. What amount of nonoperating revenues should be reported by the Enterprise Fund based on the above information?
3. What amounts should be reported as cash flows from noncapital financing activities?
4. What amounts should be reported as cash flows from capital and related financing activities?
5. What amounts should be reported as cash flows from investing activities?

## Problems

**P 12-1**  (Multiple Choice)

1. Which of the following activities would be least likely to be operated as and accounted for in an Enterprise Fund?
   a. town planning department          c. parking garage
   b. sports stadium                    d. mass transit authority
2. The city of Philaburg arranged for a 10-year, $40 million loan to finance construction of a toll bridge over the Tradewater River. Assuming that the toll bridge is accounted for as an Enterprise Fund activity and that a certain portion of the tolls collected are required to be set aside for maintaining the bridge, these resources should be accounted for in
   a. a Debt Service Fund.              d. a Capital Projects Fund.
   b. the General Fund.                 e. none of the above
   c. the Toll Bridge Enterprise Fund.
3. The city of Silerville operates a water authority that sells water to city residents. Each new customer is required to pay a $75 deposit at the time of hookup. The deposit is returnable with interest if the customer maintains a satisfactory payment record during the first two years of service. The city should record these deposits
   a. in an Expendable Trust Fund.
   b. as restricted cash and a liability payable from restricted assets in a Water Fund subfund.
   c. as unrestricted cash and a long-term liability in the Water Fund.
   d. as restricted cash and a liability payable from restricted assets in the General Fund.
   e. none of the above

Use the following facts for Questions 4 and 5.

On January 1, 19X7, Clyde County issued $100 million of 10%, 20-year bonds at 102. Interest is payable semiannually. The proceeds were restricted for the construction of a new county water purification plant for its Water Enterprise Fund.

4. The bond issue should be reflected in the Water Fund Statement of Revenues, Expenses, and Changes in Retained Earnings as
   a. revenues of $102 million.
   b. other financing sources of $102 million.
   c. revenues of $100 million.
   d. other financing sources of $100 million.
   e. none of the above

5. What effect will the bond premium have on interest expense in 19X7, assuming straight-line amortization is used where appropriate?
   a. no effect
   b. increase interest expense by $100,000
   c. decrease interest expense by $100,000
   d. none of the above

6. All Enterprise Fund residual equity transfers are reported in an Enterprise Fund's operating statement when it reports changes in
   a. total fund equity.               c. unreserved retained earnings.
   b. total retained earnings.         d. none of the above

7. Enterprise Fund operating transfers are reported in an Enterprise Fund's operating statement
   a. after net income but before the beginning fund equity.
   b. after net income and after beginning fund equity, but before residual equity transfers.
   c. as part of operating income.
   d. in a separate section following operating income and nonoperating revenues and expenses, and included in net income.
   e. as part of nonoperating income and expenses.

8. Depreciation expense on all of an Enterprise Fund's fixed assets must be reported as expenses in the fund's operating statement. However, in computing the net change in retained earnings for the year, depreciation *may* be added back to the extent that it is on fixed assets
   a. financed from restricted donations.
   b. financed from residual equity transfers.
   c. financed from intergovernmental capital grants.
   d. constructed by subdividers or financed with special assessments.
   e. all of the above
   f. none of the above

9. Enterprise Fund resources, $3,000,000, are paid yearly to the Hogan County General Fund. Assuming that these payments are payments in lieu of taxes, they should be recorded in the Enterprise Fund as
   a. expenses.                         d. reductions of revenues.
   b. expenditures.                     e. residual equity transfers out.
   c. operating transfers out.

10. Assuming that the payments in item 9 are not payments in lieu of taxes, they should be recorded in the Enterprise Fund as
    a. expenses.                        d. reductions of revenues.
    b. expenditures.                    e. residual equity transfers out.
    c. operating transfers out.

**P 12-2** (Worksheet and Statements) The city of Lenn operates its municipal airport. The trial balance of the Airport Fund as of January 1, 19X0, was as follows:

| | | |
|---|---:|---:|
| Cash .......................................................... | $ 37,000 | |
| Accounts Receivable ...................................... | 50,000 | |
| Allowance for Uncollectible Accounts ....................... | | $ 2,000 |
| Land ......................................................... | 200,000 | |
| Structures and Improvements ............................. | 700,000 | |
| Accumulated Depreciation—Structures and Improvements ...... | | 50,000 |
| Equipment ................................................ | 250,000 | |
| Accumulated Depreciation—Equipment .................... | | 90,000 |
| Vouchers Payable ......................................... | | 48,000 |
| Bonds Payable ............................................ | | 800,000 |
| Contributed Capital—Governmental Unit ................... | | 200,000 |
| Retained Earnings ........................................ | | 47,000 |
| | $1,237,000 | $1,237,000 |

The following transactions took place during the year:
1. Revenues collected in cash: aviation revenues, $340,500; concession revenues, $90,000; revenues from airport management, $30,000; revenues from sales of petroleum products (net revenue, after deducting all costs relating to the sales), $10,500.
2. Expenses, all paid in cash with the exception of $24,000, which remained unpaid at December 31, were operating, $222,000; maintenance, $75,000; general and administrative, $73,000.
3. Bad debts written off during the year, $1,900.
4. The vouchers payable outstanding on January 1, 19X0 were paid.
5. Bond principal paid during the year, $50,000, together with interest of $40,000.
6. The remaining accounts receivable outstanding on January 1, 19X0 were collected.
7. Accounts receivable on December 31, 19X0 amounted to $30,000, all applicable to aviation revenues, of which $1,400 is estimated to be uncollectible.
8. Accrued interest payable at the end of the year, $3,000.
9. Depreciation charges:

| | |
|---|---:|
| Structures and Improvements ........................ | $14,000 |
| Equipment ......................................... | 21,000 |

**Required** (a) Prepare a worksheet to reflect the beginning trial balance, the transactions and adjustments during 19X0, the revenues and expenses of the year (or closing entries), and the ending balance sheet data.

(b) Prepare a balance sheet for the Airport Fund as of December 31, 19X0.

(c) Prepare a statement of revenues, expenses, and changes in fund equity for the Airport Fund for the fiscal year ended December 31, 19X0.

**P 12-3** (Cash Flow Statement) Indicate the classification in which each of the following would be reported in a government proprietary fund cash flow statement. Use the following letters for each classification to respond:

A. Cash flows from operating activities.
B. Cash flows from noncapital financing activities.
C. Cash flows from capital and related financing activities.
D. Cash flows from investing activities.
E. None of the above.

1. Cash paid to purchase investments.
2. Cash received for the sale of equipment.
3. Cash paid for salaries.
4. Cash received from interest on investments that are restricted for use in servicing bonds that had been issued to finance construction of a building.
5. Cash paid for interest on refunding boards that were issued to provide for repayment of bonds that were issued to finance purchase of major pieces of equipment.
6. Cash paid to General Fund in an operating transfer. The General Fund budget requires these funds to be used to help finance acquisition of a fire truck.
7. Cash received from operating grants.

8. Cash received from a residual equity transfer from the General Fund to finance expansion of the physical plant.
9. Cash received from capital grants.
10. Cash paid for interest on a short-term note issued to fulfill a temporary need for operating funds.

**P 12-4** (Cash Flow Statement) The following information was derived from the accounts, financial statements, and related data for the Hestand County Electric Services Enterprise Fund for 19X2:

| | |
|---|---:|
| Sales of services to public | $800,000 |
| Cost of electricity purchases paid | 500,000 |
| Sales of services to other county departments | 100,000 |
| Salaries and wages paid | 150,000 |
| Purchases of supplies | 35,000 |
| Payment in lieu of taxes paid to county General Fund | 17,000 |
| Annual transfer from General Fund received | 70,000 |
| Residual equity transfer paid to help establish a Central Equipment Fund, the sole purpose of which is to finance fixed asset purchases | 212,000 |
| Proceeds from sale of fixed assets | 37,000 |
| Investment purchases | 25,000 |
| Interest received from investments | 10,000 |
| Interest paid on bonds issued to finance plant construction | 33,000 |
| Retirement of six-month note issued to relieve cash shortfall: | |
|   Principal | 75,000 |
|   Interest | 3,750 |
| Decrease in receivables from customers | 150,000 |
| January 1 unrestricted cash balance | 200,000 |
| January 1 restricted cash balance | 7,200 |

**Required** Prepare the 19X2 statement of cash flows for the Hestand County Electric Service Enterprise Fund. (Exclude accompanying schedules for which you do not have sufficient information.)

**P 12-5** (Cash Flow Statement) Using the following information, prepare a formal statement of cash flows for the Tignor County Water and Sewer Enterprise Fund for the year ended December 31, 1996. Schedules that would normally accompany the financial statements are not required. (Numbers given are in thousands.)

| | |
|---|---:|
| Cash received from current year's sales | $3,000 |
| Collections of prior year accounts receivable | 300 |
| Accounts receivable balance, December 31, 1996 | 150 |
| Cash purchases of inventory items | 1,200 |
| Increase in inventory | — |
| Cash paid for salaries and wages | 500 |
| Increase in accrued salaries payable | 50 |
| Payment in lieu of taxes to General Fund | 75 |
| Depreciation of fixed assets | 200 |
| Operating transfer to General Fund | 180 |
| Residual equity transfer from General Fund for purpose of financing half the cost of expanding the sewer treatment plant | 5,000 |
| Construction costs billed to the fund, half of which were paid | 7,500 |
| Issuance of bonds to finance construction costs | 5,000 |
| Federal capital grant received to assist in financing plant expansion and modernization ($2,500 of the $7,500 of construction costs billed are reimbursable under this grant) | 5,000 |
| EPA grant received for purpose of improving water quality | 800 |

| | |
|---|---:|
| Expenditure of EPA grant funds to purchase water quality monitoring equipment .................................... | 350 |
| Expenditure of EPA grant resources to pay new water quality monitor's salary and benefits (not included in salary payments listed above) .......................................... | 85 |
| Issuance of nine-month note to provide for cash shortage ....... | 600 |
| Retirement of bonds (originally issued to finance fixed asset acquisition) ........................................... | 500 |
| Payment of interest on the retired bonds .................... | 25 |
| Accrual of interest on nine-month note ..................... | 15 |
| Accrual of interest on Sewer Plant Bonds ................... | 100 |
| Proceeds from sale of investment (Investment was sold to provide cash to pay construction costs.) .......................... | 1,000 |
| Cash received for interest on investments ................... | 275 |
| Loss on sale of investment ................................ | 35 |
| Unrestricted cash balance (beginning of year) ............... | 100 |
| Restricted cash balance (beginning of year) ................. | 700 |

**P 12-6** (Operating Statement) Explain or illustrate how the following items should be reported in a proprietary fund's statement of revenues, expenses, and changes in retained earnings.
1. Depreciation on capital grant financed fixed assets.
2. Depreciation on fixed assets contributed by subdividers.
3. Residual equity transfers from other funds.
4. Cash proceeds of short-term note issuances.
5. Retirement of bonds payable of the fund.
6. Operating transfers from other funds.
7. Gain on sale of fixed assets.
8. Loss on advance refunding of bonds.
9. Restricted grants received that can be used for operations or for fixed asset acquisition—assume 30% was expended during the year to acquire fixed assets, 30% to cover operating expenses, and 40% has not been expended.
10. Entering into a capital lease with a capitalizable cost of $4,000,000 on the last day of the year. Assume an initial payment on that day of $1,000,000.

**P 12-7** (Worksheet and Statements) The city of Clifton provides electric energy for its citizens through an operating department. All transactions of the Electric Department are recorded in a self-sustaining fund supported by revenue from the sales of energy. Plant expansion is financed by the issuance of bonds that are repaid out of revenues. All cash of the electric department is held by the city treasurer. Receipts from customers and others are deposited in the treasurer's account. Disbursements are made by drawing warrants on the treasurer.

The following is the postclosing trial balance of the department as of June 30, 19X7:

| | | |
|---|---:|---:|
| Cash and Investments with City Treasurer .................... | $ 2,250,000 | |
| Due from Customers ...................................... | 2,120,000 | |
| Other Current Assets ..................................... | 130,000 | |
| Construction in Progress ................................. | 500,000 | |
| Land ................................................... | 5,000,000 | |
| Electric Plant .......................................... | 50,000,000* | |
| Accumulated Depreciation—Electric Plant .................... | | $10,000,000 |
| Accounts Payable and Accrued Liabilities ................... | | 3,270,000 |
| 5% Electric Revenue Bonds Payable ........................ | | 20,000,000 |
| Contributed Capital—Governmental Unit .................... | | 5,000,000 |
| Retained Earnings ........................................ | | 21,730,000 |
| | $60,000,000 | $60,000,000 |

*The plant is being depreciated on the basis of a 50-year composite life.

During the year ended June 30, 19X8, the department had the following transactions:

1. Sales of electric energy, $10,700,000.
2. Purchases of fuel and operating supplies, $2,950,000.
3. Construction expenditures relating to miscellaneous system improvements in progress (financed from operations), $750,000.
4. Fuel consumed, $2,790,000.
5. Miscellaneous plant additions and improvements constructed and placed in service at midyear, $1,000,000.
6. Wages and salaries paid, $4,280,000.
7. Sale at par on December 31, 19X7 of 20-year, 5% Electric Revenue Bonds, dated January 1, 19X8, with interest payable semiannually, $5,000,000.
8. Expenditures out of bond proceeds for construction of Clifton Steam Plant Unit No. 1, $2,800,000.
9. Operating materials and supplies consumed, $150,000.
10. Payments received from customers, $10,500,000.
11. Expenditures out of bond proceeds for construction of Clifton Steam Plant Unit No. 2, $2,200,000.
12. Warrants drawn on city treasurer in settlement of accounts payable, $3,045,000.
13. The Clifton Steam Plant was placed in service June 30, 19X8.
14. Interest on bonds paid during the year, $500,000.

**Required** (a) Prepare a worksheet for the Electric Department Fund showing:
   (1) The balance sheet amounts at June 30, 19X7.
   (2) The transactions for the year and closing entries. (Note: Formal journal entries are not required and interest capitalization may be ignored.)
   (3) The balance sheet amounts at June 30, 19X8.
   (b) Prepare a statement of cash flows for the Electric Department Fund for the year ended June 30, 19X8.

**P 12-8** (Bond Refunding) Prepare journal entries, including adjusting entries when needed, to record the following transactions in a government's Enterprise Fund.
   1. Issued refunding bonds at par, $10 million. The interest rate is 10%, payable annually. Bonds mature in 10 years. Bond issue costs were $200,000.
   2. Retired old debt with refunding proceeds of $9.8 million.
      Bonds payable outstanding (old), $9,300,000.
      Unamortized premium on outstanding bonds, $300,000.
      Unamortized bond issue costs on outstanding bonds, $50,000.
      Remaining term of old debt, 4 years.
   3. Annual interest payment ($1,000,000) on new bonds was made at the due date, which is year end.

**P 12-9** (Various Entries)
   1. On April 30, 19X2 the Pickens County Transit Authority leased ten buses under a 6-year, noncancellable capital lease. The capitalizable cost of the buses was $680,000 and an $80,000 down payment was made. The county does not receive title to the leased buses at the end of the lease term.
   2. Lease payments made during the fiscal year ended April 30, 19X3 totaled $130,262, including interest of $37,932.
   3. The county estimates its probable losses from claims and judgments against the Transit Authority for events occurring in 19X2–19X3 at $227,000. However, only $85,000 of this can reasonably be expected to be payable from expendable, available financial resources of the fund.

**Required** Prepare all the general journal entries, including adjusting entries, that Pickens County must make in 19X1–19X2 and 19X2–19X3 to record these transactions and events—assuming that
   (a) The Transit Authority is accounted for in an Enterprise Fund.
   (b) The Transit Authority is accounted for as a general government activity.

**P 12-10**   (Operating Statement) Using the following information, prepare the statement of revenues, expenses, and changes in fund equity for the town of Robinson for the year ended June 30, 19X6.

| | |
|---|---:|
| Charges for water services rendered | $ 1,800,000 |
| Charges for sewer services rendered | 2,000,000 |
| Interest income | 50,000 |
| Increase in fair value of investments | 12,000 |
| Proceeds of bond issuance | 13,000,000 |
| Salaries and wages | 400,000 |
| Contractual services (purchased) | 2,600,000 |
| Depreciation on capital grant financed fixed assets | 100,000 |
| Depreciation on fixed assets contributed by subdividers | 75,000 |
| Depreciation on other fixed assets | 80,000 |
| Capital grants received (all grant conditions met) | 1,500,000 |
| Operating grants received (half expended for operations and half for fixed asset purchases) | 250,000 |
| Gain on sale of equipment | 13,000 |
| Deferred interest expense adjustment (debit) (at beginning of year) | 100,000 |
| Operating transfer to General Fund | 90,000 |
| Payment in lieu of taxes to General Fund | 17,000 |
| Residual equity transfer from General Fund | 500,000 |
| Interest on short-term note payable | 5,000 |
| Payment of short-term note | 75,000 |
| Interest on bonds payable | 95,000 |
| Retained earnings, July 1, 19X5 | 22,000,000 |

Water and sewer service claims and judgments paid during the year totaled $100,000. The liability (half of which is long term) for these claims and judgments increased by $10,000 during the year.

The refunded bonds have a 5-year remaining term and the term of the new bonds is 10 years. Robinson uses the depreciation reporting option permitted by GAAP that maximizes its retained earnings balance.

**P 12-11**   (Grant Accounting) (a) Prepare journal entries, including adjusting entries when needed, to record the following transactions in a government's Enterprise Fund.
   1. Received a grant, $3,000,000, which was restricted to use for constructing a production facility.
   2. Expended half of the grant funds for the construction of the building for which the grant was received.
   (b) Prepare journal entries, including adjusting entries when needed, to record the following transactions affecting a government's Enterprise Fund.
   1. Received a grant, $3,000,000, which was restricted to use for paying the salaries of air quality monitors.
   2. Expended half of the grant funds for the salary payments for which the grant was received.

**P 12-12**   (Restricted Asset Accounting) McKenzie's Point issued $1,200,000 of 6%, 10-year serial bonds at par on July 1, 19X4. Interest is due semiannually on January 1 and July 1 each year, and one-tenth of the principal is due each July 1. The bond indenture requires that the proceeds be accounted for in a separate fund and used to construct an addition to the maintenance building for the municipal airport, which is accounted for in an Enterprise Fund. Furthermore, the bond agreement requires McKenzie's Point to set aside airport revenues of $20,000 per month plus one-sixth of the next interest payment each month in a separate fund for debt service from which debt service payments are to be made. The following also occurred during 19X4:

July 2—The city signed a contract with Keith Construction for construction of the addition, $1,200,000.

July 31—The city set aside the required amount to provide for debt service.

August 29—The city received a bill from Keith Construction for $1,200,000 upon completion of the addition. After inspection and approval, the bill was paid.

August 31, September 30, October 31, November 30, and December 31—On each of these dates the city set aside the required amounts to provide for debt service.

**Required** Assuming August 31 is the end of the fiscal year of McKenzie's Point, prepare the general journal entries, including adjusting and closing entries, for the preceding transactions. Ignore interest capitalization.

**P 12-13** (Worksheet and Financial Statements) The following information pertains to the operation of the Water Fund of the city of Marion. Included in the operations of this fund are those of a special Replacement Fund for the Water Department, the accounts of which are a part of the accounts of the Water Fund.

The balances in the accounts of this fund on January 1, 19X5, were as follows:

| | |
|---|---:|
| Cash | $ 6,126 |
| Accounts Receivable (net of $1,200 estimated to be uncollectible). | 7,645 |
| Stores | 13,826 |
| Investments—Replacement Fund | 21,700 |
| Property, Plant, and Equipment | 212,604 |
| Accumulated Depreciation | 50,400 |
| Vouchers Payable | 4,324 |
| Customer Deposits* | 1,500 |
| Replacement Fund Reserve | 21,700 |
| Retained Earnings | 21,977 |
| Bonds Payable | 60,000 |
| Contributed Capital | 102,000 |

*No restrictions are placed on deposits received or investment income thereon; interest is not paid on deposits.

The following items represent all transactions of the fund for the year ended December 31, 19X5:

| | | |
|---|---|---:|
| 1. | Services billed | $146,867 |
| 2. | Accounts collected | 147,842 |
| 3. | Uncollectible accounts of prior years written off; current provision made, $750 | 1,097 |
| 4. | Invoices and payrolls approved and vouchered for current expense | 69,826 |
| 5. | Invoices approved and vouchered for water department stores purchased | 31,424 |
| 6. | Stores issued for use in operation | 32,615 |
| 7. | Supplies secured from General Fund stores and used in operations (cash paid to General Fund) | 7,197 |
| 8. | Vouchers approved for payment of annual serial bonds maturity, including interest of $3,000 | 23,000 |
| 9. | Depreciation (replacement reserve and assets adjusted also to fully reserve and fund the accumulated depreciation) | 10,600 |
| 10. | Deposits received | 400 |
| | Deposits refunded | 240 |

11. Invoices approved and vouchered for replacement of fully
    depreciated equipment which had cost $6,200 . . . . . . . . . .        7,800
12. Invoices approved and vouchered for additions to plant . . . . .      12,460
13. Interest received on investments; none is accrued at year end .        1,102
14. Purchased securities as necessary to fully invest the Replace-
    ment Fund to the nearest whole $100 . . . . . . . . . . . . . . . .    compute
15. Approved vouchers paid (general) . . . . . . . . . . . . . . . . . .  133,316
16. Stores inventory per physical count at December 31, 19X5
    (any shortages or overages are assumed to be related to
    operating expenses) . . . . . . . . . . . . . . . . . . . . . . . . .  11,820

**Required** (a) A worksheet analysis of the beginning trial balance, transactions and adjustments during 19X5, revenues and expenses, and postclosing trial balance at December 31, 19X5, of the Water Fund of the city of Marion.

(b) A Balance Sheet of the Water Fund as of December 31, 19X5.

(c) A Statement of Revenues, Expenses, and Changes in Fund Equity for the Water Fund for the year ended December 31, 19X5. (AICPA, adapted)

# 13

# FINANCIAL REPORTING: THE CAFR AND GPFS

State and local government financial reporting is addressed by the twelfth principle set forth in the GASB *Codification,* which states in part:

### Interim and Annual Financial Reports

a. Appropriate **interim financial statements** and reports of financial position, operating results, and other pertinent information should be prepared to facilitate management control of financial operations, legislative oversight, and, where necessary or desired, for external reporting purposes.

b. A **comprehensive annual financial report [CAFR]** should be prepared and published, covering all funds and account groups of the primary government (including its blended component units) and providing an overview of all discretely presented component units of the reporting entity—including introductory section; appropriate combined, combining and individual fund statements; notes to the financial statements; required supplementary information; schedules; narrative explanations; and statistical tables. The reporting entity is the primary government (including its blended component units) and all discretely presented component units. . . .

c. **General purpose financial statements [GPFS]** of the reporting entity may be issued separately from the comprehensive annual financial report. Such statements should include the basic financial statements and notes to the financial statements that are essential to fair presentation of financial position and results of operations (and cash flows of those fund types and discretely presented component units that use proprietary fund accounting). Those statements may also be required to be accompanied by required supplementary information, essential to financial reporting of certain entities.[1]

This chapter considers interim reporting briefly, then focuses on the basics of annual financial reporting for a simple government reporting entity. The next chapter deals with the unique aspects of reporting for a government with a complex reporting entity structure and with selected budgetary reporting issues.

---

[1] GASB *Codification,* sec. 1900.100.(a–c). (Acronyms and emphasis added.)

## INTERIM REPORTING

Very few governments publish interim financial statements for external use. Rather, interim statements of governments are prepared on the budgetary basis and are designed primarily to meet the needs of administrative personnel such as the chief executive, departmental supervisors, and budget examiners, though legislators may be interested in them. Interim statements thus help determine how well the executive branch is complying with budgetary and other finance-related legal requirements. In addition, interim statements are important for controlling current operations—they disclose variations from plans that may require altering the plans or improving operating performance—and for planning future operations.

Interim balance sheets for a General Fund are mentioned in Chapter 4. Interim operating statements presented earlier include the interim budgetary comparison statement in Figure 3–10. Other interim statements commonly prepared include detailed budgetary statements and statements of cash receipts, disbursements, and balances for each fund.

The GASB recognizes the importance of good interim reporting both by including it in the Reporting Principle and in its discussion of that principle:

> Interim financial reports are comprised principally of statements that reflect current financial position at the end of a month or quarter and compare actual financial results with budgetary estimates and limitations for the month or quarter and/or for the year to date. Interim reports typically are prepared primarily for internal use. Thus, they usually are prepared on the budgetary basis and often do not include statements reporting general fixed assets or general long-term debt. Further, they may properly contain budgetary or cash flow projections and other information deemed pertinent to effective management control during the year.
>
> The key criteria by which internal interim reports are evaluated are their relevance and usefulness for purposes of management control, which include planning future operations as well as evaluating current financial status and results to date. . . . Because managerial styles and perceived information needs vary widely, however, appropriate internal interim reporting is largely a matter of professional judgment rather than one to be set forth in detail here.[2]

Interim reporting typically is for internal use, and individual managers and environments require different types of interim reports. Thus, neither the GASB nor any other recognized body has set forth what might be considered generally accepted principles of interim reporting.

## ANNUAL REPORTING

Reporting is the last phase of the annual budget and accounting cycle for which the executive branch of the government is responsible. The ideal annual financial report has two key functions. One is for the executive branch to demonstrate its compliance with finance-related legal and contractual requirements, including fund and appropriation requirements, under which the government is operated. The second function is to present audited financial statements that conform with generally accepted accounting principles. The annual financial report is designed to inform

---

[2] Ibid., sec. 1900.107–.108.

the legislative body, creditors, investors, analysts, students of public finance, political scientists, and the general public.

The GASB is emphatic that:

> Every governmental entity should prepare and publish, as a matter of public record, a comprehensive annual financial report (CAFR) that encompasses all funds and account groups of the primary government (including its blended components units). The CAFR should also encompass all discretely presented component units of the reporting entity. The CAFR should contain:
>
> a. The general purpose financial statements (GPFS) [by fund type and account group].
> b. Combining statements for the fund types of the primary government (including its blended component units). Combining statements should also be presented for the discretely presented component units.
> c. Individual fund statements and schedules for the funds of the primary government (including its blended component units).
>
> The CAFR is the governmental entity's official annual report and should also contain introductory information, schedules necessary to demonstrate compliance with finance-related legal and contractual provisions, and statistical data.[3]

Principle 12b, quoted at the beginning of the chapter, states that the reporting entity being reported upon in a CAFR (or in GPFS) includes the primary government (defined later) and discretely presented component units (defined later). Indeed, many governments have no discretely presented component units; rather they have a simple entity structure in which the primary government is the reporting entity. This chapter assumes that the term *primary government* is simply a synonym for the legal entity being reported upon. The next chapter explains (1) how a government determines if entities other than the primary government legal entity should be included in its reporting entity, (2) how the data of other included units (component units) are incorporated in the CAFR and the GPFS, and (3) how other associated organizations that are not component units (such as joint ventures) impact a primary government's CAFR.

## THE PYRAMID CONCEPT—SIMPLE ENTITY STRUCTURE

The financial statements and schedules section of the CAFR is based on a pyramid concept of reporting. In studying the financial reporting pyramid (Figure 13–1) note that:

1. The top of the pyramid represents highly aggregated, consolidated financial statements, whereas the bottom of the pyramid represents highly detailed, voluminous reports that would include the details of virtually every transaction or event of a governmental unit. The GASB requires reports and statements between these two extremes. Thus, neither "Condensed Summary Data" nor "Transaction Data" fall within the bounds of reports and statements to be prepared under generally accepted accounting principles.[4]

2. A dual external reporting approach is employed. The Comprehensive Annual Financial Report (CAFR) is the primary report, the official annual report of the governmental unit,

---

[3] Ibid., sec. 1900.109.

[4] As discussed in Chapter 15, the GASB has proposed to require entity-wide financial statements to be presented in addition to fund-based financial statements. The fund-based reporting envisioned in the GASB's proposed reporting model standard is quite similar to current reporting requirements.

FIGURE 13–1  **The Financial Reporting Pyramid**

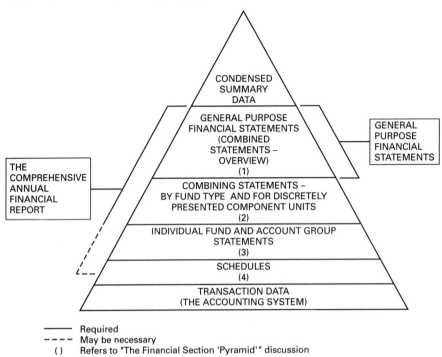

—— Required
- - - - May be necessary
( )    Refers to "The Financial Section 'Pyramid'" discussion

*Source:* Adapted from GASB *Codification*, sec. 1900.117.

whereas the General Purpose Financial Statements (GPFS) in the CAFR may be issued separately for inclusion in official statements for bond offerings and for general widespread distribution to users apt to require less detail than is contained in the CAFR, provided the GPFS refer the reader to the CAFR in case more detailed information is needed.

3. The contents of the GPFS are limited to several combined statements, whereas the CAFR includes the combined statements, combining statements, and, perhaps, individual fund and account group statements. The dashed line in Figure 13–1 indicates the area where professional judgment is to be exercised in determining when adequate disclosure has been achieved without overwhelming the user of the CAFR with excessive detail.

4. It is essential (a) to distinguish between and among combined statements, combining statements, and individual fund and account group statements and schedules and (b) to realize that the data in combined statements are more summarized than those in the combining statements, which are more summarized than those presented in the individual fund and account group statements, which are more summarized than those presented in most individual fund and account group schedules. Thus, the higher on the pyramid, the more summarized the data presented; and the lower on the pyramid, the more detailed the data presented.

The relationships between the different levels of financial statements are illustrated in Figure 13–2. (Recall that the current chapter assumes a simple entity structure, which means that this figure does not include component unit columns in the combined statements nor does it include combining component unit financial statements. These are illustrated in the next chapter.) Note that the total columns of the various combining financial statements for each fund type are reported for that fund type in the corresponding combined statement (although probably in less detail). Thus, the combined financial statements and combining financial statements clearly articulate. Furthermore, each individual fund financial statement presented will articulate with the corresponding column for that specific fund in the corresponding combining statement. Indeed, it will simply be a more detailed, or otherwise more informative, presentation of the same data.

## THE COMPREHENSIVE ANNUAL FINANCIAL REPORT (CAFR)—SIMPLE ENTITY STRUCTURE

The general outline and minimum contents of the CAFR include (1) the **Introductory** Section, (2) the **Financial** Section, and (3) the **Statistical** Section. These CAFR sections and their contents are illustrated in Figure 13–3, which should be studied now for an overview of the CAFR. It will be useful to refer to this figure and Figure 13–2 when studying specific components of the CAFR in order to visualize the relationships among the components.[5]

### The Introductory Section

The introductory section of the CAFR includes a table of contents, letter(s) of transmittal, and other material deemed appropriate by management—for example, organization chart, copy of current certificate of achievement for excellence in financial reporting awarded by the Government Finance Officers Association, roster of elected officials, and description of the government entity being reported on.

The transmittal letter from the chief finance officer is an extremely important part of the CAFR. Indeed, like the president's letter in private corporation reports, most readers direct their attention here initially for an overview of the financial position of the city at year end and the results of operations for the year. Readers also expect that the major significant events that occurred during the year, whether good or bad, will be highlighted here.

### The Financial Section—Simple Entity Structure

As illustrated in Figure 13–3, the financial section for an SLG with a simple reporting entity structure has three subsections: (1) the auditor's report, (2) the general purpose financial statements (GPFS)—the combined statements and notes to the financial statements (followed by any required supplementary information), and (3) the combining and individual fund statements and schedules.

#### The Auditor's Report

The auditor's report on the financial statements is the first item presented in the financial section of a government's CAFR. The auditor's report on the city of Orlando's financial statements for a recent fiscal year appears in Figure 13–4 (page 513). Note that this opinion is a dual opinion in that it covers both the combined statements in the GPFS and the combining and individual fund and account group statements equally. The report covers the financial and budgetary schedules

---

[5] Many governments have their CAFRs, or at least their GPFSs, available on the Internet. A search using the term *CAFR* or *Comprehensive Annual Financial Report* typically will provide a list of many from which to choose. You may find it interesting and helpful to look at several of these as you continue studying this chapter.

**FIGURE 13–2 Nature of and Interrelationships between Different Levels of Financial Statements—Simple Entity Structure**

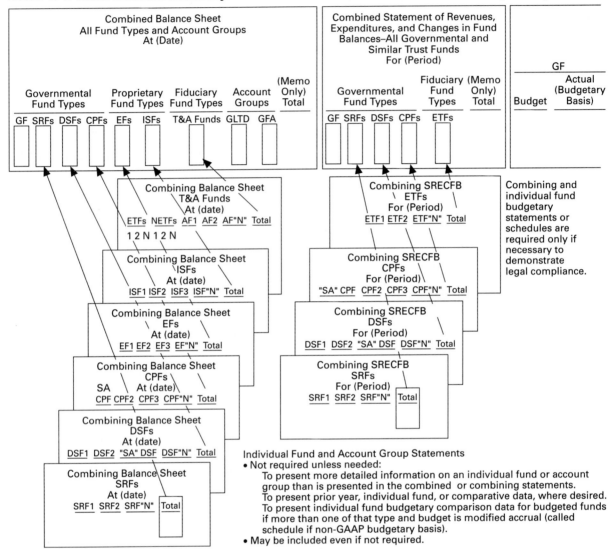

**Note:** All of the statements prepared for each level of financial statements are prepared on the GAAP basis, except for the budgetary comparison statements. The budgetary comparison statements (or schedules) are presented on the budgetary basis even if it differs from GAAP.

only as accompanying (supplemental) data presented for purposes of additional analysis.

### The Combined Statements (GPFS) and Notes

As shown in Figure 13–3, as few as five combined statements, accompanied by appropriate notes, may present fairly the financial position and results of operations of a state or local government (and the cash flows of its proprietary and non-expendable trust funds) in accordance with GAAP. Because the data in combined statements are aggregated by fund type, not by individual fund, these statements have a fund-type entity focus. This focus on fund types rather than on individual funds is reflected in Figure 13–2, which illustrates the overall structure of the various combined statements.

**FIGURE 13-2** *(Continued)*

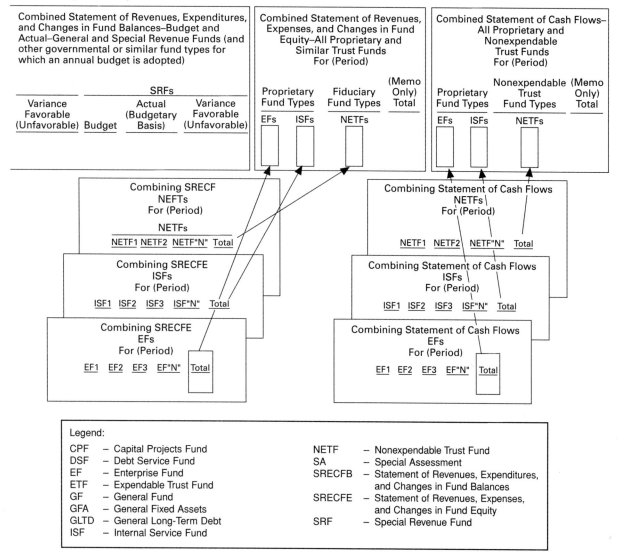

Legend:

| | | | |
|---|---|---|---|
| CPF | – Capital Projects Fund | NETF | – Nonexpendable Trust Fund |
| DSF | – Debt Service Fund | SA | – Special Assessment |
| EF | – Enterprise Fund | SRECFB | – Statement of Revenues, Expenditures, |
| ETF | – Expendable Trust Fund | | and Changes in Fund Balances |
| GF | – General Fund | SRECFE | – Statement of Revenues, Expenses, |
| GFA | – General Fixed Assets | | and Changes in Fund Equity |
| GLTD | – General Long-Term Debt | SRF | – Special Revenue Fund |
| ISF | – Internal Service Fund | | |

**Note:** A statement of changes in net assets is required also if the government has pension trust or investment trust funds.

As shown in Figures 13–2 and 13–3, the combined statements in the GPFS are:

1. Combined Balance Sheet—All Fund Types and Account Groups
2. Combined Statement of Revenues, Expenditures, and Changes in Fund Balances—All Governmental and Similar Trust Fund Types
3. Combined Statement of Revenues, Expenditures, and Changes in Fund Balances—Budget and Actual—General and Special Revenue Fund Types (and similar funds for which an annual budget is adopted)
4. Combined Statement of Revenues, Expenses, and Changes in Fund Equity (or Retained Earnings)—All Proprietary and Similar Trust Fund Types
5. Combined Statement of Cash Flows—All Proprietary and Nonexpendable Trust Fund Types
6. Combined Statement of Changes in Net Assets—Pension Trust Funds and Investment Trust Funds

FIGURE 13–3  **General Outline and Content of a CAFR—Simple Entity Structure**

---

## INTRODUCTORY SECTION

| Components Required by the GASB | Other Items Commonly Included |
| --- | --- |
| 1. Table of contents<br>2. Letter(s) of transmittal<br>3. Other material deemed appropriate by management | List of principal officials<br>Organization chart<br>GFOA certificate of achievement for excellence in financial reporting (if awarded) |

---

## FINANCIAL SECTION

| Auditor's Report | General Purpose Financial Statements (Combined Statements—Overview) | Combining and Individual Fund and Account Group Statements and Schedules |
| --- | --- | --- |
| | (1) *Combined Balance Sheet*—All Fund Types and Account Groups (Figure 13–5).<br><br>(2) *Combined Statement of Revenues, Expenditures, and Changes in Fund Balances*—All Governmental and Similar Trust Fund Types (Figure 13–6).<br><br>(3) *Combined Statement of Revenues, Expenditures, and Changes in Fund Balances—Budget and Actual*—General and Special Revenue Fund Types (and similar governmental and trust fund types for which annual budgets have been legally adopted) (Figure 13–7).<br><br>(4) *Combined Statement of Revenues, Expenses, and Changes in Fund Equity or Retained Earnings*—All Proprietary and Similar Trust Fund Types (Figure 13–8).<br><br>(5) *Combined Statement of Cash Flows*—All Proprietary and Nonexpendable Trust Fund Types (Figure 13–9).<br><br>(6) *Combined Statement of Changes in Net Assets*—All Pension Trust and Investment Trust Funds (Figure 13–10).<br><br>(7) *Notes to the financial statements* (Figure 13–11).<br>[Most Trust Fund operations may be reported in (2), (3), (4), and (5) above, as appropriate, or separately]<br><br>(8) *Required supplementary information*—For example, certain ten-year historical trend information relating to pension plans must be presented after the notes by most governments with single-employer or agent multiple-employer PERS. | (1) *Combining Statements*—by Fund Type—where a governmental unit has more than one fund of a given fund type (e.g., Figures 4–10, 4–11, 4–12, 7–10, 8–5, 8–6, 8–8, and 8–9).<br><br>(2) *Individual fund and account group statements*—where a governmental unit has only one fund of a given type and for account groups and/or where necessary to present prior year and budgetary comparisons. (These statements are optional unless circumstances make them necessary for fair presentation of the financial statements.)<br><br>(3) *Schedules*<br>(a) Schedules necessary to demonstrate compliance with finance-related legal and contractual provisions. (These schedules are required in some circumstances.)<br><br>(b) Schedules to present information spread throughout the statements that can be brought together and shown in greater detail (e.g., taxes receivable, including delinquent taxes, long-term debt; investments; and cash receipts, disbursements, and balances). (Optional schedules)<br><br>(c) Schedules to present greater detail for information reported in the statements (e.g., additional revenue sources detail and object of expenditure data by departments). (Optional schedules)<br><br>(Narrative explanations useful in understanding combining and individual fund and account group statements and schedules that are not included in the notes to the financial statements should be presented on divider pages, directly on the statements and schedules, or in a separate section.) |

---

## STATISTICAL SECTION

| Tables Covering Last Ten Fiscal Years | | Other Tables |
| --- | --- | --- |
| ■ General Government Expenditures by Function<br>■ General Revenues by Source<br>■ Property Tax Levies and Collections<br>■ Assessed and Estimated Actual Value of Taxable Property<br>■ Property Tax Rate—All Overlapping Governments | ■ Special Assessment Collections<br>■ Ratio of Net General Bonded Debt to Assessed Value and Net Bonded Debt per Capita<br>■ Ratio of Annual Debt Service for General Bonded Debt to Total General Expenditures<br>■ Revenue Bond Coverage<br>■ Property Value, Construction, and Bank Deposits | ■ Computation of Legal Debt Margin (If not presented in the GPFS)<br>■ Computation of Overlapping Debt (If not presented in the GPFS)<br>■ Demographic Statistics<br>■ Principal Taxpayers<br>■ Miscellaneous Statistics |

FIGURE 13–4  **Report of Independent Accountants**

# Coopers
# &Lybrand

**Coopers & Lybrand L.L.P.**

a professional services firm

Honorable Mayor and City Council
City of Orlando, Florida

We have audited the accompanying general purpose financial statements and the combining and individual fund and account group financial statements of the City of Orlando, Florida, as of and for the year ended September 30, 19X7, as listed in the table of contents. These financial statements are the responsibility of the City of Orlando, Florida, management. Our responsibility is to express an opinion on these financial statements based on our audit.

We conducted our audit in accordance with generally accepted auditing standards and the standards applicable to financial audits contained in *Government Auditing Standards,* issued by the Comptroller General of the United States. Those standards require that we plan and perform the audit to obtain reasonable assurance about whether the financial statements are free of material misstatement. An audit includes examining, on a test basis, evidence supporting the amounts and disclosures in the financial statements. An audit also includes assessing the accounting principles used and significant estimates made by management, as well as evaluating the overall financial statement presentation. We believe that our audit provides a reasonable basis for our opinion.

In our opinion, the general purpose financial statements referred to above present fairly, in all material respects, the financial position of the City of Orlando, Florida, as of September 30, 19X7, and the results of its operations and the cash flows of its proprietary fund types and nonexpendable trust funds for the year then ended in conformity with generally accepted accounting principles. Also, in our opinion, the combining and individual fund and account group financial statements referred to above present fairly, in all material respects, the financial position of each of the individual funds and account groups of the City of Orlando, Florida, as of September 30, 19X7, and the results of operations of such funds and the cash flows of individual proprietary fund types and nonexpendable trust funds for the year then ended in conformity with generally accepted accounting principles.

As described in Note II.E. to the general purpose financial statements, the City of Orlando, Florida, adopted Governmental Accounting Standards Board *Statement #31 and #32,* which changed its method of accounting for investments and the method of accounting and reporting the deferred compensation fund, respectively.

In accordance with *Government Auditing Standards,* we have also issued our report dated November 26, 19X7, on our consideration of the City of Orlando's internal control over financial reporting and our tests of its compliance with certain provisions of laws, regulations, contracts, and grants.

Our audit was made for the purpose of forming an opinion on the general purpose financial statements taken as a whole and on the combining and individual fund and account group financial statements. The accompanying financial information listed as supplementary information on page iii in the table of contents is presented for purposes of additional analysis and is not a required part of the financial statements of the City of Orlando, Florida. Such information has been subjected to the auditing procedures applied in the audit of the general purpose, combining and individual fund and account group financial statements and, in our opinion, is fairly presented in all material respects in relation to the financial statements of each of the respective individual funds and account groups taken as a whole.

The information presented in the Statistical Section is presented for purposes of additional analysis and is not a required part of the financial statements. Such information has not been subjected to the auditing procedures applied in the audit of the financial statements and, accordingly, we express no opinion on it.

*Coopers + Lybrand L.L.P.*

Orlando, Florida
November 26, 19X7

*Source:* Adapted from a recent city of Orlando, Florida, annual report.

As indicated in Figure 13–2, the combined balance sheet includes all fund types and account groups. Separate operating statements are required for the governmental and the proprietary fund types, however, because governmental fund operations are measured on the expenditure basis, whereas proprietary fund operations are measured on the expense basis. In the combined statements Trust Fund operations may be presented separately but are more commonly included in the appropriate governmental and/or proprietary fund statements, as illustrated in the figure.

**Combined Balance Sheet (pages 515 to 517)**    A Combined Balance Sheet is presented in Figure 13–5. Note that the data in this statement are highly summarized because the purpose of the statement is to present an overview. Note also the "Primary Government" and "Component Units" headings and the "Governmental/Downtown Development Board" and "Proprietary/Civic Facilities Authority" specific component unit subheadings. Also observe that the current year total and the prior year comparative total are labeled **"Memorandum Only"**—to signal that these totals do not purport to show data in conformity with GAAP, as do the fund type and specific component unit columns in the statement. (Discrete component unit presentation is discussed in the next chapter.)

**Combined Statement of Revenues, Expenditures, and Changes in Fund Balances (page 518)**    Several aspects of this statement, illustrated in Figure 13–6, warrant attention: (1) It includes all of the governmental (expendable) funds, the Expendable Trust Fund(s), as permitted by the GASB *Codification,* and the "Governmental" component unit (Downtown Development Board); (2) the format of the statement is one of the acceptable alternatives set forth in the *Codification*—other financing sources and uses (in this case, operating transfers) are reported together after the excess of revenues over expenditures; (3) operating transfers between the primary government and its component units are distinguished from those between funds of the primary government; and (4) the statement presents changes in total fund balances, not unreserved fund balances, and thus has no changes in reserves section.

**Combined Statement of Revenues, Expenditures, and Changes in Fund Balances—Budget and Actual (page 519)**    The budget for the city of Orlando is prepared and administered on the modified accrual basis except that budgetary basis expenditures include encumbrances outstanding at year end. Thus, the actual expenditures on the budgetary basis shown in the budgetary comparison statement in Figure 13–7 differ from those presented in the GAAP basis statement in Figure 13–6. The differences are reconciled in the budgetary statement (rather than in the notes as discussed and illustrated in Chapter 14) by reporting the GAAP-basis expenditures and adding the encumbrances outstanding at year end to arrive at the budgetary basis expenditures for the year.

Note also that Debt Service Funds are presented in the budgetary comparison statement—as are all other governmental fund types and Expendable Trust Funds—which indicates that their annual budgets are also legally adopted. Note also that budgetary comparisons are not required for discretely presented component units—and thus no "Component Units" column(s) appears on this statement. Finally, note the fund balance allocation added to the budget of each fund type. This represents Orlando's budgeted use of a portion of beginning fund balance to cover the excess of budgeted expenditures over budgeted revenues and is pre-

FIGURE 13–5

## CITY OF ORLANDO, FLORIDA
### COMBINED BALANCE SHEET
#### All Fund Types, Account Groups, and Discretely Presented Component Units
September 30, 19X7

| | Primary Government | | | | | | | | | | Component Units | | Total (Memorandum Only) |
|---|---|---|---|---|---|---|---|---|---|---|---|---|---|
| | Governmental Fund Types | | | | Proprietary Fund Types | | Fiduciary Fund Types | Account Groups | | Total (Memorandum Only) | Governmental | Proprietary | |
| | General | Special Revenue | Debt Service | Capital Projects | Enterprise | Internal Service | Trust & Agency | General Fixed Assets | General Long-Term Obligations | Primary Government | Downtown Development Board | Civic Facilities Authority | Reporting Entity |
| **Assets and Other Debits** | | | | | | | | | | | | | |
| **Current Assets** | | | | | | | | | | | | | |
| Cash and Cash Equivalents | $57,600,947 | $43,935,161 | $ — | $18,863,477 | $41,100,209 | $8,035,561 | — | $ — | $ — | $169,535,355 | $331,132 | $1,190,788 | $171,057,275 |
| Investments | — | — | — | 26,221,550 | — | — | — | — | — | 26,221,550 | — | — | 26,221,550 |
| Receivables (Net of Allowance for Uncollectibles): | | | | | | | | | | | | | |
| Accounts | 3,075,802 | 84,739 | — | 70,357 | 4,414,269 | 3,910 | — | — | — | 7,649,077 | — | 184,745 | 7,833,822 |
| Taxes | 396,599 | — | — | — | — | — | — | — | — | 396,599 | — | — | 396,599 |
| Special Assessments | 773,047 | — | — | — | — | — | — | — | — | 773,047 | — | — | 773,047 |
| Due from Other Funds | 943,749 | — | — | — | — | — | — | — | — | 943,749 | — | — | 943,749 |
| Due from Other Governments | 3,965,478 | 2,030,500 | — | 6,263,172 | 1,137,153 | 10,604 | — | — | — | 13,406,907 | 9,092 | 16,451 | 13,432,450 |
| Inventories | 893,919 | — | — | — | 480,678 | 402,050 | — | — | — | 1,776,647 | — | 41,806 | 1,818,453 |
| Land Held for Sale | 1,857,775 | — | — | — | — | — | — | — | — | 1,857,775 | — | — | 1,857,775 |
| Prepaid Items | 563,679 | 848 | — | — | 15,314 | 7,084 | — | — | — | 586,925 | 482 | — | 587,407 |
| **Total Current Assets** | 70,070,995 | 46,051,248 | — | 51,418,556 | 47,147,623 | 8,459,209 | — | — | — | 223,147,631 | 340,706 | 1,433,790 | 224,922,127 |
| **Restricted Assets** | | | | | | | | | | | | | |
| Cash and Cash Equivalents | — | — | 2,175,640 | — | 129,208,588 | 39,168,890 | 25,753,845 | — | — | 196,306,963 | — | 3,026,029 | 199,332,992 |
| Investments | — | — | 10,202,465 | — | 33,720,898 | 7,089,971 | 551,736,266 | — | — | 602,749,600 | — | 1,373,648 | 604,123,248 |
| Securities Lending Collateral | — | — | — | — | — | — | 73,622,765 | — | — | 73,622,765 | — | — | 73,622,765 |
| Accounts and Notes Receivable | — | — | — | — | 830,179 | 62,044 | 2,483,096 | — | — | 3,375,319 | — | — | 3,375,319 |
| Prepaid Items | — | — | — | — | — | 128,145 | 1,467 | — | — | 129,612 | — | — | 129,612 |
| Due from Other Governments | — | — | — | — | — | — | — | — | — | 101,224 | — | — | 101,224 |
| Inventory | — | — | — | — | 74,792 | 26,432 | 53,820 | — | — | 53,820 | — | — | 53,820 |
| Equity in SSGF Commission | — | — | — | — | — | 365,438 | — | — | — | 365,438 | — | — | 365,438 |
| Loans to Other Funds | — | — | — | — | 365,438 | 94,288,120 | — | — | — | 94,288,120 | — | — | 94,288,120 |
| Loans to Component Units | — | — | — | — | 4,009,649 | 4,009,649 | — | — | — | 4,009,649 | — | — | 4,009,649 |
| **Total Restricted Assets** | — | — | 12,378,105 | — | 163,834,457 | 145,138,689 | 653,651,259 | — | — | 975,002,510 | — | 4,399,677 | 979,402,187 |
| **Property, Plant, and Equipment** | | | | | | | | | | | | | |
| Land | — | — | — | — | 44,015,650 | 540,638 | 31,278 | 38,085,447 | — | 82,673,013 | — | 1,132,426 | 83,805,439 |
| Buildings | — | — | — | — | 277,287,441 | 263,976 | — | 62,182,800 | — | 339,734,217 | 6,303 | 5,253,079 | 344,987,296 |
| Improvements Other Than Buildings | — | — | — | — | 121,745,131 | 245,762 | 30,518 | 62,172,545 | — | 184,193,956 | — | 45,893,207 | 230,093,466 |
| Equipment | — | — | — | — | 106,551,658 | 1,616,518 | 2,431 | 23,058,699 | — | 131,229,306 | 56,655 | 1,550,053 | 132,836,014 |
| Wastewater and Stormwater Lines and Pump Stations | — | — | — | — | 229,121,703 | — | — | — | — | 229,121,703 | — | — | 229,121,703 |
| Vehicles | — | — | — | — | — | 38,361,959 | — | — | — | 38,361,959 | — | — | 38,361,959 |
| Total | — | — | — | — | 778,721,583 | 41,028,853 | 64,227 | 185,499,491 | — | 1,005,314,154 | 62,958 | 53,828,765 | 1,059,205,877 |
| Less Accumulated Depreciation | — | — | — | — | (276,538,843) | (27,658,065) | (18,155) | — | — | (304,215,063) | — | (14,248,473) | (318,463,536) |
| Construction Work in Process | — | — | — | — | 28,347,717 | 284,535 | — | 1,053,131 | — | 29,685,383 | — | — | 29,685,383 |
| **Net Property, Plant, and Equipment** | — | — | — | — | 530,530,457 | 13,655,323 | 46,072 | 186,552,622 | — | 730,784,474 | 62,958 | 39,580,292 | 770,427,724 |
| Long-Term Lease Receivable | — | — | — | — | — | — | — | — | — | — | — | 1,008,519 | 1,008,519 |
| Unamortized Bond Costs | — | — | — | — | 1,621,495 | 555,781 | — | — | — | 2,177,276 | — | — | 2,177,276 |
| Amount Available in Debt Service Funds | — | — | — | — | — | — | — | — | 11,342,801 | 11,342,801 | — | — | 11,342,801 |
| Amount to Be Provided for Retirement of Long-Term Debt | — | — | — | — | — | — | — | — | 128,725,180 | 128,725,180 | 80,606 | — | 128,805,786 |
| **Total Assets and Other Debits** | $70,070,995 | $46,051,248 | $12,378,105 | $51,418,556 | $743,134,032 | $167,809,002 | $653,697,331 | $186,552,622 | $140,067,981 | $2,071,179,872 | $484,270 | $46,422,278 | $2,118,086,420 |

(continued)

FIGURE 13–5 (Continued)

## CITY OF ORLANDO, FLORIDA
## COMBINED BALANCE SHEET
### All Fund Types, Account Groups, and Discretely Presented Component Units
### September 30, 19X7

| Liabilities, Fund Equity, and Other Credits | General | Special Revenue | Debt Service | Capital Projects | Enterprise | Internal Service | Trust & Agency | General Fixed Assets | General Long-Term Obligations | Total (Memorandum Only) Primary Government | Downtown Development Board (Governmental) | Civic Facilities Authority (Proprietary) | Total (Memorandum Only) Reporting Entity |
|---|---|---|---|---|---|---|---|---|---|---|---|---|---|
| **Current Liabilities (Payable from Current Assets)** | | | | | | | | | | | | | |
| Accounts Payable | $ 3,986,912 | $1,038,284 | $ — | $ 3,130,518 | $ 8,901,601 | $ 1,237,720 | $ — | $ — | $ — | $ 18,295,035 | $ 26,269 | $ 316,795 | $ 18,638,099 |
| Accrued Liabilities | 2,328,155 | 22,839 | — | — | 462,560 | 92,544 | — | — | — | 2,906,098 | 8,596 | 11,837 | 2,926,531 |
| Compensated Absences | 866,495 | — | — | — | 2,014,362 | 452,978 | — | — | — | 3,333,835 | 1,866 | 29,352 | 3,365,053 |
| Advance Payments | 7,388,225 | 100 | — | 3,582,093 | 996,789 | — | — | — | — | 11,967,207 | — | 20,235 | 11,987,442 |
| Due to Other Funds | — | 781,858 | — | — | 161,891 | — | — | — | — | 943,749 | — | — | 943,749 |
| Short-Term Loans from Other Funds | 1,857,775 | — | — | 3,600,000 | — | — | — | — | — | 5,457,775 | — | — | 5,457,775 |
| Other Current Liabilities | — | — | — | — | 2,031 | — | — | — | — | 2,031 | — | — | 2,031 |
| Deferred Revenue | 1,296,879 | 142,170 | — | — | — | — | — | — | — | 1,439,049 | — | — | 1,439,049 |
| **Total Current Liabilities (Payable from Current Assets)** | 17,724,441 | 1,985,251 | — | 10,312,611 | 12,539,234 | 1,783,242 | — | — | — | 44,344,779 | 36,731 | 378,219 | 44,759,729 |
| **Current Liabilities (Payable from Restricted Assets)** | | | | | | | | | | | | | |
| Obligations Under Securities Lending | | | | | | | 73,622,765 | | | 73,622,765 | | | 73,622,765 |
| Accounts Payable | | | | | 1,740,131 | 154,782 | 675,952 | | | 2,570,865 | | | 2,570,865 |
| Accrued Liabilities | | | | | | 15,994 | 23,146 | | | 39,140 | | | 39,140 |
| Compensated Absences | | | | | | 50,014 | 51,062 | | | 101,076 | | | 101,076 |
| Deferred Revenue | | | | | | 23,423 | | | | 23,423 | | | 23,423 |
| Claims Liabilities | | | | | | 16,979,849 | | | | 16,979,849 | | | 16,979,849 |
| Accrued Interest Payable | | | 1,035,304 | | 4,138,667 | 2,005,043 | | | | 7,179,014 | | 130,975 | 7,309,989 |
| Current Portion of Bonds Payable | | | | | 7,480,000 | 1,930,000 | | | 1,130,000 | 10,540,000 | | 270,000 | 10,810,000 |
| Current Portion of Loans Payable | | | | | 2,241,914 | 463,391 | | | 6,874,277 | 9,579,582 | | | 9,579,582 |
| Current Portion of Loans Payable from Primary Government | | | | | | | | | | | | 257,470 | 257,470 |
| Advance Payments | | | | | 13,243,249 | | 6,730 | | | 13,249,979 | | | 13,249,979 |
| **Total Current Liabilities (Payable from Restricted Assets)** | | | 1,035,304 | | 28,843,961 | 21,622,496 | 74,379,655 | | 8,004,277 | 133,885,693 | | 658,445 | 134,544,138 |
| **Long-Term Liabilities** | | | | | | | | | | | | | |
| Bonds Payable after One Year | | | | | 201,899,568 | 77,515,712 | | | 74,495,000 | 353,910,280 | | 3,816,548 | 357,726,828 |
| Advances from Orange County | | | | | | | | | | | | 5,159,000 | 5,159,000 |
| Loans Due after One Year | | | | | | 37,673,951 | | | | 37,673,951 | | | 37,673,951 |
| Loans from Other Funds | | | | | 33,144,689 | 1,591,825 | | | 44,514,249 | 79,250,763 | | | 79,250,763 |
| Loans from Primary Government | | | | | | | | | | | | 3,752,179 | 3,752,179 |
| Compensated Absences | | | | | | | | | 13,054,455 | 13,054,455 | 80,606 | | 13,135,061 |
| **Total Long-Term Liabilities** | | | | | 235,044,257 | 116,781,488 | | | 132,063,704 | 483,889,449 | 80,606 | 12,727,727 | 496,697,782 |
| **Total Liabilities** | $17,724,441 | $1,985,251 | $1,035,304 | $10,312,611 | $276,427,452 | $140,187,226 | $74,379,655 | $ — | $140,067,981 | $662,119,921 | $117,337 | $13,764,391 | $676,001,649 |

FIGURE 13–5 (Continued)

## CITY OF ORLANDO, FLORIDA
## COMBINED BALANCE SHEET
### All Fund Types, Account Groups, and Discretely Presented Component Units
### September 30, 19X7

|  | Governmental Fund Types — General | Special Revenue | Debt Service | Capital Projects | Proprietary Fund Types — Enterprise | Internal Service | Fiduciary Fund Types — Trust & Agency | Account Groups — General Fixed Assets | General Long-Term Obligations | Total (Memorandum Only) Primary Government | Component Units — Governmental Downtown Development Board | Proprietary Civic Facilities Authority | Total (Memorandum Only) Reporting Entity |
|---|---|---|---|---|---|---|---|---|---|---|---|---|---|
| **Fund Equity and Other Credits** | | | | | | | | | | | | | |
| Investment in General Fixed Assets | $ — | $ — | $ — | $ — | $ — | — | $ — | $186,552,622 | $ — | $186,552,622 | $62,958 | $ — | $186,615,580 |
| Contributions | — | — | — | — | 240,702,569 | 7,056,784 | 31,278 | — | — | 247,790,631 | — | 31,961,946 | 279,752,577 |
| **Retained Earnings** | | | | | | | | | | | | | |
| Reserved for Debt Service | | | | | 30,571,934 | 2,213,262 | | | | 32,785,196 | | 2,632,252 | 35,417,448 |
| Reserved for Risk Management | | | | | | 7,142,256 | | | | 7,142,256 | | | 7,142,256 |
| Reserved for Vehicle Replacement | | | | | | 7,510,449 | | | | 7,510,449 | | | 7,510,449 |
| Reserved for Capital Projects | | | | | 89,677,820 | | | | | 89,677,820 | | | 89,677,820 |
| Reserved for Renewal and Replacement | | | | | 15,179,298 | | | | | 15,179,298 | | 179,188 | 15,358,486 |
| Reserved for Contractual Obligation | | | | | | | | | | | | 11,470,678 | 11,470,678 |
| Unreserved | | | | | 90,574,959 | 3,699,025 | | | | 94,273,984 | | (13,586,177) | 80,687,807 |
| **Total Retained Earnings** | | | | | 226,004,011 | 20,564,992 | | | | 246,569,003 | | 695,941 | 247,264,944 |
| **Fund Balances** | | | | | | | | | | | | | |
| Reserved for Debt Service | | | 11,342,801 | | | | | | | 11,342,801 | | | 11,342,801 |
| Reserved for Inventories | 893,919 | | | | | | 53,820 | | | 947,739 | | | 947,739 |
| Reserved for Land Held for Sale | 1,857,775 | | | | | | | | | 1,857,775 | | | 1,857,775 |
| Reserved for Prepaid Items | 563,679 | 848 | | | | | 1,467 | | | 565,994 | | | 565,994 |
| Reserved for Contractual Obligations | | 2,581,007 | | | | | | | | 2,581,007 | | | 2,581,007 |
| Reserved for Encumbrances | 1,338,287 | 4,388,902 | | 2,835,923 | | | 126,844 | | | 8,689,956 | 2,385 | | 8,692,341 |
| Reserved for Retirement Benefits | | | | | | | 551,827,439 | | | 551,827,439 | | | 551,827,439 |
| Reserved for Disability Income | | | | | | | 4,364,783 | | | 4,364,783 | | | 4,364,783 |
| Reserved for Other Projects | | | | | | | 1,411,060 | | | 1,411,060 | | | 1,411,060 |
| **Total Reserved Fund Balance** | 4,653,660 | 6,970,757 | 11,342,801 | 2,835,923 | | | 557,785,413 | | | 583,588,554 | 2,385 | | 583,590,939 |
| Designated for Working Capital | 30,000,000 | | | | | | | | | 30,000,000 | | | 30,000,000 |
| Designated for Project Appropriation | 4,788,084 | | | | | | | | | 4,788,084 | | | 4,788,084 |
| Designated for Capital Projects | 7,000,000 | | | 38,270,022 | | | | | | 45,270,022 | | | 45,270,022 |
| Designated for Subsequent Year's Budget | | 37,095,240 | | | | | 21,500,985 | | | 58,596,225 | | | 58,596,225 |
| Undesignated | 5,904,810 | | | | | | | | | 5,904,810 | | | 5,904,810 |
| **Total Unreserved Fund Balance** | 47,692,894 | 37,095,240 | | 38,270,022 | | | 21,500,985 | | | 144,559,141 | 301,590 | | 144,860,731 |
| **Total Fund Balances** | 52,346,554 | 44,065,997 | 11,342,801 | 41,105,945 | | | 579,286,398 | | | 728,147,695 | 301,590 | | 728,451,670 |
| **Total Fund Equity and Other Credits** | 52,346,554 | 44,065,997 | 11,342,801 | 41,105,945 | 466,706,580 | 27,621,776 | 579,317,676 | 186,552,622 | | 1,409,059,951 | 366,933 | 32,657,887 | 1,442,084,771 |
| **Total Liabilities, Fund Equity, and Other Credits** | $70,070,995 | $46,051,248 | $12,378,105 | $51,418,556 | $743,134,032 | $167,809,002 | $653,697,331 | $186,552,622 | $140,067,981 | $2,071,179,872 | $484,270 | $46,422,278 | $2,118,086,420 |

The accompanying notes are an integral part of the financial statements.
*Source:* Adapted from a recent city of Orlando, Florida, annual report.

# FIGURE 13–6

## CITY OF ORLANDO, FLORIDA
### COMBINED STATEMENT OF REVENUES, EXPENDITURES, AND CHANGES IN FUND BALANCES
**All Governmental Fund Types, Expendable Trust Funds, and Discretely Presented Component Unit**
For the year ended September 30, 19X7

| | Primary Government | | | | | | Component Units | |
| --- | --- | --- | --- | --- | --- | --- | --- | --- |
| | Governmental Fund Types | | | | Fiduciary Fund Types | Total (Memorandum Only) | Governmental | Total (Memorandum Only) |
| | General | Special Revenue | Debt Service | Capital Projects | Expendable Trust | Primary Government | Downtown Development Board | Reporting Entity |
| **Revenues** | | | | | | | | |
| Property Taxes | $ 47,183,672 | $ — | $ — | $ — | $ — | $ 47,183,672 | $ 799,091 | $ 47,982,763 |
| Intergovernmental | 59,450,458 | 14,580,167 | — | 17,768,143 | 282,940 | 92,081,708 | — | 92,081,708 |
| Occupational Licenses and Franchise Fees | 19,538,786 | — | — | — | — | 19,538,786 | — | 19,538,786 |
| Utilities Services Tax | — | — | — | — | 26,838,317 | 26,838,317 | — | 26,838,317 |
| Other Licenses, Permits, and Fees | 18,927,988 | 5,998,325 | — | — | — | 24,926,313 | — | 24,926,313 |
| Fines and Forfeitures | 1,711,216 | — | — | — | — | 1,711,216 | — | 1,711,216 |
| Income on Investments | 4,586,745 | 2,732,787 | 354,552 | 1,226,194 | 8,545,666 | 17,445,944 | 25,853 | 17,471,797 |
| Employee Contributions | — | — | — | — | 4,410,573 | 4,410,573 | — | 4,410,573 |
| Special Assessments | — | — | 2,991,079 | — | — | 2,991,079 | — | 2,991,079 |
| Other | 6,228,417 | 146,013 | — | 1,058 | 830,154 | 7,205,642 | 225,544 | 7,431,186 |
| **Total Revenues** | 157,627,282 | 23,457,292 | 3,345,631 | 18,995,395 | 40,907,650 | 244,333,250 | 1,050,488 | 245,383,738 |
| **Expenditures** | | | | | | | | |
| Current Operating: | | | | | | | | |
| General Administration | 11,258,316 | — | — | — | — | 11,258,316 | — | 11,258,316 |
| Planning and Development | 7,209,826 | 5,125,323 | — | — | — | 12,335,149 | — | 12,335,149 |
| Finance | 2,580,033 | — | — | — | — | 2,580,033 | — | 2,580,033 |
| Public Works | 20,586,243 | 9,786,375 | — | — | — | 30,372,618 | — | 30,372,618 |
| Community and Youth Services | 15,773,523 | — | — | — | 1,843,239 | 17,616,762 | — | 17,616,762 |
| Centroplex | 375,961 | — | — | — | — | 375,961 | — | 375,961 |
| Police | 56,467,482 | — | — | — | 369,989 | 56,837,471 | — | 56,837,471 |
| Information Systems | 5,759,492 | — | — | — | — | 5,759,492 | — | 5,759,492 |
| Human Resources | 2,084,745 | — | — | — | — | 2,084,745 | — | 2,084,745 |
| Fire | 27,016,312 | — | — | — | — | 27,016,312 | — | 27,016,312 |
| Other Expenditures | 14,196,012 | — | — | — | 12,439 | 14,208,451 | — | 14,208,451 |
| Downtown Development Board | — | — | — | — | — | — | 1,284,146 | 1,284,146 |
| Community Redevelopment Agency | — | 1,106,788 | — | — | — | 1,106,788 | — | 1,106,788 |
| Capital Improvements | — | — | — | 37,592,447 | — | 37,592,447 | — | 37,592,447 |
| Deferred Compensation | — | — | — | — | 1,094,468 | 1,094,468 | — | 1,094,468 |
| Debt Service: | | | | | | | | |
| Principal Payments | 4,716,606 | 1,457,255 | 1,070,000 | — | — | 7,243,861 | — | 7,243,861 |
| Interest and Other | 2,091,434 | 955,582 | 1,877,911 | 42,003 | — | 4,966,930 | — | 4,966,930 |
| **Total Expenditures** | 170,115,985 | 18,431,323 | 2,947,911 | 37,634,450 | 3,320,135 | 232,449,804 | 1,284,146 | 233,733,950 |
| **Excess (Deficiency) of Revenues over Expenditures** | (12,488,703) | 5,025,969 | 397,720 | (18,639,055) | 37,587,515 | 11,883,446 | (233,658) | 11,649,788 |
| **Other Financing Sources and (Uses)** | | | | | | | | |
| Operating Transfers In | 27,897,545 | 3,320,725 | 2,894,536 | 6,648,826 | 1,100,000 | 41,861,632 | — | 41,861,632 |
| Operating Transfers (Out) | (9,069,877) | (2,476,392) | (317,966) | (1,056,931) | (24,898,244) | (37,819,410) | — | (37,819,410) |
| Operating Transfers to Primary Government | — | — | — | — | — | — | (7,500) | (7,500) |
| Operating Transfers from Primary Government | — | — | — | — | — | — | 295,192 | 295,192 |
| Operating Transfers to Component Units | (771,201) | (156,100) | — | — | — | (927,301) | — | (927,301) |
| Nonoperating Capital Transfers (Out) | (1,500) | — | — | — | — | (1,500) | — | (1,500) |
| Bond and Loan Proceeds | — | — | 3,846,888 | 45,992,140 | — | 49,839,028 | — | 49,839,028 |
| Loan Payments | — | — | — | (12,150,000) | — | (12,150,000) | — | (12,150,000) |
| Bond Issuance Costs | — | — | — | (933,208) | — | (933,208) | — | (933,208) |
| Proceeds from the Sale of Land | — | 899,425 | — | 4,514,301 | — | 5,413,726 | — | 5,413,726 |
| **Total Other Financing Sources and (Uses)** | 18,054,967 | 1,587,658 | 6,423,458 | 43,015,128 | (23,798,244) | 45,282,967 | 287,692 | 45,570,659 |
| **Excess of Revenues and Other Sources over Expenditures and Other (Uses)** | 5,566,264 | 6,613,627 | 6,821,178 | 24,376,073 | 13,789,271 | 57,166,413 | 54,034 | 57,220,447 |
| **Fund Balances at Beginning of Year, As Restated** | 46,780,290 | 37,452,370 | 4,521,623 | 16,729,872 | 54,471,411 | 159,955,566 | 249,941 | 160,205,507 |
| **Fund Balances at End of Year** | $ 52,346,554 | $44,065,997 | $11,342,801 | $41,105,945 | $68,260,682 | $217,121,979 | $ 303,975 | $217,425,954 |

The accompanying notes are an integral part of the financial statements.
*Source:* Adapted from a recent city of Orlando, Florida, annual report.

FIGURE 13–7

## CITY OF ORLANDO, FLORIDA
## COMBINED STATEMENT OF REVENUES AND EXPENDITURES—ACTUAL AND BUDGET
### PRIMARY GOVERNMENT
#### All Governmental Fund Types and Expendable Trust Funds
#### For the year ended September 30, 19X7

| | General Fund | | | | | Special Revenue Funds | | | | | Debt Service Funds | | |
|---|---|---|---|---|---|---|---|---|---|---|---|---|---|
| | Actual | Encumbrances | Budgetary Basis | Budget | Variance—Favorable (Unfavorable) | Actual | Encumbrances | Budgetary Basis | Budget | Variance—Favorable (Unfavorable) | Actual and Budgetary Basis | Budget | Variance—Favorable (Unfavorable) |
| **Revenues** | | | | | | | | | | | | | |
| Property Taxes | $ 47,183,672 | $ — | $ 47,183,672 | $ 47,253,893 | $ (70,221) | $ 14,580,167 | $ 189,265 | $ 14,769,432 | $ 20,243,579 | $ (5,474,147) | $ — | $ — | $ — |
| Intergovernmental | 59,450,458 | — | 59,450,458 | 58,907,913 | 542,545 | | | | | | — | — | — |
| Occupational Licenses and Franchise Fees | 19,538,786 | — | 19,538,786 | 19,448,149 | 90,637 | | | | | | — | — | — |
| Other Licenses, Permits, and Fees | 18,927,988 | — | 18,927,988 | 17,669,299 | 1,258,689 | 5,998,325 | — | 5,998,325 | 5,963,756 | 34,569 | — | — | — |
| Fines and Forfeitures | 1,711,216 | — | 1,711,216 | 1,969,250 | (258,034) | | | | | | — | — | — |
| Income on Investments | 4,586,745 | — | 4,586,745 | 4,838,715 | (251,970) | 2,732,787 | — | 2,732,787 | 1,623,938 | 1,108,849 | 2,991,079 | 2,991,079 | — |
| Special Assessments | | | | | | | | | | | 354,552 | 354,552 | — |
| Other | 6,228,417 | — | 6,228,417 | 6,108,599 | 119,818 | 146,013 | — | 146,013 | 181,943 | (35,930) | | | |
| **Total Revenues** | 157,627,282 | — | 157,627,282 | 156,195,818 | 1,431,464 | 23,457,292 | 189,265 | 23,646,557 | 28,013,216 | (4,366,659) | 3,345,631 | 3,345,631 | — |
| **Expenditures** | | | | | | | | | | | | | |
| Current Operating: | | | | | | | | | | | | | |
| General Administration | 11,258,316 | 818,081 | 12,076,397 | 14,274,520 | 2,198,123 | 5,125,323 | 330,627 | 5,455,950 | 13,730,158 | 8,274,208 | | | |
| Planning and Development | 7,209,826 | 12,232 | 7,222,058 | 8,312,995 | 1,090,937 | | | | | | | | |
| Finance | 2,580,033 | 82,648 | 2,662,681 | 2,712,670 | 49,989 | | | | | | | | |
| Public Works | 20,586,243 | 148,637 | 20,734,880 | 22,574,426 | 1,839,546 | 9,786,375 | 4,247,440 | 14,033,815 | 32,018,474 | 17,984,659 | | | |
| Community and Youth Services | 15,773,523 | 26,753 | 15,800,276 | 16,575,626 | 775,350 | | | | | | | | |
| Centroplex | 375,961 | — | 375,961 | 406,670 | 30,709 | | | | | | | | |
| Police | 56,467,482 | 114,896 | 56,582,378 | 57,780,080 | 1,197,702 | | | | | | | | |
| Information Systems | 5,759,492 | 36,498 | 5,795,990 | 6,318,039 | 522,049 | | | | | | | | |
| Human Resources | 2,084,745 | 30,132 | 2,114,877 | 2,177,415 | 62,538 | | | | | | | | |
| Fire | 27,016,312 | 68,410 | 27,084,722 | 27,457,547 | 372,825 | | | | | | | | |
| Other Expenditures | 14,196,012 | — | 14,196,012 | 15,004,781 | 808,769 | | | | | | | | |
| Community Redevelopment Agency | | | | | | 1,106,788 | 100 | 1,106,888 | 3,883,850 | 2,776,962 | | | |
| Debt Service | | | | | | 2,412,837 | | 2,412,837 | 2,425,824 | 12,987 | 2,947,911 | 9,961,418 | 7,013,507 |
| **Total Expenditures** | 170,115,985 | 1,338,287 | 171,454,272 | 180,563,064 | 9,108,792 | 18,431,323 | 4,578,167 | 23,009,490 | 52,058,306 | 29,048,816 | 2,947,911 | 9,961,418 | 7,013,507 |
| Excess (Deficiency) of Revenues over Expenditures | (12,488,703) | (1,338,287) | (13,826,990) | (24,367,246) | 10,540,256 | 5,025,969 | (4,388,902) | 637,067 | (24,045,090) | 24,682,157 | 397,720 | (6,615,787) | 7,013,507 |
| **Other Financing Sources and (Uses)** | | | | | | | | | | | | | |
| Operating Transfers In | 27,897,545 | — | 27,897,545 | 27,900,559 | (3,014) | 3,320,725 | — | 3,320,725 | 3,320,725 | — | 2,894,536 | 2,895,531 | (995) |
| Operating Transfers (Out) | (9,069,877) | — | (9,069,877) | (9,217,736) | 147,859 | (2,476,392) | — | (2,476,392) | (2,480,400) | 4,008 | (317,966) | (317,966) | — |
| Operating Transfers In (Out) to Component Units | | | | | | (156,100) | — | (156,100) | (156,100) | — | | | |
| Nonoperating Capital Transfers (Out) | (771,201) | — | (771,201) | (1,125,751) | 354,550 | | | | | | | | |
| Bond Proceeds | (1,500) | | (1,500) | (1,500) | — | | | | | | | | |
| Proceeds from Sale of Land | | | | | | 899,425 | | 899,425 | | 899,425 | 3,846,888 | 3,846,888 | — |
| **Total Other Financing Sources and (Uses)** | 18,054,967 | | 18,054,967 | 17,555,572 | 499,395 | 1,587,658 | | 1,587,658 | 684,225 | 903,433 | 6,423,458 | 6,424,453 | (995) |
| Excess (Deficiency) of Revenues and Other Sources over Expenditures and Other (Uses) | 5,566,264 | (1,338,287) | 4,227,977 | (6,811,674) | 11,039,651 | 6,613,627 | (4,388,902) | 2,224,725 | (23,360,865) | 25,585,590 | 6,821,178 | (191,334) | 7,012,512 |
| Fund Balance Allocation | | | | 6,811,674 | (6,811,674) | | | | 23,360,865 | (23,360,865) | | 191,334 | (191,334) |
| **Excess (Deficiency) of Revenues and Other Sources over Expenditures and Other (Uses)** | $ 5,566,264 | $ (1,338,287) | $ 4,227,977 | $ -0- | $ 4,227,977 | $ 6,613,627 | $ (4,388,902) | $ 2,224,725 | $ -0- | $ 2,224,725 | $ 6,821,178 | $ -0- | $ 6,821,178 |

The accompanying notes are an integral part of the financial statements.
*Source:* Adapted from a recent city of Orlando, Florida, annual report.

sented only in the budgetary operating statement and only because it is a budgeted amount.

**Combined Statement of Revenues, Expenses, and Changes in Retained Earnings/Fund Equity (page 520)**   This statement (Figure 13–8) resembles a combined income and retained earnings statement for a business concern, as it properly should under the GASB *Codification*. Note that (1) both "Primary Government" and "Component Unit" columns are presented, (2) operating transfers

FIGURE 13–8

**CITY OF ORLANDO, FLORIDA**
**COMBINED STATEMENT OF REVENUES, EXPENSES, AND CHANGES IN RETAINED EARNINGS/FUND BALANCES**
**All Proprietary Fund Types, Similar Trust Funds, and Discretely Presented Component Unit**
For the year ended September 30, 19X7

| | Primary Government | | | | Component Units | |
| --- | --- | --- | --- | --- | --- | --- |
| | Proprietary Fund Types | | Fiduciary | Total (Memorandum Only) | Proprietary | Total (Memorandum Only) |
| | Enterprise | Internal Service | Nonexpendable Trust | Primary Government | Civic Facilities Authority | Reporting Entity |
| **Operating Revenues** | | | | | | |
| User Charges | $ 64,785,224 | $15,905,745 | $ — | $ 80,690,969 | $ — | $ 80,690,969 |
| Fees | 16,492,993 | 13,219,017 | — | 29,712,010 | 1,795,246 | 31,507,256 |
| Facility Rental | 2,924,963 | — | — | 2,924,963 | 490,947 | 3,415,910 |
| Parking Fines | 2,365,270 | — | — | 2,365,270 | — | 2,365,270 |
| Contributions from Employees | — | — | 319,923 | 319,923 | — | 319,923 |
| Tax Increment Fees | — | — | 4,986,610 | 4,986,610 | — | 4,986,610 |
| Other | 1,104,768 | 887,170 | 19,007 | 2,010,945 | 3,344 | 2,014,289 |
| Total Operating Revenues | 87,673,218 | 30,011,932 | 5,325,540 | 123,010,690 | 2,289,537 | 125,300,227 |
| **Operating Expenses** | | | | | | |
| Salaries, Wages, and Employee Benefits | 24,686,264 | 5,026,811 | — | 29,713,075 | 516,092 | 30,229,167 |
| Contractual Services, Materials, and Supplies | 38,031,346 | 6,465,930 | 721 | 44,497,997 | 1,879,004 | 46,377,001 |
| Depreciation Expense | 26,486,412 | 5,468,979 | 2,020 | 31,957,411 | 1,332,318 | 33,289,729 |
| Insurance, Administrative, and Other | 5,072,225 | 9,994,476 | — | 15,066,701 | 802,489 | 15,869,190 |
| Disability Income Benefits | — | — | 225,997 | 225,997 | — | 225,997 |
| Total Operating Expenses | 94,276,247 | 26,956,196 | 228,738 | 121,461,181 | 4,529,903 | 125,991,084 |
| Operating Income (Loss) | (6,603,029) | 3,055,736 | 5,096,802 | 1,549,509 | (2,240,366) | (690,857) |
| **Nonoperating Revenues (Expenses)** | | | | | | |
| Income on Investments | 12,458,298 | 3,111,301 | 306,885 | 15,876,484 | 477,287 | 16,353,771 |
| Impact Fees | 12,414,294 | — | — | 12,414,294 | — | 12,414,294 |
| Interest Expense | (13,620,407) | (6,585,870) | — | (20,206,277) | (498,516) | (20,704,793) |
| Gain (Loss) on Sale of Fixed Assets | 1,825,568 | 1,764,230 | — | 3,589,798 | — | 3,589,798 |
| Total Nonoperating Revenues (Expenses) | 13,077,753 | (1,710,339) | 306,885 | 11,674,299 | (21,229) | 11,653,070 |
| Income (Loss) before Operating Transfers | 6,474,724 | 1,345,397 | 5,403,687 | 13,223,808 | (2,261,595) | 10,962,213 |
| **Operating Transfers** | | | | | | |
| Operating Transfers In | 3,464,239 | 1,589 | — | 3,465,828 | — | 3,465,828 |
| Operating Transfers (Out) | (2,078,310) | (438,863) | (4,990,877) | (7,508,050) | — | (7,508,050) |
| Operating Transfers from Primary Government | — | — | — | — | 632,109 | 632,109 |
| Operating Transfers from Component Units | 7,500 | — | — | 7,500 | — | 7,500 |
| Nonoperating Capital Transfers (Out) | (31,000) | — | — | (31,000) | — | (31,000) |
| Total Operating Transfers | 1,362,429 | (437,274) | (4,990,877) | (4,065,722) | 632,109 | (3,433,613) |
| **Net Income (Loss)** | 7,837,153 | 908,123 | 412,810 | 9,158,086 | (1,629,486) | 7,528,600 |
| Depreciation on Contributed Assets | 10,241,900 | — | — | 10,241,900 | 1,132,455 | 11,374,355 |
| Net Increase (Decrease) in Retained Earnings/ Fund Balances | 18,079,053 | 908,123 | 412,810 | 19,399,986 | (497,031) | 18,902,955 |
| **Retained Earnings/Fund Balances at Beginning of Year, As Restated** | 207,924,958 | 19,656,869 | 4,387,885 | 231,969,712 | 1,192,972 | 233,162,684 |
| **Retained Earnings/Fund Balances at End of Year** | $226,004,011 | $20,564,992 | $4,800,695 | $251,369,698 | $ 695,941 | $252,065,639 |

The accompanying notes are an integral part of the financial statements.
*Source:* Adapted from a recent city of Orlando, Florida, annual report.

are reported in a separate section before net income, and (3) Orlando chose to present its fiduciary (nonexpendable trust) fund statements with the governmental and proprietary fund statements, as appropriate, rather than separately.

**Combined Statement of Cash Flows (page 522)**      GASB *Statement Nos. 9 and 14* require a statement of cash flows to be presented for proprietary funds, nonexpendable trust funds, and discretely presented proprietary-type component units. The direct method Orlando statement (Figure 13–9) is prepared in accordance with these GASB statements.

**Combined Statement of Changes in Plan Net Assets—Pension Trust Funds (page 523)**      Governments that report defined benefit Pension Trust Funds (PTFs) in their combined balance sheet must also report PTF operating results. The city of Orlando presents a separate Combined Statement of Changes in Plan Net Assets—Firefighters, Police, and General Employees' Pension Plans (Figure 13–10). Note that although PTF assets and liabilities are included in the combined balance sheet, changes in PTF net assets cannot be included in either of the combined operating statements because it is based on a different model than either of those statements.

**The Notes to the Financial Statements**      The notes to the GPFS of a governmental unit are an integral part of the GPFS. The notes provide information that is necessary for fair presentation and appropriate understanding of the financial position and operating results of the various fund types of the government and of the financing and investing activities of its proprietary fund types, but that is not readily apparent from or cannot be included in the GPFS. The notes in a typical report are quite extensive, often as long as 25 to 50 pages, and contain significant information.

The GASB identifies numerous notes that it considers essential to fair presentation of the GPFS for all governments, and many other notes that should be presented when applicable. Most of these are identified in Figure 13–11. The distinctions between the notes in each category are not clear because (1) some notes categorized as essential do not apply to all governments, and thus may not be presented, and (2) all pertinent notes presented should be essential to fair presentation at the GPFS level. Apparently, those notes listed as essential to fair presentation of the GPFS are those thought to be applicable for the overwhelming majority of governments.

Note in reviewing Figure 13–11 that a number of the notes listed provide information that should be obvious from the combining and/or individual fund financial statements included in the CAFR. Examples include notes regarding:

- Overexpenditure of appropriations in individual funds
- Deficit fund balance or retained earnings of individual funds
- Interfund receivables and payables
- Segment information for Enterprise Funds

This duplication occurs because the GPFS and notes must be sufficiently complete to "stand alone," because they may be issued separately from the CAFR (but, if so, must indicate the availability of the CAFR for those wanting more detail).

The GASB also states that the list of notes in Figure 13–11 is not exhaustive and is not intended to replace professional judgment. Too, the Board emphasizes that the notes should not be "cluttered" with unnecessary disclosures. Indeed, the GASB is reviewing its note disclosure requirements to ensure that all of them are necessary and are presented as concisely as possible.

FIGURE 13–9

**CITY OF ORLANDO, FLORIDA**
**COMBINED STATEMENT OF CASH FLOWS**
**All Proprietary Fund Types, Nonexpendable Trust Funds, and Discretely Presented Component Unit**
For the year ended September 30, 19X7

| | Primary Government | | | | Component Units | |
| | Proprietary Fund Types | | Fiduciary Fund Type | Total (Memorandum Only) | Proprietary | Total (Memorandum Only) |
| | Enterprise | Internal Service | Nonexpendable Trust | Primary Government | Civic Facilities Authority | Reporting Entity |
|---|---|---|---|---|---|---|
| **Increase (Decrease) in Cash and Cash Equivalents:** | | | | | | |
| **Cash Flows from Operations:** | | | | | | |
| Receipts from Customers | $ 87,948,920 | $30,157,756 | $5,325,844 | $123,432,520 | $ 2,179,500 | $125,612,020 |
| Repayment of Loans to Other Funds | — | 20,394,993 | — | 20,394,993 | — | 20,394,993 |
| Repayment of Loans to Component Units | — | 239,911 | — | 239,911 | — | 239,911 |
| Loans to Other Funds and Developers | — | (14,311,933) | — | (14,311,933) | — | (14,311,933) |
| Payments to Suppliers | (36,483,555) | (13,747,655) | (231,368) | (50,462,578) | (2,541,773) | (53,004,351) |
| Payments to Employees | (18,930,399) | (3,927,346) | — | (22,857,745) | (410,085) | (23,267,830) |
| Payments to Internal Service Funds of the Primary Government and Administrative Fees | (10,241,730) | (1,414,796) | — | (11,656,526) | (238,058) | (11,894,584) |
| **Net Cash Provided By (Used In) Operating Activities** | 22,293,236 | 17,390,930 | 5,094,476 | 44,778,642 | (1,010,416) | 43,768,226 |
| **Cash Flows from Noncapital Financing Activities:** | | | | | | |
| Operating Transfers In | 3,464,239 | 1,589 | — | 3,465,828 | 632,109 | 4,097,937 |
| Operating Transfers (Out) | (2,078,310) | (438,863) | (4,990,877) | (7,508,050) | — | (7,508,050) |
| Operating Transfers from Component Units | 7,500 | — | — | 7,500 | — | 7,500 |
| (Increase) Decrease Due from Other Governments | — | — | — | — | (16,451) | (16,451) |
| Increase (Decrease) Due to Other Funds | 93,102 | — | — | 93,102 | — | 93,102 |
| Principal Paid on Bonds and Loans | — | (1,850,000) | — | (1,850,000) | — | (1,850,000) |
| Interest Paid on Bonds and Loans | — | (6,481,105) | — | (6,481,105) | — | (6,481,105) |
| **Net Cash Flows from Noncapital Financing Activities** | 1,486,531 | (8,768,379) | (4,990,877) | (12,272,725) | 615,658 | (11,657,067) |
| **Cash Flows from Capital and Related Financing Activities:** | | | | | | |
| Proceeds from Bonds, Loans, and Advances | 86,075,819 | 2,055,216 | — | 88,131,035 | 200,000 | 88,331,035 |
| Additions to Property, Plant, and Equipment | (31,316,494) | (6,807,803) | — | (38,124,297) | (1,023,789) | (39,148,086) |
| Principal Paid on Bonds, Interfund Loans, Loans, and Leases | (91,731,590) | — | — | (91,731,590) | (489,910) | (92,221,500) |
| Interest Paid on Bonds, Interfund Loans, Loans, and Leases | (13,930,986) | — | — | (13,930,986) | (503,282) | (14,434,268) |
| Proceeds from Sale of Property, Plant, and Equipment | 1,978,346 | 741,782 | — | 2,720,128 | — | 2,720,128 |
| Capital Contributions from Other Governments, Developers, and Funds | 3,850,697 | 612,707 | — | 4,463,404 | 1,017,326 | 5,480,730 |
| Impact Fees Received | 10,628,712 | — | — | 10,628,712 | — | 10,628,712 |
| Principal Paid on Long-Term Lease Receivable | — | — | — | — | 13,871 | 13,871 |
| Original Issue Discount and Bond Issuance Costs | (475,421) | — | — | (475,421) | — | (475,421) |
| **Net Cash Flows from Capital and Related Financing Activities** | (34,920,917) | (3,398,098) | — | (38,319,015) | (785,784) | (39,104,799) |
| **Cash Flows from Investing Activities:** | | | | | | |
| Purchases of Investments | (250,030,292) | (81,779,659) | — | (331,809,951) | 1,017,994 | (330,791,957) |
| Proceeds from Sales and Maturities of Investments | 250,358,014 | 81,242,519 | — | 331,600,533 | (1,099,640) | 330,500,893 |
| Interest on Investments | 12,810,177 | 3,242,287 | 306,885 | 16,359,349 | 489,664 | 16,849,013 |
| **Net Cash Flows from Investing Activities** | 13,137,899 | 2,705,147 | 306,885 | 16,149,931 | 408,018 | 16,557,949 |
| **Net Increase (Decrease) in Cash and Cash Equivalents** | 1,996,749 | 7,929,600 | 410,484 | 10,336,833 | (772,524) | 9,564,309 |
| Cash and Cash Equivalents at Beginning of Year, As Restated | 168,312,048 | 39,274,851 | 4,371,941 | 211,958,840 | 4,989,341 | 216,948,181 |
| **Cash and Cash Equivalents at End of Year** | $170,308,797 | $47,204,451 | $4,782,425 | $222,295,673 | $ 4,216,817 | $226,512,490 |
| **Classified As:** | | | | | | |
| Current Assets | $ 41,100,209 | $ 8,035,561 | $ | $ 49,135,770 | $ 1,190,788 | $ 50,326,558 |
| Restricted Assets | 129,208,588 | 39,168,890 | 4,782,425 | 173,159,903 | 3,026,029 | 176,185,932 |
| **Total** | $170,308,797 | $47,204,451 | $4,782,425 | $222,295,673 | $ 4,216,817 | $226,512,490 |
| **Reconciliation of Operating Income (Loss) to Net Cash Provided By (Used In) Operating Activities:** | | | | | | |
| **Operating Income (Loss)** | $ (6,603,029) | $ 3,055,736 | $5,096,802 | $ 1,549,509 | $(2,240,366) | $ (690,857) |
| **Adjustments Not Affecting Cash:** | | | | | | |
| Depreciation | 26,486,413 | 5,468,979 | 2,020 | 31,957,412 | 1,332,318 | 33,289,730 |
| Amortization | 696,544 | 133,679 | — | 830,223 | — | 830,223 |
| Bad Debt Expense | 357,510 | — | — | 357,510 | — | 357,510 |
| **Change in Assets and Liabilities:** | | | | | | |
| (Increase) Decrease in Accounts Receivable | 285,979 | 286 | 304 | 286,569 | (99,269) | 187,300 |
| (Increase) Decrease in Due from Other Governments | (227,084) | (30,831) | — | (257,915) | — | (257,915) |
| (Increase) Decrease in Inventory | 14,528 | 15,759 | — | 30,287 | 21,128 | 51,415 |
| (Increase) Decrease in Prepaid Items | (6,565) | 88,772 | — | 82,207 | — | 82,207 |
| (Increase) Decrease in Due from Other Funds | — | 19,267 | — | 19,267 | — | 19,267 |
| (Increase) Decrease in Loans to Other Funds | — | 6,083,060 | — | 6,083,060 | — | 6,083,060 |
| (Increase) Decrease in Loans to Component Units | — | 239,911 | — | 239,911 | — | 239,911 |
| Increase (Decrease) in Accounts Payable | 1,345,847 | 549,655 | (4,650) | 1,890,852 | (24,229) | 1,866,623 |
| Increase (Decrease) in Other Liabilities | (200) | — | — | (200) | — | (200) |
| Increase (Decrease) in Accrued Liabilities | 52,442 | 22,930 | — | 75,372 | 6,704 | 82,076 |
| Increase (Decrease) in Compensated Absences | 31,554 | (5,393) | — | 26,161 | 4,066 | 30,227 |
| Increase (Decrease) in Advance Payments | (140,703) | — | — | (140,703) | (10,768) | (151,471) |
| Increase (Decrease) in Deferred Revenue | — | 23,423 | — | 23,423 | — | 23,423 |
| Increase (Decrease) in Claims Payable | — | 1,725,697 | — | 1,725,697 | — | 1,725,697 |
| **Total Adjustments** | 28,896,265 | 14,335,194 | (2,326) | 43,229,133 | 1,229,950 | 44,459,083 |
| **Net Cash Provided By (Used In) Operating Activities** | $ 22,293,236 | $17,390,930 | $5,094,476 | $ 44,778,642 | $(1,010,416) | $ 43,768,226 |
| **Noncash Investing, Capital, and Financing Activities:** | | | | | | |
| Contributed Property, Plant, and Equipment | $ 500,382 | $ — | $ — | $ 500,382 | $ — | $ 500,382 |
| Equity in Earnings of SSGFC | — | 10,846 | — | 10,846 | — | 10,846 |
| **Total Noncash Investing, Capital, and Financing Activities** | $ 500,382 | $ 10,846 | $ –0– | $ 511,228 | $ –0– | $ 511,228 |

The accompanying notes are an integral part of the financial statements.
*Source:* Adapted from a recent city of Orlando, Florida, annual report.

FIGURE 13–10

**CITY OF ORLANDO, FLORIDA**
**COMBINED STATEMENT OF CHANGES IN PLAN NET ASSETS**
**FIREFIGHTERS', POLICE, AND GENERAL EMPLOYEES' PENSION PLANS**
For the year ended September 30, 19X7

| | Pension Trust |
|---|---|
| **Additions** | |
| **Contributions** | |
| Employer | $ 15,643,428 |
| State | 3,084,505 |
| Plan Members | 4,235,470 |
| Plan Member Buybacks | 21,497 |
| **Total Contributions** | 22,984,900 |
| **Investment Income** | |
| Net Appreciation in Fair Value of Investments | 82,871,927 |
| Interest | 10,970,136 |
| Dividends | 7,388,444 |
| Securities Lending | 3,917,933 |
| | 105,148,440 |
| Less Investment Expenses: | |
| Investment Management Fees | 1,310,651 |
| Custodian Fees | 161,773 |
| Securities Lending Expenses: | |
| Interest Expense | 3,786,551 |
| Agent Fees | 45,900 |
| **Net Investment Income** | 99,843,565 |
| **Total Additions** | 122,828,465 |
| **Deductions** | |
| Benefits | 16,856,132 |
| Refunds of Contributions | 516,806 |
| Administrative Expense | 165,783 |
| Salaries, Wages, and Employee Benefits | 25,382 |
| **Total Deductions** | 17,564,103 |
| **Net Increase** | 105,264,362 |
| **Net Assets Held in Trust For Pension Benefits** | |
| **Beginning of Year, As Restated** | 400,960,659 |
| **End of Year** | $506,225,021 |

The accompanying notes are an integral part of the financial statements.
*Source:* Adapted from a recent report of the city of Orlando, Florida.

Some of the notes typically presented by governments are very similar, if not identical, to notes presented in business financial statements. Others are unique to governments. Several of the unique notes that are discussed at different points in the book are illustrated or noted in the following sections.

FIGURE 13-11 **Common Note Disclosures**

| **Notes *Essential* to Fair Presentation of GPFS** | **Additional Note Disclosures, If Applicable, Including** |
|---|---|

**Notes *Essential* to Fair Presentation of GPFS**

1.  Summary of significant accounting policies, including
    -   Reporting entity criteria and component units
    -   Revenue recognition policies
    -   Encumbrance accounting and reporting methods
    -   Policies as to reporting infrastructure GFA
    -   Policies with regard to capitalization of interest on fixed assets
    -   Cash and cash equivalents definition for cash flow statements
    -   Policy on use of FASB guidance for proprietary activities
2.  Cash deposits with financial institutions (related legal and contractual provisions and categories of risk)
3.  Investments—including repurchase agreements (related legal and contractual provisions and categories of risk)
4.  Significant contingent liabilities
5.  Encumbrances outstanding
6.  Significant effects of subsequent events
7.  Annual pension cost and net pension obligations
8.  Material violations of finance-related legal and contractual provisions
9.  Schedule of debt service requirements to maturity
10. Commitments under noncapitalized (operating) leases
11. Construction and other significant commitments
12. Schedule of changes in general fixed assets (unless reported by including a statement of changes in general fixed assets in the GPFS)
13. Schedule of changes in general long-term debt (unless reported by including a statement of changes in general long-term debt in the GPFS)
14. Any excess of expenditures over appropriations in individual funds
15. Deficit fund balance or retained earnings of individual funds
16. Interfund receivables and payables

**Additional Note Disclosures, If Applicable, Including**

1.  Risk management activities
2.  Property taxes
3.  Segment information
4.  Condensed financial statements of discretely presented component units (complex entity structure only)
5.  Budgetary basis of accounting—including an explanation of the differences between the budgetary and GAAP bases
6.  Short-term debt instruments and liquidity
7.  Related party transactions
8.  Nature of accountability for related organizations
9.  Capital leases
10. Joint ventures and jointly governed organizations
11. Litigation, claims and judgments, compensated absences, special termination benefits, and so on
12. Debt extinguishment including advance refundings
13. Grants, entitlements, and shared revenues
14. Method of estimation of fixed asset costs
15. Fund balance designations
16. Interfund eliminations in combining statements not apparent from headings
17. Pension plans—in both separately issued plan financial statements and employer statements
18. Bond, tax, or revenue anticipation notes excluded from current liabilities (proprietary funds)
19. Financial statement inconsistencies associated with component units with different fiscal year ends
20. For separate component unit reports, the primary government in whose report it is included and the relationship
21. Reverse repurchase and dollar reverse repurchase agreements
22. Securities lending transactions
23. Special assessment debt and related activities
24. Demand bonds
25. Postemployment benefits other than pension benefits
26. Landfill closure and postclosure care
27. On-behalf payments for fringe benefits and salaries
28. Entity involvement in conduit debt obligations
29. Sponsoring government disclosures on external investment pools reported as investment trust funds
30. Contingencies
31. Other, as appropriate in the circumstances

*Source:* Adapted from GASB *Codification,* sec. 2300.106–.107.

**Deposits and Investments**     Governments have significant amounts of resources on deposit with financial institutions and invested in various types of securities. The degrees of risk associated with various deposits and investments often vary greatly among governments, among funds of the same government, or even within a single fund. Hence, the GASB requires several disclosures with respect to deposits and investments. The basic disclosure categories required are:

- Legal and contractual provisions regarding deposits and investments
- Segregation of deposits by three categories of credit risk
- Segregation of investments by three categories of credit risk
- Other specific disclosures

Repurchase agreements—in which a government buys securities and the seller agrees to buy them back later—are to be treated like other investments under this guidance, but unique disclosures are required for reverse repurchase agreements—in which the SLG sells securities it owns and agrees to buy them back at some future date. An example of a deposits and investments footnote is provided in Figure 13–12.

**Segment Information for Enterprise Funds**   The GASB also requires disclosure in the GPFS of certain specified information for certain Enterprise Funds. This segment (individual fund) information is required for each Enterprise Fund with bonds or other long-term debts outstanding, for each major nonhomogenous Enterprise Fund, and for any other Enterprise Fund that meets any one of five specified criteria that indicate that the fund may not be operating on a break-even basis, but instead may be charging users significantly less than or more than the cost of providing its services.

Enterprise Fund segment information disclosures can be accomplished in several ways. But, although the GASB permits two other approaches, it states that note disclosure is preferable. A segment information note is presented in Figure 13–13.

**Other Notes**   Several other disclosure requirements are discussed in other chapters. These include disclosures concerning

- Advance refundings and in-substance defeasance of debt (Chapter 8).
- Reconciliation of budgetary and GAAP-basis operating results or fund balances (Chapter 14, illustrated in Figures 14–5 and 14–6).
- Debt service requirements to maturity (Chapter 9, illustrated in Figure 9–8).
- Pension plans and employer pension costs (Chapter 10).

Disclosures regarding the governmental reporting entity and joint ventures are discussed in the next chapter. Also, notes illustrating the disclosure and reconciliation of (1) individual fund interfund payables and receivables, and (2) operating transfers in and out and residual equity transfers in and out are illustrated in Figures 13–14 and 13–15, respectively. Careful study of these selected notes yields many real-world insights while illustrating some of the common disclosures listed in Figure 13–11.

**The Combining and Individual Fund and Account Group Statements and Schedules**
Combining and individual fund and account group statements and schedules have been presented in the preceding chapters both as integral parts of illustrative examples and as ancillary illustrations. The GASB *Codification* observes that:

> The major differences between the GPFS and the other statements in the CAFR relate to the reporting entity focus and the reporting on finance-related legal and contractual provisions that differ from GAAP. The CAFR includes (a) both individual fund and account group data and aggregate data by fund types for the primary government (including its blended component units), and combined and combining statements for discretely presented component units, together with introductory, supplementary, and statistical information; and (b) schedules essential to demonstrate compliance with finance-related legal and contractual provisions. . . .

**FIGURE 13–12 Deposits and Investments Note**

City of Tulsa
Notes to Combined Financial Statements
June 30, 19X4
(dollar amounts expressed in thousands)

## NOTE 3. CASH AND INVESTMENTS

### A. CASH AND INVESTMENTS

The City's investments policies are governed by State Statute and City Ordinances. Permissible investments include direct obligations of the U.S. government and agency securities, certificates of deposit, and savings accounts or savings certificates of savings and loan associations, repurchase agreements, judgments, and bank or guaranteed investment contracts. Collateral is required for demand deposits, certificates of deposits and repurchase agreements at 102% of all amounts not covered by federal deposit insurance. Obligations that may be pledged as collateral are obligations of the United States and its agencies and obligations of the State and its subdivisions. The City's deposits and investments are categorized below to indicate the level of risk assumed by the City as of June 30, 19X4.

**Deposit Categories of Credit Risk (See following schedules)**
A  Insured or collateralized with securities held by the entity or by its agent in the entity's name.
B  Collateralized with securities held by the pledging financial institution's trust department or agent in the entity's name.
C  Uncollateralized

**Investment Categories of Credit Risk (See following schedules)**
1  Insured or registered or securities held by the entity or its agent in the entity's name.
2  Uninsured and unregistered, with securities held by the counterparty's trust department or agent in the entity's name.
3  Uninsured and unregistered, with securities held by the counterparty or by its trust department or agent but not in the entity's name.

**Pooled Cash and Investments**

The City's pooled cash and investments consist of deposits with financial institutions, certificates of deposits, U.S. government and agency securities, and repurchase agreements and judgments. These investments have varying maturities ranging from 30 days to 12 years. A minimum of two-thirds of pooled funds shall be invested for terms less than one year except Government National Mortgage Association Securities (limited to 10% of the portfolio) and monies accumulated for bond or building funds. Component Units comprise $97,025 and 42% of the total pooled cash and investments. The following is a schedule of the City's pooled cash and investments as of June 30, 19X4 categorized by risk:

| Deposits | Category A | B | C | Bank Balance | Carrying Amount |
|---|---|---|---|---|---|
| Cash and Certificates of deposit | $ 8,690 | | | $ 8,690 | $ 1,497 |

| Investments | Category 1 | 2 | 3 | Carrying Amount | Market Value |
|---|---|---|---|---|---|
| U.S. Govt. Obligations | $192,370 | | | $192,370 | $191,230 |
| Repurchase Agreement | 17,429 | | | 17,429 | 17,429 |
| | 209,799 | | | 209,799 | 208,659 |
| Judgments | 4,298 | | | 4,298 | 4,298 |
| | $214,097 | | | $214,097 | $212,957 |

**Non-Pooled Cash and Investments**

| Deposits | Category A | B | C | Bank Balance | Carrying Amount |
|---|---|---|---|---|---|
| Cash and Certificates of deposit: | | | | | |
| Primary Government | $ 1,462 | $1 | $ | $ 1,463 | $ 1,463 |
| Component Units | 531 | | 961 | 1,492 | 1,479 |
| | $ 1,993 | $1 | $961 | $ 2,955 | $ 2,942 |

## NOTE 3. CASH AND INVESTMENTS cont'd.

| Investments | Category 1 | 2 | 3 | Carrying Amount | Market Value |
|---|---|---|---|---|---|
| **Primary Government:** | | | | | |
| U.S. Govt. Obligations | $ | | $ 20,512 | $ 36,565 | $ 36,441 |
| Corporate Bonds | | | 21,384 | 21,384 | 20,543 |
| U.S. Agency Securities | | 1,083 | 6,524 | 7,607 | 7,667 |
| Common Stock | | | 28,936 | 28,936 | 33,550 |
| Other | | 26 | 10,658 | 10,684 | 10,655 |
| | | 1,109 | 88,014 | 105,176 | 108,856 |
| Deferred compensation mutual funds and annuities administered by independent plan administrator | | | | 13,085 | 13,085 |
| Mutual funds, including funds invested in U.S. instrumentality securities | | | | 52,105 | 56,210 |
| **TOTAL NON-POOLED INVESTMENTS PRIMARY GOVERNMENT** | | | | 170,366 | 178,151 |
| **Component Units:** | | | | | |
| U.S. government obligations | | 637 | 3,433 | 4,070 | 4,080 |
| Corporate bonds | | | 10,335 | 10,335 | 10,291 |
| U.S. Agency Securities | | | 1,609 | 1,609 | 1,526 |
| | | 637 | 15,377 | 16,014 | 15,897 |
| Mutual Fund, including funds invested in U.S. instrumentality securities Guaranteed Investment Contract | | | | 31,560 | 31,560 |
| | | | | 2,944 | 2,944 |
| **TOTAL NON-POOLED INVESTMENTS COMPONENT UNITS** | | | | 50,518 | 50,401 |
| **TOTAL NON-POOLED INVESTMENTS** | $1,746 | | $103,391 | $220,884 | $228,552 |

**SUMMARY OF CASH AND INVESTMENTS**

| | Deposits | Carrying Amount Investments | Total |
|---|---|---|---|
| Pooled | $ 1,497 | $214,097 | $215,594 |
| Non-Pooled | 2,942 | 220,884 | 223,826 |
| | $ 4,439 | $434,981 | $439,420 |

**Balance Sheet Acounts:**

| | |
|---|---|
| Unrestricted: | |
| Cash and cash equivalents | $123,774 |
| Investments | 153,329 |
| Restricted: | |
| Cash and cash equivalents | 139,744 |
| Investments | 22,573 |
| TOTAL CASH AND INVESTMENTS | $439,420 |

*Source:* Adapted from a recent report of the city of Tulsa, Oklahoma.

**FIGURE 13-13  Segment Information Note**

---

*Segment Information—Enterprise Funds (See Note X for Component Unit Segment Information)*

The City maintains four enterprises that provide water and sewer, parking, food services, and redevelopment programs. Selected financial information for business segments of Enterprise Funds for the year ended June 30, 19X4, is as follows:

| | Water and Sewer Facilities | Parking Facilities Fund | Food Services Fund | Redevelopment Program Fund | Total |
|---|---|---|---|---|---|
| Operating Revenues | $ 47,788,348 | $ 4,071,972 | $56,004 | $  11,871 | $ 51,928,195 |
| Depreciation and amortization | 7,407,796 | 314,072 | 596 | 0 | 7,722,464 |
| Operating income | 19,923,730 | 2,466,768 | (172) | (211,652) | 22,178,674 |
| Operating transfers in (out) | (6,854,570) | (2,135,064) | 0 | 1,400,334 | |
| (7,589,300) | | | | | |
| Net income (loss) | 7,086,792 | (141,222) | (172) | 1,501,495 | 8,446,893 |
| Property, plant & equipment | | | | | |
| Additions | 15,538,805 | 14,469 | 0 | 726,699 | 16,279,973 |
| Deletions | 131,369 | 0 | 0 | 0 | 131,369 |
| Net working capital | 54,033,669 | 3,914,841 | (33,800) | 8,935,579 | 66,850,289 |
| Total assets | 348,582,938 | 19,562,507 | 2,289 | 9,100,450 | 377,248,184 |
| Bonds payable and other long-term liabilities payable from other sources | 144,737,394 | 10,116,731 | 0 | 0 | 154,854,125 |
| Total equity (deficit) | $192,445,377 | $ 8,642,193 | ($31,511) | $8,935,579 | $209,991,638 |

---

*Source:* Adapted from a recent annual report of the city of Columbia, South Carolina.

The GPFS present only aggregate data for the fund types and account groups of the primary government (including its blended component units) and aggregate data for its discretely presented component units, together with notes to the financial statements that are essential to fair presentation, including disclosures of material violations of finance-related legal and contractual provisions and other important matters that are not apparent from the face of the financial statements.[6]

The entity focus of the combining and individual fund and account group statements is on the individual fund or account group—and combining statements also present total data for a fund type—whereas the GPFS entity focus is on aggregated fund type data. In summarizing its intent with respect to financial reporting under the pyramid concept, the GASB observes:

> . . . The governmental unit need go only as far down the reporting pyramid—in terms of increasing levels of detail—as necessary to report the financial position and operating results of its individual funds, account groups, and component units; to demonstrate compliance with finance-related legal and contractual requirements; and to assure adequate disclosure at the individual fund and component unit level.[7]

---

[6] Ibid., sec. 1900.113–.114.

[7] Ibid., sec. 1900.117.

**FIGURE 13–14** **Disclosure of Individual Fund Interfund Receivables and Payables**

## CITY OF TULSA
## NOTES TO COMBINED FINANCIAL STATEMENTS

June 30, 19X4
(dollar amounts expressed in thousands)

### Note 4. Interfund Receivables and Payables

Interfund receivables and payables as of June 30, 19X4 were as follows:

| Amount | Due from Other Funds | Due to Other Funds |
|---|---|---|
| $ 300 | General Fund | Agency Fund |
| 32 | General Fund | Psychological Services |
| 12 | Stormwater Management Fund | General Fund |
| 337 | 19X1–19X5 Sales Tax Fund | Stormwater Management Fund |
| 89 | 19X6–19Y1 Sales Tax Fund | Stormwater Management Fund |
| 770 | | |

| Amount | Due from Primary Government | Due to Component Units |
|---|---|---|
| 4 | General Fund | TMUA—Sewer |
| 4 | | |

| Amount | Due From Component Units | Due to Primary Governments |
|---|---|---|
| 30 | General Fund | Tulsa Airports |
| 78 | Tulsa Development Authority | Federal & State Grants |
| 45 | Agency | TMUA—Water |
| 25 | General Fund | TMUA—Water |
| 178 | | |
| $ 952 | | |

| Amount | Advances to Other Funds | Advances from Other Funds |
|---|---|---|
| 508 | General Fund | E-911 Construction Fund |
| 1,197 | General Fund | Federal and State Grants Fund |
| 543 | General Fund | Agency Fund |
| 235 | Stormwater Management | Agency Fund |
| 16,702 | Tulsa Public Facilities Authority | Capital Cost Recovery Fund |
| 19,185 | | |

| Amount | Advances to Primary Government | Advances from Component Units |
|---|---|---|
| $ 127 | Tulsa Airports | General Fund |
| 550 | TMUA—Sewer | Agency Fund |
| 223 | Tulsa Authority for the Recovery of Energy | Agency Fund |
| 656 | TMUA—Water | Agency Fund |
| $1,556 | | |

| Amount | Advances to Component Units | Advances from Primary Government |
|---|---|---|
| 538 | General Fund | Metropolitan Tulsa Transit Authority |
| 1,194 | 19X1–19X5 Sales Tax Fund | Tulsa Development Authority |
| 334 | Special Development Fund | Tulsa Parking Authority |
| 2,066 | | |
| $22,807 | | |

| Due From | | Due To | |
|---|---|---|---|
| Other Funds | $770 | Other Funds | $770 |
| Primary Government | 4 | Primary Government | 148 |
| Component Unit | 178 | Primary Government—Restricted | 30 |
| | $952 | Component Unit | 4 |
| | | | $952 |

| Advances To | | Advances From | |
|---|---|---|---|
| Other Funds | $ 2,483 | | |
| Other Funds—Restricted | 16,702 | Other Funds | $19,185 |
| Primary Government | 1,429 | Primary Government | 2,066 |
| Primary Government—Restricted | 127 | Component Units | 1,556 |
| Component Units | 2,066 | | $22,807 |
| | $22,807 | | |

*Source:* Adapted from a recent annual report of the city of Tulsa, Oklahoma.

**FIGURE 13–15  Disclosure of Interfund Transfers**

### NOTE 11. OPERATING AND RESIDUAL EQUITY TRANSFERS

**Operating transfers** among funds occur when a fund receiving revenues transfers resources to a fund where the resources are to be expended. The transfers occur only after being legally authorized by the Legislature through statute or an *Appropriation Act*. For the fiscal year ended June 30, 19X4, the operating transfers by fund are as follows:

**Operating Transfers**
*(Expressed in Thousands)*

| | General Fund | Special Revenue Funds | | | Capital Projects Fund | Debt Service Fund | Internal Service Fund | Trust Funds | Total Transfers Out |
| | | Uniform School Fund | Trans-portation Fund | Federal Retirees Settlement Fund | | | | | |
|---|---|---|---|---|---|---|---|---|---|
| **Transfers Out:** | | | | | | | | | |
| General Fund . . . . . . . . . . | $ — | $ 2,093 | $ 21,481 | $ 16,319 | $ 29,578 | $ 71,036 | 345 | $ 1,452 | $142,304 |
| Special Revenue Funds: | | | | | | | | | |
|   Uniform School Fund . . . | 19,480 | — | — | — | — | — | — | | 19,480 |
|   Transportation Fund . . . . | 22,531 | — | — | — | — | — | — | — | 22,531 |
|   Sports Authority Fund . . | — | — | — | — | 3,292 | — | — | | 3,292 |
| Capital Projects Fund . . . . . | 3,205 | — | — | — | — | — | — | — | 3,205 |
| Enterprise Funds . . . . . . . . | 17,973 | — | — | — | — | — | — | — | 17,973 |
| Internal Service Funds . . . . | 1,837 | — | — | — | — | — | — | — | 1,837 |
| Trust Funds . . . . . . . . . . . . . | 25,363 | — | — | — | — | — | — | — | 25,363 |
|   Total Transfers In . . . . | $ 90,389 | $ 2,093 | $ 21,481 | $ 16,319 | $ 32,870 | $ 71,036 | $ 345 | $ 1,452 | $ 235,985 |

In addition, the General Fund transferred $4.135 million and $363.24 million to the component units' Proprietary Funds and Colleges and Universities, respectively. Of the $4.135 million transferred to component units $1.25 millon was transferred to the Comprehensive Health Insurance Fund after their December 31, 19X3, year end.

**Residual Equity transfers** occur when nonroutine transfers are made from one fund to another. These transfers are usually made to provide funds for working capital. In addition to fund equity transfers, fixed assets with an original cost of $16 thousand and estimated accumulated depreciation of $6 thousand were transferred from the General Fixed Assets Account Group to the Internal Service Fund, resulting in a contributed capital increase of $10 thousand. For the fiscal year end June 30, 19X4, the residual equity transfers by fund are as follows:

**Residual Equity Transfers**
*(Expressed in Thousands)*

| | General Fund | Enterprise Fund | Internal Service Fund | Total Transfers |
|---|---|---|---|---|
| **Transfers Out:** | | | | |
| General Fund . . . . . . . . . . . . . . . . . . . . . . . . . . . . . | $ — | $ 3,973 | $ 22,248 | $ 26,221 |
| Uniform School Fund . . . . . . . . . . . . . . . . . . . . . . . | — | — | 117 | 117 |
| Internal Service Funds . . . . . . . . . . . . . . . . . . . . . | 439 | — | 237 | 676 |
| Enterprise Funds . . . . . . . . . . . . . . . . . . . . . . . . . . | 1,645 | — | — | 1,645 |
|   Total Transfers In . . . . . . . . . . . . . . . . . . . . . | $ 2,084 | $ 3,973 | $ 22,602 | $ 28,659 |

The Surplus Property and Fuel Dispensing Internal Service Funds have been consolidated with the General Services Internal Service Fund with a net $237 thousand residual equity transfer.

*Source:* Adapted from a recent annual report of the state of Utah.

Thus, the purpose of the combining statements, individual fund and account group statements, and schedules is to "fill the gap," so to speak, between the GPFS that "present fairly" at the fund type entity level and the need in the CAFR also to "present fairly" under the individual fund and account group entity focus. Determining which financial statements and schedules must be presented in the CAFR beyond those of the GPFS requires careful consideration of the facts of each situation and professional judgment. When all three levels are presented, the combining statements link the combined statements and the individual fund statements presented in the CAFR.

The city of Memphis, Tennessee, Combining Statement of Revenues, Expenditures, and Changes in Fund Balances for its Special Revenue Funds is presented in Figure 4–11. The total column of this *Combining* Statement of Revenues, Expenditures, and Changes in Fund Balances must articulate with the "Special Revenue Fund" column in its *Combined* Statement of Revenues, Expenditures, and Changes in Fund Balances.

Combining statements are always required where a government has more than one fund of a fund type. Combining statements also may be presented in more detail than is possible in combined statements, often in sufficient detail to present fairly and thus avoid the need for several individual fund statements.

Individual fund statements are required only if sufficient detail is not presented in combining statements or, in the case of the General Fund and the account groups, in the combined statements. They may also be needed to present budgetary comparisons in sufficient detail and/or to present prior year comparative data.

Schedules are used primarily to (1) demonstrate finance-related legal and contractual compliance, such as when the budgetary basis differs from the GAAP basis, the budget is adopted in more detail than is presented in the financial statements, or bond indentures require certain data to be presented in the CAFR; (2) present more detailed data than that appearing in the combined, combining, and individual fund and account group statements, such as detailed schedules of revenues and of expenditures; and (3) present other data management may wish to present such as cash receipts and disbursements schedules for one, some, or all funds. Schedules are not considered to be required for fair presentation in conformity with GAAP unless they are referenced in a statement or footnote. However, the notes to the financial statements (Figure 13–11) often include several schedules that are deemed essential to reporting in conformity with GAAP, and schedules demonstrating legal (particularly budgetary) compliance are often required for fair presentation.

Narrative explanations are in essence additional notes to the combining and individual fund and component unit statements and schedules. They are not called notes under the GASB's dual reporting approach so that they will not be confused with the notes to the GPFS, which are referred to as the "Notes to the Financial Statements" in the GASB *Codification*. The *Codification* summarizes the nature and role of the narrative explanations in the CAFR as follows:

> Narrative explanations of combining, individual fund, and account group statements and schedules of the primary government (including its blended component units) and of combining and individual discretely presented component units should provide information not included in the financial statements, notes to the financial statements, and schedules that is necessary (a) to assure an understanding of those statements and schedules, and (b) to demonstrate compliance with finance-related legal and contractual provisions. (In extreme cases, it may be necessary to prepare a separate legal-basis special report. . . .) The narrative explanations, including a description of the nature and purpose of the various funds, should be presented on divider pages, directly on the statements and schedules, or in a separate section.[8]

### Additional Observations on Financial Reporting—Simple Entity Structure

The GASB offers several other guidelines to financial reporting. At one point the *Codification* states that "financial statements should present data summarized appropriately to their pyramid level."[9] This is an important point because, consistent with the pyramid concept, it emphasizes that combined statements are the most

---

[8] Ibid., sec. 2200.131.
[9] Ibid., sec. 2200.110.

summarized; combining statements should articulate with, but be in more detail than, the combined statements; and individual fund and account group statements should be in more detail than combining or combined statements.

Additionally, we recommend that:

**1.** Combined statements should be in no more detail than can be presented on two pages. Some reduction is acceptable, but the published statements should be readable.

**2.** If a combining statement involves so many different funds that, after reduction, the statement would not be readily readable, a two-tier approach should be used. Under this approach the major funds of the type are presented and an "Other" column summarizes all of the other funds, which are presented in a second combining statement or schedule supporting the main combining statement.

**3.** Statements that would exceed two pages because of reporting detailed subclassifications of accounts should be restructured to present more summarized data, with the detail presented in the next lower-level statement or in a schedule(s).

The GASB *Codification* also notes that combined statements may have total columns, but they must be labeled "Memorandum Only." Also, combined or combining statements may have an "Interfund and Similar Eliminations" column; or the total may be based on such eliminations even if an eliminations column does not appear in the statement. Interfund and similar eliminations are a permissible option but, if made, must be apparent from the headings of the statement or disclosed in the notes and narrative explanations, as appropriate.

Finally, recall from prior chapters that there are several acceptable options for formats of statements of revenues, expenditures, and changes in fund balances prepared for governmental funds and similar trust funds. The GASB *Codification* illustrates one format, which is the basis for the illustrative example statement in Chapter 4 and is used by the city of Orlando, as shown in Figure 13–6. Another acceptable approach is illustrated in Chapter 7.

## Statistical Tables

The final section of the CAFR contains several types of statistical presentations. Some of the data are extracted from present and past financial statements, such as the table of General Government Expenditures by Function—Last Ten Years (Figure 13–16), to give the reader a historical and trend perspective of the government. Other data relate only to one year—such as the computation of legal debt margin and the computation of overlapping debt (Figure 13–17)—to demonstrate compliance with laws on the amount of debt that can be incurred, to indicate approximately how much more debt could be issued before reaching the legal debt ceiling, or to provide a perspective of the total local government tax load on the citizens in the government's jurisdiction. Other types of economic and demographic data are also presented in the statistical section to give the reader a perspective on such matters as employment and unemployment, the major employers and taxpayers, and the general condition of the local economy.

The GASB *Codification* specifies that certain statistical tables be included in the CAFR unless clearly inapplicable in the circumstances. These tables are listed in Figure 13–3. The GASB *Codification* also urges preparers to devise new types of statistical statements as needed.

Although space precludes illustrating all 15 of these statistical tables, examples of each of the broad types—that is, those presenting (1) ten-year data, (2) single-year data, and (3) other economic and demographic data—are included in Figures 13–16, 13–17, and 13–18, respectively.

FIGURE 13–16  Statistical Table—Ten-Year Data

**County of Los Angeles**
**General Governmental Expenditures by Function**
**Last Ten Fiscal Years (in $ thousands)**

| Function | 19W1–19W2 | 19W2–19W3* | 19W3–19W4 | 19W4–19W5 | 19W5–19W6 | 19W6–19W7 | 19W7–19W8 | 19W8–19W9 | 19W9–19X0 | 19X0–19X1 | Function |
|---|---|---|---|---|---|---|---|---|---|---|---|
| General government | $ 413,591 | $ 421,309 | $ 413,216 | $ 467,254 | $ 536,137 | $ 560,636 | $ 477,189 | $ 491,518 | $ 577,216 | $ 536,766 | General government |
| Public protection | 822,122 | 1,095,054 | 1,136,048 | 1,228,331 | 1,353,044 | 1,533,311 | 1,629,994 | 1,905,283 | 2,133,042 | 2,370,265 | Public protection |
| Public ways and facilities | 96,256 | 137,739 | 141,355 | 133,295 | 153,909 | 197,272 | 187,812 | 166,506 | 154,819 | 151,694 | Public ways and facilities |
| Health and sanitation | 337,749 | 404,132 | 409,219 | 421,168 | 474,744 | 515,070 | 549,646 | 611,299 | 683,661 | 743,398 | Health and sanitation |
| Public assistance | 547,988 | 1,604,257 | 1,760,123 | 1,910,958 | 2,102,990 | 2,257,504 | 2,307,896 | 2,486,169 | 2,737,791 | 3,084,846 | Public assistance |
| Education | 27,003 | 29,414 | 31,134 | 36,689 | 37,526 | 38,655 | 41,742 | 49,084 | 56,410 | 60,970 | Education |
| Recreation and cultural services | 67,854 | 66,778 | 71,846 | 75,072 | 78,841 | 80,446 | 85,412 | 105,757 | 112,807 | 128,445 | Recreation and cultural services |
| Debt service | 81,028 | 161,390 | 163,990 | 410,661 | 328,750 | 196,243 | 240,891 | 283,575 | 275,393 | 314,011 | Debt service |
| Capital outlay | 963 | 29,226 | 53,314 | 35,260 | 40,699 | 96,606 | 219,659 | 186,602 | 160,517 | 157,556 | Capital outlay |
| Total | $2,394,554 | $3,949,299 | $4,180,245 | $4,718,688 | $5,106,640 | $5,475,743 | $5,740,241 | $6,285,793 | $6,891,656 | $7,547,951 | Total |

Notes:
*Fiscal years prior to 19W2–W3 have not been retroactively adjusted to reflect inclusion of certain organizations, functions, and activities included in 19W1–W3. . . . Accordingly, fiscal years prior to 19W2–W3 exclude the operations of Fire Protection, Flood Control, Street Lighting, Garbage Disposal and Sewer Maintenance Special Districts, Transit and Paratransit Operations Funds, the Community Development Commission (including the Housing Authority of the County of Los Angeles), and various nonprofit corporations and joint powers authorities.

*Source:* Annual Report of the Board of Supervisors and Comprehensive Annual Financial Report, includes General, Special Revenue, Debt Service, and Capital Projects Funds.

**FIGURE 13-17  Statistical Table—Single-Year Data**

**CITY OF LOUISVILLE**
Computation of Direct and Overlapping Bonded Debt
General Obligation Bonds
June 30, 19X4

| Governmental Unit | Net General Obligation Bonded Debt Outstanding | Percentage Applicable to City of Louisville | Amount Applicable to City of Louisville |
|---|---|---|---|
| Direct debt—City of Louisville Serial Bonds .......................... | $   6,445,000 | 100.00% | $   6,445,000 |
| Overlapping debt: | | | |
| Louisville and Jefferson County Board of Education ............ | 196,575,400 | 33.83% | 66,500,811 |
| Jefferson County ................ | 172,170,000 | 33.84% | 58,262,328 |
| Total direct and overlapping debt | $375,190,400 | | $131,208,139 |

*Source:* A recent city of Louisville, Kentucky, annual report.

**FIGURE 13-18  Statistical Table—Economic and Demographic Data**

**COUNTY OF LOS ANGELES**
Principal Taxpayers
June 30, 19X1

| Taxpayers | Total Tax Levy Fiscal Year 19X0–19X1 | Percentage of Total* | Percentage of Total Tax Levy Fiscal Year 19X0–19X1 |
|---|---|---|---|
| Pacific Bell .................. | $  48,434,114 | 22.09 | 1.05 |
| Southern California Edison Co. . | 40,814,286 | 18.61 | .88 |
| GTE California, Inc. .......... | 33,068,576 | 15.08 | .71 |
| Southern California Gas Company | 20,416,080 | 9.31 | .44 |
| Hughes Aircraft Company ..... | 17,079,508 | 7.79 | .37 |
| Northrop Corporation ......... | 13,916,348 | 6.35 | .30 |
| Chevron USA Inc. ............ | 13,013,864 | 5.93 | .28 |
| Shuwa Investments Corporation | 11,824,517 | 5.39 | .26 |
| McDonnell Douglas Corp. ..... | 10,757,062 | 4.91 | .23 |
| Atlantic Richfield ............. | 9,959,110 | 4.54 | .21 |
| Total | $219,283,465 | 100.00 | 4.73 |

*Detail may not add to total due to rounding.
*Source:* Los Angeles County Treasurer-Tax Collector.

*Source:* A recent county of Los Angeles, California, annual report.

## SUPPLEMENTAL AND SPECIAL-PURPOSE REPORTING

A variety of special reports has emerged in recent years. Some are necessary because a government prepares its CAFR in accordance with GAAP but must also submit a non-GAAP report (possibly of cash receipts, disbursements, and balances) to a state agency. This type of situation is contemplated and discussed in the GASB *Codification.*

Another type of report that has emerged may be called the *condensed summary* (or *popular*) *report.* These reports are directed at the top of the financial reporting pyramid. They vary from highly condensed (even consolidated) financial statements, perhaps presented in short booklets or brochures highlighting the key aspects of a government's operating results and status, to misleading presentations of selected data of only a few of a government's funds and account groups. In other words, some appear to be sincere efforts to communicate vital data at a more condensed level than that of the GPFS, whereas others appear to hide more than they disclose.

Presentations of data more aggregated than the GPFS are not considered GAAP. At the same time, the GASB *Codification* recognizes that GAAP continually evolve and notes:

> Some governmental units have for many years published highly condensed summary financial data, usually as "popular" reports directed primarily to citizens. Often the data in such reports are presented in charts or graphs rather than in financial statements. More recently, several professional association committees and individuals have undertaken research and experimentation directed toward the design of highly condensed summary financial statements for governmental units. Such research and experimentation is encouraged, but at the present time such statements should supplement, rather than supplant, the CAFR and the separately issued GPFS. Further, the data in such highly condensed summary statements should be reconcilable with the combined, combining, and individual fund and account group statements, and the reader of such statements should be referred to the CAFR and/or the separately issued GPFS of the governmental unit.[10]

Indeed, the GASB recently sponsored a popular reporting research project and published the results of the research.[11]

Finally, the GASB *Codification* recognizes that the standards established by the Board and its predecessors are minimum standards of financial reporting, not maximum standards. Accordingly, the finance officer should assume responsibility for preparing other information needed for management, policy, and other decisions. The GASB also notes that supplementary information may be as valuable as GAAP information in meeting some information needs.

## CONCLUDING COMMENTS

The pyramid reporting concept embraced in the GASB *Codification* represents a major change in annual financial reporting by state and local governments that was implemented during the 1980s. Previously the reporting focus had been almost completely on individual fund and account group statements, with four statements

---

[10] Ibid., sec. 2700.104.

[11] Frances H. Carpenter and Florence C. Sharp, *Popular Reporting: Local Government Financial Reports to the Citizenry* (Norwalk, CT: GASB, 1992).

typically required for each fund. By requiring only two or three statements for each governmental, proprietary, and fiduciary fund, and with many separate funds reported in combining statements, the pyramid concept facilitates the streamlining of the CAFRs of many state and local governments to a fraction of their former size. Furthermore, the CAFR is far more usable and understandable than before because it permits users to begin with the combined overview statements—the general purpose financial statements (GPFS)—and proceed to the more detailed combining and individual fund and account group statements in a logical manner.

Even more important, perhaps, is the dual reporting entity focus: (1) the GPFS, which include data aggregated by fund type and account group; and (2) the other financial statements in the CAFR, which include combining and individual fund and account group data. Together they provide both overview and more detailed financial information.

The reporting changes incorporated in current GAAP are more drastic than some wanted. On the other hand, others continue to urge the GASB to develop and promulgate standards for condensed summary or even consolidated financial statements for state and local governments. Too, some consider recent changes as improvements; others see them as faulty. The GASB has recommended major changes in financial reporting for governments. Proposed changes affect the level of aggregation of financial statements, the basis of accounting used for reporting certain activities, fund definitions, and many other aspects. The key proposals are discussed in Chapter 15.

## Questions

**Q 13-1** What standard(s) are prescribed by the GASB for interim financial statements? Explain.

**Q 13-2** Distinguish between the content and purpose(s) of the general purpose financial statements (GPFS) and the comprehensive annual financial report (CAFR).

**Q 13-3** Explain the pyramid reporting concept utilized by the GASB.

**Q 13-4** Why is a good transmittal letter essential to the comprehensive annual financial report (CAFR)?

**Q 13-5** Distinguish between combined statements and combining statements.

**Q 13-6** (a) Why is the total column of the combined balance sheet (e.g., Figure 13–5) labeled "Memorandum Only"? (b) Why is it not necessary to label the total(s) column(s) of combining statements "Memorandum Only"?

**Q 13-7** Are interfund eliminations proper under generally accepted accounting principles? Explain.

**Q 13-8** What is the purpose(s) of the notes to the financial statements? The narrative explanations?

**Q 13-9** Why do the notes to the GPFS contain much information that is also reported elsewhere in the CAFR? Give some examples of this duplication.

**Q 13-10** What is the purpose(s) of schedules, as contrasted with statements? Are schedules necessary for reporting in conformity with GAAP?

**Q 13-11** What is the purpose(s) of statistical tables as contrasted with that (those) of financial statements? What are the broad types and purposes of statistical tables?

**Q 13-12** Does the GASB approve consolidated financial statements and consider them within the bounds of generally accepted accounting principles? Explain.

**Q 13-13** Referring to the auditor's report in Figure 13–4, which data are (a) included fully in the auditor's scope and depth of examination, (b) included in the scope but reported on only in relationship to the data in (a), and (c) excluded from the auditor's scope?

**Q 13-14**   How can one quickly determine, by observation, whether a statement of revenues, expenditures, and changes in fund balances explains the changes in *total* fund balances or *unreserved* fund balances?

**Q 13-15**   A Lakesiditis resident became concerned when reviewing the city of Lakesiditis annual report because the amount of property taxes reported for the General Fund in the Combined Statement of Revenues, Expenditures, and Changes in Fund Balances—All Governmental Fund Types differs significantly from the amount of actual property taxes reported for that fund in the Combined Statement of Revenues, Expenditures, and Changes in Fund Balances—Budget and Actual—General and Special Revenue Funds. The resident is certain an error has occurred and calls it to the attention of the mayor, who immediately calls in the chief accountant to explain how such an error has occurred. Can such a discrepancy exist under generally accepted accounting principles applicable to governments? Explain.

## Exercises

**E 13-1**   (Combining and Combined Financial Statements) Barkhi County's fund structure is as follows:

   General Fund
   3 Special Revenue Funds
   1 Capital Projects Fund
   2 Debt Service Funds
   4 Expendable Trust Funds
   3 Internal Service Funds
   5 Enterprise Funds
   General Fixed Assets Account Group
   General Long-Term Debt Account Group

*Required*   a.   List the combining financial statements required in the Barkhi County Comprehensive Annual Financial Report.
   b.   List the combined financial statements required in Barkhi County's General Purpose Financial Statements. Indicate the columns that should be included in each statement.

**E 13-2**   (CAFR and GPFS) Outline the required parts of a comprehensive annual financial report. Which parts are focused on individual funds and account groups? Which parts comprise general purpose financial statements? When is each part required?

## Problems

**P 13-1**   (Multiple Choice)
   1.   The proper ordering of the following statements (from highest degree of summarization to lowest degree of summarization) is
      a.   combining statements, combined statements, individual fund and account group statements.
      b.   combined statements, individual fund and account group statements, combining statements.
      c.   combined statements, combining statements, individual fund and account group statements.
      d.   individual fund and account group statements, combined statements, combining statements.
      e.   individual fund and account group statements, combining statements, combined statements.

    f. combining statements, individual fund and account group statements, combined statements.

2. Should the notes to the Simpson County General Purpose Financial Statements provide information concerning its interfund receivables and payables even if such information is contained in the combining and/or individual fund financial statements?

    a. No, because such information is not required to be included in the notes.

    b. No, because disclosure of the same information in two separate portions of the CAFR would be redundant.

    c. Yes, because the General Purpose Financial Statements and accompanying notes must be sufficiently complete to stand alone.

    d. Yes, because the GASB has ruled that interfund payable and receivable information must be presented in both portions of the CAFR financial section.

3. The principal purpose for the required footnote disclosures on government deposits and investments is

    a. to enable users to identify potential conflicts of interest.

    b. to encourage governments to obtain the highest return possible on deposits and investments.

    c. to enable users to assess the credit risk of a government's deposits and investments.

    d. to enable users to better estimate a government's future cash flows.

    e. none of the above.

4. Narrative explanations differ from notes to financial statements in that

    a. narrative explanations relate to combining and individual fund statements, whereas the notes relate to the general purpose financial statements.

    b. narrative explanations need not conform with generally accepted accounting principles, whereas the notes must conform.

    c. narrative explanations are essentially verbal in nature, whereas the notes are basically quantitative in nature.

    d. there is no difference, because narrative explanations provide essentially the same information included in the notes.

5. The statistical section of a comprehensive annual financial report (CAFR)

    a. is required for fair presentation of a government's financial position and operating results.

    b. is required in the CAFR.

    c. is composed solely of 10-year historical trend information.

    d. is an optional section of the CAFR.

    e. is required in the CAFR but, except for 10-year trend data on general government revenues and expenditures, its content is based solely on the judgment of the government's management.

    f. none of the above.

6. A combining statement differs from a combined statement in that

    a. the combining statement contains less detailed information than a combined statement.

    b. the combining statement must have "Total" columns, but "Total" columns are optional in the combined statement.

    c. the combining statement may have an "Interfund and Similar Eliminations" column, whereas the combined statement may not.

    d. the combined statement is required where the government has more than one fund of a specific fund type, whereas the combining statement need not be used if there is more than one fund of a specific fund type.

    e. none of the above.

7. Individual fund and account group statements are required to be presented

    a. in both the GPFS and the CAFR.

    b. in the GPFS, but not in the CAFR.

    c. in the CAFR, but not in the GPFS.

d. when there is more than one fund of a particular type.

e. for the General Fund.

f. more than one of the above are true.

8. Segment information for Enterprise Funds (EFs) is

a. required to be presented for each EF with long-term debt outstanding.

b. best presented in a footnote.

c. information on specific individual EFs.

d. required for each major nonhomogenous EF.

e. all of the above.

f. none of the above.

**P 13-2** (Review Problem: Error Identification and Statement Correction) The following statement was prepared by the new accountant at Fullerton City:

**Fullerton City**

Statement of Revenues, Expenses, and Changes in Fund Balance

December 31, 19X8

**Revenues:**

| | |
|---|---:|
| Property taxes | $ 600,000 |
| Sales taxes | 400,000 |
| Licenses and permits | 100,000 |
| Federal grant | 300,000 |
| Traffic violations and court costs | 50,000 |
| Internal Service Fund | 75,000 |
| Capital Projects Fund | 25,000 |
| Other | 60,000 |
| | 1,610,000 |

**Expenses:**

| | |
|---|---:|
| Salaries and wages | 645,000 |
| Contractual services | 130,000 |
| Rentals | 90,000 |
| Prior year | 40,000 |
| Debt service | 120,000 |
| Enterprise Fund | 125,000 |
| Special Revenue Fund | 160,000 |
| Property taxes | 5,000 |
| Depreciation of general fixed assets | 100,000 |
| Other | 30,000 |
| | 1,445,000 |

| | |
|---|---:|
| Profit for the year | 165,000 |
| Fund Surplus, beginning of year | 200,000 |
| Surplus receipts | 135,000 |
| Increase in Reserve for Contingencies | (100,000) |
| Fund Surplus, end of year | $ 400,000 |

**Additional Information:**

(1) The statement purports to present information for the General Fund of Fullerton City.

(2) The Property Taxes revenue figure represents (a) collections during 19X8 of 19X7 taxes that were properly recorded as revenues and receivables in 19X7, $80,000; (b) the gross property taxes levied for 19X8; and (c) a $3,000 payment on 19X9 taxes by a property owner who plans an extended vacation overseas. The

expenditure figure is for 19X7 property taxes written off during 19X8; some $20,000 of the current year property tax levy is expected to prove uncollectible. An allowance for uncollectible taxes has not been used in the past.

(3)   The Sales Taxes amount is the total of sales taxes collected during 19X8, $350,000; some $20,000 certified by the state as collected and due Fullerton City; and $30,000 estimated by the city controller to be due the city as a result of Christmas sales in November and December.

(4)   The Licenses and Permits data include $85,000 of licenses and permits collected during 19X8 and $15,000 representing the final one-third payment of 19X8 business permit applications due January 15, 19X9.

(5)   The Federal Grant amount is the total of a recently approved cost reimbursement grant to develop an improved water supply system for Fullerton City. Only $20,000 has been spent so far, as the project is still in the preliminary stages.

(6)   Traffic Violations and Court Costs includes all fines and court costs collected during 19X8, $1,000 of which was on 19X7 offenses; and $6,000 of parking tickets issued during 19X8, of which $4,000 has been collected and $2,000 appears to be uncollectible.

(7)   The Internal Service Fund amount results from the repayment of an interfund advance.

(8)   The Capital Projects Fund figure represents the balance of a Capital Projects Fund returned to the General Fund at the end of the project so the Capital Projects Fund could be terminated.

(9)   Other revenues includes (a) $15,000 arising upon reinventorying the warehouse at the beginning of 19X8; the inventory was $60,000 rather than the $45,000 reported initially; and (b) $2,000 paid the General Fund from a Special Revenue Fund in reimbursement of contractual services expenditures initially made from the former but attributable to the latter.

(10)   Salaries and Wages includes the gross pay earned by employees during 19X8 and $25,000 of 19X7 gross wages that were not recorded as 19X7 expenditures.

(11)   Contractual Services includes consultation fees paid to individuals and firms, including $8,000 attributable to an Enterprise Fund and $10,000 for services rendered in 19X7 but not recorded as 19X7 expenditures. Some $18,000 of 19X8 consulting services had been rendered, but not formally billed, at the end of 19X8.

(12)   Rentals includes the aggregate rentals paid under a lease-purchase arrangement on city buildings used to house the city shop and warehouse. If this were a private business these capital lease payments would be reported as 75% interest and 25% principal reduction.

(13)   Prior Year represents the amount paid during 19X8 on 19X7 bills that had been recognized as expenditures and liabilities in 19X7.

(14)   Debt Service Fund indicates the amount paid from the General Fund to a Debt Service Fund as the annual contribution from the former to the latter.

(15)   The Enterprise Fund amount is (a) the amount (not expected to be repaid) that was transferred from the General Fund to acquire (with other borrowings) a local electric utility, and (b) the general government electric bills totaling $35,000.

(16)   The Special Revenue Fund amount arose from a 2-year loan from the General Fund to a Special Revenue Fund.

(17)   Other expenditures includes $20,000 of encumbrances at the end of 19X8.

(18)   Surplus Receipts is the amount realized from selling (during 19X8) a house the city owned.

(19)   The beginning of the year Fund Surplus account was correct except for any errors noted in items 1 to 18.

***Required*** (a) Identify the errors in the statement of revenues, expenditures, and changes in fund balance prepared by the new accountant for the General Fund of Fullerton City and prepare a schedule showing the uncorrected amounts, corrections and reclassifications, and correct classifications and amounts.

(b) Prepare a correct statement of revenues, expenditures, and changes in fund balance for the General Fund of Fullerton City for the year ended December 31, 19X8, in acceptable form.

**P 13-3** (Notes to the Financial Statements) Obtain a recent comprehensive annual financial report (CAFR) or a set of general purpose financial statements (GPFS) of a state or local government (SLG).

*Required* Study the GPFS and related notes, make a copy of or prepare a table of contents to the notes, and answer—from a note disclosure perspective:

1. What information can one learn about the SLG from the notes that is not apparent from the face of the financial statements?
2. Pretend there were no notes. To what extent would the GPFS be less useful? Why?
3. Which notes did you find the most interesting and useful? Why?
4. Which notes did you consider less useful? Why?

**P 13-4** (CAFR Analysis) Obtain a copy of a recent comprehensive annual financial report (CAFR) of a state or local government (SLG). Evaluate the contents of the CAFR with reference to Figure 13–3. Include in your brief analysis your observations with respect to:

1. *Introductory Section*
   a. Are the components required by the GASB present?
   b. What other items are included?
   c. Overall, how useful do you think this section is to the CAFR users?
2. *Financial Section*
   a. Auditor's report
      1) Compare it to the report of independent accountants in Figure 13–4. How is it similar? Different?
      2) Do any aspects of the report differ from what you expected? Explain.
   b. General purpose financial statements (GPFS)
      1) Combined statements—Are all required GPFS present? Do you observe any statements or statement items that differ from what you expected? Explain.
      2) Notes to the financial statements—Compare the types of notes presented to those listed in Figure 13–11. What notes are presented that are not listed in Figure 13–11? What notes listed in Figure 13–11 are not presented?
   c. Combining and individual fund and account group statements and schedules
      1) Statements—Are all of the financial statements required presented? Note the specific types of Special Revenue Funds, particularly any that are different than you might expect.
      2) Schedules—What types of schedules are presented? Were any schedules presented to demonstrate legal compliance?
3. *Statistical Section*
   a. Are all of the items listed in Figure 13–3 present? What other informational presentations are included?
   b. What do you find most interesting in the statistical section? What do you consider most useful to one attempting to understand the government?

**P 13-5** (CAFR Review Project) Obtain a copy of a recent comprehensive annual financial report of a state or local government. Evaluate the report using the Government Finance Officers Association reviewers' checklist for the certificate of achievement for excellence in financial reporting. Cross-reference the checklist to the CAFR by indicating (1) in the CAFR the question number to which specific items pertain and (2) in the checklist the CAFR page number where you found the answer to the checklist question.

Prepare a 1-page summary of the major strengths and weaknesses of the CAFR that you reviewed. Also indicate any questions you have and any aspects of the report that differ from what you expected.

(***Instructor's Note:*** A copy of the GFOA checklist that has been modified for classroom use is provided in the Instructor's Manual.)

**P 13-6**   (Internet Research) Search the Internet using search terms such as *CAFR* and *comprehensive annual financial report.*

***Required***   1. List all of the CAFRs dated this year or last year that were referenced by your search.

2. Attempt to access recent CAFRs until you are able to access at least five CAFRs. Note those you accessed successfully on your list (item 1) and note those you were unable to access.

3. Print the table of contents of two CAFRs and compare them. What differences do you observe?

# 14

# FINANCIAL
# ACCOUNTING
# AND REPORTING

## Complex Reporting Entities
## and Non-GAAP Bases of
## Accounting

Up to this point, our financial reporting discussion has assumed that only data from a government's legally defined entity are included in its GAAP financial statements. We referred to this situation as a government with a simple entity structure. In practice, many SLGs have a much more complex entity structure. One basic purpose of this chapter is to discuss the unique issues and requirements involved when SLGs have a complex reporting structure.

Additionally, the illustrative examples and most of the discussion in previous chapters presume that SLGs maintain their accounts on a GAAP basis. This assumption is necessary because the objective is to teach government GAAP. Furthermore, another simplifying assumption in most of the examples is that the government adopts its budget on the GAAP basis of accounting.

More often than not, either one or both of these assumptions is not true in practice. Accordingly, a second purpose of this chapter is to address some of the accounting and reporting issues that arise when a government uses non-GAAP basis of accounting for its budget and/or maintains its accounts on a non-GAAP basis during the year and must convert to GAAP at year end.

## FINANCIAL REPORTING—COMPLEX ENTITY STRUCTURE

Many SLGs have complex entity structures and must include other government, quasi-government, or even nongovernment organizations in their financial report. Their reporting entities are not limited to their legally defined entity. They have varying degrees of authority over and/or responsibilities for other legally separate governmental, quasi-governmental, or other entities such as school districts, housing authorities, building authorities, fire districts, water districts, airport authorities, and transit authorities. At least one local government reporting entity includes a semiprofessional baseball team. Figure 14–1 illustrates some of the potential interrelationships between a local government and other associated entities.

A government (such as the City of Lubburg in Figure 14–1) that has other legally separate organizations associated with it must determine whether its reporting entity should include one or more of the associated organizations (referred to as potential component units) in addition to its own legal entity. The government's legal entity is called the primary government.

The GASB requires certain associated organizations to be included as component units of the government's reporting entity. A government financial report that erroneously includes or erroneously excludes a potential component unit from the government's reporting entity does not fairly present its financial position or results of operations.

## Reporting Entity Definition

According to the GASB *Codification*, each general purpose unit of government— that is, state, county, city, and so on—is a primary government. Some special-purpose units of government such as school districts also are primary governments. Those special purpose units that have popularly elected governing bodies, separate

FIGURE 14–1  **The Governmental Reporting Entity Issue**

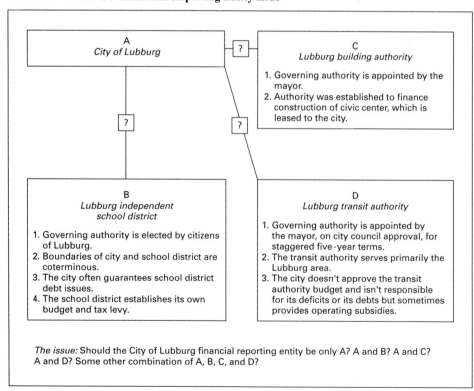

*Source:* Robert J. Freeman and Craig D. Shoulders, "Defining the Governmental Reporting Entity," *Journal of Accountancy* (October 1982), p. 52.

legal standing, and fiscal independence are primary governments. All others are not. Any organization that is legally dependent on a primary government is defined as part of that primary government. The *Codification* says that any government organization that is not a primary government should define its reporting entity and incorporate its component units into its CAFR as if it were a primary government.

A potential component unit is included in a primary government's reporting entity if the primary government is financially accountable for the potential component unit. A primary government is financially accountable for a potential component unit if the organization is fiscally dependent on the primary government. An entity is **fiscally independent** according to GASB standards if it does not require another entity's substantive approval in order to do any of the following:

- Establish its budget
- Levy taxes or set other rates or charges
- Issue bonded debt

If a primary government has substantive approval authority over one or more of these activities, the entity is **fiscally dependent** on the primary government.

A primary government also can be financially accountable for another organization even if the organization is fiscally independent. In this situation, financial accountability exists when both of the following conditions are met:

1. The primary government **either** (a) appoints (or has ex officio representation constituting) a voting majority of the potential component unit's governing body or (b) created and can unilaterally abolish the other organization, **and**

2. The primary government **either** (a) has the ability to impose its will on the potential component unit or (b) has the potential to receive specific financial benefits from or be subject to specific financial burdens because of the organization.

The conditions that indicate ability to impose will and financial benefit or burden are summarized in Figure 14–2.

An associated organization is a component unit of a primary government's reporting entity if the primary government is financially accountable for the organization. Likewise, a for-profit organization is a component unit of a primary government if the primary government holds majority ownership in the organization for the purpose of directly facilitating provision of government services. Too, a government's reporting entity should include any other potential component unit

**FIGURE 14–2  Ability to Impose Will and Financial Benefit/Burden Criteria**

- ABILITY OF A PRIMARY GOVERNMENT TO IMPOSE ITS WILL on a potential component unit exists if the primary government has the substantive authority to:
  - Remove appointed governing board members at will, or
  - Approve or require modification of the organization's budget, or
  - Approve or require modification of rate or fee changes affecting the organization's revenues, or
  - Veto, overrule, or otherwise modify other governing body decisions, or
  - Appoint, hire, reassign, or dismiss the organization's management, or
  - Take other actions that indicate its ability to impose its will on the organization

- A FINANCIAL BENEFIT OR BURDEN RELATIONSHIP exists if the primary government:
  - Has the ability to access the resources of the entity without dissolution of the entity, or
  - Is legally or otherwise obligated to finance the deficits of, or provide financial support to, the organization, or
  - Is obligated in some manner for the debt of the organization

deemed necessary to keep the reporting entity financial statements from being misleading or incomplete.

The GASB established two modifying rules with respect to the reporting entity definition that impact some governments. First, an organization may not be a component unit of two different primary governments, even if the conditions for inclusion are met for both. (However, the guidance provided does not indicate how to determine which primary government reporting entity should exclude the potential component unit based on its inclusion in the other primary government's reporting entity.) Second, the reporting entity criteria are applied from the bottom up. Assume, for example, that Organization A is a component unit of Organization B and Organization B is a component unit of Organization C. In this case, Organization A also is a component unit of Organization C because it is a component unit of one of Organization C's component units. Note that Organization A is a component unit of Organization C even if it would not otherwise meet the criteria for inclusion in Organization C's reporting entity.

## Reporting Entity Disclosures

Extensive reporting entity disclosures—including (1) the component units of a government's reporting entity, (2) the criteria used to determine which potential component units to include, and (3) other related information—are required in the notes to the financial statements. Specifically, the following disclosures are required:

1. The component units included in the reporting entity
2. The criteria used in determining the scope of the reporting entity, including the key decision criteria
3. How the component units were reported
4. How to obtain the separate financial statements of individual component units

## INTEGRATING COMPONENT UNITS INTO THE REPORTING ENTITY

Two different approaches to incorporating component unit data into a primary government's CAFR are required by the GASB. The approach used for each component unit depends upon whether the component unit is in substance part of the primary government. To be considered part of the substantive primary government, a component unit must:

• Have substantively the same governing body as the primary government's governing body. (Substantively the same governing body is interpreted to mean that at least a voting majority of the primary government governing body serves on a component unit governing body and also constitutes a voting majority of that component unit's governing body.[1]), or

• Provide services only to the primary government (meaning to the government itself, not to its constituency), or

• Benefit the primary government exclusively even though it does not provide services directly to the primary government.

---

[1] GASB, "Guide to Implementation of *Statement No. 14* on the Financial Reporting Entity" (Norwalk, Conn.: GASB, June 1994), pp. 24–25.

Note that, by definition, the overwhelming majority of component units will not meet either of the last two criteria for being part of the substantive primary government. Only certain types of organizations—such as building authorities—have the potential to meet these latter criteria. Organizations such as school districts, airport authorities, civic center commissions, transit authorities, and so on can be part of the substantive primary government only if the substantively the same governing body criterion is met. These organizations' fundamental purpose is to serve and benefit the public and entities external to the government, not the government itself.

An example may clarify the **substantively the same governing body** criterion. Assume that a city council has 7 members and a potential component unit's governing board has 5 members. For the substantively the same governing body criterion to be met, at least 4 council members must serve on the component unit governing body. If only 3 serve, the criterion would not be met. The 3 council members would represent a voting majority on the component unit board but not a voting majority of the city council. The criterion requires both. As a further example, for a state component unit to meet this criterion would require that the component unit have an extremely large governing body. At least one more than half of the state legislature would have to serve on the component unit governing body!

Financial data of component units that are defined as part of the primary government in substance are to be blended with the financial data of the primary government legal entity (as are all entities that are legally part of the primary government). All other component units—those that are not part of the substantive primary government—are discretely presented. Both blending and discrete presentation are described in the following sections.

## Blending

Blending incorporates the data of the blended component units into a report that treats the primary government legal entity and all of the blended component units as a single entity. Accordingly, the primary government obtains the data of the various component units to be blended and, if necessary, converts those data to conform with GASB standards. The data then are combined with those of the appropriate fund types and account groups of the primary government legal entity. Some blended component units may be reported as a single fund. Other blended component units must be reported in several funds and account groups. In general, blended component unit funds and account groups (classified per the GASB fund types) are reported as the same types of funds and account groups in the statements of the primary government legal entity. The single exception is that the General Fund of a blended component unit is treated as a Special Revenue Fund of the substantive primary government. This is because those resources are to be used only for the purposes of that component unit. Hence, the General Fund of the legal entity is the General Fund of the primary government of the reporting entity. Each blended component unit fund should be presented in a separate column in the pertinent combining financial statements of the reporting entity. Figure 14–3 illustrates the classification of funds for several component units of an illustrative government assuming that they are to be blended.

The GASB states that the data of the blended entity, that is, the substantive primary government, are the focal point of interest for users of a government's fi-

**FIGURE 14–3  Classification of Blended Component Unit Funds and Account Groups into Reporting Entity Fund Types and Account Groups**

Reporting Entity Funds and Account Groups

|  | GF | SRFs | CPFs | DSFs | EFs | ISFs | T&A | GFAAG | GLTDAG |
|---|---|---|---|---|---|---|---|---|---|
| Primary Government Legal Entity Funds and AGs / Blended Component Units' Funds and AGs | X | X | X | X | X | X | X | X | X |
| Transit Authority: (Enterprise Fund) |  |  |  |  | X |  |  |  |  |
| Pension Board: (Trust Fund) |  |  |  |  |  |  | X |  |  |
| School District: General Fund |  | X |  |  |  |  |  |  |  |
| Special Revenue Funds |  | X |  |  |  |  |  |  |  |
| Capital Projects Fund |  |  | X |  |  |  |  |  |  |
| Debt Service Fund |  |  |  | X |  |  |  |  |  |
| Internal Service Fund |  |  |  |  |  | X |  |  |  |
| Trust Funds |  |  |  |  |  |  | X |  |  |
| General Fixed Assets Account Group |  |  |  |  |  |  |  | X |  |
| General Long-Term Debt Account Group |  |  |  |  |  |  |  |  | X |

nancial reports. For many (if not most) governments, this entity will include only the legal entity; that is, there will be no blended component units.

## Discrete Presentation

Discrete presentation is required for most component units. The philosophy behind this reporting approach is that discretely presented component units are of secondary interest to financial statement users. Therefore, a broad overview of these component units' financial position and operating results supposedly will provide sufficient information for fair presentation within the reporting entity context. Hence, the purpose of discrete presentation is to present component unit data along with, but separate from, primary government data.

Governments must report the data of discretely presented component units in a manner that clearly indicates that they are not part of the primary government. Thus, each combined financial statement presents the primary government fund type and account group columns under a "Primary Government" heading. To the right of these columns, the "Component Units" data are presented in one or more appropriately headed additional columns. (An exception is that budgetary comparisons are not required for these component units.) A combined balance sheet with three discretely presented component units is illustrated in Figure 14–4. This illustration aggregates all three discretely presented component units in a single column. This approach is permitted on each combined financial statement. At the other extreme, each discretely presented component unit may be reported in a separate column. Various degrees of aggregation of component units are permissible between these two extremes.

**FIGURE 14-4   Reporting Entity Combined Balance Sheet (with Single Component Unit Column)**

Our City (Reporting Entity)
**Balance Sheet**
September 30, 19X1

| | Governmental Funds | | | | Proprietary Funds | | Fiduciary Funds | General Fixed Assets | General Long-Term Debt | Primary Government (Memorandum Only Totals) | | Component Units | Reporting Entity (Memorandum Only Totals) | |
|---|---|---|---|---|---|---|---|---|---|---|---|---|---|---|
| | General* | Special Revenue | Debt Service | Capital Projects | Enterprise | Internal Service | | | | 19X1 | 19X0 | | 19X1 | 19X0 |
| **ASSETS AND OTHER DEBITS:** | | | | | | | | | | | | | | |
| Cash | $1,500,000 | $1,000,000 | $100,000 | $300,000 | $685,000 | $50,000 | $330,000 | $ | $ | $3,965,000 | | $2,686,000 | $6,651,000 | |
| Investments | 475,000 | 200,000 | 75,000 | 100,000 | 160,000 | 100,000 | 350,000 | | | 1,460,000 | | 990,000 | 2,450,000 | |
| Receivables, Net | 150,000 | | | 100,000 | 500 | 300,000 | | | | 550,500 | | 169,000 | 719,500 | |
| Due from Federal Government | | | | | | | | | | | | 500,000 | 500,000 | |
| Due from Other Funds | | | | | | | | | | | | 11,000 | 11,000 | |
| Due from Component Units | 30,000 | | | | | | | | | 30,000 | | | 30,000 | |
| Inventory | | | | | | | | | | | | 53,000 | 53,000 | |
| Fixed Assets | | | | | 3,190,000 | 250,000 | 220,000 | 700,000 | | 4,360,000 | | 4,110,000 | 8,470,000 | |
| Amount Available in Debt Service Funds | | | | | | | | | 200,000 | 200,000 | | 190,000 | 390,000 | |
| Amount to Be Provided for Retirement of General Long-Term Debt | | | | | | | | | 200,000 | 200,000 | | 710,000 | 910,000 | |
| TOTAL ASSETS | $2,155,000 | $1,200,000 | $175,000 | $500,000 | $4,035,500 | $700,000 | $900,000 | $700,000 | $400,000 | $10,765,500 | | $9,419,000 | $20,184,500 | |
| **LIABILITIES AND FUND BALANCES/EQUITY** | | | | | | | | | | | | | | |
| **LIABILITIES:** | | | | | | | | | | | | | | |
| Accounts Payable | $500,000 | $400,000 | | $300,000 | $54,000 | $50,000 | $100,000 | | $ | $1,404,000 | | $940,000 | $2,344,000 | |
| Wages Payable | 300,000 | 400,000 | | 100,000 | 100,000 | 50,000 | 5,000 | | | 955,000 | | 400,000 | 1,355,000 | |
| Notes Payable | 200,000 | | | | 31,500 | | | | | 231,500 | | 1,557,000 | 1,788,500 | |
| Interest Payable | | | | | | | | | | | | 6,000 | 6,000 | |
| Contracts Payable | | | | | | | | | | | | 50,000 | 50,000 | |
| Due to Other Funds | | | | | | | | | | | | 11,000 | 11,000 | |
| Due to Primary Government | | | | | | | | | | | | 30,000 | 30,000 | |
| Deferred Revenues | 125,000 | | | | | 100,000 | 145,000 | | | 370,000 | | 307,000 | 677,000 | |
| Bonds Payable | | | | | 700,000 | 200,000 | | | 400,000 | 1,300,000 | | 1,700,000 | 3,000,000 | |
| TOTAL LIABILITIES | 1,125,000 | 900,000 | | 400,000 | 885,500 | 300,000 | 250,000 | | 400,000 | 4,260,500 | | 5,001,000 | 9,261,500 | |
| **FUND BALANCES/EQUITY:** | | | | | | | | | | | | | | |
| Investment in General Fixed Assets | | | | | | | | 700,000 | | 700,000 | | 1,500,000 | 2,200,000 | |
| Contributed Capital | | | | | 2,100,000 | 200,000 | 100,000 | | | 2,400,000 | | 935,000 | 3,335,000 | |
| Retained Earnings | | | | | 1,050,000 | 200,000 | 450,000 | | | 1,700,000 | | 514,000 | 2,214,000 | |
| Fund Balances | 1,030,000 | 300,000 | 175,000 | 100,000 | | | 100,000 | | | 1,705,000 | | 1,449,000 | 3,154,000 | |
| TOTAL FUND BALANCES/EQUITY | 1,030,000 | 300,000 | 175,000 | 100,000 | 3,150,000 | 400,000 | 650,000 | 700,000 | | 6,505,000 | | 4,418,000 | 10,923,000 | |
| TOTAL LIABILITIES AND FUND BALANCES/FUND EQUITY | $2,155,000 | $1,200,000 | $175,000 | $500,000 | $4,035,500 | $700,000 | $900,000 | $700,000 | $400,000 | $10,765,500 | | $9,419,000 | $20,184,500 | |

*Source:* Adapted from James Walter Rhea, Judith Ann Runyon, and Aristarchos Hadjieftychiou, "Case Illustration for Applying GASB Statement No. 14, 'The Financial Reporting Entity,'" (A working paper).

Consistent with the financial reporting pyramid concept discussed in Chapter 13, any component unit column in a combined statement that aggregates two or more component units must be supported in the CAFR by a corresponding combining component unit financial statement that articulates with and supports it (see Figure 14–5). This relationship parallels that between combining fund type

**FIGURE 14–5  Combining Component Unit Balance Sheet**

Our City
Component Units

**Combining Balance Sheet**
September 30, 19X1

| | *Parks and Recreation Commission* | *School District* | *Airport Authority* | *Totals* |
|---|---|---|---|---|
| **Assets and Other Debits** | | | | |
| Cash | $2,050,000 | $ 585,000 | $ 51,000 | $2,686,000 |
| Investments | 350,000 | 490,000 | 150,000 | 990,000 |
| Receivables, Net | 100,000 | 64,000 | 5,000 | 169,000 |
| Due from Federal Government | | 500,000 | | 500,000 |
| Due from Other Funds | | 11,000 | | 11,000 |
| Inventory | | 53,000 | | 53,000 |
| Fixed Assets | 1,500,000 | 1,900,000 | 710,000 | 4,110,000 |
| Amount Available in Debt Service Fund | 100,000 | 90,000 | | 190,000 |
| Amount to Be Provided for General Long-Term Debt Retirement | 400,000 | 310,000 | | 710,000 |
| Total Assets and Other Debits | $4,500,000 | $4,003,000 | $916,000 | $9,419,000 |
| **Liabilities and Fund Balances/Equity** | | | | |
| **Liabilities** | | | | |
| Accounts Payable | $ 670,000 | $ 230,000 | $ 40,000 | $ 940,000 |
| Wages Payable | 400,000 | | | 400,000 |
| Notes Payable | 525,000 | 1,025,000 | 7,000 | 1,557,000 |
| Interest Payable | | 6,000 | | 6,000 |
| Contracts Payable | | 50,000 | | 50,000 |
| Due to Other Funds | | 11,000 | | 11,000 |
| Due to Primary Government | 30,000 | | | 30,000 |
| Deferred Revenues | 300,000 | 7,000 | | 307,000 |
| Bonds Payable | 1,300,000 | 400,000 | | 1,700,000 |
| Total Liabilities | 3,225,000 | 1,729,000 | 47,000 | 5,001,000 |
| **Fund Balances/Equity** | | | | |
| Investment in General Fixed Assets | 600,000 | 900,000 | | 1,500,000 |
| Contributed Capital | 150,000 | 250,000 | 555,000 | 955,000 |
| Retained Earnings | 150,000 | 50,000 | 314,000 | 514,000 |
| Fund Balance | 375,000 | 1,074,000 | | 1,449,000 |
| Total Fund Balance/Equity | 1,275,000 | 2,274,000 | 869,000 | 4,418,000 |
| Total Liabilities and Fund Balances/Equity | $4,500,000 | $4,003,000 | $916,000 | $9,419,000 |

*Source:* Adapted from James Walter Rhea, Judith Ann Runyon, and Aristarchos Hadjieftychiou, "Case Illustration for Applying GASB *Statement No. 14,* 'The Financial Reporting Entity'," (A working paper).

financial statements and the columns for each fund type in the combined financial statements. In other words, a combining component unit financial statement consists of adjacent columns presenting data on individual component units and a total column in which the individual component unit data have been summed. This total column—perhaps in different account classification detail—is what is reported in the combined financial statement discretely presented component units column to which it relates.

The combining component unit balance sheet for the discretely presented component units reported in the combined balance sheet in Figure 14–4 is presented in Figure 14–5. Note that the data reported for the Parks and Recreation Commission and the School District in the combining component unit statements are from the "Memorandum Only" (optional) total columns from the combined financial statements in their separately issued financial reports. These data are not considered GAAP presentations in the separately issued financial statements of the individual component units, but the GASB states that they are GAAP presentations (not memorandum only) in the reporting entity financial report. Furthermore, the totals of the data of these various component units, which are presented as the component unit column in the combined statements (as in Figure 14–4), also are deemed GAAP presentations and are not labeled "Memorandum Only."

Discretely presented component units may be aggregated into a column even when the component units use different reporting models—for example, governmental fund accounting and proprietary fund accounting. When such component units are aggregated, the component unit fund equity data can be presented in the combined balance sheet using the same classifications as for the primary government. Alternatively, discretely presented component units' equity may be aggregated into other classifications such as "Fund balance—governmental fund component units," "Contributed capital—proprietary fund component units," or "Equity—component units."

Similarly, operations data for component units such as school districts that have both governmental and proprietary funds may be reported in two different ways. Under one approach, the operations data for the component unit's governmental and similar trust funds are included in the component unit column(s) of the combined statement of revenues, expenditures, and changes in fund balances for the reporting entity. Likewise, the operations data for the component unit's proprietary and similar trust funds are included in the combined statement of revenues, expenses, and changes in fund equity (retained earnings) for the reporting entity. Alternatively, the aggregated operations data of all of a discretely presented component unit's fund types may be presented in the component unit column(s) of either the combined governmental fund operating statement or the combined proprietary fund operating statement, as deemed most appropriate in the circumstances. Under this approach, the operating results of the component unit fund types that use the other method of accounting would be summarized as a single line item such as "Net income from proprietary operations" or "Excess of revenues and other financing sources over expenditures and other financing uses of governmental fund activities."

Finally, if the combining component unit financial statements are not included in the GPFS, the notes to the GPFS must include condensed financial statements for each major discretely presented component unit that has been aggregated with other component units in the combined financial statements. The minimum detail to be disclosed in such condensed financial statements is outlined in Figure 14–6.

## Other Issues

Several other issues must be addressed in combining the data of several component units into a single reporting entity report. These issues include:

- The budget basis budgetary comparison statement in the reporting entity GPFS should report the aggregation of all of the legally approved budgets, as amended, of the primary government (including blended component units) compared to related actuals. Budgetary comparison data for discretely presented component units are not required to be included.

- Any receivables and payables between blended component units or between a blended component unit and the primary government should be reclassified and reported as amounts due to and due from (or advances to and advances from) other funds. Receivables and payables between discretely presented component units or between a discretely presented component unit and the primary government should also be reclassified. They should be reported as amounts due to/from or advances to/from the primary government or discretely presented component units to distinguish them from interfund payables and receivables between entities that are part of the in-substance primary government, as illustrated in Figure 14–4.

FIGURE 14–6 **Condensed Financial Statements**

**Major Discretely Presented Component Units**

Minimum Disclosures

- **CONDENSED BALANCE SHEET**
  - Current assets (intraentity receivables separately identified)
  - Property, plant, and equipment
  - Amounts to be provided (available) for the retirement of GLTD
  - Current liabilities (intraentity payables separately identified)
  - Bonds and other long-term debts outstanding (intraentity payables separately identified)

- **CONDENSED STATEMENT OF REVENUES, EXPENSES, AND CHANGES IN EQUITY (PROPRIETARY-TYPE FUNDS)**
  - Operating revenues (intraentity sales separately identified)
  - Operating expenses
  - Operating income or loss
  - Operating grants, entitlements, and shared revenues
  - Transfers to/from the primary government and other component units
  - Tax revenues
  - Net income or loss
  - Current capital contributions

- **CONDENSED STATEMENT OF REVENUES, EXPENDITURES, AND CHANGES IN FUND BALANCES (GOVERNMENTAL-TYPE FUNDS)**
  - Revenues
  - Current expenditures
  - Capital outlay expenditures
  - Debt service expenditures
  - Transfers to/from the primary government and other component units
  - Excess (deficiency) of revenues and expenditures

- Transactions between the various component units—which typically are accounted for as revenues and expenditures or expenses by the various legally separate units during the year—must be evaluated from the perspective of being interfund transactions. Only those that qualify as quasi-external transactions should be reported as revenues, expenditures, or expenses. Other transactions should be reclassified and reported as operating or residual equity transfers, as appropriate. Assume, for example, that a city provides a grant from its General Fund to a metropolitan transit authority to subsidize its operations. The transit authority is a separate legal entity that is a component unit of the city. If the transit authority were not a component unit, the grant would be reported as expenditures in the city General Fund operating statement and as revenues by the transit authority. However, because it is a city component unit, the grant must be reported as an operating transfer in the city's CAFR.

  Operating and residual equity transfers between funds of the in-substance primary government are distinguished from those involving one or more discretely presented component units. Transfers involving discretely presented component units are reported separately as operating (or residual equity) transfers to/from discretely presented component units (or the primary government).

- The combined statements of a reporting entity may include a memorandum only total column for the primary government fund types and account groups to the left of the discretely presented component unit column(s)—as illustrated in Figure 14–4. If a primary government memorandum only total column is presented, a second memorandum only total column—aggregating the data in the primary government total column with that in the component unit column(s) may be presented as well—as is also illustrated in Figure 14–4. This reporting entity memorandum only total column cannot be presented unless the primary government total column is also presented. Recall that the component unit columns are considered GAAP presentations and thus are not labeled "Memorandum Only."

Accounting for transactions with potential component units that are excluded from the reporting entity is not affected by this guidance.

Finally, the GASB *Codification* provides guidance for primary governments with component units that have differing fiscal years. The most desirable solution from a reporting simplicity standpoint is to have component units adopt a common fiscal year. This is not always practicable or desirable for other reasons, however. When component units have differing fiscal years, the reporting entity financial statements are prepared for the primary government's fiscal year and include component unit data for the other component unit fiscal years ended either (1) during the primary government's fiscal year or (2) within the first quarter after the primary government's fiscal year end if accurate component unit data are available on a timely basis. If including component unit data for differing fiscal years results in material inconsistencies in amounts, such as in due to/from and transfer to/from amounts, the nature and amount of the transactions involved (and the inconsistencies) should be disclosed in the notes.

# SEPARATE ISSUANCE OF PRIMARY GOVERNMENT FINANCIAL STATEMENTS

The GASB acknowledges that there may be instances in which a government may find it desirable to issue a financial report that covers its primary government but does not incorporate the data of discretely presented component units. However, the Board clearly states that such a financial report does not constitute reporting in conformity with GAAP. Such reports should be viewed like other special reports.

# RELATED ORGANIZATIONS, JOINT VENTURES, AND JOINTLY GOVERNED ORGANIZATIONS

A final reporting-entity-related issue is accounting and reporting for potential component units in which an SLG participates but which are excluded from its reporting entity. Such entities are classified into three broad categories—related organizations, joint ventures, and jointly governed organizations. The three are distinguished as follows:

- Related organizations are potential component units that were excluded from the reporting entity because, although the appointment authority criterion was met, the primary government is not financially accountable for the organization—that is, the primary government does not have the ability to impose its will over the potential component unit and does not have a financial benefit or burden relationship with it.

- Joint ventures and jointly governed organizations are potential component units that are subject to the joint control of two or more other entities. Joint control implies that the primary government does not appoint a voting majority of the potential component unit governing body. (Another participant in the joint venture or jointly governed organization may appoint a voting majority of the organization's governing body, however, and may treat it as a component unit.)

- Joint ventures are distinguished from jointly governed organizations by the presence in joint ventures of an ongoing financial interest or an ongoing financial responsibility.

- An ongoing financial interest is evidenced by the primary government having an equity interest (an explicit and measurable right to joint venture net assets that is set forth in the joint venture agreement) or another arrangement under which the primary government can access the joint venture net resources.

- An ongoing financial responsibility exists if the primary government is obligated in some manner for the joint venture debts or if the joint venture cannot continue to exist without the continued financing of the primary government.

For related organizations and jointly governed organizations, a government must disclose required related party transactions information. Additionally, a government is to disclose the nature of its accountability for its related organizations.

A government is required to report its joint venture participation as follows:

- The explicit and measurable amount of any equity interest in a joint venture is reported as an asset.

- Proprietary fund joint venture investments are reported in the investing proprietary fund using the equity method.

- Governmental fund joint venture investments are reported:
  1. As governmental fund assets (or liabilities) only if they represent financial resources receivable or payable.
  2. As governmental fund revenues and expenditures only if the governmental fund revenue and expenditure recognition criteria are met.
  3. As assets in the General Fixed Assets Account Group to the extent that the equity interest of governmental fund joint venture investments exceeds the amount to be reported in the governmental funds.

- The notes to the financial statements should provide:
  1. A general description of each joint venture, including any ongoing financial interest in or responsibility for the joint venture and information on whether the joint venture is either accumulating significant financial resources or experiencing fiscal stress. (Such conditions may give rise to an additional financial benefit or burden in the future.)
  2. Any other required related party transactions information.

## USE OF NON-GAAP ACCOUNTING BASIS; YEAR-END GAAP CONVERSIONS; BUDGETARY-BASIS TO GAAP-BASIS RECONCILIATIONS

As pointed out earlier, the assumption that governments maintain their accounts on a GAAP basis during the year is not true for most governments. Instead, they make entries during the year on a non-GAAP basis of accounting. They may use (1) the cash basis, or even the cash receipts and disbursements basis; (2) a non-GAAP basis prescribed by state or local law, for example, or by the terms of an intergovernmental grant agreement; or (3) a non-GAAP budgetary basis. Each of these non-GAAP bases of accounting is discussed and illustrated in this section.

### Non-GAAP Accounting Basis Not Necessarily "Bad"

Maintaining the accounts on a non-GAAP basis during the year does not indicate improper or "bad" accounting systems or practices. Indeed, although mandatory where required by law or contract, using non-GAAP accounting procedures during the year also may be:

- Necessary to ensure adequate budgetary control during the year and proper budgetary accountability at year end.
- Useful in facilitating the preparation of special-purpose non-GAAP financial statements, schedules, and reports during the year and at year end.
- Efficient and effective in minimizing the number and types of accounting entries made—and, thus, the accounting costs incurred and errors made—during the year.

Accordingly, most SLG accounting systems are maintained on (or essentially on) a non-GAAP basis during the year. At year end, governments that maintain their accounts on a non-GAAP basis must first adjust the data in the accounts to the budgetary, grant, or other non-GAAP basis required to prepare annual **special purpose** statements, schedules, and reports on the non-GAAP basis. Then the data in the accounts are adjusted again to convert them from the non-GAAP basis to the GAAP basis in order to prepare the GAAP basis financial statements, schedules, and reports. This second adjustment process is often referred to as the **conversion to GAAP.**

This two-phase adjustment process for preparing both non-GAAP special-purpose (or supplemental) and GAAP-basis financial statements and schedules requires more analyses and adjusting entries, of course, than when the accounts are maintained on (or near) the GAAP basis during the year, as in earlier chapters. However, these more complex analyses usually are done only once a year—at year end. Also, these analyses typically are done by the government's most skilled accountants, its auditors, or both. Many of the adjusting (and readjusting or *conversion*) entries are similar—both to each other and at each year end; only a few may require complex analyses or difficult calculations. Furthermore, many SLG accountants and auditors make both sets of adjusting entries on year-end worksheets—often computer spreadsheets—and only journalize and post to the accounts those adjusting entries that would not be reversed at the beginning of the next year.

### The Two-Phase Adjustment Process

The approach to the two-phase, year-end adjustment process is essentially the same regardless of the accounting methods used during the year or the non-GAAP-basis statements to be prepared at year end before preparing the GAAP-basis financial statements for the year. The steps are:

1. *Analyze the unadjusted preclosing year-end trial balance.* Be certain you understand the accounts used during the year—including their classification and the nature and basis (e.g., cash, modified accrual, or other basis) of their unadjusted preclosing balances at year end.

2. *Determine the non-GAAP-basis rules and how they differ from the unadjusted preclosing balances.* (a) Study the legal and/or contractual non-GAAP financial reporting requirements—for example, provisions of relevant laws, grant agreements or regulations, the annual budget, bond indentures—to ensure that you understand the nature, account classification, basis, and presentation rules of the special-purpose non-GAAP financial statements, schedules, or reports that must be prepared. (b) Identify the differences between the non-GAAP basis—including account classifications—and the balances of the accounts in the unadjusted year-end preclosing trial balance.

3. *Prepare the "phase 1" adjusting entries and the required non-GAAP financial statements.* Based on your analyses and comparisons in steps 1 and 2, (a) determine the "phase 1" adjusting entries needed to adjust the account balances in the unadjusted preclosing trial balance (step 1) to the non-GAAP basis required (step 2); (b) prepare the "phase 1" adjusting entries and post them to a worksheet and/or to the accounts, as appropriate; and (c) prepare a "phase 1 adjusted" preclosing trial balance and the legally or contractually required non-GAAP statements, schedules, and reports.

4. *Identify and evaluate the differences between the non-GAAP basis and the GAAP basis.* Compare the account classifications and basis of the non-GAAP-basis data in the accounts at this point—after step 3—with the account classifications and modified accrual or accrual basis data required to prepare financial statements that conform with GAAP.

5. *Prepare the "phase 2" or "conversion to GAAP" adjusting entries and the GAAP-basis financial statements.* Based on your analyses and comparisons in step 4, (a) determine the "phase 2" adjusting entries needed to convert the non-GAAP-basis "phase 1 adjusted" account balances in the preclosing trial balance prepared at step 3 to the GAAP basis; (b) prepare the "phase 2" ("conversion to GAAP") adjusting entries and post them to a worksheet and/or to the accounts, as appropriate; and (c) prepare an adjusted ("phase 2") GAAP-basis preclosing trial balance and the GAAP-basis financial statements.

The two-phase adjustment process analytical approach and method is summarized in Figure 14–7, which also illustrates the type of year-end worksheet that is often used to facilitate the two-phase adjustment process and preparation of both the non-GAAP and GAAP financial statements. Note the logic and method illustrated in Figure 14–7 carefully because, as noted earlier, the analytical approach and related adjustment processes are essentially the same regardless of the basis—cash basis, budgetary basis, or other non-GAAP basis—on which the accounts are maintained during the year.

Some of the major considerations in applying this two-phase adjustment process approach are discussed in the remainder of this section. These considerations are discussed in the context of governmental fund accounts being maintained during the year on (1) the cash basis, (2) a legally prescribed or contractually agreed non-GAAP basis, and (3) a non-GAAP budgetary basis. For proprietary fund conversions, other non-GAAP versus GAAP differences are involved, but the analytical process is the same.

## Cash Basis

Governments that maintain their governmental fund accounts on the cash basis during the year usually have fund asset, liability, fund balance, revenue, and expenditure accounts like those illustrated in earlier chapters. However, they record revenues only when received in cash and they recognize expenditures only when cash is paid. Likewise, they typically record cash investments made but not accrued

**FIGURE 14–7  Analytical Approach and Worksheet Two-Phase Adjustment Process**

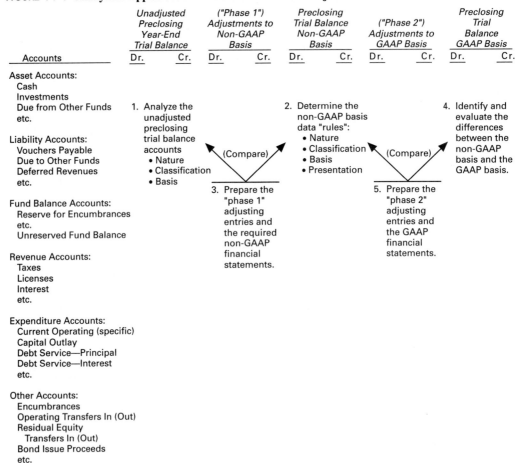

Note: This worksheet may be expanded to include columns for the year-end closing entries and postclosing trial balance.

interest receivable, and record liabilities only when notes payable are issued or retired. Thus, many accruals and deferrals may be required to adjust cash-basis data to a non-GAAP basis and/or to the GAAP basis at year end.

To simplify our discussion of the cash basis, we assume for the moment that we do not have any non-GAAP reporting requirements and thus are concerned only with adjusting the cash-basis data to the GAAP basis. No harm will be done by this momentary assumption because the non-GAAP-basis discussions later in this section may readily be related to this section.

### Revenues

Assuming that the proper amounts of cash receipts have been credited to each Revenues account during the period, adjusting those accounts to amounts properly reported as revenues on the modified accrual basis requires determining the amounts that were:

- accrued at the end of last year and are accrued at the end of this year, and
- deferred revenues at the end of last year and are deferred revenues at the end of this year.

Likewise, the amounts of related allowances for uncollectible receivables must be determined.

**Revenues Adjustments: Example 1**     To illustrate, observe this calculation to determine a revenue's amount—assuming the revenues are available and no allowance for uncollectibles adjustment is needed—for the current year:

**Revenues Example 1: Adjusting from Cash Basis to
GAAP (Modified Accrual) Basis**

| | | | |
|---|---|---:|---:|
| Revenues (Cash Basis) . . . . . . . . . . . . . . . . . . . . . . . . . . . . . . . . . . . | | | $320,000 |
| Accrued Revenues (Receivable): | | | |
|   End of this year . . . . . . . . . . . . . . . . . . . . . . . . . . . . . . . . . . . . | $25,000 | | |
|   End of last year . . . . . . . . . . . . . . . . . . . . . . . . . . . . . . . . . . . . | (15,000) | 10,000 | |
| Deferred Revenues: | | | |
|   End of this year . . . . . . . . . . . . . . . . . . . . . . . . . . . . . . . . . . . . | (22,000) | | |
|   End of last year . . . . . . . . . . . . . . . . . . . . . . . . . . . . . . . . . . . . | 16,000 | (6,000) | |
| Revenues (GAAP Basis) . . . . . . . . . . . . . . . . . . . . . . . . . . . . . . . | | | $324,000 |

Thus, of the $320,000 received in cash this year, $15,000 accrued at the end of last year should have been recognized as GAAP revenues last year. The $25,000 accrued at the end of this year should be recognized as GAAP revenues currently even though not collected. Furthermore, the $16,000 of deferred revenues at the end of last year should be recognized as GAAP revenues in the current year, but the $22,000 of deferred revenues at the end of the current year should not be recognized as revenues until next year. Thus, the adjustment process is not difficult conceptually, though determining the accrued revenues and deferred revenues at the beginning and end of the year is sometimes difficult in practice.

The general ledger adjusting entry required in this example—assuming the amounts accrued and deferred at the end of the prior year (19X0) were posted to the accounts, were not reversed, and thus are in the accounts at the end of the current year (19X1)—is:

| | | |
|---|---:|---:|
| Accrued Receivables (specify)  . . . . . . . . . . . . . . . . . . . . . . . . . . . . | $10,000 | |
|   Deferred Revenues . . . . . . . . . . . . . . . . . . . . . . . . . . . . . . . . . . . . | | $6,000 |
|   Revenues . . . . . . . . . . . . . . . . . . . . . . . . . . . . . . . . . . . . . . . . . . . . | | 4,000 |

**Revenues Adjustments: Example 2**     Property taxes levied and other receivables often are not recorded by SLGs accounting on the cash basis during the year. Indeed, any adjusting entry made at the end of the previous year may have been posted only to a worksheet; and, if posted to the accounts, it may have been reversed at the beginning of the current year. The adjustment process in this case would be like our preceding example but would also involve consideration of the need for an allowance for uncollectible accounts. Thus, if the allowance for uncollectible taxes was $4,000 at the end of last year (19X0) and should be $5,000 at the end of the current year (19X1), the net revenues adjustment required would be $3,000:

**Revenues Example 2: Adjusting from Cash Basis to**
**GAAP (Modified Accrual Basis)**

| | | |
|---|---:|---:|
| Revenues (Cash Basis) | | $320,000 |
| Accrued Revenues (Receivable): | | |
| End of this year | $25,000 | |
| End of last year | (15,000) | 10,000 |
| Deferred Revenues: | | |
| End of this year | (22,000) | |
| End of last year | 16,000 | (6,000) |
| Allowance for Uncollectible Receivables: | | |
| End of this year | (5,000) | |
| End of last year | 4,000 | (1,000) |
| Revenues (GAAP Basis) | | $323,000 |

The adjusting entry—assuming the property taxes are delinquent, reversing entries are not made, and the proper account balances from 19X0 are in the accounts—would be:

| | | |
|---|---:|---:|
| Property Taxes Receivable—Delinquent | $10,000 | |
| Deferred Revenues | | $6,000 |
| Allowance for Uncollectible Delinquent Taxes | | 1,000 |
| Revenues—Property Taxes | | 3,000 |

To adjust the property tax accounts at year end (19X1).

### Expenditures

Similarly, assuming that the proper amounts of cash disbursements have been debited to each Expenditures account during the period, adjusting those accounts to amounts properly reported as expenditures on the modified accrual basis is not difficult conceptually. However, in practice it may be difficult to determine the related accruals and other amounts. Indeed, because the available criterion applies only to revenues, adjusting expenditures is often simpler than adjusting revenues.

**Expenditures Adjustments: Example 1**     Accruals at the end of both the prior year and the current year are the primary factor in the adjustment of most cash basis Expenditures account balances to the modified accrual basis. Indeed, accruals are often the only adjustment factor. To illustrate:

**Expenditures Example 1: Adjusting from Cash Basis to**
**GAAP (Modified Accrual) Basis**

| | | |
|---|---:|---:|
| Expenditures (Cash Basis) | | $300,000 |
| Accrued Expenditures (Payable): | | |
| End of this year | $28,000 | |
| End of last year | (31,000) | (3,000) |
| Expenditures (GAAP Basis) | | $297,000 |

Thus, although $300,000 was disbursed in cash for this type of expenditure during the current year, (1) $28,000 of GAAP-basis expenditures were incurred during the year that will not be paid until next year, and (2) $31,000 was paid this year on last year's GAAP-basis expenditures.

The expenditures adjusting entry at the end of 19X1—assuming the 19X0 adjusting entry was made and was not reversed—would be:

| | | |
|---|---|---|
| Accrued Expenditures Payable ........................... | $3,000 | |
| Expenditures ........................................ | | $3,000 |

To adjust the expenditures at the end of 19X1.

**Expenditures Adjustments: Example 2**     If inventory or prepayments accounted for on the consumption method are involved, the expenditure adjustment process is more complex:

**Expenditures Example 2: Adjusting from Cash Basis to
GAAP (Modified Accrual) Basis
Inventories and Prepayments—Consumption Method**

| | | |
|---|---|---|
| Expenditures (Cash Basis) ................................ | | $300,000 |
| Accrued Expenditures (Payable): | | |
| End of this year ..................................... | $28,000 | |
| End of last year ..................................... | (31,000) | (3,000) |
| Inventories or Prepayments: | | |
| End of this year ..................................... | (10,000) | |
| End of last year ..................................... | 18,000 | 8,000 |
| Expenditures (GAAP Basis) ............................. | | $305,000 |

Thus, although the current year expenditures would have been properly reported at $297,000 in the absence of a change in the levels of inventories or prepayments, the changes in those amounts during the current year must be considered in the adjustment process. Here the $8,000 net decrease indicates that amounts paid for last year were used during this year. Had the inventory or prepayment level increased during the current year, that amount would have been deducted in determining current year expenditures under the consumption method.

The year-end 19X1 adjusting entry—assuming the 19X0 adjusting entry was properly made and not reversed—would be:

| | | |
|---|---|---|
| Accrued Expenditures Payable ........................... | $3,000 | |
| Expenditures ......................................... | 5,000 | |
| Inventories or Prepayments ............................ | | $8,000 |

To record year end 19X1 expenditures adjustments.

### Other Accounts

The revenues and expenditures adjusting entries also adjust many of the related asset and liability account balances. However, any other asset accounts—such as the Investments account and related liability accounts—should be reviewed and adjusted as needed. Also, the Encumbrances account should be reviewed as discussed in Chapter 6 and any necessary adjusting entries should be made.

### Worksheet

A worksheet similar to that presented in Figure 14–7 is essential to organizing, accomplishing, and documenting most cash-basis–GAAP-basis conversions. If only GAAP-basis statements are to be presented, only three pairs of worksheet columns would be needed because the phase 1 and phase 2 (or "Conversion to GAAP") adjustments could be made in the same columns.

### Reconciliation

If the cash-basis governmental fund statements are issued—for either external or internal use—the cash basis on which they are prepared should be described and it should be made clear that they do not purport to present fairly in conformity with GAAP. Furthermore, a brief reconciliation of the cash-basis and GAAP-basis amounts should be prepared by summarizing the cash-basis–GAAP-basis adjustments:

1. To ensure adequate disclosure in the notes to the financial statements;
2. As part of the SLG accountant's year-end adjustment-closing-statement preparation routine and/or as one of the audit procedures; or
3. To facilitate the explanation of the differences between the cash-basis amounts—with which nonaccountant managers and governing body members are apt to be more familiar, particularly when monthly or other interim reports are prepared on the cash basis—and the modified accrual basis amounts presented in the GAAP-basis financial statements.

Such cash-basis–GAAP-basis reconciliations typically are brief summaries of the differences between key statement amounts—usually ending fund balance or the excess of revenues and other financing sources over (under) expenditures and other financing uses—on each basis. They are prepared by summarizing the effects of the several (often many) adjusting entries into a few net effect categories, then adding and deducting these net effects to and from the key amount calculated using the cash basis to summarize the derivation of that amount on the GAAP basis, thus reconciling the differences.

**Reconciliation Illustrations** To illustrate cash-basis–GAAP-basis reconciliation for governmental funds, assume that (1) the amounts in the revenues and expenditures adjustment examples earlier in this section are the SLG's total revenues and expenditures for the current year; (2) the data in the "Revenues Example 1" adjustment are paired with the "Expenditures Example 1" adjustment data, as are the "Revenues Example 2" and "Expenditures Example 2" adjustment data; (3) there were no other financing sources and uses, RETs, or fund balance restatements during the year; (4) the beginning fund balance amounts were as indicated in the following table; and (5) the SLG accountant had properly calculated the following amounts.

**Revenues and Expenditures Adjustment Examples**

|  | Example No. 1 | | Example No. 2 | |
|---|---|---|---|---|
|  | Cash Basis | GAAP Basis | Cash Basis | GAAP Basis |
| Revenues . . . . . . . . . . . . . . . . . . . . . . . . . . | $320,000 | $324,000 | $320,000 | $323,000 |
| Expenditures . . . . . . . . . . . . . . . . . . . . . . . | 300,000 | 297,000 | 300,000 | 305,000 |
| Excess of Revenues over Expenditures . . . | 20,000 | 27,000 | 20,000 | 18,000 |
| Fund Balance—Beginning of Year . . . . . . . | 60,000 | 90,000 | 60,000 | 68,000 |
| Fund Balance—End of Year . . . . . . . . . . . | $ 80,000 | $117,000 | $ 80,000 | $ 86,000 |

Note that every key amount will differ between operating statements presented on the cash basis and on the GAAP (modified accrual) basis under the assumptions of either set of illustrative revenues and expenditures adjusting entries. Obviously, this might confuse many nonaccountants (and some accountants) unless the differences are adequately explained and reconciled.

Using this information and that from the illustrative revenues and expenditures adjusting entry calculations earlier in this section, we can prepare summary reconciliations of the differences between the cash basis and GAAP (modified accrual) basis amounts that reconcile either (1) the excess of revenues over expenditures amounts or (2) the ending fund balance amounts. These two reconciliation approaches are often referred to as the excess approach and the fund balance approach, respectively,

The excess approach reconciliations under both sets of adjusting entry assumptions are presented (as Example 1 and Example 2) in Figure 14–8. The fund balance approach reconciliations are presented in Figure 14–9. Only one reconciliation would be presented in practice, of course. That reconciliation would summarize the numerous cash-basis–GAAP (modified accrual) basis conversion adjustments made—which may have involved hundreds of adjusting entries—in a few categories that reconcile the differences reported in either the excess or the ending fund balance amounts under the two bases.

**Excess Reconciliation Approach**     Note that the excess reconciliation approach illustrated in Figure 14–8:

1. Begins with the "Excess of Revenues over Expenditures (Cash Basis)" amount—clearly indicating that this is a cash-basis amount; then

2. Summarizes the categories of adjustments made and their effects in the cash-basis–GAAP-basis conversion; and

3. Ends with the "Excess of Revenues over Expenditures (GAAP Basis)"—again clearly indicating that this is a GAAP (modified accrual) basis amount.

Note also that the accountant should attempt to describe the reconciling items in a manner that is understandable to the nonaccountant manager, governing body member, newspaper reporter, or other statement reader or public meeting participant.

Also observe in the reconciliations presented in Figure 14–8 that the revenues adjustments are added or deducted as in the related calculations. But the expendi-

FIGURE 14–8  **Excess Reconciliation Approach**

Cash-Basis–GAAP (Modified Accrual) Basis Reconciliation

|  | Example No. 1 | | Example No. 2 | |
|---|---|---|---|---|
| Excess of Revenues over Expenditures **(Cash Basis)** | | $20,000 | | $20,000 |
| **Revenues:** | | | | |
| Increase in accrued revenues (receivable) | $10,000 | | $10,000 | |
| Increase in deferred revenues | (6,000) | | (6,000) | |
| Increase in allowance for uncollectible receivables | — | 4,000 | (1,000) | 3,000 |
| **Expenditures:** | | | | |
| Decrease in accrued expenditures (payable) | 3,000 | | 3,000 | |
| Decrease in inventory or prepayal | — | 3,000 | (8,000) | (5,000) |
| Excess of Revenues over Expenditures **(GAAP Basis)** | | $27,000 | | $18,000 |

Note: Example No. 1 is based on the **first** revenues and expenditures adjustment to GAAP examples in the text; Example No. 2 is based on the **second** text examples of adjusting revenues and expenditures data from the cash basis to the GAAP basis.

**FIGURE 14–9 Fund Balance Reconciliation Approach**

Cash-Basis–GAAP (Modified Accrual) Basis Reconciliation

| | Example No. 1 | | Example No. 2 | |
|---|---|---|---|---|
| Revenues (**Cash Basis**—Detailed) | | $320,000 | | $320,000 |
| Expenditures (**Cash Basis**—Detailed) | | | $300,000 | 300,000 |
| Excess of Revenues over Expenditures (**Cash Basis**) ................ | | 20,000 | | 20,000 |
| Fund Balance—Beginning of Year (**Cash Basis**) ................ | | 60,000 | | 60,000 |
| **Fund Balance—End of Year (Cash Basis)** ................ | | 80,000 | | 80,000 |
| **Reconciliation to GAAP Basis:** | | | | |
| **Revenues:** | | | | |
| Increase in accrued revenues (receivable) ................ | $10,000 | | 10,000 | |
| Increase in deferred revenues .... | (6,000) | | (6,000) | |
| Increase in allowance for uncollectible receivables ....... | — | 4,000 | (1,000) | 3,000 |
| **Expenditures:** | | | | |
| Decrease in accrued expenditures (payable) ................. | 3,000 | | 3,000 | |
| Decrease in inventory or prepayal.. | — | 3,000 | (8,000) | (5,000) |
| **Fund Balance—Beginning of Year:** | | | | |
| GAAP Basis ................ | 90,000 | | 68,000 | |
| Cash Basis ................ | 60,000 | 30,000 | 60,000 | 8,000 |
| **Fund Balance—End of Year (GAAP Basis)** ............... | | $117,000 | | $ 86,000 |

tures adjustments are added or deducted oppositely because expenditures are deducted in determining the excess being reconciled.

The excess reconciliation approach is widely used in practice. This type of reconciliation typically (1) is accompanied by an explanation of the differences between the cash and GAAP bases, and (2) is presented in the notes to the financial statements or in narrative explanations of the cash-basis statements or schedules included in the CAFR, though it may also be presented in a note at the bottom of the cash-basis operating statement.

**Fund Balance Reconciliation Approach**     Whereas the excess approach reconciliation typically is presented in the notes to the financial statements or in the narrative explanations of supplemental statements and schedules, the fund balance approach reconciliation usually is presented as the concluding section of the cash-basis operating statement. Thus, the fund balance reconciliation approach illustrated in Figure 14–9 contains two distinct sections: (1) a cash-basis statement of revenues, expenditures, and changes in fund balance—in standard format but all amounts determined on the cash basis—and (2) the "Reconciliation to GAAP Basis" that concludes with "Fund Balance—End of Year" (GAAP Basis).

Note that most of the reconciling items are identical to those illustrated in Figure 14–8. However, one additional reconciling item—the difference between the cash-basis and GAAP-basis beginning fund balances amounts—usually must be included. This is because the other reconciling items explain the differences between the cash-basis and GAAP-basis amounts during the year but do not consider the cumulative differences arising in prior years as of the beginning of the current year.

The fund balance reconciliation approach is widely used where both the GAAP-basis and cash-basis operating statements are presented in the same financial report—as when the budget is enacted on the cash basis. This is because in the excess approach the GAAP and budgetary-basis (e.g., cash-basis) operating statements not only contain different revenues and expenditures amounts, but also conclude with different "Fund Balance—End of Year" amounts. This may confuse readers, who typically must turn to the notes to the financial statements to find the excess approach reconciliation—then turn back and forth between the operating statements and the notes to understand the reconciliation.

On the other hand, the fund balance approach reconciliation (Figure 14–9) is presented as an integral part of the budgetary-basis (e.g., cash-basis) operating statement, which typically is presented immediately after the similar GAAP-basis statement. Furthermore, although the revenues, expenditures, and other amounts differ from those in the GAAP-basis statement, both the budgetary-basis and GAAP-basis operating statements conclude with the same amount—"Fund Balance—End of Year" (GAAP Basis)—which facilitates reader acceptance and understanding of both statements.

## Legally Prescribed or Contractually Agreed Non-GAAP Basis

From Chapter 1 on—particularly in discussing the first GASB principle (Chapter 2) and the importance of budgetary accounting and reporting (Chapter 3)—we have often noted that non-GAAP accounting and reporting requirements may be imposed on, or agreed to by, state and local governments. Furthermore, we observed the analogy between (1) the dual income tax basis and GAAP-basis accounting and reporting requirements applicable to businesses, and (2) the dual (at least) budgetary-basis—and perhaps other non-GAAP-basis—accounting and reporting requirements and the GAAP reporting requirements applicable to SLGs. But until this chapter we have deferred discussion of non-GAAP accounting and reporting—focusing instead on GAAP-basis accounting and reporting.

Non-GAAP-basis budgetary accounting and reporting—including budgetary-basis–GAAP-basis explanations and reconciliations—are so important that they are discussed and illustrated separately in the next section of this chapter rather than here. Other types of legally prescribed and contractually agreed non-GAAP accounting and reporting requirements are considered briefly in this section.

### Legally Prescribed Non-GAAP Basis

Some states prescribe uniform fund and account group structures, charts of accounts, and financial statements for their counties, cities, towns and townships, school districts, and/or other special districts. Most of the states with such uniform accounting and reporting requirements intend for the requirements to be consistent with GAAP; and most issue detailed instruction manuals, which are updated regularly, to facilitate compliance. But a few states have uniform accounting requirements that are not consistent with GAAP.

These state-mandated non-GAAP uniform accounting and reporting requirements may intentionally differ from GAAP—as when non-GAAP fund types, account classifications, or revenue and expenditure recognition rules are specified to achieve some state purpose. But often the differences are unintentional—arising from a lack of understanding of GAAP applicable to SLGs by those who wrote the requirements or the failure to revise requirements that once were consistent with GAAP to reflect changed GASB requirements.

The analyses and procedures necessary to account and report on a state-mandated non-GAAP basis and also report on the GAAP basis are similar to those discussed and illustrated earlier in this chapter (see Figure 14–7). The most difficult steps often are understanding the legally prescribed non-GAAP accounting and reporting requirements—which may be unique to that jurisdiction—so the accounts can be maintained on and/or adjusted to the prescribed non-GAAP basis.

### Contractually Agreed Non-GAAP Basis

We have noted at several points that federal and state grantor and contracting agencies, in particular, may include non-GAAP accounting and reporting requirements in the contractual provisions of intergovernmental grants, entitlements, and research and other contracts. The SLG must agree to abide by such non-GAAP accounting and specific purpose reporting requirements as a condition of being awarded and accepting such grants, entitlements, and research or other contracts.

Such contractually agreed accounting and reporting provisions often require that specified accounts be maintained—perhaps on the encumbrances basis but with expenditures and encumbrances distinguished. Indeed, it is not uncommon for these provisions to stipulate that special purpose financial statements be issued in prescribed formats, perhaps for grant or contract periods other than the SLG's fiscal year. Furthermore, both the accounts specified and the financial statements required may focus in detail on the distinction between allowable or reimbursable grant or contract expenditures and other costs—as defined contractually or in related regulations—and unallowable or nonreimbursable expenditures and costs.

Here again the analyses and procedures necessary to account for and report on a contractually agreed non-GAAP basis and also report on the GAAP basis are similar to those discussed and illustrated earlier in this chapter (see Figure 14–7). And, as noted at "Legally Prescribed Non-GAAP Basis," the most difficult steps often are understanding the contractually agreed non-GAAP accounting and reporting requirements—which may change as related regulations are issued during the course of the grant or contract—so the accounts can be maintained on and/or adjusted to the agreed non-GAAP basis.

## Non-GAAP Budgetary Basis

We have discussed the legal and managerial significance of the SLG annual budget(s) at numerous points earlier in the text. Indeed, the annual governmental funds budget(s) is so important in the SLG environment—from both legal compliance and accountability standpoints and managerial and oversight body planning, control, and evaluation perspectives—that four of the twelve basic GASB principles establish budgetary accounting and reporting standards as an integral part of the GASB's GAAP reporting standards. Furthermore, the GASB standards require that a budgetary comparison statement for all annually budgeted governmental funds be presented—on the budgetary basis—as one of the primary financial statements in general purpose financial statements (GPFS) presented in conformity with GAAP. Thus, assuming the annual governmental fund budget(s) is enacted on a non-GAAP basis, the budgetary comparison statement is the only non-GAAP basis statement that must be presented as a primary financial statement—together with the five required GAAP basis financial statements—in GPFS presented in conformity with GAAP.[2]

### Reasons for Non-GAAP-Basis Budgets

Many SLGs prepare their annual governmental fund budget(s) on the GAAP basis because, for example:

1. They are legally required to do so by state law or local ordinance.
2. Their managers and oversight bodies want to do so for budgetary planning, control, and evaluation purposes and/or for budgetary oversight and accountability purposes.
3. Their managers and/or oversight bodies prefer to present all of the GPFS on the GAAP basis. Or perhaps they prefer not to present the budgetary comparison statement on a non-GAAP basis—with amounts that differ from those in the GAAP-basis operating statement, possibly confusing some statement users—which also requires that the budgetary-basis–GAAP-basis differences be explained and reconciled.

On the other hand, most SLGs budget on a non-GAAP basis because, for example:

1. They are legally required to do so by state law or local ordinance.
2. Their managers and/or oversight bodies want to budget—and establish budgetary control, evaluation, and accountability functions and responsibilities—on a non-GAAP basis. They may want encumbrances to be treated essentially like expenditures for budgetary control, evaluation, and accountability purposes, for example, and may not want revenues to be recognized for budgetary purposes until the cash is received (and thus can be spent).
3. Their managers and/or oversight bodies may prefer a non-GAAP budgetary approach such as just previously described because they understand the non-GAAP budgetary basis better than the GAAP basis, and believe that most nonaccountant department heads and financial statement users do also. Indeed, they may consider the interim and annual budgetary comparison statements to be more useful than the annual GAAP-basis operating statement.

### Non-GAAP Budgetary Bases

Unless a specified budgetary basis is legally required by a higher-level government, the SLG may budget in any manner that its customs and the preferences of its leadership may call for. Thus, several different non-GAAP budgetary bases are found in practice.

Most non-GAAP budgetary bases in common use are either:

- Cash basis
- Cash basis + Encumbrances
- Modified accrual basis + Encumbrances

Others are quite close to one of these bases. However, determining the budgetary basis in use is extremely difficult occasionally; and a mixed budgetary basis—where some revenues and expenditures are budgeted on one basis and others are budgeted on another basis—may also be encountered.

Cash basis accounting is discussed and illustrated earlier in this chapter. Adjustments to both the cash basis and the GAAP basis, and both cash-basis and

---

[2] GASB standards permit, but do not require, budgetary comparison statements or schedules to be presented for proprietary funds. Some governments include such comparisons.

GAAP-basis reporting—including reconciliation of the cash-basis and GAAP-basis statements—are considered there as well. The same methods and procedures are employed when the budget is enacted on the cash basis. Thus, cash-basis budgeting need not be considered further here. Accordingly, the remainder of the chapter focuses on (1) the cash basis + encumbrances and modified accrual basis + encumbrances bases, both referred to as encumbrances bases, and (2) some illustrations of non-GAAP reporting and disclosure, including budgetary-basis–GAAP-basis reconciliations.

### Encumbrances Bases

That encumbrances—the estimated cost of goods and services on order—are considered substantially equivalent to expenditures by many SLG budget officers, managers, governing body members, and others has been noted at several points earlier in the text. Encumbrances are recorded as reductions of available expenditure authority in the Expenditures Subsidiary Ledger accounts and, assuming they will be honored in the next year, as reservations of fund balance at year end. Thus, data on encumbrances are required for both budgetary and GAAP reporting purposes.

As noted in earlier chapters, GAAP standards are based on the legal definitions of expenditures and liabilities—and thus encumbrances are not reported with expenditures in GAAP operating statements or with liabilities in GAAP balance sheets. However, encumbrances may be reported with (or even as) expenditures and liabilities in budgetary-basis financial statements. Thus, encumbrances often constitute another budgetary-basis–GAAP-basis difference that requires budgetary-basis–GAAP-basis adjusting entries and causes differences between the budgetary-basis and GAAP-basis operating statements. These differences must be explained and reconciled in the financial statements and/or in the notes to the financial statements.

The two common variations of the encumbrances basis are:

- Cash basis + encumbrances—in which the SLG accounts on the cash basis, as described earlier in this chapter, but also treats encumbrances as expenditures for budgetary purposes.
- Modified accrual basis + encumbrances—in which the SLG accounts on the modified accrual basis, as discussed and illustrated in earlier chapters, but also treats encumbrances as expenditures for budgetary purposes.

It is important to identify which encumbrances basis is in use, of course, to ensure that (1) the proper amounts are in the "Preclosing Trial Balance—Non-GAAP Basis" columns of the year-end worksheet (Figure 14–7) after the "phase 1" adjustments are recorded, and (2) the "phase 2" adjustments made lead to a proper "Preclosing Trial Balance—GAAP Basis." Furthermore, one must recognize and adjust for the fact that encumbrances outstanding at year end overlap two accounting periods—either the prior year and current year or the current year and following year.

Assuming the proper amounts of encumbrances are recorded in the accounts and in the "Preclosing Trial Balance—Non-GAAP Basis" (or "Budgetary Basis" or "Encumbrances Basis") columns of a worksheet like that in Figure 14–7, the differences between the budgetary and GAAP treatments of encumbrances must be understood to complete the "phase 2" or "conversion to GAAP" adjustments. To this end, consider the following expenditures and encumbrances amounts—assuming that the expenditures resulting from the encumbrances in the next year were equal to the encumbrances recorded in the previous year:

*Expenditures + Encumbrances*
*($540,000)*

| Budgetary Basis | Encumbrances End of 19X0 ($60,000) | Expenditures During 19X1 ($500,000) | Encumbrances End of 19X1 ($40,000) | |
|---|---|---|---|---|
| | 19X0 | 19X1 | | 19X2 |
| GAAP Basis | | Expenditures during 19X1 ($560,000) | | |

The 19X1 GAAP-basis expenditures were properly computed as follows: $540,000 19X1 budgetary-basis Expenditures – $40,000 19X1 year-end Encumbrances (which are not GAAP-basis expenditures) + $60,000 19X0 Encumbrances (included in 19X0 budgetary-basis expenditures but in 19X1 GAAP-basis expenditures) = $560,000 19X1 GAAP-basis Expenditures. Or, more briefly:

| | |
|---|---|
| 19X1 Budgetary Basis Expenditures + Encumbrances .......................... | $540,000 |
| Less: 19X1 Encumbrances ................................. | (40,000) |
| Add: 19X0 Encumbrances ................................. | 60,000 |
| 19X1 GAAP-Basis Expenditures .......................... | $560,000 |

But what if the actual 19X1 expenditures are more or less than the amounts encumbered at the end of 19X0? Normally any excess is charged against a similar appropriation in the 19X1 budgetary-basis expenditure accounts, and any difference from a less-than-encumbered expenditure is credited to a similar or miscellaneous expenditure account in the 19X1 budgetary-basis expenditure accounts. Thus, the preceding calculation approach works unless another disposition is made of the difference—such as improperly crediting the less-than-encumbered difference to Revenues in the budgetary-basis accounts. In any event, such differences usually are immaterial to the governmental fund financial statements, though material differences are encountered occasionally.

In sum, the related 19X1 worksheet columns (Figure 14–7) and non-GAAP–GAAP-basis adjusting entries might appear as:

| | Preclosing Trial Balance Non-GAAP (Budgetary) Basis | | Adjustments to GAAP Basis | | Preclosing Trial Balance GAAP Basis | |
|---|---|---|---|---|---|---|
| | **Dr.** | **Cr.** | **Dr.** | **Cr.** | **Dr.** | **Cr.** |
| Expenditures and Encumbrances ........ | 540,000 | | | 540,000 (1) | — | |
| Accounts and Vouchers Payable ..... | | 140,000 | 40,000 (3) | | | 100,000 |
| Expenditures ........... | | | 540,000 (1) 20,000 (3) | | 560,000 | |
| Encumbrances ......... | | | 40,000 (2) | | 40,000 | |
| Reserve for Encumbrances ........ | | | | 40,000 (2) | | 40,000 |
| Unreserved Fund Balance ............ | | 50,000 | | 60,000 (3) | | 110,000 |

The initial Accounts and Vouchers Payable ($140,000) non-GAAP balance assumes that the 19X1 encumbrances were recorded as liabilities, whereas they should be excluded from the GAAP-basis liabilities ($100,000) reported. Similarly, the Unreserved Fund Balance ($50,000) amount was assumed to demonstrate how the change in Reserve for Encumbrances ($60,000 – $40,000 = $20,000) may be recorded net in the worksheet in deriving expenditures. The adjusting entries may be made under other logical approaches and in other sequences, of course—and may be compounded—so long as the proper amounts are extended to the "Preclosing Trial Balance—GAAP Basis" columns.

### Non-GAAP Budgetary Basis–GAAP-Basis Reconciliations

Non-GAAP budgetary basis–GAAP-basis reconciliations are similar to the cash-basis–GAAP-basis reconciliations discussed earlier and illustrated in Figures 14–8 and 14–9. Both may be presented in either the excess or fund balance approach, and may be presented either in the body of the statements and schedules or in the notes to the financial statements.

Non-GAAP budgetary basis–GAAP basis reconciliations vary more than cash-basis–GAAP-basis reconciliations, however, primarily because budgetary bases vary among governments. The only difference between the budgetary and GAAP bases in some SLGs is that encumbrances are considered tantamount to expenditures in the budgetary basis. In other SLGs there also are revenue accrual and other expenditure accrual differences between the budgetary and GAAP bases; and often some of the governmental funds are not budgeted annually.

The approach to preparing the reconciliation is the same in all cases, however. The "phase 2" adjustments from the non-GAAP-budgetary basis to the GAAP basis (see Figure 14–7) are summarized by category—such as revenue accruals, expenditure accruals, encumbrances—and presented in a condensed manner that explains the differences between (reconciles) the budgetary-basis and GAAP-basis "excess" or "fund balance" amounts.

Reconciliation presentations vary widely both because of budgetary–GAAP-basis differences and because of differing professional judgments of how reconciliations are best presented. Some governments reconcile from the budgetary basis to the GAAP basis, for example, and others reconcile from the GAAP basis to the budgetary basis. Any reasonable approach that is effective in communicating the differences between the budgetary-basis and GAAP-basis amounts seems acceptable under GAAP.

Brief budgetary-basis–GAAP-basis reconciliation examples extracted from recent annual financial reports of state and local governments are presented in Figures 14–10 and 14–11 to illustrate varying reconciliation presentations:

- "Excess" Approach Budgetary-Basis–GAAP-Basis Reconciliation Examples (Figure 14–10)

  Part I—City of Tulsa—illustrates a simple "excess" presentation reconciling differences in encumbrances, revenue accruals, and nonbudgeted funds in the notes to the financial statements.

  Part II—Hamilton County, Tennessee—demonstrates a simple "excess" presentation in the body of the budgetary operating statement—which concludes with the same GAAP-basis fund balance amount as the GAAP operating statement—where the only budgetary–GAAP-basis difference is the treatment of encumbrances.

**FIGURE 14–10  Excess Approach Budgetary-Basis–GAAP-Basis Reconciliation Examples**

**Part I—City of Tulsa**
Budget Reconciliations

[Notes to the Financial Statements]

Items required to adjust actual revenues, expenditures, and encumbrances reported on the budgetary basis to those reported on the Combined Statement of Revenues, Expenditures, and Changes in Fund Balance—All Governmental Fund Types and Expendable Trust Funds (GAAP basis) are as follows:

|  | Revenues | Expenditures | Other Financing Sources (Uses) |
|---|---|---|---|
| **General Fund** | | | |
| **Budgetary basis** | $126,084 | ($118,404) | ($10,997) |
| To adjust for revenue accruals | 2,314 | | (414) |
| To adjust for encumbrances | | 2,910 | 15 |
| **GAAP basis** | $128,398 | ($115,494) | ($11,396) |
| **Special Revenue Funds** | | | |
| **Budgetary basis** | $ 7,179 | ($ 24,721) | $14,101 |
| To adjust for revenue differences | (1,350) | | 1,358 |
| Nonbudgeted funds. | 17,667 | (14,221) | (1,019) |
| To adjust for encumbrances | | 1,820 | |
| **GAAP basis** | $ 23,496 | ($ 37,122) | ($14,440) |

**Part II—Hamilton County, Tennessee**
Combined Statement of Revenues, Expenditures, and Changes in Fund Balances—Budget and Actual
General, Special Revenue, and Debt Service Fund Types
Hamilton County, Tennessee
Year Ended June 30, 19X1

| | General Fund | | |
|---|---|---|---|
| | Budget | Actual (Non-GAAP Basis) | Variance— Favorable (Unfavorable) |
| Revenues: | | | |
| Taxes | $38,033,185 | $38,191,551 | $ 158,366 |
| Excess (deficiency) of revenues and other financing sources over (under) budgetary expenditures and other financing uses | (3,250,481) | 208,168 | 3,458,649 |
| Fund balance allocation | 3,250,481 | — | (3,250,481) |
| | — | 208,168 | $ 208,168 |
| Add encumbrances at end of year | | 812,952 | |
| Less encumbrances at beginning of year | | (753,805) | |
| Excess of revenues and other financing sources over expenditures and other financing uses—(GAAP) | | 267,315 | |
| Fund balances at beginning of year—(GAAP) | | 17,444,806 | |
| Fund balances at end of year—(GAAP) | | $17,712,121 | |

*Source:* Adapted from recent annual financial reports of the city of Tulsa, Oklahoma, and Hamilton County, Tennessee.

FIGURE 14–11 **"Fund Balance" Approach Budgetary-Basis–GAAP-Basis Reconciliation Examples**

**Part I—State of Missouri**
Notes to the Financial Statements

The following is a reconciliation of the differences between the budgetary basis and the GAAP basis.

*Budgetary Basis vs. GAAP (in thousands of dollars)*

|  | General | Special Revenue | Debt Service | Capital Projects |
|---|---|---|---|---|
| Fund Balance (Budgetary Basis) | | | | |
| June 30, 19X1 ............... | $216,968 | $287,201 | $84,675 | $ 37,873 |
| Add (Deduct): | | | | |
| Accrued Revenues ........... | 230,081 | 63,533 | 633 | 50,980 |
| Deferred Revenues .......... | (4,767) | (1,889) | — | — |
| Accrued Expenditures ....... | (275,404) | 12,434 | — | (3,027) |
| Inventory Balance .......... | 9,085 | 4,115 | — | 33,022 |
| Fund Balances of Funds Not | | | | |
| Budgeted (GAAP Basis) ...... | 38,718 | (35,761) | — | 51,183 |
| Fund Balance (GAAP Basis) | | | | |
| June 30, 19X1 .............. | $214,681 | $329,633 | $85,308 | $170,031 |

**Part II—County of Los Angeles**
Notes to the Financial Statements

The following schedule is a reconciliation of the budgetary and GAAP fund balances (in thousands).

|  | General Fund | Special Revenue Funds | Debt Service Funds |
|---|---|---|---|
| Fund balance—budgetary basis ......... | $342,357 | $308,298 | $ 21,850 |
| Encumbrances outstanding at year end ... | 115,571 | 79,195 | |
| Subtotal ...................... | 457,928 | 387,493 | 21,850 |
| Adjustments: | | | |
| Accrual of workers' compensation | | | |
| liability........................... | (64,604) | (6,610) | |
| Accrual of estimated liability for | | | |
| litigation and self-insurance claims .... | (15,350) | (9,712) | |
| Accrual of vacation and sick leave | | | |
| benefits......................... | (237) | (1,691) | |
| Accrual of amounts due from and due | | | |
| to other funds .................... | (3,748) | | |
| Change in advances to and from other | | | |
| funds............................ | 11,200 | (8,800) | |
| Change in revenue accruals ........... | (8,573) | (4,813) | 526 |
| Subtotal ...................... | 376,616 | 355,867 | 22,376 |
| Fund balance—nonbudgeted funds ...... | | 54,408 | 218,702 |
| Fund balance—GAAP basis .......... | $376,616 | $410,275 | $241,078 |

*Source:* Adapted from recent annual financial reports of the state of Missouri and the county of Los Angeles, California.

- "Fund Balance" Approach Budgetary-Basis–GAAP-Basis Reconciliation Examples (Figure 14–11)

  Part I—State of Missouri—reconciles differences involving inventory accounting and deferred revenues as well as nonbudgeted funds, encumbrances, revenue accruals, and expenditure accruals.

  Part II—County of Los Angeles—illustrates a reconciliation involving differences in accounting for claims and judgments, compensated absences, and interfund payables and receivables as well as encumbrances and revenue accruals.

Again, these examples were selected to illustrate the variety of ways—not the only ways—that budgetary-basis–GAAP-basis reconciliations may be presented in the financial statements and schedules and/or in the notes to the financial statements. No two governments are apt to present identical reconciliations, of course, but most use presentation approaches similar to those illustrated here.

## CONCLUDING COMMENTS

This chapter focuses on accounting and reporting issues that result from more complex interrelationships between entities and from the use in practice of non-GAAP bases of accounting. Chapter 13 discussed the Comprehensive Annual Financial Report and General Purpose Financial Statements for a government with a simple entity structure. This chapter discusses GAAP requirements when a reporting government has one or more other entities associated with it that might need to be included in its financial reports. Both criteria for determining which associated entities are component units and how component unit information must be reported are discussed and illustrated in some detail. Likewise, reporting and disclosure of other associated organizations that are not component units are discussed briefly.

Additionally, earlier chapters assumed for illustrative (and CPA exam) purposes that the governmental fund budget was prepared—and the accounts were maintained during the year—on the GAAP basis. But many SLGs budget on a non-GAAP budgetary basis. Likewise, most SLGs use non-GAAP accounting methods during the year for various budgetary, legal or contractual, and accounting simplification reasons. At year end, these SLGs (1) adjust the data in the accounts to the budgetary or other required non-GAAP basis in order to prepare budgetary statements and/or special purpose reports on another non-GAAP basis, then (2) adjust the non-GAAP-basis data to the GAAP basis in order to prepare the GAAP-basis financial statements. The adjusting entries made in this two-phase adjustment process may be posted to the accounts or may be posted only to the year-end worksheets.

This chapter concludes the discussion of current GAAP for state and local governments. The GASB has proposed major changes in the reporting model for these entities. In addition, the Board is considering various other more specific, topical issues. The proposed new reporting model and several of the other topics being addressed by the GASB are discussed in Chapter 15.

APPENDIX 14–1

## Financial Statement Analysis for Governmental Units*

# INTRODUCTION

Although the literature on financial statement analysis for business enterprises is well developed, a similar effort has been applied to governmental entities only since New York City's 1975 financial crisis. The major contributions to this growing literature are outlined in Table 14–l.

The literature does not provide a clear framework or order of importance for the various proposed financial condition indicators. The approach used here focuses first on overall financial condition. The overall analysis provides some ten-

TABLE 14–1   **Literature on Governmental Financial Statement Analysis**

| Author/Publisher | Year | Title | Indicators | Major Categories |
|---|---|---|---|---|
| Dearborn | 1977 | "Elements of Municipal Financial Analysis" | 6 | Liquidity, budget performance, debt |
| Municipal Finance Officers Association (MFOA) | 1978 | *Is Your City Heading for Financial Difficulty: A Guidebook for Small Cities and Other Governmental Units* | 28 | Economic vitality, financial independence & flexibility, productivity, deferral of current costs, financial management practices |
| Howell & Stamm | 1979 | *Urban Fiscal Stress* (Lexington Books) | 22 | Current expenses, intergovernmental transfers, educational expenses, debt |
| Groves & Valente (International City Management Association) | 1986 (1980) | *Evaluating Financial Condition, (Financial Trend Monitoring System)* | 36 | Revenues, expenditures, operating position, debt structure, unfunded liabilities, capital plant condition, community needs & resources |
| Zehms | 1991 | "Proposed Financial Ratios for Use in Analysis of Municipal Financial Statements" *Government Accountants Journal* (Fall 1991) 79–85 | 13 | Operating, debt, capital expenditures |
| Berne (GASB Research Study) | 1992 | *The Relationships between Financial Reporting and the Measurement of Financial Condition* | 43* | Economy & demographics, revenue base, revenues, current & capital expenditures, debt, pensions & other postemployment benefits, internal resources |
| Brown | 1993 | "The 10-Point Test of Financial Condition" | 10** | Revenues, general fund revenues, expenditures, fund balance, liquid assets, debt |
|  | 1996 | "Trends in Key Ratios Using the GFOA Financial Indicators Databases," *Government Finance Review* |  |  |

*Recommended measures.

**Dr. Brown's ten-point test and comparative ratios for cities, counties, and school districts are described more fully at his home page <http://www.smsu.edu/kwb237f>.

---

*This appendix was contributed by David R. Olson, Associate Professor of Accountancy, University of Illinois–Springfield.

tative conclusions and questions that provide direction for a more detailed analysis of general government revenues, expenditures, and debt and of major proprietary funds. After presenting a general discussion of the method of analysis, we use the city of Orlando's comprehensive annual financial report (CAFR) to illustrate how financial statement analysis can be performed on a governmental unit.

# OVERALL ANALYSIS

Traditional business financial statement analysis generally examines the profitability, solvency, and liquidity of a commercial enterprise, with an emphasis on profitability. The absence of the profit motive in government means that the analysis focuses on liquidity and solvency. Investigators are especially interested in whether and to what extent government programs create benefits that are greater than their costs. However, knowledge about the benefits of government programs must await continuing developments in the field of service efforts and accomplishments (SEA) reporting, as discussed in Chapter 15. For the present, financial statement analysis for state and local governmental units is primarily a question of the management of liquidity and solvency—the management of liquid resources in the short and long run. A government's ability to manage its liquidity and solvency depends on its ability to manage its revenues and expenditures, particularly those revenues and expenditures that are determined largely at the discretion of the government itself. This is why analysis begins with the unrestricted resources accounted for in the General Fund.

## General Fund

Most governments depend heavily on their General Fund. Indeed, the financial health of the General Fund often largely determines the financial health of the unit as a whole. As Dearborn stated in 1977, "The condition of a government's General Fund is a key indicator of financial strength or weakness. . . . Most historical financial emergencies in governments have begun with an inability to maintain liquidity in the General Fund."[1] As an example, when Standard and Poor's lowered the state of Illinois' bond rating in 1992, they cited the "continued weak financial operations and liquidity position" in the state's General Fund as the reason for their action.[2]

Most expenditures financed from the General Fund are for activities and functions that governments provide on a continuing basis over the long term. These services are usually personnel intensive and involve skilled and/or professional workers. For both of these reasons, if at all possible sufficient resources must be provided to avoid undesirable programmatic and personnel reductions.

Most governments face certain risks with respect to their principal revenue sources. Governmental revenues usually are not as stable or predictable as government expenditures. This is particularly true with income and sales tax revenues that are dependent on local (or state) economic conditions. It is also true for intergovernmental revenue. On the other hand, property tax revenue typically is a relatively stable, reliable revenue source. Management must address this long-term

[1] Philip M. Dearborn, *Elements of Municipal Financial Analysis,* memorandum of The First Boston Corporation, 1977, part I, p. 5.
[2] "Illinois Ratings on Bonds, Debt Lowered by S&P," *The Wall Street Journal,* August 10, 1992, p. A5A.

fundamental imbalance between expenditure stability and revenue instability in the governmental environment.

A healthy, positive fund balance facilitates financing fund operations while avoiding cash flow problems. A significant fund balance is good insurance against problems caused by the revenue fluctuations that can be expected over the course of several fiscal years. A significant fund balance can be used to minimize or eliminate the tax increases, spending cuts, or borrowing that would otherwise be necessary to handle significant decreases in revenues. Whereas use of fund balance during a temporary fall in revenues permits a government to sustain its program services, establishing a positive fund balance requires expenditure restraint during the periods when revenues exceed current, short-term needs. The use of the fund balance to help smooth the peaks and troughs over the business cycle is a sign of capable, forward-looking management. The lack of a healthy fund balance and/or drastic changes in fund balance are a cause for concern and need to be investigated through further analysis and by looking for management's explanation in the introductory section of the government unit's CAFR and elsewhere in the report. Groves and Valente cited the importance of the unreserved fund balance compared to net operating revenues.

> The size of a local government's fund balances can affect its ability to withstand financial emergencies. It can also affect its ability to accumulate funds for capital purchases without having to borrow. In states that allow it, jurisdictions usually try to operate each year at a small surplus to maintain positive fund balances and thus maintain adequate reserves.[3]

Three key measures that are useful in evaluating overall financial health and stability of the General Fund and the adequacy of its fund balance are the:

1. Ratio of General Fund Unreserved Fund Balance to General Fund revenues
2. Comparison of General Fund revenue growth to General Fund expenditure growth
3. Role and sustainability of operating transfers from other funds in financing General Fund operations

The ratio of General Fund Unreserved Fund Balance divided by total General Fund revenues is one of Brown's ten key ratios. In his study covering 1989–1993, Brown found average percentages for the 25th, 50th, and 75th percentile cities of 9.7%, 19.9%, and 35.3%, respectively.[4] The ability to create and preserve a healthy fund balance obviously depends on the ability to keep expenditure levels and growth in line with revenue levels and growth.

The analysis of the General Fund should also include an evaluation of the role of transfers in changing the fund balance. If an unfavorable revenue–expenditure balance is being propped up by operating transfers, then the viability of the transferor fund(s) should be investigated to determine if the transfers are sustain-

[3] Sanford M. Groves & Maureen Godsey Valente, *Evaluating Financial Condition: A Handbook for Local Government,* International City Management Association, 1986, p. 69. An earlier version by Groves entitled *Financial Trend Monitoring System: A Practitioner's Workbook for Collecting Data, Charting Trends, and Interpreting Results* was published by the ICMA in 1980.

[4] Ken W. Brown, "Trends in Key Ratios Using the GFOA Financial Indicators Databases 1989–1993," *Government Finance Review,* December 1996, p. 33. These ratios are explained in Brown's "The 10-Point Test of Financial Condition: Toward an Easy-to-Use Assessment Tool for Smaller Cities," *Government Finance Review,* December 1993, pp. 21–26.

able in the future. If the fund is being supported by debt proceeds, then such practices should be investigated for specific reasons or justification.

## Other Major Governmental Funds

Some of the other major governmental funds also should be analyzed similarly over a four-year period. Each fund should be analyzed separately using the combining or individual fund statements. Again, the focus here should be on the overall picture using the GAAP statements.

## Total Governmental Funds Revenues and Expenditures

The analysis of the General Fund and other major governmental funds should be accompanied by an overall look at the size and growth of total governmental fund revenues and expenditures reported in the combined statement of revenues, expenditures, and changes in fund balances for all governmental fund types. Many governments include the expendable trust fund (ETF) types in this statement. Including ETFs is appropriate for analysis purposes only if ETF assets may be used for governmental purposes. Some governments also include component units in this statement. Component unit amounts should be excluded from the analysis unless their financial resources are under the control of the primary government and resources can be used for primary government purposes.

Both increases and decreases over time and comparisons with other units of government are considered in this analysis. In making government-to-government comparisons, recognize that different governments have different revenue sources, different service responsibilities, and different mixes of programs. Rarely can meaningful comparisons be made between cities and counties or between school districts and state governments. However, even city-to-city or county-to-county comparisons are not appropriate without adjustments when there are significant differences in the scope of services provided. As one important example, in many communities in the eastern United States elementary and secondary education is provided by school districts that are part of city or county government and are reported as blended or discretely presented component units. In midwest and western states, school districts typically are independent governmental entities and are not included in municipal or county CAFRS. Careful reading of the introductory section and the reporting entity note to the GPFS provides important information about the scope of services provided.

## Inflation Adjustments

Analysis can, of course, be extended to cover longer periods of time. If this is done, and if there are periods of time when the inflation rate is high or changes dramatically (as in the United States in 1979–1982), it is a good idea to control for the effects of inflation. The consumer price index (CPI) for all urban consumers, though not without limitations, is the most widely used measure of inflation. The CPI can be found at the CPI home page <http://www.bls.gov/cpihome.htm> or in the annual *Economic Report of the President*[5] The inflation-adjusted results will indicate the extent to which total governmental revenues and expenditures are keeping up with inflation. The easiest and most meaningful method is to adjust (or inflate) earlier

[5] *Economic Report of the President,* February 1998, Table B-60.

years' nominal dollars to the most recent year reported. Two excellent CPI-related Internet sites that include adjustment calculators are located at <http://www.westegg.com> and <http://www.aier.org/colcalc.htm>.

## Total Governmental Funds Revenues and Expenditures per Capita

The analysis of total governmental revenue and expenditure growth is not complete without taking population into account. Groves and Valente indentify both revenues per capita and expenditures per capita as important indicators, although they suggest "net operating revenues and expenditures" as the appropriate numerators.

> As population increases, it might be expected that revenues and the need for services would increase proportionately, and therefore that the level of per capita revenues should remain at least constant in real terms. If per capita revenues are decreasing, the government may be unable to maintain existing service levels unless it finds new revenue sources or ways to save money. . . .
>
> Increasing per capita expenditures can indicate that the cost of providing services is outstripping the community's ability to pay, especially if spending is increasing faster than the resident's collective personal income. From a different perspective, if the increase in spending is greater than can be accounted for by inflation or the addition of new services, it may indicate declining productivity.[6]

The MFOA (now GFOA) Guidebook also suggests that expenditures per capita is a "broad measure of municipal productivity."[7] Both Groves and Valente and the MFOA Guidebook recommend that these indicators be computed in inflation-adjusted or real terms. One of Brown's ten key ratios calculated for cities is real revenue per capita. He calculated the 25th, 50th, and 75th percentile amounts for 1993 at $458, $585, and $784, respectively.[8]

At this point, the overall picture of financial conditions should be fairly clear, and the conclusions reached or questions raised so far should provide the perspective needed for a more detailed, micro-level analysis of general government revenues, expenditures, and debt and of major proprietary funds.

## DETAILED ANALYSIS

### Revenues

#### Major Revenue Sources

Most governmental units rely on relatively few major revenue sources, usually property, income, or sales taxes. The major sources of revenue should be analyzed for year-to-year growth or decline.

Unusual and one-time revenues or other financing sources should also be examined over time to determine if they are having significant impacts on total government revenues or on the General or major Special Revenue Funds. Heavy

---

[6] Groves & Valente, 1986, pp. 19, 48.

[7] *Is Your City Heading for Financial Difficulty: A Guidebook for Small Cities and Other Governmental Units,* Municipal Finance Officers Association, 1978, p. 17.

[8] Brown, 1996, p. 32.

reliance on one-time revenue sources can make a city vulnerable when those revenues decrease or cease to be available.[9] Significant volatility in the amount of an ongoing revenue source creates similar stress.

## Economic Factors Affecting Major Revenue Sources

The economic factors or drivers that determine the amounts and stability of major revenue sources must be analyzed carefully. This is particularly true with taxes; the analysis should also focus on the rate of taxation and the tax base. In most cases, the CAFR statistical section contains information about tax bases, such as property tax assessed valuations, retail sales, personal and business income, and employment, as well as other useful statistics. Property tax rates usually are displayed; however, other tax and fee rates may be found only by direct inquiry.

The CAFR's statistical section should also include a schedule of the ten largest taxpayers in the government's jurisdiction. Usually, these are the ten largest property taxpayers. This schedule provides an insight into the concentration of industries or companies and the related risks, particularly of single company or single industry communities.

## Restricted Revenues

Local governments typically receive restricted revenues by exercising special local taxing authority or from state or federal grant programs. State governments also can receive restricted resources on their own authority or from federal grant sources. Initially, these revenues are generally welcomed by the recipient governments as new initiatives or as enhancements to existing programs. However, Groves and Valente point out the subtle perils of relying on restricted revenues, especially those received from other governments, which is a widespread practice in local government.

> From one perspective, it would seem that many of these restrictions, especially those relating to outside funding, should not affect a local government's financial health. The government has the option of not accepting the revenue and of not providing the service. This option, however, is not always easy to exercise [because] governments develop economic and political dependencies on these revenues and on the programs they support. Moreover, many governments finance their own "essential" services with intergovernmental revenues, which makes it doubly hard to cut them out. As the percentage of restricted revenues increases, a local government loses its ability to respond to changing conditions and to citizens needs and demands. Increases in restricted revenues may also indicate overdependence on external revenues and signal a future inability to maintain service levels.[10]

Reliance on restricted revenues (and intergovernmental revenues discussed below) has generally occurred gradually and with the money coming several years before the inevitable restrictions and mandates ("strings") begin to affect decisions of recipients. A low ratio or downward trend suggests that the governmental unit has significant and/or increasing financial flexibility. This ratio is computed by taking restricted revenues (total governmental funds revenue minus total General Fund revenue) divided by total governmental funds revenue. Some governments may have restricted revenues in the General Fund; if so, these amounts need to be removed from the numerator.

---

[9] Groves & Valente, 1986, p. 32.

[10] Groves & Valente, 1986, p. 23.

### Intergovernmental Revenues

Intergovernmental revenues are those revenues raised by one government and passed along to other governmental units through grants or revenue sharing. As in the case of restricted revenue, Groves and Valente warn about the conditions or strings that attach to these revenues.

> ...conditions attached to the revenues may prove too costly, especially if these conditions are changed after the local government has already become dependent on the program. ...
>
> The primary concern in analyzing intergovernmental revenues is determining whether the local government is controlling its use of the external revenues—or whether these revenues are controlling the local government.[11]

Berne also noted the importance of intergovernmental revenues, calling them "a critical part of financial condition analysis."[12] This ratio is computed by dividing total intergovernmental revenues for all funds by total governmental funds revenue.

## Expenditures

### Major Expenditure Categories

The analysis of governmental funds expenditures is even more important than the analysis of revenues. Unfortunately, the expenditure information presented in the CAFR is usually highly aggregated. Although this analysis can help to identify expenditure areas that are large and/or growing rapidly, it is usually only suggestive. In order to scrutinize expenditures properly, the analysis must be detailed, whether expenditures are budgeted and tracked by object, program, function, or organizational unit. A detailed analysis almost always requires that budgetary reports be used, but these reports may not have been audited. In addition, it is common for analysts to have significant problems reconciling budgetary information with information in the audited CAFR. For both of these reasons, detailed expenditure analysis can easily become problematic unless the analyst has the power to compel the governmental unit under study to prepare detailed budgetary crosswalk schedules that reconcile the budgetary and GAAP amounts or to otherwise provide the data needed by the analyst.

### Capital Expenditures

While varying degrees of capital assets are necessary to provide public services, all governments have some responsibility for owning, maintaining, and replacing these assets. Because capital assets (including infrastructure) are by definition a long-term fiscal policy matter, the purpose of the capital expenditures analysis is to assess the government's long-term capital plan. In Berne's view,

> ...the underlying question is whether the infrastructure has been developed and maintained to support the level and quality of service needs and economic development demands faced by government now and in the future.[13]

---

[11] Groves & Valente, 1986, p. 26.

[12] Robert Berne, *The Relationships between Financial Reporting and the Measurement of Financial Condition,* GASB Research Report, 1992, p. 46.

[13] Berne, 1992, p. 79. Also see Attmore, Miller, & Fountain, "Governmental Capital Assets: The Challenge to Report Decision-Useful Information," *Government Finance Review,* August 1989, pp. 13–17.

Often this question is difficult to answer directly but can be examined indirectly by looking at capital expenditure levels. The introductory section of the CAFR, the budget document, and other sources should be read carefully for any information about the capital asset management plan. Governments have been known to solve short-term budgetary gaps by delaying capital expenditures. Groves and Valente and the MFOA Guidebook both suggest that a declining capital expenditure ratio may mean that the capital base is at an adequate level, with no increase needed (unlikely), or that the infrastructure is being allowed to deteriorate, with ominous future implications.[14] The capital expenditure ratio is calculated by dividing all capital expenditures made from governmental funds by total governmental funds expenditures.

### Personnel Costs

Providing government services is a labor-intensive activity, and personnel costs are a major portion of government expenditures. Managing and controlling these expenditures is one of the most important challenges facing government decision makers. Both the MFOA Guidebook and Groves and Valente suggest that the number of employees per capita is the most meaningful way to track this important cost.[15] Unfortunately, most CAFRs do not provide information on total government employment. If selected employment categories (such as police and fire protection) are provided, they might be analyzed. If details on the object of expenditure category are available in the CAFR, the result of personnel and related expenditures for all governmental funds divided by total governmental funds expenditures provides a personnel expenditure ratio that can be tracked through time.

### Debt Service Expenditures

The level of debt service expenditures is important in gauging the financial strength of any economic unit, including state and local governments. Dearborn explains why this is true.

> Debt service represents an uncontrollable cost that cannot be quickly reduced in a fiscal crisis. Therefore, the larger debt service is relative to operating expenses [expenditures], the less opportunity there is for budget reduction and the greater the risk that debt service will not be paid during a fiscal crisis. For example, if debt service represents 20% of total spending, it may be impossible from a practical standpoint to adjust other operating expenses downward fast enough to provide funds for debt service payments. On the other hand, if debt service is only 5% of total spending, the city would have greater flexibility (financially and politically) to make the necessary adjustments.[16]

Dearborn suggests that 10% is a critical proportion of debt service expenditures compared to total *General Fund* expenditures.[17] Groves and Valente compute net *governmental fund* direct debt service to net operating revenues, indicating

---

[14] Groves & Valente, 1986, p. 102; MFOA Guidebook, 1978, pp. 21–22.

[15] MFOA Guidebook, 1978, p. 17; Groves & Valente, 1986, p. 52.

[16] Dearborn, 1977, part. III, p. 4. Also see Hugh C. Sherwood, *How Corporate and Municipal Debt Is Rated: An Inside Look at Standard & Poor's Rating System,* John Wiley & Sons, 1976. On page 118, Sherwood indicates that Standard & Poor's also looks closely at debt service costs compared to revenues.

[17] Dearborn, 1977, part. III, p. 4.

that a ratio in excess of 20% should be considered a potential problem, while 10% would be considered acceptable.[18] The MFOA Guidebook suggests that a growing general government debt burden (compared to own source revenues) may unduly restrict future financial flexibility.[19]

The portion of *total governmental fund* revenues devoted to debt service is calculated by dividing total debt service expenditures for all governmental funds by total governmental funds revenues. The numerator typically includes all expenditures in debt service funds. Debt service expenditures that are separately identified in other governmental (and expendable trust) funds also should be included.

Brown identifies debt service to total revenue as a key ratio and, during the years 1989 through 1993, reported average percentages for the 25th, 50th, and 75 percentile cities of 13.4%, 6.9%, and 2.0%, respectively.[20] Caution must be exercised in using this ratio because, as Dearborn points out, there are sometimes significant confounding problems in applying the criteria, such as the use of separate capital authorities and situations in which units have different scopes of public services.

## Debt

The debt service to total revenue ratio is perhaps the best way to assess the overall burden of debt on a governmental unit. However, other indicators are also used.

### Total Debt, Debt Components, and Debt per Capita

The amount of debt is an important element of financial condition for any economic entity. This is especially true for governments. Analysis of government debt is complicated by a number of factors, however, including the various kinds of debt that are incurred[21] and the important distinctions made between general government debt and proprietary (or revenue) debt. Governments have become increasingly creative in the form and manner by which they incur indebtedness, so a comprehensive approach to debt analysis is warranted.

Although proprietary and trust fund debt is typically thought to be self-supporting, only enterprise funds that sell services or goods to the general public and are financially sound should properly be excluded from an analysis of government debt. Internal Service Fund financing ultimately depends on general government revenue sources, particularly those Internal Service Funds devoted to risk management or loan management activities for general government functions. Accordingly, the approach outlined here is much more comprehensive than many authors have suggested. This comprehensive approach starts with total long-term liabilities in the general long-term debt account group. It then considers all long-term liabilities in Internal Service, Trust, and Enterprise Funds. The total amount of long-term debt for the primary government is calculated, and each debt amount is used to calculate per capita debt.

---

[18] Groves & Valente, 1986, p. 83.

[19] MFOA Guidebook, 1978, p. 12.

[20] Brown, 1996, p. 33.

[21] See the definition of debt included in the GLTD Account Group in Chapter 9.

### Debt Compared to Assessed Valuation

When the property tax is the main revenue source pledged to repay debt, the comparison of total general obligation bonds payable to total assessed property valuations is often used in the computation of legal debt margin. This computation usually is presented in the statistical section of the CAFR.

### Unfunded Pension Liabilities

Both the MFOA Guidebook and Groves and Valente identify pension liabilities as important indicators or trends to be analyzed.[22] Similarly, Berne considers pensions "an important initial part of financial condition analysis."[23] GASB Statements Nos. 25 and 27 require that governments report annual pension costs and contributions.

### Postemployment Benefits

Postemployment benefits can include health care benefits, life insurance, and other assistance programs. Berne noted that postemployment benefits "can create significant obligations in the future."[24] GASB Statement No. 12 requires several disclosures about postemployment benefits, including expenditure and expenses if financed on a pay-as-you-go basis or, if financed on an actuarial basis, certain actuarial data.

## Major Proprietary Funds Analysis

Major proprietary funds should be analyzed separately using the combining or individual fund statements and a commercial financial statement analysis framework. Although profitability and rate of return are not generally of primary interest,[25] these funds should be managed so that financial capital is maintained.[26] Thus, operating income and net income or loss should be closely examined over time. For proprietary funds with significant amounts of long-term debt, the debt to total assets and the times interest earned ratios should be analyzed. Other financial ratios measure the level of liquidity (current ratio, acid-test ratio), the management of receivables (accounts receivable turnover), and inventories (inventory turnover).

Market pressures for efficiency are sometimes not as strong for governmental proprietary activities as they are for private, for-profit entities. Accordingly, additional analysis is needed to gain insight into efficiency and managerial performance. Governments sometimes decide to operate these funds in a manner that regularly generates losses or profits. This is why the nature and amount of operating transfers is also of particular interest: Operating transfers in suggest that the fund is being subsidized; operating transfers out suggest that the fund is generating profits that are used to support other governmental activities. Other significant nonoperating revenues and expenses must be analyzed in order to have

---

[22] MFOA Guidebook, 1978, p. 22; Groves & Valente, 1986, p. 90.

[23] Berne, 1992, p. 69.

[24] Ibid.

[25] Profitability and rate of return are appropriate indicators for those governmental activities such as government lotteries in which the goal is to make money.

[26] Groves & Valente, 1986, p. 66. The authors emphasize the importance of recovering all costs, including depreciation through user charges.

a complete picture of the fund's operations. Although the financial report may not be very helpful in this regard, the introductory section of the CAFR should be read carefully for information about proprietary functions management, changes during the year, workload or activity measures, and related issues.

## ILLUSTRATIVE ANALYSIS—CITY OF ORLANDO

To illustrate in part the types of analyses discussed, we will use the city of Orlando, Florida, as an example. We will begin with an overall analysis like the one discussed earlier.

### Overall Analysis

As a preliminary step, the introductory section of the CAFR should be read for each of the four years to be analyzed. This should provide some understanding of city management's point of view about the issues facing the governmental unit and provide the analyst with background information about the government.

#### General Fund

Table 14–2 presents the analysis of Orlando's General Fund. The data are taken from the General Fund column of the Combined Statement of Revenues, Expenditures, and Changes in Fund Balance using the modified accrual basis of accounting (see Figure 13–6, for example). The analysis is designed to evaluate the overall picture of the financial health and stability of the fund. Total revenues, total expenditures, and other significant categories (such as operating transfers) should be listed separately. The focus is on the net change in fund balance for the year and the level of fund balance throughout the four-year period.

Orlando's ratio of General Fund fund balance to General Fund revenues exceeds 30% in each year reported. This is well above the 50th percentile level reported by Brown and approaches the 75th percentile level. Maintaining this significant level of fund balance—sometimes referred to as a "rainy day fund"—will likely be vitally important if Orlando ever suffers significant revenue shortfalls or unexpected expenditure increases. Comparing Orlando's General Fund revenue growth over the four-year period with its expenditure growth for the same period does not signal any potential problems.

However, the role of transfers from other funds in financing General Fund expenditures and maintaining its healthy level of fund balance must be examined. If an unfavorable revenue–expenditure balance is being propped up by operating transfers, then the viability of the transferor fund(s) should be investigated to see if the transfers are sustainable in the future. The role of operating transfers in Orlando's General Fund is significant, particularly the large decrease in FY 19X5–19X6, followed by the large increase in 19X6–19X7. The General Fund's health is substantially determined by these transfers and depends on the stability and sustainability of this financing source in the future. Although there are several categories of operating transfers in and out, by far the largest item is an operating transfer in ($20,553,093 in FY 19X5–19X6) from the Utilities Service Tax (expendable trust) Fund. This fund accounts for taxes on electric, natural gas, LP gas, water, and telecommunications collected within the city limits. This fund and its revenue sources are examined in the next section.

TABLE 14–2

**CITY OF ORLANDO, FLORIDA**
**General Fund Analysis**
FY 19X4–19X7

| | FY 19X3–19X4 | FY 19X4–19X5 | FY 19X5–19X6 | FY 19X6–19X7 |
|---|---|---|---|---|
| Fund balance, beginning of year | $44,437,726 | $41,516,967 | $41,344,634 | * $46,780,290 |
| Revenue | $128,507,918 | $136,020,824 | $151,297,577 | $157,627,282 |
| Percent growth | | 5.85% | 11.23% | 4.18% |
| Expenditures | ($149,757,784) | ($156,370,683) | ($161,741,678) | ($170,115,985) |
| Percent growth | | 4.42% | 3.43% | 5.18% |
| Operating transfers, net | $18,329,107 | $20,177,526 | $16,575,569 | $18,054,967 |
| Percent growth | | 10.08% | (17.85%) | 8.93% |
| Other changes | | | | |
| Net change | ($2,920,759) | ($172,333) | $6,131,468 | $5,566,264 |
| Fund balance, end of year | $41,516,967 | $41,344,634 | $47,476,102 | $52,346,554 |
| Percent of revenues in end-of-year fund balance | 32.31% | 30.40% | 31.38% | 33.21% |
| [CAFR page number] | [8] | [8] | [8] | [8] |

*Fund balance was restated downward by $695,812 because of GASB Statement No. 31.

### Other Major Governmental Funds

The analysis of Orlando's largest (in expenditures) major governmental fund (after the General Fund)—the Gas Tax Revenue (special revenue) Fund—is presented in Table 14–3. Although growth in revenues, expenditures, and operating transfers has been erratic, the fund balance was approximately 200% of yearly revenues during the four-year period analyzed. This amount is clearly more than enough to avoid any liquidity problems and may suggest that the city is accumulating resources for some large expenditure projects in the future. The introductory section of the CAFR should be read carefully for management's plans in this respect.

The General Fund relies significantly on operating transfers from the Utilities Service Tax (expendable trust) Fund, as shown in Table 14–4. According to the description of the fund, its resources are "restricted by pledge to Wastewater bonds," an activity accounted for in an enterprise fund (and examined in the subsequent detailed analysis). This arrangement is somewhat unusual. Because the Wastewater Fund handles its own debt service requirements, however, the operating transfers from this fund to the General Fund appear to be secure. These resources would likely be accounted for in the General Fund were it not for the restrictions related to the Wastewater bonds.

### Total Governmental Funds Revenues and Expenditures

Orlando's total governmental funds revenues and expenditures are presented in Table 14–5. Orlando has kept total governmental expenditure growth generally in line with or below revenue growth, except for FY 19X5–19X6, when total

TABLE 14–3

**CITY OF ORLANDO, FLORIDA**
**Gas Tax Revenue (Special Revenue) Fund**
**Analysis of Fund Balance**
FY 19X4–19X7

| | *FY 19X3–19X4* | *FY 19X4–19X5* | *FY 19X5–19X6* | *FY 19X6–19X7* |
|---|---|---|---|---|
| Fund balance, beginning of year | | $13,956,977 | $16,101,924 | $20,176,223 | * $20,294,603 |
| Revenue | $8,518,246 | $10,316,158 | $10,013,984 | $10,660,690 |
| *Percent growth | | 21.11% | (2.93%) | 6.46% |
| Expenditures | ($9,250,542) | ($6,143,819) | ($9,008,081) | ($10,560,913) |
| *Percent growth | | (33.58%) | 46.62% | 17.24% |
| Operating transfers, net | $2,877,243 | ($98,040) | ($686,099) | $812,378 |
| Other changes | | | | |
| Net change | $2,144,947 | $4,074,299 | $319,804 | $912,155 |
| Fund balance, end of year | $16,101,924 | $20,176,223 | $20,496,027 | $21,206,758 |
| Percent of revenues in end-of-year fund balance | 189.03% | 195.58% | 204.67% | 198.92% |
| [CAFR page number] | [92] | [94] | [92] | [98] |

*Fund balance was restated downward by $201,424 because of GASB Statement No. 31.

expenditures increased slightly faster than total revenues. In FY 19X6–19X7, expenditures grew by over 12%. Even though total revenues jumped by over 19%, the growth in total expenditures was substantially larger than during the previous two fiscal years. This might be the beginning of an unfavorable trend.

Orlando has enjoyed substantial real growth in revenues and, except for FY 19X6–19X7, has managed to keep expenditures growing modestly in real terms. Real expenditure growth in FY 19X6–19X7 of 9.95% raises the same concern about the future mentioned in the preceding paragraph.

### Total Governmental Revenues and Expenditures per Capita

Compared to Brown's real revenue per capita statistics cited earlier, Orlando's per capita amounts seem high. This may be due in part to the high level of services needed for a community heavily affected by tourism and the entertainment industry.

### Summary: Overall Analysis

Orlando gives every indication of being a financially sound city government overall. The General Fund is well positioned to meet future unfavorable revenue or expenditure changes. Trends in total revenues and expenditures also seem to be reasonably under control, with the significant operating transfers apparently assured. The detailed analysis that follows looks more closely at revenues, expenditures, debt, and major proprietary funds. The unfavorable expenditure trends in FY 19X6–19X7 are also noted for further analysis.

TABLE 14–4

**CITY OF ORLANDO, FLORIDA**
**Utilities Services Tax (Expendable Trust) Fund**
**Analysis of Fund Balance**
FY 19X4–19X7

| | FY 19X3–19X4 | FY 19X4–19X5 | FY 19X5–19X6 | FY 19X6–19X7 |
|---|---|---|---|---|
| Fund balance, beginning of year | $13,697,208 | $13,946,325 | $13,555,087 | * $18,407,793 |
| Revenue | | | | |
| Utilities service tax | $21,631,723 | $22,606,912 | $24,825,948 | $26,838,317 |
| *Percent growth | | 4.51% | 9.82% | 8.11% |
| Income on investments | $590,154 | $701,850 | $717,065 | $1,136,830 |
| Expenditures | $0 | $0 | ($8,782) | ($11,711) |
| Operating transfers, net | ($21,972,760) | ($23,700,000) | ($20,553,093) | ($24,870,244) |
| *Percent growth | | 7.86% | (13.28%) | 21.00% |
| Other changes | | | | |
| Net change | $249,117 | ($391,238) | $4,981,138 | $3,093,192 |
| Fund balance, end of year | $13,946,325 | $13,555,087 | $18,536,225 | $21,500,985 |
| Percent of revenues in end-of-year fund balance | 64.47% | 59.96% | 74.66% | 80.11% |
| [CAFR page number] | [137] | [139] | [137] | [153] |

*Fund balance was restated downward by $128,432 because of GASB Statement No. 31.

## Detailed Analysis of Orlando

### Revenues: Major Revenue Sources

As shown in Table 14–6, Orlando's principal revenue sources have grown over the four-year period. None of the major revenue sources declined, although the two largest—intergovernmental and property taxes—grew very slowly in FY 19X5–19X6. Intergovernmental revenues increased substantially in FY 19X4–19X5 and 19X6–19X7.

- *Economic Factors Affecting Major Revenue Sources.* Orlando's second largest source of revenue, property taxes, is a direct function of assessed values and the property tax rate. Table 14–6 shows that the property tax base has expanded each year, while the rate of tax has been constant. Orlando's schedule of its ten largest taxpayers indicates that an entertainment company, Universal City, Florida Partners, is the largest single taxpayer, accounting for over 5% of the total taxable assessed value. The ten largest taxpayers, including developers, communications firms, a commercial shopping center, and a bank, pay approximately 12%–14% of the total property tax in Orlando.

- *Restricted Revenue Ratio.* Orlando's trend is erratic and may be trending upward.

- *Intergovernmental Revenue Ratio.* As noted earlier, intergovernmental revenue is Orlando's largest single revenue source. Typically, the restricted revenue ratio is higher than

TABLE 14–5

**CITY OF ORLANDO, FLORIDA**
**Total Governmental Funds, Revenues, and Expenditures Analysis**
FY 19X4–19X7

| | FY 19X3–19X4 | FY 19X4–19X5 | FY 19X5–19X6 | FY 19X6–19X7 |
|---|---|---|---|---|
| **Total Governmental Funds Revenues** | $173,634,259 | $195,346,951 | $203,975,140 | $244,333,250 |
| Growth | | 12.5% | 4.42% | 19.79% |
| Consumer Price Index | 148.2 | 152.4 | 156.9 | 160.5 |
| Real governmental funds revenue | $188,045,200 | $205,729,565 | $208,655,258 | $244,333,250 |
| Real growth | | 9.4% | 1.42% | 17.1% |
| Population | 170,780 | 170,307 | 173,122 | 176,373 |
| Total governmental funds revenues per capita | $ 1,017 | $ 1,147 | $ 1,178 | $ 1,385 |
| Real governmental funds revenue per capita | $ 1,101 | $ 1,208 | $ 1,205 | $ 1,385 |
| **Total Governmental Funds Expenditures** | $189,680,939 | $197,255,413 | $206,675,873 | $232,449,804 |
| Growth | | 3.99% | 4.78% | 12.34% |
| Real governmental funds expenditures | $205,423,689 | $207,739,461 | $211,417,958 | $232,449,804 |
| Real growth | | 1.13% | 1.77% | 9.95% |
| Total governmental funds expenditures per capita | $ 1,111 | $ 1,158 | $ 1,194 | $ 1,318 |
| Real governmental funds expenditures per capita | $ 1,203 | $ 1,220 | $ 1,221 | $ 1,318 |
| [CAFR page number] | [8, 9, 229] | [8, 9, 231] | [8, 9, 229] | [8, 9, 245] |

the intergovernmental ratio because most intergovernmental monies are for restricted purposes. However, Orlando's General Fund receives significant amounts of state sales tax revenue and a contribution from the Orlando Utilities Commission, both of which are presumably unrestricted. This makes the intergovernmental ratio higher than the restricted ratio. This relatively high level of intergovernmental revenue may be problematic for the city's future for the reasons mentioned earlier.

### Expenditures

An analysis of Orlando's major operating expenditure categories is presented in Table 14–7. Because Orlando has managed total expenditures reasonably well, it is not surprising that the operating spending categories appear to be under control. However, had the overall analysis revealed expenditure problems, this part of the analysis would be critical in identifying those program areas of excessive expenditure growth. Expenditures for the police function increased by 8.77% in FY 19X6–19X7, an increase of $4.5 million in one year. This increase and the $12.7 million increase in capital expenditures (discussed below) are two principal reasons why total expenditures increased so dramatically in FY 19X6–19X7.

- *Capital expenditure.* Orlando's capital expenditure ratio is substantial, and it increased significantly in FY 19X6–19X7. This suggests that capital assets are an increasingly important priority for the city.

- *Personnel costs.* Orlando's CAFR does not contain any information on overall levels of city government employment. The number of employees in the fire and police protection functions is included, however, and indicates that the level of employment in these two

TABLE 14–6

**CITY OF ORLANDO, FLORIDA**
**Revenues Analysis**
FY 19X4–19X7

|  | *FY 19X3–19X4* | *FY 19X4–19X5* | *FY 19X5–19X6* | *FY 19X6–19X7* |
|---|---|---|---|---|
| **Total Governmental Funds Revenues** | $ 173,634,259 | $ 195,346,951 | $ 203,975,140 | $ 244,333,250 |
| Major Sources |  |  |  |  |
| Intergovernmental | $ 62,395,519 | $ 75,145,474 | $ 75,801,967 | $ 92,081,708 |
| Growth |  | 20.43% | 0.87% | 21.48% |
| Property taxes | $ 42,770,637 | $ 44,830,696 | $ 45,086,129 | $ 47,183,672 |
| Growth |  | 4.82% | 0.57% | 4.65% |
| Utilities service tax | $ 21,631,723 | $ 22,606,912 | $ 24,825,948 | $ 26,838,317 |
| Growth |  | 4.51% | 9.82% | 8.11% |
| Other licenses, permits, and fees | $ 16,389,592 | $ 18,422,273 | $ 19,255,250 | $ 24,926,313 |
| Growth |  | 12.4% | 4.52% | 29.45% |
| Occupational licenses and franchise fees | $ 17,293,709 | $ 18,030,106 | $ 19,103,129 | $ 19,538,786 |
| Growth |  | 4.26% | 5.95% | 2.28% |
| Total general fund revenues | $ 128,507,918 | $ 136,020,824 | $ 151,297,577 | $ 157,627,282 |
| Restricted revenues percentage | 25.99% | 30.37% | 25.83% | 35.49% |
| Intergovernmental revenue percentage | 35.94% | 38.47% | 37.16% | 37.69% |
| [CAFR page number] | [8, 9] | [8, 9] | [8, 9] | [8, 9] |
| Property taxes |  |  |  |  |
| Assessed value of taxable property | $7,607,830,369 | $7,763,926,392 | $8,033,160,016 | $8,777,058,007 |
| Millage tax rates (in percent) | 0.60666 | 0.60666 | 0.60666 | 0.60666 |
| Largest taxpayers', percentage | 5.46% | 5.89% | 5.78% | 6.81% |
| Ten largest taxpayers' percentage | 12.06% | 13.05% | 12.77% | 14.70% |
| [CAFR page number] | [216, 217, 230] | [218, 219, 232] | [216, 217, 230] | [232, 233, 246] |

functions increased slightly over the first three years analyzed and then increased by nearly 3% in FY 19X6–19X7.

- *Debt service expenditures.* Orlando's debt service expenditure ratios are slightly better than the 50th percentile amounts reported by Brown. In addition, they are much better than the standards suggested in Groves & Valente and the MFOA Guidebook.

## Total Debt, Debt Components, and Debt per Capita

Table 14–8 presents Orlando's debt, pension, and postemployment benefits information. The trend in Orlando's total debt and debt per capita was downward during the three years ending in FY 19X5–19X6, followed by a modest increase in FY 19X6–19X7. Enterprise Fund debt fell in each of the years analyzed, while general long-term debt declined for three years and then rose significantly in FY 19X6–19X7.

- *Pension Liabilities.* Orlando's pension contributions were equal to annual pension costs in each of the four years, resulting in no pension liability accruing in the general long-term debt group or in any individual fund. In addition, the notes indicate that there was no unfunded pension liability at the point of transition to reporting under GASB Statement Nos. 25 and 27.

- *Postemployment Benefits.* The number of retirees and employer costs are both rising. Both should be watched in the future.

TABLE 14–7

**CITY OF ORLANDO, FLORIDA**
**Expenditures**
*FY 19X4–X7*

|  | *FY 19X3–19X4* | *FY 19X4–19X5* | *FY 19X5–19X6* | *FY 19X6–19X7* |
|---|---|---|---|---|
| **Total Governmental Funds Expenditures** | $189,680,939 | $197,255,413 | $206,675,873 | $232,449,804 |
| Major Sources |  |  |  |  |
| Police | 47,224,127 | 49,971,689 | 52,253,702 | 56,837,471 |
| Growth |  | 5.82% | 4.57% | 8.77% |
| Public works | 28,225,405 | 25,329,760 | 28,261,026 | 30,372,618 |
| Growth |  | (10.26%) | 11.57% | 7.47% |
| Fire | 23,085,919 | 23,999,306 | 25,714,668 | 27,016,312 |
| Growth |  | 3.96% | 7.15% | 5.06% |
| Community and youth services | 14,707,990 | 16,136,950 | 16,635,806 | 17,616,762 |
| Growth |  | 9.72% | 3.09% | 5.9% |
| Capital Expenditures |  |  |  |  |
| Total, capital projects funds | $ 22,291,791 | $ 24,534,037 | $ 24,915,469 | $ 37,634,450 |
| Capital outlays, general fund | 0 | 0 | 0 | 0 |
| Capital outlays, special revenue funds | 0 | 0 | 0 | 0 |
| Capital outlays, expendable trust funds | 0 | 0 | 0 | 0 |
| Total capital expenditures | $ 22,291,791 | $ 24,534,037 | $ 24,915,469 | $ 37,634,450 |
| Capital expenditure ratio | 11.75% | 12.44% | 12.06% | 16.2% |
| Employment Levels |  |  |  |  |
| Fire protection, employees, sworn | 305 | 304 | 305 | 317 |
| Fire protection, employees, civilian | 50 | 49 | 50 | 44 |
| Police protection, employees, sworn | 591 | 596 | 591 | 617 |
| Police protection, employees, reserves | 12 | 12 | 12 | 13 |
| Police protection, employees, civilian | 249 | 249 | 249 | 262 |
| Total, fire and police protection | 1,207 | 1,210 | 1,207 | 1,253 |
| Debt Service Expenditures |  |  |  |  |
| Total governmental funds: |  |  |  |  |
| Debt service–principal | $ 6,231,308 | $ 6,064,891 | $ 7,729,398 | $ 7,243,861 |
| Debt service–interest | 5,234,348 | 5,109,497 | 5,137,034 | 4,966,930 |
| Total | $ 11,465,656 | $ 11,174,388 | $ 12,866,432 | $ 12,210,791 |
| Total Governmental Funds Revenues | $173,634,259 | $195,346,951 | $203,975,140 | $244,333,250 |
| Debt Service % of Total Revenues | 6% | 5.72% | 6.31% | 5.0% |
| [CAFR page number] | [8, 9, 232] | [8, 9, 234] | [8, 9, 232] | [8, 9, 248] |

## Major Proprietary Funds

Table 14–9 presents selected information and ratio calculations for Orlando's largest Enterprise Fund and largest Internal Service Fund.

- *Wastewater System Fund.* The fund is being operated profitably due in part to large amounts of impact fees. However, operating revenues have not kept pace with operating expenses, especially in the last two fiscal years. Although interest expense appears to be covered adequately, action may be needed to bring operating revenues and expenses into line.

TABLE 14–8

## CITY OF ORLANDO, FLORIDA
### Debt Analysis
FY 19X4–19X7

|  | *FY 19X3–19X4* | *FY 19X4–19X5* | *FY 19X5–19X6* | *FY 19X6–19X7* |
|---|---|---|---|---|
| GLTDG long-term liabilities | $106,320,384 | $ 99,799,841 | $ 94,048,280 | $132,063,704 |
| Internal service long-term debt | 120,400,158 | 118,742,760 | 117,007,633 | 116,781,488 |
| Trust and agency long-term debt | 0 | 0 | 0 | 0 |
| Enterprise long-term debt | 249,671,382 | 248,322,371 | 240,576,854 | 235,044,257 |
| Total long-term debt | $476,391,924 | $466,864,972 | $451,632,767 | $483,889,449 |
| Population | 170,780 | 170,307 | 173,122 | 176,373 |
| Per capita GLTDG long-term debt | $ 623 | $ 586 | $ 543 | $ 749 |
| Per capita internal service long-term debt | 705 | 697 | 676 | 662 |
| Per capita trust & agency long-term debt | 0 | 0 | 0 | 0 |
| Per capita Enterprise long-term debt | 1,462 | 1,458 | 1,390 | 1,333 |
| Per capita Total Debt | $2,790 | $2,741 | $2,609 | $2,744 |
| [CAFR page number] | [2, 3, 4, 5] | [2, 3, 4, 5] | [2, 3, 4, 5] | [2, 3, 4, 5] |
| Pensions |  |  |  |  |
| Annual pension costs |  |  |  |  |
| General employees | $ 6,150,000 | $ 6,370,000 | $ 7,070,000 | $ 7,750,000 |
| Firefighters | 3,040,000 | 3,230,000 | 3,550,000 | 3,870,000 |
| Police | 4,310,000 | 5,550,000 | 5,630,000 | 7,110,000 |
| Total | $ 13,500,000 | $ 15,150,000 | $ 16,250,000 | $ 18,730,000 |
| Contributions Made |  |  |  |  |
| General employees | $ 6,150,000 | $ 6,370,000 | $ 7,070,000 | $ 7,750,000 |
| Firefighters | 3,040,000 | 3,230,000 | 3,550,000 | 3,870,000 |
| Police | 4,310,000 | 5,550,000 | 5,630,000 | 7,110,000 |
| Total | $ 13,500,000 | $ 15,150,000 | $ 16,250,000 | $ 18,730,000 |
| [CAFR page number] | [41] | [41] | [40] | [44] |
| Postemployment benefits |  |  |  |  |
| Total employer cost of retirees | $ 1,309,000 | $ 1,398,000 | $ 1,395,000 | $ 1,451,000 |
| Number of retirees participating | 862 | 913 | 966 | 1,017 |
| [CAFR page number] | [44] | [45] | [44] | [48] |

- *Fleet Management Fund.* This fund has also earned small net profits in three of the four years under review; operating losses have been chronic though not large. Although the fund has very little debt, action may be needed on operating revenues and/or expenses.

## Summary of Orlando's Financial Condition

The overall analysis of Orlando's financial condition reveals a city government that seems to manage its financial liquidity capably. Orlando's General Fund is financially strong and expenditure growth is in line with revenue expansion. Government-wide revenue growth has been substantially above the inflation rate, keeping pace with the city's expanding population. Government-wide expenditures exhibit

TABLE 14–9

## CITY OF ORLANDO, FLORIDA
### Proprietary Funds Analysis
FY 19X4–19X7

| | FY19X3–19X4 | FY 19X4–19X5 | FY19X5–19X6 | FY19X6–19X7 |
|---|---|---|---|---|
| **Enterprise Fund—Wastewater System** | | | | |
| Operating revenues | $ 43,904,896 | $ 42,726,429 | $ 40,253,968 | $ 40,608,586 |
| Operating expenses | 41,591,706 | 44,170,903 | 45,799,669 | 45,829,594 |
| Operating income (loss) | 2,313,190 | (1,444,474) | (5,545,701) | (5,221,000) |
| Nonoperating items | | | | |
| Investment income | $ 6,450,358 | $ 8,415,267 | $ 9,480,387 | $ 10,797,558 |
| Interest expense | (12,934,080) | (12,705,133) | (12,934,070) | (10,795,232) |
| Impact fees | 9,153,378 | 9,294,596 | 10,784,373 | 12,414,294 |
| Operating transfers in (out) | ($ 101,726) | ($ 35,600) | ($ 576,800) | ($ 109,941) |
| Net income (loss) | $ 3,823,822 | $ 3,519,383 | $ 1,691,505 | $ 8,943,457 |
| Cash & cash equivalents | $ 20,724,864 | $ 25,126,037 | $ 18,116,594 | $ 20,803,609 |
| Receivables | 2,569,837 | 1,780,970 | 2,546,591 | 2,539,287 |
| Due from other governments | $ 2,021,043 | $ 1,505,984 | $ 869,442 | $ 951,637 |
| Total current assets | 25,591,271 | 28,714,182 | 21,811,660 | 24,590,379 |
| Total restricted current assets | 141,744,728 | 151,798,355 | 164,181,247 | 158,035,832 |
| Total assets | 527,427,164 | 529,861,874 | 523,416,852 | 523,375,732 |
| Total current liabilities | $ 5,962,427 | $ 12,654,369 | $ 6,215,020 | $ 7,617,943 |
| Total current liabilities payable from restricted assets | 26,531,062 | 27,937,919 | 26,806,381 | 25,626,955 |
| Total liabilities | 233,517,467 | 237,501,283 | 223,981,963 | 216,926,266 |
| Current ratio | 4.29 | 2.27 | 3.51 | 3.23 |
| Current ratio (restricted) | 5.34 | 5.43 | 6.12 | 6.17 |
| Accounts receivable turnover | | 10.85 | 12.01 | 11.76 |
| Times interest earned | 1.30 | 1.28 | 1.13 | 1.83 |
| Total debt to total assets ratio | 0.44 | 0.45 | 0.43 | 0.41 |
| [CAFR page number] | [110–115] | [112–117] | [110–115] | [126–131] |
| **Internal Service Fund— Fleet Management** | | | | |
| Operating revenues | $ 11,307,659 | $ 11,724,558 | $ 12,335,537 | $ 14,165,988 |
| Operating expenses | 11,559,325 | 11,910,008 | 12,651,577 | 14,458,605 |
| Interest expense | 0 | 0 | 0 | 0 |
| Operating income (loss) | ($ 251,666) | ($ 185,450) | ($ 316,040) | ($ 292,617) |
| Net income (loss) | 400,690 | (279,723) | 249,585 | 1,278,766 |
| Cash & cash equivalents | $ 4,706,348 | $ 4,549,641 | $ 5,271,152 | $ 7,527,898 |
| Accounts receivable | 16,411 | 7,771 | 9,696 | 3,515 |
| Due from other governments | 4,693 | 6,221 | 6,205 | 10,604 |
| Total current assets | $ 5,115,241 | $ 4,979,082 | $ 5,845,716 | $ 7,951,151 |
| Total assets | $ 16,913,265 | $ 17,433,893 | $ 18,171,018 | $ 21,391,574 |
| Total current liabilities | $ 744,196 | $ 649,217 | $ 995,956 | $ 1,572,719 |
| Total current liabilities payable from restricted assets | 0 | 0 | 0 | $ 463,391 |
| Total liabilities | $ 744,196 | $ 649,217 | $ 995,956 | $ 3,627,935 |
| Current ratio | 6.87 | 7.67 | 5.87 | 5.06 |
| Accounts receivable turnover | | 668.14 | 825.31 | 943.77 |
| Times interest earned | 0.00 | 0.00 | 0.00 | 0.00 |
| Total debt to total assets ratio | 0.04 | 0.04 | 0.05 | 0.17 |
| [CAFR page number] | [122–127] | [124–129] | [122–127] | [138–143] |

a similar (but lower) trend. Orlando depends on intergovernmental revenues to a large extent, causing some concern about its fiscal independence. Expenditures appear to be largely under control and in line with overall revenue growth, however, with significant resources devoted to capital expenditures. The level of debt has grown recently but seems well within the city's fiscal capability. The two largest proprietary funds have been managed on a self-sustaining basis.

## Questions

**Q 14-1** (a) What is a joint venture? (b) Under what circumstances must a government apply the special joint venture accounting and disclosure requirements set forth in the GASB *Codification*? (c) What are those requirements?

**Q 14-2** The finance officer of the city of Beamstown is concerned about whether to include the City School District, the Beamstown Transit Authority, and the Beamstown-Thais County Regional Airport in the city's reporting entity. Explain how the finance director should determine which, if any, of these related entities should be included in the city's reporting entity.

**Q 14-3** If the primary government "Memorandum Only" total columns in Figure 14–4 had been omitted, what other changes would be required? Why?

**Q 14-4** Assume that in addition to the component units indicated in Figures 14–4 and 14–5, there is a blended component unit which has both governmental and proprietary funds. In the combined budgetary comparison statement for the reporting entity, which component unit budgetary comparison data should be incorporated?

**Q 14-5** Identify and explain (briefly) the various types of non-GAAP accounting methods and reporting requirements that may be encountered in SLG accounting, reporting, and auditing.

**Q 14-6** Why might an SLG properly prefer to maintain its governmental fund accounts on a non-GAAP basis during the year?

**Q 14-7** Why is it essential that the SLG accountant and auditor understand the SLG's non-GAAP special purpose reporting requirements and the basis on which its accounts are maintained during the year?

**Q 14-8** Briefly explain the two-phase adjustment process typically required for SLGs that have non-GAAP special purpose reporting requirements and also present financial statements in conformity with GAAP.

**Q 14-9** Distinguish between the cash basis of revenue and expenditure accounting and the cash receipts and disbursements basis.

**Q 14-10** Why might an SLG prepare and enact its governmental fund annual budget(s) on a non-GAAP budgetary basis?

**Q 14-11** An SLG may properly consider encumbrances to be essentially equivalent to expenditures in budgetary operating statements but may not do so in GAAP operating statements. Explain this apparent inconsistency.

**Q 14-12** What is meant by reconciling or presenting a reconciliation of non-GAAP-basis and GAAP-basis financial statements?

**Q 14-13** (a) Distinguish between the excess and fund balance reconciliation approaches. (b) What are the advantages of each approach?

## Exercises

**E 14-1** Which of the following cases meet the substantively the same governing body criterion and indicate that a component unit should be blended instead of discretely presented?
1. The city council appoints all members of the governing board of the component unit and can remove them at will (without cause).

2. The city council also serves as the governing board of the component unit.
3. The 5 city council members all serve on the governing board of the component unit. The component unit board has 12 members.
4. The 5 city council members, the city manager, and the city finance director all serve on the governing board of the component unit on an ex officio basis. The component unit board has 12 members.
5. The component unit governing body consists of 3 of the 7 elected council members of the city.

**E 14-2** Which of the following sets of circumstances require a government to treat another entity as a component unit of its reporting entity? Why?
1. The government appoints 3 of the 7 members of the governing body of the other entity, guarantees substantial portions of its debt, and must approve its tax rate.
2. The government appoints 5 of the 7 members of the governing body of the other entity, guarantees a limited portion of its debt, and does not have substantive approval authority over either its budget, its tax rate, or its debt issuances.
3. The government appoints 4 of the 7 members of the governing body of the other entity, provides in excess of 50% of its financing, but has no direct authority over its operations or budget. Also, the other entity is a not-for-profit organization.
4. The government created the organization to perform key functions that it believed could be performed more effectively by a separate organization. The government does not appoint any board members but does have substantive approval authority over the hiring of key management personnel. If desired in the future, the government can take over the entity's operations and eliminate the other entity.

## Problems

**P 14-1** (Multiple Choice)
1. A county transit authority is fiscally dependent upon the county because the transit authority—a legally separate entity–cannot set its fares without the substantive approval of the county commission. In which of the following circumstances would the transit authority be deemed financially accountable to and thus a component unit of the county?
   a. The appointment authority and ability to impose will criteria are met. There is no financial benefit or burden relationship between the county and the authority.
   b. The appointment authority and financial benefit or burden criteria are met. The county does not have the ability to impose its will on the authority.
   c. The authority has a separately elected governing board, but the ability to impose will and financial benefit or burden criteria are met.
   d. The authority would be financially accountable to the county, and thus a component unit, because it is fiscally dependent on the county—regardless of whether any other interrelationships exist.
2. In which of the following circumstances would a potential component unit always be fiscally dependent upon a city?
   a. The city is the sole source of revenue of the potential component unit.
   b. The city provides over 75% of the revenues of the potential component unit.
   c. The city provides over 50% of the revenues of the potential component unit.
   d. The city provides significant revenues to the potential component unit.
   e. none of the above.
3. Which of following statements is true?
   a. An organization can be fiscally dependent upon a primary government but not financially accountable to that primary government.
   b. An organization can be financially accountable to a primary government but not fiscally dependent upon that primary government.

    c. An organization must be fiscally dependent upon and financially accountable to a primary government in order to be a component unit of that primary government.

    d. An organization is fiscally dependent on a primary government if that primary government provides the majority of the revenues of the organization.

4. In which of the following circumstances is the appointment authority criterion met?

    a. A majority vote of the governing board is required for major decisions. A city council appoints 3 of the 8 members of the potential component unit governing board, and the city finance director and treasurer serve on the governing board by virtue of their positions with the city.

    b. A majority vote of the governing board is required for major decisions. A city council appoints 5 of the 8 members of the potential component unit governing board.

    c. A two-thirds vote of the governing board is required for major decisions. A city council appoints 5 of the 9 members of the potential component unit governing board.

    d. all of the above.

    e. both a and b.

5. In which of the following circumstances would a city be viewed as having appointed members of a potential component unit's governing body for the purposes of determining if the appointment criterion has been met?

    a. The mayor appoints members.

    b. The council and mayor jointly appoint members.

    c. The city finance director appoints members.

    d. The governing board of a city component unit (whose board is appointed by the city) appoints members.

    e. More than one of the above (specify).

6. A Downtown Development Authority was formed by a city as a separate legal entity. The authority's board consists of two members appointed by city council and four members representing major civic and business organizations in the city and appointed by those organizations. The city has no financial benefit or burden relationship with the authority, which is fiscally independent. Which of the following conditions would have to be met for the authority to be considered a component unit of the city?

    a. The authority would have to be a governmental organization, not a nonprofit entity.

    b. The city would have to have the ability to impose its will over the authority with respect to the major types and levels of activities undertaken.

    c. The city would have to be able to abolish the authority.

    d. The authority would have to serve or benefit either the city or its citizenry (including businesses within the city's jurisdiction) exclusively or almost exclusively.

    e. More than one of the above (specify).

7. If a government both created and can abolish a potential component unit, it is financially accountable for that other entity

    a. unless the potential component unit has a separately elected governing body.

    b. unless another government appoints a voting majority of the potential component unit's governing board.

    c. unless it is unlikely that the government would ever exercise its authority to abolish the potential component unit.

    d. if it has the ability to impose its will over the potential component unit or has a financial benefit or burden relationship with it.

8. A state college treats the university foundation as a component unit. The college is a component unit of the state. The foundation would be included in the state reporting entity

   a. only if financially accountable to the state government.
   b. only if fiscally dependent on the state.
   c. under no circumstances.
   d. regardless of other facts.

9. A public housing authority established as a separate legal entity by a county has a governing board appointed by the county. The county cannot remove the authority board members for any reason before the end of their 4-year terms. The county is not obligated in any manner for the authority's debt and desires for the authority to set its rents at a level that will cover all costs not subsidized by the federal or state governments. However, in each year of the authority's existence the county has provided resources to finance a portion of the authority's operating expenditures that rents and state and federal subsidies have been inadequate to cover. The housing authority is financially accountable to and a component unit of
   a. the county.
   b. the federal government.
   c. the state government.
   d. none of the other governments.

10. Assuming that a government has some discretely presented component units that have only proprietary activities and others that have only governmental fund activities, a "Component Units" column must be presented in which of the government's combined financial statements?
   a. Combined balance sheet.
   b. Combined statement of revenues, expenditures, and changes in fund balances (GAAP basis).
   c. Combined statement of revenues, expenditures, and changes in fund balances (budgetary basis).
   d. Combined statement of revenues, expenses, and changes in fund equity (or retained earnings).
   e. Combined statement of cash flows.
   f. All but one of the above (specify).

**P 14-2** (Incorporation of Component Units) Leary County officials have concluded that several legally separate entities must be included as component units of its reporting entity in its Comprehensive Annual Financial Report. Three of those entities and the funds used to account for them are:

> Puryear Corner School District
> General Fund
> Gymnasium Construction Fund
> Educational Buildings Improvement Fund
> Gymnasium Debt Service Fund
> Payroll Withholding Fund
> Deferred Compensation Fund
> Food Services Enterprise Fund
> Central Printing Services Fund
> General Long-Term Debt Account Group
> General Fixed Assets Account Group
> Erica-Leary-Austin Tri-County Airport Authority (Enterprise Fund)
> Leary County Public Employee Retirement System

The Leary County board of commissioners also serves as the governing board of the Leary County public employee retirement system and the county appoints the voting majority of the board of the airport authority. The school board is elected.

**Required** Indicate the reporting entity fund type or account group in which each of the funds and account groups listed previously for the component units of Leary County should be reported. Explain the reasons for your answer in detail.

**P 14-3** (Component Unit Identification and Reporting) The relationships between a county and several potential component units are outlined as follows.

Pat County is organized under the county executive form of government, as provided by state law. Under this form of government, the policies concerning the financial and business affairs of the county are determined by the County Board of Supervisors. The Board is composed of eight elected members who serve four-year terms. The Board appoints a county executive who is the government's chief administrative officer and executes the Board's policies and programs. All but two of the following component units issue separately audited financial statements. The School Board and Adult Detention Center do not prepare separate financial reports at this time.

| *Potential Component Unit* | *Description of Activities and Relationship to the County* |
|---|---|
| Dale City Recreation Center | Derives revenue from a special levy on personal property and real estate within the district and user fees. Assists and advises Board on management and planning of levy district and its recreation center. County appoints majority of board, guarantees debt. |
| District Home Board | Agreement between five jurisdictions. Establishes policy for operation of two district homes. Each county appoints a board member. No other formal relationships or responsibilities. |
| Northern Region Health Center Commission | County Board resolution created a commission for the operation of a nursing home pursuant to state code. Develops and establishes policies for the operation of a nursing home. Appoints two of the five board members. Another cooperating county appoints two other board members. The governor appoints the fifth member. |
| Northern Region Special Education Regional Program | Agreement between three school districts to foster cooperation in the development and delivery of special education programs and other appropriate educational services. Each district appoints one-third of the board and subsidizes one-third of any operating deficiency. |
| Adult Detention Center (ADC) | Establishes policy for operation of regional adult detention center, providing care and confinement for all County and adjoining city prisoners. Majority of Board is appointed by County; County hires management officials. |
| Park Authority | Established by County Board resolution. Acquires, develops, maintains, and operates park and recreation areas according to authority and Board comprehensive plans. Majority of County Board serves as the board of the authority. Financial benefit/burden relationship exists; Authority provides services to the County. |
| County Parkway District | Exercises the powers and duties enumerated in the state code related to the transportation improvement district. Majority of Board is appointed by County; financial benefit/burden relationship exists. |
| Pat County School Board | Board is selected by popular election. Board has no taxing authority. Most resources are provided by the county, which has budget approval authority over the school board budget. |

**Required** a. Determine which of the potential component units the county should report as component units in its financial report. Explain the basis for your decision.
b. For each component unit, indicate whether it should be blended or discretely reported. Explain.
c. For each component unit, indicate whether more detail must be presented in the county's Comprehensive Annual Financial Report than the information in the combining component unit financial statements.

**P 14-4**    (Complex Reporting Entity—Balance Sheet) Presented next is information excerpted from the balance sheets of Bunnell County and its three component units that are to be discretely presented. The component units are the Bunnell County School Board, the Bunnell County Park Authority, and the Bunnell County Adult Detention Center (ADC).

***Required***    Complete Bunnell County's Combined Balance Sheet at December 31, 20X0. Begin with the "Primary Government Memorandum Only" total column. Prepare the county's combining component unit balance sheet for the same date.

**BUNNELL COUNTY**
All Fund Types, Account Groups, and Discretely Presented
Component Units
Combined Balance Sheet
June 30, 20X0

|  | Totals (Memorandum Only) Primary Government |
|---|---|
| **ASSETS AND OTHER DEBITS** |  |
| ASSETS: |  |
| Cash and pooled investments | $159,998 |
| Restricted cash | 13,781 |
| Investments | 3,652 |
| Restricted investments | 1,250 |
| Taxes receivable, net | 2,790 |
| Accounts receivable, net | 5,619 |
| Water and sewer assessments, receivables | 43 |
| Due from other governmental units | 7,529 |
| Due from other funds | 1,701 |
| Due from component units | 196 |
| Inventory | 405 |
| Prepaid items | 594 |
| Fixed assets, net of accumulated depreciation | 141,949 |
| OTHER DEBITS: |  |
| Amount available in governmental funds for the retirement of general long-term debt | 18 |
| Amount to be provided for the retirement of general long-term debt | 160,062 |
| Total assets and other debits | $499,587 |
| **LIABILITIES, EQUITY, AND OTHER CREDITS** |  |
| LIABILITIES: |  |
| Accounts payable and accrued liabilities | $ 39,951 |
| Accrued closure liability | 2,531 |
| Due to other governmental units | 967 |
| Due to other funds | 1,701 |
| Due to component units | 1,190 |
| Deferred revenue | 61,271 |
| Bonds payable | 136,611 |
| Capital lease obligations | 40,435 |
| Compensated absences | 8,866 |
| Total liabilities | 293,523 |
| **FUND BALANCES, EQUITY, AND OTHER CREDITS**: |  |
| Contributed capital | 2,097 |
| Investment in general fixed assets | 111,147 |
| Retained earnings: |  |
| Unreserved | 16,776 |
| Fund balances: |  |
| Reserved | 20,202 |
| Unreserved: |  |
| Designated | 30,683 |
| Undesignated | 25,159 |
| Total fund balances, equity, and other credits | 206,064 |
| Total liabilities, fund balances, equity, and other credits | $499,587 |

**BUNNELL COUNTY SCHOOL BOARD**
All Fund Types and Account Groups
Combined Balance Sheet
June 30, 20X0

|  | Totals (Memorandum Only) |
|---|---|
| **ASSETS AND OTHER DEBITS** | |
| ASSETS: | |
| Cash and pooled investments | $ 56,727 |
| Accounts receivable, net | 62 |
| Due from other governmental units | 5,136 |
| Due from other funds | 5,080 |
| Inventory | 1,422 |
| Fixed assets, net of accumulated depreciation | 348,927 |
| OTHER DEBITS: | |
| Amount available in governmental funds for the retirement of general long-term debt | 1,294 |
| Amount to be provided for the retirement of general long-term debt | 145,143 |
| Total assets and other debits | $563,791 |
| **LIABILITIES, EQUITY, AND OTHER CREDITS** | |
| LIABILITIES: | |
| Accounts payable and accrued liabilities | $ 34,008 |
| Due to other governmental units | 492 |
| Due to other funds | 5,080 |
| Deferred revenues | 148 |
| Bonds payable | 124,142 |
| Special termination benefit payable | 11,646 |
| Compensated absences | 10,649 |
| Total liabilities | 186,165 |
| FUND BALANCES, EQUITY, AND OTHER CREDITS: | |
| Investment in general fixed assets | 348,927 |
| Retained earnings: | |
| Unreserved | 6,123 |
| Fund balances: | |
| Reserved | 11,380 |
| Unreserved: | |
| Designated | 11,196 |
| Total fund balances, equity, and other credits | 377,626 |
| Total liabilities, fund balances, equity, and other credits | $563,791 |

**BUNNELL COUNTY ADULT DETENTION CENTER**
All Fund Types and Account Groups
Combined Balance Sheet
June 30, 20X0

|  | Totals (Memorandum Only) |
|---|---|
| **ASSETS AND OTHER DEBITS** | |
| ASSETS: | |
| Cash and pooled investments | $20,515 |
| Due from other governmental units | 1,622 |
| Fixed assets, net of accumulated depreciation | 14,238 |
| OTHER DEBITS: | |
| Amount to be provided for the retirement of general long-term debt | 3,912 |
| Total assets and other debits | $40,287 |
| **OTHER LIABILITIES, EQUITY, AND OTHER CREDITS** | |
| LIABILITIES: | |
| Accounts payable and accrued liabilities | $ 507 |
| Due to other governmental units | 1,193 |
| Capital lease obligations | 3,120 |
| Compensated absences | 792 |
| Total liabilities | 5,612 |

| | Totals (Memorandum Only) |
|---|---|
| **FUND BALANCES AND OTHER CREDITS:** | |
| Investment in general fixed assets | $14,238 |
| Fund balances: | |
| Reserved | 555 |
| Unreserved: | |
| Designated | 18,392 |
| Undesignated | 1,490 |
| Total fund balances and other credits | 34,675 |
| Total liabilities, fund balances, and other credits | $40,287 |

### BUNNELL COUNTY PARK AUTHORITY
#### All Fund Types and Account Groups
#### Combined Balance Sheet
#### June 30, 20X0

| | Totals (Memorandum Only) |
|---|---|
| **ASSETS:** | |
| Cash and pooled investments | $ 1,435 |
| Restricted cash | 3,409 |
| Restricted investments | 3,379 |
| Accounts receivable, net | 108 |
| Deferred charge | 164 |
| Prepaid items | 77 |
| Fixed assets, net of accumulated depreciation | 61,174 |
| Total assets and other debits | $69,746 |
| **LIABILITIES:** | |
| Accounts payable and accrued liabilities | $ 2,407 |
| Due to primary government | 188 |
| Deferred revenue | 183 |
| Installment notes payable | 307 |
| Bonds payable | 20,985 |
| Total liabilities | 24,070 |
| **EQUITY:** | |
| Contributed capital | 43,665 |
| Retained earnings: | |
| Reserved for debt service | 1,322 |
| Unreserved | 689 |
| Total equity | 45,676 |
| Total liabilities and equity | $69,746 |

**P 14-5**   (Cash Basis and Conversion to GAAP Entries)

1. The cash receipts of the Robintown General Fund for January 19X1 included the following:

| | |
|---|---|
| $  800,000 | Collection of current taxes receivable |
| 150,000 | Collection of delinquent taxes receivable |
| 5,000 | Collection of interest and penalties not previously accrued |
| 6,000 | Collection of previously recorded interfund charges to departments financed by other funds for services rendered by departments financed by the General Fund—2/3 was for services rendered in 19X0, 1/3 for those in 19X1 |
| 20,000 | Payment in lieu of taxes from the city water and sewer department |
| 200,000 | Proceeds of a grant from the state to be matched equally by the city and expended for street improvements |
| 1,000 | Fines and forfeitures |
| $1,182,000 | |

2. The cash disbursements of the Robintown General Fund for the month included:

| | |
|---|---|
| $ 600,000 | Payroll |
| 200,000 | Payments on accounts outstanding at 12/31/X0 |
| 50,000 | To a Capital Projects Fund (City's contribution to project—not previously accrued) |
| 75,000 | To establish a fund to operate a new central print shop to serve town departments |
| 80,000 | For street improvements made from grant funds and matching funds; related liabilities of $32,000 remain outstanding at the end of the month |
| 20,000 | Purchase of police cars |
| 120,000 | To the Enterprise Fund to be repaid in 19X5 |
| 10,000 | For supplies ordered in December 19X0 and reappropriated for and received in 19X1 |
| $1,155,000 | |

**Required** Prepare general journal entries to record the Robintown General Fund cash receipts and disbursements for January 19X1 on the cash basis in the general ledger. December 31 is the fiscal year end. Then prepare any other General Fund general journal "conversion to GAAP" entries required to prepare GAAP-basis financial statements.

**P 14-6** (Budgetary–GAAP-Basis Adjustments and Reconciliation) The auditor has determined that the 19X8 budgetary-basis operating statement of a Special Revenue Fund of Yarborough County is correct.

**Yarborough County**
Special Revenue Fund
**Budgetary-Basis Operating Statement**
For 19X8 Fiscal Year

| | |
|---|---|
| Revenues: | |
| Property taxes | $ 700,000 |
| Sales taxes | 600,000 |
| Federal grants | 500,000 |
| Other | 200,000 |
| | 2,000,000 |
| Expenditures: | |
| Highways | 1,150,000 |
| Law enforcement | 400,000 |
| Administration | 250,000 |
| Other | 150,000 |
| | 1,950,000 |
| Excess of Revenues Over Expenditures | 50,000 |
| Fund Balance—Beginning of 19X8 | 300,000 |
| Fund Balance—End of 19X8 | $ 350,000 |

The following additional information was determined that may be relevant in the process of deriving the adjustments needed to convert the budgetary-basis operating statement data to the GAAP basis.

1. The Yarborough County governmental fund annual operating budgets are prepared—and the governmental fund accounts are maintained—using its budgetary basis under which (a) revenues are recognized only when collected, and (b) expenditures are recorded when encumbrances are incurred or when payments are made for unencumbered expenditures.
2. The GAAP-basis statements at the beginning of 19X8 indicate that total fund balance then was $275,000.
3. Accrued revenues receivable were:

| | Beginning of 19X8 | End of 19X8 |
|---|---|---|
| Property taxes (2/3 "available") ............. | $120,000 | $150,000 |
| Sales taxes ................................ | 100,000 | 45,000 |
| Federal grants .......................... | 60,000 | 20,000 |
| Other ....................................... | — | 10,000 |

4. Accrued expenditures payable were:

| | Beginning of 19X8 | End of 19X8 |
|---|---|---|
| Highways ............................. | $ 30,000 | $ 40,000 |
| Law enforcement ........................ | 50,000 | — |
| Administration ......................... | 15,000 | 5,000 |
| Other ....................................... | 20,000 | 25,000 |

5. Encumbrances outstanding were:

| | Beginning of 19X8 | End of 19X8 |
|---|---|---|
| Highways ............................. | $100,000 | $150,000 |
| Law enforcement ........................ | 175,000 | 50,000 |
| Administration ......................... | 60,000 | 30,000 |
| Other ....................................... | — | 20,000 |

6. There were no interfund transfers to or from this Special Revenue Fund during 19X8, nor were there any restatements of beginning fund balance.

**Required** (1) Prepare a GAAP-basis statement of revenues, expenditures, and changes in [total] fund balance for the Yarborough County Special Revenue Fund for the 19X8 fiscal year. (A worksheet in statement format may be substituted for a formal statement.)

(2) Prepare an excess approach budgetary-basis–GAAP-basis reconciliation to be presented in the notes to the financial statements.

(3) Prepare a fund balance approach budgetary-basis–GAAP-basis reconciliation to be added to the budgetary-basis operating statement presented previously. (You need not present the entire statement.)

**P 14-7** (Budgetary Statement) The General Fund schedule of revenues and expenditures—budgeted and actual—for the year ended December 31, 19X7, for the city of Armstrong has been competently prepared, and you may assume it is accurate. The budgetary basis employed is (1) cash receipts for revenues, and (2) cash disbursements plus encumbrances outstanding for expenditures.

**City of Armstrong**
General Fund
Schedule of Revenues and Expenditures
Budgeted and Actual
For the Year Ended December 31, 19X7
(in thousands)

| | Budget (Revised) | Actual (Budgetary Basis) | Actual (Modified Accrual Basis) |
|---|---|---|---|
| **Revenues:** | | | |
| Taxes ............................ | $ 77,500 | $ 75,300 | $ 72,500 |
| Licenses ......................... | 2,680 | 3,320 | 3,320 |
| Charges for services ............... | 9,340 | 8,400 | 8,200 |
| Fines and forfeitures .............. | 23,500 | 20,100 | 20,000 |
| Other ........................... | 1,980 | 2,880 | 980 |
| | 115,000 | 110,000 | 105,000 |

|  | Budget (Revised) | Actual (Budgetary Basis) | Actual (Modified Accrual Basis) |
|---|---|---|---|
| **Expenditures:** | | | |
| Current Operating: | | | |
| Protection of people and property ...... | 58,900 | 55,740 | 53,722 |
| Community cultural and recreation ..... | 13,900 | 11,500 | 11,400 |
| Community development and welfare ... | 11,700 | 10,900 | 9,400 |
| Transportation and related services ..... | 23,200 | 19,280 | 17,900 |
| Administration ..................... | 4,300 | 3,580 | 3,578 |
| | 112,000 | 101,000 | 96,000 |
| Capital outlay ........................ | 10,400 | 6,400 | 3,400 |
| Debt Service ......................... | 6,600 | 6,600 | 6,600 |
| | 129,000 | 114,000 | 106,000 |
| Excess of revenues over (under) | | | |
| expenditures ........................ | ($ 14,000) | ($ 4,000) | ($ 1,000) |

**Required** (a) Analyze the schedule presented carefully and respond to the following questions:
1. How might it be possible for a city to budget an excess of fund expenditures over revenues? Is that a bad practice? Is an excess of actual expenditures over revenues bad?
2. Why might the modified accrual and budgetary-basis revenue data differ somewhat with respect to taxes, charges for services, and fines and forfeitures, yet be identical for licenses and permits?
3. Why might the modified accrual and budgetary-basis expenditure amounts differ in most instances, yet agree on the debt service expenditure?

(b) After giving consideration to the following additional information, prepare a statement of revenues, expenditures, and changes in fund balance—budget and actual for the city of Armstrong General Fund for the year ended December 31, 19X7, in standard format. The following numbers are in thousands of dollars, as are the schedule and the statement you are to prepare.
1. The beginning of year fund balance was $4,000 (budgetary) and $3,000 (modified accrual).
2. A budgeted operating transfer of $20,000 was made to the General Fund from a Special Revenue Fund.

(c) Whenever the basis of the budget differs from GAAP, the GASB *Codification* requires that the difference(s) between the budgetary basis and GAAP be explained in the notes to the financial statements. Draft an appropriate note for this purpose.

**P 14-8** (Budgetary–GAAP-Basis Adjustments and Reconciliation) Unadjusted budgetary-basis balances of the operating accounts of the General Fund of Tuscahassec Independent School District at the end of 19X3 were:

**Revenues and Other Financing Sources**
| | |
|---|---|
| Property Taxes ........................................ | $ 700,000 |
| State Operating Grant ................................ | 500,000 |
| Interest ............................................... | 60,000 |
| Other .................................................. | 40,000 |
| Transfer from Special Revenue Fund ...................... | 70,000 |
| Transfer from Capital Projects Fund ...................... | 100,000 |
| | $1,470,000 |

**Expenditures and Other Financing Uses**
| | |
|---|---|
| Educational Programs ...................................... | $ 800,000 |
| Transportation ......................................... | 200,000 |
| Administration ......................................... | 150,000 |
| Other .................................................. | 50,000 |
| Transfer to Debt Service Fund ............................ | 160,000 |
| | $1,360,000 |

During the course of the 19X3 audit it was determined that:

1. The district's budgetary basis recognizes revenues and expenditures only as cash is received and disbursed, respectively, but considers encumbrances equivalent to expenditures.

2. The unadjusted budgetary-basis accounts should be adjusted, as appropriate, in view of the following information:

   a. A $7,000 other revenue was inadvertently credited to other expenditures during 19X3.

   b. In addition to the recorded encumbrances ($25,000 Educational Programs and $15,000 Administration), there were unrecorded encumbrances outstanding at year end: $40,000 Educational Programs and $35,000 Transportation.

3. The following information should be considered in deriving the budgetary-basis–GAAP-basis adjustments:

|  | | Beginning of Year | End of Year |
|---|---|---|---|
| a. | *Accrued Revenues/Receivables* | | |
| | (1)  Property taxes receivable | $120,000 | $170,000 |
| | (2)  State operating grant receivable | 90,000 | 75,000 |
| | (3)  Interest receivable | 10,000 | 15,000 |
| | (All receivables were available.) | | |
| b. | *Accrued Expenditures/Payables* | | |
| | (1)  Education programs | $ 18,000 | $ 44,000 |
| | (2)  Transportation | — | 12,000 |
| | (3)  Other | 17,000 | — |
| c. | *Reserve for Encumbrances* | | |
| | (1)  Education programs | $ 20,000 | $ 65,000 |
| | (2)  Transportation | 15,000 | 35,000 |
| | (3)  Administration | 35,000 | 15,000 |
| d. | *Other Accrued Liabilities* | | |
| | (1)  Claims and judgments (other) | | |
| |    —current liability | $ 25,000 | $ 15,000 |
| |    —noncurrent liability | 200,000 | 240,000 |
| | (2)  Compensated absences | | |
| |    —current liability | 40,000 | 70,000 |
| |    —noncurrent liability | 310,000 | 290,000 |
| | (Chargeable 7:2:1 to Education Programs, Transportation, and Administration.) | | |

   e. The beginning of 19X3 fund balance reported in the district's GAAP-basis financial statements was:

   | | |
   |---|---|
   | Reserve for Encumbrances | $ 70,000 |
   | Unreserved | 130,000 |
   | | $200,000 |

   f. There were no accumulated differences from prior years between the budgetary-basis and GAAP-basis total fund balances at the beginning of 19X3.

   g. The Special Revenue Fund and Debt Service Fund transfers were routine annual transfers; the Capital Projects Fund transfer was upon termination of the CPF.

***Required*** (1) Prepare a simplified, partial, two-phase worksheet to derive the information needed to prepare both a budgetary-basis and a GAAP-basis Statement of Revenues, Expenditures, and Changes in [Total] Fund Balance. Your worksheet should (a) list the accounts and subtotals through the Excess of Revenues and Other Financing Sources Over (Under) Expenditures and Other Financing Uses, and (b) have these columns:
(1) "Unadjusted Budgetary Basis"
(2) "Adjustments to Budgetary Basis"
(3) "Budgetary Basis"
(4) "Adjustments to GAAP Basis"
(5) "GAAP Basis"
Your adjustments should be keyed to the problem.

(2) Prepare a detailed "fund balance" approach budgetary-basis–GAAP-basis reconciliation.

(3) Prepare a summarized "excess" approach budgetary-basis–GAAP-basis reconciliation.

# CHAPTER

# 15

# CONTEMPORARY ISSUES

The current state and local government (SLG) accounting and reporting model discussed in the last 13 chapters has deep roots historically and is firmly entrenched in practice. Formalized and formally adopted in the United States by the National Committee on Municipal Accounting in the 1930s, the model has evolved in several stages during the past 60 years, most recently as the result of key pronouncements of the Governmental Accounting Standards Board (GASB). Furthermore, the GASB's agenda includes projects that could have a pervasive and dramatic impact on the SLG reporting model.

How good is the SLG model? Opinions vary. At one extreme are its staunch advocates and defenders—who point to its heritage, note that it has proven practical and workable in practice, and believe it provides information that is useful to government decision makers. At the other extreme are its staunch critics, who say that such an "old" model cannot serve today's needs—that the complexities of modern governments and of their financial transactions cannot be adequately accommodated by the model from either an accounting or a reporting standpoint—and that an entirely new SLG accounting and reporting model should be developed. As is so often the case, the truth probably lies somewhere between these extremes.

The Governmental Accounting Standards Board (GASB) is nearing completion of its SLG financial reporting model project. The Board has proposed a major change in the government financial reporting model. This proposal is emphasized in this chapter.

Other unresolved conceptual and practical issues are considered in this chapter as well. Most of these issues are pervasive in nature and are likely to have a broad impact on most government financial reports. These issues are (1) reporting service efforts and accomplishments (SEA), (2) popular reporting (3) fund structure and classification-related issues, and (4) note disclosures.

## CORE FINANCIAL STATEMENTS

After first attempting to implement GASB *Statement No. 11,* "Measurement Focus and Basis of Accounting—Governmental Fund Operating Statements," within the context of the current model, the Board decided that the most appropriate vehicle for moving governmental financial reporting forward was the financial reporting model project. The Board's Exposure Draft, "Basic Financial Statements—and Management's Discussion and Analysis—for State and Local Governments," sets forth its tentative conclusions on the reporting model.

In the exposure draft the Board proposes presentation of a government's basic financial statements using a "dual reporting perspective," or "dual perspective." One of the proposed perspectives is called the "fund perspective" or "fund-based" perspective. Though some changes are proposed in the exposure draft, the fund-based perspective would require only moderate changes from the financial statements required under current GAAP. In other words, data would be presented by fund type, with general government activities reported in governmental fund types using the flow of current financial resources (revenue and expenditure) measurement focus and modified accrual basis of accounting. Business-type activities would be reported in proprietary fund types using the flow of economic resources (revenue and expense) measurement focus and accrual basis. Data would also be presented individually for major funds.

The other perspective is new. It represents a dramatic change in financial reporting for state and local governments. This perspective—the entity-wide perspective—represents a significantly higher level of aggregation than permitted by current GAAP. Under this proposed entity-wide perspective:

- All general government activities are aggregated and are reported using the flow of economic resources (revenue and expense) measurement focus. General fixed assets and general long-term debt are aggregated along with the governmental fund data and most Internal Service Fund assets and liabilities. All general government fixed assets, including infrastructure fixed assets, are reported in the statement of net assets. Depreciation is reported in the entity-wide operating statement, and interest is reported in the same manner as for enterprise activities.

- All enterprise activities are aggregated and are reported using the flow of economic resources (revenue and expense) measurement focus. This is largely the same data presented currently in the combined statements for Enterprise Funds.

- The governmental activities and business-type activities data are then aggregated (totaled) to arrive at the primary government total data. (Discretely presented component unit data are aggregated in the entity-wide statements and are not presented in the fund perspective statements.)

Many noteworthy changes are proposed in this exposure draft. However, the most fundamental change—and the only one that is truly a change of the reporting model—is the requirement to report governmental activities (including general fixed assets and general long-term debt) in aggregated form on a revenue and expense basis. Certain changes such as capitalizing and reporting general government infrastructure fixed assets and reporting depreciation on general government fixed assets are necessitated by the model change.

Most other significant reporting changes could be implemented by the GASB even if it decided not to change the financial reporting model. In other words, these changes could be made even if the GASB were not to finalize its financial reporting model changes. Examples of such changes include:

- Requiring presentation of a management discussion and analysis
- Changing the definition of Enterprise Funds
- Changing the definition of fiduciary funds

- Identification of and separate reporting in governmental fund operating statements of extraordinary items and special items such as the sale of significant fixed assets
- Required presentation of the original budget as well as the revised budget in budgetary comparison statements
- Replacing the contributed capital versus retained earnings distinction in proprietary funds with the distinctions of amounts invested in capital assets, net of related debt; restricted fund equity; and unrestricted fund equity
- Reporting capital contributions as nonoperating revenues
- Reporting separate combined balance sheets for governmental and proprietary funds
- Defining and having more extensive reporting requirements for major funds

The Board's hope is that this dual perspective approach will meet the diverse needs of financial statement users and the broad financial reporting objectives, as outlined in Chapter 2. The fund perspective provides users with detailed fund information using traditional measurement and recognition standards. The entity-wide perspective attempts to meet several of the unanswered financial report objectives with introduction of an economic resources model. Examples of financial statements are presented in Figures 15–1 to 15–10 to illustrate the statements required by the exposure draft. The proposed **entity-wide** financial statements include:

1. Statement of Net Assets (Figure 15–1)
2. Statement of Activities (Figure 15–2)

Note a few features of the entity-wide statements because they are not familiar to you. First, the statement of net assets is essentially a balance sheet presented on a business-type basis. Equity is referred to and presented as various components of net assets with no distinction between contributed versus earned equity. Capital assets include all general government and proprietary fixed assets, including general government infrastructure. Hence, governments will have to inventory and record streets, roads, bridges, storm sewers, and so on to fully implement the requirements of this exposure draft if it is adopted.

The statement of activities (Figure 15–2) uses a program or function orientation. Under this presentation of the statement of activities, the net program costs incurred or net program revenues generated by each government program are reported—and the "excess (deficiency) of revenues over expenses" for the year is equivalent to net income in business accounting. No entity-wide statement of cash flows is proposed.

The proposed **fund perspective** financial statements include the following:

1. Balance Sheet—Governmental Funds (Figure 15–3)
2. Statement of Revenues, Expenditures, and Changes in Fund Balances—Governmental Funds (Figure 15–4)
3. Budgetary Comparison Statement—Budgetary Basis—General Fund[1] (Figure 15–5)
4. Balance Sheet—Proprietary Funds (Figure 15–6)

---

[1] Budgetary comparison statements for other major governmental funds with legally adopted annual budgets are required here only if a full CAFR is not presented.

FIGURE 15–1        **ENTITY-WIDE PERSPECTIVE**

**STATEMENT OF NET ASSETS**

| Assets and liabilities are presented in order of relative liquidity. | *Primary Government* | | | |
|---|---|---|---|---|
| | *Governmental Activities* | *Business-Type Activities* | *Total** | *Component Units* |
| **ASSETS** | | | | |
| Cash and cash equivalents | $ 13,597,899 | $ 10,279,143 | $ 23,877,042 | $ 303,935 |
| Investments | 27,365,221 | — | 27,365,221 | 7,428,952 |
| Receivables (net) | 12,833,132 | 3,609,615 | 16,442,747 | 4,042,290 |
| Internal receivables | 175,000 | — | — | — |
| Inventories | 322,149 | 126,674 | 448,823 | 83,697 |
| Capital assets, net | 170,022,760 | 151,388,751 | 321,411,511 | 37,744,786 |
| Total assets | 224,316,161 | 165,404,183 | 389,545,344 | 49,603,660 |
| **LIABILITIES** | | | | |
| Accounts payable | 6,783,310 | 751,430 | 7,534,740 | 1,803,332 |
| Internal payables | — | 175,000 | — | — |
| Deferred revenue | 1,435,599 | — | 1,435,599 | 38,911 |
| Long-term liabilities | 92,538,378 | 78,908,559 | 171,446,937 | 28,532,790 |
| Total liabilities | 100,757,287 | 79,834,989 | 180,417,276 | 30,375,033 |
| **NET ASSETS** | | | | |
| Invested in capital assets, net of related debt | 90,701,684 | 73,088,574 | 163,790,258 | 15,906,392 |
| Restricted for: | | | | |
|   Capital projects | 24,715,566 | — | 24,715,566 | 492,445 |
|   Debt service | 3,020,708 | 1,451,996 | 4,472,704 | — |
|   Community development projects | 4,811,043 | — | 4,811,043 | — |
|   Other purposes | 3,214,302 | — | 3,214,302 | — |
| Unrestricted (deficit) | (2,904,429) | 11,028,624 | 8,124,195 | 2,829,790 |
| Total net assets | $123,558,874 | $ 85,569,194 | $209,128,068 | $19,228,627 |

> The total column for the primary government is required. A total column may be presented for the reporting entity but is not required.

*After elimination of internal balances.

**5.** Statement of Revenues, Expenses, and Changes in Fund Equity—Proprietary Funds (Figure 15–7)

**6.** Statement of Cash Flows—Proprietary Funds (Figure 15–8)

**7.** Statement of Net Assets—Fiduciary Funds (Figure 15–9)

**8.** Statement of Changes in Net Assets—Fiduciary Funds (Figure 15–10)

FIGURE 15–2

# ENTITY-WIDE PERSPECTIVE
## Statement of Activities
### *Primary Government*

| Functions/Programs | Program Revenues | | | Net (Expense) Revenue | | | Component Units Net (Expense) Revenue |
|---|---|---|---|---|---|---|---|
| | Expenses | Charges for Services | Grants and Contributions | Governmental Activities | Business-Type Activities | Total | |
| **Primary government:** | | | | | | | |
| General government | $ 9,571,410 | $ 3,146,915 | $ 843,617 | $ (5,580,878) | $ — | $ (5,580,878) | |
| Public safety | 34,844,749 | 1,198,855 | 1,369,993 | (32,275,901) | | (32,275,901) | |
| Public works | 10,128,538 | 850,000 | 2,252,615 | (7,025,923) | | (7,025,923) | |
| Engineering services | 1,299,645 | 704,793 | — | (594,852) | | (594,852) | |
| Health and sanitation | 6,738,672 | 5,612,267 | 575,000 | (551,405) | | (551,405) | |
| Cemetery | 735,866 | 212,496 | | (523,370) | | (523,370) | |
| Culture and recreation | 11,532,350 | 3,995,199 | 2,450,000 | (5,087,151) | | (5,087,151) | |
| Community development | 2,919,389 | — | 2,580,000 | (339,389) | | (339,389) | |
| Interest on long-term debt | 6,068,121 | | | (6,068,121) | | (6,068,121) | |
| Water | 3,595,733 | 4,159,350 | 1,159,909 | | 1,723,526 | 1,723,526 | |
| Sewer | 4,912,853 | 7,170,533 | 486,010 | | 2,743,690 | 2,743,690 | |
| Parking facilities | 2,796,283 | 1,344,087 | — | | (1,452,196) | (1,452,196) | |
| Total primary government | $95,143,609 | $28,394,495 | $11,717,144 | (58,046,990) | 3,015,020 | (55,031,970) | |
| **Component units:** | | | | | | | |
| Landfill | $ 3,382,157 | $ 3,857,858 | $11,397 | | | | $ 487,098 |
| Public school system | 31,186,498 | 705,765 | 3,937,083 | | | | (26,543,650) |
| Total component units | $34,568,655 | $ 4,563,623 | $ 3,948,480 | | | | (26,056,552) |
| | | | | | | | |
| General revenues: | | | | | | | |
| Taxes: | | | | | | | |
| Real estate | | | | 34,168,449 | — | 34,168,449 | 21,893,273 |
| Other | | | | 13,308,487 | — | 13,308,487 | — |
| Grants and contributions not restricted to specific programs | | | | 1,457,820 | | 1,457,820 | 6,461,708 |
| Interest and investment earnings | | | | 1,958,144 | 601,349 | 2,559,493 | 881,763 |
| Miscellaneous | | | | 884,907 | 104,925 | 989,832 | 22,464 |
| Total general revenues | | | | 51,777,807 | 706,274 | 52,484,081 | 29,259,208 |
| Excess (deficiency) of revenues over expenses before special item | | | | (6,269,183) | 3,721,294 | (2,547,889) | 3,202,656 |
| Special item: | | | | | | | |
| Gain on sale of park land | | | | 2,653,488 | — | 2,653,488 | — |
| Excess (deficiency) of revenues over expenses | | | | (3,615,695) | 3,721,294 | 105,599 | 3,202,656 |
| Transfers | | | | 501,409 | (501,409) | — | — |
| Change in net assets | | | | (3,114,286) | 3,219,885 | 105,599 | 3,202,656 |
| Net assets–beginning | | | | 126,673,160 | 82,349,309 | 209,022,469 | 16,025,971 |
| Net assets–ending | | | | $123,558,874 | $85,569,194 | $209,128,068 | $19,228,627 |

> The amounts reported in the "Net (Expense) Revenue" columns are intended to give the reader an idea of the relative extent to which each function relies upon or contributes to the general revenues of the government.

FIGURE 15–3

**BALANCE SHEET**
**Governmental Funds**

| | *General Fund* | *Special Revenue Funds* | *Debt Service Funds* | *Capital Projects Funds* |
|---|---|---|---|---|
| **ASSETS** | | | | |
| Cash and cash equivalents | $3,418,485 | $ 3,797,635 | $ 842,004 | $ 1,141,648 |
| Investments | — | — | 3,141,980 | 23,729,732 |
| Receivables, net | 3,644,561 | 2,963,659 | — | 364,340 |
| Receivable from other funds | 1,370,757 | — | — | — |
| Receivable from other governments | — | 253,778 | — | 1,461,319 |
| Liens receivable | 791,926 | 3,195,745 | — | — |
| Inventories | 182,821 | — | — | — |
| Total assets | $9,408,550 | $10,210,817 | $3,983,984 | $26,697,039 |
| **LIABILITIES** | | | | |
| Accounts payable | $3,408,680 | $  366,591 | $  151,922 | $ 1,981,473 |
| Payable to other funds | — | 25,369 | — | — |
| Payable to other governments | 94,074 | — | — | — |
| Deferred revenue | 4,250,430 | 6,273,045 | — | 261,000 |
| Total liabilities | 7,753,184 | 6,665,005 | 151,922 | 2,242,473 |
| **FUND BALANCES** | | | | |
| Reserved | 1,015,039 | 1,179,752 | 3,832,062 | 6,587,305 |
| Unreserved | 640,327 | 2,366,060 | — | 17,867,261 |
| Total fund balances | 1,655,366 | 3,545,812 | 3,832,062 | 24,454,566 |
| Total liabilities and fund balances | $9,408,550 | $10,210,817 | $3,983,984 | $26,697,039 |

> A total column may be presented in any fund perspective statement but is not required. If a total column is presented, it should clearly indicate whether interfund and similar eliminations have been made.

Reviewing the financial statement examples might raise several questions. For instance,

- When considering citizen users of government financial statements, will two perspectives clarify or confuse? (The perceptions gained from the entity-wide statements often will differ dramatically from those of the major fund/fund type financial statements. One state, which would have reported several billion dollars of net assets in an entity-wide balance sheet or statement of net assets like that in Figure 15–1, reported a General Fund fund balance deficit exceeding $120 million at the same point in time.)

FIGURE 15–4        **STATEMENT OF REVENUES, EXPENDITURES,
AND CHANGES IN FUND BALANCES**
Governmental Funds

| | General Fund | Special Revenue Funds | Debt Service Funds | Capital Projects Funds |
|---|---|---|---|---|
| **REVENUES** | | | | |
| Property taxes | $29,280,163 | $      — | $ 4,605,192 | $      — |
| Other taxes | 13,025,392 | — | — | — |
| Fees and fines | 606,946 | — | — | — |
| Licenses and permits | 2,287,794 | — | — | — |
| Intergovernmental | 6,119,938 | 3,951,287 | — | 1,457,820 |
| Charges for services | 11,374,460 | 30,708 | — | — |
| Interest | 552,325 | 215,204 | 146,604 | 836,589 |
| Miscellaneous | 881,874 | 66,270 | — | 2,939 |
| Total revenues | 64,128,892 | 4,263,469 | 4,751,796 | 2,297,348 |
| **EXPENDITURES** | | | | |
| Current operating: | | | | |
| General government | 8,630,835 | 53,622 | 11,820 | 490,124 |
| Public safety | 33,729,623 | — | — | — |
| Public works | 4,975,775 | 3,721,542 | — | — |
| Engineering services | 1,299,645 | — | — | — |
| Health and sanitation | 6,070,032 | — | — | — |
| Cemetery | 706,305 | — | — | — |
| Culture and recreation | 11,411,685 | — | — | — |
| Community development | — | 2,879,389 | — | — |
| Debt service: | | | | |
| Principal | — | 75,000 | 3,375,000 | — |
| Interest and other charges | — | — | 5,215,151 | — |
| Capital outlay | — | — | — | 16,718,649 |
| Total expenditures | 66,823,900 | 6,729,553 | 8,601,971 | 17,208,773 |
| Excess (deficiency) of revenues over expenditures | (2,695,008) | (2,466,084) | (3,850,175) | (14,911,425) |
| **OTHER FINANCING SOURCES (USES)** | | | | |
| Proceeds of refunding bonds | — | — | 38,045,000 | — |
| Proceeds of long-term capital debt | — | — | — | 18,829,560 |
| Payment to bond refunding escrow agent | — | — | (37,284,144) | — |
| Transfers in | 129,323 | 134,500 | 3,991,298 | 1,269,722 |
| Transfers out | (2,163,759) | (348,046) | — | (2,273,187) |
| Total other financing sources and uses | (2,034,436) | (213,546) | 4,752,154 | 17,826,095 |
| **SPECIAL ITEM** | | | | |
| Proceeds from sale of park land | 3,476,488 | — | — | — |
| Net change in fund balance | (1,252,956) | (2,679,630) | 901,979 | 2,914,670 |
| Fund balances–beginning | 2,908,322 | 6,225,442 | 2,930,083 | 21,539,896 |
| Fund balances–ending | $ 1,655,366 | $3,545,812 | $ 3,832,062 | $24,454,566 |

FIGURE 15–5

**BUDGETARY COMPARISON STATEMENT**
**General Fund**

| | Budgeted Amounts | | Actual Amounts (Budgetary Basis) | Variance with Final Budget Positive (Negative) |
|---|---|---|---|---|
| | Original | Final | | |
| Budgetary fund balance, January 1 | $ 2,736,824 | $ 1,950,873 | $ 1,950,873 | $       — |
| Resources (inflows) | | | | |
| Property taxes | 30,124,560 | 29,959,745 | 29,280,163 | (679,582) |
| Franchise taxes | 4,546,209 | 4,528,750 | 4,055,505 | (473,245) |
| Public service taxes | 8,295,000 | 8,307,274 | 8,969,887 | 662,613 |
| Licenses and permits | 2,126,600 | 2,126,600 | 2,287,794 | 161,194 |
| Fines and forfeitures | 718,800 | 718,800 | 606,946 | (111,854) |
| Charges for services | 12,392,972 | 11,202,150 | 11,374,460 | 172,310 |
| Grants | 6,905,898 | 6,571,360 | 6,119,938 | (451,422) |
| Sale of land | 1,355,250 | 3,500,000 | 3,476,488 | (23,512) |
| Miscellaneous | 3,024,292 | 1,220,991 | 881,874 | (339,117) |
| Interest received | 1,015,945 | 550,000 | 552,325 | 2,325 |
| Transfers from other funds | 939,525 | 130,000 | 129,323 | (677) |
| Amounts available for appropriation | 74,181,875 | 70,766,543 | 69,685,576 | (1,080,967) |
| Charges to appropriations (outflows) | | | | |
| General government: | | | | |
| Legal | 665,275 | 663,677 | 632,719 | 30,958 |
| Mayor, legislative, fiduciary, and audit | 3,058,750 | 3,192,910 | 2,658,264 | 534,646 |
| Finance and accounting | 1,932,500 | 1,912,702 | 1,852,687 | 60,015 |
| City clerk and elections | 345,860 | 354,237 | 341,206 | 13,031 |
| Employee relations | 1,315,500 | 1,300,498 | 1,234,232 | 66,266 |
| Planning and economic development | 1,975,600 | 1,784,314 | 1,642,575 | 141,739 |
| Public safety: | | | | |
| Police | 19,576,820 | 20,367,917 | 20,246,496 | 121,421 |
| Fire department | 9,565,280 | 9,358,453 | 9,559,967 | (201,514) |
| EMS | 2,323,171 | 2,470,127 | 2,459,866 | 10,261 |
| Inspections | 1,585,695 | 1,585,695 | 1,533,380 | 52,315 |
| Public works: | | | | |
| Public works administration | 388,500 | 385,013 | 383,397 | 1,616 |
| Street maintenance | 2,152,750 | 2,019,166 | 2,233,362 | (214,196) |
| Street lighting | 762,750 | 742,540 | 759,832 | (17,292) |
| Traffic operations | 385,945 | 374,945 | 360,509 | 14,436 |
| Mechanical maintenance | 1,525,685 | 1,272,696 | 1,256,087 | 16,609 |
| Engineering services: | | | | |
| Engineering administration | 1,170,650 | 1,140,289 | 1,158,023 | (17,734) |
| Geographical information system | 125,625 | 119,315 | 138,967 | (19,652) |
| Health and sanitation: | | | | |
| Garbage pickup | 5,756,250 | 5,865,757 | 6,174,653 | (308,896) |
| Cemetery: | | | | |
| Personal services | 425,000 | 425,000 | 422,562 | 2,438 |
| Purchases of goods and services | 299,500 | 299,500 | 283,743 | 15,757 |
| Culture and recreation: | | | | |
| Library | 985,230 | 1,023,465 | 1,022,167 | 1,298 |
| Parks and recreation | 9,521,560 | 9,786,397 | 9,756,618 | 29,779 |
| Community communications | 552,350 | 558,208 | 510,361 | 47,847 |
| Nondepartmental: | | | | |
| Miscellaneous | — | — | 259,817 | (259,817) |
| Contingency | 2,544,049 | — | — | — |
| Transfers to other funds | 2,970,256 | 2,025,000 | 2,163,759 | (138,759) |
| Total charges to appropriations | 71,910,551 | 69,027,821 | 69,045,249 | (17,428) |
| Budgetary fund balance, December 31 | $ 2,271,324 | $ 1,738,722 | $    640,327 | ($1,098,395) |

The "Variance with Final Budget" column is not required. Governments may also choose to present a variance column to display the differences between the original and final budgets.

This statement presents only the general fund budgetary comparison—the minimum requirement when the government presents the full financial section of a CAFR. If less than the full financial section is issued, budgetary comparisons are also required for other major governmental funds for which annual budgets are adopted.

FIGURE 15–6

**BALANCE SHEET**
**Proprietary Funds**

| | Enterprise Funds | Permanent Fund Cemetery Care | Internal Service Funds |
|---|---|---|---|
| **ASSETS** | | | |
| Current assets: | | | |
| Cash and cash equivalents | $  8,785,821 | $        — | $ 3,336,099 |
| Investments | — | — | 171,708 |
| Receivables, net | 3,568,121 | — | 136,333 |
| Due from other governments | 41,494 | — | — |
| Inventories | 126,674 | — | 139,328 |
| Total current assets | 12,522,110 | — | 3,783,468 |
| Noncurrent assets: | | | |
| Restricted cash and cash equivalents | 1,493,322 | 1,062,028 | — |
| Restricted investments and accrued interest | — | 343,272 | — |
| Capital assets: | | | |
| Land | 3,835,150 | — | — |
| Buildings and equipment | 168,669,015 | — | 14,721,786 |
| Less accumulated depreciation | (21,115,414) | — | (5,781,734) |
| Capital assets, net | 151,388,751 | — | 8,940,052 |
| Total assets | $165,404,183 | $1,405,300 | $12,723,520 |
| **LIABILITIES** | | | |
| Current liabilities: | | | |
| Accounts payable | $      751,430 | $        — | $     780,570 |
| Due to other funds | 175,000 | — | 1,170,388 |
| Compensated absences | 121,677 | — | 237,690 |
| Claims and judgments | — | — | 1,687,975 |
| Bonds, notes, and loans payable | 4,304,609 | — | 249,306 |
| Total current liabilities | 5,352,716 | — | 4,125,929 |
| Noncurrent liabilities: | | | |
| Compensated absences | 486,705 | — | — |
| Claims and judgments | — | — | 5,602,900 |
| Bonds, notes, and loans payable | 73,995,568 | — | — |
| Total noncurrent liabilities | 74,482,273 | — | 5,602,900 |
| Total liabilities | 79,834,989 | — | 9,728,829 |
| **FUND EQUITY** | | | |
| Invested in capital assets, net of related debt | 73,088,574 | — | 8,690,746 |
| Restricted | 1,451,996 | 1,405,300 | — |
| Unrestricted (deficit) | 11,028,624 | — | (5,696,055) |
| Total fund equity | 85,569,194 | 1,405,300 | 2,994,691 |
| Total liabilities and fund equity | $165,404,183 | $1,405,300 | $12,723,520 |

FIGURE 15–7    **STATEMENT OF REVENUES, EXPENSES, AND CHANGES IN FUND EQUITY**

**Proprietary Funds**

| | *Enterprise Funds* | *Permanent Fund* *Cemetery Care* | *Internal Service Funds* |
|---|---|---|---|
| **OPERATING REVENUES:** | | | |
| Charges for services | $12,670,144 | $ — | $15,256,164 |
| Interest and investment revenue | — | 72,689 | — |
| Miscellaneous | 3,826 | — | 1,066,761 |
| Total operating revenues | 12,673,970 | 72,689 | 16,322,925 |
| **OPERATING EXPENSES:** | | | |
| Personal services | 4,162,907 | — | 4,157,156 |
| Contractual services | 440,454 | — | 584,396 |
| Utilities | 854,833 | — | 214,812 |
| Repairs and maintenance | 811,932 | — | 1,960,490 |
| Other supplies and expenses | 515,332 | — | 234,445 |
| Insurance claims and expenses | — | — | 8,004,286 |
| Depreciation | 1,705,189 | — | 1,707,872 |
| Total operating expenses | 8,490,647 | — | 16,863,457 |
| Operating income (loss) | 4,183,323 | 72,689 | (540,532) |
| **NONOPERATING REVENUES (EXPENSES):** | | | |
| Interest and investment revenue | 601,349 | — | 134,733 |
| Miscellaneous revenue | 104,925 | — | 20,855 |
| Capital contributions | 1,645,919 | — | 18,788 |
| Interest expense | (2,767,376) | — | (41,616) |
| Miscellaneous expense | (46,846) | — | (176,003) |
| Total nonoperating revenues (expenses) | (462,029) | — | (43,243) |
| Net income (loss) | 3,721,294 | 72,689 | (583,775) |
| Transfers out | (501,409) | (63,409) | (175,033) |
| Net change in fund equity | 3,219,885 | 9,280 | (758,808) |
| Total fund equity—beginning | 82,349,309 | 1,396,020 | 3,753,499 |
| Total fund equity—ending | $85,569,194 | $1,405,300 | $ 2,994,691 |

> Capital contributions are required to be reported as revenue rather than direct additions to fund equity.

> Transfers should be reported *after* net income.

- Which FASB standards are to be applied to general government activities in presenting the entity-wide financial statements?
- Is the dual perspective approach feasible? Cost beneficial?

The GASB exposure draft includes an extensive basis for conclusions section. Those interested in more specifics should obtain a copy of the exposure draft from the GASB.

FIGURE 15–8

**STATEMENT OF CASH FLOWS**
**Proprietary Funds**

| | Enterprise Funds | Permanent Fund<br>Cemetery Care | Internal<br>Service Funds |
|---|---|---|---|
| The direct method for reporting cash flows from operating activities is required. | | | |
| **CASH FLOWS FROM OPERATING ACTIVITIES** | | | |
| Receipts from customers | $12,745,492 | $ — | $15,326,343 |
| Payments to suppliers | (3,090,486) | — | (2,812,238) |
| Payments to employees | (4,110,883) | — | (4,209,688) |
| Claims paid to outsiders | — | — | (8,482,451) |
| Other receipts (payments) | (2,462,342) | — | 1,061,118 |
| Net cash provided by operating activities | 3,081,781 | — | 883,084 |
| **CASH FLOWS FROM NONCAPITAL FINANCING ACTIVITIES** | | | |
| Transfers to other funds | (501,409) | (63,409) | (175,033) |
| **CASH FLOWS FROM CAPITAL AND RELATED FINANCING ACTIVITIES** | | | |
| Proceeds from capital debt | 12,702,100 | — | — |
| Capital contributions | 486,010 | — | — |
| Purchases of capital assets | (4,338,751) | — | (400,086) |
| Principal paid on capital debt | (11,073,491) | — | (954,137) |
| Interest paid on capital debt | (2,646,254) | — | (35,185) |
| Other receipts (payments) | 19,174 | — | 124,985 |
| Net cash used by capital and related financing activities | (4,851,212) | — | (1,264,423) |
| **CASH FLOWS FROM INVESTING ACTIVITIES** | | | |
| Proceeds from sales and maturities of investments | — | 10,925 | 15,684 |
| Interest and dividends | 598,540 | 72,664 | 129,550 |
| Net cash provided by investing activities | 598,540 | 83,589 | 145,234 |
| Net increase (decrease) in cash and cash equivalents | (1,672,300) | 20,180 | (411,138) |
| Balances–beginning of the year | 11,951,443 | 1,041,848 | 3,747,237 |
| Balances–end of the year | $10,279,143 | $1,062,028 | $ 3,336,099 |
| **Reconciliation of Operating Income (Loss) to Net Cash Provided by Operating Activities** | | | |
| Operating income (loss) | $ 4,183,323 | $ 72,689 | $ (540,532) |
| Adjustments to reconcile operating income (loss) to net cash provided by operating activities: | | | |
| Cash flows reported in other categories: | | | |
| Interest and dividends | — | (72,664) | — |
| Depreciation expense | 1,705,189 | — | 1,707,872 |
| Change in assets and liabilities: | | | |
| Receivables, net | 654,469 | (25) | 31,941 |
| Inventories | 2,829 | — | 39,790 |
| Accounts and other payables | (384,089) | — | 475,212 |
| Accrued expenses | (3,079,940) | — | (831,199) |
| Net cash provided by operating activities | $ 3,081,781 | $ — | $ 883,084 |

**Note:** The required information about noncash investing, capital, and financing activities is not illustrated.

FIGURE 15–9

**STATEMENT OF NET ASSETS**
**Fiduciary Funds**

| | *Employee Retirement Plan* | *Private-Purpose Trusts* | *Agency Funds* |
|---|---|---|---|
| **ASSETS** | | | |
| Cash and short-term investments | $ 1,973 | $81,250 | $ 44,889 |
| Receivables: | | | |
|   Interest and dividends | 508,475 | 760 | — |
|   Other receivables | 6,826 | — | 183,161 |
|     Total receivables | 515,301 | 760 | 183,161 |
| Investments, at fair value: | | | |
|   U.S. government obligations | 13,056,037 | — | — |
|   Municipal bonds | 6,528,019 | — | — |
|   Corporate bonds | 16,320,047 | — | — |
|   Corporate stocks | 26,112,075 | — | — |
|   Other investments | 3,264,009 | — | — |
|     Total investments | 65,280,187 | — | — |
|     Total assets | 65,797,461 | 82,010 | $228,050 |
| **LIABILITIES** | | | |
| Accounts payable | — | 1,234 | $ — |
| Refunds payable and others | 1,358 | — | 228,050 |
|   Total liabilities | 1,358 | 1,234 | $228,050 |
| **NET ASSETS** | | | |
| Held in trust for pension benefits and other purposes | $65,796,103 | $80,776 | |

FIGURE 15–10

**STATEMENT OF CHANGES IN NET ASSETS**
**Fiduciary Funds**

| | *Employee Retirement Plan* | *Private-Purpose Trusts* |
|---|---|---|
| **ADDITIONS** | | |
| Contributions: | | |
|   Employer | $ 2,721,341 | $ — |
|   Plan members | 1,421,233 | — |
|     Total contributions | 4,142,574 | — |
| Investment income: | | |
|   Net appreciation (depreciation) in fair value of investments | (272,522) | — |
|   Interest | 2,460,871 | 4,560 |
|   Dividends | 1,445,273 | — |
|     Total investment income | 3,633,622 | 4,560 |
|   Less investment expense | (216,428) | — |
|     Net investment income | 3,417,194 | 4,560 |
|     Total additions | 7,559,768 | 4,560 |
| **DEDUCTIONS** | | |
| Benefits | 2,453,047 | 3,800 |
| Refunds of contributions | 464,691 | — |
| Administrative expenses | 87,532 | 678 |
|   Total deductions | 3,005,270 | 4,478 |
| Net increase | 4,554,498 | 82 |
| Net assets—beginning of the year | 61,241,605 | 80,694 |
| Net assets—end of the year | $65,796,103 | $80,776 |

> Because agency funds have no net assets and therefore no changes in net assets, they are not included in this statement.

## SERVICE EFFORTS AND ACCOMPLISHMENTS (SEA)

Another area receiving increasing attention from academe, governments, and the GASB is the reporting of service efforts and accomplishments (SEA) information. Traditional financial reporting—whether under current GAAP guidance or with the possible changes that the GASB may mandate over the next few years— is limited in what it can communicate. The growth in the scope, complexity, and size of governments in recent decades has drawn attention to these limitations and to the need of government officials to give an account of more than simply how they have raised and used financial resources.

The electorate is entitled to hold government officials responsible for the efficient use of resources in providing government services. Moreover, government officials are also accountable for whether government programs and activities are achieving the desired or planned results—and are doing so in a frugal and efficient manner. Furthermore, the electorate even has the right to hold such officials accountable for whether or not the established goals and objectives of government programs are appropriate.

Traditional financial-statement-focused reporting does not provide the information needed by the electorate to assess government performance in terms of economy, efficiency, and effectiveness. Many persons and groups think that being able to evaluate whether governments are using resources efficiently and effectively is a higher level of accountability than is the accountability for flows and balances of resources per se. They feel strongly that making progress toward appropriate measurement and reporting of indicators of the efficiency and effectiveness of government programs is of paramount importance. SLG auditors, in particular, have urged the GASB to undertake SEA-related projects. The GASB has actively encouraged and supported research in this area and has issued a statement on concepts related to service efforts and accomplishments reporting.

Although the desirability of reporting indicators of service efforts and accomplishments is logically and intuitively appealing, such reporting is subject to many potential problems. These include possible poor association of reported performance measures with goals and desired effects, manipulation of reported performance by taking actions designed to improve reported performance that do not result in improved performance, lack of comparability where governments with apparently identical programs have notably different underlying goals for the programs, difficulty of accurate measurement of some possible performance indicators, and the potential for information overload because multiple measures are typically necessary to communicate performance from different perspectives or related to different goals for a single program. Indeed, many people believe that SEA is not within the proper purview of GAAP and the GASB.

Some of the hurdles and problems that must be addressed with respect to service efforts and accomplishments reporting may be highlighted in a familiar context by considering the types of areas about which information on university student outputs was considered desirable by respondents to a National Center for Higher Education Management Systems survey. The areas are listed in Figure 15–11. Furthermore, it may be useful to consider the different types of performance indicators that might be useful, depending on the perspective from which a university's success is being viewed by a report user. The different per-

FIGURE 15–11  **Ten Outcome Areas for Higher Education**

1. **Student Knowledge and Skills Development**
   Information about student understanding, competencies, and attitudes relative to bodies of facts and principles and use of their intellectual and physical abilities.
2. **Student Educational Career Development**
   Information about student attitudes and success concerning certain academic pursuits (e.g., student educational degree aspirations and attainments).
3. **Student Educational Satisfaction**
   Information that indicates the satisfaction of students about the knowledge and skills they have acquired and their progress toward their educational and occupational career objectives.
4. **Student Occupational Career Development**
   Information about student attitudes and success concerning certain occupational goals and their job performance.
5. **Student Personal Development**
   Information about changes in students concerning the growth and maintenance of their personal life (e.g., their ability to adapt to new situations, their self-concept, etc.).
6. **Student Social/Cultural Development**
   Information about student abilities and attitudes in dealing with people and their interest in cultural activities.
7. **Community Educational Development**
   Information about the attitudes and success of nonmatriculating participants concerning their acquisition of knowledge and skills, personal and social development, and occupational career goals and performance.
8. **Community Service**
   Information about the impact of the opportunities and services provided by the institution and received by the community (e.g., agricultural extension services, cultural and recreational opportunities, etc.).
9. **Community Impact**
   Information about the impact of an institution's programs and its faculty, staff, and students (current and former) on the financial health, manpower supply, and attitudes of the community (local, state, or national).
10. **Development of New Knowledge and Art**
    Information about new knowledge and art forms created, applied, and reorganized as a result of an institution's programs and its faculty, staff, and students (current and former).

*Source:* The National Center for Higher Education Management Systems, *The Higher Education Outcome Measures Identification Study,* 1974, cited in Committee on Nonprofit Entities' Performance Measures, Government and Nonprofit Section, American Accounting Association, *Measuring the Performance of Nonprofit Organizations: The State of the Art,* 1988, pp. 88–89.

spectives and indicators in Figure 15–12 are numerous, yet are not exhaustive in scope.

Finally, the GASB research report, *Service Efforts and Accomplishments Reporting: Its Time Has Come—Elementary and Secondary Education,* recommends a set of SEA indicators for elementary and secondary schools to select from for SEA reporting purposes (see Figure 15–13). Different schools might report using

FIGURE 15–12 **Performance Indicators for Colleges and Universities**

**Resources Approach**
Student Selectivity (admission scores, acceptance rate, and yield)
Student Demand (pool of applicants, number of majors, enrollment trends)
Student Composition (ethnicity, part-time/full-time students)
Faculty Prestige
Faculty Training (% doctorate)
Faculty Composition (full-time/part-time faculty)
Faculty Teaching Loads
Size of Budget
Library Holdings
Condition and Adequacy of Equipment
Size of Endowment

**Reputational Approach**
Reputational Ranking of Programs
Reputational Ranking of Students (for example, top ten institutions with the
    enrollment of National Merit Scholars)
Reputational Ranking of Faculty's Scholarly Productivity
Relative Ranking of Resources (for example, faculty compensation and size of
    endowment)
Reputational Ranking of Institution's Prestige

**Outcomes Approach**
Faculty Scholarly Productivity (publication counts, citation index count, perceived
    reputation)
Faculty Awards and Honors
Faculty Research Support
Faculty Teaching Performance
Student Academic Achievement
Student Achievement Following Graduation
Student Placement
Alumni Satisfaction
Student Retention Rate
Student Transfer Rate to Senior Institutions
Student Graduation Rates
Student Rate of Advanced Graduate Study
Student Job Placement Rate
Employer Satisfaction
Passing Rate of Professional Certification Exams

**Value-added Approach**
Changes in Students' Cognitive Abilities (ACT-COMP)
Student Personal Development
Student Career Development
Social Benefits

*Source:* Susy S. Chan, "Service Efforts and Accomplishments of Higher Education Institutions: Issues in Measurement and Reporting," Fifth Annual University of Illinois at Chicago Governmental Accounting Symposium, 1988.

different subsets of these indicators because of differing goals, objectives, and needs.

SEA reporting continues to be experimented with and debated. No doubt SEA information will continue to evolve for budgetary, managerial, audit, and financial reporting purposes.

## FIGURE 15–13  Elementary and Secondary Education SEA Indicators

| *SEA Indicator* | *Rationale for Selecting Indicator* |
|---|---|
| *Inputs:*   Expenditures[a] (in millions) (may be also broken out by type of activity such as instructional and administrative) | |
|     Current dollars ⎫<br>    Constant dollars ⎭ | To provide a measure of resources used to provide services |
|     Total number of personnel | To provide a measure of the size of the organization |
| *Outputs:*   Number of student-days (thousands) | To provide a general measure of workload |
|     Number of students promoted/graduated | To provide a measure of students satisfactorily completing educational requirements |
|     Carnegie units as percentage required[b] (with number of required units shown parenthetically—can be reported by major subject area) | To provide an indication of courses taken by students in certain critical subject areas |
|     Absenteeism rate | To provide a measure of student participation in classes and an indication of their interest in learning |
|     Dropout rate | To indicate the school's success in keeping students actively involved in the learning process |
| *Outcomes:*   Test score results—*for each major subject area* | |
|     Average percentile on standardized tests ⎫<br>    Percentage of students above the 50th percentile[c] ⎬<br>    Percentage of students reaching their grade level of proficiency or higher ⎭ | To provide measures of student achievement in academic subjects and a comparison with expected achievement and established norms |
|     Percentage of students receiving grade-level gain on achievement test[d] (may be presented for major subject areas as well as overall) | To provide a measure of student annual progress—the indicator is also used to develop a measure of cost-effectiveness |
|     Percentage of students scoring higher than specified level of self-esteem ⎫<br>    Percentage of students achieving specified physical fitness test standards ⎬ | To provide an indication of the development of noncognitive skills and abilities generally considered as objectives of formal education |
|     Percentage of graduates gainfully employed or continuing education two years after graduation | To provide an indication of the school system's results in preparing graduates for further education or to become members of the work force |
|     Percentage of students rating as good, excellent, or improved—their own: | |
|       Work and study skills ⎫<br>      Self-discipline ⎬<br>      Interpersonal skills ⎭<br>      Knowledge gained | To provide measures of students' perceptions of their acquisition of knowledge and selected noncognitive skills and behavior |
|     Percentage of parents rating their children good, excellent, or improved in: | |
|       Work and study skills ⎫<br>      Self-discipline ⎬<br>      Interpersonal skills ⎭<br>      Knowledge gained | To provide parents' perceptions of their child's acquisition of knowledge and important noncognitive skills and behavior; to allow comparison with student perceptions; to indicate the school system's contribution to the acquisition of these skills and behavior |
| *Efficiency (input/output and input/outcome measures):* | |
|     Cost per output | |
|       Per student-day ⎫<br>      Per student promoted/graduated ⎭ | To provide an indication of the school system's technical efficiency of operation |
|     Cost per outcome | |
|       Per student achieving grade-level score gain | To provide an indication of the school system's true efficiency in achieving student outcomes |
| *Explanatory Data:* | |
|     Controllable<br>      Average number of hours per student in oversized classes (per day) | |
|     Not controllable<br>      Average daily attendance<br>      Percentage of minority students<br>      Percentage of students participating in subsidized lunch or other public welfare program<br>      Percentage of students needing special remedial programs<br>      Student mobility rate<br>      Percentage of students with English as second language<br>      Student enrollments | To provide information on factors that are likely to have some effect on student achievement and that can be important in understanding performance on output, outcome, and efficiency indicators |

[a] A clear description of which expenditures are included or excluded should be provided.

[b] One Carnegie unit equals five hours per week of instructional class time on a subject for an entire school year.

[c] The 50th percentile is the point at which one-half of the students being scored are below the score of that student or group of students.

[d] A grade-level gain is the measure of a student's progress by school year, as assessed by a test score, for example, from the 6.1 grade level to the 7.1 grade level.

## POPULAR REPORTING

Like service efforts and accomplishments reporting, another reporting development that is motivated by the desire to meet needs of users that are not met effectively by current CAFRs is popular reporting. Broadly speaking, popular reporting encompasses various attempts to communicate information about an entity in a form that is understood by a larger portion of the targeted users of government reports—especially citizens. Few citizens have ever seen a CAFR, and only a few would be able to understand its implications for their voting or other decisions. Therefore, standards-setters have for years encouraged experimentation with popular reporting.

Popular reporting takes various forms—from consolidated financial statements to financial statements limited to the total columns of the combined statements to other condensed summary financial statements to budgetary data presentations to narrative presentations supplemented with graphs and charts. Popular reporting is referred to on the financial reporting pyramid discussed in Chapter 13 as condensed summary reporting. Many believe that to develop a report that will be useful to the citizenry means developing some type of condensed summary financial report. Indeed the entity-wide statements proposed in the GASB's reporting model exposure draft might serve as the basis for popular reporting; and the popular report might include some service efforts and accomplishments (SEA) reporting. So these developments may complement each other.

Moreover, the GASB has sponsored popular reporting research, the American Institute of CPAs (AICPA) has developed guidance for auditor association with summary financial information, and the Government Finance Officers Association (GFOA) has developed an award program for innovative popular reports. Thus, considerable progress in popular reporting is expected in the next few years.

## FUND STRUCTURE AND CLASSIFICATION ISSUES

Another pervasive issue that has various implications for government financial reporting is identifying the appropriate fund structure and fund classification criteria. The most significant change in fund structure in recent decades was the elimination of the Special Assessment Fund type in the mid-1980s. This change simply required the normal fund structure to be used for the special case of special assessment projects, for which a special fund had been required in the past. In essence, it eliminated an exception to the fund structure that had been required in the past. The GASB proposes other changes in its reporting model exposure draft discussed at the beginning of this chapter.

### Number of Funds

One aspect of fund structure for which there is only minimal guidance is the issue of when should separate funds of a particular type be used. This issue many be even more critical if the GASB adopts financial reporting requirements under which only major funds are to be separately reported. This is because the current literature does not provide clear guidance as to when separate capital projects, debt service, or other funds are required. One city, for instance, has over 70 individual capital projects—several of which are financed by separate, major bond issues—but reports only one Capital Projects Fund. Other cities with similar circumstances report numerous Capital Projects Funds. Should this wide variation in practice—limited by little more than the preferences of individuals—be permitted? Or are there common guiding principles that should be established and followed with respect to how many individual funds of a particular type are appropriate in differing circumstances? If the current variation in practice were permitted and only major individual funds had to be separately reported, one potentially could manipulate which fund(s) are or are not reported by virtue of the manner in which separate funds are established.

### Proprietary or Governmental Fund?

Perhaps the most significant aspect of fund structure and classification that should be considered is whether a given program, function, or activity should be accounted for in a proprietary fund or in a governmental fund (and perhaps in the GFA and GLTD accounts). Specifically, this conceptual and practice issue may arise in two forms: (1) Enterprise Fund or governmental fund, and (2) Internal Service Fund or governmental fund. These are important issues because they will determine or impact such things as:

1. Whether the program, function, or activity is accounted for in a single proprietary fund entity or in several entities—governmental funds and account groups.
2. The measurement focus and basis of accounting used—that is, whether expenses or expenditures are measured.
3. In the case of Internal Service Funds, whether charges are borne centrally or are charged to the user agencies.
4. Rates to be charged for goods and services.

Again, this issue may become even more important if the GASB ultimately requires individual fund statements only for major funds.

### Enterprise or Governmental Fund?

The Enterprise Fund issue most often arises from the flexibility permitted in the two-part (mandatory and permissive) Enterprise Fund definition:

> Enterprise Funds—to account for operations (a) that are financed and operated in a manner similar to private business enterprises—where the intent of the governing body is that the costs (expenses, including depreciation) of providing goods or services to the general public on a continuing basis be financed or recovered primarily through user charges; or (b) where the governing body has decided that periodic determination of revenues earned, expenses incurred, and/or net income is appropriate for capital maintenance, public policy, management control, accountability, or other purposes.[2]

Part (a) of this definition, the mandatory provision, is designed to include government-owned utilities and other profitable or break-even activities. Its most critical aspect is determining the intent of the governing body. That intent may or may not have been expressed in the minutes or in discussions with knowledgeable persons. But actions can also imply intent, and if a governing board has consistently operated a function as an enterprise, setting rates to recover full cost and in other ways acting like the activity is an enterprise, it probably is one under part (a) of the definition.

---

[2] GASB *Codification*, sec. 1300.104b(1).

Changes in intent can occur when membership and attitudes of a governing board change, of course, but it clearly is not intended for an activity to be accounted for as an enterprise one year, a governmental activity the next, and so forth. When a new activity is the center of the Enterprise Fund or governmental fund issue, persuading the proper people to agree upon and document the intent of the governing board may be the best approach. On the other hand, a strong finance officer will often make such decisions, then have the council ratify them and record the ratification in the minutes.

The "permissive" part (b) of the Enterprise Fund definition is intended to cover governmental bus lines, city markets, and other activities apt to incur losses. This criterion requires positive action by a governing board—to state and document its intent that a given program, function, or activity that does not meet the usual Enterprise Fund definition is to be accounted for as an Enterprise Fund for one or more of the several possible reasons noted. In such cases the usual reason is to see how much is being lost on a full cost basis as well as to know the sources, uses, and balances of the working capital or cash devoted to the activity.

The disadvantage of this criterion is that it essentially provides governments with a "free choice"—total flexibility in deciding whether to report an activity as an Enterprise activity. Many feel that such a "free choice" criterion is no criterion at all, that it essentially says "report activities in whatever manner pleases you," and that it leads to noncomparability among governments because different governments may report identical activities in different fund types.

In an attempt to provide more consistency from year to year and greater comparability among governments, the GASB has proposed a new definition of an Enterprise Fund or activity in its reporting model exposure draft. This proposed new definition of an Enterprise Fund or activity states that an Enterprise Fund may be used to report any activity for which a fee is charged to external users for goods and services. Activities are *required to* be reported as Enterprise Funds *if* any *one* of the following criteria is met. Each of these criteria should be applied in the context of the activity's principal revenue sources.

a. The activity is financed with debt that is secured solely by a pledge of the net revenues from fees and charges of the activity. Debt that is secured by a pledge of net revenues from fees and charges and the full faith and credit of a related primary government or component unit—even if that government is not expected to make any payments—is not payable solely from fees and charges of the activity.

b. Laws or regulations require that the activity's costs of providing services, including capital costs (such as depreciation or capital debt service), be recovered with fees and charges rather than with taxes or similar revenues.

c. The pricing policies of the activity establish fees and charges designed to recover its costs, including capital costs (such as depreciation or debt service).

## Internal Service or Governmental Fund

The Internal Service Fund or governmental fund question may arise in connection with a variety of functions or activities, for example, data processing, communications, purchasing, and materials storage and handling. There are two aspects of this decision, of which the first may be the easier: (1) Internal Service Fund or governmental fund, and (2) if Internal Service Fund, which costs are to be recovered through the fund and thus constitute cost in this situation?

Whether an activity is established as an Internal Service Fund—and thus its costs are allocated to those using its goods or services—is a policy decision. Often it begins with or is made by (with approval of superiors) the chief finance officer, who seeks to obtain better accountability for the function as well as better cost control and distribution of costs to user agencies.

Although the Internal Service Fund definition does not appear at first glance to be as flexible as the Enterprise Fund definition, as it has been interpreted and applied in practice, it permits total free choice and, thus, is fraught with all the disadvantages of the permissive Enterprise Fund criterion discussed previously.

Assuming that an activity will be accounted for as an Internal Service Fund, there should be a determination of precisely which costs are to be charged to user agencies and on what basis. This should be agreed to by all agencies affected and should be documented.

## In Sum

Two significant problems arise from the proprietary fund versus governmental fund classification issue. First, the reporting of the activity will be significantly different under the two different classifications. Thus, it is important that the situations in which each reporting approach provides the most useful information be identified clearly. Current GAAP provide no such clear delineation. Indeed, the standards are weak with respect to the classification of activities as proprietary or governmental. As noted earlier, whether a government reports an activity as an enterprise activity is a matter of its own free choice unless the mandatory criterion—part (a)—is met. Furthermore, whether to use an Internal Service Fund to account for provision of goods or services to other departments of the government is a matter of totally free choice because, as interpreted and applied in practice, the standards permit use of Internal Service Funds but never require use of Internal Service Funds.

Second is the issue of comparability among governments. Assume that two governments have precisely the same activities and circumstances. Under current standards, one government might account for an activity in a proprietary fund and another account for the same (hypothetically equivalent) activity in its governmental funds and account groups. The reason is that intent is the fundamental thread that runs throughout the proprietary or governmental fund issue. And intent varies among governments and may vary within one government through time.

## NOTES TO THE FINANCIAL STATEMENTS

Under the pyramid concept explained in Chapter 13, the primary financial statement reporting focus is on the fund type data reported in the combined general purpose financial statements (GPFS). Individual fund data are not a required part of the GPFS but are to be reported in the official comprehensive annual financial report (CAFR) of the SLG unit.

The GASB *Codification* provides that the notes to the financial statements are those applicable to the GPFS; additional notes that might be necessary at the individual fund level are referred to as narrative explanations. Certain types of notes to the GPFS, some of which are individual fund disclosures, are required. Too, any other disclosures necessary in the circumstances for fair presentation of the financial statements should also be included. The importance of the notes is not diminished by the Board's proposed changes to the financial reporting model. Moreover, several additional note disclosures are proposed. The GASB *Codification* contains a checklist of note disclosures cross-referenced to the *Codification* section requiring each note. Relatively little guidance is provided as to the specific content of many of the notes, however, and practice appears to vary considerably with respect to the disclosures presented. Accounting and audit practitioners should use the GASB *Codification* checklist but also should review the notes to the financial statements in several good reports to help ensure that they do not fail to include important notes to the financial statements.

Another potential problem with respect to the notes to the financial statements—currently under consideration by the GASB—is that they tend to be quite extensive—often 25 to 45 pages or more. Some believe that while any one of the numerous notes typically found in government reports may be useful when taken by itself, it is not useful to have the extensive note disclosure currently found in most government reports. They believe that the volume of material and the number and significance of adjustments that users interpreting the financial statements must make—as a result of the notes—tend to overwhelm or confuse many readers. Others consider the level of note disclosure found in most reports both appropriate and essential. Indeed, many emphasize that full disclosure is required in SLG reporting rather than the adequate disclosure of business reporting. It is difficult to say who is correct, but clearly note disclosures should be viewed from the context of their overall impact on clarity and fair presentation, not solely on their own merits.

## CONCLUDING COMMENTS

Controversy and change frustrate some persons. Others view them as positive signs that the attention of the accounting profession—including SLG finance officers, professors, and independent public accountants—is increasingly being directed toward the improvement of state and local government accounting and financial reporting. The latter is our view, though it admittedly is frustrating to realize that some aspects of our text are apt to be outdated soon after its release and that, on some issues, we feel the "old" was better than the "new."

Accounting and reporting concepts and practices should and must evolve in all fields—business, nonprofit, and government. Through the combined efforts of the GASB and many persons and organizations, this evolution appears to be accelerating in the public sector.

## SELECTED BIBLIOGRAPHY

### Governmental Accounting Standards Board Publications

#### I. Research Reports

"The Needs of Users of Governmental Financial Reports," by Jones and Others (1985).

"Infrastructure Assets: An Assessment of User Needs and Recommendations for Financial Reporting," by Van Daniker and Kwiatkowski (1986).

"Financial Reporting Practices of Local Governments," by Ingram and Robbins (1987).

"An Empirical Study of Governmental Financial Reporting Entity Issues," by Patton (1987).

"A Study of the Usefulness of Disclosures Required by GASB Standards," by Hay (1988).

"Information Needs of College and University Financial Decision Makers," by Engstrom (1988).

"Other Postemployment Benefits in State and Local Governmental Units," by Bokemeier, Van Daniker, and Parrish (1990).

"Financial Reporting by State and Local Governments: A Survey of Preferences among Alternative Formats," by Wilson (1990).

"Popular Reporting: Local Government Financial Reports to the Citizenry," by Carpenter and Sharp (1992).

"The Relationships between Financial Reporting and the Measurement of Financial Condition," by Berne (1992).

### II. Service Efforts and Accomplishments Reporting: Its Time Has Come

"Elementary and Secondary Education," by Hatry, Alexander, and Fountain (1989).

*Executive Summary,* "Elementary and Secondary Education" (1989).

"An Overview," by Hatry, Fountain, Sullivan, and Kremer, eds. (1990).

"Water and Wastewater Treatment," by Burnaby and Herhold (1990).

"Mass Transit," by Wallace (1991).

"Sanitation Collection and Disposal," by Rubin (1991).

"Fire Department Programs," by Parry, Sharp, Vreeland, and Wallace (1991).

"Public Health," by Carpenter, Ruchala, and Waller (1991).

"Police Department Programs," by Drebin and Brannon (1992).

"Road Maintenance," by Hyman, Alfelor, and Allen (1993).

## Questions

**Q 15-1** Explain the two major financial reporting perspectives in GASB's dual perspective reporting approach.

**Q 15-2** What problems do you foresee in applying the GASB's proposed new Enterprise Fund definition in practice?

**Q 15-3** The notes to the financial statements of a government are often quite extensive. What problems are associated with the use of note disclosures to communicate information essential to fair presentation of a government's financial position and operating results? What are the advantages of such disclosures?

**Q 15-4** What are the major reporting model changes proposed by the GASB exposure draft on basic financial statements?

**Q 15-5** What do you consider to be the strengths and weaknesses of the GASB's proposed new financial reporting requirements?

## Problems

**P 15-1** Obtain a copy of a government's comprehensive annual financial report or general purpose financial statements. As best as possible from reviewing the material in the chapter or a copy of the GASB's exposure draft, convert those financial statements as necessary to develop and present the entity-wide statements proposed by the GASB. State any major assumptions made. What are the advantages and disadvantages of the proposed statements?

**P 15-2** (Research Problem) Obtain the comprehensive annual financial report (CAFR) or general purpose financial statements (GPFS) of several governments. Analyze the notes to the financial statements for each government in terms of
  a. whether the notes required are presented.
  b. understandability of the notes.
  c. consistency of notes presented by various governments and types of information presented in similar notes.
  d. the extent to which individual notes enhance your analysis and understanding of the financial statements.
  e. whether the volume of notes diminishes their value significantly.
  f. other strengths or weaknesses related to the notes.

  Prepare a 10- to 20-page report presenting your analyses and conclusions.

**P 15-3** (Research Problem) Study the GASB's statement of objectives of accounting and reporting for governmental units and compare them with the current principles and practices discussed in Chapters 2 to 14. Prepare a 10- to 20-page report analyzing the extent to which current GAAP fulfills the objectives and how well they would be fulfilled if the proposed core financial statements were presented instead.

**P 15-4** (Research Problem) Obtain a copy of several of GASB's research studies on service efforts and accomplishments. Prepare a 10- to 20-page report discussing the potential benefits and limitations of such reports. Discuss what the GASB's role should be in service efforts and accomplishments reporting.

**P 15-5** (Research Problem) Obtain a copy of a recent GASB Discussion Memorandum or Preliminary Views document and research the issues involved in depth. Prepare a 10- to 20-page report that explains and justifies the accounting and reporting alternative that you consider most appropriate.

CHAPTER

# 16

# ACCOUNTING
# FOR COLLEGES
# AND UNIVERSITIES

The development of accounting and reporting principles for colleges and universities followed a pattern almost identical to that of municipalities. A few publications on the subject appeared during the 1910–1935 era; the first attempt at standardization, undertaken cooperatively by the various regional associations of college and university business officers, was published in 1935. This was followed by a series of interpretive and advisory studies by the American Council on Education (ACE) during the 1935–1942 period.

A National Committee on the Preparation of a Manual on College and University Business Administration prepared *College and University Business Administration.* This two-volume work, published by the ACE in 1952 and 1955, respectively, was the first authoritative publication covering all areas of higher education business administration. A one-volume 1968 revised edition of *College and University Business Administration*[1] *(CUBA)* found widespread acceptance in practice and in textbooks on college and university accounting.

The AICPA Committee on College and University Accounting and Auditing prepared *Audits of Colleges and Universities,*[2] an industry audit guide issued in 1973. The audit guide basically endorsed *CUBA* as a primary authoritative source of generally accepted accounting principles.

In 1979, the FASB assumed responsibility for all nonbusiness organization (except government) accounting and reporting standards and designated those in the audit guide preferable standards pending any FASB statements on college and university accounting and reporting.[3] Pending possible FASB pronouncements related to colleges and universities, the fourth edition of *CUBA,* issued in 1982, did not include a comprehensive revision of college and university financial account-

---

[1] *College and University Business Administration,* rev. ed. (Washington, D.C.: American Council on Education, 1968). Specifically, see Part 2, "Principles of Accounting and Reporting"; Appendix A, "The Chart of Accounts"; and Appendix B, "Illustrative Forms."

[2] Committee on College and University Accounting and Auditing, American Institute of Certified Public Accountants, *Audits of Colleges and Universities* (New York: AICPA, 1973).

[3] Financial Accounting Standards Board, *Statement of Financial Accounting Standards No. 32,* "Specialized Accounting and Reporting Principles and Practices in AICPA Statements of Position and Guides on Accounting and Auditing Matters" (Stamford, Conn.: FASB, September 1979). (Rescinded by SFAS 111 in 1992).

ing and reporting principles.[4] The National Association of College and University Business Officers (NACUBO) replaced the CUBA accounting and reporting guidance in 1990 with its *Financial Accounting and Reporting Manual for Higher Education* (FARM) loose-leaf manual.[5]

In 1984 the FASB-GASB jurisdiction agreement granted the GASB authority for establishing standards for colleges and universities that are part of state and local governments. This created the possibility of different standards for government and private colleges and universities.

From 1984 to 1992, FASB standards were presumed to apply to state and local government (SLG) entities unless the GASB issued a negative standard to the contrary. One of the four GASB negative statements issued during the 1984–1992 period was directed specifically to SLG colleges and universities. FASB *Statement No. 93,* "Recognition of Depreciation by Not-for-Profit Organizations," requires nongovernmental colleges and universities to report depreciation. However, the GASB stated that government colleges and universities should not change their accounting practices as a result of FASB *Statement No. 93.*[6]

The new AICPA GAAP hierarchy that became effective in 1992 eliminated the need for GASB to issue negative standards on college and university accounting and reporting standards. However, it also left the status of the related NACUBO and AICPA guidance in doubt. But GASB *Statement No. 15,* "Governmental College and University Accounting and Financial Reporting Models,"[7] gives the guidance in the AICPA audit and accounting guide—which is based on the NACUBO literature—the highest (Rule 203) status under the new government GAAP hierarchy. A further result of GASB *Statement No. 15* is that the FASB standards on accounting for not-for-profit organizations that are discussed in Chapter 18 cannot be applied to government colleges and universities. Those standards—SFAS 116, *Accounting for Contributions Received and Contributions Made,* and SFAS 117, *Financial Statements of Not-for-Profit Organizations*—conflict with GASB *Statement No. 15.* Thus, subject to any related GASB pronouncements, the NACUBO *Financial Accounting and Reporting Manual for Higher Education (FARM)* and the AICPA audit (and accounting) guide, as amended, are the most authoritative sources of government college and university accounting and reporting principles. Accordingly, this chapter is based on those recommendations. Alternatively, government colleges and universities are permitted to use the governmental reporting standards that apply to cities, counties, states, and so on. Few government colleges choose this alternative.

As discussed in Chapter 18, FASB SFASs 116, 117, and 124 apply to all nongovernment, not-for-profit organizations—including not-for-profit colleges. These standards are illustrated in Chapter 18. The key differences between government and nongovernment colleges and universities are discussed briefly at the end of Chapter 18. Therefore, they are not emphasized here.

---

[4] National Association of College and University Business Officers, *College and University Business Administration,* 4th ed. (Washington, D.C.: NACUBO, 1982). Hereafter cited as *CUBA.*

[5] National Association of College and University Business Officers, *Financial Accounting and Reporting Manual for Higher Education* (Washington, D.C.: NACUBO, 1990). Hereafter cited as *FARM.*

[6] Governmental Accounting Standards Board, *Statement No. 8,* "Applicability of FASB *Statement No. 93,* 'Recognition of Depreciation by Not-for-Profit Organizations,' to Certain State and Local Governmental Entities" (Stamford, Conn.: GASB, January 1988).

[7] Governmental Accounting Standards Board, *Statement No. 15,* "Governmental College and University Accounting and Financial Reporting Models" (Norwalk, Conn.: GASB, October 1991).

# OVERVIEW

Government college and university accounting and reporting share numerous similarities with municipal accounting and reporting. Among the features shared with municipalities is the fund principle.

## Fund Groups

Both *FARM* and the AICPA audit guide, *Audits of Colleges and Universities,* endorse the use of the following fund groups by colleges and universities:

| *Fund Group* | *Major Subdivisions* |
|---|---|
| 1. Current Funds | Current Funds—Unrestricted |
| | Current Funds—Restricted |
| 2. Plant Funds | Unexpended Plant Funds |
| | Funds for Renewals and Replacements |
| | Funds for Retirement of Indebtedness |
| | Investment in Plant |
| 3. Loan Funds | |
| 4. Endowment and Similar Funds | Endowment Funds ("pure" or "true") |
| | Term Endowment Funds |
| | Quasi-Endowment Funds (Funds Functioning as Endowment) |
| 5. Annuity and Life Income Funds | Annuity Funds |
| | Life Income Funds |
| 6. Agency Funds | |

Because the last four fund groups are all fiduciary fund groups, college and university funds may be discussed and illustrated in three broad categories—Current Funds, Plant Funds, and Trust and Agency Funds.

These fund groups are based on the restrictions on and the purposes of the funds. A college or university may (1) establish several separate fund entities of each group, as needed, but prepare its financial reports on a fund group basis, or (2) maintain only one fund accounting entity for each fund group and account for the subfunds on an intrafund "funds within a fund" basis. Either approach is acceptable; however, within each of the fund groups each fund must, as a minimum, have separate accounts to show its fund balance and the results of its operations. These fund groups are discussed and illustrated more fully following a brief comparison of the major features of government college and university accounting and reporting with those of municipalities.

## Comparison with State and Local Government Accounting

Many of the features of government college and university accounting are similar to their counterparts in municipal accounting. Recognizing these similarities facilitates understanding government college and university accounting.

### Fund Structure

As Figure 16–1 illustrates, there are many similarities between the fund structure of colleges and universities and those of state and local governments (SLGs). For example, the Unrestricted Current Fund is essentially the same as a SLG's General Fund. Likewise, the Plant Fund for Retirement of Indebtedness is used to account for the same types of resources as a SLG Debt Service Fund. Also note the parallels between the fund structures; throughout the remainder of this chapter, and observe the similarities and differences in usage of each college and university fund compared to each SLG fund.

### Measurement Focus

As with accounting for governmental funds of SLGs, college and university accounting and reporting is concerned primarily with measuring and **reporting revenues and expenditures**—funds flows and balances—rather than determining net

**FIGURE 16–1  Summary Comparison of Fund Structures of Colleges and Universities and Municipalities**

| Primary Purpose of Funds and Account Groups | State and Local Governments | Government Colleges and Universities |
|---|---|---|
| Finance current operations | General<br>Special Revenue (and Expendable Trust) | Unrestricted Current<br>Restricted Current* |
| Fiduciary responsibilities | Nonexpendable Trust | Loan<br>Endowment and Similar:<br>  Endowment (true)<br>  Term Endowment<br>  Quasi-Endowment<br>Annuity and Life Income:<br>  Annuity<br>  Life Income |
|  | Agency | Agency |
| Acquisitions of and accountability for major fixed assets and related long-term debt | Capital Projects‡<br><br>Debt Service<br><br>General Fixed Assets/General Long-Term Debt | Plant:<br>  Unexpended<br>  For Renewals and Replacements<br>  For Retirement of Indebtedness<br>  Investment in Plant |

\* Restricted Current Funds revenue is considered realized and hence is recognized as revenue only to the extent that it has been expended for the specified purpose.

‡ Financial resources for renewals and replacements of SLG fixed assets may be accounted for in the General Fund or in Capital Projects, Expendable Trust, or Special Revenue Funds, as appropriate to the restrictions on or purpose of these resources and their materiality.

income of the organization. Thus, depreciation expense is not recorded in the Current Funds of colleges and universities (nor in governmental funds of SLGs). However, accumulated depreciation may be recorded in a university's Investment in Plant accounts in the same manner as is permitted for general fixed assets of SLGs in the General Fixed Assets Account Group. Finally, accounting and reporting for interfund transfers of colleges and universities is similar to that for SLGs; and accounting for restricted contributions and restricted investment earnings is similar to that for restricted grants in governments.

### Financial Statements

In reporting for government colleges and universities, as in SLG governmental funds:

1. Combined balance sheets and operating statements are presented.
2. Statements analyzing changes in fund balances are major operating statements for most fund groups.

Note, however, that only the Current Funds are reported in the statement of revenues, expenditures, and other changes of a government college or university.

### Budgetary Accounts and Subsidiary Ledgers

The current period expenditures of both government colleges and universities and governments are typically controlled by budgets or appropriations. Thus, budgetary accounts often are established in the Current Funds of colleges and universities as in governmental funds of governments. Both account for and report encumbrances, and government university statements setting forth detailed revenues and expenditures for the year may include budgetary comparisons as in SLG reporting.

Likewise, as in accounting for governmental funds of state and local governments, both Revenues Subsidiary Ledgers and Expenditures Subsidiary Ledgers are employed in government college and university accounting. However, this chapter focuses on general ledger accounting for transactions and events. Therefore, subsidiary ledger entries are not illustrated.

## Chapter Overview

Many of the main aspects of college and university accounting and reporting may be observed from the presentations in Figure 16–1 (discussed earlier) and Figure 16–2. Figure 16–2 provides an overview of the college and university fund structure, revenue and expenditure recognition, and interfund relationships. Study this figure now for an overview of government college and university accounting and reporting. Also refer to it in studying the remainder of the chapter to reinforce your understanding of the principles and concepts in the chapter; and use it as a basis for reviewing the chapter.

Each of the fund groups commonly found in government college and university accounting is discussed more fully in the following pages. These discussions are illustrated by means of a continuing case example. For simplicity of illustration we assume that A Government University is in its first full year of operation, though some of the physical plant was acquired in the preceding year.

**FIGURE 16-2  Government College and University Accounting Overview**

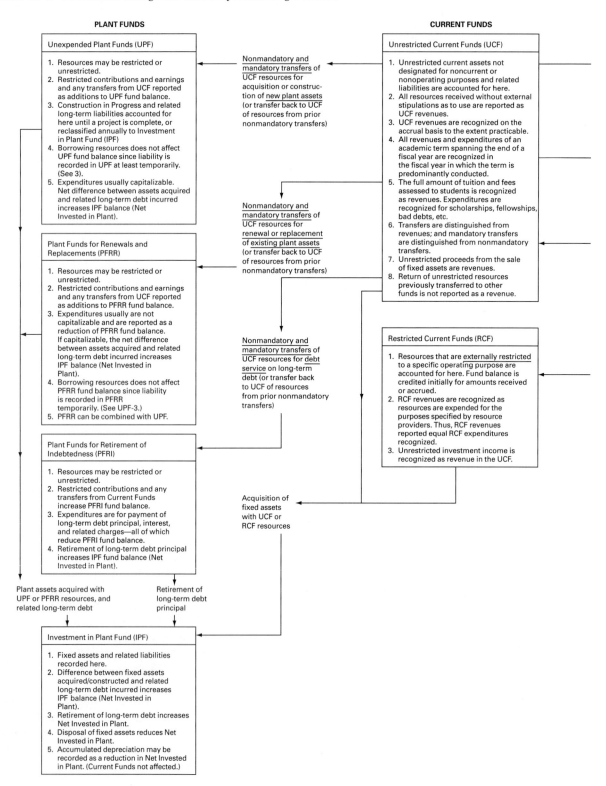

**PLANT FUNDS**

**Unexpended Plant Funds (UPF)**

1. Resources may be restricted or unrestricted.
2. Restricted contributions and earnings and any transfers from UCF reported as additions to UPF fund balance.
3. Construction in Progress and related long-term liabilities accounted for here until a project is complete, or reclassified annually to Investment in Plant Fund (IPF).
4. Borrowing resources does not affect UPF fund balance since liability is recorded in UPF at least temporarily. (See 3).
5. Expenditures usually capitalizable. Net difference between assets acquired and related long-term debt incurred increases IPF balance (Net Invested in Plant).

**Plant Funds for Renewals and Replacements (PFRR)**

1. Resources may be restricted or unrestricted.
2. Restricted contributions and earnings and any transfers from UCF reported as additions to PFRR fund balance.
3. Expenditures usually are not capitalizable and are reported as a reduction of PFRR fund balance. If capitalizable, the net difference between assets acquired and related long-term debt incurred increases IPF balance (Net Invested in Plant).
4. Borrowing resources does not affect PFRR fund balance since liability is recorded in PFRR temporarily. (See UPF-3.)
5. PFRR can be combined with UPF.

**Plant Funds for Retirement of Indebtedness (PFRI)**

1. Resources may be restricted or unrestricted.
2. Restricted contributions and any transfers from Current Funds increase PFRI fund balance.
3. Expenditures are for payment of long-term debt principal, interest, and related charges—all of which reduce PFRI fund balance.
4. Retirement of long-term debt principal increases IPF fund balance (Net Invested in Plant).

Plant assets acquired with UPF or PFRR resources, and related long-term debt

Retirement of long-term debt principal

**Investment in Plant Fund (IPF)**

1. Fixed assets and related liabilities recorded here.
2. Difference between fixed assets acquired/constructed and related long-term debt incurred increases IPF balance (Net Invested in Plant).
3. Retirement of long-term debt increases Net Invested in Plant.
4. Disposal of fixed assets reduces Net Invested in Plant.
5. Accumulated depreciation may be recorded as a reduction in Net Invested in Plant. (Current Funds not affected.)

Nonmandatory and mandatory transfers of UCF resources for acquisition or construction of new plant assets (or transfer back to UCF of resources from prior nonmandatory transfers)

Nonmandatory and mandatory transfers of UCF resources for renewal or replacement of existing plant assets (or transfer back to UCF of resources from prior nonmandatory transfers)

Nonmandatory and mandatory transfers of UCF resources for debt service on long-term debt (or transfer back to UCF of resources from prior nonmandatory transfers)

Acquisition of fixed assets with UCF or RCF resources

**CURRENT FUNDS**

**Unrestricted Current Funds (UCF)**

1. Unrestricted current assets not designated for noncurrent or nonoperating purposes and related liabilities are accounted for here.
2. All resources received without external stipulations as to use are reported as UCF revenues.
3. UCF revenues are recognized on the accrual basis to the extent practicable.
4. All revenues and expenditures of an academic term spanning the end of a fiscal year are recognized in the fiscal year in which the term is predominantly conducted.
5. The full amount of tuition and fees assessed to students is recognized as revenues. Expenditures are recognized for scholarships, fellowships, bad debts, etc.
6. Transfers are distinguished from revenues; and mandatory transfers are distinguished from nonmandatory transfers.
7. Unrestricted proceeds from the sale of fixed assets are revenues.
8. Return of unrestricted resources previously transferred to other funds is not reported as a revenue.

**Restricted Current Funds (RCF)**

1. Resources that are externally restricted to a specific operating purpose are accounted for here. Fund balance is credited initially for amounts received or accrued.
2. RCF revenues are recognized as resources are expended for the purposes specified by resource providers. Thus, RCF revenues reported equal RCF expenditures recognized.
3. Unrestricted investment income is recognized as revenue in the UCF.

FIGURE 16–2 *(Continued)*

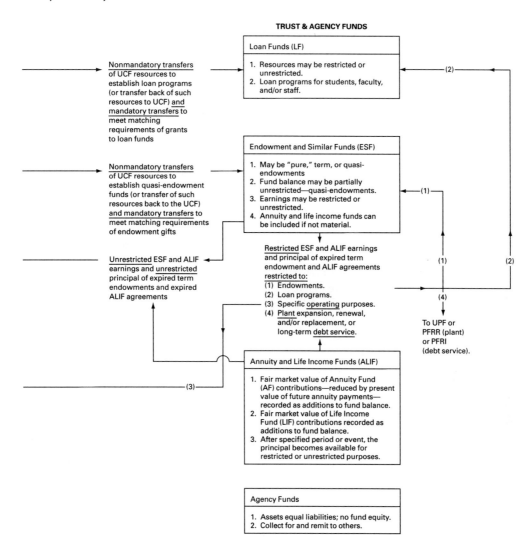

**TRUST & AGENCY FUNDS**

Loan Funds (LF)

1. Resources may be restricted or unrestricted.
2. Loan programs for students, faculty, and/or staff.

Nonmandatory transfers of UCF resources to establish loan programs (or transfer back of such resources to UCF) and mandatory transfers to meet matching requirements of grants to loan funds

Endowment and Similar Funds (ESF)

1. May be "pure," term, or quasi-endowments
2. Fund balance may be partially unrestricted—quasi-endowments.
3. Earnings may be restricted or unrestricted.
4. Annuity and life income funds can be included if not material.

Nonmandatory transfers of UCF resources to establish quasi-endowment funds (or transfer of such resources back to the UCF) and mandatory transfers to meet matching requirements of endowment gifts

Restricted ESF and ALIF earnings and principal of expired term endowment and ALIF agreements restricted to:
(1) Endowments.
(2) Loan programs.
(3) Specific operating purposes.
(4) Plant expansion, renewal, and/or replacement, or long-term debt service.

Unrestricted ESF and ALIF earnings and unrestricted principal of expired term endowments and expired ALIF agreements

To UPF or PFRR (plant) or PFRI (debt service).

Annuity and Life Income Funds (ALIF)

1. Fair market value of Annuity Fund (AF) contributions—reduced by present value of future annuity payments—recorded as additions to fund balance.
2. Fair market value of Life Income Fund (LIF) contributions recorded as additions to fund balance.
3. After specified period or event, the principal becomes available for restricted or unrestricted purposes.

Agency Funds

1. Assets equal liabilities; no fund equity.
2. Collect for and remit to others.

---

REVENUE AND EXPENDITURE RECOGNITION SUMMARY

1. All university revenues and expenditures recognized are recorded in the Current Funds.
2. Unrestricted revenues are recognized immediately as UCF revenues; UCF expenditures are recognized when liabilities to be paid from UCF resources are incurred.
3. Restricted appropriations, contributions, gifts and grants, and interest earnings are recorded as fund balance increases of the RCF, Plant Funds, or Trust Funds—depending on whether they are for operating (RCF), plant, or trust purposes.
4. RCF revenues are recognized when RCF expenditures are incurred for the specified restricted purposes.
5. Plant and Trust Funds revenues and expenditures are not recognized as university revenues or expenditures. However, unrestricted earnings and the unrestricted principal of expired term endowments and ALIF agreements are recognized as UCF revenues.

# CURRENT FUNDS

Current Funds financial resources available for current operations may be either restricted or unrestricted. Typically they may be used either for general educational purposes or for auxiliary enterprises. A careful distinction should be maintained between Unrestricted Current Funds and Restricted Current Funds, as the accounting and reporting procedures are quite different for these two subgroups of Current Funds.

## Unrestricted Current Funds

The Unrestricted Current Funds subgroup includes those financial resources of the institution that have not been restricted externally (by grantors, donors, and so on) for specific purposes and are expendable for any legal and reasonable purpose agreed upon by the governing board in carrying out the primary purposes of the institution (e.g., instruction, research, public service). Thus, the Unrestricted Current Funds are similar to the General Fund of a government. Resources restricted by donors, grantors, or outside agencies for specific current operating purposes are accounted for in the Restricted Current Funds.

Unrestricted Current Funds resources that are designated by the governing board to serve as loan or quasi-endowment funds, or to be expended for plant purposes, are transferred to the Loan, Endowment, and Plant Funds, respectively. Such unrestricted amounts are distinguished from the restricted portions of those funds by using Fund Balance—Unrestricted and Fund Balance—Restricted accounts. Unrestricted Current Funds resources that are designated by the governing board for specific current operating purposes should be accounted for in the Unrestricted Current Funds, either as formal appropriations or as allocations, designations, or reservations of the fund balance, as appropriate.

## Restricted Current Funds

The Restricted Current Funds subgroup is used to account for resources that are expendable but are restricted by donors, grantors, or other outside agencies to expenditure for specific operating purposes. Municipalities use Special Revenue Funds to account for such resources. Revenue is recognized on the same basis as that for restricted grants in SLG accounting. **Earnings of or contributions to Restricted Current Funds are not recognized as revenue when received. Instead, revenues are recognized when fund resources are expended for their intended purpose.** Amounts received or accrued are credited initially to a Fund Balance account. Prior to preparation of financial statements, an amount equal to that expended for the restricted purpose is deducted from the appropriate Fund Balance account and added to the appropriate Revenues account. Thus, Restricted Current Funds revenues and expenditures are typically equal.

The more common additions to Restricted Current Funds include (1) restricted gifts for specific operating purposes; (2) restricted endowment income; and (3) grants received from private organizations or governments for research, public service, or other specific purposes. Reductions of Restricted Current Funds fund balances result from (1) expenditures charged to the funds; (2) refunds to donors and grantors; and (3) transfers to the Unrestricted Current Funds for indirect cost recoveries on sponsored programs, if the resources were initially accounted for in the Restricted Current Funds. (Any unrestricted resources received as indirect cost recoveries may be recorded directly in the Unrestricted Current Funds.)

The Fund Balance accounts are titled according to restricted use or source, such as:

> Fund Balances:
>> Restricted Income from Endowment Funds
>> Gifts Restricted for Operating Purposes
>> Federal Government Grants for Research
>> Auxiliary Enterprises

The Fund Balance accounts may be separately titled in the general ledger, the subsidiary ledger, or in both ledgers. Furthermore, the governing board may designate portions of these balances for specific purposes or projects permissible under the restrictions placed on them. Thus, even more detailed Fund Balance accounts may be required.

## Current Funds Revenues and Expenditures

Current Funds revenues are accounted for essentially on the accrual basis and are classified by source. Typical revenue sources include:

1. Tuition and fees
2. Appropriations from various levels of government
3. Government grants and contracts
4. Private gifts, grants, and contracts
5. Endowment income
6. Sales and services of educational activities

Expenditures result from using resources of the Current Funds group to finance the current operations of a college or university. Current Funds expenditures are recognized when liabilities to be paid from the Current Funds are incurred. Current Funds expenditures are reported by function, and educational and general expenditures are reported separately from auxiliary enterprise and hospital expenditures. Functional classifications of educational and general expenditures include:

1. Instruction
2. Research
3. Public service
4. Academic support
5. Student services
6. Institutional support
7. Operation and maintenance of plant
8. Scholarships and fellowships

The major Revenues, Expenditures, and Transfers accounts recommended in *FARM* are presented in Figure 16–3. More detailed accounts would be established in practice, of course—in the general ledger, in the subsidiary ledger(s), or in both ledgers. For ease of illustration, we use only general ledger control accounts in the illustrative entries in this chapter.

**FIGURE 16–3 Classification of Current Funds Revenues, Expenditures, and Transfers**

| *Revenues* | *Expenditures and Transfers* |
|---|---|
| Tuition and Fees | Educational and General |
| Appropriations | Instruction |
| Federal | Research |
| State | Public Service |
| Local | Academic Support, e.g., |
| Grants and Contracts | Computing Services |
| Federal | Libraries |
| State | Student Services, e.g., |
| Local | Counseling and Career Guidance |
| Private Gifts, Grants, and Contracts | Dean of Students |
| Endowment Income | Financial Aid Administration |
| Sales and Services of Educational | Intramural Athletics |
| Activities, e.g., | Institutional Support, e.g., |
| Film Rentals | Legal Counsel |
| Testing Services | Alumni Office |
| Sales and Services of Auxiliary | Purchasing |
| Enterprises, e.g., | Operation and Maintenance of Plant |
| Residence Halls | Scholarships and Fellowships |
| Food Services | Mandatory Transfers |
| College Union | Nonmandatory Transfers |
| Athletic Programs | Auxiliary Enterprises, Hospitals, and Other |
| Sales and Services of Hospitals | Auxiliary Enterprises |
| Other Sources | Hospitals |
| Independent Operations | Independent Operations |

*Source:* National Association of College and University Business Officers, *Financial Accounting and Reporting Manual for Higher Education* (Washington, D.C.: NACUBO, 1990–1998).

## Transfers

Transfers of resources to or from other funds may result in nonrevenue and nonexpenditure changes in the fund balances of Current Funds. Transfers are nonloan movements of financial resources from one fund group to another in order for the resources to be used for the objectives of the recipient fund group. Transfers may involve either Unrestricted Current Funds or Restricted Current Funds, but transfers involving Unrestricted Current Funds are far more common. Whereas other governments distinguish operating and residual equity transfers, government colleges and universities distinguish **mandatory transfers** and **nonmandatory transfers.**

If the board, at its discretion, directs that a portion of the Current Funds resources be set aside for a noncurrent or nonoperating purpose, a nonmandatory (discretionary) transfer to other funds—not an expenditure—is reported as a Current Funds fund balance decrease. Likewise, the return of previously transferred resources to the Current Funds is reported as a nonmandatory transfer from other funds in the Current Funds—not as revenues. Mandatory transfers, on the other hand, are legally or contractually required transfers of Current Funds resources to other funds—such as required transfers to the Plant Funds for Retirement of Indebtedness to provide for debt service and transfers to Loan Funds required by federal grants. No mandatory transfers to the Current Funds are reported. Rather, required transfers of resources from other funds, such as the transfer of unrestricted Endowment Funds earnings—initially recorded in the Endowment Funds—to the Current Funds are recorded and reported by source of resources (e.g., endowment income).

The terms *mandatory transfer* and *nonmandatory transfer* are unique to government college and university accounting. *FARM* further defines and explains them as follows:

> Mandatory transfers. Transfers from the Current Funds group to other fund groups arising out of (1) binding legal agreements related to the financing of educational plant, such as amounts for debt retirement, interest, and required provisions for renewals and replacements of plant, not financed from other sources; and (2) grant agreements with agencies of the federal government, donors, and other organizations to match gifts and grants to loan and other funds. Mandatory transfers may be required to be made from either unrestricted or restricted current funds.
>
> Nonmandatory transfers. Transfers from the Current Funds group to other fund groups made at the discretion of the governing board to serve a variety of objectives, such as additions to loan funds, additions to quasi-endowment funds, general or specific plant additions, voluntary renewals and replacements of plant, and prepayments on debt principal.[8]

Nonmandatory transfers also may include the retransfer of resources back to the Current Funds. Both mandatory transfers and nonmandatory transfers are reported separately from revenues and expenditures in government university operating statements.

## Revenue and Expenditure Recognition Conventions— Unrestricted Current Funds

Several revenue and expenditure recognition conventions of Unrestricted Current Funds accounting should be noted. These relate to (1) tuition and fee waivers and uncollectible accounts, (2) legally restricted fees, (3) academic terms that span two fiscal years, (4) auxiliary enterprises and hospitals, (5) expired endowments and other trusts, and (6) other special considerations.

### Tuition and Fee Waivers and Uncollectible Accounts

Accounting for tuition and fees has several unique features. One is that in college and university accounting, the full amount of the standard tuition and fees is recognized as revenues. Scholarships, fellowships, bad debts, and similar items are accounted for as expenditures.

For example, assume that Harvey College has gross tuition and fee charges for 19A of $20,000,000. Harvey College grants full or partial tuition waivers totaling $600,000 for the year, and estimates that $100,000 of the 19A tuition and fees will be uncollectible. The entries in the **Unrestricted Current Funds** accounts are:

| | | |
|---|---|---|
| Accounts Receivable | $20,000,000 | |
|   Revenues—Educational and General | | $20,000,000 |
| To record tuition and fees earned. | | |
| Expenditures—Educational and General—Tuition Waivers | $ 600,000 | |
| Expenditures—Educational and General—Bad Debts | 100,000 | |
|   Accounts Receivable | | $ 600,000 |
|   Allowance for Uncollectible Accounts | | 100,000 |
| To record expenditures for tuition waivers and estimated uncollectible accounts. | | |

[8] *FARM,* ¶340–341.

### Legally Restricted Fees

Another unique feature of government college and university accounting is the reporting of specific fees and other revenue sources that are legally or contractually pledged (externally restricted) to nonoperating purposes (such as debt service or plant construction or renovation). Where the full amount of such fees or other revenue sources is externally restricted to a nonoperating purpose, they are recorded as additions to the fund balance of the appropriate fund—for example, the Plant Funds in the examples cited earlier. Neither the assets nor revenues are recorded in the Unrestricted Current Funds. On the other hand, if only part of the specific fees or other revenue sources is legally or contractually pledged for nonoperating purposes, the full amount of the fees or other revenue sources is reported as revenues in the Unrestricted Current Funds. The restricted amount is reported as a mandatory transfer to the appropriate fund—for example, the Plant Funds in the example cited earlier.

To illustrate the latter situation, assume that a college charges student fees totaling $1,000,000. Also assume that 20% of the fees are restricted to payment of debt service on bonds issued to finance modernization and expansion of the college's student activity center. The entries required in the **Unrestricted Current Funds** are:

| | | |
|---|---:|---:|
| Cash . . . . . . . . . . . . . . . . . . . . . . . . . . . . . . . . . . . . . . . . . . . . . . . . . . . | $1,000,000 | |
|    Revenues—Tuition and Fees . . . . . . . . . . . . . . . . . . . . . . . . . . . . . | | $1,000,000 |
| To record student fee revenues. | | |
| Mandatory Transfers to Plant Funds . . . . . . . . . . . . . . . . . . . . . . . | $ 200,000 | |
|    Due to Plant Funds . . . . . . . . . . . . . . . . . . . . . . . . . . . . . . . . . . . . | | $ 200,000 |
| To record required transfer of student fees restricted for debt service to the Plant Funds. | | |

Even if none of the fees were restricted to a specific purpose, the governing board might allocate part of these resources for debt service, or plant construction or renovation, or some other specific purpose. The accounting treatment would differ from the foregoing example only in that the transfer of resources to the appropriate other fund group would be a nonmandatory (not mandatory) transfer. Likewise, the return of unrestricted resources that had been transferred previously to a Quasi-Endowment Fund or to the Plant Funds, for example, should be reported as a nonmandatory transfer, not as revenues, in the Statement of Current Funds Revenues, Expenditures, and Other Changes.

### Term Spanning Two Fiscal Years

A final practice related to tuition and fees concerns tuition and fees assessed for a term of instruction that spans two fiscal years. All tuition and fees assessed for that term of instruction are reported as revenues of the fiscal year in which the term is predominantly conducted, as are all expenditures incurred to finance that term.

For instance, if Forrest College's six-week summer term begins July 15 and its fiscal year ends July 31, the term is predominantly conducted in the next fiscal year. Thus, the $1,000,000 of tuition and fees charged and collected as of July 31 and the related expenditures of $250,000 should be recorded as follows in the **Unrestricted Current Funds:**

| | | |
|---|---|---|
| Cash . . . . . . . . . . . . . . . . . . . . . . . . . . . . . . . . . . . . . . . . . . . . . . . . . | $1,000,000 | |
|   Deferred Revenues . . . . . . . . . . . . . . . . . . . . . . . . . . . . . . . . . . . | | $1,000,000 |
| To record deferred revenues for the summer term. | | |
| Deferred Expenditures . . . . . . . . . . . . . . . . . . . . . . . . . . . . . . . . . . | $ 250,000 | |
|   Cash/Inventory/Payables . . . . . . . . . . . . . . . . . . . . . . . . . . . . . . | | $ 250,000 |
| To record deferred expenditures for the summer term. | | |

These deferred revenues and expenditures should be recognized as revenues and expenditures of the next fiscal year.

### Auxiliary Enterprises and Hospitals

Auxiliary enterprises are self-sustaining activities of a university—such as residence halls, food services, and bookstores—that provide goods or services to students, faculty, or staff and charge fees, often related to costs, for the goods or services. Auxiliary enterprises may be accounted for in a separate subfund, but their operating accounts are reported as part of the Current Funds. The fixed assets and long-term debts related to auxiliary enterprises are accounted for in the Plant Funds.

Auxiliary enterprises are not reported on a revenues and expenses basis as are proprietary funds of governments, but on a revenues, expenditures, and fund balances basis like that of SLG governmental funds. Thus, the "auxiliary enterprises" revenue category is used to account for all revenues generated through the operations of auxiliary enterprises. Likewise, all auxiliary enterprise expenditures are reported as such in the Current Funds operating statement.

Government university hospitals are similar to auxiliary enterprises. Some apply government hospital GAAP (Chapter 17), but our examples assume they apply *FARM* guidelines. Thus, hospital patient service revenues (net of deductions from revenues for discounts and allowances) and hospital revenues arising from other hospital services are reported in this revenue source category in the Unrestricted Current Funds. But restricted gifts, grants, or endowment income to be used for auxiliary enterprise or hospital operations are not immediately recognized as revenues. Rather, they are initially accounted for as Restricted Current Funds fund balance increases and then are reported as Restricted Current Funds revenues upon expenditure of the restricted resources for the specified operating purpose.

### Expired Endowments and Other Trusts

The principal of some endowment gifts received by a government college or university is not expendable (nonexpendable trust) for a specified term (e.g., 20 years). In addition to these term endowments, colleges and universities sometimes receive gifts with the stipulation that a fixed payment (annuity gifts) or the income earned on the donated assets (life income gifts) be paid to a specified beneficiary for some period of time. Upon expiration of the term or conditions of these gift agreements, the principal of the gifts may be expended for either restricted or unrestricted university purposes.

If the principal of a term endowment or of an annuity or life income agreement becomes available for unrestricted use by the university when its term expires, the principal of the expired gift agreement is recognized as Unrestricted Current Funds revenues upon its expiration. But if the principal for the expired endowment, annuity, or life income agreement is restricted to a specific use, it will not be reported as revenues. Rather, it will be added to the fund balance of the appropriate restricted use fund: Restricted Current Funds (for operations), Endowment Funds (held in trust), or Plant Funds (for capital outlay or debt service). Earnings on investments of restricted assets are accounted for similarly.

### Other Special Considerations

Several other accounting practices related to operations of colleges and universities should be noted. Significant amounts of inventory should be reported in the year-end balance sheet, and Expenditures should be increased or reduced, as appropriate, by the amount of the inventory change during the year. (This compares with the consumption or use method of inventory accounting by state and local governments.) Similarly, if significant amounts of service costs benefit subsequent periods, such prepayals should be recorded as deferred charges and the Expenditures account reduced.

Also, the "Deductions from Fund Balances" account may be encountered in higher education accounting and reporting. Refunds to donors and grantors, the return of unencumbered or unexpended balances of lapsed appropriations to the state, and similar transactions are recorded and reported as deductions from fund balances rather than as expenditures.

## Budgetary Accounts

As in other state and local governments, government colleges and universities typically use fixed-dollar budgeting. Thus, it usually is necessary to maintain budgetary control accounts for a college or university in much the same manner as for other governments.

Budgetary accounts may be incorporated in the ledger of either Unrestricted or Restricted Current Funds in a manner similar to that used in the General Fund of a municipality. Slightly different account titles are commonly used by colleges or universities, as compared with municipalities. Furthermore, the difference between estimated revenues and estimated expenditures is usually carried in an Unassigned Budget Balance or Unallocated Budget Balance account—similar to the Budgetary Fund Balance account used by some governments—during the period rather than in the Fund Balance account. Budgetary accounting for colleges and universities closely parallels that of a municipal General Fund, so it is not illustrated in this chapter.

## Transactions and Entries—Unrestricted Current Funds

Assume for purposes of illustration that two Current Funds accounting entities—an Unrestricted Current Fund and a Restricted Current Fund—are in use and that most auxiliary enterprises are accounted for as part of the Unrestricted Current Fund. The following are some typical Unrestricted Current Fund transactions and the entries to record them. Transactions 10, 11, and 12 require entries not only in the Unrestricted Current Fund but also in the Plant Funds; entry 13 requires an entry in the Endowment and Similar Funds; and entry 15 corresponds with entry 3 in the Restricted Current Fund illustration.

Note that while Figure 16–3 contains an excellent classification of Current Funds Revenues, Expenditures, and Transfers accounts, our illustrative examples use an even simpler approach for ease of illustration. Both revenues and expenditures are classified simply as either (1) educational and general or (2) auxiliary enterprises. Furthermore, Revenues Subsidiary Ledger and Expenditures Subsidiary Ledger entries are not illustrated because they would be similar to those illustrated for SLG General and Special Revenue Funds; only general ledger entries are presented in the example.

### Transactions and Entries

**1.** Educational and general revenues earned during the year amounted to $2,600,000, of which $2,538,000 has been collected.

| | | |
|---|---|---|
| (1) Cash ........................................... | $2,538,000 | |
| Accounts Receivable ............................ | 62,000 | |
| **Revenues—Educational and General** ............. | | $2,600,000 |
| To record educational revenues earned. | | |

Note that the gross amount of tuition and fees is recorded as revenues without regard to the ultimate collectibility of the amounts.

**2.** It is estimated that $2,000 of this year's accounts receivables will never be collected, and $12,000 of tuition scholarships were granted.

| | | |
|---|---|---|
| (2) **Expenditures—Educational and General** ............. | $  14,000 | |
| Accounts Receivable .......................... | | $  12,000 |
| Allowance for Uncollectible Accounts ............ | | 2,000 |
| To record provision for uncollectible accounts and scholarships. | | |

**3.** Other revenues of $700,000 were collected through auxiliary enterprises.

| | | |
|---|---|---|
| (3) Cash ........................................... | $ 700,000 | |
| **Revenues—Auxiliary Enterprises** ................ | | $ 700,000 |
| To record revenues of auxiliary enterprises. | | |

**4.** Total purchases of materials and supplies for the year amounted to $600,000, of which $560,000 has been paid.

| | | |
|---|---|---|
| (4) **Inventory of Materials and Supplies** ................ | $ 600,000 | |
| Cash ........................................ | | $ 560,000 |
| Accounts Payable ............................. | | 40,000 |
| To record purchases of materials and supplies. | | |

**5.** Materials and supplies used during the year amounted to $550,000, of which $250,000 is chargeable to educational and general activities and $300,000 to auxiliary enterprises.

| | | |
|---|---|---|
| (5) Expenditures—Educational and General ............. | $ 250,000 | |
| **Expenditures—Auxiliary Enterprises** ............... | 300,000 | |
| Inventory of Materials and Supplies .............. | | $ 550,000 |
| To record cost of materials and supplies used. | | |

**6.** Salaries and wages paid amounted to $2,200,000, of which $1,920,000 is chargeable to educational and general activities and $280,000 to auxiliary enterprises.

| | | |
|---|---|---|
| (6) Expenditures—Educational and General ............. | $1,920,000 | |
| Expenditures—Auxiliary Enterprises ............... | 280,000 | |
| Cash ........................................ | | $2,200,000 |
| To record salaries and wages paid. | | |

**7.** Legal fees, insurance, interest on money borrowed temporarily for operating purposes, and telephone and Internet expenditures, all chargeable to educational and general activities, amounted to $100,000; all had been paid by the end of the year.

(7) Expenditures—Educational and General .......... $100,000
    Cash ...................................... $100,000
    To record legal and insurance expenditures, interest
    on money borrowed for operating purposes, and
    telephone and Internet expenditures.

**8.** Other expenditures chargeable to auxiliary enterprises and paid for totaled $10,000.

(8) Expenditures—Auxiliary Enterprises .............. $ 10,000
    Cash ...................................... $ 10,000
    To record expenditures of auxiliary enterprises other
    than those for materials and supplies or for salaries.

**9.** Student aid cash grants totaled $8,000.

(9) Expenditures—Educational and General .......... $ 8,000
    Cash ...................................... $ 8,000
    To record student aid granted.

**10.** Unrestricted Current Funds cash, $25,000, was transferred to the Funds for Retirement of Indebtedness—as required by the terms of the loan agreement—to pay a scheduled installment of the mortgage note carried as a liability in the Investment in Plant accounts. (See entry 1, Funds for Retirement of Indebtedness.)

(10) **Mandatory Transfers to Plant Funds** .............. $ 25,000
    Cash ...................................... $ 25,000
    To record transfer to Plant Funds to provide for
    payment of mortgage note carried as a liability in
    the Plant Funds.

**11.** A $30,000 nonmandatory transfer was made from the Unrestricted Current Fund to the Unexpended Plant Funds for the purpose of financing additions to the plant. (See entry 2, Unexpended Plant Funds.)

(11) **Nonmandatory Transfers to Plant Funds** ........... $ 30,000
    Cash ...................................... $ 30,000
    To record transfers to Plant Funds for purposes of
    making additions to plant.

**12.** Unrestricted Current Funds cash, $10,000, was spent for equipment. (See entry 1, Investment in Plant.)

(12) Expenditures—Educational and General .......... $ 10,000
    Cash ...................................... $ 10,000
    To record cost of plant additions financed from the
    Unrestricted Current Fund.

Purchases of equipment and similar items are often financed directly from Current Funds resources as assumed here. The proper handling of other more significant plant additions is (1) to transfer financial resources to the Plant Funds and (2) to record the acquisition of the asset in that fund group. If that had been done for this example, Nonmandatory Transfers to Plant Funds would have been debited instead of Expenditures.

**13.** In accordance with a resolution of the board of trustees of the university, $100,000 was transferred from the Unrestricted Current Fund to the Endowment and Similar Funds group for the purpose of establishing a fund that is to function as an endowment. (See entry 10, Endowment and Similar Funds.)

(13) Nonmandatory Transfers to Endowment
    and Similar Funds ......................... $100,000
    Cash ...................................... $100,000
    To record transfer of cash to Endowment and Similar
    Funds group for the purpose of establishing a fund
    that is to function as an endowment.

**14.** The board of trustees voted to reserve $75,000 of the Unrestricted Current Fund resources for a computer use survey during the subsequent year.

(14) **Fund Balances—Unallocated** ..................... $   75,000
    **Fund Balances—Allocated** ..................... $   75,000
    To establish a fund balance reserve for the estimated
    cost of a computer use survey to be made during
    the subsequent period.

**15.** Indirect overhead recovery on sponsored research, $8,000, was paid from the Restricted Current Fund to the Unrestricted Current Fund. (See entry 3, Restricted Current Fund.)

(15) Cash ......................................... $    8,000
    Revenues—Educational and General ........... $    8,000
    To record receipt of indirect cost recovery on
    sponsored research from the Restricted Current
    Fund.

Recall that if the reimbursement for the indirect cost recoveries is initially identified or received separately from the restricted portion of the research grant, it may be recorded directly in the Unrestricted Current Funds as revenues—rather than being recorded in the Restricted Current Funds and later reclassified.

**16.** The university borrowed $6,000 for current operations.

(16) Cash ........................................ $    6,000
    Notes Payable ............................. $    6,000
    To record issuance of note for current operations.

**17.** Accrued interest on the note at year end was $100.

(17) Expenditures—Educational and General ........... $      100
    Accrued Interest Payable .................... $      100
    To accrue interest on note.

**18.** Revenue, expenditure, and transfer accounts were closed at year end.

(18) Revenues—Educational and General .............. $2,608,000
    Revenues—Auxiliary Enterprises ................    700,000
    Expenditures—Educational and General ......... $2,302,100
    Expenditures—Auxiliary Enterprises ............    590,000
    Mandatory Transfers to Plant Funds .............     25,000
    Nonmandatory Transfers to Plant Funds ..........     30,000
    Nonmandatory Transfers to Endowment
      and Similar Funds .........................    100,000
    Fund Balances—Unallocated ..................    260,900
    To close revenues, expenditures, and transfers
    accounts at year end.

## Transactions and Entries—Restricted Current Funds

The following are typical transactions of the Restricted Current Funds and the entries made to record them. Note in studying the illustration that the Fund Balance account is used essentially like a deferred revenue account. When revenues are received but not earned, the Fund Balance account is credited instead of Revenues. Once qualifying expenditures are made, Revenue is recognized by reducing the Fund Balance account.

**Transactions and Entries**

1. Cash receipts during the year were as follows:

| | |
|---|---:|
| Federally Sponsored Research (grant) ........ | $100,000 |
| Gifts—Library Operations ................ | 200,000 |
| Endowment Income—Supplemental Salary Payments ........................... | 62,400 |
| Endowment Income—Student Aid ......... | 15,600 |
| Endowment Income—Auxiliary Enterprise .. | 9,700 |
| | $387,700 |

(See also Endowment and Similar Funds, transaction 5.)

| | | |
|---|---:|---:|
| (1) Cash ......................................... | $387,700 | |
| **Fund Balances—Grants—Federally Sponsored Research** ................................ | | $100,000 |
| **Fund Balances—Gifts—Library Operations** ........ | | 200,000 |
| **Fund Balances—Endowment Income—Supplemental Salary Payments** ........................... | | 62,400 |
| **Fund Balances—Endowment Income—Student Aid** . | | 15,600 |
| **Fund Balances—Endowment Income—Auxiliary Enterprises** ................................ | | 9,700 |
| To record resources received. | | |

(Fund Balance subsidiary ledger accounts usually show the sources and purposes of the resources received or accrued. Alternatively, a series of Fund Balances general ledger accounts may be used, as is done here for clarity of illustration.)

2. Expenditures were incurred as follows, of which $7,000 remained unpaid at year end:

| | |
|---|---:|
| Sponsored Research .................... | $ 40,000 |
| Library Operations .................... | 130,000 |
| Instruction and Departmental Research (Supplemental Salary Payments) ......... | 50,000 |
| Student Aid .......................... | 12,000 |
| Auxiliary Enterprises .................... | 2,000 |
| | $234,000 |

| | | |
|---|---:|---:|
| (2) Expenditures—Educational and General ............ | $232,000 | |
| Expenditures—Auxiliary Enterprises .............. | 2,000 | |
| Accounts Payable ............................ | | $ 7,000 |
| Cash ........................................ | | 227,000 |
| To record expenditures incurred. | | |

3. Recovery of indirect costs of $8,000, associated with the $40,000 of sponsored research expenditures, was transferred to the Unrestricted Current Fund. (See also Unrestricted Current Fund, transaction 15.)

| | | |
|---|---:|---:|
| (3) **Fund Balances—Grants—Federally Sponsored Research** ................................ | $ 8,000 | |
| Cash ........................................ | | $ 8,000 |
| To record payment to Unrestricted Current Fund of indirect cost recovery under provisions of grant. | | |

(The indirect cost recovery revenue is recognized in the Unrestricted Current Fund in entry 15. Recall that in some instances indirect cost recoveries may be recorded directly in the Unrestricted Current Fund rather than being recorded initially in the Restricted Current Fund.)

**4.** Income due from the Endowment and Similar Funds group at year end was as follows:

| | |
|---|---|
| For Supplemental Salary Payments ......... | $25,000 |
| For Student Aid ....................... | 5,000 |
| | $30,000 |

(See also Endowment and Similar Funds, transaction 9.)

| | | |
|---|---|---|
| (4) Due from Endowment and Similar Funds ........... | $ 30,000 | |
|     **Fund Balances—Endowment Income—Supplemental Salary Payments** ............................ | | $ 25,000 |
|     **Fund Balances—Endowment Income—Student Aid** . | | 5,000 |
|     To record resources due from endowment earnings. | | |

**5.** Revenue for the period was recognized and fund balances were adjusted accordingly at year end.

| | | |
|---|---|---|
| (5) **Fund Balances—Grants—Federally Sponsored Research** ................................ | $ 40,000 | |
|     **Fund Balances—Gifts—Library Operations** ......... | 130,000 | |
|     **Fund Balances—Endowment Income—Supplemental Salary Payments** ............................ | 50,000 | |
|     **Fund Balances—Endowment Income—Student Aid** ... | 12,000 | |
|     **Fund Balances—Endowment Income—Auxiliary Enterprises** ............................. | 2,000 | |
|       **Revenues—Educational and General** ............ | | $232,000 |
|       **Revenues—Auxiliary Enterprises** ............... | | 2,000 |
|     To recognize revenues to the extent that restricted resources were expended during the period. | | |

(Compare this entry to entry 2. Note again that revenues are recognized only to the extent that the restricted resources have been expended for the purposes or functions designated by donors, grantors, or outside agencies.)

**6.** Closing entries were made.

| | | |
|---|---|---|
| (6) Revenues—Educational and General .............. | $232,000 | |
|     Revenues—Auxiliary Enterprises ................. | 2,000 | |
|       Expenditures—Educational and General .......... | | $232,000 |
|       Expenditures—Auxiliary Enterprises ............ | | 2,000 |
|     To close the revenues and expenditures accounts at year end. | | |

(Obviously, the entries to close the Revenues and Expenditures accounts must be in corresponding amounts in the case of Restricted Current Funds because revenue is realized only upon expenditure of the restricted resources.)

In each preceding case, less resources were expended (and recognized as revenue) than were received or accrued. Had fund balances been brought forward from prior years, the opposite might have been true. The logic of the realization (revenue recognition) convention employed in Restricted Current Funds accounting—as required by the GASB—is that the resources have not been earned until they have been expended for their restricted purposes.

## Government University Operating Statement—Current Funds

A Statement of Current Funds Revenues, Expenditures, and Other Changes, based on the journal entries for the two Current Funds subgroups, is presented in Figure 16–4. It shows the total revenues from each source and the total expenditures

**FIGURE 16–4 Statement of Current Funds Revenues, Expenditures, and Other Changes**

A Government University
**Statement of Current Funds Revenues,**
**Expenditures, and Other Changes**
For the Year Ended October 31, 19A

|  | Total | Unrestricted | Restricted |
|---|---|---|---|
| **Revenues:** | | | |
| Tuition and fees ........................ | $1,358,000 | $1,358,000 | $ — |
| State appropriations .................... | 1,000,000 | 1,000,000 | — |
| Federal grants and contracts ............. | 40,000 | — | 40,000 |
| State grants and contracts ............... | — | — | — |
| Local government grants and contracts ..... | 132,000 | 132,000 | — |
| Private gifts, grants, and contracts ........ | 130,000 | — | 130,000 |
| Endowment income .................... | 64,000 | — | 64,000 |
| Sales and services of educational activities .. | 68,000 | 68,000 | — |
| Sales and services of auxiliary enterprises ... | 700,000 | 700,000 | — |
| Expired term endowment ................. | — | — | — |
| Other sources (if any) .................. | 50,000 | 50,000 | — |
| Total Revenues ..................... | 3,542,000 | 3,308,000 | 234,000 |
| | | | |
| **Expenditures and mandatory transfers:** | | | |
| **Educational and general:** | | | |
| Instruction ......................... | 932,000 | 882,000 | 50,000 |
| Research .......................... | 140,000 | 100,000 | 40,000 |
| Public service ...................... | 50,000 | 50,000 | — |
| Academic support ................... | 330,000 | 200,000 | 130,000 |
| Student services .................... | 150,000 | 150,000 | — |
| Institutional support ................. | 400,100 | 400,100 | — |
| Operation and maintenance of plant .... | 500,000 | 500,000 | — |
| Scholarships and fellowships .......... | 32,000 | 20,000 | 12,000 |
| Total Educational and General | | | |
| Expenditures ................... | 2,534,100 | 2,302,100 | 232,000 |
| Mandatory transfers for: | | | |
| Principal and interest .............. | 25,000 | 25,000 | — |
| Renewals and replacements ......... | — | — | — |
| Loan fund matching grant .......... | — | — | — |
| Total Educational and General .... | 2,559,100 | $2,327,100 | 232,000 |
| **Auxiliary enterprises:** | | | |
| Expenditures: ...................... | 592,000 | 590,000 | 2,000 |
| Mandatory transfers for: | | | |
| Principal and interest .............. | — | — | — |
| Renewals and replacements ......... | — | — | — |
| Total Auxiliary Enterprises ....... | 592,000 | 590,000 | 2,000 |
| Total Expenditures and Mandatory | | | |
| Transfers .................... | 3,151,100 | 2,917,100 | 234,000 |
| | | | |
| **Other transfers and additions (deductions):** | | | |
| Excess of restricted receipts over transfers to | | | |
| revenues ........................... | 175,700 | — | 175,700 |
| Nonmandatory transfer to plant funds ...... | (30,000) | (30,000) | — |
| Nonmandatory transfer to Endowment and | | | |
| Similar Funds ....................... | (100,000) | (100,000) | — |
| | | | |
| **Net Increase in Fund Balance** .............. | $ 436,600 | $ 260,900 | $175,700 |

for each major activity, both classified as to whether they pertain to Unrestricted or Restricted Current Funds.

Because detailed revenue and expenditure accounts are not used in the journal entries in this chapter, the most common accounts (see Figure 16–3) are listed in Figure 16–4. The amounts presented in the "Restricted Current Funds" columns are properly classified, as are the mandatory and nonmandatory transfers and auxiliary enterprises revenues and expenditures. The other amounts in the "Unrestricted Current Funds" columns have been allocated (arbitrarily) among the more common revenue and expenditure accounts solely for illustrative purposes. Also, some accounts with zero balances are included for illustrative purposes. Schedules of the details of the current revenues and expenditures, and of the transfers, should be prepared for internal uses. For example, details of the operations of each department should be shown, and a separate statement of revenues and expenditures should be prepared for each of the auxiliary activities.

## BALANCE SHEET—FOR A GOVERNMENT UNIVERSITY

A Balance Sheet for the university at the close of the fiscal year is presented in Figure 16–5. Data from the transactions already presented for the Unrestricted Current and Restricted Current Funds are the bases of the balance sheet for the Current Funds group. The year-end balance sheets of the other funds or fund groups (after the transactions discussed later) are added to the balance sheets of the two types of funds already discussed.

This "pancake" form of the university-wide balance sheet seems to be the preferred form, though college and university balance sheets are often presented in columnar form. Even though like balances of the several fund groups are placed on the same line using a columnar format, no total column is usually provided. This recognizes that assets and liabilities of the fund groups are in most cases subject to legal or donor restrictions and other obligations that may make it misleading to show totals for the university as a whole.

## PLANT FUNDS

As noted earlier, government college and university fixed assets and long-term debt are not accounted for in the Current Funds group. Instead, the fixed assets and long-term liabilities are accounted for in the Plant Funds group. Any financial resources that are internally designated or externally restricted either to plant expansion, renewal, or replacement or to servicing long-term debt also are accounted for in the Plant Funds.

The Plant Funds consist of four fund subgroups:

1. *Unexpended Plant Funds:* to account for resources to be used for the acquisition of institutional fixed assets.

2. *Funds for Renewals and Replacements:* to account for resources to be used for the remodeling, renovation, or replacement of existing fixed assets.

3. *Funds for Retirement of Indebtedness:* to account for resources to be used to service the debt incurred in relation to the physical plant.

4. *Investment in Plant:* to account for the institution's fixed assets, related indebtedness, and net investment in plant.

**FIGURE 16–5  Year-End Balance Sheet—All Funds**

A Government University
**Balance Sheet**
October 31, 19A

| Assets | | | Liabilities and Fund Balances | | |
|---|---:|---:|---|---:|---:|
| **Current Funds:** | | | **Current Funds:** | | |
| **Unrestricted:** | | | **Unrestricted:** | | |
| Cash | | $ 209,000 | Accounts Payable | | $ 40,000 |
| Accounts receivable, less allowance for | | | Notes Payable | | 6,000 |
| uncollectible accounts of $2,000 | | 48,000 | Interest Payable | | 100 |
| Inventory of materials and supplies | | 50,000 | Fund balances | | 260,900 |
| Total unrestricted | | 307,000 | Total unrestricted | | 307,000 |
| **Restricted:** | | | **Restricted:** | | |
| Cash | | 152,700 | Accounts payable | | 7,000 |
| Due from endowment and similar funds | | 30,000 | Fund balances | | 175,700 |
| Total restricted | | 182,700 | Total restricted | | 182,700 |
| Total Current Funds | | $ 489,700 | Total Current Funds | | $ 489,700 |
| **Loan Funds:** | | | **Loan Funds:** | | |
| Cash | | $ 25,400 | Fund balances* | | $ 99,900 |
| Loans receivable | | 49,500 | | | |
| Investments | | 25,000 | | | |
| Total Loan Funds | | $ 99,900 | Total Loan Funds | | $ 99,900 |
| **Endowment and Similar Funds:** | | | **Endowment and Similar Funds:** | | |
| Assets other than fixed assets: | | | Due to restricted current funds | | $ 30,000 |
| Cash | | $ 205,500 | Fund balances:* | | |
| Investments: | | | Endowment | $2,926,500 | |
| Preferred stocks, at fair value | $ 500,000 | | Quasi-Endowment | 100,000 | 3,026,500 |
| Common stocks, at fair value | 1,065,000 | | | | |
| Bonds, at fair value | 456,000 | | | | |
| Held in trust by others (cost and fair | | | | | |
| value, $200,000) | | 2,021,000 | | | |
| | | 2,226,500 | | | |

**Assets side:**

| | | |
|---|--:|--:|
| Fixed assets: | | |
| Land | 100,000 | |
| Buildings, less accumulated depreciation of $6,000 | 594,000 | |
| Equipment, less accumulated depreciation of $14,000 | 136,000 | |
| | 830,000 | |
| **Total Endowment and Similar Funds** | | $3,056,500 |
| **Annuity and Life Income Funds:** | | |
| Cash | $ 10,000 | |
| Investments, at fair value | 176,000 | |
| **Total Annuity and Life Income Funds** | | $ 186,000 |
| **Plant Funds:** | | |
| **Unexpended:** | | |
| Cash | $ 318,000 | |
| Investments, at fair value | 20,000 | |
| | | 338,000 |
| Total unexpended | | 338,000 |
| **For retirement of indebtedness:** | | |
| Investments, at fair value | 25,000 | |
| Sinking fund—bank trustee | 200,000 | |
| | | 225,000 |
| Total for retirement of indebtedness | | 225,000 |
| **Investment in plant:** | | |
| Land | 300,000 | |
| Buildings, less accumulated depreciation of $4,159,000** | 3,841,000 | |
| Improvements other than building, less accumulated depreciation of $600** | 11,400 | |
| Equipment, less accumulated depreciation of $1,080,400** | 728,600 | |
| Library books | 200,000 | |
| Construction in progress | 240,000 | |
| Total investment in plant | | 5,321,000 |
| **Total Plant Funds** | | $5,884,000 |

**Liabilities and Fund Balances side:**

| | | |
|---|--:|--:|
| **Total Endowment and Similar Funds** | | $3,056,500 |
| **Annuity and Life Income Funds:** | | |
| Annuities payable | | $ 162,881 |
| Fund balances—Annuities* | | 23,119 |
| **Total Annuity and Life Income Funds** | | $ 186,000 |
| **Plant Funds:** | | |
| **Unexpended:** | | |
| Accounts payable | | $ 40,000 |
| Notes payable | | 260,000 |
| Fund balances—Unrestricted* | | 18,000 |
| Fund balances—Restricted | | 20,000 |
| Total unexpended | | 338,000 |
| **For retirement of indebtedness:** | | |
| Fund balances—Restricted* | | 225,000 |
| Total for retirement of indebtedness | | 225,000 |
| **Investment in plant:** | | |
| Notes payable | | 240,000 |
| Mortgage payable | | 370,000 |
| Net invested in plant* | | 4,711,000 |
| Total investment in plant | | 5,321,000 |
| **Total Plant Funds** | | $5,884,000 |

*Statements analyzing changes in the balances of each fund group should be presented in the financial report.

**State and local government colleges and universities are not required to report accumulated depreciation on Plant Funds assets but may elect to do so.

The Unexpended Plant Funds and the Funds for Renewals and Replacements are similar to Capital Projects Funds of municipalities; the Funds for Retirement of Indebtedness compare to Debt Service Funds of municipalities; and the Investment in Plant subgroup is like a combination of the General Fixed Assets and General Long-Term Debt Account Groups of a municipality.

All but the Investment in Plant subgroup are used primarily to account for financial resources (cash, investments, and so on). Sometimes these financial resources are recorded directly in the Plant Funds, as when (1) resources are dedicated by donors for plant purposes, and (2) specific student fees are assessed under binding external agreements for plant improvement or related debt service purposes. Other restricted financial resources may come from the Endowment and Similar Funds; and unrestricted resources may be transferred to the Plant Funds from the Unrestricted Current Funds. The distinction between unrestricted and restricted (externally) resources should be maintained in the accounts and reports (1) to ensure that the restricted resources are used for the proper purposes, and (2) because the governing board can transfer unrestricted resources back to the Unrestricted Current Funds or to the Endowment and Similar Funds.

For external reporting purposes all Plant Funds subgroups may be reported either separately or combined, as long as the separate fund balances are reported. Any encumbrances outstanding should be disclosed by a Reserve for Encumbrances or in the notes to the financial statements. The results of the transactions and entries of each Plant Funds subgroup are shown in the Balance Sheet presented in Figure 16–5 and in the Statement of Changes in Fund Balances presented in Figure 16–6 (pages 652–653). Plant Funds are not reported in the university's statement of revenues and expenditures.

## Unexpended Plant Funds

The purpose of the Unexpended Plant Funds is to account for the inflows, uses, and balances of financial resources (and any related liabilities) obtained from various sources to finance the acquisition of new long-lived plant assets. Most expenditures from this fund will ultimately be capitalized in the Investment in Plant accounts.

If debt is issued to finance a project, the debt is initially accounted for in the Unexpended Plant Funds. Expenditures are debited to Construction in Progress unless they are noncapitalizable, in which case they are debited to Fund Balance.

The Construction in Progress and any related liabilities should be reclassified from the Unexpended Plant Funds to the Investment in Plant accounts either (1) at each year end, or (2) at the conclusion of the project. When this is done at the end of each year, equal amounts of Construction in Progress and liabilities are moved to the Investment in Plant accounts until all liabilities have been reclassified; thereafter, Unexpended Plant Funds fund balance is reduced. Our example assumes that the reclassification occurs at the end of each fiscal year.

Some typical Unexpended Plant Funds transactions and the related entries are given below. Transaction 3 also affects the Investment in Plant accounts.

**Transactions and Entries**

**1.** An individual donated preferred stock valued at $20,000 to finance additions to the plant.

| | | |
|---|---|---|
| (1) Investments ....................................... | $20,000 | |
|     **Fund Balances—Restricted** ...................... | | $20,000 |

    To record investments donated for the purpose of financing additions to plant. (The Fund Balances account controls accounts for separate funds or subfunds in this subgroup.)

Note that government colleges and universities must apply the GASB *Statement No. 31* guidance on accounting for investments that all other government entities must apply.

2. Cash ($30,000) was transferred from the Unrestricted Current Fund to this subgroup to finance additions to the plant. (See transaction 11, Unrestricted Current Fund.)

(2)  Cash ........................................ $ 30,000
    **Fund Balances—Unrestricted** ................... $ 30,000
    To record receipt of cash from the Unrestricted Current
    Fund for the purpose of financing additions to plant.

3. A small house trailer costing $12,000 was purchased for cash. (See transaction 2, Investment in Plant.)

(3)  **Fund Balances—Unrestricted** ..................... $ 12,000
    Cash ....................................... $ 12,000
    To record purchase of a house trailer.

4. A $500,000 loan was secured to finance a building addition.

(4)  Cash ........................................ $500,000
    **Notes Payable** .............................. $500,000
    To record borrowing to finance a building addition.

5. By year end $240,000 of capitalizable building addition expenditures had been incurred, of which $200,000 had been paid.

(5)  **Construction in Progress** ........................ $240,000
    Cash ....................................... $200,000
    Accounts Payable ........................... 40,000
    To record capitalizable construction expenditures and
    the related payments.

6. The college reclassified the construction in progress from the Unexpended Plant Fund to the Investment in Plant accounts.

(6)  **Notes Payable** ................................ $240,000
    **Construction in Progress** ...................... $240,000
    To reclassify Construction in Progress and Notes
    Payable to the Investment in Plant accounts.

A corresponding entry will be made in the Investment in Plant accounts to record the Construction in Progress and Notes Payable in that subgroup. Also note that these costs are recorded as Construction in Progress because they are capitalizable. Noncapitalizable costs would have been recorded as reductions in the fund balance of the Unexpended Plant Funds.

## Funds for Renewals and Replacements

The Funds for Renewals and Replacements are accounted for in the same way as the Unexpended Plant Funds. The only difference is that the expenditures of this fund are for renewals and replacements of plant assets, most of which are charged to Fund Balance rather than being capitalized. In practice it is often difficult to distinguish betterments and improvements, which are capitalized, and expenditures for renewals and replacements, which are not capitalized. In any event, some of the expenditures of the Funds for Renewals and Replacements may properly be capitalized in the Investment in Plant accounts.

Again, the accounting and reporting for Funds for Renewals and Replacements are identical to that for the Unexpended Plant Funds. Indeed, this plant fund

**FIGURE 16–6  Statement of Changes in Fund Balances**

A Government University
**Statement of Changes in Fund Balances**
For the Year Ended October 31, 19A

| | Current Funds | | Loan Funds | Endowment and Similar Funds | Annuity and Life Income Funds | Plant Funds | | | |
|---|---|---|---|---|---|---|---|---|---|
| | Unrestricted | Restricted | | | | Unexpended | Renewal and Replacement | Retirement of Indebtedness | Investment In Plant |
| **Revenues and other additions:** | | | | | | | | | |
| Unrestricted Current Fund revenues | $3,308,000 | | | | | | | | |
| Expired term endowment—restricted | | xxx | | | | | | | |
| State appropriations—restricted | | xxx | | | | xxx | xxx | | |
| Federal grants and contracts—restricted | | 100,000 | xx | | | | | | |
| State grants and contracts | | xxx | | | | | | | |
| Local government grants and contracts | | xxx | | | | | | | |
| Private gifts, grants, and contracts—restricted | | 200,000 | 100,000 | 2,925,000 | xxx | 20,000 | xxx | 240,000 | |
| Endowment income—restricted | | 117,700 | | | | | xxx | | |
| Investment income—restricted | | xxx | 400 | 1,500 | | xxx | xxx | xxx | |
| Interest on loans receivable | | | xxx | | | | | | |
| Proceeds from disposal of plant facilities | | | | | | | xxx | | |
| Expended for plant facilities (including $10,000 charged to current funds expenditures) | | | | | | | | | 22,000 |
| Retirement of long-term debt principal | | | | | | | | | 30,000 |
| Matured annuity and life income funds— restricted to endowment | | | | xxx | | | | | |
| Gift in excess of actuarial liability for annuity payable | | | | | 24,411 | | | | |
| **Total revenues and other additions** | 3,308,000 | 417,700 | 100,400 | 2,926,500 | 24,411 | 20,000 | —— | 240,000 | 52,000 |

| | | | | | | | | |
|---|--:|--:|--:|--:|--:|--:|--:|--:|
| **Expenditures and other deductions:** | | | | | | | | |
| Educational and general expenditures | 2,302,100 | 232,000 | | | | | | |
| Auxiliary enterprises expenditures | 590,000 | 2,000 | | | | | | |
| Indirect costs recovered | | 8,000 | | | | | | |
| Refunded to grantors | | xxx | | | | | | |
| Loan cancellations and write-offs | | | 500 | | | | | |
| Administrative and collection costs | | | xxx | | | | | |
| Adjustment of actuarial liability for annuities payable | | | | | 1,292 | | | |
| Expended for plant facilities including noncapitalized expenditures of $xxx | | | | | | 100,000 | | |
| Retirement of long-term debt principal | | | | | | | 30,000 | |
| Interest on indebtedness | | | | | | | 10,000 | |
| Disposal of plant facilities | | | | | | | | 1,000 |
| Provision for depreciation* | | | | | | | | 230,000 |
| Expired term endowments ($xxx unrestricted, $xxx restricted to accounting program and plant) | | | | xxx | | | | |
| Matured annuity and life income funds restricted to endowment | | | | | xxx | | | |
| **Total expenditures and other deductions** | 2,892,100 | 242,000 | 500 | xxx | 1,292 | 100,000 | 40,000 | 231,000 |
| **Transfers among funds—additions/(deductions):** | | | | | | | | |
| **Mandatory:** | | | | | | | | |
| Principal and interest | (25,000) | | | | | | 25,000 | |
| Renewals and replacements | (xxx) | | | | | | | |
| Loan fund matching grant | (xxx) | | xxx | | | | | |
| **Nonmandatory:** | | | | | | | | |
| Additions to plant | (30,000) | | | | | 30,000 | | |
| Quasi-endowment | (100,000) | | | 100,000 | | | | |
| **Total transfers** | (155,000) | | | 100,000 | | 30,000 | 25,000 | |
| Net increase/(decrease) for the year | 260,900 | 175,700 | 99,900 | 3,026,500 | 23,119 | 38,000 | | (179,000) |
| Fund balance at beginning of year | | | | | | | | 4,890,000 |
| **Fund balance at end of year** | $ 260,900 | $175,700 | $ 99,900 | $3,026,500 | $23,119 | $38,000 | $225,000 | $4,711,000 |

*State and local government colleges and universities are not required to report a provision for depreciation of Plant Funds assets but may elect to do so.

653

subgroup may be combined with the Unexpended Plant Funds. Thus, we assume that A Government University does not have such a fund, and we do not illustrate any transactions or entries for the Funds for Renewals and Replacements subgroup.

## Funds for Retirement of Indebtedness

The Funds for Retirement of Indebtedness subgroup is used to account for the accumulation and expenditure of financial resources to service the institution's plant-related indebtedness. Payments of debt principal, interest, and fiscal agent fees are made from this fund. These payments reduce the fund balance of the funds for Retirement of Indebtedness. When debt principal payments are made from the funds for Retirement of Indebtedness, the additional net investment of the university in fixed assets is recognized in the Net Invested in Plant account (and the liability is reduced) in the Investment in Plant subgroup. Assets of the Funds for Retirement of Indebtedness are also sometimes required to be paid into debt service sinking funds. Such payments do not reduce the fund balance of the funds for Retirement of Indebtedness; rather, they are treated as investments of this subgroup.

The following are some typical transactions of this fund and the related entries. Transactions 2 and 4 affect not only this fund but also the Investment in Plant accounts.

**Transactions and Entries**

1. A mandatory transfer of $25,000 was received from the Unrestricted Current Fund. (See entry 10, Unrestricted Current Fund.)

   | | | | |
   |---|---|---|---|
   | (1) | Cash .......................................... | $25,000 | |
   | |     Fund Balances—Restricted ..................... | | $25,000 |

   To record receipt of mandatory transfer from Unrestricted Current Fund.

2. The $25,000 received from the Unrestricted Current Fund was used to pay an installment of the mortgage note, including $5,000 interest. (See entry 4, Investment in Plant.)

   | | | | |
   |---|---|---|---|
   | (2) | Fund Balances—Restricted ...................... | $25,000 | |
   | |     Cash ....................................... | | $25,000 |

   To record payment on mortgage note, including $5,000 interest.

   Note that the mortgage payable is recorded in, and must be reduced in, the Investment in Plant subgroup.

3. A donation of $15,000 was received for the purpose of paying a $10,000 mortgage installment falling due during the current year, plus $5,000 interest.

   | | | | |
   |---|---|---|---|
   | (3) | Cash .......................................... | $15,000 | |
   | |     Fund Balances—Restricted ..................... | | $15,000 |

   To record receipt of money to pay mortgage installment falling due during the current year.

4. The money was used for this purpose. (See transaction 5, Investment in Plant.)

   | | | | |
   |---|---|---|---|
   | (4) | Fund Balances—Restricted ...................... | $15,000 | |
   | |     Cash ....................................... | | $15,000 |

   To record payment of mortgage installment: $5,000 interest and $10,000 principal.

5. A donation of $25,000 was received for the purpose of paying a mortgage installment falling due next year.

| | | |
|---|---:|---:|
| (5)  Cash ....................................... | $ 25,000 | |
|       Fund Balances—Restricted .................... | | $ 25,000 |

      To record receipt of money to pay part of mortgage
      installment falling due during the following year.

**6.** The cash received in transaction 5 was invested.

| | | |
|---|---:|---:|
| (6)  Investments .................................. | $ 25,000 | |
|       Cash ....................................... | | $ 25,000 |

      To record investing the donated cash.

**7.** A $200,000 gift was received with the stipulation that the funds be managed as a debt service sinking fund by the Last National Bank. The donor is attempting to get others to match his gesture so that a major building program may be begun.

| | | |
|---|---:|---:|
| (7) (a) Cash ..................................... | $200,000 | |
|         Fund Balances—Restricted .................. | | $200,000 |

        To record gift to be used to set up sinking fund
        at the Last National Bank.

| | | |
|---|---:|---:|
|    (b) Sinking Fund—Last National Bank .............. | $200,000 | |
|         Cash ..................................... | | $200,000 |

        To record payment to the Last National Bank to
        establish a debt service sinking fund.

## Investment in Plant

The asset accounts in the Investment in Plant subgroup contain the book values of the institutional plant properties except any that are in Endowment and Similar Funds. State and local government colleges and universities have the option of reporting depreciation on these assets. Historically, they have not done so. (We include accumulated depreciation and the periodic provision for depreciation in our examples for illustrative purposes.)

    Liabilities incurred to acquire or construct plant assets, including those arising from capital leases, also are accounted for here. Increments of Construction in Progress and related liabilities may be added each year, or the total liability and asset cost may be added here at the conclusion of the project. The net equity in fixed assets is maintained in the Net Invested in Plant account, detailed as seems necessary. For example, separate categories might be maintained for net investment from gifts; appropriations; federal, state, and local grants; Current Funds; and other funds.

    The balances in the Investment in Plant accounts at the beginning of the period were as follows:

| | Debit | Credit |
|---|---:|---:|
| Land ........................................... | $   300,000 | |
| Buildings ........................................ | 8,000,000 | |
| Accumulated Depreciation* ........................... | | $ 4,000,000 |
| Equipment ....................................... | 1,800,000 | |
| Accumulated Depreciation* ......................... | | 1,010,000 |
| Library Books ..................................... | 200,000 | |
| Mortgage Payable .................................. | | 400,000 |
| Net Invested in Plant ................................ | | 4,890,000 |
| | $10,300,000 | $10,300,000 |

*Government colleges and universities are not required to report accumulated depreciation on Plant Funds assets.

**Transactions and Entries**

**For transactions originating in:**

1. Unrestricted Current Fund (see transaction 12 in that fund): Equipment was purchased for $10,000.

   | | | |
   |---|---|---|
   | (1) Equipment . . . . . . . . . . . . . . . . . . . . . . . . . . . . . . . . . . . . | $ 10,000 | |
   | **Net Invested in Plant** . . . . . . . . . . . . . . . . . . . . . . . . | | $ 10,000 |

   To record purchase of equipment with Unrestricted Current Fund cash.

2. Unexpended Plant Funds (see transaction 3 in that fund): A house trailer costing $12,000 was purchased for cash.

   | | | |
   |---|---|---|
   | (2) Improvements Other Than Buildings . . . . . . . . . . . . . . | $ 12,000 | |
   | Net Invested in Plant . . . . . . . . . . . . . . . . . . . . . . . . | | $ 12,000 |

   To record purchase of house trailer out of the Unexpended Plant Funds.

3. Unexpended Plant Funds (see transaction 6 in that fund): Construction in Progress on a building addition and the related portion of Notes Payable issued for the building addition were reclassified to the Investment in Plant accounts.

   | | | |
   |---|---|---|
   | (3) **Construction in Progress** . . . . . . . . . . . . . . . . . . . . . . . . | $240,000 | |
   | **Notes Payable** . . . . . . . . . . . . . . . . . . . . . . . . . . . . . . . | | $240,000 |

   To reclassify Construction in Progress and Notes Payable to the Investment in Plant accounts.

4. Funds for Retirement of Indebtedness (see transaction 2 in that fund): Mortgage notes carried as a liability of the Investment in Plant subgroup $20,000 were paid from Funds for Retirement of Indebtedness. (Recall that $5,000 interest was paid also, but only the principal payment affects the Investment in Plant accounts.)

   | | | |
   |---|---|---|
   | (4) **Mortgage Payable** . . . . . . . . . . . . . . . . . . . . . . . . . . . . . | $ 20,000 | |
   | **Net Invested in Plant** . . . . . . . . . . . . . . . . . . . . . . . . | | $ 20,000 |

   To record payment of mortgage principal from the Funds for Retirement of Indebtedness.

5. Funds for Retirement of Indebtedness (see transaction 4 in that fund): An installment of the mortgage note in the amount of $10,000 was retired.

   | | | |
   |---|---|---|
   | (5) Mortgage Payable . . . . . . . . . . . . . . . . . . . . . . . . . . . . . | $ 10,000 | |
   | Net Invested in Plant . . . . . . . . . . . . . . . . . . . . . . . . | | $ 10,000 |

   To record payment of part of mortgage payable from the Retirement of Indebtedness Fund.

6. Investment in Plant Accounts: New, uninsured equipment financed from current revenues and costing $1,000 was destroyed by fire.

   | | | |
   |---|---|---|
   | (6) Net Invested in Plant . . . . . . . . . . . . . . . . . . . . . . . . . . | $ 1,000 | |
   | Equipment . . . . . . . . . . . . . . . . . . . . . . . . . . . . . . . . . | | $ 1,000 |

   To remove the original cost of equipment destroyed.

7. Investment in Plant Accounts: The provision for depreciation of the university's plant assets totaled $230,000.

   | | | |
   |---|---|---|
   | (7) Net Invested in Plant . . . . . . . . . . . . . . . . . . . . . . . . . . | $230,000 | |
   | **Accumulated Depreciation** . . . . . . . . . . . . . . . . . . . . . | | $230,000 |

   To record the provision for depreciation for the year.

Recall that recording and reporting depreciation and accumulated depreciation of Plant Funds assets is optional for government colleges and universities.

## TRUST AND AGENCY TYPE FUND GROUPS

All university resources being used in operations are accounted for in the Current Funds and Plant Funds. In addition, colleges and universities often have significant amounts of resources that are accounted for in fiduciary fund groups that are in essence trust and agency type funds. These fund groups include Loan Funds, Endowment and Similar Funds, Annuity and Life Income Funds, and Agency Funds.

Most of the assets accounted for in these fiduciary-type funds are restricted by donors. However, unrestricted resources designated by the governing board for loan or endowment purposes are accounted for in the Loan Funds and the Endowment and Similar Funds along with resources externally restricted for those purposes. Also, the assets donated in some annuity agreements are available for unrestricted use even during the term of the annuity agreement. Although accounting for these trust and agency type funds is similar to that for similar types of funds of governments, there are sufficient differences to warrant brief explanations and illustrations of each of these fund groups.

## LOAN FUNDS

Loan Funds are used to account for resources that may be loaned to students and, in some cases, to faculty and staff. If only the fund's income may be loaned, the principal is included in the Endowment and Similar Funds group and only the income is included with the Loan Funds. The fund balances of Loan Funds should be classified in appropriate ways, such as by sources of resources, purposes for which loans may be made, and restricted versus unrestricted. For example, some may come from appropriations, others from private donors, and still others from Unrestricted Current Funds set aside for this purpose by the college or university governing board. Some may be refundable to donors under specified conditions.

Loan Funds have become major activities requiring professional management at many higher education institutions. Some have raised large sums for loan purposes through gifts, and many participate in federal and state government loan programs. Both federal and state programs must be administered in accordance with many regulations and typically require the college or university to contribute a percentage of the total loan fund balance.

Covering such programs, which are subject to change, is beyond the scope of this text. Rather, because loan funds of governments were covered earlier, accounting for loan losses in colleges and universities is discussed briefly and a simplified example of a college or university Loan Fund is presented.

Loan losses may be accounted for in one of two ways. Under one method, an Allowance for Loan Losses is deducted from both the total loans and the Loan Funds Fund Balance in the year-end balance sheet. It is reversed at the start of the new year and loan losses are charged against specific Loan Funds Fund Balance accounts. Under the second method, an allowance method, estimated losses are deducted from the Loan Funds Fund Balance accounts to which they are expected to relate and an Allowance for Loan Losses is established. Loan losses incurred are charged against the allowance account.

In reviewing the following transactions assume that a Loan Fund was established to make interest-free loans and that (1) income on fund investments is to be added to the principal of the fund, and (2) the total assets of the fund, both the original principal and that from earnings, may be loaned.

**Transactions and Entries**

**1.** A donation of $100,000 was received for the purpose of making loans to students.

| (1) | Cash | $100,000 | |
| | Fund Balance—Restricted | | $100,000 |
| | To record donation received for the purpose of setting up Loan Fund. | | |

**2.** Loans of $50,000 were made.

| (2) | Loans Receivable | $ 50,000 | |
| | Cash | | $ 50,000 |
| | To record loans made. | | |

**3.** $25,000 was invested in bonds. The bonds were purchased at par plus accrued interest of $100.

| (3) | Investments | $ 25,000 | |
| | Accrued Interest on Investments Purchased | 100 | |
| | Cash | | $ 25,100 |
| | To record investments and accrued interest purchased. | | |

**4.** A $500 check in payment of bond interest was received.

| (4) | Cash | $    500 | |
| | Accrued Interest on Investments Purchased | | $    100 |
| | Fund Balance—Restricted | | 400 |
| | To record receipt of interest payment. | | |

**5.** A student died and it was decided to write off his loan of $500 as uncollectible.

| (5) | Fund Balance—Restricted | $    500 | |
| | Loans Receivable | | $    500 |
| | To write off loan as uncollectible. | | |

## ENDOWMENT AND SIMILAR FUNDS

Endowment and Similar Funds is used to account for assets that, at least at the moment, cannot be expended, although usually the income from them may be. Assets donated by outsiders fall into two categories: (1) those that have been given in perpetuity, which are accounted for in Endowment Funds, sometimes referred to as true or pure Endowment Funds; and (2) those that the donor has specified may be expended after a particular date or event, which are accounted for in Term Endowment Funds.

The appropriate policy-making body of an institution may also set aside (designate) unrestricted resources for the same purposes as those donated as endowments. These are accounted for in *Quasi-Endowment Funds* or *Funds Functioning as Endowments,* and, of course, are subject to reassignment by the authority that created them.

Donors may choose to make the income from endowment-type funds available to a university but to leave the principal in the possession and control of a trustee other than the university. Such funds usually are not included among the Endowment and Similar Funds of the university but should be disclosed in the financial statements by an appropriate note. Unrestricted income from such funds is reported as revenue in the Unrestricted Current Funds. If restricted to specific operating purposes, the income is recorded as an addition to the Restricted Current Funds fund balance. When expended, it is reported there as Endowment Income if the trust is irrevocable or as Gifts if it is a revocable trust. If the income is restricted to plant or debt service uses, it is recorded in the appropriate Plant Funds.

## Determining and Reporting Income

One of the most debated issues in Endowment Fund accounting is: What portion, if any, of net appreciation of Endowment Fund investments should be treated as additions to expendable endowment income rather than as part of the endowment principal?

Several views have found their way into practice. The alternatives range from the classical trust or fiduciary principle that includes no net appreciation of Endowment Fund assets (realized or unrealized) in expendable income (or yield) to the various total return approaches. Under the total return approaches, a prudent portion of the net appreciation is considered income and spent along with the dividends, rents, royalties, interest, and other realized revenues that constitute the yield under the classical trust principle.

Donors sometimes require gains and losses, whether realized or not, to be added to or deducted from endowment principal. State laws sometimes dictate the determination of expendable endowment income, where donor agreements are silent. When not legally or contractually required to exclude realized gains or losses or appreciation from the amount of expendable income, universities can choose the treatment that they prefer. However, for accounting and reporting purposes, gains and losses (including unrealized changes in fair value) must be reported as investment income that increases the Endowment Fund balance. Any portion of the appreciation that is expendable is moved to the appropriate recipient fund along with the balance of the expendable endowment earnings. If unrestricted, the expendable endowment earnings are reported as income in the Unrestricted Current Fund. If restricted, the earnings are reported as fund balance increases in the Restricted Current Fund, the appropriate Plant Fund, or a Trust and Agency Fund. The appropriate fund depends upon the restriction placed on use of the earnings.

## Transactions and Entries—Endowment Funds

The following transactions and entries illustrate the operation of Endowment and Similar Funds, which are similar to SLG Nonexpendable Trust Funds.

**Transactions and Entries**

1. Cash was donated by a family during the year to establish three separate endowments, as follows:

| | |
|---|---:|
| Endowment A (for Supplemental Salary Payments) | $1,000,000 |
| Endowment B (for Supplemental Salary Payments) | 600,000 |
| Endowment C (for Student Aid) | 400,000 |
| | $2,000,000 |

These endowments included a provision that any earnings in excess of $78,000 be dedicated to the athletic program, an auxiliary enterprise of the university. Furthermore, the donor stipulates that appreciation and depreciation of the assets comprising the endowment principal are to be added to or deducted from the principal. They do not affect expendable earnings.

| | | | |
|---|---|---:|---:|
| (1) | Cash | $2,000,000 | |
| | Fund Balance—Endowment A | | $1,000,000 |
| | Fund Balance—Endowment B | | 600,000 |
| | Fund Balance—Endowment C | | 400,000 |
| | To record receipt of money for the purpose of establishing three endowments. | | |

2. It was decided to invest this money in securities that were to be pooled. The following securities were acquired at the prices indicated:

| | |
|---|---:|
| Preferred stocks | $ 500,000 |
| Common stocks | 1,000,000 |
| Bonds: | |
| Par value | 200,000 |
| Premiums | 10,000 |
| Bonds: | |
| Par value | 250,000 |
| Discounts | 5,000 |
| Accrued interest on investments purchased | 1,000 |

| | | | |
|---|---|---:|---:|
| (2) | Investments in Preferred Stocks | $ 500,000 | |
| | Investments in Common Stocks | 1,000,000 | |
| | Investments in Bonds | 455,000 | |
| | Accrued Interest on Investments Purchased | 1,000 | |
| | Cash | | $1,956,000 |
| | To record purchase of pooled investments. | | |

Note that the investments are recorded at fair value.

3. Cash received on these investments for the year was as follows:

| | |
|---|---:|
| Dividends on preferred stocks | $20,000 |
| Dividends on common stocks | 59,700 |
| Interest | 9,000 |

No material amounts of investment income were accrued at year end.

| | | | |
|---|---|---:|---:|
| (3) | Cash | $ 88,700 | |
| | Income on Pooled Investments | | $ 87,700 |
| | Accrued Interest on Investments Purchased | | 1,000 |
| | To record investment income received. | | |

**4.** The fair value of the pooled investments increased by $1,000 during the year.

(4) Investments .................................... $ 1,000
       Income on Pooled Investments ................. $ 1,000
       To record increase in fair value of investments.

**5.** The earnings on Endowments A, B, and C exceeded $78,000. Thus, $78,000 was paid to the Restricted Current Funds for the primary purposes of these endowments, and the remainder of the expendable income from pooled investments was paid to the Restricted Current Funds for auxiliary enterprise purposes. (See transaction 1 and also transaction 1, Restricted Current Funds.)

(5a) Income on Pooled Investments ................... $87,700
       Cash ..................................... $87,700
       To record payment of endowment income to the
       Restricted Current Funds as follows:

| Fund | Fund Balance* | Percentage of Total | Income Apportioned |
|------|--------------|---------------------|--------------------|
| A | $1,000,000 | 50% | $39,000 |
| B | 600,000 | 30 | 23,400 |
| C | 400,000 | 20 | 15,600 |
| | $2,000,000 | 100% | 78,000 |
| Earnings | | | 87,700 |
| Balance—for auxiliary enterprises | | | $ 9,700 |

*It is assumed that market values and book values of the several funds are in this case identical.

The appreciation ($1,000) in investment values that is included in the Income on Pooled Investments account is added to the respective Fund Balance accounts using the same percentages.

(5b) Income on Pooled Investments ................... $ 1,000
       **Fund Balance—Endowment A** ................. $ 500
       **Fund Balance—Endowment B** ................. 300
       **Fund Balance—Endowment C** ................. 200
       To apportion the appreciation in fair value of
       investments to the affected Fund Balance accounts.

**6.** Common stock with a book value of $10,000 was sold for $10,500.

(6) Cash ........................................ $10,500
       Investments in Common Stock ................. $10,000
       **Fund Balance—Endowment A** ................. 250
       **Fund Balance—Endowment B** ................. 150
       **Fund Balance—Endowment C** ................. 100
       To record sale of common stock at a gain of $500 and
       the addition of its share of the gain to the balance
       of each Endowment Fund.

**7.** An individual donated common stock that had cost $65,000 (hereafter referred to as Endowment Fund D). At the time of the donation the stock had a fair value of $75,000. The income from these securities is unrestricted and may be used for any university purposes.

(7) Common Stock ............................... $75,000
       **Fund Balance—Endowment D** ................. $75,000
       To record donation of common stock at its fair value;
       the net income of Endowment D is unrestricted.

8. Another individual had a small apartment complex constructed and equipped and then turned it over to the university with the specification that the net income therefrom is to be used for student aid and for supplemental salary payments (hereafter referred to as Endowment Fund E). The total cost was $850,000, divided as follows:

| | |
|---|---|
| Land ................................. | $100,000 |
| Building ............................. | 600,000 |
| Equipment ........................... | 150,000 |

| | | |
|---|---|---|
| (8) Land ....................................... | $100,000 | |
| Building ...................................... | 600,000 | |
| Equipment .................................... | 150,000 | |
| **Fund Balance—Principal—Endowment E** ........ | | $850,000 |

To record gift of an apartment complex as an endowment, the net income of which is restricted to certain purposes.

9. Gross income from the apartments (Endowment Fund E) for the current year was $170,000; and total expenses were $120,000, exclusive of depreciation of $20,000 (building, $6,000; equipment, $14,000). No receivables or payables were outstanding at year end, and the net income of Endowment Fund E was established as a liability to the Restricted Current Fund. (See transaction 4, Restricted Current Funds.)

| | | |
|---|---|---|
| (9a) Cash ........................................ | $170,000 | |
| **Fund Balance—Earnings—Endowment E** ........ | | $170,000 |

To record revenues from the apartments.

| | | |
|---|---|---|
| (9b) **Fund Balance—Earnings—Endowment E** .......... | $120,000 | |
| Cash ...................................... | | $120,000 |

To record rental *expenses,* other than depreciation, incurred in operating the apartments.

| | | |
|---|---|---|
| (9c) **Fund Balance—Earnings—Endowment E** .......... | $ 50,000 | |
| Accumulated Depreciation—Building ........... | | $ 6,000 |
| Accumulated Depreciation—Equipment ........ | | 14,000 |
| Due to Restricted Current Funds .............. | | 30,000 |

To record depreciation expenses for Endowment E and the liability to the Restricted Current Funds for the net income of Endowment E.

10. $100,000 was received from the Unrestricted Current Fund for the purpose of establishing a fund functioning as an endowment (Quasi-Endowment Fund) in accordance with a resolution adopted by the university's board of trustees. (See transaction 13, Unrestricted Current Funds.)

| | | |
|---|---|---|
| (10) Cash ........................................ | $100,000 | |
| **Fund Balance—Quasi-Endowment—Unrestricted** .. | | $100,000 |

To record receipt of cash from the Unrestricted Current Fund for purpose of setting up a fund to function as an Endowment Fund in accordance with resolution adopted by the university's board of trustees.

11. An individual set up a trust (to be administered by the Village National Bank) in the amount of $200,000, the income from which is to go to the university.

(11) No entry, or memorandum entry. The trust would be disclosed in the notes to the financial statements.

## ANNUITY AND LIFE INCOME FUNDS

Annuity and Life Income Funds are used to account for assets given to the institution with the stipulation that the institution make certain payments to a designated recipient(s). Annuity Funds are used if the gift agreement requires a fixed-dollar payment regardless of the income of the fund. Life Income Funds are used if the amount of the payment to the beneficiary varies according to the earnings of the fund. Typically, annuity agreements also specify a certain number of years during which the beneficiary is to receive the annuity, but the period need not be fixed. Indeed, the period could be specified as the lifetime of the beneficiary. Similarly, a life income agreement usually requires payment of the income of the fund—or some portion of the income of the fund—until the death of the beneficiary or the donor. However, a life income agreement could specify that the earnings, or some portion of the earnings, be paid to the designated beneficiary for a specified number of years. After the specified payment period, the principal is transferred to the fund group specified by the donor or, if unrestricted, to the Unrestricted Current Funds.

Accounting for Annuity and Life Income Funds is similar to that for Endowment and Similar Funds. Indeed, if these funds are small, they may be reported with the Endowment and Similar Funds.

### Annuity Funds

The Internal Revenue Code and regulations state the conditions under which an annuity trust may be accepted and must be administered from an income tax standpoint, and several states also regulate annuity trusts. Too, because the institution accepts some risk by guaranteeing the beneficiary a fixed amount for a specified period, perhaps for life or even for the lifetime of two or more persons, the governing board will want assurances (1) that the assets donated should generate sufficient income to pay the specified amounts, or (2) if some of the payments must come from principal, that a significant residual balance should be available to the institution at the end of the annuity period.

When the Annuity Fund is established, the assets should be recorded at their fair value, together with any liabilities against the assets assumed by the institution. The liability for the annuity payments is recorded at its present value, based on the expected earnings rate and, if appropriate, life expectancy tables. Any difference between the assets and liabilities should be debited or credited, as appropriate, to the Annuity Funds Fund Balance account.

To illustrate Annuity Funds accounting, assume that an individual donated $20,000 of cash and $180,000 of investments to A University on January 2, 19X3 with the stipulation that she be paid $25,000 each December 31 for the next ten years. Any remaining net assets should then be used to remodel the business and public administration building. The university finance officer expects to earn at least 7% on the fund's assets during each of the next ten years. The entry to record creation of this Annuity Fund would be:

| | | | |
|---|---|---|---|
| (1) | Cash | $ 20,000 | |
| | Investments | 180,000 | |
| | **Annuities Payable** | | $175,589 |
| | **Fund Balance—Annuity** | | 24,411 |

To record *establishment* of Annuity Fund. Calculation of annuity payable: $25,000 × 7.023582, the present value of an ordinary annuity of $1 for 10 periods at 7%, is $175,589.

Investment earnings and gains are credited, and annuity payments and losses are debited, to Annuities Payable. Assuming that various investment transactions already have been recorded during the year and that the annuity payments are due each December 31, the following entries would be made on December 31, 19X3, the end of the university's fiscal year:

(2)  **Annuities Payable** . . . . . . . . . . . . . . . . . . . . . . . . . . . . . . . . . . . . . .     $25,000

       Cash (or Annuities Currently Payable) . . . . . . . . . . . . . . . . .               $25,000

       To record the annual **annuity payment.**

(3)  Investment Earnings . . . . . . . . . . . . . . . . . . . . . . . . . . . . . . . . . . . . . .     $13,000

     Investment Gains . . . . . . . . . . . . . . . . . . . . . . . . . . . . . . . . . . . . . . . .       3,000

       Investment Losses . . . . . . . . . . . . . . . . . . . . . . . . . . . . . . . . . . . . . .             $  5,000

       **Annuities Payable** . . . . . . . . . . . . . . . . . . . . . . . . . . . . . . . . . . . . . .             11,000

       To *close* the (amounts assumed) investment earnings, gains,
        and losses accounts at year end.

Because the Annuities Payable account should always be carried at the present value of the future series of required payments, the Annuities Payable account must be adjusted annually to its present value. If actuarial assumptions such as yield estimates or life expectancies are revised, the adjustment to Annuities Payable should reflect those changes. The adjustments to Annuities Payable will cause a change in the Annuity Funds Fund Balance to be reported in the Statement of Changes in Fund Balances (Figure 16–6). In this example the Annuities Payable balance at year end should be equal to the present value of the nine remaining annuity payments ($25,000 × 6.515232), or $162,881. The required adjustment to Fund Balance is the difference between the Annuities Payable balance after the preceding entries ($161,589) and the present value of the nine remaining payments. This adjustment of $1,292 is recorded as follows:

(4)  **Fund Balance—Annuity** . . . . . . . . . . . . . . . . . . . . . . . . . . . . . . . .     $1,292

       **Annuities Payable** . . . . . . . . . . . . . . . . . . . . . . . . . . . . . . . . . . . . . .           $1,292

       To *adjust Annuities Payable* to present value at year end.

The preceding approach to accounting for Annuity Funds earnings and the fund balance adjustment is consistent with the audit guide description of accounting for Annuity Funds. This approach results in reporting—in the Statement of Changes in Fund Balances—only the net adjustment to Fund Balance that results from investment earnings, interest expenses, and changes in actuarial assumptions, such as changes in the appropriate interest rate for discounting the remaining annuity payments.

However, some colleges and universities use a different accounting approach in which the income of the Annuity Funds is closed to Fund Balance. This approach would result in the last two entries in this example being as follows:

Investment Earnings . . . . . . . . . . . . . . . . . . . . . . . . . . . . . . . . . . . . . .     $13,000

Investment Gains . . . . . . . . . . . . . . . . . . . . . . . . . . . . . . . . . . . . . . . .       3,000

    Investment Losses . . . . . . . . . . . . . . . . . . . . . . . . . . . . . . . . . . . . . .           $  5,000

    Fund Balance—Annuity . . . . . . . . . . . . . . . . . . . . . . . . . . . . . . . . . .           11,000

    To *close* the investment earnings, gains, and losses accounts
     at year end.

Fund Balance—Annuity . . . . . . . . . . . . . . . . . . . . . . . . . . . . . . . . . .     $12,292

    Annuities Payable . . . . . . . . . . . . . . . . . . . . . . . . . . . . . . . . . . . . . . .           $12,292

    To *adjust Annuities Payable* to its present value at year end.

A college or university using this accounting approach still could report only the net adjustment of Fund Balance, the decrease of $1,292, in its Statement of Changes in Fund Balances. At the end of the annuity period any remaining balance should be transferred to the Plant Funds because the donor specified that it should be used to remodel the business and public administration building.

## Life Income Funds

Life Income Funds are subject to Internal Revenue Code and regulation provisions, as are Annuity Funds, and may be subject to state regulations. Because only the earnings inure to the beneficiary(ies) of Life Income Funds, and no fixed payment is guaranteed, the college or university does not have an earnings risk as in the case of Annuity Funds.

The accounting for Life Income Funds is not as complex as that for Annuity Funds. All that is involved is:

1. At its inception—record the assets at fair value and record any liabilities assumed; the difference is credited to Life Income Fund Balance.

2. During the term of the fund—record fund revenues, expenses, gains, and losses following donor instructions or, in the absence of instructions, applicable law in determining whether gains or losses affect income or the principal, and distribute the earnings to the beneficiary(ies).

3. At the end of the benefit period or upon the death of the beneficiary(ies)—distribute the net assets of the fund as specified by the donor or, in the absence of such instructions, to the Unrestricted Current Funds.

## AGENCY FUNDS

A university usually serves as a depository and fiscal agent for a number of student, faculty, and staff organizations. It holds money and other assets belonging to others in these cases; only the usual asset and liability accounts of Agency Funds need be maintained because there is no Agency Fund fund balance.

## FINANCIAL REPORTING

The three basic financial statements recommended in the NACUBO *FARM* and in the AICPA audit guide for government colleges and universities are:

1. Balance Sheet
2. Statement of Changes in Fund Balances
3. Statement of Current Funds Revenues, Expenditures, and Other Changes

Both a Balance Sheet (Figure 16–5) and a Statement of Current Funds Revenues, Expenditures, and Other Changes (Figure 16–4) have been discussed for the A Government University example. Figure 16–6 (pages 652–653) presented a Statement of Changes in Fund Balances for the example. The **boldface type** in this statement indicates accounts and amounts that are based on the data in the example. The other accounts are items commonly found in more complex situations. The funds that these items typically affect are indicated by "xxx."

In reviewing the Statement of Current Funds Revenues, Expenditures, and Other Changes (Figure 16–4), note particularly the additions to Restricted Current Funds balances—such as through gifts and investment earnings—that would be reported as revenue immediately were it not for the convention of recognizing revenue only to the extent that restricted resources are expended. Note also in the Statement of Changes in Fund Balances (Figure 16–6), that additions to the Restricted Current Funds, not revenues, are reported. Both statements report a net Fund Balance increase of $175,700 for the Restricted Current Funds because the difference between restricted receipts and restricted revenues recognized during a year is reported in the Statement of Current Funds Revenues, Expenditures, and Other Changes. Similarly, in studying the Statement of Changes in Fund Balances (Figure 16–6), note the additions to the Endowment and Similar Funds that will not be recognized as revenue until such time, if ever, that the investment earnings are expended for operating purposes.

The primary statements should be accompanied by detailed supporting schedules and footnotes appropriate to ensure full disclosure and fair presentation of the operations and balances of the various fund groups and subgroups. The NACUBO *FARM* suggests numerous supplemental schedules for consideration.

## CONCLUDING COMMENTS

Accounting and reporting for colleges and universities has evolved rapidly in recent years and may be expected to evolve still further in the future. The efforts of the AICPA, NACUBO, and other committees were extensive. Numerous major improvements in college and university accounting and reporting resulted from these joint efforts by preparers, auditors, and users of higher education financial reports.

College and university financial reporting is apt to change even more dramatically in the future. The major differences between nongovernment college and university financial reports and those of government colleges and universities are discussed and illustrated in an appendix to Chapter 18. Many are troubled by the dramatically different financial reporting requirements for private and for government colleges and universities. Too, the culmination of the GASB financial reporting model project may significantly change reporting for government universities.

## Questions

**Q 16-1** Which standards setting body has the authority for establishing GAAP for colleges and universities?

**Q 16-2** Under what circumstances are resources expendable for operating purposes accounted for in Restricted Current Funds? At what point should contributions to Restricted Current Funds be recognized as revenue?

**Q 16-3** Why is it necessary to distinguish restricted and unrestricted balances in the Endowment and Similar Funds, Loan Funds, and Plant Funds?

**Q 16-4** Student tuition, fees, and other assessments may be restricted, in whole or in part, to debt service or plant acquisition, renewal, or replacement. How should these amounts be accounted for by a college or university?

**Q 16-5** Distinguish between mandatory and nonmandatory transfers and how they are reported in higher education financial statements.

**Q 16-6** What is an auxiliary enterprise? How is it accounted for and reported on by colleges and universities?

**Q 16-7** When are earnings of Endowment and Similar Funds reported as revenue? Might the principal of such funds also be reported as revenue? Explain.

**Q 16-8** Distinguish between the key accounting aspects of Annuity Funds and Life Income Funds.

**Q 16-9** Should plant-related long-term debt and construction in progress be accounted for in the Unexpended Plant Funds or the Plant Funds for Renewal and Replacement until completion of the project, or should appropriate amounts be reclassified to the Investment in Plant accounts at the end of each year?

**Q 16-10** Distinguish between expenditures and transfers.

**Q 16-11** How should government college and university revenues and expenditures be classified for external financial reporting purposes?

**Q 16-12** Identify the required financial statements for government colleges and universities and the fund groups covered by each statement.

**Q 16-13** 1. Which of the following transactions are mandatory transfers?
   a. Endowment income earned that is not restricted for any purpose is moved to the Unrestricted Current Fund.
   b. Establishment of an endowment from unrestricted resources by order of the university board of directors.
   c. Reclassification of Unrestricted Current Fund resources as Loan Fund resources to meet the matching requirement of a gift to the Loan Funds.
   d. Reclassification of construction in progress from the Unexpended Plant Funds to the Investment in Plant subgroup.
   2. Explain how the transactions in item 1 that are not mandatory transfers should be reported.

**Q 16-14** How are uncollectible accounts for tuition and fees reported in a government university's operating statement?

**Q 16-15** In what financial statement are increases in the net assets of the Unexpended Plant Fund reported?

**Q 16-16** What are the key expenditure classifications for a university?

## Exercises

**E 16-1** (Unrestricted Current Funds Entries) Prepare the necessary journal entries to record each of the following transactions in the Unrestricted Current Funds of Dewey County College.
   1. Tuition and fees charged for the fall 19X8 semester totaled $3,700,000. $100,000 of this amount was waived as a result of scholarships and fee waivers, and $12,000 more is expected to be uncollectible.
   2. For the winter 19X9 semester Dewey College levied a general student fee of $18,000. The full amount of this fee is restricted for the purchase of computer equipment and software needed to establish computer labs at the college.
   3. What would the entries for 2 be if half of the revenue from the student fees was unrestricted as to use?

4. What would the entries for 2 be if there were no external restrictions on the use of the resources, but the board requires the fees to be set aside for purchase of computer equipment and software?
5. What would the entries for 2 be if the fees were to supplement the income of a specific auxiliary enterprise of the college?

**E 16-2** (Various Funds—Entries) Prepare all the journal entries required in all the funds/accounts of a government college or university to record the following transactions.
1. Tuition and fees assessed total $3,000,000—80% is collected, scholarships are granted for $100,000, and $50,000 is expected to prove uncollectible.
2. Revenues collected from sales and services of the university bookstore, an auxiliary enterprise, were $400,000.
3. Salaries and wages paid, $1,300,000. $85,000 of this was for employees of the university bookstore.
4. Unrestricted resources were paid to the fund to be used to service the long-term mortgage on the university's buildings, $500,000.
5. Mortgage payments totaled $480,000. $300,000 of this was for interest.
6. Restricted contributions for a specific academic program were received, $220,000.
7. Expenditures for the restricted program were incurred and paid, $100,000.
8. Equipment was purchased from resources previously set aside for that purpose, $22,000.

**E 16-3** (Grant-Related Entries) January 10, 19X8—Buchanan State College received a $100,000 grant to be used to finance a study of the effects of the Tax Reform Act of 19X6 on the economy.

During 19X8—Expenditures of $72,000 were incurred and paid on the research project.

*Required* (a) Record these transactions in the accounts of the appropriate fund groups of Buchanan State College, and explain how the effects of the transactions should be reported in the college's financial statements.
(b) Repeat requirement (a) under the assumption that the grant was to finance plant expansion.

**E 16-4** (Endowment Entries) Mr. Harvey Robinson donated $2,000,000 to the University of Aggiemania with the stipulation that earnings of the first ten years be used to endow professorships in each of the university's colleges. At the end of the ten-year period the principal of the gift will become available for unrestricted use.

*Required* (a) Prepare the entry(ies) needed in the various fund groups to record the gift, assuming a government university.
(b) Prepare the entry(ies) needed in the various fund groups to record the expiration of the term of the endowment, assuming a government university.

**E 16-5** (Plant Funds Entries)

Hitech State University issued $14,000,000 of bonds to finance construction of a new computer facility on March 25, 19X8.

The contractor billed Hitech University $3,200,000 for work completed during 19X8. The university paid all but a 5% retained percentage.

In 19X9 the contractor completed the facility and billed Hitech for $10,800,000. The university has paid all but a 5% retained percentage as of year end.

*Required* (a) Prepare the necessary journal entries for 19X8 and 19X9 to account for the preceding transactions assuming that Hitech reclassifies its Construction in Progress from the Unexpended Plant Funds at the end of each year.
(b) Prepare the necessary journal entries for the preceding transactions assuming that the university carries the construction costs in the Unexpended Plant Funds until construction is complete.
(c) What is the effect on the fund balances of the various Plant Fund subgroups under these two alternatives?

## Problems

**Note:**  Problems 16–3 to 16–7 relate to X University. These problems along with Problem 16–8 comprise a comprehensive review problem.

**P 16-1, Part I**  (Multiple Choice) (Respond assuming a government university.)

1. The current funds group of a government university includes which of the following?

| | *Annuity Funds* | *Loan Funds* |
|---|---|---|
| a. | Yes | Yes |
| b. | Yes | No |
| c. | No | No |
| d. | No | Yes |

2. For the spring semester of 19X4, Lane University assessed its students $3,400,000 (net of refunds) of tuition and fees for educational and general purposes. However, only $3,000,000 was expected to be realized because scholarships totaling $300,000 were granted to students, and tuition remissions of $100,000 were allowed to faculty members' children attending Lane. How much should Lane include in educational and general current funds revenues from student tuition and fees?
   a. $3,400,000                      c. $3,100,000
   b. $3,300,000                      d. $3,000,000

3. The following funds were among those on Key University's books at April 30, 19X4:

Funds to be used for acquisition of additional properties
   for university purposes (unexpended at 4/30/X4) . . . . . . . . .   $3,000,000
Funds set aside for debt service charges and for retirement
   of indebtedness on university properties . . . . . . . . . . . . . . .   5,000,000

   How much of the previously mentioned funds should be included in plant funds?
   a. $0                              c. $5,000,000
   b. $3,000,000                      d. $8,000,000

4. During the years ended June 30, 19X0 and 19X1, Sonata University conducted a cancer research project financed by a $2,000,000 gift from an alumnus. This entire amount was pledged by the donor on July 10, 19W9, although he paid only $500,000 at that date. The gift was restricted to the financing of this particular research project. During the 2-year research period Sonata's related gift receipts and research expenditures were as follows:

| | *Year Ended June 30* | |
|---|---|---|
| | **19X0** | **19X1** |
| Gift receipts . . . . . . . . . . . . . . . . . . | $1,200,000 | $ 800,000 |
| Cancer research expenditures . . . . | 900,000 | 1,100,000 |

   How much gift revenue should Sonata report in the restricted column of its statement of current funds revenues, expenditures, and other changes for the year ended June 30, 19X1?
   a. $0                              c. $1,100,000
   b. $800,000                        d. $2,000,000

5. On January 2, 19X2, John Reynolds established a $500,000 trust, the income from which is to be paid to Mansfield University for general operating purposes. The

Wyndham National Bank was appointed by Reynolds as trustee of the fund. What journal entry is required on Mansfield's books?

| | Dr. | Cr. |
|---|---|---|
| a. Memorandum entry only | | |
| b. Cash ..................... | $500,000 | |
|   Endowment fund balance ..... | | $500,000 |
| c. Nonexpendable endowment fund | $500,000 | |
|   Endowment fund balance ..... | | $500,000 |
| d. Expendable funds ........... | $500,000 | |
|   Endowment fund balance ..... | | $500,000 |

(AICPA, adapted)

**P 16-1, Part II** (Multiple Choice)

1. The fiscal year of Redfern University ends on June 30 of each year. In 19X6, the school's summer session started on June 20 and ended on July 30. Tuition and fees for the 19X6 summer session should be recognized as revenue
   a. entirely in the July 1, 19X5–June 30, 19X6 fiscal year.
   b. entirely in the July 1, 19X6–June 30, 19X7 fiscal year.
   c. 25% in the July 1, 19X5–June 30, 19X6 fiscal year and 75% in the July 1, 19X6–June 30, 19X7 fiscal year.
   d. in the fiscal year that payment is actually received.
   e. None of the above.
2. Loan Funds are used to account for assets that
   a. are received as loans from banks and other financial institutions for restricted uses.
   b. are received as loans from federal and state government agencies for restricted uses.
   c. are received as loans from banks and other financial institutions for general (unrestricted) uses.
   d. are received from private donors to be used to make loans to students or staff.
   e. are to be used to pay principal and interest on university long-term debt.
3. The carrying value of the Annuities Payable account in a college's Annuity Fund
   a. should be adjusted to reflect changes in actuarial assumptions such as life expectancies or yield estimates.
   b. should be adjusted only for benefit payments made and investment income earned.
   c. must be adjusted annually to the present value of the required payments.
   d. a and b.
   e. a and c.
4. Boris Badinoff gave 250,000 shares of Natasha, Inc., stock to Bullwinkle State University to endow two scholarships for outstanding students in the school's cartoon department. Dividend income received on these shares should be included in the school's
   a. Loan Fund.
   b. Unrestricted Current Funds.
   c. Restricted Current Funds.
   d. Endowment Funds.
   e. Quasi-Endowment Funds.
5. Wildcat University charges each student an annual student activity fee, which is pledged, via a written contract, for payment of debt service on the Massimino Student Center. The student activity fees, when received, should be recorded
   a. as revenues in the Restricted Current Funds.
   b. as revenues in the Unrestricted Current Funds and as mandatory transfers to the Plant Funds.

    c. as additions to the Plant Funds.

    d. as revenues in the Unrestricted Current Funds and as nonmandatory transfers to the Plant Funds.

    e. as revenues in the Restricted Current Funds and as mandatory transfers to the Plant Funds.

6. The governing board of Slippery Stone University has decided that 10% of tuition for the 19X6 academic year will be set aside for construction of a new physical science building. The designated portion of the tuition should be recorded initially in the

    a. Unrestricted Current Funds.

    b. Restricted Current Funds.

    c. Investment in Plant accounts.

    d. Unexpended Plant Funds.

    e. Quasi-Endowment Funds.

**P 16-2** (Fund Group Identification) Abbreviations such as the following are often used to identify the government college and university fund groups and subgroups:

| | |
|---|---|
| UCF—Unrestricted Current Funds | UPF—Unexpended Plant Funds |
| RCF—Restricted Current Funds | PFRR—Plant Funds for Renewals and |
| ESF—Endowment and Similar Funds |     Replacement |
| LF—Loan Funds | PRFI—Plant Funds for Retirement of |
| AF—Annuity Funds |     Indebtedness |
| LIF—Life Income Funds | IPF—Investment in Plant subgroup |

Using these abbreviations, indicate the fund group or subgroup to be used to account for each of the following items.

1. Unrestricted resources set aside to provide travel loans to students to cover reimbursable expenses incurred on job interviews
2. Fixed assets used in operations
3. Resources set aside by the board to establish a Presidential Honor Scholarship Fund
4. Short-term debt incurred to provide temporary financing for operations
5. Long-term debt related to plant assets in use
6. Fixed assets of a bookstore that is an auxiliary enterprise
7. Bond debt service sinking fund
8. Resources donated to the university with the stipulation that the donor—an active university supporter—receive $80,000 per year for the remainder of his life
9. The resources in 8 after the donor's death, assuming
    a. There are no restrictions on use of the resources
    b. The resources must be used to finance a fine arts center
10. Tuition and fees—a portion of which is required to be used for expanding the student activity center and the library
11. Construction in progress
12. Unrestricted earnings of a term endowment
13. Resources externally restricted by donors for plant additions
14. Earnings of an endowment required to be used to finance scholarships
15. Resources from a grant received to finance cancer research
16. Unrestricted resources set aside by the board of trustees of the university for plant expansion
17. Unrestricted resources set aside by the governing board to finance development of specialized governmental and nonprofit accounting courses
18. Principal of a term endowment upon expiration of the term of the endowment, assuming no restrictions on the use of the resources

**P 16-3** (Unrestricted Current Funds Entries) The trial balance of the Unrestricted Current Funds of X University, a government university, on September 1, 19X0, was as follows:

| | | |
|---|---|---|
| Cash ....................................... | $155,000 | |
| Accounts Receivable ......................... | 30,000 | |
| Allowance for Uncollectible Accounts ............ | | $ 2,000 |
| Inventory of Materials and Supplies ............. | 25,000 | |
| Vouchers Payable ........................... | | 23,000 |
| Fund Balance ............................... | | 185,000 |
| | $210,000 | $210,000 |

X University's dormitory and food service facilities are operated as auxiliary enterprises.

The following transactions took place during the current fiscal year:

1. Collections amounted to $2,270,000, distributed as follows: tuition and fees, $1,930,000; unrestricted gifts, $170,000; sales and services of educational activities, $115,000; other sources, $25,000; accounts receivable, $30,000.
2. Receivables at end of the year were $29,000, consisting entirely of tuition and fees revenues.
3. It is estimated that tuition receivable of $3,000 will never be collected.
4. Revenues from auxiliary enterprises were $300,000, all collected in cash.
5. Materials purchased during the year for cash, $500,000; on account, $50,000.
6. Materials used amounted to $510,000, distributed as follows:

| | | |
|---|---|---|
| Educational and general: | | |
| Institutional support ..................... | $ 30,000 | |
| Research .............................. | 5,000 | |
| Instruction ........................... | 305,000 | |
| Academic support ..................... | 7,000 | |
| Other .............................. | 53,000 | $400,000 |
| Auxiliary enterprises ..................... | | 110,000 |
| | | $510,000 |

7. Salaries and wages paid:

| | | |
|---|---|---|
| Educational and general: | | |
| Institutional support ..................... | $ 170,000 | |
| Research ............................. | 63,000 | |
| Instruction ......................... | 1,212,000 | |
| Academic support ..................... | 80,000 | |
| Other ............................. | 85,000 | $1,610,000 |
| Auxiliary enterprises ..................... | | 90,000 |
| | | $1,700,000 |

8. Other expenditures paid:

| | | |
|---|---|---|
| Educational and general: | | |
| Institutional support ..................... | $10,000 | |
| Research ............................. | 2,000 | |
| Instruction ......................... | 53,000 | |
| Academic support ..................... | 3,000 | |
| Other ............................. | 7,000 | $75,000 |
| Auxiliary enterprises ..................... | | 20,000 |
| | | $95,000 |

9. Interest expenditures chargeable to Institutional Support, $3,000, were paid.
10. Vouchers payable paid, $40,000.
11. A transfer of $20,000 was made to the Fund for Retirement of Indebtedness, as required by the bond indenture.

12. The board of trustees of the university passed a resolution ordering the transfer of $150,000 to a fund that is to function as an endowment, and the transfer was made.
13. $30,000 was transferred from the Unrestricted Current Fund, one-half for additions to the plant and one-half for plant renewals and replacements.

**Required** Prepare journal entries for the Unrestricted Current Funds for the 19X0–19X1 fiscal year.

**P 16-4** (Restricted Current Funds Entries) The trial balance of the Restricted Current Funds of X University on September 1, 19X0 was as follows:

| | | |
|---|---:|---:|
| Cash ............................................... | $32,000 | |
| Vouchers Payable ...................................... | | $ 2,000 |
| Fund Balance* ......................................... | | 30,000 |
| | $32,000 | $32,000 |

*The Fund Balance was from private gifts to be used only for academic support.

The following transactions took place during the current fiscal year:
1. Cash was received as follows for the purposes noted:

| | | |
|---|---:|---:|
| Educational and general: | | |
| Endowments—Institutional support and research ........................ | $ 75,000 | |
| Private gifts—Research ................. | 40,000 | |
| Federal grants—Instruction .............. | 150,000 | |
| State grant—Student services ............ | 20,000 | $285,000 |
| Auxiliary enterprises ...................... | | 130,000 |
| | | $415,000 |

2. Expenditures paid in cash:

| | | |
|---|---:|---:|
| Educational and general: | | |
| Institutional support .................... | $ 40,000 | |
| Research ............................... | 30,000 | |
| Instruction ........................... | 125,000 | |
| Student services ....................... | 20,000 | $215,000 |
| Auxiliary enterprises ..................... | | 90,000 |
| | | $305,000 |

3. Investments of $100,000 were made.

**Required** Prepare journal entries for the Restricted Current Funds for the 19X0–19X1 fiscal year.

**P 16-5** (Endowment Funds Entries) X University, a government university, had no Endowment Funds prior to September 1, 19X0. The following transactions took place in the Endowment Funds of X University during the fiscal year ended August 31, 19X1:
1. At the beginning of the year, a cash donation of $900,000 was received to establish Endowment Fund X, and another donation of $600,000, also in cash, was received for the purpose of establishing Endowment Fund Y. The income from these funds is restricted for specific purposes. It was decided to invest this money immediately; to pool the investments of both funds; and to share earnings, including any gains or losses on sales of investments, at the end of the year based on the ratio of the original contributions of each fund.
2. Securities with a par value of $1,000,000 were purchased at a premium of $10,000.
3. Securities with a par value of $191,500 were acquired at a discount of $2,000; accrued interest at date of purchase amounted to $500.
4. The university trustees voted to pool the investments of a new endowment, Endowment Fund Z, with the investments of Endowment Funds X and Y under the same conditions as applied to the latter two funds. The investments of Endowment Fund Z at the date it joined the pool at midyear amounted to $290,000 at book

value and $300,000 at market value. (Hereafter, the investment pool earnings are to be shared 9:6:3.)

5. Cash dividends received from the pooled investments during the year amounted to $70,000, and interest receipts amounted to $5,500.
6. Premiums of $500 and discounts of $100 were amortized.
7. Securities carried at $30,000 were sold at a gain of $2,400.
8. Each fund was credited with its share of the investment earnings for the year (see transactions 1 and 4).
9. A provision of Endowment Fund Y is that a minimum of $75,000 each year, whether from earnings or principal or both, is to be paid to the Restricted Current Funds to support specified institutional services and research projects. The payment was made.
10. An apartment complex comprised of land, buildings, and equipment valued at $800,000 was donated to the university, distributed as follows: land, $80,000; buildings, $500,000; equipment, $220,000. The donor stipulated that an endowment fund (designated as Endowment Fund N) should be established and that the income therefrom should be used for a restricted operating purpose.
11. $150,000 was received from Unrestricted Current Funds as a quasi-endowment (or fund functioning as an endowment) and was designated Fund O.
12. A trust fund in the amount of $350,000 (cash) was set up by a donor with the stipulation that the income was to go to the university to be used for general purposes. This fund was designated Endowment Fund P.

**Required** Prepare journal entries for the Endowment and Similar Funds group for the 19X0–19X1 fiscal year.

**P 16-6** (Annuity and Life Income Funds Entries) The following transactions affected the Annuity and Life Income Funds and the Loan Funds of X University, a government university, during the fiscal year ended August 31, 19X1:

### Annuity and Life Income Funds

1. A gift of $500,000 cash, from the Lobo family, was received by X University on September 3, 19X0. According to the terms of the bequest, the university must pay the donor, or her estate should she die, $50,000 on each August 31 for 20 years, beginning in 19X1. The balance remaining at the end of the 20-year period is to be used to supplement the income of outstanding professors at X University. The chief finance officer expects to earn an average of at least 9% on investments over the next 20 years.
2. Another gift, from the Mann family, was received, composed of:

| Assets | Donor's Cost | Fair Value |
| --- | --- | --- |
| Land . . . . . . . . . . . . . . . . . . . . . . . . . . . . . . . . | $ 50,000 | $ 70,000 |
| Building . . . . . . . . . . . . . . . . . . . . . . . . . . . . | 300,000 | 400,000 |
| Equipment . . . . . . . . . . . . . . . . . . . . . . . . . . | 80,000 | 40,000 |
| Common Stock . . . . . . . . . . . . . . . . . . . . . . | 100,000 | 90,000 |
| | $530,000 | $600,000 |

The university is to pay the income (as conventionally determined) from these assets to the donor or his spouse as long as either lives. Their combined life expectancy is 15 years according to recognized life expectancy tables.
3. The $500,000 cash received from the Lobo family was invested.
4. The Lobo investments earned $55,000 during the year, all received in cash.
5. The Mann investment earnings were (a) office complex: revenues, $900,000; expenses of $700,000, including $30,000 depreciation on the building and $4,000 depreciation on the equipment; an amount equal to net income before depreciation was received by X University; (b) common stock: dividends of $75,000, all received in cash.

6. The appropriate payments were made to the Lobo and Mann families and appropriate adjusting and closing entries, if any, were made.

### Loan Funds

1. A donation of $150,000 was received in cash for the purpose of making loans to students.
2. Cash in the amount of $50,000 was invested in bonds acquired at par.
3. Loans of $60,000 were made to students.
4. Interest on investments, $300, was received in cash.
5. Student loans of $1,000 were written off as uncollectible.

**Required** Prepare journal entries for the appropriate funds for the 19X0–19X1 fiscal year.

**P 16-7** (Plant Funds Entries) The trial balance of the Investment in Plant subgroup of X University, a government university, as of September 1, 19X0, was as follows:

| | | |
|---|---:|---:|
| Land | $ 200,000 | |
| Buildings | 3,300,000 | |
| Accumulated Depreciation—Buildings | | $ 900,000 |
| Equipment | 1,200,000 | |
| Accumulated Depreciation—Equipment | | 300,000 |
| Mortgage Payable | | 250,000 |
| Net Invested in Plant—Federal Grants | | 625,000 |
| Net Invested in Plant—Unrestricted Funds | | 525,000 |
| Net Invested in Plant—Gifts | | 2,100,000 |
| | $4,700,000 | $4,700,000 |

X University is a state university, but has elected to record accumulated depreciation of its Plant Funds fixed assets.

The following transactions took place during the year:

1. A cash donation of $40,000 was received from an individual for the purpose of financing new additions to the business and public administration building.
2. The money was invested in securities acquired at par.
3. Cash was received from the Unrestricted Current Fund as follows:

| | |
|---|---:|
| For retiring indebtedness | $20,000 |
| For plant improvements and renovations | 15,000 |
| For plant additions | 15,000 |
| | $50,000 |

4. Of the money received from the Unrestricted Current Fund, $10,000 was used to finance the acquisition of additional equipment.
5. A $1,000,000 addition to the business and public administration building was begun. Expenditures of $600,000 were incurred (and paid) by August 31, 19X1, financed by a loan (note) of $1,000,000 from the Last National Bank pending the receipt of more donations. X University's accounting policy is to reclassify construction in progress and related debt to the Investment in Plant accounts at year end.
6. $13,000 was spent in remodeling an art building classroom.
7. A cash donation of $75,000 was received for the purpose of paying part of the mortgage.
8. A mortgage installment of $35,000 ($10,000 principal and $25,000 interest) became due during the year and was paid from the above donation.
9. An uninsured piece of equipment costing $5,000 and financed from the Unrestricted Current Fund was destroyed. Related accumulated depreciation was $2,000.
10. The provision for depreciation for the year was $270,000 for buildings and $120,000 for equipment.

*Required* Prepare journal entries for the several types of Plant Funds, as needed, for the 19X0–19X1 fiscal year.

**P 16-8** (Statements) Analysis of the accounts of Jonimatt State College for the fiscal year ended June 30, 19X7 provided the following information:

| | Unrestricted | Restricted |
|---|---|---|
| Current Fund Revenues from: | | |
| Tuition and fees | $7,300,000 | |
| State appropriations | 5,920,000 | $ 413,000 |
| Federal grants and contracts | | 2,000,000 |
| Private gifts, grants, and contracts | 2,950,000 | 1,112,000 |
| Sales and services of auxiliary enterprises | 3,000,000 | |
| Sales and services of educational activities | 500,000 | |
| | | |
| Current Funds Expenditures for: | | |
| Instruction | 5,830,000 | 760,000 |
| Research | 1,200,000 | 610,000 |
| Public service | 300,000 | 2,000,000 |
| Academic support | 2,000,000 | |
| Student services | 925,000 | |
| Institutional support | 2,500,000 | |
| Operation and maintenance of plant | 3,125,000 | |
| Scholarships and fellowships | 200,000 | 155,000 |
| Auxiliary enterprises | 2,660,000 | |

Jonimatt State College has elected to report accumulated depreciation of Plant Funds assets.

**Additional Information:**

1. Earnings of the Endowment Funds included the following:

| | | |
|---|---|---|
| Unrestricted | $100,000 | |
| Restricted for: | | |
| Scholarships and fellowships | 45,000 | |
| Plant expansion | 75,000 | |
| Total | $220,000 | |

2. Contributions received during fiscal year 19X7 were for these purposes:

| | |
|---|---|
| a. Unrestricted | $2,950,000 |
| b. Scholarships and fellowships | 320,000 |
| c. Specific academic programs | 1,800,000 |
| d. Endowment | 4,300,000 |
| e. Plant expansion | 850,000 |
| f. Debt service | 40,000 |
| g. Life income trust | 160,000 |

3. Restricted investment income was earned for:

| | |
|---|---|
| a. Scholarships and fellowships | $195,000 |
| b. Specific academic programs | 250,000 |
| c. Plant expansion | 78,000 |
| d. Debt service | 30,000 |

4. Federal grants and contracts received during the year of $2,230,000 were restricted for specific operating purposes. State appropriations of $340,000 restricted to spe-

cific academic programs and $500,000 restricted to expansion of the business building also were received.

5. Jonimatt State College accounts for its investments at fair value. Realized gains on restricted endowment funds investments amounted to $50,000 during the year.

6. Proceeds of equipment sales during the year, $27,000, are unrestricted. The cost of the assets sold was $140,000, and the related accumulated depreciation was $104,000.

7. Depreciation of plant facilities for the fiscal year was $800,000.

8. $1,300,000 of plant assets were acquired during fiscal year 19X7, including $280,000 acquired with proceeds of long-term debt issued during the year and $600,000 recorded as current funds expenditures (included in previous information). The remainder of the plant assets was acquired with Unexpended Plant Fund resources. Also, the university issued $4,000,000 of bonds at par to finance construction of a new chemistry building, but construction had not begun at June 30, 19X7.

9. $300,000 of long-term debt and $340,000 of interest matured and were paid in fiscal year 19X7.

10. A $1,000,000 annuity gift was received during the year. The present value of the annuity payments was $480,144 when the gift was received. Investment income for the year was $100,000 and a $90,000 annuity payment was made as stipulated in the gift agreement. The present value of the remaining annuity payments at June 30, 19X7 was $438,158.

11. The principal of a Life Income Fund became available for endowment purposes, $500,000. In addition, two term endowments expired during 19X7. One became available for unrestricted purposes, $350,000; the other is to be used for environmental engineering research, $190,000.

12. $30,000 of a grant restricted for operating purposes that expired during the year was refunded to the federal government.

13. Transfers during fiscal year 19X7 included:
    a. $600,000 to cover scheduled debt service payments
    b. $300,000 to match restricted contributions for plant additions
    c. $100,000 that the board voted to use for plant expansion
    d. $200,000 to establish an endowment for a professorship to honor the university's first president

14. Fund balances of the various funds at the beginning of the year were:

| | |
|---|---:|
| Unrestricted Current Funds | $ 2,012,000 |
| Restricted Current Funds | 978,000 |
| Endowment and Similar Funds | 1,022,000 |
| Annuity and Life Income Funds | 702,000 |
| Unexpended Plant Funds | 320,000 |
| Retirement of Indebtedness Fund | 450,000 |
| Investment in Plant subgroup | 22,717,000 |

**Required**  (a) Prepare a Statement of Current Funds Revenues, Expenditures, and Other Changes for Jonimatt State College for the fiscal year ended June 30, 19X7.

(b) Prepare a Statement of Changes in Fund Balances for Jonimatt State College for the fiscal year ended June 30, 19X7.

# CHAPTER

# 17

# ACCOUNTING FOR HEALTH CARE ORGANIZATIONS

The scope and complexity of the health care environment have undergone swift and dramatic changes in recent years. Correspondingly, health care financial management and accounting practices have evolved rapidly and significantly to keep abreast of environmental changes in areas such as the types and levels of health care services, the way health care services are delivered and procured, the ultimate sources of financing to cover health care charges, the roles of insurance companies and governments in financing health care, and the scope and intensity of competitive pressures.

Because it is more difficult than in the past to generate cash by operations—and because government grants and gifts from philanthropists for construction have decreased, and for other reasons as well—health care entities have found it necessary to turn to the capital markets for loans for expansion. Audited financial statements are highly desirable, if not mandatory, to support borrowing activities; and auditors have therefore increasingly influenced the reporting practices of health care entities. The AICPA's audit guide, *Audits of Health Care Organizations*,[1] is now recognized to constitute, together with applicable GASB and FASB pronouncements, generally accepted accounting principles for government health care providers. As with nongovernment colleges and universities, nongovernment, not-for-profit health care organizations must report in accordance with SFASs 116, 117, and 124. The AICPA audit guide provides guidance for implementing these standards in those nongovernment not-for-profit health care organizations. Additionally, accounting and reporting standards applicable to for-profit entities vary somewhat from those for either of the other types.

GASB *Statement No. 29* prohibits government health care organizations from applying the "not-for-profit" SFASs. Therefore, this chapter emphasizes accounting and reporting for government health care organizations in accordance with GASB standards and the audit guide. The key differences in financial reporting for nongovernment, not-for-profit hospitals are highlighted briefly at the end of Chapter 18. Also, financial statements are presented at that point in accordance with SFASs 116 and 117 using the data from the illustrative example in this chapter.

---

[1] Health Care Committee and Health Care Audit Guide Task Force, American Institute of Certified Public Accountants, *Audits of Health Care Organizations* (New York: AICPA, 1997). (Including Statements of Position issued by the Auditing Standards Division and the Accounting Standards Division.) (Hereafter referred to as the *Health Care Audit Guide.*)

The same accounting and reporting principles apply to the various types of government health care providers. Those principles will be discussed and illustrated in the context of hospitals—the most familiar and most prominent health care provider organization. These principles, with slight variations for unique circumstances and transactions, apply to government nursing homes, and other government health care organizations.

Two industry professional associations—the American Hospital Association (AHA) and the Healthcare Financial Management Association (HFMA)—have been dominant forces in the development and improvement of health care financial management, accounting, and reporting. Accounting and statistical manuals, data processing services, symposiums and workshops, advisory services, and recognized journals are provided for the industry on a regular basis through these associations.[2] These organizations encourage their members to follow generally accepted accounting principles in reporting and to have annual audits. Additionally, HFMA's Principles and Practices Board issues Statements of Principles and Practices providing guidance on certain health care accounting and financial reporting issues.

Accounting for hospitals is very similar to accounting for a specialized industry in business accounting. In fact, in the absence of resources whose use is restricted by donors or grantors, the only significant differences between hospital accounting and business accounting are certain revenue recognition practices of hospitals and the absence, in government and nonprofit hospitals, of the distinction between contributed capital and retained earnings. But when donor- or grantor-restricted assets are held, government hospitals may use separate funds to account for those resources.

## FUNDS—GOVERNMENT HOSPITALS

Governmental hospital financial statements distinguish only two major classes of funds: **unrestricted** and **restricted.** Assets restricted to use for specific purposes by donors or grantors must be accounted for in one of the Restricted Funds. All other assets—including assets whose use is limited by bond indenture, governing board, or other nondonor or nongrantor restrictions—should be accounted for in the Unrestricted Fund. The segregation of donor-restricted resources is reflected in the financial statements of government hospitals primarily in four ways:

- Only transactions and events affecting the Unrestricted Fund are reported in the statement of operations.
- Changes in fund balances of Unrestricted Funds and of Restricted Funds are reported separately in the statement of changes in fund balances.
- Assets that are donor restricted for endowment purposes or for plant purposes are reported as separate line items in the balance sheet.
- The satisfaction of restrictions on the net assets of different types of Restricted Funds are reported differently in the statement of operations and in the statement of changes in fund balances because of the difference in the nature of the restrictions.

Information for some of these reporting distinctions associated with restricted assets typically is accumulated by maintaining accounts using three traditional types of restricted funds. These fund types—Specific Purpose Funds, Endowment Funds,

---

[2] *Hospitals* is the official journal of the American Hospital Association; *Healthcare Financial Management* is that of the Healthcare Financial Management Association (formerly the Hospital Financial Management Association).

and Plant Replacement and Expansion Funds—and their use are discussed later in this section.

## Unrestricted Fund

Four types of resources are accounted for in the Unrestricted Fund: (1) **current** (sometimes called **operating**), (2) **assets limited as to use,** (3) **plant,** and (4) assets held in an **agency** capacity. Assets limited as to use do not include donor-restricted resources. Resources are reported under this category to communicate that assets have been segregated and limited to a specific use based on an internal management decision (often called board designations) or as a result of external restrictions other than those imposed by the donor or grantor of the resources. The external restrictions may arise from bond indenture provisions, trust agreements, externally restricted third-party (Blue Cross, Medicare, Medicaid, etc.) reimbursement agreements, or other similar arrangements. Assets limited to use externally must be distinguished from board-designated resources either in the balance sheet or in the notes.

The limitations on the use of board-designated resources clearly are created at the board's discretion. These are unrestricted resources that the board has designated (not restricted) to be used for a specific noncurrent or nonoperating purpose. Board designations might be established, for example, for expansion of the physical plant, to retire debt, or even to serve as an endowment for the hospital. Board designation of assets for specified purposes does not change the unrestricted status of the assets.

Unlike board-designated resources, other assets limited as to use by bond indentures, third-party reimbursement arrangements, and so on, are legally restricted—just as donor-restricted assets are legally restricted. The apparent distinction between these assets and donor- or grantor-restricted resources is that the bond agreements and third-party reimbursement agreements were entered into voluntarily at the discretion of the governing board of the hospital. Also, some note that such transactions are prevalent throughout U.S. industry and are normal, recurring activities related to the general business operations of a hospital. Thus, Restricted Funds are used only to account for donor- or grantor-restricted resources.

All fixed assets are recorded in the Unrestricted Fund unless they are (1) endowment related or (2) donated fixed assets not yet placed in service. Likewise, a hospital should account for all liabilities that are incurred for the hospital's benefit in the Unrestricted Fund—unless endowment related—if the hospital is responsible for their repayment. Thus, the basic accounting equation for a government hospital Unrestricted Fund is:

$$\frac{\text{Current}}{\text{Assets}} + \frac{\text{Noncurrent}}{\text{Assets}} - \frac{\text{Current}}{\text{Liabilities}} - \frac{\text{Long-Term}}{\text{Liabilities}} = \frac{\text{Fund}}{\text{Balance}}$$

This equation varies from the business accounting equation only with respect to the presentation of equity. As noted earlier, government hospital accounting differs relatively little from basic business accounting.

## Restricted Funds

The term *restricted* is reserved for resources that are restricted as to purpose or timing of use **by donors or grantors.** Examples of purposes for which resources may be restricted are (1) specific operating purposes, (2) additions to fixed assets, and (3) endowment. Many restrictions are temporary and are removed either (1) by meeting a specific condition—as with restrictions for specific purposes—or (2) by passage of time—as with term endowments. Pure endowments—in which the endowment principal can never be expended—create permanent restrictions on those net assets. When restrictions are met, the Unrestricted Funds fund balance is increased and the Restricted Funds fund balance is decreased by the amounts released from restrictions.

Although the only explicit fund distinction required in government hospital financial statements is between Unrestricted and Restricted Funds, three categories of Restricted Funds may be used internally to account for a hospital. We discuss and illustrate these fund types because they facilitate capturing and reporting information that must be reported differently about various Restricted Fund assets and liabilities.

### Specific Purpose Funds

Funds restricted by donors or grantors to specific operating purposes typically are accounted for as restricted fund balance in the Unrestricted Fund or placed in a Specific Purpose Fund until appropriate qualifying costs are incurred. When qualifying costs are incurred, a corresponding amount of revenues for the "amount released from restrictions" also is recognized. The Restricted Fund balance of the Specific Purpose Fund (or of the Unrestricted Fund) is decreased by the same amounts. The qualifying costs incurred are also recorded as assets or expenses, as appropriate, in the Unrestricted Fund.

### Plant Replacement and Expansion Funds

Financial resources and other investments that are given to a government hospital by donors or grantors to be used only for additions to fixed assets are credited to fund balance in a Plant Replacement and Expansion Fund. When costs that satisfy the donor's terms are incurred, the fixed assets acquired and placed in service—and the related fund balance amount—should be recorded in the Unrestricted Fund by debiting the asset account and crediting the Fund Balance account. At the same time, both the assets and the fund balance of the Plant Replacement and Expansion Fund are reduced. Likewise, fixed assets donated to a government hospital and restricted to a specific use are recorded in the Plant Replacement and Expansion Fund until they are placed into service. When placed into service, they also are recorded in the Unrestricted Fund along with the related fund balance amount and are removed from the Plant Replacement and Expansion Fund.

### Endowment Funds

Endowment Funds, including income therefrom, should be accounted for in accordance with the terms of the donor. Income may be unrestricted, in which case it is reported in the Unrestricted Fund—typically as nonoperating gains. The principal of pure endowments must be maintained in perpetuity. The principal of term endowments may become available to the board for either unrestricted or restricted use when the term expires. The financial statements should disclose the essential terms of the endowment—length; uses of resources; restrictions, if any, on the use of income; and the like.

## INCOME DETERMINATION AND ASSET VALUATION FEATURES

Although government hospital accounting may be fund based, the excess of revenues over expenses of the hospital as a whole is calculated and reported. As noted earlier, this does not mean that all hospitals are profit-seeking organizations.

Rather, it reflects the predominant view that (1) hospitals are "going concerns," even if nonprofit, and (2) revenues and gains must cover all expenses and losses if the hospital's capital is to be maintained. Generally accepted accounting principles applicable to government hospitals are a blend of the principles of financial accounting for businesses and of fund accounting. Also, hospital accounting involves several unique income determination and asset valuation features. Many of these are highlighted in Figure 17–1, which summarizes government hospital revenue recognition and fund structure.

## Distinguishing Revenues and Expenses from Gains and Losses

The *Health Care Audit Guide* applies the FASB Concepts *Statement No. 6* definitions of revenues, expenses, gains, and losses. Revenues and expenses result from delivering or producing goods or services, or other "activities that constitute the entity's ongoing major or central operations."[3] Gains and losses occur casually or incidentally in relation to the provider's ongoing activities. The classification of items as revenue or gain and expense or loss, therefore, depends on the individual health care provider. The same transaction may result in reporting revenues for one health care provider and gains for another. Certain transactions such as contributions may be revenue or expense for some hospitals but gain or loss for others. For example, donors' contributions are revenues for hospitals for which fund raising is a major, ongoing activity through which resources are raised to finance the basic functions of the hospital. Hospitals that receive only occasional contributions and have no ongoing, active fund-raising function would report donations as gains.

## Classes of Revenues

Hospital revenues are classified broadly into three major categories:

1. Patient service revenues are earned in the several revenue-producing centers through rendering inpatient and outpatient services. Patient service revenues include revenues generated from (1) daily patient services such as room, board, and general nursing services; (2) other nursing services such as operating room, recovery room, and labor and delivery room nursing services; and (3) other professional services such as laboratories, radiology, anesthesiology, and physical therapy.

2. Premium fees (or subscriber fees) are revenues from agreements under which a hospital has agreed to provide any necessary patient services (perhaps from a contractually agreed set of services) for a specific fee—usually a per member per month (pmpm) fee. Because these fees are earned without regard to the patient services actually provided, they should be reported separately from patient service revenues.

3. Other revenues are those revenues that are derived from ongoing activities other than patient care and service. Major sources are (1) student tuition and fees derived from schools that a hospital operates; (2) revenues recognized when donor- or grantor-restricted resources are used for the specified operating purposes—such as research or education—that fulfill the donor or grantor restrictions; (3) revenues from gifts, grants, or endowment income restricted by donors to finance charity care, and (4) miscellaneous sources such as rentals of hospital plant, sales of scrap, cafeteria sales, sales of supplies to physicians and employees, and fees charged for copies of documents.

Patient service is the major source of revenues for most hospitals. Only the amount of patient service revenues that someone has a responsibility to pay are reported in the hospital statement of revenues and expenses. Patient service revenues

---

[3] *Health Care Audit Guide,* para. 10.2.

**FIGURE 17-1  Government Hospital Revenue and Gain Recognition**

| | | | |
|---|---|---|---|
| **THE UNRESTRICTED FUND (UF)** | | | |

**Unrestricted Fund**

| *Unrestricted "Subfund"* | *Limited Use "Subfund"* | *Unrestricted Operating Revenues* | *Typical Nonoperating Gains\** |
|---|---|---|---|
| 1. Hospital net income is determined here. | 1. UF balances that are not externally restricted but are designated by the governing board for specific purposes and assets limited to use by bond indentures, trust agreements, third-party reimbursement arrangements, etc. | 1. Net Patient Service Revenues | 1. Unrestricted Contributions |
| 2. Full accrual accounting is used, subject to restricted revenue recognition conventions. | | 2. Premium Fees | 2. Income and Gains from Unrestricted Investments |
| 3. Revenues are distinguished from gains. | | 3. Other Operating Revenues | 3. Donations of Noncash Assets |
| 4. Patient service revenue is reported net of contractual and other adjustments that reflect amounts that patients are not obligated to pay. | | • Amounts Released from Restrictions Used for Specific Operating Purposes | |
| | 2. Assets limited as to use are reported in the balance sheet after Current Assets. | • Professional Services | |
| 5. Provision of charity services does not result in revenue. | | • Tuition | |
| | | • Parking | |
| | 3. "Designation" of Unrestricted Fund (UF) fund balance can be shown. | • Cafeteria | |
| 6. All unrestricted assets and liabilities are recorded here. | | • Medical Records | |
| | | • Donation of Services | |
| | | • Etc. | |

↑ Plant and equipment purchased from the PREF is capitalized in the UF when placed in service and increases Unrestricted Fund Balance (not revenues or gains) in the UF.

↑ Unrestricted EF earnings and any principal of expired term endowments are recognized in the UF as nonoperating gains.\*

↑ Transfers (reclassifications) are recognized in the UF as (1) operating revenues, if used for operating purposes, or (2) nonoperating gains\* if unrestricted investment income.

**RESTRICTED FUNDS (RF)**
donor- or grantor-restricted contributions and related restricted interest earnings are recorded as fund balance increases. Satisfactions of restrictions are recorded as RF decreases since all "operations" are reported in the UF.

| *Plant Replacement and Expansion (PREF)* | | *Endowment (EF)* | | *Specific Purpose (SPF)* |
|---|---|---|---|---|
| 1. Contributions to the PREF are viewed as increases of hospital capital. | Endowment earnings restricted for plant placement and expansion | 1. May be permanent ("pure") or "term" endowment. | Endowment earnings restricted for a specific purpose | 1. Fund balance is decreased by "Amounts Released from Restrictions . . ." when qualifying SPF expenditures are made from UF. |
| 2. Capital outlay expenditures decrease the PREF fund balance and increase the UF fund balance when the assets are placed in service. | ← — | 2. Endowment earnings may be restricted or unrestricted. | — → | |
| 3. Unrestricted investment earnings are transferred to the UF as non-operating gains.\* | | | | 2. Unrestricted investment earnings are transferred to the UF as nonoperating gains.\* |

↑ ↑ ↑ Donor- or Grantor-Restricted Contributions—Government Grants—Restricted Investment Earnings

\*Can be revenue if a major, ongoing, central part of operations.

are reported net of charity services, contractual adjustments arising from third-party payer agreements or regulations, policy discounts extended to patients who are members of the medical profession or clergy, administrative adjustments, and any similar amounts that neither patients nor third-party payers are deemed obligated to pay. Revenues are not reduced for estimated uncollectible accounts.

Typical types of deductions from patient service revenues include (1) charity services for patients who do not pay the established rates because they are indigent, (2) policy discounts for members of groups (doctors, clergy, employees, or employees' dependents) who receive allowances in accordance with hospital policy, and (3) contractual adjustments for patients' bills that are paid to the hospital by third-party payers at lower than established rates in accordance with contracts between the hospital and third-party payers. A hospital must have established criteria to distinguish charity services from bad debts. Charity services are not reported as revenues or as receivables in the financial statements. Only services rendered under circumstances that meet the preestablished criteria for charity services should be treated as charity services. Other uncollectible amounts are reported as bad debt expense. The distinction is significant both in terms of financial reporting and funding under certain federal and state programs.

When third-party payers (usually Medicare, Medicaid, and Blue Cross) contract with hospitals to pay patients' bills, agreed reimbursement rates are likely to be based on cost or some national or regional average charge for similar hospital services. Established (standard) hospital rates are not necessarily based on cost; indeed, they are not likely to represent cost. Hence, whereas gross revenues for services rendered to Medicare and other third-party payer patients are initially recorded at standard established rates, a contractual allowance is needed to reduce gross revenues to amounts actually receivable. This internal accounting approach provides information useful for management analyses of revenue patterns and certain note disclosures—for example, the amount of charity services rendered.

To illustrate, assume that a hospital's standard gross charges for services rendered in a year total $1,000,000, but the amount it ultimately expects to collect is only $850,000. The hospital rendered $40,000 of charity services and had estimated contractual adjustments of $60,000 and estimated bad debts of $50,000. The required entries are:

**Unrestricted Fund**

| | | |
|---|---|---|
| Accounts and Notes Receivable .......................... | $1,000,000 | |
|     Patient Service Charges ............................... | | $1,000,000 |

To record gross billings for services at established rates.

| | | |
|---|---|---|
| Contractual Adjustments .................................. | $  60,000 | |
| Charity Services or **Patient Service Charges**[4] ................. | 40,000 | |
|     Allowance for Uncollectible Receivables and Third-Party | | |
|         Contractuals ........................................ | | $  60,000 |
|     Accounts and Notes Receivable ......................... | | 40,000 |

To record deductions from gross revenues and the related
  allowance.

| | | |
|---|---|---|
| Expenses—Provision for Bad Debts ....................... | $  50,000 | |
|     Allowance for Uncollectible Receivables and Third-Party | | |
|         Contractuals ........................................ | | $  50,000 |

To record estimated bad debts.

---

[4] Charity services are not revenues. Hospitals may initially record the patient services charges, however, for two reasons. First, the hospital may not know initially that an account qualifies as charity service. Second, hospitals must disclose the level of charity service provided. If a hospital does this based on standard charges for charity services provided, this method captures that information.

Note that when specific receivables are identified as not being collectible, the receivables should be written off against the allowance. The appropriate reporting of this information is:

**Balance Sheet**

| | | |
|---|---|---|
| Accounts and notes receivable | $960,000 | |
| Less: Allowance for uncollectible receivables and third-party contractuals | 110,000 | $850,000 |

**Statement of Operations**

| | |
|---|---|
| Net Patient Service Revenues | $900,000 |
| ($1,000,000 – $40,000 – $60,000) | |
| Bad Debt Expense | $ 50,000 |

## Gains

As noted earlier, gains arise from activities that are not part of a hospital's major, ongoing, or central operations. Too, whereas revenues are reported prior to deducting related costs, gains often will be reported net of such costs, for example, gains on sales of investments in securities or fixed assets. Typical gains of hospitals result from

> Sales of investments in securities
>
> Sales of fixed assets
>
> Gifts or donations (which are revenue for some hospitals)
>
> Investment income (which is revenue for some hospitals)

Whether items such as contributions and investment income are revenues or gains depends upon the definition of the mission of individual hospitals. The treatment is determined by whether fund raising (for contributions) or investment income are intended to be major ongoing sources of financing for the hospital. If so, the related amounts are revenue; otherwise they are gains.

## Donations

Government hospitals receive several kinds of donations. Unrestricted gifts, grants, and bequests typically are recorded as gains of the Unrestricted Fund. Hospitals also may receive donations in the form of professional services. For example, retired physicians or pharmacists may voluntarily work part-time in their professional capacities. Or priests and nuns who are physicians, pharmacists, or nurses may work full-time for no pay. The fair market value of donated services is recorded as other revenues if they create or enhance a nonfinancial asset, or if they meet three other conditions. These conditions are as follows:

- The service requires specialized skills.
- The volunteer possesses the specialized skills.
- The service would typically need to be bought if not contributed.

Gifts of supplies and commodities also are recorded at fair market value as other revenues or as gains.

Resources that donors require to be used for specific operating purposes increase restricted fund balance. They ordinarily are recorded as additions to fund balance in a Specific Purpose Fund, as assumed here. When the terms of the gift (or grant) are satisfied by appropriate expenditures, net assets released from restrictions should be recognized as (1) operating revenues in the Unrestricted Fund, and (2) as a decrease in Restricted Fund Balance in the Statement of Changes in

Fund Balance. "Amounts released from restrictions" is the terminology used to communicate that the restrictions on resources have been satisfied. It always results in an increase in Unrestricted Fund Balance and a decrease in Restricted Fund Balance. The increase in Unrestricted Fund Balance is reported differently in the Statement of Operations for satisfaction of different types of restrictions as shown in Figure 17–2. Donations or grants made to a government hospital for the care of charity patients should be reported as revenues as well.

When a donor specifies that resources are to be used to acquire fixed assets, such gifts increase the permanent capital, and the resources are recorded as an increase in the Plant Replacement and Expansion Fund fund balance. When construction costs are incurred, construction in progress is recorded in the Plant Replacement and Expansion Fund. When the fixed asset is placed in service, net assets released from restriction are reported as an increase in Unrestricted Fund Balance and a decrease in Restricted Fund Balance. If the donation consists of fixed assets, they are recorded directly in the Unrestricted Fund with a credit to Fund Balance unless the assets are not placed in service immediately. Donated fixed assets not placed in service immediately are initially recorded in the Plant Replacement and Expansion Fund. They are transferred to the Unrestricted Fund—increasing Unrestricted Fund fund balance—when placed in service. The rationale for not recognizing revenue or gain is that a restricted capital gift has been made. A more practical reason might be to avoid the distortion of reported revenues and gains that would result from reporting the gift of a major asset as revenues or gains.

## Timing of Revenue and Gain Recognition

A significant feature of government hospital accounting is that revenue or gain is recognized in the period in which the related assets become available for unrestricted use by the governing board or are used for the donor-specified restricted purposes. Unrestricted revenues and gains are recognized on the accrual basis. Assets restricted to use for specified purposes, such as research grants, are considered realized in the period that they are used for the restricted purpose.

Recognition of revenue or gain for donor-restricted assets is delayed for two reasons. First, it permits recognition of revenues or gains in the same period that the related costs are incurred. Second, it can be said that externally restricted resources are not truly earned until they are used for their designated purpose.

## Expense Classification

The measurement and recognition criteria for expenses and losses are generally identical to those for business entities. A key exception is that the pension expense measurement for government hospitals differs because government entities should apply GASB *Statement No. 27,* "Accounting for Pensions by State and Local Governmental Employers," rather than SFAS 87, "Employers' Accounting for Pensions." Hospital expenses are typically classified by such major functions as:

1. Nursing services
2. Other professional services
3. General services
4. Fiscal services
5. Administrative services
6. Other services

**FIGURE 17–2  Government Hospital Reporting of Restricted Cash Contributions**

| Transaction/Event | Balance Sheet | Statement of Operations | Statement of Changes in Fund Balances (FB) | Statement of Cash Flows |
|---|---|---|---|---|
| Receipt of SPF contribution | Cash included with UF cash; Restricted Fund Balance reported | | Increase in Restricted Fund FB | Noncapital Financing Activities |
| Receipt of EF or PREF contribution | Reported as Assets Restricted for Endowment (or Plant Replacement and Expansion); Restricted Fund Balance reported | | Increase in Restricted Fund FB | Noncapital Financing Activities for EF contributions received; Capital and Related Financing Activities for PREF contributions received |
| Qualifying expenditures for SPF gift incurred | | Revenues—Amount Released from Restrictions Used for Specific Programs | (1) Included in Excess of Revenues over Expenses for UF (2) Reported as decrease in FB—Amounts Released from Restrictions—for Restricted Funds | Cash payments typically are Operating Activities, but fixed asset purchases are Capital and Related Financing Activities |
| Qualifying PREF expenditures incurred, asset placed in service | Fixed asset reported; Unrestricted FB reported | No revenues reported. Amount Released from Restrictions Used for Purchase of Property and Equipment reported after Excess of Revenues and Gains over Expenses and Losses | Reported as Amounts Released from Restrictions . . .—an increase in FB for the UF and a decrease in FB for the Restricted Funds | Capital and Related Financing Activities (when cash is paid) |
| Expiration of term endowment—no purpose restriction | Becomes part of general cash or investment balance; Unrestricted FB reported | Gain—Amount Released from Restriction by Expiration of Endowment Term | Reported as Amounts Released from Restrictions . . .—an increase in FB for the UF and a decrease in FB for the Restricted Funds | |

**Legend:**

    EF   = Endowment Fund
    FB   = Fund Balance
    PREF = Plant Replacement and Expansion Fund
    SPF  = Specific Purpose Fund
    UF   = Unrestricted Fund

Each of these major expense classifications may be subclassified further according to organizational unit and object classification, thus creating a multiple classification scheme not unlike the multiple classification of expenditures used in state and local government accounting. Hospitals are permitted to use natural rather than functional expense classifications in the statement of operations. However, if functional classifications are not reported in the statement, they must be disclosed in the notes.

**Nursing services expenses** includes the nursing services provided in the various patient care facilities of a hospital—for example, medical and surgical, pediatrics, intensive care, operating rooms—as well as nursing administrative, educational, and various other related costs. **Other professional services expenses** is used to classify expenses incurred in providing other medical care to patients—such as laboratories, blood bank, radiology, pharmacy, anesthesiology, and social services—as well as expenses incurred for research, education, and administration in these areas. Care of the physical plant, dietary services, and other nonmedical services that are part of the ongoing physical operations of a hospital are classified as **general services expenses.** Expenses incurred for accounting, admitting, data processing, storerooms, and similar activities are grouped as **fiscal services expenses;** and expenses incurred by the executive office, personnel, purchasing, public relations, and the like are classified as **administrative services expenses.** Depreciation, bad debts, employee benefits, interest, taxes, insurance, and similar costs may be reported under the preceding functional classifications or may be reported as separate line items in a government hospital statement of revenues and expenses.

## Property, Plant, and Equipment

Hospital fixed assets should be recorded at historical cost or at fair value at donation in the Unrestricted Fund and depreciated. If appropriate records have not been maintained, the assets should be inventoried, appraised on the basis of historical cost (net of accumulated depreciation), and recorded. The basis of fixed asset valuation should be disclosed, of course, as should the depreciation policy.

Assets used by the hospital may be owned outright, leased from or made available by independent or related organizations, or provided by a governmental agency or hospital district. The nature of such relationships must be disclosed in the financial statements, and they should be accounted for and reported in conformity with GAAP. Specifically, the provisions of FASB *Statement No. 13,* "Accounting for Leases," as amended, should be followed in accounting for leases.

## ILLUSTRATIVE TRANSACTIONS AND ENTRIES

Accounting for the varied, complex, and voluminous transactions of a government hospital requires many subsidiary ledgers and other similar records. In this illustrative case we deal only with the general ledger accounts.

The case example presented here relates to Alzona Hospital, a medium size, government, general short-term health care facility financed from patient services fees, donations, and investment earnings. The balance sheet of Alzona Hospital at October 1, 19A, the beginning of the fiscal year to which the example relates, is presented as Figure 17–3.

**FIGURE 17–3 Beginning Balance Sheet—Government Hospital**

Alzona Hospital
**Balance Sheet**
October 1, 19A

**Assets**

Current:

| | | |
|---|---:|---:|
| Cash | | $ 215,000 |
| Investments | | 460,000 |
| Accounts and notes receivable | $ 700,000 | |
| Less: Estimated uncollectibles and allowances | 85,000 | 615,000 |
| Inventories | | 165,000 |
| Total current assets | | 1,455,000 |

Noncurrent:

| | | |
|---|---:|---:|
| Assets restricted for plant replacement and expansion* | 325,000 | |
| Assets restricted for permanent endowments* | 480,000 | |
| Total noncurrent restricted assets | 805,000 | |
| Property, plant, and equipment: | | |
| Land | 130,000 | |
| Land improvements | 80,000 | |
| Buildings | 5,000,000 | |
| Fixed equipment | 600,000 | |
| Major movable equipment | 90,000 | |
| Total property, plant, and equipment | 5,900,000 | |
| Less: Accumulated depreciation | 2,450,000 | |
| Net property, plant, and equipment | 3,450,000 | |
| Total noncurrent assets | | 4,255,000 |
| Total assets | | $5,710,000 |

**Liabilities and Fund Balances**

Current liabilities:

| | | |
|---|---:|---:|
| Notes payable | $ 150,000 | |
| Accounts payable | 175,000 | |
| Total current liabilities | 325,000 | |
| Long-term debt: | | |
| Mortgage payable | 100,000 | |
| Total Liabilities | | $ 425,000 |

Fund Balance:

Restricted for:

| | | |
|---|---:|---:|
| Specific programs | 255,000 | |
| Endowment | 480,000 | |
| Plant purposes | 325,000 | |
| Total restricted fund balance | 1,060,000 | |
| Unrestricted | 4,225,000 | |
| Total fund balance | | 5,285,000 |
| Total liabilities and fund balance | | $5,710,000 |

*See October 1, 19A trial balance for Alzona's Restricted Funds and the accompanying discussion in Figure 17–4.

**FIGURE 17–4  Restricted Funds Trial Balances**

Alzona Hospital
**Restricted Funds Trial Balances**
October 1, 19A

| Accounts | Specific Purpose Dr. | Specific Purpose Cr. | Endowment Dr. | Endowment Cr. | Plant Replacement and Expansion Dr. | Plant Replacement and Expansion Cr. |
|---|---|---|---|---|---|---|
| Cash | $ 20,000 | | $ 25,000 | | $ 25,000 | |
| Investments | 360,000 | | 475,000 | | 300,000 | |
| Due from Endowment Fund | 20,000 | | | | | |
| Due to Unrestricted Fund | | $145,000 | | | | |
| Due to Specific Purpose Fund | | | | $ 20,000 | | |
| Fund Balance | | 255,000 | | 480,000 | | 325,000 |
| Totals | $400,000 | $400,000 | $500,000 | $500,000 | $325,000 | $325,000 |

Notes:

1. Interfund payables and receivables are eliminated by assuming that payment is made. Amounts reported in the balance sheet are presented under this assumption. Thus, $20,000 of Endowment Fund cash is reported as if it were Specific Purpose Fund cash, eliminating the Due to Specific Purpose Fund in the Endowment Fund and the Due from Endowment Fund in the Specific Purpose Fund. Specific Purpose Fund cash and investments are not required to be reported separately from Unrestricted Fund assets. Therefore, the Due to Unrestricted Fund liability is eliminated against the equivalent Due from Specific Purpose Fund asset account that would appear in an Unrestricted Fund trial balance (which is not presented here) and neither is reported in the balance sheet.

2. Specific Purpose Fund cash, $20,000, is added to the cash of the Unrestricted Fund (which was $175,000 at October 1, 19A) in determining the amount to report as cash in the balance sheet. Likewise, another $20,000 of cash included in the Endowment Fund is assumed collected by the Specific Purpose Fund from the Endowment Fund to settle the interfund receivable. (See previous note.) That amount also is added to the Unrestricted Fund cash to get the amount reported as cash in the balance sheet, $215,000 ($175,000 + $20,000 + $20,000).

   Any remaining cash balances of the Endowment Fund or the Plant Replacement and Expansion Fund are reported in the restricted asset line items discussed in the next note.

3. The net assets of the Plant Replacement and Expansion Fund are required to be reported as "Assets restricted for plant replacement and expansion." The amount reported equals the fund balance of this fund.

4. The net assets of the Endowment Fund are required to be reported as "Assets restricted for endowment." The amount reported equals the fund balance of the Endowment Fund.

**Summary of Transactions and Events**

## Unrestricted Fund:

**1.** Gross charges to patients at standard established rates were $4,400,000.

| | | |
|---|---|---|
| (1) Accounts and Notes Receivable . . . . . . . . . . . . . . . . . . . | $4,400,000 | |
| **Patient Service Charges** . . . . . . . . . . . . . . . . . . . . . . . | | $4,400,000 |

To record gross billings for services at established rates.

**2.** $85,000 of receivables were written off against the prior year allowance balance—$70,000 for uncollectible accounts and $15,000 for contractual adjustments.

(2) **Allowance for Uncollectible Receivables and**
   **Third-Party Contractuals** . . . . . . . . . . . . . . . . . . . .   $   85,000
   Accounts and Notes Receivable . . . . . . . . . . . . . . . .       $   85,000
   To record write-off of receivables.

**3.** The hospital wrote off $265,000 of receivables established in 19B (entry 1) associated with Medicare, Medicaid, and insured patients due to contractual adjustments.

(3)  Contractual Adjustments . . . . . . . . . . . . . . . . . . . . . . . .   $   265,000
   Accounts and Notes Receivable . . . . . . . . . . . . . . . .       $   265,000
   To record contractual adjustments.

**4.** The hospital determined that $125,000 of the services it provided were to patients who met the hospital criteria for charity services.

(4)  Charity Services . . . . . . . . . . . . . . . . . . . . . . . . . . . . . . . .   $   125,000
   Accounts and Notes Receivable . . . . . . . . . . . . . . . .       $   125,000
   To record charity services.

Recall that charity services do not result in patient service revenues—gross or net—under the audit guide because there is no expectation of payment. If a hospital discloses the composition of its net patient service revenues in its notes, charity services are not part of that disclosure. Disclosure of the level of charity service is required—but may be in terms of revenue, cost, units, or other statistics.

**5.** Collections of accounts receivable totaled $3,800,000.

(5)  Cash . . . . . . . . . . . . . . . . . . . . . . . . . . . . . . . . . . . . . . . . . .   $3,800,000
   Accounts and Notes Receivable . . . . . . . . . . . . . . . .       $3,800,000
   To record collections of accounts receivable.

**6.** Additional accounts receivable written off as uncollectible during the year totaled $55,000.

(6)  Allowance for Uncollectible Receivables and
   Third-Party Contractuals . . . . . . . . . . . . . . . . . . . .   $   55,000
   Accounts and Notes Receivable . . . . . . . . . . . . . . . .       $   55,000
   To record write-off of accounts deemed uncollectible.

**7.** The estimated bad debts for the year totaled $120,000. Also, additional contractual adjustments related to 19B of $25,000 are expected to result from final settlements with third-party payers of their clients' accounts.

(7) **Expenses—Bad Debts** . . . . . . . . . . . . . . . . . . . . . . . . . .   $   120,000
   Contractual Adjustments . . . . . . . . . . . . . . . . . . . . . . .     25,000
   Allowance for Uncollectible Receivables and
    Third-Party Contractuals . . . . . . . . . . . . . . . . . . . .       $   145,000
   To adjust bad debt expense, deductions from gross
    revenues, and the allowance accounts to appropriate
    year-end balances.

**8.** Materials and supplies, including food, purchased on account during the year totaled $600,000. A perpetual inventory system is in use.

(8)  Inventories . . . . . . . . . . . . . . . . . . . . . . . . . . . . . . . . . . . .   $   600,000
   Accounts Payable . . . . . . . . . . . . . . . . . . . . . . . . . . .       $   600,000
   To record inventory purchases on account.

**9.** Materials and supplies were used by major functions as follows:

| | |
|---|---:|
| Nursing services . . . . . . . . . . . . . . . . . . . . . . . | $170,000 |
| Other professional services . . . . . . . . . . . . . . . | 50,000 |
| General services . . . . . . . . . . . . . . . . . . . . . | 319,000 |
| Fiscal services . . . . . . . . . . . . . . . . . . . . . . . | 8,000 |
| Administrative services . . . . . . . . . . . . . . . . . | 3,000 |
| | $550,000 |

| | | |
|---|---:|---:|
| (9) **Expenses—Nursing Services** . . . . . . . . . . . . . . . . . . . . | $ 170,000 | |
| **Expenses—Other Professional Services** . . . . . . . . . . . | 50,000 | |
| **Expenses—General Services** . . . . . . . . . . . . . . . . . . . | 319,000 | |
| **Expenses—Fiscal Services** . . . . . . . . . . . . . . . . . . . . | 8,000 | |
| **Expenses—Administrative Services** . . . . . . . . . . . . . | 3,000 | |
| Inventories . . . . . . . . . . . . . . . . . . . . . . . . . . | | $ 550,000 |
| To record inventory usage. | | |

**10.** Accounts payable paid during the year were $725,000.

| | | |
|---|---:|---:|
| (10) Accounts Payable . . . . . . . . . . . . . . . . . . . . . . . . . | $ 725,000 | |
| Cash . . . . . . . . . . . . . . . . . . . . . . . . . . . . . . . . | | $ 725,000 |
| To record payment of accounts payable. | | |

**11.** Salaries and wages paid during the year were for the following:

| | |
|---|---:|
| Nursing services . . . . . . . . . . . . . . . . . . . . . . . | $1,316,000 |
| Other professional services . . . . . . . . . . . . . . . | 828,000 |
| General services . . . . . . . . . . . . . . . . . . . . . | 389,000 |
| Fiscal services . . . . . . . . . . . . . . . . . . . . . . . | 102,000 |
| Administrative services . . . . . . . . . . . . . . . . . | 65,000 |
| | $2,700,000 |

| | | |
|---|---:|---:|
| (11) Expenses—Nursing Services . . . . . . . . . . . . . . . . . . . . | $1,316,000 | |
| Expenses—Other Professional Services . . . . . . . . . . . | 828,000 | |
| Expenses—General Services . . . . . . . . . . . . . . . . . . . | 389,000 | |
| Expenses—Fiscal Services . . . . . . . . . . . . . . . . . . . . | 102,000 | |
| Expenses—Administrative Services . . . . . . . . . . . . . | 65,000 | |
| Cash . . . . . . . . . . . . . . . . . . . . . . . . . . . . . . . . | | $2,700,000 |
| To record salaries and wages paid. | | |

**12.** Expenses, other than for salaries and materials and supplies, paid during the year were chargeable as follows:

| | |
|---|---:|
| Nursing services . . . . . . . . . . . . . . . . . . . . . . . | $ 86,000 |
| Other professional services . . . . . . . . . . . . . . . | 79,000 |
| General services . . . . . . . . . . . . . . . . . . . . . | 221,000 |
| Fiscal services . . . . . . . . . . . . . . . . . . . . . . . | 44,000 |
| Administrative services . . . . . . . . . . . . . . . . . | 327,000 |
| | $757,000 |

| | | |
|---|---:|---:|
| (12) Expenses—Nursing Services . . . . . . . . . . . . . . . . . . . . | $ 86,000 | |
| Expenses—Other Professional Services . . . . . . . . . . . | 79,000 | |
| Expenses—General Services . . . . . . . . . . . . . . . . . . . | 221,000 | |
| Expenses—Fiscal Services . . . . . . . . . . . . . . . . . . . . | 44,000 | |
| Expenses—Administrative Services . . . . . . . . . . . . . | 327,000 | |
| Cash . . . . . . . . . . . . . . . . . . . . . . . . . . . . . . . . | | $ 757,000 |
| To record expense payments. | | |

**13.** Salaries and wages accrued at year end were for the following:

| | |
|---|---:|
| Nursing services | $35,000 |
| Other professional services | 21,000 |
| General services | 19,000 |
| Fiscal services | 6,000 |
| Administrative services | 2,000 |
| | $83,000 |

| | | |
|---|---:|---:|
| (13) Expenses—Nursing Services | $35,000 | |
| Expenses—Other Professional Services | 21,000 | |
| Expenses—General Services | 19,000 | |
| Expenses—Fiscal Services | 6,000 | |
| Expenses—Administrative Services | 2,000 | |
| Accrued Salaries and Wages Payable | | $83,000 |
| To record accrued expenses at year end. | | |

**14.** Interest expense on notes payable was $8,000, of which $1,000 was accrued at year end; the principal was reduced by $20,000.

| | | |
|---|---:|---:|
| (14) Notes Payable | $20,000 | |
| Expenses—Interest | 8,000 | |
| Accrued Interest Payable | | $ 1,000 |
| Cash | | 27,000 |
| To record interest payment and accrual, and reduction of principal of notes payable. | | |

**15.** Interest earned during the year on Unrestricted Fund investments was $5,000, of which $2,000 was accrued at year end. The investments are exempt from the GASB fair value accounting requirements.

| | | |
|---|---:|---:|
| (15) Cash | $ 3,000 | |
| Accrued Interest Receivable | 2,000 | |
| Nonoperating Gains—Unrestricted Fund Investment Income | | $ 5,000 |
| To record interest earned on Unrestricted Fund investments. | | |

**16.** Unrestricted earnings on Specific Purpose Fund investments, $24,000, were received and accounted for directly in the Unrestricted Fund.

| | | |
|---|---:|---:|
| (16) Cash | $24,000 | |
| **Nonoperating Gains—Unrestricted Investment Income from Specific Purpose Fund** | | $24,000 |
| To record unrestricted interest earnings on Specific Purpose Fund investments deposited directly in the Unrestricted Fund. | | |

**17.** Professional services donated to the hospital were objectively valued and charged as follows:

| | |
|---|---:|
| Nursing services | $17,000 |
| Other professional services | 3,000 |
| | $20,000 |

| | | |
|---|---:|---:|
| (17) Expenses—Nursing Services | $17,000 | |
| Expenses—Other Professional Services | 3,000 | |
| **Revenues—Donated Services** | | $20,000 |
| To record the value of donated services received. | | |

**18.** Other revenues collected during the year were from the following:

| | |
|---|---:|
| Cafeteria sales | $45,000 |
| Television rentals | 30,000 |
| Medical record transcript fees | 15,000 |
| Vending machine commissions | 5,000 |
| | $95,000 |

| | | |
|---|---:|---:|
| (18) Cash | $ 95,000 | |
| Revenues—Cafeteria Sales | | $ 45,000 |
| Revenues—Television Rentals | | 30,000 |
| Revenues—Medical Record Transcript Fees | | 15,000 |
| Revenues—Vending Machine Commissions | | 5,000 |

To record receipt of miscellaneous revenues.

**19.** General contributions received in cash, $100,000.

| | | |
|---|---:|---:|
| (19) Cash | $ 100,000 | |
| **Nonoperating Gains—General Contributions** | | $ 100,000 |

To record receipt of unrestricted contributions.

**20.** Bonds were issued at par, $3,000,000, to be used to pay for a new building wing and to retire the mortgage payable.

| | | |
|---|---:|---:|
| (20) **Cash—Construction** | $2,900,000 | |
| **Cash—Debt Service** | 100,000 | |
| Bonds Payable | | $3,000,000 |

To record sale of bonds at par.

Note that this externally restricted cash is reported as "Assets limited as to use."

**21.** The mortgage notes (Figure 17–3) were paid and the contractor billed Alzona $2,500,000 for work completed on the new wing to date. All but a 5% retained percentage was paid.

| | | |
|---|---:|---:|
| (21) Construction in Process | $2,500,000 | |
| **Mortgage Payable** | 100,000 | |
| **Contracts Payable—Retained Percentage—Construction** | | $ 125,000 |
| **Cash—Construction** | | 2,375,000 |
| **Cash—Debt Service** | | 100,000 |

To record payment of mortgage payable and the progress billings on the building, less percentage of contract retained pending final inspection.

**22.** Equipment costing $100,000, on which there was accumulated depreciation of $60,000, was sold for $30,000.

| | | |
|---|---:|---:|
| (22) Cash | $ 30,000 | |
| Accumulated Depreciation | 60,000 | |
| Nonoperating Losses—Disposal of Fixed Assets | 10,000 | |
| Fixed Equipment | | $ 100,000 |

To record the sale of fixed equipment at a loss.

**23.** The board of directors designated $100,000 for future plant replacement and expansion. Although this action is binding on hospital management, it does not remove resources from the Unrestricted Fund.

(23) (a) **Investments—Designated for Plant Replacement** .. $100,000

    Investments ..............................         $100,000

    To reclassify investments per board designation.

(23) (b) **Fund Balance** .............................. $100,000

    **Fund Balance Designated for Plant Replacement**

      **and Expansion** .........................       $100,000

    To record the board's designation for plant
    replacement and expansion.

Note that this action creates internal "Assets limited as to use."

**24.** The charges to General Services Expenses were found to include $5,000 for major movable equipment. (No depreciation need be recorded for the current year.)

(24) Major Movable Equipment ...................... $ 5,000

    Expenses—General Services ..................     $ 5,000

    To capitalize equipment previously charged to
    expense.

**25.** Depreciation expense for the year was $300,000.

(25) Expenses—Depreciation ....................... $300,000

    Accumulated Depreciation ...................      $300,000

    To record depreciation expense.

**26.** Accrued interest on bonds payable at year end (see transaction 20) was $30,000.

(26) Expenses—Interest ........................... $ 30,000

    Accrued Interest Payable ....................      $ 30,000

    To record interest accrued at year end on bonds
    outstanding.

## Specific Purpose Fund (Transactions and entries 27 to 31 affect only the Specific Purpose Fund.)

**27.** A $400,000 grant to defray specific operating costs was received.

(27) Cash ........................................ $400,000

    **Fund Balance** ..............................      $400,000

    To record receipt of a grant to be used to pay certain
    operating costs.

Note that different gifts or grants may be required to be used for different operating purposes. Thus, several Fund Balance accounts must be maintained for the Specific Purpose Fund. We assume that the detail in this example is maintained in a Fund Balance subsidiary ledger—which is not illustrated in the example—rather than in separate general ledger Fund Balance accounts. The latter approach is illustrated in the college and university Restricted Current Funds example in Chapter 16.

**28.** Investments made during the period were $300,000.

(28) Investments ................................. $300,000

    Cash .......................................      $300,000

    To record investments during the period.

**29.** Investments maturing during the period, $150,000, had been originally purchased at par.

(29) Cash ........................................ $150,000

    Investments .................................      $150,000

    To record the maturity of investments originally
    purchased at par.

**30.** Earnings on investments, restricted to specific purposes, were $15,000. (Compare this transaction with transaction 16.)

| | | |
|---|---|---|
| (30)  Cash ........................................ | $ 15,000 | |
|        **Fund Balance** ............................. | | $ 15,000 |

To record receipt of investment income that is restricted to specific purposes.

**31.** The fair market value of Specific Purpose Fund investments on which income is restricted to a specific purpose increased by $500.

| | | |
|---|---|---|
| (31)  Investments ................................... | $   500 | |
|        Fund Balance ............................. | | $   500 |

To record the increase in the fair market value of restricted investments.

## Endowment Fund (Transactions and entries 32 to 35 affect only the Endowment Fund.)

**32.** A benefactor gave rental properties valued at $300,000, and subject to a $100,000 mortgage, to the hospital. The corpus is to be maintained intact; earnings may be used for general operating purposes.

| | | |
|---|---|---|
| (32)  Rental Properties ........................... | $300,000 | |
|        Mortgage Payable .......................... | | $100,000 |
|        Fund Balance ............................. | | 200,000 |

To record a gift of properties, subject to mortgage assumed. The corpus is to be maintained intact; earnings are not restricted as to use.

**33.** Rentals received in cash were $45,000.

| | | |
|---|---|---|
| (33)  Cash ........................................ | $ 45,000 | |
|        Rental Revenues ........................... | | $ 45,000 |

To record receipt of rentals.

**34.** Depreciation of rental property was $6,000.

| | | |
|---|---|---|
| (34)  Expenses—Depreciation ...................... | $  6,000 | |
|        Accumulated Depreciation .................. | | $  6,000 |

To record depreciation.

**35.** Other expenses related to rental property, paid in cash, were $9,000.

| | | |
|---|---|---|
| (35)  Expenses—Other ............................. | $  9,000 | |
|        Cash ...................................... | | $  9,000 |

To record payment of rental expenses.

## Plant Replacement and Expansion Fund (Transactions and entries 36 and 37 affect only the Plant Replacement and Expansion Fund.)

**36.** Earnings on Plant Replacement and Expansion Fund investments, $15,400, are restricted to plant expansion.

| | | |
|---|---|---|
| (36)  Cash ........................................ | $ 15,400 | |
|        **Fund Balance** ............................. | | $ 15,400 |

To record earnings on plant fund investments; these earnings are restricted to use for plant expansion.

**37.** The fair market value of Plant Replacement and Expansion Fund investments increased $600 during the year. Earnings are restricted for plant expansion.

| | | |
|---|---|---|
| (37) Investments .................................... | $ 600 | |
| Fund Balance ............................. | | $ 600 |
| To record increase in fair value of investments restricted to plant expansion. | | |

## Interfund (The remaining transactions and entries impact more than one fund, as indicated.)

**38.** Specific Purpose Fund investments costing $165,000 were sold for $170,000; proceeds from gains on these investments are available for unrestricted use.

**Specific Purpose Fund:**

| | | |
|---|---|---|
| (38) Cash ...................................... | $170,000 | |
| Investments ................................ | | $165,000 |
| **Due to Unrestricted Fund** .................... | | 5,000 |
| To record sale of investments at a gain and the resulting liability to the Unrestricted Fund. | | |

**Unrestricted Fund:**

| | | |
|---|---|---|
| (38) Due from Specific Purpose Fund ................. | $ 5,000 | |
| **Nonoperating Gains—Unrestricted Income from Specific Purpose Fund** ..................... | | $ 5,000 |
| To record gain on sale of Specific Purpose Fund investments and a receivable therefore. | | |

(Had the proceeds of the sale in excess of cost not been available for unrestricted use, the $5,000 would have been credited to Specific Purpose Fund Fund Balance; no entry would have been made in the Unrestricted Fund, and no gain would have been recognized at this time. The earnings would be reported as an increase in restricted fund balance in the statement of changes in fund balance.)

**39.** Cash was transferred as necessary to settle the beginning of year interfund receivables and payables.

**Unrestricted Fund:**

| | | |
|---|---|---|
| (39) Cash ....................................... | $145,000 | |
| Due from Specific Purpose Fund ............... | | $145,000 |
| To record settlement of beginning interfund balances. | | |

**Specific Purpose Fund:**

| | | |
|---|---|---|
| (39) Due to Unrestricted Fund ...................... | $145,000 | |
| Due from Endowment Fund .................. | | $ 20,000 |
| Cash ...................................... | | 125,000 |
| To record settlement of beginning interfund balances. | | |

**Endowment Fund:**

| | | |
|---|---|---|
| (39) Due to Specific Purpose Fund ................... | $ 20,000 | |
| Cash ...................................... | | $ 20,000 |
| To record settlement of beginning interfund balances. | | |

**40.** A $300,000 transfer from the Specific Purpose Fund was authorized to reimburse the Unrestricted Fund for specified expenses incurred; $200,000 of this amount was paid from the Specific Purpose Fund.

**Unrestricted Fund:**

| (40) Cash | $200,000 | |
| Due from Specific Purpose Fund | 100,000 | |
| **Revenues—Amounts Released from Restriction for Specific Programs** | | $300,000 |

To record revenue transfer.

**Specific Purpose Fund:**

| (40) **Fund Balance** | $300,000 | |
| Due to Unrestricted Fund | | $100,000 |
| Cash | | 200,000 |

To record transfer to Unrestricted Fund.

**41.** Endowment rental property earnings were established as a liability to the Unrestricted Fund.

**Endowment Fund:**

| (41) Rental Revenues | $ 45,000 | |
| Expenses—Depreciation | | $  6,000 |
| Expenses—Other | | 9,000 |
| **Due to Unrestricted Fund** | | 30,000 |

To close operating accounts and record liability to Unrestricted Fund for earnings.

**Unrestricted Fund:**

| (41) Due from Endowment Fund | $ 30,000 | |
| **Nonoperating Gains—Unrestricted Income from Endowment Fund** | | $ 30,000 |

To record net rental income due from Endowment Fund.

**42.** Major movable equipment was purchased for $18,000 from the Unrestricted Fund, which was reimbursed by the Plant Replacement and Expansion Fund.

**Unrestricted Fund:**

| (42) (a) Major Movable Equipment | $ 18,000 | |
| Cash | | $ 18,000 |

To record purchase of equipment.

| (42) (b) Cash | $ 18,000 | |
| **Amounts Released from Restrictions Used for Purchase of Property, Plant, and Equipment** | | $ 18,000 |

To record reimbursement for purchase of equipment.

Note that this amount is closed directly to Fund Balance in entry 44b. It is reported as a direct addition to Unrestricted Fund Balance and must be excluded from revenues and gains.

**Plant Replacement and Expansion Fund:**

| (42) **Fund Balance** | $ 18,000 | |
| Cash | | $ 18,000 |

To record reimbursement of the Unrestricted Fund for purchase of equipment.

**43.** Restricted earnings received on Endowment Fund investments, $25,000, were recorded as a liability to the Specific Purpose Fund.

**Endowment Fund:**

| | | | | |
|---|---|---|---|---|
| (43) | Cash ........................................ | $ | 25,000 | |
| | Due to Specific Purpose Fund ................. | | | $ 25,000 |
| | To record restricted earnings due to the Specific Purpose Fund. | | | |

**Specific Purpose Fund:**

| | | | | |
|---|---|---|---|---|
| (43) | Due from Endowment Fund .................... | $ | 25,000 | |
| | Fund Balance ............................... | | | $ 25,000 |
| | To record restricted purpose earnings due from the Endowment Fund. | | | |

# Closing:

**44.** Closing entries were made at year end:

**Unrestricted Fund:**

| | | |
|---|---|---|
| (44) (a) Patient Service Charges ...................... | $4,400,000 | |
| Revenues—Cafeteria Sales .................... | 45,000 | |
| Revenues—Television Rentals ................. | 30,000 | |
| Revenues—Medical Record Transcript Fees ...... | 15,000 | |
| Revenues—Vending Machine Commissions ...... | 5,000 | |
| Revenues—Amounts Released from Restrictions for Specific Programs .................... | 300,000 | |
| Nonoperating Gains—Unrestricted Income from Endowment Fund ................... | 30,000 | |
| Nonoperating Gains—Unrestricted Fund Investment Income ..................... | 5,000 | |
| Nonoperating Gains—Unrestricted Investment Income from Specific Purpose Fund ......... | 29,000 | |
| Revenues—Donated Services .................. | 20,000 | |
| Nonoperating Gains—General Contributions ..... | 100,000 | |
| Excess of Expenses and Losses over Revenues and Gains ............................. | 9,000 | |
| Expenses—Bad Debts ...................... | | $ 120,000 |
| Contractual Adjustments ................... | | 290,000 |
| Charity Services .......................... | | 125,000 |
| Expenses—Nursing Services ................ | | 1,624,000 |
| Expenses—Other Professional Services ........ | | 981,000 |
| Expenses—General Services ................. | | 943,000 |
| Expenses—Fiscal Services ................... | | 160,000 |
| Expenses—Administrative Services ........... | | 397,000 |
| Expenses—Interest ....................... | | 38,000 |
| Expenses—Depreciation .................... | | 300,000 |
| Nonoperating Losses—Disposal of Fixed Assets .. | | 10,000 |
| To close accounts at year end. | | |

(44) (b) Amounts Released from Restrictions Used for
Purchase of Property and Equipment ........ $18,000
Excess of Expenses and Losses over
Revenues and Gains ..................... $9,000
Fund Balance ............................. 9,000
To close the net loss to Fund Balance.

Revenues and expenses of the other funds have been closed in preceding entries or carried directly to fund balance. Thus, no closing entries are required for the Specific Purpose, Endowment, or Plant Replacement and Expansion Funds.

# FINANCIAL STATEMENTS

The financial statements that a government hospital should prepare for external use include a Balance Sheet, a Statement of Operations, a Statement of Changes in Fund Balances, and a Statement of Cash Flows. Statements should be comparative in form to provide maximum information to readers.

## Balance Sheets

Figures 17–3 (page 689) and 17–5 provide beginning and year end balance sheets for the Alzona Hospital that has been used as the example for hospital operations. Because Figure 17–3 does not contain comparative data, Figure 17–5 should be considered the better example. Note the "Assets limited as to use" section of the year end Balance Sheet (Figure 17–5). These are essentially special subfunds—cash and investments designated internally or restricted externally for specific purposes—but exclude donor- or grantor-restricted assets. The portion of assets limited as to use that is required to meet current liabilities payable from those assets ($125,000) is (1) reported as current assets and (2) then deducted from total assets limited as to use in the noncurrent assets section in deriving net noncurrent assets limited as to use. Too, the internal and external portions of assets limited as to use are distinguished. Recall that Cash includes Cash of the Unrestricted Fund and Cash of the Specific Purpose Fund, as discussed in the notes to Figure 17–4. Likewise, recall that the amounts reported as "Assets restricted for plant replacement and expansion" and "Assets restricted for endowment" are assets restricted by donors for the purposes indicated. Specific Purpose Fund net assets are not restricted for noncurrent purposes and, therefore, are not required to be reported separately from unrestricted assets.

## Statement of Operations

Alzona Hospital's Statement of Operations, Figure 17–6, is based on the operations of the Unrestricted Fund. Increases and decreases in other funds are considered changes in fund balance rather than revenues, expenses, gains, and losses. Only when these amounts affect the Unrestricted Fund are they reported as revenues, expenses, gains, and losses. (Note that amounts restricted by donors or grantors to plant expansion and replacement or permanent endowment are never recorded as revenues or gains. When resources restricted for plant purposes are expended for that purpose, the assets acquired are recorded in the Unrestricted Fund with a corresponding increase in fund balance.) This fund balance increase, "Amount released from restrictions for the purchase of property and equipment," is reported

**FIGURE 17–5  Year End Balance Sheet—Government Hospital**

Alzona Hospital
**Balance Sheet**
September 30, 19B
With Comparative Figures for September 30, 19A

|  | September 30 | |
|---|---|---|
|  | **19B** | **19A** |
| **Assets** | | |
| Current: | | |
| Cash ................................................ | $ 548,000 | $ 215,000 |
| Assets limited as to use—required for current liabilities .... | 125,000 | |
| Investments ....................................... | 445,500 | 460,000 |
| Receivables (less allowance for uncollectibles of $90,000 | | |
| for 19B and $85,000 for 19A) ....................... | 680,000 | 615,000 |
| Accrued interest receivable .......................... | 2,000 | |
| Inventory of materials and supplies .................... | 215,000 | 165,000 |
| Total current assets .............................. | 2,015,500 | 1,455,000 |
| Noncurrent: | | |
| Noncurrent investments and special funds: | | |
| Assets limited as to use for plant expansion by bond | | |
| indenture agrement .............................. | 525,000 | |
| Less assets limited as to use that are required for | | |
| current liabilities ............................... | 125,000 | |
| Noncurrent assets limited as to use ................. | 400,000 | |
| Assets restricted for plant replacement and expansion ...... | 323,000 | 325,000 |
| Assets restricted for permanent endowments ............. | 780,000 | 480,000 |
| Total noncurrent investments and special funds ......... | 1,503,000 | 805,000 |
| Property, plant, and equipment: | | |
| Land ............................................. | 130,000 | 130,000 |
| Land improvements ................................. | 80,000 | 80,000 |
| Buildings ......................................... | 5,000,000 | 5,000,000 |
| Fixed equipment ................................... | 500,000 | 600,000 |
| Major movable equipment ........................... | 113,000 | 90,000 |
| Construction in process ............................. | 2,500,000 | |
| Total property, plant, and equipment ................. | 8,323,000 | 5,900,000 |
| Less: Accumulated depreciation ..................... | 2,690,000 | 2,450,000 |
| Net property, plant, and equipment .................. | 5,633,000 | 3,450,000 |
| Total noncurrent assets ............................ | 7,136,000 | 4,255,000 |
| Total assets .................................. | $9,151,500 | $5,710,000 |
| **Liabilities and Fund Balances** | | |
| Current liabilities: | | |
| Notes payable ..................................... | $ 130,000 | $ 150,000 |
| Accounts payable .................................. | 50,000 | 175,000 |
| Accrued interest payable ............................ | 31,000 | |
| Accrued salaries and wages payable ................... | 83,000 | |
| Contracts payable, retained percentage ................. | 125,000 | |
| Total current liabilities ............................ | 419,000 | 325,000 |
| Long-term debt: | | |
| Mortgage payable .................................. | 100,000 | 100,000 |
| Bonds payable ..................................... | 3,000,000 | |
| Total liabilities ................................... | 3,519,000 | 425,000 |
| Fund balance: | | |
| Restricted for: | | |
| Specific programs ................................. | 395,500 | 255,000 |
| Plant replacement and expansion .................... | 323,000 | 325,000 |
| Endowment ...................................... | 680,000 | 480,000 |
| Total restricted fund balance ...................... | 1,398,500 | 1,060,000 |
| Unrestricted ....................................... | 4,234,000 | 4,225,000 |
| Total fund balance ................................ | 5,632,500 | 5,285,000 |
| Total liabilities and fund balance ...................... | $9,151,500 | $5,710,000 |

FIGURE 17–6 **Government Hospital Statement of Operations**

Alzona Hospital
**Statement of Operations**
For the Year Ended September 30, 19B*

**Revenues:**

| | |
|---|---:|
| Net Patient Service Revenues | $3,985,000** |
| Other Revenues: | |
|     Cafeteria sales | 45,000 |
|     Television rentals | 30,000 |
|     Medical record transcript fees | 15,000 |
|     Vending machine commissions | 5,000 |
|     Donated services | 20,000 |
|     Amounts released from restrictions for specific programs | 300,000 |
|     Total Other Operating Revenues | 415,000 |
| Total Operating Revenues | 4,400,000 |

**Expenses:**

| | |
|---|---:|
| Nursing services | 1,624,000 |
| Other professional services | 981,000 |
| General services | 943,000 |
| Fiscal services | 160,000 |
| Administrative services | 397,000 |
| Depreciation | 300,000 |
| Bad debts | 120,000 |
| Interest expense | 38,000 |
|     Total Expenses | 4,563,000 |
|         Operating Loss | (163,000) |

**Nonoperating Gains and (Losses):**

| | |
|---|---:|
| Unrestricted endowment income | 30,000 |
| Unrestricted investment income | 34,000 |
| General contributions | 100,000 |
| Loss on disposal of assets | (10,000) |
|     Total Nonoperating Gains (Losses) | 154,000 |

| | |
|---|---:|
| **Excess of Expenses and Losses over Revenues** | (9,000) |
| Amounts released from restrictions used for purchase of property and equipment | 18,000 |
| **Increase in Unrestricted Fund balance** | $ 9,000 |

* Although the hospital operated in fiscal 19A, the figures for that year's activities were not needed for the example in the chapter.

**Calculations: Patient service charges ($4,400,000) less charity services ($125,000) and contractual adjustments ($290,000).

after the performance measurement in the Statement of Operations (Figure 17–6) and in the Statement of Changes in Fund Balances (Figure 17–7).

The statement of operations illustrates some of the points made earlier. Notice that patient service revenues are reported at the net amount that patients or

**FIGURE 17–7  Government Hospital Statement of Changes in Fund Balances**

Alzona Hospital
**Statement of Changes in Fund Balances**
For the Year Ended September 30, 19B

| | *Unrestricted* | *Restricted* |
|---|---|---|
| Fund balance, October 1, 19A .......................... | $4,225,000 | $1,060,000 |
| Excess of expenses and losses over revenues and gains ....... | (9,000) | |
| Restricted grants and contributions ...................... | | 600,000 |
| Restricted investment income .......................... | | 56,500 |
| Amounts released from restrictions used for specific programs* ....................................... | | (300,000) |
| Amounts released from restrictions used for purchase of property and equipment .......................... | 18,000 | (18,000) |
| Fund balance, September 30, 19B ....................... | $4,234,000 | $1,398,500 |

*Note that this amount does not have to be added to the Unrestricted Fund here because it is already included in revenues (see Figure 17–6) and thus in the "Excess of expenses and losses over revenues and gains."

third-party payees are obligated to pay—that is, net of deductions from revenues. Too, bad debts are reported as expenses. Also note (1) the distinction between patient service revenues, other revenues, and nonoperating gains, (2) the sources of revenues and gains, and (3) the distinction between expenses and losses. Finally, observe the strong similarity of this statement and a typical business organization's income statement.

## Statement of Changes in Fund Balances

The Statement of Changes in Fund Balances distinguishes the Unrestricted and Restricted Funds of a government hospital. The three Restricted Funds typically are reported in the aggregate as in Figure 17–7. Note the reporting of the aggregate changes in the Unrestricted Fund fund balance resulting from the excess of revenues and gains over (under) expenses and losses. This summary reporting of these changes is employed because the detail is presented in the Statement of Operations. Finally, observe that investment income restricted for a specific operating purpose by donors and grantors is reported as a direct increase in fund balance of the appropriate Restricted Funds. However, unrestricted investment income of the Restricted Funds is reported as nonoperating gains in the Statement of Operations (Figure 17–6).

## Statement of Cash Flows

The Statement of Cash Flows, Figure 17–8, is conventional for enterprise-type organizations. Note that it reports all cash flows for the hospital—whether affecting the Unrestricted Fund cash balance, the cash included in assets limited as to use, or cash of donor-restricted funds. The cash balances reported in the cash flow statement are the beginning and ending balances of the sum of the cash reflected in those three different classifications.

FIGURE 17–8  **Statement of Cash Flows for Government Hospital**

Alzona Hospital
**Statement of Cash Flows**
For the Year Ended September 30, 19B

**Cash flows from operating activities:**

| | | |
|---|---:|---:|
| Cash received from patients ............................... | $3,800,000 | |
| Cash received from other revenues ......................... | 95,000 | |
| Cash paid to suppliers of goods and services ................ | (1,477,000) | |
| Cash paid to employees ................................... | (2,700,000) | |
|     Net cash flows from operating activities ................. | | ($282,000) |

**Cash flows from noncapital financing activities:**

| | | |
|---|---:|---:|
| Cash paid to retire note ................................. | (20,000) | |
| Cash paid for interest ................................... | (7,000) | |
| Cash received from unrestricted contributions ............. | 100,000 | |
| Cash received from specific purpose gifts .................. | 400,000 | |
|     Net cash flows from noncapital financing activities ......... | | 473,000 |

**Cash flows from capital and related financing activities:**

| | | |
|---|---:|---:|
| Cash received from issuing bonds ......................... | 3,000,000 | |
| Cash paid to retire mortgage ............................. | (100,000) | |
| Cash paid to purchase fixed assets ........................ | (2,398,000) | |
| Cash received from sale of equipment ...................... | 30,000 | |
|     Net cash flows from capital and related financing activities ... | | 532,000 |

**Cash flows from investing activities:**

| | | |
|---|---:|---:|
| Cash paid for investments ............................... | (300,000) | |
| Cash received from sale of investments ..................... | 320,000 | |
| Cash received from investment earnings .................... | 82,400 | |
| Cash received from rent of Endowment Fund properties ....... | 45,000 | |
| Cash paid for Endowment Fund expenses .................... | (9,000) | |
|     Net cash flows from investing activities .................. | | 138,400 |
| **Net increase in cash** ...................................... | | 861,400 |
| Cash, October 1, 19A ..................................... | | 245,000* |
| Cash, September 30, 19B .................................... | | $1,106,400* |

**Reconciliation of Net Cash Flows from Operating Activities to**
  **Loss from Operations:**

| | | |
|---|---:|---:|
| Loss from operations .................................... | ($ 163,000) | |
| Adjustments to reconcile net cash flows from operating | | |
|   activities and operating loss: | | |
|       Depreciation ..................................... | 300,000 | |
|       Interest expense ................................... | 38,000 | |
|       Increase in inventory .............................. | (50,000) | |
|       Increase in accounts receivable ...................... | (65,000) | |
|       Increase in salaries payable ......................... | 83,000 | |
|       Decrease in accounts payable ........................ | (125,000) | |
|       Amounts released from restrictions used for specific | | |
|         programs ........................................ | (300,000) | |
| Net cash flows from operating activities ...................... | ($ 282,000) | |

Significant noncash financing and investing activities:

| | | |
|---|---:|---:|
|   Equity in property donated for endowment .................. | $ 200,000 | |

    *\* The cash balance is comprised of:*

| | *October 1, 19A* | *September 30, 19B* |
|---|---:|---:|
| *Unrestricted Fund cash account balance* ............... | *$175,000* | *$ 363,000* |
| *Cash in assets limited as to use* ...................... | *—* | *525,000* |
| *Specific Purpose Fund cash* ......................... | *20,000* | *130,000* |
| *Endowment Fund cash* ............................. | *25,000* | *66,000* |
| *Plant Replacement and Expansion Fund cash* .......... | *25,000* | *22,400* |
|     *Total* ........................................ | *$245,000* | *$1,106,400* |

## CONCLUDING COMMENTS

Health care accounting and reporting has evolved over the past 50 years to adapt to the ever-changing health care environment. Today, health care accounting and reporting is very similar to accounting and reporting for business enterprises. However, because of the many unique features of the health care environment, health care financial management and accounting practices have several unique features.

The most significant unique features of government health care accounting compared to business accounting are (1) various unique income determination features, and (2) the inclusion of the statement of changes in fund balances in the basic financial statements. This chapter dealt specifically with reporting for *government* hospitals. Chapter 18 discusses and illustrates accounting and reporting for nongovernment, not-for-profit entities. Voluntary health and welfare and other nonprofit organizations provide the context for most of that chapter. But financial reporting for not-for-profit hospitals is discussed briefly at the end of Chapter 18 by drawing on your knowledge of government hospital accounting and the nongovernment, not-for-profit organization guidance in the first part of that chapter.

## Questions

**Q 17-1**   What is the accounting equation for the Unrestricted Fund of a government hospital?

**Q 17-2**   What Unrestricted Fund treatment is accorded amounts released from restrictions used for specific operating purposes?

**Q 17-3**   What is the difference between resources designated by hospital boards for specific purposes and those designated by outside donors for specific purposes? What are the differing accounting effects?

**Q 17-4**   A government hospital provides services with a standard charge of $5,000. Because of a contract with an insurance company, it only bills and collects $4,000 for the services. What amount of patient service revenues should be reported in the statement of operations? Why?

**Q 17-5**   What are premium fee revenues? When should they be recognized as revenues?

**Q 17-6**   Why is it important to distinguish between internal and external assets limited as to use? (Define these terms in your answer.)

**Q 17-7**   List the principal classifications of hospital revenues.

**Q 17-8**   Why should hospitals report only the net amount of patient service revenue in their statements of revenues and expenses? Why are bad debts treated differently than such items as contractual adjustments?

**Q 17-9**   Identify the required financial statements for a government hospital.

**Q 17-10**   Diagnostic and analysis equipment developed by the federal government at a cost of $1,000,000 per unit was donated to Peoples' Hospital for medical and research use. Similar equipment is available from a commercial supplier at a cost of $600,000 new or for $400,000 if used and of about the same age as that received. The hospital will use the equipment extensively, but the administrator doubts that it will be replaced when it is worn out or obsolete due to its high cost. (a) Should the contribution be accounted for as either revenue or gain or contributed capital by the hospital? Explain. (b) Should depreciation be recorded and, if so, on what cost basis?

**Q 17-11**   (a) Should depreciation be charged on the fixed assets of a hospital if these assets have been financed from contributions but are intended to be replaced from hospital revenues? (b) Assume that the replacement of the fixed assets is intended to be financed from contributions. Should depreciation be charged on such fixed assets?

**Q 17-12** A government hospital's assets include:
  a. $2,000,000 set aside by the hospital board as an endowment to support research for curing the common cold;
  b. $25,000,000 donated by various individuals and organizations to finance construction and equipping of a cancer treatment and research center;
  c. $3,500,000 from a bond issue to finance expansion of the maternity wing; and
  d. $1,000,000 received from Blue Cross–Blue Shield (BCBS) as part of the hospital's reimbursement for services rendered to BCBS insurees. The reimbursement agreement with BCBS requires that this portion of the reimbursement be used for plant replacement and expansion.

  How should these resources be reported in the hospital's balance sheet? How do they affect restricted fund balances?

**Q 17-13** Identify the key differences between government health care accounting and commercial accounting.

**Q 17-14** (a) What is a term endowment? (b) How should a hospital account for the receipt of a term endowment? (c) How should a hospital account for the resources of a term endowment when the term of the endowment expires?

**Q 17-15** Certain financial resources are required to be used to acquire or construct a fixed asset. When the asset has been completed and placed in service, what is the impact on the Statement of Operations and the Statement of Changes in Fund Balances?

**Q 17-16** Following are various types of revenues, gains, and other amounts that may be received or accrued by a government hospital. For each type of revenue or gain, indicate whether it should typically be classified as:
  1. Patient service revenue (P)
  2. Other operating revenue (O)
  3. Nonoperating gain (N)
  4. none of the above (X)

  _____ a. Unrestricted income from Endowment Funds
  _____ b. Operating room charges
  _____ c. Gains from sale of land owned by the hospital
  _____ d. General nursing service charges
  _____ e. Harrimon Foundation grant received by hospital in recognition of outstanding past service to community
  _____ f. Room and board charges
  _____ g. Cafeteria sales
  _____ h. Professional services donated to the hospital
  _____ i. Sales of scrap materials
  _____ j. Tuition and fees from an affiliated nursing school
  _____ k. Contractual Medicare allowances
  _____ l. Physical therapy fees
  _____ m. Interest on Unrestricted Fund investments
  _____ n. Nursing salaries
  _____ o. Rockefeller Foundation grant received by hospital for medical research

## Exercises

**E 17-1** A hospital has the following assets among others:
  1. Investments of $2 million from a donation made specifically for the purpose of defraying part of the costs of enlarging the hospital's pediatric center.
  2. Cash and investments totaling $750,000 that the hospital board has designated for use for the expansion of the pediatric center.

3. $1.5 million restricted by donors to be used to supplement the operating budget of the hospital's cancer treatment center.

4. $2 million restricted by third party reimbursement agreements to be used to replace certain equipment.

***Required*** Show how these amounts should be reported in the hospital's balance sheet.

**E 17-2** A government hospital received two gifts in 20X0. The first gift was for $3,000,000. Its use was restricted to a specific operating purpose. Costs incurred during the year that qualified for use of the resources of the gift amounted to $1,250,000. The second gift was for $8,000,000 and was restricted for a capital project. $2,000,000 of construction costs were incurred on the project in 20X0. Explain or illustrate how these transactions should be reported in the hospital's statement of operations and in its statement of changes in fund balance for 20X0.

## Problems

**P 17-1** (Multiple Choice)

1. A gift to a government hospital that is restricted by the donor to use for a specific program should be credited directly to
   a. restricted fund balance.
   b. deferred revenue.
   c. revenue.
   d. unrestricted fund balance.

2. Donated medicines that normally would be purchased by a government hospital should be recorded at fair market value and should be credited directly to
   a. other operating revenue.
   b. nonoperating gain.
   c. fund balance.
   d. deferred revenue or gain.

3. On July 1, 19X1, Lilydale Hospital's board of trustees designated $200,000 for expansion of outpatient facilities. The $200,000 is expected to be expended in the fiscal year ending June 30, 19X4. In Lilydale's balance sheet at June 30, 19X2, this cash should be classified as
   a. assets limited as to use.
   b. a restricted noncurrent asset.
   c. an unrestricted current asset.
   d. an unrestricted noncurrent asset.

4. During the year ended December 31, 19X1, Melford Hospital received the following donations stated at their respective fair values:

   | | |
   |---|---|
   | Employee services from members of a religious group ...... | $100,000 |
   | Medical supplies from an association of physicians. These supplies were restricted for indigent care, and were used for such purpose in 19X1 ................. | 30,000 |

   How much revenue or gain from donations should Melford report in its 19X1 statement of revenues and expenses?
   a. $0
   b. $30,000
   c. $100,000
   d. $130,000

5. Glenmore County Hospital's property, plant, and equipment (net of depreciation) consists of the following:

   | | |
   |---|---|
   | Land ............................................. | $   500,000 |
   | Buildings ......................................... | 10,000,000 |
   | Movable Equipment ................................ | 2,000,000 |

What amount should be included in the restricted funds?
a. $0
b. $2,000,000
c. $10,500,000
d. $12,500,000

6. Which of the following would normally be included in other operating revenues of a government hospital?
   a. unrestricted interest income from an endowment fund
   b. an unrestricted gift
   c. donated services
   d. both b and c

7. Which of the following would be included in the fund balance of the Unrestricted Fund of a government hospital?
   a. permanent endowments
   b. unexpired term endowments
   c. board-designated funds originating from previously accumulated income
   d. plant expansion and replacement funds (restricted by donors)

Items 8 and 9 are based on the following data:

Under Abbey Hospital's established rate structure, the hospital would have earned patient service revenue of $6,000,000 for the year ended December 31, 19X3. However, Abbey did not expect to collect this amount because of charity allowances of $1,000,000 and discounts of $500,000 to third-party payers. In May 19X3, Abbey purchased bandages from Lee Supply Co. at a cost of $1,000. However, Lee notified Abbey that the invoice was being canceled and that the bandages were being donated to Abbey.

8. For the year ended December 31, 19X3, how much should Abbey report as patient service revenue in its statement of revenues and expenses?
   a. $6,000,000
   b. $5,500,000
   c. $5,000,000
   d. $4,500,000

9. For the year ended December 31, 19X3, Abbey should report the donation of bandages as
   a. a $1,000 reduction in operating expenses.
   b. nonoperating gain of $1,000.
   c. other operating revenue of $1,000.
   d. a memorandum entry only.

10. Which of the following is excluded from the excess of revenues and gains over expenses and losses?
    a. Amounts released from restrictions—Expiration of term endowments
    b. Amounts released from restrictions—Purchase of fixed assets
    c. Amounts released from restrictions—Used for specific programs
    d. Change in fair value of unrestricted investments

11. A government hospital's restricted funds include assets that are legally restricted by
    a. bond indentures.
    b. donors and grantors.
    c. third-party reimbursement arrangements.
    d. the hospital's governing board.
    e. all of the above.
    f. a, b, and c.

12. Donations received by a government hospital that are restricted for fixed asset acquisition should be reported as revenue in the statement of revenues and expenses in the period
    a. in which the contributions are unconditionally pledged.
    b. in which the donations are received.

    c. in which qualifying fixed assets are acquired.

    d. none of the above.

    (AICPA adapted)

**P 17-2**   (Reporting Classifications)

*Government Hospital Financial Reporting Classifications*

| *Balance Sheet* | | *Statement of Operations* | |
|---|---|---|---|
| CA | Current Assets | PSR | Patient Service Revenues |
| ALU | Assets Limited as to Use | OOR | Other Operating Revenues |
| PPE | Property, Plant, and Equipment | NG | Nonoperating Gains |
| IA | Intangible Assets | NSE | Nursing Services Expenses |
| OA | Other Assets | OPE | Other Professional Services Expenses |
| CL | Current Liabilities | GSE | General Services Expenses |
| LTL | Long-Term Liabilities | FSE | Fiscal Services Expenses |
| FB | Fund Balance | ASE | Administrative Services Expenses |
| | | OE | Other Expenses |

Using the preceding abbreviations, indicate how each of the following items should be reported in these hospital financial statements. If none of the preceding items is appropriate, explain how the item should be reported.

  1. Anesthesiology expenses

  2. Qualifying expenses under a restricted grant

  3. Provision for bad debts

  4. Fixed asset (currently in use) purchased from donor-restricted resources

  5. Expiration of term endowments—restricted to use for plant expansion

  6. Gain on sale of equipment

  7. Admitting office expenses

  8. Donated services

  9. Bond sinking fund

 10. Cash and investments set aside by board to finance cancer research

 11. Emergency services expenses

 12. Unrestricted contributions

 13. Bonds payable (issued to finance construction underway)

 14. Provision for depreciation

 15. Gift restricted for operations

 16. Intensive care expenses

 17. Power plant expenses

 18. Income and gain from board-designated funds

 19. Dietary service expenses

 20. Interest expense

**P 17-3, Part I**   (Fixed Asset Related Entries) Pinckney County Hospital entered into the following transactions in 19X8:

    April 1—Purchased incubators for the nursery for $47,300 from unrestricted resources. (Assume straight-line depreciation on all hospital fixed assets.)

    July 1—Issued $10,000,000 of 10%, 20-year bonds at par to finance construction of a major hospital addition. Construction is to begin early in 19X9, but bond market conditions are expected to become much less desirable over the next few months. The proceeds are invested in securities that also yield 10% interest.

    October 31—Sold a kidney dialysis machine for $19,000 halfway through its useful life. The machine originally cost $25,000 and was expected to have a $10,000 salvage value.

    December 31—(a) The incubators have a five-year useful life. (b) The first semi-annual interest payment on the bonds is made.

***Required*** Prepare all entries required on the preceding dates for these transactions. (Assume straight-line depreciation.)

**P 17-3, Part II** (Selected Revenue-Related Entries)
1. Svoboda County Regional Medical Center's gross charges for services rendered to patients in 19X8 were $82,000,000. Of this, $2,500,000 was for services rendered to individuals who were certified by the county as having no means to pay. Also, contractual adjustments granted on services rendered to insured patients and Medicare patients during 19X8 totaled $4,800,000 by December 31, 19X8, and it was estimated that another $350,000 of contractual adjustments would be made associated with those services. In addition, the hospital estimated that it will incur bad debt losses of approximately $3,200,000 associated with the services rendered in 19X8.
2. Svoboda County Regional Medical Center received $875,000 of donations in 19X8 to be used to cover the cost of charity services provided to patients who do not have sufficient means to pay for the needed medical care.

***Required*** (a) Prepare the general journal entries that Svoboda County Regional Medical Center should make to record these transactions.
(b) Prepare the portion(s) of the Svoboda County Regional Medical Center's statement of operations affected by these transactions.

**P 17-4** (Donation-Related Entries) Miss Jenny Russ donated $3,000,000 to Broadus Memorial Hospital on June 17, 19X8.
1. Assume that no restrictions are placed on the use of the donated resources.
   a. Prepare the required June 17, 19X8 entry.
   b. Prepare any entries necessary in 19X9 if $400,000 of the gift is used to finance hospital operating expenses.
2. Assume that the donation was restricted to leukemia research.
   a. Prepare the required June 17, 19X8 entry.
   b. Prepare any entries required in 19X9 as a result of spending $400,000 for leukemia research during 19X9.
3. Assume that the donation was restricted for use in adding a pediatrics intensive care unit to the hospital.
   a. Prepare the required June 17, 19X8 entry.
   b. Prepare any entries required in 19X9 if $400,000 of the gift is used to begin constructing the intensive care unit.

***Required*** Explain or illustrate how each of the three situations described previously would be reported in Broadus Memorial Hospital's financial statements in 19X8 and in 19X9.

**P 17-5** (Various Entries) The following transactions and events relate to the operation of a government hospital.
A. Prepare journal entries to record the effects of these transactions and events in the general ledger accounts of the appropriate fund(s). Explanations of entries may be omitted, but indicate the fund in which each is made.
   1. Total billings for patient services rendered, $85,000; it was estimated that bad debt losses on these billings would be $1,000 and that contractual adjustments would amount to $6,000.
   2. A transfer from the Heart Research Fund to the Unrestricted Fund was authorized, $15,000, to defray such expenses previously recorded in the Unrestricted Fund. The cash will be transferred later in the year.
   3. An item of fixed equipment (cost, $8,000; accumulated depreciation, $5,000) was sold for $1,000.
   4. Depreciation expense on buildings was recognized, $18,000.
   5. Earnings of the Endowment Fund are restricted to use for intern education. The net income of the Endowment Fund (revenues, $18,000; expenses, $4,000) was established as a liability to the appropriate fund.
   6. Unrestricted income on Endowment Fund investments, $3,500, was received and recorded directly in the Unrestricted Fund.

7. An $11,000 designation of the Unrestricted Fund fund balance was authorized to partially fund depreciation expense.

8. Of the billings for patient services rendered (see item 1), $1,000 was written off, $600 of which was related to charity cases.

B. Explain how each of the preceding transactions affects the statement of operations.

**P 17-6** (Operating Statement) The following selected information was taken from the books and records of Glendora Hospital (a government hospital) as of and for the year ended June 30, 19X2:

- Patient service revenues totaled $16,000,000, with associated allowances for contractual adjustments ($2,400,000) and uncollectible accounts ($1,000,000). Other operating revenues aggregated $346,000, and included $160,000 from Specific Purpose Funds. Revenue of $6,000,000 recognized under cost reimbursement agreements is subject to audit and retroactive adjustments by third-party payers. Estimated retroactive adjustments under these agreements have been included in allowances.
- Unrestricted gifts and bequests of $410,000 were received.
- Unrestricted income from endowment funds totaled $160,000.
- Income from board-designated funds aggregated $82,000.
- Operating expenses totaled $13,270,000, and included $500,000 for depreciation computed on the straight-line basis. However, accelerated depreciation is used to determine reimbursable costs under certain third-party reimbursement agreements. Net cost reimbursement revenue amounting to $220,000, resulting from the difference in depreciation methods, was deferred to future years.
- Fixed asset acquisitions during the year totaled $1,300,000.
- Endowment earnings restricted to artificial heart implant research were $250,000.
- Also included in operating expenses are pension costs of $100,000, in connection with a noncontributory pension plan covering substantially all of Glendora's employees.

*Required*   Prepare a formal statement of revenues and expenses for Glendora Hospital for the year ended June 30, 19X2.

(AICPA, adapted)

**P 17-7** (Worksheet with Correcting Entries) Following is Esperanza Hospital's postclosing trial balance at December 31, 19X6.

**ESPERANZA HOSPITAL**
**Trial Balance**
December 31, 19X6

| | *Debit* | *Credit* |
|---|---|---|
| Cash . . . . . . . . . . . . . . . . . . . . . . . . . . . . . . . . . . . . . . . . . . . . . . . . . . . . . | $   60,000 | |
| Investment in U.S. Treasury Bills . . . . . . . . . . . . . . . . . . . . . . . . . . . . | 400,000 | |
| Investment in Corporate Bonds  . . . . . . . . . . . . . . . . . . . . . . . . . . . . | 500,000 | |
| Interest Receivable . . . . . . . . . . . . . . . . . . . . . . . . . . . . . . . . . . . . . . | 10,000 | |
| Accounts Receivable  . . . . . . . . . . . . . . . . . . . . . . . . . . . . . . . . . . . | 50,000 | |
| Inventory . . . . . . . . . . . . . . . . . . . . . . . . . . . . . . . . . . . . . . . . . . . . . . | 30,000 | |
| Land  . . . . . . . . . . . . . . . . . . . . . . . . . . . . . . . . . . . . . . . . . . . . . . . . . | 100,000 | |
| Building . . . . . . . . . . . . . . . . . . . . . . . . . . . . . . . . . . . . . . . . . . . . . . . | 800,000 | |
| Equipment  . . . . . . . . . . . . . . . . . . . . . . . . . . . . . . . . . . . . . . . . . . . | 170,000 | |
| Accumulated Depreciation . . . . . . . . . . . . . . . . . . . . . . . . . . . . . . . | | $  410,000 |
| Accounts Payable . . . . . . . . . . . . . . . . . . . . . . . . . . . . . . . . . . . . . . | | 20,000 |
| Notes Payable . . . . . . . . . . . . . . . . . . . . . . . . . . . . . . . . . . . . . . . . . | | 70,000 |
| Endowment Fund Balance . . . . . . . . . . . . . . . . . . . . . . . . . . . . . . . . | | 520,000 |
| Other Fund Balances . . . . . . . . . . . . . . . . . . . . . . . . . . . . . . . . . . . | | 1,100,000 |
| | $2,120,000 | $2,120,000 |

Esperanza, which is a government hospital, did not maintain its books in conformity with the principles of hospital fund accounting. Effective January 1, 19X7, Esperanza's board of trustees voted to adjust the December 31, 19X6 general ledger balances, and to establish separate funds for the Unrestricted Funds, the Endowment Fund, and the Plant Replacement and Expansion Fund.

**Additional account information:**
- *Investment in corporate bonds* pertains to the amount required to be accumulated under a board policy to invest cash equal to accumulated depreciation until it is needed for asset replacement. The $500,000 balance at December 31, 19X6, is less than the full amount required because of errors in computation of building depreciation for past years. Included in the accumulated depreciation is a correctly computed amount of $90,000 applicable to equipment.

- *Endowment Fund balance* has been credited with the following:

| | |
|---|---:|
| Donor's bequest of cash | $300,000 |
| Gains on sales of securities | 100,000 |
| Interest and dividends earned in 19X4, 19X5, and 19X6 | 120,000 |
| Total | $520,000 |

The terms of the bequest specify that the principal, plus all gains on sales of investments, are to remain fully invested in U.S. government or corporate securities. At December, 31, 19X6, $400,000 was invested in U.S. Treasury bills. The bequest further specifies that interest and dividends earned on investments are to be used for payment of current operating expenses.

- *Land* comprises the following:

| | |
|---|---:|
| Donation of land in 19W0, at appraised value | $ 40,000 |
| Appreciation in fair value of land as determined by independent appraiser ten years later in 19X0 | 60,000 |
| Total | $100,000 |

- *Building* comprises the following:

| | |
|---|---:|
| Hospital building completed 40 years ago (as of the beginning of 19X7), when operations were started (estimated useful life 50 years), at cost | $720,000 |
| Installation of elevator 20 years ago (as of the beginning of 19X7) (estimated useful life 20 years), at cost | 80,000 |
| Total | $800,000 |

*Required*  A.  Using a worksheet with the following column headings, enter the adjustments necessary to restate the general ledger account balances properly. Distribute the adjusted balances to establish the separate fund accounts, and complete the worksheet. Formal journal entries are not required, but supporting computations should be referenced to the worksheet adjustments.

| *Column Headings* | *Column Numbers* |
|---|---|
| Trial balance—December 31, 19X6 | 1–2 |
| Adjustments | 3–4 |
| Unrestricted Fund | 5–6 |
| Endowment Fund | 7–8 |
| Plant Replacement and Expansion Fund | 9–10 |

B.  Explain how Restricted Fund resources and transactions should be reported in Esperanza's financial statements.
(AICPA, adapted)

**P 17-8** Joshua Regional Hospital, a government hospital, provided the following information from its records.
    1. Fund balances:

| | |
|---|---:|
| Unrestricted Fund | $ 8,000,000 |
| Specific Purpose Fund | 3,000,000 |
| Endowment Fund | 25,000,000 |
| Plant Replacement and Expansion Fund | 6,000,000 |

    2. Other information:
        a. Assets of the Unrestricted Fund include:
            (1) Fixed assets of $30,000,000
            (2) Cash restricted to fixed asset acquisition by insurance company contracts of $1,500,000
        b. Term endowments total $5,500,000; the remaining endowments were permanent endowments.

*Required* Prepare the fund balance section of the balance sheet for this government hospital.

**P 17-9** (Statement of Operations) Based on the following information, prepare a statement of operations for Hudgins County (government) Hospital for the year ended December 31, 20X1:

| | |
|---|---:|
| Patient service charges | $14,000,000 |
| Premium fees earned | 5,000,000 |
| Restricted contributions for heart research | 20,000,000 |
| Medical record transcript fees | 75,000 |
| Cafeteria sales | 150,000 |
| Restricted contributions for specialized equipment purchases | 6,500,000 |
| Unrestricted income from endowments | 1,000,000 |
| Donated services | 330,000 |
| Donated materials | 88,000 |
| Unrestricted contributions | 550,000 |
| Nursing services expenses | 7,850,000 |
| Other professional services expense | 5,400,000 |
| General services expenses | 3,210,000 |
| Fiscal services expenses | 300,000 |
| Administrative expenses | 900,000 |
| Interest expense | 440,000 |
| Depreciation expense | 1,200,000 |
| Bad debt expense | 430,000 |
| Charity services | 375,000 |
| Contractual adjustments | 950,000 |
| Equipment purchases paid from donor-restricted resources | 3,750,300 |

Also, a term endowment restricted to heart research expired during the year. The foregoing expenses include $800,000 payable from donor-restricted resources.

**P 17-10** (General Journal/Ledger Entries) Prepare general ledger entries to record the following transactions.
    1. Patient service charges totaled $8,000,000; 1% is expected to be uncollectible and 0.5% is expected to be charity services; $880,000 of contractual adjustments are expected to be made.
    2. Received premium fees for the month, $100,000. Only half of the covered patients actually received any treatments during the month.
    3. Received contributions for a restricted program, $2,000,000.
    4. Incurred expenses for the restricted program, $1,200,500.
    5. Received contributions restricted for use for purchase of MRI equipment, $600,000.
    6. Purchased MRI equipment, $480,000.
    7. Received contribution in the form of a term endowment, $300,000.

# 18

# NON-SLG NOT-FOR-PROFIT ORGANIZATIONS: SFAS 116 AND 117 APPROACH

The previous chapters of this text dealt with accounting and financial reporting for various types of government entities—primarily state and local government entities. Some of these entities, notably hospitals and colleges and universities, have nongovernment, not-for-profit counterparts. This chapter explains and illustrates the basic financial reporting principles and practices that apply to all **nongovernment,** not-for-profit organizations. The principles are discussed and illustrated in the context of voluntary health and welfare organizations (VHWOs) and other not-for-profit organizations (ONPOs). ONPOs are not-for-profit organizations other than health care organizations, colleges and universities, and VHWOs. The same basic principles apply to nongovernment health care organizations and to nongovernment colleges and universities. Separate appendices address not-for-profit colleges and universities and not-for-profit health care organizations.

Accounting standards for VHWOs and ONPOs have evolved through several stages since the 1960s. Industry organizations took the initial steps. The AICPA began to play a central role in accounting standards for these organizations beginning in the mid-1960s.[1] In 1979 the FASB assumed responsibility for setting accounting and reporting standards for all nonbusiness organizations except governments. The Board accepted responsibility in FASB *Statement*

---

[1] Key documents in the progression of VHWO and ONPO accounting guidance include:

- National Health Council and National Assembly for Social Policy and Development, *Standards of Accounting and Financial Reporting for Voluntary Health and Welfare Organizations* (Washington, D.C., 1964); National Health Council, National Assembly for National Voluntary Health and Social Welfare Organizations, and United Way of America, *Standards of Accounting and Financial Reporting for Voluntary Health and Welfare Organizations,* 3rd ed. (Washington, D.C., 1988).

- Committee on Voluntary Health and Welfare Organizations, American Institute of Certified Public Accountants, *Audits of Voluntary Health and Welfare Organizations* (New York: AICPA, 1974), hereafter cited as VHWO audit guide.

- Accounting Standards Division, American Institute of Certified Public Accountants, *Statement of Position 78–10,* "Accounting Principles and Reporting Practices for Certain Nonprofit Organizations" (New York: AICPA, December 31, 1978), hereafter cited as SOP 78–10.

*No. 32*[2] for the specialized accounting and reporting principles and practices in various AICPA SOPs, audit guides, and accounting guides.

The primary current authoritative guidance for all nongovernment, not-for-profit organizations, including VHWOs and ONPOs, was established in June 1993. At that time the FASB issued SFAS No. 116, "Accounting for Contributions Received and Contributions Made,"[3] and SFAS No. 117, "Financial Statements of Not-for-Profit Organizations."[4] These standards apply to all **nongovernment,** not-for-profit organizations except those that operate for the direct economic benefit of their members. (Such member benefit organizations as credit unions, rural electric cooperatives, and employee benefit plans are to be accounted for like their private-sector counterparts.) These two FASB statements required major changes in financial reporting for nongovernment, not-for-profit organizations. In 1996, the AICPA issued an audit and accounting guide, *Audits of Not-for-Profit Organizations,*[5] which incorporates the requirements of SFASs 116 and 117 and provides additional implementation guidance. This guide applies to all **nongovernment** VHWOs and ONPOs (and colleges and universities).

As noted in earlier chapters, the GASB has primary standards-setting authority for all state and local government organizations, including government VHWOs, colleges and universities, hospitals, and other nonprofit organizations. The GASB prohibits **government** not-for-profit organizations from applying SFAS No. 116 and SFAS No. 117—and other statements issued solely for not-for-profit organizations—in GASB *Statement No. 29,* "The Use of Not-for-Profit Accounting and Financial Reporting Principles by Governmental Entities."[6] Depending on the circumstances, government not-for-profits are to apply either the governmental model or the guidance in the pertinent AICPA industry audit and accounting guide or SOP—modified to conform with GASB standards. For *government* VHWOs, *Audits of Voluntary Health and Welfare Organizations* provides the predominant reporting guidance. Likewise, for *government* ONPOs, SOP 78–10, "Accounting Principles and Practices for Certain Nonprofit Organizations," is the source of most guidance.

This chapter first discusses the requirements of SFAS Nos. 116 and 117 for **nongovernment** VHWOs and ONPOs. The key provisions of those standards are then illustrated. Financial statements based on the guidelines of SFAS Nos. 116 and 117 are then presented for the illustrative organization.

Finally, Appendix 18–1 discusses financial reporting for nongovernment, not-for-profit colleges and universities. Appendix 18–2 addresses financial reporting for nongovernment, not-for-profit health care organizations.

---

[2] Financial Accounting Standards Board, *Statement of Financial Accounting Standards No. 32,* "Specialized Accounting and Reporting Principles and Practices in AICPA Statements of Position and Guides on Accounting and Auditing Matters" (Stamford, Conn.: FASB, September 1979). The FASB rescinded SFAS No. 32 in November 1992 (*Statement of Financial Accounting Standards No. 111,* "Rescission of FASB Statement No. 32 and Technical Corrections"). The FASB considered SFAS No. 32 unnecessary under the new GAAP hierarchy (discussed in Chapter 1) adopted by the AICPA in *Statement on Auditing Standards No. 69.*

[3] Financial Accounting Standards Board, *Statement of Financial Accounting Standards No. 116,* "Accounting for Contributions Received and Contributions Made" (Stamford, Conn.: FASB, June 1993).

[4] Financial Accounting Standards Board, *Statement of Financial Accounting Standards No. 117,* "Financial Statements of Not-for-Profit Organizations" (Stamford, Conn.: FASB, June 1993).

[5] Auditing Standards Board, American Institute of Certified Public Accountants, *Audits of Not-for-Profit Organizations* (New York: AICPA, 1996).

[6] GASB, *Statement No. 29,* "The Use of Not-for-Profit Accounting and Financial Reporting Principles by Governmental Entities" (Stamford, Conn.: GASB, August, 1995).

# CLASSIFICATION OF ORGANIZATIONS

Properly classifying nonprofit organizations as governmental or nongovernmental is essential because government VHWOs and ONPOs must not apply SFAS Nos. 116 and 117, whereas nongovernment VHWOs and ONPOs are required to report in accordance with these SFASs. Too, nongovernment entities need not apply GASB standards, although government entities must do so. The definition of a government was discussed in Chapter 1 (see Figure 1–5).

Likewise, properly identifying the type of not-for-profit organization—VHWO versus ONPO—is important because of the differences in the accounting and financial reporting principles that apply to each. Proper classification is particularly important for government not-for-profit organizations. It is sometimes difficult to distinguish VHWOs from ONPOs. The focus in this decision typically is on whether the organization is a VHWO because ONPOs are defined as all nonprofit organizations other than hospitals (and similar health care institutions), colleges and universities, and VHWOs.

## Voluntary Health and Welfare Organizations

Voluntary health and welfare organizations are formed to provide various kinds of health, welfare, and community services voluntarily (for no fee or a low fee) to various segments of society. VHWOs are tax exempt, organized for the public benefit, supported largely by public contributions, and operated on a not-for-profit basis. Thus, the features that distinguish VHWOs (from ONPOs) are:

1. Their purpose—to meet a community health, welfare, or other social service need;
2. Their voluntary nature—no fee is charged, or only a very small fee in proportion to the services provided is charged; and
3. Their relationship to resource providers—providers of resources are not the primary recipients of services or benefits of a VHWO.

Some ONPOs may provide services similar to those provided by certain VHWOs. But ONPOs finance the services with user charges or membership fees charged to the primary recipients of the services.

The United Way—or another federated community contribution solicitation and allocation organization—is active in most cities and is perhaps the most widely recognized type of VHWO in the United States. Numerous other VHWOs exist in most cities, however, such as the Boy Scouts and Girl Scouts, the American Heart Association, the YMCA and YWCA, and various mental health associations. Many of these organizations are financed wholly or partly by allocations from the United Way or equivalent organizations. Among the many types of services provided through VHWOs are child care for working mothers, family counseling, nutritious meals and recreation for the elderly, care and treatment of persons with mental and/or physical handicaps, protection of children from parental or other abuse, halfway houses for criminal or drug offenders, and sheltered workshops for citizens who are impaired physically and/or mentally. Most VHWOs charge modest fees to those who can afford to pay them, using a sliding fee schedule based on family size and income.

## Other Nonprofit Organizations

The **other** nonprofit organizations include all nonprofit organizations except (1) hospitals, colleges and universities, state and local governments, and voluntary health and welfare organizations, and (2) those nonprofit organizations that operate essentially as business enterprises for the direct economic benefit of their members or stockholders. Thus, the term **other** not-for-profit organizations is used to designate the following types of organizations and other truly nonprofit organizations:

Cemetery organizations
Civic organizations
Fraternal organizations
Libraries
Museums
Other cultural institutions
Performing arts organizations
Political parties
Private and community foundations
Private elementary and secondary schools
Professional associations
Religious organizations
Research and scientific organizations
Zoological and botanical societies

Member benefit organizations should be accounted for like their private-sector counterparts.

## CLASSES OF NET ASSETS

SFAS No. 117 does not require nonprofit organizations to report their resources by fund. The accounting equation is Assets = Liabilities + Net Assets. The standards require that net assets (assets less liabilities) be reported in three classes. These three classes are

*Unrestricted net assets*—the portion of net assets not temporarily or permanently restricted. (This category may include assets that previously were temporarily restricted, but the donor stipulation has been met, removing the restriction.)

*Temporarily restricted net assets*—the portion of net assets whose use is limited by donor-imposed restrictions on the timing of and/or purpose of use of the donated resources.

*Permanently restricted net assets*—the portion of net assets whose use is limited by donor-imposed restrictions that are permanent in nature; that is, restrictions that cannot be fulfilled by either passage of time or by actions of the organization.

SFAS No. 117 also requires changes in net assets to be reported for each of the net asset classes.

## BASIS OF ACCOUNTING

Both VHWOs and ONPOs are required to report their financial statements on the economic resources measurement focus and the accrual basis of accounting—that is, accounting for revenues and expenses. It is acceptable to keep the accounts on some other basis, such as the cash basis, and make period-end adjustments to convert them to GAAP.

# FUND ACCOUNTING

Neither SFAS No. 117 nor predecessor documents require fund accounting to be used. However, many VHWOs and ONPOs receive grants and contributions restricted for specific purposes and use fund accounting to facilitate observing and demonstrating accountability for such restrictions. The more significant the amount of restricted financial resources held by an organization, the more useful fund accounting is in enhancing fiscal control and accountability.

Some ONPOs use fund accounting even though normally they do not have significant amounts of restricted financial resources. Fund accounting is typically used by such organizations as private schools and religious organizations, for instance, because it is a well-established practice in those industries. Other ONPOs may use fund accounting because (1) they have material amounts of property, plant, and equipment, and/or (2) depreciation is not provided for in budgeting but capital additions are budgeted. Using fund accounting when an organization has material amounts of property, plant, and equipment and a significant portion of its total equity results from its net investment in those assets may permit clearer presentation of the financial resources available to finance ongoing services in the financial statements.

No specific fund structure is required for VHWOs or ONPOs by the VHWO audit guide or by SOP 78–10 for organizations that use fund accounting. Also, reporting by funds is not permitted in place of aggregated reporting. Thus, fund accounting and reporting are not illustrated in this chapter.

# SFAS 117 FINANCIAL STATEMENTS

The financial statements required by SFAS 117 are the

1. Statement of Financial Position (Balance Sheet);
2. Statement of Activities; and
3. Statement of Cash Flows.

Additionally, VHWOs must present a Statement of Functional Expenses. Each of the basic financial statements is discussed and illustrated and the underlying principles are explained in the following sections.

## Balance Sheet

SFAS No. 117 does not prescribe a specific balance sheet format. The standard does not require, nor does it prohibit, reporting an organization's data disaggregated by funds. Its unique and minimum requirements are that aggregated totals of assets, liabilities, and net assets be reported. Also, net assets must be reported in the three classes described earlier—unrestricted, temporarily restricted, and permanently restricted. Otherwise, the aggregation and presentation of assets and liabilities are similar to that for for-profit organizations. (See Figure 18–4.) The AICPA audit and accounting guide, *Audits of Not-for-Profit Organizations,* provides guidance on reporting for specific assets and liabilities, including those discussed here.

### Investments

Investments of nongovernment VHWOs and nongovernment ONPOs are recorded initially at cost, except that donated securities are recorded at their fair market value at the date of the gift. Thereafter, the audit guide requires nonprofits to report the fair value of their investments in equity securities with readily determinable fair values and of their investments in debt securities.[7] Other investments may be accounted for at cost (or lower of cost or market) or at market value. All of the other investments should be accounted for on the same basis. The net change in market value of investments is classified as unrestricted unless restricted by donor stipulation or law.

### Pledges

Under SFAS No. 116, organizations should **recognize pledges** receivable in the accounts **if** the pledges are **unconditional** promises to give. An unconditional promise to give is one that is not subject to provisions (conditions) that release the donor from the obligation to give based on occurrence or nonoccurrence of a future and uncertain event. A conditional promise to give is considered unconditional if the likelihood of not meeting the condition is remote (slight). Furthermore, promises to give must be distinguished from other nonbinding statements of donors that might express donor intentions but not constitute a promise to give.

For pledges that are to be collected within one year, the net expected unconditional pledge collections are recognized as assets and contributions. Pledges expected to be collected over longer periods should be recorded as assets and contributions at their present value. Conditional promises to give are not reported as receivables but are disclosed in the notes. Support is recognized when the condition(s) is met.

### Fixed Assets

Fixed assets of VHWOs are recorded at cost or, if donated, at fair market value at donation. If historical cost or fair market value data are not available, fixed asset costs may be estimated. In such cases the valuation method(s) used should be disclosed in the notes to the financial statements.

Donated fixed assets to be used in operations are reported as contributions. If they are to be sold or held to produce income, the fixed assets affect the net asset class that is consistent with any donor restrictions on use of the proceeds. For instance, fixed asset contributions are reported as unrestricted revenue if the income and/or sale proceeds are unrestricted. Similarly, fixed asset contributions are reported as temporarily restricted revenues if the income and/or sale proceeds are restricted as to use.

Depreciation expense and accumulated depreciation are recorded for exhaustible fixed assets in operating use or held to produce income. Depreciation is not recorded on fixed assets held for sale.

### Collections

Some not-for-profit organizations have assets that qualify as collections. Collections are defined in SFAS No. 116 as:

> Works of art, historical treasures or similar assets that are (a) held for public exhibition, education, or research in furtherance of public service rather than financial gain, (b) protected, kept unencumbered, cared for and preserved, and (c) subject to an organizational policy that requires the proceeds of items that are sold to be used to acquire other items for collections.[8]

---

[7] Financial Accounting Standards Board, *Statement of Financial Accounting Standards No. 124,* "Accounting for Certain Investments Held by Not-for-Profit Organizations" (Norwalk, Conn: FASB, November 1995), para. 3.

[8] SFAS No. 116, para. 11.

Not-for-profit organizations must capitalize works of art, historical treasures, and similar assets that do not meet the criteria for a collection. For collections three accounting options are permitted:

1. Not capitalizing any collections.
2. Capitalizing collections acquired after adoption of SFAS No. 116 but not those acquired prior to that date.
3. Capitalizing all collections regardless of when acquired.

Organizations that capitalize collections, under either of the last two options, report donated collections as assets at fair value and as contributions—increasing the appropriate net asset class. If collections are not capitalized, contributions are not reported for donated collections, but are disclosed in the notes to the financial statements.

### Trusts and Similar Agreements

Irrevocable trusts and similar agreements established to benefit a not-for-profit organization, but held by a third party, should be recognized as assets and contributions unless the third party has the discretion to provide the resources, or earnings thereon, to some other entity. If the third party has such discretion, assets and contributions are recognized as the third party makes resources available to the organization. Revocable trusts and similar agreements are treated as conditional promises to give.

Irrevocable perpetual trusts established for the sole benefit of a not-for-profit organization increase permanently restricted net assets. Term endowments of which the principal can be expended after the end of a specified term and many similar arrangements increase temporarily restricted net assets.

## Operating Statement

The major nongovernment ONPO or VHWO operating statement is the Statement of Activities. Figure 18–1 summarizes the format of the operating statement. **Revenues** and gains are reported **by source. Expenses,** classified between program services and supporting services, are reported **by function.** Also note in Figure 18–1 that changes in each of the three classes of net assets are reported separately. A columnar approach is acceptable as well.

SFAS No. 117 allows significant flexibility regarding what, if any, bottom line measurement of operations that an organization presents. Although some organizations may view the change in net assets or change in unrestricted net assets to be appropriate and adequate measurements of operations, other measures may be presented by organizations that deem them necessary. For instance, changes in unrestricted net assets may be distinguished between operating activities (as defined by the organization) and nonoperating activities. This flexibility permits reporting of an operating subtotal such as "changes in unrestricted net assets from operating activities." The standard even permits presentation of a separate statement of operations—but the statement must also report the total changes in unrestricted net assets for the period. Hospitals, for instance, report a statement of operations. Extraordinary items, gains or losses on discontinued operations, and cumulative effects of changes in accounting principles are reported separately as the last items before the "Change in Unrestricted Net Assets" regardless of the format or intermediate operating measures that are used.

Figure 18–1 also reflects that all expenses are reported as changes in unrestricted net assets. When restrictions on temporarily restricted net assets are met by

FIGURE 18–1  **Statement of Activities**
**Format and Content**

Not-for-Profit Organization
**Statement of Activities**
For Fiscal Year 19XX

**Changes in unrestricted net assets:**
Revenues and gains
   Contributions (unrestricted support) ...................... xx
   Other revenues (by source) ............................. xx
   Gains (may be reported net) ............................ xx
     Total unrestricted revenues and gains .................... xxx
Net assets released from temporary restrictions:
   Satisfaction of program restrictions ........................ xx
   Satisfaction of fixed asset acquisition restrictions ............. xx
   Expiration of time restrictions ........................... xx
     Total net assets released from temporary restrictions ....... xx
Expenses and losses:
   Program services (listed by function) ..................... xx
   Supporting Services:
     Management and general ............................. xx
     Fund raising ...................................... xx
     Membership development ............................ xx
   Direct benefits provided to donors ....................... xx
   Losses (may be reported net) .......................... xx
   Total expenses and losses ............................. xxx
     Increase (decrease) in unrestricted net assets .............. xx
**Changes in temporarily restricted net assets:**
   Restricted contributions (support) ........................ xx
   Restricted income, gain, or loss on
     investment of donor-restricted net assets ................. xx
   Net assets released from restrictions ....................... (xx)
     Increase (decrease) in temporarily restricted net assets ....... xx
**Changes in permanently restricted net assets:**
   Restricted contributions (support) ........................ xx
   Permanently restricted income, gain, or loss on investment of
     donor-restricted resources ........................... xx
     Increase (Decrease) in permanently restricted net assets ...... xx
**Increase (Decrease) in net assets** ......................... xxx

Net assets at beginning of year .............................. xxx

Net assets at end of year ................................... xxx

incurring expenses or costs for the temporarily restricted purpose or by passage of time, the release of net assets from restrictions is reported as an addition to unrestricted net assets and as a deduction from temporarily restricted net assets. Any related expenses are, of course, reported as deductions from unrestricted net assets.

### Revenues and Expenses Reported at Gross Amounts

Revenues and expenses of not-for-profit organizations must be reported at gross (rather than net) amounts. Gains and losses may be reported net of related amounts. Revenues and expenses result from transactions that are part of an organization's ongoing major or central activities. Gains and losses result from transactions that are considered peripheral or incidental for the organization. Therefore, a particular type of transaction—such as a special fund-raising event—may be reported as revenue by one not-for-profit organization and as a gain by another.

Note also that revenues and gains, as well as losses, must be classified as changes in either unrestricted, temporarily restricted, or permanently restricted net assets. The classification depends on the existence and nature of donor restrictions. As noted earlier, all expenses are reported as changes in unrestricted net assets.

### Contributions

Contributions are a significant revenue source for most VHWOs and ONPOs. These entities often refer to contributions as public support. SFAS No. 116 defines a contribution as follows:

> An *unconditional* transfer of cash or other assets to an entity or a settlement or cancellation of its liabilities in a *voluntary nonreciprocal transfer by another entity acting other than as owner.*[9]

The key features that distinguish contributions from other transactions such as exchange transactions and agency transactions are:

- Unconditional—not subject to future and uncertain event(s) that could require return of assets or reinstatement of liabilities
- Nonreciprocal—nothing of value given in return for the contribution
- Voluntary
- Contributor is not acting as owner (i.e., not an ownership investment)

SFAS No. 116 requires contributions to be recognized as revenues in the period that they are received or unconditionally promised. Contributions are to be recognized at this point even if the use of the resources is restricted. Transactions such as grants, membership dues, and sponsorships should be evaluated carefully to determine if they are contributions or if they are agency or exchange transactions (or part contribution and part exchange transaction). Different revenue recognition guidance applies to exchange transactions than to contributions.

Unrestricted contributions are reported as unrestricted revenues in the "Changes in Unrestricted Net Assets" section of the statement of activities. Restricted contributions are reported as revenue under "Changes in Temporarily Restricted Net Assets" if the restriction is temporary or under "Changes in Permanently Restricted Net Assets" if the restriction is permanent.

An alternative treatment of temporarily restricted contributions and temporarily restricted investment earnings is permitted (not required) when the use restrictions on part (or all) of the restricted contributions or restricted investment earnings are met in the same period that the revenues are recognized. Under the alternative treatment, these portions of the restricted contributions and restricted investment earnings are reported as changes in unrestricted net assets, provided the alternative treatment is applied consistently to both revenue sources from period to period and the policy is disclosed. Organizations that do not adopt this policy report the restricted revenues as increases in temporarily restricted net assets and also report the satisfaction of the restrictions as both a decrease in temporarily restricted net assets and an increase in unrestricted net assets.

---

[9] Ibid., para. 5. (Emphasis added.)

### Pledges, Membership Dues, and Other Fees

As noted earlier, not-for-profit organizations record unconditional pledges receivable as assets and as contributions revenue when the pledge is made. Conditional pledges and conditional transfers of assets (that meet the other criteria for contributions) are recognized as contributions revenue when the conditions are met. Unconditional pledges, even if not restricted as to use, are reported as restricted support unless the donor(s) specifies that the contributions are intended to support the current year. In other words, a time restriction (for use in subsequent periods) is implied for pledges unless explicitly contradicted by the donor(s).

Membership dues of some organizations are exchange transactions for which benefits or services are made available by the organization. Dues of other organizations are contributions. Dues of still other organizations are part exchange transactions (to the extent benefits or services are provided) and part contributions. Membership dues representing exchange transactions are recognized as revenue over the period(s) that the benefits are provided. Those dues representing contributions should be recognized as revenue when received. Lifetime membership dues and nonrefundable initiation fees are reported as revenue when they become receivable if future fees are assessed to cover the costs of future services provided to members. If not, lifetime membership dues and nonrefundable initiation fees are unearned exchange revenues that will be recognized over future periods—determined by such factors as the average duration of membership or other appropriate factors.

### Special Fund-Raising Events

Not-for-profit organizations often hold special fund-raising events to generate contributions. Examples include dinners, bazaars, and concerts. Revenues from these events should be reported at the gross amount unless the event is incidental or peripheral. If the special event is incidental or peripheral, gains, not revenues, should be reported. Gains from special fund-raising events may be reported gross or net of direct costs of holding the event.

Direct costs of holding special fund-raising events that are reported gross may be reported as an expense deduction from the revenues—just as cost of goods sold is deducted from sales. Alternatively, the direct costs may be reported in the expenses section of the statement of activities. The cost of benefits such as meals that are provided to contributors may be reported as part of a separate line item that identifies such costs. Other direct costs such as advertising should be included in fund-raising expenses. If special event gains are reported net instead of at the gross amount, the direct costs of holding the special event should be disclosed parenthetically.

### Investment Income and Gains/Losses

Investment income reported and gains and losses recognized on investment transactions are determined partly by the investment valuation method(s) used. Where the fair value method of investment accounting is used, the changes in fair value, as well as interest and dividends, are reported as changes in unrestricted net assets unless those amounts are temporarily or permanently restricted by law or donor stipulation. Restricted income, including gains and losses, is reported as changes in temporarily or permanently restricted net assets, as appropriate.

### Donated Materials, Facilities, and Services

The fair market value of significant amounts of materials donated to not-for-profit organizations should be reported as contributions when the materials are received. Expenses should be reported when the materials are used or sold. The same is true for donated (free) use of facilities and other assets.

Donated services should also be reported both as contributions and as assets or expense if the following conditions are met. The services either:

**a.** create or enhance nonfinancial assets *or:*

**b.** 1. require specialized skills (e.g., accounting, medicine, plumbing),
    2. are provided by individuals with those skills, *and*
    3. would typically have to be purchased if they were not donated to the organization.

These criteria are rather restrictive and preclude recording most volunteer services; for example, in fund raising or in assisting staff work with agency clients.

### Net Assets Released from Restrictions

Perhaps the most unique reporting feature of nongovernment, not-for-profit organizations is the "Net assets released from restrictions," which is reported when donor restrictions on resource use have been met (whether by passage of time or by incurring costs for the restricted use). It is presented as an addition to unrestricted net assets and a deduction from temporarily restricted net assets. The increase is not considered revenue in reporting changes in unrestricted net assets. Revenues—for the temporarily restricted contributions and other temporarily restricted resources—were recognized as changes in temporarily restricted net assets when the revenue recognition criteria were met. Likewise, the deduction from temporarily restricted net assets is not an expense. (All expenses are reported as changes in unrestricted net assets.) The increase reported in the changes in unrestricted net assets essentially communicates that temporarily restricted resources have been used to finance either current expenses—if the restriction was met by passage of time or by incurring current expenses—or future years' expenses (if the restriction was met by acquiring fixed assets or retiring fixed asset-related debt). The deduction reported as a change in temporarily restricted net assets simply reflects the reduction in those net assets. Use restrictions are deemed to have been met to the extent that costs have been incurred during the period for the restricted use—whether or not restricted resources actually were used for payment.

Recall from the discussion on contributions that if temporary restrictions are met in the same period that temporarily restricted contributions or investment earnings are recognized as revenues, those contributions and investment earnings—to the extent that restrictions are satisfied—may be reported as revenues in the changes in unrestricted net assets. If this policy is adopted, the organization will not report net assets released from temporary restrictions for those amounts.

### Expenses

Expenses of nongovernment VHWOs and ONPOs are always reported as changes in unrestricted net assets. The expenses should be categorized appropriately between (1) **program expenses,** which relate directly to the primary missions of the organization, and (2) **supporting services,** which do not relate directly to the primary missions and include such costs as general administration, membership development, and fund raising. Furthermore, the expenses are to be reported by major programs or functions within these two categories. (See Figure 18–5)

Accounting for expenses during the year may center on departmental responsibility and type (object) of expense incurred rather than on functions. Furthermore, some personnel may work in more than one function and some expenses may involve several functions. In such cases it is necessary to maintain time and activity records by functions, and other records where appropriate, so that all expenses can be assigned, directly or by allocation, to the functions of the organization. If such records are not maintained during the year, it may be difficult and costly—if not impossible—to classify expenses properly by function at year end as required by GAAP.

**Program Services** Program services expenses are those that relate directly to the primary missions of the organization. Such expenses should be classified by functions using terms that best convey the primary thrust of programs of the organization. Program services expenses include both direct expenses that are clearly identifiable with the program or function and rational and systematic allocations of indirect costs.

Some not-for-profit organizations remit a portion of their receipts to an affiliated state or national organization. Where practicable, these payments should be allocated to functional classifications. If not allocable, or if some portion is not allocable, it should be reported as a separate line item under supporting services.

**Supporting Services** Supporting services expenses do not relate directly to the primary missions of the organization and include management and general, fund-raising, and other costs not associated directly with rendering program services. Analysts and regulators pay close attention to the relationship of supporting services expenses to program services expenses and total expenses. In particular, fund-raising costs are often compared among organizations and for individual organizations through time.

*Management and General Costs.* Management and general costs are not identifiable with a specific program or fund-raising activity but relate to the organization's existence and effectiveness. They include such costs as board meetings, business management, record keeping, budgeting, accounting, and overall direction and leadership. To the extent that some of these costs are directly related to the primary programs, they should be allocated to those programs in a systematic and rational manner.

*Fund-Raising and Other Supporting Services.* Fund-raising costs are incurred to induce contributions of money, securities, real estate or other properties, materials, or time to the organization. Fund-raising efforts and costs vary widely among the many types of not-for-profit organizations, but fund-raising costs such as the following are often incurred: mailing lists, printing, mailing, personnel, occupancy, newspaper and other media advertising, and costs of unsolicited merchandise sent to encourage contributions. Some organizations combine fund-raising efforts with educational materials or program services. In such cases, the combined costs incurred must be allocated appropriately among fund-raising and the various program functions so that each is reflected appropriately in the organization's operating statement.

Fund-raising costs paid directly by a contributor should be recorded by the organization as both a contribution and a fund-raising expense. As noted earlier, when fund-raising banquets, dinner parties, theater parties, merchandise auctions or drawings, and similar events are ongoing and major activities, the gross proceeds of such functions are reported as revenue. The direct costs of the fund-raising merchandise, meals, or other direct benefits to donors should be reported as well. These direct costs may be displayed as a deduction from the special event revenues or be reported in the expenses section of the statement. If reported in the expenses section, the direct costs of benefits (unless peripheral or incidental), such as meals provided at a fund-raising banquet, may be included in a separate line item called "Benefits provided to donors." Other direct costs such as promotional costs are included in fund-raising expenses.

### Statement of Cash Flows

SFAS No. 117 also requires nongovernment, not-for-profit organizations to present a Statement of Cash Flows—in accordance with the requirements of SFAS No. 95, "Statement of Cash Flows." The most unique items reflected in this statement, compared to a typical business cash flow statement, are:

- Reporting of contributions and investment earnings that are restricted for capital-asset–related, endowment, or other long-term purposes as financing activities
- Reporting of changes in cash restricted for long-term purposes (and thus excluded from current assets and from cash and cash equivalents) as investing activities

These uniquenesses are illustrated in the statement of cash flows (see Figure 18–6) presented for the illustrative example later in the chapter.

### Statement of Functional Expenses

VHWOs are required to present a Statement of Functional Expenses (illustrated later in Figure 18–7). This statement presents a detailed analysis of the expenses section of the statement of activities by object class or type of expense. Note that (1) the headings correspond to the "Program Services" and "Supporting Services" expense categories of the Statement of Activities and that (2) a "Total expenses before depreciation" subtotal is presented, followed by "Depreciation of buildings, improvements, and equipment" and "Total expenses." The detailed statement of functional expenses is optional for ONPOs.

## NONGOVERNMENT VHWO AND ONPO ACCOUNTING AND REPORTING ILLUSTRATION

This section presents illustrative transactions and entries for a VHWO or ONPO. The trial balance of the Illustrative Nongovernment VHWO/ONPO at December 31, 19X0 is presented in Figure 18–2.

### Summary of Transactions and Entries

Transactions and entries of the illustrative entity are presented in this section. The entries illustrate most of the principles discussed thus far. Note that we record contributions revenue as support in the illustration. Under SFASs 116 and 117, support is reported as revenues. Support results from nonreciprocal transactions—it is essentially a synonym for contributions.

FIGURE 18–2  **Nongovernment VHWO/ONPO General Ledger Trial Balance**

Illustrative VHWO/ONPO
**Beginning Trial Balance**
January 1, 19X1

|  | *Debit* | *Credit* |
|---|---:|---:|
| Cash | $ 125,000 | |
| Pledges Receivable | 50,000 | |
| Allowance for Uncollectible Pledges | | $    4,000 |
| Accrued Interest Receivable | 2,000 | |
| Inventory of Materials | 3,000 | |
| Investments | 90,000 | |
| Cash Restricted for Plant Purposes | 150,000 | |
| Investments Restricted for Plant Purposes | 120,000 | |
| Cash Restricted for Endowment | 132,000 | |
| Investments Restricted for Endowment | 313,000 | |
| Land | 50,000 | |
| Buildings and Improvements | 420,000 | |
| Accumulated Depreciation—Buildings and Improvements | | 140,000 |
| Equipment | 200,000 | |
| Accumulated Depreciation—Equipment | | 85,000 |
| Vouchers Payable | | 28,000 |
| Mortgage Payable | | 205,000 |
| Unrestricted Net Assets | | 417,000 |
| Temporarily Restricted Net Assets—Education | | 24,000 |
| Temporarily Restricted Net Assets—Research | | 15,000 |
| Temporarily Restricted Net Assets—Term Endowments | | 100,000 |
| Temporarily Restricted Net Assets—Plant Purposes | | 270,000 |
| Temporarily Restricted Net Assets—Pledged for Future Years | | 22,000 |
| Permanently Restricted Net Assets | | 345,000 |
| | $1,655,000 | $1,655,000 |

## Current Unrestricted Fund

**1.** Unrestricted gifts and pledges of prior years that donors designated for 19X1 were re-classified as unrestricted net assets because the time restriction is met.

| (1) **Temporarily Restricted Net Assets—Reclassifications** | | |
|---|---:|---:|
| **Out** | $22,000 | |
| **Unrestricted Net Assets—Reclassifications In** | | $22,000 |

To record reclassification of temporarily restricted net assets as unrestricted net assets.

This reclassification entry is made because the implied (or expressed) time restriction has been met. The reclassification accounts are reported as "Net assets released from restrictions."

**2.** Unrestricted cash gifts of $5,000 available for use in 19X1 and $10,000 designated by donors to be used to finance operations in 19X2 were received.

| (2) Cash | $15,000 | |
|---|---:|---:|
| **Unrestricted Support—Contributions** | | $ 5,000 |
| **Restricted Support—Contributions** | | 10,000 |

To record cash gifts received in 19X1 for 19X1 and 19X2.

The restricted support (or restricted revenue) account is used to record temporarily restricted contributions that are to be reported as changes in temporarily restricted net assets. The restriction is a time restriction in this case.

3. Unrestricted pledges of $250,000 were received in 19X1, of which $50,000 is designated by donors for use during 19X2 and $200,000 is designated to support 19X1 operations. Ten percent of the pledges are expected to be uncollectible.

| (3) **Pledges Receivable** ............................. | $250,000 | |
|---|---|---|
|    **Allowance for Uncollectible Pledges** ............. | | $ 25,000 |
|    Unrestricted Support—Contributions ............ | | 180,000 |
|    Restricted Support—Contributions ............... | | 45,000 |

To record pledges received in 19X1 for 19X1 and 19X2 and the estimated uncollectibles.

4. Pledges receivable of $205,000 were collected in 19X1 and pledges of $18,000 were written off as uncollectible.

| (4) Cash ........................................ | $205,000 | |
|---|---|---|
|    Allowance for Uncollectible Pledges .............. | 18,000 | |
|     Pledges Receivable ........................... | | $223,000 |

To record collection and write-off of pledges receivable.

5. Land and a building were donated to the organization in 19X1 and held for resale. The fair value of the land and building when donated was $150,000. There are no restrictions on the donated property or its sale proceeds.

| (5) **Land and Buildings Held for Resale** ............... | $150,000 | |
|---|---|---|
|     Unrestricted Support—Contributions ............ | | $150,000 |

To record donated land and building held for resale.

6. The donated land and building were sold for $150,000.

| (6) Cash ........................................ | $150,000 | |
|---|---|---|
|     Land and Building Held for Resale .............. | | $150,000 |

To record sale of land and building held for resale.

7. Investment income of $20,000 on unrestricted investments and $14,000 of unrestricted investment income from endowments were received. Interest accrued at the end of 19X0 was also received, $2,000.

| (7) Cash ........................................ | $ 36,000 | |
|---|---|---|
|     Accrued Interest Receivable ................... | | $ 2,000 |
|     Unrestricted Revenues—Investment Income ....... | | 34,000 |

To record investment income available for unrestricted purposes.

8. A fund-raising banquet was held. Proceeds were $75,000 and related direct costs of $25,000 for the meals and gratuities were incurred and paid.

| (8) (a) Cash ........................................ | $ 75,000 | |
|---|---|---|
|      **Unrestricted Support—Special Events** .......... | | $ 75,000 |

To record ticket sales from fund-raising dinner.

| (8) (b) **Expenses—Direct Costs of Special Events** ........ | $ 25,000 | |
|---|---|---|
|      Cash ..................................... | | $ 25,000 |

To record direct costs incurred for fund-raising dinner.

9. Donated materials and contributed use of facilities that are recordable in 19X1 were:
   a. Materials, $10,000 (40% unused at year end; 60% used on fund-raising projects)
   b. Facilities, $8,000 (60% used for research offices; 40% for record keeping)

| (9) (a) Inventory of Materials . . . . . . . . . . . . . . . . . . . . . . . . | $4,000 | |
|---|---|---|
| Expenses—Fund-Raising . . . . . . . . . . . . . . . . . . . . . | 6,000 | |
| **Unrestricted Support—Donated Materials** . . . . . . | | $10,000 |
| To record donated materials. | | |

| (9) (b) Expenses—Research . . . . . . . . . . . . . . . . . . . . . . . . . | $4,800 | |
|---|---|---|
| Expenses—Management and General . . . . . . . . . . . | 3,200 | |
| **Unrestricted Support—Donated Facilities** . . . . . . . | | $ 8,000 |
| To record donated facilities. | | |

**10.** Donated services that are recordable include the time of:

a. A CPA, who audited the agency at no cost, $6,000;

b. An attorney, who did necessary legal work at no cost, $1,000; and

c. A physician, who assisted in a research project, $3,000.

| (10) Expenses—Management and General . . . . . . . . . . . . | $7,000 | |
|---|---|---|
| Expenses—Research . . . . . . . . . . . . . . . . . . . . . . . . | 3,000 | |
| **Unrestricted Support—Donated Services** . . . . . . . . | | $10,000 |
| To record donated services. | | |

**11.** Annual membership dues of $17,300 were billed and collected for 19X1. The dues constitute an exchange transaction for this organization.

| (11) Cash . . . . . . . . . . . . . . . . . . . . . . . . . . . . . . . . . . . . . . . . | $17,300 | |
|---|---|---|
| **Unrestricted Revenues—Membership Dues** . . . . . . . | | $17,300 |
| To record collection of dues. | | |

**12.** Salaries and wages paid during 19X1 totaled $85,000 and $3,000 was accrued at year end, allocated as follows:

| Management and General . . . . . . . . . . . . . . . . | $30,000 |
|---|---|
| Fund-Raising . . . . . . . . . . . . . . . . . . . . . . . . . . | 15,000 |
| Education . . . . . . . . . . . . . . . . . . . . . . . . . . . . . | 27,000 |
| Research . . . . . . . . . . . . . . . . . . . . . . . . . . . . . . | 16,000 |
| Total . . . . . . . . . . . . . . . . . . . . . . . . . . . . . | $88,000 |

| (12) Expenses—Management and General . . . . . . . . . . . . . | $30,000 | |
|---|---|---|
| Expenses—Fund-Raising . . . . . . . . . . . . . . . . . . . . . . | 15,000 | |
| Expenses—Education . . . . . . . . . . . . . . . . . . . . . . . | 27,000 | |
| Expenses—Research . . . . . . . . . . . . . . . . . . . . . . . . . | 16,000 | |
| Cash . . . . . . . . . . . . . . . . . . . . . . . . . . . . . . . . . . . . . | | $85,000 |
| Accrued Salaries Payable . . . . . . . . . . . . . . . . . . . . . | | 3,000 |
| To record salaries and wages for 19X1. | | |

**13.** Other 19X1 expenses, payments, and vouchers were:

| | Expenses Incurred | Amounts Paid | Unpaid at Year End |
|---|---|---|---|
| Vouchers Payable, January 1, 19X1 . . . . . . . . . | | $ 17,000 | |
| Management and General Expenses . . . . . . . . | $ 98,000 | 98,000 | |
| Fund Raising Expenses . . . . . . . . . . . . . . . . . . . | 67,000 | 60,000 | $ 7,000 |
| Education Expenses . . . . . . . . . . . . . . . . . . . . | 85,000 | 80,000 | 5,000 |
| Research Expenses . . . . . . . . . . . . . . . . . . . . . | 50,000 | 48,000 | 2,000 |
| Materials Purchased . . . . . . . . . . . . . . . . . . . . | | 800 | |
| Total . . . . . . . . . . . . . . . . . . . . . . . . . . . . . . | $300,000 | $303,800 | $14,000 |

|  |  |  |
|---|---|---|
| (13) Vouchers Payable ............................. | $ 17,000 |  |
| Inventory of Materials .......................... | 800 |  |
| Expenses—Management and General ............. | 98,000 |  |
| Expenses—Fund-Raising ........................ | 67,000 |  |
| Expenses—Education .......................... | 85,000 |  |
| Expenses—Research .......................... | 50,000 |  |
| Cash ..................................... |  | $303,800 |
| Vouchers Payable ........................... |  | 14,000 |
| To record various expenses incurred during 19X1 and payments of vouchers payable. |  |  |

**14.** The board of directors designated $50,000 of investments to be used as an endowment, the earnings of which will be used to finance research.

|  |  |  |
|---|---|---|
| (14) Unrestricted Net Assets ........................ | $ 50,000 |  |
| **Unrestricted Net Assets—Designated for Endowment** ............................... |  | $ 50,000 |
| To record board designation of fund balance. |  |  |

Note that board designation of assets for a specific purpose does not change the classification of net assets from unrestricted to restricted.

**15.** Restricted gifts and pledges of prior years designated by donors for use in 19X1 to finance certain research programs have met the time restrictions imposed by donors.

(15) No entry is required at this time. Although the time restriction has been met, these assets are not reclassified as unrestricted net assets at this time because there is another temporary restriction—that is, the resources must be used for certain research programs. The resources will not be reclassified as unrestricted until this use restriction is fulfilled.

**16.** Cash gifts of $30,000 and pledges of $100,000 (collectible over the next year), both restricted to use for certain education efforts, were received. Ten percent of the pledges are estimated to be uncollectible.

|  |  |  |
|---|---|---|
| (16) Cash ........................................ | $ 30,000 |  |
| Pledges Receivable ............................ | 100,000 |  |
| Allowance for Uncollectible Pledges ............. |  | $ 10,000 |
| Restricted Support—Contributions .............. |  | 120,000 |
| To record gifts and pledges restricted to education. |  |  |

**17.** Pledges of $80,000 for restricted purposes were collected and $7,000 of restricted pledges were written off as uncollectible.

|  |  |  |
|---|---|---|
| (17) Cash ........................................ | $ 80,000 |  |
| Allowance for Uncollectible Pledges .............. | 7,000 |  |
| Pledges Receivable .......................... |  | $ 87,000 |
| To record collection and write-off of pledges receivable. |  |  |

**18.** Investment income of $20,500 on investments of restricted contributions was received. The income also is restricted by the donors: $10,000 is restricted to certain education efforts and $10,500 to certain research projects.

|  |  |  |
|---|---|---|
| (18) Cash ........................................ | $ 20,500 |  |
| Restricted Revenues—Investment Income ........ |  | $ 20,500 |
| To record investment earnings restricted for operating uses. |  |  |

The distinction between investment income restricted for education and that restricted for research is assumed to be maintained in subsidiary ledger accounts in this illustration.

**19.** Education expenses of $70,000 for purposes specified by donors were incurred and paid, as were $18,000 of research expenses.

| (19) (a) Expenses—Education ........................ | $ 70,000 | |
|---|---|---|
| Expenses—Research ........................ | 18,000 | |
| Cash ..................................... | | $ 88,000 |
| To record expenses for education and research. | | |

When temporarily restricted resources are available to finance a specific program, qualifying costs are presumed to be met from those resources. This releases the temporarily restricted resources as early as possible. Also recall that all expenses are reported as changes in unrestricted net assets.

| (19) (b) Temporarily Restricted Net Assets— | | |
|---|---|---|
| Reclassifications Out ..................... | $ 88,000 | |
| Unrestricted Net Assets—Reclassifications In .. | | $ 88,000 |
| To record reclassifications of net assets upon satisfaction of temporary restrictions. | | |

**20.** Cash gifts of $55,000 were received to endow (permanently) one of the education programs provided by the organization.

| (20) Cash Restricted for Endowment ................. | $ 55,000 | |
|---|---|---|
| Permanently Restricted Support—Contributions ... | | $ 55,000 |
| To record gifts received for endowment purposes. | | |

**21.** Endowment Fund investment earnings that are restricted by donor stipulation to increasing the permanent endowment base were received, $10,500.

| (21) Cash Restricted for Endowment ................. | $ 10,500 | |
|---|---|---|
| Permanently Restricted Revenues— | | |
| Investment Income ........................ | | $ 10,500 |
| To record investment income restricted to endowment. | | |

**22.** Endowment Fund investments that cost $13,000 were sold for $14,400. By donor stipulation, realized gains and losses on this endowment must be added to or deducted from permanent endowment principal.

| (22) Cash Restricted for Endowment .................. | $ 14,400 | |
|---|---|---|
| Investments Restricted for Endowment .......... | | $ 13,000 |
| Permanently Restricted Gain—Gain on Sale | | |
| of Investments ............................ | | 1,400 |
| To record sale of investments. | | |

Again, recall that the various restrictions on the use of resources assumedly are being accounted for in subsidiary ledger accounts.

**23.** Cash gifts of $100,000 restricted for acquisition of fixed assets were received in 19X1.

| (23) Cash Restricted for Plant Purposes ................ | $100,000 | |
|---|---|---|
| Restricted Support—Contributions ............. | | $100,000 |
| To record restricted contributions for capital additions. | | |

**24.** Equipment costing $140,000 was acquired using donated resources restricted for that purpose.

| (24) (a) Equipment ................................. | $140,000 | |
|---|---|---|
| Cash Restricted for Plant Purposes ........... | | $140,000 |
| To record purchase of equipment with restricted resources. | | |

(24) (b) Temporarily Restricted Net Assets—
Reclassifications Out ..................... $140,000
Unrestricted Net Assets—Reclassifications In .. $140,000
To record reclassification of net assets upon
satisfaction of temporary restrictions.

The illustrative organization does not have a policy of implying a time restriction on fixed assets acquired with restricted resources. Likewise, the donor did not specify that the fixed assets had to be held and used for a certain minimum period of time. Hence, the only requirement to satisfy the restriction was to purchase the fixed asset. That is why the reclassification entry occurs at this time. If the fixed assets were required by donors to be used a certain number of years, the reclassification would be allocated over those years.

**25.** Depreciation expense for 19X1 on plant assets was $30,000 ($14,000 on buildings and $16,000 on equipment), allocated as follows:

| | |
|---|---:|
| Management and General ................ | $13,000 |
| Research ............................... | 12,000 |
| Education .............................. | 2,000 |
| Fund-Raising .......................... | 3,000 |

(25) Expenses—Management and General ............ $ 13,000
Expenses—Research .......................... 12,000
Expenses—Education .......................... 2,000
Expenses—Fund-Raising ....................... 3,000
Accumulated Depreciation—Buildings and
Improvements ............................. $ 14,000
Accumulated Depreciation—Equipment ........ 16,000
To record depreciation of plant assets.

If explicit donor stipulations require certain depreciable fixed assets to be used for a certain period of time, reclassification of a proportional amount of those fixed assets costs from temporarily restricted to unrestricted net assets must be recorded. Likewise, if the organization has a policy of implying a time restriction on donated or donor-financed fixed assets, reclassification of net assets equal to the depreciation expense on those fixed assets must be recorded at this time. The illustrative organization does not imply such a time restriction.

**26.** Investment income of $15,000 was earned on restricted investments ($12,000 was received). The income is restricted by donors for fixed asset purchases.

(26) Cash Restricted for Plant Purposes ............... $ 12,000
Interest Receivable Restricted for Plant Purposes .... 3,000
Restricted Revenues—Investment Income ........ $ 15,000
To record investment earnings.

**27.** Mortgage payments of $60,000, of which $20,000 was for interest, matured and were paid from resources restricted for that purpose.

(27) (a) Mortgage Payable ......................... $ 40,000
Expenses—Interest .......................... 20,000
Cash Restricted for Plant Purposes ........... $ 60,000
To record mortgage payments.

(27) (b) Temporarily Restricted Net Assets—
Reclassifications Out .................... $ 60,000
Unrestricted Net Assets—Reclassifications In .. $ 60,000
To record reclassification of net assets upon
satisfaction of temporary restrictions.

**28.** A $200,000 building addition was completed and paid for using $100,000 of contributions received previously for that purpose and $100,000 of unrestricted resources.

| | | | |
|---|---|---|---|
| (28) (a) | Buildings and Improvements ................... | $200,000 | |
| | Cash Restricted for Plant Purposes ........... | | $100,000 |
| | Cash ..................................... | | 100,000 |
| | To record building addition. | | |
| (28) (b) | Temporarily Restricted Net Assets— | | |
| |    Reclassifications Out ..................... | $100,000 | |
| | Unrestricted Net Assets—Reclassifications In  .. | | $100,000 |
| | To record reclassification of temporarily restricted net assets. | | |

**29.** Equipment that had been used in operations was sold for $40,000. The cost of the equipment was $75,000, and related accumulated depreciation at the date of sale was $45,000. The proceeds from the sales are not restricted.

| | | | |
|---|---|---|---|
| (29) | Cash ........................................ | $ 40,000 | |
| | Accumulated Depreciation—Equipment ........... | 45,000 | |
| | Equipment .................................... | | $ 75,000 |
| | Unrestricted Gain—Gain on Sale of Equipment ... | | 10,000 |
| | To record sale of equipment. | | |

**30.** A ten-year term endowment with a balance of $100,000 expired; $65,000 of the expired term endowment must be used for capital outlay; but the remainder is unrestricted.

| | | | |
|---|---|---|---|
| (30) (a) | Cash Restricted for Plant Purposes ............. | $ 65,000 | |
| | Cash ..................................... | 35,000 | |
| | Cash Restricted for Endowment ............. | | $100,000 |
| | To record reclassification of assets of expired term endowment that are restricted to capital outlay. | | |
| (30) (b) | Temporarily Restricted Net Assets— | | |
| |    Reclassifications Out ..................... | $ 35,000 | |
| | Unrestricted Net Assets—Reclassifications In  .. | | $ 35,000 |
| | To record reclassification of temporarily restricted net assets. | | |

**31.** The accounts were closed at year end.

| | | | |
|---|---|---|---|
| (31) (a) | Unrestricted Support—Contributions ........... | $335,000 | |
| | Unrestricted Support—Donated Materials ....... | 10,000 | |
| | Unrestricted Support—Donated Facilities ........ | 8,000 | |
| | Unrestricted Support—Donated Services ........ | 10,000 | |
| | Unrestricted Support—Special Events ........... | 75,000 | |
| | Unrestricted Revenues—Membership Dues ...... | 17,300 | |
| | Unrestricted Revenues—Investment Income ..... | 34,000 | |
| | Unrestricted Gain—Gain on Sale of Equipment  .. | 10,000 | |
| | Unrestricted Net Assets—Reclassifications In  .... | 445,000 | |
| | Expenses—Education ..................... | | $184,000 |
| | Expenses—Research ...................... | | 103,800 |
| | Expenses—Management and General ......... | | 151,200 |
| | Expenses—Fund-Raising ................... | | 91,000 |
| | Expenses—Direct Costs of Special Events ..... | | 25,000 |
| | Expenses—Interest ...................... | | 20,000 |
| | Unrestricted Net Assets ................... | | 369,300 |
| | To close changes in unrestricted net assets. | | |

| (31) (b) | Restricted Support—Contributions . . . . . . . . . . . . | $275,000 | |
|---|---|---|---|
| | Restricted Revenues—Investment Income . . . . . . . | 35,500 | |
| | Temporarily Restricted Net Assets . . . . . . . . . . . . . | 134,500 | |
| | Temporarily Restricted Net Assets— Reclassifications Out . . . . . . . . . . . . . . . . . . . . | | $445,000 |
| | To close changes in temporarily restricted net assets. | | |
| (31) (c) | Permanently Restricted Support—Contributions . . | $ 55,000 | |
| | Permanently Restricted Revenues— Investment Income . . . . . . . . . . . . . . . . . . . . . | 10,500 | |
| | Permanently Restricted Gain—Gain on Sale of Investments . . . . . . . . . . . . . . . . . . . . . . . . | 1,400 | |
| | Permanently Restricted Net Assets . . . . . . . . . . | | $ 66,900 |
| | To close changes in permanently restricted net assets. | | |

## Illustrative Nongovernment VHWO/ONPO Financial Statements

The financial statements for 19X1 for the illustrative nongovernment VHWO/ONPO include the balance sheet, the statement of activities, the statement of cash flows, and the statement of functional expenses. Recall that the statement of functional expenses is required if the illustrative organization is a VHWO. If the organization is an ONPO, it is an optional statement. A postclosing trial balance is presented in Figure 18–3. The closing entries for the illustration are useful for tracing amounts from the entries to the statement of activities in Figure 18–5.

### Balance Sheet

The balance sheet in Figure 18–4 closely resembles that of a business organization. Two matters are worthy of special attention. First, financial resources restricted for long-term purposes should not be reported as cash and cash equivalents. They should be reported as noncurrent assets if a classified balance sheet is presented. Therefore, for example, the beginning and ending cash balances reported in Figure 18–4 are the sums of the unrestricted cash and the cash restricted for specific current purposes—education and research. The financial resources restricted for plant purposes in the trial balance are reported as "Assets restricted for plant purposes" in the balance sheet. Likewise, the financial resources restricted for endowment in the trial balance are reported as "Assets restricted for endowment" in the balance sheet. The three classes of net assets—unrestricted, temporarily restricted, and permanently restricted—are reported as required by SFAS No. 117.

### Operating Statement

The operating statement in Figure 18–5—the Statement of Activities—follows the format illustrated in Figure 18–1. The amount reported for contributions under "Changes in Unrestricted Net Assets" is the sum of the balances of the Unrestricted Support accounts for contributions, donated materials, donated facilities, and donated services [closing entry 31 (a)]. Note also:

- The reporting of special events
- The reporting of all expenses as changes in unrestricted net assets
- The functional reporting of program services and supporting services

FIGURE 18–3  **Nongovernment VHWO/ONPO End of 19X1 Trial Balance**

Illustrative VHWO/ONPO
**Postclosing Trial Balance**
December 31, 19X1

| | *Debit* | *Credit* |
|---|---|---|
| Cash | $ 227,000 | |
| Pledges Receivable | 90,000 | |
| Allowance for Uncollectible Pledges | | $ 14,000 |
| Inventory of Materials | 7,800 | |
| Investments | 90,000 | |
| Cash Restricted for Plant Purposes | 27,000 | |
| Cash Restricted for Endowment | 111,900 | |
| Investments Restricted for Plant Purposes | 120,000 | |
| Investments Restricted for Endowment | 300,000 | |
| Interest Receivable Restricted for Plant Purposes | 3,000 | |
| Land | 50,000 | |
| Buildings and Improvements | 620,000 | |
| Accumulated Depreciation—Buildings and Improvements | | 154,000 |
| Equipment | 265,000 | |
| Accumulated Depreciation—Equipment | | 56,000 |
| Vouchers Payable | | 25,000 |
| Accrued Salaries Payable | | 3,000 |
| Mortgage Payable | | 165,000 |
| Unrestricted Net Assets | | 786,300 |
| Temporarily Restricted Net Assets—Time Restricted | | 55,000 |
| Temporarily Restricted Net Assets—Research | | 7,500 |
| Temporarily Restricted Net Assets—Education | | 84,000 |
| Temporarily Restricted Net Assets—Plant Purposes | | 150,000 |
| Permanently Restricted Net Assets | | 411,900 |
| | $1,911,700 | $1,911,700 |

- "The reporting of net assets released from restrictions" as an increase in unrestricted net assets and a corresponding decrease in temporarily restricted net assets—thus having a zero net effect on changes in (total) net assets

### Statement of Cash Flows

Figure 18–6, the Statement of Cash Flows, is quite similar to a business cash flow statement. Note the key modifications as you review the statement. These are:

- Classification of contributions and earnings that are restricted for plant and endowment purposes as financing activities,
- Classification of the decrease in cash restricted for long-term purposes as an investing activity, and
- Reconciliation of operating cash flows with the change in net assets instead of with net income.

**FIGURE 18–4 Nongovernment VHWO/ONPO Comparative Balance Sheet**

Illustrative VHWO/ONPO
**Balance Sheet**
December 31, 19X1 and 19X0

| **Assets** | *19X1* | *19X0* |
|---|---:|---:|
| Cash (and cash equivalents) ............................. | $ 227,000 | $ 125,000 |
| Pledges receivable* (less allowance for uncollectibles of $14,000 in 19X1 and $4,000 in 19X0) .................. | 76,000 | 46,000 |
| Accrued interest receivable .............................. | — | 2,000 |
| Inventory of materials and supplies ....................... | 7,800 | 3,000 |
| Investments .......................................... | 90,000 | 90,000 |
| Assets restricted for plant purposes ...................... | 150,000 | 270,000 |
| Land ................................................ | 50,000 | 50,000 |
| Buildings and improvements (net of accumulated depreciation of $140,000 and $154,000) .................. | 466,000 | 280,000 |
| Equipment (net of accumulated depreciation of $56,000 and $85,000) ........................................... | 209,000 | 115,000 |
| Assets restricted for endowment ......................... | 411,900 | 445,000 |
| Total Assets ...................................... | $1,687,700 | $1,426,000 |

**Liabilities and Net Assets**

| | *19X1* | *19X0* |
|---|---:|---:|
| Liabilities: | | |
| Vouchers payable ...................................... | $ 25,000 | $ 28,000 |
| Accrued salaries payable ............................... | 3,000 | — |
| Mortgage payable ..................................... | 165,000 | 205,000 |
| Total liabilities ................................... | 193,000 | 233,000 |
| Net Assets: | | |
| Permanently restricted .................................. | 411,900 | 345,000 |
| Temporarily restricted: | | |
| For research ........................................ | 7,500 | 15,000 |
| For education ....................................... | 84,000 | 24,000 |
| For plant assets ..................................... | 150,000 | 270,000 |
| For endowment ...................................... | — | 100,000 |
| For future years .................................... | 55,000 | 22,000 |
| Total temporarily restricted net assets ................. | 296,500 | 431,000 |
| Unrestricted: | | |
| Designated for capital additions ......................... | — | 100,000 |
| Designated for endowment ............................. | 50,000 | — |
| Invested in fixed assets .............................. | 560,000 | 240,000 |
| Undesignated ....................................... | 176,300 | 77,000 |
| Total unrestricted net assets ......................... | 786,300 | 417,000 |
| Total net assets ............................... | 1,494,700 | 1,193,000 |
| Total Liabilities and Net Assets ......................... | $1,687,700 | $1,426,000 |

*Recall that pledges receivables are permitted to be reported at net realizable value only if they are for a period of one year or less as in the illustration. Otherwise, these receivables should be reported at their present value.

FIGURE 18–5  **Nongovernment VHWO/ONPO Operating Statement**

Illustrative VHWO/ONPO
**Statement of Activities**
For the Year Ended December 31, 19X1

**Changes in Unrestricted Net Assets:**

Revenues and gains:

| | | |
|---|---:|---:|
| Contributions (net of estimated uncollectible pledges of $20,000)* | | $   363,000 |
| Special events | $75,000 | |
| Less: Direct costs of special events | 25,000 | 50,000 |
| Membership dues | | 17,300 |
| Investment income** | | 34,000 |
| Gain on sale of equipment | | 10,000 |
| Total revenues and gains | | 474,300 |
| Net assets released from restrictions | | 445,000 |
| Increase in unrestricted net assets | | 919,300 |

Expenses:

Program Services:

| | |
|---|---:|
| Research | 103,800 |
| Education | 184,000 |
| Total program services | 287,800 |

Supporting Services:

| | |
|---|---:|
| Management and general | 171,200 |
| Fund raising | 91,000 |
| Total supporting services | 262,200 |
| Total expenses | 550,000 |
| Net increase in unrestricted net assets | 369,300 |

**Changes in Temporarily Restricted Net Assets:**

| | |
|---|---:|
| Contributions | 275,000 |
| Investment income** | 35,500 |
| Net assets released from restrictions | (445,000) |
| Decrease in temporarily restricted net assets | (134,500) |

**Changes in Permanently Restricted Net Assets:**

| | |
|---|---:|
| Contributions | 55,000 |
| Investment income permanently restricted by donors | 10,500 |
| Realized gains on sale of investments** | 1,400 |
| Increase in permanently restricted net assets | 66,900 |
| **Increase in net assets** | 301,700 |
| Net assets, January 1 | 1,193,000 |
| Net assets, December 31 | $1,494,700 |

*Contributions may be reported at the net realizable value of pledges (plus other contributions) only if pledges are to be collected within a year. Otherwise, the present value, not the net realizable value, of the pledges should be included in contributions.

**The illustration assumes that the carrying value of investments equals their fair value at year end. If not, unrealized gains or losses on investments reported at fair value would be reported.

**FIGURE 18-6  Nongovernment VHWO/ONPO Statement of Cash Flows**

Illustrative VHWO/ONPO
**Statement of Cash Flows**
For the Year Ended December 31, 19X1

| | |
|---|---:|
| **Cash flows from operating activities:** | |
| Cash received from contributors ................................ | $330,000 |
| Cash received from sale of assets donated for resale ............... | 150,000 |
| Cash received from special events .............................. | 50,000 |
| Cash received from membership dues .......................... | 17,300 |
| Interest and dividends received ................................ | 56,500 |
| Interest paid .................................................. | (20,000) |
| Cash paid to employees and suppliers ......................... | (476,800) |
| Net cash provided by operating activities ..................... | 107,000 |
| **Cash flows from investing activities:** | |
| Purchase of buildings and improvements ...................... | (200,000) |
| Purchase of equipment ........................................ | (140,000) |
| Proceeds from sale of equipment ............................. | 40,000 |
| Proceeds from sale of investments ........................... | 14,400 |
| Decrease in cash invested in assets restricted for plant | |
|     and endowment purposes* ........................... | 143,100 |
| Net cash used by investing activities ......................... | (142,500) |
| **Cash flows from financing activities:** | |
| Proceeds from contributions restricted for: | |
|     Investment in endowment ................................ | 55,000 |
|     Investment in plant .................................... | 100,000 |
| Interest and dividends restricted to reinvestment ................. | 22,500 |
| Payment of mortgage notes payable .......................... | (40,000) |
| Net cash provided by financing activities .................... | 137,500 |
| **Net increase in cash** ....................................... | 102,000 |
| Cash at the beginning of the year ............................. | 125,000 |
| Cash at the end of the year ................................... | $227,000 |
| **Reconciliation of change in net assets and** | |
|   **cash provided by operating activities:** | |
| Change in net assets .......................................... | $301,700 |
| Adjustments to reconcile change in net assets to net | |
|   cash provided by operating activities: | |
|     Depreciation expense .................................... | 30,000 |
|     Increase in pledges receivable ........................... | (30,000) |
|     Decrease in interest receivable ........................... | 2,000 |
|     Increase in inventory .................................... | (4,800) |
|     Decrease in vouchers payable ............................ | (3,000) |
|     Increase in salaries payable .............................. | 3,000 |
|     Gain on sale of equipment ............................... | (10,000) |
|     Gain on sale of long-term investments .................... | (1,400) |
|     Contributions restricted for long-term investment ................. | (155,000) |
|     Interest and dividends restricted for long-term investment ........... | (25,500) |
|     Net cash provided by operating activities ..................... | $107,000 |

*In practice this cash probably would have been invested, then later the investments would have been sold. Therefore, this amount normally would have been reflected in the difference between cash used to purchase investments and cash received from sale of investments.

## Statement of Functional Expenses

The Statement of Functional Expenses in Figure 18–7 is a basic, required financial statement of VHWOs and presents the expenses incurred for each program or function in detail by object class. Again, this statement is optional for ONPOs.

**FIGURE 18–7 Statement of Functional Expenses**

Illustrative VHWO/ONPO
**Statement of Functional Expenses**
For the Year Ended December 31, 19X1

| | Program Services | | | Supporting Services | | | |
|---|---|---|---|---|---|---|---|
| | *Research* | *Education* | *Total* | *Management and General* | *Fund-Raising* | *Total* | *Total Expenses* |
| Salaries ................. | $ 16,000 | $ 27,000 | $ 43,000 | $ 30,000 | $15,000 | $ 45,000 | $ 88,000 |
| Employee health and retirement benefits ............ | 1,289 | 3,340 | 4,629 | 4,648 | 1,284 | 5,932 | 10,561 |
| Payroll taxes, etc. ........... | 644 | 1,670 | 2,314 | 2,324 | 642 | 2,966 | 5,280 |
| Total Salaries and Related Expenses .............. | 17,933 | 32,010 | 49,943 | 36,972 | 16,926 | 53,898 | 103,841 |
| Professional fees and contract service payments ......... | 34,996 | 90,710 | 125,706 | 13,428 | 2,283 | 15,711 | 141,417 |
| Supplies ................. | 4,852 | | 4,852 | 9,296 | 6,000 | 15,296 | 20,148 |
| Telephone and Internet ...... | 1,245 | 1,670 | 2,915 | 7,747 | 5,965 | 13,712 | 16,627 |
| Postage and shipping ........ | 1,192 | 1,670 | 2,862 | 6,714 | 8,015 | 14,729 | 17,591 |
| Occupancy ............... | 10,000 | | 10,000 | 15,494 | 7,707 | 23,201 | 33,201 |
| Rental of equipment ........ | 322 | 835 | 1,157 | 1,549 | 4,567 | 6,116 | 7,273 |
| Local transportation ........ | 966 | 2,505 | 3,471 | 11,879 | 8,563 | 20,442 | 23,913 |
| Conferences, conventions, meetings ............... | 2,577 | 6,680 | 9,257 | 19,626 | 3,711 | 23,337 | 32,594 |
| Printing and publications .... | 1,289 | 3,340 | 4,629 | 7,231 | 18,268 | 25,499 | 30,128 |
| Awards and grants .......... | 16,106 | 41,747 | 57,853 | | | | 57,853 |
| Interest .................. | | | | 20,000 | | 20,000 | 20,000 |
| Meals ................... | | | | | 20,000 | 20,000 | 20,000 |
| Gratuities ................ | | | | | 5,000 | 5,000 | 5,000 |
| Miscellaneous ............ | 322 | 833 | 1,155 | 8,264 | 5,995 | 14,259 | 15,414 |
| Total Expenses before Depreciation .......... | 91,800 | 182,000 | 273,800 | 158,200 | 113,000 | 271,200 | 545,000 |
| Depreciation of buildings, improvements, and equipment ............... | 12,000 | 2,000 | 14,000 | 13,000 | 3,000 | 16,000 | 30,000 |
| Total Expenses .......... | 103,800 | 184,000 | 287,800 | 171,200 | 116,000 | 287,200 | 575,000 |
| Less: Expenses deducted directly from revenues ..... | | | | | (25,000) | (25,000) | (25,000) |
| Total expenses reported by function ............... | $103,800 | $184,000 | $287,800 | $171,200 | $91,000 | $262,200 | $550,000 |

# CONCLUDING COMMENTS

VHWOs and ONPOs encompass a myriad of diverse types of not-for-profit organizations. Some of these organizations are government entities; many are not. This chapter discussed the accounting and reporting standards applicable to nongovernment VHWOs and ONPOs. Those applicable to government VHWOs and ONPOs differ dramatically and are not covered because they are significantly less common. Significant differences also exist in the accounting and financial reporting for nongovernment and for government health care organizations and colleges and universities. The key differences in accounting for nongovernment, not-for-profit colleges and universities and health care entities compared to government ones are discussed in Appendices 18–1 and 18–2.

Chapter 19 addresses financial reporting for the federal government. Chapter 20 deals with auditing in the government and not-for-profit environments.

## APPENDIX 18–1:

## Nongovernment, Not-for-Profit University Reporting

This chapter discusses nongovernment, not-for-profit reporting standards in the context of voluntary health and welfare organizations and other nonprofit organizations. Chapters 16 and 17 discussed accounting and reporting for government colleges and universities and for government hospitals, respectively. Nongovernment, not-for-profit colleges and universities and nongovernment, not-for-profit health care organizations must apply the same FASB not-for-profit guidance as nongovernmental VHWOs and ONPOs. However, they have transactions such as patient service revenues of hospitals that VHWOs and ONPOs do not have. Therefore, this appendix illustrates briefly the application of SFAS 116 and SFAS 117 to nongovernment colleges and universities. The next appendix illustrates the application of that FASB guidance to nongovernment hospitals.

The differences between financial reporting for government and nongovernment colleges and universities are far more dramatic than those between government and nongovernment hospitals, voluntary health and welfare organizations, and other nonprofit organizations. The more important differences include:

- Different financial statements are required—Nongovernment, not-for-profit colleges and universities are required to present a balance sheet, statement of activities, and statement of cash flows instead of the statements illustrated for a government university.

- Different entity focus in the financial statements—Whereas the financial statements of a government university are clearly fund based and need not present entity-wide totals, the minimum requirement for a nongovernment, not-for-profit institution is the presentation of the aggregated, entity-wide totals.

- Different measurement focus—Nongovernment, not-for-profit colleges and universities must report changes in economic resources (revenues and expenses) instead of changes in current fund financial resources (revenues and expenditures).

- Tuition revenues of nongovernment colleges are reported net of reductions such as scholarships and fellowships awarded by the institution.

- Different recognition criteria for restricted grants, contributions, investment income, and other restricted inflows—Nongovernment, not-for-profit institutions should recognize revenues for these items when they become unconditional or are earned, as appropriate. Government institutions recognize revenues on those restricted for current fund purposes when expended for that purpose. They recognize revenues for term endowments and similar agreements when they become available for unrestricted use or when used for the restricted current fund purpose. Most amounts restricted for plant asset or permanent endowment purposes are not reported as revenues by a government college or university.

- Differences in reporting equity—Nongovernment, not-for-profit organizations must report the university's equity categorized into three classes of net assets (discussed in this chapter)—unrestricted, temporarily restricted, and permanently restricted. The relationships between the fund balances reported for A Government University in Chapter 16 and the net asset classes that would be reported if the university were a not-for-profit institution are shown in Figure 18–8.

**FIGURE 18–8  Derivation of Net Asset Classes from Fund Balances**

*Unrestricted Net Assets*
*$5,089,900*

(1) Fund balance of Unrestricted Current Fund, $260,900
(2) Fund balance—unrestricted of Unexpended Plant Fund, $18,000
(3) Fund balance—unrestricted of Plant Fund for Retirement of Indebtedness (none for this university)
(4) Fund balance—unrestricted of Loan Funds (none for this university)
(5) Fund balance—unrestricted of Annuity and Life Income Funds (none for this university)
(6) Fund balance—unrestricted of Endowment and Similar Funds, $100,000
(7) Net invested in plant, $4,711,000*

*Temporarily Restricted*
*Net Assets*
*$543,719*

(1) Fund balance—temporarily restricted of Unrestricted Current Fund (equal to pledges receivable not specifically designated for current period)—none in this example
(2) Fund balance of Restricted Current Fund, $175,700
(3) Fund balance—restricted of Unexpended Plant Fund, $20,000
(4) Fund balance—donor-restricted of Plant Fund for Retirement of Indebtedness, $225,000
(5) Fund balance—donor-restricted of Loan Funds, $99,900
(6) Fund balance—donor-restricted of Annuity and Life Income Funds, $23,119
(7) Fund balances—temporarily restricted of Endowment and Similar Funds (none for this university)

*Permanently Restricted*
*Net Assets*
*$3,126,500*

(1) Fund balance—restricted for endowment of Endowment and Similar Funds, $2,926,500
(2) Trust administered by Village National Bank (Endowment Fund transaction 11), $200,000

*If a donor has specified that the organization must use the fixed asset for some minimal time period, the asset is classified as temporarily restricted during that period. Likewise, organizations are permitted to adopt a policy of implying a time restriction for donated fixed assets equal to their estimated useful lives. Organizations with this policy classify the book value of donated fixed assets and fixed assets acquired with donor-restricted resources as temporarily restricted during their useful lives. If donors stipulate that a donated fixed asset must be kept by and used by an organization in perpetuity or that, if sold, proceeds from the sale must be reinvested in fixed assets, those fixed assets should be classified as permanently restricted.

Many of these and other differences can be observed by comparing the balance sheet (Figure 18–9) and the statement of activity (Figure 18–10) prepared under the assumption in this chapter that the illustrative university is a private, not-for-profit university with the financial statements presented in Chapter 16 for A Government University. (See Figure 16–5, page 646; Figure 16–4, pages 648–649; and Figure 16–6, pages 652–653.) A statement of cash flows also would be required for a private, not-for-profit university. That statement is not presented here because there is not a similar statement to which to compare it for A Government University. Too, the cash flow statement would resemble closely the nongovernment, not-for-profit cash flow statements presented for other nongovernment, not-for-profit entities in Figures 18–6 and 18–14.

FIGURE 18–9  **Nongovernment, Nonprofit University Balance Sheet**

A Nongovernment, Nonprofit University
**Balance Sheet**
October 31, 19A

**Assets**

| | |
|---|---:|
| Cash (and cash equivalents) | $ 509,700 |
| Accounts receivable (less allowance for uncollectibles of $2,000) | 48,000 |
| Inventory of materials and supplies | 50,000 |
| Assets restricted for annuity agreements | 186,000 |
| Assets restricted for loan programs | 99,900 |
| Assets restricted for plant purposes | 545,000 |
| Assets restricted for endowment | 3,126,500 |
| Land | 300,000 |
| Building and improvements (net of accumulated depreciation of $4,159,600) | 3,852,400 |
| Equipment (net of accumulated depreciation of $1,080,400) | 728,600 |
| Library books | 200,000 |
| Construction in progress | 240,000 |
| Total assets | $9,886,100 |

**Liabilities and Net Assets**

| | |
|---|---:|
| Accounts payable | $    47,000 |
| Interest payable | 100 |
| Accounts payable from restricted assets | 40,000 |
| Annuities payable | 162,881 |
| Mortgages and other notes payable | 876,000 |
| Total liabilities | 1,125,981 |
| Net Assets: | |
| Permanently restricted | 3,126,500 |
| Temporarily restricted | 543,719 |
| Unrestricted: | |
| Net invested in fixed assets | 4,711,000 |
| Other | 378,900 |
| Total unrestricted net assets | 5,089,900 |
| Total net assets | 8,760,119 |
| Total liabilities and net assets | $9,886,100 |

FIGURE 18–10  **Nongovernment, Nonprofit University Operating Statement**

A Nongovernment, Nonprofit University
**Statement of Activity**
For the Year Ended October 31, 19A

*Operating revenues, gains, and net assets released from restrictions:*

Revenues and gains:

| | |
|---|---|
| Tuition and fees | $1,326,000 |
| State appropriations | 1,000,000 |
| Unrestricted local gifts, grants, and contracts | 124,000 |
| Sales and services of educational activities | 68,000 |
| Sales and services of auxiliary enterprises | 700,000 |
| Other revenues and gains (if any) | 50,000 |
| Total revenues and gains | 3,268,000 |

Net assets released from restrictions for operating use by satisfying use restrictions on:

| | |
|---|---|
| Federal grants | 48,000 |
| Local gifts and grants, | 2,000 |
| Private gifts and grants | 130,000 |
| Endowment income | 62,000 |
| Total net assets released from use or term restrictions for operating purposes | 242,000 |
| Total operating revenues, gains, and reclassifications | 3,510,000 |

Expenses:

Educational and general:

| | |
|---|---|
| Instruction | 932,000 |
| Research | 140,000 |
| Public service | 50,000 |
| Academic support | 330,000 |
| Student services | 150,000 |
| Institutional support | 400,000 |
| Operation and maintenance of plant | 490,000 |
| Depreciation | 230,000 |
| Total educational and general expenses | 2,722,000 |
| Auxiliary enterprises | 592,000 |
| Total operating expenses | 3,314,000 |
| Excess of operating revenues, gains, and reclassifications over operating expenses | 196,000 |

Nonoperating changes in unrestricted net assets:

| | |
|---|---|
| Interest expense | (10,100) |
| Fire loss | (1,000) |
| Net assets released from restrictions for plant asset-related purposes | 15,000 |
| Changes in unrestricted net assets from nonoperating activities | 3,900 |
| Net increase in unrestricted net assets | 199,900 |

Changes in Temporarily Restricted Net Assets:

| | |
|---|---|
| Contributions | 584,411 |
| Restricted federal grants | 100,000 |
| Endowment income | 117,700 |
| Restricted losses of loan fund | (500) |
| Restricted interest income | 400 |
| Change in value of annuity agreement | (1,292) |
| Net assets released from restrictions | (257,000) |
| Increase in temporarily restricted net assets | 543,719 |

Changes in Permanently Restricted Net Assets:

| | |
|---|---|
| Contributions | 3,125,000 |
| Realized gains on sale of investments | 500 |
| Unrealized gains on investments | 1,000 |
| Increase in permanently restricted net assets | 3,126,500 |
| Increase in net assets | 3,870,119 |
| Net assets, November 1, 19Z | 4,890,000 |
| Net assets, October 31, 19A | $8,760,119 |

APPENDIX 18–2:

# Nongovernment, Nonprofit Hospital Reporting

Like colleges and universities, nongovernment, not-for-profit health care organizations are required to follow the guidance of SFASs 116 and 117 for financial reporting purposes. The AICPA *Health Care Audit Guide* provides implementation guidance to assist those organizations to comply with those standards. Chapter 17 on accounting for health care organizations dealt solely with government health care organizations. This chapter discussed and illustrated the requirements of SFASs 116 and 117 but not the unique practices or transactions affecting health care organizations. This appendix discusses and illustrates the application of those standards to nongovernment, not-for-profit hospitals (hereafter, NFP hospitals).

First, note that there are far more similarities in accounting and reporting government versus NFP hospitals than there are differences. For instance, all of the following are accounted for and reported in virtually the same manner:

- Patient service revenues
- Charity services
- Deductions from revenues of various types
- Premium fee revenues
- Other revenues—such as cafeteria sales, medical record transcript fees, and unrestricted contributions
- Most expenses
- Net assets released from restrictions used for operations
- Net assets released from restrictions used for plant purposes
- Assets limited as to use
- Assets restricted for noncurrent purposes, such as endowment or plant purposes
- Classification of fixed assets as unrestricted

The key differences in reporting government hospitals and NFP hospitals are that NFP hospitals:

- Report net assets classified into the three categories required by SFAS 117 instead of as restricted versus unrestricted fund balance
- Present a statement of changes in net assets instead of a statement of changes in fund balances
- Report restricted contributions and restricted investment income as revenues (changes in temporarily or permanently restricted net assets) in the period unconditionally pledged or received
- Apply FASB cash flow statement guidance instead of GASB guidance
- Exclude some items from the performance measurement in the statement of operations that government hospitals include—for example, unrealized gains or losses on other than trading securities

Most of these similarities and differences are readily observable by comparing the financial statements in this appendix—Figures 18–11, 18–12, 18–13, and 18–14—with those in Chapter 17. The appendix statements are based on the same transactions and assumptions used in the government hospital illustration in Chapter 17.

FIGURE 18–11 **Year-End Balance Sheet—Nongovernment, Nonprofit Hospital**

Alzona Hospital
**Balance Sheet**
September 30, 19B
With Comparative Figures for September 30, 19A

| | September 30 | |
|---|---|---|
| | **19B** | **19A** |
| **Assets** | | |
| Current: | | |
| Cash | $ 548,000 | $ 215,000 |
| Assets limited as to use—required for current liabilities .... | 125,000 | |
| Receivables (less allowance for uncollectibles of $90,000 | | |
| for 19B and $85,000 for 19A) | 680,000 | 615,000 |
| Investments | 345,500 | 460,000 |
| Accrued interest receivable | 2,000 | |
| Inventory of materials and supplies | 215,000 | 165,000 |
| Total current assets | 1,915,500 | 1,455,000 |
| Noncurrent: | | |
| Noncurrent investments and special funds: | | |
| Assets limited as to use by internal designation | 100,000 | |
| Assets limited as to use for plant expansion by bond | | |
| indenture agreement | 525,000 | |
| Less assets limited as to use that are required for | | |
| current liabilities | 125,000 | |
| Noncurrent assets limited as to use externally | 400,000 | |
| Assets restricted for plant replacement and expansion | 323,000 | 325,000 |
| Assets restricted for permanent endowments | 780,000 | 480,000 |
| Total noncurrent investments and special funds | 1,603,000 | 805,000 |
| Property, plant, and equipment: | | |
| Land | 130,000 | 130,000 |
| Land improvements | 80,000 | 80,000 |
| Buildings | 5,000,000 | 5,000,000 |
| Fixed equipment | 500,000 | 600,000 |
| Major movable equipment | 113,000 | 90,000 |
| Construction in progress | 2,500,000 | |
| Total property, plant, and equipment | 8,323,000 | 5,900,000 |
| Less: Accumulated depreciation | 2,690,000 | 2,450,000 |
| Net property, plant, and equipment | 5,633,000 | 3,450,000 |
| Total noncurrent assets | 7,236,000 | 4,255,000 |
| Total assets | $9,151,500 | $5,710,000 |
| **Liabilities and Net Assets** | | |
| Current liabilities: | | |
| Notes payable | $ 130,000 | $ 150,000 |
| Accounts payable | 50,000 | 175,000 |
| Accrued interest payable | 31,000 | |
| Accrued salaries and wages payable | 83,000 | |
| Contracts payable, retained percentage | 125,000 | |
| Total current liabilities | 419,000 | 325,000 |
| Long-term debt: | | |
| Mortgage payable | 100,000 | 100,000 |
| Bonds payable | 3,000,000 | |
| Total liabilities | 3,519,000 | 425,000 |
| Net assets: | | |
| Unrestricted | 4,234,000 | 4,225,000 |
| Temporarily restricted by donors or grantors | 718,500 | 580,000 |
| Permanently restricted by donors | 680,000 | 480,000 |
| Total net assets | 5,632,500 | 5,285,000 |
| Total liabilities and net assets | $9,151,500 | $5,710,000 |

FIGURE 18–12 **Nongovernment, Nonprofit Hospital Operating Statement**

Alzona Hospital
**Statement of Operations**
For the Year Ended September 30, 19B

Unrestricted revenues, gains, and other support:

| | |
|---|---:|
| Net patient service revenue | $3,985,000 |
| Other operating revenues | 115,000 |
| Unrestricted contributions | 100,000 |
| Unrestricted investment income | 64,000 |
| Net assets released from restrictions for operating use | 300,000 |
| Total operating revenues, gains, and net assets released from restrictions for operating use | 4,564,000 |

Expenses and losses:

| | |
|---|---:|
| Nursing services | 1,624,000 |
| Other professional services | 981,000 |
| General services | 943,000 |
| Fiscal services | 160,000 |
| Administrative services | 397,000 |
| Depreciation | 300,000 |
| Bad debts | 120,000 |
| Interest | 38,000 |
| Loss on disposal of fixed assets | 10,000 |
| Total expenses and losses | 4,573,000 |

| | |
|---|---:|
| Excess (Deficiency) of revenues, gains, and other support over expenses and losses | (9,000) |
| Net assets released from restrictions for plant asset purposes | 18,000 |
| Increase in unrestricted net assets | $    9,000 |

FIGURE 18–13 **Nongovernment, Nonprofit Hospital Statement of Changes in Net Assets***

Alzona Hospital
**Statement of Changes in Net Assets**
For the Year Ended September 30, 19B

| | Unrestricted | Temporarily Restricted | Permanently Restricted | Total |
|---|---:|---:|---:|---:|
| Balance, October 1, 19A | $4,225,000 | $580,000 | $480,000 | $5,285,000 |
| Operating loss | (9,000) | | | (9,000) |
| Contributions | | 400,000 | 200,000 | 600,000 |
| Restricted investment income | | 56,500 | | 56,500 |
| Net assets released from restrictions | 18,000 | (318,000) | | (300,000) |
| Changes in net assets | 9,000 | 138,500 | 200,000 | 347,500 |
| Balance, September 30, 19B | $4,234,000 | $718,500 | $680,000 | $5,632,500 |

*Note that this statement would, in this case, be identical to the statement of changes in fund balances, Figure 17–7, if the two middle columns were combined and the total column omitted.

**FIGURE 18-14  Nongovernment, Nonprofit Hospital Statement of Cash Flows***

Alzona Hospital
**Statement of Cash Flows**
For the Year Ended September 30, 19B

**Cash flows from operating activities:**

| | | |
|---|---:|---:|
| Cash received from patients. . . . . . . . . . . . . . . . . . . . . . . . | $3,800,000 | |
| Cash received from other revenues. . . . . . . . . . . . . . . . . . . | 95,000 | |
| Cash received from contributions . . . . . . . . . . . . . . . . . . . | 500,000 | |
| Cash paid to suppliers and employees. . . . . . . . . . . . . . . . | (4,177,000) | |
| Cash received from investment earnings. . . . . . . . . . . . . . | 97,000 | |
| Cash paid for interest . . . . . . . . . . . . . . . . . . . . . . . . . . . . | (7,000) | |
| Net cash flows from operating activities . . . . . . . . . . . . | | 308,000 |

**Cash flows from investing activities:**

| | | |
|---|---:|---:|
| Cash paid for property, plant, and equipment. . . . . . . . . . . | (2,398,000) | |
| Net increase in cash invested in assets limited as to use . . . | (525,000) | |
| Net increase in cash invested in assets restricted for | | |
| endowment and plant purposes . . . . . . . . . . . . . . . . . . . . . | (4,000) | |
| Proceeds from sale of equipment . . . . . . . . . . . . . . . . . . . . | 30,000 | |
| Cash paid for investments . . . . . . . . . . . . . . . . . . . . . . . . . . | (300,000) | |
| Cash received from sale of investments . . . . . . . . . . . . . . . | 320,000 | |
| Net cash used in investing activities. . . . . . . . . . . . . . . . . | | (2,877,000) |

**Cash flows from financing activities:**

| | | |
|---|---:|---:|
| Cash received from issuing bonds . . . . . . . . . . . . . . . . . . . . | 3,000,000 | |
| Cash paid to retire debt . . . . . . . . . . . . . . . . . . . . . . . . . . . | (120,000) | |
| Cash received from investment earnings restricted for | | |
| plant purposes and restricted endowment revenues. . . . . | 22,000 | |
| Net cash flows from financing activities. . . . . . . . . . . . . . | | 2,902,000 |

| | | |
|---|---:|---:|
| **Net increase in cash**. . . . . . . . . . . . . . . . . . . . . . . . . . . . . . | | 333,000 |
| Cash balance, October 1, 19A. . . . . . . . . . . . . . . . . . . . . . . . | | 215,000 |
| Cash balance, September 30, 19B . . . . . . . . . . . . . . . . . . . . . | | $ 548,000 |

**Reconciliation of change in net assets to cash provided**
  **by operating activities:**

| | | |
|---|---:|---:|
| Change in net assets. . . . . . . . . . . . . . . . . . . . . . . . . . . . . . | $347,500 | |
| Adjustments to reconcile change in net assets to net cash provided | | |
| by operating activities: | | |
| Depreciation expense. . . . . . . . . . . . . . . . . . . . . . . . . . . . . | 300,000 | |
| Increase in accounts receivable . . . . . . . . . . . . . . . . . . . . . | (65,000) | |
| Increase in interest receivable . . . . . . . . . . . . . . . . . . . . . . | (2,000) | |
| Increase in inventory . . . . . . . . . . . . . . . . . . . . . . . . . . . . . | (50,000) | |
| Decrease in accounts payable . . . . . . . . . . . . . . . . . . . . . . . | (125,000) | |
| Increase in salaries and wages payable . . . . . . . . . . . . . . . | 83,000 | |
| Increase in interest payable . . . . . . . . . . . . . . . . . . . . . . . . | 31,000 | |
| Loss on disposal of fixed assets . . . . . . . . . . . . . . . . . . . . . | 10,000 | |
| Gain on sale of investments. . . . . . . . . . . . . . . . . . . . . . . . . | (5,000) | |
| Contributions restricted for permanent endowment . . . . . . | (200,000) | |
| Investment income—unrealized or restricted for long-term | (16,500) | |
| Net cash provided by operating activities . . . . . . . . . . . . | $ 308,000 | |

*Note that although there are major differences between this statement and Figure 17–8, the differences would be the same for any other government versus nongovernment entity of any type. The differences are not unique to hospitals.

## Questions

**Q 18-1**   Some VHWOs and ONPOs are required to follow the guidance of SFAS Nos. 116 and 117. Others are not permitted to do so. Why do different standards apply? Which organizations must apply the SFASs? What guidance must the other organizations apply?

**Q 18-2**   What are the basic financial statements required for nongovernment ONPOs?

**Q 18-3**   Neither VHWOs nor ONPOs are required to use fund accounting. The accountants for a newly established ONPO have asked your advice in establishing its accounting system. Specifically, they ask you: "What is fund accounting and how do we know if we should use it?" Respond.

**Q 18-4**   Identify and distinguish between the three classes of net assets required by SFAS 117.

**Q 18-5**   When should a nongovernment ONPO recognize contributions that are restricted by donors for fixed asset acquisitions?

**Q 18-6**   Inexhaustible collections of ONPOs are not required to be capitalized, much less depreciated. Why is this so, and what accounting and reporting recognition, if any, is given such inexhaustible collections?

**Q 18-7**   Gifts, contributions, and bequests to VHWOs and ONPOs may be restricted to use for specified operating or capital outlay purposes. Explain how restricted contributions, and so on, are accounted for (a) at receipt, and (b) upon expenditure, by nongovernment VHWOs.

**Q 18-8**   When nongovernment VHWOs and ONPOs hold fund-raising events such as banquets, auctions, and bazaars, the gross receipts often must be reported as revenues. Explain or illustrate how the direct costs of these special fund-raising events are to be reported. Also, may these nongovernment organizations report the special event using the net method?

**Q 18-9**   Donated services are sometimes given accounting recognition—and at other times are not given accounting recognition—in the accounts and statements of VHWOs and ONPOs. Explain why some are given accounting recognition and others are not. (Do not list the criteria.)

**Q 18-10**  Some VHWOs and ONPOs combine educational and program brochures with their fund-raising mailings and charge part or all of the cost of the mailings to program services. Why? Also, is this permitted by GAAP?

**Q 18-11**  A nongovernment VHWO receives pledges from donors for contributions to be received annually over the next three years. When should these contributions be recognized as revenues? As changes in which net asset class? How should the amount of revenues be measured?

**Q 18-12**  What is the difference between conditional and unconditional pledges? What effect does this have on revenue recognition?

**Q 18-13**  What is the difference between restricted and unrestricted contributions? What effect do restrictions have on revenue recognition?

**Q 18-14**  How do nongovernment, not-for-profit hospitals measure and report patient service revenues? How does this differ from government hospitals?

**Q 18-15**  What are the major differences between government college and university reporting and nongovernment college and university reporting?

## Exercises

**E 18-1**   Record the following transactions in the accounts of a nongovernment VHWO or ONPO.
1. Unconditional pledges made to the organization during the year total $1,000,000 unrestricted and $500,000 restricted to a specific program. All of the restricted

pledges are collected during the year. 75% of the unrestricted pledges are collected. 20% of the uncollected pledges outstanding at year end are expected to be uncollectible.

2. Cash gifts of $300,000 are received during the year. These gifts are restricted for permanent endowment purposes.
3. $222,000 of qualifying costs are incurred for the program for which restricted pledges were received.
4. Conditional pledges made to the organization during the year total $90,000 (unrestricted). None were collected during the year.

**E 18-2**   Record the following transactions in the accounts of a nongovernment VHWO or ONPO.

1. Purchased supplies on account, $50,000.
2. Used supplies costing $40,000.
3. Purchased equipment costing $16,000 using donor-restricted resources.
4. Issued $1,000,000 of bonds at par.
5. Sold land that had cost $33,000 for $45,000.
6. Received interest earned on investment of donor-restricted resources, $6,000. The donor did not specify that the interest income be used for the same purpose stipulated for the principal of the gift, but the organization traditionally has done so and plans to in this case.

## Problems

**P 18-1**   (Multiple Choice)

1. Securities donated to a voluntary health and welfare organization should be recorded at the
   a. donor's recorded amount.
   b. fair market value at the date of the gift.
   c. fair market value at the date of the gift, or the donor's book value, whichever is lower.
   d. fair market value at the date of the gift, or the donor's book value, whichever is higher.

   Items 2 and 3 are based on the following data:

   The Charles Vernon Eames Community Service Center is a nongovernment voluntary health and welfare organization financed by contributions from the general public. During 19X3, unrestricted pledges of $900,000 were received, half of which were payable in 19X3, with the other half payable in 19X4 for use in 19X4. It was estimated that 10% of these pledges would be uncollectible. In addition, Louease Jones, a social worker on the center's permanent staff, contributed an additional 800 hours of her time to the center at no charge. Jones's annual salary is $20,000 based on a workload of 2,000 hours.

2. How much should the center report as contributions revenue for 19X3 from the pledges?
   a. $0              c. $810,000
   b. $405,000        d. $413,000
3. How much should the center record in 19X3 for contributed service expense?
   a. $8,000          c. $800
   b. $4,000          d. $0
4. Cura Foundation, a nongovernment voluntary health and welfare organization supported by contributions from the general public, included the following costs in its statement of functional expenses for the year ended December 31, 19X3:

| | |
|---|---|
| Fund Raising ..................................... | $500,000 |
| Administrative (including data processing) .............. | 300,000 |
| Research ........................................ | 100,000 |

Cura's functional expenses for 19X3 program services were
a. $900,000.
b. $500,000.
c. $300,000.
d. $100,000.

5. The permanently restricted net assets of an ONPO include net assets from which of the following?

| | Term Endowment Gifts | Fixed Asset Restricted Gifts |
|---|---|---|
| a. | No | No |
| b. | No | Yes |
| c. | Yes | Yes |
| d. | Yes | No |

6. During the years ended June 30, 19X0 and 19X1, a nongovernment ONPO conducted a cancer research project financed by a $2,000,000 restricted gift. This entire amount was pledged by the donor on July 10, 19W9, although he paid only $500,000 at that date. During the 2-year research period the ONPO-related gift receipts and research expenses were as follows:

| | Year Ended June 30 | |
|---|---|---|
| | *19X0* | *19X1* |
| Gift receipts | $1,200,000 | $ 800,000 |
| Cancer research expenses | 900,000 | 1,100,000 |

How much support should the ONPO report in its statement of activity for the year ended June 30, 19X1?
a. $0
b. $800,000
c. $1,100,000
d. $2,000,000

7. What amount of net assets released from restrictions should the ONPO in item 6 report in its statement of activity for 19X1?
a. $0
b. $800,000
c. $1,100,000
d. $2,000,000

8. A nongovernment voluntary health and welfare organization received an unconditional pledge in 19X0 from a donor specifying that the amount pledged be used in 19X2. The donor paid the pledge in cash in 19X1. The pledge should be reflected in
a. temporarily restricted net assets in the balance sheet at the end of 19X0, and in unrestricted net assets at the end of 19X1.
b. temporarily restricted net assets in the balance sheet at the end of 19X0 and 19X1, and in unrestricted net assets at the end of 19X2.
c. in unrestricted net assets at the end of 19X0.
d. none of the above.
(Items 1–8, AICPA, adapted)

9. VHWO financial statements are prepared under which basis of accounting?
   a. cash
   b. accrual
   c. modified accrual
   d. cost
   e. Modified cash
10. The primary financial statement(s) required to be prepared by other nonprofit organizations do not include a
    a. balance sheet.
    b. statement of cash flows.
    c. statement of functional expenses.
    d. statement of activity.
    e. both b and c.
11. On December 31, 19X7, the Greater Ottumnwa (Iowa) United Fund had $150,000 in pledges receivable from 19X7 pledges, all of which were receivable during 19X8. During the past five years, this nongovernment agency has collected an average of 90% of all pledges. With respect to the agency's 19X7 financial statements, what amount of contributions revenue should be recognized for the pledges?
    a. $0          c. $150,000
    b. $135,000    d. none of the above
12. Unconditional promises to give that are restricted for the purpose of acquiring fixed assets should be recognized as contributions revenue by nongovernment VHWOs and ONPOs in the period(s) that
    a. the unconditional promises are made.
    b. the promised amounts are received.
    c. the donated resources are used to acquire the fixed assets.
    d. the assets purchased with the donated resources are used.
13. A nongovernment ONPO incurred expenses for its public service programs. The ONPO had resources available from prior year donations that were restricted by donors to finance expenses for these public service programs. Which of the following is (are) true?
    a. The ONPO should recognize the expenses as decreases in temporarily restricted net assets—because they are financed from temporarily restricted net assets.
    b. The ONPO should recognize contributions revenue in the current year as an increase in unrestricted net assets.
    c. This transaction will reduce temporarily restricted net assets.
    d. The ONPO should recognize contributions revenue in the current year as an increase in temporarily restricted net assets.
    e. Two or more of the preceding statements are true. Specify the correct choices.
14. Which of the following would not affect a nongovernment ONPO statement of activity?
    a. depreciation expense
    b. expenditure of restricted contributions for the restricted purpose in the current year (but cash was received in a prior year)
    c. gain on the sale of investments
    d. purchase of fixed assets from restricted donations
    e. none of the above

**P 18-2** (Donation-Related Entries) Mr. Larry Leininger donated $3,000,000 to a nongovernment VHWO on June 17, 19X8.
   1. Assume that no restrictions are placed on the use of the donated resources.
      a. Prepare the required June 17, 19X8 entry.
      b. Prepare any entries necessary in 19X9 if $400,000 of the gift is used to finance VHWO operating expenses.

2. Assume that the donation was restricted to research.
    a. Prepare the required June 17, 19X8 entry.
    b. Prepare any entries required in 19X9 as a result of spending $400,000 for research during 19X9.
3. Assume that the donation was restricted for fixed asset acquisitions.
    a. Prepare the required June 17, 19X8 entry.
    b. Prepare any entries required in 19X9 if $400,000 of the gift is used to begin constructing a new building.
4. Explain or illustrate how each of the three preceding situations would be reported in the nongovernment VHWO's financial statements in 19X8 and in 19X9.

**P 18-3, Part I** (Fixed-Asset–Related Entries) The Perfater Society entered into the following transactions in 19X8:

April 1—Purchased equipment with donor-restricted resources for $47,300. The equipment has a 5-year useful life.

July 1—Issued $10,000,000 of 10%, 20-year bonds at par to finance construction of a major building addition.

During 19X8—$800,000 of contributions to be used to service the bonds were received. Interest and 5% of the principal are due each June 30.

October 31—Sold machinery for $19,000 halfway through its useful life. The machine originally cost $25,000 and was expected to have a $10,000 salvage value. (Assume straight-line depreciation.)

December 31—The first semiannual interest payment on the bonds was made.

*Required* Prepare all entries required on the preceding dates to record these transactions, assuming that the Perfater Society is a nongovernment ONPO and that December 31 is the end of the fiscal year.

**P 18-3, Part II** (Endowment Entries) P. S. Callahan, a noted philanthropist, donated $2,000,000 to the Neuland Community Center with the stipulation that the first 10 years of earnings be used to endow specific programs of the organization. At the end of the 10-year period, half of the principal of the gift will become available for unrestricted use and half for capital additions.

*Required* (a) Assume that the Neuland Center is a nongovernment VHWO.
    (1) Prepare the entry(ies) to record the gift.
    (2) Prepare the entry(ies) to record the expiration of the term of the endowment.
(b) Describe how this gift should be reported in the statement of activity:
    (1) When received.
    (2) When the term expires.

**P 18-4** (Classification of Net Assets) A nongovernment VHWO or ONPO has the following resources:

| | |
|---|---:|
| Resources restricted for use in future years but not restricted to a specific purpose | $ 1,300,000 |
| Unrestricted resources designated for plant expansion | 3,000,000 |
| Unrestricted, undesignated resources | 9,000,000 |
| Resources restricted by donors for: | |
|   Scholarships | 4,000,000 |
|   Research | 10,000,000 |
|   Plant expansion | 5,000,000 |
|   Term endowments | 2,000,000 |
|   Permanent endowments | 50,000,000 |
| Resources invested in fixed assets (net of related accumulated depreciation and debt) | 17,000,000 |
| Resources restricted by bond indenture for plant expansion | 4,500,000 |

Additional information provided indicates that land with a recorded value of $1,500,000 must be used for the purposes of the organization in perpetuity.

**Required**   Prepare the net assets section of the balance sheet for this nongovernment VHWO or ONPO.

**P 18-5**   (ONPO Balance Sheet) The bookkeeper of the West Texas Zoological and Botanical Society, a nongovernment ONPO, prepared the following balance sheet:

**West Texas Zoological and Botanical Society**
**Balance Sheet**
December 31, 19X5

**Assets**

| | |
|---|---:|
| Cash | $   350,000 |
| Accounts receivable | 120,000 |
| Allowance for doubtful accounts | (20,000) |
| Pledges receivable | 700,000 |
| Allowance for doubtful pledges | (100,000) |
| Inventories | 300,000 |
| Investments | 15,000,000 |
| Land | 1,000,000 |
| Buildings and improvements | 35,000,000 |
| Equipment | 2,000,000 |
| Accumulated depreciation | (10,000,000) |
| Other assets | 150,000 |
| | $44,500,000 |

**Liabilities and Fund Balance**

| | |
|---|---:|
| Accounts payable | $   525,000 |
| Accrued expenses payable | 100,000 |
| Unearned revenue—unrestricted (exchange transactions) | 75,000 |
| Deferred support—restricted | 4,500,000 |
| Deferred capital contributions | 1,200,000 |
| Long-term debt | 6,000,000 |
| | 12,400,000 |
| Fund Balance: | |
|    Invested in plant | 22,000,000 |
|    Endowment | 2,850,000 |
|    Restricted—specific programs | 1,000,000 |
|    Unrestricted | 6,250,000 |
| | 32,100,000 |
| | $44,500,000 |

**Additional information:**
(1) The Endowment Fund consists solely of investments, except for $50,000 of cash, and has no liabilities.
(2) Restricted operating gifts include $115,000 cash, the pledges receivable, and $25,000 of accounts payable, in addition to investments.

**Required**   Prepare in good form a corrected balance sheet for the West Texas Zoological and Botanical Society, a nongovernment ONPO, at December 31, 19X5.

**P 18-6**   (Various VHWO Entries) Prepare the general journal entries needed to record the following transactions and events in the general ledger accounts of the Cecil Helping Hand Institute, a nongovernment VHWO.
   1. Contributions were received as follows:

a. Cash:

| | |
|---|---|
| $ 700,000 | for general operations |
| 600,000 | for building addition |
| 200,000 | for aid to the elderly |
| 500,000 | as an endowment, the income to be used for |
| $2,000,000 | assisting handicapped persons |

b. Pledges:

| | |
|---|---|
| $ 750,000 | for aid to the handicapped |
| 950,000 | for building additions |
| 150,000 | for general operations in future years |
| $1,850,000 | |

Experience indicates that 10% of the pledges will prove uncollectible.

2. A building addition was completed at a cost of $1,500,000. The $600,000 received in item 1 was paid the contractor, and the balance is owed on a 5-year, 12% note.
3. Expenditures, all paid, were made as follows:

| From: | For: | Amount |
|---|---|---|
| Unrestricted Resources | Fund Raising ...................... | $100,000 |
| | General and Administrative ........... | 80,000 |
| | Aid to Children (Program A) ......... | 320,000 |
| | | $500,000 |

| From: | For: | Amount |
|---|---|---|
| Restricted Resources | Aid to Elderly (Program B) ........... | $ 200,000 |
| | Aid to Handicapped (Program C) ...... | 400,000 |
| | 1/10 of the note principal ............. | 90,000 |
| | and six months' interest ............ | 54,000 |
| | Endowment Investments ............. | 450,000 |
| | | $1,194,000 |

4. Equipment costing $300,000 was purchased from unrestricted resources.
5. An older piece of equipment, original cost $100,000, accumulated depreciation $65,000, was sold for $40,000. The cash received was unrestricted.
6. A lot and building, estimated fair market value $850,000, were donated to the institute on the condition that they be sold and the proceeds used for Program D, which serves physically and mentally handicapped babies and children.
7. The lot and building (6) sold immediately for $850,000.
8. Investment earnings were accrued and received as follows:

| | | |
|---|---|---|
| Earnings on unrestricted investments .................... | $ 40,000 | accrued |
| Restricted earnings on program-restricted investments ...... | 60,000 | accrued |
| Restricted earnings on endowment investments [Restricted: see 1 above] ........................... | 65,000 | cash |
| Unrestricted earnings on investments restricted for plant purposes ..................................... | 35,000 | cash |
| | $200,000 | |

9. A fund-raising bazaar, tasting bee, and banquet were held. All $300,000 of gross receipts were unrestricted. Costs incurred—including food, gifts, kitchen help, and waiters—totaled $60,000. They would have been higher but the hotel waived its normal charge ($10,000) and a local supermarket donated food and other merchandise valued at $7,500.
10. To ensure that the babies, young children, and elderly clients are receiving proper medical attention, a local doctor gives each a thorough physical examination annually. He has a young child in one of the VHWO programs and refuses to accept payment for his services, conservatively valued at $30,000. Similarly, a clinical psychologist, who also has a child in the program, ensures that each child is properly

tested (e.g., intelligence, aptitudes, progress) on a timely basis. His time would be conservatively valued at $15,000. Both the doctor and the psychologist have assigned duties, keep regular hours, maintain case records on each child, and call to the attention of institute staff members each child's status, potential, and psychological or medical needs. Both of their time is spent approximately 30% on Program A clients, 20% on Program B clients, and 50% on Program C clients.

11. The family that donated the lot and building (in item 7) also donated land and a small building adjacent to the institute offices for use as an infant nursery and playground. The land and building are conservatively appraised at:

| | |
|---|---|
| Land | $100,000 |
| Building | 250,000 |
| | $350,000 |

However, there is a 6%, $50,000 mortgage note payable on the building, which the institute assumed.

**P 18-7** (Nongovernment VHWO Operating Statement and Balance Sheet) Following is the adjusted trial balance of the Community Association for Handicapped Children, a nongovernment voluntary health and welfare organization, at June 30, 19X4:

Community Association for Handicapped Children<br>Adjusted Trial Balance*<br>June 30, 19X4

| | Dr. | Cr. |
|---|---|---|
| Cash | $ 49,000 | |
| Bequest receivable | 5,000 | |
| Pledges receivable | 12,000 | |
| Accrued interest receivable | 1,000 | |
| Investments (at cost, which approximates market) | 100,000 | |
| Accounts payable and accrued expenses | | $ 51,000 |
| Unearned exchange revenue | | 2,000 |
| Allowance for uncollectible pledges | | 3,000 |
| Fund balances, July 1, 19X3: | | |
| Designated | | 12,000 |
| Undesignated | | 26,000 |
| Restricted | | 3,000 |
| Unrestricted endowment income | | 20,000 |
| Contributions | | 315,000 |
| Membership dues | | 25,000 |
| Program service fees | | 30,000 |
| Investment income | | 10,000 |
| Deaf children's program | 120,000 | |
| Blind children's program | 150,000 | |
| Management and general services | 49,000 | |
| Fund-raising services | 9,000 | |
| Provision for uncollectible pledges | 2,000 | |
| | $497,000 | $497,000 |

*Other information:
1. Investments of permanent endowment, $500,000
2. Equipment, $150,000
3. Accumulated depreciation, $50,000
4. Note payable for equipment, $12,000
5. Current-year depreciation, management and general, $6,000

***Required*** (a) Prepare a statement of activity for the year ended June 30, 19X4.

(b) Prepare a balance sheet as of June 30, 19X4. (AICPA, adapted)

**P 18-8** (Nongovernment ONPO/VHWO Statement of Activities) The following information for 20X1 was derived from the records of a nongovernment ONPO or VHWO:

| | |
|---|---:|
| Unrestricted contributions | $ 5,000,000 |
| Unrestricted contributions (intended to finance next year) | 700,000 |
| Contributions restricted for specific programs | 2,300,000 |
| Contributions restricted for permanent endowments | 4,000,000 |
| Contributions restricted for term endowments | 600,000 |
| Contributions restricted for plant assets | 11,000,000 |
| Special event revenues | 3,000,000 |
| Unrestricted investment income of permanent endowments | 3,000,000 |
| Investment income restricted for plant purposes | 2,700,000 |
| Restricted gain on sale of investments of permanent endowments | 950,000 |
| Membership dues (not contributions) | 1,800,000 |
| Expenses for research programs for which donor-restricted resources are available | 3,500,000 |
| Expenses for other research programs | 1,750,000 |
| Purchase of fixed assets from donor-restricted resources | 7,000,000 |
| Expiration of term endowments (unrestricted) | 1,200,000 |
| Expenses for community service programs | 3,000,000 |
| Special events—Direct costs | 2,100,000 |
| Expenses for fund raising | 1,000,000 |
| Expenses for administrative functions | 700,000 |
| Beginning unrestricted net assets | 3,000,000 |
| Beginning temporarily restricted net assets | 9,400,000 |
| Beginning permanently restricted net assets | 22,000,000 |

***Required*** Prepare a statement of activity for this nongovernment, not-for-profit organization for 20X1. Special events are part of the major or central ongoing activities of the entity.

**P 18-9** (General Journal Entries—Nongovernment ONPO) Prepare journal entries to record the following transactions for a nongovernment ONPO.

1. Unrestricted cash gifts that were received last year but designated for use in the current year totaled $50,000.
2. Unrestricted pledges of $600,000 were received. Donors specified that $450,000 of this was intended to finance current-year operations (even though part of those donations may not be collected until early next year). Ten percent (10%) of pledges typically prove uncollectible.
3. Pledges receivable of $480,000 were collected during the year; $7,000 of pledges were written off as uncollectible.
4. Donations of materials totaled $22,000; $5,000 of the materials were on hand at year end.
5. Membership dues of $400,000 were collected during the year. Members receive only nominal or no benefits in exchange for their dues.
6. Cash gifts to finance specific community outreach projects were received, $30,000.
7. Expenses were incurred for those specific community outreach projects—salaries, $3,000; equipment rental, $15,000. Management decided to pay these costs from unrestricted (rather than restricted) resources.
8. Cash gifts restricted to finance construction of a recreation center were received, $500,000. An additional amount was pledged and is expected to be collected in full in the next fiscal year, $2,200,000. No construction costs had been incurred by year end.

**P 18-10**   (Nongovernment ONPO Statement of Activities) The following information was drawn from the accounts and records of the Kindness Cooperative, a nongovernment ONPO. The balances are as of December 31, 20X0 unless otherwise noted.

| | |
|---|---:|
| Unrestricted Support—Contributions | $335,000,000 |
| Unrestricted Support—Donated Materials | 10,000,000 |
| Unrestricted Support—Donated Facilities | 8,000,000 |
| Unrestricted Support—Donated Services | 10,000,000 |
| Unrestricted Support—Special Events | 75,000,000 |
| Unrestricted Revenues—Membership Dues | 17,300,000 |
| Unrestricted Revenues—Investment Income | 34,000,000 |
| Unrestricted Gain—Gain on Sale of Equipment | 10,000,000 |
| Expenses—Education | 184,000,000 |
| Expenses—Research | 103,800,000 |
| Expenses—Management and General | 151,200,000 |
| Expenses—Fund Raising | 91,000,000 |
| Expenses—Direct Costs of Special Events | 25,000,000 |
| Expenses—Interest | 20,000,000 |
| Restricted Support—Contributions | 275,000,000 |
| Restricted Revenues—Investment Income | 35,500,000 |
| Permanently Restricted Support—Contributions | 55,000,000 |
| Permanently Restricted Revenues—Investment Income | 10,500,000 |
| Permanently Restricted Gain | 1,400,000 |
| Unrestricted Net Assets, January 1, 20X0 | 750,000,000 |
| Temporarily Restricted Net Assets, January 1, 20X0 | 250,000,000 |
| Permanently Restricted Net Assets, January 1, 20X0 | 300,000,000 |

In addition to the unrestricted contributions of $335 million, $100 million of unrestricted pledges outstanding at the beginning of 20X0 were collected during the year. All the expenses for research were financed from resources restricted for specific research projects. $110 million of construction expenditures and equipment purchases were financed from resources restricted for those purposes.

**Required**   Prepare the Kindness Cooperative's Statement of Activities for 20X0 in good form.

# CHAPTER

# 19

# FEDERAL GOVERNMENT ACCOUNTING

The federal government of the United States is engaged in an unparalleled number and variety of functions, programs, and activities both here and abroad. It is by far the country's biggest employer and also its biggest consumer. Federal disbursements were $591 billion during 1980, up about twelvefold from 1950, and exceeded $1,600,000,000,000 ($1.6 trillion) during fiscal year 1997. Federal disbursements for fiscal year 2003 are expected to be just under $2 trillion.

Federal accounting, like that of state and local governments, is heavily influenced by law and regulation. It serves as a major tool of fund and appropriation control at both the central government and agency levels. But it is noticeably different in that (1) the agency[1] is generally considered the primary accounting entity, (2) agency accounting provides—via dual-track systems—for both budgetary and proprietary accounting and reporting, and (3) accounting is concerned with both budgetary and proprietary accountability for the federal government as a whole and of individual agencies.

Thus, the accounting system of the federal government is composed of many sets of systems and subsystems. Complete financial data are to be maintained for each agency by its system; financial reports are to be prepared by the agency. Financial reports for the federal government as a whole are compiled by the Office of Management and Budget (OMB) and the Department of the Treasury from the central accounts and from agency reports or electronic data provided by the agency.

## THE FEDERAL FINANCIAL MANAGEMENT ENVIRONMENT

The importance of budgeting, accounting, and reporting to governmental financial management and accountability was recognized by those drafting the Constitution of the United States. Thus, they included a mandate (Article I, Section 9) that:

> No money shall be drawn from the treasury, but in consequence of appropriations made by law; and a regular statement and account of the receipts and expenditures of all public money shall be published from time to time.

---

[1] The term *agency* is used in this chapter to refer to departments, establishments, commissions, boards, or organizational entities thereof, such as a bureau.

From the outset, therefore, financial management was seen as a shared function of the legislative and executive branches of the federal government. Then, as now, the "power of the purse string" was vested in Congress, whereas the executive branch was charged with administering the activities of the federal government and reporting on its stewardship both to the Congress and to the public.

## Accounting and Financial Reporting Roles and Responsibilities

Several federal organizations have significant influence on financial management directives, requirements, and trends. However, in the financial management component of accounting and financial reporting, responsibilities center primarily around three oversight agencies—the Department of the Treasury, the Office of Management and Budget, and the General Accounting Office (Comptroller General)—the Federal Accounting Standards Advisory Board, and the individual agencies. Figure 19–1 contains a summary of these responsibilities, which are discussed in the following sections.

### Department of the Treasury

The Department of the Treasury, in the executive branch, is headed by the Secretary of the Treasury. The Treasury acts as both chief accountant and banker for the federal government. The Treasury's functions include:

- Central accounting and reporting for the federal government as a whole, including development of government-wide consolidated financial statements.

FIGURE 19–1   **Federal Accounting and Financial Reporting Roles and Responsibilities—A Summary**

| Oversight Agencies | Department of the Treasury | Office of Management and Budget | General Accounting Office |
|---|---|---|---|
| | Cash receipts/disbursements; central proprietary accounting and reporting; SGL; prepare and present (with OMB coordination) audited, government-wide financial statements; debt management | Budget preparation; apportionment; central budgetary accounting and reporting; form and content of financial statements | Prescribe accounting and auditing standards and audit agency financial statements |

Federal Accounting Standards Advisory Board

Develop and recommend accounting and financial reporting principles, standards, and related requirements

Federal Agencies

Maintain adequate accounting systems; implement and operate the SGL; and prepare and submit proprietary and budget execution reports required by oversight agencies

- Cash receipt and disbursement management—including supervising the federal depository system and disbursing cash for virtually all civilian agencies.
- Management of the public debt—including the scheduling of borrowing to meet current needs, repayment of debt principal, and meeting interest requirements.
- Supervision of agency borrowing from the Treasury.
- Maintenance of the government-wide Standard General Ledger (SGL).

Numerous directives issued by the Secretary of the Treasury affect federal accounting and reporting, the most comprehensive being the *Treasury Financial Manual.* This manual includes agency proprietary reporting requirements as well as agency requirements to implement the SGL.

### Office of Management and Budget (OMB)

An agency within the Executive Office of the President, the OMB has broad financial management powers as well as the responsibility of preparing the executive budget. Among the accounting and financial reporting duties assigned the OMB are:

- To apportion enacted appropriations among the agencies and establish reserves in anticipation of cost savings, contingencies, and so on.
- To set forth the requirements for accounting and reporting on budget execution.
- To prescribe the form and content of financial statements consistent with applicable accounting principles, standards, and requirements.
- To provide guidance on all matters related to budget preparation and execution.

Numerous bulletins, circulars, and other directives relating to federal budgeting, accounting, and reporting that are required to be followed by agencies have been issued by the OMB.

### General Accounting Office (GAO)

A multitude of roles and responsibilities have been assigned to the GAO—headed by the Comptroller General of the United States—since its inception in 1921. The primary responsibilities of the GAO are assisting the Congress in the general oversight of the executive branch and serving as the independent legislative auditor of the federal government. The GAO's two primary responsibilities related to accounting and financial reporting are:

1. *Prescribing principles and standards for federal agency accounting and financial reporting, internal control, accounting systems, and auditing.* This is done largely through the *General Accounting Office Policy and Procedures Manual for Guidance of Federal Agencies,* published in loose-leaf form and updated periodically.

2. *Auditing the financial statements of federal agencies.* In recent years, the GAO has begun auditing agency financial statements for the purpose of rendering opinions on their fair presentation with the goal of being able to audit the consolidated financial statements of the overall federal government within the next few years.

### Federal Accounting Standards Advisory Board (FASAB)

The Federal Accounting Standards Advisory Board (FASAB), created by a joint agreement between the Treasury, OMB, and GAO, began operations in early 1991. Its purpose is to develop and recommend accounting principles and standards to be followed by federal agencies. Upon approval by the heads of the Treasury, OMB, and GAO, the OMB and GAO issue these principles and standards.

The FASAB is a nine-member board with one representative each from the Treasury, OMB, GAO, the Congressional Budget Office, civil agencies, and defense and international agencies, and three representatives from outside the federal government. The chairperson is a nonfederal member. The FASAB has a staff director and dedicated full-time staff.

As of mid-1998, the FASAB's approved concept statements and standards included:

**CONCEPT STATEMENTS**

1. "Objectives of Federal Financial Reporting"
2. "Entity and Display"

**STANDARDS**

1. "Accounting for Selected Assets and Liabilities"
2. "Accounting for Direct Loans and Loan Guarantees"
3. "Accounting for Inventory and Related Property"
4. "Managerial Cost Accounting Concepts and Standards"
5. "Accounting for Liabilities of the Federal Government"
6. "Accounting for Property, Plant, and Equipment"
7. "Accounting for Revenue and Other Financing Sources"
8. "Supplementary Stewardship Reporting"
9. "Deferral of the Effective Date of Managerial Cost Accounting Standards for the Federal Government in SFFAS No. 4"

In addition, three exposure drafts were outstanding covering amendments to accounting for property, plant, and equipment; accounting for internal use software; and federal government-wide supplementary stewardship reporting. Finally, the FASAB is involved in other projects. The most notable of these projects are accounting for social insurance (such as social security), accounting for natural resources, and requirements for discussion and analysis related to agencies' annual financial statements.

### Federal Agencies

The effectiveness of federal financial management depends upon the individual federal agencies. Similarly, federal budgeting, accounting, and reporting can be no better than that of the related agency systems and subsystems upon which the central systems depend. Among the many accounting-related functions and activities of agencies are these:

- To prepare agency budget requests for submission to the President through the OMB.
- To establish and maintain effective systems of accounting and financial reporting and internal control, in conformity with the principles and standards prescribed by the GAO.
- To implement and operate the SGL. The SGL Board, comprised of agency representatives, maintains account definitions, transactions, and crosswalks to reports.
- To prepare and submit proprietary reports and budget execution reports in accordance with the accounting and reporting requirements of the oversight agencies.

Most federal agencies have an **Inspector General** (IG) or similar internal audit and investigation officer who continually studies and evaluates the agency's activities. Each IG must prepare a semiannual report on audit findings and forward it to appropriate congressional committees. Most Inspector Generals are involved in the audit of the financial statements of the agency.

## Overview

Responsibility for accounting and financial reporting principles, standards, and related requirements in the federal sector is not as simple or clear cut as those in the private or state and local government sectors. The Congress, through legislation, has established numerous guidelines for accounting and financial reporting. As discussed throughout this chapter, responsibility for developing, promulgating, and implementing accounting and financial reporting principles, standards, and requirements within the guidelines set forth in law is shared within the federal government. The two major categories of principles, standards, and requirements are budgetary and proprietary.

Although budgetary accounting and financial reporting guidelines have not traditionally been labeled as principles and standards, there are significant requirements that direct its practices in the federal sector. Budgetary requirements are developed and promulgated by OMB. Implementation mandates are also set by OMB, but it is the agencies that must actually implement the mandates received from OMB. Also, Treasury sets forth several requirements to help implement fiscal reporting and management in the federal government and provide support for the SGL Board. Moreover, GAO also issues requirements consistent with OMB directives.

Proprietary principles, standards, and requirements are required by law to be promulgated by GAO. The current process, however, calls for the principles and standards to be developed by the FASAB; approved by the heads of OMB, Treasury, and GAO; and promulgated by OMB and GAO. GAO also develops and promulgates requirements such as those for accounting systems and internal controls. OMB is required by law to promulgate the requirements for the form and content of financial statements. In addition, the Treasury implements the principles, standards, and requirements by directing agencies to provide it with financial statements periodically and annually. (Most agencies provide trial balances to the Treasury, which provide the information needed to prepare the consolidated financial statements.)

Agencies sometimes engage in transactions not yet addressed by a FASAB standard. For such transactions, agencies must use the following hierarchy (Level 1 has the greatest authority) to select the appropriate accounting treatment:

1. Individual standards agreed to by the Director of OMB, the Comptroller General, and the Secretary of the Treasury (and published by OMB and the GAO)

2. Interpretations related to the SFFASs issued by OMB in accordance with the procedures outlined in OMB Circular A-134, "Financial Accounting Principles and Standards"

3. Requirements contained in OMB's Form and Content Bulletin in effect for the period covered by the financial statements

4. Accounting principles published by other authoritative standards-setting bodies and other authoritative sources (a) in the absence of other guidance in the first three parts of this hierarchy, and (b) if the use of such accounting principles improves the meaningfulness of the financial statements

## THE BUDGETARY PROCESS

The budgetary process in the federal government along with the related budgetary accounting is far more complex than in a municipality. (Although the process involves many intricate steps and is multifaceted, only those major processes impacting accounting are covered here.) The following primary reasons highlight the differences and the complexity of the federal budget process:

- Agency authority to incur obligations for future disbursement is usually not directly based on estimates of revenues, either at the agency or overall federal level.

- Budget authority to incur obligations is granted by the Congress under three types—appropriations, contract authority, or borrowing authority. Still further, appropriations can be one-year, multiyear or no-year, or permanent authorizations. Contract and borrowing authority can also contain various year limitations. Additional authority may be derived from collections from performing services to other agencies and the public.

- The process of spending budget authority is divided into five clearly distinct steps, most of which are closely monitored for legal and regulatory compliance. The five steps are: apportionment, allotment, commitment, obligation, and expended appropriation.

## The Budget Cycle

The federal budget cycle, like that of state and local governments, has four phases: (1) formulation, (2) approval, (3) execution, and (4) reporting. (Auditing is included in the fourth phase; however, discussions of it are omitted in this text.)

### Formulation and Approval

Budget formulation begins in the executive branch and ends when the budget is formally presented to the Congress. Budget preparation and presentation of the budget to the Congress is a presidential responsibility. Preparation requires continuous exchange of information, proposals, evaluations, and policy determinations among the President, central financial agencies, and operating agencies.

Budget approval is a congressional function. The Congressional Budget Act of 1974 created the present procedure by which the Congress determines the annual federal budget. At the beginning of consideration, by concurrent resolution, it establishes target levels for overall expenditures, budget authority, budget outlays, broad functional expenditure categories, revenues, the deficit, and the public debt.

An appropriation is contained in an act passed by the Congress that becomes a public law. There are about 13 major laws passed through the normal congressional budget process each year containing between 1,200 and 1,400 individual appropriations. Congressional appropriations are not based directly on expended appropriations (i.e., receipt of goods or services), but on authority to obligate the federal government ultimately to make disbursements.

### Execution

When an appropriation bill becomes law, an appropriation warrant is drawn by the Treasury and forwarded to the agency. The agency sends a request for apportionment to the OMB. The OMB makes apportionments to the agency, reserving appropriations for contingency, savings, timing, or policy reasons. The agency carries on its programs with the apportioned appropriations through allotments for programs and activities; committing, obligating, and expending money; and providing services. It reports to the OMB on its activities and uses of budgetary authority. The agencies prepare vouchers for expended appropriations and submit them to the Treasury or disbursement officers for payment.

An explanation of each aspect of budget execution with respect to basic operating appropriations follows.

**Warrants**     A warrant is a document required by law as a means of verification of an appropriation amount contained in a public law. A warrant is signed by the Secretary of the Treasury (or by the Secretary's designee). The warrant contains the amount of the appropriation and is the primary source of recognition by an agency in its accounts for the budget resources awarded to it. Treasury or the disbursing agent maintains central control by limiting an agency to a line of credit for disbursements not to exceed the amount of the warrant.

**Apportionment**     Apportionments are divisions, or portions, of appropriations granted agency heads by OMB. Apportionments are required by law to prevent obligation or use of an appropriation at a rate that might result in a deficiency or a supplemental appropriation. Apportionments divide appropriation amounts available for use by specific time periods, activities, projects, types of uses, or combinations thereof. The most common apportionments are divisions based on time periods, usually quarterly. An agency will record its entire appropriation in its accounts when it receives a warrant from the Treasury. However, it can only use the amount of the apportionment received from OMB. The total apportionments granted for each appropriation cannot exceed the amount of the appropriation. (Note that apportionments by time periods are the equivalent of allotments for SLGs, as discussed in Chapter 6.) Apportionment control is maintained centrally by OMB "after the fact"—it is monitored from the monthly budget execution reports submitted by agencies.

**Allotment**     An allotment is budget authority in the form of apportionments delegated by the agency head to subordinate managers for use. Suballotments are further divisions of budget authority to lower management levels. The total allotments per apportionment cannot exceed the amount of the apportionment and the total suballotments cannot exceed the total of their related allotment amount. (Note that allotments in federal government terminology are like SLG allocations discussed in Chapter 6.)

**Commitment**     A commitment is a preliminary, administrative reservation of budget authority (allotment or suballotment) for the order of goods and services for program purposes. It is a charge to an allotment account based on a preliminary estimate. A commitment is usually a request within an agency for the purchase of items, travel, or other related purposes. Commitment accounting is not required by law, regulation, or directive from oversight agencies. However, it is a useful planning tool that agencies employ to reserve appropriation authority prior to obligation. Indeed, commitments might be thought of as pre-encumbrances.

**Obligation**     An obligation is a formal reservation of budget authority. It is a formal charge to an allotment or related commitment with the latest estimate of the cost of goods or services being purchased. Obligations for the purchase of goods and services are required by regulations and directives from the oversight agencies. Obligations represent orders for the acquisition of goods and/or services for program purposes and compare to encumbrances in SLG budgetary accounting.

**Expended Appropriations**     Expended appropriations represent the amount of goods and/or services received and accepted or program costs incurred. It is the formal use of budget authority in an actual amount and either (1) it releases the related prior obligation or (2) in cases where obligations are not required, for example, in payroll in some agencies, it is a charge to the related allotment. Expended appropriations are equivalent to expenditures in state and local government accounting. When expended appropriations are incurred for budgetary accounting purposes, an agency also recognizes a financing source, called Appropriations Used, for proprietary accounting purposes.

**Expired Authority**     Expired authority represents unexpended, unobligated (i.e., unused) appropriation authority of prior years. Expended appropriations against prior year obligations that exceed the previously obligated amount are charged against this expired authority. Expired authority is canceled at the end of the fifth year after the authority first became expired.

One aspect of the preceding description bears repetition and emphasis: Only part of an agency's annual obligational authority is available to it at any time—the apportioned part. The agency head (or designee), in turn, allots its apportioned obligation authority to subordinate managers to operate their programs and/or organizational subunits. Only allotted apportionments may be obligated by organizations within an agency.

## Reporting

Budget execution is reported periodically and annually to OMB. For each category of appropriation or other budget authority, agencies report the amount of authority, the amount of expended appropriations, the amount of obligations, the amount of apportionments unobligated (unused budget authority), and the amounts of outlays (essentially disbursements) incurred. OMB reports centrally for the overall government on an obligations and outlay basis each year in the annual budget proposal submitted to the Congress by the President. The annual budget proposal contains the current year's projected amounts along with summary amounts of actuals (total obligations and total outlays) for preceding years. Although OMB reports amounts related to the budget, both proposed and prior years' actuals, the Treasury reports periodic and annual amounts of actual disbursements.

## Exceeding Budget Authority

Numerous laws and regulations highlight the impropriety of exceeding budget authority. Budget authority is considered exceeded when any of the four following events occur:

1. An apportionment exceeds an appropriation.
2. An allotment exceeds an appropriation or an apportionment.
3. An obligation exceeds an allotment, apportionment, or appropriation.
4. An expended appropriation exceeds an appropriation, an apportionment, or an allotment.

Note that commitments are not considered formal use of budget authority.

Laws and regulations provide for criminal penalties for those responsible (the agency head or the managers responsible for allotments and suballotments) when authority is exceeded. In addition, agency management is required to submit reports to the President and the Congress when budget authority is exceeded. The Congress makes the decision whether to provide for a deficiency appropriation to make up the amounts exceeded and the administrative and judicial process determines any punishment.

# ACCOUNTING PRINCIPLES AND STANDARDS FOR FEDERAL AGENCIES

Accounting principles and standards for federal agencies set forth requirements for preparing basic financial statements. Agencies are required to prepare six basic year-end financial statements. They are:

1. Balance Sheet
2. Statement of Net Cost
3. Statement of Changes in Net Position
4. Statement of Budgetary Resources
5. Statement of Financing
6. Statement of Custodial Activity

## The Federal Model

The federal model of accounting is different than the private or state and local government models. It contains what is referred to as a dual-track system. This dual-track system contains a complete set of self-balancing accounts for both budgetary and proprietary amounts. Each set of self-balancing accounts reflects an accounting equation.

The budgetary equation is: Budgetary Resources = Status of Authority. The components of each side of the equation are:

| **Budgetary Resources** | = **Status of Authority** |
| --- | --- |
| Appropriations | Unapportioned Appropriations (Authority) |
| + Borrowing Authority | + Apportionments |
| + Contract Authority | + Allotments |
| + Reimbursable Authority | + Commitments |
| (between agencies) | + Obligations |
| + Collections from Other | + Expended Appropriations (Authority) |
| Sources | + Expired Authority |

The proprietary equation is the private-sector equation of: Assets = Liabilities + Equity (called net position in federal government accounting). However, because of the processes in the federal government and the need to account for appropriations, there are several unique variations to this equation that do not exist in the private sector. The primary variations deal with the cash account and disbursements, net position accounts, and the unique nature of and interrelationships between the components of net position. These key variations are discussed in the following sections.

### Cash and Disbursements

Although agencies have small balances of cash for imprest funds and in rare cases significant balances, the predominant amount is represented by a line of credit with the Treasury (or, in the case of the Department of Defense, a disbursing agent) in the amount of the warrants it has received. This line of credit is referred to as Fund Balance with Treasury and is handled as cash in a bank account would be by a business. To use this line of credit, the normal process is for an agency to complete a request for payment to the Treasury. When the request for payment is forwarded to the Treasury, a liability account, Disbursements in Transit, is recognized. When the agency receives the completed request back from the Treasury indicating that checks have been written and mailed (referred to as an accomplished request), the agency reduces the liability account Disbursements in Transit and the Fund Balance with Treasury for the same amount.

### Net Position

The Net Position of the U.S. Government (or an agency) represents the net assets of the federal government or the agency and is equal to the difference between the assets and liabilities of the agency. Net position is composed of three items:

1. Cumulative results of operations
2. Unexpended appropriations
3. Trust Fund balances

The first two of these are illustrated in Figure 19–2 and discussed in the chapter.

**Cumulative Results of Operations**   The Cumulative Results of Operations is defined as the net difference between (1) expenses and losses from the inception of an agency or activity and (2) financing sources (i.e., appropriations used and revenues) and gains from the inception of an agency or activity (whether financed from appropriations, revenues, reimbursements, or any combination) to the reporting date. For a revolving fund or business-type activity (with no trust assets), this portion of net position is essentially the same as the total equity of a business. The Unexpended Appropriations would be zero. If an agency is financed exclusively or almost exclusively with appropriations, this component will be the difference between the cumulative expended appropriations of the agency over the years and the cumulative expenses and losses over the same period.

**Unexpended Appropriations**   Unexpended appropriations—the budgetary fund balance of an agency—represents amounts of obligational authority (appropriations) that have neither been expended nor withdrawn as of the reporting date. To the extent that unused appropriations have not been withdrawn, this portion of the net position of the agency equals the sum of the unapportioned appropriations, unallotted apportionments, unobligated allotments, obligations at the reporting date, and expired authority. If an agency is operated solely on a business-type basis and receives no appropriations, this component of net position will be zero.

### Changes in Net Position

The causes of changes in each of the two most common components of net position are illustrated in Figure 19–3. The most significant ones are discussed in the following sections. The changes in net position are recorded in separate temporary accounts as necessary for proper reporting.

**Enacting Appropriations**   Perhaps the most difficult to understand feature of federal agency accounting is the interrelationships among appropriations and the various components of net position. These interrelationships can be explained best in a simplified context. Therefore, assume that an agency is financed solely from appropriations. How would a $1,000,000 appropriation affect the net position components of the agency?

FIGURE 19–2  **Components of Net Position of a Federal Agency**

| SOME AGENCIES HAVE | ALL AGENCIES HAVE |
|---|---|
| Unexpended Appropriations (results from appropriation-financed activities) | Cumulative Results of Operations |
| Represents valid unused appropriation authority that carries over to the next fiscal year or other reporting period. | Net assets of an agency other than Fund Balance with Treasury associated with unexpended budget authority or net assets held in trust. |

FIGURE 19–3 **Changes in Components of Net Position of U.S. Government**

| Cumulative Results of Operations | Unexpended Appropriations |
|---|---|

- - - - - - - - - - - - **Increases** - - - - - - - - - - - - - - - - - - - - - - - - - - - **Increases** - - - - - - - - - - - -

(1) Financing sources:
    (a) Expended appropriations
       (appropriations used)
    (b) Operating revenues from
       businesslike activities
    (c) Reimbursements from other agencies
(2) Gains
(3) Initial investments made to begin
    operations or a new activity of a
    revolving fund or businesslike activities

(1) Appropriation authority
    granted for the fiscal year

- - - - - - - - - - - - **Decreases** - - - - - - - - - - - - - - - - - - - - - - - - - - - **Decreases** - - - - - - - - - - -

(1) Expenses
(2) Losses
(3) Amounts representing initial invest-
    ments in revolving funds or businesslike
    activities are returned to investor agency
    or entity or otherwise transferred out.

(1) Expended appropriations
(2) Withdrawal of unexpended and/or
    unobligated appropriation authority.

First, when the appropriation is made, it increases the Unexpended Appropriations component of net position, as indicated in Figure 19–4. From the perspective of the agency, appropriations increase net position (although the net position of the consolidated federal government entity does not change). If a portion of this appropriation authority is withdrawn by the OMB or the Congress before it is used, the Unexpended Appropriations account is reduced by that amount.

**Incurring Expended Appropriations**    When expended appropriations are incurred, the proprietary accounts are affected in three ways. First, the Unexpended Appropriations account is reduced reflecting the decrease in unused obligational authority. At the same time, a temporary account, Appropriations Used, is increased by the same amount. The Appropriations Used account is reported in the statement of changes in net position as a financing source and is closed to cumulative results of operations. Finally, either (a) fixed assets, inventory, or other assets are capitalized, or (b) expenses are recorded in the amount of the expended appropriations.

**Incurring Unfunded Expenses**    Not all expenses result in recognition of appropriations used in the same year. Agencies incur some expenses that will be funded in future years for budgetary purposes. Appropriations used will be recognized in that future year. Examples of unfunded expenses include pension costs, contingent liabilities, and employees' annual leave earned but not taken. Most agencies incur at least one unfunded expense, that of the annual leave benefits earned by employees. In most agencies these expenses are immaterial to the total expenses; however, in smaller, service-oriented agencies, these can be material. Recognition of unfunded expenses is the same as in the private sector. The expense is debited and a liability is credited.

Figure 19–4 illustrates the interrelationships between the components of net position. These relationships are illustrated further in accounting for an illustrative federal agency.

**FIGURE 19–4  Interrelationship of Net Position of U.S. Government Components (For Agency Financed Solely by Annual Appropriations)**

| Transaction | Cumulative Results of Operations | Unexpended Appropriations |
|---|---|---|
| Appropriation granted | | + |
| Expenditure incurred to finance operating expense | − Operating Expense + Report Appropriations Used as financing source in statement of changes in net position | − |
| Expenditure incurred to acquire fixed asset, inventory, etc. | + Report Appropriations Used as financing source in statement of changes in net position | − |
| Fixed asset depreciated or other assets expensed | − Depreciation (or other) expense | |
| Unfunded expenses, e.g., employees' annual leave | − | |
| Unobligated appropriations are withdrawn | | − |
| Year end balance | Equal to book values of nonmonetary assets less the liability for unfunded expenses | Equals sum of obligations outstanding (undelivered orders) and expired authority |

## Standard General Ledger

The Government Wide Standard General Ledger (SGL) was developed in 1986 and issued as a requirement to all agencies by the three oversight agencies in 1988. The SGL has perhaps been the most influential requirement inducing agencies to implement the dual-track federal model, which was first required by the 1984 Title 2. Treasury oversees an SGL Board made up of members representing the major federal agencies. The Board maintains and updates the SGL.

The SGL contains approximately 200 separate accounts in its chart of accounts. The principal SGL accounts, account definitions, transactions, and crosswalks to reports are organized as follows:

| | |
|---|---|
| 1000s | Asset Accounts |
| 2000s | Liability Accounts |
| 3000s | Net Position Accounts |
| 4000s | Budgetary Accounts |
| 5000s | Revenues and Other Credits in the Statement of Operations |
| 6000s | Expenses |
| 7000s | Gains and Losses |

Because this chapter is a summary overview of federal accounting, we will use only 22 of the SGL accounts, 8 budgetary and 14 proprietary, and we will assume budgetary authority is granted only in the form of a one-year operating appropriation. The eight budgetary accounts are as follows.

Budgetary Resources (Normal Debit Balance):
Other Appropriations Realized

Status of Authority (Normal Credit Balances):
Authority Available for Apportionment
Apportionment Available for Distribution
Allotment Available for Commitment/Obligation

FIGURE 19–5  **The Use of Budget Authority and Closings of Budget Accounts**

**The Flow of Entries to Record Basic Transactions Involving Status of Unexpired Appropriations**

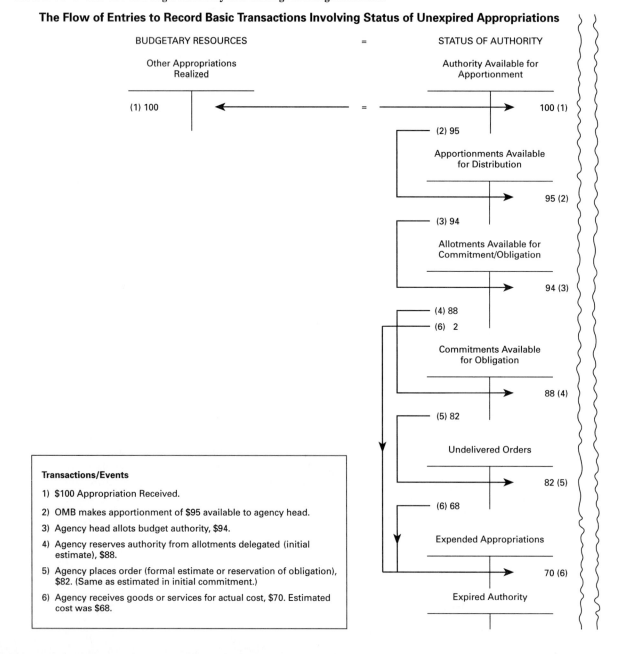

BUDGETARY RESOURCES          =          STATUS OF AUTHORITY

Other Appropriations Realized                 Authority Available for Apportionment

(1) 100          =          100 (1)

(2) 95

Apportionments Available for Distribution

95 (2)

(3) 94

Allotments Available for Commitment/Obligation

94 (3)

(4) 88
(6)  2

Commitments Available for Obligation

88 (4)

(5) 82

Undelivered Orders

82 (5)

(6) 68

Expended Appropriations

70 (6)

Expired Authority

**Transactions/Events**

1) $100 Appropriation Received.

2) OMB makes apportionment of $95 available to agency head.

3) Agency head allots budget authority, $94.

4) Agency reserves authority from allotments delegated (initial estimate), $88.

5) Agency places order (formal estimate or reservation of obligation), $82. (Same as estimated in initial commitment.)

6) Agency receives goods or services for actual cost, $70. Estimated cost was $68.

Commitment Available for Obligation
Undelivered Orders
Expended Appropriations
Expired Authority

Figure 19–5 shows the effect on the accounts when budgetary authority is granted, delegated, and used as well as the closing entries involved. Note that

FIGURE 19–5 *(Continued)*

**Budgetary Closing Entries**

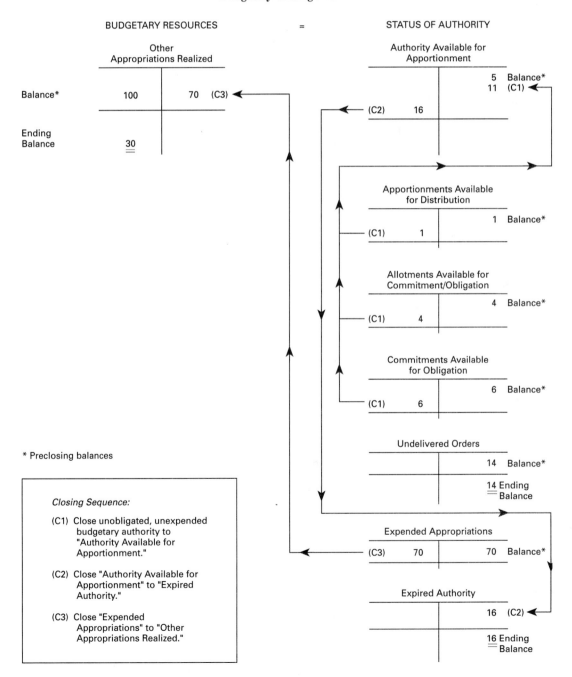

Expended Appropriations is closed to the Budgetary Resources account, Other Appropriations Realized, and that Undelivered Orders (encumbered amounts) is not closed. The remaining Status accounts are closed into the Expired Authority account making its balance equal to the unobligated, unexpended appropriation authority that has not been canceled.

Figure 19–6 contains a graphic illustration of the proprietary accounts used. As with the budgetary accounts, the account titles are those required in the SGL.

Integration of both budgetary and proprietary accounts is an important concept required when implementing the SGL. Integration occurs when entries are required in both budgetary and proprietary accounts as a result of the same transaction. For example, when an agency receives a warrant as a result of the passage of an appropriation bill into law, the agency makes entries in both the budgetary and proprietary accounts, as follows:

| | | |
|---|---|---|
| **Budgetary:** | Other Appropriations Realized . . . . . . . . . . . . . . . XXX | |
| | Authority Available for Apportionment . . . . . . . | XXX |
| **Proprietary:** | Fund Balance with Treasury . . . . . . . . . . . . . . . . . . XXX | |
| | Unexpended Appropriations . . . . . . . . . . . . . . . | XXX |

The case illustration at the end of this chapter will show other example entries required by both tracks as a result of the same transaction.

**FIGURE 19–6 Overview of the Federal Government Proprietary Accounting Equation**

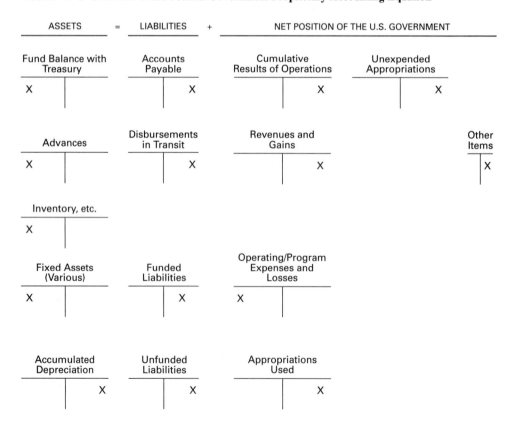

## Funds and the Federal Entity

Fund structures employed in federal government accounting may be broadly classified as (1) funds derived from general taxing and revenue powers and from business operations, also known as federal or government-owned funds, and (2) funds held by the government in the capacity of custodian or trustee, sometimes referred to as not government-owned or Trust and Agency funds. Six types of funds are employed within these two broad categories.

| *Government-owned or Federal Funds* | *Trust or Custodian Funds* |
|---|---|
| General Fund | Trust Funds |
| Special Funds | Deposit Funds |
| Revolving Funds | |
| Management Funds | |

However, in the federal sector, the fund type or the specific fund does not influence accounting or financial reporting as it does in the state and local government sector. The federal entity instead is twofold. For budgetary purposes, the entity is each appropriation or other budget authority granted by the Congress. Budget execution reports are required for each appropriation. Thus, each appropriation for each specific year has a complete SGL. The proprietary entity is broader, although it can also be each appropriation. The Treasury requires approximately between 650 and 750 complete sets of the primary proprietary financial statements each year. These sets include many single-year appropriations as well as consolidated statements of agencies and departments. The SGL is designed to separately maintain two proprietary accounts, Fund Balance with Treasury and Unexpended Appropriations, on an appropriation basis by year in the subsidiary accounts.

## Financial Reporting

Federal financial reporting includes both agency-level and government-wide statements. In 1990, the Congress passed the Chief Financial Officers Act (CFO Act), which, among other provisions, established financial statement and audit requirements for certain federal agencies. In 1994, the Congress passed the Government Management Reform Act extending the financial statement and audit requirements of the CFO Act to all major agencies and making them permanent requirements. These acts also require preparation of annual government-wide audited financial statements. Specifically, each major agency was to submit agency-level financial statements covering fiscal year 1996 to the director of the OMB by March 1, 1997. Consolidated, government-wide, audited financial statements for fiscal year 1997 were to be presented to the President and the Congress by March 1, 1998. Subsequent fiscal years' financial statements are to be provided on the same basic schedule.

### Agency Level

Although agency managers determine the internal reports needed, there are six basic statements required at least annually of all federal agencies. Two additional proprietary statements are optional but preferred. The statements are:

1. Balance Sheet
2. Statement of Net Cost

**3.** Statement of Changes in Net Position

**4.** Statement of Budgetary Resources

**5.** Statement of Financing

**6.** Statement of Custodial Activity

The first four statements are illustrated in the final section of this chapter. Other financial reports are required by the Congress, its committees, or the central oversight agencies.

### Government-wide Statements

The first four financial statements required for each agency also are to be presented annually on a government-wide basis. The government-wide statements are required to include all of its departments, agencies, and other units.

In preparing the government-wide statements, all interdepartmental and interagency balances and transactions are eliminated. Depreciation is recorded for agency fixed assets on which depreciation is not reported by the agencies. Any other adjustments needed to report the consolidated entity's financial statements from the perspective of the U.S. government as a single entity are made as well.

## FEDERAL AGENCY ACCOUNTING AND REPORTING ILLUSTRATED

This section of the chapter contains (1) a case illustration of federal agency accounting and (2) illustrative agency financial statements. The case is designed to illustrate the major federal accounting principles and standards. Those interested in more in-depth and specific coverage of federal government accounting may wish to review the United States Standard General Ledger developed by the Treasury and the prescribed financial report formats established by the OMB.

In the case illustration, we initially demonstrate how the agency would maintain budgetary accountability in its accounting system. Next, the simultaneous maintenance of proprietary information is illustrated. Then various transactions of the agency are presented with both budgetary and proprietary entries being made as needed. The accounts are closed at year end in a manner that highlights the relationship between the budgetary accounts and the proprietary accounts. Finally, illustrative financial statements are presented for the agency.

Although specific methods of accounting vary among agencies, as do their functions and financing methods, the approach illustrated is typical and serves to highlight the major aspects of federal agency accounting and reporting.

### A Case Illustration

In order to illustrate the principal aspects of federal agency accounting, assume that (1) an agency began the 19X0–X1 fiscal year with the trial balance in Figure 19–7; and (2) its activities are financed solely through a single-year appropriation. To simplify the illustration, we also (1) assume that general ledger control accounts similar to those in Figures 19–5 and 19–6 are employed, (2) limit our presentation to general ledger entries, and (3) in order to demonstrate the entire cycle, make summary entries where similar transactions typically recur throughout the year. The agency's functions primarily entail rendering services to the public.

FIGURE 19–7  **Beginning Trial Balance**

XYZ Agency

**Trial Balance**

October 1, 19X0

**Budgetary Accounts**

| | | |
|---|---|---|
| Other Appropriations Realized . . . . . . . . . . . . . . . . . . . . . . . . . . . | $ 13,000 | |
| Authority Available for Apportionment . . . . . . . . . . . . . . . . . . . . | | $    — |
| Apportionment Available for Distribution . . . . . . . . . . . . . . . . . . | | — |
| Allotments Available for Commitment/Obligation . . . . . . . . . . . | | — |
| Commitments Available for Obligation . . . . . . . . . . . . . . . . . . . . | | — |
| Undelivered Orders . . . . . . . . . . . . . . . . . . . . . . . . . . . . . . . . . . . . | | — |
| Expended Appropriations . . . . . . . . . . . . . . . . . . . . . . . . . . . . . . . | | — |
| Expired Authority . . . . . . . . . . . . . . . . . . . . . . . . . . . . . . . . . . . . . | | 13,000 |
| | $ 13,000 | $ 13,000 |

**Proprietary Accounts**

| | | |
|---|---|---|
| Fund Balance with Treasury—19X0 . . . . . . . . . . . . . . . . . . . . . . . | $ 62,200 | |
| Fund Balance with Treasury—19X1 . . . . . . . . . . . . . . . . . . . . . . . | — | |
| Advances to Others . . . . . . . . . . . . . . . . . . . . . . . . . . . . . . . . . . . . | 800 | |
| Inventory for Agency Operations . . . . . . . . . . . . . . . . . . . . . . . . . | 17,000 | |
| Equipment . . . . . . . . . . . . . . . . . . . . . . . . . . . . . . . . . . . . . . . . . . . | 20,000 | |
| Accumulated Depreciation on Equipment . . . . . . . . . . . . . . . . . . | | $   8,000 |
| Disbursements in Transit . . . . . . . . . . . . . . . . . . . . . . . . . . . . . . . | | 12,000 |
| Accounts Payable . . . . . . . . . . . . . . . . . . . . . . . . . . . . . . . . . . . . . | | 30,000 |
| Accrued Funded Payroll and Benefits . . . . . . . . . . . . . . . . . . . . . | | 8,000 |
| Accrued Unfunded Annual Leave . . . . . . . . . . . . . . . . . . . . . . . . | | 50,000 |
| Unexpended Appropriations—19X0 . . . . . . . . . . . . . . . . . . . . . . | | 13,000 |
| Unexpended Appropriations—19X1 . . . . . . . . . . . . . . . . . . . . . . | | — |
| Cumulative Results of Operations . . . . . . . . . . . . . . . . . . . . . . . . | 21,000 | |
| | $121,000 | $121,000 |

## Maintaining Agency Budgetary Control

Budgetary control is maintained on a fixed-dollar basis for operations of the federal government agencies, as is true with state and local governments. However, as indicated in Figure 19–8, the means for implementing budgetary control in the accounting system tends to be somewhat more complex than with SLGs.

Budgetary accounting and proprietary accounting are shown simultaneously in this illustration using the dual-track approach required for federal agencies.

### Summary of Transactions and Events/Entries

**1.** Congress enacted appropriations that included $225,000 for XYZ Agency. The agency received an appropriation warrant in that amount from the Treasury.

**Proprietary Entry**

| | | |
|---|---|---|
| (1a)  Fund Balance with Treasury—19X1 . . . . . . . . . . . . . . . . . . . | $225,000 | |
|      Unexpended Appropriations—19X1 . . . . . . . . . . . . . . . . . | | $225,000 |
|     To record receipt of appropriation warrant. | | |

This proprietary entry establishes the agency's line of credit with the Treasury as an asset of the agency and the related net position increase. Recall that you may wish to think of the Fund Balance with Treasury as if it were a Cash account.

FIGURE 19–8  **Maintaining Budgetary Accountability for a Federal Agency**

| Event | Effect on Budgetary Accounts | | | | | |
|-------|------------------------------|---|---|---|---|---|
| | *Authority Available for Apportionment* | *Apportionments Available for Distribution* | *Allotments Available for Commitment/ Obligation* | *Commitments Available for Obligation* | *Undelivered Orders* | *Expended Appropriations* |
| 1. Congress enacts appropriations | + | | | | | |
| 2. OMB apportions appropriation authority to agencies | – | + | | | | |
| 3. Agency directors allot apportionments to various purposes | | – | + | | | |
| 4. Goods/services are requested for order | | | – | + | | |
| 5. Goods are ordered or contracts for services are signed | | | | – | + | |
| 6. Expenditures are incurred upon receipt of goods or services | | | | | – | + |

**Budgetary Entry**

(1b)  Other Appropriations Realized . . . . . . . . . . . . . . . . . . . . . . . . $225,000

            Authority Available for Apportionment . . . . . . . . . . . . . . . $225,000

        To record receipt of budgetary authority.

This budgetary-track entry establishes initial accountability for the agency's appropriation for the fiscal year.

The budgetary accounting and control mechanism appears more complex in the federal government in part because not all of the appropriations adopted by the Congress serve as valid expenditure authority for the various agencies. Instead, as mentioned earlier, the OMB apportions part of the appropriation authority to the agencies initially. Thus, it is necessary to distinguish between appropriations (Authority Available for Apportionment) and apportionments (Apportionments Available for Distribution) of the federal agency just as we distinguish between Unallotted Appropriations and Allotments in state and local governments (see

Chapter 6). However, not all of the apportionments are typically available to agency field offices for any purpose because the agency head will normally make allotments of the apportionments. Therefore, a federal agency must also distinguish between Apportionments Available for Distribution and allotments. (The allotments account is called Allotments Available for Commitment/Obligation.) Hence, only the balance in Allotments Available for Commitment/Obligation provides valid budgetary authority against which field offices can obligate the agency. The next two transactions and entries illustrate the reclassification of appropriations as apportionments and allotments are made.

**2.** The OMB apportioned $220,000 of the congressional appropriation, reserving $5,000 for possible cost savings and contingencies. The apportionments were distributed as follows:

| | |
|---|---:|
| First quarter | $ 68,000 |
| Second quarter | 58,000 |
| Third quarter | 44,000 |
| Fourth quarter | 50,000 |
| | $220,000 |

**Proprietary Entry**—None
**Budgetary Entry**

| | | | |
|---|---|---:|---:|
| (2a) | Authority Available for Apportionment | $68,000 | |
| | Apportionment Available for Distribution | | $68,000 |
| | To record OMB apportionment of appropriation for the first quarter. | | |

Note that only the $68,000 balance in Apportionment Available for Distribution can be allotted, committed, or obligated during the first quarter. Similar entries would be made as additional apportionments are made:

**Proprietary Entry**—None
**Budgetary Entry**

| | | | |
|---|---|---:|---:|
| (2b) | Authority Available for Apportionment | $152,000 | |
| | Apportionment Available for Distribution | | $152,000 |
| | To record OMB apportionments of appropriation for the remaining quarters. | | |

Entry 2b is a summary entry. In practice an entry would be made each quarter; the $152,000 is the total of the apportionments made during the last three quarters. Subsequent transactions will assume that the entire $220,000 has been apportioned.

**3.** Administrative allotments made by the agency head were distributed as follows:

| | |
|---|---:|
| Salaries and benefits | $135,000 |
| Materials and supplies | 40,000 |
| Fixed assets | 12,000 |
| Travel | 2,000 |
| Other | 25,000 |
| | $214,000 |

**Proprietary Entry**—None
**Budgetary Entry**

| | | | |
|---|---|---:|---:|
| (3) | Apportionment Available for Distribution | $214,000 | |
| | Allotments Available for Commitment/Obligation | | $214,000 |
| | To record allotments of apportioned appropriations. | | |

The subsequent accounting for obligations (encumbrances) and expended appropriations incurred by a federal agency against its allotments differs from the treatment illustrated in state and local government accounting. Separate encumbrance and expenditure accounts are used in state and local government accounting, and their total is subtracted from allotments to determine the unencumbered balance still available for encumbrance and expenditure for a particular purpose. In federal agency accounting, however, this unencumbered balance is maintained in a single account, the Allotments Available for Commitment/Obligation account, or in that account and a Commitments Available for Obligation account, which may be used to formally capture purchase requests prior to orders being approved and placed. Too, the encumbrances of a federal agency are referred to as obligations and recorded in an account called Undelivered Orders. The recording of commitments, obligations, and expended appropriations of a federal agency is illustrated in the next three transactions.

**4.** Preliminary requests were made within the agency for the purchase of $37,000 of supplies and for equipment expected to cost $11,000.

**Proprietary Entry**—None
**Budgetary Entry**

| | | | |
|---|---|---|---|
| (4) | Allotments Available for Commitment/Obligation . . . . . . . . | $48,000 | |
| | Commitments Available for Obligation . . . . . . . . . . . . . . | | $48,000 |
| | To record purchase requisitions being processed within the agency. | | |

Note that this entry reduces the Allotments Available for Commitment/Obligation by the estimated cost of the purchase request, leaving the unobligated (unencumbered), uncommitted balance of the allotments (or the unused expenditure authority) in the account.

**5.** Purchase orders were approved and placed for materials estimated to cost $37,000—all of which had been previously committed in that amount.

**Proprietary Entry**—None
**Budgetary Entry**

| | | | |
|---|---|---|---|
| (5) | Commitments Available for Obligation . . . . . . . . . . . . . . . . | $37,000 | |
| | Undelivered Orders . . . . . . . . . . . . . . . . . . . . . . . . . . . . . | | $37,000 |
| | To record purchase orders outstanding. | | |

**6.** Materials estimated to cost $30,000 were received; the invoice was for $30,500.

**Budgetary Entry**

| | | | |
|---|---|---|---|
| (6a) | Undelivered Orders . . . . . . . . . . . . . . . . . . . . . . . . . . . . . | $30,000 | |
| | Allotments Available for Commitment/Obligation . . . . . . . . | 500 | |
| | Expended Appropriations . . . . . . . . . . . . . . . . . . . . . . . . . | | $30,500 |
| | To record expenditure of budgetary authority. | | |

Note that the actual cost of the materials purchased is reflected as Expended Appropriations, whereas the estimated cost is removed from the Undelivered Orders (encumbrances) account.

## Maintaining Agency Accrual Accounting Information

The preceding entries demonstrate how budgetary control is maintained in the agency's accounting records. However, as stated earlier, the agencies are also required to account for and report their activities in proprietary accounts. Therefore, in addition to the budgetary accounting entries illustrated earlier, the agency must record the following entries:

**Proprietary Entry**

(6b)  Inventory of Materials and Supplies . . . . . . . . . . . . . . . . . . .     $30,500

        Accounts Payable . . . . . . . . . . . . . . . . . . . . . . . . . . . . . . .             $30,500

        To record materials received.

(6c)  Unexpended Appropriations—19X1 . . . . . . . . . . . . . . . . . .     $30,500

        Appropriations Used . . . . . . . . . . . . . . . . . . . . . . . . . . . .             $30,500

        To record Appropriations Used resulting from purchase of inventory.

The first preceding entry records the materials purchased as inventory and the related payable. The second entry records the use of appropriations as discussed earlier. Subsequently, the cost of materials used is recorded as an expense of the agency. No budgetary entry is necessary when the expense is recorded.

**7.** Materials costing $25,000 were used by the agency.

**Proprietary Entry**

(7)  Operating/Program Expenses—Materials and Supplies . . . .     $25,000

        Inventory of Materials and Supplies . . . . . . . . . . . . . . . . .             $25,000

        To record cost of materials used.

**Budgetary Entry—None**

## Other Miscellaneous Transactions and Entries During the Year

Various other transactions entered into by the agency are recorded in this section. Notice that budgetary entries and proprietary entries often are required simultaneously.

**8.** The Treasury notified the agency that the checks ordered but not issued in fiscal year 19X0 (Disbursements in Transit in the beginning trial balance—$12,000) were issued in 19X1.

**Proprietary Entry**

(8)  Disbursements in Transit . . . . . . . . . . . . . . . . . . . . . . . . . . .     $12,000

        Fund Balance with Treasury—19X0 . . . . . . . . . . . . . . . . .             $12,000

        To record notification of issuance of checks requested in 19X0.

**Budgetary Entry—None**

**9.** Travel orders in the amount of $1,200 were issued.

**Proprietary Entry—None**
**Budgetary Entry**

(9)  Allotments Available for Commitment/Obligation . . . . . . . .     $ 1,200

        Undelivered Orders . . . . . . . . . . . . . . . . . . . . . . . . . . . . . .             $ 1,200

        To record approval of travel orders.

**10.** Checks for travel advances totaling $1,000 were requested from the Treasury.

**Proprietary Entry**

(10)  Advances to Others . . . . . . . . . . . . . . . . . . . . . . . . . . . . . . .     $ 1,000

        Disbursements in Transit . . . . . . . . . . . . . . . . . . . . . . . . . .             $ 1,000

        To record request to the Treasury for travel advances.

**Budgetary Entry—None**

**11.** Travel vouchers for $1,050 were received, including $880 to which advances were to be applied. Travel orders had not been issued (in transaction 9) for $50 of the travel costs.

**Proprietary Entry**

(11a) Operating/Program Expenses—Travel ................. $ 1,050

    Advances to Others ................................         $ 880

    Accounts Payable .................................         170

    To record travel expenses incurred.

(11b) Unexpended Appropriations—19X1 ................... $ 1,050

    Appropriations Used .............................         $ 1,050

    To record financing source for unexpended appropriations
    used to finance operating expenses.

**Budgetary Entry**

(11c) Allotments Available for Commitment/Obligation ........ $ 50

    Undelivered Orders ................................ 1,000

    Expended Appropriations ..........................         $ 1,050

    To record expenditure of budgetary authority for travel costs.

**12.** Checks to pay the travel claims were ordered from the Treasury.

**Proprietary Entry**

(12)   Accounts Payable ................................... $ 170

    Disbursements in Transit ..........................         $ 170

    To record order of checks from the Treasury to settle
    accounts payable.

**Budgetary Entry—None**

**13.** The Advances to Others related to the prior fiscal year were repaid by employees, $800.

**Proprietary Entry**

(13)   Fund Balance with Treasury—19X0 ................... $ 800

    Advances to Others ...............................         $ 800

    To record collection of unused advances.

**Budgetary Entry—None**

**14.** The Treasury notified the agency that the checks ordered to date, $1,170, were issued.

**Proprietary Entry**

(14)   Disbursements in Transit ........................... $ 1,170

    Fund Balance with Treasury .......................         $ 1,170

    To record issuance of checks by the Treasury.

**Budgetary Entry—None**

**15.** The agency incurred rental expenses, $13,000, utility costs, $8,200, and other miscellaneous expenses totaling $3,500 during the year. These items had not been obligated previously.

**Proprietary Entry**

(15a) Operating/Program Expenses—Rent ................... $13,000

    Operating/Program Expenses—Utilities ................ 8,200

    Operating/Program Expenses—Miscellaneous ........... 3,500

    Accounts Payable .................................         $24,700

    To record various expenses incurred.

(15b) Unexpended Appropriations—19X1 ................... $24,700

    Appropriations Used .............................         $24,700

    To record financing source for unexpended appropriations
    used to finance various operating expenses.

**Budgetary Entry**

(15c) Allotments Available for Commitment/Obligation  . . . . . . . .    $ 24,700

      Expended Appropriations  . . . . . . . . . . . . . . . . . . . . . . . . . .    $ 24,700

    To record expenditure of budgetary authority for various
    operating expenses.

**16.** Purchase orders were approved and placed for equipment estimated to cost $10,200—which had been previously committed at $10,500.

**Proprietary Entry**—None

**Budgetary Entry**

(16)  Commitments Available for Obligation  . . . . . . . . . . . . . . . .    $ 10,500

      Allotments Available for Obligation/Commitment  . . . . . .    $    300

      Undelivered Orders  . . . . . . . . . . . . . . . . . . . . . . . . . . . . . .    10,200

    To record purchase orders outstanding.

**17.** The equipment was received, together with an invoice for $10,000.

**Proprietary Entry**

(17a) Equipment  . . . . . . . . . . . . . . . . . . . . . . . . . . . . . . . . . . . . .    $ 10,000

      Accounts Payable  . . . . . . . . . . . . . . . . . . . . . . . . . . . . . . . .    $ 10,000

    To record acquisition of equipment.

(17b) Unexpended Appropriations—19X1  . . . . . . . . . . . . . . . . . .    $ 10,000

      Appropriations Used  . . . . . . . . . . . . . . . . . . . . . . . . . . . . . .    $ 10,000

    To record financing source for unexpended appropriations
    used to purchase equipment.

**Budgetary Entry**

(17c) Undelivered Orders  . . . . . . . . . . . . . . . . . . . . . . . . . . . . . . .    $ 10,200

      Allotments Available for Commitment/Obligation  . . . . . .    $    200

      Expended Appropriations  . . . . . . . . . . . . . . . . . . . . . . . . . .    10,000

    To record expenditure of budgetary authority.

**18.** Salaries and wages totaling $134,000 were paid during the year, including the agency's share of related payroll expenses. $8,000 of this amount was accrued at the beginning of the year. (Withholding deductions and the use of the disbursements in transit account are omitted for purposes of this illustration.)

**Proprietary Entry**

(18a) Accrued Funded Payroll and Benefits  . . . . . . . . . . . . . . . . .    $  8,000

      Operating/Program Expenses—Salaries and Benefits  . . . . . .    126,000

      Fund Balance with Treasury—19X0  . . . . . . . . . . . . . . . . . .    $  8,000

      Fund Balance with Treasury—19X1  . . . . . . . . . . . . . . . . . .    126,000

    To record payment of payroll.

(18b) Unexpended Appropriations—19X1  . . . . . . . . . . . . . . . . . .    $126,000

      Appropriations Used  . . . . . . . . . . . . . . . . . . . . . . . . . . . . . .    $126,000

    To record financing source for unexpended appropriations
    used to finance payroll expenses.

**Budgetary Entry**

(18c) Allotments Available for Commitment/Obligation  . . . . . . . .    $126,000

      Expended Appropriations  . . . . . . . . . . . . . . . . . . . . . . . . . .    $126,000

    To record expenditure of budgetary authority for
    payroll costs.

**19.** Commitments were placed for contractual services estimated at $3,000.

**Proprietary Entry**—None
**Budgetary Entry**

| | | | |
|---|---|---|---|
| (19) | Allotments Available for Commitment/Obligation ........ | $ 3,000 | |
| | Commitments Available for Obligation .............. | | $ 3,000 |
| | To record commitment for contract request. | | |

**20.** A contract was approved for the services requested in transaction 19.

**Proprietary Entry**—None
**Budgetary Entry**

| | | | |
|---|---|---|---|
| (20) | Commitments Available for Obligation ................ | $ 3,000 | |
| | Undelivered Orders .................................. | | $ 3,000 |
| | To record approval of contract for services. | | |

**21.** The contracted services were received, $3,000.

**Proprietary Entry**

| | | | |
|---|---|---|---|
| (21a) | Operating/Program Expenses—Contractual Services ...... | $ 3,000 | |
| | Accounts Payable ................................. | | $ 3,000 |
| | To record receipt of contractual services. | | |
| (21b) | Unexpended Appropriations—19X1 .................. | $ 3,000 | |
| | Appropriations Used ............................. | | $ 3,000 |
| | To record financing source for unexpended appropriations used to finance contractual services expense. | | |

**Budgetary Entry**

| | | | |
|---|---|---|---|
| (21c) | Undelivered Orders ................................ | $ 3,000 | |
| | Expended Appropriations .......................... | | $ 3,000 |
| | To record expended appropriations for contractual services. | | |

**22.** Checks to pay all accounts payable except that for the contractual services were requested from the Treasury, $95,200.

**Proprietary Entry**

| | | | |
|---|---|---|---|
| (22) | Accounts Payable .................................. | $95,200 | |
| | Disbursements in Transit .......................... | | $95,200 |
| | To record request for the Treasury to pay accounts payable. | | |

**Budgetary Entry**—None

**23.** Treasury notified the agency that checks totaling $85,000 were issued, including $30,000 relating to accounts payable outstanding at the beginning of the fiscal year.

**Proprietary Entry**

| | | | |
|---|---|---|---|
| (23) | Disbursements in Transit ........................... | $85,000 | |
| | Fund Balance with Treasury—19X0 ................. | | $30,000 |
| | Fund Balance with Treasury—19X1 ................. | | 55,000 |
| | To record issuance of checks by the Treasury. | | |

**Budgetary Entry**—None

**24.** Depreciation on agency equipment amounted to $2,500.

**Proprietary Entry**

| | | | |
|---|---|---|---|
| (24) | Operating/Program Expenses—Depreciation ........... | $ 2,500 | |
| | Accumulated Depreciation ........................ | | $ 2,500 |
| | To record depreciation of equipment. | | |

**Budgetary Entry**—None

**25.** Salaries and benefits (other than annual leave) amounting to $7,000 were accrued at year end.

**Proprietary Entry**

| | | |
|---|---|---|
| (25a) Operating/Program Expenses—Salaries and Benefits . . . . . . | $ 7,000 | |
|     Accrued Funded Payroll . . . . . . . . . . . . . . . . . . . . . . . . . . | | $ 7,000 |
|     To accrue payroll at year end. | | |
| (25b) Unexpended Appropriations—19X1 . . . . . . . . . . . . . . . . . . | $ 7,000 | |
|     Appropriations Used . . . . . . . . . . . . . . . . . . . . . . . . . . . . | | $ 7,000 |
|     To accrue financing source for unexpended appropriations used to finance accrual of payroll expenses. | | |

**Budgetary Entry**

| | | |
|---|---|---|
| (25c) Allotments Available for Commitment/Obligation . . . . . . . . | $ 7,000 | |
|     Expended Appropriations . . . . . . . . . . . . . . . . . . . . . . . . | | $ 7,000 |
|     To record accrual of expended appropriations against budgetary authority for payroll. | | |

**26.** The liability for accrued annual leave increased $10,000 during the year.

**Proprietary Entry**

| | | |
|---|---|---|
| (26)  Operating/Program Expenses—Salaries and Benefits . . . . . . | $10,000 | |
|     Accrued Unfunded Annual Leave Liability . . . . . . . . . . . . | | $10,000 |
|     To accrue annual leave earned in excess of leave used. | | |

**Budgetary Entry**—None

## Closing Entries

The closing process for a federal agency entails closing both budgetary and proprietary accounts. The preclosing balance for the illustrative agency at September 30, 19X1 (Figure 19–9) provides the account balance information needed for the closing entries. The closing entries for the budgetary accounts and for the proprietary accounts for the illustrative agency are presented in the following separate sections.

### Budgetary Accounts

Unexpended appropriation authority is retained by law by the agency until canceled. The purpose of this retention is for:

**A.** Expended appropriations resulting from prior year obligations to be charged against the Undelivered Orders balance established in the prior year.

**B.** Any excess of actual over estimated cost of expended appropriations from prior year obligations to be charged against expired appropriation authority from the prior year.

Hence, note that the unobligated, unexpended appropriations are closed to an account called Expired Authority. Also note that Expended Appropriations are closed to Other Appropriations Realized—Leaving the unexpended balance of Appropriations in that Budgetary Resources account.

| | | |
|---|---|---|
| (27a) Apportionment Available for Distribution . . . . . . . . . . . . . . | $ 6,000 | |
|     Allotments Available for Commitment/Obligation . . . . . . . . | 4,050 | |
|     Commitments Available for Obligation . . . . . . . . . . . . . . . . | 500 | |
|     Authority Available for Apportionment . . . . . . . . . . . . . . | | $10,550 |
|     To close apportionments, allotments, and commitments. | | |

FIGURE 19–9 **Preclosing Trial Balance**

XYZ Agency

**Preclosing Trial Balance**

September 30, 19X1

**Budgetary Accounts**

| | | |
|---|---|---|
| Other Appropriations Realized . . . . . . . . . . . . . . . . . . . . . . . . . | $238,000 | |
| Authority Available for Apportionment . . . . . . . . . . . . . . . . . . . | | $   5,000 |
| Apportionment Available for Distribution . . . . . . . . . . . . . . . . . | | 6,000 |
| Allotments Available for Commitment/Obligation . . . . . . . . . . | | 4,050 |
| Commitments Available for Obligation . . . . . . . . . . . . . . . . . . . | | 500 |
| Undelivered Orders . . . . . . . . . . . . . . . . . . . . . . . . . . . . . . . . . . | | 7,200 |
| Expended Appropriations . . . . . . . . . . . . . . . . . . . . . . . . . . . . . | | 202,250 |
| Expired Authority . . . . . . . . . . . . . . . . . . . . . . . . . . . . . . . . . . . | | 13,000 |
| | $238,000 | $238,000 |

**Proprietary Accounts**

| | | |
|---|---|---|
| Fund Balance with Treasury—19X0 . . . . . . . . . . . . . . . . . . . . . . | $ 13,000 | |
| Fund Balance with Treasury—19X1 . . . . . . . . . . . . . . . . . . . . . . | 42,830 | |
| Advances to Others . . . . . . . . . . . . . . . . . . . . . . . . . . . . . . . . . . | 120 | |
| Inventory for Agency Operations . . . . . . . . . . . . . . . . . . . . . . . | 22,500 | |
| Equipment . . . . . . . . . . . . . . . . . . . . . . . . . . . . . . . . . . . . . . . . . | 30,000 | |
| Accumulated Depreciation on Equipment . . . . . . . . . . . . . . . . | | $ 10,500 |
| Disbursements in Transit . . . . . . . . . . . . . . . . . . . . . . . . . . . . . | | 10,200 |
| Accounts Payable . . . . . . . . . . . . . . . . . . . . . . . . . . . . . . . . . . . | | 3,000 |
| Accrued Funded Payroll and Benefits . . . . . . . . . . . . . . . . . . . | | 7,000 |
| Accrued Unfunded Annual Leave . . . . . . . . . . . . . . . . . . . . . . . | | 60,000 |
| Unexpended Appropriations—19X0 . . . . . . . . . . . . . . . . . . . . . | | 13,000 |
| Unexpended Appropriations—19X1 . . . . . . . . . . . . . . . . . . . . . | | 22,750 |
| Cumulative Results of Operations . . . . . . . . . . . . . . . . . . . . . . | 21,000 | |
| Net Results of Operations . . . . . . . . . . . . . . . . . . . . . . . . . . . . . | | — |
| Appropriations Used . . . . . . . . . . . . . . . . . . . . . . . . . . . . . . . . . | | 202,250 |
| Operating/Program Expenses—Salaries and Benefits . . . . . . . . | 143,000 | |
| Operating/Program Expenses—Materials and Supplies . . . . . . . | 25,000 | |
| Operating/Program Expenses—Rent . . . . . . . . . . . . . . . . . . . . . | 13,000 | |
| Operating/Program Expenses—Utilities . . . . . . . . . . . . . . . . . . | 8,200 | |
| Operating/Program Expenses—Depreciation . . . . . . . . . . . . . . | 2,500 | |
| Operating/Program Expenses—Travel . . . . . . . . . . . . . . . . . . . | 1,050 | |
| Operating/Program Expenses—Contractual Services . . . . . . . . | 3,000 | |
| Operating/Program Expenses—Miscellaneous . . . . . . . . . . . . . | 3,500 | |
| | $328,700 | $328,700 |

| | | |
|---|---|---|
| (27b) Authority Available for Apportionment . . . . . . . . . . . . . . . . . | $ 15,550* | |
| Expired Authority . . . . . . . . . . . . . . . . . . . . . . . . . . . . . . . | | $ 15,550 |
| To close expired appropriation authority. | | |

*(Note that a balance was left in Authority Available for Apportionment for illustrative purposes. The OMB normally must apportion the full amount of an agency's appropriations.)

| | | |
|---|---|---|
| (27c) Expended Appropriations . . . . . . . . . . . . . . . . . . . . . . . . . . . . | $202,250 | |
| Other Appropriations Realized . . . . . . . . . . . . . . . . . . . . . | | $202,250 |
| To close expended appropriations. | | |

### Proprietary Accounts

Expended Appropriations and the budgetary accounts were closed separately to emphasize better the complete separation of budgetary and proprietary accounting. The proprietary accounts must also be closed.

**28.** The proprietary accounts are closed with the following entries:

| | | |
|---|---|---:|
| (28a) Appropriations Used .............................. | $202,250 | |
| Net Results of Operations ......................... | | $ 3,000 |
| Operating/Program Expenses—Salaries and Benefits .... | | 143,000 |
| Operating/Program Expenses—Materials and Supplies .. | | 25,000 |
| Operating/Program Expenses—Rent ................. | | 13,000 |
| Operating/Program Expenses—Utilities .............. | | 8,200 |
| Operating/Program Expenses—Depreciation .......... | | 2,500 |
| Operating/Program Expenses—Travel ............... | | 1,050 |
| Operating/Program Expenses—Contractual Services .... | | 3,000 |
| Operating/Program Expenses—Miscellaneous .......... | | 3,500 |
| To close proprietary accounts to net results of operations. | | |
| (28b) Net Results of Operations .......................... | $ 3,000 | |
| Cumulative Results of Operations .................. | | $ 3,000 |
| To close the net operating loss. | | |

## Reporting

As noted earlier, the principal financial statements prepared for federal agencies include the following:

**1.** Balance Sheet (Figure 19–10)

**FIGURE 19–10  Federal Agency Balance Sheet**

XYZ Agency
**Comparative Balance Sheet**
September 30 of Fiscal Years 19X1 and 19X0

| | September 30 of Fiscal Year 19X1 | | September 30 of Fiscal Year 19X0 | |
|---|---:|---:|---:|---:|
| **Assets** | | | | |
| Fund Balance with Treasury—19X0 ...................... | | $13,000 | | $ 62,200 |
| Fund Balance with Treasury—19X1 ...................... | | 42,830 | | — |
| Advance to Others ...................................... | | 120 | | 800 |
| Inventory for Agency Operation .......................... | | 22,500 | | 17,000 |
| Equipment ............................................. | $30,000 | | $20,000 | |
| Less Accumulated Depreciation ........................ | (10,500) | 19,500 | (8,000) | 12,000 |
| Total Assets .......................................... | | $97,950 | | $ 92,000 |
| **Liabilities and Net Position** | | | | |
| **Liabilities** | | | | |
| Liabilities Covered by Budgetary Resources | | | | |
| Disbursements in Transit .............................. | $10,200 | | $12,000 | |
| Accounts Payable .................................... | 3,000 | | 30,000 | |
| Accrued Funded Payroll and Benefits ................... | 7,000 | $20,200 | 8,000 | 50,000 |
| Liabilities Not Covered by Budgetary Resources | | | | |
| Accrued Unfunded Annual Leave ....................... | | 60,000 | | 50,000 |
| Total Liabilities ..................................... | | $80,200 | | $100,000 |
| **Net Position** | | | | |
| Unexpended Appropriations—19X0 ...................... | 13,000 | | 13,000 | |
| Unexpended Appropriations—19X1 ...................... | 22,750 | | — | |
| Cumulative Results of Operations ........................ | (18,000) | | (21,000) | |
| Total Net Position of the U.S. Government ............... | | 17,750 | | (8,000) |
| Total Liabilities and Net Position ......................... | | $97,950 | | $ 92,000 |

**2.** Statement of Net Cost (Figure 19–11)

**3.** Statement of Changes in Net Position (Figure 19–12)

**4.** Statement of Budgetary Resources (Figure 19–13)

**FIGURE 19–11  Federal Agency Statement of Net Cost**

XYZ Agency
**Statement of Net Cost**
For Year Ended September 30 of Fiscal Year 19X1

**Program A:**
**Operating/Program Expenses**

| | | |
|---|--:|--:|
| Depreciation on Equipment | $   2,500 | |
| Payroll and Benefits | 143,000 | |
| Contractual Services | 3,000 | |
| Materials and Supplies Used | 25,000 | |
| Travel Expense | 1,050 | |
| Rent Expense | 13,000 | |
| Utilities Expense | 8,200 | |
| Miscellaneous Expense | 3,500 | |
| Total Operating/Program Expenses | | $199,250 |
| Less Earned Revenues | | — |
| Net Program Costs* | | 199,250 |
| Costs Not Assigned to Programs | | — |
| Less Earned Revenues Not Attributed to Programs | | — |
| Deferred Maintenance (Note X) | | |
| Net Costs of Operations | | $199,250 |

*This section is repeated for each program.

**FIGURE 19–12  Federal Agency Statement of Changes in Net Position**

XYZ Agency
**Statement of Changes in Net Position**
For Year Ended September 30 of Fiscal Year 19X1

| | |
|---|--:|
| Net Costs of Operations | $199,250 |
| Financing Sources (other than exchange revenues) | |
| Appropriations Used | 202,250 |
| Taxes (and other nonexchange revenues) | — |
| Donations | — |
| Net Results of Operations | 3,000 |
| Prior Period Adjustments | — |
| Net Change in Cumulative Results of Operations | 3,000 |
| Increase in Unexpended Appropriations | 22,750 |
| Change in Net Position | 25,750 |
| Net Position, September 30, 19X0 | (8,000) |
| Net Position, September 30, 19X1 | $ 17,750 |

FIGURE 19–13  **Federal Agency Report on Budgetary Resources**

XYZ Agency
**Statement of Budgetary Resources**
Fiscal Year End 19X1

| Part I: | Budgetary Resources | |
|---|---|---|
| | Appropriations realized | $225,000 |
| | Plus other authority | —0— |
| | Less withdrawals | —0— |
| | Total Budgetary Authority | $225,000 |

| Part II: | Status of Authority | |
|---|---|---|
| | Obligations incurred | $209,450[a] |
| | Plus unobligated balances available | —0— |
| | Plus unobligated balances not available | 15,550[b] |
| | Total Budgetary Authority | $225,000 |

| Part III: | Relationship of Obligations to Outlays to Expended Appropriations | |
|---|---|---|
| | Obligations incurred | $209,450 |
| | Less obligations not yet disbursed | (27,280)[c] |
| | Outlays | 182,170[d] |
| | Plus changes in funded liabilities | 20,080[c] |
| | Expended Appropriations | $202,250 |

[a] Expended Appropriations plus Undelivered Orders.
[b] Increase in Expired Authority.
[c] Computations:

| | |
|---|---|
| Disbursements in Transit | $10,200 |
| Accounts Payable | 3,000 |
| Accrued Funded Payroll and Benefits | 7,000 |
| Undelivered Orders | 7,200 |
| | 27,400 |
| Less: Advances | (120) |
| Obligations not yet disbursed | 27,280 |
| Less: Undelivered Orders | (7,200) |
| Change in Funded Liabilities | $20,080 |

[d] Proposed changes would conclude this report at this point.

**5.** Statement of Financing

**6.** Statement of Custodial Activity

The preclosing trial balance in Figure 19–9 should facilitate your transition from the journal entries to the financial statements presented for our illustrative agency. The Treasury consolidates the financial statements from the various federal agencies along with data from central accounting records to prepare the consolidated financial statements of the U.S. government. These include the first three statements—the balance sheet or statement of financial position, the statement of net cost, and the statement of changes in net position. The most recently available U.S. consolidated financial statements are presented in Figures 19–14 to 19–16. Although it is beyond the scope of this chapter to discuss the many eliminations, adjustments, and additions made in preparing the consolidated statements from the federal agency statements, some of the adjustments and eliminations are obvious when you compare the illustrative agency statements (Figures 19–10 to 19–12) with the consolidated statements. For example, note the absence of Unexpended Appropriations as a component of net position. Also note that Appropriations Used is not a financing source in the consolidated statement of changes in net position. Likewise, the change in Unexpended Appropriations does not appear in the consolidated statement.

**FIGURE 19–14  U.S. Government Statement of Financial Position**

U.S. Government
**Consolidated Statement of Financial Position**
As of September 30 (Unaudited)
(in billions of dollars)

|  | 1996 | 1995 |
|---|---|---|
| **Assets** | | |
| Cash and other monetary assets | 193.4 | 193.5 |
| Accounts and loans receivable | 171.7 | 161.8 |
| Taxes receivable* | 33.8 | 46.2 |
| Inventories and related properties | 232.1 | 219.9 |
| Property, plant, and equipment | 969.1 | 934.4 |
| Other assets | 123.8 | 133.6 |
| Total assets | 1,723.9 | 1,689.4 |
| **Liabilities and Net Position** | | |
| Accounts payable | 161.8 | 153.6 |
| Federal debt securities held by the public | 3,730.0 | 3,603.3 |
| Pensions and other actuarial liabilities | 1,651.5 | 1,628.2 |
| Environmental liabilities | 246.5 | 227.2 |
| Other liabilities | 283.6 | 228.7 |
| Total liabilities | 6,073.4 | 5,841.0 |
| Net position | –4,349.5 | –4,151.6 |

*Taxes receivable for individual and corporate income taxes, net of allowances for loss, are reported by the Internal Revenue Service.

**FIGURE 19–15  U.S. Government Statement of Net Cost**

U.S. Government
**Consolidated Statement of Net Cost**
For the Year Ended September 30 (Unaudited)
(in billions of dollars)

| *Costs of Government Functions* | Gross Costs 1996 | 1995 | Exchange Revenues 1996 | 1995 | Net Costs 1996 | 1995 |
|---|---|---|---|---|---|---|
| National defense | 230.2 | 194.6 | 9.4 | 11.1 | 220.8 | 183.5 |
| Human resources: | | | | | | |
| Education, training, employment, and social services | 54.5 | 82.5 | 1.6 | 3.2 | 52.9 | 79.3 |
| Health | 132.9 | 132.2 | 5.4 | 4.8 | 127.5 | 127.4 |
| Medicare | 224.7 | 211.1 | 20.3 | 21.2 | 204.4 | 189.9 |
| Income security | 227.8 | 186.0 | 11.8 | 10.6 | 216.0 | 175.4 |
| Social security | 380.8 | 364.1 | 1.1 | — | 379.7 | 364.1 |
| Veterans' benefits and services | 13.3 | 81.0 | 3.6 | 3.7 | 9.7 | 77.3 |
| Subtotal | 1,034.0 | 1,056.9 | 43.8 | 43.5 | 990.2 | 1,013.4 |
| Physical resources: | | | | | | |
| Energy | 31.2 | 15.1 | 14.0 | 10.2 | 17.2 | 4.9 |
| Natural resources and environment | 29.8 | 23.8 | 3.0 | 2.9 | 26.8 | 20.9 |
| Commerce and housing credit | 73.2 | 70.0 | 66.2 | 68.9 | 7.0 | 1.1 |
| Transportation | 53.7 | 37.4 | 2.1 | 2.5 | 51.6 | 34.9 |
| Community and regional development | 8.1 | 13.7 | .9 | 1.5 | 7.2 | 12.2 |
| Subtotal | 196.0 | 160.0 | 86.2 | 86.0 | 109.8 | 74.0 |
| Net Interest: | | | | | | |
| Interest on the public debt | 241.7 | 234.3 | — | — | 241.7 | 234.3 |
| Other | .1 | .1 | — | — | .1 | .1 |
| Subtotal | 241.8 | 234.4 | — | — | 241.8 | 234.4 |
| Other functions: | | | | | | |
| International affairs | 20.8 | 19.3 | 6.0 | 2.7 | 14.8 | 16.6 |
| General science, space, and technology | 16.5 | 17.9 | — | .1 | 16.5 | 17.8 |
| Agriculture | 16.7 | 7.0 | 2.8 | 2.9 | 13.9 | 4.1 |
| Administration of justice | 21.5 | 16.9 | 1.0 | 1.1 | 20.5 | 15.8 |
| General government | 26.7 | 50.3 | 8.5 | 8.8 | 18.2 | 41.5 |
| Subtotal | 102.2 | 111.4 | 18.3 | 15.6 | 83.9 | 95.8 |
| Total | 1,804.2 | 1,757.3 | 157.7 | 156.2 | 1,646.5 | 1,601.1 |

FIGURE 19–16  **U.S. Government Statement of Changes in Net Position**

U.S. Government
**Consolidated Statement of Changes in Net Position**
For the Year Ended September 30 (Unaudited)
(in billions of dollars)

|  | 1996 | 1995 |
|---|---|---|
| Net cost of government operations | –1,646.5 | –1,601.1 |
| Less financing sources from nonexchange revenues: | | |
| From income taxes: | | |
| Individual | 656.4 | 590.2 |
| Corporate | 171.8 | 157.0 |
| From employment taxes and contributions: | | |
| Social security | 371.4 | 355.0 |
| Medicare | 105.0 | 96.0 |
| Unemployment insurance | 28.6 | 28.9 |
| From other taxes and governmental receipts: | | |
| Excise taxes | 54.0 | 57.5 |
| Estate and gift taxes | 17.2 | 14.8 |
| Customs duties | 18.7 | 19.3 |
| Miscellaneous | 25.5 | 27.3 |
| Total nonexchange revenues | 1,448.6 | 1,346.0 |
| Net results of operations | –197.9 | –255.1 |
| Prior period adjustments | — | 109.7* |
| Change in net position | –197.9 | –145.4 |
| Net position, beginning of period | –4,151.6 | –4,006.2 |
| Net position, end of period | –4,349.5 | –4,151.6 |

*Prior period adjustments consist of environmental clean-up cost of –$227.2 billion; Bureau of Indian Affairs, –$1.6 billion; defense inventories and fixed assets, –$82.4 billion; and depreciation, $420.9 billion.

## CONCLUDING COMMENTS

The federal government is the largest, most complex entity in the United States. Accordingly, the accounting and reporting systems of the various agencies must meet the many multifaceted needs of both internal and external persons and groups. The discussion of the financial management structure of the federal government in the first part of this chapter indicates the many agencies involved in helping meet those needs.

Federal agency accounting and reporting are the focus of the latter part of this chapter. These agencies are significant reporting entities; furthermore, the reports for the government as a whole must be derived from the accounts and reports of the various agencies. Each agency's accounting and reporting systems must provide both information needed by the agency's management and that needed to ensure and demonstrate compliance with budgetary and other legal requirements.

Federal government accounting integrates accrual basis accounting and budgetary accounting in a unique manner. Some aspects of federal agency accounting are unique to the federal government; others are somewhat similar to state and local government accounting and other aspects are similar to business accounting. This chapter discusses and illustrates the basic principles and concepts that federal agencies are required to apply.

## Questions

**Q 19-1** Explain the meaning of the following terms in federal accounting:
a. Apportionment
b. Allotment
c. Obligation
d. Commitment
e. Expended Appropriations
f. Obligations Incurred
g. Fund Balance with Treasury

**Q 19-2** List the types of financial statements issued annually by federal agencies.

**Q 19-3** Describe the components of the net position of the U.S. government.

**Q 19-4** Compare the manner in which budgetary accounting is accomplished in a federal agency with that of a municipality.

**Q 19-5** What are the principal duties of the Federal Accounting Standards Advisory Board?

**Q 19-6** Describe the function of a federal agency's inspector general. To whom and in what manner does the agency inspector general report?

**Q 19-7** What are the key functions and responsibilities of the General Accounting Office?

**Q 19-8** When a federal agency purchases a fixed asset, what are the impacts on the components of net position? On the statement of changes in net position?

**Q 19-9** What is expired authority? What is its primary purpose?

## Problems

**P 19-1** (Multiple Choice)
1. Formal notification that Congress has enacted an appropriation for an agency requires recognition by the agency in
   a. budgetary accounts only.
   b. proprietary accounts only.
   c. both budgetary and proprietary accounts.
   d. neither budgetary or proprietary accounts. (No entry is required until apportionments are made.)
2. Primary responsibility with respect to accounting for agency resources and expended appropriations rests with
   a. each individual agency.
   b. the Department of the Treasury.
   c. the General Accounting Office.
   d. the Office of Management and Budget.
   e. the Federal Accounting Standards Advisory Board.
3. A federal agency's accounting system does *not* need to include information pertaining to
   a. expended appropriations.
   b. fixed assets.
   c. obligations.
   d. expenses.
   e. all of the above must be included.

4. In 19X5, the U.S. Weather Service purchased a parcel of land near Carmel, California, with $850,000 of appropriated funds with the intention of constructing a facility thereon. The effect of this transaction on Cumulative Results of Operations is
   a. no change.
   b. increase it by $850,000.
   c. no change, but Unexpended Appropriations would be decreased by $850,000.
   d. none of the above.

5. An appropriation that has expired
   a. is reported by a federal agency as authority available for apportionment.
   b. is reported by a federal agency as unexpended appropriations.
   c. is reported by a federal agency as unobligated allotments.
   d. is not reported by a federal agency in any of its net position accounts.

6. Direct labor costs incurred by a federal agency during a period will be reflected in the agency's budgetary accounts as
   a. a debit to Expended Appropriations and credit to Cash
   b. a debit to Expended Appropriations and credit to Cumulative Results of Operations
   c. a debit to Allotments Available for Obligation and credit to Expended Appropriations
   d. a debit to Undelivered Orders and credit to Expended Appropriations

7. On June 1, 19X7, the Department of Labor ordered $10,000 worth of stationery and office supplies from an authorized contractor. At the time of the purchase order, this transaction should be recorded by the agency as
   a. a $10,000 debit to current assets and a $10,000 credit to liabilities.
   b. a $10,000 debit to Allotments Available for Obligation and a $10,000 credit to Undelivered Orders.
   c. a $10,000 debit to Expended Appropriations and a $10,000 credit to Cumulative Results of Operations.
   d. a $10,000 debit to Allotments Available for Obligation and a $10,000 credit to Expended Appropriations.
   e. a $10,000 debit to Authority Available for Apportionment and a $10,000 credit to Expended Appropriations.

8. Authority Available for Apportionment is reclassified as Apportionments Available for Distribution when
   a. the Office of Management and Budget releases enacted appropriations to the federal agency.
   b. the appropriate agency officials assign appropriations to various departments within the agency.
   c. purchase orders are approved and sent to suppliers of goods.
   d. suppliers are paid for goods furnished to an agency.
   e. assets are returned by a federal agency to the Treasury.

9. Certain proprietary financial statements are required as indicated in the chapter. These statements are required to be prepared and presented for
   a. each federal agency, but not for the federal government as a whole.
   b. for the government as a whole, but not for each agency.
   c. each federal agency and for the federal government as a whole.
   d. none of the above.

**P 19-2** (Budgetary Accounting) Prepare the general journal entries required to record each of the following transactions.
1. The Interstate Fur Trading Commission received a warrant from the Treasury for a $2,000,000 appropriation from the Congress for the fiscal year beginning October 1, 19X7.
2. The OMB apportioned the commission $500,000 of its appropriation.

3. The commission head allotted $400,000 to specific purposes.
4. Salaries incurred and paid for the quarter totaled $120,000.
5. Purchase orders for equipment estimated to cost $50,000 were requested.
6. Equipment estimated to cost $33,000 was ordered.
7. The equipment was received along with an invoice for its cost, $32,890.

**P 19-3** (Expended Appropriations and Net Position) Prepare the general journal entries to adjust and close the Environmental Enhancement Agency's accounts at year end assuming the agency is financed solely from appropriations.

| | |
|---|---|
| Appropriations expended for operating costs | $3,700,000 |
| Appropriations expended for inventory | 400,000 |
| Appropriations expended for property, plant, and equipment | 1,200,000 |
| Depreciation expense | 250,000 |
| Cost of inventory used during the period | 420,000 |
| Expired authority for the year | 212,000 |
| Undelivered orders at year end | 185,000 |

**P 19-4** (Various Transactions) Record the following transactions and events of Able Agency, which occurred during the month of October 19X6:
1. Able Agency received a warrant for its fiscal 19X7 appropriation of $2,500,000.
2. The Office of Management and Budget apportioned $600,000 to Able Agency for the first quarter of the 19X7 fiscal year.
3. Able Agency's chief executive allotted $500,000 of the first-quarter appropriation apportionment.
4. Obligations incurred during the month for equipment, materials, and program costs amounted to $128,000.
5. Goods and services ordered during the prior year—and to be charged to obligations carried over from the 19X6 fiscal year—were received:

| | Obligated For | Actual Cost |
|---|---|---|
| Materials | $20,000 | $21,000 |
| Program A costs | 7,000 | 6,200 |
| Program B costs | 3,000 | 2,500 |
| | $30,000 | $29,700 |

6. Goods and services ordered during October 19X6 were received and vouchered:

| | Obligated For | Actual Cost |
|---|---|---|
| Materials | $ 6,000 | $ 5,000 |
| Equipment | 10,000 | 10,000 |
| Program A costs | 30,000 | 32,000 |
| Program B costs | 80,000 | 81,000 |
| | $126,000 | $128,000 |

7. Depreciation for the month of October was estimated at $200, chargeable to Overhead.
8. Materials issued from inventory during October were for: Program A, $18,000; Program B, $7,000; and general (Overhead), $3,000.
9. Liabilities placed in line for payment by the U.S. Treasurer totaled $145,000.
10. Other accrued expenses at October 31, 19X6, not previously recorded, were Program A, $1,000; Program B, $6,000; and general (Overhead), $1,500.

**P 19-5** **Following is the September 30, 19X8 trial balance for ABC Agency.**

**ABC AGENCY**
**Postclosing Trial Balance**
September 30 of Fiscal Year 19X8
(Amounts in thousands of dollars)

| | | |
|---|---:|---:|
| Budgetary Accounts: | | |
| Other Appropriations Realized ......................... | $ 18 | |
| Expired Authority ..................................... | | $ 18 |
| | $ 18 | $ 18 |
| Proprietary Accounts: | | |
| Fund Balance with Treasury—19X8 ..................... | $168 | |
| Advances to Others ................................ | 15 | |
| Inventory for Agency Operations ...................... | 75 | |
| Equipment .......................................... | 300 | |
| Accumulated Depreciation on Equipment ................ | | $135 |
| Disbursements in Transit ............................. | | 30 |
| Accounts Payable .................................... | | 60 |
| Accrued Funded Payroll and Benefits ................... | | 75 |
| Accrued Unfunded Annual Leave ....................... | | 210 |
| Unexpended Appropriations—19X8 ..................... | | 18 |
| Cumulative Results of Operations ..................... | | 30 |
| | $558 | $558 |

The agency applies the following accounting policies:

• Commitment accounting is used only for fixed assets, inventories for agency operations, and services.

• Salaries and benefits do not have undelivered orders placed in advance of expending the appropriation for them.

• All disbursements except for salaries, benefits, and advances to others must have accounts payable established first.

Following are transactions during fiscal year 19X9. All are in thousands of dollars.

1. The agency received an appropriation warrant from the Treasury in the amount of $30,000, notifying it that its appropriation had been enacted in that amount. The enabling legislation specified that $9,000 was for salaries and benefits, $6,000 was for travel, and $15,000 was for fixed assets, materials, and services.

2. OMB apportioned the entire appropriation during the year.

3. The agency head allotted $8,700 for salaries and benefits, $6,000 for travel, and $14,450 for fixed assets, inventory, and supplies.

4. The Treasury notified the agency that the checks ordered but not issued in fiscal year 19X8 were issued.

5. a. Travel orders in the amount of $5,400 were issued.
   b. Checks for travel advances totaling $3,000 were requested from the Treasury.
   c. Travel vouchers in the amount of $5,700 were received, including $5,250 related to $5,325 of the travel for which orders had been issued. Advances of $2,970 were to be applied.
   d. Checks to pay the travel claims were ordered from the Treasury.
   e. The advances related to fiscal year 19X8 were repaid by employees.
   f. The Treasury notified the agency that checks ordered in (b) and (d) were issued.

6. a. The agency head allotted the remaining payroll budget.
   b. Payroll paid during the year, including the agency's share of expenses, amounted to $9,015. Ignore withholding deductions and omit going through the disbursements in transit account. Remember that $75 was included in year 19X8 Expended Appropriations and is accrued.

7. a. Commitments were placed for $14,450 of fixed assets, inventory, and services.
   b. The agency head allotted an additional $300 for fixed assets, inventory, and services.
   c. Orders were placed for $14,700 of fixed assets, inventory, and services. Of those, $14,250 had previously been committed in the amount of $14,400. Due to failure to follow procedures, the remaining $450 had not been previously committed.
   d. Orders in (c) were received and approved, as follows:

|  | Estimate | Actual |
| --- | --- | --- |
| Equipment | $ 3,000 | $ 3,300 |
| Inventory | 600 | 540 |
| Services Used | 10,875 | 10,800 |
|  | $14,475 | $14,640 |

   e. Checks for accounts payable of $14,100 were requested from the Treasury during the year, including those related to fiscal year 19X8. The Treasury notified the agency that checks amounting to $13,980 were issued during fiscal year 19X9, including those relating to fiscal year 19X8 accounts payable.

8. The following year-end information was compiled.
   a. Depreciation on equipment amounted to $45.
   b. Salaries and benefits other than annual leave to be accrued amounted to $60.
   c. According to a report from the payroll department, the annual leave liability at fiscal year end was $219.
   d. A physical count of inventory indicated that $164 of inventory had been used.

**Required** (a) Prepare the general journal entries required for ABC Agency for fiscal year 19X9.
   (b) Post the entries to T-accounts.
   (c) Prepare a preclosing trial balance for September 30, 19X9.
   (d) Close the accounts.

**P 19-6** Using the information from Problem 19-5, prepare the four financial statements illustrated in the chapter for federal agencies:
   a. Balance sheet
   b. Statement of net cost
   c. Statement of changes in net position
   d. Statement of budgetary resources

Auditing is the process of collecting and evaluating evidence to formulate an independent, professional opinion or other judgment about assertions made by management. The auditing process should be conducted in accordance with standards adopted to assure audit quality; and the auditor's opinion or other judgment relates to the degree of correspondence with established criteria, such as generally accepted accounting principles, laws and regulations, contractual agreements, or other criteria agreed upon with users of the audit report.

The typical readers of financial statements or operational reports issued by management have no opportunity to review the operations or balances in question or to assess the credibility of management's representations, and few could do a good job given the opportunity. The auditor's examination provides an expert's independent, professional judgment on the matters covered in the audit report. The purpose of the auditor's opinion is to add credibility to those representations properly made by management and to reduce the credibility of those that the auditor does not consider appropriate. These representations may take the form of financial statements, other reports on the activities of organizations in conducting programs assigned by legislative action or financed by intergovernmental grants, or implied representations regarding the carrying out of basic managerial responsibilities. For example, management is responsible for compliance with legal requirements, for maintaining adequate internal controls, and for conducting programs economically and efficiently. The auditor may be asked to give an opinion or to present other findings on such matters even when management's representation is an implied one.

## OVERVIEW

This chapter is intended to familiarize the reader with the major unique aspects of government auditing. An overview of the nature, purpose, and scope of government auditing is presented first. This overview is followed by a summary of generally accepted governmental auditing standards (GAGAS) established by the U.S. General Accounting Office (GAO). Finally, the concept and framework of a *single audit* are explained.

### What Is an Audit?

Although there are several specific types of audits, most audits can be visualized generally as illustrated in Figure 20–1:

FIGURE 20–1  **The Audit Process**

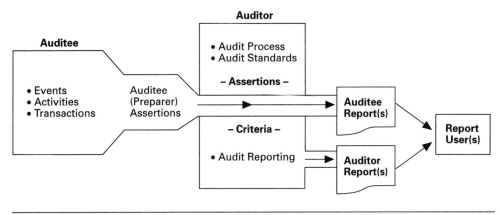

1. An *auditee* is considered accountable for certain events, activities, and transactions—and makes assertions, either directly or indirectly, regarding such accountability.

2. The *auditor* compares the auditee's assertions against established criteria—following an appropriate audit process and standards—and reports an opinion or other judgment based on the result of the audit.

3. The audit report *users* are provided information by both the auditee (assertions) and the auditor (opinion or other judgment) to use in making their evaluations and decisions regarding the auditee's accountability.

## Classifications of Audits

The term **preaudit** refers to the internal procedures used to control the accuracy of the collecting and recording of revenues and the incurring and recording of expenditures and disbursements. Preaudit work is part of the accounting and control processes and therefore is **not** included in the definition of **auditing** as that term is used here. **Postaudits**—examinations conducted after transactions and events have occurred—are the principal focus of this chapter.

Audits may be classified as internal or external on the basis of the relationship of the auditor to the agency being examined. Management customarily uses **internal auditors**—who are employees of the agency being audited—to review the operations of the agency, including employee compliance with managerial policies, and to report to management on these matters. The internal auditor's responsibility is ordinarily to top management of the agency.

**External auditors** are independent of the auditee agency and are responsible to the legislative body, the public, and other governmental units. External auditors typically express an opinion—primarily for the benefit of third parties—concerning the fairness of financial statements. However, their audit scope may extend beyond financial statements.

GAGAS (the GAO audit standards) further subdivide audits into four categories:

### Financial Audits

a. **Financial statement audits**—provide reasonable assurance about whether the financial statements of an audited entity present fairly the financial position, the results of operations, and cash flows or changes in financial position in accordance with generally accepted accounting principles. Financial statement audits also include audits of financial statements prepared in conformity with any of several other comprehensive bases of accounting (OCBOA) discussed in auditing standards issued by the American Institute of Certified Public Accountants (AICPA).

b. **Financial related audits—include determining whether** (1) financial information is presented in accordance with established or stated criteria, (2) the entity has adhered to specific financial compliance requirements, or (3) the entity's internal control structure over financial reporting and/or safeguarding assets is suitably designed and implemented to achieve the control objectives.

For example, financial related audits may include audits of the following:

- Segments of financial statements; financial information (for example, statement of revenue and expenses, statement of cash receipts and disbursements, statement of fixed assets); budget requests; and variances between estimated and actual financial performance.
- Internal controls over compliance with laws and regulations, such as those governing the (1) bidding for, (2) accounting for, and (3) reporting on grants and contracts (including proposals, amounts billed, amounts due on termination claims, and so forth).
- Internal controls over financial reporting and/or safeguarding assets, including controls using computer-based systems.
- Compliance with laws and regulations and allegations of fraud.

**Performance Audits**

a. **Economy and efficiency audits**—include determining (1) whether the entity is acquiring, protecting, and using its resources (such as personnel, property, and space) economically and efficiently, (b) the causes of inefficiencies or uneconomical practices, and (c) whether the entity has complied with laws and regulations concerning matters of economy and efficiency.

b. **Program audits**—include determining (1) the extent to which the desired results or benefits established by the legislature or other authorizing body are being achieved, (b) the effectiveness of the organizations, programs, activities, or functions, and (c) whether the entity has complied with significant laws and regulations applicable to the program.[1]

The purposes of each type of audit identified by the GAO have to do with an evaluation of the responsibility and accountability of public officials. **Financial audits**—financial statement audits and financial related audits—deal with compliance with fiscal requirements. **Performance audits**—economy and efficiency audits and program audits—emphasize managerial effectiveness. An audit intended to fulfill all these purposes or objectives is referred to as a *comprehensive audit.*

Few (if any) audits of governments today are intended to include all aspects of the comprehensive audit in depth. Rather, audits increasingly are designed to meet the specific needs of agency managers, other governments, investors, and the public in a given situation. Thus, whereas some attention may be given to all areas of the comprehensive audit, one aspect may receive the principal thrust of the audit effort while the others receive secondary attention. The **primary thrust** of most contemporary **general audits** of governments is on the financial statements—the **financial and compliance (fiscal)** aspects. Indeed, most state and local governments are subject to the requirements of the Single Audit Act of 1984, as amended in 1996, which focuses on the financial statement audit with specific additional re-

---

[1] Adapted from Comptroller General of the United States, *Government Auditing Standards* (Washington, D.C.: U.S. General Accounting Office, 1994), pp. 12–16. (Emphasis added.) Hereafter cited as the GAO Audit Standards.

quirements with respect to internal control over—and compliance with the provisions of—federal financial assistance programs. However, **special audits** are often directed toward the efficiency and economy or program results (effectiveness) aspects. These various audit aspects (or thrusts) are not mutually exclusive but overlap significantly. The alternative thrusts of public sector auditing and the overlapping nature of these alternative audit thrusts are illustrated in Figure 20–2.

Financial audits are performed by independent public accountants and auditors or by state auditors, whereas performance audits typically are performed by internal audit divisions of a government or by a subunit of a state audit organization. Relatively little performance auditing is conducted by independent public accounting firms. The U.S. General Accounting Office (GAO) has also developed auditing standards for performance audits (summarized later in the chapter) and has published guidelines for conducting performance audit (or review) engagements. The primary focus of this chapter, however, is on *external auditing*—particularly *single audits;* in-depth discussion of performance auditing is beyond the scope of the chapter.

**FIGURE 20–2  Alternative Thrusts of Public Sector Auditing**

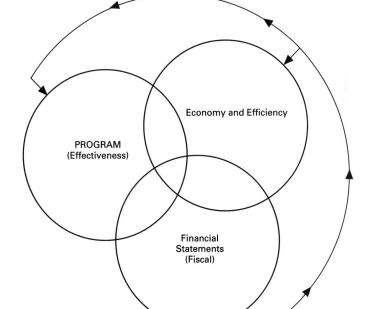

*Most authorities believe that the *minimum* acceptable scope of contemporary public sector audits should include in-depth consideration of the financial and compliance (fiscal) aspects plus review and comment upon significant aspects relative to the economy and efficiency and program results (effectiveness) aspects that come to the auditor's attention during the course of the fiscal audit work. Most state and local government audits require significant internal control and compliance testing because they are subject to the requirements of the Single Audit Act, discussed later.

## Management's Representations

An organization's management is responsible for recording, processing, and reporting on financial and other economic transactions, events, and balances. The reports generated by management contain various representations and assertions about the events summarized. The auditors' responsibilities are to collect objective data that allow them to express an opinion on the accuracy and reliability of the explicit and implicit representations and assertions contained in a given report. If it does not publicly address itself to the other matters, management implicitly asserts that it has complied with the law, has achieved agency and program objectives or has made reasonable progress toward them, and has operated economically and efficiently. Although these representations may not be as specific as those regarding finances, they can be evaluated—and the auditor's opinion may be as useful as if specific representations had been made.

## Classification of External Auditors

External audits are performed by persons who are independent of the administrative organization of the unit audited. There are three groups of independent auditors: (1) those who are officials of the governmental unit being examined, (2) those who are officials of a government other than the one being examined, and (3) independent public accountants and auditors.

Most states and a few municipalities have an independent auditor either elected by the people or appointed by the legislative body. In such cases the auditor is responsible directly to the legislative body or to the people, not to the chief executive or anyone else in the executive branch of the government. Election of the independent auditor works well in some jurisdictions, but in others only minimal qualifications are needed to seek the office and the auditor may be elected "on the coattails" of the governor. The elected auditor's independence and effectiveness are impaired significantly in the latter situation.

The term *auditor* is sometimes applied to the principal accounting officer of a state or county. In such cases the auditor is not, of course, an independent external auditor.

State audit agencies in some states are responsible for auditing local governmental units, either at or without the request of the units. Such audit agencies do not necessarily audit any of the state agencies, though some do. Most local governmental audits are done by independent certified public accountants, however, and state agencies increasingly are concerning themselves with (1) setting standards for the scope and minimum procedures of local government audits in their jurisdiction, (2) reviewing reports prepared by independent auditors to ensure compliance with the standards, (3) performing "spot check" or test audit procedures where audit coverage appears to be insufficient, and (4) accumulating reliable and useful statewide statistics on local government finance.

## The Audit Contract

To ensure that there is no misunderstanding as to the nature, scope, or other aspects of the independent auditor's engagement, the contract should be in written form. Frequently, correspondence is simply exchanged, though formal contracts are generally considered preferable. Among the matters to be covered in the contract are (1) the type and purpose of the audit—including a clear specification of the audit scope, any limitation of the scope, the parties at interest, and whether or not a single audit is to be preformed; (2) the exact departments, funds, agencies, and the like to be audited; (3) the period the audit is to cover; (4) approximate beginning and completion dates and the date of delivery of the report; (5) the number of copies of the report; (6) the information and assistance that the auditee will provide for the auditor; (7) the means of handling unexpected problems, such as the discovery of fraud, which require a more extensive audit than was agreed upon, and the manner by which—and to whom—the auditor is to report any fraud, malfeasance, and so on, discovered; (8) the terms of compensation and reimbursement of the auditor's expenses; and (9) the place at which the audit work will be done.

Preliminary steps in the audit of an organization that uses fund accounting include familiarization with the nature of the organization, investigation of its system of internal control, and familiarization with the appropriate principles of accounting and financial reporting. The auditor must also become knowledgeable of the legal and contractual provisions that govern the agency's fiscal and reporting activities. These include the restrictions governing its revenues and expenditures and those controlling its funds and budget practices. An understanding of the requirements of the Single Audit Act of 1984, as amended, and related implementation guidance is essential as well if the audit is to be a single audit. Some of these preliminary steps, or portions of them, often must be taken before the auditor can determine whether to accept the engagement or before the terms of the engagement may be intelligently agreed upon.

## AUDITING STANDARDS

Audit procedures must be distinguished from audit standards. Standards are guidelines that deal with overall audit quality, whereas procedures are the actual work that is performed. Standards govern the auditor's judgment in deciding which procedures will be used, the way they will be used, when they will be used, and the extent to which they will be used. No listing of audit procedures is attempted here. Many of the procedures for a government audit are essentially the same as those for the examination of a profit-seeking organization; however, the procedures used must be tailored to the characteristics of the organization, which include legal requirements and restrictions, generally accepted accounting principles, and the objectives of the audit.

In conducting audits of governments, auditors must comply with both generally accepted auditing standards (GAAS) established by the AICPA and generally accepted government auditing standards (GAGAS)—the GAO audit standards established by the Comptroller General. GAGAS incorporate but go beyond GAAS. This section provides an overview of GAAS and GAGAS.

### AICPA Auditing Standards—GAAS

The general membership of the American Institute of Certified Public Accountants (AICPA) has approved a set of standards of quality for the performance of an audit. These ten standards apply to all audits—whether private sector or public sector:

- **General Standards**
  1. The audit is to be performed by a person or persons having **adequate technical training and proficiency** as an auditor.
  2. In all matters relating to the assignment an **independence** in mental attitude is to be maintained by the auditor or auditors.

3. **Due professional care** is to be exercised in the performance of the examination and the preparation of the report.

- **Standards of Field Work**
    1. The **work** is to be **adequately planned and assistants,** if any, are to be **properly supervised.**
    2. A **sufficient understanding of the internal control structure** is to be obtained to plan the audit and to determine the nature, timing, and extent of the tests to be performed.
    3. **Sufficient competent evidential matter** is to be obtained through inspection, observation, inquiries, and confirmations to afford a reasonable basis for an opinion regarding the financial statements under examination.
- **Standards of Reporting**
    1. The report shall state **whether** the **financial statements** are presented in accordance with **generally accepted accounting principles.**
    2. The report shall **identify** those **circumstances** in which such **principles** have **not** been **consistently observed** in the current period in relation to the preceding period.
    3. Informative **disclosures** in the financial statements are to be regarded as reasonably adequate unless otherwise stated in the report.
    4. The report shall either contain an expression of **opinion** regarding the financial statements, taken as a whole, **or an assertion** to the effect **that an opinion cannot be expressed.** When an overall opinion cannot be expressed, the reasons therefore should be stated. In all cases where an auditor's name is associated with financial statements the report should contain a clear-cut indication of the character of the auditor's examination, if any, and the degree of responsibility he is taking.[2]

In addition to these ten broad standards, auditors are provided more detailed guidance in *Statements on Auditing Standards* (SASs) issued by the AICPA Auditing Standards Board (ASB). For some special types of audits, including government audits, specific recommended procedures are set forth in AICPA Audit Guides and Statements of Position (SOPs). In the remainder of this chapter, reference to GAAS includes all of these sources and levels of audit standards.

The AICPA audit standards—GAAS—are applicable to examinations of financial statements of organizations that use fund accounting, but some interpretation seems desirable. For example, an auditor may have adequate technical training and proficiency to audit a profit-seeking enterprise but lack the knowledge of governmental accounting or of the laws of a specific government necessary for an adequate audit of a government. If so, the auditor should acquire the necessary knowledge or refuse the engagement. Additional guidance and interpretation are provided by the governmental auditing standards set forth by the Comptroller General of the United States, known as the GAO audit standards or GAGAS.

## Government (GAO) Auditing Standards—GAGAS Overview

Though there are many similarities between auditing profit-seeking and governmental organizations, there are also many differences. Furthermore, there was no comprehensive statement of generally accepted government auditing standards prior to issuance of *Standards for Audit of Governmental Organizations, Programs, Activities & Functions*[3] by the Comptroller General of the United States in 1972. Those standards were designed because:

---

[2] American Institute of Certified Public Accountants, *Codification of Statements on Auditing Standards* (New York: AICPA, 1997), par. 150.02. (Emphasis added.)

[3] Comptroller General of the United States, *Standards for Audit of Governmental Organizations, Programs, Activities & Functions* (Washington, D.C.: U.S. General Accounting Office, 1972).

Public officials, legislators, and the general public want to know whether governmental funds are handled properly and in compliance with existing laws and whether governmental programs are being conducted efficiently, effectively, and economically. They also want to have this information provided, or at least concurred in, by someone who is not an advocate of the program but is independent and objective.

This demand for information has widened the scope of governmental auditing so that such auditing no longer is a function concerned primarily with financial operations. Instead, governmental auditing now is also concerned with whether governmental organizations are achieving the purposes for which programs are authorized and funds are made available, are doing so economically and efficiently, and are complying with applicable laws and regulations. The standards contained in this statement were developed to apply to audits of this wider scope.[4]

The GAO audit standards are intended to be applied in audits of all governmental organizations, programs, activities, and functions—whether they are performed by auditors employed by federal, state, or local governments; independent public accountants; or others qualified to perform parts of the audit work contemplated under the standards. Similarly, they are intended to apply to both internal audits and audits of contractors, grantees, and other external organizations performed by or for a governmental agency. Too, federal legislation requires that (1) the federal inspectors general comply with the GAO audit standards in audits of federal agencies and (2) the GAO audit standards be followed by those conducting audits of state and local governments under the Single Audit Act (discussed later in this chapter). Several state and local government audit agencies have adopted these standards, and the AICPA has issued guidance to its members, discussed later in this chapter, concerning the GAO audit standards.

The GAO auditing standards set forth by the Comptroller General recognize and incorporate the standards of the AICPA. The AICPA standards are recognized as being necessary and appropriate to financial statement audits, but insufficient for the broader scope of governmental auditing. Thus, as noted earlier, the GAO audit standards incorporate the AICPA audit standards and add additional auditing standards that are unique to public sector auditing.

The governmental auditing standards are built around the four categories of postaudits discussed earlier, which include the three elements of a comprehensive audit illustrated in Figure 20–2. Again, these four categories are: (1) financial statement audits, (2) financial related audits, (3) economy and efficiency audits, and (4) program audits. Provision for such a broad audit scope as the comprehensive audit is not intended to imply that all audits are or should be of such an extensive scope. Indeed, the introduction to the original *Standards* publication notes that:

> Auditors may perform audits that are a combination of the above or audits that include only some aspects of one of the above. It is not intended, or even feasible or desirable, that every audit include all of the above.
>
> The above expansion of governmental auditing highlights the importance of a clear understanding of the audit scope by all interested parties. This takes on added importance when contracting and/or arranging for audits. The engagement agreement should specify the scope of the work to be performed to avoid misunderstandings.[5]

Because the standards are structured so that any one of the four categories of audits can be performed separately, if desired, it is essential (1) that audit contracts

[4] Ibid., p. i.
[5] Ibid., pp. 1–6.

or letters of engagement specifically identify the scope of the audit and (2) that the auditor's report clearly indicate the scope of the audit as well. Obviously, in the governmental environment an audit is not necessarily synonymous with a financial audit—because the scope of audit engagements varies considerably.

## GAO Auditing Standards (GAGAS) Summary

The GAO audit standards (GAGAS), as stated in the 1994 revision,[6] are summarized in Figure 20–3.

FIGURE 20–3  **Government (GAO) Auditing Standards—GAGAS**

**SCOPE OF AUDIT WORK**

| ▪ **Financial Audits**<br>—Financial Statement Audits<br>—Financial Related Audits | ▪ **Performance Audits**<br>—Economy and Efficiency Audits<br>—Program Audits |
|---|---|

**GENERAL STANDARDS**

| ▪ Qualifications<br>▪ Independence | ▪ Due Professional Care<br>▪ Quality Control |
|---|---|

**FIELD WORK AND REPORTING STANDARDS**

| FINANCIAL AUDITS | PERFORMANCE AUDITS |
|---|---|
| ▪ **Field Work Standards**<br>—Planning<br>—Irregularities, Illegal Acts, and Other Noncompliance<br>—Internal Controls<br>—Working Papers<br>—Financial Related Audits<br>▪ **Reporting Standards**<br>—Communication with Audit Committees or Other Responsible Individuals<br>—Report Compliance with Generally Accepted Government Auditing Standards<br>—Report on Compliance with Laws and Regulations and on Internal Controls<br>—Privileged and Confidential Information<br>—Report Distribution<br>—Reporting on Finance-Related Audits | ▪ **Field Work Standards**<br>—Planning<br>—Supervision<br>—Compliance with Laws and Regulations<br>—Management Controls<br>—Evidence<br>▪ **Reporting Standards**<br>—Form<br>—Timeliness<br>—Report Contents<br>—Report Presentation<br>—Report Distribution |

*Source:* Comptroller General of the United States, *Government Auditing Standards* (Washington, D.C.: U.S. General Accounting Office, 1994).

---

[6] Comptroller General of the United States, *Government Auditing Standards* (Washington, D.C.: U.S. General Accounting Office, 1994).

Among the particularly significant aspects of the GAO government auditing standards, or GAGAS, are that:

1. The AICPA auditing standards, or GAAS, are adopted and incorporated into GAGAS.
2. GAGAS include additional supplemental standards for government audits.
3. The GAGAS supplemental field work and reporting standards for financial audits require that
   - audit planning must consider the requirements of all levels of governments.
   - the auditor's report must include a statement that the audit was made in accordance with generally accepted *government* auditing standards (GAGAS).
   - the auditor must make written reports on the auditor's
     — tests of compliance with applicable laws and regulations, and
     — understanding of the entity's internal control structure and the assessment of control risk made as part of a financial audit.
4. GAGAS also require specified types of continuing professional education by auditors of state and local government.

## AUDITING PROCEDURES

Whereas audit standards provide guidelines for what an audit should accomplish, audit procedures are specific tests and other activities performed to accomplish those objectives. An authoritative coverage of government auditing procedures is contained in *Audits of State and Local Governmental Units (ASLGU),*[7] an AICPA industry audit and accounting guide. The auditor should be thoroughly familiar with the latest revision of this guide. In addition, several states and state CPA societies prescribe or recommend minimum audit programs or procedures. Audit guides are also available for some federal programs. These should be studied carefully by the auditor in formulating an audit program. Finally, guidelines are available for those performing financial and compliance audits, economy and efficiency audits, and program audits. Several of these are cited in the following sections.

## THE FINANCIAL STATEMENT (FISCAL) AUDIT

The usual purpose of a financial statement audit is to determine whether the financial statements of the government being audited fairly present the financial position and operating results of the funds and account groups of a government (and the changes in financial position of its proprietary funds) in accordance with GAAP. In making this determination, the auditor must, among other things, ascertain whether the entity has complied with laws and regulations applicable to transactions and events for which noncompliance might have a material effect on the entity's financial statements. Legal compliance is considered an integral part both of managerial responsibility and accountability and of the fiscal audit of governments. The financial statement audit must be concerned with the possibility that noncompliance might create contingent or actual liabilities—or invalidate receivables—that are material to the entity's financial statements. The legal constraints under which governments operate and control orientation of governmental accounting systems

---

[7] Government Accounting and Auditing Committee, American Institute of Certified Public Accountants, *Audits of State and Local Governmental Units* (New York: AICPA, 1998). Hereafter cited as *ASLGU.*

have been commented upon at numerous points throughout this book. Obviously, the accountability process is incomplete if the audit of the financial statements does not include the legal compliance aspects within its scope or these are not included in the auditor's report.

## Auditing Standards

The AICPA standards are designed for the financial aspects of the financial statement audit and, as noted earlier, are incorporated in the GAO audit standards. The laws, regulations, and other legal constraints under which the government operates establish the standards against which legal compliance is measured.

## Audit Procedures

The procedures commonly employed in financial statement auditing are covered adequately in most auditing textbooks. But they usually must be adapted to the G&NP environment.

Specific guidance for audits of governments, hospitals, colleges and universities, voluntary health and welfare organizations, and other nonprofit organizations is available in the several AICPA audit guides for these types of organizations, cited at various points in this text. The most detailed guidance to the procedural aspects of fiscal audits generally is contained in *ASLGU,* the state and local government audit guide. This guide covers topics such as audit standards to be applied, audit procedures to be followed, audit reports to be prepared, planning the audit, audit workpapers, compliance with legal and regulatory requirements, study of internal control, and tests of account balances.

The procedures involved in auditing legal compliance will vary with the circumstances. The auditor must determine the legal provisions of laws, ordinances, bond indentures, grants, and so on that are applicable in the situation. The auditor then determines the extent to which they have been complied with and the adequacy of the disclosure in the financial statements in this regard. The auditor must also obtain reasonable assurance that the auditee has not incurred significant unrecorded liabilities through failure to comply with, or through violation of, pertinent laws and regulations.

## The Audit Report

The auditor's report on a financial statement audit of a government is similar to an auditor's report for the audit of corporate financial statements, as is seen in Figure 13–4, the auditor's report on the city of Orlando, Florida, financial statements. The key differences in an auditor's report on the examination of government financial statements result from (1) the need to follow generally accepted governmental auditing standards (GAGAS) as well as GAAS and (2) the different levels of financial statements—combined, combining, and individual fund and account group statements—as discussed in Chapter 13. Because an auditor can assume differing levels of responsibility for differing levels of financial statements, the audit report must clearly indicate the responsibility assumed for the different levels of financial statements as well as for any accompanying information. The GASB position on the degree of responsibility that auditors should accept for different levels of financial statements is that:

> The general purpose financial statements (GPFS) . . . are designed to present fairly the financial position of the fund types and account groups, the results of operations by

fund type, and the changes in financial position of the proprietary funds in conformity with generally accepted accounting principles. Thus, the GPFS comprise the minimum acceptable scope of annual audits.

It is recommended that the scope of the annual audit also encompass the combining and individual financial statements of the funds and account groups. . . .[8]

Thus, the GASB clearly would approve of audit reports like that in Figure 13–4 in which the auditor accepts full responsibility for all levels of statements presented.

As noted earlier, GAGAS also require the auditor to issue written reports regarding auditee internal control and compliance with applicable laws and regulations. Although these are not opinion reports, they can be very important to grantors and others who attempt to evaluate the auditee entity's management style and abilities.

Finally, although the independent auditor is engaged primarily to render an opinion on the financial statements, one of the auditor's most valuable services can be to provide analyses and recommendations on related matters learned of during the examination. This additional information typically is presented in a letter to responsible officials known as the *management letter.* In the management letter the auditor provides discussions, analyses, and recommendations on operational matters such as accounting systems and procedures, including internal accounting and administrative controls; protection, utilization, and disposition of assets; number of funds; cash management; organizational arrangements; and insurance and bonding practices.

# THE SINGLE AUDIT

The $1.3+ trillion of federal grants to, and contracts with, state and local governments, universities, hospitals, and other not-for-profit organizations each year has led to greater scrutiny of the use of federal financial assistance and the method of auditing entities for compliance with grant provisions and other federal requirements. These factors resulted in the development of the concept known as the **single audit.** Several states also require the auditor to include *state* financial aid programs in the scope of single audits.

To illustrate the single audit concept, consider Figure 20–4, which presents one way that a state or local government might be viewed from a financial standpoint.

- The rectangle represents a government entity—for which the basic financial statements are prepared by fund type and account group. Its top part is assumed to be nonfederal resources used to finance the government's expenditures; the bottom portion of the diagram represents resources provided to the SLG by the federal government, that is, federal financial assistance.

- Each circle in this section of the diagram is assumed to be resources received from a separate federal financial assistance *program.* Most governments receive resources from various programs.

- Smaller circles for individual grants or contracts might also be drawn within each program circle. Governments may have literally hundreds of individual grants and contracts, several of which may be provided under the same federal financial assistance program.

- Two or more programs that are closely related and subject to common compliance requirements are called a *cluster* of programs.

---

[8] GASB *Codification,* Appendix D, pars. 103–104.

FIGURE 20–4 A State or Local Government: Federal vs. Nonfederal Resources

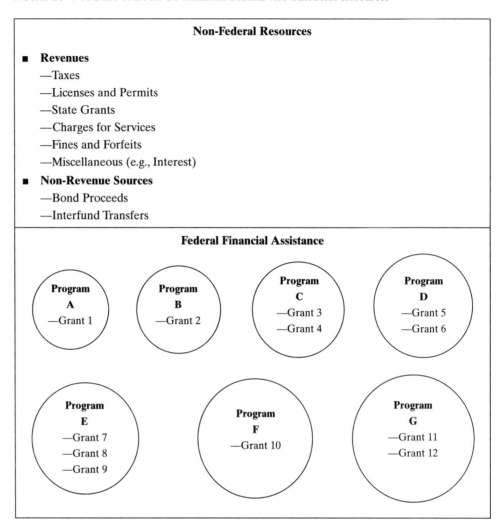

## Grant by Grant Audits

Before the single audit concept was developed, federal agencies responsible for the various federal financial assistance programs typically required nonfederal recipients of program grants or contracts to have an audit conducted of each grant or contract. Each of these numerous special audits was designed to ensure that resources provided to the recipient under a specific grant or contract had been used only for purposes allowable under that grant or contract and that the recipient had complied with any other legal requirements and agency regulations related to the program.

As a result of this grant by grant, contract by contract, or program by program approach to auditing federal financial assistance programs, state and local governments (and other nonfederal organizations that received federal assistance) were subjected to numerous different audits by various federal and state audit agencies and independent public accountants. Most of the audits were limited in scope to different facets of the organization's operations, such as a research grant, the food stamp program, or a day care center. In other words, such audits typically covered only one of the many grants or programs (circles) in the bottom portion of Figure 20–4.

The basic notion of the single audit is that one audit can provide both (1) a basis for an opinion on the recipient entity's financial statements and (2) a basis for determining whether federal financial assistance program resources are being used appropriately and in accordance with legal and contractual requirements.

One disadvantage of the single audit approach from the perspective of some grantor agencies, however, is that the grantor agencies do not receive as much information about the grant programs as they do when separate grant audits are performed. As a result, some grantor agencies require work to be done that goes beyond the single audit requirements. Grantor agencies have the right to require such additional work when necessary to fulfill their oversight responsibilities as long as they pay the additional audit costs. Thus, whereas most federal financial assistance is audited using the single audit concept discussed here, some grant by grant and program by program audits are still performed either in addition to the single audit or instead of a single audit under some of the options and exceptions permitted by the Single Audit Act of 1984, as amended in 1996. Too, some state audit agencies perform grant by grant audits on selected state assistance programs.

## Purposes of a Single Audit

Congress stated that the purposes of the Single Audit Act are to:

- Improve the financial management and accountability of state and local governments (SLGs) and nonprofit organizations (NPOs) with respect to federal financial assistance programs;
- Establish uniform requirements for audits of federal financial assistance provided to state and local governments and nonprofit organizations;
- Promote the efficient and effective use of audit resources; and
- Ensure that federal departments and agencies rely upon and use audit work done pursuant to the Act to the maximum extent practicable.

Under the Act, a single audit is to achieve several audit objectives:

- **Related to the Entity as a Whole**—both parts of the box representing the SLG or NPO in Figure 20–4—The audit should be designed to determine whether the basic financial statements fairly present the financial position and results of operations in accordance with GAAP (or the non-GAAP basis indicated). This also includes:
  —Determining whether the government or other nonprofit organization has complied with laws and regulations with which noncompliance may have a material effect on the financial statements of the entity.
  —Studying and evaluating internal controls of the entity to determine the nature, extent, and timing of the auditing procedures necessary to express an opinion on the entity's financial statements.
- **Related to All Federal Financial Assistance Programs**—The audit should determine whether:
  —The supplementary schedule of expenditures of federal awards is fairly stated in all material respects in relation to the basic financial statements taken as a whole. (An example schedule of federal expenditures of federal awards is presented in Figure 20–9.)
  —The government or NPO has established internal control systems, including both accounting and administrative controls, to provide reasonable assurance that federal monies are managed in compliance with applicable laws and regulations.
  —The SLG or NPO has complied with the laws and regulations that may have a material effect on each major federal assistance program.

## Single Audit Overview

The single audit incorporates both GAAS and GAGAS—and also requires additional audit procedures and reports with respect to federal financial assistance (FFA) programs. Four illustrations have proven helpful in overviewing the single audit before studying its details:

Figure 20–5: GAAS—GAGAS—Single Audit Relationships

Figure 20–6: Levels of Reporting in Single Audits

Figure 20–7: Applicability of the Single Audit Act and OMB Circular A-133

Figure 20–8: GAAS, Governmental Audit Standards, and Single Audit—SASs 68 and 74

Figure 20–5 illustrates how GAGAS incorporates but adds requirements beyond GAAS, and how a single audit incorporates GAGAS (including GAAS) and adds requirements beyond GAGAS. Figure 20–6 indicates from an audit reporting perspective how the single audit encompasses and goes beyond the requirements of GAAS and GAGAS. (The bottom of the pyramid diagram indicates the additional single audit reports required.)

**FIGURE 20–5  GAAS—GAGAS—Single Audit Relationships**

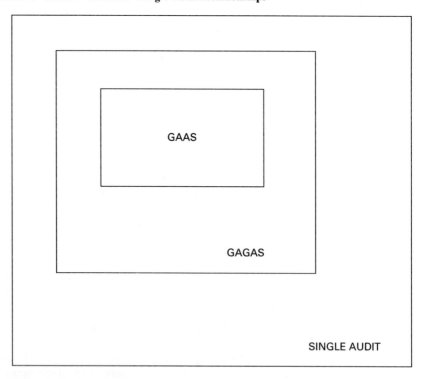

■  GAGAS incorporates GAAS – and includes
      additional requirements

■  SINGLE AUDIT incorporates GAGAS – and
      includes additional requirements

FIGURE 20-6  **Levels of Reporting Single Audits**

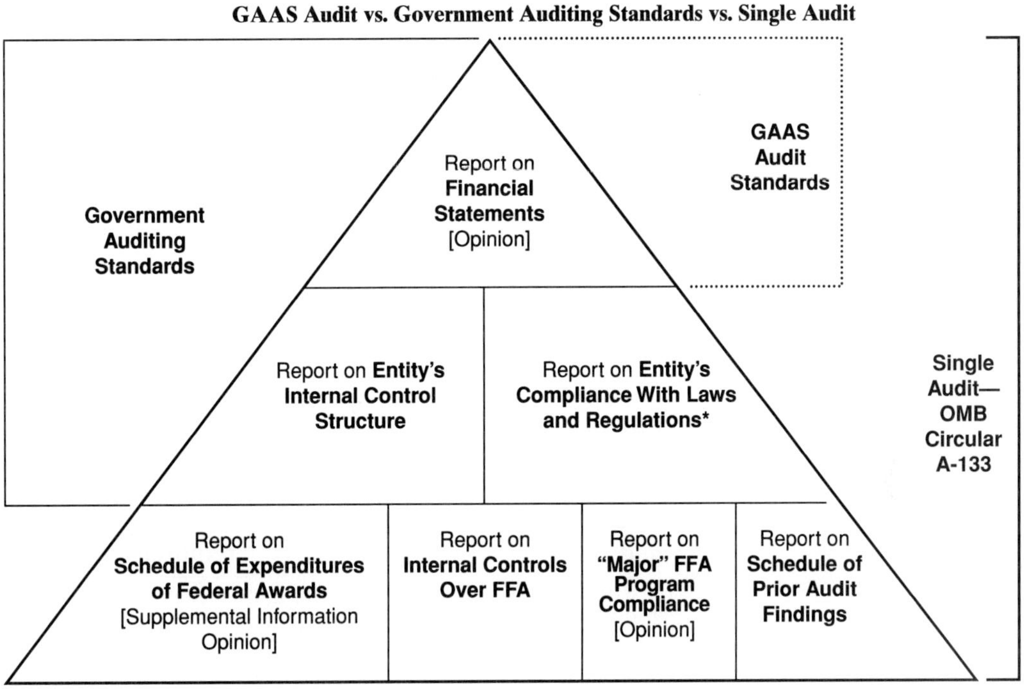

**GAAS Audit vs. Government Auditing Standards vs. Single Audit**

*A report on illegal acts may also be required.
*Source:* Adapted from American Institute of Certified Public Accountants, *Audits of State and Local Governmental Units* (New York: AICPA, 1994).

Figure 20-7 summarizes the applicability of the Single Audit Act and OMB Circular A-133. Figure 20-8 provides a more detailed overview of the single audit processes and reports. Too, Figure 20-8 is designed to be referred to often as the single audit section of this chapter is studied and reviewed.

## Applicability of the Single Audit Act

The Single Audit Act of 1984—as amended in 1996 and implemented by OMB Circular A-133—generally requires SLGs and nonprofit organizations that expend $300,000 or more of federal financial assistance in a fiscal year to have a single audit for that fiscal year. This $300,000 expenditure threshold amount may be increased by the OMB but may not be decreased.

The Act permits some exceptions to these requirements. Specifically, a series of audits of the SLG's or NPO's individual departments, agencies, and establishments for the same fiscal year satisfies the audit requirements of the Act—providing all operations are included. Too, in some circumstances, the SLG or NPO may have a *program-specific audit* of the federal financial assistance (FFA) program(s) rather than a single audit.

Finally, SLGs and NPOs that expend less than $300,000 in federal financial assistance in any fiscal year are exempt from the single audit requirements—as well as other federal audit requirements—for that year. However, these governments

FIGURE 20–7  **Applicability of the Single Audit Act and OMB Circular A-133**

```
┌─────────────────────────┐                    ┌─────────────────────────┐
│ Did the non-Federal     │        No          │ No single audit or      │
│ entity expend $300,000* │ ─────────────────► │ program-specific audit  │
│ or more of federal      │                    │ required—only GAAS and  │
│ awards?                 │                    │ GAGAS required.         │
└─────────────────────────┘                    └─────────────────────────┘
            │
           Yes
            │
            ▼
┌─────────────────────────┐
│ Did the non-federal     │
│ entity                  │
│ (1) expend federal      │
│     awards under only   │
│     one federal         │        Yes         ┌─────────────────────────┐
│     program—which does  │ ─────────────────► │ A program-specific      │
│     not require a       │                    │ audit is required.      │
│     financial statement │                    └─────────────────────────┘
│     audit,              │
│ (2) meet other          │
│     requirements, and   │
│ (3) properly elect a    │
│     program-specific    │
│     audit?              │
└─────────────────────────┘
            │
            No
            │
            ▼
┌─────────────────────────┐
│ A single audit is       │
│ required.               │
└─────────────────────────┘
```

*The OMB can raise this expenditure threshold in the future but may not lower it.

must keep adequate accounting records and make them available for inspection and audit upon request.

The applicability of the Single Audit Act, as amended in 1996, and OMB Circular A-133 are summarized in Figure 20–7 and illustrated in more detail in Figure 20–8.

## Federal Financial Assistance/Awards Defined

Federal financial assistance is defined in the Act as assistance provided by a federal agency—that nonfederal entities receive or administer—in the form of grants, contracts, cooperative agreements, loans, loan guarantees, property, interest subsidies, insurance, food commodities, or direct appropriations—including both direct federal awards received and those received indirectly (*pass through*) from other SLGs.[9] Direct cash assistance to individuals is not considered federal financial assistance under the Act. In sum, federal financial assistance is defined to include all assistance provided by federal agencies to state or local governments, even if that aid is subsequently passed on to other governments, organizations, or individuals. Federal financial awards are defined by OMB Circular A-133 as including both

---

[9] Single Audit Act of 1984, as amended in 1996.

# FIGURE 20–8  GAAS, Governmental Audit Standards, and Single Audits

## Auditor Reports Required

- GAAS—1
- Government Audit Standards—1, 2, 3, (7) [GAGAS]
- Single Audit—1, 2, 3, 4, 5, 6, (7)

Financial Audit

Single Audit *

### Basic Financial Statements

| Accounts | GF | SRFs | CPFs | EFs | ... | Total |
|---|---|---|---|---|---|---|
| | | | | | | (Memo Only) |
| | Included in the above are | | | | | |
| | G1 nm | G3 M | G5 M | G6 nm | | |
| | G2 nm | G4 nm | | | | |

### Internal Control Structure

"Detailed Study" Test Controls (50%/25% Rule)

| No Requirements | | | | |
|---|---|---|---|---|
| nm | nm | M | M | M |
| No Requirements | | | Audit(s) | |

**Legend**

M = Major FFA Program
nm = Nonmajor FFA Program
G = Grant

### Schedule of Expenditures of Federal Awards

| | Expenditures |
|---|---|
| **Agency 1** | |
| **Program A** | |
| Grant 1 | xx |
| Grant n | xx |
| **Program B** | |
| ~~~ ~~~ ~~~ ~~~ | xx |
| **Agency N** | |
| **Program A** | |
| ~~~ ~~~ ~~~ ~~~ | |
| **Total** | XX |

\* Additional Requirements beyond Financial Audit

## AUDITOR REPORTS

### I. For the Entity

1. **Financial Statements**
   [Auditor Opinion (or Disclaimer)]

2. **Internal Accounting Control**
   [overall—based on financial statement audit: SASs 55, 60, 78, and GAGAS]

3. **Compliance**
   [overall—based on financial statement audit: SASs 53, 54, 68, and 74]

### II. For the Federal Programs

4. **Schedule of Expenditures of Federal Awards**
   [Auditor "Supplemental Information" Opinion]

5. **Internal Control over Federal Programs**

6. **Compliance** [with Federal program rules and regulations—including a Schedule of Findings and Questioned Costs and a Summary Schedule of Prior Audit Findings] M—Specific Requirements
   [Auditor Opinion (or Disclaimer)]

7. **Fraud, irregularities, etc.** [if any noted]

**Notes**: Auditor reports 2 and 3 are usually combined, as are reports 5 and 6. Alternatively, auditor reports 2 and 5 may be combined, as can be reports 3 and 6.

I. For the Entity
2. Internal Accounting Control—report "material weaknesses" and "reportable conditions."
3. Compliance—report "material" noncompliance
II. For the Federal Programs
5. Internal Control over Federal Programs—"materiality" based on programs.
6. Compliance—report "material" noncompliance.

federal financial assistance (including loans) and cost-reimbursement-type contracts. A schedule of expenditures of federal awards is illustrated in Figure 20–9.

## Auditee Responsibilities

The auditee government or nonprofit organization is required to:

1. Identify in its accounts all federal awards received and expended and the federal programs under which they were received.

2. Maintain internal controls over federal programs that provide reasonable assurance that the auditee is managing federal awards in compliance with laws, regulations, and the provisions of contracts or grant agreements that could have a material effect on each of its federal programs.

3. Comply with laws, regulations, and the provisions of contracts or grant agreements related to each of its federal programs.

**FIGURE 20–9  Schedule of Expenditures of Federal Awards**

A City
**Schedule of Expenditures of Federal Awards**
Year Ended June 30, 19X4

| *Federal Grantor/ Program Title/Grant Number* | *Federal CFDA Number* | *Expenditures* |
|---|---|---|
| MAJOR PROGRAMS: | | |
| U.S. Department of Housing and Urban Development: | | |
| Community Development Block Grant | | |
| B-94-MC-12-0026 | 14.218 | |
| B-93-MC-12-0026 | 14.218 | $  517,690 |
| B-92-MC-12-0026 | 14.218 | 364,132 |
| B-90-MC-12-0026 | 14.218 | 147,900 |
| | | 1,029,722 |
| | | |
| U.S. Department of Justice/Office of National Drug Control: | | |
| High Intensity Drug Trafficking Area Grant; Southeast | | |
| Florida Regional Task Force Program | | |
| 93-HJ-H3-K042 | 16.580 | 273,117 |
| 94-HJ-I4-K005 | 16.580 | |
| GE-3-M24 | 16.580 | 52,416 |
| | | 325,533 |
| Total major programs | | 1,355,255 |
| NON-MAJOR PROGRAM: | | |
| U.S. Department of Agriculture: | | |
| Pass through Florida Department of Education; Summer | | |
| Food Service Program | | |
| 04-984 | 10.559 | 27,743 |
| Total nonmajor program | | 27,743 |
| Total federal financial assistance | | $1,382,998 |

See notes to schedule of federal financial assistance.

4. Prepare appropriate financial statements, including the schedule of expenditures of federal awards.

5. Ensure that the audits required are properly performed and the audit reports are submitted when due.

6. Follow up and take corrective action on audit findings, which includes preparing a summary schedule of prior audit findings and a corrective action plan.

## Auditor Responsibilities: Scope of the Single Audit

OMB Circular A-133 summarizes the auditor's responsibilities—and the scope of the single audit—in six topic areas: (a) general, (b) financial statements, (c) internal control, (d) compliance, (e) audit follow-up, and (f) data collection form. These six topic areas include:

1. **General.**
    (a) The audit must be conducted in accordance with GAGAS.
    (b) The audit must cover the entire operations of the auditee. (At the option of the auditee, the audit may include a series of audits covering all its departments, agencies, and other organizational units that expended or administered federal awards during the fiscal year.)
    (c) The financial statements and schedule of expenditures of federal awards must be for the same fiscal year.

2. **Financial Statements.** The auditor is required to determine:
    (a) Whether the auditee's financial statements are presented fairly in all material respects in conformity with generally accepted accounting principles, and
    (b) Whether the schedule of expenditures of federal awards is presented fairly in all material respects in relation to the auditee's financial statements taken as a whole.

3. **Internal Control.** The A-133 guidance on internal control is relatively specific:
    (a) In addition to the requirements of GAGAS, the auditor must perform procedures to obtain an understanding of the internal control over federal programs sufficient to plan the audit to support a low assessed level of control risk for major programs.
    (b) Except as provided in 3(c), the auditor must:
        (i) Plan the testing of internal control over major programs to support a low assessed level of control risk for the assertions relevant to the compliance requirements for each major program; and
        (ii) Perform testing of internal control as planned in paragraph 3(b)(i).
    (c) When internal controls over some or all of the compliance requirements for a major program are likely to be ineffective in preventing or detecting noncompliance, the planning and performing of testing described in paragraph 3(b) are not required for those compliance requirements. However, the auditor must report a reportable condition (including whether any such condition is a material weakness), assess the related control risk at the maximum, and consider whether additional compliance tests are required because of ineffective internal control.

4. **Compliance.**
    (a) In addition to the requirements of GAGAS, the auditor must determine whether the auditee has complied with laws, regulations, and the provisions of contracts or grant agreements that may have a direct and material effect on each of its major programs.
    (b) The principal compliance requirements applicable to most federal programs and the compliance requirements of the largest federal programs are included in the OMB *compliance supplement.*
        • An audit of the compliance requirements related to federal programs contained in the compliance supplement will meet the requirements of A-133.
        • Where there have been changes to the compliance requirements and the changes are not reflected in the compliance supplement, the auditor must determine the current compliance requirements and modify the audit procedures accordingly.

(c) For federal programs not covered in the compliance supplement, the auditor should use the types of compliance requirements contained in the compliance supplement as guidance for identifying the types of compliance requirements to test, and determine the requirements governing the federal program by reviewing the provisions of contracts and grant agreements and the laws and regulations referred to in the contracts and grant agreements.

(d) The compliance testing must include tests of transactions and other auditing procedures necessary to provide the auditor sufficient evidence to support an opinion on compliance.

5. **Audit Follow-up.** The auditor is required to:

(a) Follow up on prior audit findings, perform procedures to assess the reasonableness of the summary schedule of prior audit findings, and

(b) Report—as a current year audit finding—when the auditor concludes that the summary schedule of prior audit findings materially misrepresents the status of any prior audit finding. (The auditor must perform audit follow-up procedures regardless of whether a prior audit finding relates to a major program in the current year.)

6. **Data Collection Form.** The auditor must complete and sign specified sections of the data collection form (Appendix 20–2).

These scope elements permeate the single audit planning, performance, and reporting processes discussed and illustrated in this chapter.

## Auditing Standards, Guidance, and Relationships

Several sources of guidance are available to those conducting a single audit. Such guidance typically is available in publications, loose-leaf services, and on the Internet. (For example, much guidance is available at http://www.financenet.com.) The Single Audit Act requires generally accepted governmental auditing standards (GAGAS) to be applied in conducting audits under the Act. The Act defines GAGAS as "the standards for audit of governmental organizations, programs, activities, and functions, issued by the Comptroller General."[10] These standards are in *Standards for Audit of Governmental Organizations, Programs, Activities, and Functions*—commonly referred to as the "GAO Audit Standards," or simply as the "Yellow Book"—that are summarized earlier in this chapter.

As noted in Figures 20–5, 20–6, and 20–8, the requirements of the Single Audit Act go beyond those of GAAS and GAGAS. For example, the level of compliance auditing and internal control study and evaluation is much more extensive than that required by GAGAS for a financial statement audit. Thus, auditors who conduct single audits must be familiar with the act and related implementation guidance provided in OMB Circular A-133 as well as with GAGAS and the OMB A-133 Compliance Supplement—which summarizes relevant federal rules and regulations and includes suggested compliance auditing procedures. Too, the AICPA state and local government audit guide (ASLGU) and related statements of position (SOPs) and the OMB A-133 "questions and answers" publication provide extensive implementation guidance based upon the Act, OMB Circular A-133, and extensive consultations with representatives of the OMB, the GAO, and the inspectors general.

Two other sources of implementation guidance are the President's Council on Integrity and Efficiency (PCIE) and the auditee's cognizant agency. The PCIE is composed of the federal inspectors general and is responsible for overseeing implementation of the single audit. The PCIE issues statements of position on issues related to the single audit occasionally as questions and problems arise.

---

[10] Single Audit Act of 1984, sec. 7501(7).

Federal *cognizant agencies* are federal agencies assigned by the OMB to oversee implementation of the single audit. Cognizant agencies are assigned for states and local governments that expend more than $25 million of federal financial assistance annually. (Other governments are under the general oversight of the federal agency or department from which they receive the most *direct* assistance in a particular year.) OMB Circular A-133 places the following **responsibilities** on **cognizant agencies:**

1. Provide technical audit advice and liaison to auditees and auditors.

2. Consider auditee requests for extensions to the report submission due date. (The cognizant agency for audit may grant extensions for good cause.)

3. Obtain or conduct quality control reviews of selected audits made by nonfederal auditors; and, when appropriate, provide the results to other interested organizations.

4. Promptly inform other affected federal agencies and appropriate federal law enforcement officials of any direct reporting by the auditee or its auditor of irregularities or illegal acts, as required by GAGAS or laws and regulations.

5. Advise the auditor and, where appropriate, the auditee of any deficiencies found in the audits when the deficiencies require corrective action by the auditor. (Major inadequacies or repetitive substandard performance by auditors are referred to appropriate state licensing agencies and professional bodies for disciplinary action.)

6. Coordinate audits or reviews made by or for federal agencies that are in addition to single audits and program-specific audits, so that additional audits or reviews build upon these audits.

7. Coordinate a management decision for audit findings that affect the federal programs of more than one agency.

8. Coordinate the audit work and reporting responsibilities among auditors to achieve the most cost-effective audit.

9. For biennial audits consider auditee requests to qualify as a "low-risk auditee."[11]

In view of the oversight, technical assistance, and quality control responsibilities of cognizant agencies, auditors often seek the advice or concurrence of the cognizant agency when planning and conducting a single audit. In addition to the federal cognizant agencies, some states assign cognizant agencies to local governments in the state—particularly to those that have no federal cognizant agency.

## Major Federal Financial Assistance Program (MFAP)

The Single Audit Act does not modify the auditing procedures designed to determine whether the entity's financial statements fairly present its financial position and operating results. However, it requires that extensive work be performed by the auditor to determine (1) whether laws and grant provisions that might have a material effect on major federal financial assistance programs have been complied with and (2) whether internal control systems have been established over federal financial assistance programs to ensure that the resources are expended in accordance with applicable laws and grant provisions. Because the audit focus is on *major* programs, it is important to understand the Act's definition of a *major federal financial assistance program* (MFAP)—and to recall that the OMB Circular A-133 federal financial assistance definition includes cost-type contracts in defining federal financial awards subject to single audit.

---

[11] Office of Management and Budget (OMB), Circular No. A-133, "Audits of State and Local Governments," April 22, 1997, pp. 18–19. (Emphasis added.)

The auditor uses a four-step **risk-based approach** to determine which federal programs are **major** programs. This approach includes consideration of program size, the current and prior audit experience, oversight by federal agencies and pass-through entities, and the inherent risk of the federal program, and is summarized in Figure 20–10.

**Step 1.** The auditor identifies the larger federal programs, which are called **Type A** programs. Type A programs are defined as federal programs with federal awards expended during the audit period of the *larger of:*

- $300,000 or 3% (.03) of total federal awards expended in the case of an auditee for which total federal awards expended equal or exceed $300,000 but are less than or equal to $100 million.
- $3 million or three-tenths of 1% (.003) of total federal awards expended in the case of an auditee for which total federal awards expended exceed $100 million but are less than or equal to $10 billion.
- $30 million or fifteen-hundredths of 1% (.0015) of total federal awards expended in the case of an auditee for which total federal awards expended exceed $10 billion.

The smaller federal programs that are not Type A programs are called **Type B** programs.

FIGURE 20–10  **Risk-Based Approach Major Program Determination**

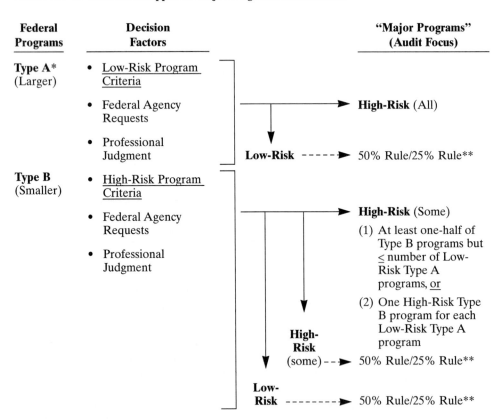

*Each Type A program must be considered a major program at least once every three years.
**At least *50%* of total federal program expenditures must be audited as major programs—*except* only *25%* of total federal program expenditures of auditees meeting specific *low-risk auditee criteria* must be audited as major programs.

**Step 2.**  The auditor then identifies **low-risk** Type A programs:

- Type A programs considered low risk
  (1) have been audited as a major program in at least one of the last two years audited, and
  (2) in the most recent audit period, had no audit findings that must be reported.
- The auditor may use judgment. For example, most audit findings from questioned costs, fraud, and audit follow-up for the summary schedule of prior audit findings do not preclude a Type A program from being considered low risk.
- The auditor also considers the federal program risk criteria specified in OMB Circular A-133, results of audit follow-up, and whether any changes in personnel or systems affecting a Type A program have significantly increased risk.
- Finally, the auditor considers any federal agency requests and applies professional judgment in determining whether a Type A program is low risk.

Regardless of the auditor's judgments, however, the OMB may approve a federal awarding agency's request that a Type A program at certain recipients may not be considered low risk.

**Step 3.**  The auditor identifies **high-risk** Type B programs using professional judgment and the federal program risk criteria in OMB A-133. These criteria are summarized in Figure 20–11. Note also that:

- If the auditor selects Option 2 under Step 4 below, he or she is not required to identify more high-risk Type B programs than the number of low-risk Type A programs.
- Except for known reportable conditions in internal control or significant compliance problems, a single program risk criteria would not usually cause a Type B program to be considered high risk.

The auditor is not expected to perform risk assessments on relatively small federal programs. Thus, the auditor is only required to perform risk assessments on Type B programs that exceed the larger of:

- $100,000 or three-tenths of 1% (.003) of total federal awards expended when the auditee has less than or equal to $100 million in total federal awards expended.
- $300,000 or three-hundredths of 1% (.0003) of total federal awards expended when the auditee has more than $100 million in total federal awards expended.

**Step 4.**  At a minimum, the *auditor is required to audit all of the following as major programs:*

- All Type A programs, except the auditor may exclude any Type A programs identified as low risk under Step 2.
- High-risk Type B programs as identified under either of the following two options:
  (1) Option 1.  At least one-half of the Type B programs identified as high risk under Step 3, except the auditor is not required to audit more high-risk Type B programs than the number of low-risk Type A programs identified as low risk under Step 2.
  (2) Option 2.  One high-risk Type B program for each Type A program identified as low risk under Step 2.
  The OMB encourages auditors identifying which high-risk Type B programs to audit as major, under either Option 1 or 2, to use an approach that provides an opportunity for different high-risk Type B programs to be audited as major over a period of time.
- Such additional programs as may be necessary to comply with the **percentage of coverage rule.** This may require the auditor to audit more programs as major than the number of Type A programs.

The **percentage of coverage rule** requires that programs classified as major federal programs, in the aggregate, encompass at least **50%** of total federal awards expended. If the auditee meets the criteria for a **low-risk auditee,** the major federal programs audited must, in the aggregate, encompass at least **25%** of total federal awards expended. The low-risk auditee criteria are summarized in Figure 20–12.

**FIGURE 20–11 Criteria for Federal Program Risk**

(a) **General.** The auditor's risk assessment should be based on an overall evaluation of the risk of noncompliance occurring that could be material to the federal program. The auditor should use judgment and consider criteria—such as described in (b), (c), and (d)—to identify risk in federal programs. Also, as part of the risk analysis, the auditor may wish to discuss a particular federal program with auditee management and the federal grantor agency or pass-through entity.

(b) **Current and prior audit experience.**

(1) Weaknesses in internal control over federal programs may indicate high risk.

- A federal program administered under multiple internal control structures may have high risk.
- When significant parts of a federal program are passed through to subrecipients, a weak system for monitoring subrecipients indicates high risk.
- The extent to which computer processing is used to administer federal programs, as well as the complexity of that processing, should be considered in assessing risk. New and recently modified computer systems may also indicate risk.

(2) Prior audit findings may indicate high risk, particularly when the situations identified in the audit findings could have a significant impact on a federal program or have not been corrected.

(3) Federal programs not recently audited as major programs may have higher risk than federal programs recently audited as major programs without audit findings.

(c) **Oversight exercised by federal agencies and pass-through entities.**

(1) Oversight exercised by federal agencies or pass-through entities could indicate risk. For example, recent monitoring reviews performed by an oversight entity that disclosed significant problems would indicate high risk.

(2) Federal agencies, with the concurrence of OMB, may identify federal programs that are high risk. (OMB provides this identification in the compliance supplement.)

(d) **Inherent risk of the federal program.**

(1) The nature of a federal program may indicate risk. Consideration should be given to the complexity of the program and the extent to which the federal program contracts for goods and services.

(2) The phase of a federal program in its life cycle at the federal agency may indicate risk.

- For example, a new federal program with new or interim regulations may have higher risk than an established program with time-tested regulations.
- Also, significant changes in the federal programs, laws, regulations, or the provisions of contracts or grant agreements may increase risk.

(3) The phase of a federal program in its life cycle at the auditee may indicate risk. For example, during the first and last years that an auditee participates in a federal program, the risk may be high due to startup or closeout of program activities and staff.

(4) Type B programs with larger federal awards expended would be higher risk than programs with substantially smaller federal awards expended.

A significant **first-year audit** deviation from use of risk criteria is permitted. For first-year audits, the auditor may elect to determine major programs as all Type A grants plus any Type B programs necessary to meet the percentage of coverage rule. Under this option, the auditor would consider the larger programs to be the major programs and would not be required to perform the risk assessment procedures discussed in Steps 2 and 3.

- A first-year audit is the first year the entity is audited under OMB Circular A-133 or the first year of a change of auditors.
- To ensure that a frequent change of auditors does not preclude audit of high-risk Type B programs, the OMB prohibits this first-year audit election by an auditee more than once every three years.

FIGURE 20–12  **Criteria for Low-Risk Auditee**

An auditee that meets all of the following conditions for each of the preceding two years (or, in the case of biennial audits, preceding two audit periods) qualifies as a **low-risk auditee** eligible for reduced audit coverage.

(a) **Single audits performed.** Single audits were performed on an annual basis in accordance with the provisions of OMB Circular A-133. (A nonfederal entity that has biennial audits does not qualify as a low-risk auditee unless agreed to in advance by the cognizant agency or the oversight agency for audit.)

(b) **Auditor's opinions unqualified.** The auditor's opinions on the financial statements and the schedule of expenditures of federal awards were unqualified. (However, the cognizant or oversight agency for audit may judge that an opinion qualification does not affect the management of federal awards and may provide a waiver.

(c) **No GAGAS IC material weaknesses.** There were no deficiencies in internal control that were identified as material weaknesses under the requirements of GAGAS. (However, the cognizant oversight agency for audit may judge that any identified material weaknesses do not affect the management of the federal awards and may provide a waiver.)

(d) **No Type A program findings.** None of the federal programs had audit findings from any of the following in either of the preceding two years (or, in the case of biennial audits, preceding two audit periods) in which they were classified as Type A programs:

(1) Internal control deficiencies identified as material weaknesses.

(2) Noncompliance with the provisions of laws, regulations, contracts, or grant agreements that have a material effect on the Type A programs.

(3) Known or likely questioned costs that exceed 5% of the total federal awards expended for Type A programs during the year.

## Schedule of Findings and Questioned Costs

The auditor's report on compliance is accompanied by a schedule of findings and questioned costs. OMB Circular A-133 defines **questioned cost** as follows:

> **Questioned cost** means a cost that is questioned by the auditor because of an audit finding:
> - Which resulted from a violation or possible violation of a provision of a law, regulation, contract, grant, cooperative agreement, or other agreement or document governing the use of Federal funds, including funds used to match Federal funds;
> - Where the costs, at the time of an audit, are not supported by adequate documentation; or
> - Where the costs incurred appear unreasonable and do not reflect the actions a prudent person would take in the circumstances.[12]
>
> In general, the criteria for determining and reporting questioned costs are as follows:
> a. **Unallowable costs**—Certain costs specifically unallowable under the general and special award conditions or agency instructions (including, but not limited to, pregrant and postgrant costs and costs in excess of the approved grant budget either by category or in total)
> b. **Undocumented costs**—Costs charged to the grant for which adequate detailed documentation does not exist (for example, documentation demonstrating their relationship to the grant or the amounts involved)

---

[12] OMB Circular A-133, par. 105.

c. **Unapproved costs**—Costs that are not provided for in the approved grant budget, or for which the grant or contract provisions or applicable cost principles require the awarding agency's approval, but for which the auditor finds no evidence of approval

d. **Unreasonable costs**—Costs incurred that may not reflect the actions a prudent person would take in the circumstances, or costs resulting from assigning an unreasonably high valuation to in-kind contributions.[13]

More specifically, *ASLGU* (1994) states that:

The schedule of findings and questioned costs should contain a summary of all reportable instances (findings) of noncompliance and should identify total amounts questioned, if any, for each federal financial assistance program. *Government Auditing Standards* . . . suggests that well-developed findings, which provide sufficient information to federal, state, and local officials to permit timely and proper corrective action, generally consist of statements of the following:

- The condition (what is)
- Criteria (what should be)
- Effect (the difference between what is and what should be)
- Cause (why it happened)

However, the auditor may not be able to fully develop all of these points, given the scope and purpose of single audits.[14]

## Illegal Acts

In addition to the internal control evaluation and compliance testing required in a single audit, the auditor is required to report any illegal acts discovered during the audit. The auditor is not required to test for illegal acts. But if the auditor becomes aware of situations or transactions that could be indicative of fraud, abuse, or illegal expenditures, additional audit steps and procedures should be applied to determine whether such irregularities have occurred. Both *ASLGU* and the GAO audit standards contain specific guidance as to the steps to be taken if such situations or transactions are discovered, which is relatively rare.

## Subrecipients

SLGs that receive federal financial assistance and pass through $300,000 or more of it in a fiscal year to a subrecipient must:

- *Identify Federal Awards.* Identify federal awards made by informing each subrecipient of the CFDA title and number, award name and number, award year, if the award is R&D, and the name of the federal agency. When some of this information is not available, the pass-through entity shall provide the best information available to describe the federal award.

---

[13] *ASLGU* (1994), pars. 24.31–24.32.
[14] Ibid., par. 24.38.

- ***Advise Subrecipients.*** Advise subrecipients of requirements imposed on them by federal laws, regulations, and the provisions of contracts or grant agreements as well as any supplemental requirements imposed by the pass-through entity.

- ***Monitor Subrecipient Activities.*** Monitor the activities of subrecipients as necessary to ensure that federal awards are used for authorized purposes in compliance with laws, regulations, and the provisions of contracts or grant agreements and that performance goals are achieved.

- ***Ensure Audit Requirements Are Met.*** Ensure that subrecipients expending $300,000 or more in federal awards during the subrecipient's fiscal year have met the audit requirements of OMB Circular A-133 for that fiscal year.

- ***Issue Management Decision.*** Issue a management decision on audit findings within six months after receipt of the subrecipient's audit report and ensure that the subrecipient takes appropriate and timely corrective action.

- ***Consider Adjusting Own Records.*** Consider whether subrecipient audits necessitate adjustment of the pass-through entity's own records.

- ***Require Access.*** Require each subrecipient to permit the pass-through entity and auditors to have access to the records and financial statements as necessary for the pass-through entity to monitor the subrecipient's activities.

OMB Circular A-133 does not permit pass-through entities to recover single audit costs to monitor subrecipients expending less than $300,000 annually. However, it does permit pass-through entities to arrange for—and be reimbursed for—agreed upon procedures engagements that address specified compliance requirements of subrecipients.

*ASLGU* (1994) observes that:

> Those primary recipient's responsibilities may be discharged by (a) relying on independent audits performed of the subrecipient, performed in accordance with OMB Circular A-102 or A-133 (or, in some cases, Circular A-110), (b) relying on appropriate procedures performed by the primary recipient's internal audit or program management personnel, (c) expanding the scope of the independent financial and compliance audit of the primary recipient to encompass testing of subrecipients' charges, or (d) a combination of those procedures.
>
> The primary recipient is also responsible for (a) reviewing audit and other reports submitted by subrecipients and identifying questioned costs and other findings pertaining to the federal financial assistance passed through to the subrecipients and (b) properly accounting for and pursuing resolution of questioned costs and ensuring that prompt and appropriate corrective action is taken in instances of material noncompliance with laws and regulations.[15]

Additionally, *ASLGU* notes that subrecipient noncompliance can result in questioned costs for the primary recipient. Thus, the primary recipient controls established to monitor subrecipient compliance should be studied and evaluated.

Specific instances of subrecipient noncompliance need not be included in the primary recipient's audit report. However, the auditor should consider whether reported subrecipient exceptions, or events, or indications of material weaknesses in the primary recipient's monitoring system could materially affect any major federal financial assistance program of the primary recipient.

---

[15] Ibid., pars. 23.28–23.29.

## Auditor Reports—Single Audit

Audit reports prepared at the completion of the audit should meet the requirements of the Single Audit Act, as amended, and OMB Circular A-133. The auditor's report(s) may be in the form of either combined or separate reports and is required to state that the audit was conducted in accordance with OMB Circular A-133 and include the following:

A. **Opinion on Financial Statements and on Schedule of Expenditures of Federal Awards.** Two auditor opinions must be reported: (1) an opinion (or disclaimer of opinion) as to whether the financial statements are presented fairly in all material respects in conformity with generally accepted accounting principles and (2) an opinion (or disclaimer of opinion) as to whether the schedule of expenditures of federal awards is presented fairly in all material respects in relation to the financial statements taken as a whole.

B. **Report(s) on Internal Controls.** A report(s) on internal control—related to (1) the financial statements and (2) the major programs—must describe the scope of testing of internal controls and the results of the tests, and, where applicable, refer to the separate schedule of findings and questioned costs.

C. **Report(s) on Compliance.** A report(s) must be made on (1) compliance with laws, regulations, and the provisions of contracts or grant agreements—noncompliance with which could have a material effect on the financial statements. (2) The report(s) must also:
   - include an opinion (or disclaimer of opinion) as to whether the auditee complied with laws, regulations, and the provisions of contracts or grant agreements, which could have a direct and material effect on each major program, and
   - where applicable, refer to the separate schedule of findings and questioned costs.

D. **Schedule of Findings and Questioned Costs.** A schedule of findings and questioned costs should include these three components:
   1. A summary of the auditor's results, which should include:
      (a) The type of report the auditor issued on the financial statements of the auditee (i.e., unqualified opinion, qualified opinion, adverse opinion, or disclaimer of opinion).
      (b) Where applicable, a statement that reportable conditions in internal control were disclosed by the audit of the financial statements and whether any such conditions were material weaknesses.
      (c) A statement as to whether the audit disclosed any noncompliance that is material to the financial statements of the auditee.
      (d) Where applicable, a statement that reportable conditions in internal control over major programs were disclosed by the audit and whether any such conditions were material weaknesses.
      (e) The type of report the auditor issued on compliance for major programs (i.e., unqualified opinion, qualified opinion, adverse opinion, or disclaimer of opinion).
      (f) A statement as to whether the audit disclosed any audit findings that the auditor is required to report under A-133.
      (g) An identification of major programs.
      (h) The dollar threshold used to distinguish between Type A and Type B programs.
      (i) A statement as to whether the auditee qualified as a low-risk auditee.
   2. Findings relating to the financial statements, which are required to be reported in accordance with GAGAS.
   3. Findings and questioned costs for federal awards.

The several types of single audit findings—and the detail that must be reported—are summarized in Figures 20–13 and 20–14, respectively.

The single audit report is required to include several components that can either be bound into a single report or presented together as separate documents.

**FIGURE 20–13  Types of Single Audit Findings**

OMB Circular A-133 requires the auditor to report the following as audit findings in a schedule of findings and questioned costs.

1. **Reportable conditions in internal control over major programs.** The auditor's determination of whether a deficiency in internal control is a reportable condition for the purpose of reporting an audit finding is in relation to a type of compliance requirement for a major program or an audit objective identified in the compliance supplement. The auditor shall identify reportable conditions that are individually or cumulatively material weaknesses.

2. **Material noncompliance with the provisions of laws, regulations, contracts, or grant agreements related to a major program.** The auditor's determination of whether a noncompliance with the provisions of laws, regulations, contracts, or grant agreements is material for the purpose of reporting an audit finding is in relation to a type of compliance requirement for a major program or an audit objective identified in the compliance supplement.

3. **Known questioned costs that are greater than $10,000 for a type of compliance requirement for a major program.** Known questioned costs are those specifically identified by the auditor. In evaluating the effect of questioned costs on the opinion on compliance, the auditor considers the best estimate of total costs questioned (likely questioned costs), not just the questioned costs specifically identified (known questioned costs). The auditor shall also report known questioned costs when likely questioned costs are greater than $10,000 for a type of compliance requirement for a major program.

4. **Known questioned costs that are greater than $10,000 for a federal program that is not audited as a major program.** Except for audit follow-up, the auditor is not required to perform audit procedures for a nonmajor federal program; thus, the auditor will normally not find questioned costs for a program that is not audited as a major program. However, if the auditor becomes aware of questioned costs for a federal program that is not audited as a major program (e.g., as part of audit follow-up or other audit procedures) and the known questioned costs are greater than $10,000, then the auditor shall report this as an audit finding.

5. **The circumstances concerning why the auditor's report on compliance for major programs is other than an unqualified opinion**—unless such circumstances are otherwise reported as audit findings in the schedule of findings and questioned costs for federal awards.

6. **Known fraud affecting a federal award**—unless such fraud is otherwise reported as an audit finding in the schedule of findings and questioned costs for federal awards.

7. **Instances where the results of audit follow-up procedures disclosed that the summary schedule of prior audit findings prepared by the auditee materially misrepresents the status of any prior audit finding.**

The required components, as well as any report needed on illegal acts, are summarized in Figure 20–15 and categorized in terms of whether they relate to the entity as a whole or only to its federal financial assistance programs. The types of procedures performed and reports issued are summarized by audit type in Figure 20–16. Finally, note that three of the reports—those on the examination of the financial statements, the schedule of federal financial assistance, and compliance for MFAPs—require expression of an opinion by the auditor. The others do not.

**FIGURE 20–14 Audit Findings Detail: Single Audit**

OMB Circular A-133 states that audit findings must be presented in sufficient detail (1) for the auditee to prepare a corrective action plan and take corrective action and (2) for federal agencies and pass-through entities to arrive at a management decision. The following specific information shall be included, as applicable, in audit findings:

1. Federal program and specific federal award identification—including the *Catalog of Federal Domestic Assistance* (CFDA) title and number, federal award number and year, name of federal agency, and name of the applicable pass-through entity.

2. The criteria or specific requirement upon which the audit finding is based—including statutory, regulatory, or other citation.

3. The condition found—including facts that support the deficiency identified in the audit finding.

4. Identification of questioned costs and how they were computed.

5. Information to provide proper perspective for judging the prevalence and consequences of the audit findings, such as whether the audit findings represent an isolated instance or a systemic problem. Where appropriate, instances identified shall be related to the universe and the number of cases examined and be quantified in terms of dollar value.

6. The possible asserted effect—to provide sufficient information to the auditee and federal agency, or pass-through entity in the case of a subrecipient, to permit them to determine the cause and effect to facilitate prompt and proper corrective action.

7. Recommendations to prevent future occurrences of the deficiency identified in the audit finding.

8. Views of responsible officials of the auditee when there is disagreement with the audit findings (to the extent practical).

**FIGURE 20–15 Single Audit Reports**

| *For the Organization or Other Entity:* | *For Its Federal Financial Assistance Programs:* |
|---|---|
| ■ A report on an examination of the general purpose or basic financial statements of the entity as a whole, or the department, agency, or establishment covered by the audit. Includes opinion on fairness of presentation of financial statements. (GAAS) | ■ A report on a supplementary schedule of the entity's federal financial assistance award programs, showing total expenditures for each federal assistance award program. Includes opinion on whether fairly stated relative to the GPFS taken as a whole. |
| ■ A report on internal accounting control based solely on a study and evaluation made as a part of the audit of the general purpose or basic financial statements. (GAGAS) | ■ A report on internal controls related to the major federal award programs. |
| ■ A report on compliance with laws and regulations that may have a material effect on the financial statements. (GAGAS) | ■ A report on compliance with specific program requirements, including related federal laws and regulations, including, where appropriate, reference to the schedule of findings and questioned costs. Includes auditor opinion(s) on whether MFAPs were administered in compliance with those specific program laws and regulations for which noncompliance could have a material effect on the allowability of program expenditures. |
| A report on illegal acts, or indications of such acts, when discovered (a written report is required). Normally, such reports are issued separately and only if such irregularities are discovered. | |

FIGURE 20–16  **Audit and Reporting Requirements Under the Single Audit Act and OMB Circular A-133**

| Type of Audit | Procedures Performed | Report Issued |
|---|---|---|
| **GAAS** (only) | 1. Audit of the financial statements in accordance with generally accepted auditing standards | ■ Opinion on the financial statements<br>■ Report on supplementary schedule of federal financial assistance |
| **GAGAS** (includes GAAS) | 2. Audit of the financial statements in accordance with Government Auditing Standards | ■ Report on compliance with laws and regulations that may have a material effect on the financial statements<br>■ Report on internal control structure-related matters based solely on an assessment of control risk performed as part of the audit of the financial statements |
| **Single Audit** (includes GAAS and GAGAS) | 3. Obtain an understanding of the internal controls over major federal financial assistance programs, assess control risk, and perform tests of controls | ■ Report on internal controls over major federal financial assistance programs (MFAPs) |
| | 4. Audit of compliance with specific requirements applicable to major federal financial assistance programs as defined by the Single Audit Act or OMB Circular A-133 | ■ Opinion on compliance with specific requirements applicable to *each* major federal financial assistance program<br>■ Schedule of findings and questioned costs<br>■ Report if summary schedule of prior audit findings materially misrepresents the status of any prior audit finding |
| | 5. Perform follow-up procedures related to the summary schedule of prior audit findings. | |

*Source:* Adapted from Auditing Standards Board, American Institute of Certified Public Accountants, *Statements on Auditing Standards 68 and 74,* "Compliance Auditing Applicable to Governmental Entities and Other Recipients of Governmental Financial Assistance" (New York: AICPA, 1991 and 1995).

## Auditee Reporting Responsibilities

The auditee is responsible for assembling a single audit reporting package that includes the:

1. Financial statements
2. Schedule of expenditures of federal awards
3. Summary schedule of prior audit findings
4. Auditor's report(s)—including the schedule and findings and questioned costs
5. Corrective action plan

One copy of this reporting package, as well as a uniform data collection form, must be sent to the Federal Audit Clearinghouse of the U.S. Bureau of the Census. In addition, wherever there are audit findings, copies of the reporting package must be:

- provided to the clearinghouse for each federal agency that made findings-related awards directly to the auditee, and
- sent to each pass-through entity that made findings-related awards indirectly to the auditee.

### Other Matters

This discussion explains the general requirements and framework of a single audit under the Single Audit Act, as amended, and Circular A-133. More detailed guidance is included in the Act, OMB Circular A-133, the GAO audit standards and other GAO publications, *ASLGU,* AICPA Statements of Position (SOPs) on single audits, OMB and PCIE "question and answer" (Q&A) publications, and the literature of certain federal agencies other than the OMB and GAO. Practitioners continue to raise numerous questions regarding implementation as they conduct single audits. In response to these questions and concerns, the AICPA, OMB, GAO, and the President's Council on Integrity and Efficiency continue to study, discuss, and interpret the Act and the related guidance and to provide additional guidance on implementing the specific requirements of the Act and regulations.

## CONCLUDING COMMENTS

Both the theory and the practice of governmental auditing are evolving rapidly. The Single Audit Act was the most important development in governmental auditing in the 1980s. This Act, as amended, and OMB Circular A-133 require that governmental and nonprofit audits go significantly beyond the traditional fiscal audit in evaluating legal compliance and internal controls for federal financial assistance award programs.

The Single Audit Act has had a significant impact on the audit profession—including internal, external, and governmental auditors. The Act covers all 50 states, most of the 80,000 plus local governmental units, and many nonprofit organizations. Indeed, whereas public accountants perform fewer than 5,000 audits of publicly held corporations each year, they perform several times as many single audits under OMB Circular A-133.

The single audit concept and guidance continue to evolve as new issues and concerns are raised. This evolution is critical to the long-term success of the single audit concept because, although the concept is sound, some are not satisfied with the single audit as it exists today. Some federal agencies are concerned that the single audit does not provide sufficient information for them to fulfill their oversight roles. Also, some cognizant agents are concerned that not enough compliance testing is being done under the single audit concept. These and other concerns must be addressed as the single audit concept and practices evolve.

### APPENDIX 20–1

### Glossary

This glossary of governmental audit terminology is adapted from the "Definitions" section of OMB Circular A-133—Revised June 24, 1997—"Audits of States, Local Governments, and Non-Profit Organizations."

**Auditee** means any nonfederal entity that expends federal awards which must be audited under Circular A-133.

**Auditor** means an auditor, that is, a public accountant or a federal, state, or local government audit organization, which meets the general standards specified in generally accepted government auditing standards (GAGAS). The term *auditor* does not include internal auditors of nonprofit organizations.

**Audit finding** means deficiencies which the auditor is required to report in the schedule of findings and questioned costs.

**CFDA number** means the number assigned to a federal program in the *Catalog of Federal Domestic Assistance (CFDA)*.

**Cluster of programs** means a grouping of closely related programs that share common compliance requirements. The types of clusters of programs are research and development (R&D), student financial aid (SFA), and other clusters. "Other clusters" are as defined by the Office of Management and Budget (OMB) in the compliance supplement or as designated by a state for federal awards the state provides to its subrecipients that meet the definition of a cluster of programs.

**Cognizant agency for audit** means the federal agency designated to carry out the responsibilities described in Circular A-133.

**Compliance supplement** refers to the *Circular A-133 Compliance Supplement,* included as Appendix B to Circular A-133, or such documents as OMB or its designee may issue to replace it. This document is available from the Government Printing Office, Superintendent of Documents, Washington, D.C. 20402–9325. (Also available at the OMB Website.)

**Corrective action** means action taken by the auditee that:

(1) Corrects identified deficiencies;

(2) Produces recommended improvements; or

(3) Demonstrates that audit findings are either invalid or do not warrant auditee action.

**Federal awarding agency** means the federal agency that provides an award directly to the recipient.

**Federal financial assistance** means assistance that nonfederal entities receive or administer in the form of grants, loans, loan guarantees, property (including donated surplus property), cooperative agreements, interest subsidies, insurance, food commodities, direct appropriations, and other assistance, but does not include amounts received as reimbursement for services rendered to individuals.

**Federal program** means:

(1) All federal awards to a nonfederal entity assigned a single number in the *CFDA*.

(2) When no *CFDA* number is assigned, all federal awards from the same agency made for the same purpose should be combined and considered one program.

(3) Notwithstanding paragraphs (1) and (2) of this definition, a cluster of programs. The types of clusters of programs are:

(i)   Research and development (R&D);

(ii)  Student financial aid (SFA); and

(iii) "Other clusters," as described in the definition of cluster of programs in this section.

**GAGAS** means generally accepted government auditing standards issued by the Comptroller General of the United States, which are applicable to financial audits.

**Internal control** means a process, effected by an entity's management and other personnel, designed to provide reasonable assurance regarding the achievement of objectives in the following categories:

(1) Effectiveness and efficiency of operations;

(2) Reliability of financial reporting; and

(3) Compliance with applicable laws and regulations.

**Internal control pertaining to the compliance requirements for federal programs (internal control over federal programs)** means a process—effected by an entity's management and other personnel—designed to provide reasonable assurance regarding the achievement of the following objectives for federal programs:

(1) Transactions are properly recorded and accounted for to:

(i)   Permit the preparation of reliable financial federal reports;

(ii)  Maintain accountability over assets; and

(iii) Demonstrate compliance with laws, regulations, and other compliance requirements.

(2) Transactions are executed in compliance with:
  (i) Laws, regulations, and the provisions of contracts or grant agreements that could have a direct and material effect on a federal program; and
  (ii) Any other laws and regulations that are identified in the compliance supplement.
(3) Funds, property, and other assets are safeguarded against loss from unauthorized use or disposition.

**Major programs** means a federal program determined by the auditor to be a major program in accordance with Circular A-133 guidelines or a program identified as a major program by a federal agency or pass-through entity.

**Management decision** means the evaluation by the federal awarding agency or pass-through entity of the audit findings and corrective action plan and the issuance of a written decision as to what corrective action is necessary.

**OMB** means the Executive Office of the President, Office of Management and Budget.

**Oversight agency for audit** means the federal awarding agency that provides the predominant amount of direct funding to a recipient not assigned a cognizant agency for audit. When there is no direct funding, the federal agency with the predominant indirect funding shall assume the oversight responsibilities.

**Pass-through entity** means a nonfederal entity that provides a federal award to a subrecipient to carry out a federal program.

**Program-specific audit** means an audit of one federal program (rather than a single audit) as provided for in Circular A-133.

**Questioned cost** means a cost that is questioned by the auditor because of an audit finding:
(1) Which resulted from a violation or possible violation of a provision of a law, regulation, contract, grant, cooperative agreement, or other agreement or document governing the use of federal funds, including funds used to match federal funds;
(2) Where the costs, at the time of the audit, are not supported by adequate documentation; or
(3) Where the costs incurred appear unreasonable and do not reflect the actions a prudent person would take under the circumstances.

**Recipient** means a nonfederal entity that expends federal awards received directly from a federal awarding agency to carry out a federal program.

**Single audit** means an audit which includes both the entity's financial statements and the federal awards as described in Circular A-133.

**Subrecipient** means a nonfederal entity that expends federal awards received from a pass-through entity to carry out a federal program but does not include an individual that is a beneficiary of such a program. A subrecipient may also be a recipient of other federal awards directly from a federal awarding agency.

**Types of compliance requirements** refers to the types of compliance requirements listed in the compliance supplement. Examples include activities allowed or unallowed; allowable costs/cost principles; cash management; eligibility; matching, level of effort, earmarking; and reporting.

## APPENDIX 20–2

## Data Collection Form for Reporting on Audits of States, Local Governments, and Nonprofit Organizations

Office of Management and Budget (OMB) Form SF-SAC, "Data Collection Form for Reporting on Audits of States, Local Governments, and Non-Profit Organizations" is reproduced on pages 831–833:

- to illustrate how the results of a single audit (or program-specific audit) are summarized in a brief uniform informational report, and
- as a succinct summary of many of the discussions and illustrations in this chapter.

OMB No. 0348-0057

FORM **SF-SAC**
(8-97)

U.S. DEPARTMENT OF COMMERCE - BUREAU OF THE CENSUS
ACTING AS COLLECTING AGENT FOR
OFFICE OF MANAGEMENT AND BUDGET

**Data Collection Form for Reporting on**

## AUDITS OF STATES, LOCAL GOVERNMENTS, AND NON-PROFIT ORGANIZATIONS

▶ Complete this form, as required by OMB Circular A-133, "Audits of States, Local Governments, and Non-Profit Organizations."

**RETURN TO** | **Single Audit Clearinghouse**
**1201 E. 10th Street**
**Jeffersonville, IN 47132**

| **PART I** | **GENERAL INFORMATION** *(To be completed by auditee, except for Item 7)* |
|---|---|

**1.** Fiscal year ending date for this submission

Month / Day / Year

**2.** Type of Circular A-133 audit

1 ☐ Single audit   2 ☐ Program-specific audit

**3.** Audit period covered

1 ☐ Annual   3 ☐ Other – _____ Months
2 ☐ Biennial

**FEDERAL GOVERNMENT USE ONLY**

**4.** Date received by Federal clearinghouse

**5.** Employer Identification Number (EIN)

**a.** Auditee EIN [ | | | | | | | | | ]   **b.** Are multiple EINs covered in this report?   1 ☐ Yes   2 ☐ No

**6. AUDITEE INFORMATION**

**a.** Auditee name

**b.** Auditee address *(Number and street)*

City

State          ZIP Code

**c.** Auditee contact
Name

Title

**d.** Auditee contact telephone
(    ) –

**e.** Auditee contact FAX *(Optional)*
(    ) –

**f.** Auditee contact E-mail *(Optional)*

**7. AUDITOR INFORMATION** *(To be completed by auditor)*

**a.** Auditor name

**b.** Auditor address *(Number and street)*

City

State          ZIP Code

**c.** Auditor contact
Name

Title

**d.** Auditor contact telephone
(    ) –

**e.** Auditor contact FAX *(Optional)*
(    ) –

**f.** Auditor contact E-mail *(Optional)*

**g. AUDITEE CERTIFICATION STATEMENT–** This is to certify that, to the best of my knowledge and belief, the auditee has: (1) Engaged an auditor to perform an audit in accordance with the provisions of OMB Circular A-133 for the period described in Part I, Items 1 and 3; (2) the auditor has completed such audit and presented a signed audit report which states that the audit was conducted in accordance with the provisions of the Circular; and, (3) the information included in **Parts I, II,** and **III** of this data collection form is accurate and complete. I declare that the foregoing is true and correct.

Signature of certifying official   Date
Month / Day / Year

Name/Title of certifying official

**g. AUDITOR STATEMENT–** The data elements and information included in this form are limited to those prescribed by OMB Circular A-133. The information included in Parts II and III of the form, except for Part III, Items 5 and 6, was transferred from the auditor's report(s) for the period described in Part I, Items 1 and 3, and is **not a substitute** for such reports. The auditor has not performed any auditing procedures since the date of the auditor's report(s). A copy of the reporting package required by OMB Circular A-133, which includes the complete auditor's report(s), is available in its entirety from the auditee at the address provided in Part I of this form. As required by OMB Circular A-133, the information in **Parts II** and **III** of this form was entered in this form by the auditor based on information included in the reporting package. The auditor has not performed any additional auditing procedures in connection with the completion of this form.

Signature of auditor   Date
Month / Day / Year

EIN: ☐☐☐☐☐☐☐☐☐

**8.** Indicate whether the auditee has either a Federal cognizant or oversight agency for audit.　*(Mark (X) one box)*

₁☐ Cognizant agency　　　₂☐ Oversight agency

**9.** Name of Federal cognizant or oversight agency for audit　*(Mark (X) one box)*

01☐ African Development Foundation
02☐ Agency for International Development
10☐ Agriculture
11☐ Commerce
94☐ Corporation for National and Community Service
12☐ Defense
84☐ Education
81☐ Energy
66☐ Environmental Protection Agency

83☐ Federal Emergency Management Agency
34☐ Federal Mediation and Conciliation Service
39☐ General Services Administration
93☐ Health and Human Services
14☐ Housing and Urban Development
03☐ Institute for Museum Services
04☐ Inter-American Foundation
15☐ Interior

16☐ Justice
17☐ Labor
43☐ National Aeronautics and Space Administration
89☐ National Archives and Records Administraton
05☐ National Endowment for the Arts
06☐ National Endowment for the Humanities
47☐ National Science Foundation
07☐ Office of National Drug Control Policy

08☐ Peace Corps
59☐ Small Business Administration
96☐ Social Security Administration
19☐ State
20☐ Transportation
21☐ Treasury
82☐ United States Information Agency
64☐ Veterans Affairs
☐ Other – *Specify:*

---

**PART II　　FINANCIAL STATEMENTS** *(To be completed by auditor)*

**1.** Type of audit report　*(Mark (X) one box)*
₁☐ Unqualified opinion　　₂☐ Qualified opinion　　₃☐ Adverse opinion　　₄☐ Disclaimer of opinion

**2.** Is a "going concern" explanatory paragraph included in the audit report?　₁☐ Yes　₂☐ No

**3.** Is a reportable condition disclosed?　₁☐ Yes　₂☐ No – *SKIP to Item 5*

**4.** Is any reportable condition reported as a material weakness?　₁☐ Yes　₂☐ No

**5.** Is a material noncompliance disclosed?　₁☐ Yes　₂☐ No

---

**PART III　　FEDERAL PROGRAMS** *(To be completed by auditor)*

**1.** Type of audit report on major program compliance
₁☐ Unqualified opinion　　₂☐ Qualified opinion　　₃☐ Adverse opinion　　₄☐ Disclaimer of opinion

**2.** What is the dollar threshold to distinguish Type A and Type B programs §___ .520(b)?
$

**3.** Did the auditee qualify as a low-risk auditee (§___ .530)?
₁☐ Yes　　₂☐ No

**4.** Are there any audit findings required to be reported under §___ .510(a)?
₁☐ Yes　₂☐ No

**5.** Which Federal Agencies are required to receive the reporting package?　*(Mark (X) all that apply)*

01☐ African Development Foundation
02☐ Agency for International Development
10☐ Agriculture
11☐ Commerce
94☐ Corporation for National and Community Service
12☐ Defense
84☐ Education
81☐ Energy
66☐ Environmental Protection Agency

83☐ Federal Emergency Management Agency
34☐ Federal Mediation and Conciliation Service
39☐ General Services Administration
93☐ Health and Human Services
14☐ Housing and Urban Development
03☐ Institute for Museum Services
04☐ Inter-American Foundation
15☐ Interior

16☐ Justice
17☐ Labor
43☐ National Aeronautics and Space Administration
89☐ National Archives and Records Administraton
05☐ National Endowment for the Arts
06☐ National Endowment for the Humanities
47☐ National Science Foundation
07☐ Office of National Drug Control Policy

08☐ Peace Corps
59☐ Small Business Administration
96☐ Social Security Administration
19☐ State
20☐ Transportation
21☐ Treasury
82☐ United States Information Agency
64☐ Veterans Affairs
00☐ None
☐ Other – *Specify:*

FORM SF-SAC (8-97)

832

EIN:

## PART III — FEDERAL PROGRAMS-Continued

### 6. FEDERAL AWARDS EXPENDED DURING FISCAL YEAR

| CFDA number [1] (a) | Name of Federal program (b) | Amount expended (c) |
|---|---|---|
| | | $ |
| | | $ |
| | | $ |
| | | $ |
| | | $ |
| | | $ |
| | | $ |
| | | $ |
| | | $ |
| **TOTAL FEDERAL AWARDS EXPENDED →** | | $ |

### 7. AUDIT FINDINGS AND QUESTIONED COSTS

| Major program (a) | Type of compliance requirement [2] (b) | Amount of questioned costs (c) | Internal control findings [3] (d) | Audit finding reference number(s) (e) |
|---|---|---|---|---|
| 1 ☐ Yes  2 ☐ No | | $ | 1 ☐ A  3 ☐ C  2 ☐ B | |
| 1 ☐ Yes  2 ☐ No | | $ | 1 ☐ A  3 ☐ C  2 ☐ B | |
| 1 ☐ Yes  2 ☐ No | | $ | 1 ☐ A  3 ☐ C  2 ☐ B | |
| 1 ☐ Yes  2 ☐ No | | $ | 1 ☐ A  3 ☐ C  2 ☐ B | |
| 1 ☐ Yes  2 ☐ No | | $ | 1 ☐ A  3 ☐ C  2 ☐ B | |
| 1 ☐ Yes  2 ☐ No | | $ | 1 ☐ A  3 ☐ C  2 ☐ B | |
| 1 ☐ Yes  2 ☐ No | | $ | 1 ☐ A  3 ☐ C  2 ☐ B | |
| 1 ☐ Yes  2 ☐ No | | $ | 1 ☐ A  3 ☐ C  2 ☐ B | |
| 1 ☐ Yes  2 ☐ No | | $ | 1 ☐ A  3 ☐ C  2 ☐ B | |

*IF ADDITIONAL LINES ARE NEEDED, PLEASE PHOTOCOPY THIS PAGE, ATTACH ADDITIONAL PAGES TO THE FORM, AND SEE INSTRUCTIONS*

[1] Or other identifying number when the Catalog of Federal Domestic Assistance (CFDA) number is not available.

[2] Type of compliance requirement *(Enter the letter(s) of all that apply to audit findings and questioned costs reported for each Federal program.)*

A. Activities allowed or unallowed
B. Allowable costs/cost principles
C. Cash management
D. Davis - Bacon Act
E. Eligibility
F. Equipment and real property management
G. Matching, level of effort, earmarking
H. Period of availability of funds
I. Procurement
J. Program income
K. Real property acquisition and relocation assistance
L. Reporting
M. Subrecipient monitoring
N. Special tests and provisions
O. None

[3] Type of internal control findings *(Mark (X) all that apply)*

A. Material weaknesses    B. Reportable conditions    C. None reported

## Questions

**Q 20-1** Compare the responsibilities of a municipality's officers and its independent auditor for the financial report.

**Q 20-2** Explain how both program size and related risk factors affect the decision as to which federal award programs are considered major programs.

**Q 20-3** What are the responsibilities of the government being audited with respect to the single audit report?

**Q 20-4** A municipality requires auditors to submit bids as to how much they would charge for the annual audit. The audit contract is awarded to the lowest bidder. What might be wrong with this method of engaging auditors?

**Q 20-5** What advantages accrue to the auditee and auditor if the auditee subject to single audit qualifies as a low-risk auditee? What criteria must be met?

**Q 20-6** The comptroller of D City is responsible for approval of all city receipts and disbursements. The city council takes the position that, because the comptroller is auditing both receipts and disbursements for accuracy and legality, no additional audit by independent accountants is necessary. What position would you, a new council member, take?

**Q 20-7** The state auditor has for years been responsible for examinations of the financial operations of all state agencies. A bill is under consideration to make the state auditor the chief accounting officer of the state as well. You are testifying before a legislative committee that is considering the bill. What is the tenor of your testimony?

**Q 20-8** Auditing has been defined as the process of collecting and evaluating evidence in order to formulate an opinion about assertions made by management. What assertions does the external auditor address in an opinion as the result of a fiscal audit? What assertions does the external auditor address in giving an opinion as the result of a performance audit? What assertions does the external auditor address in giving an opinion as the result of a compliance audit of a MFAP?

**Q 20-9** Describe the nature of a single audit of a state or local government.

**Q 20-10** When is a state or local government required to have a single audit performed?

**Q 20-11** Distinguish between major federal financial assistance award programs and nonmajor federal financial assistance award programs. Why is this distinction important?

**Q 20-12** What reports are required to be presented as a result of a single audit?

**Q 20-13** What is a cognizant agency? What are its responsibilities? Which federal agency would be the cognizant agency for smaller governments such as the city of Providence, Kentucky, which has a population of approximately 4,500?

**Q 20-14** What is the OMB Compliance Supplement? What is its purpose?

**Q 20-15** Distinguish between the internal control evaluation required for MFAPs and for non-MFAPs. What level of internal control evaluation is required if a government has no MFAPs?

**Q 20-16** Distinguish the compliance audit requirements for MFAPs from those for non-MFAPs. What requirements apply if there are no MFAPs?

**Q 20-17** What types of audit findings might result from a single audit? Explain.

## Problems

**P 20-1** (Multiple Choice)
  1. A performance audit is concerned with which of the following issues?
     a. The minimization of expenditures for agency programs
     b. The extent to which agency programs met their objectives

    c. The extent to which agency programs produced benefits greater than or equal to their cost

    d. All of the above

    e. a and c

2. Generally accepted governmental auditing standards are issued by the
    a. Office of Management and Budget.
    b. General Accounting Office.
    c. Governmental Accounting Standards Board.
    d. Auditing Standards Board.
    e. Department of the Treasury.

3. In performing audits under the Single Audit Act, auditors must comply with
    a. generally accepted auditing standards (GAAS).
    b. generally accepted governmental auditing standards (GAGAS).
    c. both GAAS and GAGAS.
    d. neither GAAS nor GAGAS, because the provisions of the Act override both.

4. Which of the following would not be an element of a single audit?
    a. determination of whether the government's financial statements are fairly presented
    b. determination of whether the government has established adequate internal control systems
    c. determination of whether the government has complied with laws and regulations relating to major federal financial assistance programs
    d. determination of whether the government has accurately listed the federal financial assistance it has expended during the period in its schedule of expenditures of federal awards
    e. none of the above

5. During the 19X9 fiscal year, the city of Metropolis Human Services Department received a $210,000 federal grant. The only other Metropolis department or agency that received a federal grant during the fiscal year was its Police Department, which received a $95,000 federal grant. The city of Metropolis
    a. is exempt from all auditing requirements for the 19X9 fiscal year.
    b. is exempt from audit requirements for the 19X9 fiscal year but is required to keep adequate accounting records and to make them available for inspection and audit upon request.
    c. must either have a single audit or, at the grantor's option, a program-specific audit for the 19X9 fiscal year.
    d. must have a single audit for the 19X9 fiscal year.
    e. none of the above.

6. The city of Tampando learned in December 19X6 that it was being awarded a $9,000,000 cost-reimbursement grant from the U.S. Department of Transportation to lengthen the main runway at the Tampando International Airport. The city paid $9,000,000 for the construction on November 15, 19X7 and received the $9,000,000 from the Department of Transportation on January 2, 19X8. Tampando's fiscal year runs from January 1 to December 31, and its financial statements are prepared according to generally accepted accounting principles. For the purpose of the Single Audit Act, the city would recognize the grant expenditures in

    a. 19X6.                             c. 19X8.

    b. 19X7.                            d. Either of the three is acceptable.

7. The state of Oklabraska received a total of $325,000 in federal financial assistance during its 19X8 fiscal year. It passed on $30,000 of these grants to the city of Lineman to help finance a pilot police training program. The city of Lineman also received $200,000 in financial assistance directly from federal government agencies during fiscal 19X8. Which government(s) would be required to have a single audit for the 19X8 fiscal year?

  a. the state of Oklabraska only
  b. the city of Lineman only
  c. both the state of Oklabraska and the city of Lineman
  d. neither the state of Oklabraska nor the city of Lineman

8. The city of Celtics received $7,000,000 in federal financial assistance and incurred $6,000,000 in federal financial assistance program expenditures during fiscal 19X8. The city of Lakers received $12,000,000 in federal financial assistance and made $11,500,000 in federal financial assistance program expenditures during fiscal 19X8. During the fiscal year, each city received $310,000 for, and expended $290,000 on, a driver safety education program financed by the U.S. Department of Transportation. This program would constitute a major federal assistance program

  a. for Celtics, but not for Lakers.            c. for both Celtics and Lakers.
  b. for Lakers, but not for Celtics.            d. for neither Celtics nor Lakers.

9. Cognizant agencies are assigned to

  a. state governments.                          d. both a and b.
  b. large local governments.                    e. both b and c.
  c. small governments.                          f. all governments.

10. The city of Lukeville has three major federal assistance programs with the following expenditures in 19X7:

| Program | Expenditures |
|---------|-------------:|
| A       | $2,000,000   |
| B       | 1,000,000    |
| C       | 500,000      |

  If the city has total federal assistance expenditures for 19X7 of $5,500,000, Lukeville's single audit should include a study and evaluation of internal controls of the type conducted when intending to rely upon those controls to reduce substantive testing for which programs?

  a. Program A                                   d. Both A and B
  b. Program B                                   e. All three programs
  c. Program C

**P 20-2**  (Single Audit) The A City schedule of expenditures of federal awards is presented in Figure 20–9. Assuming A City is not a low-risk auditee and this is the first year under new auditors, what level of internal control and compliance auditing work should be performed for each of the city's programs? Justify your response.

**P 20-3**  (Single Audit) Following are the expenditures incurred in 19X2 and 19X3 by Thompson County under each of its federal assistance programs.

| Federal Program | Grant | 19X2 Expenditures | 19X3 Expenditures |
|---------|-------|------------------:|------------------:|
| A       | 1     | $  180,000        | $  40,000         |
|         | 2     | 75,000            | 120,000           |
|         | 3     | 60,000            | 100,000           |
| B       |       | 271,000           | 250,000           |
| C       |       | 3,000,000         | 220,000           |
| D       |       | 500,000           | —                 |
| E       | 1     | 80,000            | 80,000            |
|         | 2     | 130,000           | 110,000           |
| Total   |       | $4,296,000        | $920,000          |

*Required* (1) Which of Thompson County's federal financial assistance programs are Type A federal assistance programs in 19X2? In 19X3?

(2) What level of internal control study and evaluation must be performed for each major program in 19X2 under the single audit requirements? In 19X3?

(3) What level of compliance auditing is required for each major program in 19X2 under the single audit requirements? In 19X3?

(4) How would your responses to requirements 1–3 of Problem 20–3 differ if the expenditures data were for a nonprofit organization subject to OMB Circular A-133?

**P 20-4** (Major Program Determination) Sharendale County expended $7,000,000 of federal financial assistance during 19X9 in the following programs:

| Federal Programs | Expenditures | Risk-Assessment |
|---|---|---|
| A | $1,100,000 | Low |
| B | 1,500,000 | High |
| C | 900,000 | High |
| D | 2,500,000 | Low |
| E | 800,000 | Low |
| F | 200,000 | — |
| | $7,000,000 | |

*Required* (1) Assume that Sharendale County is **not** a low-risk auditee and programs A to E had been audited as major programs in one of the two prior years. Which programs will probably be selected as major programs this year?

(2) Assume that Sharendale County is a low-risk auditee and programs A to E had been audited as major programs in one of the two prior years. Which programs will probably be selected as major programs this year?

**P 20-5** (Major Program Determination) A government receives and expends funds under several federal programs during 20X0. The programs and amounts expended follow:

| | |
|---|---|
| Program A | $90,000 |
| Program B | $500,000 |
| Program C | $1,000,000 |
| Program D | $250,000 |
| Program E | $180,000 |
| Program F | $700,000 |
| Program G | $220,000 |
| Program H | $150,000 |
| Program I | $230,000 |
| Program J | $275,000 |

Programs C and J have been audited as major programs (with no audit findings) in the past two years.

*Required* Which programs would you treat as major programs in a single audit for 20X0 if the government is not a low-risk auditee? Document the basis for your decision including any risk assessments that you would conduct. (Indicate programs that you have assessed as high risk—i.e., assume that some are high risk and indicate which ones you assume are.)

**P 20-6** (Research Project—Single Audit) Obtain a copy of a recent single audit report and evaluate it in terms of the requirements for single audit reports discussed in this chapter. Prepare a brief report (3–8 pages) summarizing your analyses, findings, and conclusions, and attach a photocopy of any unusual or otherwise noteworthy examples.

**P 20-7** (Research Project—Audit Guide) Obtain a copy of the AICPA Audit and Accounting Guide, *Audits of State and Local Governmental Units (1998),* and determine which of the illustrative audit's reports in Appendix A relate to the various sections of Figure 20–6, "Levels of Reporting in Governmental Single Audits." Prepare a brief report (3–8 pages) summarizing your analyses and conclusions.

**P 20-8** (Research Project—Internet) Search the Internet for single audit information. Write a brief paper (3–8 pages) summarizing your research and findings, and attach copies of the most useful home page sites and selected other pages.

# INDEX

## A

Accountability
  in budgeting process, 91
  classification of fixed assets and,
    351–352, 355
  external restrictions on, 7
  internal requirements for, 7
  as primary consideration in
    G&NP accounting, 11
  of primary government, 553
  state and local government, 26–28
  in Trust and Agency Fund ac-
    counting, 394–395
Accounting. *See also* Financial re-
    porting; Financial statement(s)
  objectives of, 5–6, 10–11
  regulation of, 5
  as service function, 7
Accounting entity concept, 11
Accounting equation
  federal government
    budgetary, 766
    proprietary, 766, 772
  government hospital Unrestricted
    Fund, 680
  state and local government
    fiduciary fund, 37
    General Fixed Assets Account
      Group, 36, 353
    General Fund, 113
    General Long-Term Debt Ac-
      count Group, 36, 369–370
    governmental (expendable)
      funds, 36
    government hospital Unre-
      stricted Fund, 680
    proprietary (nonexpendable)
      funds, 37
    Special Revenue Funds, 113
Accounting principles. *See also* Ac-
    crual basis accounting; Gener-
    ally accepted accounting
    principles (GAAP); Govern-
    mental Accounting Standards
    Board (GASB) principles
  change in
    expenditure accounting, 238–239

revenue accounting, 198–199
college and university, 627–628
federal government, 760–761, 762,
  765–774
  federal model of accounting,
    766–769
  financial reporting, 759–762, 765,
    773–774, 785–790
  fund accounting, 773
  Government Wide Standard
    General Ledger (SGL),
    769–773
health and welfare organizations,
  678–679
sources of G&NP, 11–17
state and local government, 13,
  14–16, 32–56
  changes in, 198–199, 238–239
  Enterprise Funds, 461–462
  evolution of, 57–60
  Internal Service Funds, 427–434
for voluntary health and welfare
  organizations and other not-
  for-profit organizations, 11, 13,
  714–715, 717
Accounting Principles Board (APB)
  Financial Accounting Standards
    Board as successor to, 13
  *Opinion 20,* 12
Accounts payable, between component units and primary government, 551
Accounts receivable
  between component units and pri-
    mary government, 551
  unbilled, adjusting entries
    for, 473
Accounts receivable turnover, 581
Accrual basis accounting
  described, 46–48
  federal government, 778–779
  modified, 47–48, 91, 170–171
  for revenue recognition, 47,
    170–171
  for VHWOs and ONPOs, 717
Acid-test ratio, 581
Activity
  defined, 242

expenditure classification by,
  242–244
Adjusting entries
  expenditure-related, 229–238
    claims and judgments, 232–234,
      237
    compensated absences,
      236–238
    debt service, 230–231
    encumbrances, 230
    inventory, 223, 559
    non-GAAP to GAAP account-
      ing, 558–559
    pension plan contributions,
      237–238
  non-GAAP to GAAP accounting
    basis, 554–555, 560–561,
    566
  expenditures, 558–559
  revenues, 557–558
  revenue-related, 557–558
  state and local government,
    124–125
    Enterprise Fund, 466, 468, 472,
      473
    Pension Trust Fund, 412
Administrative involvement, 186,
  186*n*
Administrative services expenses,
  688
Administrators, as users of financial
  reports, 28, 31
Advance refundings, 332–333, 335,
  336–338, 525
Advances from (Fund) account, 136,
  429, 528
Advances to (Fund) account, 135,
  136, 429, 528
Agency Funds
  college and university, 629, 665
  federal government, 773–774
  state and local government, 37, 39,
    401–408
    accountability focus of, 394–395
    budgets and, 74
    combining Trust Fund annual
      statements with, 416, 417
    Enterprise Funds and, 462

858 *Index*